The SportingNews

COMPLETE
BASEBALL
RECORD BOOK

2002 EDITION

Editor/Complete Baseball Record Book

CRAIG CARTER

ON THE COVER: Barry Bonds. Photos by John Cordes for THE SPORTING NEWS.

Spine photo of Ichiro Suzuki by Albert Dickson/THE SPORTING NEWS.

Back cover photo of Rickey Henderson by Todd Warshaw for THE SPORTING NEWS.

ISBN: 0-89204-668-0

10 9 8 7 6 5 4 3 2 1

CONTENTS

REGULAR SEASON

Service
    Individual 14
    Club 16
League 19
Batting
    Individual 20
    Club 48
    League 68
Baserunning
    Individual 72
    Club 74
    League 76
Pitching
    Individual 77
    Club 93
    League 96
Fielding
    Individual 98
    Club 120
    League 124
Miscellaneous
    Individual 126
    Club 128
    League 137
Non-Playing Personnel 139
Yearly Leaders 140
Career Milestones 170
General Reference...........................182
American League Team Records 228
National League Team Records 282
Index...543

DIVISION SERIES

Service
    Individual 340
    Club 341
Batting
    Individual 344
    Club 351
Baserunning
    Individual 362
    Club 363
Pitching
    Individual 365
    Club 370
Fielding
    Individual 371
    Club 380
Miscellaneous................................384
Non-Playing Personnel 386
General Reference...........................387
Index...546

CHAMPIONSHIP SERIES

Service
    Individual 394
    Club 396
Batting
    Individual 400
    Club 408
Baserunning
    Individual 422
    Club 423
Pitching
    Individual 425
    Club 430
Fielding
    Individual 432
    Club 442
Miscellaneous................................447
Non-Playing Personnel 450
General Reference...........................451
Index...548

WORLD SERIES

Service
    Individual 462
    Club 463
Batting
    Individual 466
    Club 474
Baserunning
    Individual 483
    Club 484
Pitching
    Individual 486
    Club 490
Fielding
    Individual 491
    Club 499
Miscellaneous................................502
Non-Playing Personnel 504
General Reference...........................505
Index...549

ALL-STAR GAME

Service...522
Batting
    Individual 523
    Club 526
Baserunning..................................528
Pitching 529
Fielding
    Individual 531
    Club 534
Miscellaneous................................536
Non-Playing Personnel 537
General Reference...........................538
Index...551

A NOTE ABOUT THE 2002 EDITION

Regular readers and users of the Complete Baseball Record Book will note a few changes to this year's edition. By making these few additions to the book, we hope to make it easier to use and make more timely information more accessible.

Just below, you can follow through a primer on how to locate records in this book. Keeping all of these pages updated and organized is the monumental task of editor Craig Carter. The primer should make finding exactly the information you're seeking much easier.

Following that, you'll find a quick statistical breakdown of the season just past and the upcoming season. It's our way of highlighting what a terrific year it was for baseball records in 2000, and our way of previewing and preparing you for what records to keep an eye on.

We hope you like the changes. You're always welcome to send me feedback at smeyerhoff@sportingnews.com.

Steve Meyerhoff
Editorial Director, Books
The Sporting News

HOW TO LOCATE A RECORD IN THE COMPLETE BASEBALL RECORD BOOK

The huge volume of records in this edition necessitates an understanding of the basic methods with which the entries are organized. An explanation of the basic system and an example will follow.

1. Sections are first divided into the following (columnwise in order):

- Regular Season
- Championship Series
- All-Star Game
- Division Series
- World Series

2. Within each of the sections in part 1 above are the following categories (columnwise in order):

- Service
- Pitching
- Non-Playing Personnel (includes managers and umpires)
- Batting
- Fielding
- General Reference
- Baserunning
- Miscellaneous

In addition, the Regular Season section has the following sections:

- Yearly Leaders (Year-by-year leaders in various offensive and defensive categories)
- Career Milestones (Career leaders in various offensive and defensive categories)
- American League Team Records (Team-by-team records for each A.L. club)
- National League Team Records (Team-by-team records for each N.L. club)

3. Within the first five categories in part 2 above are the following designations indicating to whom the records apply (in order):

- Individual
- Club
- League

To look up a record, first select one bulleted title from each of the three sections above that best describe the record you desire. For example, if you want to find the player with the most home runs in World Series history, you will select the following from each section:

Section 1	Section 2	Section 3
• World Series	• Batting	• Individual

Once you find the items that best describe each of the three sections above, refer to the vertical gray tabs on the sides of each page, which look like the following:

The tabs are aligned according to the sections listed in part 1 above. All Regular Season records have aligned vertical tabs near the top of the page, Division Series records have a tab in the middle edge, etc.

Use the tabs to navigate your way into the general area you want to be in the book. From this point, you will rely on black and gray horizontal bars on the pages to further locate exactly where you want to be. The black bars will guide you into more specific categories and the gray bars will let you get even more specific.

Once you are into a section, you need to further isolate the record you want. For this book, we generally try to sequence most of our records according to the order you would likely see them listed in a line of averages as follows:

Batting: Normally have their games played listed first, followed by batting and slugging average, runs, hits, singles, doubles, triples, home runs, grand slams, total bases, long hits and extra bases, runs batted in, bases on balls, strikeouts, sacrifice hits and flies, hit by pitch and grounding into double plays. (There are more records, but these are the most common ones and are generally arranged with the more important ones listed first.)

Baserunning: Stolen bases, caught stealing and, for club and league records, left on bases.

Pitching: Games, games started, games finished, complete games, innings, games won, saves, games lost, at-bats and plate appearances, runs, earned runs, ERA, shutouts and scoreless innings, 1-0 games, hits, home runs, long hits, bases on balls, strikeouts, hit batsmen, wild pitches, sacrifice hits and flies, and balks.

Fielding: Games, average, putouts, assists, chances accepted, errors and double plays.

The above are not all the categories in the book, but are the most common subjects. Note that within these categories can be found further divisions of categories such as records for rookies, righthanders, switch-hitters, etc.

Example
To find the record for most regular season home runs by a rookie:
1. Determine which section you need (in this example it is Regular Season), which category within the Regular Season section you need (in this case it is Batting) and whether you are looking for an Individual, Club or League record (in this case it is an Individual record).
2. Locate the vertical tab indicating you are in the Regular Season, Individual Batting section (this section runs from page 20 through 47.
3. Find the horizontal black bar labeled "Home Runs" (which can be found on page 30). Then find the horizontal gray bar labeled "Season" (which can be found on page 31). The record for most home runs by a rookie in the regular season can be found in this section.

NOTES ON MAJOR LEAGUE RECORDS

Records noted in this book refer to the following leagues: M.L.—major leagues, 1876 to date; N.L.—National League, 1876 to date; A.A.—American Association, 1882 to 1891; U.A.—Union Association, 1884; P.L.—Players League, 1890; A.L.—American League, 1901 to date. This book does not include the Federal League of 1914 and 1915 as a major league.

Two games in one day (a.m. and p.m.) are included with doubleheader records.

American League and National League records are listed for 8-, 10-, 12-, 14- and 16-club leagues unless the number achieved with a larger number of clubs is lower than that of the record for a smaller number of clubs.

References to 8-, 10-, 12-, 14- and 16-club leagues refer to the following years:

	National League	American League
8-club league	1901-1961	1901-1960
10-club league	1962-1968	1961-1968
12-club league	1969-1992	1969-1976
14-club league	1993-1997	1977-present
16-club league	1998-present	

In years when many games were canceled because of work stoppages (1972, 1981, 1994 and 1995), club and league records for fewest are omitted.

EXPLANATION OF CONFUSING STATISTICAL TERMS

Most categorical titles used in the *Complete Baseball Record Book* are understood by most readers. The following terms, however, merit clarification:

Long hits are simply extra-base hits (doubles, triples and home runs). **Extra bases on long hits** refers to the number of bases a batter advances beyond first base on a hit (one extra base on a double, two on a triple and three on a home run). Extra-base hits are called long hits in this book because it sounds cumbersome to refer to the complementary category as "extra bases on extra-base hits."

Chances offered equals the sum of putouts, assists and errors. **Chances accepted** equals the sum of putouts and assists. Dividing chances accepted by chances offered results in fielding percentage.

Section 2
• Batting

Section 3
• Individual

Section 1
• World Series

WORLD SERIES   Individual batting

A LOOK BACK...AND A LOOK AHEAD

Bonds Sets Many Records in Memorable 2001 Season

Barry Bonds enjoyed one of the greatest seasons in major league history in 2001, as he set a number of slugging records. The San Francisco outfielder's most notable feats were setting major league records with 73 home runs, compiling a slugging percentage of .863 and collecting 177 bases on balls. Following are some of the records Bonds set in 2001:

Highest slugging percentage, career (minimum 15 years)—.585, broke Rogers Hornsby's N.L. record of .578.
Highest slugging percentage, season—.863, broke Babe Ruth's (New York A.L., 1920) M.L. record of .847.
Most home runs by lefthander, career—567, broke Willie McCovey's N.L. record of 521.
Most home runs, season—73, broke Mark McGwire's (St. Louis, 1998) M.L. record of 70.
Most home runs by lefthander at home, season—37, broke Ted Kluszewski's (Cincinnati, 1954) M.L. record of 34.
Most home runs on road, season—36, broke M.L. mark of 32 held by Babe Ruth (New York A.L., 1927) and Mark McGwire (St. Louis, 1998).
Most consecutive years with 30 or more home runs—10, broke N.L. mark of 9 he shared with Eddie Mathews and Mike Schmidt.
Most home runs by lefthander, two consecutive seasons—122, broke Ted Kluszewski's (Cincinnati, 1954-55) N.L. record of 96.
Most home runs by lefthander, one month—17, tied M.L. mark held by Babe Ruth (New York A.L., September, 1923). Bonds hit his 17 in May.
Most home runs in two straight games—5, tied M.L. mark held by many players. Bonds hit three on May 19 and two on May 20.
Most home runs in three straight games—6, tied M.L. mark held by many players. Bonds hit one on May 18, three on May 19, two on May 20 and one on May 21. This comprises two streaks of six homers during three-game spans.
Most home runs in six straight games—9, broke N.L. mark of 8 held by George Kelly (New York, 1924), Walker Cooper (New York, 1947), Willie Mays (New York, 1955) and Graig Nettles (San Diego, 1984). Bonds hit homers on May 17, 18, 19 (3), 20 (2), 21 and 22. During this span, he also tied various M.L. and N.L. records for most homers in two consecutive games, three consecutive games and five consecutive games.
Most long hits, season—107, tied Chuck Klein's (Philadelphia, 1930) N.L. record.
Most extra bases on long hits, season—255, broke Babe Ruth's (New York A.L., 1921) M.L. record of 253.
Most bases on balls, season—177, broke Babe Ruth's (New York A.L., 1923) M.L. record of 170.
Most years leading league in bases on balls—7, broke N.L. mark of 6 he shared with Mel Ott.
Most intentional bases on balls, career—355, increased his own M.L. record.

Rookies Pujols & Suzuki Enter Record Book

A pair of rookies—St. Louis Cardinals infielder/outfielder Albert Pujols and Seattle Mariners outfielder Ichiro Suzuki—had record-breaking seasons in 2001. Both set a number of rookie records in helping their teams reach the playoffs.

Suzuki won the American League batting crown with a .350 mark, joining Tony Oliva (.323 with Minnesota in 1964) as the only rookies in modern major league history to win batting titles. He became only the second player to win both the Rookie of the Year and Most Valuable Player awards in the same season, joining Fred Lynn of Boston in 1975. Suzuki set the following marks in 2001:

Most at-bats by rookie, season—692, broke Nomar Garciaparra's (Boston, 1997) A.L. record of 684.
Most at-bats by lefthander, season—692, broke Don Mattingly's (New York, 1986) A.L. record of 677.
Most hits by rookie, season—242, broke Lloyd Waner's (Pittsburgh, 1927) M.L. record of 223.
Most games with one or more hits, season—135, tied M.L. mark held by Rogers Hornsby (St. Louis, 1922), Chuck Klein (Philadelphia, 1930), Wade Boggs (Boston, 1985) and Derek Jeter (New York A.L., 1999).
Most singles, and most singles by lefthander, season—192, broke Wade Boggs' (Boston, 1985) A.L. record of 187.
Most singles by rookie, season—192, broke Harvey Kuenn's (Detroit, 1953) A.L. record of 167.

Pujols belted 37 home runs for the Cardinals, falling one short of Wally Berger's National League record of 38, set in 1930. But Pujols did set a number of marks in the following categories:

Most total bases by rookie, season—360, broke Dick Allen's (Philadelphia, 1964) N.L. record of 352.
Most long hits by rookie, season—88, broke Johnny Frederick's (Brooklyn, 1929) N.L. record of 82.
Most runs batted in by rookie, season—130, broke Wally Berger's (Boston, 1930) N.L. record of 119.

Gwynn, McGwire & Ripken Retire Following 2001 Season

Three superstars of the baseball world—Tony Gwynn of the San Diego Padres, Mark McGwire of the St. Louis Cardinals and Cal Ripken Jr. of the Baltimore Orioles—retired following the 2001 season. Their names dot the record books with their many feats.

Gwynn, who holds many records for the Padres franchise, won eight National League batting titles and batted over .300 (minimum 50 games) for 17 consecutive years. He retires with the 17th-highest hit total (3,141) in major league history, his singles total of 2,378 is eighth best, and he ranks 17th all-time with 543 doubles.

McGwire, who became the first major league player to hit 70 home runs in a season, holds major league records for most home runs by a righthanded batter (70 with St. Louis in 1998) and most home runs by a rookie (49 with Oakland in 1987). He finished his career with the fifth-highest home run total (583) and his 67 multiple home run games is second only to Babe Ruth (72).

Ripken holds many Orioles franchise records and is best-remembered for breaking Lou Gehrig's consecutive-games streak of 2,130. Ripken finished his streak with 2,632 consecutive games played. In addition, the Orioles superstar ranks 13th on the all-time hit list (3,184), and his 431 home runs ranks 30th.

Following is a comparison of each player's major batting statistics:

Player, Team	Y	G	AB	R	H	2B	3B	HR	RBI	Avg.	BB	SO	SB
Tony Gwynn, Padres	20	2440	9288	1383	3141	543	85	135	1138	.338	790	434	319
Mark McGwire, A's, Cardinals	16	1874	6187	1167	1626	252	6	583	1414	.263	1317	1596	12
Cal Ripken Jr., Orioles	21	3001	11551	1647	3184	603	44	431	1695	.276	1129	1305	36

Mariners Win Major League Record-Tying 116 Games

The Seattle Mariners won a major league record-tying 116 games in 2001. The victory total matched the record set 95 years earlier by the Chicago Cubs, and broke the American League mark set by the Yankees in 1998. The chart below ranks all teams with 105 or more victories in the regular season and shows that a great regular-season win total doesn't necessarily guarantee success in the postseason.

Club	Year	W	L	Pct.	World Series performance
Chicago Cubs	1906	116	36	.763	Lost 4-2 to Chicago White Sox
Seattle Mariners	**2001**	**116**	**46**	**.716**	**Lost 4-1 to New York Yankees in Championship Series**
New York Yankees	1998	114	48	.704	Won 4-0 vs. San Diego Padres
Cleveland Indians	1954	111	43	.721	Lost 4-0 to New York Giants
Pittsburgh Pirates	1909	110	42	.724	Won 4-3 vs. Detroit Tigers
New York Yankees	1927	110	44	.714	Won 4-0 vs. Pittsburgh Pirates
New York Yankees	1961	109	53	.673	Won 4-1 vs. Cincinnati Reds
Baltimore Orioles	1969	109	53	.673	Lost 4-1 to New York Mets
Baltimore Orioles	1970	108	54	.667	Won 4-1 vs. Cincinnati Reds
Cincinnati Reds	1975	108	54	.667	Won 4-3 vs. Boston Red Sox
New York Mets	1986	108	54	.667	Won 4-3 vs. Boston Red Sox
Chicago Cubs	1907	107	45	.704	Won 4-0 vs. Detroit Tigers (one tie)
Philadelphia Athletics	1931	107	45	.704	Lost 4-3 to St. Louis Cardinals
New York Yankees	1932	107	47	.695	Won 4-0 vs. Chicago Cubs
New York Giants	1904	106	47	.693	No World Series played
New York Yankees	1939	106	45	.702	Won 4-0 vs. Cincinnati Reds
St. Louis Cardinals	1942	106	48	.688	Won 4-1 vs. New York Yankees
Atlanta Braves	1998	106	56	.654	Lost 4-2 to San Diego Padres in Championship Series
New York Giants	1905	105	48	.686	Won 4-1 vs. Philadelphia Athletics
Boston Red Sox	1912	105	47	.691	Won 4-3 vs. New York Giants (one tie)
St. Louis Cardinals	1943	105	49	.682	Lost 4-1 to New York Yankees
St. Louis Cardinals	1944	105	49	.682	Won 4-2 vs. St. Louis Browns
Brooklyn Dodgers	1953	105	49	.682	Lost 4-2 to New York Yankees

Bonds Closes in on 500-500 Power-Speed Milestone

With 567 home runs and 484 stolen bases, Barry Bonds is within 16 steals of becoming the first player to collect 500 career home runs and stolen bases. This is a remarkable achievement considering Bonds is the lone member of the 400-400 club and there are only three players—including Bonds' father Bobby and godfather Willie Mays—in the 300-300 club. Following are members of the 400-400, 300-300 and 250-250 clubs, and a list of current players with a chance to join the 250-250 club in 2002. Current players are listed in boldface and 2001 home run and stolen base totals are listed in parentheses.

400-400 CLUB

Player	Years	Games	HR	'01 HR	SB	'01 SB
Barry Bonds	16	2296	567	(73)	484	(13)

300-300 CLUB

Player	Years	Games	HR	'01 HR	SB	'01 SB
Willie Mays	22	2992	660		338	
Bobby Bonds	14	1849	332		461	
Andre Dawson	21	2627	438		314	

250-250 CLUB

Player	Years	Games	HR	'01 HR	SB	'01 SB
Don Baylor	19	2292	338		285	
Rickey Henderson	**23**	**2979**	**290**	**(8)**	**1395**	**(25)**
Ryne Sandberg	16	2164	282		344	
Eric Davis	**17**	**1626**	**282**	**(4)**	**349**	**(1)**
Joe Morgan	22	2649	268		689	
Vada Pinson	18	2469	256		305	
Kirk Gibson	17	1635	255		284	
Robin Yount	20	2856	251		271	

CLOSING IN ON 250-250 CLUB IN 2002

Player	Years	Games	HR	'01 HR	SB	'01 SB
Sammy Sosa	**13**	**1725**	**450**	**(64)**	**231**	**(0)**
Ron Gant	**14**	**1713**	**302**	**(10)**	**239**	**(5)**
Larry Walker	**13**	**1527**	**309**	**(38)**	**209**	**(14)**
Ray Lankford	**12**	**1528**	**226**	**(19)**	**254**	**(10)**
Brady Anderson	**14**	**1800**	**209**	**(8)**	**311**	**(12)**

Sosa Belts 60 Homers for Third Time

Chicago Cubs outfielder Sammy Sosa clubbed 64 home runs in 2001 to became the first player to hit 60 home runs in a season three times. Oddly, he has failed to lead the league in homers in any of his 60-homer seasons. Of the 34 instances when players have hit 50 or more home runs in a season, half of them have come in the last dozen years, while six of the eight 60-homer seasons have come in the last four seasons. Following are charts showing players with 60 and 50 or more home runs during a season. Names in bold are those occurring in 1990 or later.

60 OR MORE HOME RUNS

HR	Player, Club, League	Year
73	**Barry Bonds, San Francisco N.L.**	**2001**
70	**Mark McGwire, St. Louis N.L.**	**1998**
66	**Sammy Sosa, Chicago N.L.**	**1998**
65	**Mark McGwire, St. Louis N.L.**	**1999**
64	**Sammy Sosa, Chicago N.L.**	**2001**
63	**Sammy Sosa, Chicago N.L.**	**1999**
61	Roger Maris, New York A.L.	1961
60	Babe Ruth, New York A.L.	1927

50-59 HOME RUNS

HR	Player, Club, League	Year
59	Babe Ruth, New York A.L.	1921
58	Jimmie Foxx, Philadelphia A.L.	1932
58	Hank Greenberg, Detroit A.L.	1938
58	Mark McGwire, Oak. A.L. (34)-St.L. N.L. (24)	1997
57	**Luis Gonzalez, Arizona N.L.**	**2001**
56	Ken Griffey Jr., Seattle A.L.	1997

HR	Player, Club, League	Year
56	**Ken Griffey Jr., Seattle A.L.**	**1998**
56	Hack Wilson, Chicago N.L.	1930
54	Babe Ruth, New York A.L.	1920
54	Babe Ruth, New York A.L.	1928
54	Ralph Kiner, Pittsburgh N.L.	1949
54	Mickey Mantle, New York A.L.	1961
52	Mickey Mantle, New York A.L.	1956
52	Willie Mays, San Francisco N.L.	1965
52	George Foster, Cincinnati N.L.	1977
52	**Mark McGwire, Oakland A.L.**	**1996**
52	**Alex Rodriguez, Texas A.L.**	**2001**
51	Ralph Kiner, Pittsburgh N.L.	1947
51	Johnny Mize, New York N.L.	1947
51	Willie Mays, New York N.L.	1955
51	**Cecil Fielder, Detroit A.L.**	**1990**
50	Jimmie Foxx, Boston A.L.	1938
50	**Albert Belle, Cleveland A.L.**	**1995**
50	**Brady Anderson, Baltimore A.L.**	**1996**
50	**Greg Vaughn, San Diego N.L.**	**1998**
50	**Sammy Sosa, Chicago N.L.**	**2000**

Clemens Ties A.L. Record with 16 Straight Victories

Yankees pitcher Roger Clemens tied the American League record for most consecutive victories in a season with 16 in 2001. He became the fifth A.L. hurler to win 16 in a row, joining Walter Johnson (Washington, 1912), Joe Wood (Boston, 1912), Lefty Grove (Philadelphia, 1931) and Schoolboy Rowe (Detroit, 1934). Following is a chart of Clemens' 16 consecutive victories, showing the opponents, scores and his pitching line for each game.

Date	Opponent	Result	IP	H	R	ER	BB	SO
May 26	At Cleveland	Won, 12-5	7.0	8	5	5	2	8
June 2	Cleveland	Won, 9-4	6.0	9	4	4	3	6
June 7	Baltimore	Won, 4-0	8.0	3	0	0	2	10
June 13	Montreal N.L.	Won, 9-3	8.0	7	3	3	1	6
June 18	At Detroit	Won, 10-1	7.0	7	1	0	3	7
June 23	At Tampa Bay	Won, 2-1	6.0	5	1	1	3	8
June 29	Tampa Bay	Won, 7-5	6.2	8	4	3	0	8
July 4	At Baltimore	Won, 4-3	6.2	5	2	2	1	6
July 18	At Detroit	Won, 8-5	5.2	9	5	5	3	3
July 23	Toronto	Won, 7-2	6.2	7	2	2	1	8
July 28	At Toronto	Won, 12-1	5.2	1	0	0	3	8
Aug. 15	Tampa Bay	Won, 10-3	7.0	4	2	2	3	8
Aug. 25	At Anaheim	Won, 7-5	7.0	7	2	2	2	4
Aug. 31	At Boston	Won, 3-1	7.0	7	1	1	0	10
Sept. 5	At Toronto	Won, 4-3	7.1	6	2	2	4	5
Sept. 19	At Chicago A.L.	Won, 6-3	6.1	5	3	2	2	1

Rickey Henderson Continues to Add to His Records

Rickey Henderson continued his assault on the record books in 2001. Not only is he the all-time base-stealing champion, but Henderson has now scored more runs (2,248) and received more bases on balls (2,141) than any player in baseball history. Henderson, playing in his 23rd major league season, finished the season ninth on the all-time list with 2,979 games played and 12th in at-bats with 10,710. He also became the 25th player in major league history to collect 3,000 hits.

Henderson, of course, is most known for his base-stealing exploits. He set the all-time stolen base record ten years ago and continues to add to the total. He's now at 1,395. Henderson is also the career leader in caught stealing with 333.

In addition to his speed totals, Henderson added to his record total of leadoff home runs. He now has led off 79 games with a home run.

Brewers Teammates Club Three Home Runs in Same Game

Milwaukee Brewers teammates Jeromy Burnitz and Richie Sexson became the first pair of teammates to each hit three home runs in the same game on September 25. The unique feat occurred in a 9-4 Brewers victory at Arizona. Burnitz belted his homers in the second, fourth and sixth innings and Sexson hit his in the fourth, sixth and ninth innings. Their home runs accounted for all the homers in the game and the pair drove in eight of the nine Milwaukee runs.

To give more perspective to this achievement, consider that not only was this the first time teammates belted three homers in the same game, but never before had two opponents hit three home runs in the same game. The chart below shows the fastest, in terms of calendar days, any team has had a pair of three-homer players.

Year	Club	League	Days Elapsed	Date of First Occurrence	Player	Date of Second Occurrence	Player
2001	Milwaukee Brewers ..........N.L.		0	September 25	Jeromy Burnitz	September 25	Richie Sexson
1930	New York Yankees .............A.L.		1	May 21	Babe Ruth	May 22	Lou Gehrig
1998	Chicago Cubs....................N.L.		3	June 15	Sammy Sosa	June 18	Brant Brown
1986	Baltimore Orioles ..............A.L.		4	June 8	Lee Lacy	June 12	Juan Beniquez
1932	Philadelphia A's ................A.L.		5	July 10	Jimmie Foxx	July 15	Al Simmons
1950	Brooklyn Dodgers ..............N.L.		5	August 26	Roy Campanella	August 31	Gil Hodges
1950	New York Yankees ...........A.L.		5	September 10	Joe DiMaggio	September 15	Johnny Mize
1982	California Angels ..............A.L.		5	August 3	Doug DeCinces	August 8	Doug DeCinces

Brewers Strike Out More Than They Hit Safely in 2001

Milwaukee Brewers batters struck out 1,399 times in 2001, shattering the major league record of 1,268, set by the 1996 Detroit Tigers. Not only did they set a new club strikeout record, but the Brewers became the first team in major league history collect more strikeouts than hits. The Brewers gathered 1,378 hits, a total which was 21 fewer than their strikeout total. Only four other times in major league history has a club even come within 100 hits of equaling their strikeout total. Below are charts showing the clubs with the most strikeouts in history and a comparison of teams whose strikeouts most closely approached their hit totals.

TOP 15 SINGLE-SEASON STRIKEOUT TEAMS

Year	Club	League	B.A.	Hits	HR	Strikeouts	Hits Minus Strikeouts
2001	**Milwaukee Brewers** .............N.L.	....	**.251**	**1378**	**209**	**1399**	**-21**
2001	**San Diego Padres** ...................N.L.	....	**.252**	**1379**	**161**	**1273**	**106**
1996	Detroit Tigers ...................A.L.		.256	1413	204	1268	145
2000	St. Louis Cardinals .........N.L.		.270	1481	235	1253	228
2000	Milwaukee Brewers .........N.L.		.246	1366	177	1245	121
1998	Arizona Diamondbacks.............N.L.		.246	1353	159	1239	114
1998	Chicago Cubs...................N.L.		.264	1494	212	1223	271
1968	New York Mets.................N.L.		.228	1252	81	1203	49
1999	St. Louis Cardinals .........N.L.		.262	1461	194	1202	259
1999	Pittsburgh Pirates............N.L.		.259	1417	171	1197	220

CLUBS WHOSE STRIKEOUT TOTALS MOST CLOSELY APPROACHED THEIR HIT TOTALS

Year	Club	League	B.A.	Hits	HR	Strikeouts	Hits Minus Strikeouts
2001	**Milwaukee Brewers** ............N.L.	....	**.251**	**1378**	**209**	**1399**	**-21**
1968	New York Mets.................N.L.		.228	1252	81	1203	49
1969	San Diego Padres...............N.L.		.225	1203	99	1143	60
1965	New York Mets.................N.L.		.221	1202	107	1129	73
1963	New York Mets.................N.L.		.219	1168	96	1078	90
1965	Washington Senators.............A.L.		.228	1227	136	1125	102
2001	**San Diego Padres** ..................N.L.		**.252**	**1379**	**161**	**1273**	**106**
1998	Arizona Diamondbacks.............N.L.		.246	1353	159	1239	114
2000	Milwaukee Brewers .........N.L.		.246	1366	177	1245	121
1964	Washington Senators.............A.L.		.231	1246	125	1124	122

Padres Held Hitless Twice in 2001

The San Diego Padres tied a major league record in 2001 by being victimized by no-hitters twice, joining several clubs to have been no-hit twice in a season. Florida's A.J. Burnett held the Padres hitless at San Diego on May 12, and Bud Smith of St. Louis also held the team hitless in San Diego on September 3. Prior to the Padres' "feat," the last major league team to be held hitless twice in a season was the 1996 Colorado Rockies.

At the other end of the spectrum, the New York Yankees extended their major league record of not being held hitless in a game to 43 consecutive years. The last time they were victims of a no-hit game of nine or more innings was September 20, 1958, when Hoyt Wilhelm of the Baltimore Orioles held them hitless.

Moving from a hitting to a pitching perspective, the New York Mets staff in 2001 continued its streak of never pitching a no-hit game. The Mets have now been in existence for 40 years and have yet to hold another team hitless. The team has not been around long enough yet to challenge the major league record for most years without holding a team hitless. The Philadelphia Phillies went from 1907 through 1963—57 years—without pitching a no-hit game.

Raines Duo Becomes Second Father-Son Playing Teammates

Tim Raines Sr. and Tim Raines Jr. became only the second father-son duo to play together in the major leagues when they played for the Baltimore Orioles versus Toronto on October 3. Tim Jr. played center field and went 2-for-4 for the Orioles, while his father Tim Sr. went 0-for-1 with a sacrifice fly as a pinch-hitter and designated hitter for Baltimore. It marked the first time since the Griffeys—Ken Sr. and Ken Jr.—played as teammates for the Seattle Mariners in 1990 and 1991. The Griffey's last appeared in the same game on May 31, 1991, at Texas, with Ken Sr. starting in left field and going 0-for-3, and Ken Jr. starting in center field and going 0-for-2.

Tim Sr. and Tim Jr. played in four games together, but failed to hit safely in the same game on any of the four occasions. The Griffeys hit safely in the same game a number of times, doing so for the last time on May 28, 1991 in a game against Kansas City. In that game, Ken Sr. collected a pinch single and Ken Jr. started in center field and hit a single and double.

Burks, McGriff & McGwire Homer in Most Ballparks

Three players in 2001—Ellis Burks of the Cleveland Indians, Fred McGriff of the Tampa Bay Devil Rays and Chicago Cubs, and Mark McGwire of the St. Louis Cardinals—increased their total of different major league ballparks in which they homered, tying them for the major league record with 39.

Each player has homered in all but four of the 43 most recent traditional stadiums in use. All three have homered in each of the following 34 parks:

Edison International Field of Anaheim
Memorial Stadium, Baltimore
Oriole Park at Camden Yards, Baltimore
Fenway Park, Boston
Old Comiskey Park, Chicago
New Comiskey Park, Chicago
Municipal Stadium, Cleveland
Jacobs Field, Cleveland
Tiger Stadium, Detroit
Comerica Park, Detroit
Kauffman Stadium, Kansas City
Humphrey Metrodome, Minnesota

Yankee Stadium, New York
Network Associates Coliseum, Oakland
Kingdome, Seattle
Arlington Stadium, Texas
Exhibition Stadium, Toronto
SkyDome, Toronto
Turner Field, Atlanta
Wrigley Field, Chicago
Cinergy Field, Cincinnati
Coors Field, Colorado
Pro Player Stadium, Florida
Astrodome, Houston

Enron Field, Houston
Dodger Stadium, Los Angeles
County Stadium, Milwaukee
Olympic Stadium, Montreal
Shea Stadium, New York
Veterans Stadium, Philadelphia
Three Rivers Stadium, Pittsburgh
Busch Stadium, St. Louis
Qualcomm Stadium, San Diego
3Com Park, San Francisco

In addition, each player has homered in five of the following stadiums:

Ballpark	When opened or closed	Ellis Burks	Fred McGriff	Mark McGwire
Safeco Field, Seattle	July, 1999	No	Yes	No
Tropicana Field, Tampa Bay	1998	Yes	Yes	No
The Ballpark in Arlington, Texas	1994	No	Yes	Yes
Bank One Ballpark, Arizona	1998	Yes	No	Yes
Fulton County Stadium, Atlanta	Closed following 1996 season	Yes	Yes	No
Mile High Stadium, Colorado	Closed following 1994 season	Yes	Yes	No
Miller Park, Milwaukee	2001	No	No	Yes
PNC Park, Pittsburgh	2001	No	No	Yes
Pacific Bell Park, San Francisco	2000	Yes	No	Yes

These Players Homered in Non-Traditional Stadiums

While three players have homered in as many as 39 major league ballparks, some players can boast they've homered in ballparks that even Ellis Burks, Fred McGriff and Mark McGwire have not hit them in. Over the past six years, major league games have been played in such locations as Las Vegas; Monterrey, Mexico; Honolulu; Tokyo, Japan and San Juan, Puerto Rico. And some major leaguers have hit as many as three homers in these non-traditional stadiums used by the major leagues.

Following is the list of non-traditional stadiums used for major league games in the past six years, followed by a list of players who have homered in these parks:

Ballpark, City	Games	Year	Homers	Homers by players
Cashman Field, Las Vegas	6	1996	23	Oakland (10)—Scott Brosius 3, Geronimo Berroa 2, Phil Plantier 2, Terry Steinbach 2, Matt Stairs. Detroit (8)—Bobby Higginson 3, Travis Fryman 2, Chad Curtis, Cecil Fielder, Melvin Nieves. Toronto (5)—Domingo Cedeno, Carlos Delgado, Alex Gonzalez, John Olerud, Ed Sprague.
Monterrey Stadium, Mexico	3	1996	9	San Diego (8)—Ken Caminiti 3, Steve Finley, John Flaherty, Joey Hamilton, Brian Johnson, Greg Vaughn. New York N.L. (1)—Andy Tomberlin.
Aloha Stadium, Hawaii	3	1997	1	St. Louis (1)—Ron Gant.
Tokyo Dome, Japan	2	2000	4	Chicago N.L. (2)—Shane Andrews, Mark Grace. New York N.L. (2)—Benny Agbayani, Mike Piazza.
Hiram Bithorn Stadium, San Juan, P.R.	1	2001	2	Toronto (2)—Tony Batista, Shannon Stewart.

Olerud Becomes Second Player to Hit for Cycle for A.L. & N.L.

Seattle Mariners first baseman John Olerud in 2001 joined Bob Watson as the only players in major league history to hit for the cycle in both the American and National leagues. After hitting for the cycle as a member of the New York Mets against Montreal on September 11, 1997, Olerud hit for the cycle for the Mariners against San Diego on June 16, 2001.

Watson had performed the feat for the Houston Astros of the National League in 1977 and the Boston Red Sox of the American League in 1979.

Prior to Olerud, the last player to twice hit for the cycle was George Brett of the Kansas City Royals, who performed the feat in 1979 and 1990. The 1979 game lasted 16 innings. The last player to twice hit for the cycle in nine-inning games was Chris Speier, who performed the feat for the Montreal Expos in 1978 and the San Francisco Giants in 1988.

Cy Young Winners Clemens & Johnson Continue Strikeout Feats

Roger Clemens climbed the strikeout ladder in 2001, settling into third place with an American League record 3,717. The Yankees fireballer struck out 213 during the season, giving him an American League-record 11 years with 200 or more strikeouts, and extending his A.L. record to 16 consecutive years with 100 or more whiffs. Clemens passed Walter Johnson (3,508) early in the season to earn the league record and now trails only Nolan Ryan (5,714) and Steve Carlton (4,136) in career strikeouts. In addition, Clemens compiled a 20-3 record and 3.51 ERA in earning an unprecedented sixth Cy Young Award.

Leaping from 12th to ninth place on the all-time strikeout list, Arizona's Randy Johnson struck out 372 batters in 2001. Johnson tied Amos Rusie and Sandy Koufax with his third career 300-whiff season. Johnson also tied a National League record by striking out 20 batters in a game on May 8 when he pitched the first nine innings of an 11-inning game against the Cincinnati Reds. Two months after his 20-strikeout performance, the Diamondbacks lefthander made his only relief appearance of the season and set a major league record by striking out 16 San Diego Padres over the last seven innings of a nine-inning game. Curt Schilling started the game on July 18, but the contest was suspended in the top of the third when two electrical explosions knocked out the lights in left field. Johnson entered the game the next day when it was resumed and completed the game with his record-breaking performance.

In collecing 372 strikeouts during the season—11 short of Nolan Ryan's (California, 1973) modern major league mark—Johnson struck out 10 or more batters in a game 23 times, tying a big league record he shared with Ryan (1973). Johnson has collected 23 10-strikeout games in each of the last three seasons. Johnson's feats, along with his 21-6 record and league-leading 2.49 ERA, earned him his third straight Cy Young Award and the fourth of his career.

Dawson, Smith & Trammell Are Leading Candidates for 2002 Hall of Fame

Three candidates are expected to lead the balloting in the 2002 Hall of Fame voting. Andre Dawson, an outfielder who played the majority of his career with the Montreal Expos and Chicago Cubs; Ozzie Smith, a shortstop for the San Diego Padres and St. Louis Cardinals; and Alan Trammell, a shortstop who spent his entire 20-year career with the Detroit Tigers, lead the list of players who became eligible for the 2002 election by the Baseball Writers' Association of America. This edition of the Complete Baseball Record Book will be published before the winners of the election are announced.

Following is a list of players who become eligible for the Hall of Fame for the first time in the next five years. These are not complete lists, but include the players expected to be the leading first-time eligible candidates for those years. Any player trying to make a comeback will move back his time of first-year eligibility.

2002 LEADING CANDIDATES

Batter (M.L. seasons)	G	AB	R	H	2B	3B	HR	RBI	Avg.	BB	SO	SB	PO	A	E	Avg.
Andre Dawson (21)	2627	9927	1373	2774	503	98	438	1591	.279	589	1509	314	5158	157	93	.983
Ozzie Smith (19)	2573	9396	1257	2460	402	69	28	793	.262	1072	589	580	4249	8375	281	.978
Alan Trammell (20)	2293	8288	1231	2365	412	55	185	1003	.285	850	874	236	3448	6265	235	.976

2003 LEADING CANDIDATES

Pitcher (M.L. seasons)	W	L	Pct.	ERA	G	GS	CG	ShO	Sv.	IP	H	R	ER	BB	SO
Lee Smith (16)	68	87	.439	2.95	943	6	0	0	471	1213.0	1048	435	397	452	1195
Fernando Valenzuela (15)	158	133	.543	3.49	402	375	112	31	2	2669.1	2435	1164	1036	1038	1918

Batter (M.L. seasons)	G	AB	R	H	2B	3B	HR	RBI	Avg.	BB	SO	SB	PO	A	E	Avg.
Eddie Murray (21)	3026	11336	1627	3255	560	35	504	1917	.287	1333	1516	110	21372	1874	169	.993
Ryne Sandberg (16)	2164	8385	1318	2386	403	76	282	1061	.285	761	1260	344	3893	6648	120	.989

2004 LEADING CANDIDATES

Pitcher (M.L. seasons)	W	L	Pct.	ERA	G	GS	CG	ShO	Sv.	IP	H	R	ER	BB	SO
Dennis Eckersley (24)	197	171	.535	3.50	1071	361	100	20	390	3285.2	3076	1382	1278	738	2401
Jimmy Key (15)	186	117	.614	3.51	470	389	34	13	10	2591.2	2518	1104	1010	668	1538
Dennis Martinez (23)	245	193	.559	3.70	692	562	122	30	8	4000.0	3897	1835	1643	1165	2149
Bob Tewksbury (13)	110	102	.519	3.92	302	277	31	7	1	1806.2	2043	884	787	292	812

Batter (M.L. seasons)	G	AB	R	H	2B	3B	HR	RBI	Avg.	BB	SO	SB	PO	A	E	Avg.
Joe Carter (16)	2189	8422	1170	2184	432	53	396	1445	.259	527	1387	231	5890	281	118	.981
Paul Molitor (21)	2683	10835	1782	3319	605	114	234	1307	.306	1094	1244	504	3506	3241	208	.970
Tom Pagnozzi (12)	927	2896	247	733	153	11	44	320	.253	189	450	18	4382	407	38	.992
Terry Pendleton (15)	1893	7032	851	1897	356	39	140	946	.270	486	979	127	1386	3889	238	.957
Juan Samuel (16)	1720	6081	873	1578	287	102	161	703	.259	440	1442	396	3572	3287	188	.973

2005 LEADING CANDIDATES

Pitcher (M.L. seasons)	W	L	Pct.	ERA	G	GS	CG	ShO	Sv.	IP	H	R	ER	BB	SO
Tom Candiotti (16)	151	164	.479	3.73	451	410	68	11	0	2725.0	2662	1299	1130	883	1735
Mark Langston (16)	179	158	.531	3.97	457	428	81	18	0	2962.2	2723	1438	1306	1289	2464
Jeff Montgomery (13)	46	52	.469	3.27	700	1	0	0	304	868.2	785	347	316	296	733

Batter (M.L. seasons)	G	AB	R	H	2B	3B	HR	RBI	Avg.	BB	SO	SB	PO	A	E	Avg.
Wade Boggs (18)	2440	9180	1513	3010	578	61	118	1014	.328	1412	745	24	2115	4304	232	.965
Chili Davis (19)	2436	8673	1240	2380	424	30	350	1372	.274	1194	1698	142	2566	77	80	.971
Jeff King (11)	1201	4262	600	1091	222	18	154	709	.256	442	584	75	4604	1841	107	.984
Willie McGee (18)	2201	7649	1010	2254	350	94	79	856	.295	448	1238	352	4294	136	108	.976
Terry Steinbach (14)	1546	5369	638	1453	273	21	162	745	.271	418	938	23	7849	651	100	.988

2006 LEADING CANDIDATES

Pitcher (M.L. seasons)	W	L	Pct.	ERA	G	GS	CG	ShO	Sv.	IP	H	R	ER	BB	SO
Orel Hershiser (18)	204	150	.576	3.48	510	466	68	25	5	3130.1	2939	1366	1211	1007	2014

Batter (M.L. seasons)	G	AB	R	H	2B	3B	HR	RBI	Avg.	BB	SO	SB	PO	A	E	Avg.
Albert Belle (12)	1539	5853	974	1726	389	21	381	1239	.295	683	961	88	2642	91	66	.976
Will Clark (15)	1976	7173	1186	2176	440	47	284	1205	.303	937	1190	67	16695	1294	136	.992
Gary Gaetti (20)	2507	8951	1130	2280	443	39	360	1341	.255	634	1602	96	2607	4624	237	.968

Major Leagues Witness Five Years of Interleague Play

Major League Baseball completed its fifth season of interleague play in 2001. National League teams hold a 597-595 edge in games played against the American League. Following are team-vs.-team interleague records from 1997 through 2001:

AMERICAN LEAGUE

A.L. team vs.	Ari.	Atl.	Chi.	Cin.	Col.	Fla.	Hou.	L.A.	Mil.	Mon.	N.Y.	Phi.	Pit.	St.L.	S.D.	S.F.	W	L	Pct.
Oakland	9-3	—	—	—	9-7	—	—	9-7	—	—	—	—	—	—	11-5	12-14	50	36	.581
New York	—	8-8	—	—	—	8-6	—	—	—	9-6	15-9	8-7	—	—	—	—	48	36	.571
Chicago	—	—	13-11	9-2	—	—	7-5	—	8-4	—	—	—	6-5	5-10	—	—	48	37	.565
Cleveland	—	—	6-2	13-11	—	—	7-8	—	7-5	—	—	—	7-8	8-3	—	—	48	37	.565
Milwaukee*	—	—	1-2	0-3	—	—	2-1	—	—	—	—	—	2-1	3-0	—	—	8	7	.533
Seattle	7-5	—	—	—	10-6	—	—	8-8	—	—	—	—	—	—	12-14	7-9	44	42	.512
Detroit	1-2	2-1	5-3	6-6	—	1-2	2-7	—	6-6	0-3	3-0	2-1	7-5	8-6	—	—	43	42	.506
Texas	10-6	—	—	—	8-8	—	3-3	7-9	—	—	—	—	—	—	8-8	7-9	43	43	.500
Anaheim	5-7	—	—	—	12-4	—	—	13-13	—	—	—	—	—	—	7-9	5-11	42	44	.488
Minnesota	—	—	5-10	8-7	—	—	8-6	—	5-5	—	—	—	8-7	6-9	—	—	40	44	.476
Boston	—	9-15	—	—	—	9-6	—	—	—	8-7	7-8	7-9	—	—	—	—	40	45	.471
Toronto	—	9-6	—	—	—	4-11	—	—	—	16-9	3-12	7-8	—	—	—	—	39	46	.459
Baltimore	—	8-7	—	—	—	4-11	—	—	—	6-9	5-11	14-10	—	—	—	—	37	48	.435
Kansas City	1-2	—	6-9	3-5	—	4-11	—	5-7	—	—	—	—	9-8	9-6	—	—	37	48	.435
Tampa Bay	—	3-9	—	—	—	7-15	—	—	—	5-7	5-7	8-4	—	—	—	—	28	42	.400
Totals	33-25	39-46	36-37	39-34	39-25	33-51	33-41	37-37	31-27	44-41	38-47	46-39	39-34	39-34	38-36	31-43	595	597	.499

*Milwaukee was an American League club in 1997.

NATIONAL LEAGUE

N.L. team vs.	Ana.	Bal.	Bos.	Chi.	Cle.	Det.	K.C.	Mil.*	Min.	N.Y.	Oak.	Sea.	T.B.	Tex.	Tor.	W	L	Pct.
Florida	—	11-4	6-9	—	—	2-1	—	—	—	6-8	—	—	15-7	—	11-4	51	33	.607
San Francisco	11-5	—	—	—	—	—	—	—	—	—	14-12	9-7	—	9-7	—	43	31	.581
Houston	—	—	5-7	8-7	7-2	11-4	1-2	6-8	—	—	—	—	3-3	—	—	41	33	.554
New York	—	11-5	8-7	—	—	0-3	—	—	—	9-15	—	—	7-5	—	12-3	47	38	.553
Atlanta	—	7-8	15-9	—	—	1-2	—	—	—	8-8	—	—	9-3	—	6-9	46	39	.541
Chicago	—	—	—	11-13	2-6	3-5	9-6	2-1	10-5	—	—	—	—	—	—	37	36	.507
Los Angeles	13-13	—	—	—	—	—	—	—	—	—	7-9	8-8	—	9-7	—	37	37	.500
San Diego	9-7	—	—	—	—	—	—	—	—	—	5-11	14-12	—	8-8	—	36	38	.486
Montreal	—	9-6	7-8	—	—	3-0	—	—	—	6-9	—	—	7-5	—	9-16	41	44	.482
St. Louis	—	—	—	10-5	3-8	6-8	6-9	0-3	9-6	—	—	—	—	—	—	34	39	.466
Pittsburgh	—	—	—	5-6	8-7	5-7	8-9	1-2	7-8	—	—	—	—	—	—	34	39	.466
Cincinnati	—	—	—	2-9	11-13	6-6	5-3	3-0	7-8	—	—	—	—	—	—	34	39	.466
Milwaukee	—	—	—	4-8	5-7	6-6	7-5	—	5-5	—	—	—	—	—	—	27	31	.466
Philadelphia	—	10-14	9-7	—	—	1-2	—	—	—	7-8	—	—	4-8	—	8-7	39	46	.459
Arizona	7-5	—	—	—	—	2-1	2-1	—	—	—	3-9	5-7	—	6-10	—	25	33	.431
Colorado	4-12	—	—	—	—	—	—	—	—	—	7-9	6-10	—	8-8	—	25	39	.391
Totals	44-42	48-37	45-40	37-48	37-48	42-43	48-37	7-8	44-40	36-48	36-50	42-44	42-28	43-43	46-39	597	595	.501

*Milwaukee was an American League club in 1997; Brewers have a total interleague record of 35-38, .479.

REGULAR SEASON

Service (Individual, Club, League)

Batting (Individual, Club, League)

Baserunning (Individual, Club, League)

Pitching (Individual, Club, League)

Fielding (Individual, Club, League)

Miscellaneous (Individual, Club, League)

Non-Playing Personnel

Yearly Leaders

Career Milestones

General Reference

American League Team Records

National League Team Records

INDIVIDUAL SERVICE

ALL PLAYERS
YEARS

Most years played

M.L.—27—Nolan Ryan, New York N.L., California A.L., Houston N.L., Texas A.L.; 1966 through 1993, except 1967 (14 in N.L., 13 in A.L.), 807 games.

A.L.—25—Eddie Collins, Philadelphia, Chicago, 1906 through 1930, 2,826 games.

N.L.—24—Pete Rose, Cincinnati, Philadelphia, Montreal, 1963 through 1986, 3,562 games.

For complete lists of 20-year players and pitchers, see page 170.

Most consecutive years played

M.L.—26—Nolan Ryan, New York N.L., California A.L., Houston N.L., Texas A.L.; 1968 through 1993 (13 in N.L., 13 in A.L.), 805 games.

A.L.—25—Eddie Collins, Philadelphia, Chicago, 1906 through 1930, 2,826 games.

N.L.—24—Pete Rose, Cincinnati, Philadelphia, Montreal, 1963 through 1986, 3,562 games.

Most years with one club

A.L.—23

Brooks Robinson, Baltimore, 1955 through 1977, 2,896 games.

Carl Yastrzemski, Boston, 1961 through 1983, 3,308 games.

N.L.—22

Cap Anson, Chicago, 1876 through 1897, 2,253 games.

Mel Ott, New York, 1926 through 1947, 2,730 games.

Stan Musial, St. Louis, 1941 through 1963, except 1945 in military service, 3,026 games.

Most consecutive years with one club

A.L.—23

Brooks Robinson, Baltimore, 1955 through 1977, 2,896 games.

Carl Yastrzemski, Boston, 1961 through 1983, 3,308 games.

N.L.—22

Cap Anson, Chicago, 1876 through 1897, 2,253 games.

Mel Ott, New York, 1926 through 1947, 2,730 games.

(Military service in 1945 interrupted a 22-year streak by Stan Musial, who played for St. Louis from 1941 through 1963, 3,026 games.)

BY POSITION (EXCEPT PITCHERS)

Most years by first baseman

N.L.—22—Willie McCovey, San Francisco, San Diego, 1959 through 1980, 2,045 games.

A.L.—20—Joe Judge, Washington, Boston, 1915 through 1934, 2,084 games.

Most years by second baseman

M.L.—22—Joe Morgan, Houston N.L., Cincinnati N.L., San Francisco N.L., Philadelphia N.L., Oakland A.L., 1963 through 1984, 2,527 games.

A.L.—21—Eddie Collins, Philadelphia, Chicago, 1908 through 1928, 2,651 games.

N.L.—21—Joe Morgan, Houston, Cincinnati, San Francisco, Philadelphia, 1963 through 1983, 2,427 games.

Most years by third baseman

A.L.—23—Brooks Robinson, Baltimore, 1955 through 1977, 2,870 games.

N.L.—18—Mike Schmidt, Philadelphia, 1972 through 1989, 2,212 games.

Most years by shortstop

M.L.—20

Bill Dahlen, Chicago N.L., Brooklyn N.L., New York N.L., Boston N.L., 1891 through 1911, except 1910, 2,139 games.

Bobby Wallace, St. Louis N.L., St. Louis A.L., 1899 through 1918, 1,828 games.

Luke Appling, Chicago A.L., 1930 through 1950, except 1944 in military service, 2,218 games.

Alan Trammell, Detroit, 1977 through 1996, 2,139 games.

A.L.—20

Luke Appling, Chicago, 1930 through 1950, except 1944 in military service, 2,219 games.

Alan Trammell, Detroit, 1977 through 1996, 2,139 games.

N.L.—20—Bill Dahlen, Chicago, Brooklyn, New York, Boston, 1891 through 1911, except 1910, 2,139 games.

N.L. since 1900—19

Rabbit Maranville, Boston, Pittsburgh, Chicago, Brooklyn, St. Louis, 1912 through 1931, except 1924, 2,153 games.

Dave Concepcion, Cincinnati, 1970 through 1988, 2,178 games.

Chris Speier, San Francisco, Montreal, St. Louis, Chicago, 1971 through 1989, 1,888 games.

Ozzie Smith, San Diego, St. Louis, 1978 through 1996, 2,511 games.

Most years by outfielder

A.L.—24—Ty Cobb, Detroit, Philadelphia, 1905 through 1928, 2,938 games.

N.L.—22—Willie Mays, New York Giants, San Francisco, New York Mets, 1951 through 1973, except 1953 in military service, 2,843 games.

Most years by catcher

M.L.—25—Deacon McGuire, Toledo, Cleveland, Rochester, Washington A.A.; Detroit, Philadelphia, Washington, Brooklyn N.L.; Detroit, New York, Boston, Cleveland A.L., 1884 through 1912, except 1889, 1908, 1909, 1911, 1,608 games.

A.L.—24—Carlton Fisk, Boston, Chicago, 1969 through 1993, except 1970, 2,226 games.

N.L.—21—Bob O'Farrell, Chicago, St. Louis, New York, Cincinnati, 1915 through 1935, 1,338 games.

YOUNGEST AND OLDEST PLAYERS

Youngest player, game

N.L.—15 years, 10 months, 11 days—Joe Nuxhall, Cincinnati, June 10, 1944 (pitcher).

A.L.—16 years, 8 months, 5 days—Carl Scheib, Philadelphia, September 6, 1943, second game (pitcher).

Oldest player, game

A.L.—59 years, 2 months, 18 days—Satchel Paige, Kansas City, September 25, 1965 (pitcher).

N.L.—52 years, 29 days—Jim O'Rourke, New York, September 22, 1904 (catcher).

LEAGUES AND CLUBS

Most leagues played for, career

4— Held by 20 players. Last time—Lave Cross, A.A., P.L., N.L., A.L., 1887 through 1907, 21 years, 2,259 games.

Most leagues played for, season

3— Willie Murphy, 1884, N.L., A.A., U.A.
Walter Prince, 1884, N.L., A.A., U.A.
George Strief, 1884, A.A., U.A., N.L.

Most clubs played for, career

M.L.—12

Deacon McGuire, Toledo, Cleveland, Rochester, Washington, A.A.; Detroit, Philadelphia, Washington, Brooklyn N.L.; Detroit, New York, Boston, Cleveland A.L.; 1884 to 1912, except 1889, 1909, 1911.

Mike Morgan, Oakland A.L., New York A.L., Toronto A.L., Seattle A.L., Baltimore A.L., Los Angeles N.L., Chicago N.L., St. Louis N.L., Cincinnati N.L., Minnesota A.L., Texas A.L., Arizona N.L., 1978 through 2001, except 1980, 1981 and 1984, 21 years.

N.L.—9—Dan Brouthers, Troy, Buffalo, Detroit, Boston, Brooklyn, Baltimore, Louisville, Philadelphia, New York, 1879 through 1889, 1892 through 1896, 1904, 17 years.

N.L. since 1899—7

Jack Barry, Washington, Boston, Philadelphia, Chicago, Cincinnati, St. Louis, New York, 1899 through 1908, 10 years.

Joe Schultz Sr., Boston, Brooklyn, Chicago, Pittsburgh, St. Louis, Philadelphia, Cincinnati, 1912 through 1925, except 1914, 1917 and 1918, 11 years.

Frank J. Thomas, Pittsburgh, Cincinnati, Chicago, Milwaukee, New York, Philadelphia, Houston, 1951 through 1966, 16 years.

A.L.—8—Juan Beniquez, Boston, Texas, New York, Seattle, California, Baltimore, Kansas City, Toronto, 1971 through 1988, except 1973, 17 years.

Most clubs played for, season

M.L.—4—Held by many players. Last player—Dave Martinez, Tampa Bay A.L., Chicago N.L., Texas A.L., Toronto A.L., 132 games, 2000.

N.L.—4—Tom Dowse, Louisville, Cincinnati, Philadelphia, Washington, 63 games, 1892.

A.L.—4

Frank Huelsman, Chicago, Detroit, St. Louis, Washington, 112 games, 1904.

Paul Lehner, Philadelphia, Chicago, St. Louis, Cleveland, 65 games, 1951.

Ted Gray, Chicago, Cleveland, New York, Baltimore, 14 games, 1955.

Most clubs played for, one day

N.L.—2

Max Flack, Chicago, St. Louis, May 30 a.m., p.m., 1922.

Cliff Heathcote, St. Louis, Chicago, May 30 a.m., p.m., 1922.

Joel Youngblood, New York, Montreal, August 4, 1982.

POSITIONS

Most positions played, season

N.L.—9

Sport McAllister, Cleveland, 110 games, 1899.

Jimmy M.T. Walsh, Philadelphia, 84 games, 1911.

Gene Paulette, St. Louis, 125 games, 1918.

Jose Oquendo, St. Louis, 148 games, 1988.

A.L.—9

Sam Mertes, Chicago, 129 games, 1902.

Jack Rothrock, Boston, 117 games, 1928.

Bert Campaneris, Kansas City, 144 games, 1965.

Cesar Tovar, Minnesota, 157 games, 1968.

Scott Sheldon, Texas, 58 games, 2000.

Shane Halter, Detroit, 105 games, 2000.

Most positions played, game

A.L.—9

Bert Campaneris, Kansas City, September 8, 1965; played 8.2 innings of 13-inning game.

Cesar Tovar, Minnesota, September 22, 1968.

Scott Sheldon, Texas, September 6, 2000; played six innings of nine-inning game.

Shane Halter, Detroit, October 1, 2000.

PITCHERS
YEARS

Most years pitched

M.L.—27—Nolan Ryan, New York N.L., California A.L., Houston N.L., Texas A.L., 1966 through 1993, except 1967, 807 games.

A.L.—23—Early Wynn, Washington, Cleveland, Chicago, 1939, 1941 through 1963, except 1945, in military service, 691 games.

N.L.—22—Steve Carlton, St. Louis, Philadelphia, San Francisco, 1965 through 1986, 695 games.

For a complete list of 20-year pitchers, see page 170.

Most consecutive years pitched

M.L.—26—Nolan Ryan, New York N.L., California A.L., Houston N.L., Texas A.L., 1968 through 1993.

A.L.—22

Samuel P. Jones, Cleveland, Boston, New York, St. Louis, Washington, Chicago, 1914 through 1935.

(Military service in 1918 interrupted a 22-year streak by Herb Pennock, who pitched for Philadelphia, Boston and New York from 1912 through 1934; military service in 1945 interrupted a 22-year streak by Early Wynn, who pitched for Washington, Cleveland and Chicago from 1941 through

1963; military service in 1943 and 1944 interrupted a 22-year streak by Red Ruffing, who pitched for Boston, New York and Chicago from 1924 through 1947.)

N.L.—22—Steve Carlton, St. Louis, Philadelphia, San Francisco, 1965 through 1986.

Most years pitched with one club

A.L.—21

Walter Johnson, Washington, 1907 through 1927, 802 games.

Ted Lyons, Chicago, 1923 through 1946, except 1943,1944, 1945, in military service, 594 games.

N.L.—21—Phil Niekro, Milwaukee, Atlanta, 1964 through 1983, 1987, 740 games.

Most consecutive years pitched with one club

A.L.—21

Walter Johnson, Washington, 1907 through 1927, 802 games. (Military service from 1943 through 1945 interrupted a 21-year streak by Ted Lyons, who pitched for Chicago from 1923 through 1946, 594 games.)

N.L.—20

Phil Niekro, Milwaukee, Atlanta, 1964 through 1983, 739 games. (Military service from 1943 through 1945 interrupted a 20-year streak for Warren Spahn, who pitched for Boston and Milwaukee from 1942 through 1964, 714 games.)

YOUNGEST AND OLDEST PITCHERS

Youngest pitcher, game

N.L.—15 years, 10 months, 11 days—Joe Nuxhall, Cincinnati, June 10, 1944.

A.L.—16 years, 8 months, 5 days—Carl Scheib, Philadelphia, September 6, 1943, second game.

Oldest pitcher, game

A.L.—59 years, 2 months, 18 days—Satchel Paige, Kansas City, September 25, 1965.

N.L.—50 years, 2 days—Jack Quinn, Cincinnati, July 7, 1933.

LEAGUES AND CLUBS

Most leagues pitched in

4— Jersey Bakely, A.A., U.A., N.L., P.L.

Ed Crane, U.A., N.L., P.L., A.A.

Frank Foreman, U.A., A.A., N.L., A.L.

Con Murphy, U.A., N.L., P.L., A.A.

Most clubs pitched on

M.L.—12—Mike Morgan, Oakland A.L., New York A.L., Toronto A.L., Seattle A.L., Baltimore A.L., Los Angeles N.L., Chicago N.L., St. Louis N.L., Cincinnati N.L., Minnesota A.L., Texas A.L., Arizona N.L., 1978 through 2001, except 1980, 1981 and 1984, 21 years, 568 games.

A.L.—7

Ken Sanders, Kansas City No. 1, 1964, Boston, Kansas City No. 1, 1966, Oakland, 1968, Milwaukee 1970, 1971, 1972, Minnesota, 1973, Cleveland, 1973, 1974, California, 1974, Kansas City No. 2, 1976, 9 years, 348 games. (Note: Oakland considered part of Kansas City No. 1 franchise and is not considered as separate club).

Ken Brett, Boston, Milwaukee, New York, Chicago, California, Minnesota, Kansas City, 1967, 1969 through 1972, 1976 through 1981, 11 years, 238 games.

Mike Morgan, Oakland, New York, Toronto, Seattle, Baltimore, Minnesota, Texas, 1978, 1979, 1982, 1983, 1985 through 1988, 1998, 1999, 10 years, 209 games.

N.L.—7—Mike Maddux, Philadelphia, Los Angeles, San Diego, New York, Pittsburgh, Montreal, Houston, 1986 through 1995, 1998 through 2000, 13 years, 407 games.

Most clubs pitched on, season

M.L.—4

Willis Hudlin, Cleveland A.L., Washington A.L., St. Louis A.L., New York N.L., 19 games, 1940.

Ted Gray, Chicago A.L., Cleveland A.L., New York A.L., Baltimore A.L., 14 games, 1955.

Mike Kilkenny, Detroit A.L., Oakland A.L., San Diego N.L., Cleveland A.L., 29 games, 1972.

A.L.—4—Ted Gray, Chicago, Cleveland, New York, Baltimore, 14 games, 1955.

N.L.—3—Held by many pitchers. Last pitcher—Willie Banks, Chicago, Los Angeles, Florida, 25 games, 1995.

CLUB SERVICE

PLAYERS USED

Most players used, season
A.L.—56—Philadelphia, 1915.
N.L.—56—San Diego, 2000.

Fewest players used, season
A.L.—18—Boston, 1904.
N.L. —20—Chicago, 1905.

Most players used, nine-inning game
A.L.—27—Kansas City vs. California, September 10, 1969.
N.L.—25
St. Louis vs. Los Angeles, April 16, 1959.
Milwaukee vs. Philadelphia, September 26, 1964.
Philadelphia vs. Chicago, September 27, 1981, second game.

Most players used, extra-inning game
A.L.—30—Oakland vs. Chicago, September 19, 1972, 15 innings.
N.L.—27
Philadelphia vs. St. Louis, September 13, 1974, 17 innings.
Chicago vs. Pittsburgh, September 21, 1978, 14 innings.
Chicago vs. Houston, September 2, finished September 3, 1986, 18 innings.
Los Angeles vs. San Francisco, September 28, 1986, 16 innings.

Most players used by both clubs, nine-inning game
N.L.—45—Chicago 24, Montreal 21, September 5, 1978.
A.L.—42
Oakland 24, Kansas City 18, September 20, 1975.
Boston 24, Detroit 18, September 15, 2000.
Detroit 23, Minnesota 19, October 1, 2000.

Most players used by both clubs, extra-inning game
A.L.—54—Seattle 29, Texas 25, September 25, 1992, 16 innings.
N.L.—53—Chicago 27, Houston 26, September 2, finished September 3, 1986, 18 innings.

Most players used, doubleheader (18 innings)
A.L.—41—Chicago vs. Oakland, September 7, 1970.
N.L.—41—San Diego vs. San Francisco, May 30, 1977.

Most players used, doubleheader (more than 18 innings)
N.L.—42
St. Louis vs. Brooklyn, August 29, 1948, 19 innings.
Montreal vs. Pittsburgh, September 5, 1975, 19 innings.
A.L.—Less than nine-inning record.

Most players used by both clubs, doubleheader (18 innings)
N.L.—74—San Diego 41, San Francisco 33, May 30, 1977.
A.L.—70—Oakland 36, Texas 34, September 7, 1975.

Most players used by both clubs, doubleheader (more than 18 innings)
N.L.—74—Montreal 42, Pittsburgh 32, September 5, 1975, 19 innings.
A.L.—73—Washington 37, Cleveland 36, September 14, finished September 20, 1971, 29 innings.

PINCH-HITTERS

Most pinch-hitters used, nine-inning game
N.L.—9
Los Angeles vs. St. Louis, September 22, 1959.
Montreal vs. Pittsburgh, September 5, 1975, second game.
Atlanta vs. Montreal, September 21, 1993.
A.L.—8—Baltimore vs. Chicago, May 28, 1954, first game.

Most pinch-hitters used, extra-inning game
A.L.—10—Oakland vs. Chicago, September 19, 1972, 15 innings.
N.L.—9
San Francisco vs. Los Angeles, September 28, 1986, 16 innings.
St. Louis vs. Cincinnati, September 25, 1997, 14 innings.

Most pinch-hitters used by both clubs, nine-inning game
N.L.—13—Atlanta 9, Montreal 4, September 21, 1993.
A.L.—10—Baltimore 6, New York 4, April 26, 1959, second game.

Most pinch-hitters used by both clubs, extra-inning game
N.L.—14
New York 7, Chicago 7, May 2, 1956, 17 innings.
San Francisco 9, Los Angeles 5, September 28, 1986, 16 innings.
A.L.—14—Oakland 10, Chicago 4, September 19, 1972, 15 innings.

Most pinch-hitters used, doubleheader (18 innings)
A.L.—10
New York vs. Boston, September 6, 1954.
Baltimore vs. Washington, April 19, 1959.
N.L.—10
St. Louis vs. Chicago, May 11, 1958.
St. Louis vs. Pittsburgh, July 13, 1958.

Most pinch-hitters used, doubleheader (more than 18 innings)
N.L.—15—Montreal vs. Pittsburgh, September 5, 1975, 19 innings.
A.L.—9—New York vs. Washington, August 14, 1960, 24 innings.

Most pinch-hitters used by both clubs, doubleheader (18 innings)
N.L.—15—Milwaukee 8, San Francisco 7, August 30, 1964.
A.L.—14—New York 10, Boston 4, September 6, 1954.

Most pinch-hitters used by both clubs, doubleheader (more than 18 innings)
N.L.—19—Montreal 15, Pittsburgh 4, September 5, 1975, 19 innings.
A.L.—17—New York 9, Washington 8, August 14, 1960, 24 innings.

Most pinch-hitters used, inning
N.L.—6
San Francisco vs. Pittsburgh, May 5, 1958, ninth inning.
San Diego vs. San Francisco, September 16, 1986, ninth inning.
Atlanta vs. Montreal, September 21, 1993, seventh inning.
A.L.—6—Detroit vs. New York, September 5, 1971, seventh inning.

Most consecutive pinch-hitters used, inning
N.L.-A.L.—5—Made in many innings.
Last N.L. time—Chicago vs. Pittsburgh, September 20, 1996, eighth inning.
Last A.L. time—New York vs. Milwaukee, September 22, 1987, first game, eighth inning.

Most pinch-hitters used by both clubs, inning
A.L.—8—Chicago 5, Baltimore 3, May 18, 1957, seventh inning.
N.L.—8
Philadelphia 5, St. Louis 3, April 30, 1961, eighth inning.
New York 5, San Francisco 3, September 16, 1966, ninth inning.

PINCH-RUNNERS

Most pinch-runners used, inning
A.L.—4
Chicago vs. Minnesota, September 16, 1967, ninth inning.
Oakland vs. Chicago, September 24, 1975, seventh inning.
Texas vs. California, September 10, 1987, ninth inning.
N.L.—4
Montreal vs. St. Louis, September 26, 1977, ninth inning.
San Diego vs. Cincinnati, August 10, 1978, seventh inning.

Most pinch-runners used by both clubs, inning
N.L.—5—Pittsburgh 3, New York 2, September 21, 1981, ninth inning.
A.L.—4—Occurred in many innings.

INFIELDERS

Most first basemen used, nine-inning game
A.L.—5—Chicago vs. New York, June 25, 1953.
N.L.—3—Made in many games.

Most first basemen used, extra-inning game
N.L.—4
  Philadelphia vs. Milwaukee, July 23, 1964, 10 innings.
  Cincinnati vs. Chicago, May 28, 2001, 13 innings.
A.L.—4
  Detroit vs. Philadelphia, September 30, 1907, 17 innings.
  Texas vs. Oakland, June 29, 1978, 10 innings.

Most first basemen used by both clubs, nine-inning game
A.L.—6—Chicago 5, New York 1, June 25, 1953.
N.L.—5
  Los Angeles 3, New York 2, September 12, 1966.
  Cincinnati 3, New York 2, August 24, 1968.
  Houston 3, San Diego 2, September 7, 1974.

Most first basemen used by both clubs, extra-inning game
N.L.—6—Cincinnati 4, Chicago 2, May 28, 2001, 13 innings.
A.L.—Less than nine-inning record.

Most second basemen used, nine-inning game
A.L.-N.L.—4—Made in many games.

Most second basemen used, extra-inning game
A.L.—6—Oakland vs. Chicago, September 19, 1972, 15 innings.
N.L.—5—New York vs. Cincinnati, July 20, 1954, 13 innings.

Most second basemen used by both clubs, nine-inning game
A.L.—6
  Oakland 4, Cleveland 2, May 5, 1973.
  Oakland 4, Cleveland 2, May 6, 1973, first game.
  Oakland 4, Cleveland 2, May 6, 1973, second game.
N.L.—5
  Brooklyn 4, New York 1, April 21, 1948.
  Chicago 4, New York 1, August 21, 1952, second game.
  Houston 3, St. Louis 2, June 15, 1975.

Most second basemen used by both clubs, extra-inning game
A.L.—8—Oakland 6, Chicago 2, September 19, 1972, 15 innings.
N.L.—7—New York 5, Cincinnati 2, July 20, 1954, 13 innings.

Most third basemen used, game
N.L.—5
  Atlanta vs. Philadelphia, April 21, 1966.
  Philadelphia vs. Pittsburgh, August 6, 1971.
A.L.—4—Held by many clubs.

Most third basemen used by both clubs, game
N.L.—7—Philadelphia 5, Pittsburgh 2, August 6, 1971.
A.L.—6
  Detroit 3, Cleveland 3, July 10, 1969, 11 innings.
  Minnesota 3, Cleveland 3, July 27, 1969.
  Boston 3, Milwaukee 3, September 14, 1976.

Most shortstops used, nine-inning game
A.L.—4
  New York vs. Washington, September 5, 1954.
  Minnesota vs. Oakland, September 22, 1968.
N.L.—4—San Francisco vs. Cincinnati, September 4, 1989.

Most shortstops used, extra-inning game
N.L.—5
  Philadelphia vs. Cincinnati, May 8, 1949, 12 innings.
  San Francisco vs. Los Angeles, September 28, 1986, 16 innings.
A.L.—4
  Detroit vs. New York, July 28, 1957, second game, 15 innings.
  Baltimore vs. New York, September 26, 1958, 12 innings.
  Texas vs. Seattle, September 25, 1992, 16 innings.

Most shortstops used by both clubs, nine-inning game
A.L.—6—Detroit 3, Washington 3, September 21, 1968.
N.L.—5
  Cincinnati 3, Houston 2, July 13, 1969.
  Montreal 3, Pittsburgh 2, October 1, 1969.
  San Francisco 4, Cincinnati 1, September 4, 1989.

Most right fielders used, nine-inning game
A.L.—4—Baltimore vs. Washington, September 25, 1955.
N.L.—4
  Philadelphia vs. St. Louis, June 2, 1928.
  Los Angeles vs. Houston, June 10, 1962, first game.

Most right fielders used, extra-inning game
A.L.—6—Kansas City vs. California, September 8, 1965, 13 innings.
N.L.—5—New York vs. Cincinnati, July 22, 1986, 14 innings.

Most right fielders used by both clubs, nine-inning game
N.L.—6—Los Angeles 4, Houston 2, June 10, 1962, first game.
A.L.—5—Occurred in many games.

Most right fielders used by both clubs, extra-inning game
N.L.—8—San Francisco 4, Los Angeles 4, September 28, 1986, 16 innings.
A.L.—7—Kansas City 6, California 1, September 8, 1965, 13 innings.

Most center fielders used, game
A.L.—5—Minnesota vs. Oakland, September 22, 1968.
N.L.—4
  Boston vs. Brooklyn, April 25, 1917, 12 innings.
  Cincinnati vs. St. Louis, May 30, 1942, second game.
  Philadelphia vs. St. Louis, September 25, 1966, 13 innings.
  Houston vs. Chicago, September 2, finished September 3, 1986, 18 innings.
  Philadelphia vs. Cincinnati, July 20, 1987, 11 innings.

Most center fielders used by both clubs, nine-inning game
A.L.—7—Minnesota 5, Oakland 2, September 22, 1968.
N.L.—6—Cincinnati 4, St. Louis 2, May 30, 1942, second game.

Most center fielders used by both clubs, extra-inning game
N.L.—7—Houston 4, Chicago 3, September 2, finished September 3, 1986, 18 innings.
A.L.—Less than nine-inning record.

Most left fielders used, nine-inning game
A.L.—5—Seattle vs. Oakland, September 11, 1992.
N.L.—4
  Brooklyn vs. Philadelphia, September 26, 1946.
  Los Angeles vs. New York, June 4, 1966.
  Chicago vs. Philadelphia, September 21, 1977.

Most left fielders used, extra-inning game
N.L.—5—Philadelphia vs. Milwaukee, July 23, 1964, 10 innings.
A.L.—4
  Boston vs. Chicago, August 16, 1916, first game, 16 innings.
  New York vs. Boston, September 26, 1953, 11 innings.

Most left fielders used by both clubs, nine-inning game
N.L.—6—New York 3, San Francisco 3, September 22, 1963.
A.L.—6
  Oakland 4, Cleveland 2, July 20, 1974.
  Seattle 5, Oakland 1, September 11, 1992.

Most left fielders used by both clubs, extra-inning game
N.L.—7—Los Angeles 4, St. Louis 3, May 12, 1962, 15 innings.
A.L.—6
  Minnesota 3, Baltimore 3, April 16, 1961, second game, 11 innings.
  Minnesota 3, Oakland 3, September 6, 1969, 18 innings.

Most catchers used, game
N.L.—4
  Boston vs. New York, October 6, 1929.
  Brooklyn vs. St. Louis, May 5, 1940.
  New York vs. St. Louis, September 12, 1962.
A.L.—4
  Minnesota vs. California, September 27, 1967.
  Kansas City vs. Chicago, September 21, 1973, 12 innings.

REGULAR SEASON *Club service*

Most catchers used by both clubs, game

A.L.—6

Chicago 3, Philadelphia 3, July 10, 1926.
Chicago 3, New York 3, September 10, 1955, 10 innings.
California 3, Oakland 3, September 28, 1969, 11 innings.
Kansas City 4, Chicago 2, September 21, 1972, 12 innings.

N.L.—6

Boston 4, New York 2, October 6, 1929.
Brooklyn 4, St. Louis 2, May 5, 1940.
New York 3, Chicago 3, May 2, 1956, 17 innings.
New York 4, St. Louis 2, September 2, 1962.

Most pitchers used, season

A.L.—29—California, 1996.
N.L.—29—San Diego, 2000.

Fewest pitchers used, season

A.L.—5—Boston, 1904.
N.L.—5—Boston, 1901.

Most relief appearances, season

N.L.—491—Montreal, 2001.
A.L.—483—Cleveland, 2001.

Most pitchers used, nine-inning game

A.L.—9

St. Louis vs. Chicago, October 2, 1949, first game.
Chicago vs. Cleveland, September 14, 1997.

N.L.—9

Montreal vs. Chicago, September 10, 1996.
St. Louis vs. Los Angeles, September 8, 2001.

Most pitchers used, extra-inning game

A.L.—11—Seattle vs. Texas, September 25, 1992, 16 innings.
N.L.—10

Chicago vs. Pittsburgh, April 20, finished August 11, 1986, 17 innings.
Colorado vs. Atlanta, August 22, 2000, 12 innings.

Most pitchers used by both clubs, nine-inning game

N.L.—15

St. Louis 8, Cincinnati 7, September 7, 1993, first game.
Montreal 8, Atlanta 7, September 27, 1996.
Arizona 8, Milwaukee 7, September 7, 1999.

A.L.—15—Detroit 8, Minnesota 7, October 1, 2000.

Most pitchers used by both clubs, extra-inning game

A.L.—18

Washington 9, Cleveland 9, September 14, finished September 20, 1971, 20 innings.
Seattle 9, Oakland 9, September 20, 1997, 15 innings.

N.L.—18—Houston 10, Chicago 8, September 28, 1995, 11 innings.

Most pitchers used by winning club, shutout game

A.L.—8—Boston vs. Baltimore, October 3, 1999, 10 innings (won 1-0).

N.L.—6

Los Angeles vs. Milwaukee, October 3, 1965 (won 3-0).
Florida vs. Chicago, May 15, 1994 (won 3-0).
St. Louis vs. Pittsburgh, May 17, 1994 (won 2-0).
St. Louis vs. Philadelphia, April 19, 1996 (won 1-0).

Most pitchers used by winning club, no-hit game

A.L.—4

Oakland vs. California, September 28, 1975 (won 5-0).
Baltimore vs. Oakland, July 13, 1991 (won 2-0).

N.L.—3—Atlanta vs. San Diego, September 11, 1991 (won 1-0).

Most pitchers used, doubleheader (18 innings)

N.L.—13—San Diego vs. San Francisco, May 30, 1977.
A.L.—12

Cleveland vs. Detroit, September 7, 1959.
California vs. Detroit, September 30, 1967.

Most pitchers used, doubleheader (more than 18 innings)

N.L.—13—Milwaukee vs. Philadelphia, May 12, 1963, 23 innings.
A.L.—13—Baltimore vs. Texas, August 13, 1991, 21 innings.

Most pitchers used by both clubs, doubleheader (18 innings)

N.L.—22—Milwaukee 11, New York 11, July 26, 1964.
A.L.—21—Detroit 11, Kansas City 10, July 23, 1961.

Most pitchers used by both clubs, doubleheader (more than 18 innings)

A.L.—22—Washington 12, Cleveland 10, September 14, finished September 20, 1971, 29 innings.
N.L.—20—St. Louis 12, Cincinnati 8, July 1, 1956, 19 innings.

Most pitchers used, inning

A.L.—6—Oakland vs. Cleveland, September 3, 1983, ninth inning.
N.L.—5—Occurred in many innings. Last time—Philadelphia vs. Atlanta, April 8, 1999, eighth inning.

Most pitchers used by both clubs, inning

N.L.—8—Los Angeles 5, New York 3, August 26, 1987, eighth inning.
A.L.—7

Chicago 4, Baltimore 3, July 16, 1955, ninth inning.
Baltimore 4, Boston 3, June 20, 1975, ninth inning.
Oakland 6, Cleveland 1, September 3, 1983, ninth inning.

FRANCHISE LONGEVITY

Most years in same city by a franchise

N.L.—126—Chicago, 1876 through 2001 (consecutive).
A.L.—101—Boston, Chicago, Cleveland, Detroit, 1901 through 2001 (consecutive).

LEAGUE SERVICE

ALL PLAYERS

Most players, season (since 1900)
N.L. (16-club league)—699 in 2000.
N.L. (14-club league)—588 in 1995, 1997.
N.L. (12-club league)—491 in 1990.
N.L. (10-club league)—373 in 1967.
A.L. (14-club league)—610 in 2000.
A.L. (12-club league)—440 in 1969.
A.L. (10-club league)—369 in 1962.
A.L. (8-club league)—323 in 1955.
N.L. (8-club league)—333 in 1946.

Most players in 150 or more games, season (since 1900)
A.L. (14-club league)—46 in 1998.
A.L. (12-club league)—32 in 1976.
A.L. (10-club league)—30 in 1962.
A.L. (8-club league)—19 in 1921, 1936.
N.L. (16-club league)—42 in 1998.
N.L. (12-club league)—40 in 1978, 1979.
N.L. (10-club league)—34 in 1965.
N.L. (8-club league)—23 in 1953.

Fewest players, season (since 1900)
A.L. (12-club league)—412 in 1976.
A.L. (8-club league)—166 in 1904.
N.L. (12-club league)—420 in 1979.
N.L. (8-club league)—188 in 1905.

Most players playing in all games, season (since 1900)
N.L.—10 in 1932.
A.L.—10 in 1933.

Fewest players playing in all games, season
A.L.—0—1910, 1963.
N.L.—0—1914.

Most players with two or more clubs, season (since 1900)
N.L.—48 in 1998.
A.L.—47 in 1952.

Fewest players with two or more clubs, season (since 1900)
A.L.—2 in 1940.
N.L.—5 in 1935.

Most players with three or more clubs, season (since 1900)
A.L.—4 in 1952.
N.L.—3 in 1919.

PITCHERS

Most pitchers in league, season
N.L. (16-club league)—341 in 2000.
N.L. (14-club league)—290 in 1995.
N.L. (12-club league)—228 in 1990.
N.L. (10-club league)—167 in 1967.
N.L. (8-club league)—152 in 1946.
A.L. (14-club league)—303 in 2000.
A.L. (12-club league)—189 in 1970.
A.L. (10-club league)—170 in 1962.
A.L. (8-club league)—141 in 1946, 1955.

Most pitchers in league, one day
N.L.—72—September 7, 1964.
A.L.—62—August 9, 1970.

Most pitchers in both leagues, one day
121—September 7, 1964, 72 in N.L. (10 games), 49 in A.L. (eight games).

INDIVIDUAL BATTING

GAMES

Most games, career

N.L.—3,562—Pete Rose, Cincinnati, Philadelphia, Montreal, 24 years, 1963 through 1986.

A.L.—3,308—Carl Yastrzemski, Boston, 23 years, 1961 through 1983.

For a complete list of players playing in 2,400 games in career, see page 170.

Most consecutive games, career

A.L.—2,632—Cal Ripken Jr., Baltimore, May 30, 1982 through September 19, 1998.

N.L.—1,207—Steve Garvey, Los Angeles, San Diego, September 3, 1975, through July 29, 1983, first game.

For a complete list of players playing in 500 consecutive games in career, see page 170.

Most consecutive games from start of career

N.L.—424—Ernie Banks, Chicago, September 17, 1953, through August 10, 1957.

A.L.—394—Al Simmons, Philadelphia, April 15, 1924, through July 20, 1926.

Most games played, season

N.L.—165—Maury Wills, Los Angeles, 1962.
A.L.—164—Cesar Tovar, Minnesota, 1967.

Most games played with two clubs, season

N.L.—164—Frank Taveras, Pittsburgh, New York, 1979.
A.L.—160
Julio Cruz, Seattle, Chicago, 1983.
Cecil Fielder, Detroit, New York, 1996.

Most games by rookie, season

A.L.—162
Jake Wood, Detroit, 1961.
Bobby Knoop, Los Angeles, 1964.
George Scott, Boston, 1966.
N.L.—162
Dick Allen, Philadelphia, 1964.
Johnny Ray, Pittsburgh, 1982.
Jeff Conine, Florida, 1993.

Most games by righthander, season

N.L.—164
Jose Pagan, San Francisco, 1962.
Ron Santo, Chicago, 1965.
Frank Taveras, Pittsburgh, New York, 1979.
A.L.—164—Cesar Tovar, Minnesota, 1967.

Most games by lefthander, season

N.L.—164—Billy Williams, Chicago, 1965.
A.L.—163
Leon Wagner, Cleveland, 1964.
Al Oliver, Texas, 1980.
Greg Walker, Chicago, 1985.

Most games by switch-hitter, season

N.L.—165—Maury Wills, Los Angeles, 1962.
A.L.—163
Don Buford, Chicago, 1966.
Tony Fernandez, Toronto, 1986.

Most games by pinch-hitter, season

N.L.—95—Lenny Harris, New York, 2001.
A.L.—81—Elmer Valo, New York, Washington, 1960.

Most years leading league in games

A.L.—9—Cal Ripken Jr., Baltimore, 1983 (tied), 1984 (tied), 1987, 1989 (tied), 1991 (tied), 1992, 1993, 1996, 1997 (tied).
N.L.—6
Ernie Banks, Chicago, 1954 (tied), 1955 (tied), 1957 (tied), 1958, 1959 (tied), 1960.
Steve Garvey, Los Angeles, 1977 (tied), 1978 (tied), 1980, 1981 (tied), 1982 (tied), San Diego, 1985 (tied).

Most years played all club's games

A.L.—15—Cal Ripken Jr., Baltimore, 1983 through 1997 (consecutive).

N.L.—10—Pete Rose, Cincinnati, 1965, 1972, 1974, 1975, 1976, 1977, Philadelphia, 1979, 1980, 1981, 1982.

Most consecutive years played all club's games

A.L.—15—Cal Ripken Jr., Baltimore, 1983 through 1997.
N.L.—7—Steve Garvey, Los Angeles, 1976 through 1982.

Most years playing 150 or more games

N.L.—17—Pete Rose, Cincinnati, Philadelphia, 1963 through 1983, except 1964, 1967, 1968, 1981.
A.L.—15—Cal Ripken Jr., Baltimore, 1982 through 1998, except 1994 and 1995.

Most consecutive years playing 150 or more games

N.L.—13—Willie Mays, New York, San Francisco, 1954 through 1966.
A.L.—12—Cal Ripken Jr., Baltimore, 1982 through 1993.

Most years playing 100 or more games

N.L.—23—Pete Rose, Cincinnati, Philadelphia, Montreal, 1963 through 1985.
A.L.—22—Carl Yastrzemski, Boston, 1961 through 1983, except 1981.

Most consecutive years playing 100 or more games

N.L.—23—Pete Rose, Cincinnati, Philadelphia, Montreal, 1963 through 1985.
A.L.—20—Carl Yastrzemski, Boston, 1961 through 1980.

Fewest games for leader, season

N.L.—152
Stan Hack, Chicago, 1938.
Billy Herman, Chicago, 1938.
A.L.—154—Held by many players.

BATTING AVERAGE

Highest average, career (15 or more seasons)

A.L.—.367—Ty Cobb, Detroit, Philadelphia, 24 years, 1905 through 1928 (11,429 at-bats, 4,191 hits).

N.L.—.359—Rogers Hornsby, St. Louis, New York, Boston, Chicago, 19 years, 1915 through 1933 (8,058 at-bats, 2,895 hits).

For a complete list of players with .300 career batting averages with 1,500 or more hits, see page 171.

Highest average, season (100 or more games)

N.L.—.438—Hugh Duffy, Boston, 124 games, 1894.
N.L. since 1900—.424—Rogers Hornsby, St. Louis, 143 games, 1924.
A.L.—.422—Nap Lajoie, Philadelphia, 131 games, 1901.

Highest average for non-leader, season (100 or more games)

A.L.—.408—Joe Jackson, Cleveland, 147 games, 1911.
N.L.—.406—Fred Clarke, Louisville, 129 games, 1897.
N.L. since 1900—.393—Babe Herman, Brooklyn, 153 games, 1930.

Highest average by rookie, season (100 or more games)

N.L.—.373—George Watkins, St. Louis, 119 games, 1930.
A.L.—.350—Ichiro Suzuki, Seattle, 157 games, 2001.

League leader in batting average, rookie season

N.L.—.356—Abner Dalrymple, Milwaukee, 60 games, 1878.
A.L.—.323—Tony Oliva, Minnesota, 161 games, 1964.
.350—Ichiro Suzuki, Seattle, 157 games, 2001.

Highest average by righthander, season (100 or more games)

N.L.—.438—Hugh Duffy, Boston, 124 games, 1894.
N.L. since 1900—.424—Rogers Hornsby, St. Louis, 143 games, 1924.
A.L.—.422—Nap Lajoie, Philadelphia, 131 games, 1910.

Highest average by lefthander, season (100 or more games)
N.L.—.432—Willie Keeler, Baltimore, 128 games, 1897.
A.L.—.41979—George Sisler, St. Louis, 142 games, 1922.
(Ty Cobb batted .41962 for Detroit in 146 games in 1911.)
N.L. since 1900—.401—Bill Terry, New York, 154 games, 1930.

Highest average by switch-hitter, season (100 or more games)
N.L.—.373—George Davis, New York, 133 games, 1893.
A.L.—.365—Mickey Mantle, New York, 144 games, 1957.
N.L. since 1900—.353—Willie McGee, St. Louis 152, games, 1985.

Highest average by first baseman, season (100 or more games)
A.L.—.420—George Sisler, St. Louis, 142 games, 1922; 141 games at first base.
N.L.—.401—Bill Terry, New York, 154 games, 1930; 154 games at first base.

Highest average by second baseman, season (100 or more games)
N.L.—.424—Rogers Hornsby, St. Louis, 143 games, 1924; 143 games at second base.
A.L.—.422—Nap Lajoie, Philadelphia, 131 games, 1901; 130 games at second base.

Highest average by third baseman, season (100 or more games)
A.L.—.390—George Brett, Kansas City, 117 games, 1980; 112 games at third base.
N.L.—.390—John McGraw, Baltimore, 118 games, 1899; 118 games at third base.
N.L. since 1900—.379—Fred Lindstrom, New York, 148 games, 1930; 148 games at third base.

Highest average by shortstop, season (100 or more games)
N.L.—.397—Hughey Jennings, Baltimore, 129 games, 1896; 129 games at shortstop.
A.L.—.388—Luke Appling, Chicago, 138 games, 1936; 137 games at shortstop.
N.L. since 1900—.385—Arky Vaughan, Pittsburgh, 137 games, 1935; 137 games at shortstop.

Highest average by outfielder, season (100 or more games)
N.L.—.438—Hugh Duffy, Boston, 124 games, 1894; 123 games in outfield.
A.L.—.420—Ty Cobb, Detroit, 146 games, 1911; 146 games in outfield.
N.L. since 1900—.398—Lefty O'Doul, Philadelphia, 154 games, 1929; 154 games in outfield.

Highest average by catcher, season (100 or more games)
A.L.—.362—Bill Dickey, New York, 112 games, 1936; caught in 107 games.
N.L.—.362—Mike Piazza, Los Angeles, 152 games, 1997; caught in 139 games.

Highest average by pitcher, season (only for games as a pitcher)
A.L.—.440—Walter Johnson, Washington, 36 games, 1925; pitched 30 games.
N.L.—.406—Jack Bentley, New York, 52 games, 1923; pitched 31 games.

Most years leading league in batting average
A.L.—12—Ty Cobb, Detroit, 1907, 1908, 1909, 1910, 1911, 1912, 1913, 1914, 1915, 1917, 1918, 1919.
N.L.—8
Honus Wagner, Pittsburgh, 1900, 1903, 1904, 1906, 1907, 1908, 1909, 1911.
Tony Gwynn, San Diego, 1984, 1987, 1988, 1989, 1994, 1995, 1996, 1997.

For a complete list of triple crown winners, see page 182.

Most consecutive years leading league in batting average
A.L.—9—Ty Cobb, Detroit, 1907 through 1915.
N.L.—6—Rogers Hornsby, St. Louis, 1920 through 1925.

Most years batting .400 or over (50 or more games)
N.L.—3
Jesse Burkett, Cleveland, St. Louis, 1895, 1896, 1899.
Rogers Hornsby, St. Louis, 1922, 1924, 1925.
A.L.—3—Ty Cobb, Detroit, 1911, 1912, 1922.

Most consecutive years batting .400 or over (50 or more games)
N.L.—2
Jesse Burkett, Cleveland, 1895, 1896.
Rogers Hornsby, St. Louis, 1924, 1925.
A.L.—2—Ty Cobb, Detroit, 1911, 1912.

For a complete list of .400 hitters, see page 182.

Most years batting .300 or over (50 or more games)
A.L.—23—Ty Cobb, Detroit, Philadelphia, 1906 through 1928.
N.L.—18—Cap Anson, Chicago, 1876 through 1897, except 1877, 1879, 1891 and 1892.
N.L. since 1900—18—Tony Gwynn, San Diego, 1983 through 1999, 2001.

For a complete list of batters hitting .300 or better 10 or more times, see page 171.

Most consecutive years batting .300 or over (50 or more games)
A.L.—23—Ty Cobb, Detroit, Philadelphia, 1906 through 1928.
N.L.—17
Honus Wagner, Louisville, Pittsburgh, 1897 through 1913.
Tony Gwynn, San Diego, 1983 through 1999.

Most consecutive years batting .300 or over from start of career (50 or more games)
N.L.—17—Honus Wagner, Louisville, Pittsburgh, 1897 through 1913.
N.L. since 1900—12
Paul Waner, Pittsburgh, 1926 through 1937.
(Military service in 1945 interrupted a 16-year streak by Stan Musial, who batted .300 for St. Louis from 1942 through 1958.)
A.L.—11
Al Simmons, Philadelphia, Chicago, 1924 through 1934.
(Military service from 1943 through 1945 and most of 1952 and 1953 interrupted a 15-year streak by Ted Williams, who batted .300 for Boston from 1939 through 1958.)

Most years batting .300 or over by pitcher
A.L.—8—Red Ruffing, Boston, New York, 1928, 1929, 1930, 1931, 1932, 1935, 1939, 1941.
N.L.—5—Jack Stivetts, Boston, 1892, 1893, 1894, 1896, 1897.

Highest average over five consecutive seasons (100 or more games)
N.L.—.4024—Rogers Hornsby, St. Louis, 1921 through 1925.
A.L.—.3965—Ty Cobb, Detroit, 1909 through 1913.

Highest average over four consecutive seasons (100 or more games)
N.L.—.4039—Rogers Hornsby, St. Louis, 1922 through 1925.
A.L.—.4019—Ty Cobb, Detroit, 1910 through 1913.

Highest average over three consecutive seasons (100 or more games)
A.L.—.4084—Ty Cobb, Detroit, 1911, 1912, 1913.
N.L.—.40647—Willie Keeler, Baltimore, 1895, 1896, 1897.
N.L. since 1900—.405—Rogers Hornsby, St. Louis, 1923, 1924, 1925.

Highest average over two consecutive seasons (100 or more games)
N.L.—.417—Jesse Burkett, Cleveland, 1895, 1896.
A.L.—.415—Ty Cobb, Detroit, 1911, 1912.
N.L. since 1900—.413—Rogers Hornsby, St. Louis, 1924, 1925.

Lowest average, season (150 or more games)
A.L.—.182—Monte Cross, Philadelphia, 153 games, 1904.
N.L.—.201—Dal Maxvill, St. Louis, 152 games, 1970.

Lowest average for leader, season (100 or more games)
A.L.—.301—Carl Yastrzemski, Boston, 157 games, 1968.
N.L.—.313—Tony Gwynn, San Diego, 133 games, 1988.

SLUGGING AVERAGE

Highest slugging average, career (15 or more years)
M.L.—.690—Babe Ruth, Boston A.L., New York A.L., Boston N.L., 22 years, 1914 through 1935.
A.L.—.692—Babe Ruth, Boston, New York, 21 years, 1914 through 1934.
N.L.—.585—Barry Bonds, Pittsburgh, San Francisco, 16 years, 1986 through 2001.

For a complete list of career slugging averages of players with 4,000 or more total bases, see page 172.

Highest slugging average, season (100 or more games)
N.L.—.863—Barry Bonds, San Francisco, 153 games, 2001.
A.L.—.847—Babe Ruth, New York, 142 games, 1920.

Highest slugging average by rookie, season (100 or more games)
N.L.—.621—George Watkins, St. Louis, 119 games, 1930.
A.L.—.618—Mark McGwire, Oakland, 151 games, 1987.

Highest slugging average by righthander, season (100 or more games)
N.L.—.756—Rogers Hornsby, St. Louis, 138 games, 1925.
A.L.—.749—Jimmie Foxx, Philadelphia, 154 games, 1932.

Highest slugging average by lefthander, season (100 or more games)
N.L.—.863—Barry Bonds, San Francisco, 153 games, 2001.
A.L.—.847—Babe Ruth, New York, 142 games, 1920.

Highest slugging average by switch-hitter, season
A.L.—.705—Mickey Mantle, New York, 150 games, 1956.
N.L.—.633—Chipper Jones, Atlanta, 157 games, 1999.

Most years leading league in slugging average (100 or more games)
A.L.—13—Babe Ruth, Boston, New York, 1918 through 1931, except 1925. (Played only 95 games in 1918, short season due to war.)
N.L.—9—Rogers Hornsby, St. Louis, Boston, Chicago, 1917, 1920, 1921, 1922, 1923, 1924, 1925, 1928, 1929.

Lowest slugging average, season (150 or more games)
N.L.—.223—Dal Maxvill, St. Louis, 152 games, 1970.
A.L.—.243—George McBride, Washington, 156 games, 1914.

Lowest leading slugging average, season (100 or more games)
N.L.—.436—Hy Myers, Brooklyn, 133 games, 1919.
A.L.—.466—Elmer Flick, Cleveland, 131 games, 1905.

AT-BATS AND PLATE APPEARANCES
CAREER AND SEASON

Most at-bats, career
N.L.—14,053—Pete Rose, Cincinnati, Philadelphia, Montreal, 24 years, 1963 through 1986.
A.L.—11,988—Carl Yastrzemski, Boston, 23 years, 1961 through 1983.

For a complete list of players with 9,000 or more career at-bats, see page 172.

Most plate appearances, career
N.L.—15,890—Pete Rose, Cincinnati, Philadelphia, Montreal, 24 years, 1963 through 1986.
A.L.—13,990—Carl Yastrzemski, Boston, 23 years, 1961 through 1983.

Most at-bats, season
A.L.—705—Willie Wilson, Kansas City, 161 games, 1980.
N.L.—701—Juan Samuel, Philadelphia, 160 games, 1984.

Most plate appearances, season
N.L.—773—Lenny Dykstra, Philadelphia, 161 games, 1993.
A.L.—758—Wade Boggs, Boston, 161 games, 1985.

Most at-bats by rookie, season
N.L.—701—Juan Samuel, Philadelphia, 160 games, 1984.
A.L.—692—Ichiro Suzuki, Seattle, 157 games, 2001.

Most at-bats by righthander, season
N.L.—701—Juan Samuel, Philadelphia, 160 games, 1984.
A.L.—692—Bobby Richardson, New York, 161 games, 1962.

Most at-bats by lefthander, season
N.L.—698—Matty Alou, Pittsburgh, 162 games, 1969.
A.L.—692—Ichiro Suzuki, Seattle, 157 games, 2001.

Most at-bats by switch-hitter, season
A.L.—705—Willie Wilson, Kansas City, 161 games, 1980.
N.L.—695—Maury Wills, Los Angeles, 165 games, 1962.

Most at-bats by pinch-hitter, season
N.L.—83—Lenny Harris, New York, 95 games, 2001.
A.L.—72—Dave Philley, Baltimore, 79 games, 1961.

Most years leading league in at-bats
A.L.—7—Doc Cramer, Philadelphia, Boston, Washington, Detroit, 1933, 1934, 1935, 1938, 1940, 1941, 1942.
N.L.—4—
Abner Dalrymple, Chicago, 1880, 1882, 1884, 1885.
Pete Rose, Cincinnati, 1965, 1972, 1973, 1977.

Most consecutive years leading league in at-bats
N.L.—3—
Sparky Adams, Chicago, 1925, 1926, 1927.
Dave Cash, Philadelphia, 1974, 1975, 1976.
A.L.—3—
Doc Cramer, Philadelphia, 1933, 1934, 1935.
Doc Cramer, Boston, Washington, Detroit, 1940, 1941, 1942.
Bobby Richardson, New York, 1962, 1963, 1964.

Most years with 600 or more at-bats
N.L.—17—Pete Rose, Cincinnati, 1963 through 1978, except 1964, 1967, Philadelphia, 1979, 1980, 1982.
A.L.—13—Cal Ripken Jr., Baltimore, 1983 through 1993, except 1988; 1996 through 1998.

Most consecutive years with 600 or more at-bats
N.L.—13—Pete Rose, Cincinnati, Philadelphia, 1968 through 1980.
A.L.—12—Nellie Fox, Chicago, 1951 through 1962.

Fewest at-bats, season (150 or more games)
N.L.—362—Jim Eisenreich, Philadelphia, 153 games, 1993.
A.L.—389—Tom McCraw, Chicago, 151 games, 1966.

Fewest at-bats for leader, season
N.L.—585—Spike Shannon, New York, 155 games, 1907.
A.L.—588—Ty Cobb, Detroit, 152 games, 1917.

GAME AND INNING

Most at-bats, nine-inning game
N.L.—8—Held by 18 players. Last player—Barry McCormick, Chicago, June 29, 1897.
N.L. since 1900—7—Held by many players.
A.L.—7—Held by many players.

Most at-bats, extra-inning game
N.L.—11—
Carson Bigbee, Pittsburgh, August 22, 1917, 22 innings.
Charlie Pick, Boston, May 1, 1920, 26 innings.
Tony Boeckel, Boston, May 1, 1920, 26 innings.
Ralph Garr, Atlanta, May 4, 1973, 20 innings.
Dave Schneck, New York, September 11, 1974, 25 innings.
Dave Cash, Montreal, May 21, 1977, 21 innings.
A.L.—11—
Johnny Burnett, Cleveland, July 10, 1932, 18 innings.
Ed Morgan, Cleveland, July 10, 1932, 18 innings.
Irv Hall, Philadelphia, July 21, 1945, 24 innings.
Bobby Richardson, New York, June 24, 1962, 22 innings.
Cecil Cooper, Milwaukee, May 8, completed May 9, 1984, 25 innings.
Julio Cruz, Chicago, May 8, completed May 9, 1984, 25 innings.
Carlton Fisk, Chicago, May 8, completed May 9, 1984, 25 innings.
Rudy Law, Chicago, May 8, completed May 9, 1984, 25 innings.

Most times faced pitcher as batsman, nine-inning game
N.L. before 1900—8—Held by many players.

N.L. since 1900—8
  Russ Wrightstone, Philadelphia, August 25, 1922.
  Frank Parkinson, Philadelphia, August 25, 1922.
  Taylor Douthit, St. Louis, July 6, 1929, second game.
  Mike Cameron, Cincinnati, May 19, 1999.
A.L.—8
  Clyde Vollmer, Boston, June 8, 1950.
  Darryl Hamilton, Milwaukee, August 28, 1992.

Most times faced pitcher as batsman, extra-inning game
N.L.—12
  Felix Millan, New York, September 11, 1974, 25 innings.
  John Milner, New York, September 11, 1974, 25 innings.
A.L.—12
  Harold Baines, Chicago, May 8, completed May 9, 1984, 25 innings.
  Carlton Fisk, Chicago, May 8, completed May 9, 1984, 25 innings.
  Rudy Law, Chicago, May 8, completed May 9, 1984, 25 innings.

Most times faced pitcher with no official at-bats, game
N.L.—6
  Pop Smith, Boston, April 17, 1890 (5 bases on balls, 1 hit by pitch).
  Walt Wilmot, Chicago, August 22, 1891 (6 bases on balls).
  Miller Huggins, St. Louis, June 1, 1910 (4 bases on balls, 1 sacrifice hit, 1 sacrifice fly).
  Billy Urbanski, Boston, June 13, 1934 (4 bases on balls, 2 sacrifice hits).
A.L.—6—Jimmie Foxx, Boston, June 16, 1938 (6 bases on balls).

Most at-bats, doubleheader (18 innings)
N.L.—13
  Rabbit Maranville, Pittsburgh, August 8, 1922.
  Billy Herman, Chicago, August 21, 1935.
A.L.—13—Dave Philley, Chicago, May 30, 1950.

Most at-bats, doubleheader (more than 18 innings)
A.L.—14
  Rick Monday, Kansas City, June 17, 1967, 28 innings.
  Ramon Webster, Kansas City, June 17, 1967, 28 innings.
N.L.—14
  Jesus Alou, San Francisco, May 31, 1964, 32 innings.
  Joe Christopher, New York, May 31, 1964, 32 innings.
  Jim Hickman, New York, May 31, 1964, 32 innings.
  Ed Kranepool, New York, May 31, 1964, 32 innings.
  Roy McMillan, New York, May 31, 1964, 32 innings.
  Frank J. Thomas, New York, May 31, 1964, 32 innings.

Most times faced pitcher as batsman, inning
A.A.—3—Larry Murphy, Washington, June 17, 1891, first inning.
N.L. before 1900—3—Held by 10 players.
N.L. since 1900—3
  Marty Callaghan, Chicago, August 25, 1922, fourth inning.
  Billy Cox, Pee Wee Reese and Duke Snider, Brooklyn, May 21, 1952, first inning.
  Gil Hodges, Brooklyn, August 8, 1954, eighth inning.
  Dusty Baker, Atlanta, September 20, 1972, second inning.
  Mariano Duncan and Luis Quinones, Cincinnati, August 3, 1989, first inning.
  Stan Javier, San Francisco, July 15, 1997, seventh inning.
A.L.—3
  Ted Williams, Boston, July 4, 1948, seventh inning.
  Sammy White, Gene Stephens, Tom Umphlett, Johnny Lipon and George Kell, Boston, June 18, 1953, seventh inning.
  Darryl Hamilton, Texas, April 19, 1996, eighth inning.

RUNS
CAREER AND SEASON

Most runs, career
M.L.—2,248—Rickey Henderson, Oakland A.L., New York A.L., Toronto A.L., San Diego N.L., Anaheim A.L., New York N.L., Seattle A.L., 23 years, 1979 through 2001 (1,899 in A.L., 349 in N.L.).
A.L.—2,245—Ty Cobb, Detroit, Philadelphia, 24 years, 1905 through 1928.

N.L.—2,165—Pete Rose, Cincinnati, Philadelphia, Montreal, 24 years, 1963 through 1986.

For a complete list of players with 1,500 or more career runs, see page 172.

Most runs, season
N.L.—196—Billy Hamilton, Philadelphia, 131 games, 1894.
A.L.—177—Babe Ruth, New York, 152 games, 1921.
N.L. since 1900—158—Chuck Klein, Philadelphia, 156 games, 1930.

Most runs by rookie, season
A.A.—152—Mike Griffin, Baltimore, 136 games, 1887.
N.L.—135—Roy Thomas, Philadelphia, 148 games, 1899.
N.L. since 1900—133—Lloyd Waner, Pittsburgh, 150 games, 1927.
A.L.—132—Joe DiMaggio, New York, 138 games, 1936.

Most runs by righthander, season
N.L.—167—Joe Kelley, Baltimore, 129 games, 1894.
N.L. since 1900—156—Rogers Hornsby, Chicago, 156 games, 1929.
A.L.—152—Al Simmons, Philadelphia, 138 games, 1930.

Most runs by lefthander, season
N.L.—196—Billy Hamilton, Philadelphia, 131 games, 1894.
A.L.—177—Babe Ruth, New York, 152 games, 1921.
N.L. since 1900—158—Chuck Klein, Philadelphia, 156 games, 1930.

Most runs by switch-hitter, season
N.L.—140—Max Carey, Pittsburgh, 155 games, 1922.
A.L.—138—Roberto Alomar, Cleveland, 159 games, 1999.

Most years leading league in runs
A.L.—8—Babe Ruth, Boston, New York, 1919, 1920, 1921, 1923, 1924, 1926, 1927, 1928.
N.L.—5
  George Burns, New York, 1914, 1916, 1917, 1919, 1920.
  Rogers Hornsby, St. Louis, New York, Chicago, 1921, 1922, 1924 (tied), 1927 (tied), 1929.
  Stan Musial, St. Louis, 1946, 1948, 1951 (tied), 1952 (tied), 1954 (tied).

Most consecutive years leading league in runs
N.L.—3
  King Kelly, Chicago, 1884, 1885, 1886.
  Chuck Klein, Philadelphia, 1930, 1931 (tied), 1932.
  Duke Snider, Brooklyn, 1953, 1954 (tied), 1955.
  Pete Rose, Cincinnati, 1974, 1975, 1976.
A.L.—3
  Ty Cobb, Detroit, 1909, 1910, 1911.
  Eddie Collins, Philadelphia, 1912, 1913, 1914.
  Babe Ruth, Boston, 1919, New York, 1920, 1921 and New York, 1926, 1927, 1928.
  Ted Williams, Boston, 1940, 1941, 1942 (military service from 1943 through 1945 interrupted a five-year streak by Williams of Boston, who led in runs from 1940 through 1947).
  Mickey Mantle, New York, 1956, 1957, 1958.

Most years with 150 or more runs
A.L.—6—Babe Ruth, New York, 1920, 1921, 1923, 1927, 1928, 1930.
N.L.—4—Billy Hamilton, Philadelphia, Boston, 1894, 1895, 1896, 1897.
N.L. since 1900—2—Chuck Klein, Philadelphia, 1930, 1932.

Most years scoring 100 or more runs
N.L.—15—Hank Aaron, Milwaukee, Atlanta, 1955 through 1970, except 1968.
A.L.—13—Lou Gehrig, New York, 1926 through 1938.

Most consecutive years scoring 100 or more runs
A.L.—13—Lou Gehrig, New York, 1926 through 1938.
N.L.—13—Hank Aaron, Milwaukee, Atlanta, 1955 through 1967.

Fewest runs for leader, season
N.L.—89—Gavvy Cravath, Philadelphia, 150 games, 1915.
A.L.—92—Harry H. Davis, Philadelphia, 149 games, 1905.

Fewest runs, season (150 or more games)
A.L.—25—Leo Cardenas, California, 150 games, 1972.
N.L.—32—Mike Doolan, Philadelphia, 151 games, 1913.

GAME AND INNING

Most runs, game

A.A.—7—Guy Hecker, Louisville, August 15, 1886, second game.
N.L.—6
Jim Whitney, Boston, June 9, 1883.
Cap Anson, Chicago, August 24, 1886.
Mike Tiernan, New York, June 15, 1887.
King Kelly, Boston, August 27, 1887.
Ezra Sutton, Boston, August 27, 1887.
Jimmy Ryan, Chicago, July 25, 1894.
Bobby Lowe, Boston, May 3, 1895.
Ginger Beaumont, Pittsburgh, July 22, 1899.
Mel Ott, New York, August 4, 1934, second game; April 30,
    1944, first game.
Frank Torre, Milwaukee, September 2, 1957, first game.
Edgardo Alfonzo, New York, August 30, 1999.
A.L.—6
Johnny Pesky, Boston, May 8, 1946.
Spike Owen, Boston, August 21, 1986.

Most runs by pitcher, game

A.A.—7—Guy Hecker, Louisville, August 15, 1886, second game.
N.L.—5—Nig Cuppy, Cleveland, August 9, 1895.
N.L. since 1900—4—Held by many pitchers. Last pitcher—Jim
    Tobin, Boston, September 12, 1940, first game.
A.L.—4—Held by many pitchers. Last pitcher—Billy Hoeft,
    Detroit, May 5, 1956.

Most runs, two consecutive games (18 innings)

A.A.—11—Guy Hecker, Louisville, August 12, August 15, second game, 1886.
A.L.—9
Mel Almada, Washington, July 25, 25, 1937.
Mark McGwire, Oakland, June 27, 28, 1987.
N.L.—9
Herman Long, Boston, May 30, 30, 1894.
Jimmy Ryan, Chicago, July 24, 25, 1894.
Bill Dahlen, Chicago, September 20, 21, 1894.
N.L. since 1900—8
Kiki Cuyler, Pittsburgh, June 20, 22, 1925.
Johnny Frederick, Brooklyn, May 17, 18, 1929.
Mel Ott, New York, August 4, second game, August 5, 1934.
Chuck Klein, Chicago, August 21, 21, 1935.
Stan Musial, St. Louis, May 19, 20, 1948.

Most runs, doubleheader (18 innings)

N.L.—9—Herman Long, Boston, May 30, 1894.
A.L.—9—Mel Almada, Washington, July 25, 1937.
N.L. since 1900—8—Chuck Klein, Chicago, August 21, 1935.

Most consecutive games scoring one or more runs, season

N.L.—24—Billy Hamilton, Philadelphia, July 6 through August
    2, 1894 (35 runs).
A.L.—18
Red Rolfe, New York, August 9 through August 25, second
    game, 1939 (30 runs).
Kenny Lofton, Cleveland, August 15 through September 3,
    2000 (26 runs).
N.L. since 1900—17—Ted Kluszewski, Cincinnati, August 27
    through September 13, 1954 (24 runs).

Most times with five or more runs in one game, career

M.L.—6
George Gore, Chicago N.L., 1880, 1881, 1882 (2), 1883, New
    York P.L. 1890.
Jimmy Ryan, Chicago N.L., 1887, 1889, 1891, 1894 (2), 1897.
Willie Keeler, Baltimore N.L., 1895 (2), 1897 (2), Brooklyn
    N.L., 1901, 1902.
N.L.—6
Jimmy Ryan, Chicago, 1887, 1889, 1891, 1894 (2), 1897.
Willie Keeler, Baltimore, Brooklyn, 1895 (2), 1897 (2), 1901,
    1902.
N.L. since 1900—3
Mel Ott, New York, 1934, 1944 (2).
Willie Mays, New York, San Francisco, 1954, 1964 (2).
A.L.—3
Lou Gehrig, New York, 1928, 1936 (2).
Jimmie Foxx, Philadelphia, Boston, 1932, 1935, 1939.

Most times with five or more runs in one game, season

N.L.—2—Held by many players.
N.L. since 1900—2
Kiki Cuyler, Pittsburgh, May 12, second game, June 20, 1925.
Mel Ott, New York, April 30, first game, June 12, 1944.
Phil Weintraub, New York, April 30, first game, June 12, 1944.
Willie Mays, San Francisco, April 24, September 19, 1964.
A.L.—2—Lou Gehrig, New York, May 3, July 28, 1936.

Most runs, inning

A.L.—3—Sammy White, Boston, June 18, 1953, seventh inning.
N.L.—3
Tommy Burns, Chicago, September 6, 1883, seventh inning.
Ned Williamson, Chicago, September 6, 1883, seventh inning.
N.L. since 1900—2—Held by many players.

HITS

CAREER AND SEASON

Most hits, career

N.L.—4,256—Pete Rose, Cincinnati, Philadelphia, Montreal, 24
    years, 1963 through 1986.
A.L.—4,191—Ty Cobb, Detroit, Philadelphia, 24 years, 1905
    through 1928.

**For a complete list of players with 2,500 or
more career hits, see page 172.**

Most hits by pinch-hitter, career

N.L.—151—Lenny Harris, Cincinnati, Los Angeles, New York,
    Colorado, Arizona, 13 years, 1989 through 2001, 667 games.
A.L.—107—Gates Brown, Detroit, 13 years, 1963 through
    1975, 525 games.

**Most hits, season (Except 1887, when bases on balls counted
as hits)**

A.L.—257—George Sisler, St. Louis, 154 games, 1920.
N.L.—254
Lefty O'Doul, Philadelphia, 154 games, 1929.
Bill Terry, New York, 154 games, 1930.

Most hits by rookie, season

A.L.—242—Ichiro Suzuki, Seattle, 157 games, 2001.
N.L.—223—Lloyd Waner, Pittsburgh, 150 games, 1927.

**For a complete list of rookies with 200 or
more hits, see page 182.**

Most hits by righthander, season

A.L.—253—Al Simmons, Philadelphia, 153 games, 1925.
N.L.—250—Rogers Hornsby, St. Louis, 154 games, 1922.

Most hits by lefthander, season

A.L.—257—George Sisler, St. Louis, 154 games, 1920.
N.L.—254
Lefty O'Doul, Philadelphia, 154 games, 1929.
Bill Terry, New York, 154 games, 1930.

Most hits by switch-hitter, season

N.L.—230—Pete Rose, Cincinnati, 160 games, 1973.
A.L.—230—Willie Wilson, Kansas City, 161 games, 1980.

**Switch-hitters with 100 or more hits from each side of plate,
season**

N.L.—Garry Templeton, St. Louis, 154 games, 1979 (111 hits
    lefthanded, 100 hits righthanded).
A.L.—Willie Wilson, Kansas City, 161 games, 1980 (130 hits
    lefthanded, 100 hits righthanded).

Most hits by pinch-hitter, season

N.L.—28—John Vander Wal, Colorado, 92 games, 1995.
A.L.—24—Dave Philley, Baltimore, 79 games, 1961.

Most years leading league in hits

A.L.—8—Ty Cobb, Detroit, 1907, 1908, 1909, 1911, 1912,
    1915, 1917, 1919 (tied).
N.L.—7
Pete Rose, Cincinnati, 1965, 1968 (tied), 1970 (tied), 1972,
    1973, 1976, Philadelphia, 1981.

Tony Gwynn, San Diego, 1984, 1986, 1987, 1989, 1994, 1995 (tied), 1997.

Most consecutive years leading league in hits
N.L.—3
Ginger Beaumont, Pittsburgh, 1902, 1903, 1904.
Rogers Hornsby, St. Louis, 1920, 1921, 1922.
Frank McCormick, Cincinnati, 1938, 1939, 1940 (tied).
A.L.—3
Ty Cobb, Detroit, 1907, 1908, 1909.
Tony Oliva, Minnesota, 1964, 1965, 1966.
Kirby Puckett, Minnesota, 1987 (tied), 1988, 1989.

Most games with one or more hits, season
N.L.—135
Rogers Hornsby, St. Louis, 154 games, 1922.
Chuck Klein, Philadelphia, 156 games, 1930.
A.L.—135
Wade Boggs, Boston, 161 games, 1985.
Derek Jeter, New York, 158 games, 1999.
Ichiro Suzuki, Seattle, 157 games, 2001.

Most years with 200 or more hits, career
N.L.—10—Pete Rose, Cincinnati, 1965, 1966, 1968, 1969, 1970, 1973, 1975, 1976, 1977, Philadelphia, 1979.
A.L.—9—Ty Cobb, Detroit, 1907, 1909, 1911, 1912, 1915, 1916, 1917, 1922, 1924.

For a complete list of players collecting 200 or more hits four or more times, see page 173.

Most consecutive years with 200 or more hits, career
N.L.—8—Willie Keeler, Baltimore, Brooklyn, 1894 through 1901.
A.L.—7—Wade Boggs, Boston, 1983 through 1989.
N.L. since 1900—5—Chuck Klein, Philadelphia, 1929 through 1933.

Most hits, two consecutive seasons
N.L.—485—Rogers Hornsby, St. Louis, 235 in 1921, 250 in 1922.
A.L.—475—Ty Cobb, Detroit, 248 in 1911, 227 in 1912.

Fewest hits, season (150 or more games)
N.L.—80—Dal Maxvill, St. Louis, 152 games, 1970.
A.L.—82—Eddie Brinkman, Washington, 154 games, 1965.

Fewest hits for leader, season
N.L.—171—Sherry Magee, Philadelphia, 146 games, 1914.
A.L.—177—Bert Campaneris, Oakland, 159 games, 1968.

Most at-bats in hitless season
N.L.—70—Bob Buhl, Milwaukee, Chicago, 35 games, 1962.
A.L.—61—Bill Wight, Chicago, 30 games, 1950.

GAME AND DOUBLEHEADER

Most hits, nine-inning game
N.L.—7
Wilbert Robinson, Baltimore, June 10, 1892, first game (6 singles, 1 double; consecutive).
Rennie Stennett, Pittsburgh, September 16, 1975 (4 singles, 2 doubles, 1 triple; consecutive).
A.L.—6—Held by many players.

For a complete list of players with six or more hits in a game, see page 191.

Most hits, extra-inning game
A.L.—9—Johnny Burnett, Cleveland, July 10, 1932, 18 innings (7 singles, 2 doubles).
N.L.—6—Less than nine-inning record.

Most times reached base, nine-inning game (batting 1.000)
N.L.—8—Piggy Ward, Cincinnati, June 18, 1893 (2 singles, 5 bases on balls, 1 hit by pitch).
N.L. since 1900—7
Cliff Heathcote, Chicago, August 25, 1922 (3 singles, 2 doubles, 2 bases on balls).
Cookie Lavagetto, Brooklyn, September 23, 1939, first game (4 singles, 1 double, 1 triple, 1 base on balls).

Mel Ott, New York, April 30, 1944, first game (2 singles, 5 bases on balls).
Rennie Stennett, Pittsburgh, September 16, 1975 (4 singles, 2 doubles, 1 triple).
Sean Casey, Cincinnati, May 19, 1999 (2 singles, 2 home runs, 3 bases on balls).
A.L.—7—Ben Chapman, New York, May 24, 1936 (2 doubles, 5 bases on balls).

Most times reached base, extra-inning game (batting 1.000)
N.L.—9—Max Carey, Pittsburgh, July 7, 1922, 18 innings (5 singles, 1 double, 3 bases on balls).
A.L.—7
Cesar Gutierrez, Detroit, June 21, 1970, second game, 12 innings (6 singles, 1 double).
Tim Raines Sr., Chicago, April 20, 1994, 12 innings (3 singles, 4 bases on balls).

Most clubs with one or more hits, one day
N.L.—2—Joel Youngblood, New York, Montreal, August 4, 1982.

Most hits in first major league game, nine innings
N.L.—5—Fred Clarke, Louisville, June 30, 1894 (4 singles, 1 triple).
N.L. since 1900—4
Casey Stengel, Brooklyn, September 17, 1912 (4 singles).
Ed Freed, Philadelphia, September 11, 1942 (1 single, 2 doubles, 1 triple).
Willie McCovey, San Francisco, July 30, 1959 (2 singles, 2 triples; consecutive).
Mack Jones, Milwaukee, July 13, 1961 (3 singles, 1 double).
Delino DeShields, Montreal, April 9, 1990 (3 singles, 1 double).
A.L.—4
Ray Jansen, St. Louis, September 30, 1910 (4 singles; only game in major league career).
Art Shires, Chicago, August 20, 1928 (3 singles, 1 triple).
Russ Van Atta, New York, April 25, 1933 (4 singles).
Forrest Jacobs, Philadelphia, April 13, 1954 (4 singles).
Ted Cox, Boston, September 18, 1977 (3 singles, 1 double; consecutive).
Kirby Puckett, Minnesota, May 8, 1984 (4 singles).
Billy Bean, Detroit, April 25, 1987 (2 singles, 2 doubles).

Most hits in first major league game, extra innings
A.L.—5—Cecil Travis, Washington, May 16, 1933, 12 innings (5 singles).
N.L.—Less than nine-inning record.

Most hits by pitcher, game
A.A.—6—Guy Hecker, Louisville, August 15, 1886, second game.
N.L.-A.L.—5—Held by many pitchers.
N.L.—Last pitcher—Pete Donohue, Cincinnati, May 22, 1925 (4 singles, 1 home run).
A.L.—Last pitcher—Mel Stottlemyre, New York, September 26, 1964 (4 singles, 1 double).

Most hits, opening day of season
N.L.-A.L.—5—Held by many players.
N.L.—Last player—Craig Biggio, Houston, April 3, 2001 (5 singles).
A.L.—Last player—Nellie Fox, Chicago, April 10, 1959, 14 innings (3 singles, 1 double, 1 home run).

Most hits comprising all of club's hits, game
A.L.—4—Kid Elberfeld, New York, August 1, 1903 (4 singles).
N.L.—4—Billy Williams, Chicago, September 5, 1969 (2 doubles, 2 home runs).

Most at-bats with no hits, extra-inning game
N.L.—11—Charles Pick, Boston, May 1, 1920, 26 innings.
A.L.—10—George Kell, Detroit, July 21, 1945, 24 innings.

Most times with six hits in six times at bat in game, career
M.L.—2
Ed Delahanty, Cleveland, P.L., June 2, 1890; Philadelphia, N.L., June 16, 1894.
Jim Bottomley, St. Louis N.L., September 16, 1924; August 5, 1931, second game.
Doc Cramer, Philadelphia A.L., June 20, 1932; July 13, 1935.
N.L.—2—Jim Bottomley, St. Louis, September 16, 1924; August 5, 1931, second game.
A.L.—2—Doc Cramer, Philadelphia, June 20, 1932; July 13, 1935.

Most times with five or more hits in one game, career
A.L.—14—Ty Cobb, Detroit, Philadelphia, 1908 to 1927.
N.L.—10—Pete Rose, Cincinnati, Philadelphia, 1965 to 1986.

Most times with five hits in one game, by pitcher, career
3—Jim Callahan, Chicago N.L., 1897, Chicago A.L., 1902, 1903.

Most times with five or more hits in one game, season
N.L.—4
Willie Keeler, Baltimore, July 17, August 14, September 3, September 6, first game, 1897.
Stan Musial, St. Louis, April 30, May 19, June 22, September 22, 1948.
Tony Gwynn, San Diego, April 18, April 30, July 27, August 4, 1993.
A.L.—4—Ty Cobb, Detroit, May 7, July 7, second game, July 12, July 17, 1922.

Most hits, doubleheader
A.A.—9—Fred Carroll, Pittsburgh, July 5, 1886.
N.L.—9
Wilbert Robinson, Baltimore, June 10, 1892.
Joe Kelley, Baltimore, September 3, 1894 (consecutive).
Fred Lindstrom, New York, June 25, 1928.
Bill Terry, New York, June 18, 1929.
A.L.—9
Ray Morehart, Chicago, August 31, 1926.
George Case, Washington, July 4, 1940.
Pete Runnels, Boston, August 30, 1960, 25 innings.
Lee Thomas, Los Angeles, September 5, 1961.

Most hits by pinch-hitter, doubleheader
N.L.-A.L.—2—Held by many pinch-hitters.

Most hits in first doubleheader in majors
N.L.-A.L.—6—Held by many players.

Most hits, two consecutive doubleheaders
A.L.—14—Ty Cobb, Detroit, July 17 (7), 19 (7), 1912.
N.L.—14—Bill White, St. Louis, July 17 (8), 18 (6), 1961.

Most at-bats with no hits, doubleheader (nine-inning games)
A.L.—11—Albie Pearson, Los Angeles, July 1, 1962.
N.L.—Held by many players.

Most at-bats with no hits, doubleheader (over 18 innings)
A.L.—13—Brian L. Hunter, Detroit, June 20, 1998, 26 innings.
N.L.—12—Red Schoendienst, St. Louis, June 9, 1947, 24 innings.

HITTING FOR CYCLE
(Single, double, triple, home run in game)
Most times hitting for cycle, career
M.L.—3
John Reilly, Cincinnati A.A., 1883 (2), Cincinnati N.L., 1890.
Bob Meusel, New York A.L., 1921, 1922, 1928.
Babe Herman, Brooklyn N.L., 1931 (2), Chicago N.L., 1933.
A.L.—3—Bob Meusel, New York, 1921, 1922, 1928.
N.L.—3—Babe Herman, Brooklyn, 1931 (2), Chicago, 1933.

For a complete list of players hitting for cycle, see page 189.

Hitting for cycle in American and National leagues
Bob Watson, Houston N.L., June 24, 1977; Boston A.L., September 15, 1979.
John Olerud, New York N.L., September 11, 1997; Seattle A.L., June 16, 2001.

Most times hitting for cycle, season
A.A.—2
John, Reilly, Cincinnati, 1883.
Tip O'Neill, St. Louis, 1887.
N.L.—2—Babe Herman, Brooklyn, 1931.
A.L.—1—Held by many players.

INNING

Most hits, inning
A.L.—3—Gene Stephens, Boston, June 18, 1953, seventh inning (2 singles, 1 double).

N.L.—3
Tommy Burns, Chicago, September 6, 1883, seventh inning (2 doubles, 1 home run).
Fred Pfeffer, Chicago, September 6, 1883, seventh inning (2 singles, 1 double).
Ned Williamson, Chicago, September 6, 1883, seventh inning (2 singles, 1 double).

Most hits in one inning of first major league game
A.L.—2
Billy Martin, New York, April 18, 1950, eighth inning.
Russ Morman, Chicago, August 3, 1986, fourth inning.
Chad Kreuter, Texas, September 14, 1988, fifth inning.
N.L.—1—Held by many players.

Most times with two hits in one inning, game
N.L.—2
Max Carey, Pittsburgh, June 22, 1925, first and eighth innings (2 singles in each inning).
Rennie Stennett, Pittsburgh, September 16, 1975, first inning (single and double); fifth inning (double and single).
A.L.—2
Johnny Hodapp, Cleveland, July 29, 1928, second and sixth innings (2 singles in each inning).
Sherm Lollar, Chicago, April 23, 1955, second inning (single and home run); sixth inning (2 singles).

Most times reached first base safely, inning
N.L.—3
Ned Williamson, Chicago, September 6, 1883, seventh inning.
Tommy Burns, Chicago, September 6, 1883, seventh inning.
Fred Pfeffer, Chicago, September 6, 1883, seventh inning.
Herman Long, Boston, June 18, 1894, a.m. game, first inning.
Bobby Lowe, Boston, June 18, 1894, a.m. game, first inning.
Hugh Duffy, Boston, June 18, 1894, a.m. game, first inning.
Pee Wee Reese, Brooklyn, May 21, 1952, first inning.
A.L.—3
Sammy White, Boston, June 18, 1953, seventh inning.
Gene Stephens, Boston, June 18, 1953, seventh inning.
Tommy Umphlett, Boston, June 18, 1953, seventh inning.

BATTING STREAKS

Most consecutive hits, season (bases on balls shown in streak)
A.L.—12
Pinky Higgins, Boston, June 19, 19, 21, 21, 1938 (2 B.B.).
Walt Dropo, Detroit, July 14, 15, 15, 1952 (0 B.B.).
N.L.—10
Ed Delahanty, Philadelphia, July 13, 13, 14, 1897 (1 B.B.).
Jake Gettman, Washington, September 10, 11, 11, 1897 (0 B.B.).
Ed Konetchy, Brooklyn, June 28, second game, June 29, July 1, 1919 (0 B.B.).
Kiki Cuyler, Pittsburgh, September 18, 19, 21, 1925 (1 B.B.).
Chick Hafey, St. Louis, July 6, second game, July 8, 9, 1929 (2 B.B.).
Joe Medwick, St. Louis, July 19, 19, 21, 1936 (1 B.B.).
Buddy Hassett, Boston, June 9, second game, June 10, 14, 1940 (1 B.B.).
Woody Williams, Cincinnati, September 5, second game, September 6, 6, 1943 (1 B.B.).
Bip Roberts, Cincinnati, September 19, 20, 22, second game, 23 1992 (1 B.B.).

Most consecutive times reached base safely, season
A.L.—16—Ted Williams, Boston, September 17 (1), 18 (1), 20 (1), 21 (4), 22 (4), 23 (5), 1957 (2 singles, 4 home runs, 9 bases on balls, 1 hit by pitch).
N.L.—15
Barry Bonds, San Francisco, August 31 (1), September 1 (5), 2 (4), 4 (5), 1998 (5 singles, 2 doubles, 2 home runs, 6 bases on balls).
John Olerud, New York, September 16 (1), 18 (5), 20 (4), 22 (1), 1998 (6 singles, 1 double, 2 home runs, 6 bases on balls).

Most consecutive hits from start of career
A.L.—6—Ted Cox, Boston, September 18, 19, 1977.

Most consecutive hits by pinch-hitter, career
N.L.—9—Dave Philley, Philadelphia, September 9 through September 28, 1958; April 16, 1959.

Most consecutive hits by pinch-hitter, season
N.L.—8
Dave Philley, Philadelphia, September 9 through September 28, 1958.
Rusty Staub, New York, June 11 through June 26, first game, 1983 (1 hit by pitch during streak).
A.L.—7
Bill Stein, Texas, April 14 through May 25, 1981.
Randy Bush, Minnesota, July 5 through August 19, 1991.

Most consecutive games batted safely during season
A.L.—56—Joe DiMaggio, New York, May 15 through July 16, 1941.
N.L.—44
Willie Keeler, Baltimore, April 22 through June 18, 1897.
Pete Rose, Cincinnati, June 14 through July 31, 1978.

Most consecutive games batted safely by rookie, season
N.L.—34—Benito Santiago, San Diego, August 25 through October 2, 1987.
A.L.—30—Nomar Garciaparra, Boston, July 26 through August 29, 1997.

Most consecutive games batted safely by righthander, season
A.L.—56—Joe DiMaggio, New York, May 15 through July 16, 1941.
N.L.—42—Bill Dahlen, Chicago, June 20 through August 6, 1894.
N.L. since 1900—34—Benito Santiago, San Diego, August 25 through October 2, 1987.

For a complete list of players with 30-game batting streaks, see page 182. For a detailed breakdown of Joe DiMaggio's 56-game hitting streak, see page 197.

Most consecutive games batted safely by lefthander, season
N.L.—44—Willie Keeler, Baltimore, April 22 to June 18, 1897.
A.L.—41—George Sisler, St. Louis, July 27 to September 17, 1922.
N.L. since 1900—37—Tommy Holmes, Boston, June 6, first game, to July 8, second game, 1945.

Most consecutive games batted safely by switch-hitter, season
N.L.—44—Pete Rose, Cincinnati, June 14 through July 31, 1978.
A.L.—27—Jose Offerman, Kansas City, July 11 through August 7, 1998.

Most consecutive games batted safely from start of season
N.L.—44—Willie Keeler, Baltimore, April 22 through June 18, 1897.
A.L.—34—George Sisler, St. Louis, April 14 through May 19, 1925.
N.L. since 1900—25—Charlie Grimm, Pittsburgh, April 17 through May 16, 1923.

Most 20-game batting streaks, career
N.L.—8—Willie Keeler, Baltimore, Brooklyn, 1894, 1896, 1897, 1898 (2), 1899, 1900, 1902.
N.L. since 1900—7—Pete Rose, Cincinnati, Philadelphia, 1967, 1968, 1977 (2), 1978, 1979, 1982.
A.L.—7—Ty Cobb, Detroit, Philadelphia, 1911, 1912, 1917, 1918, 1920, 1926, 1927.

Most 20-game batting streaks, season
A.L.—3—Tris Speaker, Boston, 1912.
N.L.—2—Held by many players. Last player—Steve Garvey, Los Angeles, 1978.

Most hits in two consecutive nine-inning games
N.L.—12—Cal McVey, Chicago, July 22 (6), 25 (6), 1876.
N.L. since 1900—10—Rennie Stennett, Pittsburgh, September 16 (7), 17 (3), 1975.
A.L.—10—Kirby Puckett, Minnesota, August 29 (4), 30 (6), 1987.

Most hits in two consecutive extra-inning games
A.L.—11—Johnny Burnett, Cleveland, July 9, second game (2), 10 (9), 1932, 27 innings.
N.L.—10—Roberto Clemente, Pittsburgh, August 22 (5), 23 (5), 1970, 25 innings.

Most hits by pitcher in two consecutive games
A.A.—10—Guy Hecker, Louisville, August 12, 15, second game, 1886.
A.L.—8—George Earnshaw, Philadelphia, June 9, 12, second game, 1931.
N.L. since 1900—8—Kirby Higbe, Brooklyn, August 11, 17, first game, 1941.

Most hits in three consecutive games
N.L.—15—Cal McVey, Chicago, July 20, 22, 25, 1876.
N.L. since 1900—14
Mike Benjamin, San Francisco, June 11, 13, 14, 1995.
A.L.—13
Joe Cronin, Washington, June 19, 21, 22, 1933.
Walt Dropo, Detroit, July 14, 15, 15, 1952.
Tim Salmon, California, May 10, 11, 13, 1994.

Most hits in four consecutive games
N.L.—18—Cal McVey, Chicago, July 20, 22, 25, 27, 1876.
N.L. since 1900—16—Milt Stock, Brooklyn, June 30, July 1, 2, 3, 1925.
A.A.—17—Guy Hecker, Louisville, August 8, 10, 12, 15, second game, 1886.
A.L.—15
Joe Cronin, Washington, June 18, second game, 19, 21, 22, 1933.
Joe Cronin, Washington, June 19, 21, 22, 23, 1933.
John Lewis Jr., Washington, July 25, 25, 27, 28, 1937.
Walt Dropo, Detroit, July 14, 15, 15, 16, 1952.
Johnny Damon, Kansas City, July 18, 19, 20, 21, 2000.

Most consecutive games with three or more hits, season
A.L.—6—George Brett, Kansas City, May 8, 9, 10, 11, 12, 13, 1976.

SINGLES

Most singles, career
N.L.—3,215—Pete Rose, Cincinnati, Philadelphia, Montreal, 24 years, 1963 through 1986.
A.L.—3,052—Ty Cobb, Detroit, Philadelphia, 24 years, 1905 through 1928.

For a complete list of players with 2,000 or more career singles, see page 173.

Most singles, season
N.L.—202—Willie Keeler, Baltimore, 128 games, 1898.
N.L. since 1900—198—Lloyd Waner, Pittsburgh, 150 games, 1927.
A.L.—192—Ichiro Suzuki, Seattle, 157 games, 2001.

Most singles by rookie, season
N.L.—198—Lloyd Waner, Pittsburgh, 150 games, 1927.
A.L.—192—Ichiro Suzuki, Seattle, 157 games, 2001.

Most singles by righthander, season
N.L.—178—Curt Flood, St. Louis, 162 games, 1964.
A.L.—174—Al Simmons, Philadelphia, 153 games, 1925.

Most singles by lefthander, season
N.L.—202—Willie Keeler, Baltimore, 128 games, 1898.
N.L. since 1900—198—Lloyd Waner, Pittsburgh, 150 games, 1927.
A.L.—192—Ichiro Suzuki, Seattle, 157 games, 2001.

Most singles by switch-hitter, season
A.L.—184—Willie Wilson, Kansas City, 161 games, 1980.
N.L.—181—Pete Rose, Cincinnati, 160 games, 1973.

Most years leading league in singles
A.L.—8—Nellie Fox, Chicago, 1952, 1954, 1955, 1956, 1957, 1958, 1959, 1960.
N.L.—7—Tony Gwynn, San Diego, 1984, 1986 (tied), 1987, 1989, 1994, 1995, 1997.

Most consecutive years leading league in singles
A.L.—7—Nellie Fox, Chicago, 1954, 1955, 1956, 1957, 1958, 1959, 1960.
N.L.—4—Brett Butler, San Francisco, 1990, Los Angeles, 1991, 1992, 1993.

Fewest singles, season (150 or more games)
N.L.—49—Barry Bonds, San Francisco, 153 games, 2001.
A.L.—53—Mark McGwire, Oakland, 154 games, 1991.

Fewest singles by leader, season
A.L.—129—Don Buford, Chicago, 155 games, 1965.
N.L.—127—Enos Slaughter, St. Louis, 152 games, 1942.

Most singles, nine-inning game
M.L.—6—Held by many players.
Last N.L. player—Dave Bancroft, New York, June 28, 1920.
Last A.L. player—Floyd Robinson, Chicago, July 22, 1962.

Most singles, extra-inning game
A.L.—7—Johnny Burnett, Cleveland, July 10, 1932, 18 innings.
N.L.—6—Held by many players. Last player—Willie Davis, Los Angeles, May 24, 1973, 19 innings.

Most singles in a game, each batting in three runs
N.L.-A.L.—1—Held by many players.
Last N.L. player—Willie Montanez, Philadelphia, September 8, 1974, eighth inning.
Last A.L. player—Ernest Riles, Milwaukee, June 5, 1985, third inning.

Most singles, doubleheader
N.L.-A.L.—8—Held by many players.
Last A.L. player—Earl Averill, Cleveland, May 7, 1933.
Last N.L. player—Ken Hubbs, Chicago, May 20, 1962.

Most singles, inning
N.L.-A.L.—2—Held by many players.

DOUBLES
CAREER AND SEASON

Most doubles, career
A.L.—793—Tris Speaker, Boston, Cleveland, Washington, Philadelphia, 22 years, 1907 through 1928.
N.L.—746—Pete Rose, Cincinnati, Philadelphia, Montreal, 24 years, 1963 through 1986.

For a complete list of players with 450 or more career doubles, see page 173.

Most doubles, season
A.L.—67—Earl Webb, Boston, 151 games, 1931.
N.L.—64—Joe Medwick, St. Louis, 155 games, 1936.

Most doubles by rookie, season
N.L.—52—Johnny Frederick, Brooklyn, 148 games, 1929.
A.L.—47—Fred Lynn, Boston, 145 games, 1975.

Most doubles by righthander, season
A.L.—64—George Burns, Cleveland, 151 games, 1926.
N.L.—64—Joe Medwick, St. Louis, 155 games, 1936.

Most doubles by lefthander, season
A.L.—67—Earl Webb, Boston, 151 games, 1931.
N.L.—62—Paul Waner, Pittsburgh, 154 games, 1932.

Most doubles by switch-hitter, season
N.L.—55—Lance Berkman, Houston, 156 games, 2001.
A.L.—47—John Anderson, Milwaukee, 138 games, 1901.

Most doubles by catcher, season
A.L.—45—Ivan Rodriguez, Texas, 146 games, 1996 (had two additional doubles as a designated hitter).
N.L.—40
Johnny Bench, Cincinnati, 154 games, 1968; caught 154 games.
Terry Kennedy, San Diego, 153 games, 1982; caught 139 games (had two additional doubles as first baseman).

Most years leading league in doubles
N.L.—8
Honus Wagner, Pittsburgh, 1900, 1901 (tied), 1902, 1904, 1906, 1907, 1908, 1909.
Stan Musial, St. Louis, 1943, 1944, 1946, 1948, 1949, 1952, 1953, 1954.
A.L.—8—Tris Speaker, Boston, 1912, Cleveland, 1914, 1916 (tied), 1918, 1920, 1921, 1922, 1923.

Most consecutive years leading league in doubles
N.L.—4—Honus Wagner, Pittsburgh, 1906, 1907, 1908, 1909.
A.L.—4—Tris Speaker, Cleveland, 1920, 1921, 1922, 1923.

Most years with 50 or more doubles, career
A.L.—5—Tris Speaker, Boston, 1912, Cleveland, 1920, 1921, 1923, 1926.
N.L.—3
Paul Waner, Pittsburgh, 1928, 1932, 1936.
Stan Musial, St. Louis, 1944, 1946, 1953.

Fewest doubles, season (150 or more games)
N.L.—5—Dal Maxvill, St. Louis, 152 games, 1970.
A.L.—6—Billy Purtell, Chicago, Boston, 151 games, 1910.

Fewest doubles for leader, season
A.L.—32
Sal Bando, Oakland, 162 games, 1973.
Pedro Garcia, Milwaukee, 160 games, 1973.
N.L.—34—Hank Aaron, Milwaukee, 153 games, 1956.

GAME AND INNING

Most doubles, game
N.L.—4—20 times (held by 20 players). Last player—Jeff Bagwell, Houston, June 14, 1996.
A.L.—4—22 times (held by 21 players). Last players—Johnny Damon, Kansas City, July 18, 2000; Shannon Stewart, Toronto, July 18, 2000.
A.A.—4—2 times (held by 2 players).

Most consecutive doubles, nine-inning game
N.L.—4
Frank Bonner, Baltimore, August 4, 1894.
Joe Kelley, Baltimore, September 3, 1894, second game.
Dick Bartell, Philadelphia, April 25, 1933.
Ernie Lombardi, Cincinnati, May 8, 1935, first game.
Bill Werber, Cincinnati, May 13, 1940.
Willie Jones, Philadelphia, April 20, 1949.
Billy Williams, Chicago, April 9, 1969.
A.L.—4
Bill Werber, Boston, July 17, 1935, first game.
Mike Kreevich, Chicago, September 4, 1937.
Johnny Lindell, New York, August 17, 1944.
Lou Boudreau, Cleveland, July 14, 1946, first game.
Vic Wertz, Cleveland, September 26, 1956.
Bill Bruton, Detroit, May 19, 1963.
Dave Duncan, Baltimore, June 30, 1975, second game.
Sandy Alomar Jr., Cleveland, June 6, 1997.

Most doubles, opening game of season
A.L.—4—Frank Dillon, Detroit, April 25, 1901.
N.L.—4—Jim Greengrass, Cincinnati, April 13, 1954.

Most doubles by pitcher, game
N.L.—3
George Hemming, Baltimore, August 1, 1895.
Andy Messersmith, Los Angeles, April 25, 1975.
A.L.—3
George Mullin, Detroit, April 27, 1903.
Walter Johnson, Washington, July 29, 1917.
Babe Ruth, Boston, May 9, 1918, 10 innings.
George Uhle, Cleveland, June 1, 1923.
Red Ruffing, Boston, May 25, 1929, second game.
Don Ferrarese, Cleveland, May 26, 1959.

Most doubles, each batting in three runs, game
N.L.—2
Bob Gilks, Cleveland, August 5, 1890 (1 in second, 1 in eighth).
Harry Davis, New York, June 27, 1896 (1 in fifth, 1 in ninth).
William Douglass, Philadelphia, July 11, 1898 (1 in second, 1 in sixth).
Gavvy Cravath, Philadelphia, August 8, 1915 (1 in fourth, 1 in eighth).
A.L.—1—Held by many players.

Most doubles, doubleheader
A.L.—6—Hank Majeski, Philadelphia, August 27, 1948.
N.L.—5
Chick Hafey, Cincinnati, July 23, 1933.
Joe Medwick, St. Louis, May 30, 1935.
Red Schoendienst, St. Louis, June 6, 1948.
Mike Ivie, San Diego, May 30, 1977.

Most doubles in two consecutive games
N.L.—6
Cap Anson, Chicago, July 3, 4, a.m. game, 1883.
Sam Thompson, Philadelphia, June 29, July 1, 1895, 22 innings.
Red Schoendienst, St. Louis, June 5, 6, first game, 1948.
A.L.—5
Joe Dugan, Philadelphia, September 24, 25, 1920.
Earl Sheely, Chicago, May 20, 21, 1926.
Hank Majeski, Philadelphia, August 27, 28, 1948.
Kirby Puckett, Minnesota, May 13, 14, 1989.

Most doubles in three consecutive games
N.L.—8—Red Schoendienst, St. Louis, June 5, 6, 6, 1948.
A.L.—7
    Joe Dugan, Philadelphia, September 23, 24, 25, 1920.
    Earl Sheely, Chicago, May 20, 21, 22, 1926.

Most doubles by pinch-hitter, three consecutive games
N.L.—3
    Bert Haas, Brooklyn, September 18, 19, 20, 1937.
    Doug Clemens, Philadelphia, June 6, 6, 7, 1967.
    Bob Robertson, Pittsburgh, July 18, 19, 20, 1974.
A.L.—Never accomplished.

Most doubles, inning
N.L.-A.L.—2—Held by many players.
Last N.L. player—Jeff Kent, San Francisco, May 10, 2001, sixth inning.
Last A.L. players—Jose Guillen, Tampa Bay, May 28, 2000, eighth inning; Ivan Rodriguez, Texas, June 14, 2000, fourth inning; Frank Thomas, Chicago, September 3, 2000, first inning; Tim Salmon, Anaheim, September 23, 2000, second inning.

Most doubles by pitcher, inning
N.L.—2
    Fred Goldsmith, Chicago, September 6, 1883, seventh inning.
    Hank Borowy, Chicago, May 5, 1946, first game, seventh inning.
A.L.—2
    Joe Wood, Boston, July 4, 1913, a.m. game, fourth inning.
    Ted Lyons, Chicago, July 28, 1935, first game, second inning.

TRIPLES
CAREER AND SEASON

Most triples, career
M.L.—312—Sam Crawford, Cincinnati N.L., Detroit A.L., 19 years, 1899 through 1917 (62 in N.L. and 250 in A.L.).
A.L.—298—Ty Cobb, Detroit, Philadelphia, 24 years, 1905 through 1928.
N.L.—252—Honus Wagner, Louisville, Pittsburgh, 21 years, 1897 through 1917.
N.L. since 1900—231—Honus Wagner, Pittsburgh, 18 years, 1900 through 1917.

For a complete list of players with 150 or more career triples, see page 173.

Most triples with bases filled, career
A.L.—8—Shano Collins, Chicago, Boston, 1910, 1915, 1916, 1918 (3), 1920 (2).
N.L.—7—Stan Musial, St. Louis, 1946, 1947 (2), 1948, 1949, 1951, 1954.

Most triples, season
N.L.—36—Owen Wilson, Pittsburgh, 152 games, 1912.
A.L.—26
    Joe Jackson, Cleveland, 152 games, 1912.
    Sam Crawford, Detroit, 157 games, 1914.

Most triples by rookie, season
N.L.—28—Jimmy Williams, Pittsburgh, 153 games, 1899.
N.L. since 1900—22—Paul Waner, Pittsburgh, 144 games, 1926.
A.L.—19—Joe Cassidy, Washington, 154 games, 1904.
(Home Run Baker collected 19 triples in 148 games in 1909. Baker, however, had 31 at-bats in nine games in 1908. During this period there was no rookie qualification rule.)

Most triples by righthander, season
N.L.—33—Perry Werden, St. Louis, 124 games, 1893.
N.L. since 1900—26—Kiki Cuyler, Pittsburgh, 153 games, 1925.
A.L.—23—Jimmy Williams, Baltimore, 125 games, 1902.

Most triples by lefthander, season
N.L.—36—Owen Wilson, Pittsburgh, 152 games, 1912.
A.L.—26
    Joe Jackson, Cleveland, 152 games, 1912.
    Sam Crawford, Detroit, 157 games, 1914.

Most triples by switch-hitter, season
N.L.—26—George Davis, New York, 133 games, 1893.
A.L.—21—Willie Wilson, Kansas City, 141 games, 1985.

N.L. since 1900—19
    Max Carey, 153 games, 1923.
    Garry Templeton, St. Louis, 154 games, 1979.

Most triples with bases filled, season
N.L.—3
    George J. Burns, New York, 154 games, 1914.
    Ted Sizemore, Los Angeles, 159 games, 1969.
    Manny Sanguillen, Pittsburgh, 138 games, 1971.
    Alfredo Griffin, Los Angeles, 95 games, 1988.
A.L.—3
    Shano Collins, Chicago, 103 games, 1918.
    Elmer Valo, Philadelphia, 150 games, 1949.
    Jackie Jensen, Boston, 151 games, 1956.

Most years leading league in triples (since 1900)
M.L.—6—Sam Crawford, Cincinnati N.L., 1902; Detroit A.L., 1903, 1910, 1913, 1914, 1915.
A.L.—5
    Sam Crawford, Detroit, 1903, 1910, 1913, 1914, 1915.
    Willie Wilson, Kansas City, 1980 (tied), 1982, 1985, 1987, 1988 (tied).
N.L.—5—Stan Musial, St. Louis, 1943, 1946, 1948, 1949 (tied), 1951 (tied).

Most consecutive years leading league in triples (since 1900)
A.L.—4—Lance Johnson, Chicago, 1991 (tied), 1992, 1993, 1994.
N.L.—3—Garry Templeton, St. Louis, 1977, 1978, 1979.

Most years with 20 or more triples
M.L.—5—Sam Crawford, Cincinnati N.L., 1902; Detroit A.L., 1903, 1912, 1913, 1914.
A.L.—4
    Sam Crawford, Detroit, 1903, 1912, 1913, 1914.
    Ty Cobb, Detroit, 1908, 1911, 1912, 1917.
N.L.—2—Held by many players. Last player—Stan Musial, St. Louis, 1943, 1946.

Most at-bats without a triple, season
A.L.—646—Cal Ripken Jr., Baltimore, 162 games, 1989.
N.L.—643—Sammy Sosa, Chicago, 159 games, 1998.

Fewest triples for league leader, season
A.L.—8—Del Unser, Washington, 153 games, 1969.
N.L.—10
    Johnny Callison, Philadelphia, 157 games, 1962.
    Willie Davis, Los Angeles, 157 games, 1962.
    Bill Virdon, Pittsburgh, 156 games, 1962.
    Maury Wills, Los Angeles, 165 games, 1962.
    Dickie Thon, Houston, 136 games, 1982.

GAME AND INNING

Most triples, game
A.A.—4—George Strief, Philadelphia, June 25, 1885.
N.L.—4—Bill Joyce, New York, May 18, 1897.
N.L. since 1900—3—Held by many players. Last players—Shawon Dunston, Chicago, July 28, 1990; Herm Winningham, Cincinnati, August 15, 1990, 12 innings.
A.L.—3—Held by many players. Last player—Lance Johnson, Chicago, September 23, 1995.

Most triples, first major league game
A.L.—2
    Ed Irvin, Detroit, May 18, 1912 (only major league game).
    Roy Weatherly, Cleveland, June 27, 1936.
N.L.—2
    Willie McCovey, San Francisco, July 30, 1959.
    John Sipin, San Diego, May 24, 1969 (only major league triples).

Most triples by pitcher, game
N.L.—3—Jouett Meekin, New York, July 4, 1894, first game.

Most consecutive triples, nine-inning game
N.L.-A.L.—3—Held by many players.
Last N.L. player—Roberto Clemente, Pittsburgh, September 8, 1958.
Last A.L. player—Ben Chapman, Cleveland, July 3, 1939.

Most triples with bases filled, game
N.L.—2
    Sam Thompson, Detroit, May 7, 1887.
    Heinie Reitz, Baltimore, June 4, 1894, 1 in third inning, 1 in seventh inning.

Willie Clark, Pittsburgh, September 17, 1898, second game, 1 in first inning, 1 in seventh inning.
Bill Bruton, Milwaukee, August 2, 1959, second game, 1 in first inning, 1 in sixth inning.
A.L.—2
Elmer Valo, Philadelphia, May 1, 1949, first game, 1 in third inning, 1 in seventh inning.
Duane Kuiper, Cleveland, July 27, 1978, second game, 1 in first inning, 1 in fifth inning.

Most times with three triples in one game, career
N.L.—3
John Reilly, Cincinnati, 1890, 1891.
George Davis, Cleveland, New York, 1891, 1894.
Bill Dahlen, Chicago, 1896, 1898.
Dave Brain, St. Louis, Pittsburgh, 1905 (2).
A.L.—1—Held by many players.

Most times with three triples in one game, season
N.L.—2—Dave Brain, St. Louis, May 29, 1905; Pittsburgh, August 8, 1905.
A.L.—1—Held by many players.

Hitting triple and home run in first major league game
A.L.—Hank Arft, St. Louis, July 27, 1948.
N.L.—Lloyd Merriman, Cincinnati, April 24, 1949, first game.
Frank Ernaga, Chicago, May 24, 1957.
Ken Caminiti, Houston, July 16, 1987.

Hitting triple and home run with bases filled, game
N.L.—Dennis Brouthers, Detroit, May 17, 1887.
Kid Nichols, Boston, September 19, 1892.
Jake Stenzel, Pittsburgh, July 15, 1893.
Del Bissonette, Brooklyn, April 21, 1930.
Eddie Phillips, Pittsburgh, May 28, 1931.
Luis Olmo, Brooklyn, May 18, 1945.
Robin Jennings, Cincinnati, August 31, 2001.
A.L.—George Sisler, St. Louis, July 11, 1925.
Harry Heilmann, Detroit, July 26, 1928, second game.

Most triples, doubleheader
A.A.—4—Billy Hamilton, Kansas City, June 28, 1889.
N.L.—4—Mike Donlin, Cincinnati, September 22, 1903.
A.L.—3—Held by many players.

Most triples in five consecutive games
N.L.—6—Owen Wilson, Pittsburgh, June 17, 18, 19, 20, 20 (2), 1912.

Most triples, inning
N.L.—2
Joe Hornung, Boston, May 6, 1882, eighth inning.
Heinie Peitz, St. Louis, July 2, 1895, first inning.
Frank Shugart, Louisville, July 30, 1895, fifth inning.
Buck Freeman, Boston, July 25, 1900, first inning.
Bill Dahlen, Brooklyn, August 30, 1900, eighth inning.
Curt Walker, Cincinnati, July 22, 1926, second inning.
A.A.—2
Harry Wheeler, Cincinnati, June 28, 1882, 11th inning.
Harry Stovey, Philadelphia, August 18, 1884, eighth inning.
A.L.—2
Al Zarilla, St. Louis, July 13, 1946, fourth inning.
Gil Coan, Washington, April 21, 1951, sixth inning.

HOME RUNS
CAREER

Most home runs, career
M.L.—755—Hank Aaron, Milwaukee N.L., Atlanta N.L., Milwaukee A.L., 23 years, 1954 through 1976 (733 in N.L.; 22 in A.L.).
N.L.—733—Hank Aaron, Milwaukee, Atlanta, 21 years, 1954 through 1974.
A.L.—708—Babe Ruth, Boston, New York, 21 years, 1914 through 1934.

For a complete list of players with 300 or more career home runs, see page 174.

Most home runs with one club, career
N.L.—733—Hank Aaron, Milwaukee, Atlanta, 21 years, 1954 through 1974.
A.L.—659—Babe Ruth, New York, 15 years, 1920 through 1934.

Most home runs by righthander, career
M.L.—755—Hank Aaron, Milwaukee N.L., Atlanta N.L., Milwaukee A.L., 23 years, 1954 through 1976 (733 in N.L.; 22 in A.L.).
N.L.—733—Hank Aaron, Milwaukee, Atlanta, 21 years, 1954 through 1974.
A.L.—573—Harmon Killebrew, Washington, Minnesota, Kansas City, 22 years, 1954 through 1975.

Most home runs by lefthander, career
M.L.—714—Babe Ruth, Boston A.L., New York A.L., Boston N.L., 22 years, 1914 through 1935 (708 in A.L.; 6 in N.L.).
A.L.—708—Babe Ruth, Boston, New York, 21 years, 1914 through 1934.
N.L.—567—Barry Bonds, Pittsburgh, San Francisco, 16 years, 1986 through 2001.

Most home runs by switch-hitter, career
A.L.—536—Mickey Mantle, New York, 18 years, 1951 through 1968.
N.L.—247—Bobby Bonilla, Pittsburgh, New York, Florida, Los Angeles, Atlanta, St. Louis, 15 years, 1986 through 2001, except 1996.

Most home runs by pinch-hitter, career
M.L.—20—Cliff Johnson, Houston N.L., New York A.L., Cleveland A.L., Chicago N.L., Oakland A.L., Toronto A.L., 1974 (5), 1975, 1976, 1977 (3), 1978 (2), 1979, 1980 (3), 1981, 1983, 1984, 1986.
N.L.—18—Jerry Lynch, Cincinnati, Pittsburgh, 1957 (3), 1958, 1959, 1961 (5), 1962, 1963 (4), 1964, 1965, 1966.
A.L.—16—Gates Brown, Detroit, 1963, 1964, 1965, 1966 (2), 1968 (3), 1970, 1971 (2), 1972, 1974 (3), 1975.

For a complete list of players with 10 or more career pinch-hit home runs, see page 174.

Most home runs leading off game, career
M.L.—79—Rickey Henderson, Oakland A.L., New York A.L., Toronto A.L., San Diego N.L., Anaheim A.L., New York N.L., Seattle A.L., 23 years, 1979 through 2001 (72 in A.L., 7 in N.L.).
A.L.—72—Rickey Henderson, Oakland, New York, Toronto, Anaheim, Seattle, 20 years, 1979 through 2000, except 1996 and 1999.
N.L.—30—Bobby Bonds, San Francisco, St. Louis, Chicago, 1968 through 1974, nine years, 1980 through 1981.

Most home runs in extra innings, career
N.L.—22—Willie Mays, New York Giants, San Francisco, New York Mets, 22 years, 1951 through 1973, except 1953 in military service.
A.L.—16—Babe Ruth, Boston, New York, 21 years, 1914 through 1934.

Most home runs in opening games of season, career
M.L.—8—Frank Robinson, Cincinnati N.L., 1959, 1961, 1963; Baltimore A.L., 1966, 1969, 1970; California A.L., 1973; Cleveland A.L., 1975 (5 in A.L., 3 in N.L.).
N.L.—7
Eddie Mathews, Milwaukee, 1954 (2), 1958 (2), 1959, 1961, 1965.
Willie Mays, New York, 1954; San Francisco, 1962, 1963, 1964 (2), 1966, 1971.
A.L.—7—Ken Griffey Jr., Seattle, 1990, 1993, 1995, 1997 (2), 1998, 1999.

Most home runs by first baseman, career
M.L.—566—Mark McGwire, Oakland A.L., St. Louis N.L., 16 years, 1986 through 2001 (349 in A.L., 217 in N.L.).
A.L.—493—Lou Gehrig, New York, 17 years, 1923 through 1939.
N.L.—439—Willie McCovey, San Francisco, San Diego, 22 years, 1959 through 1980.

Most home runs by second baseman, career
N.L.—277—Ryne Sandberg, Philadelphia, Chicago, 16 years, 1981 through 1997, except 1995.
A.L.—246—Joe Gordon, New York, Cleveland, 11 years, 1938 through 1950, except 1944, 1945 in military service.

Most home runs by third baseman, career
N.L.—509—Mike Schmidt, Philadelphia, 18 years, 1972 through 1989.
A.L.—319—Graig Nettles, Minnesota, Cleveland, New York, 16 years, 1968 through 1983.

Most home runs by shortstop, career
A.L.—345—Cal Ripken Jr., Baltimore, 16 years, 1981 through 1996.
N.L.—277—Ernie Banks, Chicago, nine years, 1953 through 1961.

Most home runs by outfielder, career
M.L.—692—Babe Ruth, Boston A.L., New York A.L., Boston N.L., 17 years, 1918 through 1935 (686 in A.L.; 6 in N.L.).
A.L.—686—Babe Ruth, Boston, New York, 17 years, 1918 through 1934.
N.L.—661—Hank Aaron, Milwaukee, Atlanta, 21 years, 1954 through 1974.

Most home runs by catcher, career
A.L.—351—Carlton Fisk, Boston, Chicago, 24 years, 1969 through 1993, except 1970.
N.L.—327—Johnny Bench, Cincinnati, 17 years, 1967 through 1983.

Most home runs by pitcher, career
A.L.—36—Wes Ferrell, Cleveland, Boston, Washington, New York, 13 years, 1927 through 1939. (Also one home run as pinch-hitter, 1935; one home run as pitcher, Boston N.L., 1941).
N.L.—35—Warren Spahn, Boston, Milwaukee, New York, San Francisco, 21 years, 1942 through 1965, except 1943, 1944, 1945 in military service.

Most major league ballparks, one or more home runs, career (since 1900)
M.L.—39
  Ellis Burks, Boston A.L., Chicago A.L., Colorado N.L., San Francisco N.L., Cleveland A.L., 15 years, 1987 through 2001.
  Fred McGriff, Toronto A.L., San Diego N.L., Atlanta N.L., Tampa Bay A.L., Chicago N.L., 16 years, 1986 through 2001.
  Mark McGwire, Oakland A.L., St. Louis N.L., 16 years, 1986 through 2001.
A.L.—30—Rafael Palmeiro, Texas, Baltimore, 13 years, 1989 through 2001.
N.L.—29—Mike Piazza, Los Angeles, Florida, New York, 10 years, 1992 through 2001.

Most consecutive at-bats without hitting a home run, career
N.L.—3,347—Tommy Thevenow, St. Louis, Philadelphia, Pittsburgh, Cincinnati, Boston, September 24, 1926 through October 2, 1938 (end of career).
A.L.—3,278—Eddie Foster, Washington, Boston, St. Louis, April 20, 1916 through August 5, 1923 (end of career).

SEASON

Most home runs, season
N.L.—73—Barry Bonds, San Francisco, 153 games, 2001.
A.L.—61—Roger Maris, New York, 161 games, 1961.

For a complete list of players with 40 or more home runs in a season, see page 182. For complete lists of players combining power and speed (40 HRs, 40 SBs; 30 HRs, 30 SBs; 50 HRs, 20 SBs and 20 HRs, 50 SBs) during a season, see page 188. For detailed breakdowns of Barry Bonds' 73-homer season, Mark McGwire's 70-homer season, Roger Maris' 61-homer season and Babe Ruth's 60-homer season, see page 193.

Most home runs for runner-up, season
N.L.—66—Sammy Sosa, Chicago, 159 games, 1998.
A.L.—54—Mickey Mantle, New York, 153 games, 1961.

Most years leading league in home runs
A.L.—12—Babe Ruth, Boston, New York, 1918 (tied), 1919, 1920, 1921, 1923, 1924, 1926, 1927, 1928, 1929, 1930, 1931 (tied).

N.L.—8—Mike Schmidt, Philadelphia, 1974, 1975, 1976, 1980, 1981, 1983, 1984 (tied), 1986.

Most consecutive years leading league in home runs
N.L.—7—Ralph Kiner, Pittsburgh, 1946, 1947 (tied), 1948 (tied), 1949, 1950, 1951, 1952 (tied).
A.L.—6—Babe Ruth, New York, 1926 through 1931 (tied in 1931).

Most home runs by rookie, season
A.L.—49—Mark McGwire, Oakland, 151 games, 1987.
N.L.—38
  Wally Berger, Boston, 151 games, 1930.
  Frank Robinson, Cincinnati, 152 games, 1956.

Most home runs by righthander, season
N.L.—70—Mark McGwire, St. Louis, 155 games, 1998.
A.L.—58
  Jimmie Foxx, Philadelphia, 154 games, 1932.
  Hank Greenberg, Detroit, 155 games, 1938.

Most home runs by lefthander, season
N.L.—73—Barry Bonds, San Francisco, 153 games, 2001.
A.L.—61—Roger Maris, New York, 161 games, 1961.

Most home runs by switch-hitter, season
A.L.—54—Mickey Mantle, New York, 153 games, 1961.
N.L.—45—Chipper Jones, Atlanta, 157 games, 1999.

Most home runs by pinch-hitter, season
N.L.—7
  Dave Hansen, Los Angeles, 2000.
  Craig Wilson, Pittsburgh, 2001.
A.L.—5—Joe Cronin, Boston, 1943.

Most home runs leading off game, season
A.L.—12—Brady Anderson, Baltimore, 149 games, 1996 (50 home runs for season).
N.L.—11—Bobby Bonds, San Francisco, 160 games, 1973 (39 home runs for season).

Most home runs by first baseman, season
N.L.—69—Mark McGwire, St. Louis, 155 games, 1998, 151 games at first base (also had one home run as pinch-hitter).
A.L.—58—Hank Greenberg, Detroit, 155 games, 1938, 154 games at first base.

Most home runs by second baseman, season
N.L.—42
  Rogers Hornsby, St. Louis, 154 games, 1922, 154 games at second base.
  Dave Johnson, Atlanta, 157 games, 1973, 156 games at second base (also had one home run as pinch-hitter).
A.L.—36—Bret Boone, Seattle, 158 games, 2001, 156 games at second base (also had one home run as pinch-hitter).

Most home runs by third baseman, season
N.L.—48—Mike Schmidt, Philadelphia, 150 games, 1980, 149 games at third base.
A.L.—46—Troy Glaus, Anaheim, 159 games, 2000, 156 games at third base (also had one home run as designated hitter).

Most home runs by shortstop, season
A.L.—52—Alex Rodriguez, Texas, 162 games, 2001, 161 games at shortstop.
N.L.—47—Ernie Banks, Chicago, 154 games, 1958, 154 games at shortstop.

Most home runs by outfielder, season
N.L.—71—Barry Bonds, San Francisco, 153 games, 2001, 143 games in outfield (also had one home run as pinch-hitter and one home run as designated hitter).
A.L.—61—Roger Maris, New York, 161 games, 1961, 160 games in outfield.

Most home runs by catcher, season
N.L.—41—Todd Hundley, New York, 153 games, 1996, caught 150 games.
  (Roy Campanella, Brooklyn, 1953, had 40 home runs in 140 games as a catcher and one additional home run as a pinch-hitter; Johnny Bench, Cincinnati, 1970, had 38 home runs in 139 games as a catcher and seven additional home runs as an outfielder and first baseman.)
A.L.—35—Ivan Rodriguez, Texas, 144 games, 1999, caught 141 games.

(Carlton Fisk, Chicago, 1985, had 33 home runs in 130 games as a catcher and four additional home runs as a designated hitter.)

Most home runs by pitcher, season (only those hit as pitcher)
A.L.—9—Wes Ferrell, Cleveland, 48 games, 1931, pitched 40 games.
N.L.—7
Don Newcombe, Brooklyn, 57 games, 1955, pitched 34 games.
Don Drysdale, Los Angeles, 47 games, 1958, pitched 44 games.
Don Drysdale, Los Angeles, 58 games, 1965, pitched 44 games.
Mike Hampton, Colorado, 42 games, 2001, pitched 32 games.

Most home runs against one club, season
A.L.—14—Lou Gehrig, New York vs. Cleveland, 1936 (6 at New York, 8 at Cleveland).
N.L.—13
Hank Sauer, Chicago vs. Pittsburgh, 1954 (8 at Chicago, 5 at Pittsburgh).
Joe Adcock, Milwaukee vs. Brooklyn, 1956 (5 at Milwaukee, 7 at Brooklyn, 1 at Jersey City).

Most at-bats without a home run, season
N.L.—672—Rabbit Maranville, Pittsburgh, 155 games, 1922.
A.L.—658—Doc Cramer, Boston, 148 games, 1938.

Fewest home runs by leader, season
N.L.—7—Red Murray, New York, 149 games, 1909.
A.L.—7
Sam Crawford, Detroit, 152 games, 1908.
Bob Roth, Chicago, Cleveland, 109 games, 1915.

HOME AND ROAD

Most home runs hit at home, season
A.L.—39—Hank Greenberg, Detroit, 1938.
N.L.—38—Mark McGwire, St. Louis, 1998.

Most home runs hit at home by righthander, season
A.L.—39—Hank Greenberg, Detroit, 1938.
N.L.—38—Mark McGwire, St. Louis, 1998.

Most home runs hit at home by lefthander, season
N.L.—37—Barry Bonds, San Francisco, 2001.
A.L.—32
Babe Ruth, New York, 1921.
Kenny Williams, St. Louis, 1922.

Most home runs hit at home by switch-hitter, season
A.L.—27—Mickey Mantle, New York, 1956.
N.L.—25—Chipper Jones, Atlanta, 1999.

Most home runs hit at home against one club, season
A.L.—10—Gus Zernial, Philadelphia vs. St. Louis, 1951.
N.L.—9—Stan Musial, St. Louis vs. New York, 1954.

Most home runs hit on road, season
N.L.—36—Barry Bonds, San Francisco, 2001.
A.L.—32—Babe Ruth, New York, 1927.

Most home runs hit on road by righthander, season
N.L.—32—Mark McGwire, St. Louis, 1998.
A.L.—28
Harmon Killebrew, Minnesota, 1962.
George Bell, Toronto, 1987.
Mark McGwire, Oakland, 1996.

Most home runs hit on road by lefthander, season
N.L.—36—Barry Bonds, San Francisco, 2001.
A.L.—32—Babe Ruth, New York, 1927.

Most home runs hit on road by switch-hitter, season
A.L.—30—Mickey Mantle, New York, 1961.
N.L.—23—Howard Johnson, New York, 1987.

Most home runs hit on road against one club, season
A.L.—10—Harry Heilmann, Detroit at Philadelphia, 1922.
N.L.—9
Joe Adcock, Milwaukee at Brooklyn, 1954.
Willie Mays, New York at Brooklyn, 1955.

Most major league ballparks, one or more home runs, season
N.L.—18
Sammy Sosa, Chicago, 1998 (homered in 16 N.L. parks and 2 A.L. parks).

Mike Piazza, New York, 2000 (homered in 14 N.L. parks, 3 A.L. parks and one park in Japan).
A.L.—16
Ken Griffey Jr., Seattle, 1998 (homered in 13 A.L. parks and 3 N.L. parks).
Juan Gonzalez, Texas, 1999 (homered in 13 A.L. parks and 3 N.L. parks).

Most years hitting home runs in all parks, career
A.L.—11—Babe Ruth, Boston, New York, 1919, 1920, 1921, 1923, 1924, 1926, 1927, 1928, 1929, 1930, 1931.
N.L.—9—Hank Aaron, Milwaukee, Atlanta, 1954, 1955, 1956, 1957, 1958, 1959, 1960, 1963, 1966.

50, 40, 30 AND 20 IN SEASON

Most years with 50 or more home runs
M.L.—4
Babe Ruth, New York A.L., 1920, 1921, 1927, 1928.
Mark McGwire, Oakland A.L., 1996; Oakland A.L. and St. Louis N.L., 1997; St. Louis N.L., 1998, 1999.
Sammy Sosa, Chicago N.L., 1998, 1999, 2000, 2001.
A.L.—4—Babe Ruth, New York, 1920, 1921, 1927, 1928.
N.L.—4—Sammy Sosa, Chicago, 1998, 1999, 2000, 2001.

Most consecutive years with 50 or more home runs
M.L.—4
Mark McGwire, Oakland A.L., 1996, Oakland A.L. and St. Louis N.L., 1997, St. Louis N.L., 1998, 1999.
Sammy Sosa, Chicago, 1998, 1999, 2000, 2001.
N.L.—4—Sammy Sosa, Chicago, 1998, 1999, 2000, 2001.
A.L.—2
Babe Ruth, New York, 1920, 1921 and 1927, 1928.
Ken Griffey Jr., Seattle, 1997, 1998.

Most years with 40 or more home runs
A.L.—11—Babe Ruth, New York, 1920, 1921, 1923, 1924, 1926, 1927, 1928, 1929, 1930, 1931, 1932.
N.L.—8—Hank Aaron, Milwaukee, Atlanta, 1957, 1960, 1962, 1963, 1966, 1969, 1971, 1973.

For a complete list of players with 40 or more home runs in a season, see page 182.

Most consecutive years with 40 or more home runs
A.L.—7—Babe Ruth, New York, 1926 through 1932.
N.L.—5
Ralph Kiner, Pittsburgh, 1947 through 1951.
Duke Snider, Brooklyn, 1953 through 1957.

Most years with 30 or more home runs
N.L.—15—Hank Aaron, Milwaukee, Atlanta, 1957 through 1973, except 1964, 1968.
A.L.—13—Babe Ruth, New York, 1920 through 1933, except 1925.

Most consecutive years with 30 or more home runs
A.L.—12—Jimmie Foxx, Philadelphia, Boston, 1929 through 1940.
N.L.—10—Barry Bonds, Pittsburgh, San Francisco, 1992 through 2001.

Hitting 20 or more home runs for two leagues, season
Mark McGwire, Oakland A.L., 34, St. Louis N.L., 24, 1997.

Most years with 20 or more home runs
N.L.—20—Hank Aaron, Milwaukee, Atlanta, 1955 through 1974.
A.L.—16
Babe Ruth, Boston, New York, 1919 through 1934.
Ted Williams, Boston, 1939, 1940, 1941, 1942, 1946, 1947, 1948, 1949, 1950, 1951, 1954, 1955, 1956, 1957, 1958, 1960.
Reggie Jackson, Oakland, Baltimore, New York, California, 1968 through 1980, 1982, 1984, 1985.

Most consecutive years with 20 or more home runs
N.L.—20—Hank Aaron, Milwaukee, Atlanta, 1955 through 1974.
A.L.—16—Babe Ruth, Boston, New York, 1919 through 1934.

TWO CONSECUTIVE SEASONS

Most home runs, two consecutive seasons
N.L.—135—Mark McGwire, St. Louis, 70 in 1998, 65 in 1999.
A.L.—114—Babe Ruth, New York, 60 in 1927, 54 in 1928.

Most home runs by righthander, two consecutive seasons
N.L.—135—Mark McGwire, St. Louis, 70 in 1998, 65 in 1999.
A.L.—106—Jimmie Foxx, Philadelphia, 58 in 1932, 48 in 1933.

Most home runs by lefthander, two consecutive seasons
N.L.—122—Barry Bonds, San Francisco, 49 in 2000, 73 in 2001.
A.L.—114—Babe Ruth, New York, 60 in 1927, 54 in 1928.

Most home runs by switch-hitter, two consecutive seasons
A.L.—94—Mickey Mantle, New York, 40 in 1960, 54 in 1961.
N.L.—81—Chipper Jones, Atlanta, 45 in 1999, 36 in 2000.

MONTH AND WEEK

Most home runs, one month (from first through last day of month)
N.L.—20—Sammy Sosa, Chicago, June 1998.
A.L.—18—Rudy York, Detroit, August 1937.

Most home runs by righthander, one month
N.L.—20—Sammy Sosa, Chicago, June 1998.
A.L.—18—Rudy York, Detroit, August 1937.

Most home runs by lefthander, one month
A.L.—17—Babe Ruth, New York, September 1927.
N.L.—17—Barry Bonds, San Francisco, May 2001.

Most home runs by switch-hitter, one month
A.L.—16—Mickey Mantle, New York, May 1956.
N.L.—14—Ken Caminiti, San Diego, August 1996.

Most home runs in March
N.L.—2—Vinny Castilla, Colorado, March 1998.
A.L.—1—Held by many players.

Most home runs in April
A.L.—13—Ken Griffey Jr., Seattle, April 1997.
N.L.—13—Luis Gonzalez, Arizona, April 2001.

Most home runs through April 30
A.L.—13—Ken Griffey Jr., Seattle, 1997.
N.L.—13—Luis Gonzalez, Arizona, April 2001.

Most home runs in May
N.L.—17—Barry Bonds, San Francisco, May 2001.
A.L.—16—Mickey Mantle, New York, May 1956.

Most home runs through May 31
N.L.—28—Barry Bonds, San Francisco, 2001.
A.L.—24—Ken Griffey Jr., Seattle, 1997.

Most home runs in June
N.L.—20—Sammy Sosa, Chicago, June 1998.
A.L.—15
  Babe Ruth, New York, June 1930.
  Bob Johnson, Philadelphia, June 1934.
  Roger Maris, New York, June 1961.

Most home runs through June 30
N.L.—39—Barry Bonds, San Francisco, 2001.
A.L.—32—Ken Griffey Jr., Seattle, 1994.

Most home runs in July
A.L.—16—Albert Belle, Chicago, July 1998.
N.L.—16—Mark McGwire, St. Louis, July 1999.

Most home runs through July 31
N.L.—45
  Mark McGwire, St. Louis, 1998.
  Barry Bonds, San Francisco, 2001.
A.L.—41
  Babe Ruth, New York, 1928.
  Jimmie Foxx, Philadelphia, 1932.

Most home runs in August
A.L.—18—Rudy York, Detroit, August 1937.
N.L.—17
  Willie Mays, San Francisco, August 1965.
  Sammy Sosa, Chicago, August 2001.

Most home runs through August 31
N.L.—57—Barry Bonds, San Francisco, 2001.
A.L.—51—Roger Maris, New York, 1961.

Most home runs in September
A.L.—17
  Babe Ruth, New York, September 1927.
  Albert Belle, Cleveland, September 1995.
N.L.—16—Ralph Kiner, Pittsburgh, September 1949.

Most home runs through September 30
N.L.—70—Mark McGwire, St. Louis, 1998.
A.L.—60
  Babe Ruth, New York, 1927.
  Roger Maris, New York, 1961.

Most home runs in October
N.L.—5
  Richie Sexson, Milwaukee, October 2001.
  Sammy Sosa, Chicago, October 2001.
A.A.—4—John Milligan, St. Louis, October 1889.
A.L.—4
  Gus Zernial, Chicago, October 1950.
  George Brett, Kansas City, October 1985.
  Ron Kittle, Chicago, October 1985.
  Wally Joyner, California, October 1987.
  Jose Cruz Jr., Toronto, October 2001.

Most home runs in one week (Sunday through Saturday)
A.L.—10—Frank Howard, Washington, May 12 through 18, 1968, six games.
N.L.—8
  Ralph Kiner, Pittsburgh, September 7 through 13, 1947, seven games.
  Ted Kluszewski, Cincinnati, July 1, first game, through 7, 1956, seven games.
  Nate Colbert, San Diego, July 30, first game, through August 5, 1972, nine games.

GAME, DOUBLEHEADER, INNING

Most home runs, game
N.L.—4
  Bobby Lowe, Boston, May 30, 1894, p.m. game (consecutive).
  Ed Delahanty, Philadelphia, July 13, 1896.
  Chuck Klein, Philadelphia, July 10, 1936, 10 innings.
  Gil Hodges, Brooklyn, August 31, 1950.
  Joe Adcock, Milwaukee, July 31, 1954.
  Willie Mays, San Francisco, April 30, 1961.
  Mike Schmidt, Philadelphia, April 17, 1976, 10 innings (consecutive).
  Bob Horner, Atlanta, July 6, 1986.
  Mark Whiten, St. Louis, September 7, 1993, second game.
A.L.—4
  Lou Gehrig, New York, June 3, 1932 (consecutive).
  Pat Seerey, Chicago, July 18, 1948, first game, 11 innings.
  Rocky Colavito, Cleveland, June 10, 1959 (consecutive).

For a complete list of players with three or more home runs in a game, see page 184.

Most home runs by pitcher, game
A.A.—3—Guy Hecker, Louisville, August 15, 1886, second game.
N.L.—3—Jim Tobin, Boston, May 13, 1942.
A.L.—2—Held by many pitchers. Last pitcher—Sonny Siebert, Boston, September 2, 1971.

Most home runs, first game in major leagues
A.A.—2—Charlie Reilly, Columbus, October 9, 1889 (on third and fifth times at bat).
A.L.—2
  Bob Nieman, St. Louis, September 14, 1951 (on first two times at bat).
  Bert Campaneris, Kansas City, July 23, 1964 (on first and fourth times at bat).
  Mark Quinn, Kansas City, September 14, 1999, second game (on third and fourth times at bat).
N.L.—1—Held by many players.

Most home runs, opening game of season
A.L.—3—George Bell, Toronto, April 4, 1988.
N.L.—3—Karl Rhodes, Chicago, April 4, 1994.

Most inside-the-park home runs, game

N.L.—3—Tom McCreery, Louisville, July 12, 1897.
N.L.-A.L. since 1900—2—Held by many players.
Last N.L. player—Hank Thompson, New York (at Polo Grounds), August 16, 1950.
Last A.L. player—Greg Gagne, Minnesota (at Metrodome), October 4, 1986.

Most home runs in extra innings, game

N.L.—2
   Art Shamsky, Cincinnati, August 12, 1966, 10th and 11th innings (consecutive).
   Ralph Garr, Atlanta, May 17, 1971, 10th and 12th innings (consecutive).
A.L.—2
   Vern Stephens, St. Louis, September 29, 1943, first game, 11th and 13th innings (consecutive).
   Willie Kirkland, Cleveland, June 14, 1963, second game, 11th and 19th innings.
   Mike Young, Baltimore, May 28, 1987, 10th and 12th innings (consecutive).

Home run winning longest extra-inning game

A.L.—Harold Baines, Chicago, 25 innings, 0 on base, Chicago won vs. Milwaukee, 7-6, May 8, completed May 9, 1984.
N.L.—Rick Dempsey, Los Angeles, 22 innings, 0 on base, Los Angeles won vs. Montreal, 1-0, August 23, 1989.

Home run winning longest 1-0 game

N.L.—Rick Dempsey, Los Angeles, August 23, 1989, 22 innings.
A.L.—Bill Skowron, New York, April 22, 1959, 14 innings.

Home run by pitcher winning 1-0 extra-inning complete game

A.L.—Tom Hughes, Washington, August 3, 1906, 10 innings.
   Red Ruffing, New York, August 13, 1932, 10 innings.
N.L.—Never accomplished—(Johnny Klippstein, Cincinnati, on August 6, 1962, hit home run in 13th inning, after relieving Bob Purkey, who had pitched first 10 innings).

Home run in first major league at-bat

*On first pitch †Not first plate appearance ‡Pitcher

A.A.—George Tebeau, Cincinnati, April 16, 1887.
   Mike Griffin, Baltimore, April 16, 1887.

Total number of players: 2

A.L.—Luke Stuart, St. Louis, August 8, 1921.
   Earl Averill, Cleveland, April 16, 1929.
   Ace Parker, Philadelphia, April 30, 1937.
   Gene Hasson, Philadelphia, September 9, 1937, first game.
   Bill Lefebvre, Boston, June 10, 1938.*‡
   Hack Miller, Detroit, April 23, 1944, second game.
   Eddie Pellagrini, Boston, April 22, 1946.
   George Vico, Detroit, April 20, 1948.*
   Bob Nieman, St. Louis, September 14, 1951.
   Bob Tillman, Boston, May 19, 1962.†
   John Kennedy, Washington, September 5, 1962, first game.
   Buster Narum, Baltimore, May 3, 1963.‡
   Gates Brown, Detroit, June 19, 1963.
   Bert Campaneris, Kansas City, July 23, 1964.*
   Bill Roman, Detroit, September 30, 1964, second game.
   Brant Alyea, Washington, September 12, 1965.*
   John Miller, New York, September 11, 1966.
   Rick Renick, Minnesota, July 11, 1968.
   Joe Keough, Oakland, August 7, 1968, second game.
   Gene Lamont, Detroit, September 2, 1970, second game.
   Don Rose, California, May 24, 1972.*‡
   Reggie J. Sanders, Detroit, September 1, 1974.
   Dave McKay, Minnesota, August 22, 1975.
   Al Woods, Toronto, April 7, 1977.
   Dave Machemer, California, June 21, 1978.
   Gary Gaetti, Minnesota, September 20, 1981.
   Andre David, Minnesota, June 29, 1984, first game.
   Terry Steinbach, Oakland, September 12, 1986.
   Jay Bell, Cleveland, September 29, 1986.*
   Junior Felix, Toronto, May 4, 1989.*
   Jon Nunnally, Kansas City, April 29, 1995.
   Carlos Lee, Chicago, May 7, 1999.
   Esteban Yan, Tampa Bay, June 4, 2000.*‡

Total number of players: 33

N.L.—Joe Harrington, Boston, September 10, 1895.
   Bill Duggleby, Philadelphia, April 21, 1898 (grand slam).‡
   Johnny Bates, Boston, April 12, 1906.
   Walter Mueller, Pittsburgh, May 7, 1922.
   Clise Dudley, Brooklyn, April 27, 1929.*‡
   Gordon Slade, Brooklyn, May 24, 1930.
   Eddie Morgan, St. Louis, April 14, 1936.*
   Ernie Koy, Brooklyn, April 19, 1938.
   Emmett Mueller, Philadelphia, April 19, 1938.
   Clyde Vollmer, Cincinnati, May 31, 1942, second game.*
   Paul Gillespie, Chicago, September 11, 1942.
   Buddy Kerr, New York, September 8, 1943.
   Whitey Lockman, New York, July 5, 1945.
   Dan Bankhead, Brooklyn, August 26, 1947.‡
   Les Layton, New York, May 21, 1948.
   Ed Sanicki, Philadelphia, September 14, 1949.
   Ted Tappe, Cincinnati, September 14, 1950, first game.
   Hoyt Wilhelm, New York, April 23, 1952.‡
   Wally Moon, St. Louis, April 13, 1954.
   Chuck Tanner, Milwaukee, April 12, 1955.*
   Bill White, New York, May 7, 1956.
   Frank Ernaga, Chicago, May 24, 1957.
   Don Leppert, Pittsburgh, June 18, 1961, first game.
   Cuno Barragan, Chicago, September 1, 1961.
   Benny Ayala, New York, August 27, 1974.
   John Montefusco, San Francisco, September 3, 1974.†‡
   Jose Sosa, Houston, July 30, 1975.‡
   Johnnie LeMaster, San Francisco, September 2, 1975.
   Tim Wallach, Montreal, September 6, 1980.†
   Carmelo Martinez, Chicago, August 22, 1983.†
   Mike Fitzgerald, New York, September 13, 1983.
   Will Clark, San Francisco, April 8, 1986.
   Ricky Jordan, Philadelphia, July 17, 1988.†
   Jose Offerman, Los Angeles, August 19, 1990.
   Dave Eiland, San Diego, April 10, 1992.‡
   Jim Bullinger, Chicago, June 8, 1992, first game.*‡
   Jay Gainer, Colorado, May 14, 1993.*
   Mitch Lyden, Florida, June 16, 1993.
   Garey Ingram, Los Angeles, May 19, 1994.
   Jermaine Dye, Atlanta, May 17, 1996.
   Dustin Hermanson, Montreal, April 16, 1997.
   Brad Fullmer, Montreal, September 2, 1997.
   Marlon Anderson, Philadelphia, September 8, 1998.
   Guillermo Mota, Montreal, June 9, 1999.
   Alex Cabrera, Arizona, June 26, 2000.
   Keith McDonald, St. Louis, July 4, 2000.
   Chris Richard, St. Louis, July 17, 2000.*
   Gene Stechschulte, St. Louis, April 17, 2001.*‡ (Was a pitcher batting as a pinch-hitter.)

Total number of players: 48

Players hitting a pinch home run in first major league at-bat

N.L.—Eddie Morgan, St. Louis, April 14, 1936, seventh inning.
   Les Layton, New York, May 21, 1948, ninth inning.
   Ted Tappe, Cincinnati, September 14, 1950, first game, eighth inning.
   Chuck Tanner, Milwaukee, April 12, 1955, eighth inning.
   Marlon Anderson, Philadelphia, September 8, 1998, seventh inning.
   Gene Stechschulte, St. Louis, April 17, 2001, sixth inning.
A.L.—Ace Parker, Philadelphia, April 30, 1937, ninth inning.
   John Kennedy, Washington, September 5, 1962, first game, sixth inning.
   Gates Brown, Detroit, June 19, 1963, fifth inning.
   Bill Roman, Detroit, September 30, 1964, second game, seventh inning.
   Brant Alyea, Washington, September 12, 1965, sixth inning.
   Joe Keough, Oakland, August 7, 1968, second game, eighth inning.
   Al Woods, Toronto, April 7, 1977, fifth inning.

Home run in first two major league at-bats

A.L.—Bob Nieman, St. Louis, September 14, 1951 (first two plate appearances).
N.L.—Keith McDonald, St. Louis, July 4, July 6, 2000 (first two plate appearances).

Most home runs, doubleheader (homering in each game)
N.L.—5
Stan Musial, St. Louis, May 2, 1954.
Nate Colbert, San Diego, August 1, 1972.
A.L.—4
Earl Averill, Cleveland, September 17, 1930.
Jimmie Foxx, Philadelphia, July 2, 1933, 19 innings.
Jim Tabor, Boston, July 4, 1939.
Gus Zernial, Chicago, October 1, 1950.
Charlie Maxwell, Detroit, May 3, 1959 (consecutive).
Roger Maris, New York, July 25, 1961.
Rocky Colavito, Detroit, August 27, 1961.
Harmon Killebrew, Minnesota, September 21, 1963.
Bobby Murcer, New York, June 24, 1970 (consecutive).
Graig Nettles, New York, April 14, 1974.
Otto Velez, Toronto, May 4, 1980, 19 innings.
Al Oliver, Texas, August 17, 1980.

Most home runs by pinch-hitter, doubleheader
A.L.—2—Joe Cronin, Boston, June 17, 1943.
N.L.—2—Hal Breeden, Montreal, July 13, 1973.

Most home runs, inning
A.A.—2—Ed Cartwright, St. Louis, September 23, 1890, third inning.
P.L.—2—Lou Bierbauer, Brooklyn, July 12, 1890, third inning.
A.L.—2
Kenny Williams, St. Louis, August 7, 1922, sixth inning.
Bill Regan, Boston, June 16, 1928, fourth inning.
Joe DiMaggio, New York, June 24, 1936, fifth inning.
Al Kaline, Detroit, April 17, 1955, sixth inning.
Jim Lemon, Washington, September 5, 1959, third inning.
Joe Pepitone, New York, May 23, 1962, eighth inning.
Rick Reichardt, California, April 30, 1966, eighth inning.
Cliff Johnson, New York, June 30, 1977, eighth inning.
Ellis Burks, Boston, August 27, 1990, fourth inning.
Carlos Baerga, Cleveland, April 8, 1993, seventh inning.
Joe Carter, Toronto, October 3, 1993, second inning.
Dave Nilsson, Milwaukee, May 17, 1996, sixth inning.
Mark McGwire, Oakland, September 22, 1996, fifth inning.
N.L.—2
Charley Jones, Boston, June 10, 1880, eighth inning.
Bobby Lowe, Boston, May 30, 1894, p.m. game, third inning.
Jake Stenzel, Pittsburgh, June 6, 1894, third inning.
Hack Wilson, New York, July 1, 1925, second game, third inning.
Hank Leiber, New York, August 24, 1935, second inning.
Andy Seminick, Philadelphia, June 2, 1949, eighth inning.
Sid Gordon, New York, July 31, 1949, second game, second inning.
Willie McCovey, San Francisco, April 12, 1973, fourth inning and June 27, 1977, sixth inning.
John Boccabella, Montreal, July 6, 1973, first game, sixth inning.
Lee May, Houston, April 29, 1974, sixth inning.
Andre Dawson, Montreal, July 30, 1978, third inning and September 24, 1985, fifth inning.
Ray Knight, Cincinnati, May 13, 1980, fifth inning.
Von Hayes, Philadelphia, June 11, 1985, first inning.
Dale Murphy, Atlanta, July 27, 1989, sixth inning.
Jeff Bagwell, Houston, June 24, 1994, sixth inning.
Jeff King, Pittsburgh, August 8, 1995, second inning and April 30, 1996, fourth inning.
Sammy Sosa, Chicago, May 16, 1996, seventh inning.
Mike Lansing, Montreal, May 7, 1997, sixth inning.
Gary Sheffield, Florida, July 13, 1997, fourth inning.
Fernando Tatis, St. Louis, April 23, 1999, third inning.
Eric Karros, Los Angeles, August 22, 2000, sixth inning.

THREE AND TWO IN GAME

Most times hitting three or more home runs in a game, career
M.L.—6—Johnny Mize, St. Louis N.L., 1938 (2), 1940 (2), New York N.L., 1947, New York A.L., 1950.
N.L.—5
Johnny Mize, St. Louis, 1938 (2), 1940 (2); New York, 1947.
Sammy Sosa, Chicago, 1996, 1998, 2001 (3).
A.L.—5—Joe Carter, Cleveland, 1986, 1987, 1989 (2); Toronto, 1993.

For a complete list of players with three or more home runs in a game, see page 184.

Most times hitting three or more home runs in a game, season
N.L.—3—Sammy Sosa, August 9, August 22, September 23, 2001.
A.L.—2
Ted Williams, Boston, May 8, June 13, 1957.
Doug DeCinces, California, August 3, August 8, 1982.
Joe Carter, Cleveland, June 24, July 19, 1989.
Cecil Fielder, Detroit, May 6, June 6, 1990.
Geronimo Berroa, Oakland, May 22, August 12, 1996.

Most times hitting three home runs in a doubleheader, career (homering in both games)
A.L.—7—Babe Ruth, New York, 1920, 1922, 1926, 1927, 1930, 1933 (2).
N.L.—5—Mel Ott, New York, 1929, 1931, 1932, 1933, 1944.

Most times hitting three consecutive home runs in a game, career
4—Johnny Mize, St. Louis, N.L., 1938, 1940, New York, N.L., 1947, New York A.L., 1950.

Most times hitting three or more consecutive home runs in a game, career
N.L.—3
Johnny Mize, St. Louis, 1938, 1940, New York, 1947.
Sammy Sosa, Chicago, 1996, 2001 (2).
A.L.—3—Cecil Fielder, Detroit, 1990 (2), 1996.

Most times hitting two or more home runs in a game, career
M.L.—72—Babe Ruth, Boston A.L., New York A.L., Boston N.L., 22 years, 1914 through 1935 (71 in A.L., 1 in N.L.).
A.L.—71—Babe Ruth, Boston, New York, 21 years, 1914 through 1934.
N.L.—63—Willie Mays, New York Giants, San Francisco, New York Mets, 22 years, 1951 through 1973, except 1953 in military service.

For a complete list of players with 25 or more multiple-home run games, see page 174.

Most times hitting two or more home runs in a game, season
A.L.—11—Hank Greenberg, Detroit, 1938.
N.L.—11—Sammy Sosa, Chicago, 1998.

Most times pitcher hitting two home runs in a game, career
A.L.—5—Wes Ferrell, Cleveland, Boston, 1931, 1934 (2), 1935, 1936.
N.L.—3—Don Newcombe, Brooklyn, 1955 (2), 1956.

Most times pitcher hitting two home runs in a game, season
A.L.—2
Wes Ferrell, Boston, 1934.
Jack Harshman, Baltimore, 1958.
Dick Donovan, Cleveland, 1962.
N.L.—2
Don Newcombe, Brooklyn, 1955.
Tony Cloninger, Atlanta, 1966.
Rick Wise, Philadelphia, 1971.

Most games hitting home runs from both sides of plate, career
M.L.—11—Eddie Murray, Baltimore A.L., 1977, 1979, 1981, 1982 (2), 1985, 1987 (2); Los Angeles N.L., 1990 (2); Cleveland A.L., 1994.
A.L.—10—Mickey Mantle, New York, 1955 (2), 1956 (2), 1957, 1958, 1959, 1961, 1962, 1964.
N.L.—10—Ken Caminiti, Houston, 1994; San Diego, 1995 (3), 1996 (4), 1998; Houston, 1999.

For a complete list of players hitting home runs from both sides of plate in a game, see page 187.

Most games hitting home runs from both sides of plate, season
N.L.—4—Ken Caminiti, San Diego, 1996.
A.L.—3—Tony Clark, Detroit, 1998.

Hitting home runs from both sides of plate, inning
A.L.—Carlos Baerga, Cleveland, April 8, 1993, seventh inning.
N.L.—Never accomplished.

CONSECUTIVE AND
IN CONSECUTIVE GAMES

Most consecutive home runs, game
N.L.—4
Bobby Lowe, Boston, May 30, 1894, p.m. game.
Mike Schmidt, Philadelphia, April 17, 1976, 10 innings.
A.L.—4
Lou Gehrig, New York, June 3, 1932.
Rocky Colavito, Cleveland, June 10, 1959.

Most consecutive home runs, two games (*also base on balls)
A.L.—4
Jimmie Foxx, Philadelphia, June 7 (1), 8 (3), 1933.
Hank Greenberg, Detroit, July 26 (2), 27 (2), 1938.
Charlie Maxwell, Detroit, May 3, first game (1), 3, second game (3), 1959.
Willie Kirkland, Cleveland, July 9, second game (3), 13 (1), 1961 (also two bases on balls and one sacrifice hit).
Mickey Mantle, New York, July 4, second game (2), 6 (2), 1962.
Bobby Murcer, New York, June 24, first game (1), 24, second game (3), 1970.*
Mike Epstein, Oakland, June 15 (2), 16 (2), 1971.
Don Baylor, Baltimore, July 1 (1), 2 (3), 1975.*
Larry Herndon, Detroit, May 16 (1), 18 (3), 1982.
Bo Jackson, Kansas City, July 17 (3), August 26 (1), 1990.
Bobby Higginson, Detroit, June 30 (3), July 1 (1), 1997.*
Manny Ramirez, Cleveland, September 15 (3), 16 (1), 1998.
N.L.—4
Bill Nicholson, Chicago, July 22 (1), 23, first game (3), 1944.*
Ralph Kiner, Pittsburgh, August 15 (1), 16 (3), 1947.*
Ralph Kiner, Pittsburgh, September 11 (2), 13 (2), 1949.
Stan Musial, St. Louis, July 7, second game (1), 8 (3), 1962.*
Art Shamsky, Cincinnati, August 12 (3), 14 (1), 1966.
Deron Johnson, Philadelphia, July 10, second game (1), 11 (3), 1971.
Mike Schmidt, Philadelphia, July 6 (1), 7 (3), 1979.
Benito Santiago, Philadelphia, September 14 (1), 15 (3), 1996.*
Barry Bonds, San Francisco, May 19 (2), 20 (2), 2001.*

Most consecutive home runs, three games (*also base on balls)
A.L.—4
Johnny Blanchard, New York, July 21 (1), 22 (1), 26 (2), 1961.
Jeff Manto, Baltimore, June 8 (1), 9 (2), 10 (1), 1995.*
N.L.—Never accomplished.

Most consecutive home runs, four games
A.L.—4—Ted Williams, Boston, September 17, 20, 21, 22, 1957 (four bases on balls in streak).
N.L.—Never accomplished.

Most home runs in consecutive at-bats as a pinch-hitter
N.L.—3
Lee Lacy, Los Angeles, May 2, 6, 17, 1978 (includes one base on balls during streak).
Del Unser, Philadelphia, June 30, July 5, 10, 1979.
A.L.—2
Ray Caldwell, New York, June 10, 11, 1915.
Joe Cronin, Boston, June 17, first game, 17, second game, 1943.
Charlie Keller, New York, September 12, 14, 1948.
Del Wilber, Boston, May 6, 10, 1953.
Ted Williams, Boston, September 17, 20, 1957 (includes one base on balls during streak).
Johnny Blanchard, New York, July 21, 22, 1961.
Chuck Schilling, Boston, April 30, May 1, 1965.
Ray Barker, New York, June 20, 22, first game, 1965.
Curt Motton, Baltimore, May 15, 17, 1968.
Gates Brown, Detroit, August 9, 11, first game, 1968.
Gary Alexander, Cleveland, July 5, 6, 1980.
Daryl Sconiers, California, April 30, May 7, 1983.
Alex Sanchez, Detroit, July 20, 23, 1985.
Randy Bush, Minnesota, June 20, 23, 1986.
Jeromy Burnitz, Milwaukee, August 2, 3, 1997.

Most consecutive games hitting home run in each game
N.L.—8—Dale Long, Pittsburgh, May 19, 20, first game, 20, second game, 22, 23, 25, 26, 28, 1956 (eight home runs).
A.L.—8
Don Mattingly, New York, July 8 (2), 9, 10, 11, 12, 16 (2), 17, 18, 1987 (10 home runs).

Ken Griffey Jr., Seattle, July 20, 21, 22, 23, 24, 25, 27, 28, 1993 (eight home runs).

Most consecutive games hitting home runs from both sides of plate
A.L.—2—Eddie Murray, Baltimore, May 8, 9, 1987.
N.L.—2—Ken Caminiti, San Diego, September 16, 17, 1995.

Most consecutive games hitting home run by pitcher
N.L.—4—Ken Brett, Philadelphia, June 9, 13, 18, 23, 1973.
A.L.—2—Held by many pitchers.

Most home runs, two consecutive days
A.L.—6
Babe Ruth, New York, May 21 (3), 21 (0), 22 (2), 22, 1930, four games.
Tony Lazzeri, New York, May 23, 23 (2), 24 (3), 1936, three games.
N.L.—6—Ralph Kiner, Pittsburgh, September 11, 11 (3), 12 (2), 1947, three games.

Most home runs, first two major league games
A.A.—3—Charlie Reilly, Columbus, October 9 (2), 10, 1889.
N.L.—3—Joe Cunningham, St. Louis, June 30, July 1 (2), 1954.
A.L.—2
Earl Averill, Cleveland, April 16, 17, 1929.
Bob Nieman, St. Louis, September 14 (2), 15 (0), 1951.
Bert Campaneris, Kansas City, July 23 (2), 24 (0), 1964.
Curt Blefary, Baltimore, April 14 (0), 17 (2), 1965.
Joe Lefebvre, New York, May 22, 23, 1980.
Dave Stapleton, Boston, May 30 (0), 31 (2), 1980.
Tim Laudner, Minnesota, August 28, 29, 1981.
Alvin Davis, Seattle, April 11, 13, 1984.
Sam Horn, Boston, July 25, 26, 1987.
Mark Quinn, Kansas City, September 14 (2), 15 (0), 1999.

Most home runs in two straight games (homering in each game)
N.L.—5
Cap Anson, Chicago, August 5 (2), 6 (3), 1884.
Ralph Kiner, Pittsburgh, August 15 (2), 16 (3), 1947.
Ralph Kiner, Pittsburgh, September 11 (3), 12 (2), 1947.
Don Mueller, New York, September 1 (3), 2 (2), 1951.
Stan Musial, St. Louis, May 2, first game (3), 2, second game (2), 1954.
Joe Adcock, Milwaukee, July 30, 31 (4), 1954.
Billy Williams, Chicago, September 8 (2), 10 (3), 1968.
Nate Colbert, San Diego, August 1, first game (2), second game (3), 1972.
Mike Schmidt, Philadelphia, April 17 (4), 18, 1976.
Dave Kingman, Chicago, July 27 (2), 28 (3), 1979.
Gary Carter, New York, September 3 (3), 4 (2), 1985.
Barry Larkin, Cincinnati, June 27 (2), 28 (3), 1991.
Geoff Jenkins, Milwaukee, April 28 (3), 29 (2), 2001.
Barry Bonds, San Francisco, May 19 (3), 20 (2), 2001.
A.L.—5
Ty Cobb, Detroit, May 5 (3), 6 (2), 1925.
Tony Lazzeri, New York, May 23, second game (2), 24 (3), 1936.
Carl Yastrzemski, Boston, May 19 (3), 20 (2), 1976.
Mark McGwire, Oakland, June 27 (3), 28 (2), 1987.
Joe Carter, Cleveland, July 18 (2), 19 (3), 1989.
Mark McGwire, Oakland, June 10 (2), 11 (3), 1995.
Albert Belle, Cleveland, September 18 (2), 19 (3), 1995.
Matt Williams, Cleveland, April 25 (3), 26 (2), 1997.
Manny Ramirez, Cleveland, September 15 (3), 16 (2), 1998.

Most home runs in three straight games (homering in each game)
A.L.—6
Tony Lazzeri, New York, May 23, 23 (2), 24 (3), 1936.
Gus Zernial, Philadelphia, May 13, second game (2), 15 (2), 16 (2), 1951.
Manny Ramirez, Cleveland, September 15 (3), 16 (2), 17, 1998.
N.L.—6
Ralph Kiner, Pittsburgh, August 14, 15 (3), 16 (3), 1947, also September 10 (2), 11, 11 (3), 1947.
Frank Thomas, New York, August 1 (2), 2 (2), 3 (2), 1962.
Lee May, Cincinnati, May 24 (2), 25 (2), 28 (2), 1969.
Mike Schmidt, Philadelphia, April 17 (4), 18, 20, 1976.
Barry Bonds, San Francisco, May 18, 19 (3), 20 (2), 2001.
Barry Bonds, San Francisco, May 19 (3), 20 (2), 21, 2001.

Most home runs in four straight games (homering in each game)
N.L.—8—Ralph Kiner, Pittsburgh, September 10 (2), 11, 11 (3), 12 (2), 1947.
A.L.—7
Tony Lazzeri, New York, May 21, 23, 23 (2), 24 (3), 1936.
Gus Zernial, Philadelphia, May 13, second game (2), 15 (2), 16 (2), 17, 1951.
Frank Howard, Washington, May 12 (2), 14 (2), 15, 16 (2), 1968.

Players hitting home runs in first four games of season
N.L.—4
Willie Mays, San Francisco, April 6, 7, 8, 10, 1971.
Mark McGwire, St. Louis, March 31, April 2, 3, 4, 1998.
A.L.—Never accomplished.

Most home runs in five straight games (homering in each game)
A.L.—8
Frank Howard, Washington, May 12 (2), 14 (2), 15, 16 (2), 17, 1968.
Frank Howard, Washington, May 14 (2), 15, 16 (2), 17, 18 (2), 1968.
N.L.—8
Barry Bonds, San Francisco, May 17, 18, 19 (3), 20 (2), 21, 2001.
Barry Bonds, San Francisco, May 18, 19 (3), 20 (2), 21, 22, 2001.

Most home runs in six straight games (homering in each game)
A.L.—10—Frank Howard, Washington, May 12 (2), 14 (2), 15, 16 (2), 17, 18 (2), 1968.
N.L.—9—Barry Bonds, San Francisco, May 17, 18, 19 (3), 20 (2), 21, 22, 2001.

Most home runs in seven straight games (homering in each game)
A.L.—9—Don Mattingly, New York, July 8 (2), 9, 10, 11, 12, 16 (2), 17, 1987.
N.L.—7—Dale Long, Pittsburgh, May 19, 20, 20, 22, 23, 25, 26, 1956.

Most homers in eight straight games (homering in each game)
A.L.—10—Don Mattingly, New York, July 8 (2), 9, 10, 11, 12, 16 (2), 17, 18, 1987.
N.L.—8—Dale Long, Pittsburgh, May 19, 20, 20, 22, 23, 25, 26, 28, 1956.

GRAND SLAMS

Most grand slams, career
A.L.—23—Lou Gehrig, New York, 17 years, 1923 through 1939.
N.L.—18—Willie McCovey, San Francisco, San Diego, 22 years, 1959 through 1980.

For a complete list of players with 10 or more career grand slams, see page 175.

Most grand slams by pinch-hitter, career
A.L.—3—Rich Reese, Minnesota, August 3, 1969, June 7, 1970, July 9, 1972.
N.L.—3
Ron Northey, St. Louis, September 3, 1947; May 30, 1948, second game; Chicago, September 18, 1950.
Willie McCovey, San Francisco, June 12, 1960; September 10, 1965; San Diego, May 30, 1975.

Most grand slams, season
A.L.—6—Don Mattingly, New York, 141 games, 1987.
N.L.—5—Ernie Banks, Chicago, 154 games, 1955.

Most grand slams by pinch-hitter, season
N.L.—2
Dave Johnson, Philadelphia, April 30, June 3, 1978.
Mike Ivie, San Francisco, May 28, June 30, first game, 1978.
A.L.—2—Darryl Strawberry, New York, May 2, August 4, 1998.

Most grand slams in one month
A.L.—3
Rudy York, Detroit, May 16, 22, 30, first game, 1938.
Jim Northrup, Detroit, June 24 (2), 29, 1968.

Larry Parrish, Texas, July 4, 7, 10, first game, 1982.
Mike Blowers, Seattle, August 3, 14, 18, 1995.
Shane Spencer, New York, September 18, 24, 27, 1998.
N.L.—3
Eric Davis, Cincinnati, May 1, 3, 30, 1987.
Mike Piazza, Los Angeles, April 9, 10, 24, 1998.
Devon White, Milwaukee, May 10, 15, 20, 2001.

Most grand slams in one week (Sunday through Saturday)
A.L.—3
Jim Northrup, Detroit, June 24 (2), 29, 1968. (Lou Gehrig, New York, hit grand slams on Saturday, August 29, Monday, August 31, Tuesday, September 1, 1931, second game.)
Larry Parrish, Texas, July 4, 7, 10, first game, 1982.
N.L.—2—Held by many players. Last players—Fernando Tatis, St. Louis, April 23 (2), 1999; Robin Ventura, New York, May 20, first and second games, 1999.

Most grand slams in one game
A.L.—2
Tony Lazzeri, New York, May 24, 1936, second and fifth innings.
Jim Tabor, Boston, July 4, 1939, second game, third and sixth innings.
Rudy York, Boston, July 27, 1946, second and fifth innings.
Jim Gentile, Baltimore, May 9, 1961, first and second innings.
Jim Northrup, Detroit, June 24, 1968, fifth and sixth innings.
Frank Robinson, Baltimore, June 26, 1970, fifth and sixth innings.
Robin Ventura, Chicago, September 4, 1995, fourth and fifth innings.
Chris Hoiles, Baltimore, August 14, 1998, third and eighth innings.
Nomar Garciaparra, Boston, May 10, 1999, first and eighth innings.
N.L.—2
Tony Cloninger, Atlanta, July 3, 1966, first and fourth innings.
Fernando Tatis, St. Louis, April 23, 1999, both in third inning.

Most grand slams, inning
N.L.—2—Fernando Tatis, St. Louis, April 23, 1999, third inning.
A.L.—1—Held by many players.

Most grand slams in first major league game
N.L.—1
Bill Duggleby, Philadelphia, April 21, 1898, second inning (on first at-bat).
Bobby Bonds, San Francisco, June 25, 1968, sixth inning (on third at-bat).
A.L.—Never accomplished.

Most grand slams, two straight games (homering in each game)
N.L.—2
Jimmy Bannon, Boston, August 6, 7, 1894.
Jim Sheckard, Brooklyn, September 23, 24, 1901.
Phil Garner, Pittsburgh, September 14, 15, 1978.
Fred McGriff, San Diego, August 13, 14, 1991.
Eric Davis, Cincinnati, May 4, 5, 1996.
Mike Piazza, Los Angeles, April 9, 10, 1998.
Sammy Sosa, Chicago, July 27, 28, 1998.
Robin Ventura, New York, May 20, first game, second game, 1999.
A.L.—2
Babe Ruth, New York, September 27, 29, 1927; also August 6, second game, August 7, first game, 1929.
Bill Dickey, New York, August 3, second game, 4, 1937.
Jimmie Foxx, Boston, May 20, 21, 1940.
Jim Busby, Cleveland, July 5, 6, 1956.
Brooks Robinson, Baltimore, May 6, 9, 1962.
Willie Aikens, California, June 13, second game, 14, 1979.
Greg Luzinski, Chicago, June 8, 9, 1984.
Rob Deer, Milwaukee, August 19, 20, 1987.
Mike Blowers, Seattle, May 16, 17, 1993.
Dan Gladden, Detroit, August 10, 11, 1993.
Ken Griffey Jr., Seattle, April 29, 30, 1999.
Albert Belle, Baltimore, June 14, 15, 2000.

Hitting grand slam in both games of doubleheader

N.L.—Robin Ventura, New York, May 20, first game, second game, 1999.
A.L.—Never accomplished.

TOTAL BASES
CAREER AND SEASON

Most total bases, career

M.L.—6,856—Hank Aaron, Milwaukee N.L., Atlanta N.L., Milwaukee A.L., 23 years, 1954 through 1976 (6,591 in N.L., 265 in A.L.).
N.L.—6,591—Hank Aaron, Milwaukee, Atlanta, 21 years, 1954 through 1974.
A.L.—5,862—Ty Cobb, Detroit, Philadelphia, 24 years, 1905 through 1928.

For a complete list of players with 4,000 or more career total bases, see page 175.

Most total bases, season

A.L.—457—Babe Ruth, New York, 152 games, 1921.
N.L.—450—Rogers Hornsby, St. Louis, 154 games, 1922.

For a complete list of players with 400 or more total bases in a season, see page 189.

Most total bases by rookie, season

A.L.—374
Hal Trosky, Cleveland, 154 games, 1934.
Tony Oliva, Minnesota, 161 games, 1964.
N.L.—360—Albert Pujols, St. Louis, 161 games, 2001.

Most total bases by righthander, season

N.L.—450—Rogers Hornsby, St. Louis, 154 games, 1922.
A.L.—438—Jimmie Foxx, Philadelphia, 154 games, 1932.

Most total bases by lefthander, season

A.L.—457—Babe Ruth, New York, 152 games, 1921.
N.L.—445—Chuck Klein, Philadelphia, 156 games, 1930.

Most total bases by switch-hitter, season

A.L.—376—Mickey Mantle, New York, 150 games, 1956.
N.L.—369—Rip Collins, St. Louis, 154 games, 1934.

Most years leading league in total bases

N.L.—8—Hank Aaron, Milwaukee, 1956, 1957, 1959, 1960, 1961, 1963, Atlanta, 1967, 1969.
A.L.—6
Ty Cobb, Detroit, 1907, 1908, 1909, 1911, 1915, 1917.
Babe Ruth, Boston, 1919, New York, 1921, 1923, 1924, 1926, 1928.
Ted Williams, Boston, 1939, 1942, 1946, 1947, 1949, 1951.

Most consecutive years leading league in total bases

N.L.—4
Honus Wagner, Pittsburgh, 1906, 1907, 1908, 1909.
Chuck Klein, Philadelphia, 1930, 1931, 1932, 1933.
A.L.—3
Ty Cobb, Detroit, 1907, 1908, 1909.
Jim Rice, Boston, 1977, 1978, 1979.
(Military service from 1943 through 1945 interrupted a three-year streak by Ted Williams of Boston, who led in total bases from 1942 through 1947.)

Most years with 400 or more total bases

A.L.—5—Lou Gehrig, New York, 1927, 1930, 1931, 1934, 1936.
N.L.—3—Chuck Klein, Philadelphia, 1929, 1930, 1932.

For a complete list of players with 400 or more total bases in a season, see page 189.

Most consecutive years with 400 or more total bases

A.L.—2
Lou Gehrig, New York, 1930, 1931.
Jimmie Foxx, Philadelphia, 1932, 1933.
N.L.—2
Chuck Klein, Philadelphia, 1929, 1930.
Todd Helton, Colorado, 2000, 2001.

Most years with 300 or more total bases

N.L.—15—Hank Aaron, Milwaukee, Atlanta, 1955 through 1971, except 1964, 1970.
A.L.—13—Lou Gehrig, New York, 1926 through 1938.

Most consecutive years with 300 or more total bases

A.L.—13—Lou Gehrig, New York, 1926 through 1938.
N.L.—13—Willie Mays, New York, San Francisco, 1954 through 1966.

Fewest total bases, season (150 or more games)

N.L.—89—Dal Maxvill, St. Louis, 152 games, 1970.
A.L.—114—Eddie Brinkman, Washington, 154 games, 1965.

Fewest total bases for leader

N.L.—237—Honus Wagner, Pittsburgh, 140 games, 1906.
A.L.—260—George Stone, St. Louis, 154 games, 1905.

GAME AND INNING

Most total bases, game

N.L.—18—Joe Adcock, Milwaukee, July 31, 1954 (4 home runs, 1 double).
A.L.—16
Ty Cobb, Detroit, May 5, 1925 (3 home runs, 1 double, 2 singles).
Lou Gehrig, New York, June 3, 1932 (4 home runs).
Jimmie Foxx, Philadelphia, July 10, 1932, 18 innings (3 home runs, 1 double, 2 singles).
Pat Seerey, Chicago, July 18, 1948, first game, 11 innings (4 home runs).
Rocky Colavito, Cleveland, June 10, 1959 (4 home runs).
Fred Lynn, Boston, June 18, 1975 (3 home runs, 1 triple, 1 single).

Most total bases by pitcher, nine-inning game

A.A.—15—Guy Hecker, Louisville, August 15, 1886, second game (3 home runs, 3 singles).
N.L.—12—Jim Tobin, Boston, May 13, 1942 (3 home runs).
A.L.—10
Lewis Wiltse, Philadelphia, August 10, 1901, second game (2 triples, 2 doubles).
Babe Ruth, Boston, May 9, 1918, 10 innings (1 single, 3 doubles, 1 triple).
Red Ruffing, New York, June 17, 1936, first game (2 singles, 2 home runs).
Jack Harshman, Baltimore, September 23, 1958 (2 home runs, 1 double).

Most total bases, doubleheader

N.L.—22—Nate Colbert, San Diego, August 1, 1972.
A.L.—21
Jimmie Foxx, Philadelphia, July 2, 1933, 19 innings.
Al Oliver, Texas, August 17, 1980.

Most total bases, two consecutive games

A.L.—25—Ty Cobb, Detroit, May 5, 6, 1925.
N.L.—25—Joe Adcock, Milwaukee, July 30, 31, 1954.

Most total bases, inning

N.L.-A.L.—8—Held by many players.

LONG HITS
CAREER AND SEASON

Most long hits, career

M.L.—1,477—Hank Aaron, Milwaukee N.L., Atlanta N.L., Milwaukee A.L., 1954 through 1976 (1,429 in N.L., 48 in A.L.; 624 doubles, 98 triples, 755 home runs).
N.L.—1,429—Hank Aaron, Milwaukee, Atlanta, 21 years, 1954 through 1974 (600 doubles, 96 triples, 733 home runs).
A.L.—1,350—Babe Ruth, Boston, New York, 21 years, 1914 through 1934 (506 doubles, 136 triples, 708 home runs).

For a complete list of players with 800 or more career long hits, see page 175.

Most long hits, season

A.L.—119—Babe Ruth, New York, 152 games, 1921 (44 doubles, 16 triples, 59 home runs).

N.L.—107
  Chuck Klein, Philadelphia, 156 games, 1930 (59 doubles, 8 triples, 40 home runs).
  Barry Bonds, San Francisco, 153 games, 2001 (32 doubles, 2 triples, 73 home runs).

For a complete list of players with 100 or more long hits in a season, see page 189.

Most long hits by rookie, season
A.L.—89—Hal Trosky, Cleveland, 154 games, 1934 (45 doubles, 9 triples, 35 home runs).
N.L.—88—Albert Pujols, St. Louis, 161 games, 2001 (47 doubles, 4 triples, 37 home runs).

Most long hits by righthander, season
A.L.—103
  Hank Greenberg, Detroit, 154 games, 1937 (49 doubles, 14 triples, 40 home runs).
  Albert Belle, Cleveland, 143 games, 1995 (52 doubles, 1 triple, 50 home runs).
N.L.—103—Sammy Sosa, Chicago, 160 games, 2001 (34 doubles, 5 triples, 64 home runs).

Most long hits by lefthander, season
A.L.—119—Babe Ruth, New York, 152 games, 1921 (44 doubles, 16 triples, 59 home runs).
N.L.—107
  Chuck Klein, Philadelphia, 156 games, 1930 (59 doubles, 8 triples, 40 home runs).
  Barry Bonds, San Francisco, 153 games, 2001 (32 doubles, 2 triples, 73 home runs).

Most long hits by switch-hitter, season
N.L.—94—Lance Berkman, Houston, 156 games, 2001 (55 doubles, 5 triples, 34 home runs).
A.L.—79—Mickey Mantle, New York, 150 games, 1956 (22 doubles, 5 triples, 52 home runs).

Most years leading league in doubles, triples and home runs in same season
A.A.—1—Tip O'Neill, St. Louis, 123 games, 1887 (46 doubles, 24 triples, 13 home runs. Also led in batting, .492).
N.L.-A.L.—Never accomplished.

Twenty or more doubles, triples and homers in one season
N.L.—Buck Freeman, Washington, 155 games, 1899 (20 doubles, 26 triples, 25 home runs).
  Frank Schulte, Chicago, 154 games, 1911 (30 doubles, 21 triples, 21 homers).
  Jim Bottomley, St. Louis, 149 games, 1928 (42 doubles, 20 triples, 31 homers).
  Willie Mays, New York, 152 games, 1957 (26 doubles, 20 triples, 35 homers).
A.L.—Jeff Heath, Cleveland, 151 games, 1941 (32 doubles, 20 triples, 24 homers).
  George Brett, Kansas City, 154 games, 1979 (42 doubles, 20 triples, 23 homers).

Most years leading league in long hits
N.L.—7
  Honus Wagner, Pittsburgh, 1900, 1902, 1903, 1904, 1907, 1908, 1909.
  Stan Musial, St. Louis, 1943, 1944, 1946, 1948, 1949, 1950, 1953.
A.L.—7—Babe Ruth, Boston, New York, 1918, 1919, 1920, 1921, 1923, 1924, 1928.

Most consecutive years leading league in long hits
A.L.—4—Babe Ruth, Boston, New York, 1918, 1919, 1920, 1921.
N.L.—3—Held by many players. Last player—Duke Snider, Brooklyn, 1954, 1955 (tied), 1956.

Fewest long hits, season (150 or more games)
N.L.—7—Dal Maxvill, St. Louis, 152 games, 1970 (5 doubles, 2 triples).
A.L.—10
  Luis Gomez, Toronto, 153 games, 1978 (7 doubles, 3 triples).
  Felix Fermin, Cleveland, 156 games, 1989 (9 doubles, 1 triple).

Fewest long hits for leader
N.L.—50—Sherry Magee, Philadelphia, 154 games, 1906 (36 doubles, 8 triples, 6 home runs).
A.L.—54—Sam Crawford, Detroit, 156 games, 1915 (31 doubles, 19 triples, 4 home runs).

Most consecutive games with one or more long hits, season
N.L.—14—Paul Waner, Pittsburgh, June 3 through 19, 1927 (12 doubles, 4 triples, 4 home runs).
A.L.—11—Jesse Barfield, Toronto, August 17 through 27, 1985 (8 doubles, 3 triples, 1 home run).

Most consecutive long hits, season
A.L.—7
  Elmer Smith, Cleveland, September 4, 5, 5, 1921 (3 doubles, 4 home runs; 2 bases on balls in streak).
  Earl Sheely, Chicago, May 20, 21, 1926 (6 doubles, 1 home run; 1 sacrifice hit in streak).
N.L.—6—Larry Walker, Colorado, May 21, 22, 1996 (2 doubles, 3 triples, 1 home run in streak).

GAME AND INNING

Most long hits, game
A.A.—5—George Strief, Philadelphia, June 25, 1885 (4 triples, 1 double; consecutive).
N.L.—5
  George Gore, Chicago, July 9, 1885 (2 triples, 3 doubles; consecutive).
  Larry Twitchell, Cleveland, August 15, 1889 (1 double, 3 triples, 1 home run).
  Joe Adcock, Milwaukee, July 31, 1954 (4 home runs, 1 double; consecutive).
  Willie Stargell, Pittsburgh, August 1, 1970 (3 doubles, 2 home runs).
  Steve Garvey, Los Angeles, August 28, 1977 (3 doubles, 2 home runs; consecutive).
A.L.—5—Lou Boudreau, Cleveland, July 14, 1946, first game (4 doubles, 1 home run).

Most long hits, opening game of season
N.L.—4
  George Myers, Indianapolis, April 20, 1888 (3 doubles, 1 home run).
  Billy Herman, Chicago, April 14, 1936 (3 doubles, 1 home run).
  Jim Greengrass, Cincinnati, April 13, 1954 (4 doubles).
A.L.—4
  Frank Dillon, Detroit, April 25, 1901 (4 doubles).
  Don Baylor, Baltimore, April 6, 1973 (2 doubles, 1 triple, 1 home run).

Most long hits by pitcher, nine-inning game
A.A.—4—Bob Caruthers, St. Louis, August 16, 1886 (2 home runs, 1 triple, 1 double).
A.L.—4—Lewis Wiltse, Philadelphia, August 10, 1901, second game (2 triples, 2 doubles).
N.L.—3—Held by many players—Last pitcher—Andy Messersmith, Los Angeles, April 25, 1975 (3 doubles).

Most long hits by pitcher, extra-inning game
A.L.—4—Babe Ruth, Boston, May 9, 1918, 10 innings (3 doubles, 1 triple).

Most games with four or more long hits, career
A.L.—5
  Lou Gehrig, New York, 1926, 1928, 1930, 1932, 1934.
  Joe DiMaggio, New York, 1936, 1937, 1941, 1948, 1950.
N.L.—4—Willie Stargell, Pittsburgh, 1965, 1968, 1970, 1973.

Most games with four long hits, season
A.A.—2—Henry Larkin, Philadelphia, June 16, July 29, 1885.
A.L.—2
  George H. Burns, Cleveland, June 19, first game, July 23, 1924.
  Jimmie Foxx, Philadelphia, April 24, July 2, second game, 1933.
N.L.—2
  Joe Medwick, St. Louis, May 12, August 4, 1937.
  Billy Williams, Chicago, April 9, September 5, 1969.

Most long hits, doubleheader (nine-inning games)
N.L.—6
  Joe Medwick, St. Louis, May 30, 1935 (5 doubles, 1 triple).
  Red Schoendienst, St. Louis, June 6, 1948 (5 doubles, 1 home run).

REGULAR SEASON Individual batting

A.L.—6

John Stone, Detroit, April 30, 1933 (4 doubles, 2 home runs).
Hank Majeski, Philadelphia, August 27, 1948 (6 doubles).
Hal McRae, Kansas City, August 27, 1974 (5 doubles, 1 home run).
Al Oliver, Texas, August 17, 1980 (1 double, 1 triple, 4 home runs).

Most long hits, doubleheader (more than 18 innings)

N.L.—6

Chick Hafey, St. Louis, July 28, 1928, 21 innings (4 doubles, 2 home runs).
Mel Ott, New York, June 19, 1929, 20 innings (4 doubles, 2 home runs).
Dusty Rhodes, New York, 20 innings, August 29, 1954 (2 doubles, 2 triples, 2 home runs).

A.L.—6—Jimmie Foxx, Philadelphia, July 2, 1933, 19 innings (1 double, 1 triple, 4 home runs).

Most long hits in two consecutive games

N.L.—7

Ed Delahanty, Philadelphia, July 13, 14, 1896 (2 doubles, 1 triple, 4 home runs).
Red Schoendienst, St. Louis, June 5, 6, first game, 1948 (6 doubles, 1 home run).
Joe Adcock, Milwaukee, July 30, 31, 1954 (2 doubles, 5 home runs).
Larry Walker, Colorado, May 21, 22, 1996 (2 doubles, 3 triples, 2 home runs).

A.L.—7—Earl Sheely, Chicago, May 20, 21, 1926 (6 doubles, 1 home run).

Most long hits in three consecutive games

N.L.—9—Red Schoendienst, St. Louis, June 5, 6, 6, 1948 (8 doubles, 1 home run).
A.L.—8—Earl Sheely, Chicago, May 20, 21, 22, 1926 (7 doubles, 1 home run).

Most long hits, inning

N.L.—3—Tommy Burns, Chicago, September 6, 1883, seventh inning (2 doubles, 1 home run).
A.L.-N.L. since 1900—2—Held by many players.

Most long hits by pitcher, inning

N.L.—2

Fred Goldsmith, Chicago, September 6, 1883, seventh inning (2 doubles).
William Terry, Chicago, May 19, 1895, third inning (1 home run, 1 double).
Hank Borowy, Chicago, May 5, 1946, first game, seventh inning (2 doubles).

A.L.—2

Joe Wood, Boston, July 4, 1913, a.m. game, fourth inning (2 doubles).
Bob Shawkey, New York, July 12, 1923, third inning (1 triple, 1 double).
Ted Lyons, Chicago, July 28, 1935, first game, second inning (2 doubles).

EXTRA BASES ON LONG HITS

Most extra bases on long hits, career

M.L.—3,085—Hank Aaron, Milwaukee N.L., Atlanta N.L., Milwaukee A.L., 23 years, 1954 through 1976 (2,991 in N.L., 94 in A.L.).
N.L.—2,991—Hank Aaron, Milwaukee, Atlanta, 21 years, 1954 through 1974.
A.L.—2,902—Babe Ruth, Boston, New York, 21 years, 1914 through 1934.

For a complete list of players with 1,500 or more career extra bases on long hits, see page 175.

Most extra bases on long hits, season

N.L.—255—Barry Bonds, San Francisco, 153 games, 2001.
A.L.—253—Babe Ruth, New York, 152 games, 1921.

Most extra bases on long hits by rookie, season

A.L.—183—Mark McGwire, Oakland, 151 games, 1987.
N.L.—169—Wally Berger, Boston, 151 games, 1930.

Most extra bases on long hits by righthander, season

N.L.—236—Sammy Sosa, Chicago, 160 games, 2001.
A.L.—225—Jimmie Foxx, Philadelphia, 154 games, 1932.

Most extra bases on long hits by lefthander, season

N.L.—255—Barry Bonds, San Francisco, 153 games, 2001.
A.L.—253—Babe Ruth, New York, 152 games, 1921.

Most extra bases on long hits by switch-hitter, season

A.L.—190—Mickey Mantle, New York, 153 games, 1961.
N.L.—178—Chipper Jones, Atlanta, 157 games, 1999.

Most years leading league in extra bases on long hits

A.L.—9—Babe Ruth, Boston, New York, 1918, 1919, 1920, 1921, 1923, 1924, 1926, 1928, 1929.
N.L.—7—Mike Schmidt, Philadelphia, 1974, 1975, 1976, 1980, 1981, 1982, 1986.

Most consecutive years leading league in extra bases on long hits

A.L.—4—Babe Ruth, Boston, New York, 1918, 1919, 1920, 1921.
N.L.—3—Held by many players. Last player—Mike Schmidt, Philadelphia, 1980, 1981, 1982.

Most years with 200 or more extra bases on long hits

A.L.—4—Babe Ruth, New York, 1920, 1921, 1927, 1928.
N.L.—3—Sammy Sosa, Chicago, 1998, 1999, 2001.

Most consecutive years with 200 or more extra bases on long hits

M.L.—3—Mark McGwire, Oakland A.L. and St. Louis N.L., 1997; St. Louis N.L., 1998, 1999.
A.L.—2—Babe Ruth, New York, 1920, 1921, also 1927, 1928.
N.L.—2

Mark McGwire, St. Louis, 1998, 1999.
Sammy Sosa, Chicago, 1998, 1999.

Most years with 100 or more extra bases on long hits

N.L.—19—Hank Aaron, Milwaukee, Atlanta, 1955 through 1973.
A.L.—16—Ted Williams, Boston, 1939, 1940, 1941, 1942, 1946, 1947, 1948, 1949, 1950, 1951, 1954, 1955, 1956, 1957, 1958, 1960.

Most consecutive years with 100 or more extra bases on long hits

N.L.—19—Hank Aaron, Milwaukee, Atlanta, 1955 through 1973.
A.L.—14—Lou Gehrig, New York, 1925 through 1938.
(Military service from 1943 through 1945 and most of 1952 and 1953 interrupted a 15-year streak by Ted Williams of Boston, who compiled 100 extra bases on long hits from 1939 through 1958.)

Fewest extra bases on long hits, season (150 or more games)

N.L.—9—Dal Maxvill, St. Louis, 152 games, 1970.
A.L.—11—Mike Tresh, Chicago, 150 games, 1945.

Fewest extra bases on long hits by leader

N.L.—74

Harry Lumley, Brooklyn, 131 games, 1906.
Honus Wagner, Pittsburgh, 137 games, 1909.
A.L.—80—Sam Crawford, Detroit, 144 games, 1907.

Most extra bases on long hits, game

N.L.—13—Joe Adcock, Milwaukee, July 31, 1954 (4 home runs, 1 double).
A.L.—12

Lou Gehrig, New York, June 3, 1932 (4 home runs).
Pat Seerey, Chicago, July 18, 1948, first game, 11 innings (4 home runs).
Rocky Colavito, Cleveland, June 10, 1959 (4 home runs).

Most extra bases on long hits, doubleheader (each game nine innings)

N.L.—15

Stan Musial, St. Louis, May 2, 1954.
Nate Colbert, San Diego, August 1, 1972.
A.L.—15—Al Oliver, Texas, August 17, 1980.

Most extra bases on long hits, doubleheader (more than 18 innings)

A.L.—15—Jimmie Foxx, Philadelphia, July 2, 1933, 19 innings.
N.L.—13—Ralph Kiner, Pittsburgh, September 11, 1947, 22 innings.

Most extra bases on long hits, two consecutive games

A.L.—17—Tony Lazzeri, New York, May 23, second game, May 24, 1936 (5 home runs, 1 triple).

N.L.—17—Joe Adcock, Milwaukee, July 30, July 31, 1954 (5 home runs, 2 doubles).

Most extra bases on long hits, inning
N.L.-A.L.—6—Held by many players.

Most runs batted in, career
M.L.—2,297—Hank Aaron, Milwaukee N.L., Atlanta N.L., Milwaukee A.L., 23 years, 1954 through 1976 (2,202 in N.L., 95 in A.L.).
N.L.—2,202—Hank Aaron, Milwaukee, Atlanta, 21 years, 1954 through 1974.
A.L.—2,192—Babe Ruth, Boston, New York, 21 years, 1914 through 1934.

For a complete list of players with 1,200 or more career runs batted in, see page 176.

Most runs batted in, season
N.L.—191—Hack Wilson, Chicago, 155 games, 1930.
A.L.—184—Lou Gehrig, New York, 155 games, 1931.

Most runs batted in by rookie, season
A.L.—145—Ted Williams, Boston, 149 games, 1939.
N.L.—130—Albert Pujols, St. Louis, 161 games, 2001.

Most runs batted in by righthander, season
N.L.—191—Hack Wilson, Chicago, 155 games, 1930.
A.L.—183—Hank Greenberg, Detroit, 154 games, 1937.

Most runs batted in by lefthander, season
A.L.—184—Lou Gehrig, New York, 155 games, 1931.
N.L.—170—Chuck Klein, Philadelphia, 156 games, 1930.

Most runs batted in by switch-hitter, season
A.L.—130—Mickey Mantle, New York, 150 games, 1956.
N.L.—130—Ken Caminiti, San Diego, 146 games, 1996.

Most runs batted in by catcher, season
N.L.—142—Roy Campanella, Brooklyn, 144 games, 1953; caught 140 games.
A.L.—133—Bill Dickey, New York, 140 games, 1937; caught 137 games.

Most years leading league in runs batted in
A.L.—6—Babe Ruth, Boston, New York, 1919, 1920, 1921, 1923, 1926, 1928 (tied).
N.L.—4
Rogers Hornsby, St. Louis, 1920 (tied), 1921, 1922, 1925.
Hank Aaron, Milwaukee, Atlanta, 1957, 1960, 1963, 1966.
Mike Schmidt, Philadelphia, 1980, 1981, 1984 (tied), 1986.

For a complete list of triple crown winners, see page 182.

Most consecutive years leading league in runs batted in
A.L.—3
Ty Cobb, Detroit, 1907, 1908, 1909.
Babe Ruth, Boston, New York, 1919, 1920, 1921.
Cecil Fielder, Detroit, 1990, 1991, 1992.
N.L.—3
Honus Wagner, Pittsburgh, 1907, 1908, 1909.
Rogers Hornsby, St. Louis, 1920 (tied), 1921, 1922.
Joe Medwick, St. Louis, 1936, 1937, 1938.
George Foster, Cincinnati, 1976, 1977, 1978.

Most years with 100 or more runs batted in
A.L.—13
Babe Ruth, Boston, New York, 1919 through 1933, except 1922 and 1925.
Lou Gehrig, New York, 1926 through 1938.
Jimmie Foxx, Philadelphia, Boston, 1929 through 1941.
N.L.—11—Hank Aaron, Milwaukee, Atlanta, 1955, 1957, 1959, 1960, 1961, 1962, 1963, 1966, 1967, 1970, 1971.

Most consecutive years with 100 or more runs batted in
A.L.—13
Lou Gehrig, New York, 1926 through 1938.
Jimmie Foxx, Philadelphia, Boston, 1929 through 1941.

N.L.—8
Mel Ott, New York, 1929 through 1936.
Willie Mays, San Francisco, 1959 through 1966.

Most years with 150 or more runs batted in
A.L.—7—Lou Gehrig, New York, 1927, 1930, 1931, 1932, 1934, 1936, 1937.
N.L.—2
Hack Wilson, Chicago, 1929, 1930.
Sammy Sosa, Chicago, 1998, 2001.

Most consecutive years with 150 or more runs batted in
A.L.—3
Babe Ruth, New York, 1929, 1930, 1931.
Lou Gehrig, New York, 1930, 1931, 1932.
N.L.—2—Hack Wilson, Chicago, 1929, 1930.

Fewest runs batted in, season (150 or more games)
N.L.—20—Richie Ashburn, Philadelphia, 153 games, 1959.
A.L.—20—Alvaro Espinoza, New York, 150 games, 1990.

Fewest runs batted in by leader, season (since 1920)
N.L.—94
George Kelly, New York, 155 games, 1920.
Rogers Hornsby, St. Louis, 149 games, 1920.
A.L.—105—Al Rosen, Cleveland, 148 games, 1952.

Most consecutive games with one or more runs batted in, season
N.L.—17—Oscar Grimes, Chicago, June 27 through July 23, 1922 (27 runs batted in).
A.L.—13
Taffy Wright, Chicago, May 4 through May 20, 1941 (22 runs batted in).
Mike Sweeney, Kansas City, June 23 through July 4, 1999 (19 runs batted in).

Most runs batted in, game
N.L.—12
Jim Bottomley, St. Louis, September 16, 1924.
Mark Whiten, St. Louis, September 7, 1993, second game.
A.L.—11—Tony Lazzeri, New York, May 24, 1936.

Most runs batted in by pitcher, game
N.L.—9
Henry Staley, Boston, June 1, 1893*
Tony Cloninger, Atlanta, July 3, 1966.
A.L.—7—Vic Raschi, New York, August 4, 1953.
*RBIs not officially adopted until 1920.

Most runs batted in accounting for all club's runs, nine-inning game
N.L.—8—George Kelly, New York vs. Cincinnati, June 14, 1924 (New York won, 8-6).
A.L.—8—Bob Johnson, Philadelphia vs. St. Louis, June 12, 1938 (Philadelphia won, 8-3).

Most runs batted in accounting for all club's runs, extra-inning game
A.L.—9—Mike Greenwell, Boston vs. Seattle, September 2, 1996, 10 innings (Boston won, 9-8).
N.L.—Less than nine-inning record.

Most runs batted in, two consecutive games
A.L.—15—Tony Lazzeri, New York, May 23, second game (4), May 24 (11), 1936.
N.L.—13
Nate Colbert, San Diego, August 1, first game (5), August 1, second game (8), 1972.
Mark Whiten, St. Louis, September 7, first game (1), September 7, second game (12), 1993.

Most runs batted in, doubleheader
N.L.—13
Nate Colbert, San Diego, August 1, 1972.
Mark Whiten, St. Louis, September 7, 1993.
A.L.—11
Earl Averill, Cleveland, September 17, 1930, 17 innings.
Jim Tabor, Boston, July 4, 1939, 18 innings.
Boog Powell, Baltimore, July 6, 1966, 20 innings.

Most runs batted in, inning

N.L.—8—Fernando Tatis, St. Louis, April 23, 1999, third inning.

A.A.—7—Ed Cartwright, St. Louis, September 23, 1890, third inning.*

A.L.—6

Bob Johnson, Philadelphia, August 29, 1937, first game, first inning.

Tom McBride, Boston, August 4, 1945, second game, fourth inning.

Joe Astroth, Philadelphia, September 23, 1950, sixth inning.

Gil McDougald, New York, May 3, 1951, ninth inning.

Sam Mele, Chicago, June 10, 1952, fourth inning.

Jim Lemon, Washington, September 5, 1959, third inning.

Carlos Quintana, Boston, July 30, 1991, third inning.

Matt Stairs, Oakland, July 5, 1996, first inning.

Matt Williams, Cleveland, August 27, 1997, fourth inning.

*RBIs not officially adopted until 1920.

Most runs batted in, two consecutive innings (at least one each inning)

A.L.—8

Jim Gentile, Baltimore, May 9, 1961, first and second innings.

Jim Northrup, Detroit, June 24, 1968, fifth and sixth innings.

Frank Robinson, Baltimore, June 26, 1970, fifth and sixth innings.

Robin Ventura, Chicago, September 4, 1995, fourth and fifth innings.

N.L.—7

Kid Nichols, Boston, September 19, 1892, fifth and sixth innings.

Tony Piet, Pittsburgh, July 28, 1932, second game, second and third innings.

Johnny Rucker, New York, September 29, 1940, second and third innings.

Del Ennis, Philadelphia, July 27, 1950, seventh and eighth innings.

Earl Torgeson, Boston, June 30, 1951, seventh and eighth innings.

Ralph Kiner, Pittsburgh, July 4, 1951, second game, third and fourth innings.

Joe Morgan, Cincinnati, August 19, 1974, second and third innings.

Most runners left on base, game

N.L.—12—Glenn Beckert, Chicago, September 16, 1972.

A.L.—11

Frank Isbell, Chicago, August 10, 1901.

John Donahue, Chicago, June 23, 1907, 12 innings.

George Wright, Texas, August 12, 1984, 11 innings.

GAME-WINNING RBIs (1980-1988)

Most game-winning RBIs, career

N.L.—129—Keith Hernandez, St. Louis, New York, 1980 through 1988.

A.L.—117—Eddie Murray, Baltimore, 1980 through 1988.

Most game-winning RBIs, season

N.L.—24—Keith Hernandez, New York, 158 games, 1985.

A.L.—23—Mike Greenwell, Boston, 158 games, 1988.

Most game-winning RBIs by pitcher, season

N.L.—3

Rick Mahler, Atlanta, 39 games, 1985.

Rick Rhoden, Pittsburgh, 35 games, 1985.

(Tim Leary of Los Angeles had 3 in 1988, but 1 came as a pinch-hitter.)

A.L.—Never accomplished.

Most game-winning RBIs by rookie, season

A.L.—14

Jose Canseco, Oakland, 157 games, 1986.

Wally Joyner, California, 154 games, 1986.

Mark McGwire, Oakland, 151 games, 1987.

N.L.—13

Juan Samuel, Philadelphia, 160 games, 1984.

Darryl Strawberry, New York, 122 games, 1983.

Fewest game-winning RBIs in a season (150 or more games)

N.L.—0

Alan Wiggins, San Diego, 158 games, 1984.

Rafael Palmeiro, Chicago, 152 games, 1988.

A.L.—1

Jackie Gutierrez, Boston, 151 games, 1984.

Tony Phillips, Oakland, 154 games, 1984.

Steve Lombardozzi, Minnesota, 156 games, 1986.

Dick Schofield, California, 155 games, 1988.

Most game-winning RBIs, doubleheader

N.L.-A.L.—2—Held by many players.

Most consecutive games with game-winning RBI, season

A.L.—5—Kirk Gibson, Detroit, July 13 through 20, 1986.

N.L.—4

Johnny Ray, Pittsburgh, September 18 through 21, 1984.

Milt Thompson, Philadelphia, August 19 through 21, second game, 1987.

Ozzie Smith, St. Louis, September 8 through 11, 1988.

Most consecutive victories with game-winning RBI, season

N.L.—6—Johnny Ray, Pittsburgh, September 13 through 21, 1984 (two losses in streak).

A.L.—5—Kirk Gibson, Detroit, July 13 through 20, 1986 (no losses in streak).

BASES ON BALLS

Most bases on balls, career

M.L.—2,141—Rickey Henderson, Oakland A.L., New York A.L., Toronto A.L., San Diego N.L., Anaheim A.L., New York N.L., Seattle A.L., 23 years, 1979 through 2001 (1,757 in A.L., 384 in N.L.).

A.L.—2,042—Babe Ruth, Boston, New York, 21 years, 1914 through 1934.

N.L.—1,799—Joe Morgan, Houston, Cincinnati, San Francisco, Philadelphia, 21 years, 1963 through 1983.

For a complete list of players with 1,000 or more career bases on balls, see page 176.

Most bases on balls, season

N.L.—177—Barry Bonds, San Francisco, 153 games, 2001.

A.L.—170—Babe Ruth, New York, 152 games, 1923.

Most bases on balls by rookie, season

A.L.—107—Ted Williams, Boston, 149 games, 1939.

N.L.—100—Jim Gilliam, Brooklyn, 151 games, 1953.

Most bases on balls by righthander, season

N.L.—162—Mark McGwire, St. Louis, 155 games, 1998.

A.L.—151—Eddie Yost, Washington, 152 games, 1956.

Most bases on balls lefthander, season

N.L.—177—Barry Bonds, San Francisco, 153 games, 2001.

A.L.—170—Babe Ruth, New York, 152 games, 1923.

Most bases on balls by switch-hitter, season

A.L.—146—Mickey Mantle, New York, 144 games, 1957.

N.L.—126—Chipper Jones, Atlanta, 157 games, 1999.

Most bases on balls by pinch-hitter, season

N.L.—20—Matt Franco, New York, 88 games, 1999.

A.L.—18—Elmer Valo, New York, Washington, 81 games, 1960.

Most years leading league in bases on balls

A.L.—11—Babe Ruth, New York, 1920, 1921, 1923, 1924, 1926, 1927, 1928, 1930, 1931, 1932, 1933.

N.L.—7—Barry Bonds, Pittsburgh, San Francisco, 1992, 1994, 1995, 1996, 1997, 2000, 2001.

Most consecutive years leading league in bases on balls

A.L.—4

Babe Ruth, New York, 1930 through 1933.

Ted Williams, Boston, 1946 through 1949 (military service from 1943 through 1945 interrupted a six-year streak by Williams of Boston, who led in bases on balls from 1941 through 1949).

N.L.—4—Barry Bonds, San Francisco, 1994 through 1997.

Most years with 100 or more bases on balls

A.L.—13—Babe Ruth, Boston, New York, 1919, 1920, 1921, 1923, 1924, 1926, 1927, 1928, 1930, 1931, 1932, 1933, 1934.

N.L.—10—Mel Ott, New York, 1929, 1930, 1932, 1936, 1937, 1938, 1939, 1940, 1941, 1942.

Most consecutive years with 100 or more bases on balls
A.L.—8—Frank Thomas, Chicago, 1991 through 1998.
N.L.—7—Mel Ott, New York, 1936 through 1942.

Fewest bases on balls, season (150 or more games)
A.L.—10—Ozzie Guillen, Chicago, 150 games, 1996.
N.L.—12—Hal Lanier, San Francisco, 151 games, 1968.

Fewest bases on balls by leader, season
N.L.—69—Hack Wilson, Chicago, 142 games, 1926.
A.L.—89—Whitey Witt, New York, 140 games, 1922.

Most consecutive bases on balls
A.L.—7
  Billy Rogell, Detroit, August 17, second game, August 18, August 19, first game, 1938.
  Jose Canseco, Oakland, August 4, 5, 1992.
N.L.—7
  Mel Ott, New York, June 16, 17, 18, 1943.
  Eddie Stanky, New York, August 29, 30, 1950.

Most consecutive games with one or more bases on balls
A.L.—22—Roy Cullenbine, Detroit, July 2 through July 22, 1947 (34 bases on balls).
N.L.—16—Jack Clark, St. Louis, July 18 through August 10, 1987 (28 bases on balls).
A.A.—16—Yank Robinson, St. Louis, September 15 through October 2, 1888 (23 bases on balls).

Most bases on balls, nine-inning game
N.L.—6—Walt Wilmot, Chicago, August 22, 1891 (consecutive).
A.L.—6—Jimmie Foxx, Boston, June 16, 1938 (consecutive).
N.L. since 1900—5—Held by many players. Last player—Vince Coleman, New York, August 10, 1992.

Most bases on balls, extra-inning game
A.L.—6—Andre Thornton, Cleveland, May 2, 1984, 16 innings.
N.L.—6—Jeff Bagwell, Houston, August 20, 1999, 16 innings.

Most bases on balls drawn by pitcher, game
A.A.—4—Joe Miller, Philadelphia, September 13, 1886.
A.L.—4
  Urban Faber, Chicago, June 18, 1915 (consecutive).
  Chuck Stobbs, Boston, June 8, 1950 (consecutive).
N.L.—3—Held by many pitchers.

Most bases on balls, first major league game
A.L.—4
  Otto Saltzgaver, New York, April 12, 1932.
  Milt Galatzer, Cleveland, June 25, 1933, first game.
N.L.—3—Held by many players.

Most times receiving five bases on balls in one game, career
N.L.—4—Mel Ott, New York, 1929, 1933, 1943, 1944.
A.L.—2—Max Bishop, Philadelphia, 1929, 1930.

Most bases on balls, doubleheader
A.L.—8—Max Bishop, Philadelphia, May 21, 1930; Boston, July 8, 1934.
N.L.—6
  Mel Ott, New York, October 5, 1929.
  Johnny Mize, St. Louis, August 26, 1939.
  Mel Ott, New York, April 30, 1944.
  Clay Dalrymple, Philadelphia, July 4, 1967, 19 innings.
  Cleon Jones, New York, June 25, 1971.
  Jack Clark, St. Louis, July 8, 1987, 19 innings.

Most bases on balls, inning
N.L.-A.L.—2—Held by many players.

Most times receiving two bases on balls in one inning, career
A.L.—4—George Selkirk, New York, 1936 (2), 1938, 1940.
N.L.—2—Eddie Stanky, New York, 1950 (2).

Most times receiving two bases on balls in one inning, season
A.L.—2
  George Selkirk, New York, June 24, August 28, second game, 1936.
  Skeeter Webb, Chicago, July 30, September 3, 1940.
N.L.—2—Eddie Stanky, New York, June 27, August 22, 1950.

INTENTIONAL (SINCE 1955)

Most intentional bases on balls, career
N.L.—355—Barry Bonds, Pittsburgh, San Francisco, 16 years, 1986 through 2001.

A.L.—229—George Brett, Kansas City, 21 years, 1973 through 1993.

Most intentional bases on balls, season
N.L.—45—Willie McCovey, San Francisco, 149 games, 1969.
A.L.—33
  Ted Williams, Boston, 132 games, 1957.
  John Olerud, Toronto, 158 games, 1993.

Most intentional bases on balls by rookie, season
A.L.—16—Alvin Davis, Seattle, 152 games, 1984.
N.L.—14—Willie Montanez, Philadelphia, 158 games, 1971.

Most intentional bases on balls by righthander, season
N.L.—37—Sammy Sosa, Chicago, 160 games, 2001.
A.L.—29
  Frank Howard, Washington, 161 games, 1970.
  Frank Thomas, Chicago, 145 games, 1995.

Most intentional bases on balls by lefthander, season
N.L.—45—Willie McCovey, San Francisco, 149 games, 1969.
A.L.—33
  Ted Williams, Boston, 132 games, 1957.
  John Olerud, Toronto, 158 games, 1993.

Most intentional bases on balls by switch-hitter, season
N.L.—26—Tim Raines Sr., Montreal, 139 games, 1987.
A.L.—25—Eddie Murray, Baltimore, 162 games, 1984.

Most years leading league in intentional bases on balls
N.L.—7—Barry Bonds, Pittsburgh, San Francisco, 1992 through 1998.
A.L.—6—Wade Boggs, Boston, 1987, 1988 (tied), 1989, 1990, 1991, 1992.

Most consecutive years leading league in intentional bases on balls
N.L.—7—Barry Bonds, Pittsburgh, San Francisco, 1992 through 1998.
A.L.—6—Wade Boggs, Boston, 1987, 1988 (tied), 1989, 1990, 1991, 1992.

Most years with 10 or more intentional bases on balls
N.L.—16—Hank Aaron, Milwaukee, Atlanta, 1957 through 1973, except 1964.
A.L.—11—George Brett, Kansas City, 1979 through 1991, except 1981, 1984.

Most at-bats with no intentional bases on balls, season
A.L.—691—Kirby Puckett, Minnesota, 161 games, 1985.
N.L.—690—Neifi Perez, Colorado, 157 games, 1999.

Most intentional bases on balls, nine-inning game
A.L.-N.L.—3—Held by many players.

Most intentional bases on balls, extra-inning game
N.L.—5—Andre Dawson, Chicago, May 22, 1990, 16 innings.
A.L.—4
  Roger Maris, New York, May 22, 1962, 12 innings.
  Manny Ramirez, Boston, June 5, 2001, 18 innings.

STRIKEOUTS
CAREER AND SEASON

Most strikeouts, career
A.L.—2,597—Reggie Jackson, Kansas City, Oakland, Baltimore, New York, California, 21 years, 1967 through 1987.
N.L.—1,936—Willie Stargell, Pittsburgh, 21 years, 1962 through 1982.

For a complete list of players with 1,200 or more career strikeouts, see page 177.

Fewest strikeouts, career (14 or more seasons; excludes pitchers)
A.L.—113—Joe Sewell, Cleveland, New York, 14 years, 1920 through 1933, 1,903 games.
N.L.—173—Lloyd Waner, Pittsburgh, Boston, Cincinnati, Philadelphia, Brooklyn, 18 years, 1927 through 1945, except 1943, 1,993 games.

Most strikeouts, season
N.L.—189—Bobby Bonds, San Francisco, 157 games, 1970.
A.L.—186—Rob Deer, Milwaukee, 134 games, 1987.

Most strikeouts by rookie, season
A.L.—185—Pete Incaviglia, Texas, 153 games, 1986.
N.L.—168—Juan Samuel, Philadelphia, 160 games, 1984.

Most strikeouts by righthander, season
N.L.—189—Bobby Bonds, San Francisco, 157 games, 1970.
A.L.—186—Rob Deer, Milwaukee, 134 games, 1987.

Most strikeouts by lefthander, season
A.L.—185—Jim Thome, Cleveland, 156 games, 2001.
N.L.—167—Jim Edmonds, St. Louis, 152 games, 2000.

Most strikeouts by switch-hitter, season
A.L.—160—Mickey Tettleton, Baltimore, 135 games, 1990.
N.L.—146—Todd Hundley, New York, 153 games, 1996.

Most strikeouts by pitcher, season (since 1900)
A.L.—65—Wilbur Wood, Chicago, 49 games, 1972.
N.L.—62—Jerry Koosman, New York, 35 games, 1968.

Most years leading league in strikeouts
A.L.—7—Jimmie Foxx, Philadelphia, Boston, 1929, 1930 (tied), 1931, 1933, 1935, 1936, 1941.
N.L.—6—Vince DiMaggio, Boston, Pittsburgh, Philadelphia, 1937, 1938, 1942, 1943, 1944, 1945.

Most consecutive years leading league in strikeouts
A.L.—4—Reggie Jackson, Oakland, 1968 through 1971.
N.L.—4
    Hack Wilson, Chicago, 1927 through 1930.
    Vince DiMaggio, Pittsburgh, Philadelphia, 1942 through 1945.
    Juan Samuel, Philadelphia, 1984 through 1987.

Most years with 100 or more strikeouts
A.L.—18—Reggie Jackson, Oakland, Baltimore, New York, California, 1968 through 1980, 1982 through 1986.
N.L.—13—Willie Stargell, Pittsburgh, 1965 through 1976, 1979.

Most consecutive years with 100 or more strikeouts
A.L.—13—Reggie Jackson, Oakland, Baltimore, New York, 1968 through 1980.
N.L.—12—Willie Stargell, Pittsburgh, 1965 through 1976.

Fewest strikeouts, season (150 or more games)
A.L.—4
    Joe Sewell, Cleveland, 155 games, 1925.
    Joe Sewell, Cleveland, 152 games, 1929.
N.L.—5—Charlie Hollocher, Chicago, 152 games, 1922.

Fewest strikeouts by rookie, season (150 or more games)
N.L.—17—Buddy Hassett, Brooklyn, 156 games, 1936.
A.L.—25—Tom Oliver, Boston, 154 games, 1930.

Fewest strikeouts by righthander, season (150 or more games)
N.L.—8—Emil Verban, Philadelphia, 155 games, 1947.
A.L.—9
    Stuffy McInnis, Boston, 152 games, 1921.
    Lou Boudreau, Cleveland, 152 games, 1948.

Fewest strikeouts by lefthander, season (150 or more games)
A.L.—4
    Joe Sewell, Cleveland, 155 games, 1925.
    Joe Sewell, Cleveland, 152 games, 1929.
N.L.—5—Charlie Hollocher, Chicago, 152 games, 1922.

Fewest strikeouts by switch-hitter, season (150 or more games)
N.L.—10—Frankie Frisch, St. Louis, 153 games, 1927.
A.L.—23—Buck Weaver, Chicago, 151 games, 1920.

Fewest strikeouts by leader, season
N.L.—63—George Grantham, Chicago, 127 games, 1924.
A.L.—66
    Jimmie Foxx, Philadelphia, 153 games, 1930.
    Ed Morgan, Cleveland, 150 games, 1930.

Most years leading league in fewest strikeouts (150 or more games)
A.L.—11—Nellie Fox, Chicago, 1952 through 1962.
N.L.—4
    Stan Musial, St. Louis, 1943, 1948, 1952, 1956 (tied).
    Dick Groat, Pittsburgh, St. Louis, 1955, 1958, 1964, 1965 (tied).

Most consecutive games with no strikeouts, season
A.L.—115—Joe Sewell, Cleveland, May 17 through September 19, 1929 (437 at-bats).

N.L.—77—Lloyd Waner, Pittsburgh, Boston, Cincinnati, April 24 through September 16, 1941 (219 at-bats).

GAME AND INNING

Most strikeouts, nine-inning game (*consecutive)
N.L.—5
    Oscar Walker, Buffalo, June 20, 1879.*
    Pete Dowling, Louisville, August 15, 1899.*
    Floyd Young, Pittsburgh, September 29, 1935, second game.*
    Bob Sadowski, Milwaukee, April 20, 1964.*
    Dick Allen, Philadelphia, June 28, 1964, first game.*
    Ron Swoboda, New York, June 22, 1969, first game.*
    Steve Whitaker, San Francisco, April 14, 1970.*
    Dick Allen, St. Louis, May 24, 1970.*
    Bill Russell, Los Angeles, June 9, 1971.*
    Jose Mangual, Montreal, August 11, 1975.*
    Frank Taveras, New York, May 1, 1979.*
    Dave Kingman, New York, May 28, 1982.*
    Darryl Strawberry, Los Angeles, May 1, 1991.*
    Delino DeShields, Montreal, September 17, 1991, second game.*
    Scott Rolen, Philadelphia, August 23, 1999.*
    Richie Sexson, Milwaukee, May 29, 2001.*
A.L.—5
    Lefty Grove, Philadelphia, June 10, 1933, first game.*
    Johnny Broaca, New York, June 25, 1934.*
    Chet Laabs, Detroit, October 2, 1938, first game.*
    Larry Doby, Cleveland, April 25, 1948.*
    Jim Landis, Chicago, July 28, 1957.*
    Bob Allison, Minnesota, September 2, 1965.*
    Reggie Jackson, Oakland, September 27, 1968.*
    Ray Jarvis, Boston, April 20, 1969.*
    Rick Monday, Oakland, April 29, 1970.*
    Frank Howard, Washington, September 19, 1970, first game.*
    Don Buford, Baltimore, August 26, 1971.*
    Rick Manning, Cleveland, May 15, 1977.*
    Bo Jackson, Kansas City, April 18, 1987.*
    Rob Deer, Milwaukee, August 8, 1987, first game.*
    Joey Meyer, Milwaukee, September 20, 1988.*
    Phil Bradley, Baltimore, September 7, 1989, first game.
    Bernie Williams, New York, August 21, 1991.*
    Phil Plantier, Boston, October 1, 1991.*
    Bob Hamelin, Kansas City, May 24, 1995.*
    Danny Bautista, Detroit, May 28, 1995.
    Jose Canseco, Oakland, July 16, 1997.*
    Jim Thome, Cleveland, April 9, 2000.
    John Jaha, Oakland, April 20, 2000.*

Most strikeouts, extra-inning game
A.L.—6
    Carl Weilman, St. Louis, July 25, 1913, 15 innings (consecutive).
    Rick Reichardt, California, May 31, 1966, 17 innings.
    Billy Cowan, California, July 9, 1971, 20 innings.
    Cecil Cooper, Boston, June 14, 1974, 15 innings.
    Sam Horn, Baltimore, July 17, 1991, 15 innings.
    Alex Gonzalez, Toronto, September 9, 1998, 13 innings (consecutive).
N.L.—6—Don Hoak, Chicago, May 2, 1956, 17 innings.

Most times with four or more strikeouts in a game, career
M.L.—17—Rob Deer, San Francisco N.L., 1985 (1); Milwaukee A.L., 1986 (1), 1987 (3), 1989 (2), 1990 (3); Detroit A.L., 1991 (3), 1992 (1), 1993 (3).
N.L.—13—Dick Allen, Philadelphia, 1964 (2), 1966, 1968 (7), 1969 (2), St. Louis, 1970.
A.L.—16—Rob Deer, Milwaukee A.L., 1986 (1), 1987 (3), 1989 (2), 1990 (3); Detroit A.L., 1991 (3), 1992 (1), 1993 (3).

Most times with four or more strikeouts in a game, season
N.L.—7—Dick Allen, Philadelphia, April 13, May 1, 9, June 29, July 16, 21, August 19, 1968.
A.L.—5
    Reggie Jackson, Oakland, April 7, second game, April 21, May 18, June 4, September 21, first game, 1971.
    Bobby Darwin, Minnesota, May 12, 13, June 23, July 14, August 6, first game, August 10, 1972.

Most strikeouts, first major league game
N.L.—4
   Billy Sunday, Chicago, May 22, 1883.
   Wes Bales, Atlanta, August 7, 1966.
A.A.—4—Hercules Burnett, Louisville, June 26, 1888.
A.L.—4
   Rollie Naylor, Philadelphia, September 14, 1917.
   Sam Ewing, Chicago, September 11, 1973.

Most strikeouts, doubleheader
N.L.—7—Mike Vail, New York, September 26, 1975, 24 innings.
A.L.—7
   Pat Seerey, Chicago, July 24, 1948, 19 innings.
   Dave Nicholson, Chicago, June 12, 1963, 17 innings.
   Frank Howard, Washington, July 9, 1965, 18 innings.
   Bill Melton, Chicago, July 24, 1970, 18 innings.

Most strikeouts, two consecutive games (18 innings)
A.L.—8
   Rick Monday, Oakland, April 28 (3), 29 (5), 1970.
   Gorman Thomas, Milwaukee, July 27, second game (4), 28
      (4), 1975.
   Jay Buhner, Seattle, August 23 (4), 24 (4), 1990.
   Jose Canseco, Oakland, July 14 (3), 16 (5), 1997.
N.L.—8
   Wayne Twitchell, Philadelphia, May 16 (4), 22 (4), 1973.
   Ruppert Jones, San Diego, July 16 (4), 17 (4), 1982.

Most strikeouts, two consecutive games (more than 18 innings)
N.L.—9
   Eric Davis, Cincinnati, April 24 (4), 25 (5), 1987 (21 innings).
   Jack Clark, San Diego, June 11 (5), 13 (4), 1989 (21 innings).
A.L.—8
   Pedro Ramos, Cleveland, August 19, 23, 1963 (22 innings).
   Roy Smalley, Minnesota, August 28, 29, 1976 (26 innings).

Most strikeouts, three consecutive games
N.L.—10
   Adolfo Phillips, Chicago, June 8 (2), 10 (5), 11 (3), 1966.
   Wayne Twitchell, Philadelphia, May 16 (4), 22 (4), 27 (2), 1973.
   Andujar Cedeno, San Diego, July 5, 10 innings (2), 6, 12
      innings (5), 7 (3), 1995.
A.L.—10
   Bill Melton, Chicago, July 24 (4), 24 (3), 28 (3), 1970.
   Dick Drago, Kansas City, September 5 (3), 10, second game
      (4), 17 (3), 1970.
   Jim Fuller, Baltimore, September 5 (3), 27 (4), 28, first game
      (3), 1973.
   Gorman Thomas, Milwaukee, July 27, second game (4), 28
      (4), 29 (2), 1975.
   Jay Buhner, Seattle, August 23 (4), 24 (4), 25 (2), 1990.

Most strikeouts, four consecutive games
N.L.—12—Adolfo Phillips, Chicago, June 7 (2), 8 (2), 10 (5),
   11 (3), 1966.
A.L.—12
   Jim Hannan, Washington, July 24 (4), 29 (2), August 3 (3), 8
      (3), 1968.
   Bill Melton, Chicago, July 23 (2), 24 (4), 24 (3), 28 (3), 1970.

Ten or more consecutive strikeouts, season (consecutive plate appearances)
N.L.—
   12—Sandy Koufax, Brooklyn, June 24 to September 24, sec-
      ond game, 1955 (12 at-bats for season, 12 strikeouts).
   10—Tommie Sisk, Pittsburgh, July 27 (2), August 1 (3), 6
      (4), 12 (1), 1966.
A.L.—
   11—Dean Chance, Los Angeles, July 24 (1), 30 (2), August 4,
      first game (3), 9 (4), 13 (1), 1965.
   10—Joe Grzenda, Washington, April 7 (2), 22 (1), May 26
      (4), June 13 (1), 16 (1), August 3 (1), 1970.

Most consecutive strikeouts, season (not consecutive plate appearances)
N.L.—14
   Bill Hands, Chicago, June 9, second game through July 11, 1968,
      second game (also one base on balls and two sacrifice hits).
   Juan Eichelberger, San Diego, June 30 through August 15,
      1980 (also one sacrifice hit).

A.L.—13—Jim Hannan, Washington, July 24 through August
   13, 1968 (also two bases on balls).

Most strikeouts, inning
A.L.-N.L.—2—Held by many players.

SACRIFICE HITS

Most sacrifices, career
A.L.—511—Eddie Collins, Philadelphia, Chicago, 25 years,
   1906 through 1930.
N.L.—392—Jake Daubert, Brooklyn, Cincinnati, 15 years, 1910
   through 1924.

Most sacrifices, season (including sacrifice scoring flies)
A.L.—67—Ray Chapman, Cleveland, 156 games, 1917.
N.L.—46—Jim Sheckard, Chicago, 148 games, 1909.

Most sacrifices, season (excludes sacrifice flies)
A.L.—46—Bill Bradley, Cleveland, 139 games, 1907.
N.L.—43—Kid Gleason, Philadelphia, 155 games, 1905.

Most sacrifices by rookie, season (includes sacrifice scoring flies)
A.L.—39—Emory Rigney, Detroit, 155 games, 1922.
N.L.—31—Ozzie Smith, San Diego, 159 games, 1978.

Most sacrifices by rookie, season (since 1931; excludes sacrifice flies)
A.L.—28—Joe Hoover, Detroit, 144 games, 1943.
N.L.—28
   Jackie Robinson, Brooklyn, 151 games, 1947.
   Ozzie Smith, San Diego, 159 games, 1978.

Most sacrifices by righthander, season
A.L.—67—Ray Chapman, Cleveland, 156 games, 1917
   (includes a few sacrifice scoring flies).
N.L.—43—Kid Gleason, Philadelphia, 155 games, 1905 (does
   not include sacrifice flies).

Most sacrifices by lefthander, season
A.L.—52—Bob Ganley, Washington, 150 games, 1908 (includes
   a few sacrifice scoring flies).
N.L.—46—Jim Sheckard, Chicago, 148 games, 1909 (includes
   a few sacrifice scoring flies).

Most sacrifices by switch-hitter, season
A.L.—52—Donie Bush, Detroit, 157 games, 1909 (includes a
   few sacrifice scoring flies).
N.L.—35—Leo Magee, St. Louis, 142 games, 1914 (includes
   sacrifice flies).

Most years leading league in sacrifices
A.L.—6—Mule Haas, Philadelphia, Chicago, 1930, 1931, 1932,
   1933, 1934, 1936.
N.L.—4—Otto Knabe, Philadelphia, 1907, 1908, 1910, 1913.

Most consecutive years leading league in sacrifices
A.L.—5—Mule Haas, Philadelphia, Chicago, 1930 through
   1934.
N.L.—2—Held by many players. Last player—Jay Bell,
   Pittsburgh, 1990, 1991.

Most at-bats with no sacrifice hits, season
N.L.—701—Juan Samuel, Philadelphia, 160 games, 1984.
A.L.—672—Garret Anderson, Anaheim, 161 games, 2001.

Fewest sacrifices for leader, season (excludes sacrifice flies)
A.L.—13
   Billy Martin, Detroit, 131 games, 1958.
   Tony Kubek, New York, 132 games, 1959.
   Jim Landis, Chicago, 149 games, 1959.
   Al Pilarcik, Baltimore, 130 games, 1959.
   Vic Power, Minnesota, 138 games, 1963.
   Paul Blair, Baltimore, 150 games, 1969.
   Denny McLain, Detroit, 42 games, 1969.
N.L.—13—Maury Wills, Los Angeles, 148 games, 1961.

Most sacrifice hits, game
A.L.—4
   Red Killefer, Washington, August 27, 1910, first game.
   Jack Barry, Boston, August 21, 1916.
   Ray Chapman, Cleveland, August 31, 1919.
   Felix Fermin, Cleveland, August 22, 1989, 10 innings.

N.L.—4

Jake Daubert, Brooklyn, August 15, 1914, second game.
Cy Seymour, Cincinnati, July 25, 1902.

Most sacrifice hits, doubleheader

N.L.—6—Jake Daubert, Brooklyn, August 15, 1914.
A.L.—5—Red Killefer, Washington, August 27, 1910.

Most sacrifice hits, inning

A.L.—2—Al Benton, Detroit, August 6, 1941, third inning.
N.L.—1—Held by many players.

SACRIFICE FLIES

Most sacrifice flies, career

M.L.—128—Eddie Murray, Baltimore A.L., Los Angeles N.L., New York N.L., Cleveland A.L., Anaheim A.L., 21 years, 1977 through 1997 (92 in A.L., 36 in N.L.).
A.L.—123—Robin Yount, Milwaukee, 20 years, 1974 through 1993.
N.L.—113—Hank Aaron, Milwaukee, Atlanta, 21 years, 1954 through 1974.

Most sacrifice flies, season

N.L.—19—Gil Hodges, Brooklyn, 154 games, 1954. (Pie Traynor, Pittsburgh, N.L., 144 games, 1928, had 31 sacrifice flies, advancing runners to second base, third base and home.)
A.L.—17

Roy White, New York, 147 games, 1971.
Bobby Bonilla, Baltimore, 159 games, 1996.

Most sacrifice flies by rookie, season

N.L.—13—Willie Montanez, Philadelphia, 158 games, 1971.
A.L.—13—Gary Gaetti, Minnesota, 145 games, 1982.

Most sacrifice flies by righthander, season

N.L.—19—Gil Hodges, Brooklyn, 154 games, 1954.
A.L.—16

Chick Gandil, Washington, 145 games, 1914.
Juan Gonzalez, Cleveland, 140 games, 2001.

Most sacrifice flies by lefthander, season

A.L.—16—Sam Crawford, Detroit, 157 games, 1914.
N.L.—14—J.T. Snow, San Francisco, 155 games, 2000.

Most sacrifice flies by switch-hitter, season

A.L.—17

Roy White, New York, 147 games, 1971.
Bobby Bonilla, Baltimore, 159 games, 1996.
N.L.—15

Bobby Bonilla, Pittsburgh, 160 games, 1990.
Howard Johnson, New York, 156 games, 1991.

Most years leading league in sacrifice flies

A.L.—4—Brooks Robinson, Baltimore, 1962 (tied), 1964, 1967 (tied), 1968 (tied).
N.L.—3

Ron Santo, Chicago, 1963, 1967, 1969.
Johnny Bench, Cincinnati, 1970, 1972, 1973 (tied).

Most at-bats with no sacrifice flies, season

N.L.—680

Pete Rose, Cincinnati, 160 games, 1973.
Frank Taveras, Pittsburgh, New York, 164 games, 1979.
A.L.—680—Kirby Puckett, Minnesota, 161 games, 1986.

Most sacrifice flies, game

N.L.—3

Harry Steinfeldt, Chicago, May 5, 1909.
Ernie Banks, Chicago, June 2, 1961.
Vince Coleman, St. Louis, May 1, 1986.
Candy Maldonado, San Francisco, August 29, 1987.
A.L.—3

Bob Meusel, New York, September 15, 1926.
Russ Nixon, Boston, August 31, 1965, second game.
Don Mattingly, New York, May 3, 1986.
George Bell, Toronto, August 14, 1990.
Chad Kreuter, Detroit, July 30, 1994.
Juan Gonzalez, Texas, July 3, 1999.

HIT BY PITCH

Most hit by pitch, career

A.L.—267—Don Baylor, Baltimore, Oakland, California, New York, Boston, Minnesota, 19 years, 1970 through 1988.
N.L.—243—Ron Hunt, New York, Los Angeles, San Francisco, Montreal, St. Louis, 12 years, 1963 through 1974.

Most hit by pitch, season

N.L.—50—Ron Hunt, Montreal, 152 games, 1971.
A.L.—35—Don Baylor, Boston, 160 games, 1986.

Most hit by pitch by rookie, season

A.A.—29—Tommy Tucker, Baltimore, 136 games, 1887.
A.L.—21—David Eckstein, Anaheim, 153 games, 2001.
N.L.—20—Frank Robinson, Cincinnati, 152 games, 1956.

Most hit by pitch by righthander, season

N.L.—50—Ron Hunt, Montreal, 152 games, 1971.
A.L.—35—Don Baylor, Boston, 160 games, 1986.

Most hit by pitch by lefthander, season

N.L.—31—Steve Evans, St. Louis, 151 games, 1910.
A.L.—22—Brady Anderson, Baltimore, 149 games, 1996.

Most hit by pitch for switch-hitter, season

N.L.—25—F.P. Santangelo, Montreal, 130 games, 1997.
A.L.—15—Gene Larkin, Minnesota, 149 games, 1988.

Most years leading league in hit by pitch

A.L.—10—Minnie Minoso, Cleveland, Chicago, 1951, 1952, 1953, 1954, 1956, 1957, 1958, 1959, 1960, 1961.
N.L.—7—Ron Hunt, San Francisco, Montreal, St. Louis, 1968, 1969, 1970, 1971, 1972, 1973, 1974.

Most consecutive years leading league in hit by pitch

N.L.—7—Ron Hunt, San Francisco, Montreal, St. Louis, 1968 through 1974.
A.L.—6—Minnie Minoso, Chicago, Cleveland, 1956 through 1961.

Most at-bats with no hit by pitch, season

A.L.—689—Sandy Alomar Sr., California, 162 games, 1971.
N.L.—662

Hugh Critz, Cincinnati, New York, 152 games, 1930.
Granny Hamner, Philadelphia, 154 games, 1949.

Fewest hit by pitch for leader, season

A.L.—5

Frank Crosetti, New York, 138 games, 1934.
Frank Pytlak, Cleveland, 91 games, 1934.
N.L.—6

Buddy Blattner, New York, 126 games, 1946.
Andre Dawson, Montreal, 151 games, 1980.
Dan Driessen, Cincinnati, 154 games, 1980.
Tim Foli, Pittsburgh, 127 games, 1980.
Greg Luzinski, Philadelphia, 106 games, 1980.
Elliott Maddox, New York, 130 games, 1980.
Pete Rose, Philadelphia, 162 games, 1980.

Most hit by pitch, nine-inning game

A.A.—3—5 times (held by 5 players).
N.L.—3—15 times (held by 12 players). Last player—Richard Hidalgo, Houston, April 19, 2000.
A.L.—3—5 times (held by 5 players). Last player—Damion Easley, Detroit, May 31, 1999.

Most hit by pitch, extra-inning game

N.L.—3—Ron Hunt, San Francisco, April 29, 1969, 13 innings.
A.L.—3

Jake Stahl, Washington, April 15, 1904, 10 innings.
Craig Kusick, Minnesota, August 27, 1975, 11 innings.

Most times hit by pitch three times in a game, career

N.L.—3—Hughie Jennings, Baltimore, 1894, 1896, 1898.
N.L. since 1900—2—Frank Chance, Chicago, 1902, 1904.
A.L.—1—Held by five players.

Most hit by pitch, doubleheader

N.L.—5—Frank Chance, Chicago, May 30, 1904.
A.L.—3

Bert Daniels, New York, June 20, 1913.
Al Smith, Chicago, June 21, 1961.

Most hit by pitch, inning
N.L.—2
   Willard Schmidt, Cincinnati, April 26, 1959, third inning.
   Frank Thomas, New York, April 29, 1962, first game, fourth inning.
   Andres Galarraga, Colorado, July 12, 1996, seventh inning.
A.L.—2—Brady Anderson, Baltimore, May 23, 1999, first inning.

GROUNDING INTO DOUBLE PLAYS

Most grounding into double plays, career
A.L.—350—Cal Ripken Jr., Baltimore, 21 years, 1981 through 2001.
N.L.—305—Hank Aaron, Milwaukee, Atlanta, 21 years, 1954 through 1974.

Most grounding into double plays, season
A.L.—36—Jim Rice, Boston, 159 games, 1984.
N.L.—30—Ernie Lombardi, Cincinnati, 129 games, 1938.

Most grounding into double plays by rookie, season
A.L.—27
   Billy Johnson, New York, 155 games, 1943.
   Al Rosen, Cleveland, 155 games, 1950.
N.L.—21—Albert Pujols, St. Louis, 161 games, 2001.

Most grounding into double plays by righthander, season
A.L.—36—Jim Rice, Boston, 159 games, 1984.
N.L.—30—Ernie Lombardi, Cincinnati, 129 games, 1938.

Most grounding into double plays by lefthander, season
A.L.—32—Ben Grieve, Oakland, 158 games, 2000.
N.L.—26
   Willie Montanez, Philadelphia, San Francisco, 156 games, 1975.
   Dave Parker, Cincinnati, 160 games, 1985.

Most grounding into double plays by switch-hitter, season
A.L.—29—Dave Philley, Philadelphia, 151 games, 1952.
N.L.—29—Ted Simmons, St. Louis, 161 games, 1973.

Most years leading league in grounding into double plays
N.L.—4—Ernie Lombardi, Cincinnati, New York, 1933, 1934, 1938, 1944.
A.L.—4—Jim Rice, Boston, 1982, 1983 (tied), 1984, 1985.

Fewest grounding into double plays, season (150 or more games)
N.L.—0
   Augie Galan, Chicago, 154 games, 1935.
   Craig Biggio, Houston, 162 games, 1997.
A.L.—0—Dick McAuliffe, Detroit, 151 games, 1968.

Fewest grounding into double plays by rookie, season (150 or more games)
N.L.—3—Vince Coleman, St. Louis, 151 games, 1985.
A.L.—3—Ichiro Suzuki, Seattle, 157 games, 2001.

Fewest grounding into double plays by righthander, season (150 or more games)
N.L.—0—Craig Biggio, Houston, 162 games, 1997.
A.L.—2
   Cesar Tovar, Minnesota, 157 games, 1968.
   Mark Belanger, Baltimore, 152 games, 1975.

Fewest grounding into double plays by lefthander, season (150 or more games)
A.L.—0—Dick McAuliffe, Detroit, 151 games, 1968.
N.L.—2
   Lou Brock, St. Louis, 155 games, 1965.
   Lou Brock, St. Louis, 157 games, 1969.
   Will Clark, San Francisco, 150 games, 1987.
   Brett Butler, San Francisco, 157 games, 1988.

Fewest grounding into double plays by switch-hitter, season (150 or more games)
N.L.—0—Augie Galan, Chicago, 154 games, 1935.
A.L.—1—Willie Wilson, Kansas City, 154 games, 1979.

Fewest grounding into double plays for leader, season
N.L.—19
   Andy Seminick, Philadelphia, 124 games, 1946.
   George Kurowski, St. Louis, 146 games, 1947.
   Andy Pafko, Chicago, 129 games, 1947.
A.L.—21
   Brooks Robinson, Baltimore, 158 games, 1967.
   John Olerud, Seattle, 159 games, 2001.

Most years leading league in fewest grounding into double plays (150 or more games)
N.L.—6—Richie Ashburn, Philadelphia, Chicago, 1951, 1952, 1953, 1954, 1958, 1960 (tied).
A.L.—2—Held by 10 players. Last player—Willie Wilson, Kansas City, 1979, 1980.

Most grounding into double plays, nine-inning game
A.L.—4—Goose Goslin, Detroit, April 28, 1934 (consecutive).
N.L.—4—Joe Torre, New York, July 21, 1975 (consecutive).

Most grounding into double plays, two consecutive games
N.L.—5—Zeke Bonura, New York, July 8 (3), second game, July 9 (2), 1939.
A.L.—4—Held by many players.

Most grounding into infield triple plays, game or season
N.L.-A.L.—1—Held by many players.

REACHING ON ERRORS OR INTERFERENCE

Most times reaching base on error, game (fair-hit balls)
P.L.—4—Mike Griffin, Philadelphia, June 23, 1890.
N.L.—3
   George Gore, New York, August 15, 1887.
   Bill McKechnie, New York, May 9, 1916.
   Al Lopez, Boston, July 16, 1936.
   Jerry Grote, New York, September 5, 1975.
A.L.—3
   Phil Bradley, Baltimore, August 4, 1989.
   Ray Durham, Chicago, April 22, 1998.

Most times reaching base on error, inning (fair-hit balls)
A.L.—2
   Emory Rigney, Detroit, August 21, 1922, sixth inning.
   Fred Spurgeon, Cleveland, April 14, 1925, eighth inning.
   Johnny Bassler, Detroit, June 17, 1925, sixth inning.
   Sam Rice, Washington, July 10, 1926, eighth inning.
N.L.—2—Stu Martin, St. Louis, June 22, 1940, sixth inning.

Most times reaching base on catcher's interference, season
A.L.—8—Roberto Kelly, New York, 152 games, 1992.
N.L.—7—Dale Berra, Pittsburgh, 161 games, 1983.

Most times reaching base on catcher's interference, game
N.L.—2
   Ben Geraghty, Brooklyn, April 26, 1936.
   Pat Corrales, Philadelphia, September 29, 1965.
A.L.—2
   Dan Meyer, Seattle, May 3, 1977.
   Bob Stinson, Seattle, July 24, 1979.

CLUB BATTING

GAMES

Most games, league
N.L.—18,627—Chicago, 126 years, 1876 to date.
A.L.—15,718—Detroit, 101 years, 1901 to date.

Most games, season
N.L.—165
Los Angeles, 1962 (3 playoffs).
San Francisco, 1962 (3 playoffs).
A.L.—164
Cleveland, 1964 (2 tied).
New York, 1964, 1968 (2 tied).
Minnesota, 1967 (2 tied).
Detroit, 1968 (2 tied).

Fewest games, season
A.L.—147—Cleveland, 1945 (2 tied, 9 unplayed).
N.L.—149—Philadelphia, 1907 (2 tied, 7 unplayed), 1934 (5 unplayed).

Most games, one day
N.L.—3
Brooklyn and Pittsburgh, September 1, 1890 (Brooklyn won 3).
Baltimore and Louisville, September 7, 1896 (Baltimore won 3).
Pittsburgh and Cincinnati, October 2, 1920 (Cincinnati won 2).
A.L.—2—Made on many days.

Most doubleheaders, season
A.L.—44—Chicago, 1943. (Won 11, lost 10, split 23).
N.L.—43—Philadelphia, 1943. (Won 11, lost 14, split 18).

Fewest doubleheaders, season
A.L.-N.L.—0—Held by many clubs.
Last A.L. clubs—Anaheim, Boston, New York, Seattle, Tampa Bay, 2001.
Last N.L. clubs—Colorado, Los Angeles, New York, San Francisco, 2001.

Most consecutive doubleheaders played, season
N.L.—9—Boston, September 4 through September 15, 1928.
A.L.—8—Washington, July 27 through August 5, 1909.

Most consecutive games between same clubs, season
A.L.—11—Detroit vs. St. Louis, September 8 through 14, 1904.
N.L.—10—Chicago vs. Philadelphia, August 7 through 16, 1907.

Most consecutive doubleheaders between same clubs, season
A.L.—5—Philadelphia vs. Washington, August 5, 7, 8, 9, 10, 1901.
N.L.—4—New York vs. Boston, September 10, 11, 13, 14, 1928.

BATTING AVERAGE

Highest batting average, season
N.L.—.343—Philadelphia, 132 games, 1894.
N.L. since 1900—.319—New York, 154 games, 1930.
A.L.—.316—Detroit, 154 games, 1921.

Highest batting average for pennant winner, season
N.L.—.328—Baltimore, 129 games, 1894.
N.L. since 1900—.314—St. Louis, 154 games, 1930.
A.L.—.307—New York, 155 games, 1927.

Highest batting average for an outfield, season
N.L.—.405—Philadelphia, 132 games, 1894.
A.L.—.367—Detroit, 156 games, 1925.
N.L. since 1900—.350—Chicago, 156 games, 1929.

Most years leading league in batting average (since 1900)
N.L.—22—St. Louis, 1915, 1920, 1921, 1934, 1938, 1939, 1942, 1943, 1944, 1946, 1949, 1952, 1954, 1956, 1957, 1963, 1971, 1975, 1979, 1980, 1985, 1992.
A.L.—21—Boston, 1903, 1938, 1939, 1941, 1942, 1944, 1946, 1949, 1950, 1964, 1967, 1975, 1979, 1981, 1984, 1985, 1987, 1988, 1989, 1990, 1997.

Most consecutive years leading league in batting average
N.L.—7—Colorado, 1995 through 2001.
A.L.—5—Philadelphia, 1910 through 1914.

Most players batting .400 or over, season (50 or more games)
N.L.—3—Philadelphia, 1894.
N.L. since 1900—1—St. Louis, 1922, 1924, 1925; New York, 1930.
A.L.—1—Philadelphia, 1901; Detroit, 1911, 1912, 1922, 1923; Cleveland, 1911; St. Louis, 1920, 1922; Boston, 1941.

Most players batting .300 or over, season (50 or more games)
A.L.—10—Philadelphia, 1927.
N.L.—10—St. Louis, 1930.

Lowest batting average, season
N.L.—.207—Washington, 136 games, 1888.
A.L.—.212—Chicago, 156 games, 1910.
N.L. since 1900—.213—Brooklyn, 154 games, 1908.

Lowest batting average for a pennant winner, season
A.L.—.228—Chicago, 154 games, 1906; last in batting.
N.L.—.242—New York, 162 games, 1969; tied for seventh in batting.

Lowest batting average for club leader, season
A.L.—.240—Oakland, 163 games, 1968.
N.L.—.254—Pittsburgh, 157 games, 1907; St. Louis, 157 games, 1915.

SLUGGING AVERAGE

Highest slugging average, season
A.L.—.489—New York, 155 games, 1927.
N.L.—.483—Colorado, 162 games, 2001.

Most years leading league in slugging average (since 1900)
A.L.—30—New York, 1901 (franchise in Baltimore), 1920, 1921, 1923, 1924, 1926, 1927, 1928, 1930, 1931, 1936, 1937, 1938, 1939, 1943, 1944, 1945, 1947, 1948, 1951, 1953, 1954, 1955, 1956, 1957, 1958, 1960, 1961, 1962, 1986.
N.L.—20—New York/San Francisco, 1904, 1905, 1908, 1910, 1911, 1919, 1923, 1924, 1927, 1928, 1935, 1945, 1947, 1948, 1952, 1961, 1962, 1963, 1989, 1993.

Most consecutive years leading in slugging (since 1900)
A.L.—6—New York, 1953 through 1958.
N.L.—5—Colorado, 1995 through 1999.

Lowest slugging average, season (150 or more games)
A.L.—.261—Chicago, 156 games, 1910.
N.L.—.274—Boston, 155 games, 1909.

AT-BATS AND PLATE APPEARANCES

Most at-bats, season
A.L.—5,781—Boston, 162 games, 1997.
N.L.—5,767—Cincinnati, 163 games, 1968.

Fewest at-bats, season
N.L.—4,725—Philadelphia, 149 games, 1907.
A.L.—4,827—Chicago, 153 games, 1913.

Most at-bats, nine-inning game
N.L.—66—Chicago vs. Buffalo, July 3, 1883.
N.L. since 1900—58
New York vs. Philadelphia, September 2, 1925, second game.
New York vs. Philadelphia, July 11, 1931, first game.
A.L.—57—Milwaukee vs. Toronto, August 28, 1992.

Most at-bats, extra-inning game
A.L.—95—Chicago vs. Milwaukee, May 8, finished May 9, 1984, 25 innings.
N.L.—89—New York vs. St. Louis, September 11, 1974, 25 innings.

Most plate appearances, nine-inning game
N.L.—71—Chicago vs. Louisville, June 29, 1897.
N.L. since 1900—66
Philadelphia vs. Chicago, August 25, 1922.
St. Louis vs. Philadelphia, July 6, 1929, second game.
A.L.—65—Milwaukee vs. Toronto, August 28, 1992.

Most plate appearances, extra-inning game
A.L.—104—Chicago vs. Milwaukee, May 8, finished May 9, 1984, 25 innings.
N.L.—103—New York vs. St. Louis, September 11, 1974, 25 innings.

Fewest at-bats, nine-inning game (batting nine times)
A.L.—23
  Chicago vs. St. Louis, May 6, 1917.
  Cleveland vs. Chicago, May 9, 1961.
  Detroit vs. Baltimore, May 6, 1968.
N.L.—24
  Cincinnati vs. Brooklyn, July 22, 1911.
  Boston vs. Cincinnati, May 15, 1951.
  Pittsburgh vs. Chicago, May 12, 1955.

Fewest at-bats, nine-inning game (batting eight times)
A.L.—19—Baltimore vs. Kansas City, September 12, 1964.
N.L.—21—Pittsburgh vs. St. Louis, September 8, 1908.

Most at-bats by both clubs, nine-inning game
N.L.—106—Chicago 64, Louisville 42, July 22, 1876.
N.L. since 1900—99
  New York 56, Cincinnati 43, June 9, 1901.
  New York 58, Philadelphia 41, July 11, 1931, first game.
A.L.—96—Cleveland 51, Philadelphia 45, April 29, 1952.

Most at-bats by both clubs, extra-inning game
N.L.—175—New York 89, St. Louis 86, September 11, 1974, 25 innings.
A.L.—175—Chicago 95, Milwaukee 80, May 8, finished May 9, 1984, 25 innings.

Most plate appearances by both clubs, nine-inning game
N.L.—125—Philadelphia 66, Chicago 59, August 25, 1922.
A.L.—108—Cleveland 58, Philadelphia 50, April 29, 1952.

Most plate appearances by both clubs, extra-inning game
N.L.—202—New York 103, St. Louis 99, September 11, 1974, 25 innings.
A.L.—198—Chicago 104, Milwaukee 94, May 8, finished May 9, 1984, 25 innings.

Fewest at-bats by both clubs, nine-inning game
N.L.—48
  Boston 25, Philadelphia 23, April 22, 1910.
  Brooklyn 24, Cincinnati 24, July 22, 1911.
A.L.—46—Kansas City 27, Baltimore 19, September 12, 1964.

Most at-bats, doubleheader (18 innings)
A.L.—99—New York vs. Philadelphia, June 28, 1939.
N.L.—98—Pittsburgh vs. Philadelphia, August 8, 1922.

Fewest at-bats, doubleheader
A.L.—50—Boston vs. Chicago, August 28, 1912.
N.L.—52—Brooklyn vs. St. Louis, July 24, 1909.

Most at-bats by by both clubs, doubleheader (18 innings)
N.L.—176—Pittsburgh 98, Philadelphia 78, August 8, 1922.
A.L.—172—Boston 89, Philadelphia 83, July 4, 1939.

Most at-bats by by both clubs, doubleheader (more than 18 innings)
N.L.—234—New York 119, San Francisco 115, May 31, 1964, 32 innings.
A.L.—215—Kansas City 112, Detroit 103, June 17, 1967, 28 innings.

Fewest at-bats by both clubs, doubleheader
N.L.—109—St. Louis 57, Brooklyn 52, July 24, 1909.
A.L.—111—Cleveland 56, Chicago 55, May 28, 1916.

Most plate appearances, inning
A.L.—23—Boston vs. Detroit, June 18, 1953, seventh inning.
N.L.—23—Chicago vs. Detroit, September 6, 1883, seventh inning.
N.L. since 1900—21—Brooklyn vs. Cincinnati, May 21, 1952, first inning.

Most batters facing pitcher three times, inning (club)
N.L.—5—Chicago vs. Detroit, September 6, 1883, seventh inning.
A.L.—5—Boston vs. Detroit, June 18, 1953, seventh inning.
N.L. since 1900—3—Brooklyn vs. Cincinnati, May 21, 1952, first inning.

SEASON AND MONTH

Most runs, season
N.L.—1,220—Boston, 133 games, 1894.
A.L.—1,067—New York, 155 games, 1931.
N.L. since 1900—1,004—St. Louis, 154 games, 1930.

Most runs by pennant winner, season
N.L.—1,170—Baltimore, 129 games, 1894.
A.L.—1,065—New York, 155 games, 1936.
N.L. since 1900—1,004—St. Louis, 154 games, 1930.

Most runs at home, season (since 1900)
N.L.—658—Colorado, 81 games, 1996.
A.L.—625—Boston, 77 games, 1950.

Most runs on road, season (since 1900)
A.L.—591—New York, 78 games, 1930.
N.L.—492—Chicago, 78 games, 1929.

Most runs against one club, season (since 1900)
N.L.—218—Chicago vs. Philadelphia, 24 games, 1930 (117 at home, 101 at Philadelphia).
A.L.—216—Boston vs. St. Louis, 22 games, 1950 (118 at home, 98 at St. Louis).

Most players scoring 100 or more runs, season
N.L.—7—Boston, 1894.
A.L.—6—New York, 1931.
N.L. since 1900—6—Brooklyn, 1953.

Fewest runs, season
N.L.—372—St. Louis, 154 games, 1908.
A.L.—380—Washington, 156 games, 1909.

Fewest runs scored by leader, season
N.L.—590—St. Louis, 157 games, 1915.
A.L.—622—Philadelphia, 152 games, 1905.

Fewest runs by pennant winner, season
A.L.—550—Boston, 156 games, 1916.
N.L.—571—Chicago, 155 games, 1907.

Most runs scored, month (since 1900)
A.L.—275—New York, August 1938, 36 games.
N.L.—260—New York, June 1929, 33 games.

GAME AND DOUBLEHEADER—ONE CLUB

Most runs, game
N.L.—36—Chicago vs. Louisville (7), June 29, 1897.
A.L.—29
  Boston vs. St. Louis (4), June 8, 1950.
  Chicago vs. Kansas City (6), April 23, 1955.
N.L. since 1900—28—St. Louis vs. Philadelphia (7), July 6, 1929, second game.

Most runs, opening game of season
P.L.—23—Buffalo vs. Cleveland, April 19, 1890 (23-2).
A.L.—21—Cleveland vs. St. Louis, April 14, 1925 (21-14).
N.L.—19—Philadelphia vs. Boston, April 19, 1900, 10 innings (19-17).

Most runs scored by infielders, game
N.L.—16
  Chicago vs. Philadelphia, June 29, 1897.
  Chicago vs. Boston, July 3, 1945.
A.L.—16—Boston vs. St. Louis, June 8, 1950.

Most runs scored by outfielders, game
A.A.—14—Kansas City vs. Philadelphia, September 30, 1888.
N.L.—14
  New York vs. Cincinnati, June 9, 1901.
  New York vs. Brooklyn, April 30, 1944, first game.
A.L.—11
  Chicago vs. Philadelphia, September 11, 1936.
  New York vs. Washington, August 12, 1953.

Biggest run deficit overcome to win game
A.L.—12
  Detroit vs. Chicago, June 18, 1911, at Detroit.

Chicago	7	0	0	3	3	0	2	0	0—15
Detroit	0	1	0	0	4	3	0	5	3—16

Philadelphia vs. Cleveland, June 15, 1925, at Philadelphia.

Cleveland	0	4	2	2	4	2	1	0	0—15
Philadelphia	0	1	1	0	0	1	1	13	x—17

Seattle vs. Cleveland, August 5, 2001, at Cleveland, 11 innings.

Seattle	0	4	8	0	2	0	0	0	0	0—14
Cleveland	0	0	0	2	0	0	3	4	5	0 1—15

N.L.—11

St. Louis vs. New York, June 15, 1952, first game, at New York.

St. Louis	0	0	0	0	7	0	3	2	2—14
New York	0	5	6	0	0	0	0	0	1—12

Philadelphia vs. Chicago, April 17, 1976, at Chicago, 10 innings.

Philadelphia	0	1	0	1	2	0	3	5	3	3—18
Chicago	0	7	5	1	0	0	0	2	1—16

Houston vs. St. Louis, July 18, 1994, at Houston.

St. Louis	3	4	4	0	0	0	0	1—12
Houston	0	0	0	2	2	11	0	0	x—15

Most runs scored by two players, game

N.L.—12—Boston vs. Pittsburgh, August 27, 1887 (King Kelly 6, Ezra Sutton 6).
N.L. since 1900—11
New York vs. Brooklyn, April 30, 1944, first game (Mel Ott 6, Joe Medwick 5).
New York vs. Brooklyn, April 30, 1944, first game (Mel Ott 6, Phil Weintraub 5).
A.L.—10
Cleveland vs. Baltimore, September 2, 1902 (Harry Bay 5, Bill Bradley 5).
Chicago vs. Kansas City, April 23, 1955 (Chico Carrasquel 5, Minnie Minoso 5).

Longest extra-inning game without a run

N.L.—24 innings—New York vs. Houston, April 15, 1968.
A.L.—20 innings—California vs. Oakland, July 9, 1971.

Most players scoring six runs, game

N.L.—2—Boston vs. Pittsburgh, August 27, 1887 (King Kelly, Ezra Sutton).
N.L. since 1900—1
New York vs. Philadelphia, August 4, 1934, second game (Mel Ott).
New York vs. Brooklyn, April 30, 1944, first game (Mel Ott).
Milwaukee vs. Chicago, September 2, 1957, first game (Frank Torre).
New York vs. Houston, August 30, 1999 (Edgardo Alfonzo).
A.L.—1
Boston vs. Chicago, May 8, 1946 (Johnny Pesky).
Boston vs. Cleveland, August 21, 1986 (Spike Owen).

Most players scoring five or more runs, game

N.L.—3
Chicago vs. Cleveland, July 24, 1882.
Boston vs. Philadelphia, June 20, 1883.
Boston vs. Pittsburgh, August 27, 1887.
New York vs. Brooklyn, April 30, 1944, first game.
Chicago vs. Boston, July 3, 1945.
A.L.—2
Cleveland vs. Baltimore, September 2, 1902.
Chicago vs. Kansas City, April 23, 1955.

Most players scoring four or more runs, game

N.L.—6
Chicago vs. Cleveland, July 24, 1882.
Chicago vs. Louisville, June 29, 1897.
N.L. since 1900—4—St. Louis vs. Philadelphia, July 6, 1929, second game.
A.L.—4—Boston vs. St. Louis, June 8, 1950.

Most players scoring three or more runs, game

N.L.—9—Chicago vs. Buffalo, July 3, 1883.
A.L.—7—Boston vs. St. Louis, June 8, 1950.
N.L. since 1900—6—New York vs. Philadelphia, September 2, 1925, second game.

Most players scoring two or more runs, game

N.L.—10—Chicago vs. Louisville, June 29, 1897.
N.L. since 1900—9
St. Louis vs. Chicago, April 16, 1912.
Chicago vs. Philadelphia, August 25, 1922.
St. Louis vs. Philadelphia, July 6, 1929, second game.
Chicago vs. Colorado, August 18, 1995.

A.L.—9
Boston vs. Philadelphia, May 2, 1901.
New York vs. Cleveland, July 14, 1904.
Cleveland vs. Boston, July 7, 1923, first game.
New York vs. Chicago, July 26, 1931, second game.
New York vs. Philadelphia, May 24, 1936.
Boston vs. Philadelphia, June 29, 1950.

Most players scoring one or more runs, game

N.L.—13
Cincinnati vs. Boston, June 4, 1911.
New York vs. Boston, June 20, 1912.
Philadelphia vs. Chicago, August 25, 1922.
San Francisco vs. San Diego, June 23, 1986.
A.L.—13
Washington vs. St. Louis, July 10, 1926.
New York vs. St. Louis, August 7, 1949, first game.
Oakland vs. Kansas City, September 20, 1975.

Clubs scoring 20 or more runs (most times)

N.L.—41—Chicago, 1876 to date.
A.L.—22—New York, 1903 to date.
N.L. since 1900—15—Brooklyn, 1900 through 1957.

Clubs scoring 20 or more runs (most times), season

N.L.—8—Boston, 1894.
N.L. since 1900—3—Philadelphia, 1900.
A.L.—3
New York, 1939.
Boston, 1950.

Most runs, doubleheader

N.L.—43—Boston vs. Cincinnati, August 21, 1894.
A.L.—36—Detroit vs. St. Louis, August 14, 1937.
N.L. since 1900—34—St. Louis vs. Philadelphia, July 6, 1929.

Longest doubleheader without scoring a run

N.L.—27 innings
St. Louis vs. New York, July 2, 1933.
New York vs. Philadelphia, October 2, 1965.
A.L.—18 innings—Held by many clubs. Last doubleheader—Cleveland vs. Boston, September 26, 1975.

Most runs, two consecutive games

N.L.—53—Chicago, July 22, 25, 1876.
A.L.—49—Boston vs. St. Louis, June 7, 8, 1950.
N.L. since 1900—45—Pittsburgh, June 20, 22, 1925.

Most runs, three consecutive games

N.L.—71—Chicago, July 20, 22, 25, 1876.
A.L.—56—Boston vs. St. Louis, June 7, 8, 9, 1950.

Most runs, four consecutive games

N.L.—88—Chicago, July 20, 22, 25, 27, 1876.
A.L.—65—Boston, June 5, 6, 7, 8, 1950.

GAME AND DOUBLEHEADER—BOTH CLUBS

Most runs, game

N.L.—49—Chicago 26, Philadelphia 23, August 25, 1922.
A.L.—36—Boston 22, Philadelphia 14, June 29, 1950.

Most runs, opening game of season

N.L.—36—Philadelphia 19, Boston 17, April 19, 1900, 10 innings.
A.L.—35—Cleveland 21, St. Louis 14, April 14, 1925.

Most players scoring six or more runs, game

N.L.—2—Boston 2 (King Kelly, Ezra Sutton), Pittsburgh 0, August 27, 1887.
A.L.—1
Boston 1 (Johnny Pesky), Chicago 0, May 8, 1946.
Boston 1 (Spike Owen), Cleveland 0, August 21, 1986.

Most players scoring five or more runs, game

N.L.—3
Chicago 3, Cleveland 0, July 24, 1882.
Boston 3, Philadelphia 0, June 20, 1883.
Boston 3, Pittsburgh 0, August 27, 1887.
New York 3, Brooklyn 0, April 30, 1944, first game.
Chicago 3, Boston 0, July 3, 1945.
A.L.—2
Cleveland 2, Baltimore 0, September 2, 1902.
Chicago 2, Kansas City 0, April 23, 1955.

Most players scoring four or more runs, game
N.L.—6
    Chicago 6, Cleveland 0, July 24, 1882.
    Chicago 6, Louisville 0, June 29, 1897.
N.L. since 1900—4—St. Louis 4, Philadelphia 0, July 6, 1929, second game.
A.L.—4—Boston 4, St. Louis 0, June 8, 1950.

Most players scoring three or more runs, game
N.L.—9—Chicago 9, Buffalo 0, July 3, 1883.
A.L.—7—Boston 7, St. Louis 0, June 8, 1950.
N.L. since 1900—6
    New York 6, Philadelphia 0, September 2, 1925, second game.
    Cincinnati 6, Colorado 1, May 19, 1999.

Most players scoring two or more runs, game
N.L.—16—Chicago 9, Philadelphia 7, August 25, 1922.
A.L.—13
    Boston 9, Philadelphia 4, May 2, 1901.
    Boston 9, Philadelphia 4, June 29, 1950.

Most players scoring one or more runs, game
N.L.—22—Philadelphia 13, Chicago 9, August 25, 1922.
A.L.—18
    Boston 10, Philadelphia 8, June 29, 1950.
    Oakland 9, Texas 9, May 5, 2000.

Most runs, doubleheader
A.L.—54—Boston 35, Philadelphia 19, July 4, 1939.
N.L.—54—Boston 43, Cincinnati 11, August 21, 1894.
N.L. since 1900—50
    Brooklyn 26, Philadelphia 24, May 18, 1929.
    St. Louis 34, Philadelphia 16, July 6, 1929.

Fewest runs, doubleheader
N.L.—1
    Boston 1, Pittsburgh 0, September 4, 1902.
    Philadelphia 1, Boston 0, September 5, 1913.
A.L.—2
    Washington 1, St. Louis 1, September 25, 1904.
    Philadelphia 1, Boston 1, June 1, 1909.
    Philadelphia 1, Boston 1, September 11, 1909.
    Los Angeles 1, Detroit 1, August 18, 1964.
    Washington 1, Kansas City 1, May 2, 1967.
    Baltimore 2, Boston 0, September 2, 1974.

INNING

Most runs, inning
N.L.—18—Chicago vs. Detroit, September 6, 1883, seventh inning.
A.L.—17—Boston vs. Detroit, June 18, 1953, seventh inning.
N.L. since 1900—15—Brooklyn vs. Cincinnati, May 21, 1952, first inning.

Most runs by both clubs, inning
A.L.—19—Cleveland 13, Boston 6, April 10, 1977, eighth inning.
A.A.—19—Washington 14, Baltimore 5, June 17, 1891, first inning.
N.L.—18—Chicago 18, Detroit 0, September 6, 1883, seventh inning.
N.L. since 1900—17—Boston 10, New York 7, June 20, 1912, ninth inning.

Most runs, two consecutive innings
N.L.—21—Pittsburgh vs. Boston, June 6, 1894; 12 in third inning, 9 in fourth inning.

A.L.—19
    Boston vs. Philadelphia, May 2, 1901; 9 in second inning, 10 in third inning.
    Boston vs. Detroit, June 18, 1953; 2 in sixth inning, 17 in seventh inning.
    Milwaukee vs. California, July 8, 1990; 6 in fourth inning, 13 in fifth inning.
N.L. since 1900—18—Montreal vs. San Francisco, May 7, 1997; 5 in fifth inning, 13 in sixth inning.

Most runs, extra inning
A.L.—12—Texas vs. Oakland, July 3, 1983, 15th inning.

N.L.—10
    Kansas City vs. Detroit, July 21, 1886, 11th inning.
    Boston vs. New York, June 17, 1887, a.m. game, 10th inning.
    Cincinnati vs. Brooklyn, May 15, 1919, 13th inning.

Most runs by both clubs, extra inning
A.L.—12
    Minnesota 11, Oakland 1, June 21, 1969, 10th inning.
    Texas 12, Oakland 0, July 3, 1983, 15th inning.
N.L.—11
    New York 8, Pittsburgh 3, June 15, 1929, 14th inning.
    New York 6, Brooklyn 5, April 24, 1955, 10th inning.
    New York 6, Chicago 5, June 30, 1979, 11th inning.

Most runs scored at start of game with none out
N.L.—9—Philadelphia vs. New York, August 13, 1948.
A.L.—8
    Cleveland vs. Baltimore, July 6, 1954.
    New York vs. Baltimore, April 24, 1960.
    New York vs. Baltimore, September 25, 1990.
    Cleveland vs. Kansas City, May 9, 1995.

Most runs scored at start of inning with none out
N.L.—13—Chicago vs. Detroit, September 6, 1883, seventh inning.
A.L.—11—Detroit vs. New York, June 17, 1925, sixth inning.
N.L. since 1900—12—Brooklyn vs. Philadelphia, May 24, 1953, eighth inning.

Most runs scored in inning with two out
A.L.—13
    Cleveland vs. Boston, July 7, 1923, first game, sixth inning.
    Kansas City vs. Chicago, April 21, 1956, second inning.
N.L.—12
    Brooklyn vs. Cincinnati, May 21, 1952, first inning.
    Brooklyn vs. Cincinnati, August 8, 1954, eighth inning.

Most runs scored in inning with none on base and two out
N.L.—12—Brooklyn vs. Cincinnati, August 8, 1954, eighth inning.
A.L.—10—Chicago vs. Detroit, September 2, 1959, second game, fifth inning.

Most runs scored by pinch-hitters, inning
N.L.—3
    Boston vs. Philadelphia, April 19, 1900, ninth inning.
    Brooklyn vs. Philadelphia, September 9, 1926, ninth inning.
    San Francisco vs. Pittsburgh, May 5, 1958, ninth inning.
A.L.—3
    Chicago vs. Philadelphia, September 19, 1916, ninth inning.
    Philadelphia vs. Detroit, September 18, 1940, second game, ninth inning.
    Cleveland vs. Detroit, August 7, 1941, ninth inning.

Most runs scored by pinch-runners, inning
A.L.—3
    Chicago vs. Minnesota, September 16, 1967, ninth inning.
    Chicago vs. Oakland, May 19, 1968, second game, fifth inning.
    Oakland vs. California, May 7, 1975, seventh inning.
N.L.—2—Made in many innings.

Most players scoring two or more runs in one inning
N.L.—7—Chicago vs. Detroit, September 6, 1883, seventh inning.
N.L. since 1900—6
    Brooklyn vs. Cincinnati, May 21, 1952, first inning.
    Cincinnati vs. Houston, August 3, 1989, first inning.
A.L.—5
    New York vs. Washington, July 6, 1920, fifth inning.
    New York vs. Boston, June 21, 1945, fifth inning.
    Boston vs. Philadelphia, July 4, 1948, seventh inning.
    Cleveland vs. Philadelphia, June 18, 1950, second game, first inning.
    Boston vs. Detroit, June 18, 1953, seventh inning.

Clubs scoring in every inning of nine-inning game
A.A.—9
    Louisville vs. Pittsburgh, September 22, 1882.
    Columbus vs. Pittsburgh, June 14, 1883.
    Kansas City vs. Brooklyn, May 20, 1889.
N.L.—9
    Cleveland vs. Boston, August 15, 1889.
    Washington vs. Boston, June 22, 1894.

Cleveland vs. Philadelphia, July 12, 1894.
Chicago vs. Louisville, June 29, 1897.
New York vs. Philadelphia, June 1, 1923.
St. Louis vs. Chicago, September 13, 1964.
Colorado vs. Chicago, May 5, 1999.
A.L.—8
Boston vs. Cleveland, September 16, 1903, did not bat in ninth.
Cleveland vs. Boston, July 7, 1923, first game, did not bat in ninth.
New York vs. St. Louis, July 26, 1939, did not bat in ninth.
Chicago vs. Boston, May 11, 1949, did not bat in ninth.
Kansas City vs. Oakland, September 14, 1998, did not bat in ninth.

Most innings scored in by both clubs, nine-inning game
N.L.—15
Philadelphia 8, Detroit 7, July 1, 1887.
Washington 9, Boston 6, June 22, 1894.
A.A.—15—Kansas City 9, Brooklyn 6, May 20, 1889.
P.L.—15—New York 8, Chicago 7, May 23, 1890.
A.L.—14
Baltimore 8, Philadelphia 6, May 7, 1901.
St. Louis 7, Detroit 7, April 23, 1927.
Detroit 7, Chicago 7, July 2, 1940.
N.L. since 1900—14
New York 9, Philadelphia 5, June 1, 1923.
Pittsburgh 8, Chicago 6, July 6, 1975.
Los Angeles 8, Chicago 6, May 5, 1976.
Colorado 8, Los Angeles 6, June 30, 1996.

Most consecutive innings scoring runs
A.L.—17—Boston, September 15 (last 3 innings), September 16 (8 innings), September 17 (first 6 innings), 1903, 3 games.
N.L.—14
Pittsburgh, July 31 (last 5 innings), August 1 (8 innings), August 2 (first inning), 1894, 3 games.
New York, July 18 (last 3 innings), July 19 (8 innings), July 20 (first 3 innings), 1949, 3 games.
Colorado, May 4 (last 4 innings), May 5 (9 innings), May 7 (first inning), 1999, 3 games.

Most times scoring 10 or more runs in one inning
N.L.—30—Chicago, 1876 to date.
A.L.—27—Boston, 1901 to date.
N.L. since 1900—19—Brooklyn-Los Angeles, 1900 through 1957 in Brooklyn, 1958 to date in Los Angeles.

Most innings scoring 10 or more runs, season
N.L.—5—Boston, 1894.
A.L.—3—Washington, 1930.
N.L. since 1900—3—Brooklyn, 1943.

Most innings scoring 10 or more runs in same game
N.L.—2
Chicago vs. Philadelphia, August 25, 1922; 10 in second, 14 in fourth inning.
St. Louis vs. Philadelphia, July 6, 1929, second game; 10 in first, 10 in fifth inning.
Brooklyn vs. Pittsburgh, July 10, 1943; 10 in first, 10 in fourth inning.
A.L.—1—Made in many games.

Most innings with both clubs scoring 10 or more runs in same game (each club scoring)
A.A.—2—St. Louis, 12 in fifth; Baltimore, 10 in eighth; May 12, 1887.
A.L.—2—Philadelphia, 11 in third; New York, 10 in fifth; June 3, 1933.
N.L.—Never accomplished.

FIRST THROUGH 26TH INNINGS

Most runs, first inning
N.L.—16—Boston vs. Baltimore, June 18, 1894, a.m. game.
N.L. since 1900—15—Brooklyn vs. Cincinnati, May 21, 1952.
A.L.—14—Cleveland vs. Philadelphia, June 18, 1950, second game.

Most runs by both clubs, first inning
A.A.—19—Washington 14, Baltimore 5, June 17, 1891.
A.L.—16—Oakland 13, California 3, July 5, 1996.
N.L.—16—Boston 16, Baltimore 0, June 18, 1894, a.m. game.
N.L. since 1900—15—Brooklyn 15, Cincinnati 0, May 21, 1952.

Most runs, second inning
N.L.—13
New York vs. Cleveland, July 19, 1890, first game.
Atlanta vs. Houston, September 20, 1972.
San Diego vs. Pittsburgh, May 31, 1994.
A.L.—13—Kansas City vs. Chicago, April 21, 1956.

Most runs by both clubs, second inning
A.L.—14
Philadelphia 10, Detroit 4, September 23, 1913.
New York 11, Detroit 3, August 28, 1936, second game.
N.L.—13
New York 13, Cleveland 0, July 19, 1890, first game.
Chicago 10, Philadelphia 3, August 25, 1922.
Brooklyn 11, New York 2, April 29, 1930.
Atlanta 13, Houston 0, September 20, 1972.

Most runs, third inning
N.L.—14—Cleveland vs. Washington, August 7, 1889.
N.L. since 1900—13—San Francisco vs. St. Louis, May 7, 1966.
A.L.—12—New York vs. Washington, September 11, 1949, first game.

Most runs by both clubs, third inning
N.L.—14—Cleveland 14, Washington 0, August 7, 1889.
N.L. since 1900—13
San Francisco 13, St. Louis 0, May 7, 1966.
St. Louis 7, Atlanta 6, August 21, 1973.
A.L.—13—Boston 8, Detroit 5, July 2, 1995.

Most runs, fourth inning
N.L.—15—Hartford vs. New York, May 13, 1876.
N.L. since 1900—14—Chicago vs. Philadelphia, August 25, 1922.
A.L.—13—Chicago vs. Washington, September 26, 1943, first game.

Most runs by both clubs, fourth inning
N.L.—15
Hartford 15, New York 0, May 13, 1876.
Chicago 14, Philadelphia 1, August 25, 1922.
A.L.—13—Chicago 13, Washington 0, September 26, 1943, first game.

Most runs, fifth inning
A.L.—14—New York vs. Washington, July 6, 1920.
N.L.—13—Chicago vs. Pittsburgh, August 16, 1890.
N.L. since 1900—12
New York vs. Boston, September 3, 1926.
Cincinnati vs. Atlanta, April 25, 1977.
Montreal vs. Chicago, September 24, 1985.

Most runs by both clubs, fifth inning
N.L.—16—Brooklyn 11, New York 5, June 3, 1890.
N.L. since 1900—15
Brooklyn 10, Cincinnati 5, June 12, 1949.
Philadelphia 9, Pittsburgh 6, April 16, 1953.
A.L.—16—New York 10, Cleveland 6, August 3, 1986.

Most runs, sixth inning
P.L.—14—Philadelphia vs. Buffalo, June 26, 1890.
A.L.—13
Cleveland vs. Boston, July 7, 1923, first game.
Detroit vs. New York, June 17, 1925.
N.L.—13—Montreal vs. San Francisco, May 7, 1997.

Most runs by both clubs, sixth inning
A.L.—15
Philadelphia 10, New York 5, September 5, 1912, first game.
Detroit 10, Minnesota 5, June 13, 1967.
N.L.—15—New York 10, Cincinnati 5, June 12, 1979.

Most runs, seventh inning
N.L.—18—Chicago vs. Detroit, September 6, 1883.
N.L. since 1900—13—San Francisco vs. San Diego, July 15, 1997.
A.L.—17—Boston vs. Detroit, June 18, 1953.

Most runs by both clubs, seventh inning
N.L.—18—Chicago 18, Detroit 0, September 6, 1883.
A.L.—17—Boston 17, Detroit 0, June 18, 1953.

Most runs, eighth inning
A.L.—16—Texas vs. Baltimore, April 19, 1996.
N.L.—13—Brooklyn vs. Cincinnati, August 8, 1954.

Most runs by both clubs, eighth inning
A.L.—19—Cleveland 13, Boston 6, April 10, 1977.
N.L.—14
New York 11, Pittsburgh 3, May 25, 1954.
Brooklyn 13, Cincinnati 1, August 8, 1954.
Atlanta 9, San Diego 5, April 27, 1975, first game.
Colorado 8, Los Angeles 6, June 29, 1996.

Most runs, ninth inning
N.L.—14—Baltimore vs. Boston, April 24, 1894.
N.L. since 1900—12—San Francisco vs. Cincinnati, August 23, 1961.
A.L.—13
California vs. Texas, September 14, 1978.
Detroit vs. Texas, August 8, 2001.

Most runs by both clubs, ninth inning
N.L.—17—Boston 10, New York 7, June 20, 1912.
A.L.—15—Toronto 11, Seattle 4, July 20, 1984.

Most runs scored in ninth inning with two out
A.L.—9
Cleveland vs. Washington, May 23, 1901 (won 14-13).
Boston vs. Milwaukee, June 2, 1901 (won 13-2).
Cleveland vs. New York, August 4, 1929, second game (won 14-6).
N.L.—7
Chicago vs. Cincinnati, June 29, 1952, first game (won 9-8).
San Francisco vs. Pittsburgh, May 1, 1973 (won 8-7).

Most runs scored in ninth inning with two out and none on base
A.L.—9
Cleveland vs. Washington, May 23, 1901 (won 14-13).
Boston vs. Milwaukee, June 2, 1901 (won 13-2).
N.L.—7
Chicago vs. Cincinnati, June 29, 1952, first game (won 9-8).
Pittsburgh vs. Houston, July 28, 2001, a.m. game (won 9-8).

Most runs, 10th inning
A.L.—11—Minnesota vs. Oakland, June 21, 1969.
N.L.—10—Boston vs. New York, June 17, 1887, a.m. game.
N.L. since 1900—9
Cincinnati vs. Philadelphia, August 24, 1947, first game.
San Diego vs. Philadelphia, May 28, 1995.

Most runs by both clubs, 10th inning
A.L.—12—Minnesota 11, Oakland 1, June 21, 1969.
N.L.—11—New York 6, Brooklyn 5, April 24, 1955.

Most runs, 11th inning
N.L.—10—Kansas City vs. Detroit, July 21, 1886.
N.L. since 1900—9—San Diego vs. Colorado, June 28, 1994, second game.
A.L.—8
Philadelphia vs. Detroit, May 1, 1951.
Texas vs. Seattle, September 23, 1991.

Most runs by both clubs, 11th inning
A.L.—11—Seattle 6, Boston 5, May 16, 1969.
N.L.—11
New York 6, Chicago 5, June 30, 1979.
Pittsburgh 6, Chicago 5, April 21, 1991.

Most runs, 12th inning
A.L.—11—New York vs. Detroit, July 26, 1928, first game.
N.L.—9—Chicago vs. Pittsburgh, July 23, 1923.

Most runs by both clubs, 12th inning
A.L.—11
New York 8, Detroit 3, May 14, 1923.
New York 11, Detroit 0, July 26, 1928, first game.
N.L.—9
Chicago 9, Pittsburgh 0, July 23, 1923.
New York 8, Brooklyn 1, May 30, 1940, second game.
Houston 8, Cincinnati 1, June 2, 1966.
San Diego 5, Houston 4, July 5, 1969.

Most runs, 13th inning
N.L.—10—Cincinnati vs. Brooklyn, May 15, 1919.
A.L.—9—Cleveland vs. Detroit, August 5, 1933, first game.

Most runs, 14th inning
N.L.—8—New York vs. Pittsburgh, June 15, 1929.

A.L.—7
Cleveland vs. St. Louis, June 3, 1935.
Detroit vs. Milwaukee, May 27, 1991.

Most runs, 15th inning
A.L.—12—Texas vs. Oakland, July 3, 1983.
N.L.—7—St. Louis vs. Boston, September 28, 1928.

Most runs, 16th inning
A.L.—8—Chicago vs. Washington, May 20, 1920.
N.L.—5
Cincinnati vs. New York, August 20, 1973.
Houston vs. Cincinnati, April 8, 1988.

Most runs, 17th inning
N.L.—7—New York vs. Pittsburgh, July 16, 1920.
A.L.—6—New York vs. Detroit, July 20, 1941.

Most runs, 18th inning
N.L.—5—Chicago vs. Boston, May 14, 1927.
A.L.—4—Minnesota vs. Seattle, July 19, 1969.

Most runs, 19th inning
N.L.—5—New York vs. Atlanta, July 4, 1985.
A.L.—4—Cleveland vs. Detroit, April 27, 1984.

Most runs by both clubs, 19th inning
N.L.—7—New York 5, Atlanta 2, July 4, 1985.
A.L.—5—Chicago 3, Boston 2, July 13, 1951.

Most runs, 20th inning
N.L.—4—Brooklyn vs. Boston, July 5, 1940.
A.L.—3
Boston vs. Seattle, July 27, 1969.
Washington vs. Cleveland, September 14, second game, finished September 20, 1971.

Most runs by both clubs, 20th inning
N.L.—4—Brooklyn 4, Boston 0, July 5, 1940.
A.L.—4
Boston 3, Seattle 1, July 27, 1969.
Washington 3, Cleveland 1, September 14, second game, finished September 20, 1971.

Most runs, 21st inning
A.L.—4—Chicago vs. Cleveland, May 26, finished May 28, 1973.
N.L.—3—San Diego vs. Montreal, May 21, 1977.

Most runs by both clubs, 21st inning
A.L.—6—Milwaukee 3, Chicago 3, May 8, finished May 9, 1984.
N.L.—3—San Diego 3, Montreal 0, May 21, 1977.

Most runs, 22nd inning
A.L.—2—New York vs. Detroit, June 24, 1962.
N.L.—1
Brooklyn vs. Pittsburgh, August 22, 1917.
Chicago vs. Boston, May 17, 1927.

Most runs, 23rd inning
N.L.—2—San Francisco vs. New York, May 31, 1964, second game.
A.L.—0
Boston vs. Philadelphia, September 1, 1906.
Philadelphia vs. Boston, September 1, 1906.
Detroit vs. Philadelphia, July 21, 1945.
Philadelphia vs. Detroit, July 21, 1945.

Most runs, 24th inning
A.L.—3—Philadelphia vs. Boston, September 1, 1906.
N.L.—1—Houston vs. New York, April 15, 1968.

Most runs, 25th inning
N.L.—1—St. Louis vs. New York, September 11, 1974.
A.L.—1—Chicago vs. Milwaukee, May 8, finished May 9, 1984.

Most runs, 26th inning
N.L.—0
Boston vs. Brooklyn, May 1, 1920.
Brooklyn vs. Boston, May 1, 1920.
A.L.—No 26-inning game.

GAMES BEING SHUT OUT

Most games shut out, season
N.L.—33—St. Louis, 1908.
A.L.—30—Washington, 1909 (includes 1 tie).

Most consecutive games shut out, season
A.L.—4
Boston, August 2 through 6, 1906.
Philadelphia, September 23 through 25, 1906.
St. Louis, August 25 through 30, 1913.
Washington, September 19, 20, 21, 22, 1958.
Washington, September 1, 2, 4, 5, 1964.
N.L.—4
Boston, May 19 through 23, 1906.
Cincinnati, July 30 through August 3, 1908.
Cincinnati, July 31 through August 3, 1931.
Houston, June 20, 21, 22, 23, first game, 1963.
Houston, September 9, 10, 11, 11, 1966.
Chicago, June 16, 16, 19, 20, 1968.

Most games shut out, season (league champion)
N.L.—17—Los Angeles, 1966.
A.L.—16—Chicago, 1906 (includes two ties).

Most consecutive innings shut out by opponent, season
A.L.—48—Philadelphia, September 22 (last seven innings) through September 26 (first five innings), 1906.
N.L.—48—Chicago, June 15 (last eight innings) through June 21 (first two innings), 1968.

Most consecutive games without being shut out, league
A.L.—308—New York, August 3, 1931 through August 2, 1933.
N.L.—208—Cincinnati, April 3, 2000 through May 23, 2001.

Fewest games shut out, season (150 or more games)
A.L.—0—New York, 156 games, 1932.
N.L.—0—Cincinnati, 163 games, 2000.

HITS
SEASON

Most hits, season
N.L.—1,783—Philadelphia, 156 games, 1930.
A.L.—1,724—Detroit, 154 games, 1921.

Fewest hits, season
N.L.—1,044—Brooklyn, 154 games, 1908.
A.L.—1,061—Chicago, 156 games, 1910.

Most players with 200 or more hits, season
N.L.—4—Philadelphia, 1929.
A.L.—4—Detroit, 1937.

Most players with 100 or more hits, season
N.L.—9—Pittsburgh, 1921, 1972, 1976; Philadelphia, 1923; New York, 1928; St. Louis, 1979; Arizona, 2001; Florida, 2001.
A.L.—9—Philadelphia, 1925; Detroit, 1934, 1980; Baltimore, 1973; Kansas City, 1974, 1977, 1980, 1982, 1989; Oakland, 1975; Texas, 1976, 1978, 1996, 1999; Chicago, 1977; New York, 1977, 1993; California, 1978, 1982, 1988; Milwaukee, 1978, 1991, 1992; Toronto, 1983, 1988, 1992; Boston, 1984, 1991, 1999; Minnesota, 1989, 1991; Cleveland, 1997; Seattle, 2001.

Fewest players with 100 or more hits, season
N.L.—0—New York, 1972.
A.L.—2—Washington, 1965.

GAME

Most hits, nine-inning game
N.L.—36—Philadelphia vs. Louisville, August 17, 1894.
N.L. since 1900—31—New York vs. Cincinnati, June 9, 1901.
A.L.—31—Milwaukee vs. Toronto, August 28, 1992.

Most hits by both clubs, nine-inning game
N.L.—51—Philadelphia 26, Chicago 25, August 25, 1922.
A.L.—45
Philadelphia 27, Boston 18, July 8, 1902.
Detroit 28, New York 17, September 29, 1928.

Most hits, extra-inning game
A.L.—33—Cleveland vs. Philadelphia, July 10, 1932, 18 innings.
N.L.—Less than nine-inning record.

Most hits by both clubs, extra-inning game
A.L.—58—Cleveland 33, Philadelphia 25, July 10, 1932, 18 innings.
N.L.—52—New York 28, Pittsburgh 24, June 15, 1929, 14 innings.

Most hits by pinch-hitters, nine-inning game
N.L.—6—Brooklyn vs. Philadelphia, September 9, 1926.
A.L.—4
Cleveland vs. Chicago, April 22, 1930.
Philadelphia vs. Detroit, September 18, 1940, second game.
Detroit vs. Chicago, April 22, 1953.
Kansas City vs. Detroit, September 1, 1958, a.m. game.
Cleveland vs. Boston, September 21, 1967.
Oakland vs. Detroit, August 30, 1970.
Chicago vs. Oakland, September 7, 1970, second game.
Boston vs. New York, September 8, 1995.

Most hits by infield, game
N.L.—18—Boston vs. St. Louis, May 31, 1897.
A.L.—16—Boston vs. St. Louis, June 8, 1950.
N.L. since 1900—16—Pittsburgh vs. Chicago, September 16, 1975.

Most hits by outfield, game
N.L.—16—New York vs. Cincinnati, June 9, 1901.
A.L.—12
Baltimore vs. Detroit, June 24, 1901.
Detroit vs. Washington, July 30, 1917.
Cleveland vs. Philadelphia, April 29, 1952.
Boston vs. Baltimore, July 11, 1969, second game.

Most hits in shutout loss
N.L.—14—New York vs. Chicago, September 14, 1913 (15 total bases; lost 7-0).
A.L.—14—Cleveland vs. Washington, July 10, 1928, second game (16 total bases; lost 9-0).

Most hits in extra-inning shutout loss
N.L.—15
Boston vs. Pittsburgh, July 10, 1901, 12 innings (16 total bases; lost 1-0).
Boston vs. Pittsburgh, August 1, 1918, 21 innings (15 total bases; lost 2-0).
A.L.—15—Boston vs. Washington, July 3, 1913, 15 innings (19 total bases; lost 1-0).

Most consecutive hits, game
N.L.—12
St. Louis vs. Boston, September 17, 1920, fourth and fifth innings.
Brooklyn vs. Pittsburgh, June 23, 1930, sixth and seventh innings.
A.L.—10
Boston vs. Milwaukee, June 2, 1901, ninth inning.
Detroit vs. Baltimore, September 20, 1983, first inning (one walk during streak).
Toronto vs. Minnesota, September 4, 1992, second inning.

Fewest hits, game
N.L., U.A., A.A., A.L.—0—Made in many games.

Fewest hits, extra-inning game
A.A.—0—Toledo vs. Brooklyn, October 4, 1884, 10 innings.
N.L.—0
Philadelphia vs. New York, July 4, 1908, a.m. game, 10 innings.
Chicago vs. Cincinnati, May 2, 1917, 10 innings.
Chicago vs. Cincinnati, August 19, 1965, first game, 10 innings.
N.L.—1—Milwaukee vs. Pittsburgh, May 26, 1959, 13 innings.
A.L.—1
Cleveland vs. Chicago, September 6, 1903, 10 innings.
Boston vs. St. Louis, September 18, 1934, 10 innings.
Los Angeles vs. New York, May 22, 1962, 12 innings.

Fewest hits by both clubs, nine-inning game
N.L.—1—Los Angeles 1, Chicago 0, September 9, 1965.
A.A.—2—Philadelphia 1, Baltimore 1, August 20, 1886.
A.L.—2
Cleveland 1, Washington 1, July 27, 1915.
Cleveland 1, St. Louis 1, April 23, 1952.
Chicago 1, Baltimore 1, June 21, 1956.

Baltimore 1, Kansas City 1, September 12, 1964.
Baltimore 2, Detroit 0, April 30, 1967, first game.

Most games held hitless, season
A.A.—2—Pittsburgh 1884.
N.L.—2—Providence 1885; Boston 1898; Philadelphia 1960;
Chicago 1965; Cincinnati 1971; Colorado 1996; San Diego
2001.
A.L.—2—Cleveland 1910; Chicago 1917; Philadelphia 1923;
Detroit 1967, 1973; California 1977.

**Most consecutive years without being held hitless in a game
(nine or more innings)**
A.L.—43—New York, 1959 through 2001.
N.L.—40—St. Louis, 1920 through 1959.

Most games held to one hit, season
A.L.—5
St. Louis, 1910.
Cleveland, 1915.
N.L.—4—New York, 1965.

Most players with six hits in a nine-inning game
A.A.—2—Cincinnati vs. Pittsburgh, September 12, 1883.
N.L.—2—Baltimore vs. St. Louis, September 3, 1897.
A.L.—1—Made in many games.

Most players with five or more hits in a game
N.L.—4—Philadelphia vs. Louisville, August 17, 1894.
N.L. since 1900—3
New York vs. Cincinnati, June 9, 1901.
New York vs. Philadelphia, June 1, 1923.
A.L.—3
Detroit vs. Washington, July 30, 1917.
Cleveland vs. Philadelphia, July 10, 1932, 18 innings.
Washington vs. Cleveland, May 16, 1933, 12 innings.
Chicago vs. Philadelphia, September 11, 1936.

**Most players for both clubs with five or more hits, nine-inning
game**
N.L.—4—Philadelphia 4, Louisville 0, August 17, 1894.
N.L. since 1900—3
New York 3, Cincinnati 0, June 9, 1901.
New York 3, Philadelphia 0, June 1, 1923.
A.L.—3
Detroit 3, Washington 0, July 30, 1917.
Washington 3, Cleveland 0, May 16, 1933, 12 innings.
Chicago 3, Philadelphia 0, September 11, 1936.

**Most players for both clubs with five or more hits, extra-
inning game**
A.L.—5—Cleveland 3, Philadelphia 2, July 10, 1932, 18 innings.

Most players with four or more hits, nine-inning game
N.L.—7—Chicago vs. Cleveland, July 24, 1882.
N.L. since 1900—5—San Francisco vs. Los Angeles, May 13, 1958.
A.L.—4
Detroit vs. New York, September 29, 1928.
Chicago vs. Philadelphia, September 11, 1936.
Boston vs. St. Louis, June 8, 1950.
Milwaukee vs. Toronto, August 28, 1992.

**Most players for both clubs with four or more hits, nine-inning
game**
N.L.—7—Chicago 7, Cleveland 0, July 24, 1882.
N.L. since 1900—5
St. Louis 4, Philadelphia 1, July 6, 1929, second game.
San Francisco 5, Los Angeles 0, May 13, 1958.
A.L.—4
Detroit 4, New York 0, September 29, 1928.
Chicago 4, Philadelphia 0, September 11, 1936.
Boston 4, St. Louis 0, June 8, 1950.
Milwaukee 4, Toronto 0, August 28, 1992.

Most players with three or more hits, nine-inning game
N.L.—8—Chicago vs. Detroit, September 6, 1883.
N.L. since 1900—7
Pittsburgh vs. Philadelphia, June 12, 1928.
Cincinnati vs. Houston, August 3, 1989.
A.L.—7
New York vs. Philadelphia, June 28, 1939, first game.
Chicago vs. Kansas City, April 23, 1955.

Most players with two or more hits, nine-inning game
A.A.—10—Brooklyn vs. Philadelphia, June 25, 1885.
N.L.—10
Pittsburgh vs. Philadelphia, August 7, 1922.
New York vs. Philadelphia, September 2, 1925, second game.
A.L.—9—Held by many clubs.

Most players with one or more hits, nine-inning game
N.L.—14
San Francisco vs. San Diego, June 23, 1986.
Chicago vs. Colorado, August 18, 1995.
Florida vs. Atlanta, September 24, 1996.
A.L.—14—Cleveland vs. St. Louis, August 12, 1948, second game.

**Most players for both clubs with one or more hits, nine-inning
game**
N.L.—23—St. Louis 13, Philadelphia 10, May 11, 1923.
A.L.—22—New York 12, Cleveland 10, July 18, 1934.

**Most consecutive games with each player collecting one or
more hits**
N.L.—5—Pittsburgh, August 5, 7, 8, 9, 10, 1922.

DOUBLEHEADER AND CONSECUTIVE GAMES

Most hits, doubleheader
N.L.—46—Pittsburgh vs. Philadelphia, August 8, 1922.
A.L.—43—New York vs. Philadelphia, June 28, 1939.

Most hits by both clubs, doubleheader
N.L.—73
Washington 41, Philadelphia 32, July 4, 1896.
St. Louis 43, Philadelphia 30, July 6, 1929.
A.L.—65—Boston 35, Philadelphia 30, July 4, 1939.

Most hits by pitchers, doubleheader
A.L.—8—New York vs. Cleveland, June 17, 1936.

Fewest hits, doubleheader
A.L.—2—Cleveland vs. Boston, April 12, 1992.
N.L.—3
Brooklyn vs. St. Louis, September 21, 1934.
New York vs. Philadelphia, June 21, 1964.

Fewest hits by both clubs, doubleheader
A.L.—11—Detroit 7, St. Louis 4, May 30, 1914.
N.L.—12
Chicago 6, Pittsburgh 6, September 3, 1905.
St. Louis 6, Brooklyn 6, July 24, 1909.

Most hits, two consecutive games
N.L.—55—Philadelphia vs. Louisville, August 16, 17, 1894.
A.L.—51—Boston vs. St. Louis, June 7, 8, 1950.
N.L. since 1900—49—Pittsburgh vs. Philadelphia, August 7, 8,
first game, 1922.

Most hits by pitchers, two consecutive games
N.L.—9—Chicago, May 19, 20, 1895.

Fewest hits, two consecutive nine-inning games
A.A.—2—Baltimore vs. St. Louis/Louisville, July 28 (1), July 29
(1), 1886.
N.L.—2
New York vs. Providence, June 17 (1), June 18 (1), 1884.
Cincinnati vs. Brooklyn, July 5 (1), July 6 (1), 1900.
Boston vs. New York, September 28, second game (1);
September 30, first game (1), 1916.
New York vs. Milwaukee, September 10 (1), September 11
(1), 1965.
Los Angeles vs. Houston, September 26 (0), September 27
(2), 1981.
A.L.—2
New York vs. Cleveland, September 25 (1), September 26 (1),
1907.
St. Louis vs. Washington, September 25, second game (1),
vs. Philadelphia, September 27, (1), first game, 1910.
Chicago vs. Washington, August 10 (1), August 11 (1), 1917.
Milwaukee vs. Kansas City, June 18 (2), June 19 (0), 1974.
Cleveland vs. Boston, April 12, first game (0), April 12, second
game (2), 1992.
Detroit vs. Texas, May 3 (1), May 4 (1), 1996.

INNING

Most hits, inning
N.L.—18—Chicago vs. Detroit, September 6, 1883, seventh inning.
N.L. since 1900—16—Cincinnati vs. Houston, August 3, 1989, first inning.
A.L.—14—Boston vs. Detroit, June 18, 1953, seventh inning.

Most hits by pinch-hitters, inning
N.L.—4
Chicago vs. Brooklyn, May 21, 1927, second game, ninth inning.
Philadelphia vs. Pittsburgh, September 12, 1974, eighth inning.
A.L.—4
Philadelphia vs. Detroit, September 18, 1940, second game, ninth inning.
Texas vs. Kansas City, June 8, 1995, eighth inning.
Boston vs. New York, September 8, 1995, eighth inning.

Most consecutive hits, inning
N.L.—10
St. Louis vs. Boston, September 17, 1920, fourth inning.
St. Louis vs. Philadelphia, June 12, 1922, sixth inning.
Chicago vs. Boston, September 7, 1929, first game, fourth inning.
Brooklyn vs. Pittsburgh, June 23, 1930, sixth inning.
A.L.—10
Boston vs. Milwaukee, June 2, 1901, ninth inning.
Detroit vs. Baltimore, September 20, 1983, first inning (one walk during streak).
Toronto vs. Minnesota, September 4, 1992, second inning.

Most consecutive hits by pinch-hitters, inning
N.L.-A.L.—3—Made in many innings.
Last N.L. time—Pittsburgh vs. San Francisco, July 2, 1961, first game, eighth inning.
Last A.L. time—Boston vs. New York, September 8, 1995, eighth inning.

Most consecutive hits before first out of game
N.L.—8
Philadelphia vs. Chicago, August 5, 1975 (4 singles, 2 doubles, 2 home runs).
Pittsburgh vs. Atlanta, August 26, 1975 (7 singles, 1 triple).
A.L.—8
Oakland vs. Chicago, September 27, 1981, first game (8 singles).
New York vs. Baltimore, September 25, 1990 (6 singles, 2 home runs).

Most batters reaching first base safely, inning
A.L.—20—Boston vs. Detroit, June 18, 1953, seventh inning.
N.L.—20—Chicago vs. Detroit, September 6, 1883, seventh inning.
N.L. since 1900—19—Brooklyn vs. Cincinnati, May 21, 1952, first inning.

Most consecutive batters reaching base safely, inning
N.L.—19—Brooklyn vs. Cincinnati, May 21, 1952, first inning.
A.L.—13—Kansas City vs. Chicago, April 21, 1956, second inning.

Most batters reaching base safely three times, inning
N.L.—3
Chicago vs. Detroit, September 6, 1883, seventh inning.
Boston vs. Baltimore, June 18, 1894, a.m. game, first inning.
N.L. since 1900—1—Brooklyn vs. Cincinnati, May 21, 1952, first inning.
A.L.—3—Boston vs. Detroit, June 18, 1953, seventh inning.

Most players making two or more hits, inning
N.L.—7—Cincinnati vs. Houston, August 3, 1989, first inning.
A.L.—5
Philadelphia vs. Boston, July 8, 1902, sixth inning.
New York vs. Philadelphia, September 10, 1921, ninth inning.

SINGLES

Most singles, season
N.L.—1,338—Philadelphia, 132 games, 1894.
A.L.—1,298—Detroit, 154 games, 1921.
N.L. since 1900—1,297—Pittsburgh, 155 games, 1922.

Fewest singles, season
A.L.—811—Baltimore, 162 games, 1968.
N.L.—843—New York, 156 games, 1972.

Most singles, game
N.L.—28
Philadelphia vs. Louisville, August 17, 1894.
Boston vs. Baltimore, April 20, 1896.
A.L.—26—Milwaukee vs. Toronto, August 28, 1992.
N.L. since 1900—23
New York vs. Chicago, September 21, 1931.
New York vs. Atlanta, July 4, 1985, 19 innings.

Most singles by both clubs, nine-inning game
N.L.—37—Baltimore 21, Washington 16, August 8, 1896.
N.L. since 1900—36—New York 22, Cincinnati 14, June 9, 1901.
A.L.—36—Chicago 21, Boston 15, August 15, 1922.

Most singles by both clubs, extra-inning game
A.L.—42—Oakland 25, Texas 17, July 1, 1979, 15 innings.
N.L.—Less than nine-inning record.

Most singles, inning
N.L.—12—Cincinnati vs. Houston, August 3, 1989, first inning.
A.L.—11—Boston vs. Detroit, June 18, 1953, seventh inning.

Most consecutive singles, inning
N.L.—10—St. Louis vs. Boston, September 17, 1920, fourth inning.
A.L.—8
Washington vs. Cleveland, May 7, 1951, fourth inning.
Oakland vs. Chicago, September 27, 1981, first game, first inning.
Baltimore vs. Texas, May 18, 1990, first inning.

DOUBLES

Most doubles, season
N.L.—373—St. Louis, 154 games, 1930.
A.L.—373—Boston, 162 games, 1997.

Fewest doubles, season
N.L.—110—Brooklyn, 154 games, 1908.
A.L.—116—Chicago, 156 games, 1910.

Most consecutive years leading league in doubles
A.L.—8—Cleveland, 1916 through 1923.
N.L.—5—St. Louis, 1920 through 1924.

Most doubles, game
N.L.—14—Chicago vs. Buffalo, July 3, 1883.
N.L. since 1900—13—St. Louis vs. Chicago, July 12, 1931, second game.
A.L.—12
Boston vs. Detroit, July 29, 1990.
Cleveland vs. Minnesota, July 13, 1996.

Most doubles by pinch-hitters, game
A.L.—3
Cleveland vs. Washington, June 27, 1948, first game.
Chicago vs. New York, May 7, 1971.
N.L.—3—San Francisco vs. Pittsburgh, May 5, 1958.

Most doubles by both clubs, game
N.L.—23—St. Louis 13, Chicago 10, July 12, 1931, second game.
A.L.—18—Cleveland 12, Minnesota 6, July 13, 1996.

Most doubles, doubleheader
N.L.—17—St. Louis vs. Chicago, July 12, 1931.
A.L.—14—Philadelphia vs. Boston, July 8, 1905.

Most doubles by both clubs, doubleheader
N.L.—32—St. Louis 17, Chicago 15, July 12, 1931.
A.L.—26—Philadelphia 14, Boston 12, July 8, 1905.

Most doubles with bases filled, game
N.L.-A.L.—2—Made in many games.

Most doubles with bases filled by both clubs, game
N.L.-A.L.—2—Made in many games.

Most doubles, inning
N.L.—7—Boston vs. St. Louis, August 25, 1936, first game, first inning.
A.L.—6—Washington vs. Boston, June 9, 1934, eighth inning.

Most consecutive doubles, inning
A.L.—5—Washington vs. Boston, June 9, 1934, eighth inning.
N.L.—4—Held by many clubs. Last time—Philadelphia vs. Cincinnati, May 4, 2000, first inning.

Most players with two doubles, inning
N.L.—3—Boston vs. St. Louis, August 25, 1936, first game, first inning.
A.L.—2
New York vs. Boston, July 3, 1932, sixth inning.
Toronto vs. Baltimore, June 26, 1978, second inning.

TRIPLES

Most triples, season
N.L.—153—Baltimore, 129 games, 1894.
N.L. since 1900—129—Pittsburgh, 152 games, 1912.
A.L.—112
Baltimore, 134 games, 1901.
Boston, 141 games, 1903.

Fewest triples, season
A.L.—11—Baltimore, 162 games, 1998.
N.L.—14
Los Angeles, 162 games, 1986.
New York, 163 games, 1999.

Most consecutive years leading league in triples
A.L.—7—Washington, 1931 through 1937 (tied 1934).
N.L.—6—Pittsburgh, 1932 through 1937.

Most triples, game
N.L.—9—Baltimore vs. Cleveland, September 3, 1894, first game.
N.L. since 1900—8—Pittsburgh vs. St. Louis, May 30, 1925, second game.
A.L.—6
Chicago vs. Milwaukee, September 15, 1901; second game.
Chicago vs. New York, September 17, 1920.
Detroit vs. New York, June 17, 1922.

Most triples by both clubs, game
N.L.—11—Baltimore 9, Cleveland 2, September 3, 1894, first game.
N.L. since 1900—9
Pittsburgh 6, Chicago 3, July 4, 1904, p.m. game.
Pittsburgh 8, St. Louis 1, May 30, 1925, second game.
A.L.—9—Detroit 6, New York 3, June 17, 1922.

Most triples with bases filled, game
N.L.—2
Detroit vs. Indianapolis, May 7, 1887.
Pittsburgh vs. Brooklyn, September 17, 1898.
Chicago vs. Philadelphia, May 14, 1904.
Brooklyn vs. St. Louis, August 25, 1917, first game.
Cincinnati vs. Brooklyn, September 25, 1925.
Pittsburgh vs. St. Louis, September 10, 1938.
Chicago vs. Boston, June 12, 1936.
Brooklyn vs. Philadelphia, May 24, 1953, both in eighth inning.
Milwaukee vs. St. Louis, August 2, 1959, second game.
Montreal vs. Cincinnati, September 1, 1979.
New York vs. Colorado, June 6, 1994.
A.A.—2—Kansas City vs. Philadelphia, August 22, 1889.
A.L.—2
Boston vs. St. Louis, August 16, 1926, second game.
Philadelphia vs. Washington, April 26, 1928.
Philadelphia vs. Washington, May 1, 1949, first game.
Detroit vs. New York, June 9, 1950.
Cleveland vs. New York, July 27, 1978, second game.

Most bases-filled triples by both clubs, game (each club connecting)
N.L.—2—Made in many games. Last time—Chicago 1, St. Louis 1, April 22, 1938.
A.L.—2—Made in many games. Last time—Washington 1, New York 1, July 4, 1950, first game.

Longest extra-inning game without a triple
N.L.—26 innings—Brooklyn vs. Boston, May 1, 1920.

A.L.—25 innings
Milwaukee vs. Chicago, May 8, finished May 9, 1984.
Chicago vs. Milwaukee, May 8, finished May 9, 1984.

Longest extra-inning game without a triple by either club
N.L.—25 innings—New York 0, St. Louis 0, September 11, 1974.
A.L.—25 innings—Milwaukee 0, Chicago 0, May 8, finished May 9, 1984.

Most triples, doubleheader
N.L.—9
Baltimore vs. Cleveland, September 3, 1894.
Cincinnati vs. Chicago, May 27, 1922.
A.L.—9—Chicago vs. Milwaukee, September 15, 1901.

Most triples by both clubs, doubleheader
N.L.—11—Baltimore 9, Cleveland 2, September 3, 1894.
N.L. since 1900—10
Cincinnati 9, Chicago 1, May 27, 1922.
New York 7, Pittsburgh 3, July 30, 1923.
A.L.—10—Chicago 9, Milwaukee 1, September 15, 1901.

Most triples, inning
A.L.—5—Chicago vs. Milwaukee, September 15, 1901, second game, eighth inning.
N.L.—4
Boston vs. Troy, May 6, 1882, eighth inning.
Baltimore vs. St. Louis, July 27, 1892, seventh inning.
St. Louis vs. Chicago, July 2, 1895, first inning.
Chicago vs. St. Louis, April 17, 1899, fourth inning.
Brooklyn vs. Pittsburgh, August 23, 1902, third inning.
Cincinnati vs. Boston, July 22, 1926, second inning.
New York vs. Pittsburgh, July 17, 1936, first inning.

Most consecutive triples, inning
A.L.—4—Boston vs. Detroit, May 6, 1934, fourth inning.
N.L.—3—Made in many innings. Last times—Chicago vs. Philadelphia, April 25, 1981, fourth inning; Montreal vs. San Diego, May 6, 1981, ninth inning.

HOME RUNS
SEASON AND MONTH

Most home runs, season
A.L.—264—Seattle, 162 games, 1997 (131 at home, 133 on road).
N.L.—249—Houston, 162 games, 2000 (135 at home, 114 on road).

For a complete list of home runs by club each year beginning in 1901, see page 198.

Fewest home runs, season
N.L.—9—Pittsburgh, 157 games, 1917.
A.L.—3—Chicago, 156 games, 1908.

Most home runs by pinch-hitters, season
N.L.—14
Arizona, 2001.
San Francisco, 2001.
A.L.—11—Baltimore, 1982.

Most home runs at home, season
N.L.—149—Colorado, 1996, 81 games.
A.L.—134—Toronto, 2000, 81 games.

Most home runs on road, season
N.L.—138—San Francisco, 2001, 81 games.
A.L.—136—Baltimore, 1996, 81 games.

Most home runs against one club, season
A.L.—48—New York vs. Kansas City, 1956.
N.L.—44—Cincinnati vs. Brooklyn, 1956.

Most years leading league in home runs (since 1900)
A.L.—34—New York.
N.L.—28—New York/San Francisco (24 by N.Y., 4 by S.F.).

Most consecutive years leading league or tied in home runs
A.L.—12—New York, 1936 through 1947.
N.L.—7—Brooklyn, 1949 through 1955 (1954 tied).

Most years with 200 or more home runs
A.L.—6
   Detroit, 209 in 1962; 202 in 1985; 225 in 1987; 209 in 1991;
   204 in 1996; 212 in 1999.
   Cleveland, 207 in 1995; 218 in 1996; 220 in 1997; 209 in
   1999; 221 in 2000; 212 in 2001.
N.L.—5
   Colorado, 200 in 1995; 221 in 1996; 239 in 1997; 223 in
   1999; 213 in 2001.
   New York/San Francisco, 221 in 1947; 204 in 1962; 205 in
   1987; 226 in 2000; 235 in 2001 (1 with New York, 4 with
   San Francisco).

Most consecutive years with 200 or more home runs
A.L.—4—Seattle, 245 in 1996; 264 in 1997; 234 in 1998; 244
   in 1999.
N.L.—3—Colorado, 200 in 1995; 221 in 1996; 239 in 1997.

Most years with 100 or more home runs (since 1900)
A.L.—76—New York.
N.L.—65—New York/San Francisco (26 by N.Y., 39 by S.F.).

Most consecutive years with 100 or more home runs
A.L.—35—Boston, 1946 through 1980.
N.L.—29
   New York/San Francisco, 1945 through 1957 in New York,
   1958 through 1973 in San Francisco.
   Cincinnati, 1952 through 1980.

Most home runs by two players, season
A.L.—115—New York, 1961 (Maris 61, Mantle 54).
N.L.—110—San Francisco, 2001 (Bonds 73, Aurilia 37).

Most home runs by three players, season
A.L.—143—New York, 1961 (Maris 61, Mantle, 54, Skowron,
   28).
N.L.—132—San Francisco, 2001 (Bonds 73, Aurilia 37, Kent
   22).

Most players with 50 or more home runs, season
A.L.—2—New York, 1961 (Maris 61, Mantle 54).
N.L.—1—Held by many clubs.

Most players with 40 or more home runs, season
N.L.—3
   Atlanta, 1973 (Johnson 43, Evans 41, Aaron 40).
   Colorado, 1996 (Galarraga 47, Burks 40, Castilla 40).
   Colorado, 1997 (Walker 49, Galarraga 41, Castilla 40).
A.L.—2
   New York, 1927 (Ruth 60, Gehrig 47), 1930 (Ruth 49, Gehrig
   41), 1931 (Ruth 46, Gehrig 46), 1961 (Maris 61, Mantle 54).
   Detroit, 1961 (Colavito 45, Cash 41).
   Boston, 1969 (Petrocelli 40, Yastrzemski 40).
   Seattle, 1996 (Griffey 49, Buhner 44).
   Seattle, 1997 (Griffey 56, Buhner 40).
   Seattle, 1998 (Griffey 56, Rodriguez 42).
   Seattle, 1999 (Griffey 48, Rodriguez 42).
   Toronto, 1999 (Delgado 44, Green 42).
   Toronto, 2000 (Delgado 41, Batista 41).
   Texas, 2001 (A. Rodriguez 52, Palmeiro 47).

Most players with 30 or more home runs, season
N.L.—4—Los Angeles, 1977, 1997; Colorado, 1995, 1996, 1997,
   1999; Atlanta, 1998.
A.L.—4—Anaheim, 2000; Toronto, 2000.

Most players with 20 or more home runs, season
A.L.—7
   Baltimore, 1996.
   Toronto, 2000.
N.L.—6—Milwaukee, 1965.

Most home runs, one month
A.L.—58—Baltimore, May, 1987.
N.L.—55
   New York, July, 1947.
   St. Louis, April, 2000.

GAME

Most home runs, game
A.L.—10—Toronto vs. Baltimore, September 14, 1987.
N.L.—9—Cincinnati vs. Philadelphia, September 4, 1999.

Most home runs by both clubs, game
A.L.—12—Detroit 7, Chicago 5, May 28, 1995.
N.L.—11
   Pittsburgh 6, Cincinnati 5, August 12, 1966, 13 innings.
   Chicago 7, New York 4, June 11, 1967, second game.
   Chicago 6, Cincinnati 5, July 28, 1977, 13 innings.
   Chicago 6, Philadelphia 5, May 17, 1979, 10 innings.

Most home runs, night game
A.L.—10—Toronto vs. Baltimore, September 14, 1987.
N.L.—9—Cincinnati vs. Philadelphia, September 4, 1999.

Most home runs by both clubs, nine-inning night game
A.L.—11
   New York 6, Detroit 5, June 23, 1950.
   Toronto 10, Baltimore 1, September 14, 1987.
   Cleveland 8, Milwaukee 3, April 25, 1997.
N.L.—10
   Cincinnati 8, Milwaukee 2, August 18, 1956.
   Cincinnati 7, Atlanta 3, April 21, 1970.
   Cincinnati 9, Philadelphia 1, September 4, 1999.

Most home runs by pinch-hitters, game
A.L.-N.L.—2—Held by many clubs.

Most home runs by pinch-hitters for both clubs, game
N.L.—3
   Philadelphia 2, St. Louis 1, June 2, 1928.
   St. Louis 2, Brooklyn 1, July 21, 1930, first game.
A.L.—2—Made in many games. Last times—Cleveland 1,
   Minnesota 1, May 7, 1989, first game; New York 1, Chicago 1,
   June 22, 1989.

Most home runs, opening game of season
N.L.—6—New York vs. Montreal, April 4, 1988.
A.L.—5
   New York vs. Philadelphia, April 12, 1932.
   Boston vs. Washington, April 12, 1965.
   Milwaukee vs. Boston, April 10, 1980.
   Cleveland vs. Texas, April 27, 1995 (game was not Texas'
   opener).

Most home runs by both clubs, opening game of season
A.L.—7
   New York 5, Philadelphia 2, April 12, 1932.
   Boston 5, Washington 2, April 12, 1965.
   Milwaukee 5, Boston 2, April 10, 1980.
   Cleveland 5, Texas 2, April 27, 1995 (game was not Texas'
   opener).
   Milwaukee 4, California 3, April 2, 1996.
N.L.—7
   New York 6, Montreal 1, April 4, 1988.
   Atlanta 4, Chicago 3, April 5, 1988.
   Atlanta 5, San Francisco 2, April 2, 1996.

Most home runs by first-game players for both clubs, game
N.L.—2—Brooklyn 1 (Ernie Koy), Philadelphia 1 (Emmett
   Mueller), April 19, 1938 (each in first inning).

Most home runs, game (no other runs)
A.L.—6—Oakland vs. Minnesota, August 3, 1991.
N.L.—5
   New York vs. Chicago, June 16, 1930.
   St. Louis vs. Brooklyn, September 1, 1953.
   Cincinnati vs. Milwaukee, April 16, 1955.
   Chicago vs. Pittsburgh, April 21, 1964.
   Pittsburgh vs. Los Angeles, May 7, 1973.
   Colorado vs. San Francisco, May 9, 1994.
   Atlanta vs. Colorado, April 19, 1998, first game.

Most home runs by both clubs, game (no other runs)
Both leagues—5—Baltimore A.L. 3, Atlanta N.L. 2, June 5,
   1998.
N.L.—5
   San Francisco 3, Milwaukee 2, August 30, 1962.
   Montreal 3, San Diego 2, May 16, 1986.
A.L.—4
   Cleveland 4, New York 0, August 2, 1956.
   New York 4, Baltimore 0, May 13, 1973, first game.

Most home runs, shutout game (no other runs)
A.L.—4
Cleveland vs. New York, August 2, 1956.
New York vs. Baltimore, May 13, 1973, first game.
N.L.—3
St. Louis vs. New York, July 19, 1923.
Philadelphia vs. Cincinnati, August 27, 1951, second game.
San Francisco vs. Milwaukee, August 14, 1964.
Cincinnati vs. Pittsburgh, September 25, 1968.
New York vs. Philadelphia, June 29, 1971.
New York vs. Pittsburgh, September 17, 1971.
New York vs. Cincinnati, August 29, 1972.
San Francisco vs. Philadelphia, September 4, 2000.

Most home runs with none on bases, nine-inning game
A.L.—7—Boston vs. Toronto, July 4, 1977 (8 home runs in game by Boston).
N.L.—6
New York vs. Philadelphia, August 13, 1939, first game (7 home runs in game by New York).
New York vs. Cincinnati, June 24, 1950 (7 home runs in game by New York).
Atlanta vs. Chicago, August 3, 1967 (7 home runs in game by Atlanta).
Chicago vs. San Diego, August 19, 1970 (7 home runs in game by Chicago).

Most home runs with none on bases, by both clubs, game
A.L.—10—Detroit 5, Chicago 5, May 28, 1995.
N.L.—7
Chicago 6, San Diego 1, August 19, 1970.
Pittsburgh 4, Chicago 3, June 7, 1976.
Philadelphia 5, Colorado 2, May 8, 1999.

Most home runs by infield, game (excluding battery)
N.L.—6
Milwaukee vs. Brooklyn, July 31, 1954.
Montreal vs. Atlanta, July 30, 1978.
A.L.—5
New York vs. Philadelphia, June 3, 1932.
New York vs. Philadelphia, May 24, 1936.
Cleveland vs. Philadelphia, June 18, 1941.
Boston vs. St. Louis, June 8, 1950.

Most home runs by outfield, game
N.L.—6
Cincinnati vs. Milwaukee, August 18, 1956.
San Francisco vs. Milwaukee, April 30, 1961.
A.L.—5
New York vs. Chicago, July 28, 1940, first game.
Cleveland vs. New York, July 13, 1945.
Cleveland vs. Baltimore, June 10, 1959.
New York vs. Boston, May 30, 1961.

Most times with five or more home runs in game, season
A.L.—8—Boston, 1977.
N.L.—6—New York, 1947.

Most players with three or more home runs in game, season
N.L.—4
Brooklyn, 1950 (Snider, Campanella, Hodges, Brown).
Cincinnati, 1956 (Bell, Bailey, Kluszewski, Thurman).
Milwaukee, 2001 (Burnitz 2, Jenkins, Sexson).
A.L.—3
Cleveland, 1987 (Snyder, Carter, Jacoby).
Oakland, 1996 (Berroa 2, Young).
Seattle, 1996 (Wilson, Griffey, Martinez).

Most times with two or more homers by one player in a game, season
A.L.—24—New York, 1961.
N.L.—24—Atlanta, 1966.

Most players with three or more home runs, game
N.L.—2—Milwaukee vs. Arizona, September 25, 2001.
A.L.—1—Held by many clubs.

Most players with three or more home runs by both clubs, game
N.L.—2—Milwaukee 2, Arizona 0, September 25, 2001.
A.L.—1—Occurred in many games.

Most players with two or more home runs, game
N.L.—3
Pittsburgh vs. St. Louis, August 16, 1947.
Chicago vs. St. Louis, April 16, 1955, 14 innings.
New York vs. Pittsburgh, July 8, 1956, first game.
Cincinnati vs. Milwaukee, August 18, 1956.
Philadelphia vs. New York, September 8, 1998.
Colorado vs. Montreal, August 14, 1999.
Houston vs. Chicago, September 9, 2000.
A.L.—3
Boston vs. St. Louis, June 8, 1950.
New York vs. Boston, May 30, 1961.
Toronto vs. Baltimore, September 14, 1987.
Toronto vs. California, July 14, 1990.
Detroit vs. Chicago, May 28, 1995.
Seattle vs. Milwaukee, July 31, 1996.
Anaheim vs. Tampa Bay, April 21, 2000.
Minnesota vs. Milwaukee N.L., July 12, 2001.

Most players with two or more homers by both clubs, game
N.L.—4
Pittsburgh 3, St. Louis 1, August 16, 1947.
Colorado 3, Montreal 1, August 14, 1999.
A.L.—4—Detroit 3, Chicago 1, May 28, 1995.

Most players with one or more home runs, game
N.L.—8—Cincinnati vs. Philadelphia, September 4, 1999 (9 home runs in game by Cincinnati).
A.L.—7
Baltimore vs. Boston, May 17, 1967 (7 home runs in game by Baltimore).
Oakland vs. California, June 27, 1996 (8 home runs in game by Oakland).
Detroit vs. Toronto, June 20, 2000 (8 home runs in game by Detroit).

Most players with one or more home runs by both clubs, game
N.L.—9
New York 5, Brooklyn 4, September 2, 1939, first game.
New York 6, Pittsburgh 3, July 11, 1954, first game.
Chicago 5, Pittsburgh 4, April 21, 1964.
Cincinnati 6, Atlanta 3, April 21, 1970.
Los Angeles 5, Atlanta 4, April 24, 1977.
Cincinnati 5, Chicago 4, July 28, 1977, 13 innings.
Cincinnati 8, Philadelphia 1, September 4, 1999.
A.L.—9
New York 5, Detroit 4, June 23, 1950.
Minnesota 5, Boston 4, May 25, 1965.
Baltimore 7, Boston 2, May 17, 1967.
California 5, Cleveland 4, August 30, 1970.
Boston 5, Milwaukee 4, May 22, 1977, first game.
California 5, Oakland 4, April 23, 1985.
Detroit 7, Toronto 2, June 20, 2000.

Longest extra-inning game without a home run by either club
N.L.—26 innings—Boston 0, Brooklyn 0, May 1, 1920.
A.L.—24 innings
Boston 0, Philadelphia 0, September 1, 1906.
Detroit 0, Philadelphia 0, July 21, 1945.

DOUBLEHEADER AND CONSECUTIVE GAMES

Most home runs, doubleheader
A.L.—13—New York vs. Philadelphia, June 28, 1939.
N.L.—12—Milwaukee vs. Pittsburgh, August 30, 1953.

Most home runs both clubs, doubleheader
N.L.—15—Milwaukee 9, Chicago 6, May 30, 1956.
A.L.—14—New York 9, Philadelphia 5, May 22, 1930.

Most home runs by pinch-hitters, doubleheader
N.L.—3—Montreal vs. Atlanta, July 13, 1973.
A.L.—2—Made in many doubleheaders.

Most home runs by pinch-hitters for both clubs, doubleheader
N.L.—4—St. Louis 2, Brooklyn 2, July 21, 1930.
A.L.—2—Made in many doubleheaders.

Most consecutive games with one or more home runs

A.L.—25

New York, June 1, second game, through June 29, second game, 1941 (40 home runs).

Detroit, May 25 through June 19, 1994 (46 home runs).

N.L.—25—Atlanta, April 18 through May 13, 1998 (45 home runs).

Most home runs in consecutive games in which homers were hit

A.L.—50—Oakland, July 2 through July 27, 1996 (23 games).

N.L.—45—Atlanta, April 18 through May 13, 1998 (25 games).

Most consecutive games with one or more homers, start of season

N.L.—13—Chicago, April 13 through May 2, second game, 1954 (28 home runs).

A.L.—10—New York, April 5 through April 16, 1999 (16 home runs).

Most consecutive games with two or more home runs, season

A.L.—9

Cleveland, May 13, first game, through May 21, 1962 (28 home runs).

Baltimore, May 8 through May 16, 1987 (29 home runs).

Baltimore, August 3 through August 11, 1996 (23 home runs).

N.L.—8—Milwaukee, July 19 through July 26, 1956 (20 home runs).

Most home runs, two consecutive games (connecting each game)

N.L.—14—Cincinnati, September 4, 5, 1999.

A.L.—13—New York, June 28, 28, 1939.

Most home runs, three consecutive games

A.L.—16—Boston, June 17 through June 19, 1977.

N.L.—15

Los Angeles, June 29, 30, July 1, 1996.

Cincinnati, September 3, 4, 5, 1999.

Cincinnati, September 4, 5, 6, 1999.

Most home runs, four consecutive games

N.L.—18—Houston, August 13 through August 16, 2000.

A.L.—18

Boston, June 16 through June 19, 1977.

Oakland, June 25 through June 29, 1996.

Most home runs, five consecutive games

A.L.—21—Boston, June 14 through June 19, 1977.

N.L.—19—New York, July 7 through July 11, first game, 1954.

Most home runs, six consecutive games

A.L.—24—Boston, June 17 through June 22, 1977.

N.L.—22—New York, July 6 through July 11, first game, 1954.

Most home runs, seven consecutive games

A.L.—26—Boston, June 16 through June 22, 1977.

N.L.—24—New York, July 5, second game through July 11, first game, 1954.

Most home runs, eight consecutive games

A.L.—29—Boston, June 14 through June 22, 1977.

N.L.—26—New York, July 5, first game through July 11, first game, 1954.

Most home runs, nine consecutive games

A.L.—30

Boston June 14 through June 23, 1977.

Boston, June 16 through June 24, 1977.

N.L.—27—New York, July 4, second game through July 11, first game, 1954.

Most home runs, 10 consecutive games

A.L.—33—Boston, June 14 through June 24, 1977.

N.L.—28—New York, July 4, first game through July 11, first game, 1954.

INNING

Most home runs, inning

A.L.—5—Minnesota vs. Kansas City, June 9, 1966, seventh inning.

N.L.—5

New York vs. Cincinnati, June 6, 1939, fourth inning.

Philadelphia vs. Cincinnati, June 2, 1949, eighth inning.

San Francisco vs. Cincinnati, August 23, 1961, ninth inning.

For complete lists of clubs with four or more home runs in an inning and three or more consecutive home runs in an inning, see page 201.

Most home runs by pinch-hitters, inning

N.L.—2

New York vs. St. Louis, June 20, 1954, sixth inning (Hofman, Rhodes).

San Francisco vs. Milwaukee, June 4, 1958, 10th inning, (Sauer, Schmidt; consecutive).

Los Angeles vs. Chicago, August 8, 1963, fifth inning (Howard, Skowron; consecutive).

Los Angeles vs. St. Louis, July 23, 1975, ninth inning (Crawford, Lacy; consecutive).

New York vs. San Francisco, May 4, 1991, ninth inning (Sasser, Carreon; consecutive).

Cincinnati vs. Atlanta, June 22, 1995, eighth inning (Anthony, Taubensee).

New York vs. St. Louis, May 11, 1997, ninth inning (Everett, Huskey; consecutive).

A.L.—2

New York vs. Kansas City, July 23, 1955, ninth inning (Cerv, Howard).

Baltimore vs. Boston, August 26, 1966, ninth inning (Roznovsky, Powell; consecutive).

Seattle vs. New York, April 27, 1979, eighth inning (Stinson, Meyer).

Minnesota vs. Oakland, May 16, 1983, ninth inning (Engle, Hatcher).

Baltimore vs. Cleveland, August 12, 1985, ninth inning (Gross, Sheets; consecutive).

Texas vs. Boston, September 1, 1986, ninth inning (McDowell, Porter; consecutive).

Boston vs. Chicago, September 19, 1997, ninth inning (Pride, Hatteberg).

Most home runs by both clubs, inning

A.L.—5

St. Louis 3, Philadelphia 2, June 8, 1928, ninth inning.

Detroit 4, New York 1, June 23, 1950, fourth inning.

Minnesota 5, Kansas City 0, June 9, 1966, seventh inning.

Baltimore 4, Boston 1, May 17, 1967, seventh inning.

Minnesota 4, Oakland 1, May 16, 1983, ninth inning.

Cleveland 3, Milwaukee 2, April 25, 1997, fourth inning.

Detroit 3, Baltimore 2, April 7, 2000, fifth inning.

N.L.—5

New York 5, Cincinnati 0, June 6, 1939, fourth inning.

Philadelphia 5, Cincinnati 0, June 2, 1949, eighth inning.

New York 3, Boston 2, July 6, 1951, third inning.

Cincinnati 3, Brooklyn 2, June 11, 1954, seventh inning.

San Francisco 5, Cincinnati 0, August 23, 1961, ninth inning.

Philadelphia 3, Chicago 2, April 17, 1964, fifth inning.

Chicago 3, Atlanta 2, July 3, 1967, first inning.

Pittsburgh 3, Atlanta 2, August 1, 1970, seventh inning.

Cincinnati 3, Chicago 2, July 28, 1977, first inning.

San Francisco 3, Atlanta 2, May 25, 1979, fourth inning.

Cincinnati 4, Atlanta 1, June 19, 1994, first inning.

San Francisco 3, Pittsburgh 2, July 27, 1997, ninth inning.

Colorado 3, St. Louis 2, July 31, 1999, third inning.

Most consecutive home runs, inning

N.L.—4—Milwaukee vs. Cincinnati, June 8, 1961, seventh inning.

A.L.—4

Cleveland vs. Los Angeles, July 31, 1963, second game, sixth inning.

Minnesota vs. Kansas City, May 2, 1964, 11th inning.

For a complete list of clubs with three or more consecutive home runs in an inning, see page 202.

Most home runs with two out, inning
N.L.—5—New York vs. Cincinnati, June 6, 1939, fourth inning.
A.L.—4—Boston vs. Detroit, July 18, 1998, fourth inning.

Most home runs with none on base, inning
N.L.—4—New York vs. Philadelphia, August 13, 1939, first game, fourth inning.
A.L.—4
Cleveland vs. Los Angeles, July 31, 1963, second game, sixth inning (consecutive).
Minnesota vs. Kansas City, May 2, 1964, 11th inning (consecutive).
Minnesota vs. Kansas City, June 9, 1966, seventh inning (also one home run with one on base).
Boston vs. New York, June 17, 1977, first inning.
Boston vs. Toronto, July 4, 1977, eighth inning.
Boston vs. Milwaukee, May 31, 1980, fourth inning.
Minnesota vs. New York, May 2, 1992, fifth inning.
Baltimore vs. California, September 5, 1995, second inning.
Seattle vs. Oakland, September 21, 1996, third inning.

Most home runs, start of game
N.L.—3—San Diego vs. San Francisco, April 13, 1987 (Wynne, Gwynn, Kruk).
A.A.—2
Boston vs. Baltimore, June 25, 1891 (Brown, Joyce).
Philadelphia vs. Boston, August 21, 1891 (McTamany, Larkin).
A.L.—2—Held by many clubs. Last clubs: Oakland vs. Kansas City, May 16, 2000 (Long, Velarde); Chicago vs. Kansas City, July 4, 2000 (Durham, Valentin).

Most times with three consecutive home runs in an inning (league)
N.L.—15—New York/San Francisco, 1932, 1939 (2), 1948, 1949, 1953, 1954, 1956 in New York, 1963, 1969, 1982, 1998, 1999 (2), 2001 in San Francisco.
A.L.—7—Cleveland, 1902, 1939, 1950, 1951, 1962, 1963, 1970.

For a complete list of clubs with three or more consecutive home runs in an inning, see page 202.

Most times with three or more home runs in an inning, season
N.L.—5
New York, 1954.
Chicago, 1955.
A.L.—5—Baltimore, 1996.

Most times hitting two or more consecutive home runs, season
A.L.—18—Seattle, 161 games, 1996.
N.L.—15
Cincinnati, 155 games, 1956.
St. Louis, 162 games, 2000.

GRAND SLAMS

Most grand slams, season
A.L.—14—Oakland, 2000.
N.L.—12
Atlanta, 1997.
St. Louis, 2000.

Most grand slams by pinch-hitters, season
N.L.—3
San Francisco, 1973 (Arnold, Bonds, Goodson).
Chicago, 1975 (Summers, LaCock, Hosley).
San Francisco, 1978 (Ivie 2, Clark).
Philadelphia, 1978 (Johnson 2, McBride).
A.L.—3—Baltimore, 1982 (Ayala, Ford, Crowley).

Most grand slams, game
A.L.—2
Chicago vs. Detroit, May 1, 1901 (Hoy, MacFarland).
Boston vs. Chicago, May 13, 1934 (Walters, Morgan).
New York vs. Philadelphia, May 24, 1936 (Lazzeri 2).
Boston vs. Philadelphia, July 4, 1939, second game (Tabor 2).
Boston vs. St. Louis, July 27, 1946 (York 2).
Detroit vs. Philadelphia, June 11, 1954, first game (Boone, Kaline).

Baltimore vs. New York, April 24, 1960 (Pearson, Klaus).
Boston vs. Chicago, May 10, 1960 (Wertz, Repulski).
Baltimore vs. Minnesota, May 9, 1961 (Gentile 2).
Minnesota vs. Cleveland, July 18, 1962 (Allison, Killebrew).
Detroit vs. Cleveland, June 24, 1968 (Northrup 2).
Baltimore vs. Washington, June 26, 1970 (Frank Robinson 2).
Milwaukee vs. Chicago, June 17, 1973 (Porter, Lahoud).
Milwaukee vs. Boston, April 12, 1980 (Cooper, Money).
California vs. Detroit, April 27, 1983 (Lynn, Sconiers).
Boston vs. Detroit, August 7, 1984, first game (Buckner, Armas).
California vs. Oakland, July 31, 1986 (Downing, Boone).
Baltimore vs. Texas, August 6, 1986 (Sheets, Dwyer).
Boston vs. Baltimore, June 10, 1987 (Burks, Barrett).
New York vs. Toronto, June 29, 1989 (Mattingly, Winfield).
Cleveland vs. Minnesota, April 22, 1988 (Snyder, Carter).
Boston vs. New York, May 2, 1995 (Valentin, Vaughn).
Chicago vs. Texas, September 4, 1995 (Ventura 2).
Chicago vs. Detroit, May 19, 1996 (Ventura, Lewis).
Baltimore vs. Cleveland, August 14, 1998 (Hoiles 2).
Boston vs. Seattle, May 10, 1999 (Garciaparra 2).
New York vs. Toronto, September 14, 1999 (Williams, O'Neill).
Cleveland vs. Toronto, September 24, 1999 (Ramirez, Roberts).
Seattle vs. Chicago, August 8, 2000, first game (Buhner, Martinez).
N.L.—2
Chicago vs. Pittsburgh, August 16, 1890, (Burns, Kittredge).
Brooklyn vs. Cincinnati, September 23, 1901 (Kelley, Sheckard).
Boston vs. Chicago, August 12, 1903, second game (Stanley, Moran).
Philadelphia vs. Boston, April 28, 1921 (Miller, Meadows).
New York vs. Philadelphia, September 5, 1924, second game (Kelly, Jackson).
Pittsburgh vs. St. Louis, June 22, 1925 (Grantham, Traynor).
St. Louis vs. Philadelphia, July 6, 1929, second game (Bottomley, Hafey).
Pittsburgh vs. Philadelphia, May 1, 1933 (Vaughan, Grace).
Boston vs. Philadelphia, April 30, 1938 (Moore, Maggert).
New York vs. Brooklyn, July 4, 1938, second game (Bartell, Mancuso).
New York vs. St. Louis, July 13, 1951 (Westrum, Williams).
Cincinnati vs. Pittsburgh, July 29, 1955 (Thurman, Burgess).
Atlanta vs. San Francisco, July 3, 1966 (Cloninger 2).
Houston vs. New York, July 30, 1969, first game (Menke, Wynn).
San Francisco vs. Montreal, April 26, 1970, first game (McCovey, Dietz).
Pittsburgh vs. Chicago, September 14, 1982 (Hebner, Madlock).
Los Angeles vs. Montreal, August 23, 1985 (Guerrero, Duncan).
Atlanta vs. Houston, May 2, 1987 (Nettles, James).
Chicago vs. Houston, June 3, 1987 (Dayett, Moreland).
Cincinnati vs. Chicago, April 24, 1993 (Sabo, Oliver).
Pittsburgh vs. St. Louis, April 16, 1996 (Merced, Bell).
Montreal vs. Colorado, April 28, 1996 (Fletcher, Segui).
Florida vs. San Diego, April 28, 1997 (Alou, Sheffield).
Atlanta vs. Philadelphia, July 14, 1997 (Spehr, Klesko).
Philadelphia vs. San Francisco, August 18, 1997 (McMillon, Lieberthal).
San Francisco vs. Los Angeles, September 19, 1998 (Mueller, Kent).
St. Louis vs. Los Angeles, April 23, 1999 (Tatis 2).
Cincinnati vs. Montreal, August 21, 1999 (Boone, Taubensee).
Los Angeles vs. Florida, May 21, 2000 (Beltre, Green).

Most grand slams by both clubs, game (each club connecting)
A.L.—3—Baltimore 2 (Sheets, Dwyer), Texas 1 (Harrah), August 6, 1986.
N.L.—3—Chicago 2 (Dayett, Moreland), Houston 1 (Hatcher), June 3, 1987.

Most grand slams by pinch-hitters for both clubs, game
N.L.—2—New York 1 (Crawford), Boston 1 (Bell), May 26, 1929.
A.L.—1—Held by many clubs.

Most grand slams, doubleheader
N.L.-A.L.—2—Made in many doubleheaders.
Last N.L. time—New York vs. Milwaukee, May 20, 1999.
Last A.L. time—Baltimore vs. Chicago, August 14, 1976.

Most grand slams by both clubs, doubleheader
N.L.—3—Cincinnati 2, Atlanta 1, September 12, 1974.
A.L.—2—Last time—Seattle 2, Chicago 0, August 8, 2000.

Most grand slams, two consecutive games (connecting each game)
N.L.—3
Brooklyn, September 23 (2), September 24 (1), 1901.
Pittsburgh, June 20 (1), June 22 (2), 1925.
Los Angeles, May 20 (1), May 21 (2), 2000.
A.L.—3
Milwaukee, April 10 (1), April 12 (2), 1980.
Chicago, May 18 (1), May 19 (2), 1996.
Seattle, August 7 (1), August 8, first game (2), 2000.

Most consecutive games, one or more grand slams
A.L.—3
Milwaukee, April 7, 8, 9, 1978. (first three games of season.)
Detroit, August 10, 11, 12, 1993.
N.L.—2—Held by many clubs.

Most grand slams, inning
A.L.—2
Minnesota vs. Cleveland, July 18, 1962, first inning (Allison, Killebrew).
Milwaukee vs. Boston, April 12, 1980, second inning (Cooper, Money).
Baltimore vs. Texas, August 6, 1986, fourth inning (Sheets, Dwyer).
N.L.—2
Chicago vs. Pittsburgh, August 16, 1890, fifth inning (Burns, Kittredge).
Houston vs. New York, July 30, 1969, first game, ninth inning (Menke, Wynn).
St. Louis vs. Los Angeles, April 23, 1999, third inning (Tatis 2).

Most grand slams by both clubs, inning
N.L.—2
Chicago 2 (Burns, Kittredge), Pittsburgh 0, August 16, 1890, fifth inning.
New York 1 (Irvin), Chicago 1 (Walker), May 18, 1950, sixth inning.
Houston 2 (Menke, Wynn), New York 0, July 30, 1969, first game, ninth inning.
Atlanta 1 (Evans), Cincinnati 1, (Geronimo), September 12, 1974, first game, second inning.
Chicago 1 (Sandberg), Pittsburgh 1 (King), September 9, 1992, sixth inning.
St. Louis 2 (Tatis 2), Los Angeles 0, April 23, 1999, third inning.
A.L.—2
Washington 1 (Tasby), Boston 1 (Pagliaroni), June 18, 1961, first game, ninth inning.
Minnesota 2 (Allison, Killebrew), Cleveland 0, July 18, 1962, first inning.
Milwaukee 2 (Cooper, Money), Boston 0, April 12, 1980, second inning.
Cleveland 1 (Orta), Texas 1 (Sundberg), April 14, 1980, first inning.
Baltimore 2 (Sheets, Dwyer), Texas 0, August 6, 1986, fourth inning.
Interleague—2—Anaheim A.L. 1 (Fielder), Arizona N.L. 1 (Benitez), June 9, 1998, third inning.

TOTAL BASES

Most total bases, season
N.L.—2,748—Colorado, 162 games, 2001.
A.L.—2,741—Seattle, 161 games, 1996.

Fewest total bases, season
N.L.—1,358—Brooklyn, 154 games, 1908.
A.L.—1,310—Chicago, 156 games, 1910.

Most total bases, game
A.L.—60—Boston vs. St. Louis, June 8, 1950.
N.L.—58—Montreal vs. Atlanta, July 30, 1978.

Most total bases by both clubs, nine-inning game
N.L.—81—Cincinnati 55, Colorado 26, May 19, 1999.
A.L.—77—New York 50, Philadelphia 27, June 3, 1932.

Most total bases by both clubs, extra-inning game
N.L.—97—Chicago 49, Philadelphia 48, May 17, 1979, 10 innings.
A.L.—85—Cleveland 45, Philadelphia 40, July 10, 1932, 18 innings.

Most total bases, doubleheader
A.L.—87—New York vs. Philadelphia, June 28, 1939.
N.L.—73—Milwaukee vs. Pittsburgh, August 30, 1953.

Most total bases by both clubs, doubleheader
A.L.—114—New York 73, Philadelphia 41, May 22, 1930.
N.L.—108—St. Louis 62, Philadelphia 46, July 6, 1929.

Most total bases, two consecutive games
A.L.—102—Boston vs. St. Louis, June 7 (42), June 8 (60), 1950.
N.L.—89—Pittsburgh, June 20 (46), June 22 (43), 1925.

Most total bases, inning
N.L.—29—Chicago vs. Detroit, September 6, 1883, seventh inning.
N.L. since 1900—27—San Francisco vs. Cincinnati, August 23, 1961, ninth inning.
A.L.—25—Boston vs. Philadelphia, September 24, 1940, first game, sixth inning.

LONG HITS

Most long hits, season
A.L.—607—Seattle, 161 games, 1996 (343 doubles, 19 triples, 245 home runs).
N.L.—598—Colorado, 162 games, 2001 (324 doubles, 61 triples, 213 home runs).

Fewest long hits, season
A.L.—179—Chicago, 156 games, 1910 (116 doubles, 56 triples, 7 home runs).
N.L.—182—Boston, 155 games, 1909 (124 doubles, 43 triples, 15 home runs).

Most long hits, game
A.L.—17—Boston vs. St. Louis, June 8, 1950.
N.L.—16—Chicago vs. Buffalo, July 3, 1883.
N.L. since 1900—15
Philadelphia vs. Chicago, June 23, 1986.
Cincinnati vs. Colorado, May 19, 1999.

Most long hits by both clubs, game
N.L.—24—St. Louis 13, Chicago 11, July 12, 1931, second game.
A.L.—21—Chicago 11, Detroit 10, May 28, 1995.

Longest game without a long hit
N.L.—26 innings—Brooklyn vs. Boston, May 1, 1920.
A.L.—19 innings—Detroit vs. New York, August 23, 1968, second game.

Longest game without a long hit by either club
A.L.—18 innings—Chicago 0, New York 0, August 21, 1933.
N.L.—17 innings—Boston 0, Chicago 0, September 21, 1901.

Most long hits, doubleheader
N.L.—21—Baltimore vs. Cleveland, September 3, 1894.
N.L. since 1900—18—Chicago vs. St. Louis, July 12, 1931.
A.L.—18
New York vs. Washington, July 4, 1927.
New York vs. Philadelphia, June 28, 1939.

Most long hits by both clubs, doubleheader
N.L.—35—Chicago 18, St. Louis 17, July 12, 1931.
A.L.—28—Boston 16, Detroit 12, May 14, 1967.

Longest doubleheader without a long hit
A.L.—26—Cleveland vs. Detroit, August 6, 1968.

Most long hits, inning
N.L.—8—Chicago vs. Detroit, September 6, 1883, seventh inning.
N.L. since 1900—7
Boston vs. St. Louis, August 25, 1936, first game, first inning.
Philadelphia vs. Cincinnati, June 2, 1949, eighth inning.
Philadelphia vs. Cincinnati, July 6, 1986, third inning.
A.L.—7
St. Louis vs. Washington, August 7, 1922, sixth inning.
Boston vs. Philadelphia, September 24, 1940, first game, sixth inning.
New York vs. St. Louis, May 3, 1951, ninth inning.

EXTRA BASES ON LONG HITS

Most extra bases on long hits, season
A.L.—1,146—Seattle, 162 games, 1997.
N.L.—1,108—Houston, 162 games, 2000.

Fewest extra bases on long hits, season
A.L.—249—Chicago, 156 games, 1910.
N.L.—255—Boston, 155 games, 1909.

Most extra bases on long hits, game
A.L.—32—Boston vs. St. Louis, June 8, 1950.
N.L.—30—Montreal vs. Atlanta, July 30, 1978.

Most extra bases on long hits by both clubs, nine-inning game
A.L.—45—Detroit 24, Chicago 21, May 28, 1995.
N.L.—40
Milwaukee 27, Brooklyn 13, July 31, 1954.
Chicago 26, New York 14, June 11, 1967, second game.

Most extra bases on long hits by both clubs, extra-inning game
N.L.—47—Philadelphia 24, Chicago 23, May 17, 1979, 10 innings.
A.L.—Less than nine-inning record.

Most extra bases on long hits, doubleheader
A.L.—44—New York vs. Philadelphia, June 28, 1939.
N.L.—41—Milwaukee vs. Pittsburgh, August 30, 1953.

Most extra bases on long hits, two consecutive games
A.L.—51—Boston vs. St. Louis, June 7 (19), 8 (32), 1950.
N.L.—44—Milwaukee vs. Brooklyn, July 31 (27), August 1 (17), 1954.

Most extra bases on long hits, inning
N.L.—18—Philadelphia vs. Cincinnati, June 2, 1949, eighth inning.
A.L.—17—Boston vs. Philadelphia, September 24, 1940, first game, sixth inning.

RUNS BATTED IN

Most runs batted in, season
A.L.—995—New York, 155 games, 1936.
N.L.—942—St. Louis, 154 games, 1930.

Fewest runs batted in, season (since 1920)
N.L.—354—Philadelphia, 151 games, 1942.
A.L.—424—Texas, 154 games, 1972.

Most players with 100 or more runs batted in, season
A.L.—5—New York, 1936.
N.L.—4—Pittsburgh, 1925; Chicago, 1929; Philadelphia, 1929; Colorado, 1996, 1997, 1999; Arizona, 1999.

Most runs batted in, game
A.L.—29—Boston vs. St. Louis, June 8, 1950.
N.L.—26
New York vs. Brooklyn, April 30, 1944, first game.
Chicago vs. Colorado, August 18, 1995.

Most runs batted in by both clubs, nine-inning game
N.L.—43—Chicago 24, Philadelphia 19, August 25, 1922.
A.L.—35—Boston 21, Philadelphia 14, June 29, 1950.

Most runs batted in by both clubs, extra-inning game
N.L.—45—Philadelphia 23, Chicago 22, May 17, 1979, 10 innings.
A.L.—Less than nine-inning record.

Longest game without a run batted in by either club
N.L.—19 innings—Cincinnati 0, Brooklyn 0, September 11, 1946.
A.L.—18 innings
Washington 0, Detroit 0, July 16, 1909.
Washington 0, Chicago 0, May 15, 1918.

Most runs batted in, doubleheader
A.L.—34—Boston vs. Philadelphia, July 4, 1939.
N.L.—31—St. Louis vs. Philadelphia, July 6, 1929.

Most runs batted in by both clubs, doubleheader
A.L.—49—Boston 34, Philadelphia 15, July 4, 1939.
N.L.—45—St. Louis 31, Philadelphia 14, July 6, 1929.

Most runs batted in, two consecutive games
A.L.—49—Boston vs. St. Louis, June 7 (20), 8 (29), 1950.
N.L.—39—Pittsburgh, June 20 (19), June 22 (20), 1925.

Most runs batted in, inning
A.L.—17—Boston vs. Detroit, June 18, 1953, seventh inning.
N.L.—15
Chicago vs. Detroit, September 6, 1883, seventh inning.
Brooklyn vs. Cincinnati, May 21, 1952, first inning.

GAME-WINNING RBIs (1980-1988)

Most game-winning RBIs, season
N.L.—102—New York, 1986 (108 games won).
A.L.—99—Oakland, 1988 (104 games won).

Fewest game-winning RBIs, season
A.L.—48—Baltimore, 1988 (54 games won).
N.L.—51—Atlanta, 1988 (54 games won).

Most games won without game-winning RBIs, season
A.L.—12—Detroit, 1980 (84 games won).
N.L.—12—Houston, 1980 (93 games won).

Fewest games won without game-winning RBIs, season
A.L.—0—New York, 1982 (79 games won).
N.L.—1
Pittsburgh, 1985 (57 games won).
Chicago, 1987 (76 games won).

BASES ON BALLS

Most bases on balls, season
A.L.—835—Boston, 155 games, 1949.
N.L.—732—Brooklyn, 155 games, 1947.

Fewest bases on balls, season
N.L.—283—Philadelphia, 153 games, 1920.
A.L.—356—Philadelphia, 156 games, 1920.

Most bases on balls, nine-inning game
A.A.—19—Louisville vs. Cleveland, September 21, 1887.
A.L.—18
Detroit vs. Philadelphia, May 9, 1916.
Cleveland vs. Boston, May 20, 1948.
N.L.—17
Chicago vs. New York, May 30, 1887, a.m. game.
Brooklyn vs. Philadelphia, August 27, 1903.
New York vs. Brooklyn, April 30, 1944, first game.

Most bases on balls by both clubs, nine-inning game
A.L.—30—Detroit 18, Philadelphia 12, May 9, 1916.
N.L.—26—Houston 13, San Francisco 13, May 4, 1975, second game.

Most bases on balls, extra-inning game
A.L.—20—Boston vs. Detroit, September 17, 1920, 12 innings.
N.L.—16—Cincinnati vs. Atlanta, October 1, 1978, 14 innings.

Most bases on balls by both clubs, extra-inning game
A.L.—30—Washington 19, Cleveland 11, September 14, 1971, 20-inning suspended game; completed September 20.
N.L.—25
Chicago 15, Cincinnati 10, August 9, 1942, first game, 18 innings.
San Diego 13, Chicago 12, June 17, 1974, 13 innings.

Most bases on balls, nine-inning game being shut out
A.L.—11—St. Louis vs. New York, August 1, 1941.
N.L.—9—Cincinnati vs. St. Louis, September 1, 1958, first game.

Most bases on balls, extra-inning shutout game
N.L.—10—Chicago vs. Cincinnati, August 19, 1965, first game, 10 innings.
A.L.—Less than nine-inning record.

Longest game without a base on balls
N.L.—22 innings—Los Angeles vs. Montreal, August 23, 1989.
A.L.—20 innings—Philadelphia vs. Boston, July 4, 1905, p.m. game.

Longest game without a base on balls by either club
A.L.—13 innings
Washington 0, Detroit 0, July 22, 1904.
Boston 0, Philadelphia 0, September 9, 1907.
N.L.—12 innings—Chicago 0, Los Angeles 0, July 27, 1980.

Most bases on balls, doubleheader
N.L.—25—New York vs. Brooklyn, April 30, 1944.
A.L.—23—Cleveland vs. Philadelphia, June 18, 1950.

Most bases on balls by both clubs, doubleheader
N.L.—42—Houston 21, San Francisco 21, May 4, 1975.

A.L.—32

Baltimore 18, Chicago 14, May 28, 1954.
Detroit 20, Kansas City 12, August 1, 1962.

Fewest bases on balls by both clubs, doubleheader
N.L.—1

Cincinnati 1, Brooklyn 0, August 6, 1905.
Cincinnati 1, Pittsburgh 0, September 7, 1924.
Brooklyn 1, St. Louis 0, September 22, 1929.
A.L.—2

Philadelphia 2, Detroit 0, August 28, 1908, 20 innings.
Philadelphia 1, Chicago 1, July 12, 1912.
Cleveland 2, Chicago 0, September 6, 1930.

Longest doubleheader without a base on balls
N.L.—27 innings—St. Louis vs. New York, July 2, 1933.
A.L.—20 innings—Detroit vs. Philadelphia, August 28, 1908.

Most bases on balls, two consecutive games
A.L.—29—Detroit vs. Philadelphia, May 9, 10, 1916.
N.L.—25—New York vs. Brooklyn, April 30, 30, 1944.

Most bases on balls by both clubs, two consecutive games
A.L.—48—Detroit 29, Philadelphia 19, May 9, 10, 1916.

Most bases on balls, inning
A.L.—11—New York vs. Washington, September 11, 1949, first game, third inning.
N.L.—9—Cincinnati vs. Chicago, April 24, 1957, fifth inning.

Most consecutive bases on balls, inning
A.L.—7—Chicago vs. Washington, August 28, 1909, first game, second inning.
N.L.—7—Atlanta vs. Pittsburgh, May 25, 1983, third inning.

Most bases on balls by pinch-hitters, inning
N.L.—3

Pittsburgh vs. Philadelphia, June 3, 1911, ninth inning.
Brooklyn vs. New York, April 22, 1922, seventh inning.
Boston vs. Brooklyn, June 2, 1932, first game, ninth inning.
Chicago vs. Philadelphia, July 29, 1947, seventh inning.
Philadelphia vs. Pittsburgh, July 18, 1997, sixth inning.
A.L.—3

Baltimore vs. Washington, April 22, 1955, seventh inning.
Washington vs. Boston, May 14, 1961, second game, ninth inning (consecutive).

Most consecutive bases on balls by pinch-hitters, inning
N.L.—3

Brooklyn vs. New York, April 22, 1922, seventh inning.
Boston vs. Brooklyn, June 2, 1932, first game, ninth inning.
A.L.—3—Washington vs. Boston, May 14, 1961, second game, ninth inning.

Most players with two bases on balls, inning
A.L.—4—New York vs. Washington, September 11, 1949, first game, third inning.
N.L.—2—Made in many innings.

Most consecutive bases on balls at start of game
N.L.—5—New York vs. Cincinnati, June 16, 1941.
A.L.—4

Philadelphia vs. Boston, April 21, 1946.
Toronto vs. Texas, April 18, 1997.

INTENTIONAL (SINCE 1955)

Most intentional bases on balls, season
N.L.—102—Pittsburgh, 163 games, 1979.
A.L.—79—Minnesota, 162 games, 1965.

Fewest intentional bases on balls, season
A.L.—10—Kansas City, 162 games, 1961.
N.L.—22

Los Angeles, 154 games, 1958.
Pittsburgh, 163 games, 1998.

Most intentional bases on balls, nine-inning game
N.L.—6—San Francisco vs. St. Louis, July 19, 1975.
A.L.—5

California vs. New York, May 10, 1967.
Washington vs. Cleveland, September 2, 1970.
Oakland vs. Cleveland, July 16, 1991.

Most intentional bases on balls, extra-inning game
N.L.—7

New York vs. Chicago, May 2, 1956, 17 innings.
Houston vs. Philadelphia, July 15, 1984, 16 innings.
Chicago vs. Cincinnati, May 22, 1990, 16 innings.
A.L.—5

Chicago vs. Washington, June 29, 1958, second game, 11 innings.
Minnesota vs. Milwaukee, May 12, 1972, 22-inning suspended game; completed May 13.
New York vs. California, August 29, 1978, 11 innings.

Most intentional bases on balls by both clubs, nine-inning game
A.L.—6—California 5, New York 1, May 10, 1967.
N.L.—6—San Francisco 6, St. Louis 0, July 19, 1975.

Most intentional bases on balls by both clubs, extra-inning game
N.L.—11—New York 7, Chicago 4, May 2, 1956, 17 innings.
A.L.—7

Minnesota 5, Milwaukee 2, May 12, 1972, 22-inning suspended game; completed May 13.
New York 4, Baltimore 3, May 1, 1996, 15 innings.

Most intentional bases on balls, inning
N.L.-A.L.—3—Made in many innings.

STRIKEOUTS

Most strikeouts, season
N.L.—1,399—Milwaukee, 162 games, 2001.
A.L.—1,268—Detroit, 162 games, 1996.

Fewest strikeouts, season
N.L.—308—Cincinnati, 153 games, 1921.
A.L.—326—Philadelphia, 155 games, 1927.

Most strikeouts, nine-inning game
A.L.—20

Seattle vs. Boston, April 29, 1986.
Detroit vs. Boston, September 18, 1996.
N.L.—20—Houston vs. Chicago, May 6, 1998.
U.A.—19—Boston vs. Chicago, July 7, 1884.

Most strikeouts by both clubs, nine-inning game
A.L.—31—Texas 18, Seattle 13, July 13, 1997.
U.A.—29

Boston 19, Chicago 10, July 7, 1884.
St. Louis 18, Boston 11, July 19, 1884.
N.L.—29—Boston 19, Providence 10, June 7, 1884.
N.L. since 1900—28—Cincinnati 15, San Diego 13, September 15, 1972.

Most strikeouts, extra-inning game
A.L.—26—California vs. Oakland, July 9, 1971, 20 innings.
N.L.—22

New York vs. San Francisco, May 31, 1964, second game, 23 innings.
Cincinnati vs. Los Angeles, August 8, 1972, 19 innings.

Most strikeouts by both clubs, extra-inning game
A.L.—43—California 26, Oakland 17, July 9, 1971, 20 innings.
N.L.—40—San Francisco 20, San Diego 20, June 19, 2001, 15 innings.

Most strikeouts by pinch-hitters, nine-inning game
A.L.—5—Detroit vs. New York, September 8, 1979.
N.L.—4

Brooklyn vs. Philadelphia, April 27, 1950.
Philadelphia vs. Milwaukee, September 16, 1960.
Chicago vs. New York, September 21, 1962.
Chicago vs. New York, May 3, 1969.
Cincinnati vs. Houston, September 27, 1969.
Montreal vs. Philadelphia, June 24, 1972.

Most strikeouts by pinch-hitters from both clubs, nine-inning game
A.L.—5

New York 4, Boston 1, July 4, 1955, first game.
Washington 4, Cleveland 1, May 1, 1957.
Detroit 4, Cleveland 1, August 4, 1967.
Detroit 5, New York 0, September 8, 1979.

N.L.—4—Made in many games. Last time—Montreal 4, Philadelphia 0, June 24, 1972.

Most consecutive strikeouts, game

N.L.—10—San Diego vs. New York, April 22, 1970; 1 in sixth inning, 3 in seventh, eighth and ninth innings.

A.L.—8

Boston vs. California, July 9, 1972; 2 in first inning, 3 in second and third innings.

Milwaukee vs. California, August 7, 1973; 1 in first inning, 3 in second and third innings, 1 in fourth inning.

Seattle vs. Boston, April 29, 1986; 3 in fourth and fifth innings, 2 in sixth inning.

Most consecutive strikeouts at start of game

N.L.—9—Cleveland vs. New York, August 28, 1884.

N.L. since 1900—8—Los Angeles vs. Houston, September 23, 1986.

A.L.—7—Texas vs. Chicago, May 28, 1986.

Longest extra-inning game without a strikeout

N.L.—17

New York vs. Cincinnati, June 26, 1893.

Cincinnati vs. New York, August 27, 1920, first game.

A.L.—16—Cleveland vs. New York, June 7, 1936.

Longest extra-inning game without a strikeout, both clubs

A.L.—12—Chicago 0, St. Louis 0, July 7, 1931.

N.L.—10—Boston 0, New York 0, April 19, 1928.

Most strikeouts, inning (*consecutive)

A.A.—4—Pittsburgh vs. Philadelphia, September 30, 1885, seventh inning.

N.L.—4

Chicago vs. New York, October 4, 1888, fifth inning.*

Cincinnati vs. New York, May 15, 1906, fifth inning.*

St. Louis vs. Chicago, May 27, 1956, first game, sixth inning.*

Milwaukee vs. Cincinnati, August 11, 1959, first game, sixth inning.

Cincinnati vs. Los Angeles, April 12, 1962, third inning.*

Philadelphia vs. Los Angeles, April 17, 1965, second inning.*

Pittsburgh vs. St. Louis, June 7, 1966, fourth inning.

Montreal vs. Chicago, July 31, 1974, first game, second inning.*

Pittsburgh vs. Atlanta, July 29, 1977, sixth inning.

Chicago vs. Cincinnati, May 17, 1984, third inning.*

Chicago vs. Houston, September 3, 1986, fifth inning.

St. Louis vs. Atlanta, August 22, 1989, fifth inning.

San Francisco vs. Cincinnati, June 4, 1990, seventh inning.

Chicago vs. Atlanta, June 7, 1995, ninth inning.

San Diego vs. Colorado, September 19, 1995, sixth inning.

Chicago vs. Colorado, July 25, 1996, ninth inning.

Atlanta vs. New York, September 13, 1996, ninth inning.

Montreal vs. Florida, September 16, 1998, fourth inning.*

Chicago vs. Florida, April 28, 1999, seventh inning.

San Diego vs. San Francisco, July 22, 1999, seventh inning.

San Francisco vs. Montreal, August 17, 1999, seventh inning.*

Milwaukee vs. Montreal, May 5, 2000, ninth inning.

Florida vs. Cincinnati, July 22, 2001, seventh inning.

A.L.—4

Boston vs. Washington, April 15, 1911, fifth inning.

Philadelphia vs. Cleveland, June 11, 1916, sixth inning.*

Chicago vs. Los Angeles, May 18, 1961, seventh inning.

Washington vs. Cleveland, September 2, 1964, seventh inning.

California vs. Baltimore, May 29, 1970, fourth inning.*

Seattle vs. Cleveland, July 21, 1978, fifth inning.*

Baltimore vs. Texas, August 2, 1987, second inning.*

New York vs. Texas, July 4, 1988, first inning.

Boston vs. Seattle, September 9, 1990, first inning.

Detroit vs. Cleveland, May 14, 1994, ninth inning.

Toronto vs. Kansas City, September 3, 1996, fourth inning.

Detroit vs. Chicago, July 21, 1997, seventh inning.*

Tampa Bay vs. Oakland, July 27, 1998, fourth inning.

New York vs. Anaheim, May 12, 1999, third inning.

Kansas City vs. Boston, August 10, 1999, ninth inning.

Detroit vs. Anaheim, August 15, 1999, first inning.*

Texas vs. Cleveland, April 16, 2000, third inning.*

Texas vs. Oakland, June 30, 2001, seventh inning.

Most strikeouts by pinch-hitters, inning (*consecutive)

A.L.—3

Philadelphia vs. Washington, September 3, 1910, eighth inning.*

Chicago vs. Boston, June 5, 1911, ninth inning.*

Detroit vs. Cleveland, September 19, 1945, eighth inning.*

Philadelphia vs. Cleveland, September 9, 1952, ninth inning.*

Cleveland vs. New York, May 12, 1953, eighth inning.*

New York vs. Philadelphia, September 24, 1954, ninth inning.*

Detroit vs. Cleveland, August 4, 1967, eighth inning.

California vs. Minnesota, May 17, 1971, ninth inning.*

Cleveland vs. Detroit, June 25, 1975, ninth inning.

Detroit vs. New York, September 8, 1979, ninth inning.

N.L.—3

Pittsburgh vs. Cincinnati, June 5, 1953, ninth inning.*

Cincinnati vs. Brooklyn, August 8, 1953, ninth inning.

St. Louis vs. Cincinnati, May 10, 1961, ninth inning.

Cincinnati vs. Houston, June 2, 1966, eighth inning.*

Atlanta vs. Houston, June 18, 1967, eighth inning.*

Cincinnati vs. Houston, September 27, 1969, eighth inning.

St. Louis vs. Montreal, July 4, 1970, eighth inning.

Philadelphia vs. Pittsburgh, July 6, 1970, ninth inning.

Most strikeouts, doubleheader (18 innings)

N.L.—26

Philadelphia vs. New York, September 9, 1970.

San Diego vs. New York, May 29, 1971.

San Francisco vs. Houston, September 5, 1971.

A.L.—25—Los Angeles vs. Cleveland, July 31, 1963.

Most strikeouts, doubleheader (more than 18 innings)

N.L.—31

Pittsburgh vs. Philadelphia, September 22, 1958, 23 innings.

New York vs. Philadelphia, October 2, 1965, 27 innings.

A.L.—27—Cleveland vs. Boston, August 25, 1963, 24 innings.

Most strikeouts by both clubs, doubleheader (18 innings)

N.L.—41

Philadelphia 26, New York 15, September 9, 1970.

San Diego 26, New York 15, May 29, 1971.

Chicago 21, New York 20, September 15, 1971.

A.L.—40—Cleveland 23, Los Angeles 17, September 29, 1962.

Most strikeouts by both clubs, doubleheader (more than 18 innings)

N.L.—51—New York 30, Philadelphia 21, September 26, 1975, 24 innings.

A.L.—48—Detroit 24, Kansas City 24, June 17, 1967, 28 innings.

Longest doubleheader without a strikeout

N.L.—21—Pittsburgh vs. Philadelphia, July 12, 1924.

A.L.—20—Boston vs. St. Louis, July 28, 1917.

Fewest strikeouts by both clubs, doubleheader

A.L.—1—Cleveland 1, Boston 0, August 28, 1926.

N.L.—2

Brooklyn 2, New York 0, August 13, 1932.

Pittsburgh 2, St. Louis 0, September 6, 1948.

Most strikeouts, two consecutive nine-inning games

A.L.—36—Seattle vs. Boston, April 29 (20), April 30 (16), 1986.

N.L.—29—San Diego vs. New York, April 21 (10), April 22 (19), 1970.

Most strikeouts, two consecutive games (more than 18 innings)

N.L.—31

Pittsburgh vs. Philadelphia, September 22, first game, 14 innings (21); September 22, second game, nine innings (10), 1958, 23 innings.

New York vs. Philadelphia, October 2, first game, nine innings (10), October 2, second game, 18 innings (21), 1965, 27 innings.

A.L.—Less than nine-inning record.

SACRIFICE HITS

Most sacrifice hits, season (includes sacrifice scoring flies)

A.L.—310—Boston, 157 games, 1917.

N.L.—270—Chicago, 158 games, 1908.

Most sacrifice hits, season (no sacrifice flies)

N.L.—231—Chicago, 154 games, 1906.

A.L.—207—Chicago, 154 games, 1906.

Fewest sacrifice hits, season (no sacrifice flies)
A.L.—16
  Detroit, 162 games, 1998.
  New York, 162 games, 2000.
N.L.—29—San Diego, 162 games, 2001.

Most sacrifices, game (includes sacrifice flies)
A.L.—8
  New York vs. Boston, May 4, 1918 (two sacrifice scoring flies).
  Chicago vs. Detroit, July 11, 1927.
  St. Louis vs. Cleveland, July 23, 1928.
  Texas vs. Chicago, August 1, 1977.
N.L.—8—Cincinnati vs. Philadelphia, May 6, 1926.

Most sacrifices by both clubs, game (includes sacrifice flies)
A.L.—11—Washington 7, Boston 4, September 1, 1926.
N.L.—9
  New York 5, Chicago 4, August 29, 1921.
  Cincinnati 8, Philadelphia 1, May 6, 1926.
  San Francisco 6, San Diego 3, May 23, 1970, 15 innings (no sacrifice flies in game).

Longest extra-inning game without a sacrifice
A.L.—24 innings—Detroit vs. Philadelphia, July 21, 1945.
N.L.—23 innings—Brooklyn vs. Boston, June 27, 1939.

Longest extra-inning game without a sacrifice by either club
N.L.—19 innings—Philadelphia 0, Cincinnati 0, September 15, 1950, second game.
A.L.—18 innings—Washington 0, St. Louis 0, June 20, 1952.

Most sacrifices, doubleheader (includes sacrifice flies)
A.L.—10—Detroit vs. Chicago, July 7, 1921.
N.L.—9—Held by many clubs.

Most sacrifices by both clubs, doubleheader (includes sacrifice flies)
A.L.—13—Boston 9, Chicago 4, July 17, 1926.

Fewest sacrifices, doubleheader
N.L.-A.L.—0—Made in many doubleheaders.

Longest doubleheader without a sacrifice by either club
N.L.—28 innings—Cincinnati 0, Philadelphia 0, September 15, 1950.
A.L.—18 innings—Made in many doubleheaders.

Most sacrifice hits, inning (no sacrifice flies)
A.L.—3
  Cleveland vs. St. Louis, July 10, 1949, fifth inning.
  Detroit vs. Baltimore, July 12, 1970, first game, second inning (consecutive).
  Oakland vs. Kansas City, June 26, 1977, first game, fifth inning.
  Cleveland vs. Chicago, June 8, 1980, sixth inning (consecutive).
  Seattle vs. California, April 29, 1984, sixth inning.
N.L.—3
  Chicago vs. Milwaukee, August 26, 1962, sixth inning (consecutive).
  Philadelphia vs. Los Angeles, September 23, 1967, seventh inning (consecutive).
  Los Angeles vs. San Francisco, May 23, 1972, sixth inning.
  Houston vs. San Diego, April 29, 1975, seventh inning.
  Houston vs. Atlanta, July 6, 1975, ninth inning.

SACRIFICE FLIES

Most run-scoring sacrifice flies, season
A.L.—77—Oakland, 162 games, 1984.
N.L.—75—Colorado, 162 games, 2000.

Fewest sacrifice flies, season
N.L.—19—San Diego, 161 games, 1971.
A.L.—23—California, 161 games, 1967.

Most run-scoring sacrifice flies, game
A.L.—5—Seattle vs. Oakland, August 7, 1988.
N.L.—4
  New York vs. San Francisco, July 26, 1967.
  New York vs. Philadelphia, September 23, 1972.
  St. Louis vs. Cincinnati, September 2, 1980.
  Cincinnati vs. Houston, May 5, 1982.
  San Francisco vs. New York, August 29, 1987.

  Pittsburgh vs. Philadelphia, September 9, 1988.
  San Francisco vs. San Diego, September 14, 1988.
  Montreal vs. Florida, May 24, 1994.
  Houston vs. Pittsburgh, May 9, 1995.
  Houston vs. Philadelphia, September 8, 1995.
  San Diego vs. Colorado, July 3, 2001.

Most run-scoring sacrifice flies by both clubs, game
A.L.—5
  Boston 3, Washington 2, August 31, 1965, second game.
  Oakland 3, Texas 2, June 29, 1979.
  Cleveland 4, Seattle 1, June 1, 1980.
  Cleveland 4, Texas 1, August 13, 1980.
  Seattle 5, Oakland 0, August 7, 1988.
  Toronto 4, Chicago 1, August 14, 1990.
  New York 3, Milwaukee 2, August 1, 1994.
  Boston 3, Kansas City 2, August 27, 2000.
N.L.—5
  St. Louis 4, Cincinnati 1, September 2, 1980.
  Los Angeles 3, San Francisco 2, April 15, 1984, 11 innings.
  San Francisco 3, Atlanta 2, June 28, 1988.
  San Francisco 4, San Diego 1, September 14, 1988.
  San Francisco 3, Colorado 2, October 1, 1995.
  Cincinnati 3, Pittsburgh 2, April 29, 2000.

Most run-scoring sacrifice flies, inning
A.L.—3
  Chicago vs. Cleveland, July 1, 1962, second game, fifth inning.
  New York vs. Detroit, June 29, 2000, fourth inning.
  New York vs. Anaheim, August 19, 2000, third inning.
N.L.—2—Made in many innings.

HIT BY PITCH

Most hit by pitch, season
N.L.—148—Baltimore, 154 games, 1898.
N.L. since 1900—100—Houston, 162 games, 1997.
A.L.—92—Toronto, 162 games, 1996.

Fewest hit by pitch, season
A.L.—5—Philadelphia, 154 games, 1937.
N.L.—9
  Philadelphia, 152 games, 1939.
  San Diego, 162 games, 1969.

Most hit by pitch, nine-inning game
A.A.—6—Brooklyn vs. Baltimore, April 25, 1887.
A.L.—6—New York vs. Washington, June 20, 1913, second game.
N.L.—6—Louisville vs. St. Louis, July 31, 1897, first game.
N.L. since 1900—5—Atlanta vs. Cincinnati, July 2, 1969.

Most hit by pitch, extra-inning game
N.L.—6—New York vs. Chicago, June 16, 1893, 11 innings.

Most hit by pitch by both clubs, nine-inning game
N.L.—8
  Washington 5, Pittsburgh 3, May 9, 1896.
  Louisville 6, St. Louis 2, July 31, 1897, first game.
N.L. since 1900—6—Brooklyn 4, New York 2, July 17, 1900.
A.L.—7
  Detroit 4, Washington 3, August 24, 1914, second game.
  Minnesota 4, Kansas City 3, April 13, 1971.
  Kansas City 5, Texas 2, September 3, 1989.

Most hit by pitch, inning
N.L.—4—Boston vs. Pittsburgh, August 19, 1893, first game, second inning.
N.L. since 1900—3
  New York vs. Pittsburgh, September 25, 1905, first inning.
  Chicago vs. Boston, September 17, 1928, ninth inning.
  Philadelphia vs. Cincinnati, May 15, 1960, first game, eighth inning.
  Atlanta vs. Cincinnati, July 2, 1969, second inning.
  Cincinnati vs. Pittsburgh, May 1, 1974, first inning, consecutive.
  St. Louis vs. Montreal, August 15, 1992, first inning.
  Houston vs. Los Angeles, September 13, 1997, first inning.
  Florida vs. Houston, August 3, 1999, eighth inning.

A.L.—3
  New York vs. Washington, June 20, 1913, second game, first inning.
  Cleveland vs. New York, August 25, 1921, eighth inning.
  Boston vs. New York, June 30, 1954, third inning.
  Baltimore vs. California, August 9, 1968, seventh inning.
  California vs. Chicago, September 10, 1977, first inning, consecutive.
  California vs. Cleveland, July 8, 1988, fourth inning.
  Oakland vs. Minnesota, September 28, 1988, second inning.

GROUNDING INTO DOUBLE PLAYS

Most grounding into double plays, season
A.L.—174—Boston, 162 games, 1990.
N.L.—166—St. Louis, 154 games, 1958.

Fewest grounding into double plays, season
N.L.—75—St. Louis, 155 games, 1945.
A.L.—79—Kansas City, 161 games, 1967.

Most grounding into double plays, game
N.L.—7—San Francisco vs. Houston, May 4, 1969.
A.L.—6
  Washington vs. Cleveland, August 5, 1948.
  Boston vs. California, May 1, 1966, first game.
  Baltimore vs. Kansas City, May 6, 1972.
  Cleveland vs. New York, April 29, 1975.
  Toronto vs. Minnesota, August 29, 1977, first game, 10 innings.
  Milwaukee vs. Chicago, May 8, finished May 9, 1984, 25 innings.
  Boston vs. Minnesota, July 18, 1990.

Most grounding into double plays by both clubs, nine-inning game
A.L.—9
  Boston 6, California 3, May 1, 1966, first game.
  Boston 6, Minnesota 3, July 18, 1990.
N.L.—8—Boston 5, Chicago 3, September 18, 1928.

Most grounding into double plays by both clubs, extra-inning game
N.L.—9—Los Angeles 5, New York 4, May 24, 1973, 19 innings.
A.L.—Less than nine-inning record.

REACHING BASE ON ERRORS

Most times reaching first base on error, game
N.L.—10—Chicago vs. Cleveland, July 24, 1882.
A.L.—8—Detroit vs. Chicago, May 6, 1903.

Most times reaching first base on error by both clubs, game
N.L.—16—Chicago 10, Cleveland 6, July 24, 1882.
A.L.—12—Detroit 8, Chicago 4, May 6, 1903.

Most times reaching first base on error, inning
N.L.—4—St. Louis vs. Pittsburgh, August 5, 1901, eighth inning.
A.L.—4—St. Louis vs. Boston, June 8, 1911, fourth inning.

LEAGUE BATTING

GAMES

Most games, season (since 1900)
N.L. (16-club league)—1,298 in 1998 (includes interleague games).
N.L. (14-club league)—1,135 in 1993.
N.L. (12-club league)—974 in 1983.
N.L. (10-club league)—813 in 1965, 1968.
N.L. (8-club league)—625 in 1914, 1917.
A.L. (14-club league)—1,135 in 1982, 1983.
A.L. (12-club league)—973 in 1969, 1970, 1974.
A.L. (10-club league)—814 in 1964.
A.L. (8-club league)—631 in 1914.

Fewest games, season (since 1900, except 1918)
A.L.—608 in 1933.
N.L.—608 in 1934.

Most times two games in one day, season
A.L.—153 in 1943.
N.L.—146 in 1943.

BATTING AVERAGE

Highest batting average, season (since 1900)
N.L.—.303 in 1930.
A.L.—.29244 in 1921.

Lowest batting average, season (since 1900)
A.L.—.23011 in 1968.
N.L.—.23895 in 1908.

Most .400 batsmen, season (qualifiers for batting championship)
N.L.—3 in 1894.
A.L.—2 in 1911, 1922.
N.L. since 1900—1 in 1922, 1924, 1925, 1930.

Most clubs batting .300 or over, season (since 1900)
N.L.—6 in 1930.
A.L.—4 in 1921.

Most .300 batsmen, season (qualifiers for batting championship)
N.L.—33 in 1930.
A.L.—26 in 1924.

Fewest .300 batsmen, season (qualifiers for batting title)
A.L.—1 in 1968.
N.L.—4 in 1907.

SLUGGING AVERAGE

Highest slugging average, season (since 1900)
N.L.—.448 in 1930.
A.L.—.445 in 1996.

Lowest slugging average, season (since 1900)
N.L.—.306 in 1908.
A.L.—.312 in 1910.

AT-BATS

Most at-bats, season (since 1900)
N.L. (16-club league)—89,011 in 1999.
N.L. (14-club league)—77,711 in 1996.
N.L. (12-club league)—66,700 in 1977.
N.L. (10-club league)—55,449 in 1962.
N.L. (8-club league)—43,891 in 1936.
A.L. (14-club league)—79,090 in 1996.
A.L. (12-club league)—66,276 in 1973.
A.L. (10-club league)—55,239 in 1962.
A.L. (8-club league)—43,747 in 1930.

Most players with 600 or more at-bats, season (since 1900)
A.L.—22 in 1998.
N.L.—19 in 1962.

RUNS

Most runs, season (since 1900)
N.L. (16-club league)—12,976 in 2000.
N.L. (14-club league)—10,623 in 1996.
N.L. (12-club league)—8,771 in 1970, 1987.
N.L. (10-club league)—7,278 in 1962.
N.L. (8-club league)—7,025 in 1930.
A.L. (14-club league)—12,208 in 1996.
A.L. (12-club league)—8,314 in 1973.
A.L. (10-club league)—7,342 in 1961.
A.L. (8-club league)—7,009 in 1936.

Fewest runs, season (since 1900)
N.L.—4,136 in 1908.
A.L.—4,272 in 1909.

Most players with 100 or more runs, season (since 1900)
N.L.—31 in 1999.
A.L.—29 in 1999.

Most runs in league, one day
N.L.—159—August 7, 1894.
A.L.—128—May 30, 1932.
N.L. since 1900—123—August 18, 1995.

Most runs by both leagues, one day
221 on July 3, 1999; 111 in N.L. (9 games); 110 in A.L. (8 games).

Most players scoring five or more runs in a game, season (since 1900)
N.L.—7 in 1930.
A.L.—5 in 1939.

Most games with 20 or more runs, league
N.L.—1876 to date—263.
N.L. since 1900 to date—99.
A.L.—1901 to date—107.

Most games with 20 or more runs, season
N.L.—32 in 1894.
N.L. since 1900—5 in 1900, 1925.
A.L.—5 in 1923, 1999, 2000.

Most innings with 10 or more runs, season
N.L.—12 in 1894.
N.L. since 1900—6 in 1922.
A.L.—7 in 1999.

HITS

Most hits, season (since 1900)
N.L. (16-club league)—23,880 in 1999.
N.L. (14-club league)—20,427 in 1993.
N.L. (12-club league)—17,465 in 1977.
N.L. (10-club league)—14,453 in 1962.
N.L. (8-club league)—13,260 in 1930.
A.L. (14-club league)—21,922 in 1996.
A.L. (12-club league)—17,193 in 1973.
A.L. (10-club league)—14,068 in 1962.
A.L. (8-club league)—12,657 in 1962.

Fewest hits, season (since 1900)
N.L.—9,566 in 1907.
A.L.—9,719 in 1908.

Most players with 200 or more hits, season
N.L.—12 in 1929 and 1930.
A.L.—9 in 1936 and 1937.

Most players with five or more hits in a game, season (since 1900)
N.L.—27 in 1930.
A.L.—22 in 1936.

Fewest players with five or more hits in a game, season (since 1900)
N.L.—1 in 1914.
A.L.—2 in 1913, 1914, 1963.

Most hits in league, one day
A.L.—190, July 10, 1932.
N.L.—183, July 21, 1963.

Most hits by both leagues, one day
347 on July 3, 1999; 177 in N.L. (9 games); 170 in A.L. (8 games).

SINGLES

Most singles, season (since 1900)
N.L. (16-club league)—15,856 in 1999.
N.L. (14-club league)—14,370 in 1993.
N.L. (12-club league)—12,564 in 1980.
N.L. (10-club league)—10,476 in 1922.
N.L. (8-club league)—9,476 in 1962.
A.L. (14-club league)—15,072 in 1980.
A.L. (12-club league)—12,729 in 1974.
A.L. (10-club league)—9,878 in 1962.
A.L. (8-club league)—9,214 in 1921.

Fewest singles, season (since 1900)
N.L.—7,466 in 1956.
A.L.—7,573 in 1959.

DOUBLES

Most doubles, season (since 1900)
N.L. (16-club league)—4,632 in 2000.
N.L. (14-club league)—3,907 in 1997.
N.L. (12-club league)—3,126 in 1987.
N.L. (8-club league)—2,386 in 1930.
A.L. (14-club league)—4,269 in 2000.
A.L. (12-club league)—2,624 in 1973.
A.L. (8-club league)—2,400 in 1936.

Fewest doubles, season (since 1900)
N.L.—1,148 in 1907.
A.L.—1,348 in 1910.

Most players with 40 or more doubles, season (since 1900)
A.L.—15 in 2000.
N.L.—12 in 1920.

TRIPLES

Most triples, season (since 1900)
A.L.—694 in 1921.
N.L.—685 in 1912.

Fewest triples, season (since 1900)
A.L.—267 in 1959.
N.L.—323 in 1942.

Most players with 20 or more triples (since 1900)
A.L.—4 in 1912.
N.L.—3 in 1911, 1912.

HOME RUNS
SEASON

Most home runs, season
N.L. (16-club league)—3,005 in 2000.
N.L. (14-club league)—2,220 in 1996.
N.L. (12-club league)—1,824 in 1987.
N.L. (10-club league)—1,449 in 1962.
N.L. (8-club league)—1,263 in 1955.
A.L. (14-club league)—2,742 in 1996.
A.L. (12-club league)—1,746 in 1970.
A.L. (10-club league)—1,552 in 1962.
A.L. (8-club league)—1,091 in 1959.

Most home runs by both leagues, season
5,693 in 2000 (16-club N.L., 14-club A.L.)—3,005 in N.L., 2,688 in A.L.
4,962 in 1996 (14-club leagues)—2,742 in A.L., 2,220 in N.L.

4,458 in 1987 (14-club A.L., 12-club N.L.)—2,634 in A.L., 1,824 in N.L.
3,429 in 1970 (12-club leagues)—1,746 in A.L., 1,683 in N.L.
3,001 in 1962 (10-club leagues)—1,552 in A.L., 1,449 in N.L.

Fewest home runs, season (since 1900)
A.L.—101 in 1907.
N.L.—126 in 1906.

Most home runs by pinch-hitters, season
N.L. (16-club league)—95 in 2001.
N.L. (14-club league)—75 in 1995.
N.L. (12-club league)—57 in 1986.
N.L. (10-club league)—45 in 1962.
N.L. (8-club league)—42 in 1958.
A.L. (14-club league)—53 in 1980.
A.L. (10-club league)—50 in 1961.
A.L. (8-club league)—29 in 1953.

Most home runs by pinch-hitters in both leagues, season
131 in 2001 (16-club N.L., 14-club A.L.)—95 in N.L., 36 in A.L.
117 in 1996 (14-club leagues)—74 in N.L., 43 in A.L.
95 in 1970 (12-club leagues)—49 in A.L., 46 in N.L.
84 in 1962 (10-club leagues)—45 in N.L., 39 in A.L.

Most clubs with 100 or more home runs, season
N.L. (16-club league)—16 in 1998 through 2001.
N.L. (14-club league)—14 in 1996, 1997.
N.L. (12-club league)—11 in 1970, 1986, 1987.
N.L. (10-club league)—10 in 1962.
N.L. (8-club league)—8 in 1956, 1958, 1959, 1961.
A.L. (14-club league)—14 in 1977, 1982, 1985 through 1988, 1990, 1993, 1995 through 2001.
A.L. (12-club league)—11 in 1970, 1973.
A.L. (10-club league)—10 in 1964.
A.L. (8-club league)—8 in 1958, 1960.

Most players with 50 or more home runs, season
N.L.—3 in 1998, 2001.
A.L.—2 in 1938, 1961, 1996.

Most players with 40 or more home runs, season
N.L. (16-club league)—9 in 2000.
N.L. (14-club league)—8 in 1996.
N.L. (8-club league)—6 in 1954, 1955.
A.L. (14-club league)—8 in 1996, 1998.
A.L. (10-club league)—6 in 1961.
A.L. (8-club league)—3 in 1936.

Most players with 30 or more home runs, season
N.L. (16-club league)—25 in 2001.
N.L. (14-club league)—21 in 1996.
N.L. (12-club league)—12 in 1970.
N.L. (10-club league)—10 in 1965.
A.L. (14-club league)—23 in 2000.
A.L. (12-club league)—10 in 1969.
A.L. (10-club league)—9 in 1964.

Most players with 20 or more home runs, season
N.L. (16-club league)—54 in 1999.
N.L. (14-club league)—36 in 1997.
N.L. (12-club league)—29 in 1970.
N.L. (10-club league)—25 in 1962.
N.L. (8-club league)—23 in 1956.
A.L. (14-club league)—51 in 1987.
A.L. (12-club league)—25 in 1970.
A.L. (10-club league)—25 in 1964.
A.L. (8-club league)—18 in 1959.

Most players hitting home runs in all parks, season (eight-club league)
N.L.—11 in 1956 (8 parks, excluding Jersey City; 5 of 11 connected there).
A.L.—7 in 1953 (8 parks).

Most players hitting home runs in all parks, season (10-club league)
A.L.—4 in 1962.
N.L.—3 in 1963.

Most players hitting home runs in all parks, season (12-club league)
N.L.—3 in 1970.
A.L.—1 in 1975.

ONE DAY

Most players with two or more home runs in a game, season
N.L. (16-club league)—201 in 1999.
N.L. (14-club league)—137 in 1996.
N.L. (12-club league)—110 in 1987.
N.L. (8-club league)—84 in 1955.
A.L. (14-club league)—180 in 1996.
A.L. (10-club-league)—98 in 1964.
A.L. (8-club league)—62 in 1960.

Fewest players with two or more home runs in a game, season
N.L.—0 in 1907, 1918.
A.L.—0 in 1908, 1915.

Most players with two or more home runs in a game, one day
A.L. (14-club league)—6—August 2, 1983; May 8, 1987.
A.L. (10-club league)—5—June 11, 1961; May 20, 1962.
A.L. (8-club league)—4—April 30, 1933; May 30, 1956.
N.L. (16-club league)—6—July 31, 1999.
N.L. (14-club league)—5—July 14, 1996.
N.L. (12-club league)—5—May 8, 1970.
N.L. (10-club league)—5—June 5, 1966.
N.L. (8-club league)—5—August 16, 1947.

Most players with two home runs in a game both leagues, one day
8 on May 19, 1999; 5 in A.L., 3 in N.L.

Most players with three or more home runs in a game, season
N.L.—16 in 2001.
A.L.—11 in 1996.

Most players from both leagues with three homers in a game, season
22 in 2001; 16 in N.L., 6 in A.L.

Most times with five or more home runs in a game, season (club)
N.L. (16-club league)—30 in 1999.
N.L. (8-club league)—15 in 1954.
A.L. (14-club league)—27 in 1999.
A.L. (12-club league)—8 in 1969.
A.L. (8-club league)—8 in 1950.

Most times with three or more home runs in an inning, season (club)
A.L. (14-club league)—24 in 2000.
A.L. (10-club league)—10 in 1961, 1962.
A.L. (8-club league)—5 in 1936, 1947, 1953, 1954, 1956, 1957, 1959.
N.L. (16-club league)—21 in 2000.
N.L. (14-club league)—18 in 1996.
N.L. (8-club league)—13 in 1954, 1955.

Most home runs by pitchers, one day
A.L.—4—July 31, 1935.
N.L.—3—June 3, 1892; May 13, 1942; July 2, 1961; June 23, 1971.

Most home runs by pinch-hitters, one day
N.L.—4—June 2, 1928; July 21, 1930.
A.L.—4—June 28, 1987.

Most home runs in league, one day
A.L.—36—April 7, 2000 (7 games).
N.L.—34—May 21, 2000 (8 games).

Most home runs by both leagues, one day
57—April 7, 2000; 36 in A.L. (7 games), 21 in N.L. (8 games).

GRAND SLAMS

Most grand slams, season
A.L. (14-club league)—89 in 2000.
A.L. (10-club league)—48 in 1961.
A.L. (8-club league)—37 in 1938.
N.L. (16-club league)—87 in 2000.
N.L. (14-club league)—60 in 1996.
N.L. (12-club league)—49 in 1970.
N.L. (10-club league)—37 in 1962.
N.L. (8-club league)—35 in 1950.

Most grand slams by both leagues, season
176 in 2000 (16-club N.L., 14-club A.L.)—89 in A.L.; 87 in N.L.
141 in 1996 (14-club leagues)—81 in A.L.; 60 in N.L.
88 in 1970 (12-club leagues)—49 in N.L.; 39 in A.L.
77 in 1961 (10-club A.L., 8-club N.L.)—48 in A.L.; 29 in N.L.

Fewest grand slams, season
A.L.—0 in 1918 (Short season because of war).
N.L.—1 in 1920.
A.L.—1 in 1907, 1909, 1915.

Fewest grand slams by both leagues, season
3—1907 (2 in N.L., 1 in A.L.).

Most grand slams by pinch-hitters, season
A.L. (14-club league)—5 in 1982, 1988.
A.L. (10-club league)—7 in 1961.
A.L. (8-club league)—5 in 1953.
N.L. (12-club league)—9 in 1978.
N.L. (8-club league)—4 in 1959.

Most grand slams by pinch-hitters in both leagues, season
(14-club A.L.; 12-club N.L.)—13 in 1978 (9 in N.L.; 4 in A.L.).
(12-club leagues)—9 in 1973 (6 in N.L.; 3 in A.L.).
(8-club leagues)—8 in 1953 (5 in A.L.; 3 in N.L.).

Most grand slams, one day
N.L.—4—May 21, 2000.
A.L.—4—July 22, 2000.

Most grand slams by both leagues, one day
6—May 21, 2000 (4 in N.L., 2 in A.L.).

TOTAL BASES

Most total bases, season (since 1900)
N.L. (16-club league)—38,305 in 2000.
N.L. (14-club league)—31,708 in 1996.
N.L. (12-club league)—26,743 in 1987.
N.L. (10-club league)—21,781 in 1962.
N.L. (8-club league)—19,572 in 1930.
A.L. (14-club league)—35,195 in 1996.
A.L. (12-club league)—25,281 in 1973.
A.L. (10-club league)—21,762 in 1962.
A.L. (8-club league)—18,427 in 1936.

Most players with 300 or more total bases, season (since 1900)
A.L.—22 in 2000.
N.L.—20 in 1999, 2001.

Most players with 400 or more total bases, season
N.L.—4 in 2001.
A.L.—2 in 1927, 1936.

LONG HITS AND EXTRA BASES ON LONG HITS

Most long hits, season (since 1900)
N.L. (16-club league)—8,169 in 2000.
N.L. (14-club league)—6,555 in 1997.
N.L. (12-club league)—5,385 in 1987.
N.L. (10-club league)—3,977 in 1962.
N.L. (8-club league)—3,903 in 1930.
A.L. (14-club league)—7,377 in 2000.
A.L. (12-club league)—4,611 in 1970.
A.L. (10-club league)—4,190 in 1962.
A.L. (8-club league)—3,706 in 1936.

Most extra bases on long hits, season (since 1900)
N.L. (16-club league)—14,711 in 2000.
N.L. (14-club league)—11,366 in 1997.
N.L. (12-club league)—9,468 in 1987.
N.L. (10-club league)—7,328 in 1962.
N.L. (8-club league)—6,312 in 1930.
A.L. (14-club league)—13,273 in 1996.
A.L. (12-club league)—8,476 in 1970.
A.L. (10-club league)—7,694 in 1962.
A.L. (8-club league)—5,842 in 1940.

RUNS BATTED IN

Most runs batted in, season
N.L. (16-club league)—12,321 in 1999.
N.L. (14-club league)—9,987 in 1996.
N.L. (12-club league)—8,233 in 1987.
N.L. (10-club league)—6,760 in 1962.
N.L. (8-club league)—6,582 in 1930.
A.L. (14-club league)—11,583 in 1996.
A.L. (12-club league)—7,769 in 1973.
A.L. (10-club league)—6,842 in 1961.
A.L. (8-club league)—6,520 in 1936.

Most players with 100 or more runs batted in, season
A.L.—32 in 1999.
N.L.—27 in 1999.

BASES ON BALLS

Most bases on balls, season (since 1900)
N.L. (16-club league)—9,735 in 2000.
N.L. (14-club league)—7,704 in 1997.
N.L. (12-club league)—6,919 in 1970.
N.L. (10-club league)—5,265 in 1962.
N.L. (8-club league)—4,537 in 1950.
A.L. (14-club league)—8,592 in 1996.
A.L. (12-club league)—7,032 in 1969.
A.L. (10-club league)—5,902 in 1961.
A.L. (8-club league)—5,627 in 1949.

Fewest bases on balls, season (since 1900)
A.L. (12-club league)—6,128 in 1976.
A.L. (8-club league)—3,797 in 1922.
N.L. (12-club league)—5,793 in 1988.
N.L. (8-club league)—2,906 in 1921.

Most players with 100 or more bases on balls, season
A.L.—10 in 2000.
N.L.—7 in 2000.

INTENTIONAL (SINCE 1955)

Most intentional bases on balls, season
N.L.—865 in 2001 (16-club league).
A.L.—743 in 1993 (14-club league).

Fewest intentional bases on balls, season
A.L.—420 in 1998 (14-club league).
N.L.—626 in 1991 (12-club league).

STRIKEOUTS

Most strikeouts, season (since 1900)
N.L. (16-club league)—17,908 in 2001.
N.L. (14-club league)—15,320 in 1997.
N.L. (12-club league)—11,657 in 1987.
N.L. (10-club league)—9,649 in 1965.
N.L. (8-club league)—6,824 in 1960.
A.L. (14-club league)—14,617 in 1997.
A.L. (12-club league)—10,957 in 1970.
A.L. (10-club league)—9,956 in 1964.
A.L. (8-club league)—6,081 in 1959.

Fewest strikeouts, season (since 1900)
A.L. (8-club league)—3,245 in 1924.
A.L. (12-club league)—9,143 in 1976.
N.L. (8-club league)—3,359 in 1926.
N.L. (12-club league)—9,602 in 1976.

Most players with 100 or more strikeouts, season
N.L.—42 in 2001.
A.L.—38 in 1997.

SACRIFICE HITS AND FLIES

Most sacrifices including scoring flies, season (since 1900)
A.L.—1,731 in 1917.
N.L.—1,655 in 1908.

Most sacrifices with no sacrifice flies, season
A.L.—1,349 in 1906.
N.L.—1,349 in 1907.

Fewest sacrifices with no sacrifice flies, season
N.L.—510 in 1957.
A.L.—531 in 1958.

Most sacrifice flies, season
N.L. (16-club league)—809 in 2000.
N.L. (14-club league)—701 in 1993.
N.L. (12-club league)—589 in 1988.
N.L. (8-club league)—425 in 1954.
A.L. (14-club league)—765 in 1979.
A.L. (12-club league)—624 in 1976.
A.L. (10-club league)—448 in 1961.
A.L. (8-club league)—370 in 1954.

Fewest sacrifice flies, season
A.L. (14-club league)—629 in 1987.
A.L. (12-club league)—484 in 1969.
A.L. (10-club league)—348 in 1967.
A.L. (8-club league)—312 in 1959.
N.L. (16-club league)—691 in 1998.
N.L. (14-club league)—643 in 1997.
N.L. (12-club league)—430 in 1969.
N.L. (10-club league)—363 in 1966.
N.L. (8-club league)—304 in 1959.

HIT BY PITCH

Most hit by pitch, season
N.L. (16-club league)—969 in 2001.
N.L. (14-club league)—773 in 1997.
N.L. (12-club league)—443 in 1969.
N.L. (8-club league)—415 in 1903.
A.L. (14-club league)—921 in 2001.
A.L. (8-club league)—464 in 1911.

Fewest hit by pitch, season
A.L. (8-club league)—132 in 1947.
A.L. (14-club league)—372 in 1982.
N.L. (8-club league)—157 in 1943.
N.L. (12-club league)—249 in 1984.
N.L. (14-club league)—567 in 1993.
N.L. (16-club league)—824 in 1998.

GROUNDING INTO DOUBLE PLAYS

Most grounding into double plays, season
N.L. (16-club league)—1,978 in 2000.
N.L. (14-club league)—1,699 in 1996.
N.L. (12-club league)—1,547 in 1971.
N.L. (10-club league)—1,251 in 1962.
N.L. (8-club league)—1,047 in 1958.
A.L. (14-club league)—1,968 in 1980.
A.L. (12-club league)—1,608 in 1973.
A.L. (10-club league)—1,256 in 1961.
A.L. (8-club league)—1,181 in 1950.

Fewest grounding into double plays, season
N.L. (8-club league)—820 in 1945.
N.L. (12-club league)—1,198 in 1991.
A.L. (8-club league)—890 in 1945.
A.L. (12-club league)—1,440 in 1976.

INDIVIDUAL BASERUNNING

STOLEN BASES

Most stolen bases, career
M.L.—1,395—Rickey Henderson, Oakland A.L., New York A.L., Toronto A.L., San Diego N.L., Anaheim A.L., New York N.L., Seattle A.L., 23 years, 1979 through 2001 (1,262 in A.L., 133 in N.L.).
A.L.—1,262—Rickey Henderson, Oakland, New York, Toronto, Anaheim, Seattle, 20 years, 1979 through 2000, except 1996 and 1999.
N.L.—938—Lou Brock, Chicago, St. Louis, 19 years, 1961 through 1979.

For a complete list of players with 400 or more career stolen bases, see page 177.

Highest stolen base percentage, career (minimum 300 attempts)
M.L.—.853—Tony Womack, Pittsburgh N.L., Arizona N.L., 1993 through 2001, except 1995.
N.L.—.857—Tim Raines Sr., Montreal N.L., 1979 through 1990, 2001. Note: The reason Raines holds the N.L. record but not the M.L. record is that his A.L. stolen base percentage lowers his total major league percentage to .847.
A.L.—.833—Willie Wilson, Kansas City, Oakland, 1976 through 1992.

Most consecutive stolen bases with no caught stealing, career
N.L.—50—Vince Coleman, St. Louis, September 18, 1988 through July 26, 1989.
A.L.—40—Tim Raines Sr., Chicago, July 23, 1993 through August 4, 1995.

Most stolen bases, season
A.A.—156—Harry Stovey, Philadelphia, 130 games, 1888.
A.L.—130—Rickey Henderson, Oakland, 149 games, 1982 (42 caught stealing).
N.L.—118—Lou Brock, St. Louis, 153 games, 1974 (33 caught stealing).

For complete lists of players combining power and speed (40 HRs, 40 SBs; 30 HRs, 30 SBs; 50 HRs, 20 SBs and 20 HRs, 50 SBs) during a season, see page 188.

Most stolen bases by rookie, season
N.L.—110—Vince Coleman, St. Louis, 151 games, 1985.
A.A.—98—Mike Griffin, Baltimore, 136 games, 1887.
A.L.—66—Kenny Lofton, Cleveland, 148 games, 1992.

Most stolen bases with no caught stealing, season
N.L.—21—Kevin McReynolds, New York, 147 games, 1988.
A.L.—20—Paul Molitor, Toronto, 115 games, 1994.

Most years leading league in stolen bases
A.L.—12—Rickey Henderson, Oakland, New York, 1980 through 1991, except 1987; 1998.
N.L.—10—Max Carey, Pittsburgh, 1913, 1915, 1916, 1917, 1918, 1920, 1922, 1923, 1924, 1925.

Most consecutive years leading league in stolen bases
A.L.—9—Luis Aparicio, Chicago, Baltimore, 1956 through 1964.
N.L.—6
Maury Wills, Los Angeles, 1960 through 1965.
Vince Coleman, St. Louis, 1985 through 1990.

Most years with 50 or more stolen bases
A.L.—13—Rickey Henderson, Oakland, New York, Toronto, 1980 through 1993, except 1987 and 1992; 1998.
N.L.—12—Lou Brock, St. Louis, 1965 through 1976.

Most consecutive years with 50 or more stolen bases
N.L.—12—Lou Brock, St. Louis, 1965 through 1976.
A.L.—7—Rickey Henderson, Oakland, New York, 1980 through 1986.

Fewest stolen bases for leader, season
A.L.—15—Dom DiMaggio, Boston, 141 games, 1950.
N.L.—16—Stan Hack, Chicago, 152 games, 1938.

Most at-bats with no stolen bases, season
A.L.—677—Don Mattingly, New York, 162 games, 1986 (0 caught stealing).
N.L.—662—Pete Rose, Cincinnati, 162 games, 1975 (1 caught stealing).

Most years with no stolen bases (150 or more games)
M.L.—4
Deron Johnson, Cincinnati N.L., Philadelphia N.L., Chicago A.L., Boston A.L., 1965, 1970, 1971, 1975 (3 in N.L., 1 in A.L.).
Ken Singleton, Baltimore A.L., 1977, 1980, 1982, 1983.
Cecil Fielder, Detroit A.L., 1990, 1991, 1992, 1993.
A.L.—4
Ken Singleton, Baltimore, 1977, 1980, 1982, 1983.
Cecil Fielder, Detroit A.L., 1990, 1991, 1992, 1993.
N.L.—3
Dal Maxvill, St. Louis, 1967, 1968, 1970.
Deron Johnson, Cincinnati, Philadelphia, 1965, 1970, 1971.

Most stolen bases, game
N.L.—7
George Gore, Chicago, June 25, 1881.*
Billy Hamilton, Philadelphia, August 31, 1894, second game.
A.L.—6—Eddie Collins, Philadelphia, September 11, 1912; also September 22, 1912, first game.
N.L. since 1900—6
Otis Nixon, Atlanta, June 16, 1991.
Eric Young, Colorado, June 30, 1996.
*Stolen bases not officially compiled until 1886.

Most stolen bases, two consecutive games
N.L.—8—Walt Wilmot, Chicago, August 6 (4), August 7 (4), 1894.
A.L.—7
Eddie Collins, Philadelphia, September 10 (1), September 11 (6), 1912.
Amos Otis, Kansas City, April 30 (3), May 1 (4), 1975, 13 innings.
Rickey Henderson, Oakland, July 3 (4), 15 innings; July 4 (3), 1983.

Most stolen bases, inning
N.L.—3—Held by many players. Last player—Eric Young, Colorado, June 30, 1996, third inning.
A.L.—3—Held by many players. Last player—Chris Stynes, Kansas City, May 12, 1996, first inning.

Most stolen bases by pinch-runner, inning
N.L.—2
Bill O'Hara, New York, September 1, 1909, sixth inning.
Bill O'Hara, New York, September 2, 1909, ninth inning.
Sandy Piez, New York, July 6, 1914, second game, ninth inning.
Jake Pitler, Pittsburgh, May 24, 1918, ninth inning.
Dave Concepcion, Cincinnati, July 7, 1974, first game, seventh inning.
Ron LeFlore, Montreal, October 5, 1980, eighth inning.
A.L.—2
Ray Dowd, Philadelphia, July 9, 1919, second game, ninth inning.
Allan Lewis, Kansas City, July 15, 1967, seventh inning.
Bert Campaneris, Oakland, October 4, 1972, fourth inning.
Don Hopkins, Oakland, April 20, 1975, second game, seventh inning.

Appearing as a pinch-runner and pinch-hitter in the same game (different innings)
A.L.—Pat Collins, St. Louis, June 8, 1923 (pinch-runner in third inning, pinch-hitter in ninth inning).

STEALS OF HOME

Most times stole home, career
A.L.—50—Ty Cobb, Detroit, Philadelphia, 24 years, 1905 through 1928.

N.L.—33—Max Carey, Pittsburgh, Brooklyn, 20 years, 1910 through 1929.

For a complete list of players with 10 or more career steals of home, see page 177.

Most times stole home, season
A.L.—8—Ty Cobb, Detroit, 140 games, 1912 (61 stolen bases).
N.L.—7—Pete Reiser, Brooklyn, 122 games, 1946 (34 stolen bases).

Most times stole way from first to home in an inning, career
A.L.—4—Ty Cobb, Detroit, 1909, 1911, 1912 (2).
N.L.—3—Honus Wagner, Pittsburgh, 1902, 1907, 1909.
N.L.—Last player—Eric Young, Colorado, June 30, 1996, third inning.
A.L.—Last player—Chris Stynes, Kansas City, May 12, 1996, first inning.

Most times stole home, game
N.L.—2
Honus Wagner, Pittsburgh, June 20, 1901.
Ed Konetchy, St. Louis, September 30, 1907.
Joe Tinker, Chicago, June 28, 1910.
Larry Doyle, New York, September 18, 1911.
Sherry Magee, Philadelphia, July 20, 1912.
Doc Gautreau, Boston, September 3, 1927, first game.
A.L.—2
Joe Jackson, Cleveland, August 11, 1912.
Guy Zinn, New York, August 15, 1912.
Eddie Collins, Philadelphia, September 6, 1913.
Bill Barrett, Chicago, May 1, 1924.
Vic Power, Cleveland, August 14, 1958, 10 innings.

CAUGHT STEALING AND CAUGHT OFF BASE

Most caught stealing, career
M.L.—333—Rickey Henderson, Oakland A.L., New York A.L., Toronto A.L., San Diego N.L., Anaheim A.L., New York N.L., Seattle A.L., 23 years, 1979 through 2001 (291 in A.L., 42 in N.L.).
N.L.—307—Lou Brock, Chicago, St. Louis, 19 years, 1961 through 1979.
A.L.—291—Rickey Henderson, Oakland, New York, Toronto, Anaheim, Seattle, 20 years, 1979 through 2000, except 1996 and 1999.

Most caught stealing, season
A.L.—42—Rickey Henderson, Oakland, 149 games, 1982 (130 stolen bases).
N.L.—36—Miller Huggins, St. Louis, 148 games, 1914 (32 stolen bases).

Most caught stealing by rookie, season
N.L.—25—Vince Coleman, St. Louis, 151 games, 1985 (110 stolen bases).
A.L.—21—Mike Edwards, Oakland, 142 games, 1978 (27 stolen bases).

Most years leading league in caught stealing
N.L.—7
Maury Wills, Los Angeles, Pittsburgh, Montreal, 1961, 1962 (tied), 1963, 1965, 1966, 1968, 1969.
Lou Brock, Chicago, St. Louis, 1964, 1967, 1971, 1973, 1974, 1976, 1977 (tied).
A.L.—6—Minnie Minoso, Chicago, Cleveland, 1952, 1953, 1954, 1957, 1958, 1960.

Fewest caught stealing with 50 or more stolen bases, season
N.L.—2—Max Carey, Pittsburgh, 155 games, 1922 (51 stolen bases).
A.L.—8
Luis Aparicio, Chicago, 153 games, 1960 (51 stolen bases).
Bert Campaneris, Oakland, 135 games, 1969 (62 stolen bases).
Amos Otis, Kansas City, 147 games, 1971 (52 stolen bases).
Willie Wilson, Kansas City, 137 games, 1983 (59 stolen bases).
Rickey Henderson, Oakland, Toronto, 134 games, 1993 (53 stolen bases).
Vince Coleman, Kansas City, 104 games, 1994 (50 stolen bases).

Fewest caught stealing, season (150 or more games)
N.L.-A.L.—0—Held by many players.

Fewest caught stealing for leader, season
A.L.—9
Hoot Evers, Detroit, 143 games, 1950 (5 stolen bases).
Jim Rivera, Chicago, 139 games, 1956 (20 stolen bases).
N.L.—10—Willie Mays, New York, 152 games, 1956 (40 stolen bases).

Most consecutive games with no caught stealing, career
M.L.—1,206—Gus Triandos, New York A.L., Baltimore A.L., Detroit A.L., Philadelphia N.L., Houston N.L., August 3, 1953 through August 15, 1965 (1 stolen base).
A.L.—1,079—Gus Triandos, New York, Baltimore, Detroit, August 3, 1953 through September 28, 1963 (1 stolen base).
N.L.—592—Frank Torre, Milwaukee, Philadelphia, April 20, 1956 through August 10, 1962 (4 stolen bases).

Most caught stealing, nine-inning game
N.L.-A.L.—3—Held by many players.

Most caught stealing, extra-inning game
N.L.—4—Robby Thompson, San Francisco, June 27, 1986, 12 innings.

Most caught off base, game
A.A.—3—John Stricker, Philadelphia, August 29, 1883.
N.L.—3—Ben Kauff, New York, May 26, 1916.

Most times out for being hit by batted ball, game
N.L.—2—Walt Wilmot, Chicago, September 30, 1890.
A.L.—2—Ernie Shore, Boston, July 28, 1917, second game.

Most caught stealing, inning
A.L.—2
Don Baylor, Baltimore, June 15, 1974, ninth inning.
Roberto Kelly, New York, April 17, 1990, second inning.
N.L.—2
Jim Morrison, Pittsburgh, June 15, 1987, eighth inning.
Paul Noce, Chicago, June 26, 1987, third inning.
Donell Nixon, San Francisco, July 6, 1988, sixth inning.
Tony Fernandez, San Diego, June 26, 1992, fifth inning.
Eric Young, Colorado, May 1, 1993, eighth inning.
Phil Plantier, San Diego, September 25, 1993, fifth inning.
Derek Bell, Houston, June 19, 1995, fourth inning.
Larry Walker, Colorado, April 30, 1998, eighth inning.

CLUB BASERUNNING

STOLEN BASES

Most stolen bases, season
A.A.—638—Philadelphia, 137 games, 1887.
N.L.—426—New York, 136 games, 1893.
N.L. since 1900—347—New York, 154 games, 1911.
A.L.—341—Oakland, 161 games, 1976.

Most players with 50 or more stolen bases, season
A.L.—3—Oakland, 161 games, 1976. Bill North (75), Bert
Campaneris (54), Don Baylor (52).
N.L.—3—San Diego, 163 games, 1980. Gene Richards (61),
Ozzie Smith (57), Jerry Mumphrey (52).

Most years leading league in stolen bases (since 1900)
A.L.—30—Chicago.
N.L.—21
Brooklyn-Los Angeles (12-Brooklyn, 9-Los Angeles).
St. Louis.

Fewest stolen bases, season
A.L.—13—Washington, 154 games, 1957.
N.L.—17—St. Louis, 157 games, 1949.

Most stolen bases, game
A.A.—19—Philadelphia vs. Syracuse, April 22, 1890.
N.L.—17—New York vs. Pittsburgh, May 23, 1890.
A.L.—15—New York vs. St. Louis, September 28, 1911.
N.L. since 1900—11
New York vs. Boston, June 20, 1912.
St. Louis vs. Pittsburgh, August 13, 1916, second game, five
innings.

Most stolen bases by both clubs, game
A.A.—21—Philadelphia 19, Syracuse 2, April 22, 1890.
N.L.—20—New York 17, Pittsburgh 3, May 23, 1890.
N.L. since 1900—14—New York 9, Boston 5, June 20, 1912.
A.L.—15
New York 15, St. Louis 0, September 28, 1911.
St. Louis 8, Detroit 7, October 1, 1916.

Most triple steals, game
A.L.—2—Philadelphia vs. Cleveland, July 25, 1930, first and
fourth innings.
N.L.—1—Made in many games.

Most triples steals by both clubs, game
A.L.—2—Philadelphia 2, Cleveland 0, July 25, 1930.
N.L.—1—Made in many games.

Longest game without a stolen base
N.L.—26 innings—Boston vs. Brooklyn, May 1, 1920.
A.L.—24 innings
Detroit vs. Philadelphia, July 21, 1945.
Philadelphia vs. Detroit, July 21, 1945.

Longest game without a stolen base by either club
A.L.—24 innings—Detroit 0, Philadelphia 0, July 21, 1945.
N.L.—23 innings—San Francisco 0, New York 0, May 31, 1964,
second game.

Most stolen bases, inning
A.L.—8—Washington vs. Cleveland, July 19, 1915, first inning.
N.L.—8—Philadelphia vs. New York, July 7, 1919, first game,
ninth inning.

STEALS OF HOME

Most times stole home, season
A.L.—18—New York, 153 games, 1912 (245 stolen bases).
N.L.—17
Chicago, 157 games, 1911 (214 stolen bases).
New York, 154 games, 1912 (319 stolen bases).

Most times stole home, game
N.L.—3
St. Louis vs. Boston, September 30, 1907.
Chicago vs. Boston, August 23, 1909.
New York vs. Pittsburgh, September 18, 1911.

A.L.—3
Chicago vs. St. Louis, July 2, 1909.
New York vs. Philadelphia, April 17, 1915.

Most times stole home by both clubs, game
A.L.—3
Chicago 3, St. Louis 0, July 2, 1909.
New York 3, Philadelphia 0, April 17, 1915.
Detroit 2, St. Louis 1, April 22, 1924.
N.L.—3
St. Louis 3, Boston 0, September 30, 1907.
Chicago 3, Boston 0, August 23, 1909.
New York 3, Pittsburgh 0, September 18, 1911.

Most times stole home, inning
N.L.—2—Made in many innings. Last time—St. Louis vs.
Brooklyn, September 19, 1925, seventh inning.
A.L.—2—Made in many innings. Last time—Oakland vs.
Kansas City, May 28, 1980, first inning.

CAUGHT STEALING

Most caught stealing, season (since 1920)
N.L.—149—Chicago, 154 games, 1924.
A.L.—123—Oakland, 161 games, 1976.

Fewest caught stealing, season
N.L.—8—Milwaukee, 154 games, 1958 (26 stolen bases).
A.L.—11
Kansas City, 155 games, 1960 (16 stolen bases).
Cleveland, 161 games, 1961 (34 stolen bases).

Most caught stealing, game
N.L.—8—Baltimore vs. Washington, May 11, 1897.
N.L. since 1900—6—St. Louis vs. Brooklyn, August 23, 1909,
second game.
A.L.—6
St. Louis vs. Philadelphia, May 12, 1915.
Chicago vs. Philadelphia, June 18, 1915.

Most caught stealing, inning
A.A.—3—Cincinnati vs. Philadelphia, July 26, 1887, third
inning.
A.L.—3—Detroit vs. New York, August 3, 1914, second inning.
N.L.—2—Made in many innings.

LEFT ON BASE

Most left on base, season
A.L.—1,334—St. Louis, 157 games, 1941.
N.L.—1,328—Cincinnati, 162 games, 1976.

Fewest left on base, season
A.L.—925—Kansas City, 154 games, 1957.
N.L.—964—Chicago, 154 games, 1924.

Most left on base, nine-inning game
A.L.—20—New York vs. Boston, September 21, 1956.
A.A.—18—Baltimore vs. Cincinnati, July 7, 1891.
N.L.—18
Boston vs. Baltimore, August 15, 1897.
Pittsburgh vs. Cincinnati, September 8, 1905.
Boston vs. St. Louis, July 11, 1923.
St. Louis vs. Philadelphia, September 15, 1928, second game.
New York vs. Philadelphia, August 7, 1943.
St. Louis vs. Cincinnati, June 10, 1944.
St. Louis vs. Philadelphia, September 14, 1950.
Pittsburgh vs. Boston, June 5, 1951.
Atlanta vs. Los Angeles, June 23, 1986.

Most left on base, nine-inning shutout defeat
N.L.—16—St. Louis vs. Philadelphia, May 24, 1994.
A.L.—16—Seattle vs. Toronto, May 7, 1998.

Most left on base, extra-inning shutout defeat
N.L.—16—St. Louis vs. Cincinnati, August 30, 1989, 13
innings.
A.L.—Less than nine-inning record.

Most left on base by both clubs, nine-inning game

N.L.—30
  Brooklyn 16, Pittsburgh 14, June 30, 1893.
  New York 17, Philadelphia 13, July 18, 1943, first game.
A.L.—30
  New York 15, Chicago 15, August 27, 1935, first game.
  Los Angeles 15, Washington 15, July 21, 1961.

Most left on base, extra-inning game

N.L.—27—Atlanta vs. Philadelphia, May 4, 1973, 20 innings.
A.L.—25
  Washington vs. Cleveland, September 14, 1971; 20-inning
    suspended game completed September 20.
  Kansas City vs. Texas, June 6, 1991, 18 innings.

Most left on base by both clubs, extra-inning game

N.L.—45—New York 25, St. Louis 20, September 11, 1974, 25
  innings.
A.L.—45—Kansas City 25, Texas 20, June 6, 1991, 18 innings.

Fewest left on base, nine-inning game

A.L.-N.L.—0—Made in many games.

Fewest left on base, extra-inning game

A.L.—0—Philadelphia vs. New York, June 22, 1929, second
  game, 14 innings.
N.L.—No game over nine innings with none left on base.

Fewest left on base by both clubs, extra-inning game

N.L.—3—Chicago 2, Cincinnati 1, May 2, 1917, 10 innings.
A.L.—4—Made in many games.

Fewest left on base by both clubs, nine-inning game

N.L.—1—Los Angeles 1, Chicago 0, September 9, 1965.
A.L.—2—Made in many games. Last time—Cleveland 1,
  Oakland 1, July 19, 1974.

Fewest left on base, two consecutive games

A.L.—2
  Washington, May 27 (2), May 29 (0), 1952, 18 innings.
  Chicago vs. California, September 18 (1), September 19 (1),
    1971, 17 innings.
N.L.—2
  San Francisco, May 6 (2), May 7 (0), 1960, 16 innings.
  San Francisco, June 13 (1), 10 innings, June 14 (1), 8 innings,
    1963, 18 innings.

Most left on base, doubleheader (18 innings)

A.L.—30—Philadelphia vs. St. Louis, June 12, 1949.
N.L.—29
  St. Louis vs. Philadelphia, September 15, 1928.
  Philadelphia vs. Milwaukee, May 15, 1955.

Most left on base, doubleheader (more than 18 innings)

A.L.—34—Cleveland vs. New York, August 18, 1943, 21.1
  innings.
N.L.—33—Florida vs. Pittsburgh, August 18, 1995, 22 innings.

Most left on base by both clubs, doubleheader (18 innings)

N.L.—49—Brooklyn 25, Pittsburgh 24, July 24, 1926.
A.L.—49—New York 27, Chicago 22, August 27, 1935.

Fewest left on base, doubleheader

A.L.—3—Washington vs. New York, August 6, 1963, 17 innings.
N.L.—3—San Francisco vs. Houston, September 24, 1978, 16
  innings.

Fewest left on base by both clubs, doubleheader

N.L.—10—St. Louis 6, Boston 4, July 19, 1924.
A.L.—13—Chicago 9, Philadelphia 4, July 18, 1918.

LEAGUE BASERUNNING

STOLEN BASES

Most stolen bases, season (since 1900)
N.L. (16-club league)—1,959 in 1999.
N.L. (12-club league)—1,851 in 1987.
N.L. (8-club league)—1,691 in 1911.
A.L.—1,810 in 1912.

Fewest stolen bases, season (since 1900)
A.L. (8-club league)—278 in 1950.
A.L. (12-club league)—863 in 1970.
N.L. (8-club league)—337 in 1954.
N.L. (12-club league)—817 in 1969.

CAUGHT STEALING

Most caught stealing, season
A.L. (14-club league)—936 in 1977.
A.L. (12-club league)—867 in 1976.
A.L. (8-club league)—707 in 1920.
N.L. (12-club league)—870 in 1983.
N.L. (8-club league)—517 in 1925.

Fewest caught stealing, season
N.L. (8-club league)—218 in 1953.
N.L. (10-club league)—409 in 1962.
N.L. (12-club league)—492 in 1971.
A.L. (8-club league)—231 in 1950.
A.L. (10-club league)—270 in 1963.
A.L. (12-club league)—539 in 1972.

LEFT ON BASE

Most left on base, season (since 1900)
N.L. (16-club league)—18,939 in 2000.
N.L. (14-club league)—16,195 in 1997.
N.L. (12-club league)—14,468 in 1975.
N.L. (10-club league)—11,416 in 1962.
N.L. (8-club league)—9,424 in 1945.
A.L. (14-club league)—16,711 in 1996.
A.L. (12-club league)—13,925 in 1973.
A.L. (10-club league)—11,680 in 1961.
A.L. (8-club league)—9,628 in 1936.

Fewest left on base, season (since 1900)
N.L. (8-club league)—8,254 in 1920.
N.L. (10-club league)—10,994 in 1966.
N.L. (12-club league)—13,295 in 1988.
N.L. (16-club league)—18,444 in 1998.
A.L. (8-club league)—8,619 in 1958.
A.L. (10-club league)—10,668 in 1966.
A.L. (12-club league)—13,494 in 1976.

INDIVIDUAL PITCHING

GAMES

Most games pitched, career
M.L.—1,131—Jesse Orosco, New York N.L., Los Angeles, N.L., Cleveland A.L., Milwaukee A.L., Baltimore A.L., St. Louis N.L., 22 years, 1979 through 2001, except 1980 (663 in A.L., 468 in N.L.).
N.L.—1,050—Kent Tekulve, Pittsburgh, Philadelphia, Cincinnati, 16 years, 1974 through 1989.
A.L.—869—Dennis Eckersley, Cleveland, Boston, Oakland, 20 years, 1975 through 1984, 1987 through 1995, 1998.

> **For a complete list of pitchers with 700 or more career games pitched, see page 177.**

Most games pitched with one club
A.L.—802—Walter Johnson, Washington, 21 years, 1907 through 1927.
N.L.—802—Roy Face, Pittsburgh, 15 years, 1953 through 1968, except 1954.

Most complete doubleheaders pitched, career
M.L.—5—Joe McGinnity, Baltimore A.L., 1901 (2); New York N.L., 1903 (3).
N.L.—3—Joe McGinnity, New York, 1903.
A.L.—2—Held by many pitchers.

Most games pitched, season
N.L.—106—Mike G. Marshall, Los Angeles, 1974 (208 innings).
A.L.—90—Mike G. Marshall, Minnesota, 1979 (143 innings).

Most games pitched by rookie, season
A.L.—88—Sean Runyan, Detroit, 1998 (0 complete, 50.1 innings).
N.L.—78—Tim Burke, Montreal, 1985 (0 complete, 120.1 innings).

Most years leading league in games
M.L.—7—Joe McGinnity, Brooklyn N.L., Baltimore A.L., New York N.L., 1900, 1901, 1903, 1904, 1905, 1906, 1907.
N.L.—6—Joe McGinnity, Brooklyn, New York, 1900, 1903, 1904, 1905, 1906, 1907.
A.L.—6—Fred Marberry, Washington, 1924, 1925, 1926, 1928, 1929, 1932.

Fewest games pitched by leader, season
A.L.—40—Joe Haynes, Chicago, 1942 (103 innings).
N.L.—41
Ray Kremer, Pittsburgh, 1924 (259 innings).
Johnny Morrison, Pittsburgh, 1924 (238 innings).

Most complete doubleheaders pitched, season
N.L.—3—Joe McGinnity, New York, August 1, 8, 31, 1903 (won 3).
A.L.—2
Joe McGinnity, Baltimore, 1901 (split 2).
Mule Watson, Philadelphia, 1918 (split 1, lost 1 game and tied 1 in other doubleheader).

Most times pitched opening game of season
M.L.—16—Tom Seaver, New York N.L., Cincinnati N.L., Chicago A.L., 1968 through 1979, 1981 1983, 1985, 1986 (14 in N.L., 2 in A.L.; started 16, won seven, lost two).
N.L.—15—Steve Carlton, St. Louis, Philadelphia, 1965, 1972 through 1986, except 1976 (started 14, won three, lost nine).
A.L.—14
Walter Johnson, Washington, 1910 through 1926, except 1911, 1922, 1925 (started 14, won nine, lost five).
Jack Morris, Detroit, Minnesota, Toronto, 1980 through 1993 (started 14, won eight, lost six).

GAMES STARTED

Most games started, career
M.L.—818—Cy Young, Cleveland N.L., St. Louis N.L., Boston A.L., Cleveland A.L., Boston N.L., 22 years, 1890 through 1911 (460 in N.L., 358 in A.L.).

N.L.—677—Steve Carlton, St. Louis, Philadelphia, San Francisco, 22 years, 1965 through 1986.
A.L.—666—Walter Johnson, Washington, 21 years, 1907 through 1927.

> **For a complete list of pitchers with 500 or more career games started, see page 178.**

Most season-opening games started
M.L.—16—Tom Seaver, New York N.L., Cincinnati N.L., Chicago A.L., 1968 through 1979, 1981, 1983, 1985, 1986 (14 in N.L., 2 in A.L.).
A.L.—14
Walter Johnson, Washington, 1910 through 1926, except 1911, 1922, 1925.
Jack Morris, Detroit, Minnesota, Toronto, 1980 through 1993.
N.L.—14
Tom Seaver, New York, Cincinnati, 1968 through 1979, 1981, 1983.
Steve Carlton, Philadelphia, 1972 through 1986, except 1976.

Most consecutive starting assignments, career (since 1900)
M.L.—595—Nolan Ryan, California A.L., Houston N.L., Texas A.L., July 30, 1974 through 1993 (313 in A.L., 282 in N.L.).
N.L.—534—Steve Carlton, St. Louis, Philadelphia, San Francisco, May 15, 1971 through 1986.
A.L.—532—Roger Clemens, Boston, Toronto, New York, July 26, 1984 through 2001.

Most games started, season
N.L.—74—Will White, Cincinnati, 1879 (pitched 75 games).
A.L.—51—Jack Chesbro, New York, 1904 (pitched 55 games).
N.L. since 1900—48—Joe McGinnity, New York, 1903 (pitched 55 games).

Most years leading league in games started
N.L.—6—Robin Roberts, Philadelphia, 1950 (tied), 1951, 1952, 1953, 1954, 1955.
A.L.—5
Bob Feller, Cleveland, 1940, 1941, 1946, 1947, 1948.
Early Wynn, Washington, Cleveland, Chicago, 1943 (tied), 1951 (tied), 1954, 1957, 1959 (tied).

Most games started with none complete, season
N.L.—37—Steve Bedrosian, Atlanta, 1985.
A.L.—35—Rick Helling, Texas, 2000.

Most games taken out as starting pitcher, season
N.L.—37—Steve Bedrosian, Atlanta, 1985 (started 37).
A.L.—36—Stan Bahnsen, Chicago, 1972 (started 41).

GAMES RELIEVED

Most games as relief pitcher, career
M.L.—1,127—Jesse Orosco, New York N.L., Los Angeles, N.L., Cleveland A.L., Milwaukee A.L., Baltimore A.L., St. Louis N.L., 22 years, 1979 through 2001, except 1980 (663 in A.L., 464 in N.L.).
N.L.—1,050—Kent Tekulve, Pittsburgh, Philadelphia, Cincinnati, 16 years, 1974 through 1989.
A.L.—807—Sparky Lyle, Boston, New York, Texas, Chicago, 15 years, 1967 through 1982, except 1981.

Most consecutive appearances as relief pitcher, career
N.L.—1,050—Kent Tekulve, Pittsburgh, Philadelphia, Cincinnati, May 20, 1974 through July 16, 1989.
A.L.—807—Sparky Lyle, Boston, New York, Texas, Chicago, July 4, 1967 through September 9, 1980; August 23, 1982 through September 27, second game, 1982.

Most games pitched, none of which were starts, career
N.L.—1,050—Kent Tekulve, Pittsburgh, Philadelphia, Cincinnati, May 20, 1974 through July 16, 1989.
A.L.—807—Sparky Lyle, Boston, New York, Texas, Chicago, July 4, 1967 through September 9, 1980; August 23, 1982 through September 27, second game, 1982.

Most games as relief pitcher, season
N.L.—106—Mike G. Marshall, Los Angeles, 1974 (started none, 208 innings).
A.L.—89
Mike G. Marshall, Minnesota, 1979 (141 innings; also started one game—two innings).
Mark Eichhorn, Toronto, 1987, started none (127.2 innings).

Most games pitched, none of which were starts, season
N.L.—106—Mike G. Marshall, Los Angeles, 1974 (finished 83, 208 innings).
A.L.—89—Mark Eichhorn, Toronto, 1987 (finished 27, 127.2 innings).

Most consecutive games pitched as relief pitcher
N.L.—13—Mike G. Marshall, Los Angeles, June 18 through July 3, first game, 1974 (26.2 innings).
A.L.—13—Dale Mohorcic, Texas, August 6 through 20, 1986 (14 innings).

GAMES FINISHED

Most games finished, career
M.L.—802—Lee Smith, Chicago N.L., Boston A.L., St. Louis N.L., New York A.L., Baltimore A.L., California A.L., Cincinnati N.L., Montreal N.L., 18 years, 1980 through 1997 (581 in N.L., 221 in A.L.).
N.L.—638—Kent Tekulve, Pittsburgh, Philadelphia, Cincinnati, 16 years, 1974 through 1989.
A.L.—599—Sparky Lyle, Boston, New York, Texas, Chicago, 15 years, 1967 through 1982, except 1981.

Most games finished, season
A.L.—84—Mike G. Marshall, Minnesota, 1979 (90 games).
N.L.—83—Mike G. Marshall, Los Angeles 1974 (106 games).

Most years leading league in games finished
M.L.—5
Fred Marberry, Washington, 1924, 1925, 1926, 1928, 1929.
Mike G. Marshall, Montreal N.L., Los Angeles N.L., 1971, 1972, 1973, 1974, Minnesota A.L., 1979.
A.L.—5—Fred Marberry, Washington, 1924, 1925, 1926, 1928, 1929.
N.L.—4
Ace Adams, New York, 1942, 1943, 1944, 1945.
Roy Face, Pittsburgh, 1958, 1960, 1961, 1962.
Mike G. Marshall, Montreal, Los Angeles, 1971, 1972, 1973, 1974.

COMPLETE GAMES

Most complete games, career
M.L.—751—Cy Young, Cleveland N.L., St. Louis N.L., Boston A.L., Cleveland A.L., Boston N.L., 22 years, 1890 through 1911 (428 in N.L., 323 in A.L.).
N.L.—557—Pud Galvin, Buffalo, Pittsburgh, St. Louis, 12 years, 1879 through 1892, except 1886, 1890.
A.L.—531—Walter Johnson, Washington, 21 years, 1907 through 1927.
N.L. since 1900—436—Grover Alexander, Philadelphia, Chicago, St. Louis, 20 years, 1911 through 1930.

For a complete list of pitchers with 300 or more career complete games, see page 178.

Most complete games by righthander, career
N.L.—557—Pud Galvin, Buffalo, Pittsburgh, St. Louis, 12 years, 1879 through 1892, except 1886, 1890.
A.L.—531—Walter Johnson, Washington, 21 years, 1907 through 1927.
N.L. since 1900—436—Grover Alexander, Philadelphia, Chicago, St. Louis, 20 years, 1911 through 1930.

Most complete games by lefthander, career
A.L.—387—Eddie Plank, Philadelphia, St. Louis, 16 years, 1901 through 1917, except 1915.

N.L.—382—Warren Spahn, Boston, Milwaukee, New York Mets, San Francisco, 21 years, 1942 through 1965, except 1943, 1944, 1945 in military service.

Most complete games, season
N.L.—74—Will White, Cincinnati, 1879; pitched in 75 games.
A.L.—48—Jack Chesbro, New York, 1904; pitched in 55 games.
N.L. since 1900—45—Vic Willis, Boston, 1902; pitched in 51 games.

Most consecutive complete games pitched, season (since 1900)
N.L.—39—Jack W. Taylor, St. Louis, April 15 through October 6, first game, 1904 (352 innings, including two games finished in relief).
A.L.—37—Bill Dinneen, Boston, April 16 through October 10, first game, 1904 (337 innings).

Most years leading league in complete games
N.L.—9—Warren Spahn, Boston, Milwaukee, 1949, 1951, 1957, 1958, 1959, 1960 (tied), 1961, 1962, 1963.
A.L.—6—Walter Johnson, Washington, 1910, 1911, 1913, 1914, 1915, 1916.

Most complete games by rookie, season
N.L.—67—Jim Devlin, Louisville, 1876 (67 games).
N.L. since 1900—41—Irv Young, Boston, 1905 (43 games).
A.L.—36—Roscoe Miller, Detroit, 1901 (38 games).

Fewest complete games for leader, season
N.L.—6—Curt Schilling, Arizona, 2001.
A.L.—7—David Wells, Toronto, 1999.

Most games pitched, none of which were complete, season
N.L.—106—Mike G. Marshall, Los Angeles, 1974, started none (208 innings).
A.L.—90—Mike G. Marshall, Minnesota, 1979, started one (143 innings).

INNINGS

Most innings pitched, career
M.L.—7,377—Cy Young, Cleveland N.L., St. Louis N.L., Boston A.L., Cleveland A.L., Boston N.L., 22 years, 1890 through 1911 (4,143 in N.L., 3,234 in A.L.).
A.L.—5,924—Walter Johnson, Washington, 21 years, 1907 through 1927.
N.L.—5,246—Warren Spahn, Boston, Milwaukee, New York Mets, San Francisco, 21 years, 1942 through 1965, except 1943, 1944, 1945 in military service.

For a complete list of pitchers with 3,500 or more career innings, see page 178.

Most consecutive innings without relief, career (since 1900)
N.L.—1,727—Jack W. Taylor, Chicago, St. Louis, June 20, 1901, second game, through August 9, 1906 (203 games, 188 complete innings, 15 finished).

Most innings as relief pitcher, career
M.L.—1,870—Hoyt Wilhelm, New York Giants N.L., St. Louis N.L., Cleveland A.L., Baltimore A.L., Chicago A.L., California A.L., Atlanta N.L., Chicago N.L., Los Angeles N.L., 21 years, 1952 through 1972 (916 in N.L., 954 in A.L.).
N.L.—1,436.1—Kent Tekulve, Pittsburgh, Philadelphia, Cincinnati, 16 years, 1974 through 1989.
A.L.—1,265—Sparky Lyle, Boston, New York, Texas, Chicago, 15 years, 1967 through 1982, except 1981.

Most years leading league in innings pitched
N.L.—7—Grover Alexander, Philadelphia, Chicago, 1911, 1912 (tied), 1914, 1915, 1916, 1917, 1920.
A.L.—5
Walter Johnson, Washington, 1910, 1913, 1914, 1915, 1916.
Bob Feller, Cleveland, 1939, 1940, 1941, 1946, 1947.

Most innings pitched, season
N.L.—683—Will White, Cincinnati, 75 games, 1879.
A.L.—464—Ed Walsh, Chicago, 66 games, 1908.
N.L. since 1900—434—Joe McGinnity, New York, 55 games, 1903.

Most innings pitched by rookie, season (since 1900)
N.L.—378—Irv Young, Boston, 43 games, 1905.
A.L.—316—Reb Russell, Chicago, 43 games, 1913.

Most innings pitched as relief pitcher, season
N.L.—208—Mike G. Marshall, Los Angeles, 1974, pitched 106 games as relief pitcher.
A.L.—168.1—Bob Stanley, Boston, 1982, pitched 48 games as relief pitcher. (Bill Campbell, Minnesota, pitched 167.2 innings, rounded to 168, as a relief pitcher in 1976.)

Fewest innings pitched by leader, season
A.L.—231.2—David Wells, Toronto, 34 games, 1999.
N.L.—249.2—Frank Viola, New York, 35 games, 1990.

Most consecutive innings without relief, season (since 1900)
N.L.—352—Jack W. Taylor, St. Louis, April 15 through October 6, first game, 1904 (complete season, 39 complete games and two games finished).
A.L.—337—Bill Dinneen, Boston, April 16 through October 10, first game, 1904 (complete season, 37 complete games).

Most years with 200 or more innings pitched
M.L.—19
Cy Young, Cleveland N.L., St. Louis N.L., Boston A.L., Cleveland A.L., 1891 through 1909 (10 in N.L., 9 in A.L.).
Phil Niekro, Milwaukee, N.L., Atlanta N.L., New York A.L., Cleveland A.L., 1967 through 1986, except 1981 (16 in N.L., 3 in A.L.).
A.L.—18—Walter Johnson, Washington, 1908 through 1926, except 1920.
N.L.—17—Warren Spahn, Boston, Milwaukee, 1947 through 1963.

Most years with 300 or more innings pitched
M.L.—16—Cy Young, Cleveland N.L., St. Louis N.L., Boston A.L., 1891 through 1907, except 1906 (10 in N.L., 6 in A.L.).
N.L.—12—Kid Nichols, Boston, 1890 through 1899, 1901, 1904.
N.L. since 1900—11—Christy Mathewson, New York, 1901, 1903, 1904, 1905, 1907, 1908, 1910, 1911, 1912, 1913, 1914.
A.L.—9—Walter Johnson, Washington, 1910 through 1918.

Most consecutive years with 300 or more innings (since 1900)
A.L.—9—Walter Johnson, Washington, 1910 through 1918.
N.L.—7—Grover Alexander, Philadelphia, 1911 through 1917.

Most years with 400 or more innings pitched (since 1900)
N.L.—2—Joe McGinnity, New York, 1903 (434), 1904 (408).
A.L.—2—Ed Walsh, Chicago, 1907 (419), 1908 (464).

Most innings pitched, game
N.L.—26
Leon Cadore, Brooklyn, May 1, 1920 (1-1 tie).
Joe Oeschger, Boston, May 1, 1920 (1-1 tie).
A.L.—24
Jack Coombs, Philadelphia, September 1, 1906 (won 4-1).
Joe Harris, Boston, September 1, 1906 (lost 4-1).

Most innings pitched as relief pitcher finishing game
N.L.—18.1—George Zabel, Chicago, June 17, 1915 (Chicago 4, Brooklyn 3, 19 innings).
A.L.—17—Eddie Rommel, Philadelphia, July 10, 1932 (Philadelphia 18, Cleveland 17, 18 innings).

WINNING PERCENTAGE

Highest percentage of games won, career (200 or more decisions)
A.L.—.690—Whitey Ford, New York, 16 years, 1950 through 1967, except 1951, 1952 in military service (won 236, lost 106).
N.L.—.665—Christy Mathewson, New York, Cincinnati, 17 years, 1900 through 1916 (won 373, lost 188).

Highest percentage of games won, season (70 or more decisions)
N.L.—.833—Hoss Radbourn, Providence, 1884 (won 60, lost 12).

Highest percentage of games won, season (34 or more decisions)
A.L.—.886—Lefty Grove, Philadelphia, 1931 (won 31, lost 4).

N.L.—.824
Jack Chesbro, Pittsburgh, 1902 (won 28, lost 6).
Dazzy Vance, Brooklyn, 1924 (won 28, lost 6).

Highest percentage of games won, season (20 or more victories)
A.L.—.893—Ron Guidry, New York, 1978 (won 25, lost 3).
N.L.—.880
Fred Goldsmith, Chicago, 1880 (won 22, lost 3).
Preacher Roe, Brooklyn, 1951 (won 22, lost 3).

Highest percentage of games won, season (16 or more decisions)
N.L.—.947—Roy Face, Pittsburgh, 1959 (won 18, lost 1).
A.L.—.938—Johnny Allen, Cleveland, 1937 (won 15, lost 1).

Most years leading league in winning percentage (15 or more victories)
A.L.—5—Lefty Grove, Philadelphia, Boston, 1929, 1930, 1931, 1933, 1939.
N.L.—3—Ed Reulbach, Chicago, 1906, 1907, 1908.

GAMES WON
CAREER

Most games won, career
M.L.—511—Cy Young, Cleveland N.L., St. Louis N.L., Boston A.L., Cleveland A.L., Boston N.L., 22 years, 1890 through 1911 (289 in N.L., 222 in A.L.).

For a complete list of pitchers with 200 or more career victories, see page 178.

Most games won by righthander, career
A.L.—417—Walter Johnson, Washington, 21 years, 1907 through 1927.
N.L.—373
Christy Mathewson, New York, Cincinnati, 17 years, 1900 through 1916.
Grover Alexander, Philadelphia, Chicago, St. Louis, 20 years, 1911 through 1930.

Most games won by lefthander, career
N.L.—363—Warren Spahn, Boston, Milwaukee, New York, San Francisco, 21 years, 1942 through 1965, except 1943, 1944, 1945 in military service.
A.L.—305—Eddie Plank, Philadelphia, St. Louis, 16 years, 1901 through 1917, except 1915.

Most games won as relief pitcher, career
M.L.—124—Hoyt Wilhelm, New York N.L., St. Louis N.L., Cleveland A.L., California A.L., Atlanta N.L., Baltimore A.L., Chicago A.L., Chicago N.L., Los Angeles N.L., 21 years, 1952 through 1972 (73 in A.L., 51 in N.L.).
N.L.—96—Roy Face, Pittsburgh, Montreal, 16 years, 1953 through 1969, except 1954 (lost 82).
A.L.—87—Sparky Lyle, Boston, New York, Texas, Chicago, 15 years, 1967 through 1982, except 1981 (lost 67).

Most games won from one club, career
N.L.—70—Grover Alexander, Philadelphia, Chicago, St. Louis, vs. Cincinnati, 20 years, 1911 through 1930.
A.L.—66—Walter Johnson, Washington, vs. Detroit, 21 years, 1907 through 1927.

Most season-opening games won, career
A.L.—9—Walter Johnson, Washington, 1910, 1913, 1914, 1915, 1916, 1917, 1919, 1924, 1926 (all complete; seven shutouts).
N.L.—8—Grover Alexander, Philadelphia, Chicago, St. Louis, 1914, 1915, 1916, 1917, 1921, 1922, 1925, 1929 (seven complete; one shutout).

SEASON AND MONTH

Most games won by righthander, season
N.L.—60—Hoss Radbourn, Providence, 1884 (lost 12).
A.L.—41—Jack Chesbro, New York, 1904 (lost 13).

N.L. since 1900—37—Christy Mathewson, New York, 1908 (lost 11).

For a complete list of 20-game winners each season, see page 211.

Most games won by lefthander, season

A.A.—46—Matt Kilroy, Baltimore, 1887 (lost 20).
N.L.—42—Charles Baldwin, Detroit, 1886 (lost 14).
A.L.—31—Lefty Grove, Philadelphia, 1931 (lost 4).
N.L. since 1900—27
Sandy Koufax, Los Angeles, 1966 (lost 9).
Steve Carlton, Philadelphia, 1972 (lost 10).

Most games won as relief pitcher, season

N.L.—18—Roy Face, Pittsburgh, 1959 (lost 1).
A.L.—17
John Hiller, Detroit, 1974 (lost 14).
Bill Campbell, Minnesota, 1976 (lost 5).

Fewest games won by leader, season

N.L.—18—Rick Sutcliffe, Chicago, 1987 (lost 10).
A.L.—18
Whitey Ford, New York, 1955 (lost 7).
Bob Lemon, Cleveland, 1955 (lost 10).
Frank Sullivan, Boston, 1955 (lost 13).
Chuck Estrada, Baltimore, 1960 (lost 11).
Jim Perry, Cleveland, 1960 (lost 10).

Most years leading league in games won

N.L.—8—Warren Spahn, Boston, Milwaukee, 1949, 1950, 1953 (tied), 1957, 1958 (tied), 1959 (tied), 1960 (tied), 1961 (tied).
A.L.—6
Walter Johnson, Washington, 1913, 1914, 1915, 1916, 1918, 1924.
Bob Feller, Cleveland, 1939, 1940, 1941, 1946 (tied), 1947, 1951.

Most games won by rookie, season

N.L.—47—Al Spalding, Chicago, 1876 (lost 13).
N.L. since 1900—28—Grover Alexander, Philadelphia, 1911 (lost 13).
A.L.—24—Edgar Summers, Detroit, 1908 (lost 12).

Most games won from one club, season

N.L.—12—Hoss Radbourn, Providence vs. Cleveland, 1884 (lost 1).
N.L. since 1900—9—Ed Reulbach, Chicago vs. Brooklyn, 1908 (lost 0).
A.L.—9
Frank Smith, Chicago vs. Washington, 1904 (lost 1).
Ed Walsh, Chicago vs. New York, 1908 (lost 1), and vs. Boston, 1908 (lost 0).
Walter Johnson, Washington vs. Chicago, 1912 (lost 1).

Most games won, one month

N.L.—15—John Clarkson, Chicago, June 1885 (lost 1).
N.L. since 1900—9
Christy Mathewson, New York, August 1903 (lost 1).
Christy Mathewson, New York, August, 1904 (lost 1).
Grover Alexander, Chicago, May 1920 (lost 0).
A.L.—10—Rube Waddell, Philadelphia, July 1902 (lost 1, tied 1).

20 AND 30-WIN SEASONS

Most years winning 30 or more games

N.L.—7—Kid Nichols, Boston, 1891, 1892, 1893, 1894, 1896, 1897, 1898.
N.L. since 1900—4—Christy Mathewson, New York, 1903, 1904, 1905, 1908.
A.L.—2
Cy Young, Boston, 1901, 1902.
Walter Johnson, Washington, 1912, 1913.

For a complete list of pitchers with two or more 30-victory seasons, see page 179.

Most years winning 20 or more games

M.L.—16—Cy Young, Cleveland N.L., 1891, 1892, 1893, 1894, 1895, 1896, 1897, 1898; St. Louis, N.L., 1899, 1900; Boston A.L., 1901, 1902, 1903, 1904, 1907, 1908 (10 in N.L., 6 in A.L.).

For a complete list of 20-game winners each season, see page 211. For a complete list of pitchers with five or more 20-victory seasons, see page 179.

Most years winning 20 or more games by righthander

N.L.—13—Christy Mathewson, New York, 1901, 1903, 1904, 1905, 1906, 1907, 1908, 1909, 1910, 1911, 1912, 1913, 1914.
A.L.—12—Walter Johnson, Washington, 1910, 1911, 1912, 1913, 1914, 1915, 1916, 1917, 1918, 1919, 1924, 1925.

Most years winning 20 or more games by lefthander

N.L.—13—Warren Spahn, Boston, Milwaukee, 1947, 1949, 1950, 1951, 1953, 1954, 1956, 1957, 1958, 1959, 1960, 1961, 1963.
A.L.—8—Lefty Grove, Philadelphia, Boston, 1927, 1928, 1929, 1930, 1931, 1932, 1933, 1935.

Most consecutive years winning 20 or more games

M.L.—14—Cy Young, Cleveland N.L., St. Louis N.L. Boston A.L., 1891 through 1904 (10 in N.L., 4 in A.L.).
N.L.—12—Christy Mathewson, New York, 1903 through 1914.
A.L.—10—Walter Johnson, Washington, 1910 through 1919.

Most consecutive years winning 20 or more games from start of career

N.L.—10—Kid Nichols, Boston, 1890 through 1899.
A.L.—3—Vean Gregg, Cleveland, 1911, 1912, 1913.

DOUBLEHEADER

Most complete-game doubleheaders won, career

N.L.—3—Joe McGinnity, New York, 1903 (lost 0).
A.L.—2—Ed Walsh, Chicago, 1905, 1908 (lost 0).

For a complete list of pitchers with two complete-game victories in one day, see page 209.

Most complete-game doubleheaders won, season

N.L.—3—Joe McGinnity, New York, 1903.
A.L.—1—Held by many pitchers. Last pitcher—Dutch Levsen, Cleveland vs. Boston, August 28, 1926.

CONSECUTIVE

Most consecutive games won, career

N.L.—24—Carl Hubbell, New York, July 17, 1936, through May 27, 1937 (16 in 1936, 8 in 1937).
A.L.—20—Roger Clemens, Toronto, New York, June 3, 1998 through June 1, 1999 (15 with Toronto in 1998, 5 with New York in 1999).

Most consecutive games won from start of career as starting pitcher

N.L.—12—George Wiltse, New York, May 29 through September 15, 1904.
A.L.—9—Whitey Ford, New York, July 17 through September 24, second game, 1950.

Most consecutive games won from start of career as relief pitcher

N.L.—12—Butch Metzger, San Francisco, 1974 (1), San Diego, 1975 (1), 1976 (10), September 21, 1974 through August 8, 1976.
A.L.—9
Joe Pate, Philadelphia, April 15 through August 10, 1926.
Jeff Zimmerman, Texas, April 14 through August 2, 1999.

Most consecutive games won from one club, career

N.L.—24—Christy Mathewson, New York, vs. St. Louis, June 16, 1904 through September 15, 1908.
A.L.—23—Carl Mays, Boston, New York, vs. Philadelphia, August 30, 1918 through July 24, 1923.

Most consecutive games won, season

N.L.—19
  Tim Keefe, New York, June 23 through August 10, 1888.
  Rube Marquard, New York, April 11 through July 3, first game, 1912.
A.L.—16
  Walter Johnson, Washington, July 3, second game, through August 23, first game, 1912.
  Joe Wood, Boston, July 8 through September 15, second game, 1912.
  Lefty Grove, Philadelphia, June 8 through August 19, 1931.
  Schoolboy Rowe, Detroit, June 15 through August 25, 1934.
  Roger Clemens, New York, May 26 through September 19, 2001.

For a complete list of pitchers with 12 consecutive victories in one season, see page 210.

Most consecutive games won by relief pitcher, season

N.L.—17—Roy Face, Pittsburgh, April 22 through August 30, second game, 1959.
A.L.—12—Luis Arroyo, New York, July 1 through September 9, 1961.

Most consecutive games won from start of season

N.L.—19—Rube Marquard, New York, April 11 through July 3, 1912, first game.
A.L.—15
  Johnny Allen, Cleveland, April 23, 1937, through September 30, 1937, first game.
  Dave McNally, Baltimore, April 12 through July 30, 1969.

Most consecutive games won by rookie, season

N.L.—17—Pat Luby, Chicago, August 6, second game, through October 3, 1890.
N.L. since 1900—12—George Wiltse, New York, May 29 through September 15, 1904.
A.L.—12
  Atley Donald, New York, May 9 through July 25, 1939.
  Russ Ford, New York, August 9 through October 6, 1910.

Most consecutive games won by rookie as starting pitcher, season

N.L.—17—Pat Luby, Chicago, August 6, second game, through October 3, 1890.
N.L. since 1900—12—George Wiltse, New York, May 29 through September 15, 1904.
A.L.—12—Atley Donald, New York, May 9 through July 25, 1939.

Most consecutive games won by rookie as relief pitcher, season

N.L.—10
  Eddie Yuhas, St. Louis, June 5 through September 25, 1952 (end of season).
  Butch Metzger, San Diego, April 20 through August 8, 1976.
A.L.—9
  Joe Pate, Philadelphia, April 15 through August 10, 1926.
  Jeff Zimmerman, Texas, April 14 through August 2, 1999.

Most consecutive games won by a relief pitcher making consecutive appearances during club's winning streak

A.L.—3
  Hal White, Detroit, September 26, second game, 27 28, 1950, 5.1 innings.
  Grant Jackson, Baltimore, September 29, 30, October 1, 1974, 5.1 innings.
  Sparky Lyle, New York, August 29, 30, 31, 1977, 7.2 innings.
  Chuck McElroy, California, June 10, 11, 12, 1996, three innings.
  John Frascatore, Toronto, June 29, 30, July 1, 1999, 2.1 innings.
N.L.—3
  Mike G. Marshall, Los Angeles, June 21, 22, 23, 1974, 7 innings.
  Gene Garber, Philadelphia, May 15, second game, 16, 17, 1975, 5.2 innings.
  Al Hrabosky, St. Louis, July 12, 13, 17, 1975, five innings.
  Kent Tekulve, Pittsburgh, May 6, 7, 9, 1980, 5.1 innings.
  Mitch Williams, Philadelphia, August 4, 6, 7, 1991, four innings.

Most consecutive games won, end of season

N.L.—17—Pat Luby, Chicago, August 6, second game, through October 3, 1890.

N.L. since 1900—16—Carl Hubbell, New York, July 17 through September 23, 1936.
A.L.—15
  Alvin Crowder, Washington, August 2 through September 25, 1932.
  Roger Clemens, Toronto, June 3 through September 21, 1998.

SAVES (SINCE 1969)

Most saves, career

M.L.—478—Lee Smith, Chicago N.L., Boston A.L., St. Louis N.L., New York A.L., Baltimore A.L., California A.L., Cincinnati N.L., Montreal N.L., 18 years, 1980 through 1997 (347 in N.L., 131 in A.L.).
N.L.—422—John Franco, Cincinnati, New York, 18 years, 1984 through 2001.
A.L.—324—Dennis Eckersley, Cleveland, Boston, Oakland, 20 years, 1975 through 1984, 1987 through 1995, 1998.

For a complete list of pitchers with 150 or more career saves, see page 179.

Most saves, season

A.L.—57—Bobby Thigpen, Chicago, 1990.
N.L.—53
  Randy Myers, Chicago, 1993.
  Trevor Hoffman, San Diego, 1998.

Most saves by rookie, season

A.L.—37—Kazuhiro Sasaki, Seattle, 2000.
N.L.—36—Todd Worrell, St. Louis, 1986.

GAMES LOST

Most games lost, career

M.L.—313—Cy Young, Cleveland N.L., St. Louis N.L., Boston A.L., Cleveland A.L., Boston N.L., 22 years, 1890 through 1911 (172 in N.L., 141 in A.L.).
A.L.—279—Walter Johnson, Washington, 21 years, 1907 through 1927.
N.L.—268—Pud Galvin, Buffalo, Pittsburgh, St. Louis, 12 years, 1879 through 1892, except 1886 and 1890.
N.L. since 1900—251—Eppa Rixey, Philadelphia, Cincinnati, 21 years, 1912 through 1933, except 1918 in military service.

Most games lost by righthander, career

A.L.—279—Walter Johnson, Washington, 21 years, 1907 through 1927.
N.L.—268—Pud Galvin, Buffalo, Pittsburgh, St. Louis, 12 years, 1879 through 1892, except 1886 and 1890.
N.L. since 1900—230—Phil Niekro, Milwaukee, Atlanta, 21 years, 1964 through 1983, 1987.

Most games lost by lefthander, career

N.L.—251—Eppa Rixey, Philadelphia, Cincinnati, 21 years, 1912 through 1933, except 1918 in military service.
A.L.—221—Frank Tanana, California, Boston, Texas, Detroit, New York, 1973 through 1993, 21 years.

Most consecutive games lost, career

N.L.—27—Anthony Young, New York, May 6, 1992 through July 24, 1993 (14 in 1992, 13 in 1993).
A.L.—19—Jack Nabors, Philadelphia, April 28 through September 28, 1916.

Most consecutive games lost to one club, career

N.L.—13—Don Sutton, Los Angeles vs. Chicago, April 23, 1966 through July 24, 1969 (start of career).
A.L.—10—Dave Morehead, Boston vs. Los Angeles, July 28, 1963 through September 28, 1965 (start of career).

Most consecutive games lost from start of career

A.L.—16—Terry Felton, Minnesota, April 18, 1980, second game, through September 12, 1982.
A.A.—10—Charlie Stecher, Philadelphia, September 6 through October 9, 1890.

Most games lost, season
N.L.—48—John F. Coleman, Philadelphia, 1883 (won 11).
N.L. since 1900—29—Vic Willis, Boston, 1905 (won 12).
A.L.—26
  Jack Townsend, Washington, 1904 (won five).
  Bob Groom, Washington, 1909 (won six).

Most years leading league in games lost
N.L.—4—Phil Niekro, Atlanta, 1977 (tied), 1978, 1979, 1980.
A.L.—4
  Bobo Newsom, St. Louis, Washington, Detroit, Philadelphia, 1934, 1935, 1941, 1945.
  Pedro Ramos, Washington, Minnesota, 1958, 1959, 1960, 1961.

Fewest games lost for leader, season
A.L.—14
  Ted Gray, Detroit, 1951 (won seven).
  Alex Kellner, Philadelphia, 1951 (won 11).
  Bob Lemon, Cleveland 1951 (won 17).
  Billy Pierce, Chicago, 1951 (won 15).
  Duane Pillette, St. Louis, 1951 (won six).
  Dizzy Trout, Detroit, 1951 (won nine).
N.L.—15
  Don Carman, Philadelphia, 1989 (won five).
  Orel Hershiser, Los Angeles, 1989 (won 15).
  Ken Hill, St. Louis, 1989 (won seven).
  Tom Candiotti, Los Angeles, 1992 (won 11).
  Orel Hershiser, Los Angeles, 1992 (won 10).

Most games lost as relief pitcher, season
N.L.—16—Gene Garber, Atlanta, 1979 (won six).
A.L.—14
  Darold Knowles, Washington, 1970 (won two).
  John Hiller, Detroit, 1974 (won 17).
  Mike G. Marshall, Minnesota, 1979 (won 10, also lost one game as starter).

Most games lost by rookie, season
N.L.—34
  Jim Devlin, Louisville, 1876 (won 30).
  Bobby Mathews, New York, 1876 (won 21).
N.L. since 1900—25—Harry McIntire, Brooklyn, 1906 (won eight).
A.L.—26—Bob Groom, Washington, 1909 (won six).

Most games lost to one club, season (since 1900)
N.L.—7—Held by seven pitchers. Last time—Cal McLish, Cincinnati vs. Pittsburgh, 1960 (won none).
A.L.—7—Held by 4 pitchers. Last time—Camilo Pascual, Washington vs. New York, 1956 (won none).

Most consecutive games lost, season
A.L.—19—Jack Nabors, Philadelphia, April 28 through September 28, 1916.
N.L.—18
  Cliff Curtis, Boston, June 13, first game, through September 20, first game, 1910.
  Roger Craig, New York, May 4 through August 4, 1963.

For a complete list of pitchers with 12 consecutive games lost in one season, see page 210.

Most consecutive games lost by rookie, season
N.L.—16—Charles Dean, Cincinnati, July 11 through September 12, 1876.
N.L. since 1900—14—Anthony Young, New York, May 6 through September 29, 1992.
A.L.—13
  Guy Morton, Cleveland, June 24 through September 20, 1914.
  Terry Felton, Minnesota, April 17 through September 12, 1982.

Most consecutive games lost from start of season
A.L.—14
  Joe Harris, Boston, May 10 through July 25, 1906.
  Matt Keough, Oakland, April 15 through August 8, 1979.
N.L.—13—Anthony Young, New York, April 9 through July 24, 1993.

Most consecutive games lost at end of season
A.L.—19—Jack Nabors, Philadelphia, April 28 through September 28, 1916.

N.L.—18—Cliff Curtis, Boston, June 13, first game, through September 20, 1910, first game.

AT-BATS AND PLATE APPEARANCES

Most at-bats, career
A.L.—21,663—Walter Johnson, Washington, 21 years, 1907 through 1927.
N.L.—19,778—Warren Spahn, Boston, Milwaukee, New York, San Francisco, 21 years, 1942 through 1965, except 1943, 1944, 1945 in military service.

Most at-bats, season
N.L.—2,808—Will White, Cincinnati, 75 games, 683 innings, 1879.
N.L. since 1900—1,658—Joe McGinnity, New York, 55 games, 434 innings, 1903.
A.L.—1,690—Ed Walsh, Chicago, 66 games, 464 innings, 1908.

Most years leading league in at-bats
N.L.—6—Grover Alexander, Philadelphia, Chicago, 1911, 1914, 1915, 1916, 1917, 1920.
A.L.—4
  Ed Walsh, Chicago, 1908, 1910, 1911, 1912.
  Walter Johnson, Washington, 1913, 1914, 1915, 1916.
  Bob Lemon, Cleveland, 1948, 1950, 1952, 1953.

Most consecutive years leading league in at-bats
A.L.—4—Walter Johnson, Washington, 1913, 1914, 1915, 1916.
N.L.—4
  Grover Alexander, Philadelphia, 1914, 1915, 1916, 1917.
  Robin Roberts, Philadelphia, 1952, 1953, 1954, 1955.

Fewest official at-bats for leader, season
A.L.—942—Jim Bunning, Detroit, 250 innings, 1959.
N.L.—1,009—Dave Koslo, New York, 265 innings, 1946.

Most at-bats, game
N.L.—66—George Derby, Buffalo, July 3, 1883.
N.L. since 1900—49—Bill Phillips, Cincinnati, June 24, 1901, second game.
A.L.—53—Roy Patterson, Chicago, May 5, 1901.

Most men facing pitcher, nine-inning game
N.L.—67—George Derby, Buffalo, July 3, 1883.
N.L. since 1900—55—Bill Phillips, Cincinnati, June 24, 1901, second game.
A.L.—57—Roy Patterson, Chicago, May 5, 1901.

Most men facing pitcher, inning
N.L.—22—Tony Mullane, Baltimore, June 18, 1894, a.m. game, first inning.
N.L. since 1900—16—Hal Kelleher, Philadelphia, May 5, 1938, eighth inning.
A.L.—16
  Merle Adkins, Boston, July 8, 1902, sixth inning.
  Lefty O'Doul, Boston, July 7, 1923, first game, sixth inning.
  Howard Ehmke, Boston, September 28, 1923, sixth inning.

RUNS

Most runs allowed, career
M.L.—3,303—Pud Galvin, Buffalo N.L., Pittsburgh A.A., Pittsburgh N.L., Pittsburgh P.L., St. Louis N.L., 14 years, 1879 through 1892.
A.L.—2,117—Red Ruffing, Boston, New York, Chicago, 22 years, 1924 through 1947, except 1943, 1944.
N.L.—2,037—Burleigh Grimes, Pittsburgh, Brooklyn, New York, Boston, St. Louis, Chicago, 19 years, 1916 through 1934.

For a complete list of pitchers allowing 1,800 or more career runs, see page 179.

Most runs allowed, season
N.L.—544—John F. Coleman, Philadelphia, 63 games, 538 innings, 1883.
N.L. since 1900—224—Bill Carrick, New York, 45 games, 342 innings, 1900.
A.L.—219—Joe McGinnity, Baltimore, 48 games, 378 innings, 1901.

Most years leading league in runs allowed

N.L.—3
   Burleigh Grimes, Brooklyn, Pittsburgh, 1923, 1924, 1928.
   Robin Roberts, Philadelphia, 1955, 1956, 1957.
   Phil Niekro, Atlanta, 1977, 1978, 1979.
   Rick Mahler, Atlanta, Cincinnati, 1986, 1988, 1989.
A.L.—3—Wilbur Wood, Chicago, 1972, 1973, 1975.

Fewest runs allowed for leader, season

N.L.—102—George Smith, New York, Philadelphia, 196 innings, 1919.
A.L.—108—Jim Bagby, Cleveland, 280 innings, 1918.

Most runs allowed, game

N.L.—35—Dave Rowe, Cleveland, July 24, 1882.
N.L. since 1900—21—Harley Parker, Cincinnati, June 21, 1901.
A.L.—24—Al Travers, Detroit, May 18, 1912 (only major league game).

Fewest runs allowed, doubleheader

N.L.—0—Ed Reulbach, Chicago, September 26, 1908.
A.L.—1
   Ed Walsh, Chicago, September 29, 1908.
   Carl Mays, Boston, August 30, 1918.

Most runs allowed, inning

N.L.—16—Tony Mullane, Baltimore, June 18, 1894, a.m. game, first inning.
N.L. since 1900—12—Hal Kelleher, Philadelphia, May 5, 1938, eighth inning.
A.L.—13—Lefty O'Doul, Boston, July 7, 1923, first game, sixth inning.

EARNED RUNS

Most earned runs allowed, season (since 1900)

A.L.—186—Bobo Newsom, St. Louis, 330 innings, 1938.
N.L.—155—Guy Bush, Chicago, 225 innings, 1930.

Most years leading league in earned runs allowed

N.L.—3
   Burleigh Grimes, Brooklyn, 1922, 1924, 1925.
   Murry Dickson, St. Louis, Pittsburgh, 1948, 1951, 1952 (tied).
   Robin Roberts, Philadelphia, 1955, 1956, 1957.
   Jack Fisher, New York, 1964 (tied), 1965 (tied), 1967.
A.L.—3
   Bobo Newsom, St. Louis, Washington, Philadelphia, 1938, 1942, 1945.
   Wilbur Wood, Chicago, 1972, 1973, 1975.

Fewest earned runs for leader, season

A.L.—83
   Willie Adams, Philadelphia, 169 innings, 1918.
   Hooks Dauss, Detroit, 250 innings, 1918.
N.L.—85
   Pete Schneider, Cincinnati, 217 innings, 1918.
   Art Nehf, Boston, 284 innings, 1918.
   Wilbur Cooper, Pittsburgh, 287 innings, 1919.

EARNED-RUN AVERAGE

Lowest earned-run average, career (300 or more games won)

A.L.—2.47—Walter Johnson, Washington, 802 games, 21 years, 1907 through 1927. (Johnson's record includes 520 total runs in 1,729 innings from 1907 through 1912, a period in which earned runs were not compiled. Had earned runs been compiled for that period, Johnson's earned-run average would be even lower.)
N.L.—2.61—Grover Alexander, Philadelphia, Chicago, St. Louis, 696 games, 20 years, 1911 through 1930. (Alexander's record includes 133 total runs in 366 innings in 1911, a year in which earned runs were not compiled. Had earned runs been compiled that year, Alexander's earned-run average would be even lower.)

For a complete list of pitchers with career earned-run averages of 3.50 or lower with 3,000 or more innings, see page 180.

Lowest earned-run average, career (200 or more games won)

A.L.—2.47—Walter Johnson, Washington, 802 games, 21 years, 1907 through 1927. (Johnson's record includes 520 total runs in 1,729 innings from 1907 through 1912, a period in which earned runs were not compiled. Had earned runs been compiled for that period, Johnson's earned-run average would be even lower.)
N.L.—2.61—Grover Alexander, Philadelphia, Chicago, St. Louis, 696 games, 20 years, 1911 through 1930. (Alexander's record includes 133 total runs in 366 innings in 1911, a year in which earned runs were not compiled. Had earned runs been compiled that year, Alexander's earned-run average would be even lower.)

Lowest earned-run average, career (2,000 or more innings)

N.L.—2.33—Hippo Vaughn, Chicago, 2,217 innings, 305 games, nine years, 1913 through 1921.
A.L.—2.47—Walter Johnson, Washington, 5,924 innings, 802 games, 21 years, 1907 through 1927. (Johnson's record includes 520 total runs in 1,729 innings from 1907 through 1912, a period in which earned runs were not compiled. Had earned runs been compiled for that period, Johnson's earned-run average would be even lower.)

Lowest earned-run average, season (300 or more innings)

N.L.—1.12—Bob Gibson, St. Louis, 305 innings, 1968.
A.L.—1.14—Walter Johnson, Washington, 346 innings, 1913.

Lowest earned-run average by righthander, season (300 or more innings)

N.L.—1.12—Bob Gibson, St. Louis, 305 innings, 1968.
A.L.—1.14—Walter Johnson, Washington, 346 innings, 1913.

Lowest earned-run average by lefthander, season (300 or more innings)

N.L.—1.66—Carl Hubbell, New York, 309 innings, 1933.
A.L.—1.75—Babe Ruth, Boston, 324 innings, 1916.

Lowest earned-run average, season (200 or more innings)

A.L.—1.00—Dutch H. Leonard, Boston, 225 innings, 1914.
N.L.—1.12—Bob Gibson, St. Louis, 305 innings, 1968.

Most years leading league in lowest earned-run average

A.L.—9—Lefty Grove, Philadelphia, Boston, 1926, 1929, 1930, 1931, 1932, 1935, 1936, 1938, 1939.
N.L.—5
   Grover Alexander, Philadelphia, Chicago, 1915, 1916, 1917, 1919, 1920.
   Sandy Koufax, Los Angeles, 1962, 1963, 1964, 1965, 1966.

Most consecutive years leading league in lowest earned-run average

N.L.—5—Sandy Koufax, Los Angeles, 1962, 1963, 1964, 1965, 1966.
A.L.—4—Lefty Grove, Philadelphia, 1929, 1930, 1931, 1932.

Highest earned-run average for leader, season

A.L.—3.20—Early Wynn, Cleveland, 214 innings, 1950.
N.L.—3.08—Bill Walker, New York, 178 innings, 1929.

SHUTOUTS

Most shutouts won or tied by righthander, career

A.L.—110—Walter Johnson, Washington, 21 years, 1907 through 1927.
N.L.—90—Grover Alexander, Philadelphia, Chicago, St. Louis, 20 years, 1911 through 1930.

For a complete list of pitchers with 40 or more career shutouts, see page 180.

Most shutouts won or tied by lefthander, career

A.L.—64—Eddie Plank, Philadelphia, St. Louis, 16 years, 1901 through 1917, except 1915.
N.L.—63—Warren Spahn, Boston, Milwaukee, New York, San Francisco, 21 years, 1942 through 1965, except 1943, 1944, 1945 in military service.

Most shutouts won from one club, career

A.L.—23—Walter Johnson, Washington vs. Philadelphia, 21 years, 1907 through 1927.

N.L.—20—Grover Alexander, Philadelphia, Chicago, St. Louis vs. Cincinnati, 20 years, 1911 through 1930.

Most shutouts lost, career

A.L.—65—Walter Johnson, Washington, 21 years, 1907 through 1927 (won 109, tied 1).

N.L.—40—Christy Mathewson, New York, Cincinnati, 17 years, 1900 through 1916 (won 83).

Most shutouts won or tied in season openers

A.L.—7—Walter Johnson, Washington, 1910 to 1926.

N.L.—3

Rip Sewell, Pittsburgh, 1943, 1947, 1949.
Chris Short, Philadelphia, 1965, 1968, 1970.
Rick Mahler, Atlanta, 1982, 1986, 1987.

Most shutouts won or tied by righthander, season

N.L.—16

George Bradley, St. Louis, 1876.
Grover Alexander, Philadelphia, 1916.

A.L.—13—Jack Coombs, Philadelphia, 1910.

Most shutouts won or tied by lefthander, season

A.A.—12—Ed Morris, Pittsburgh, 1886.

N.L.—11—Sandy Koufax, Los Angeles, 1963.

A.L.—9

Babe Ruth, Boston, 1916.
Ron Guidry, New York, 1978.

Most shutouts participated in, season

N.L.—20—Grover Alexander, Philadelphia, 1916 (won 16, lost 4).

A.L.—18—Ed Walsh, Chicago, 1908 (won 12, lost 6).

Most shutouts lost, season

N.L.—14—Jim Devlin, Louisville, 1876 (won 5).

N.L. since 1900—11—Art Raymond, St. Louis, 1908 (won 5).

A.L.—10—Walter Johnson, Washington, 1909 (won 4).

Most years leading league in shutouts won or tied

N.L.—7—Grover Alexander, Philadelphia, Chicago, 1911 (tied), 1913, 1915, 1916, 1917, 1919, 1921 (tied).

A.L.—7—Walter Johnson, Washington, 1911 (tied), 1913, 1914, 1915, 1918 (tied), 1919, 1924.

Most shutouts won or tied by rookie, season

N.L.—16—George Bradley, St. Louis, 1876.

N.L. since 1900—8—Fernando Valenzuela, Los Angeles, 1981.

A.L.—8

Russ Ford, New York, 1910.
Reb Russell, Chicago, 1913.

Most years with 10 or more shutouts won or tied

A.L.—2—Ed Walsh, Chicago, 1906, 1908.

N.L.—2—Grover Alexander, Philadelphia, 1915, 1916.

Most clubs shut out (won or tied), season

N.L. (10-club league)—8—Bob Gibson, St. Louis, 1968.

N.L. (8-club league)—7

Pud Galvin, Buffalo, 1884.
Christy Mathewson, New York, 1907.
Grover Alexander, Philadelphia, 1913 and 1916; also with Chicago, 1919.

A.L. (12-club league)—8—Nolan Ryan, California, 1972.

A.L. (8-club league)—7

Cy Young, Boston, 1904.
Jack Coombs, Philadelphia, 1910.

Most shutouts won from one club, season

N.L.—5

Charles Baldwin, Detroit vs. Philadelphia, 1886.
Grover Alexander, Philadelphia vs. Cincinnati, 1916.
Larry Jaster, St. Louis vs. Los Angeles, 1966, consecutive.

A.L.—5—Tom Hughes, Washington vs. Cleveland, 1905.

A.A.—5—Tony Mullane, Cincinnati vs. New York, 1887.

Most shutouts lost to one club, season

N.L.—5—Jim Devlin, Louisville vs. Hartford, 1876.

A.L.—5—Walter Johnson, Washington vs. Chicago, 1909.

N.L. since 1900—4—Irv Young, Boston vs. Pittsburgh, 1906.

Most shutouts won or tied, one month

A.L.—6

Doc White, Chicago, September, 1904.
Ed Walsh, Chicago, August, 1906; September, 1908.

N.L.—5

George Bradley, St. Louis, May, 1876.
Tommy Bond, Hartford, June, 1876.
Pud Galvin, Buffalo, August, 1884.
Ben Sanders, Philadelphia, September, 1888.
Don Drysdale, Los Angeles, May, 1968.
Bob Gibson, St. Louis, June, 1968.
Orel Hershiser, Los Angeles, September, 1988.

Most shutouts lost, one month

A.L.—5—Walter Johnson, Washington, July, 1909.

N.L.—4

Jim Devlin, Louisville, June, 1876.
Fred Fitzsimmons, New York, September, 1934.
Jim McAndrew, New York, August, 1968.

Fewest shutouts pitched by leader, season

A.L.-N.L.—3—Held by many pitchers.

Pitching shutout in first major league game (nine innings)

N.L.—Held by 38 pitchers. Last pitcher—Mark Brownson, Colorado, July 21, 1998.

A.L.—Held by 35 pitchers. Last pitcher—Mike Norris, Oakland, April 10, 1975.

Most shutouts, first two major league games

N.L.—2

Al Spalding, Chicago, April 25, 27, 1876.
Jim Hughes, Baltimore, April 18, 22, 1898.
Al Worthington, New York, July 6, 11, 1953.
Karl Spooner, Brooklyn, September 22, 26, 1954.

A.L.—2

Joe Doyle, New York, August 25, first game; August 30, first game, 1906.
John Marcum, Philadelphia, September 7, September 11, second game, 1933.
Dave Ferriss, Boston, April 29, first game, May 6, first game, 1945.
Tom Phoebus, Baltimore, September 15, first game, September 20, 1966.

Most shutouts won or tied, four consecutive days

A.L.—3

Jimmy Dygert, Philadelphia, October 1, 3, 4, second game, 1907.
Walter Johnson, Washington, September 4, 5, 7, first game, 1908.

N.L.—2—held by many pitchers.

Most shutouts won or tied, five consecutive days

N.L.—3

George Bradley, St. Louis, July 11, 13, 15, 1876.
John Clarkson, Chicago, May 21, 22, 25, 1885.

Most consecutive shutouts won or tied, season

N.L.—6—Don Drysdale, Los Angeles, May 14, 18, 22, 26, 31, June 4, 1968.

A.L.—5—Doc White, Chicago, September 12, 16, 19, 25, 30, 1904.

Most consecutive shutouts lost, season

N.L.—4—Jim McAndrew, New York, July 21, first game; August 4, second game; August 10, second game; August 17, 1968.

A.L.—2—Held by many pitchers.

Most doubleheader shutouts

N.L.—1—Ed Reulbach, Chicago vs. Brooklyn, September 26, 1908 (won 5-0, 3-0).

A.L.—None.

Longest complete shutout game pitched

N.L.—18 innings

Monte Ward, Providence, August 17, 1882 (won 1-0).
Carl Hubbell, New York, July 2, 1933, first game (won 1-0).

A.L.—18 innings

Ed Summers, Detroit, July 16, 1909 (0-0 tie).
Walter Johnson, Washington, May 15, 1918 (won 1-0).

CONSECUTIVE SCORELESS INNINGS

Most consecutive scoreless innings by righthander, season
N.L.—59—Orel Hershiser, Los Angeles, from sixth inning, August 30 through 10th inning, September 28, 1988.
A.L.—55.2—Walter Johnson, Washington, from second inning, April 10 through third inning, May 14, 1913 (includes two relief appearances).

Most consecutive scoreless innings by lefthander, season
N.L.—45.1—Carl Hubbell, New York, from seventh inning, July 13 through fifth inning, August 1, 1933 (includes two relief appearances).
A.L.—45—Doc White, Chicago, September 12 through September 30, 1904.

Most consecutive scoreless innings from start of career
N.L.—25—George McQuillan, Philadelphia, from first inning, May 8, through ninth inning, September 29, first game, 1907.
A.L.—22—Dave Ferriss, Boston, from first inning, April 29, through fourth inning, May 13, 1945.

Most consecutive scoreless innings, game
N.L.—21—Joe Oeschger, Boston, May 1, 1920; sixth through 26th innings.
A.L.—20—Joe Harris, Boston, September 1, 1906; fourth through 23rd innings.

1-0 GAMES

Most 1-0 games won, career
A.L.—38—Walter Johnson, Washington, 21 years, 1907 through 1927.
N.L.—17—Grover Alexander, Philadelphia, Chicago, St. Louis, 20 years, 1911 through 1930.

For a complete list of pitchers with 10 or more career 1-0 victories, see page 180.

Most 1-0 complete games won, season
A.L.—5
    Reb Russell, Chicago, 1913.
    Walter Johnson, Washington, 1913, 1919.
    Joe Bush, Boston, 1918.
    Dean Chance, Los Angeles, 1964 (also one incomplete game).
N.L.—5—Carl Hubbell, New York, 1933.

Most years leading league in 1-0 games won
A.L.—8—Walter Johnson, Washington, 1913 (tied), 1914, 1915 (tied), 1919, 1920 (tied), 1922, 1923 (tied), 1926 (tied).
N.L.—4
    Grover Alexander, Philadelphia, Chicago, 1913 (tied), 1916 (tied), 1917 (tied), 1922 (tied).
    Bill C. Lee, Chicago, Philadelphia, Boston, 1934 (tied), 1936, 1944 (tied), 1945 (tied).

Most 1-0 games won from one club, season
A.L.—3
    Stan Coveleski, Cleveland vs. Detroit, 1917.
    Walter Johnson, Washington vs. Philadelphia, 1919.
    Jim Bagby Jr., Cleveland vs. Detroit, 1943.
N.L.—2—Held by many pitchers.

Most 1-0 games lost, career
A.L.—26—Walter Johnson, Washington, 21 years, 1907 through 1927 (won 38).
N.L.—13—Lee Meadows, St. Louis, Philadelphia, Pittsburgh, 15 years, 1915 through 1929 (won 7).

Most 1-0 games lost, season
A.L.—5
    Bill Donovan, Detroit, 1903 (won 1).
    Jack Warhop, New York, 1914 (won 0).
N.L.—5
    George McQuillan, Philadelphia, 1908 (won 2).
    Roger Craig, New York, 1963 (won 0).
    Jim Bunning, Philadelphia, 1967 (won 1).
    Ferguson Jenkins, Chicago, 1968. (won 0).

Most 1-0 games lost to one club, season
A.L.—3—Jack Warhop, New York vs. Washington, 1914.
N.L.—2—Held by many pitchers.

HITS

Most hits allowed, career
M.L.—7,078—Cy Young, Cleveland N.L., St. Louis N.L., Boston A.L., Cleveland A.L., Boston N.L., 22 years, 1890 through 1911 (4,282 in N.L., 2,796 in A.L.).
N.L.—5,490—Pud Galvin, Buffalo, Pittsburgh, St. Louis, 12 years, 1879 through 1892, except 1886, 1890.
N.L. since 1900—4,868—Grover Alexander, Philadelphia, Chicago, St. Louis, 20 years, 1911 through 1930.
A.L.—4,920—Walter Johnson, Washington, 21 years, 1907 through 1927.

For a complete list of pitchers with 4,000 or more career hits allowed, see page 180.

Most hits allowed, season
N.L.—809—John F. Coleman, Philadelphia, 63 games, 548 innings, 1883.
N.L. since 1900—415—Bill Carrick, New York, 45 games, 342 innings, 1900.
A.L.—401—Joe McGinnity, Baltimore, 48 games, 378 innings, 1901.

Fewest hits allowed for leader, season
N.L.—230—Andy Benes, San Diego, 231.1 innings, 1992.
A.L.—243—Mel Stottlemyre, New York, 279 innings, 1968.

Most years leading league in hits allowed
N.L.—5—Robin Roberts, Philadelphia, 1952, 1953, 1954, 1955, 1956.
A.L.—4—Jim Kaat, Minnesota, Chicago, 1965, 1966, 1967, 1975.

Most consecutive hitless innings, season
A.L.—23—Cy Young, Boston, from seventh inning, April 25 through sixth inning, May 11, 1904. (Note: On April 30 Young relieved in third inning after another pitcher had given up hits in that inning.)
N.L.—21—Johnny Vander Meer, Cincinnati, from first inning, June 11 through third inning, June 19, first game, 1938.

Most consecutive batsmen retired, season
N.L.—41—Jim Barr, San Francisco, August 23 (last 21), August 29 (first 20), 1972.
A.L.—38—David Wells, New York, May 12 (last 10), May 17 (all 27), May 23 (first 1), 1998.

Most hits allowed, game
N.L.—36—John Wadsworth, Louisville, August 17, 1894.
N.L. since 1900—26—Harley Parker, Cincinnati, June 21, 1901.
A.L.—26
    Hod Lisenbee, Philadelphia, September 11, 1936.
    Al Travers, Detroit, May 18, 1912 (only major league game).

Most hits allowed, extra-inning game
A.L.—29—Eddie Rommel, Philadelphia, July 10, 1932, pitched last 17 innings of 18-inning game.
N.L.—23—Jeff Pfeffer, Brooklyn, June 1, 1919, 18 innings.

Most hits allowed, two consecutive games
N.L.—48—Jim Callahan, Chicago, September 6 (25), September 11, first game (23), 1900.

Most hits allowed, nine-inning shutout game
N.L.—14—Larry Cheney, Chicago vs. New York, September 14, 1913 (won 7-0).
A.L.—14—Milt Gaston, Washington vs. Cleveland, July 10, 1928, second game (won 9-0).

Fewest hits allowed, first major league game (nine innings)
N.L.—0—Charles L. Jones, Cincinnati, October 15, 1892.
N.L. since 1900—1
    Juan Marichal, San Francisco, July 19, 1960 (single in eighth inning).
    Jimmy Jones, San Diego, September 21, 1986 (triple in third inning).

A.L.—1

Addie Joss, Cleveland, April 26, 1902 (single in seventh inning).
Mike Fornieles, Washington, September 2, 1952, second game (single in second inning).
Billy Rohr, Boston, April 14, 1967 (single with two out in ninth inning).

Fewest hits allowed, opening game of season (nine innings)

A.L.—0—Bob Feller, Cleveland, April 16, 1940.
N.L.—1—Held by many pitchers. Last pitcher—Lon Warneke, Chicago, April 17, 1934. (Leon Ames, New York, allowed no hits in 9.1 innings on April 15, 1909, but lost on seven hits in 13 innings.)

Fewest hits allowed, doubleheader (18 innings)

A.A.—3—Tim Keefe, New York, July 4, 1883.
N.L.—6

Fred Toney, Cincinnati, July 1, 1917.
Herman Bell, St. Louis, July 19, 1924.

A.L.—7

Frank Owen, Chicago, July 1, 1905.
Ed Walsh, Chicago, September 29, 1908.

Fewest hits allowed, two consecutive games (18 innings)

N.L.—0—Johnny Vander Meer, Cincinnati, June 11, 15, 1938.
A.L.—1—Howard Ehmke, Boston, September 7 (0), September 11 (1), 1923.
U.A.—1—Ed Cushman, Milwaukee, September 28 (0), October 4 (1), 1884.
A.A.—2—Tom Ramsey, Louisville, July 29 (1), July 31 (1), 12 innings, 1886.

Fewest hits allowed, three consecutive complete games

N.L.—3—Johnny Vander Meer, Cincinnati, June 5 (3), June 11 (0), June 15 (0), 1938.
A.L.—5—Held by many pitchers.

Most hits allowed, inning

N.L.—13—George Weidman, Detroit, September 6, 1883, seventh inning.
A.L.—12—Merle Adkins, Boston, July 8, 1902, sixth inning.
N.L. since 1900—11—Reggie Grabowski, Philadelphia, August 4, 1934, second game, ninth inning.

Most consecutive hits allowed from start of game

N.L.—7—Bill Bonham, Chicago, August 5, 1975 (3 singles, 2 doubles, 2 homers).
A.L.—5

Frank Tanana, California, May 18, 1980 (1 single, 2 doubles, 2 triples).
Luis Leal, Toronto, June 2, 1980 (2 singles, 3 doubles).
Ross Baumgarten, Chicago, September 27, 1981, first game (5 singles).

Most consecutive hits allowed, game

A.L.—10—Bill Reidy, Milwaukee, June 2, 1901, ninth inning.
N.L.—10—Heinie Meine, Pittsburgh, June 23, 1930, sixth inning.

NO-HIT AND ONE-HIT GAMES

Most no-hitters pitched, career (nine or more innings)

M.L.—7—Nolan Ryan, California A.L., 1973 (2), 1974, 1975; Houston N.L., 1981; Texas A.L., 1990, 1991.
A.L.—6—Nolan Ryan, California, 1973 (2), 1974, 1975; Texas, 1990, 1991.
N.L.—4—Sandy Koufax, Los Angeles, 1962, 1963, 1964, 1965.

For a complete list of no-hitters, see page 204.

Most no-hit games, season

N.L.—2

Johnny Vander Meer, Cincinnati, June 11, 15, 1938 (consecutive).
Jim Maloney, Cincinnati, June 14, first 10 innings of 11-inning game; August 19, 1965, first game, 10 innings.

A.L.—2

Allie Reynolds, New York, July 12, September 28, first game, 1951.
Virgil Trucks, Detroit, May 15, August 25, 1952.
Nolan Ryan, California, May 15, July 15, 1973.

Most consecutive no-hit games

N.L.—2—Johnny Vander Meer, Cincinnati, June 11, 15, 1938.
A.L.—Never accomplished.

Longest no-hit complete game

A.A.—10 innings—Sam Kimber, Brooklyn vs. Toledo, October 4, 1884.
N.L.—10 innings

George Wiltse, New York vs. Philadelphia, July 4, 1908, a.m. game.
Fred Toney, Cincinnati vs. Chicago, May 2, 1917.
Jim Maloney, Cincinnati vs. Chicago, August 19, 1965, first game.

A.L.—9—Held by many pitchers.

Longest one-hit complete game

N.L.—12.2 innings—Harvey Haddix, Pittsburgh vs. Milwaukee, May 26, 1959 (one double).
A.L.—10

Doc White, Chicago vs. Cleveland, September 6, 1903 (one double).
Bobo Newsom, St. Louis vs. Boston, September 18, 1934 (one single).
Bert Blyleven, Texas vs. Oakland, June 21, 1976 (one single).

Most low-hit (no-hit and one-hit) games, career (nine or more innings)

M.L.—19—Nolan Ryan, New York N.L., California A.L., Houston N.L., Texas A.L., 1966, 1968 through 1992 (6 no-hit, 9 one-hit in A.L.; 1 no-hit, 3 one-hit in N.L.).
A.L.—15—Nolan Ryan, California, Texas, 1972 through 1979, 1989 through 1992 (6 no-hit, 9 one-hit).
N.L.—8

Hoss Radbourn, Buffalo, Providence, Boston, Cincinnati, 1880 through 1889, 1891 (1 no-hit, 7 one-hit).
Jim Maloney, Cincinnati, 1960 through 1970 (3 no-hit, 5 one-hit).

Most low-hit (no-hit and one-hit) games, season (nine or more innings)

U.A.—4—Hugh Daily, Chicago, 1884.
N.L.—4—Grover Alexander, Philadelphia, 1915.
A.L.—3

Addie Joss, Cleveland, 1907.
Bob Feller, Cleveland, 1946.
Virgil Trucks, Detroit, 1952.
Nolan Ryan, California, 1973.
Dave Stieb, Toronto, 1988.

Most consecutive one-hit games

U.A.—2—Hugh Daily, Chicago, July 7, 10, 1884.
N.L.—2

Charlie Buffinton, Philadelphia, August 6, 9, 1887.
Rube Marquard, New York, August 28, September 1, second game, 1911.
Lon Warneke, Chicago, April 17, 22, 1934 (his first two games of season).
Morton Cooper, St. Louis, May 31, first game, June 4, 1943.

A.A.—2—Tom Ramsey, Louisville, July 29, 31, 12 innings, 1886.

A.L.—2

Whitey Ford, New York, September 2, 7, 1955.
Sam McDowell, Cleveland, April 25, May 1, 1966.
Dave Stieb, Toronto, September 24, 30, 1988.

SINGLES, DOUBLES AND TRIPLES

Most singles allowed, game

N.L.—28—John Wadsworth, Louisville, August 17, 1894.
A.L.—23—Charles Baker, Cleveland, April 28, 1901.

Most singles allowed, inning

N.L.—10—Reggie Grabowski, Philadelphia, August 4, 1934, second game, ninth inning.

A.L.—10—Eldon Auker, Detroit, September 29, 1935, second game, second inning.

Most doubles allowed, game
N.L.—14—George Derby, Buffalo, July 3, 1883.
A.L.—8—Ed LaFitte, Detroit, October 8, 1911, first game.

Most doubles allowed, inning
A.L.—6—Lefty Grove, Boston, June 9, 1934, eighth inning.
N.L.—5—Duke Esper, Washington, April 21, 1894, second inning.

Most triples allowed, game
N.L.—9—Mike Sullivan, Cleveland, September 3, 1894, first game.
A.L.—6—Al Travers, Detroit, May 18, 1912.

Most triples allowed, inning
A.L.—4
Fred Marberry, Detroit, May 6, 1934, fourth inning.
Al Travers, Detroit, May 18, 1912, fifth inning.
N.L.—3—Held by many pitchers.

HOME RUNS

Most home runs allowed, career
M.L.—505—Robin Roberts, Philadelphia N.L., Baltimore A.L., Houston N.L., Chicago N.L., 19 years, 1948 through 1966 (418 in N.L., 87 in A.L.).
N.L.—434—Warren Spahn, Boston, Milwaukee, New York, San Francisco, 21 years, 1942 through 1965, except 1943, 1944, 1945 in military service.
A.L.—422—Frank Tanana, California, Boston, Texas, Detroit, New York, 21 years, 1973 through 1993.

Most grand slams allowed, career
M.L.—10—Nolan Ryan, New York N.L., California A.L., Houston N.L., Texas A.L., 1970, 1972, 1973, 1977, 1984, 1985, 1988, 1990, 1992 (2) (6 in A.L., 4 in N.L.).
A.L.—9—Ned Garver, St. Louis, Detroit, Kansas City, 1949, 1950 (2), 1951, 1952, 1954, 1955 (2), 1959.
N.L.—9—Jerry Reuss, St. Louis, Houston, Pittsburgh, Los Angeles, 1971 (2), 1972, 1973, 1974, 1976 (2), 1979, 1980.

For a complete list of pitchers with seven or
more career grand slams allowed, see
page 181.

Most home runs allowed, season
A.L.—50—Bert Blyleven, Minnesota, 36 games, 271.2 innings, 1986.
N.L.—48—Jose Lima, Houston, 33 games, 196.1 innings, 2000.

Most home runs allowed, season (vs. one club)
A.L.—15—Jim Perry, Cleveland vs. New York, 1960.
N.L.—13
Warren Hacker, Chicago vs. Brooklyn, 1956.
Warren Spahn, Milwaukee vs. Chicago, 1958.

Most grand slams allowed, season
N.L.—4
Tug McGraw, Philadelphia, 1979.
Chan Ho Park, Los Angeles, 1999.
Matt Clement, San Diego, 2000.
A.L.—4
Ray Narleski, Detroit, 1959.
Mike Schooler, Seattle, 1992.

Fewest home runs allowed, season (most innings)
A.L.—0—Allen Sothoron, St. Louis, Boston, Cleveland, 29 games, 178 innings, 1921.
N.L.—1—Eppa Rixey, Cincinnati, 40 games, 301 innings, 1921.

Fewest home runs allowed, season (since 1950; 250 or more innings)
N.L.—5
Bob Veale, Pittsburgh, 39 games, 266 innings, 1965.
Ron Reed, Atlanta, St. Louis, 34 games, 250 innings, 1975.
A.L.—6—Mike Garcia, Cleveland, 45 games, 259 innings, 1954.

Most years leading league in home runs allowed
M.L.—7—Ferguson Jenkins, Chicago N.L., Texas A.L., 1967, 1968 (tied), 1971, 1972, 1973, 1975, 1979 (5 in N.L., 2 in A.L.).
N.L.—5
Robin Roberts, Philadelphia, 1954, 1955, 1956, 1957, 1960.
Ferguson Jenkins, Chicago, 1967, 1968 (tied), 1971, 1972, 1973.
A.L.—3
Pedro Ramos, Washington, Minnesota, 1957, 1958, 1961.
Denny McLain, Detroit, 1966, 1967, 1968.

Most years allowing 30 or more home runs
M.L.—9—Robin Roberts, Philadelphia N.L., Baltimore A.L., 1953, 1954, 1955, 1956, 1957, 1958, 1959, 1960, 1963.
N.L.—8—Robin Roberts, Philadelphia, 1953, 1954, 1955, 1956, 1957, 1958, 1959, 1960.
A.L.—4
Mudcat Grant, Cleveland, Minnesota, 1961, 1963, 1964, 1965.
Denny McLain, Detroit, Washington, 1966, 1967, 1968, 1971.
Jack Morris, Detroit, 1982, 1983, 1986, 1987.

Most home runs allowed, game
N.L.—7—Charlie Sweeney, St. Louis, June 12, 1886.
N.L. since 1900—6
Larry Benton, New York, May 12, 1930.
Hollis Thurston, Brooklyn, August 13, 1932, first game.
Wayman Kerksieck, Philadelphia, August 13, 1939, first game.
A.L.—6
Al Thomas, St. Louis, June 27, 1936.
George Caster, Philadelphia, September 24, 1940, first game.

Most home runs allowed, inning
N.L.—4
Bill Lampe, Boston, June 6, 1894, third inning.
Larry Benton, New York, May 12, 1930, seventh inning.
Wayman Kerksieck, Philadelphia, August 13, 1939, first game, fourth inning.
Charlie Bicknell, Philadelphia, June 6, 1948, first game, sixth inning.
Ben Wade, Brooklyn, May 28, 1954, eighth inning.
Mario Soto, Cincinnati, April 29, 1986, fourth inning.
John Smoltz, Atlanta, June 19, 1994, first inning.
Jose Lima, Houston, April 27, 2000, first inning.
Andy Benes, St. Louis, July 23, 2000, second inning.
Phil Norton, Chicago, August 8, 2000, fourth inning.
Steve Trachsel, New York, May 17, 2001, third inning.
Alan Embree, San Francisco, May 20, 2001, seventh inning.
A.L.—4
George Caster, Philadelphia, September 24, 1940, first game, sixth inning.
Cal McLish, Cleveland, May 22, 1957, sixth inning.
Paul Foytack, Los Angeles, July 31, 1963, second game, sixth inning (consecutive).
Catfish Hunter, New York, June 17, 1977, first inning.
Mike Caldwell, Milwaukee, May 31, 1980, fourth inning.
Scott Sanderson, New York, May 2, 1992, fifth inning.
Brian Anderson, California, September 5, 1995, second inning.
Dave Telgheder, Oakland, September 21, 1996, third inning.
Dave Burba, Cleveland, June 29, 2001, fourth inning.
Pat Mahomes, Texas, August 17, 2001, sixth inning.

Most consecutive home runs allowed, inning
A.L.—4—Paul Foytack, Los Angeles, July 31, 1963, second game, sixth inning.
N.L.—3—Held by many pitchers. Last pitchers—Jimmy Haynes, Milwaukee, July 12, 2001, third inning; Brian Anderson, Arizona, July 22, 2001, fifth inning; Kevin Jarvis, San Diego, August 3, 2001, sixth inning; Dave Mlicki, Houston, September 29, 2001, first inning.

LONG HITS AND TOTAL BASES

Most long hits allowed, game
N.L.—16—George Derby, Buffalo, July 3, 1883.
A.L.—10—Dale Gear, Washington, August 10, 1901, second game.

Most total bases allowed, game

N.L.—55—Bill Rhodes, Louisville, June 18, 1893.
N.L. since 1900—39—Dummy Taylor, New York, September 23, 1903.
A.L.—41—Dale Gear, Washington, August 10, 1901, second game.

Most total bases allowed, inning

N.L.—23—Bill Rhodes, Louisville, June 18, 1893, first inning.
N.L. since 1900—20—John Smoltz, Atlanta, June 19, 1994, first inning.
A.L.—22—George Caster, Philadelphia, September 24, 1940, first game, sixth inning.

BASES ON BALLS

Most bases on balls, career

M.L.—2,795—Nolan Ryan, New York N.L., California A.L., Houston N.L., Texas A.L., 27 years, 1966, 1968 through 1993 (1,655 in A.L., 1,140 in N.L.).
A.L.—1,775—Early Wynn, Washington, Cleveland, Chicago, 23 years, 1939, 1941, through 1963, except 1945 in military service.
N.L.—1,717—Steve Carlton, St. Louis, Philadelphia, San Francisco, 22 years, 1965 through 1986.

For a complete list of pitchers with 1,200 or more career bases on balls allowed, see page 181.

Most bases on balls, season

N.L.—276—Amos Rusie, New York, 64 games, 1890.
N.L. since 1900—185—Sam Jones, Chicago, 242 innings, 1955.
A.L.—208—Bob Feller, Cleveland, 278 innings, 1938.

Most intentional bases on balls, season

N.L.—23
Mike Garman, St. Louis, 66 games, 79 innings, 1975.
Dale Murray, Cincinnati, New York, 68 games, 119 innings, 1978.
Kent Tekulve, Pittsburgh, 85 games, 128.2 innings, 1982.
A.L.—19—John Hiller, Detroit, 59 games, 150 innings, 1974.

Most years leading league in bases on balls

M.L.—8—Nolan Ryan, California A.L., 1972 through 1978, except 1975; Houston N.L., 1980, 1982.
A.L.—6—Nolan Ryan, California, 1972, 1973, 1974, 1976, 1977, 1978.
N.L.—5—Amos Rusie, New York, 1890, 1891, 1892, 1893, 1894.
N.L. since 1900—4
Jimmy Ring, Philadelphia, 1922, 1923, 1924, 1925.
Kirby Higbe, Chicago, Philadelphia, Pittsburgh, Brooklyn, 1939, 1940, 1941, 1947.
Sam Jones, Chicago, St. Louis, San Francisco, 1955, 1956, 1958, 1959.
Bob Veale, Pittsburgh, 1964, 1965 (tied), 1967, 1968.

Fewest bases on balls, season (250 or more innings)

N.L.—18—Babe Adams, Pittsburgh, 263 innings, 1920.
A.L.—28—Cy Young, Boston, 380 innings, 1904.

Most consecutive innings with no bases on balls, season

A.L.—84.1—Bill Fischer, Kansas City, August 3 through September 30, 1962.
N.L.—72.1—Greg Maddux, Atlanta, June 20, third inning, through August 12, second inning, 2001.

Most consecutive innings with no bases on balls from start of season

N.L.—52—Grover Alexander, Chicago, April 18 through May 17, 1923.

Most bases on balls, nine-inning game

N.L.—16
Bill George, New York, May 30, 1887, first game.
George Van Haltren, Chicago, June 27, 1887.
N.L. since 1900—14—Henry Mathewson, New York, October 5, 1906.
P.L.—16—Henry Gruber, Cleveland, April 19, 1890.
A.L.—16—Bruno Haas, Philadelphia, June 23, 1915 (his first major league game).

Most bases on balls, extra-inning game

A.L.—16—Tommy Byrne, St. Louis, August 22, 1951, 13 innings.
N.L.—13
Cy Seymour, New York, May 24, 1899, 10 innings.
Bud Podbielan, Cincinnati, May 18, 1953, 10 innings.

Most bases on balls, shutout game

A.L.—11
Lefty Gomez, New York, August 1, 1941.
Mel Stottlemyre, New York, May 21, 1970; pitched first 8.1 innings.
N.L.—9—Vinegar Bend Mizell, St. Louis, September 1, 1958, first game.

Most bases on balls, shutout game (more than nine innings)

N.L.—10
Jim Maloney, Cincinnati, August 19, 1965, first game, 10 innings.
J.R. Richard, Houston, July 6, 1976, 10 innings.
A.L.—Less than nine-inning game.

Longest game without a base on balls

N.L.—21 innings—Babe Adams, Pittsburgh, July 17, 1914.
A.L.—20 innings—Cy Young, Boston, July 4, 1905, p.m. game.

Fewest bases on balls, doubleheader (18 innings)

A.A.—0—Guy Hecker, Louisville, July 4, 1884.
A.L.—1—Ed Walsh, Chicago, September 29, 1908.
N.L.—1—Grover Alexander, Philadelphia, September 23, 1916; September 3, 1917.

Most bases on balls, inning

A.L.—8—Bill Gray, Washington, August 28, 1909, first game, second inning.
N.L.—7
George Keefe, Washington, May 1, 1889, fifth inning.
Tony Mullane, Baltimore, June 18, 1894, a.m. game, first inning.
Bob Ewing, Cincinnati, April 19, 1902, fourth inning. (His first major league game.)

Most consecutive bases on balls, inning

A.L.—7—Bill Gray, Washington, August 28, 1909, first game, second inning.
N.L.—6—Bill Kennedy, Brooklyn, August 31, 1900, second inning.

Most consecutive bases on balls, from start of game

N.L.—4—Johnny Vander Meer, Cincinnati, June 16, 1941.
A.L.—4
Jim Bagby Jr., Boston, April 21, 1946, second game.
Roger Pavlik, Texas, April 18, 1997.
Bartolo Colon, Cleveland, June 29, 2000.

STRIKEOUTS
CAREER

Most strikeouts, career

M.L.—5,714—Nolan Ryan, New York N.L., California A.L., Houston N.L., Texas A.L., 27 years, 1966, 1968 through 1993 (3,355 in A.L., 2,359 in N.L.).
N.L.—4,000—Steve Carlton, St. Louis, Philadelphia, San Francisco, 22 years, 1965 through 1986.
A.L.—3,717—Roger Clemens, Boston, Toronto, New York, 18 years, 1984 through 2001.

For a complete list of pitchers with 2,000 or more career strikeouts, see page 181.

Most strikeouts by righthanded pitcher, career

M.L.—5,714—Nolan Ryan, New York N.L., California A.L., Houston N.L., Texas A.L., 27 years, 1966, 1968 through 1993 (3,355 in A.L., 2,359 in N.L.).
A.L.—3,717—Roger Clemens, Boston, Toronto, New York, 18 years, 1984 through 2001.
N.L.—3,272—Tom Seaver, New York, Cincinnati, 17 years, 1967 through 1983.

Most strikeouts by lefthanded pitcher, career

N.L.—4,000—Steve Carlton, St. Louis, Philadelphia, San Francisco, 22 years, 1965 through 1986.
A.L.—2,679—Mickey Lolich, Detroit, 13 years, 1963 through 1975.

SEASON

Most strikeouts, season
A.A.—505—Matt Kilroy, Baltimore, 65 games, 570 innings, 1886.
N.L.—411—Hoss Radbourn, Providence, 72 games, 679 innings, 1884.
N.L. since 1900—382—Sandy Koufax, Los Angeles, 43 games, 336 innings, 1965.
A.L.—383—Nolan Ryan, California, 41 games, 326 innings, 1973.

Most strikeouts by righthanded pitcher, season
U.A.—483—Hugh Daily, Chicago, Pittsburgh, Washington, 58 games, 501 innings, 1884.
N.L.—411—Hoss Radbourn, Providence, 72 games, 679 innings, 1884.
N.L. since 1900—319—Curt Schilling, Philadelphia, 35 games, 254.1 innings, 1997.
A.L.—383—Nolan Ryan, California, 41 games, 326 innings, 1973.

Most strikeouts by lefthanded pitcher, season
A.A.—505—Matt Kilroy, Baltimore, 65 games, 570 innings, 1886.
N.L.—382—Sandy Koufax, Los Angeles, 43 games, 336 innings, 1965.
A.L.—349—Rube Waddell, Philadelphia, 46 games, 384 innings, 1904.

Most strikeouts by relief pitcher, season
A.L.—181—Dick Radatz, Boston, 1964, 79 games, 157 innings.
N.L.—153—Dick Selma, Philadelphia, 1970, 73 games, 134 innings.

Most strikeouts by rookie, season (since 1900)
N.L.—276—Dwight Gooden, New York, 218 innings, 1984.
A.L.—245—Herb Score, Cleveland, 227 innings, 1955.

Fewest strikeouts for leader, season
A.L.—113
Cecil Hughson, Boston, 281 innings, 1942.
Bobo Newsom, Washington, 214 innings, 1942.
N.L.—133—Rube Waddell, Pittsburgh, 213 innings, 1900.

Most years leading league in strikeouts
A.L.—12—Walter Johnson, Washington, 1910, 1912, 1913, 1914, 1915, 1916, 1917, 1918, 1919, 1921, 1923, 1924.
N.L.—7—Dazzy Vance, Brooklyn, 1922 through 1928.

Most consecutive years leading league in strikeouts
A.L.—8—Walter Johnson, Washington, 1912 through 1919.
N.L.—7—Dazzy Vance, Brooklyn, 1922 through 1928.

Most years with 100 or more strikeouts
M.L.—24—Nolan Ryan, New York N.L., California A.L., Houston N.L., Texas A.L., 1968 through 1992, except 1969 (12 in N.L., 12 in A.L.).
A.L.—18—Walter Johnson, Washington, 1908 through 1926, except 1920.
N.L.—18—Steve Carlton, St. Louis, Philadelphia, 1967 through 1984.

Most consecutive years with 100 or more strikeouts
M.L.—23—Nolan Ryan, New York N.L., California A.L., Houston N.L., Texas A.L., 1970 through 1992 (11 in N.L., 12 in A.L.).
N.L.—18—Steve Carlton, St. Louis, Philadelphia, 1967 through 1984.
A.L.—16—Roger Clemens, Boston, Toronto, New York, 1986 through 2001.

Most years with 200 or more strikeouts
M.L.—15—Nolan Ryan, California A.L., Houston N.L., Texas A.L., 1972 through 1974, 1976 through 1980, 1982, 1985, 1987 through 1991.
A.L.—11—Roger Clemens, Boston, Toronto, New York, 1986 through 1992, 1996 through 1998, 2001.
N.L.—10—Tom Seaver, New York, Cincinnati, 1968 through 1976, 1978.

Most consecutive years with 200 or more strikeouts
N.L.—9—Tom Seaver, New York, 1968 through 1976.

A.L.—7
Rube Waddell, Philadelphia, St. Louis, 1902 through 1908.
Walter Johnson, Washington, 1910 through 1916.
Roger Clemens, Boston, 1986 through 1992.

Most years with 300 or more strikeouts
A.L.—6—Nolan Ryan, California, 1972 (329), 1973 (383), 1974 (367), 1976 (327), 1977 (341); Texas, 1989 (301).
N.L.—3
Amos Rusie, New York, 1890 (345), 1891 (321), 1892 (303).
Sandy Koufax, Los Angeles, 1963 (303), 1965 (382), 1966 (317).
Randy Johnson, Arizona, 1999 (364), 2000 (347), 2001 (372).

Most years with 400 or more strikeouts
M.L.—1
Fred Shaw, Detroit N.L., Boston U.A., 1884.
Hugh Daily, Chicago U.A., Pittsburgh U.A., Washington U.A., 1884.
Hoss Radbourn, Providence N.L., 1884.
Charlie Buffinton, Boston N.L., 1884.
Matt Kilroy, Baltimore A.A., 1886.
Tom Ramsey, Louisville A.A., 1886.
A.A.—1
Matt Kilroy, Baltimore, 1886.
Tom Ramsey, Louisville, 1886.
U.A.—1—Hugh Daily, Chicago, Pittsburgh, Washington, 1884.
N.L.—1
Hoss Radbourn, Providence, 1884.
Charlie Buffinton, Boston, 1884.

GAME AND INNING

Most strikeouts, nine-inning game
A.L.—20
Roger Clemens, Boston, April 29, 1986.
Roger Clemens, Boston, September 18, 1996.
N.L.—20—Kerry Wood, Chicago, May 6, 1998.
U.A.—19—Hugh Daily, Chicago, July 7, 1884.

Most strikeouts, extra-inning game
A.L.—21—Tom Cheney, Washington, September 12, 1962, 16 innings.
N.L.—20—Randy Johnson, Arizona, May 8, 2001 (pitched first nine innings of 11-inning game).

Most strikeouts by righthanded pitcher, nine-inning game
A.L.—20
Roger Clemens, Boston, April 29, 1986.
Roger Clemens, Boston, September 18, 1996.
N.L.—20—Kerry Wood, Chicago, May 6, 1998.

Most strikeouts by lefthanded pitcher, nine-inning game
N.L.—19—Steve Carlton, St. Louis, September 15, 1969.
A.L.—19
Randy Johnson, Seattle, June 24, 1997.
Randy Johnson, Seattle, August 8, 1997.

Most strikeouts by righthanded pitcher, extra-inning game
A.L.—21—Tom Cheney, Washington, September 12, 1962, 16 innings.
N.L.—Less than nine-inning record.

Most strikeouts by lefthanded pitcher, extra-inning game
N.L.—20—Randy Johnson, Arizona, May 8, 2001 (pitched first nine innings of 11-inning game).
A.L.—Less than nine-inning record.

Most strikeouts, nine-inning night game
A.L.—20
Roger Clemens, Boston, April 29, 1986.
Roger Clemens, Boston, September 18, 1996.
N.L.—19—Steve Carlton, St. Louis, September 15, 1969.

Most strikeouts by losing pitcher, nine-inning game
N.L.—19—Steve Carlton, St. Louis, September 15, 1969 (lost 4-3).
A.L.—19—Randy Johnson, Seattle, June 24, 1997 (lost 4-1).
U.A.—18
Fred Shaw, Boston, July 19, 1884 (lost 1-0).
Henry Porter, Milwaukee, October 3, 1884 (lost 5-4).
A.A.—17—Guy Hecker, Louisville, August 26, 1884 (lost 4-3).

Most strikeouts by losing pitcher, extra-inning game

A.L.—19—Nolan Ryan, California, August 20, 1974, 11 innings (lost 1-0).

N.L.—18

Warren Spahn, Boston, June 14, 1952, 15 innings (lost 3-1).
Jim Maloney, Cincinnati, June 14, 1965, 11 innings (lost 1-0).

Most strikeouts, first major league game (since 1900)

N.L.—15

Karl Spooner, Brooklyn, September 22, 1954.
J.R. Richard, Houston, September 5, 1971, second game.

A.L.—12

Elmer Myers, Philadelphia, October 6, 1915, second game.
Steve Woodard, Milwaukee, July 28, 1997, first game.

Most strikeouts by relief pitcher, game

N.L.—16—Randy Johnson, Arizona, July 18, finished July 19, 2001, last seven innings of nine-inning game.

A.L.—15—Walter Johnson, Washington, July 25, 1913, last 11.1 innings of 15-inning game.

14—Denny McLain, Detroit, June 15, 1965, 6.2 innings of nine-inning game.

Most times with 15 or more strikeouts in game, career

M.L.—26—Nolan Ryan, New York N.L., California A.L., Houston N.L., Texas A.L., 27 years, 1966 through 1993, except 1967 (23 in A.L., 3 in N.L.).

A.L.—23—Nolan Ryan, California, 1972 (4), 1973 (2), 1974 (6), 1976 (3), 1977 (2), 1978 (1), 1979 (1); Texas, 1989 (1), 1990 (2), 1991 (1).

N.L.—8—Sandy Koufax, Brooklyn, Los Angeles, 1959 (2), 1960 (2), 1961 (1), 1962 (2), 1966 (1).

Most times with 10 or more strikeouts in game, career

M.L.—215—Nolan Ryan, New York N.L., California A.L., Houston N.L., Texas A.L., 27 years, 1966 through 1993, except 1967 (148 in A.L., 67 in N.L.).

A.L.—148—Nolan Ryan, California, Texas, 13 years, 1972 through 1979, 1989 through 1993.

N.L.—97—Sandy Koufax, Brooklyn, Los Angeles, 12 years, 1955 through 1966.

Most times with 10 or more strikeouts in game, season

A.L.—23—Nolan Ryan, California, 1973.

N.L.—23—Randy Johnson, Arizona, 1999, 2000, 2001.

Most strikeouts, inning (*consecutive)

A.A.—4—Bobby Mathews, Philadelphia, September 30, 1885, seventh inning.

N.L.—4

Ed Crane, New York, October 4, 1888, fifth inning.*
George Wiltse, New York, May 15, 1906, fifth inning.*
Jim Davis, Chicago, May 27, 1956, first game, sixth inning.*
Joe Nuxhall, Cincinnati, August 11, 1959, first game, sixth inning.
Pete Richert, Los Angeles, April 12, 1962, third inning.*
Don Drysdale, Los Angeles, April 17, 1965, second inning.*
Bob Gibson, St. Louis, June 7, 1966, fourth inning.
Bill Bonham, Chicago, July 31, 1974, first game, second inning.*
Phil Niekro, Atlanta, July 29, 1977, sixth inning.
Mario Soto, Cincinnati, May 17, 1984, third inning.
Mike Scott, Houston, September 3, 1986, fifth inning.
Paul Assenmacher, Atlanta, August 22, 1989, fifth inning.
Tim Birtsas, Cincinnati, June 4, 1990, seventh inning.
Mark Wohlers, Atlanta, June 7, 1995, ninth inning.
Bruce Ruffin, Colorado, July 25, 1996, ninth inning.
Derek Wallace, New York, September 13, 1996, ninth inning.
Kirt Ojala, Florida, September 16, 1998, fourth inning*
Archie Corbin, Florida, April 28, 1999, seventh inning.
Jerry Spradlin, San Francisco, July 22, 1999, seventh inning.
Steve Kline, Montreal, August 17, 1999, seventh inning.*
Frankie Rodriguez, Cincinnati, July 22, 2001, seventh inning.

A.L.—4

Walter Johnson, Washington, April 15, 1911, fifth inning.
Guy Morton, Cleveland, June 11, 1916, seventh inning.
Ryne Duren, Los Angeles, May 18, 1961, seventh inning.
Lee Stange, Cleveland, September 2, 1964, seventh inning.
Mike Cuellar, Baltimore, May 29, 1970, fourth inning.*

Mike Paxton, Cleveland, July 21, 1978, fifth inning.*
Bobby Witt, Texas, August 2, 1987, second inning.*
Charlie Hough, Texas, July 4, 1988, first inning.
Matt Young, Seattle, September 9, 1990, first inning.
Paul Shuey, Cleveland, May 14, 1994, ninth inning.
Kevin Appier, Kansas City, September 3, 1996, fourth inning.*
Wilson Alvarez, Chicago, July 21, 1997, seventh inning.*
Blake Stein, Oakland, July 27, 1998, fourth inning.
Chuck Finley, Anaheim, May 12, 1999, third inning.
Tim Wakefield, Boston, August 10, 1999, ninth inning.
Chuck Finley, Anaheim, August 15, 1999, first inning.*
Chuck Finley, Cleveland, April 16, 2000, third inning.*
Erik Hiljus, Oakland, June 30, 2001, seventh inning.

Three strikeouts on nine pitched balls, inning

A.L.—Rube Waddell, Philadelphia, July 1, 1902, third inning.
Hollis Thurston, Chicago, August 22, 1923, 12th inning.
Lefty Grove, Philadelphia, August 23, 1928, second inning.
Lefty Grove, Philadelphia, September 27, 1928, seventh inning.
Billy Hoeft, Detroit, September 7, 1953, second game, seventh inning.
Jim Bunning, Detroit, August 2, 1959, ninth inning.
Al Downing, New York, August 11, 1967, first game, second inning.
Nolan Ryan, California, July 9, 1972, second inning.
Ron Guidry, New York, August 7, 1984, second game, ninth inning.
Jeff Montgomery, Kansas City, April 29, 1990, eighth inning.

N.L.—Pat Ragan, Brooklyn, October 5, 1914, second game, eighth inning.
Hod Eller, Cincinnati, August 21, 1917, ninth inning.
Joe Oeschger, Boston, September 8, 1921, first game, fourth inning.
Dazzy Vance, Brooklyn, September 14, 1924, third inning.
Warren Spahn, Boston, July 2, 1949, second inning.
Sandy Koufax, Los Angeles, June 30, 1962, first inning.
Sandy Koufax, Los Angeles, April 18, 1964, third inning.
Bob Bruce, Houston, April 19, 1964, eighth inning.
Nolan Ryan, New York, April 19, 1968, third inning.
Bob Gibson, St. Louis, May 12, 1969, seventh inning.
Milt Pappas, Chicago, September 24, 1971, fourth inning.
Lynn McGlothen, St. Louis, August 19, 1975, second inning.
Bruce Sutter, Chicago, September 8, 1977, ninth inning.
Jeff Robinson, Pittsburgh, September 7, 1987, eighth inning.
Rob Dibble, Cincinnati, June 4, 1989, eighth inning.
Andy Ashby, Philadelphia, June 15, 1991, fourth inning.
David Cone, New York, August 30, 1991, fifth inning.
Pete Harnisch, Houston, September 6, 1991, seventh inning.
Trevor Wilson, San Francisco, June 7, 1992, ninth inning.
Mel Rojas, Montreal, May 11, 1994, ninth inning.
Mike Magnante, Houston, August 22, 1997, ninth inning.
Randy Johnson, Arizona, August 23, 2001, sixth inning.

CONSECUTIVE AND IN CONSECUTIVE GAMES

Most consecutive strikeouts, game

N.L.—10—Tom Seaver, New York, April 22, 1970, 1 in sixth inning, 3 in seventh inning, 3 in eighth inning, 3 in ninth inning.

A.L.—8

Nolan Ryan, California, July 9, 1972, 2 in first inning, 3 in second inning, 3 in third inning.
Nolan Ryan, California, July 15, 1973, 1 in first inning, 3 in second inning, 3 in third inning, 1 in fourth inning.
Ron Davis, New York, May 4, 1981, 2 in seventh inning, 3 in eighth inning, 3 in ninth inning.
Roger Clemens, Boston, April 29, 1986, 3 in fourth inning, 3 in fifth inning, 2 in sixth inning.
Blake Stein, Kansas City, June 17, 2001, 1 in first inning, 3 in second inning, 3 in third inning, 1 in fourth inning.

Most consecutive strikeouts, first major league game
A.L.—7—Sammy Stewart, Baltimore, September 1, 1978, second game, 3 in second inning, 3 in third inning, 1 in fourth inning.
N.L.—6
　Karl Spooner, Brooklyn, September 22, 1954, 3 in seventh inning, 3 in eighth inning.
　Pete Richert, Los Angeles, April 12, 1962, 1 in second inning, 4 in third inning, 1 in fourth inning (first six batters he faced in majors).

Most consecutive strikeouts by relief pitcher, game
A.L.—8—Ron Davis, New York, May 4, 1981, 2 in seventh inning, 3 in eighth inning, 3 in ninth inning.
N.L.—6
　Jack Meyer, Philadelphia, September 22, 1958, first game, 3 in 12th inning, 3 in 13th inning (first six batters he faced).
　Pete Richert, Los Angeles, April 12, 1962, 1 in second inning, 4 in third inning, 1 in fourth inning (first six batters he faced in majors).
　Ron Perranoski, Los Angeles, September 12, 1966, 3 in fifth inning, 3 in sixth inning (first six batters he faced).
　Dick Kelley, Atlanta, September 8, 1967, 2 in sixth inning, 3 in seventh inning, 1 in eighth inning.
　Joe Hoerner, St. Louis, June 1, 1968, 3 in ninth inning, 3 in 10th inning.
　Don Gullett, Cincinnati, August 23, 1970, second game, 3 in sixth inning, 3 in seventh inning (first 6 batters he faced).
　Bruce Sutter, Chicago, September 8, 1977, 3 in eighth inning, 3 in ninth inning (first 6 batters he faced).
　Willie Hernandez, Philadelphia, July 3, 1983, 3 in eighth inning, 3 in ninth inning (all 6 batters he faced).
　Joe Price, Cincinnati, May 8, 1985, 3 in eighth inning, 3 in ninth inning.
　Randy Myers, Cincinnati, September 8, 1990, 2 in seventh inning, 3 in eighth inning, 1 in ninth inning (first 6 batters he faced).
　Rob Dibble, Cincinnati, April 23, 1991, 3 in eighth inning, 3 in ninth inning.
　Scott Williamson, Cincinnati, May 27, 1999, 3 in eighth inning, 3 in ninth inning.

Most consecutive strikeouts from start of game
N.L.—9—Mickey Welch, New York, August 28, 1884.
N.L. since 1900—8—Jim Deshaies, Houston, September 23, 1986.
A.L.—7—Joe Cowley, Chicago, May 28, 1986.

Most strikeouts, two consecutive games
U.A.—34—Fred Shaw, Boston, July 19 (18), 21 (16), 1884, 19 innings.
N.L.—33—Kerry Wood, Chicago, May 6 (20), 11 (13), 1998, 16 innings.
A.L.—32
　Luis Tiant, Cleveland, June 29, first game (13), July 3 (19), 1968, 19 innings.
　Nolan Ryan, California, August 7 (13), 12 (19), 1974, 17.2 innings.
　Randy Johnson, Seattle, August 8 (19), 15 (13), 1997, 17 innings.
　Pedro Martinez, Boston, May 6 (17), 12 (15), 2000, 18 innings.

Most strikeouts, three consecutive games
U.A.—48—Fred Shaw, Boston, July 16, 19, 21, 1884, 28 innings.
A.L.—47—Nolan Ryan, California, August 12 (19), 16 (9), 20 (19), 1974, 27.1 innings.
N.L.—43
　Dwight Gooden, New York, September 7 (11), 12 (16), 17 (16), 1984, 26 innings.
　Randy Johnson, Arizona, June 25 (14), 30 (17), July 5 (12), 1999, 25 innings.
　Randy Johnson, Arizona, April 28 (12), May 3 (11), 8 (20), 2001, 24 innings.
　Randy Johnson, Arizona, May 3 (11), 8 (20), 13 (12), 2001, 24 innings.

HIT BATSMEN

Most hit batsmen, career
A.L.—206—Walter Johnson, Washington, 21 years, 1907 through 1927.

N.L.—195—Emerson Hawley, St. Louis, Pittsburgh, Cincinnati, New York, 9 years, 1892 through 1900.
N.L. since 1900—154—Don Drysdale, Brooklyn, Los Angeles, 14 years, 1956 through 1969.

Most hit batsmen, season
A.A.—54—Phil Knell, Columbus, 58 games, 1891.
N.L.—41—Joe McGinnity, Brooklyn, 45 games, 1900.
A.L.—31—Chick Fraser, Philadelphia, 39 games, 1901.

Fewest hit batsmen for leader, season
A.L.—6—Held by five pitchers. Last pitchers—Spud Chandler, New York, 1940; Al Smith, Cleveland, 1940.
N.L.—6—Held by five pitchers. Last pitchers—Rex Barney, Brooklyn, 1948; Sheldon Jones, New York, 1948; Kent Peterson, Cincinnati, 1948.

Most years leading league in hit batsmen
A.L.—6—Howard Ehmke, Detroit, Boston, Philadelphia, 1920, 1921 (tied), 1922, 1923 (tied), 1925, 1927.
N.L.—5—Don Drysdale, Los Angeles, 1958, 1959, 1960, 1961, 1965 (tied).

Most innings with no hit batsmen, season
A.L.—327—Alvin Crowder, Washington, 50 games, 1932.
N.L.—323—Sandy Koufax, Los Angeles, 41 games, 1966.

Most innings allowing no hit batsmen over three consecutive seasons
N.L.—755—Larry Benton, New York, Cincinnati, 1928, 1929, 1930.
A.L.—569—Bill Wight, Chicago, Boston, 1949, 1950, 1951.

Most hit batsmen, nine-inning game
A.A.—6—Ed Knouff, Baltimore, April 25, 1887.
N.L.—6—John Grimes, St. Louis, July 31, 1897, first game.
N.L. since 1900—4—Held by nine pitchers. Last pitcher—Pedro Astacio, Colorado, April 22, 2001.
A.L.—4—Held by 14 pitchers. Last pitcher—Scott Schoeneweis, Anaheim, June 7, 2001.

Most hit batsmen, two consecutive games
N.L.—9—Sam Shaw, Chicago, June 13 (5), June 16 (4), 1893.

Longest game without a hit batsman
N.L.—26 innings
　Leon Cadore, Brooklyn, May 1, 1920.
　Joe Oeschger, Boston, May 1, 1920.
A.L.—21 innings—Ted Lyons, Chicago, May 24, 1929.

Most hit batsmen, inning (*consecutive)
A.L.—3
　Bert Gallia, Washington, June 20, 1913, second game, first inning.
　Harry Harper, New York, August 25, 1921, eighth inning.
　Tom Morgan, New York, June 30, 1954, third inning.
　Wilbur Wood, Chicago, September 10, 1977, *first inning.
　Bud Black, Cleveland, July 8, 1988, fourth inning.
　Bert Blyleven, Minnesota, September 28, 1988, second inning.
　Steve Sparks, Anaheim, May 22, 1999, third inning.
N.L.—3
　Pat Luby, Chicago, September 5, 1890, sixth inning.
　Emerson Hawley, St. Louis, July 4, 1894, first game, *first inning.
　Emerson Hawley, Pittsburgh, May 9, 1896, seventh inning.
　Walter Thornton, Chicago, May 18, 1898, *fourth inning.
　Deacon Phillippe, Pittsburgh, September 25, 1905, first inning.
　Ray Boggs, Boston, September 17, 1928, ninth inning.
　Raul Sanchez, Cincinnati, May 15, 1960, first game, eighth inning.
　Dock Ellis, Pittsburgh, May 1, 1974, *first inning.
　Mark Gardner, Montreal, August 15, 1992, first inning.
　Tom Candiotti, Los Angeles, September 13, 1997, first inning.
　C.J. Nitkowski, Houston, August 3, 1998, *eighth inning.

WILD PITCHES

Most wild pitches, career
M.L.—277—Nolan Ryan, New York N.L., California A.L., Houston N.L., Texas A.L., 27 years, 1966, 1968 through 1993.
A.L.—206—Jack Morris, Detroit, Minnesota, Toronto, Cleveland, 18 years, 1977 through 1994.
N.L.—200—Phil Niekro, Milwaukee, Atlanta, 21 years, 1964 through 1983, 1987.

Most wild pitches, season
N.L.—64—Bill Stemmyer, Boston, 41 games, 1886.
N.L. since 1900—30—Leon Ames, New York, 263 innings, 1905.
A.L.—26—Juan Guzman, Toronto, 221 innings, 1993.

Fewest wild pitches by leader, season
N.L.—6
Kirby Higbe, Brooklyn, 211 innings, 1946.
Charley Schanz, Philadelphia, 116 innings, 1946.
A.L.—7—Held by eight pitchers. Last pitchers—George
Earnshaw, Philadelphia, 1928; Joe Shaute, Cleveland, 1928.

Most years leading league in wild pitches
M.L.—6
Nolan Ryan, California A.L., Houston N.L., Texas A.L., 1972,
1977, 1978, 1981, 1986, 1989.
Larry Cheney, Chicago N.L., Brooklyn N.L., 1912, 1913, 1914,
1916, 1917 (tied), 1918.
Jack Morris, Detroit A.L., Minnesota A.L., Cleveland A.L.,
1983, 1984, 1985, 1987, 1991, 1994 (tied).
N.L.—6—Larry Cheney, Chicago, Brooklyn, 1912, 1913, 1914,
1916, 1917 (tied), 1918.
A.L.—6—Jack Morris, Detroit, Minnesota, Cleveland, 1983,
1984, 1985, 1987, 1991, 1994 (tied).

Most innings with no wild pitches, season
N.L.—340—Joe McGinnity, New York, 1906.
A.L.—327—Alvin Crowder, Washington, 1932.

Most innings with no wild pitches or hit batsmen, season
A.L.—327—Alvin Crowder, Washington, 1932.
N.L.—268—Jesse Barnes, Boston, 1924.

Most wild pitches, game
N.L.—10—Johnny Ryan, Louisville, July 22, 1876.
N.L. since 1900—6
J.R. Richard, Houston, April 10, 1979.
Phil Niekro, Atlanta, August 4, 1979, second game.
Bill Gullickson, Montreal, April 10, 1982.
A.L.—5
Charlie Wheatley, Detroit, September 27, 1912.
Jack Morris, Detroit, August 3, 1987, 10 innings.

Most wild pitches, first major league game
A.A.—5—Tom Seymour, Pittsburgh, September 23, 1882 (his
only game in majors).
N.L.—5
Mike Corcoran, Chicago, July 15, 1884 (his only M.L. game).
George Winkelman, Washington, August 2, 1886.

Most wild pitches, opening game of season
N.L.—4—Larry Cheney, Chicago, April 14, 1914.

Longest game without a wild pitch
N.L.—26 innings—Leon Cadore, Brooklyn, May 1, 1920.
A.L.—24 innings
Jack Coombs, Philadelphia, September 1, 1906.
Joe Harris, Boston, September 1, 1906.

Most wild pitches, inning
P.L.—5—Bert Cunningham, Buffalo, September 15, 1890, second
game, first inning.
A.L.—4—Walter Johnson, Washington, September 21, 1914,
fourth inning.
N.L.—4—Phil Niekro, Atlanta, August 4, 1979, second game,
fifth inning.

SACRIFICE HITS

Most sacrifices allowed, season (sacrifice hits and sacrifice flies)
A.L.—54
Stan Coveleski, Cleveland, 316 innings, 1921.
Eddie Rommel, Philadelphia, 298 innings, 1923.
N.L.—49
Eppa Rixey, Philadelphia, 284 innings, 1920.
Jack Scott, Philadelphia, 233 innings, 1927.

Most sacrifice hits allowed, season (no sacrifice flies)
N.L.—35—Ed Brandt, Boston, 283 innings, 1933.
A.L.—28—Earl Whitehill, Detroit, 272 innings, 1931.

Fewest sacrifice hits allowed by leader, season (no sacrifice flies)
A.L.—8
Hector Carrasco, Minnesota-Boston, 78.2 innings, 2000.
Mike Mussina, Baltimore, 237.2 innings, 2000.
N.L.—13
Johnny Antonelli, San Francisco, 242 innings, 1958.
Dick Farrell, Philadelphia, 94 innings, 1958.
Ron Kline, Pittsburgh, 237 innings, 1958.

Most innings by pitcher allowing no sacrifice hits, season
N.L.—183—Carl Willey, New York, 30 games, 1963.

Most years leading league in most sacrifices allowed
N.L.—3—Eppa Rixey, Philadelphia, Cincinnati, 1920, 1921, 1928.
A.L.—3—Earl Whitehill, Detroit, Washington, 1931, 1934, 1935.

SACRIFICE FLIES

Most sacrifice flies allowed, career
M.L.—141—Jim Kaat, Washington A.L., Minnesota A.L.,
Chicago A.L., Philadelphia N.L., New York A.L., St. Louis N.L.,
25 years, 1959 through 1983 (108 in A.L., 33 in N.L.).
A.L.—108—Jim Kaat, Washington, Minnesota, Chicago, New
York, 19 years, 1959 through 1975, 1979 through 1980.
N.L.—95—Bob Gibson, St. Louis, 17 years, 1959 through 1975.

Most sacrifice flies allowed, season
A.L.—17
Larry Gura, Kansas City, 200.1 innings, 1983.
Jaime Navarro, Milwaukee, 214.1 innings, 1993.
N.L.—15—Randy Lerch, Philadelphia, 214 innings, 1979.

Most innings by pitcher allowing no sacrifice flies, season
N.L.—284—Phil Niekro, Atlanta, 40 games, 1969.

BALKS

Most balks, season
A.L.—16—Dave Stewart, Oakland, 275.2 innings, 1988.
N.L.—11—Steve Carlton, Philadelphia, 251 innings, 1979.

Most balks, game
N.L.—5—Bob Shaw, Milwaukee, May 4, 1963.
A.L.—4
Vic Raschi, New York, May 3, 1950.
Bobby Witt, Texas, April 12, 1988.
Rick Honeycutt, Oakland, April 13, 1988.
Gene Walter, Seattle, July 18, 1988.
John Dopson, Boston, June 13, 1989.

Most balks, inning
A.L.—3
Milt Shoffner, Cleveland, May 12, 1930, third inning.
Don Heinkel, Detroit, May 3, 1988, sixth inning.
N.L.—3
Jim Owens, Cincinnati, April 24, 1963, second inning.
Bob Shaw, Milwaukee, May 4, 1963, third inning.
Jim Gott, Pittsburgh, August 6, 1988, eighth inning.

CLUB PITCHING

COMPLETE GAMES

Most complete games, season
A.L.—148—Boston, 157 games, 1904.
N.L.—146—St. Louis, 155 games, 1904.

Fewest complete games, season
A.L.—1—Tampa Bay, 162 games, 2001.
N.L.—2
Milwaukee, 162 games, 1998.
Milwaukee, 161 games, 1999.
Milwaukee, 163 games, 2000.

Most consecutive games, none complete
A.L.—152—Tampa Bay, April 14 through October 7, 2001.
N.L.—139—New York, September 5, 1998 through August 14, 1999.

INNINGS

Most innings, season
A.L.—1,507—New York, 164 games, 1964.
N.L.—1,493—Pittsburgh, 163 games, 1979.

Most pitchers with 300 or more innings, season
N.L.—3—Boston, 1905, 1906.
A.L.—3—Detroit, 1904.

GAMES WON

Most games won by two pitchers on same club, season
N.L.—77—Providence 1884 (Hoss Radbourn, 60, Charlie Sweeney, 17).
N.L. since 1900—68—New York, 1904 (Joe McGinnity, 35, Christy Mathewson, 33).
A.L.—64—New York, 1904 (Jack Chesbro, 41, Jack Powell, 23).

Most pitchers winning 20 or more games, season (since 1900)
A.L.—4
Chicago, 1920.
Baltimore, 1971.
N.L.—3
Pittsburgh, 1902.
Chicago, 1903.
New York, 1904, 1905, 1913, 1920.
Cincinnati, 1923.

Most consecutive years with pitchers winning 20 or more games
A.L.—13—Baltimore, 1968 through 1980.
N.L.—12—New York, 1903 through 1914.

Most consecutive years without pitchers winning 20 or more games
N.L.—32—Philadelphia, 1918 through 1949.
A.L.—27
California/Anaheim, 1975 through 2001.
Cleveland, 1975 through 2001.

SAVES

Most saves, season
A.L.—68—Chicago, 162 games, 1990.
N.L.—61—Montreal, 163 games, 1993.

Fewest saves, season
A.L.—11—Toronto, 162 games, 1979.
N.L.—13
Chicago, 162 games, 1971.
St. Louis, 156 games, 1972.

GAMES LOST

Most pitchers losing 20 or more games, season (since 1900)
N.L.—4—Boston, 1905, 1906.
A.L.—3
Washington, 1904.
St. Louis, 1905.
Philadelphia, 1916.

AT-BATS AND PLATE APPEARANCES

Most at-bats allowed, season
A.L.—5,770—Oakland, 162 games, 1997.
N.L.—5,763—Philadelphia, 156 games, 1930.

Fewest at-bats allowed, season
A.L.—4,933—Cleveland, 147 games, 1945.
N.L.—5,062—Philadelphia, 155 games, 1947.

Most opponents' men facing pitcher, season
A.L.—6,660—Oakland, 162 games, 1997.
N.L.—6,574—Colorado, 162 games, 1999.

Fewest opponents' men facing pitcher, season
A.L.—5,653—St. Louis, 155 games, 1936.
N.L.—5,684—Brooklyn, 154 games, 1956.

RUNS, EARNED RUNS AND ERA

Most runs allowed, season
N.L.—1,199—Philadelphia, 156 games, 1930.
A.L.—1,103—Detroit, 162 games, 1996.

Fewest runs allowed, season
N.L.—379—Chicago, 154 games, 1906.
A.L.—408—Philadelphia, 153 games, 1909.

Most earned runs allowed, season
N.L.—1,024—Philadelphia, 156 games, 1930.
A.L.—1,015—Detroit, 162 games, 1996.

Fewest earned runs allowed, season
N.L.—332—Philadelphia, 153 games, 1915.
A.L.—343—Chicago, 156 games, 1917.

Lowest earned-run average, season
A.L.—2.16—Chicago, 156 games, 1917.
N.L.—2.18—Philadelphia, 153 games, 1915.

Highest earned-run average, season
N.L.—6.70—Philadelphia, 156 games, 1930.
A.L.—6.38—Detroit, 162 games, 1996.

SHUTOUTS

Most shutout games participated in, season
A.L.—47—Chicago, 1910 (won 22, lost 24, tied 1).
N.L.—47—New York, 1968 (won 25, lost 22).

Fewest shutout games participated in, season
A.L.—4—Texas, 2001 (won 3, lost 1).
N.L.—5
Colorado, 1999 (won 2, lost 3).
San Francisco, 1999 (won 3, lost 2).
Houston, 2000 (won 2, lost 3).

Most shutout games won or tied, season
N.L.—32—Chicago, 1907, 1909.
A.L.—32—Chicago, 1906 (including 2 ties).

Fewest shutout games won or tied, season (150 or more games)
N.L.—0
Brooklyn, 1898.
Washington, 1898.

St. Louis, 1898.
Cleveland, 1899.
Colorado, 1993.
A.L.—1
Chicago, 1924.
Washington, 1956.
Seattle, 1977.
Baltimore, 1996.
Oakland, 1997.
Anaheim, 2001.
Kansas City, 2001.

Most shutouts won from one club, season
N.L.—10—Pittsburgh vs. Boston, 1906 (lost 1).
A.L.—8
Chicago vs. Boston, 1906 (lost 1).
Cleveland vs. Washington, 1956 (lost 0).
Oakland vs. Cleveland 1968 (lost 1).

Most consecutive shutout games won, season
N.L.—6—Pittsburgh, June 2 through 6, 1903 (51 innings).
A.L.—5
Baltimore, September 2 through 6, 1974 (45 innings).
Baltimore, September 26 through October 1, 1995 (45 innings).

Largest score, shutout day game
N.L.—28-0—Providence vs. Philadelphia, August 21, 1883.
N.L. since 1900—22-0—Pittsburgh vs. Chicago, September 16, 1975.
A.L.—21-0
Detroit vs. Cleveland, September 15, 1901, eight innings.
New York vs. Philadelphia, August 13, 1939, second game, eight innings.

Largest score, shutout night game
N.L.—19-0
Pittsburgh vs. St. Louis, August 3, 1961, at St. Louis.
Los Angeles vs. San Diego, June 28, 1969, at San Diego.
A.L.—17-0—Los Angeles vs. Washington, August 23, 1963, at Washington.

Most runs, doubleheader shutout
A.L.—26—Detroit vs. St. Louis, September 22, 1936 (12-0, 14-0).
N.L.—19—New York vs. Cincinnati, July 31, 1949 (10-0, 9-0).

Doubleheader shutouts since 1900
N.L.—Occurred 101 times. Last time—September 29, 1987, St. Louis vs. Montreal (St. Louis won, 1-0 and 3-0).
A.L.—Occurred 89 times. Last time—June 26, 1988, Minnesota vs. Oakland (Minnesota won, 11-0 and 5-0).

Most consecutive innings shut out opponent, season
N.L.—56—Pittsburgh, June 1 (last two innings) through June 9 (first three innings), 1903.
A.L.—54—Baltimore, September 1, (last inning) through September 7 (first eight innings), 1974.

1-0 GAMES

Most 1-0 games won, season
A.L.—11—Washington, 1914 (lost 4).
N.L.—10—Pittsburgh, 1908 (lost 1).

Fewest 1-0 games won, season
N.L.-A.L.—0—Held by many clubs.
N.L.—Last clubs—Colorado, Milwaukee, St. Louis, 2001.
A.L.—Last clubs—Boston, Chicago, Cleveland, Kansas City, Texas, 2001.

Most 1-0 games lost, season
N.L.—10—Pittsburgh, 1914; Chicago, 1916; Philadelphia, 1967.
A.L.—9—New York, 1914; Chicago, 1968.

Fewest 1-0 games lost, season
N.L.-A.L.—0—Held by many clubs.
N.L.—Last clubs—Chicago, Cincinnati, Houston, Montreal, Philadelphia, St. Louis, 2001.
A.L.—Last clubs—Chicago, Detroit, Minnesota, New York, Oakland, Seattle, 2001.

Most consecutive 1-0 games won, season
A.L.—3—Chicago, April 25, 26, 27, 1909.
N.L.—3—St. Louis, August 31, second game (five innings), September 1, 1, 1917.

Most consecutive 1-0 games lost, season
N.L.—3
Brooklyn, September 7, 7, 8 (11 innings), 1908.
Pittsburgh, August 31, second game (five innings), September 1, 1, 1917.
Philadelphia, May 11, 12, 13, 1960.
A.L.—3
St. Louis, April 25, 26, 27, 1909.
Washington, May 7, 8, 10 (11 innings), 1909.

Most 1-0 games won from one club, season
N.L.—4—Held by four clubs. Last club—Cincinnati vs. Brooklyn, 1910.
A.L.—4—Held by four clubs. Last club—Detroit vs. Boston, 1917.

Winning two 1-0 games in one day
N.L.—12 times. Last time—Pittsburgh vs. St. Louis, October 3, 1976.
A.L.—1 time—Baltimore vs. Boston, September 2, 1974.

HITS AND HOME RUNS

Most hits allowed, season
N.L.—1,993—Philadelphia, 156 games, 1930.
A.L.—1,776—St. Louis, 155 games, 1936.

Fewest hits allowed, season
A.L.—1,087—Cleveland, 162 games, 1968.
N.L.—1,174—Pittsburgh, 153 games, 1909.

Most home runs allowed, season
A.L.—241—Detroit, 162 games, 1996.
N.L.—239—Colorado, 162 games, 2001.

Most home runs allowed at home, season
N.L.—159—at Colorado, 81 games, 1999.
A.L.—132—at Kansas City, 81 games, 1964.

Most grand slams allowed, season
A.L.—14—Detroit, 162 games, 1996.
N.L.—12—Montreal, 162 games, 2000.

Fewest grand slams allowed, season
N.L.-A.L.—0—Held by many clubs.
N.L.—Last club—Cincinnati, 1999.
A.L.—Last club—Texas, 1999.

NO-HIT AND ONE-HIT GAMES

Most no-hit games, season
A.A.—2—Louisville 1882; Columbus 1884; Philadelphia 1888.
A.L.—2—Boston 1904; Cleveland 1908; Chicago 1914; Boston 1916; St. Louis 1917; New York 1951; Detroit 1952; Boston 1962; California 1973.
N.L.—2—Brooklyn 1906; Cincinnati 1938; Brooklyn 1956; Milwaukee 1960; Cincinnati 1965; Chicago 1972.

Most consecutive years with no-hit games by pitchers
N.L.—4—Los Angeles, 1962, 1963, 1964, 1965.
A.L.—3
Boston, 1916, 1917, 1918.
Cleveland, 1946, 1947, 1948.
Baltimore, 1967, 1968, 1969.
California, 1973, 1974, 1975.

Most consecutive years without no-hit games by pitchers
N.L.—57—Philadelphia, 1907 through 1963.
A.L.—39—Detroit, 1913 through 1951.

Most one-hit games, season
A.L.—5—Baltimore, 1964.
N.L.—4
Chicago, 1906, 1909.
Philadelphia, 1907, 1911, 1915, 1979.

Most consecutive one-hit nine-inning games
N.L.—2
   Providence vs. New York, June 17, 18, 1884.
   Brooklyn vs. Cincinnati, July 5, 6, 1900.
   New York vs. Boston, September 28, second game, 30, first game, 1916.
   Milwaukee vs. New York, September 10, 11, 1965.
   New York vs. Chicago, Philadelphia, May 13, 15, 1970.
   Houston vs. Philadelphia, New York, June 18, 19, 1972.
   Chicago vs. Cincinnati, Milwaukee, June 24, 25, 2001.
A.L.—2
   Cleveland vs. New York, September 25, 26, 1907.
   Washington vs. Chicago, August 10, 11, 1917.
   Texas vs. Detroit, May 3, 4, 1996.

BASES ON BALLS

Most bases on balls, season
A.L.—827—Philadelphia, 154 games, 1915.
N.L.—737—Colorado, 162 games, 1999.

Fewest bases on balls, season
N.L.—295—New York, 153 games, 1921.
A.L.—359—Detroit, 158 games, 1909.

Most intentional bases on balls, season
N.L.—116—San Diego, 162 games, 1974.
A.L.—94—Seattle, 163 games, 1980.

Fewest intentional bases on balls, season
N.L.—9—Los Angeles, 162 games, 1974.
A.L.—16
   Minnesota, 162 games, 1973.
   New York, 159 games, 1976.
   Minnesota, 162 games, 2001.

STRIKEOUTS

Most strikeouts, season
N.L.—1,344—Chicago, 162 games, 2001.
A.L.—1,266—New York, 161 games, 2001.

Fewest strikeouts, season
A.L.—356—Boston, 154 games, 1930.
N.L.—357—New York, 153 games, 1921.

HIT BATSMEN AND WILD PITCHES

Most hit batsmen, season
A.L.—93—Boston, 161 games, 2001.
N.L.—85—Pittsburgh, 134 games, 1895.
N.L. since 1900—77—Cincinnati, 162 games, 1997.

Fewest hit batsmen, season
A.L.—5—St. Louis, 154 games, 1945.
N.L.—10—St. Louis, 155 games, 1948.

Most wild pitches, season
N.L.—96—Cincinnati, 163 games, 2000.
A.L.—94—Texas, 162 games, 1986.

Fewest wild pitches, season
N.L.—9—Cincinnati, 155 games, 1944.
A.L.—10
   St. Louis, 154 games, 1930.
   Cleveland, 153 games, 1943.

SACRIFICE HITS AND FLIES

Most sacrifice hits allowed, season
N.L.—112—San Diego, 162 games, 1975.
A.L.—110—Kansas City, 158 games, 1960.

Fewest sacrifice hits allowed, season
A.L.—26—Boston, 162 games, 1998.
N.L.—44—Montreal, 156 games, 1972.

Most sacrifice flies allowed, season
N.L.—79—Pittsburgh, 154 games, 1954.
A.L.—73
   Cleveland, 163 games, 1984.
   Texas, 162 games, 2001.

Fewest sacrifice flies allowed, season
N.L.—17—San Francisco, 162 games, 1963.
A.L.—17—Detroit, 164 games, 1968.

BALKS

Most balks, season
A.L.—76—Oakland, 162 games, 1988.
N.L.—41—Montreal, 163 games, 1988.

Fewest balks season
A.L.-N.L.—0—Held by many clubs.

Most balks, nine-inning game
N.L.—6—Milwaukee vs. Chicago, May 4, 1963.
A.L.—5
   Milwaukee vs. New York, April 10, 1988.
   Oakland vs. Seattle, April 13, 1988.

Most balks by both clubs, nine-inning game
N.L.—7
   Pittsburgh 4, Cincinnati 3, April 13, 1963.
   Milwaukee 6, Chicago 1, May 4, 1963.
A.L.—6
   Milwaukee 5, New York 1, April 10, 1988.
   Chicago 4, California 2, April 12, 1988.

LEAGUE PITCHING

COMPLETE GAMES AND INNINGS

Most complete games, season
A.L.—1,100 in 1904.
N.L.—1,089 in 1904.

Fewest complete games, season
N.L.—96 in 2001.
A.L.—103 in 2001.

Most pitchers with 300 or more innings, season
A.L.—12 in 1904.
N.L.—10 in 1905.

GAMES WON AND LOST

Most pitchers winning 20 or more games, season (since 1900)
A.L. (12-club league)—12 in 1973.
A.L. (8-club league)—10 in 1907, 1920.
N.L.—9
  in 1903 (8-club league).
  in 1969 (12-club league).

Fewest pitchers winning 20 or more games, season (since 1900)
N.L.—0 in 1931, 1983, 1987.
A.L.—0 in 1955, 1960, 1982.

Most pitchers losing 20 or more games, season
N.L.—8 in 1905.
A.L.—7 in 1904.

RUNS, EARNED RUNS AND ERA

Most runs, season
N.L. (16-club league)—13,021 in 2000.
N.L. (14-club league)—10,623 in 1996.
N.L. (12-club league)—8,771 in 1970, 1987.
N.L. (10-club league)—7,278 in 1962.
N.L. (8-club league)—7,025 in 1930.
A.L. (14-club league)—12,208 in 1996.
A.L. (12-club league)—8,314 in 1973.
A.L. (10-club league)—7,342 in 1961.
A.L. (8-club league)—7,009 in 1936.

Fewest runs, season
N.L.—4,136 in 1908.
A.L.—4,272 in 1909.

Most earned runs, season
N.L. (16-club league)—11,884 in 2000.
N.L. (14-club league)—9,500 in 1996.
N.L. (12-club league)—7,878 in 1987.
N.L. (10-club league)—6,345 in 1962.
N.L. (8-club league)—6,046 in 1930.
A.L. (14-club league)—11,241 in 1996.
A.L. (12-club league)—7,376 in 1973.
A.L. (10-club league)—6,451 in 1961.
A.L. (8-club league)—6,120 in 1936.

Fewest earned runs, season
N.L.—3,258 in 1916.
A.L.—3,414 in 1914.

Lowest earned-run average, season
N.L.—2.62 in 1916.
A.L.—2.73 in 1914.

Highest earned-run average, season
A.L.—5.04 in 1936.
N.L.—4.97 in 1930.

SHUTOUTS

Most shutouts, season
A.L. (12-club league)—193 in 1972.
A.L. (10-club league)—154 in 1968.

A.L. (8-club league)—146 in 1909.
N.L. (10-club league)—185 in 1968.
N.L. (8-club league)—164 in 1908.

Most extra-inning shutouts, season
A.L.—12 in 1918 (8-club league).
  in 1976 (12-club league).
N.L. (12-club league)—12 in 1976.
N.L. (10-club league)—11 in 1965.
N.L. (8-club league)—8 in 1908, 1909, 1910.

Fewest shutouts, season
A.L. (8-club league)—41 in 1930.
A.L. (10-club league)—100 in 1961.
A.L. (14-club league)—79 in 1996.
N.L. (8-club league)—48 in 1925.
N.L. (10-club league)—95 in 1962.
N.L. (12-club league)—98 in 1987.
N.L. (14-club league)—110 in 1993.

Most shutouts, one day
N.L.—5 on July 13, 1888 (six games).
  June 24, 1892 (eight games).
  July 21, 1896 (seven games).
  July 8, 1907 (five games).
  September 7, 1908 (eight games).
  September 9, 1916 (seven games).
  May 31, 1943 (eight games).
  June 17, 1969 (nine games).
  August 9, 1984 (six games).
A.L.—5 on September 7, 1903 (eight games).
  August 5, 1909 (six games).
  May 6, 1945 (eight games).
  June 4, 1972 (nine games).

Most shutouts in both leagues, one day
8—June 4, 1972, 5 in A.L. (nine games), 3 in N.L. (seven games).

1-0 GAMES

Most 1-0 games, season
N.L. (10-club league)—44 in 1968.
N.L. (8-club league)—43 in 1907.
A.L. (12-club league)—42 in 1971.
A.L. (8-club league)—41 in 1908.

Fewest 1-0 games, season
A.L. (8-club league)—4 in 1930, 1936.
A.L. (14-club league)—6 in 1996.
N.L. (8-club league)—5 in 1932, 1956.
N.L. (10-club league)—13 in 1962.
N.L. (12-club league)—13 in 1983, 1990.
N.L. (14-club league)—22 in 1993.
N.L. (16-club league)—13 in 1999 (includes 12 intraleague plus one interleague game).

Most 1-0 games, one day
A.L.—3—May 14, 1914; July 17, 1962.
N.L.—3—July 4, 1918; September 12, 1969; September 1, 1976.

NO-HIT AND ONE-HIT GAMES

Most no-hit games of nine or more innings, season
M.L.—8
  in 1884 (4 in A.A., 2 in N.L., 2 in U.A.).
  in 1990 (6 in A.L., 2 in N.L.).
A.L. (14-club league)—6 in 1990.
A.L. (8-club league)—5 in 1917.
N.L. (12-club league)—5 in 1969.
N.L. (8-club league)—4 in 1880.

Fewest no-hit games, season
N.L.—0—Made in many seasons. Last season—2000.
A.L.—0—Made in many seasons. Last season—2000.

Most no-hit games, one day
N.L.—2 on April 22, 1898.
A.L.—1—Made on many days.

Most one-hit games of nine or more innings, season
A.L. (14-club league)—13 in 1979, 1988.
A.L. (8-club league)—12 in 1910, 1915.
N.L. (10-club league)—13 in 1965.
N.L. (8-club league)—12 in 1906, 1910.

Fewest one-hit games of nine or more innings, season
A.L. (14-club league)—3—1998.
A.L. (8-club league)—0—1922, 1926, 1927, 1930.
N.L. (12-club league)—4—1980, 1987.
N.L. (8-club league)—0—1924, 1929, 1932, 1952.

HOME RUNS

Most pitchers allowing 30 or more home runs, season
A.L.—18 in 1987 (14-club league).
N.L.—14 in 1999, 2000 (16-club league).

BASES ON BALLS

Most bases on balls, season
N.L. (16-club league)—9,847 in 2000.
N.L. (14-club league)—7,807 in 1997.
N.L. (12-club league)—6,919 in 1970.
N.L. (10-club league)—5,265 in 1962.
N.L. (8-club league)—4,537 in 1950.
A.L. (14-club season)—8,592 in 1996.
A.L. (12-club league)—7,032 in 1969.
A.L. (10-club league)—5,902 in 1961.
A.L. (8-club league)—5,627 in 1949.

Fewest bases on balls, season
N.L.—2,906 in 1921.
A.L.—3,797 in 1922.

Most intentional bases on balls, season (since 1955)
N.L. (12-club league)—862 in 1973.
N.L. (10-club league)—804 in 1967.
N.L. (8-club league)—504 in 1956.
A.L. (12-club league)—668 in 1969.
A.L. (10-club league)—534 in 1965.
A.L. (8-club league)—353 in 1957.

STRIKEOUTS

Most strikeouts, season
N.L. (16-club league)—17,930 in 2001.
N.L. (14-club league)—15,497 in 1997.
N.L. (12-club league)—11,657 in 1987.
N.L. (10-club league)—9,649 in 1965.
N.L. (8-club league)—6,824 in 1960.
A.L. (14-club league)—14,474 in 2001.
A.L. (12-club league)—10,957 in 1970.
A.L. (10-club league)—9,956 in 1964.
A.L. (8-club league)—6,081 in 1959.

Most pitchers with 300 or more strikeouts, season
A.A.—6 in 1884.
N.L.—4 in 1884.
N.L. since 1900—2 in 1997.
U.A.—3 in 1884.
A.L.—2 in 1971.

Most pitchers with 200 or more strikeouts, season
N.L.—12 in 1969.
A.L.—7 in 1967, 1973, 1986.

Most pitchers with 100 or more strikeouts, season
N.L.—59 in 1998.
A.L.—44 in 1998.

Fewest strikeouts, season
A.L.—3,245 in 1924.
N.L.—3,359 in 1926.

HIT BATSMEN

Most hit batsmen, season
N.L. (16-club league)—892 in 2000.
N.L. (14-club league)—769 in 1997.
N.L. (12-club league)—443 in 1969.
N.L. (8-club league)—415 in 1903.
A.L. (14-club league)—766 in 1998.
A.L. (12-club league)—439 in 1969.
A.L. (8-club league)—435 in 1909.

Fewest hit batsmen, season
A.L.—132 in 1947.
N.L.—157 in 1943.

WILD PITCHES AND BALKS

Most wild pitches, season
N.L. (16-club league)—953 in 2001.
N.L. (14-club league)—782 in 1996.
N.L. (12-club league)—648 in 1969.
N.L. (10-club league)—550 in 1965.
N.L. (8-club league)—356 in 1961.
A.L. (14-club league)—937 in 2001.
A.L. (12-club league)—636 in 1969.
A.L. (10-club league)—513 in 1966.
A.L. (8-club league)—325 in 1936.

Fewest wild pitches, season
A.L.—166 in 1931.
N.L.—174 in 1943.

Most balks, season
A.L. (14-club league)—558 in 1988.
A.L. (12-club league)—60 in 1976.
A.L. (10-club league)—51 in 1966.
N.L. (12-club league)—366 in 1988.
N.L. (10-club league)—147 in 1963.

Fewest balks, season
N.L.—13 in 1936, 1946, 1956.
A.L.—18 in 1933, 1941.

INDIVIDUAL FIELDING

FIRST BASEMEN
GAMES AND INNINGS

Most games, career
M.L.—2,413—Eddie Murray, Baltimore A.L., Los Angeles N.L., New York N.L., Cleveland A.L., 1977 through 1996, 20 years.
N.L.—2,247—Jake Beckley, Pittsburgh, New York, Cincinnati, St. Louis, 1888 through 1907, except 1890, 19 years.
N.L. since 1900—2,131—Charlie Grimm, St. Louis, Pittsburgh, Chicago, 1918 through 1936, 19 years.
A.L.—2,227—Mickey Vernon, Washington, Cleveland, Boston, 1939 through 1958, except 1944, 1945 in military service, 18 years.

Most consecutive games, career
A.L.—885—Lou Gehrig, New York, June 2, 1925, through September 27, 1930.
N.L.—652—Frank McCormick, Cincinnati, April 19, 1938, through May 24, 1942, second game.

Most games, season
A.L.—162
Norm Siebern, Kansas City, 1962.
Bill Buckner, Boston, 1985.
Carlos Delgado, Toronto, 2000.
N.L.—162
Bill White, St. Louis, 1963.
Ernie Banks, Chicago, 1965.
Steve Garvey, Los Angeles, 1976, 1979, 1980; San Diego, 1985.
Pete Rose, Philadelphia, 1980, 1982.
Jeff Bagwell, Houston, 1996.
Eric Karros, Los Angeles, 1997.

Most years leading league in most games
N.L.—9—Steve Garvey, Los Angeles, 1975, 1976, 1977, 1978, 1979, 1980 (tied), 1981; San Diego, 1984, 1985.
A.L.—7—Lou Gehrig, New York, 1926, 1927, 1928 (tied), 1932, 1936, 1937, 1938.

Fewest games for leader, season
A.L.—121—Vic Power, Cleveland, 1959.
N.L.—134—Ed Bouchee, Philadelphia, 1959.

Most innings played, game
N.L.—26
Walter Holke, Boston, May 1, 1920.
Ed Konetchy, Brooklyn, May 1, 1920.
A.L.—25—Ted Simmons, Milwaukee, May 8, finished May 9, 1984 (fielded 24.1 innings).

AVERAGE

Highest fielding average, career (1,000 or more games)
M.L.—.996
J.T. Snow, New York A.L., California A.L., San Francisco N.L., 1992 through 2001, 10 years, 1,190 games.
Wes Parker, Los Angeles, 1964 through 1972, nine years, 1,108 games.
Steve Garvey, Los Angeles, San Diego, 1972 through 1987, 16 years, 2,059 games.
N.L.—.996
Wes Parker, Los Angeles, 1964 through 1972, nine years, 1,108 games.
Steve Garvey, Los Angeles, San Diego, 1972 through 1987, 16 years, 2,059 games.
A.L.—.996—Don Mattingly, New York, 1983 through 1995, 13 years, 1,634 games.

Highest fielding average, season (150 or more games)
N.L.—1.000—Steve Garvey, San Diego, 159 games, 1984.
A.L.—.999—Stuffy McInnis, Boston, 152 games, 1921.

Highest fielding average, season (100 or more games)
N.L.—1.000—Steve Garvey, San Diego, 159 games, 1984.
A.L.—.999
Stuffy McInnis, Boston, 152 games, 1921.
Jim Spencer, California, Texas, 125 games, 1973.
Scott Spiezio, Anaheim, 105 games, 2001.

Most years leading league in fielding (100 or more games)
N.L.—9—Charlie Grimm, Pittsburgh, Chicago, 1920, 1922 (tied), 1923, 1924, 1928 (tied), 1930, 1931, 1932 (tied), 1933.
A.L.—6
Joe Judge, Washington, 1923, 1924 (tied), 1925, 1927, 1929, 1930.
Don Mattingly, New York, 1984 (tied), 1985, 1986 (tied), 1987, 1992, 1993.

Most consecutive years leading league in fielding (100 or more games)
N.L.—5—Ted Kluszewski, Cincinnati, 1951, 1952, 1953, 1954, 1955.
A.L.—4
Chick Gandil, Cleveland, Chicago, 1916, 1917, 1918, 1919.
Don Mattingly, New York, 1984 (tied), 1985, 1986 (tied), 1987.

Lowest fielding average for leader, season (100 or more games)
N.L.—.978—Alex McKinnon, St. Louis, 100 games, 1885.
A.L.—.981—John Anderson, Milwaukee, 125 games, 1901.
N.L. since 1900—.986
Dan McGann, St. Louis, 113 games, 1901.
Kitty Bransfield, Pittsburgh, 100 games, 1902.

Lowest fielding average, season (100 or more games)
N.L.—.954—Alex McKinnon, New York, 112 games, 1884.
N.L. since 1900—.970—Jack Doyle, New York, 130 games, 1900.
A.L.—.972
Harry Davis, Philadelphia, 100 games, 1903.
Pat Newnam, St. Louis, 103 games, 1910.

PUTOUTS

Most putouts, career
M.L.—23,696—Jake Beckley, Pittsburgh N.L., Pittsburgh P.L., New York N.L., Cincinnati N.L., St. Louis N.L., 1888 through 1907, 20 years.
N.L.—22,438—Jake Beckley, New York, Pittsburgh, Cincinnati, St. Louis, 1888 through 1907, except 1890, 19 years.
N.L. since 1900—20,700—Charlie Grimm, St. Louis, Pittsburgh, Chicago, 1918 through 1936, 19 years.
A.L.—19,754—Mickey Vernon, Washington, Cleveland, Boston, 1939 through 1958, except 1944, 1945 in military service, 18 years.

Most putouts, season
A.L.—1,846—Jiggs Donahue, Chicago, 157 games, 1907.
N.L.—1,759—George Kelly, New York, 155 games, 1920.

Most years leading league in putouts
N.L.—6
Jake Beckley, Pittsburgh, Cincinnati, St. Louis, 1892, 1894, 1895, 1900, 1902, 1904.
Frank McCormick, Cincinnati, 1939, 1940, 1941, 1942, 1944, 1945.
Steve Garvey, Los Angeles, San Diego, 1974, 1975, 1976, 1977, 1978, 1985.
A.L.—4—Wally Pipp, New York, 1915, 1919, 1920, 1922.

Fewest putouts, season (150 or more games)
A.L.—1,154—Tino Martinez, New York, 154 games, 2000.
N.L.—1,162—Gordy Coleman, Cincinnati, 150 games, 1961.

Fewest putouts for leader, season
A.L.—971—Vic Wertz, Cleveland, 133 games, 1956.
N.L.—1,127—Ed Bouchee, Philadelphia, 134 games, 1959.

Most putouts, nine-inning game
A.L.—22
Tom Jones, St. Louis, May 11, 1906.
Hal Chase, New York, September 21, 1906, first game.
Don Mattingly, New York, July 20, 1987.
Alvin Davis, Seattle, May 28, 1988.
N.L.—22—Ernie Banks, Chicago, May 9, 1963.

Most putouts, extra-inning game
N.L.—42—Walter Holke, Boston, May 1, 1920, 26 innings.
A.L.—32
Mike Epstein, Washington, June 12, 1967, 22 innings.
Rod Carew, California, April 13, finished April 14, 1982, 20 innings.

Fewest putouts, nine-inning game
A.A.—0—Al McCauley, Washington, August 6, 1891.
A.L.—0
  Bud Clancy, Chicago, April 27, 1930.
  Rudy York, Detroit, June 18, 1943.
  Frank Robinson, Baltimore, July 1, 1971.
  Gene Tenace, Oakland, September 1, 1974.
N.L.—0
  Rip Collins, St. Louis, August 21, 1935.
  Rip Collins, Chicago, June 29, 1937.
  Dolph Camilli, Philadelphia, July 30, 1937.
  Earl Torgeson, Boston, May 30, 1947, first game.
  Gary Thomasson, San Francisco, July 31, 1977.
  Len Matuszek, Philadelphia, June 1, 1984.
  Franklin Stubbs, Houston, July 25, 1990.

ASSISTS

Most assists, career
M.L.—1,865—Eddie Murray, Baltimore A.L., Los Angeles N.L.,
  New York N.L., Cleveland A.L., 1977 through 1996, 20 years.
N.L.—1,662—Keith Hernandez, St. Louis, New York, 1974
  through 1989, 16 years.
A.L.—1,444—Mickey Vernon, Washington, Cleveland,
  Washington, Boston, 1939 through 1958, except 1944, 1945
  in military service, 18 years.

Most assists, season
A.L.—184—Bill Buckner, Boston, 162 games, 1985.
N.L.—180—Mark Grace, Chicago, 153 games, 1990.

Most years leading league in assists
N.L.—8—Fred Tenney, Boston, 1899, 1901, 1902, 1903, 1904,
  1905, 1906, 1907.
A.L.—6
  George Sisler, St. Louis, 1919, 1920, 1922, 1924, 1925, 1927.
  Vic Power, Kansas City, Cleveland, Minnesota, 1955, 1957,
    1959, 1960, 1961, 1962.
  Rafael Palmeiro, Texas, Baltimore, 1989, 1992, 1993, 1995,
    1996, 1998.

Fewest assists, season (150 or more games)
N.L.—54—Jim Bottomley, St. Louis, 154 games, 1926.
A.L.—58—Lou Gehrig, New York, 154 games, 1931.

Fewest assists for leader, season
N.L.—83—Herm Reich, Chicago, 85 games, 1949.
A.L.—85—Wally Pipp, New York, 134 games, 1915.

Most assists, nine-inning game
N.L.—8—Bob Robertson, Pittsburgh, June 21, 1971.
A.L.—7—George Stovall, St. Louis, August 7, 1912.

Most assists, extra-inning game
N.L.—8—Bob Skinner, Pittsburgh, July 22, 1954, 14 innings.
A.L.—7—Ferris Fain, Philadelphia, June 9, 1949, 12 innings.

Most assists, doubleheader
A.L.—8
  Charlie Carr, Detroit, June 26, 1904.
  George Sisler, St. Louis, September 12, 1926.
  Rudy York, Chicago, September 27, 1947.
  Jim Spencer, California, August 25, 1970, 21 innings.
N.L.—8
  Gil Hodges, Brooklyn, July 24, 1952, 20 innings.
  Dale Long, Pittsburgh, May 1, 1955.

Most consecutive games with one or more assists, season
A.L.—16—Vic Power, Cleveland, June 9 through June 25, 1960
  (29 assists).
N.L.—14—Bill Terry, New York, May 13, through May 27, 1930
  (16 assists).

Most assists, inning
A.L.—3
  Dick Stuart, Boston, June 28, 1963, first inning.
  Jim Maler, Seattle, April 29, 1982, third inning.
N.L.—3
  Andre Thornton, Chicago, August 22, 1975, fifth inning.
  Leon Durham, Chicago, July 22, 1986, first inning.
  Mark Grace, Chicago, May 23, 1990, fourth inning.

  Phil Stephenson, San Diego, August 23, 1992, fourth inning.
  Will Clark, San Francisco, May 2, 1992, fourth inning.
  George Crowe, Boston, August 7, 1952, first game, fourth
    inning.
  Tony Bartirome, Pittsburgh, September 12, 1952, second
    game, fifth inning.
  Orestes Destrade, Florida, May 13, 1993, fourth inning.
  Derrek Lee, Florida, June 2, 1998, second inning.

CHANCES ACCEPTED AND OFFERED

Most chances accepted, career
M.L.—25,000—Jake Beckley, Pittsburgh N.L., Pittsburgh P.L.,
  New York N.L., Cincinnati N.L., St. Louis N.L., 1888 through
  1907, 20 years.
N.L.—23,687—Jake Beckley, Pittsburgh, New York, Cincinnati,
  St. Louis, 1888 through 1907, except 1890, 19 years.
N.L. since 1900—21,914—Charlie Grimm, St. Louis,
  Pittsburgh, Chicago, 1918 through 1936, 19 years.
A.L.—21,198—Mickey Vernon, Washington, Cleveland, Boston, 1939
  through 1958, except 1944, 1945 in military service, 18 years.

Most chances accepted, season
A.L.—1,986—Jiggs Donahue, Chicago, 157 games, 1907.
N.L.—1,862—George Kelly, New York, 155 games, 1920.

Most years leading league in chances accepted
N.L.—6
  Jake Beckley, Pittsburgh, Cincinnati, St. Louis, 1892, 1894,
    1895, 1900, 1902, 1904.
  Bill Terry, New York, 1927 (tied), 1928, 1929, 1930, 1932, 1934.
A.L.—4—Wally Pipp, New York, 1915, 1919, 1920, 1922.

Fewest chances accepted, season (150 or more games)
A.L.—1,242—Tino Martinez, New York, 154 games, 2000.
N.L.—1,251—Deron Johnson, Philadelphia, 154 games, 1970.

Fewest chances accepted by leader, season
A.L.—1,048
  Bill Skowron, New York, 120 games, 1956.
  Vic Wertz, Cleveland, 133 games, 1956.
N.L.—1,222—Ed Bouchee, Philadelphia, 134 games, 1959.

Most chances accepted, nine-inning game
A.L.-N.L.—22—Held by many first basemen.
A.L.—Last first baseman—Alvin Davis, Seattle, May 28, 1988
  (22 putouts).
N.L.—Last first baseman—Ernie Banks, Chicago, May 9, 1963
  (22 putouts).

Most chances accepted, extra-inning game
N.L.—43—Walter Holke, Boston, May 1, 1920, 26 innings.
A.L.—34
  Rudy York, Detroit, July 21, 1945, 24 innings.
  Mike Epstein, Washington, June 12, 1967, 22 innings.
  Rod Carew, California, April 13, finished April 14, 1982, 20
    innings.

Most chances accepted, doubleheader (18 innings)
A.L.—38—Hal Chase, New York, August 5, 1905.
N.L.—35—Hal Chase, New York, August 26, 1919.

Most chances accepted, two consecutive games
N.L.—39—Harvey Cotter, Chicago, July 10, 1924, second
  game; July 11, 1924.
A.L.—38—Hal Chase, New York, August 5, 5, 1905.

Fewest chances offered, game
A.A.—0
  Guy Hecker, Louisville, October 9, 1887, fielded eight innings.
  Al McCauley, Washington, August 6, 1891.
A.L.—0
  Bud Clancy, Chicago, April 27, 1930.
  Norm Cash, Detroit, June 27, 1963, fielded eight innings.
  Gene Tenace, Oakland, September 1, 1974.
N.L.—0—Rip Collins, Chicago, June 29, 1937.

Fewest chances offered, doubleheader (18 innings)
N.L.—7
  Cap Anson, Chicago, July 19, 1896.
  Frank Bowerman, Pittsburgh, August 19, 1899.

N.L. since 1900—8
Eddie Waitkus, Chicago, May 31, 1948.
George Crowe, Cincinnati, June 2, 1957.
A.L.—9—Hank Greenberg, Detroit, August 26, 1935.

Fewest chances offered, two consecutive games (18 innings)
A.L.—6—Dick Kryhoski, New York, April 29 (3), 30 (3), 1949.
N.L.—7
Cap Anson, Chicago, July 19 (5), 19 (2), 1896.
Frank Bowerman, Pittsburgh, August 19 (5), 19 (2), 1899.
Phil Cavarretta, Chicago, April 25 (6), 26 (1), 1935.

Fewest chances offered, two consecutive games (17 innings)
A.L.—5—Gene Tenace, Oakland, August 31 (5), September 1 (0), 1974.

ERRORS

Most errors, career
N.L.—568—Cap Anson, Chicago, 1879 through 1897, 19 years.
A.L.—285—Hal Chase, New York, Chicago, 1905 through 1914, 10 years, 1,175 games.
N.L. since 1900—252—Fred Tenney, Boston, New York, 1900 through 1911, except 1910, 11 years.

Most errors, season
U.A.—62—Joe Quinn, St. Louis, 100 games, 1884.
N.L.—58—Cap Anson, Chicago, 108 games, 1884.
N.L. since 1900—43—Jack Doyle, New York, 130 games, 1900.
A.L.—41—Jerry Freeman, Washington, 154 games, 1908.

Most years leading league in errors
M.L.—7—Dick Stuart, Pittsburgh N.L. 1958 (tied), 1959, 1960 (tied), 1961, 1962 (tied); Boston, A.L., 1963, 1964.
N.L.—5
Cap Anson, Chicago, 1882, 1884, 1885, 1886, 1892.
Dick Stuart, Pittsburgh, 1958 (tied), 1959, 1960 (tied), 1961, 1962 (tied).
Willie McCovey, San Francisco, 1967 (tied), 1968, 1970, 1971, 1977.
A.L.—5
Hal Chase, New York, Chicago, 1905, 1909, 1911, 1912 (tied), 1913.
George Sisler, St. Louis, 1916, 1917, 1924, 1925, 1927.
Ferris Fain, Philadelphia, 1947 (tied), 1948, 1949, 1950, 1952.
Mo Vaughn, Boston, 1992, 1993, 1994 (tied), 1996, 1997.

Fewest errors, season (150 or more games)
N.L.—0—Steve Garvey, San Diego, 159 games, 1984.
A.L.—1—Stuffy McInnis, Boston, 152 games, 1921.

Fewest errors for leader, season
A.L.—10
Vic Power, Kansas City, 144 games, 1955.
Gus Triandos, Baltimore, 103 games, 1955.
N.L.—12
Fred McGriff, San Diego, 151 games, 1992.
Eddie Murray, New York, 154 games, 1992.

Most consecutive errorless games, career
N.L.—193—Steve Garvey, San Diego, June 26, second game, 1983 through April 14, 1985 (1,623 chances accepted).
A.L.—178—Mike Hegan, Milwaukee, Oakland, September 24, 1970, through May 20, 1973 (758 chances accepted).

Most consecutive errorless games, season
N.L.—159—Steve Garvey, San Diego, April 3 through September 29, 1984 (entire season; 1,319 chances accepted).
A.L.—119—Stuffy McInnis, Boston, May 31, first game, through October 2, 1921 (1,300 chances accepted).

Most consecutive chances accepted without an error, career
A.L.—1,700—Stuffy McInnis, Boston, Cleveland, May 31, 1921, first game, through June 2, 1922, 163 games (1,300 in 1921, 400 in 1922).
N.L.—1,633—Steve Garvey, San Diego, June 26, first game, 1983 through April 15, 1985 (255 in 1983, 1,319 in 1984, 59 in 1985).

Most consecutive chances accepted without an error, season
N.L.—1,319—Steve Garvey, San Diego, April 3 through September 29, 1984 (entire season; 159 games).

A.L.—1,300—Stuffy McInnis, Boston, May 31, first game, through October 2, 1921, 119 games.

Most errors, nine-inning game
A.A.—5—Lew Brown, Louisville, September 10, 1883.
U.A.—5
John Gorman, Kansas City, June 28, 1884.
Joe Quinn, St. Louis, July 4, 1884.
N.L.—5
John Carbine, Louisville, April 29, 1876.
George Zettlein, Philadelphia, June 22, 1876.
Everett Mills, Hartford, October 7, 1876.
Tom Esterbrook, Buffalo, July 27, 1880.
Roger Connor, Troy City, May 27, 1882.
N.L. since 1900—4
John Menefee, Chicago, October 6, 1901.
Johnny Lush, Philadelphia, June 11, 1904, and September 15, 1904, second game.
Fred Tenney, Boston, July 12, 1905, first game.
Todd Zeile, Philadelphia, August 7, 1996.
A.L.—4
Hal Chase, Chicago, July 23, 1913.
George Sisler, St. Louis, April 14, 1925.
Jimmy Wasdell, Washington, May 3, 1939.
Glenn Davis, Baltimore, April 18, 1991.

Most errors, two consecutive games
A.A.—8—Lew Brown, Louisville, September 9, 10, 1883.

Longest errorless game
N.L.—26 innings
Walter Holke, Boston, May 1, 1920.
Ed Konetchy, Brooklyn, May 1, 1920.
A.L.—25 innings—Ted Simmons, Milwaukee, May 8, finished May 9, 1984 (fielded 24.1 innings).

Most errors, inning
N.L.—3
Dolph Camilli, Philadelphia, August 2, 1935, first inning.
Al Oliver, Pittsburgh, May 23, 1969, fourth inning.
Jack Clark, St. Louis, May 25, 1987, second inning.
A.L.—3
George Metkovich, Boston, April 17, 1945, seventh inning.
Tom McCraw, Chicago, May 3, 1968, third inning.
Willie Upshaw, Toronto, July 1, 1986, fifth inning.

DOUBLE PLAYS

Most double plays, career
M.L.—2,044—Mickey Vernon, Washington A.L., Cleveland A.L., Boston A.L., Milwaukee N.L., 1939 through 1959, except 1944, 1945 in military service, 19 years, 2,237 games (2,041 in A.L., 3 in N.L.).
A.L.—2,041—Mickey Vernon, Washington, Cleveland, Boston, 1939 through 1958, except 1944, 1945 in military service, 18 years, 2,227 games.
N.L.—1,708—Charlie Grimm, St. Louis, Pittsburgh, Chicago, 1918 through 1936, 19 years, 2,132 games.

Most double plays, season
A.L.—194—Ferris Fain, Philadelphia, 150 games, 1949.
N.L.—182—Donn Clendenon, Pittsburgh, 152 games, 1966.

Most unassisted double plays, season
A.L.—8—Jim Bottomley, St. Louis, 140 games, 1936.
N.L.—8—Bill White, St. Louis, 151 games, 1961.

Most years leading league in double plays
N.L.—6—Keith Hernandez, St. Louis, New York, 1977, 1979, 1980, 1981, 1983, 1984.
A.L.—4
Stuffy McInnis, Philadelphia, Boston, 1912, 1914, 1919, 1920 (tied).
Wally Pipp, New York, 1915, 1916, 1917 (tied), 1920 (tied).
Cecil Cooper, Milwaukee, 1980, 1981, 1982, 1983.

Fewest double plays, season (150 or more games)
N.L.—82—Mark Grace, Chicago, 156 games, 1998.
A.L.—87—Lou Gehrig, New York, 155 games, 1926.

Fewest double plays for leader, season
A.L.—98—Vic Power, Cleveland, 121 games, 1959.
N.L.—109—Bill White, St. Louis, 123 games, 1960.

Most double plays, game
N.L.—7—Curt Blefary, Houston, May 4, 1969.
A.L.—6
Jimmie Foxx, Philadelphia, August 24, 1935, 15 innings.
Ferris Fain, Philadelphia, September 1, 1947, second game.
George Vico, Detroit, May 19, 1948.
Eddie Robinson, Cleveland, August 5, 1948.
Lee Thomas, Los Angeles, August 23, 1963.
Bob Oliver, Kansas City, May 14, 1971.
John Mayberry, Kansas City, May 6, 1972.
Bob Oliver, New York, April 29, 1975.
Rod Carew, Minnesota, August 29, 1977, first game, 10 innings.

Most double plays started, nine-inning game
A.L.—3
Lu Blue, Detroit, September 8, 1922.
Walt Judnich, St. Louis, September 6, 1947.
Vic Power, Philadelphia, September 26, 1954.
Pete O'Brien, Texas, May 22, 1984.
N.L.—3
Frank Hurst, Philadelphia, September 17, 1930.
Tommie Aaron, Milwaukee, May 27, 1962.

Most unassisted double plays, game
N.L.—2—Held by 15 first basemen. Last first baseman Dave Kingman, New York, July 25, 1982.
A.L.—2—Held by 13 first basemen. Last first baseman—Dave Martinez, Chicago, June 21, 1997.

Most double plays, doubleheader (18 innings)
N.L.—8—Ray Sanders, St. Louis, June 11, 1944.
A.L.—8
Walt Judnich, St. Louis, September 16, 1947.
Walt Dropo, Boston, June 25, 1950.

Most double plays, doubleheader (more than 18 innings)
A.L.—10—Mickey Vernon, Washington, August 18, 1943, 23 innings.

For a complete list of players turning unassisted triple plays, see page 220.

SECOND BASEMEN
GAMES AND INNINGS

Most games, career
A.L.—2,651—Eddie Collins, Philadelphia, Chicago, 21 years, 1908 through 1928.
N.L.—2,427—Joe Morgan, Houston, Cincinnati, San Francisco, Philadelphia, 21 years, 1963 through 1983.

Most consecutive games, career
A.L.—798—Nellie Fox, Chicago, August 7, 1955 through September 3, 1960.
N.L.—443—Dave Cash, Pittsburgh, Philadelphia, September 20, 1973 through August 5, 1976.

Most games, season
A.L.—162
Jake Wood, Detroit, 1961.
Bobby Grich, Baltimore, 1973.
N.L.—163—Bill Mazeroski, Pittsburgh, 1967.

Most years leading league in games
A.L.—8—Nellie Fox, Chicago, 1952, 1953, 1954, 1955, 1956, 1957, 1958, 1959.
N.L.—8—Craig Biggio, Houston, 1992, 1993, 1994, 1995, 1996, 1997, 1998, 2001.

Fewest games for leader, season
A.L.—133—Frank LaPorte, St. Louis, 1911.
N.L.—134—George Cutshaw, Pittsburgh, 1917.

Most innings played, game
N.L.—26
Charlie Pick, Boston, May 1, 1920.
Ivy Olson, Brooklyn, May 1, 1920.
A.L.—25
Julio Cruz, Chicago, May 8, finished May 9, 1984.
Jim Gantner, Milwaukee, May 8, finished May 9, 1984 (fielded 24.1 innings).

AVERAGE

Highest fielding average, career (1,000 or more games)
N.L.—.989
Ryne Sandberg, Philadelphia, Chicago, 16 years, 1981 through 1997, except 1995, 1,995 games.
Tom Herr, St. Louis, Philadelphia, New York, San Francisco, 13 years, 1979 through 1991, 1,343 games.
Mickey Morandini, Philadelphia, Chicago, 11 years, 1990 through 2000, 1,210 games.
A.L.—.987—Roberto Alomar, Toronto, Baltimore, Cleveland, 11 years, 1991 through 2001, 1,557 games.

Highest fielding average, season (150 or more games)
N.L.—.996—Jose Oquendo, St. Louis, 150 games, 1990.
A.L.—.995—Bobby Grich, Baltimore, 162 games, 1973.

Highest fielding average, season (100 or more games)
A.L.—.997—Bobby Grich, California, 116 games, 1985.
N.L.—.997—Bret Boone, Cincinnati, 136 games, 1997.

Most years leading league in fielding (100 or more games)
A.L.—9—Eddie Collins, Philadelphia, Chicago, 1909, 1910, 1914, 1915, 1916, 1920, 1921, 1922, 1924.
N.L.—7—Red Schoendienst, St. Louis, New York, Milwaukee, 1946, 1949, 1953, 1955, 1956, 1957 (tied), 1958.

Most consecutive years leading league in fielding (100 or more games)
N.L.—6—Claude Ritchey, Pittsburgh, 1902, 1903, 1904 (tied), 1905, 1906, 1907.
A.L.—4—Charlie Gehringer, Detroit, 1934 (tied), 1935, 1936, 1937.

Lowest fielding average for leader, season (100 or more games)
N.L.—.928—Charley Bassett, Indianapolis, 119 games, 1887.
N.L. since 1900—.953—John Miller, Pittsburgh, 150 games, 1909.
A.L.—.960—Jimmy Williams, New York, 132 games, 1903.

Lowest fielding average, season (100 or more games)
N.L.—.893—Fred Pfeffer, Chicago, 109 games, 1885.
A.L.—.914—Frank Truesdale, St. Louis, 122 games, 1910.
N.L. since 1900—.927—John Farrell, St. Louis, 118 games, 1903.

PUTOUTS

Most putouts, career
A.L.—6,526—Eddie Collins, Philadelphia, Chicago, 1908 through 1928, 21 years.
N.L.—5,541—Joe Morgan, Houston, Cincinnati, San Francisco, Philadelphia, 1963 through 1983, 21 years.

Most putouts, season
A.A.—525—John McPhee, Cincinnati, 140 games, 1886.
A.L.—484—Bobby Grich, Baltimore 160 games, 1974.
N.L.—466—Billy Herman, Chicago, 153 games, 1933.

Most years leading league in putouts
A.L.—10—Nellie Fox, Chicago, 1952, 1953, 1954, 1955, 1956, 1957, 1958, 1959, 1960, 1961.
N.L.—7
Fred Pfeffer, Chicago, 1884, 1885, 1886, 1887, 1888, 1889, 1891.
Billy Herman, Chicago, Brooklyn, 1933, 1935, 1936, 1938, 1939, 1940 (tied), 1942.

Fewest putouts, season (150 or more games)
A.L.—230—Luis Rivas, Minnesota, 150 games, 2001.
N.L.—260
John Miller, Pittsburgh, 150 games, 1909.
Jose Vidro, Montreal, 153 games, 2000.

Fewest putouts for leader, season
A.L.—285—Damion Easley, Detroit, 140 games, 1998.
N.L.—292—Larry Doyle, New York, 144 games, 1909.

Most putouts, nine-inning game
A.A.—12—Lou Bierbauer, Philadelphia, June 22, 1888.
A.L.—12—Bobby Knoop, California, August 30, 1966.
N.L.—11
  Sam Wise, Washington, May 9, 1893.
  John McPhee, Cincinnati, April 21, 1894.
  Nap Lajoie, Philadelphia, April 25, 1899.
  Billy Herman, Chicago, June 28, 1933, first game.
  Gene Baker, Chicago, May 27, 1955.
  Charlie Neal, Los Angeles, July 2, 1959.
  Julian Javier, St. Louis, June 27, 1964.

Most putouts, extra-inning game
N.L.—15—Jake Pitler, Pittsburgh, August 22, 1917, 22 innings.
A.L.—12
  Billy Gardner, Baltimore, May 21, 1957, 16 innings.
  Vern Fuller, Cleveland, April 11, 1969, 16 innings.

Longest game with no putouts
A.L.—15 innings
  Steve Yerkes, Boston, June 11, 1913.
  Denny Doyle, California, June 14, 1974.
N.L.—12 innings—Ken Boswell, New York, August 7, 1972
  (none out in 13th inning).

Most putouts, two consecutive nine-inning games
A.A.—19—Bill Greenwood, Rochester, July 15, 16, 1890.

Most putouts, doubleheader (18 innings)
N.L.—16
  Fred Pfeffer, Chicago, May 31, 1897.
  Billy Herman, Chicago, June 28, 1933.
A.L.—15—Cass Michaels, Washington, July 30, 1950.

Longest doubleheader with no putouts
A.L.—21.1 innings—Eddie Foster, Washington, July 5, 1917.
N.L.—18 innings
  Claude Ritchey, Pittsburgh, September 2, 1901.
  Gene DeMontreville, Boston, September 20, 1901.
  Johnny Evers, Boston, August 3, 1916.
  John Rawlings, Boston, September 10, 1917.
  Lee Magee, Cincinnati, August 18, 1918.
  Buck Herzog, Boston, June 2, 1919.
  Milt Stock, Brooklyn, August 10, 1925.
  Rogers Hornsby, Boston, September 10, 1928.
  Bama Rowell, Boston, July 4, 1941.
  Bill Rigney, New York, September 1, 1947.
  Connie Ryan, Philadelphia, June 14, 1953.
  Tony Taylor, Philadelphia, August 9, 1960.
  Jerry Buchek, New York, May 28, 1967.

ASSISTS

Most assists, career
A.L.—7,630—Eddie Collins, Philadelphia, Chicago, 21 years, 1908 through 1928.
N.L.—6,738—Joe Morgan, Houston, Cincinnati, San Francisco, Philadelphia, 1963 through 1983, 21 years.

Most assists, season
N.L.—641—Frankie Frisch, St. Louis, 153 games, 1927.
A.L.—572—Oscar Melillo, St. Louis, 148 games, 1930.

Most years leading league in assists
N.L.—9—Bill Mazeroski, Pittsburgh, 1958, 1960, 1961, 1962, 1963, 1964, 1966, 1967, 1968.
A.L.—7—Charlie Gehringer, Detroit, 1927, 1928, 1933, 1934, 1935, 1936, 1938.

Fewest assists, season (150 or more games)
A.L.—310—Joey Cora, Seattle, Cleveland, 151 games, 1998.
N.L.—358—Tony Taylor, Philadelphia, 150 games, 1964.

Fewest assists for leader, season
N.L.—381—Emil Verban, Philadelphia, 138 games, 1946.
A.L.—396—Nellie Fox, Chicago, 154 games, 1956.

Most years with 500 or more assists
A.L.—6—Charlie Gehringer, Detroit, 1928, 1929, 1930, 1933, 1934, 1936.
N.L.—6—Ryne Sandberg, Chicago, 1983, 1984, 1985, 1988, 1991, 1992.

Most assists, nine-inning game
N.L.—12
  Monte Ward, Brooklyn, June 10, 1892, first game.
  Jim Gilliam, Brooklyn, July 21, 1956.
  Ryne Sandberg, Chicago, June 12, 1983.
  Glenn Hubbard, Atlanta, April 14, 1985.
  Juan Samuel, Philadelphia, April 20, 1985.
A.L.—12
  Don Money, Milwaukee, June 24, 1977.
  Tony Phillips, Oakland, July 6, 1986.
  Harold Reynolds, Seattle, August 27, 1986.

Most assists, extra-inning game
N.L.—15—Lave Cross, Philadelphia, August 5, 1897, 12 innings.
N.L. since 1900—13—Morrie Rath, Cincinnati, August 26, 1919, 15 innings.
A.L.—13
  Bobby Avila, Cleveland, July 1, 1952, 19 innings.
  Willie Randolph, New York, August 25, 1976, 19 innings.

CHANCES ACCEPTED AND OFFERED

Most chances accepted, career
A.L.—14,156—Eddie Collins, Philadelphia, Chicago, 1908 through 1928, 21 years.
N.L.—12,279—Joe Morgan, Houston, Cincinnati, San Francisco, Philadelphia, 1963 through 1983, 21 years.

Most chances accepted, season
N.L.—1,037—Frankie Frisch, St. Louis, 153 games, 1927.
A.L.—988—Nap Lajoie, Cleveland, 156 games, 1908.

Most years leading league in chances accepted
A.L.—9—Nellie Fox, Chicago, 1952, 1953, 1954, 1955, 1956, 1957, 1958, 1959, 1960.
N.L.—8—Bill Mazeroski, Pittsburgh, 1958, 1960, 1961, 1962, 1963, 1964, 1966, 1967.

Fewest chances accepted, season (150 or more games)
A.L.—553—Joey Cora, Seattle, Cleveland, 151 games, 1998.
N.L.—671—Mickey Morandini, Chicago, 151 games, 1998.

Fewest chances accepted by leader, season
N.L.—686—John Miller, Pittsburgh, 150 games, 1909.
A.L.—697—Eddie Collins, Philadelphia, 132 games, 1911.

Most years with 900 or more chances accepted
N.L.—5—Billy Herman, Chicago, 1932, 1933, 1935, 1936, 1938.
A.L.—4—Charlie Gehringer, Detroit, 1929, 1930, 1933, 1936.

Most chances accepted, nine-inning game
A.A.—18—Clarence Childs, Syracuse, June 1, 1890.
N.L.—18—Terry Harmon, Philadelphia, June 12, 1971.
A.L.—17
  Jimmie Dykes, Philadelphia, August 28, 1921.
  Nellie Fox, Chicago, June 12, 1952.

Most chances accepted, extra-inning game
N.L.—21—Eddie Moore, Boston vs. Chicago, May 17, 1927, 22 innings.
A.L.—20—Willie Randolph, New York, August 25, 1976, 19 innings.

Most chances accepted, doubleheader (18 innings)
N.L.—26—Frank Parkinson, Philadelphia, September 5, 1922.
A.L.—24—Cass Michaels, Washington, July 30, 1950.

Most chances accepted, doubleheader (more than 18 innings)
A.L.—26—Jerry Remy, California, June 25, 1977.
N.L.—Less than 18-inning record.

Longest game with no chances offered
A.L.—15 innings—Steve Yerkes, Boston, June 11, 1919.
N.L.—12 innings—Ken Boswell, New York, August 7, 1972 (none out in 13th inning).

Most chances accepted, two consecutive games (18 innings)

A.A.—31—Bill Greenwood, Rochester, July 15, 16, 1890.

N.L.—28

Fred Pfeffer, Chicago, August 13, 14, 1884.
Monte Ward, New York, July 18, 19, first game, 1893.

A.L.—28—Bobby Doerr, Boston, May 30, second game, June 3, first game, 1946.

N.L. since 1900—26

Frank Parkinson, Philadelphia, September 5, 5, 1922.
Emil Verban, Philadelphia, August 1, 2, 1947.

Most chances accepted, two consecutive games (more than 18 innings)

A.L.—34—Jackie Hayes, Chicago, July 14, 15, 1932, 22 innings.

N.L.—Record is less than record for nine-inning-games.

Fewest chances offered, doubleheader

N.L.—1—Buck Herzog, Boston, June 2, 1919.

A.L.—1—Eddie Foster, Washington, July 5, 1917, 21.1 innings.

Fewest chances offered, two consecutive games

N.L.—1

Buck Herzog, Boston, April 28, 30, 1919, 19 innings, also June 2, 2, 1919, 18 innings.
Jerry Buchek, New York, May 28, second game, 29, 1967, 17 innings.

A.L.—1

Bobby Young, St. Louis, April 19, 20, 1951, 17 innings.
Bobby Avila, Cleveland, April 19, 20, first game, 1952, 18 innings.
Eddie Foster, Washington, July 5, 5, 1917, 21.1 innings.

Fewest chances offered, three consecutive games

N.L.—3—Eddie Stanky, Boston, April 25, 26, 27, 1949, 26 innings.

A.L.—4—Held by many second basemen.

Fewest chances offered, four consecutive games

N.L.—5—Buck Herzog, Boston, June 2, 2, 3, 3, 1919, 37 innings.

A.L.—6—Held by many second basemen.

ERRORS

Most errors, career

M.L.—828—Fred Pfeffer, Troy N.L., Chicago N.L., Chicago P.L., Louisville N.L., New York N.L., 16 years, 1882 through 1897 (654 in N.L., 74 in P.L.)

N.L.—754—Fred Pfeffer, Troy, Chicago, Louisville, New York, 1882 through 1897, except 1890, 15 years.

N.L. since 1900—443—Larry Doyle, New York, Chicago, 1907 through 1920, 14 years.

A.L.—435—Eddie Collins, Philadelphia, Chicago, 1908 through 1928, 21 years.

Most errors, season

N.L.—88

Charles Smith, Cincinnati, 80 games, 1880.
Bob Ferguson, Philadelphia, 85 games, 1883.

N.L. since 1900—55—George Grantham, Chicago, 150 games, 1923.

A.A.—87

Yank Robinson, St. Louis, 129 games, 1886.
Bill McClellan, Brooklyn, 136 games, 1887.

A.L.—61

Kid Gleason, Detroit, 136 games, 1901.
Hobe Ferris, Boston, 138 games, 1901.

Most years leading league in errors

N.L.—5—Fred Pfeffer, Chicago, 1884, 1885, 1886, 1887, 1888.

N.L. since 1900—4

Billy Herman, Chicago, 1932, 1933, 1937, 1939.
Glenn Beckert, Chicago, 1966, 1967, 1969, 1970 (tied).

M.L. since 1900—4—Tito Fuentes, San Francisco N.L., 1971, 1972; San Diego N.L., 1976; Detroit A.L., 1977.

A.L.—4

Bill Wambsganss, Cleveland, Boston, 1917, 1919, 1920, 1924.
Joe Gordon, New York, 1938, 1941, 1942, 1943 (tied).
Harold Reynolds, Seattle, 1987, 1988, 1989, 1990 (tied).

Fewest errors, season (150 or more games)

N.L.—3—Jose Oquendo, St. Louis, 150 games, 1990.

A.L.—5

Jerry Adair, Baltimore, 153 games, 1964.
Bobby Grich, Baltimore, 162 games, 1973.
Roberto Alomar, Toronto, 150 games, 1992.
Roberto Alomar, Cleveland, 157 games, 2001.

Fewest errors for leader, season

N.L.—13—Luis Castillo, Florida, 133 games, 2001.

A.L.—14—Hector Lopez, Kansas City, 96 games, 1958.

Most consecutive errorless games, career

N.L.—123—Ryne Sandberg, Chicago, June 21, 1989 through May 17, 1990 (577 chances accepted).

A.L.—104—Roberto Alomar, Toronto, June 21, 1994 through July 3, 1995 (482 chances accepted).

Most consecutive errorless games, season

N.L.—90—Ryne Sandberg, Chicago, June 21 through October 1, 1989 (430 chances accepted).

A.L.—86—Rich Dauer, Baltimore, April 10 through September 29, 1978 (418 chances accepted).

Most consecutive chances accepted without an error, season

N.L.—479—Manny Trillo, Philadelphia, April 8 (part) through July 31 (part), 1982, 91 games.

A.L.—425—Rich Dauer, Baltimore, April 10 through September 30 (part), 1978, 87 games.

Most errors, nine-inning game

N.L.—9—Andy Leonard, Boston, June 14, 1876.

N.L. since 1900—4—Held by six second basemen. Last player—Casey Wise, Chicago, May 3, 1957.

A.L.—5

Charles Hickman, Washington, September 29, 1905.
Nap Lajoie, Philadelphia, April 22, 1915.

Longest errorless game

N.L.—25 innings

Felix Millan, New York, September 11, 1974.
Ted Sizemore, St. Louis, September 11, 1974.

A.L.—25 innings

Julio Cruz, Chicago, May 8, finished May 9, 1984.
Jim Gantner, Milwaukee, May 8, finished May 9, 1984 (fielded 24.1 innings).

Most errors, two consecutive games

N.L.—11—Andy Leonard, Boston, June 10, 14, 1876.

Most errors, three consecutive games

N.L.—13—Andy Leonard, Boston, June 10, 14, 15, 1876.

Most errors, inning

N.L.—3

Bid McPhee, Cincinnati, September 23, 1894, first game, second inning.
Claude Ritchey, Pittsburgh, September 22, 1900, sixth inning.
Bama Rowell, Boston, September 25, 1941, third inning.
Eddie Stanky, Chicago, June 20, 1943, first game, eighth inning.
George Hausmann, New York, August 13, 1944, second game, fourth inning.
Kermit Wahl, Cincinnati, September 18, 1945, first game, 11th inning.
Davey Lopes, Los Angeles, June 2, 1973, first inning.
Ted Sizemore, St. Louis, April 17, 1975, sixth inning.

A.L.—3

Del Pratt, St. Louis, September 1, 1914, second game, fourth inning.
Bill Wambsganss, Cleveland, May 15, 1923, fourth inning.
Bobby Doerr, Boston, May 11, 1949, second inning.
Tim Cullen, Washington, August 30, 1969, eighth inning (consecutive).

DOUBLE PLAYS

Most double plays, career

N.L.—1,706—Bill Mazeroski, Pittsburgh, 17 years, 1956 through 1972.

A.L.—1,568—Nellie Fox, Philadelphia, Chicago, 17 years, 1947 through 1963.

Most double plays, season

N.L.—161—Bill Mazeroski, Pittsburgh, 162 games, 1966.
A.L.—150—Gerry Priddy, Detroit, 157 games, 1950.

Most years leading league in double plays

N.L.—8—Bill Mazeroski, Pittsburgh, 1960, 1961, 1962, 1963, 1964, 1965, 1966, 1967.
A.L.—5

Nap Lajoie, Cleveland, 1903, 1906, 1907, 1908, 1909 (tied).
Eddie Collins, Philadelphia, Chicago, 1909 (tied), 1910, 1912, 1916, 1919.
Bucky Harris, Washington, 1921, 1922, 1923, 1924 (tied), 1925.
Bobby Doerr, Boston, 1938, 1940, 1943, 1946, 1947.
Nellie Fox, Chicago, 1954, 1956, 1957, 1958, 1960.

Fewest double plays, season (150 or more games)

N.L.—65

George Hausmann, New York, 154 games, 1945.
Jose Oquendo, St. Louis, 150 games, 1990.
A.L.—65—Luis Rivas, Minnesota, 150 games, 2001.

Fewest double plays for leader, season

N.L.—81—Rogers Hornsby, St. Louis, 154 games, 1922.
A.L.—84—Charlie Gehringer, Detroit, 121 games, 1927.

Most double plays, nine-inning game

A.L.—6—Bobby Knoop, California, May 1, 1966, first game.
N.L.—5—Held by many second basemen. Last player—Teddy Martinez, Los Angeles, August 21, 1977.

Most double plays, extra-inning game

A.L.—6—Joe Gordon, Cleveland, August 31, 1949, first game, 14 innings.
N.L.—6—Felix Millan, Atlanta, August 5, 1971, 17 innings.

Most double plays started, game

A.L.—5—Gerry Priddy, Detroit, May 20, 1950.
N.L.—4

Fred Dunlap, Detroit, June 11, 1887.
Frank Gustine, Pittsburgh, August 22, 1940, second game.
Emil Verban, Philadelphia, July 18, 1947.
Red Schoendienst, St. Louis, August 20, 1954.
Felix Millan, Atlanta, August 5, 1971, 17 innings.

Most unassisted double plays, game

N.L.—2

Dave Force, Buffalo, September 15, 1881.
Claude Ritchey, Louisville, July 9, 1899, first game.
A.L.—2—Mike Edwards, Oakland, August 10, 1978.

Most doubles plays, doubleheader

A.L.—8

Bobby Doerr, Boston, June 25, 1950.
Bobby Knoop, California, May 1, 1966.
N.L.—6—Held by many second basemen.

For a complete list of players turning unassisted triple plays, see page 220.

THIRD BASEMEN
GAMES AND INNINGS

Most games, career

A.L.—2,870—Brooks Robinson, Baltimore, 1955 through 1977, 23 years.
N.L.—2,212—Mike Schmidt, Philadelphia, 1972 through 1989, 18 years.

Most consecutive games, career

A.L.—576—Eddie Yost, Washington, July 3, 1951, to May 11, 1955.
N.L.—364—Ron Santo, Chicago, April 19, 1964 through May 31, 1966.

Most games, season

N.L.—164—Ron Santo, Chicago, 1965.
A.L.—163—Brooks Robinson, Baltimore, 1961, 1964.

Most years leading league in most games

A.L.—8—Brooks Robinson, Baltimore, 1960, 1961, 1962, 1963, 1964, 1966 (tied), 1968 (tied), 1970.
N.L.—7—Ron Santo, Chicago, 1961 (tied), 1963, 1965, 1966, 1967, 1968, 1969 (tied).

Fewest games for leader, season

N.L.—111—Art Whitney, Boston, 1934.
A.L.—131—George Kell, Philadelphia, Detroit, 1946.

Most innings played, game

N.L.—26

Tony Boeckel, Boston, May 1, 1920.
Jimmy Johnston, Brooklyn, May 1, 1920.
A.L.—25

Vance Law, Chicago, May 8, finished May 9, 1984.
Randy Ready, Milwaukee, May 8, finished May 9, 1984 (fielded 24.1 innings).

AVERAGE

Highest fielding average, career (1,000 or more games)

A.L.—.971—Brooks Robinson, Baltimore, 1955 through 1977, 23 years, 2,870 games.
N.L.—.970—Ken Reitz, St. Louis, San Francisco, Chicago, Pittsburgh, 1972 through 1982, 11 years, 1,321 games.

Highest fielding average, season (100 or more games)

A.L.—.991—Steve Buechele, Texas, 111 games, 1991.
N.L.—.983—Heinie Groh, New York, 145 games, 1924.

Highest fielding average, season (150 or more games)

A.L.—.989—Don Money, Milwaukee, 157 games, 1974.
N.L.—.980

Ken Reitz, St. Louis, 157 games, 1977.
Robin Ventura, New York, 160 games, 1999.

Most years leading league in fielding (100 or more games)

A.L.—11—Brooks Robinson, Baltimore, 1960, 1961, 1962, 1963, 1964, 1966, 1967, 1968, 1969 (tied), 1972, 1975.
N.L.—6

Heinie Groh, Cincinnati, New York, 1915 (tied), 1917, 1918, 1922, 1923, 1924.
Ken Reitz, St. Louis, Chicago, 1973, 1974, 1977, 1978, 1980, 1981.

Most consecutive years leading in fielding (100 or more games)

A.L.—6—Willie Kamm, Chicago, 1924 through 1929.
N.L.—4—Willie Jones, Philadelphia, 1953 through 1956.

Lowest fielding average for leader, season (100 or more games)

N.L.—.891—Ned Williamson, Chicago, 111 games, 1885.
N.L. since 1900—.917

Bobby Lowe, Boston, 111 games, 1901.
Charlie Irwin, Cincinnati, Brooklyn, 131 games, 1901.
A.L.—.936—Bill Bradley, Cleveland, 133 games, 1901.

Lowest fielding average, season (100 or more games)

N.L.—.836—Charles Hickman, New York, 118 games, 1900.
A.L.—.860—Hunter Hill, Washington, 135 games, 1904.

PUTOUTS

Most putouts, career

A.L.—2,697—Brooks Robinson, Baltimore, 1955 through 1977, 23 years.
N.L.—2,288—Pie Traynor, Pittsburgh, 1921 through 1937, except 1936, 16 years.

Most putouts, season

A.A.—252—Denny Lyons, Philadelphia, 137 games, 1887.
N.L.—252—Jimmy Collins, Boston, 142 games, 1900.
A.L.—243—Willie Kamm, Chicago, 155 games, 1928.

Most years leading league in putouts

A.L.—8—Eddie Yost, Washington, Detroit, 1948, 1950, 1951, 1952, 1953, 1954 (tied), 1956, 1959.
N.L.—7

Pie Traynor, Pittsburgh, 1923, 1925, 1926, 1927, 1931, 1933, 1934.
Willie Jones, Philadelphia, 1949, 1950, 1952, 1953, 1954, 1955, 1956.
Ron Santo, Chicago, 1962, 1963, 1964, 1965, 1966, 1967, 1969.

Fewest putouts for leader, season
N.L.—107—Mike Lowell, Florida, 144 games, 2001.
A.L.—111—Joe Randa, Kansas City, 137 games, 2001.

Fewest putouts, season (150 or more games)
N.L.—77—Chipper Jones, Atlanta, 152 games, 1997.
A.L.—79—Travis Fryman, Cleveland, 154 games, 2000.

Most putouts, nine-inning game
N.L.—10—Willie Kuehne, Pittsburgh, May 24, 1889.
N.L. since 1900—9—Pat Dillard, St. Louis, June 18, 1900.
A.L.—9
　Bill Bradley, Cleveland, September 21, 1901, first game; also
　　May 13, 1909.
　Harry Riconda, Philadelphia, July 5, 1924, second game.
　Ossie Bluege, Washington, June 18, 1927.
　Ray Boone, Detroit, April 24, 1954.

Longest game with no putouts
N.L.—20 innings—Lew Malone, Brooklyn, April 30, 1919.
A.L.—18.2 innings—Vern Stephens, Boston, July 13, 1951.

Most consecutive games with no putouts
A.L.—10—Felix Torres, Los Angeles, June 14 through June 23,
　1963.
N.L.—8—Ken Boyer, St. Louis, August 4, first game through
　August 11, 1963.

ASSISTS

Most assists, career
A.L.—6,205—Brooks Robinson, Baltimore, 23 years, 1955
　through 1977.
N.L.—5,045—Mike Schmidt, Philadelphia, 18 years, 1972
　through 1989.

Most assists, season
A.L.—412—Graig Nettles, Cleveland, 158 games, 1971.
N.L.—404—Mike Schmidt, Philadelphia, 162 games, 1974.

Most years leading league in assists
A.L.—8—Brooks Robinson, Baltimore, 1960, 1963, 1964, 1966,
　1967, 1968, 1969, 1974.
N.L.—7
　Ron Santo, Chicago, 1962, 1963, 1964, 1965, 1966, 1967, 1968.
　Mike Schmidt, Philadelphia, 1974, 1976, 1977, 1980, 1981,
　　1982, 1983.

Fewest assists, season (150 or more games)
A.L.—221
　Harry Lord, Chicago, 150 games, 1913.
　Dean Palmer, Texas, 154 games, 1996.
N.L.—238—Chipper Jones, Atlanta, 156 games, 1999.

Fewest assists for leader, season
N.L.—227—Art Whitney, Boston, 111 games, 1934.
A.L.—258—Ossie Bluege, Washington, 134 games, 1930.

Most assists, nine-inning game
N.L.—11
　Deacon White, Buffalo, May 16, 1884.
　Jerry Denny, New York, May 29, 1890.
　Damon Phillips, Boston, August 29, 1944.
　Chris Sabo, Cincinnati, April 7, 1988.
A.L.—11
　Ken McMullen, Washington, September 26, 1966, first game.
　Mike Ferraro, New York, September 14, 1968.

Most assists, extra-inning game
N.L.—12—Bobby Byrne, Pittsburgh, June 8, 1910, second
　game, 11 innings.
A.L.—11
　Home Run Baker, New York, May 24, 1918, 19 innings.
　Doug DeCinces, California, May 7, 1983, 12 innings.

Most innings with no assists, extra-inning game
A.L.—17—Toby Harrah, Texas, September 17, 1977.

CHANCES ACCEPTED AND OFFERED

Most chances accepted, career
A.L.—8,902—Brooks Robinson, Baltimore, 1955 through 1977,
　23 years.

N.L.—6,636—Mike Schmidt, Philadelphia, 1972 through 1989,
　18 years.

Most chances accepted, season
A.L.—603—Harlond Clift, St. Louis, 155 games, 1937.
N.L.—601—Jimmy Collins, Boston, 151 games, 1899.
N.L. since 1900—583—Tommy Leach, Pittsburgh, 146 games,
　1904.

Most years leading league in chances accepted
N.L.—9—Ron Santo, Chicago, 1961, 1962, 1963, 1964, 1965,
　1966, 1967, 1968, 1969 (tied).
A.L.—8
　Home Run Baker, Philadelphia, New York, 1909, 1910, 1912,
　　1913, 1914, 1917, 1918, 1919.
　Brooks Robinson, Baltimore, 1960, 1963, 1964, 1966, 1967,
　　1968, 1969, 1974.

Fewest chances accepted, season (150 or more games)
N.L.—318—Chipper Jones, Atlanta, 152 games, 1997.
A.L.—326—Dean Palmer, Texas, 154 games, 1996.

Fewest chances accepted for leader, season
N.L.—332—Art Whitney, Boston, 111 games, 1934.
A.L.—372—Robin Ventura, Chicago, 150 games, 1996.

Most chances accepted, nine-inning game
A.L.—13—Wid Conroy, Washington, September 25, 1911.
N.L.—13
　Bill Kuehne, Pittsburgh, May 24, 1889.
　Jerry Denny, New York, May 19, 1890.
　Bill Shindle, Baltimore, September 28, 1893.
　Bill Joyce, Washington, May 26, 1894.
　Art Devlin, New York, May 23, 1908, first game.
　Tony Cuccinello, Brooklyn, July 12, 1934, first game.
　Roy Hughes, Chicago, August 29, 1944, second game.

Most chances accepted, extra-inning game
N.L.—16—Jerry Denny, Providence, August 17, 1882, 18
　innings.
N.L. since 1900—14—Don Hoak, Cincinnati, May 4, 1958,
　second game, 14 innings.
A.L.—14
　Jimmy Collins, Boston, June 21, 1902, 15 innings.
　Ben Dyer, Detroit, July 16, 1919, 14 innings.

Most chances accepted, two consecutive games
N.L.—23—Joe Farrell, Detroit, June 30, July 1, 1884.
N.L. since 1900—18
　Harry Steinfeldt, Cincinnati, June 14, 16, 1902.
　Bobby Byrne, Pittsburgh, June 15, 17, 1910.
　Eddie Zimmerman, Brooklyn, July 4, 4, 1911.
　Babe Pinelli, Cincinnati, July 11, second game, July 13, 1925.
　Lee Handley, Pittsburgh, June 15, 16, first game, 1946.
A.L.—18
　Hobe Ferris, St. Louis, July 12, 13, 1909, first game.
　Terry Turner, Cleveland, May 21, June 1, 1916, first game.
　Aaron Ward, New York, April 20, 21, 1921.

Most chances accepted, doubleheader
N.L.—18—Eddie Zimmerman, Brooklyn, July 4, 1911.
A.L.—16—Billy Purtell, Chicago, July 14, 1909.

Longest game with no chances offered
N.L.—15 innings
　Harry Steinfeldt, Chicago, August 22, 1908.
　Heinie Groh, Cincinnati, August 26, 1919, second game.
　Tony Boeckel, Boston, June 16, 1921; also September 12,
　　1921, first game.
A.L.—15 innings—Toby Harrah, Cleveland, June 20, 1980.

Longest doubleheader with no chances offered
A.L.—21.2 innings—Billy Gardner, Cleveland, August 23, 1920.
N.L.—19 innings—Tony Boeckel, Boston, July 26, 1922.

ERRORS

Most errors, career
M.L.—780—Arlie Latham, St. Louis A.A., Chicago P.L.,
　Cincinnati N.L., St. Louis N.L., 1883 through 1896, 14 years.
N.L.—533—Jerry Denny, Providence, St. Louis, Indianapolis,
　New York, Cleveland, Philadelphia, Louisville, 1881 through
　1894, except 1892, 13 years.

N.L. since 1900—324—Pie Traynor, Pittsburgh, 1921 through 1935, 1937, 16 years, 1,864 games.

A.L.—359—Jimmy Austin, New York, St. Louis, 1909 through 1922, 1925, 1926, 1929, 17 years, 1,433 games.

Most errors, season

N.L.—91—Charles Hickman, New York, 118 games, 1900.

A.L.—64—Sammy Strang, Chicago, 137 games, 1902.

Most years leading league in errors

N.L.—5—Pie Traynor, Pittsburgh, 1926, 1928 (tied), 1931, 1932, 1933.

A.L.—5—Jim Tabor, Boston, 1939, 1940 (tied), 1941, 1942, 1943 (tied).

Fewest errors, season (150 or more games)

A.L.—5—Don Money, Milwaukee, 157 games, 1974.

N.L.—8—Ken Reitz, St. Louis, 150 games, 1980.

Fewest errors for leader, season

N.L.—16

Eddie Mathews, Milwaukee, 147 games, 1957.

Gene Freese, Pittsburgh, 74 games, 1957.

A.L.—17—Cecil Travis, Washington, 56 games, 1946.

Most errors, game

U.A.—6—Jim Donnelly, Kansas City, July 16, 1884.

A.A.—6

Joe Moffett, Toledo, August 2, 1884.

Joe Werrick, Louisville, July 28, 1888.

Billy Alvord, Toledo, May 22, 1890.

N.L.—6—Joe Mulvey, Philadelphia, July 30, 1884.

N.L. since 1900—5—Dave Brain, Boston, June 11, 1906.

A.L.—4—Held by 22 third basemen. Last third basemen—Mike Blowers, New York, May 3, 1990; Edgar Martinez, Seattle, May 6, 1990.

Most consecutive errorless games, career

N.L.—99—John Wehner, Pittsburgh, August 2, 1992 through September 29, 2000 (202 chances accepted; played other positions during streak).

A.L.—88—Don Money, Milwaukee, September 28, 1973, second game through July 16, 1974 (261 chances accepted).

Most consecutive errorless games, season

A.L.—86—Don Money, Milwaukee, April 5 through July 16, 1974 (257 chances accepted).

N.L.—85—Jeff Cirillo, Colorado, June 20 through October 7, 2001 (228 chances accepted).

N.L.—57—Bob Aspromonte, Houston, July 14 through September 18, 1962, second game (145 chances accepted).

Most consecutive chances accepted without an error, career

A.L.—261—Don Money, Milwaukee, September 28, 1973, first game, through July 16, 1974, 88 games.

Most consecutive chances accepted without an error, season

A.L.—257—Don Money, Milwaukee, April 5 through July 16, 1974, 88 games.

N.L.—228—Jeff Cirillo, Colorado, June 20 through October 7, 2001, 85 games.

Longest errorless game

N.L.—26 innings

Tony Boeckel, Boston, May 1, 1920.

Jimmy Johnston, Brooklyn, May 1, 1920.

A.L.—25 innings—Vance Law, Chicago, May 8, finished May 9, 1984.

Most errors, doubleheader (since 1900)

N.L.—5

Bill Bradley, Chicago, May 30, 1900.

Tommy Leach, Pittsburgh, August 20, 1903.

A.L.—4—Held by many third basemen. Last third baseman—Herb Plews, Washington, June 3, 1958.

Most errors, two consecutive games

A.A.—9—Tom Esterbrook, New York, July 15, 26, 1883.

Most errors, inning

N.L.—4

Lew Whistler, New York, June 19, 1891, fourth inning.

Bob Brenly, San Francisco, September 14, 1986, fourth inning.

A.L.—4—Jimmy Burke, Milwaukee, May 27, 1901, fourth inning.

DOUBLE PLAYS

Most double plays, career

A.L.—618—Brooks Robinson, Baltimore, 23 years, 1955 through 1977.

N.L.—450—Mike Schmidt, Philadelphia, 18 years, 1972 through 1989.

Most double plays, season

A.L.—54—Graig Nettles, Cleveland, 158 games, 1971.

N.L.—45

Darrell Evans, Atlanta, 160 games, 1974.

Jeff Cirillo, Milwaukee, 149 games, 1998.

Most years leading league in double plays

N.L.—6

Heinie Groh, Cincinnati, New York, 1915, 1916, 1918, 1919, 1920 (tied), 1922.

Ron Santo, Chicago, 1961, 1964, 1966, 1967, 1968 (tied), 1971.

Mike Schmidt, Philadelphia, 1978, 1979, 1980, 1982 (tied), 1983, 1987.

A.L.—5

Jimmy Austin, New York, St. Louis, 1909, 1911, 1913, 1915, 1917.

Ken Keltner, Cleveland, 1939, 1941, 1942, 1944, 1947.

Frank Malzone, Boston, 1957, 1958, 1959, 1960, 1961.

Fewest double plays, season (150 or more games)

N.L.—10

Bob Aspromonte, Houston, 155 games, 1964.

Chipper Jones, Atlanta, 156 games, 1999.

A.L.—17

Max Alvis, Cleveland, 156 games, 1965.

Wade Boggs, Boston, 151 games, 1988.

Dean Palmer, Texas, 154 games, 1996.

Fewest double plays for leader, season

N.L.—17

Joe Stripp, Brooklyn, 140 games, 1933.

Johnny Vergez, New York, 123 games, 1933.

Whitey Kurowski, St. Louis, 138 games, 1946.

Jim Tabor, Philadelphia, 124 games, 1946.

A.L.—23—Marty McManus, Detroit, 130 games, 1930.

Most unassisted double plays, season

A.L.—4—Joe Dugan, New York, 148 games, 1924.

N.L.—3

Harry Wolverton, Philadelphia, 34 games, 1902.

Heinie Groh, Cincinnati, 131 games, 1915.

Most double plays, game

N.L.—4

Pie Traynor, Pittsburgh, July 9, 1925, first game.

Johnny Vergez, Philadelphia, August 15, 1935.

Edgardo Alfonzo, New York, May 14, 1997.

A.L.—4

Andy Carey, New York, July 31, 1955, second game.

Felix Torres, Los Angeles, August 23, 1963.

Ken McMullen, Washington, August 13, 1965.

Scott Brosius, New York, July 6, 2000.

Most double plays started, nine-inning game

N.L.—4

Pie Traynor, Pittsburgh, July 9, 1925, first game.

Johnny Vergez, Philadelphia, August 15, 1935.

A.L.—4

Felix Torres, Los Angeles, August 23, 1963.

Ken McMullen, Washington, August 13, 1965.

Scott Brosius, New York, July 6, 2000.

Most unassisted double plays, game

N.L.-A.L.—1—Held by many third basemen.

Most unassisted double plays, two consecutive games

A.L.—2

Jim Delahanty, Detroit, August 28, 29, 1911.

Marv Owen, Detroit, April 28, 29, 1934.

N.L.—2—Harry Wolverton, Philadelphia, July 25, 26, 1902.

SHORTSTOPS
GAMES AND INNINGS

Most games, career
A.L.—2,581—Luis Aparicio, Chicago, Baltimore, Boston, 1956 through 1973, 18 years.
N.L.—2,511—Ozzie Smith, San Diego, St. Louis, 1978 through 1996, 19 years.

Most consecutive games, career
A.L.—2,216—Cal Ripken, Baltimore, July 1, 1982 through July 14, 1996.
N.L.—584—Roy McMillan, Cincinnati, September 16, 1951, first game, through August 6, 1955.

Most games, season
N.L.—165—Maury Wills, Los Angeles, 1962.
A.L.—163—Tony Fernandez, Toronto, 1986.

Most games by lefthanded shortstop, season
N.L.—73—Billy Hulen, Philadelphia, 1896.

Most years leading league in games
A.L.—12—Cal Ripken, Baltimore, 1983, 1984, 1987, 1988, 1989, 1990, 1991, 1992, 1993, 1994, 1995, 1996.
N.L.—6
  Mickey Doolan, Philadelphia, 1906, 1909, 1910, 1911, 1912, 1913.
  Arky Vaughan, Pittsburgh, 1933 (tied), 1934, 1936, 1938, 1939, 1940.
  Roy McMillan, Cincinnati, Milwaukee, 1952, 1953, 1954 (tied), 1956, 1957, 1961.

Fewest games for leader, season
N.L.—141—Rabbit Maranville, Pittsburgh, 1923.
A.L.—142—Luis Aparicio, Chicago, 1957.

Most innings played, game
N.L.—26
  Chuck Ward, Brooklyn, May 1, 1920.
  Rabbit Maranville, Boston, May 1, 1920.
A.L.—25—Robin Yount, Milwaukee, May 8, finished May 9, 1984, fielded 24.1 innings.

AVERAGE

Highest fielding average, career (1,000 or more games)
A.L.—.983—Omar Vizquel, Seattle, Cleveland, 13 years, 1989 through 2000, 1,764 games.
N.L.—.980—Larry Bowa, Philadelphia, Chicago, 1970 through 1985, 16 years, 2,222 games.

Highest fielding average, season (150 or more games)
A.L.—.996—Cal Ripken, Baltimore, 161 games, 1990.
N.L.—.994—Rey Ordonez, New York, 154 games, 1999.

Highest fielding average, season (100 or more games)
A.L.—.996—Cal Ripken, Baltimore, 161 games, 1990.
N.L.—.994—Rey Ordonez, New York, 154 games, 1999.

Most years leading league in fielding (100 or more games)
A.L.—8
  Everett Scott, Boston, New York, 1916, 1917, 1918, 1919, 1920, 1921, 1922, 1923, consecutive.
  Lou Boudreau, Cleveland, 1940, 1941, 1942, 1943, 1944, 1946, 1947, 1948.
  Luis Aparicio, Chicago, Baltimore, 1959, 1960, 1961, 1962, 1963, 1964, 1965, 1966, consecutive.
N.L.—7—Ozzie Smith, San Diego, St. Louis, 1981, 1982, 1984, 1985, 1986, 1987, 1991. (Note: Smith also led N.L. shortstops in fielding in the strike-shortened 1994 season, when he played in 96 games.)

Most consecutive years leading league in fielding (100 or more games)
A.L.—8
  Everett Scott, Boston, New York, 1916 through 1923.
  Luis Aparicio, Chicago, Baltimore, 1959 through 1966.
N.L.—5—Hughie Jennings, Baltimore, 1894 through 1898.

N.L. since 1900—4
  Eddie R. Miller, Boston, Cincinnati, 1940 through 1943.
  Ozzie Smith, St. Louis, 1984 through 1987.

Lowest fielding average for leader (100 or more games)
N.L.—.900
  Jack Glasscock, Indianapolis, 109 games, 1888.
  Arthur Irwin, Philadelphia, 121 games, 1888.
N.L. since 1900—.936—Tommy Corcoran, Cincinnati, 150 games, 1904.
A.L.—.934
  Freddy Parent, Boston, 139 games, 1903.
  Monte Cross, Philadelphia, 138 games, 1903.

Lowest fielding average, season (100 or more games)
A.L.—.861—Bill Keister, Baltimore, 114 games, 1901.
N.L.—.884—Tom Burns, Chicago, 111 games, 1885.
N.L. since 1900—.891—Otto Krueger, St. Louis, 107 games, 1902.

PUTOUTS

Most putouts, career
N.L.—5,133—Rabbit Maranville, Boston, Pittsburgh, Chicago, Brooklyn, St. Louis, 1912 through 1931, except 1924, 19 years.
A.L.—4,548—Luis Aparicio, Chicago, Baltimore, Boston, 1956 through 1973, 18 years.

Most putouts, season
N.L.—425—Hughie Jennings, Baltimore, 131 games, 1895.
A.L.—425—Donie Bush, Detroit, 157 games, 1914.
N.L. since 1900—407—Rabbit Maranville, Boston, 156 games, 1914.

Most years leading league in putouts
N.L.—6—Rabbit Maranville, Boston, Pittsburgh, 1914, 1915 (tied), 1916, 1917, 1919, 1923.
A.L.—6—Cal Ripken, Baltimore, 1984, 1985, 1988, 1989, 1991, 1992.

Fewest putouts, season (150 or more games)
N.L.—180
  Larry Bowa, Philadelphia, 156 games, 1976.
  Mark Grudzielanek, Montreal, 153 games, 1996.
A.L.—212
  Gary DiSarcina, California, 150 games, 1996.
  Derek Jeter, New York, 150 games, 2001.

Fewest putouts for leader, season
N.L.—230—Barry Larkin, Cincinnati, 151 games, 1996.
A.L.—248—Joe DeMaestri, Kansas City, 134 games, 1957.

Most putouts, nine-inning game
N.L.—11
  Shorty Fuller, New York, August 20, 1895.
  Hod Ford, Cincinnati, September 18, 1929.
A.L.—11—John Cassidy, Washington, August 30, 1904, first game.

Most putouts, opening game of season (nine innings)
N.L.—9—Bill Dahlen, Brooklyn, April 19, 1900.

Most putouts in extra-inning game
N.L.—14—Monte Cross, Philadelphia, July 7, 1899, 11 innings.
A.L.—Less than nine-inning game.

Most putouts with no assists, game
N.L.—9—Buck Herzog, Cincinnati, May 26, 1916.

ASSISTS

Most assists, career
N.L.—8,375—Ozzie Smith, San Diego, St. Louis, 1978 through 1996, 19 years.
A.L.—8,016—Luis Aparicio, Chicago, Baltimore, Boston, 1956 through 1973, 18 years.

Most assists, season
N.L.—621—Ozzie Smith, San Diego, 158 games, 1980.
A.L.—583—Cal Ripken, Baltimore, 162 games, 1984.

Most years leading league in assists

N.L.—8—Ozzie Smith, San Diego, 1979, 1980, 1981; St. Louis, 1982, 1985, 1987, 1988, 1989.
A.L.—7
Luke Appling, Chicago, 1933, 1935, 1937, 1939, 1941, 1943, 1946.
Luis Aparicio, Chicago, 1956, 1957, 1958, 1959, 1960, 1961, 1968.
Cal Ripken Jr., Baltimore, 1983, 1984, 1986, 1987, 1989, 1991, 1993.

Fewest assists, season (150 or more games)

A.L.—343—Derek Jeter, New York, 150 games, 2001.
N.L.—374—Kevin Elster, New York, 150 games, 1989.

Most years with 500 or more assists

N.L.—8—Ozzie Smith, San Diego, 1978, 1979, 1980, St. Louis, 1982, 1983, 1985, 1987, 1988.
A.L.—6—Donie Bush, Detroit, 1909, 1911, 1912, 1913, 1914, 1915.

Fewest assists for leader, season

A.L.—438—Joe Sewell, Cleveland, 137 games, 1928.
N.L.—440—Johnny Logan, Milwaukee, 129 games, 1957.

Most assists, nine-inning game

N.L.—14—Tommy Corcoran, Cincinnati, August 7, 1903.
A.L.—13
Bobby Reeves, Washington, August 7, 1927.
Alex Gonzalez, Toronto, April 26, 1996.

Most assists, extra-inning game

A.L.—15—Rick Burleson, California, April 13, finished April 14, 1982, 20 innings.
N.L.—14
Herman Long, Boston, May 6, 1892, 14 innings.
Bud Harrelson, New York, May 24, 1973, 19 innings.

Longest game played with no assists

N.L.—17 innings—Jack Coffey, Boston, July 26, 1909.
A.L.—13 innings—Rick Burleson, Boston, June 29, 1979.

CHANCES ACCEPTED AND OFFERED

Most chances accepted, career

N.L.—12,624—Ozzie Smith, San Diego, St. Louis, 1978 through 1996, 19 years.
A.L.—12,564—Luis Aparicio, Chicago, Baltimore, Boston, 1956 through 1973, 18 years.

Most chances accepted, season

N.L.—984—Dave Bancroft, New York, 156 games, 1922.
A.L.—969—Donie Bush, Detroit, 157 games, 1914.

Most years leading league in chances accepted

N.L.—8—Ozzie Smith, San Diego, St. Louis, 1978, 1980, 1981, 1983, 1985, 1987, 1988, 1989.
A.L.—7—Luis Aparicio, Chicago, 1956, 1957, 1958, 1959, 1960, 1961, 1968.

Fewest chances accepted, season, 150 or more games

A.L.—555—Derek Jeter, New York, 150 games, 2001.
N.L.—609—Kevin Elster, New York, 150 games, 1989.

Fewest chances accepted by leader in chances accepted, season

N.L.—683—Mark Grudzielanek, Montreal, 156 games, 1997.
A.L.—695—Luis Aparicio, Chicago, 142 games, 1957.

Most chances accepted in nine-inning game

N.L.—19
Danny Richardson, Washington, June 20, 1892, first game.
Eddie Joost, Cincinnati, May 7, 1941.
A.L.—17—Bobby Wallace, St. Louis, June 10, 1902.

Most chances accepted in extra-inning game

N.L.—21—Eddie R. Miller, Boston, June 27, 1939, 23 innings.
A.L.—18
Freddy Parent, Boston, July 9, 1902, 17 innings.
Chico Carrasquel, Chicago, July 13, 1951, 19 innings.
Skeeter Webb, Detroit, July 21, 1945, 24 innings.
Pete Runnels, Washington, June 3, 1952, 17 innings.
Ron Hansen, Chicago, August 29, 1965, first game, 14 innings.

Most chances accepted in doubleheader

N.L.—25—Danny Richardson, Washington, June 20, 1892.
N.L. since 1900—24
Heinie Sand, Philadelphia, July 4, 1924.
Dave Bancroft, Boston, July 31, 1926.
A.L.—24
George McBride, Washington, August 19, 1908.
Roger Peckinpaugh, New York, September 8, 1919.
Topper Rigney, Boston, July 15, 1926.

Most chances accepted in doubleheader, more than 18 innings

A.L.—28—Ron Hansen, Chicago, August 29, 1965, 23 innings.
N.L.—26—Arky Vaughan, Pittsburgh, August 22, 1940, 21 innings.

Most chances accepted in three consecutive games

A.L.—37—Wally Gerber, St. Louis, May 27, 29, 30, first game, 1923.
N.L.—35
George Davis, New York, May 23, 24, 25, 1899.
George Davis, New York, July 19, 20, 21, 1900.

Most chances accepted in four consecutive games

A.L.—48—Wally Gerber, St. Louis, May 27, 29, 30, 30, 1923.
N.L.—45—George Davis, New York, May 23, 24, 25, 26, 1899.
N.L. since 1900—44—George Davis, New York, July 18, 19, 20, 21, 1900.

Longest game with no chances offered

A.L.—12 innings
John Gochnaur, Cleveland, July 14, 1903.
Billy Rogell, Detroit, June 16, 1937, fielded 11.2 innings.
N.L.—12 innings—Irv Ray, Boston, August 15, 1888.
N.L. since 1900—11.2 innings—Eddie Feinberg, Philadelphia, May 19, 1939.

Fewest chances offered, opening game of season

A.L.—0—Frankie Crosetti, New York, April 16, 1940, 9.2 innings.
N.L.—0—Honus Wagner, Pittsburgh, April 14, 1910, nine innings.

Fewest chances offered, doubleheader

A.L.—0—Toby Harrah, Texas, June 25, 1976, 18 innings.
N.L.—1—Travis Jackson, New York, May 30, 1934, 18 innings.

Fewest chances offered, two consecutive games

A.L.—0
Tom Tresh, New York, July 31, August 1, 1968, 18 innings.
Toby Harrah, Texas, June 25, 25, 1976, 18 innings.
N.L.—1
Travis Jackson, New York, May 30, 1934, 18 innings.
Chico Fernandez, Philadelphia, May 7, 8, 1957, 18 innings.
Mike Fischlin, Houston, June 18, 20, 1978, 18 innings.

Fewest chances offered, three consecutive games

A.L.—0—Tom Tresh, New York, July 30, 31, August 1, 1968, 26 innings.
N.L.—3—Chico Fernandez, Philadelphia, May 5, second game, 7, 8, 1957, 27 innings.

ERRORS

Most errors, career

M.L.—1,037—Herman Long, Kansas City A.A., Boston N.L., New York A.L., Detroit A.L., 1889 through 1903, 15 years.
N.L.—972—Bill Dahlen, Chicago, Brooklyn, New York, Boston, 1891 through 1911, except 1910, 20 years, 2,139 games.
N.L. since 1900—676—Honus Wagner, Pittsburgh, 1901 through 1917, 17 years, 1,887 games.
A.L.—689—Donie Bush, Detroit, Washington, 1908 through 1921, 14 years, 1,866 games.

Most errors, season

P.L.—115—Bill Shindle, Philadelphia, 132 games, 1890.
N.L.—106—Joe Sullivan, Washington, 127 games, 1893.
N.L. since 1900—81—Rudy Hulswitt, Philadelphia, 138 games, 1903.
A.L.—95—John Gochnaur, Cleveland, 128 games, 1903.

Fewest errors, season (150 or more games)

A.L.—3
Cal Ripken, Baltimore, 161 games, 1990.
Omar Vizquel, Cleveland, 156 games, 2000.
N.L.—4—Rey Ordonez, New York, 154 games, 1999.

Fewest errors for leader, season
N.L.—21—Mariano Duncan, Los Angeles, 67 games, 1987.
A.L.—21—Cristian Guzman, Minnesota, 118 games, 2001.

Most years leading league in errors
N.L.—6
   Dick Groat, Pittsburgh, St. Louis, 1955, 1956, 1959, 1961,
      1962, 1964.
   Rafael Ramirez, Atlanta, 1981, 1982, 1983, 1984 (tied), 1985,
      Houston, 1989.
A.L.—5—Luke Appling, Chicago, 1933, 1935, 1937, 1939, 1946.

Most errors, nine-inning game
N.L.—7—Jimmy Hallinan, New York, July 29, 1876.
N.L. since 1900—5
   Charlie Babb, New York, August 24, 1903, first game; also
      with Brooklyn, June 20, 1904.
   Phil Lewis, Brooklyn, July 20, 1905.
A.A.—7—Germany Smith, Brooklyn, June 17, 1885.
A.L.—5—Donie Bush, Detroit, August 25, 1911, first game.

Most errors, extra-inning game
A.L.—6—Bill O'Neill, Boston, May 21, 1904, 13 innings.
N.L.—5—Held by many shortstops.

Most errors, opening game of season (nine innings)
N.L.—5—Dasher Troy, New York, May 1, 1883.
N.L. since 1900—4
   Lou Stringer, Chicago, April 15, 1941.
   Pokey Reese, Cincinnati, March 31, 1998.
A.L.—3—Held by many shortstops.

Most errors, first major league game
N.L.—4—Lou Stringer, Chicago, April 15, 1941.
A.L.—3—Held by many shortstops.

Most errors, two consecutive nine-inning games
A.A.—10—Germany Smith, Brooklyn, June 16, 17, 1885.
N.L.—9—Fred Pfeffer, Troy, September 7, 9, 1882.
A.L.—6—Juan Beniquez, Boston, July 13, 14, 1972.

Most errors, doubleheader (18 innings)
P.L.—9—Ed Delahanty, Cleveland, July 4, 1890.
N.L.—7—Bill Shindle, Baltimore, April 23, 1892.
N.L. since 1900—6—Sammy Strang, Chicago, October 8, 1900.
A.L.—5
   John Gochnaur, Cleveland, September 10, 1902.
   Al Brancato, Philadelphia, September 13, 1940.
   Zoilo Versalles, Minnesota, July 5, 1963.

Longest errorless game
N.L.—26 innings—Rabbit Maranville, Boston, May 1, 1920.
A.L.—25 innings—Robin Yount, Milwaukee, May 8, finished
   May 9, 1984, fielded 24.1 innings.

Most consecutive errorless games, career
N.L.—101—Rey Ordonez, New York, June 14, 1999 through
   March 29, 2000 (418 chances accepted).
A.L.—95—Cal Ripken, Baltimore, April 14 through July 27,
   1990 (429 chances accepted).

Most consecutive errorless games, season
N.L.—100—Rey Ordonez, New York, June 14 through October
   4, 1999 (411 chances accepted).
A.L.—95
   Cal Ripken, Baltimore, April 14 through July 27, 1990 (429
      chances accepted).
   Omar Vizquel, Cleveland, September 26, 1999 through July
      21, 2000 (428 chances accepted).

Most consecutive chances accepted without an error, career
A.L.—431—Cal Ripken, Baltimore, April 14 to July 28, first
   game, 1990.
N.L.—419—Rey Ordonez, New York, June 13 (part) through
   March 29, 2000.

Most consecutive chances accepted without an error, season
A.L.—431—Cal Ripken, Baltimore, April 14 to July 28, first
   game, 1990.
N.L.—412—Rey Ordonez, New York, June 13 (part) through
   October 4, 1999.

Most errors, inning
N.L.—4
   Shorty Fuller, Washington, August 17, 1888, second inning.
   Lennie Merullo, Chicago, September 13, 1942, second game,
      second inning.
A.L.—4—Ray Chapman, Cleveland, June 20, 1914, fifth inning.

DOUBLE PLAYS

Most double plays, career
N.L.—1,590—Ozzie Smith, San Diego, St. Louis, 1978 through
   1996, 19 years.
A.L.—1,565—Cal Ripken Jr., Baltimore, 1981 through 1996, 16
   years.

Most double plays, season
A.L.—147—Rick Burleson, Boston, 155 games, 1980.
N.L.—137—Bobby Wine, Montreal, 159 games, 1970.

Most years leading league in double plays
A.L.—8—Cal Ripken, Baltimore, 1983, 1984, 1985, 1989, 1991,
   1992, 1994, 1995.
N.L.—5
   Mickey Doolan, Philadelphia, 1907, 1909 (tied), 1910, 1911, 1913.
   Dick Groat, Pittsburgh, St. Louis, 1958, 1959, 1961, 1962, 1964.
   Ozzie Smith, San Diego, St. Louis, 1980, 1984 (tied), 1986
      (tied), 1987, 1991.

Fewest double plays, season (150 or more games)
A.L.—60—Jackie Gutierrez, Boston, 150 games, 1984.
N.L.—63—Kevin Elster, New York, 150 games, 1989.

Fewest double plays for leader, season
N.L.—79—Ozzie Smith, St. Louis, 150 games, 1991.
A.L.—81—Roger Peckinpaugh, Washington, 155 games, 1924.

Most double plays, nine-inning game
A.L.—5—29 times. Held by 26 shortstops. Last shortstop—
   Alex Rodriguez, Texas, May 22, 2001.
N.L.—5—18 times. Held by 18 shortstops. Last shortstop—
   Dave Concepcion, Cincinnati, June 25, 1975.

Most double plays, extra-inning game
A.L.—6—Bert Campaneris, Oakland, September 13, 1970, first
   game, 11 innings.
N.L.—6
   Ozzie Smith, San Diego, August 25, 1979, 19 innings.
   Rafael Ramirez, Atlanta, June 27, 1982, 14 innings.

Most double plays started, game
A.L.—5
   Charley O'Leary, Detroit, July 23, 1905.
   John P. Sullivan, Washington, August 13, 1944, second game.
   Jim Fregosi, California, May 1, 1966, first game.
N.L.—4
   Larry Kopf, Boston, April 28, 1922.
   Jimmy E. Cooney, Chicago, June 13, 1926.
   Billy Myers, Cincinnati, June 4, 1939.
   Alvin Dark, New York, July 21, 1955.
   Don Kessinger, July 21, 1971.

Most unassisted double plays, game
A.L.—2—Lee Tannehill, Chicago, August 4, 1911, first game.
N.L.—1—Held by many shortstops.

For a complete list of players turning unassisted triple plays, see page 220.

OUTFIELDERS
GAMES AND INNINGS

Most games, career
A.L.—2,938—Ty Cobb, Detroit, Philadelphia, 1905 through
   1928, 24 years.
N.L.—2,843—Willie Mays, New York Giants, San Francisco,
   present New York Mets, 1951 through 1973, 22 years, except
   1953 in military service.

Most consecutive games played, career

N.L.—897—Billy Williams, Chicago, September 22, 1963 through June 13, 1969.

A.L.—511—Clyde Milan, Washington, August 12, 1910, through October 3, 1913, second game.

Most games, season

A.L.—163—Leon Wagner, Cleveland, 1964.

N.L.—164—Billy Williams, Chicago, 1965.

Most years leading league in games played

N.L.—6

George J. Burns, New York, Cincinnati, 1914 (tied), 1916 (tied), 1919, 1920 (tied), 1922, 1923 (tied).

Billy Williams, Chicago, 1964 (tied), 1965, 1966, 1967, 1968, 1970 (tied).

Dale Murphy, Atlanta, 1982 (tied), 1983 (tied), 1984 (tied), 1985, 1987, 1988.

A.L.—5—Rocky Colavito, Cleveland, Detroit, 1959, 1961, 1962, 1963, 1965.

Fewest games for leader, season

A.L.—147—Ted Williams, Boston, 1951.

N.L.—149

Max Carey, Pittsburgh, 1924.

Chet Ross, Boston, 1940.

Most innings played, game

N.L.—26

Walt Cruise, Boston, May 1, 1920.

Les Mann, Boston, May 1, 1920.

Bernie Neis, Brooklyn, May 1, 1920.

Ray Powell, Boston, May 1, 1920.

Zack Wheat, Brooklyn, May 1, 1920.

A.L.—25

Harold Baines, Chicago, May 8, finished May 9, 1984.

Rudy Law, Chicago, May 8, finished May 9, 1984.

Ben Oglivie, Milwaukee, May 8, finished May 9, 1984 (fielded 24.1 innings).

AVERAGE

Highest fielding average, career (1,000 or more games)

M.L.—.995—Darryl Hamilton, Milwaukee A.L., Texas A.L., San Francisco N.L., Colorado N.L., New York N.L., 13 years, 1988, 1990 through 2001, 1,233 games.

N.L.—.993—Terry Puhl, Houston, 14 years, 1977 through 1990, 1,299 games.

A.L.—.991

Mickey Stanley, Detroit, 15 years, 1964 through 1978, 1,290 games.

Joe Rudi, Kansas City, Oakland, California, Boston, 16 years, 1967 through 1982, 1,195 games.

Amos Otis, Kansas City, 14 years, 1970 through 1983, 1,845 games.

Highest fielding average, season (150 or more games)

N.L.—1.000

Danny Litwhiler, Philadelphia, 151 games, 1942.

Curt Flood, St. Louis, 159 games, 1966.

Terry Puhl, Houston, 152 games, 1979.

Brett Butler, Los Angeles, 161 games, 1991.

Brett Butler, Los Angeles, 155 games, 1993.

Luis Gonzalez, Arizona, 161 games, 2001.

A.L.—1.000

Rocky Colavito, Cleveland, 162 games, 1965.

Brian Downing, California, 158 games, 1982.

Most years leading league in fielding (100 or more games; 162-game season, 108 or more games)

A.L.—5—Amos Strunk, Philadelphia, Boston, Chicago, 1912, 1914, 1917 (tied), 1918, 1920.

N.L.—4

Joe Hornung, Boston, 1881, 1882, 1883, 1887.

Steve Brodie, Boston, Pittsburgh, Baltimore, 1890, 1891, 1897, 1899.

N.L. since 1900—3

Stan Musial, St. Louis, 1949, 1954, 1961.

Tony Gonzalez, Philadelphia, 1962, 1964, 1967.

Pete Rose, Cincinnati, 1970, 1971 (tied), 1974.

Most consecutive years leading league in fielding (100 or more games)

A.L.—3—Gene Woodling, New York, 1951 (tied), 1952, 1953 (tied).

N.L.—3—Joe Hornung, Boston, 1881, 1882, 1883.

N.L. since 1900—2—Held by many outfielders. Last outfielder—Pete Rose, Cincinnati, 1970, 1971 (tied).

Lowest fielding average for leader (100 or more games)

N.L.—.941—Pete Gillespie, New York, 102 games, 1885.

N.L. since 1900—.968

Red Murray, New York, 143 games, 1912.

Max Carey, Pittsburgh, 150 games, 1912.

Zack Wheat, Brooklyn, 120 games, 1912.

A.L.—.959—Chick Stahl, Boston, 130 games, 1901.

Lowest fielding average, season (100 or more games)

N.L.—.843—Jack Manning, Philadelphia, 103 games, 1884.

N.L. since 1900—.900—Mike Donlin, Cincinnati, 118 games, 1903.

A.L.—.872—Bill O'Neill, Washington, 112 games, 1904.

PUTOUTS

Most putouts, career

N.L.—7,095—Willie Mays, New York Giants, San Francisco, New York Mets, 1951 through 1973, except 1953 in military service, 22 years.

A.L.—6,794—Tris Speaker, Boston, Cleveland, Washington, Philadelphia, 1907 through 1928, 22 years.

Most putouts, season

N.L.—547—Taylor Douthit, St. Louis, 154 games, 1928.

A.L.—512—Chet Lemon, Chicago, 149 games, 1977.

Most years leading league in putouts

N.L.—9

Max Carey, Pittsburgh, 1912, 1913, 1916, 1917, 1918, 1921, 1922, 1923, 1924.

Richie Ashburn, Philadelphia, 1949, 1950, 1951, 1952, 1953, 1954, 1956, 1957, 1958.

A.L.—7—Tris Speaker, Boston, Cleveland, 1909, 1910, 1913, 1914, 1915, 1918, 1919.

Fewest putouts, season (150 or more games)

A.L.—182—Ed Hahn, Chicago, 156 games, 1907.

N.L.—210—Sam Thompson, Philadelphia, 151 games, 1892.

N.L. since 1900—217—Al Martin, Pittsburgh, 152 games, 1996.

Fewest putouts for leader, season

A.L.—319—Tris Speaker, Boston, 142 games, 1909.

N.L.—321—Roy Thomas, Philadelphia, 139 games, 1904.

Most years with 500 or more putouts

N.L.—4—Richie Ashburn, Philadelphia, 1949, 1951, 1956, 1957.

A.L.—1

Dom DiMaggio, Boston, 1948.

Chet Lemon, Chicago, 1977.

Dwayne Murphy, Oakland, 1980.

Most years with 400 or more putouts

N.L.—9—Richie Ashburn, Philadelphia, 1949, 1950, 1951, 1952, 1953, 1954, 1956, 1957, 1958.

A.L.—5

Chet Lemon, Chicago, Detroit, 1977, 1979, 1983, 1984, 1985.

Kirby Puckett, Minnesota, 1984, 1985, 1986, 1988, 1989.

Most putouts by center fielder, nine-inning game

N.L.—12—Earl Clark, Boston, May 10, 1929.

A.L.—12—Lyman Bostock, Minnesota, May 25, 1977, second game.

Most putouts by center fielder, extra-inning game

A.L.—12

Harry Bay, Cleveland, July 19, 1904, 12 innings.

Ruppert Jones, Seattle, May 16, 1978, 16 innings.

Rick Manning, Milwaukee, July 11, 1983, 15 innings.

Gary Pettis, California, June 4, 1985, 15 innings.

Oddibe McDowell, Texas, July 20, 1985, 15 innings.

N.L.—12

Carden Gillenwater, Boston, September 11, 1946, 17 innings.

Lloyd Merriman, Cincinnati, September 7, 1951, 18 innings.

Garry Maddox, Philadelphia, June 10, 1984, 12 innings.

Most putouts by left fielder, nine-inning game
N.L.—11
Dick Harley, St. Louis, June 30, 1898.
Topsy Hartsel, Chicago, September 10, 1901.
A.L.—11
Paul Lehner, Philadelphia, June 25, 1950, second game.
Willie Horton, Detroit, July 18, 1969.

Most putouts by left fielder, extra-inning game
A.L.—12
Tom McBride, Washington, July 2, 1948, 12 innings.
Rickey Henderson, New York, September 11, 1988, 18 innings.
Darin Erstad, Anaheim, July 24, 2000, 12 innings.
N.L.—Less than nine-inning record.

Most putouts by right fielder, nine-inning game
A.L.—11—Tony Armas, Oakland, June 12, 1982.
N.L.—10—Bill Nicholson, Chicago, September 17, 1945.

Most putouts by right fielder, extra-inning game
N.L.—12—Rolando Roomes, Cincinnati, July 28, 1989, 17 innings.
A.L.—Less than nine-inning record.

Most putouts by center fielder, doubleheader (18 innings)
N.L.—18—Lloyd Waner, Pittsburgh, June 26, 1935.
A.L.—17—Lyman Bostock, Minnesota, May 25, 1977.

Most consecutive putouts, game
A.L.—7—Ben Chapman, Boston, June 25, 1937 (right field).
N.L.—6—Edd Roush, Cincinnati, July 4, 1919, a.m. game (center field).

ASSISTS

Most assists, career
A.L.—450—Tris Speaker, Boston, Cleveland, Washington, Philadelphia, 1907 through 1928, 22 years.
N.L.—356—Jimmy Ryan, Chicago, 1885 through 1900, except 1890, 15 years.
N.L. since 1900—339—Max Carey, Pittsburgh, Brooklyn, 1910 through 1929, 20 years.

Most assists, season
N.L.—45—Hardy Richardson, Buffalo, 78 games, 1881.
N.L. since 1900—44—Chuck Klein, Philadelphia, 156 games, 1930.
A.L.—35
Sam Mertes, Chicago, 123 games, 1902.
Tris Speaker, Boston, 142 games, 1909, also 153 games, 1912.

Most years leading league in assists
A.L.—7—Carl Yastrzemski, Boston, 1962, 1963, 1964 (tied), 1966, 1969, 1971, 1977.
N.L.—5—Roberto Clemente, Pittsburgh, 1958, 1960, 1961, 1966, 1967.

Fewest assists, season (150 or more games)
A.L.—1
Harmon Killebrew, Minnesota, 157 games, 1964.
Albert Belle, Chicago, 154 games, 1997.
N.L.—2
Lenny Dykstra, Philadelphia, 160 games, 1993.
Brian McRae, Chicago, 155 games, 1996.
Barry Bonds, San Francisco, 155 games, 1998.

Fewest assists for leader, season
A.L.—13
Ken Berry, California, 116 games, 1972.
Carlos May, Chicago, 145 games, 1972.
N.L.—14
Bill Bruton, Milwaukee, 141 games, 1954.
Don Mueller, New York, 153 games, 1954.
Frank Thomas, Pittsburgh, 153 games, 1954.
Barry Bonds, Pittsburgh, 150 games, 1990.
Kevin McReynolds, New York, 144 games, 1990.

Most assists, nine-inning game
N.L.—4
Harry Schafer, Boston, September 26, 1877.
Bill Crowley, Buffalo, May 24, 1880.
Bill Crowley, Buffalo, August 27, 1880.
Fred Clarke, Pittsburgh, August 23, 1910.

A.L.—4
James W. Holmes, Chicago, August 21, 1903.
Lee Magee, New York, June 28, 1916.
Happy Felsch, Chicago, August 14, 1919.
Bob Meusel, New York, September 5, 1921, second game.
Sam Langford, Cleveland, May 1, 1928.

Most assists, extra-inning game
N.L.—4—Dusty Miller, May 30, 1895, second game, 11 innings.
A.L.—3—Held by many outfielders.

Most assists by outfielder to catcher, game
N.L.—3
Dummy Hoy, Washington, June 19, 1899.
Jim Jones, New York, June 30, 1902.
Jack McCarthy, Chicago, April 26, 1905.
A.L.—2—Held by many outfielders.

Most assists, inning
A.L.-N.L.—2—Held by many outfielders.

CHANCES ACCEPTED AND OFFERED

Most chances accepted, career
N.L.—7,290—Willie Mays, New York Giants, San Francisco, New York Mets, 1951 through 1973, except 1953 in military service, 22 years.
A.L.—7,244—Tris Speaker, Boston, Cleveland, Washington, Philadelphia, 1907 through 1928, 22 years.

Most chances accepted, season
N.L.—557—Taylor Douthit, St. Louis, 154 games, 1928.
A.L.—524—Chet Lemon, Chicago, 149 games, 1977.

Most years leading league in chances accepted
N.L.—9
Max Carey, Pittsburgh, 1912, 1913, 1916, 1917, 1918, 1921, 1922, 1923, 1924.
Richie Ashburn, Philadelphia, 1949, 1950, 1951, 1952, 1953, 1954, 1956, 1957, 1958.
A.L.—8—Tris Speaker, Boston, Cleveland, 1909, 1910, 1912, 1913, 1914, 1915, 1918, 1919.

Fewest chances accepted, season (150 or more games)
A.L.—206—Ed Hahn, Chicago, 156 games, 1907.
N.L.—222—Al Martin, Pittsburgh, 152 games, 1996.

Fewest chances accepted for leader, season
A.L.—333—Sam Crawford, Detroit, 144 games, 1907.
N.L.—342—Roy Thomas, Philadelphia, 139 games, 1904.

Most chances accepted by center fielder, nine-inning game
N.L.—13—Earl Clark, Boston, May 10, 1929.
A.L.—12
Happy Felsch, Chicago, June 23, 1919.
Johnny Mostil, Chicago, May 22, 1928.
Lyman Bostock, Minnesota, May 25, 1977, second game.

Most chances accepted by center fielder, extra-inning game
A.L.—12
Harry Bay, Cleveland, July 19, 1904, 12 innings.
Ruppert Jones, Seattle, May 16, 1978, 16 innings.
Rick Manning, Milwaukee, July 11, 1983, 15 innings.
Gary Pettis, California, June 4, 1985, 15 innings.
Oddibe McDowell, Texas, July 20, 1985, 15 innings.
N.L.—12
Carden Gillenwater, Boston, September 11, 1946, 17 innings.
Lloyd Merriman, Cincinnati, September 7, 1951, 18 innings.
Garry Maddox, Philadelphia, June 10, 1984, 12 innings.

Most chances accepted by left fielder, nine-inning game
N.L.—11
Joe Hornung, Boston, September 23, 1881.
Dick Harley, St. Louis, June 30, 1898.
Topsy Hartsel, Chicago, September 10, 1901.
A.L.—11
Paul Lehner, Philadelphia, June 25, 1950, second game.
Willie Horton, Detroit, July 18, 1969.

Most chances accepted by left fielder, extra-inning game
A.L.—12—Tom McBride, Washington, July 2, 1948, 12 innings.
N.L.—Less than nine-inning record.

Most chances accepted by right fielder, nine-inning game
A.L.—12—Tony Armas, Oakland, June 12, 1982.
N.L.—11—Harry Schafer, Boston, September 26, 1877.
N.L. since 1900—10
Greasy Neale, Cincinnati, July 13, 1920.
Casey Stengel, Philadelphia, July 30, 1920.
Bill Nicholson, Chicago, September 17, 1945.
Bake McBride, Philadelphia, September 8, 1978, second game.
Raul Mondesi, Los Angeles, September 25, 1995.
Jeromy Burnitz, Milwaukee, September 17, 2001.

Most chances accepted by center fielder, doubleheader
N.L.—18—Lloyd Waner, Pittsburgh, June 26, 1935.
A.L.—17—Lyman Bostock, Minnesota, May 25, 1977.

Most chances accepted by center fielder, two consecutive games
A.L.—21—Happy Felsch, Chicago, June 23, 24, 1919.
N.L.—20—Earl Clark, Boston, May 10, 11, 1929.

Longest game with no chances offered
A.L.—22 innings
Bill Bruton, Detroit, June 24, 1962.
Cap Peterson, Washington, June 12, 1967.
N.L.—18 innings
Lance Richbourg, Boston, May 14, 1927.
Art Shamsky, Cincinnati, July 19, 1966.

Longest season-opening game with no chances offered
A.L.—14 innings
Charlie Hemphill, New York, April 14, 1910.
Clyde Engle, New York, April 14, 1910.
N.L.—13 innings
Buck Herzog, New York, April 15, 1909.
Bill O'Hara, New York, April 15, 1909.

Longest game with no chances offered by center fielder
A.L.—22 innings—Bill Bruton, Detroit, June 24, 1962.
N.L.—17.1 innings—Ernie Orsatti, St. Louis, July 2, 1933, first game.

Longest game with no chances offered by left fielder
N.L.—16 innings—Joe Delahanty, St. Louis, July 19, 1908.
A.L.—16 innings
Bob L. Johnson, Philadelphia, June 5, 1942.
Pat Mullin, Detroit, May 9, 1952.

Longest game with no chances offered by right fielder
A.L.—22 innings—Cap Peterson, Washington, June 12, 1967.
N.L.—18 innings
Lance Richbourg, Boston, May 14, 1927.
Art Shamsky, Cincinnati, July 19, 1966.

Longest doubleheader with no chances offered
A.L.—24 innings—Roger Maris, New York, August 6, 1961.
N.L.—21 innings—Dain Clay, Cincinnati, September 21, 1944.

Most consecutive games with no chances offered
A.L.—7—Baby Doll Jacobson, Boston, June 18, 19, 20, 21, 24, 25, 25, 1926, 64.1 innings (right field).
N.L.—6—Wildfire Schulte, Chicago, June 25, 25, 26, 27, 28, 29, 1912 (right field).

ERRORS

Most errors, career
M.L.—384—Dummy Hoy, Washington N.L., Buffalo P.L., St. Louis A.A., Cincinnati N.L., Louisville N.L., Chicago A.L., 1888 through 1902, except 1900, 14 years.
N.L.—347—George Gore, Chicago, New York, St. Louis, 1879 through 1892, except 1890, 13 years.
N.L. since 1900—235—Max Carey, Pittsburgh, Brooklyn, 1910 through 1929, 20 years.
A.L.—271—Ty Cobb, Detroit, Philadelphia, 1905 through 1928, 24 years.

Most errors, season
P.L.—52—Ed Beecher, Buffalo, 125 games, 1890.
N.L.—47—George Van Haltren, Baltimore, Pittsburgh, 143 games, 1892.
N.L. since 1900—36—Cy Seymour, Cincinnati, 135 games, 1903.
A.L.—31—Roy C. Johnson, Detroit, 146 games, 1929.

Most years leading league in errors
N.L.—7—Lou Brock, Chicago, St. Louis, 1964, 1965, 1966, 1967, 1968 (tied), 1972, 1973 (tied).
A.L.—5
Burt Shotton, St. Louis, Washington, 1912 (tied), 1914, 1915 (tied), 1916, 1918.
Reggie Jackson, Oakland, Baltimore, 1968, 1970, 1972, 1975, 1976 (tied).

Fewest errors, season (150 or more games)
N.L.—0
Danny Litwhiler, Philadelphia, 151 games, 1942.
Curt Flood, St. Louis, 159 games, 1966.
Terry Puhl, Houston, 152 games, 1979.
Brett Butler, Los Angeles, 161 games, 1991.
Brett Butler, Los Angeles, 155 games, 1993.
Luis Gonzalez, Arizona, 161 games, 2001.
A.L.—0
Rocky Colavito, Cleveland, 162 games, 1965.
Brian Downing, California, 158 games, 1982.

Fewest errors for leader, season
N.L.—8—David Justice, Atlanta, 140 games, 1992.
A.L.—8
Albert Belle, Chicago, 159 games, 1998.
Kenny Lofton, Cleveland, 154 games, 1998.

Most errors, nine-inning game
A.A.—5—Jim Clinton, Baltimore, May 3, 1884.
U.A.—5—Fred Tenney, Washington, May 29, 1884.
A.L.—5—Kip Selbach, Baltimore, August 19, 1902.
N.L.—5
Jack Manning, Boston, May 1, 1876.
Pop Snyder, Louisville, July 29, 1876.
Jim O'Rourke, Boston, June 21, 1877.
Charlie Bennett, Milwaukee, June 15, 1878.
Mike Dorgan, New York, May 24, 1884.
Mike Tiernan, New York, May 16, 1887.
Marty Sullivan, Chicago, May 18, 1887.
N.L. since 1900—4—Fred Nicholson, Boston, June 16, 1922.

Longest errorless game
N.L.—26 innings
Walt Cruise, Boston, May 1, 1920.
Les Mann, Boston, May 1, 1920.
Bernie Neis, Brooklyn, May 1, 1920.
Ray Powell, Boston, May 1, 1920.
Zack Wheat, Brooklyn, May 1, 1920.
A.L.—25 innings
Harold Baines, Chicago, May 8, finished May 9, 1984.
Rudy Law, Chicago, May 8, finished May 9, 1984.
Ben Oglivie, Milwaukee, May 8, finished May 9, 1984 (fielded 24.1 innings).

Most consecutive errorless games, season
A.L.—162—Rocky Colavito, Cleveland, April 13 through October 3, 1965 (274 chances accepted).
N.L.—161
Brett Butler, Los Angeles, April 10 through October 6, 1991 (380 chances accepted).
Luis Gonzalez, Arizona, April 3 through October 7, 2001 (288 chances accepted).

Most consecutive errorless games, career
M.L.—392—Darren Lewis, Oakland A.L., San Francisco N.L., August 21, 1990 through June 29, 1994 (938 chances accepted).
N.L.—369—Darren Lewis, San Francisco, July 13, 1991 through June 29, 1994 (905 chances accepted).
A.L.—244—Brian Downing, California, May 25, 1981 through July 21, 1983, second game (471 chances accepted).

Most consecutive chances accepted without an error, career
M.L.—938—Darren Lewis, Oakland A.L., San Francisco N.L., August 21, 1990 through June 29, 1994, 392 games.
N.L.—905—Darren Lewis, San Francisco, July 13, 1991 through June 29, 1994, 369 games.
A.L.—573—Ken Griffey Jr., Seattle, April 16, 1992 through August 8, 1993, 236 games.

Most errors, inning

N.L.—3
  George Gore, Chicago, August 8, 1883, first inning.
  Larry Herndon, San Francisco, September 6, 1980, fourth inning.
A.A.—3—Jim Donahue, Kansas City, July 4, 1889, p.m. game, first inning.
A.L.—3
  Kip Selbach, Washington, June 23, 1904, eighth inning.
  Harry Bay, Cleveland, June 29, 1905, second game, ninth inning.
  Harry Heilmann, Detroit, May 22, 1914, first inning.
  Herschel Bennett, St. Louis, April 14, 1925, eighth inning.
  Scott Lusader, Detroit, September 9, 1989, first inning.

DOUBLE PLAYS

Most double plays, career

A.L.—135—Tris Speaker, Boston, Cleveland, Washington, Philadelphia, 1907 through 1928, 22 years.
N.L.—86—Max Carey, Pittsburgh, Brooklyn, 1910 through 1929, 20 years.

Most unassisted double plays, career

A.L.—6—Tris Speaker, Boston, Cleveland, 1909 (1), 1910 (1), 1914 (2), 1918 (2).
N.L.—2—Held by many outfielders.

Most double plays, season

A.L.—15—Happy Felsch, Chicago, 125 games, 1919.
N.L.—12—Mel Ott, New York, 149 games, 1929.

Most unassisted double plays, season

A.L.—2
  Socks Seybold, Philadelphia, August 15, September 10, first game, 1907.
  Tris Speaker, Boston, April 21, August 8, 1914.
  Tris Speaker, Cleveland, April 18, April 29, 1918.
  Jose Cardenal, Cleveland, June 8, July 16, 1968.
N.L.—2—Adam Comorosky, Pittsburgh, May 31, June 13, 1931.

Most years leading league in double plays

A.L.—5—Tris Speaker, Boston, Cleveland, 1909, 1912, 1914, 1915, 1916.
N.L.—4—Willie Mays, New York Giants, San Francisco, 1954, 1955, 1956, 1965.

Fewest double plays, season (150 or more games)

N.L.-A.L.—0—Held by many outfielders.
N.L.—Last outfielder—Shawn Green, Los Angeles, 159 games, 2001.
A.L.—Last outfielder—Magglio Ordonez, Chicago, 155 games, 2001.

Fewest double plays for leader, season

N.L.—3
  Brett Butler, Los Angeles, 161 games, 1991.
  Willie McGee, San Francisco, 128 games, 1991.
A.L.—4—Held by 19 players. Last outfielders—Tony Armas, Oakland, 112 games, 1977; Roy White, New York, 135 games, 1977.

Most double plays started, game

A.A.—3—Candy Nelson, New York, June 9, 1887.
N.L.—3—Jack McCarthy, Chicago, April 26, 1905.
A.L.—3—Ira Flagstead, Boston, April 19, 1926, p.m. game.

Most unassisted double plays, game

N.L.-A.L.—1—Held by many outfielders.
N.L.—Last outfielder—Andy Van Slyke, Pittsburgh, July 7, 1992, sixth inning.
A.L.—Last outfielder—Brian McRae, Kansas City, August 23, 1992, eighth inning.

Most triple plays started, season

A.L.—2—Charlie Jamieson, Cleveland, May 23, June 9, 1928.
N.L.—1—Held by many outfielders.

CATCHERS
GAMES AND INNINGS

Most games, career

A.L.—2,226—Carlton Fisk, Boston, Chicago, 1969 through 1993, except 1970, 24 years.
N.L.—2,056—Gary Carter, Montreal, New York, San Francisco, Los Angeles, 1974 through 1992, 19 years.

Most consecutive games, career

A.L.—312—Frankie Hayes, St. Louis, Philadelphia, Cleveland, October 2, second game, 1943 through April 21, 1946.
N.L.—233—Ray Mueller, Cincinnati, July 31, 1943, through May 5, 1946, except 1945 in military service.

Most games, season

N.L.—160—Randy Hundley, Chicago, 1968.
A.L.—155
  Jim Sundberg, Texas, 1975.
  Frankie Hayes, Philadelphia, 1944.

Most games by lefthanded catcher, season

N.L.—105—Jack Clements, Philadelphia, 1891.
A.L.—23—Jiggs Donahue, St. Louis, 1902.

Most games catching all club's games, season

N.L.—155—Ray Mueller, Cincinnati, 1944 (135 complete games).
A.L.—155—Frankie Hayes, Philadelphia, 1944 (135 complete games).

Most consecutive games, season

A.L.—155—Frankie Hayes, Philadelphia, April 18 through October 1, second game, 1944 (135 complete).
N.L.—155—Ray Mueller, Cincinnati, April 18 through October 1, 1944 (135 complete).

Most games by rookie, season

N.L.—154—Johnny Bench, Cincinnati, 1968.
A.L.—150—Buck Rodgers, Los Angeles, 1962.

Most years leading league in games

A.L.—8—Yogi Berra, New York, 1950, 1951, 1952, 1953, 1954, 1955, 1956, 1957.
N.L.—6—Gary Carter, Montreal, 1977, 1978, 1979, 1980, 1981, 1982.

Most years with 100 or more games

M.L.—15—Bob Boone, Philadelphia N.L., California A.L., Kansas City A.L., 1973, 1974, 1976 through 1980, 1982 through 1989.
A.L.—13—Bill Dickey, New York, 1929 through 1941.
N.L.—13—Johnny Bench, Cincinnati, 1968 through 1980.

Most consecutive years with 100 or more games

A.L.—13—Bill Dickey, New York, 1929 through 1941.
N.L.—13—Johnny Bench, Cincinnati, 1968 through 1980.

Fewest games for leader, season

N.L.—96—Ernie Lombardi, New York, 1945.
A.L.—98—Jake Early, Washington, 1942.

Most innings caught, game

A.L.—25—Carlton Fisk, Chicago, May 8, finished May 9, 1984.
N.L.—24
  Hal King, Houston, April 15, 1968.
  Jerry Grote, New York, April 15, 1968 (caught 23.1 innings).

Most innings caught, doubleheader

A.L.—29—Ossee Schreckengost, Philadelphia, July 4, 1905.
N.L.—27
  Bill Fischer, Chicago, June 28, 1916.
  Gus Mancuso, New York, July 2, 1933.

AVERAGE

Highest fielding average, career (1,000 or more games)

A.L.—.993
  Elston Howard, New York, Boston, 1955 through 1968, 14 years, 1,138 games.
  Bill Freehan, Detroit, 1961, 1963 through 1976, 15 years, 1,581 games.

N.L.—.992—Johnny Edwards, Cincinnati, St. Louis, Houston, 1961 through 1974, 14 years, 1,392 games.

Highest fielding average, season (100 or more games)

A.L.—1.000—Buddy Rosar, Philadelphia, 117 games, 1946.
N.L.—1.000—Charles Johnson, Florida, 123 games, 1997.

Highest fielding average, season (150 or more games)

N.L.—.996—Randy Hundley, Chicago, 152 games, 1967.
A.L.—.995—Jim Sundberg, Texas, 150 games, 1979.

Most years leading league in fielding (100 or more games)

A.L.—8—Ray Schalk, Chicago, 1913, 1914, 1915, 1916, 1917, 1920, 1921, 1922.
N.L.—7—Gabby Hartnett, Chicago, 1925, 1928, 1930, 1934, 1935, 1936, 1937.

Most consecutive years leading league in fielding (100 or more games)

A.L.—6—Bill Freehan, Detroit, 1965, 1966, 1967 (tied), 1968, 1969 (tied), 1970.
N.L.—4
Johnny Kling, Chicago, 1902 through 1905.
Gabby Hartnett, Chicago, 1934 through 1937.

Lowest average for leader, season (100 or more games, since 1900)

A.L.—.954—Mike Powers, Philadelphia, 111 games, 1901.
N.L.—.958—Gabby Hartnett, Chicago, 110 games, 1925.

Lowest fielding average, season (100 or more games)

A.L.—.934—Sam Agnew, St. Louis, 102 games, 1915.
N.L. since 1900—.947—Red Dooin, Philadelphia, 140 games, 1909.

PUTOUTS

Most putouts, career

N.L.—11,785—Gary Carter, Montreal, New York, San Francisco, Los Angeles, 1974 through 1992, 19 years.
A.L.—11,369—Carlton Fisk, Boston, Chicago, 1969 through 1993, except 1970, 24 years.

Most putouts, season

N.L.—1,135—Johnny Edwards, Houston, 151 games, 1969.
A.L.—1,051—Dan Wilson, Seattle, 144 games, 1997.

Fewest putouts, season (150 or more games)

N.L.—471—Ray Mueller, Cincinnati, 155 games, 1944.
A.L.—575—Mike Tresh, Chicago, 150 games, 1945.

Most years leading league in putouts

A.L.—9—Ray Schalk, Chicago, 1913, 1914, 1915, 1916, 1917, 1918, 1919, 1920, 1922.
N.L.—8—Gary Carter, Montreal, 1977, 1978, 1979, 1980, 1981, 1982; New York, 1985, 1988.

Fewest putouts for leader, season

N.L.—409—Gabby Hartnett, Chicago, 110 games, 1925.
A.L.—446—Birdie Tebbetts, Detroit, 97 games, 1942.

Most putouts, nine-inning game

N.L.—20
Jerry Grote, New York, April 22, 1970 (19 strikeouts).
Sandy Martinez, Chicago, May 6, 1998 (20 strikeouts).
A.L.—20
Rich Gedman, Boston, April 29, 1986 (20 strikeouts).
Dan Wilson, Seattle, August 8, 1997 (19 strikeouts).

Most putouts, extra-inning game

N.L.—22
Bob Schmidt, San Francisco, June 22, 1958, first game, 14 innings (19 strikeouts).
Tom Haller, San Francisco, May 31, 1964, second game, 23 innings (22 strikeouts).
Steve Yeager, Los Angeles, August 8, 1972, 19 innings (22 strikeouts).
A.L.—21
Ellie Rodriguez, California, June 14, 1974, 15 innings (20 strikeouts).
Dan Wilson, Seattle, March 31, 1996, 12 innings (21 strikeouts).

Longest game with no putouts

A.L.—14 innings
Wally Schang, Boston, September 13, 1920.
Gene Desautels, Cleveland, August 11, 1942, first game.
N.L.—13 innings
Jimmie Wilson, Philadelphia, August 31, 1927, first game.
Hal Finney, Pittsburgh, September 22, 1931.

Most consecutive putouts, game

N.L.—10—Jerry Grote, New York, April 22, 1970; 1 in sixth inning, 3 in seventh inning, 3 in eighth inning, 3 in ninth inning (10 strikeouts).
A.L.—8
Mike Brumley Sr., Washington, September 4, 1965; 3 in first inning, 3 in second inning, 2 in third inning (8 strikeouts).
John Stephenson, California, July 9, 1972; 2 in first inning, 3 in second inning, 3 in third inning (8 strikeouts).
Art Kusnyer, California, July 15, 1973; 1 in first inning, 3 in second inning, 3 in third inning, 1 in fourth inning (8 strikeouts).
Rich Gedman, Boston, April 29, 1986; 3 in fourth inning, 3 in fifth inning, 2 in sixth inning (8 strikeouts).
Bill Haselman, Boston, September 18, 1996; 2 in fourth inning, 3 in fifth inning, 3 in sixth inning (8 strikeouts).

Most consecutive putouts from start of game

N.L.—9
Art Wilson, New York, May 30, 1911, a.m. game (4 strikeouts, 3 fouled out, 1 tagged out, 1 forced out).
John Bateman, Houston, July 14, 1968, second game (9 strikeouts).
A.L.—8—Mike Brumley Sr., Washington, September 4, 1965 (8 strikeouts).

Most putouts, two consecutive games

A.L.—36—Rich Gedman, Boston, April 29 (20), April 30 (16), 1986 (36 strikeouts).
N.L.—31—Jerry Grote, New York, April 21 (11), April 22 (20), 1970 (29 strikeouts).

Most putouts, doubleheader (18 innings)

N.L.—25—John Bateman, Houston, September 10, 1968 (22 strikeouts).
A.L.—25—Hank Severeid, St. Louis, July 13, 1920 (21 strikeouts).

Most fouls caught, game

N.L.—6—Wes Westrum, New York, August 24, 1949.
A.L.—6—Sherm Lollar, Chicago, April 10, 1962.

Most fouls caught, inning

N.L.—3
Mickey Owen, Brooklyn, August 4, 1941, third inning.
Wes Westrum, New York, August 24, 1949, ninth inning.
Wes Westrum, New York, September 23, 1956, fifth inning.
A.L.—3—Matt Batts, Detroit, August 2, 1953, second game, fourth game.

ASSISTS

Most assists, career

M.L.—1,835—Deacon McGuire, Toledo, Cleveland, Rochester, Washington A.A., Detroit, Philadelphia, Washington, Brooklyn N.L., Detroit, New York, Boston, Cleveland A.L., 1884 through 1912, except 1889, 1908, 1909, 1911, 25 years.
A.L.—1,810—Ray Schalk, Chicago, 1912 through 1928, 17 years.
N.L.—1,593—Red Dooin, Philadelphia, Cincinnati, New York, 1902 through 1916, 15 years.

Most assists, season

N.L.—214—Pat Moran, Boston, 107 games, 1903.
A.L.—212—Oscar Stanage, Detroit, 141 games, 1911.

Fewest assists, season (150 or more games)

N.L.—59—Randy Hundley, Chicago, 152 games, 1967.
A.L.—68—Brad Ausmus, Detroit, 150 games, 2000.

Most years leading league in assists

N.L.—6
Gabby Hartnett, Chicago, 1925, 1927, 1928 (tied), 1930, 1934, 1935.
Del Crandall, Milwaukee, 1953, 1954, 1957, 1958, 1959, 1960.

A.L.—6—Jim Sundberg, Texas, 1975, 1976, 1977, 1978, 1980, 1981.

Fewest assists for leader, season
N.L.—52—Phil Masi, Boston, 95 games, 1945.
A.L.—58—Terry Kennedy, Baltimore, 142 games, 1987.

Most assists, nine-inning game
N.L.—9—Mike Hines, Boston, May 1, 1883.
A.L.—8—Wally Schang, Boston, May 12, 1920.
N.L. since 1900—7
  Ed McFarland, Philadelphia, May 7, 1901.
  Fred Jacklitsch, Brooklyn, April 21, 1903.
  Bill Bergen, Brooklyn, August 23, 1909, second game.
  Jimmy Archer, Pittsburgh, May 24, 1918.
  Bert Adams, Philadelphia, August 21, 1919.

Most assists, inning
A.A.—3—Jocko Milligan, Philadelphia, July 26, 1887, third inning.
A.L.—3
  Les Nunamaker, New York, August 3, 1914, second inning.
  Ray Schalk, Chicago, September 30, 1921, eighth inning.
  Bill Dickey, New York, May 13, 1929, sixth inning.
  Jim Sundberg, Texas, September 3, 1976, fifth inning.
N.L.—3
  Bruce Edwards, Brooklyn, August 15, 1946, fourth inning.
  Jim Campbell, Houston, June 16, 1963, second game, third inning.

CHANCES ACCEPTED AND OFFERED

Most chances accepted, career
N.L.—12,988—Gary Carter, Montreal, New York, San Francisco, Los Angeles, 1974 through 1992, 19 years.
A.L.—12,417—Carlton Fisk, Boston, Chicago, 1969 through 1993, except 1970, 24 years.

Most chances accepted, season
N.L.—1,214—Johnny Edwards, Houston, 151 games, 1969.
A.L.—1,044—Bill Freehan, Detroit, 138 games, 1968.

Most years leading league in chances accepted
A.L.—8
  Ray Schalk, Chicago, 1913, 1914, 1915, 1916, 1917, 1919, 1920, 1922.
  Yogi Berra, New York, 1950, 1951, 1952, 1954, 1955, 1956, 1957, 1959.
N.L.—8—Gary Carter, Montreal, 1977, 1978, 1979, 1980, 1981, 1982, New York, 1985, 1988.

Fewest chances accepted, season (150 or more games)
N.L.—536—Ray Mueller, Cincinnati, 155 games, 1944.
A.L.—677—Mike Tresh, Chicago, 150 games, 1945.

Fewest chances accepted by leader, season
N.L.—474—Ernie Lombardi, New York, 96 games, 1945.
A.L.—515—Birdie Tebbetts, Detroit, 97 games, 1942.

Most chances accepted, nine-inning game
U.A.—23—George Bignell, Milwaukee, October 3, 1884 (18 strikeouts).
N.L.—22—Sandy Nava, Providence, June 7, 1884 (19 strikeouts).
N.L. since 1900—20
  Jerry Grote, New York, April 22, 1970 (19 strikeouts).
  Sandy Martinez, Chicago, May 6, 1998 (20 strikeouts).
A.L.—20
  Ellie Rodriguez, California, August 12, 1974 (19 strikeouts).
  Rich Gedman, Boston, April 29, 1986 (20 strikeouts).
  Bill Haselman, Boston, September 18, 1996 (20 strikeouts).
  Dan Wilson, Seattle, August 8, 1997 (19 strikeouts).

Most chances accepted, extra-inning game
A.L.—25—Mike Powers, Philadelphia, September 1, 1906, 24 innings (18 strikeouts).
N.L.—24—Steve Yeager, Los Angeles, August 8, 1972, 19 innings (24 strikeouts).

Most chances accepted, doubleheader (18 innings)
A.L.—27—Hank Severeid, St. Louis, July 13, 1920 (21 strikeouts).
N.L.—26—John Bateman, Houston, September 10, 1968 (22 strikeouts).

Most chances accepted, two consecutive nine-inning games
A.L.—37—Rich Gedman, Boston, April 29, 30, 1986 (36 strikeouts).
N.L.—31—Jerry Grote, New York, April 21, 22, 1970 (29 strikeouts).

Most chances accepted, inning
N.L.—5—Joe Garagiola, St. Louis, June 17, 1949, eighth inning (3 putouts, 2 assists).
A.L.—4—Held by many catchers. Last catcher—Lance Parrish, Detroit, July 28, 1979, seventh inning (2 putouts, 2 assists).

Longest game with no chances offered
A.L.—14 innings—Gene Desautels, Cleveland, August 11, 1942, first game.
N.L.—13 innings—Jimmie Wilson, Philadelphia, August 31, 1927, first game.

Fewest chances offered, doubleheader
N.L.—0—Harry McCurdy, St. Louis, July 10, 1923.
A.L.—2
  Yam Yaryan, Chicago, May 26, 1921.
  Hank Severeid, St. Louis, September 5, 1921.
  Luke Sewell, Cleveland, August 28, 1926.

Fewest chances offered, two consecutive games
A.L.—0—Cy Perkins, Philadelphia, September 16, 17, 1922.
N.L.—0
  Harry McCurdy, St. Louis, July 10, 1923.
  Andy Seminick, Cincinnati, September 15, 16, 1953.

ERRORS

Most errors, career (since 1900)
N.L.—234—Ivy Wingo, St. Louis, Cincinnati, 1911 through 1929, except 1927, 1928, 17 years.
A.L.—218—Wally Schang, Philadelphia, Boston, New York, St. Louis, Detroit, 1913 through 1931, 19 years.

Most years leading league in errors
N.L.—7—Ivy Wingo, St. Louis, Cincinnati, 1912 (tied), 1913, 1916, 1917, 1918, 1920, 1921.
A.L.—6—Birdie Tebbetts, Detroit, Boston, 1939, 1940 (tied), 1942 (tied), 1947, 1948, 1949.

Most errors, season
N.L.—94—Nat Hicks, New York, 45 games, 1876.
N.L. since 1900—40—Red Dooin, Philadelphia, 140 games, 1909.
A.A.—85—Ed Whiting, Baltimore, 72 games, 1882.
A.L.—41—Oscar Stanage, Detroit, 141 games, 1911.

Fewest errors, season (150 or more games)
N.L.—4—Randy Hundley, Chicago, 152 games, 1967.
A.L.—4—Jim Sundberg, Texas, 150 games, 1979.

Fewest errors, season (100 or more games)
A.L.—0—Buddy Rosar, Philadelphia, 117 games, 1946.
N.L.—0—Charles Johnson, Florida, 123 games, 1997.

Fewest errors for leader, season
A.L.—7—Rick Ferrell, St. Louis, 137 games, 1933.
N.L.—9—Hank Foiles, Pittsburgh, 109 games, 1957.

Most errors, nine-inning game (all fielding errors)
N.L.—7
  Jack Rowe, Buffalo, May 16, 1883.
  Dickie Lowe, Detroit, June 26, 1884.
N.L. since 1900—4—Gabby Street, Boston, June 7, 1905.
A.A.—7—Billy Taylor, Baltimore, May 29, 1886, a.m. game.
A.L.—4
  John Peters, Cleveland, May 16, 1918.
  Lena Styles, Philadelphia, July 29, 1921.
  Bill Moore, Boston, September 26, 1927, second game.

Most errors, doubleheader
A.A.—8—Jim Donahue, Kansas City, August 31, 1889.
N.L.—8—Lew Graulich, Philadelphia, September 19, 1891.
N.L. since 1900—4—Held by many catchers.
A.L.—4—Held by many catchers.

Most errors, inning
N.L.—4—Doggie Miller, St. Louis, May 24, 1895, second inning.

N.L. since 1900—3—Jeff Reed, Montreal, July 28, 1987, seventh inning.
A.L.—3
Jeff Sweeney, New York, July 10, 1912, first inning.
John Peters, Cleveland, May 16, 1918, first inning.

Longest errorless game
A.L.—24 innings
Mike R. Powers, Philadelphia, September 1, 1906.
Buddy Rosar, Philadelphia, July 21, 1945.
Bob Swift, Detroit, July 21, 1945.
N.L.—24 innings
Hal King, Houston, April 15, 1968.
Jerry Grote, New York, April 15, 1968 (caught 23.1 innings).

Most consecutive errorless games, career
N.L.—172—Charles Johnson, Florida, June 24, 1996 through September 28, 1997 (1,291 chances accepted).
A.L.—159—Rick Cerone, New York, Boston, July 5, 1987 through May 8, 1989 (896 chances accepted).

Most consecutive errorless games, season
N.L.—123—Charles Johnson, Florida, April 1 through September 28, 1997 (entire season; 973 chances accepted).
A.L.—117—Buddy Rosar, Philadelphia, April 16 through September 29, 1946, first game (605 chances accepted).

Most consecutive errorless games, start of career
A.L.—93—Frankie Pytlak, Cleveland, April 22, 1932, through May 5, 1934.

Most consecutive chances accepted without an error, career
N.L.—1,294—Charles Johnson, Florida, June 23, 1996 through September 28, 1997.
A.L.—950—Yogi Berra, New York, 148 games, July 28, 1957, second game, through May 10, 1959, second game.

Most consecutive chances accepted without an error, season
A.L.—605—Buddy Rosar, Philadelphia, 117 games, April 16 through September 29, 1946, first game.
N.L.—973—Charles Johnson, Florida, 123 games, April 1 through September 28, 1997.

PASSED BALLS

Most passed balls, season
N.L.—99
Pop Snyder, Boston, 58 games, 1881.
Michael P. Hines, Boston, 56 games, 1883.
N.L. since 1900—29—Frank Bowerman, New York, 73 games, 1900.
A.L.—35—Geno Petralli, Texas, 63 games, 1987.

Most years leading league in passed balls
N.L.—9—Ernie Lombardi, Cincinnati, Boston, New York, 1932, 1935, 1936 (tied), 1937, 1938, 1939, 1940 (tied), 1941, 1945.
A.L.—5—Rick Ferrell, St. Louis, Washington, 1931 (tied), 1939, 1940, 1944, 1945.

Fewest passed balls, season (150 or more games)
N.L.—1—Gary Carter, Montreal, 152 games, 1978.
A.L.—3—Brad Ausmus, Detroit, 150 games, 2000.

Fewest passed balls, season (100 or more games)
N.L.—0
Al Todd, Pittsburgh, 128 games, 1937.
Al Lopez, Pittsburgh, 114 games, 1941.
Johnny Bench, Cincinnati, 121 games, 1975.
Benito Santiago, San Diego, 103 games, 1992.
A.L.—0—Bill Dickey, New York, 125 games, 1931.

Fewest passed balls for leader, season
A.L.—6
Mickey Cochrane, Philadelphia, 117 games, 1931.
Charlie F. Berry, Boston, 102 games, 1931.
Rick Ferrell, St. Louis, 108 games, 1931.
N.L.—7—Held by five catchers.

Most passed balls, game
A.A.—12—Gid Gardner, Washington, May 10, 1884.
N.L.—10—Pat Dealey, Boston, May 1886.

N.L. since 1900—6
Harry Vickers, Cincinnati, October 4, 1902.
Jerry Goff, Houston, May 12, 1996.
A.L.—6—Geno Petralli, Texas, August 30, 1987.

Most passed balls, two consecutive games
N.L.—13—Pete Hotaling, Worcester, September 20, 21, 1881.

Longest game with no passed balls
A.L.—25 innings—Carlton Fisk, Chicago, May 8, finished May 9, 1984.
N.L.—24 innings
Hal King, Houston, April 15, 1968.
Jerry Grote, New York, April 15, 1968 (caught 23.1 innings).

Most passed balls, inning
A.A.—5—Dan Sullivan, St. Louis, August 9, 1885, third inning.
N.L.—4—Ray Katt, New York, September 10, 1954, eighth inning.
A.L.—4—Geno Petralli, Texas, August 22, 1987, seventh inning.

DOUBLE PLAYS

Most double plays, career
A.L.—217—Ray Schalk, Chicago, 1912 through 1928, 17 years.
N.L.—163—Gabby Hartnett, Chicago, New York, 1922 through 1941, 20 years.

Most unassisted double plays, career
A.L.—2—Held by many catchers.

Most double plays, season
A.L.—29—Frankie Hayes, Philadelphia, Cleveland, 151 games, 1945.
N.L.—23—Tom Haller, Los Angeles, 139 games, 1968.

Most unassisted double plays, season
A.L.—2
Frank Crossin, St. Louis, 1914.
Jorge Posada, New York, 2000.
N.L.—1—Held by many catchers.

Most years leading league in double plays
N.L.—6—Gabby Hartnett, Chicago, 1925 (tied), 1927, 1930 (tied), 1931, 1934, 1935.
A.L.—6—Yogi Berra, New York, 1949, 1950, 1951, 1952, 1954, 1956.

Fewest double plays for leader, season
N.L.—8
Phil Masi, Boston/Pittsburgh, 81 games, 1949.
Clyde McCullough, Pittsburgh, 90 games, 1949.
A.L.—8
Mike DiFelice, Tampa Bay, 84 games, 1998.
A.J. Hinch, Oakland, 118 games, 1998.

Most double plays, nine-inning game
N.L.—3
Jack O'Neill, Chicago, April 26, 1905.
Shanty Hogan, New York, August 19, 1931.
Ebba St. Claire, Boston, August 5, 1951.
Damian Miller, Arizona, May 25, 1999.
A.L.—3
Charlie F. Berry, Chicago, May 17, 1932.
J.C. Martin, Chicago, June 23, 1963, first game.
Earl Battey, Minnesota, August 11, 1966.
Ed Herrmann, Chicago, July 4, 1972.
Rick Dempsey, Baltimore, June 1, 1977.

Most double plays, extra-inning game
N.L.—3
Bob O'Farrell, Chicago, July 9, 1919, second game, 10.1 innings.
Ron Hodges, New York, April 23, 1978, 11.2 innings.
A.L.—3—Billy Sullivan, Chicago, July 25, 1912, 10 innings.

Most double plays started, game
N.L.—3
J. Shanty Hogan, New York, August 19, 1931.
Damian Miller, Arizona, May 25, 1999.
A.L.—2—Held by many catchers.

Most unassisted double plays, game
A.L.-N.L.—1—Held by many players.

BASERUNNERS VS. CATCHERS

Most stolen bases off catcher, game
A.A.—19—Grant Briggs, Syracuse, April 22, 1890.
N.L.—17—Doggie Miller, Pittsburgh, May 23, 1890.
N.L. since 1900—11—Bill Fischer, St. Louis, August 13, 1916, second game, five innings.
A.L.—13—Branch Rickey, New York, June 28, 1907.

Most stolen bases off catcher, inning
A.L.—8—Steve O'Neill, Cleveland, July 19, 1915, first inning.
N.L.—8—Mike Gonzalez, New York, July 7, 1919, first game, ninth inning.

Most runners caught stealing, nine-inning game
N.L.—8—Duke Farrell, Washington, May 11, 1897.
N.L. since 1900—6—Bill Bergen, Brooklyn, August 23, 1909, second game.
A.L.—6—Wally Schang, Philadelphia, May 12, 1915.

Most runners caught stealing, inning
A.A.—3—Jocko Milligan, Philadelphia, July 26, 1887, third inning.
A.L.—3—Les Nunamaker, New York, August 3, 1914, second inning.
N.L.—2—Held by many catchers.

NO-HITTERS CAUGHT

Most no-hit victories caught, career (entire game; nine or more innings)
Both leagues—3—Jeff Torborg, Los Angeles N.L., 1965, 1970; California A.L., 1973.
N.L.—3
  Roy Campanella, Brooklyn, 1952, 1956 (2).
  Del Crandall, Milwaukee, 1954, 1960 (2).
  Alan Ashby, Houston, 1979, 1981, 1986.
  Charles Johnson, Florida, 1996, 1997, 2001.
A.L.—3
  Bill Carrigan, Boston, 1911, 1916 (2).
  Ray Schalk, Chicago, 1914, 1917, 1922 (Note: In addition, Schalk caught a no-hitter that was broken up in the 10th inning in 1914).
  Val Picinich, Philadelphia, 1916, Washington, 1920, Boston, 1923.
  Luke Sewell, Cleveland, 1931, Chicago, 1935, 1937.
  Jim Hegan, Cleveland, 1947, 1948, 1951.

PITCHERS
GAMES AND INNINGS

Most games pitched, career
M.L.—1,131—Jesse Orosco, New York N.L., Los Angeles, N.L., Cleveland A.L., Milwaukee A.L., Baltimore A.L., St. Louis N.L., 22 years, 1979 through 2001, except 1980 (663 in A.L., 468 in N.L.).
N.L.—1,050—Kent Tekulve, Pittsburgh, Philadelphia, Cincinnati, 16 years, 1974 through 1989.
A.L.—869—Dennis Eckersley, Cleveland, Boston, Oakland, 20 years, 1975 through 1987 through 1995, 1998.

Most games pitched, season
N.L.—106—Mike Marshall, Los Angeles, 208 innings, 1974.
A.L.—90—Mike Marshall, Minnesota, 143 innings, 1979.

Most years leading league in games pitched
M.L.—7—Joe McGinnity, Brooklyn N.L., Baltimore A.L., New York N.L., 1900, 1901, 1903, 1904, 1905, 1906, 1907.
N.L.—6—Joe McGinnity, Brooklyn, New York, 1900, 1903, 1904, 1905, 1906, 1907.
A.L.—6—Firpo Marberry, Washington, 1924, 1925, 1926, 1928, 1929, 1932.

Fewest games for leader, season
A.L.—40—Joe Haynes, Chicago, 1942 (103 innings).
N.L.—41
  Ray Kremer, Pittsburgh, 1924 (259 innings).
  Johnny Morrison, Pittsburgh, 1924 (238 innings).

Most innings pitched, game
N.L.—26 innings
  Leon Cadore, Brooklyn, May 1, 1920.
  Joe Oeschger, Boston, May 1, 1920.
A.L.—24 innings
  Jack Coombs, Philadelphia, September 1, 1906.
  Joe Harris, Boston, September 1, 1906.

AVERAGE

Highest fielding average with most chances accepted, season
N.L.—1.000—Randy Jones, San Diego, 1976, 40 games; 31 putouts, 81 assists, 112 chances accepted.
A.L.—1.000—Walter Johnson, Washington, 1913, 48 games; 21 putouts, 82 assists, 103 chances accepted.

Most years with highest average and most chances accepted, season
N.L.—4
  Claude Passeau, Philadelphia, Chicago, 1939, 1942, 1943, 1945.
  Larry Jackson, St. Louis, Chicago, Philadelphia, 1957, 1964, 1965, 1968.
A.L.—3—Walter Johnson, Washington, 1913, 1917, 1922 (tied).

PUTOUTS

Most putouts, career (since 1900)
N.L.—422—Greg Maddux, Chicago, Atlanta, 1986 through 2001, 16 years.
A.L.—387—Jack Morris, Detroit, Minnesota, Toronto, Cleveland, 1977 through 1994, 18 years.

Most putouts, season
N.L.—52—Al Spalding, Chicago, 60 games, 1876.
A.L.—49
  Nick Altrock, Chicago, 38 games, 1904.
  Mike Boddicker, Baltimore, 34 games, 1984.
N.L. since 1900—41—Kevin Brown, Los Angeles, 35 games, 1999.

Most years leading league in putouts
N.L.—7—Greg Maddux, Chicago, 1989, 1990, 1991, 1992; Atlanta, 1993, 1996, 1998 (tied).
A.L.—5—Bob Lemon, Cleveland, 1948, 1949, 1952, 1953, 1954.

Fewest putouts for leader, season
N.L.—14
  Howie Camnitz, Pittsburgh, 38 games, 1910.
  Art Nehf, New York, 37 games, 1922.
  Tony Kaufmann, Chicago, 37 games, 1922.
A.L.—16—Roxie Lawson, Detroit, 27 games, 1937.

Most putouts, nine-inning game
N.L.—7—Greg Maddux, Chicago, April 29, 1990.
A.L.—6
  Bert Blyleven, Cleveland, June 24, 1984.
  Eric King, Detroit, July 8, 1986.

Most putouts, extra-inning game
A.L.—7—Dick Fowler, Philadelphia, June 9, 1949, 12 innings.
N.L.—Less than nine-inning record.

Most putouts, inning
A.L.—3
  Jim Bagby Jr., Boston, September 26, 1940, fourth inning.
  Bob Heffner, Boston, June 28, 1963, first inning.
  Jim Beattie, New York, September 13, 1978, second inning.
  Roger Clemens, Boston, June 27, 1992, sixth inning.
N.L.—3
  Rick Reuschel, Chicago, April 25, 1975, third inning.
  Ed Lynch, Chicago, July 22, 1986, first inning.
  Mike Harkey, Chicago, May 23, 1990, fourth inning.
  Bill Swift, San Francisco, May 2, 1992, fourth inning.
  Mike Hartley, Los Angeles, April 13, 1991, sixth inning.
  Jeff Innis, New York, July 20, 1991, seventh inning.
  Jack Armstrong, Florida, May 13, 1993, fourth inning.
  Brian Meadows, Florida, June 2, 1998, second inning.

ASSISTS

Most assists, career (since 1900)
N.L.—1,489—Christy Mathewson, New York, Cincinnati, 1900 through 1916, 17 years.
A.L.—1,337—Walter Johnson, Washington, 1907 through 1927, 21 years.

Most assists, season
A.L.—227—Ed Walsh, Chicago, 56 games, 1907.
N.L.—168—John Clarkson, Boston, 72 games, 1889.
N.L. since 1900—141—Christy Mathewson, New York, 56 games, 1908.

Most years leading league in assists
N.L.—8—Greg Maddux, Chicago, Atlanta, 1990, 1992, 1993, 1995, 1996, 1998, 2000, 2001.
A.L.—6—Bob Lemon, Cleveland, 1948, 1949, 1951, 1952, 1953, 1956.

Fewest assists for leader, season
A.L.—42—Mark Langston, California, 33 games, 1990.
N.L.—47
Ron Darling, New York, 36 games, 1985.
Ron Darling, New York, 34 games, 1986.
Bob Knepper, Houston, 40 games, 1986.
Fernando Valenzuela, Los Angeles, 34 games, 1986.

Most assists, nine-inning game
N.L.—11—Rip Sewell, Pittsburgh, June 6, 1941, second game.
A.L.—11
Al Orth, New York, August 12, 1906.
Ed Walsh, Chicago, April 19, 1907.
Ed Walsh, Chicago, August 12, 1907.
George McConnell, New York, September 2, 1912, second game.
Mellie Wolfgang, Chicago, August 29, 1914.

Most assists, extra-inning game
N.L.—12—Leon Cadore, Brooklyn, May 1, 1920, 26 innings.
A.L.—12
Nick Altrock, Chicago, June 7, 1908, 10 innings.
Ed Walsh, Chicago, July 16, 1907, 13 innings.

Most assists, inning
N.L.-A.L.—3—Held by many pitchers.

CHANCES ACCEPTED AND OFFERED

Most chances accepted, career (since 1900)
N.L.—1,761—Christy Mathewson, New York, Cincinnati, 1900 through 1916, 17 years.
A.L.—1,606—Walter Johnson, Washington, 1907 through 1927, 21 years.

Most chances accepted, season
A.L.—262—Ed Walsh, Chicago, 56 games, 1907.
N.L.—206—John Clarkson, Boston, 72 games, 1889.
N.L. since 1900—168—Christy Mathewson, New York, 56 games, 1908.

Most years leading league in chances accepted
N.L.—12—Greg Maddux, Chicago, Atlanta, 1989 through 2001, except 1997 (tied in 1999).
A.L.—8—Bob Lemon, Cleveland, 1948 through 1956, except 1955.

Fewest chances accepted for leader, season
A.L.—61—Charles Nagy, Cleveland, 34 games, 1997.
N.L.—67
Paul Minner, Chicago, 31 games, 1953.
Robin Roberts, Philadelphia, 44 games, 1953.
Jim Hearn, New York, 39 games, 1955.

Most chances accepted, nine-inning game
A.L.—13
Nick Altrock, Chicago, August 6, 1904 (3 putouts, 10 assists).
Ed Walsh, Chicago, April 19, 1907 (2 putouts, 11 assists).
N.L.—12—Rip Sewell, Pittsburgh, June 6, 1941, second game (1 putout, 11 assists).

Most chances accepted, extra-inning game
A.L.—15—Ed Walsh, Chicago, July 16, 1907, 13 innings.
N.L.—13—Leon Cadore, Brooklyn, May 1, 1920, 26 innings.

Most chances accepted, two consecutive games
A.L.—20—Ed Walsh, Chicago, April 13, 19, 1907 (2 putouts, 18 assists).

Most chances accepted, inning
N.L.—4—Phil Regan, Chicago, June 6, 1969, sixth inning (1 putout, 3 assists).
A.L.—3—Held by many pitchers.

Longest game with no chances offered
N.L.—20 innings—Milt Watson, Philadelphia, July 17, 1918.
A.L.—15 innings—Red Ruffing, New York, July 23, 1932, first game.

Fewest chances offered, two consecutive games (more than 18 innings)
A.A.—0—Jack Neagle, Pittsburgh, July 13, 17, 1884, 12 innings each.
N.L.-A.L.—1—Held by many pitchers.

Fewest chances offered, doubleheader
A.A.—1—Toad Ramsey, Louisville, July 5, 1886 (1 putout).
N.L.—3
Joe McGinnity, New York, August 1, 1903 (1 putout, 1 assist, 1 error).
Grover Alexander, Philadelphia, September 3, 1917 (1 putout, 2 assists).
Hi Bell, St. Louis, July 19, 1924 (1 putout, 2 assists).
A.L.—3—Ed Walsh, Chicago, September 29, 1908 (3 assists).

ERRORS

Most errors, career (since 1900)
N.L.—64—Hippo Vaughn, Chicago, 1913 through 1921, nine years.
A.L.—55—Ed Walsh, Chicago, 1904 through 1916, 13 years.

Most errors, season
A.A.—63—Tim Keefe, New York, 68 games, 1883.
N.L.—28—Jim Whitney, Boston, 63 games, 1881.
N.L. since 1900—17—Doc Newton, Cincinnati, Brooklyn, 33 games, 1901.
A.L.—15
Jack Chesbro, New York, 55 games, 1904.
Rube Waddell, Philadelphia, 46 games, 1905.
Ed Walsh, Chicago, 62 games, 1912.

Most years leading league in errors
N.L.—5
Hippo Vaughn, Chicago, 1914, 1915 (tied), 1917 (tied), 1919, 1920.
Warren Spahn, Boston, Milwaukee, 1949 (tied), 1950, 1952 (tied), 1954 (tied), 1964 (tied).
A.L.—4
Allen Sothoron, St. Louis, 1917, 1918 (tied), 1919, 1920.
Nolan Ryan, California, 1975, 1976, 1977 (tied), 1978.

Fewest errors for leader, season
N.L.-A.L.—4—Held by many pitchers.

Most errors, game
N.L.—5—Ed Doheny, New York, August 15, 1899.
N.L. since 1900—4
Doc Newton, Cincinnati, September 13, 1900, first game.
Lave Winham, Pittsburgh, September 21, 1903, first game.
A.L.—4—Buster Ross, Boston, May 17, 1925.

Most errors, inning
N.L.—3
Cy Seymour, New York, May 21, 1898, sixth inning.
Jaime Navarro, Chicago, August 18, 1996, third inning.
A.L.—3
Tommy John, New York, July 27, 1988, fourth inning.
Mike Sirotka, Chicago, April 9, 1999, fifth inning.

Longest errorless game
N.L.—26 innings
Leon Cadore, Brooklyn, May 1, 1920.
Joe Oeschger, Boston, May 1, 1920.

A.L.—24 innings
Jack Coombs, Philadelphia, September 1, 1906.
Joe Harris, Boston, September 1, 1906.

Most consecutive errorless games, career
N.L.—546—Lee Smith, Chicago, St. Louis, July 5, 1982 through September 22, 1992 (93 chances accepted).
A.L.—470—Dennis Eckersley, Oakland, May 1, 1987 through May 4, 1995 (76 chances accepted).

Most consecutive chances accepted without an error, career
N.L.—273—Claude Passeau, Chicago, September 21, first game, 1941 through May 20, 1946, 145 games.
A.L.—230—Rick Langford, Oakland, April 13, 1977 to October 2, 1980, 142 games.

Most consecutive errorless games, season
A.L.—88—Wilbur Wood, Chicago, April 10 through September 29, 1968 (32 chances accepted).
N.L.—84—Ted Abernathy, Chicago, April 12 through October 3, 1965 (52 chances accepted).

DOUBLE PLAYS

Most double plays, career
M.L.—83—Phil Niekro, Milwaukee N.L., Atlanta N.L., New York A.L., Cleveland A.L., Toronto A.L., 1964 through 1987, 24 years.
N.L.—82—Warren Spahn, Boston, Milwaukee, New York, San Francisco, 1942 through 1965, except 1943, 1944, 1945 in military service, 21 years.
A.L.—78—Bob Lemon, Cleveland, 1946 through 1958, 13 years.

Most unassisted double plays, career
N.L.—2
Tex Carleton, Chicago, Brooklyn, 1935, 1940.
Claude Passeau, Philadelphia, Chicago, 1938, 1945.
A.L.—1—Held by many pitchers.

Most double plays, season
A.L.—15—Bob Lemon, Cleveland, 41 games, 1953.

N.L.—12
Art Nehf, New York, 40 games, 1920.
Curt Davis, Philadelphia, 51 games, 1934.
Randy Jones, San Diego, 40 games, 1976.

Most years leading league in double plays
N.L.—5
Bucky Walters, Philadelphia, Cincinnati, 1937, 1939, 1941 (tied), 1943 (tied), 1944 (tied).
Warren Spahn, Milwaukee, 1953 (tied), 1956, 1960 (tied), 1961 (tied), 1963.
Greg Maddux, Chicago, Atlanta, 1987, 1990, 1991 (tied), 1994 (tied), 1996.
A.L.—4—Willis Hudlin, Cleveland, 1929, 1930, 1931, 1934.

Fewest double plays for leader, season
N.L.—4
Bud Black, San Francisco, 1992.
Doug Drabek, Pittsburgh, 1992.
Omar Olivares, St. Louis, 1992.
A.L.—5—Held by many pitchers.

Most double plays started, game
A.L.—4
Milt Gaston, Chicago, May 17, 1932.
Hal Newhouser, Detroit, May 19, 1948.
N.L.—3—Held by 5 pitchers. Last pitcher—Gene Conley, Milwaukee, July 19, 1957.

Most unassisted double plays, game
N.L.—1—Held by many pitchers. Last pitcher—Jim McAndrew, New York, August 17, 1968.
A.L.—1—Held by many pitchers. Last pitcher—Clay Parker, Detroit, August 10, 1990.

Most triple plays started, season
N.L.—2—Wilbur Cooper, Pittsburgh, July 7, August 21, 1920.
A.L.—1—Held by many pitchers.

CLUB FIELDING

AVERAGE

Highest fielding average, season
N.L.—.989—New York, 163 games, 1999.
A.L.—.988—Cleveland, 162 games, 2000.

Lowest fielding average, season (since 1900)
A.L.—.928—Detroit, 136 games, 1901.
N.L.—.936—Philadelphia, 155 games, 1904.

Most consecutive years leading league in fielding
A.L.—6—Boston, 1916 through 1921.
N.L.—6—St. Louis, 1984 through 1989.

PUTOUTS

Most putouts, season
A.L.—4,520—New York, 164 games, 1964.
N.L.—4,480—Pittsburgh, 163 games, 1979.

Fewest putouts, season
N.L.—3,887—Philadelphia, 149 games, 1907.
A.L.—3,907—Cleveland, 147 games, 1945.

Most players with one or more putouts, nine-inning game
A.L.—14—New York vs. Cleveland, July 17, 1952, first game.
N.L.—13
St. Louis vs. Los Angeles, April 13, 1960.
Chicago vs. New York, August 8, 1965, second game.

Most players from both clubs with one or more putouts, nine-inning game
A.L.—22—New York 14, Cleveland 8, July 17, 1952, first game.
N.L.—22—Chicago 13, New York 9, August 8, 1965, second game.

Most putouts by infield, nine-inning game
A.L.—26—Seattle vs. New York, May 28, 1988.
N.L.—25
Chicago vs. Philadelphia, September 24, 1927.
Pittsburgh vs. New York, June 6, 1941, second game.
St. Louis vs. Boston, July 17, 1947.
Chicago vs. Pittsburgh, May 9, 1963.

Most putouts by infielders from both clubs, nine-inning game
N.L.—46
Cincinnati 24, New York 22, May 7, 1941.
St. Louis 25, Boston 21, July 17, 1947.
A.L.—45
Detroit 24, Washington 21, September 15, 1945, second game.
Boston 24, Cleveland 21, July 11, 1977.

Fewest putouts by infield, nine-inning game
A.L.—3
St. Louis vs. New York, July 20, 1945, second game.
Boston vs. Seattle, April 29, 1986.
N.L.—3—New York vs. San Diego, April 22, 1970.

Most putouts by outfield, nine-inning game
N.L.—19—Pittsburgh vs. Cincinnati, July 5, 1948, second game.
A.L.—19—Minnesota vs. Toronto, July 7, 1994.

Most putouts by outfielders from both clubs, nine-inning game
N.L.—30—Chicago 16, Philadelphia 14, August 7, 1953.
A.L.—29—Washington 17, St. Louis 12, May 3, 1939.

Most putouts by outfield, extra-inning game
N.L.—23
Brooklyn vs. Boston, May 1, 1920, 26 innings.
Chicago vs. Boston, May 17, 1927, 22 innings.
A.L.—22—Chicago vs. Washington, May 15, 1918, 18 innings.

Most putouts by outfielders from both clubs, extra-inning game
N.L.—42—New York 21, Pittsburgh 21, July 17, 1914, 21 innings.
A.L.—38—Washington 20, St. Louis 18, July 19, 1924, 16 innings.

Longest game with no putouts by outfield
N.L.—13 innings
New York vs. Brooklyn, April 15, 1909.
St. Louis vs. Philadelphia, August 13, 1987.
A.L.—11 innings—St. Louis vs. Cleveland, April 23, 1905.

Fewest putouts by outfielders from both clubs, nine-inning game
A.A.—1—St. Louis 1, New York 0, June 30, 1886.
N.L.—1—Pittsburgh 1, Brooklyn 0, August 26, 1910.
A.L.—2—New York 2, Detroit 0, May 9, 1930.

Most putouts by outfield, doubleheader (18 innings)
N.L.—27—Pittsburgh vs. Cincinnati, July 5, 1948.
A.L.—24—Detroit vs. Philadelphia, June 28, 1931.

Most putouts by outfield, doubleheader (more than 18 innings)
N.L.—29—Boston vs. New York, September 3, 1933, 23 innings.
A.L.—Less than for 18 innings.

Most putouts by outfielders from both clubs, doubleheader
N.L.—47—Pittsburgh 26, Boston 21, June 26, 1935.
A.L.—43—Detroit 24, Philadelphia 19, June 28, 1931.

ASSISTS

Most assists, season
N.L.—2,293—St. Louis, 154 games, 1917.
A.L.—2,446—Chicago, 157 games, 1907.

Fewest assists, season
N.L.—1,437—Philadelphia, 156 games, 1957.
A.L.—1,439—Chicago, 161 games, 1997.

Most consecutive years leading league in assists
A.L.—6—Chicago, 1905 through 1910.
N.L.—6—New York, 1933 through 1938.

Most assists, nine-inning game
N.L.—28—Pittsburgh vs. New York, June 7, 1911.
A.L.—27—St. Louis vs. Philadelphia, August 16, 1919.

Most assists by both clubs, nine-inning game
A.L.—44—Cleveland 22, St. Louis 22, May 27, 1909.
N.L.—43—Brooklyn 24, New York 19, April 21, 1903.

Most assists, extra-inning game
N.L.—41—Boston vs. Brooklyn, May 1, 1920, 26 innings.
A.L.—38
Detroit vs. Philadelphia, July 21, 1945, 24 innings.
Washington vs. Chicago, June 12, 1967, 22 innings.

Most assists by both clubs, extra-inning game
N.L.—72—Boston 41, Brooklyn 31, May 1, 1920, 26 innings.
A.L.—72—Detroit 38, Philadelphia 34, July 21, 1945, 24 innings.

Most players with one or more assists, nine-inning game
A.L.—11
Washington vs. Philadelphia, October 3, 1920.
Boston vs. Philadelphia, May 1, 1929.
Washington vs. Baltimore, April 29, 1956, first game.
Chicago vs. Kansas City, September 22, 1970, second game.
N.L.—11—Brooklyn vs. Philadelphia, April 22, 1953.

Most assists, two consecutive games
N.L.—48—Boston vs. New York, June 24, 25, 1918.
A.L.—43—Washington vs. St. Louis, August 19, 20, 1923.

Fewest assists, game
A.L.—0
St. Louis vs. Cleveland, August 8, 1943, second game (fielded eight innings).
Cleveland vs. New York, July 4, 1945, first game.
New York vs. Cleveland, September 11, 1995.
N.L.—0
New York vs. Philadelphia, June 25, 1989.
Cincinnati vs. Colorado, August 20, 1997.

Fewest assists by both clubs, nine-inning game
A.L.—5
Baltimore 3, Cleveland 2, August 31, 1955.
Boston 4, New York 1, August 9, 1992.
N.L.—6
Chicago 5, Philadelphia 1, May 2, 1957.
San Francisco 3, Philadelphia 3, May 13, 1959.

Fewest assists, two consecutive nine-inning games
N.L.—5—Chicago vs. Philadelphia, Brooklyn, August 23 (1), 24 (4), 1932.
A.L.—7
    Chicago vs. Boston, June 11 (2), 11 (5), 1960, 17 innings.
    Kansas City vs. Milwaukee, California, April 16 (3), April 17 (4), 1970, 18 innings.

Most assists, doubleheader (nine-inning games)
N.L.—42—New York vs. Boston, September 30, 1914.
A.L.—41
    Boston vs. Detroit, September 20, 1927.
    Boston vs. Washington, September 26, 1927.

Most assists by both clubs, doubleheader (nine-inning games)
N.L.—70—Brooklyn 36, Philadelphia 34, September 5, 1922.
A.L.—68
    Detroit 34, Philadelphia 34, September 5, 1901.
    Cleveland 35, Boston 33, September 7, 1935.
    St. Louis 39, Boston 29, July 23, 1939.

Fewest assists, doubleheader (nine-inning games)
A.L.—8
    Philadelphia vs. New York, July 7, 1946.
    Minnesota vs. Los Angeles, July 19, 1961, 17.2 innings.
N.L.—7—New York vs. San Diego, May 29, 1971.

Fewest assists by both clubs, doubleheader
N.L.—22—Milwaukee 14, Philadelphia 8, September 12, 1954.
A.L.—25—Washington 13, New York 12, July 4, 1931.

Most assists by infield, nine-inning game
A.L.—22—Seattle vs. New York, May 28, 1988.
N.L.—21
    New York vs. Pittsburgh, July 13, 1919.
    Philadelphia vs. Boston, May 30, 1931, p.m. game.
    Brooklyn vs. Pittsburgh, August 18, 1935, second game.

Most assists by infielders from both clubs, nine-inning game
N.L.—38—Brooklyn 20, Cincinnati 18, June 10, 1917.
A.L.—35
    Detroit 19, Cleveland 16, April 18, 1924.
    Chicago 18, Boston 17, September 17, 1945, second game.

Fewest assists by infield, nine-inning game
N.L.—0
    Pittsburgh vs. Chicago, July 19, 1902.
    New York vs. Philadelphia, July 29, 1934, first game.
    Chicago vs. Cincinnati, April 26, 1935.
    Cincinnati vs. Brooklyn, August 6, 1938.
    Boston vs. Pittsburgh, June 17, 1940, first game.
    New York vs. Chicago, May 6, 1953.
    Philadelphia, vs. Chicago, May 2, 1957.
    Houston vs. Cincinnati, September 10, 1968, first game.
    Pittsburgh vs. Montreal, September 17, 1977.
    New York vs. Philadelphia, June 25, 1989.
A.L.—0
    Boston vs. Chicago, August 13, 1924, first game.
    Cleveland vs. New York, July 4, 1945, first game.
    St. Louis vs. New York, July 20, 1945, second game.
    Washington vs. St. Louis, May 20, 1952.
    New York vs. Cleveland, September 11, 1995.

Fewest assists by infielders from both clubs, nine-inning game
A.L.—2—Philadelphia 2, Washington 0, May 5, 1910,
    Washington fielded only eight innings.
N.L.—2—Chicago 2, Philadelphia 0, May 2, 1957.

Most assists by outfield, game
N.L.—5—Pittsburgh vs. Philadelphia, August 23, 1910.
A.L.—5
    New York vs. Boston, September 5, 1921, second game.
    Cleveland vs. St. Louis, May 1, 1928.

Most assists from outfielder to catcher with runner thrown out, game
N.L.—3
    Washington vs. Indianapolis, June 19, 1889.
    New York vs. Boston, June 30, 1902.
    Chicago vs. Pittsburgh, April 26, 1905.
    St. Louis vs. San Francisco, July 7, 1975.
A.L.—2—Made in many games.

Longest game with no outfield assists
N.L.—26 innings—Boston vs. Brooklyn, May 1, 1920.
A.L.—24 innings
    Boston vs. Philadelphia, September 1, 1906.
    Philadelphia vs. Detroit, July 21, 1945.

Longest game with no outfield assists by either club
N.L.—24 innings—Houston 0, New York 0, April 15, 1968.
A.L.—22 innings—Chicago 0, Washington 0, June 12, 1967.

Most assists, inning
A.L.—10
    Cleveland vs. Philadelphia, August 17, 1921, first inning.
    Boston vs. New York, May 10, 1952, fifth inning.
N.L.—8—Boston vs. Philadelphia, May 1, 1911, fourth inning.

CHANCES ACCEPTED AND OFFERED

Most chances accepted, season
A.L.—6,655—Chicago, 157 games, 1907.
N.L.—6,508—Chicago, 162 games, 1977.

Fewest chances accepted, season
A.L.—5,470—Cleveland, 147 games, 1945.
N.L.—5,545—Philadelphia, 154 games, 1955.

Most chances accepted, nine-inning game
N.L.—55—Pittsburgh vs. New York, June 7, 1911.
A.L.—54—St. Louis vs. Philadelphia, August 16, 1919.

Most chances accepted, extra-inning game
N.L.—119—Boston vs. Brooklyn, May 1, 1920, 26 innings.
A.L.—110—Detroit vs. Philadelphia, July 21, 1945, 24 innings.

Most chances accepted by both clubs, nine-inning game
N.L.—98
    Brooklyn 50, New York 48, April 21, 1903.
    New York 52, Cincinnati 46, May 15, 1909.
A.L.—98—Cleveland 49, St. Louis 49, May 7, 1909.

Most chances accepted by infield, nine-inning game
A.L.—48—Seattle vs. New York, May 28, 1988.
N.L.—45
    New York vs. Pittsburgh, July 13, 1919.
    Chicago vs. Philadelphia, September 24, 1927.
    Chicago vs. Pittsburgh, May 9, 1963.

Most chances accepted by infielders from both clubs, nine-inning game
N.L.—78—Cincinnati 41, New York 37, May 7, 1941.
A.L.—76—Boston 43, Cleveland 33, June 24, 1931.

Fewest chances offered to infield, nine-inning game
A.L.—3—St. Louis vs. New York, July 20, 1945, second game.
N.L.—4—New York vs. San Diego, April 22, 1970.

Fewest chances offered to infielders from both clubs, nine-inning game
A.L.—18—Cleveland 9, Baltimore 9, August 31, 1955.
N.L.—19—Chicago 10, Philadelphia 9, May 2, 1957.

Most chances accepted by outfield, game
N.L.—20—Pittsburgh vs. Cincinnati, July 5, 1948, second game.
A.L.—18
    Cleveland vs. St. Louis, September 28, 1929.
    New York vs. Boston, October 1, 1933.
    Philadelphia vs. Boston, May 27, 1941, second game.
    New York vs. Cleveland, June 26, 1955, second game.

Most chances accepted by outfielders from both clubs, game
A.L.—30—Washington 17, St. Louis 13, May 3, 1939.
N.L.—30—Chicago 16, Philadelphia 14, August 7, 1953.

Most chances accepted by outfield, extra-inning game
N.L.—24
    Brooklyn vs. Boston, May 1, 1920, 26 innings.
    Chicago vs. Boston, May 17, 1927, 22 innings.
A.L.—22—Chicago vs. Washington, May 15, 1918, 18 innings.

Most chances accepted by outfielders from both clubs, extra-inning game
N.L.—43—New York 22, Pittsburgh 21, July 17, 1914, 21 innings.
A.L.—40—Washington 21, St. Louis 19, July 19, 1924, 16 innings.

Fewest chances offered to outfield, nine-inning game
N.L.—0—Made in many games.
A.L.—0—Made in many games.

Longest game with no outfield chances offered
N.L.—13 innings—St. Louis vs. Philadelphia, August 13, 1987.
A.L.—11 innings—St. Louis vs. Cleveland, April 23, 1905.

Fewest chances offered to outfielders from both clubs, nine-inning game
A.A.—2—St. Louis 2, New York 0, June 30, 1886.
N.L.—2
Pittsburgh 1, Brooklyn 1, August 26, 1910.
Cincinnati 1, New York 1, May 7, 1941.
A.L.—3
St. Louis 2, Chicago 1, April 24, 1908.
New York 2, Boston 1, May 4, 1911.
New York 2, Detroit 1, May 9, 1930.

Fewest chances offered to outfield, two consecutive games
U.A.—0—Milwaukee vs. Boston, October 4, 5, 1884.
A.L.—1—St. Louis, April 16, 10 innings, April 17, 1908.
N.L.—2—Held by many clubs.

Most chances accepted by outfield, doubleheader
N.L.—28—Pittsburgh vs. Cincinnati, July 5, 1948.
A.L.—24
Detroit vs. Philadelphia, June 28, 1931.
Philadelphia vs. Boston, May 27, 1941.

Most chances accepted by outfielders from both clubs, doubleheader
N.L.—48—Pittsburgh 26, Boston 22, June 26, 1935.
A.L.—44—Detroit 24, Philadelphia 20, June 28, 1931.

ERRORS

Most errors, season
N.L.—867—Washington, 122 games, 1886.
N.L. since 1900—408—Brooklyn, 155 games, 1905.
A.L.—425—Detroit, 136 games, 1901.

Fewest errors, season
N.L.—68—New York, 163 games, 1999.
A.L.—72—Cleveland, 162 games, 2000.

Most errorless games, season
A.L.—104—Baltimore, 162 games, 1998.
N.L.—104—New York, 163 games, 1999.

Most consecutive years leading league in errors
N.L.—7—Philadelphia, 1930 through 1936.
A.L.—6
Philadelphia, 1936 through 1941.
St. Louis, 1948 through 1953.

Most years leading league with fewest errors
N.L. since 1900—21—Cincinnati.

Most errors, game
N.L.—24—Boston vs. St. Louis, June 14, 1876.
N.L. since 1900—11
St. Louis vs. Pittsburgh, April 19, 1902.
Boston vs. St. Louis, June 11, 1906.
St. Louis vs. Cincinnati, July 3, 1909, second game.
A.L.—12
Detroit vs. Chicago, May 1, 1901.
Chicago vs. Detroit, May 6, 1903.

Most errors by both clubs, game
N.L.—40—Boston 24, St. Louis 16, June 14, 1876.
N.L. since 1900—15
St. Louis 11, Pittsburgh 4, April 19, 1902.
Boston 10, Chicago 5, October 3, 1904.
A.L.—18—Chicago 12, Detroit 6, May 6, 1903.

Longest game with no errors
A.L.—22 innings
Chicago vs. Washington, June 12, 1967.
Washington vs. Chicago, June 12, 1967.
N.L.—21 innings
Boston vs. Pittsburgh, August 1, 1918.
Chicago vs. Philadelphia, July 17, 1918.

Philadelphia vs. Chicago, July 17, 1918 (fielded 20 innings;
Chicago scored winning run with none out in 21st inning).
San Francisco vs. Cincinnati, September 1, 1967.
San Diego vs. Montreal, May 21, 1977.

Longest game with no errors by either club
A.L.—22—Chicago 0, Washington 0, June 12, 1967.
N.L.—21—Chicago 0, Philadelphia 0, July 17, 1918
(Philadelphia fielded 20 innings; Chicago scored winning run
with none out in 21st inning).

Most consecutive errorless games, season
N.L.—16—St. Louis, July 30 through August 16, 1992.
A.L.—15—Texas, August 4, through 19, 1996.

Most errors, doubleheader (since 1900)
N.L.—17
Cincinnati vs. Brooklyn, September 13, 1900.
Chicago vs. Cincinnati, October 8, 1900.
St. Louis vs. Cincinnati, July 3, 1909.
A.L.—16—Cleveland vs. Washington, September 21, 1901.

Most errors by both clubs, doubleheader (since 1900)
N.L.—25—Chicago 17, Cincinnati 8, October 8, 1900.
A.L.—22—Cleveland 16, Washington 6, September 21, 1901.

Longest doubleheader without an error
A.L.—27 innings—Detroit vs. New York, August 23, 1968, (first
game, Detroit fielded eight innings; second game 19 innings).
N.L.—25 innings—Philadelphia vs. Cincinnati, July 8, 1924.

Longest doubleheader without an error by either club
A.L.—24 innings
New York 0, Philadelphia 0, July 4, 1925.
Washington 0, New York 0, August 14, 1960.
N.L.—20 innings
Boston 0, Chicago 0, September 18, 1924.
New York 0, Chicago 0, August 27, 1951.

Most errors by infield, nine-inning game
N.L.—17—Boston vs. St. Louis, June 14, 1876.
A.L.—10—Detroit vs. Chicago, May 1, 1901.

Most errors by infielders from both clubs, nine-inning game
N.L.—22—Boston 17, St. Louis 5, June 14, 1876.
A.L.—13—Chicago 8, Detroit 5, May 6, 1903.

Longest game without an error by infield
A.L.—25—Chicago vs. Milwaukee, May 8, finished May 9, 1984.
N.L.—24—Houston vs. New York, April 15, 1968.

Most errors by outfield, nine-inning game
N.L.—11—Boston vs. Hartford, May 1, 1876.
N.L. since 1900—4—Made in many games. Last time—San
Francisco vs. Los Angeles, July 4, 1971.
A.L.—5—Baltimore vs. St. Louis, August 19, 1902.

Most errors, inning (since 1900)
A.L.—7—Cleveland vs. Chicago, September 20, 1905, eighth
inning.
N.L.—6—Pittsburgh vs. New York, August 20, 1903, first game,
first inning.

PASSED BALLS

Most passed balls, season
N.L.—167—Boston, 98 games, 1883.
N.L. since 1900—42
Boston, 156 games, 1905.
Atlanta, 162 games, 1967.
A.L.—73—Texas, 162 games, 1987.

Fewest passed balls, season
A.L.—0—New York, 155 games, 1931.
N.L.—2
Boston, 153 games, 1943.
New York, 162 games, 1980.
San Diego, 162 games, 1992.

Most passed balls, game
A.A.—12—Washington vs. New York, May 10, 1884.
N.L.—10—Boston vs. Washington, May 3, 1886.

N.L. since 1900—6
Cincinnati vs. Pittsburgh, October 4, 1902.
Houston vs. Montreal, May 12, 1996.
A.L.—6—Texas vs. Detroit, August 30, 1987.

Most passed balls by both clubs, game
A.A.—14—Washington 12, New York 2, May 10, 1884.
N.L.—11—Troy 7, Cleveland 4, June 16, 1880.
N.L. since 1900—6
Cincinnati 6, Pittsburgh 0, October 4, 1902.
Houston 6, Montreal 0, May 12, 1996.
A.L.—6—Texas 6, Detroit 0, August 30, 1987.

Longest game with no passed balls
N.L.—26 innings
Boston vs. Brooklyn, May 1, 1920.
Brooklyn vs. Boston, May 1, 1920.
A.L.—25 innings
Chicago vs. Milwaukee, May 8, finished May 9, 1984.
Milwaukee vs. Chicago, May 8, finished May 9, 1984 (fielded 24.1 innings).

Longest game with no passed balls by either club
N.L.—26 innings—Boston 0, Brooklyn 0, May 1, 1920.
A.L.—25 innings—Chicago 0, Milwaukee 0, May 8, finished May 9, 1984 (Milwaukee fielded 24.1 innings).

DOUBLE PLAYS

Most double plays, season
A.L.—217—Philadelphia, 154 games, 1949.
N.L.—215—Pittsburgh, 162 games, 1966.

Most years with 200 or more double plays
A.L.—3—Philadelphia, 1949 (217), 1950 (208), 1951 (204).
N.L.—1
Pittsburgh, 1966 (215).
Colorado, 1997 (202).

Fewest double plays, season (A.L. since 1912; N.L. since 1919)
A.L.—74—Boston, 151 games, 1913.
N.L.—94—Pittsburgh, 153 games, 1935.

Most times with five or more double plays in a game, season
N.L.—3—New York, 1950.
A.L.—3
Cleveland, 1970.
Kansas City, 1971.

Most double plays, game
A.L.—7—New York vs. Philadelphia, August 14, 1942.
N.L.—7
Houston vs. San Francisco, May 4, 1969.
Atlanta vs. Cincinnati, June 27, 1982, 14 innings.
St. Louis vs. Pittsburgh, June 16, 1994, 10 innings.

Most double plays by both clubs, nine-inning game
A.L.—10—Minnesota 6, Boston 4, July 18, 1990.
N.L.—9
Chicago 5, Cincinnati 4, July 3, 1929.
Los Angeles 5, Pittsburgh 4, April 15, 1961.

Most double plays by both clubs, extra-inning game
N.L.—10
Boston 5, Cincinnati 5, June 7, 1925, 12 innings.
Cincinnati 6, New York 4, May 1, 1955, 16 innings.
A.L.—9—California 5, Baltimore 4, May 19, 1988, first game, 10 innings.

Most unassisted double plays, game
N.L.-A.L.—2—Made in many games.

Most unassisted double plays by both clubs, game
N.L.-A.L.—2—Made in many games.

Most double plays, doubleheader
A.L.—10—Washington vs. Chicago, August 18, 1943, 22.1 innings.
N.L.—9—St. Louis vs. Cincinnati, June 11, 1944, 18 innings.

Most double plays by both clubs, doubleheader
N.L.—13
New York 7, Philadelphia 6, September 28, 1939.
Pittsburgh 8, St. Louis 5, September 6, 1948.
A.L.—12
Philadelphia 9, Cleveland 3, September 14, 1931.
Boston 7, Chicago 5, September 15, 1947.
New York 7, Kansas City 5, July 31, 1955.
California 8, Boston 4, May 1, 1966.
California 7, Baltimore 5, May 19, 1988, 19 innings.

Most consecutive games with one or more double plays
A.L.—25
Boston, May 7 through June 4, second game, 1951 (38 double plays).
Cleveland, August 21, second game, through September 12, 1953 (38 double plays).
N.L.—23—Brooklyn, August 7, second game, through August 27, 1952 (36 double plays).

Most consecutive games with one or more double or triple plays
N.L.—26—New York, August 21 through September 16, second game, 1951 (44 double plays, 1 triple play).
A.L.—25
Boston, May 7 through June 4, second game, 1951 (38 double plays).
Cleveland, August 21, second game, through September 12, 1953 (38 double plays).

Most double plays, two consecutive nine-inning games
N.L.—10—New York vs. Brooklyn, August 12, 13, first game, 1932.
A.L.—10
Detroit vs. Boston, May 18 (4), 19 (6), 1948.
Cleveland vs. Kansas City, May 3 (5); vs. Chicago, May 5 (5), 1970.
Kansas City vs. Baltimore, May 5 (4), 6 (6), 1972.

Most double plays, three consecutive games (making at least one each game)
N.L.—13—San Francisco, April 24 through April 26, 1987.
A.L.—12
Boston, June 25 through June 27, 1950.
New York, April 19 through April 21, 1952.
Chicago, September 2 through September 3, second game, 1973.

Most double plays, four consecutive games (making at least one each game)
N.L.—15—San Francisco, April 24 through April 27, 1987.
A.L.—14
Chicago, July 12 through July 14, 1951.
New York, April 18 through April 21, 1952.

TRIPLE PLAYS

Most triple plays, season
A.A.—3
Cincinnati, 1882.
Rochester, 1890.
A.L.—3—Detroit, 1911; Boston, 1924, 1979; Oakland, 1979.
N.L.—3—Philadelphia, 1964; Chicago, 1965.

Most triple plays, game
A.L.—2—Minnesota vs. Boston, July 17, 1990, fourth and eighth innings.
N.L.—1—Held by many clubs.

Most triple plays by both clubs, game
A.L.—2—Minnesota 2, Boston 0, July 17, 1990.
N.L.—1—Made in many games.

Most consecutive games with triple play
A.L.—2—Detroit vs. Boston, June 6, 7, 1908.
N.L.—1—Held by many clubs.

LEAGUE FIELDING

GAMES

Most catchers catching 100 or more games, season
A.L. (14-club league)—12 in 1985, 1990.
A.L. (10-club league)—9 in 1966.
A.L. (8-club league)—8 in 1921, 1952.
N.L. (12-club league)—12 in 1987.
N.L. (10-club league)—9 in 1965, 1966.
N.L. (8-club league)—8 in 1931, 1941.

Fewest catchers catching 100 or more games, season (since 1890)
A.L.—0 in 1902, 1903, 1942.
N.L.—0 in 1893, 1896, 1900, 1945.

AVERAGE

Highest fielding percentage, season
A.L.—.982 in 1996, 1997, 2000.
N.L.—.982 in 2001.

Lowest fielding percentage, season (since 1900)
A.L.—.937 in 1901.
N.L.—.949 in 1903.

PUTOUTS

Most putouts, season (since 1900)
N.L. (16-club league)—69,720 in 1998.
N.L. (14-club league)—60,867 in 1996.
N.L. (12-club league)—52,630 in 1982.
N.L. (10-club league)—44,042 in 1968.
N.L. (8-club league)—33,724 in 1917.
A.L. (14-club league)—61,146 in 1991.
A.L. (12-club league)—52,510 in 1969.
A.L. (10-club league)—43,847 in 1964.
A.L. (8-club league)—33,830 in 1916.

Fewest putouts, season (since 1900)
A.L. (8-club league)—32,235 in 1938.
A.L. (12-club league)—51,821 in 1975.
A.L. (14-club league)—60,155 in 1979.
N.L. (8-club league)—32,296 in 1906.
N.L. (12-club league)—52,000 in 1978.
N.L. (14-club league)—60,767 in 1997.
N.L. (16-club league)—69,223 in 2001.

Most outfielders with 400 or more putouts, season
A.L.—5 in 1979, 1980, 1984, 1985, 1986, 1992.
N.L.—5 in 1992.

ASSISTS

Most assists, season (since 1900)
N.L. (16-club league)—27,513 in 1998.
N.L. (14-club league)—24,442 in 1993.
N.L. (12-club league)—22,341 in 1980.
N.L. (10-club league)—18,205 in 1968.
N.L. (8-club league)—16,759 in 1920.
A.L. (14-club league)—25,626 in 1980.
A.L. (12-club league)—21,786 in 1976.
A.L. (10-club league)—17,269 in 1961.
A.L. (8-club league)—17,167 in 1910.

Fewest assists, season (since 1900)
A.L. (8-club league)—13,219 in 1958.
A.L. (12-club league)—21,001 in 1971.
A.L. (14-club league)—23,063 in 1997.
N.L. (8-club league)—13,345 in 1956.
N.L. (12-club league)—20,351 in 1990.
N.L. (14-club league)—24,198 in 1997.
N.L. (16-club league)—26,279 in 2001.

Most first basemen with 100 or more assists, season
A.L.—7 in 1985, 1986.
N.L.—8 in 1997, 1998.

Most second basemen with 500 or more assists, season
N.L.—4 in 1924.
A.L.—3 in 1930.

Most shortstops with 500 or more assists, season
N.L.—5 in 1978.
A.L.—5 in 1979.

CHANCES ACCEPTED

Most chances accepted, season (since 1900)
N.L. (16-club league)—97,233 in 1998.
N.L. (14-club league)—85,296 in 1993.
N.L. (12-club league)—74,930 in 1980.
N.L. (10-club league)—62,247 in 1968.
N.L. (8-club league)—50,419 in 1920.
A.L. (14-club league)—86,621 in 1980.
A.L. (12-club league)—74,191 in 1976.
A.L. (10-club league)—60,997 in 1964.
A.L. (8-club league)—50,870 in 1910.

Fewest chances accepted, season (since 1900)
A.L. (8-club league)—46,086 in 1938.
A.L. (12-club league)—72,875 in 1971.
A.L. (14-club league)—83,658 in 1997.
N.L. (8-club league)—46,404 in 1955.
N.L. (12-club league)—73,273 in 1970.
N.L. (14-club league)—84,965 in 1997.
N.L. (16-club league)—95,502 in 2001.

ERRORS

Most errors, season (since 1900)
A.L.—2,889 in 1901.
N.L.—2,590 in 1904.

Fewest errors, season (since 1900)
A.L. (8-club league)—1,002 in 1958.
A.L. (10-club league)—1,261 in 1964.
A.L. (12-club league)—1,512 in 1971.
A.L. (14-club league)—1,560 in 1997.
N.L. (8-club league)—1,082 in 1956.
N.L. (10-club league)—1,389 in 1968.
N.L. (12-club league)—1,401 in 1992.
N.L. (14-club league)—1,677 in 1997.
N.L. (16-club league)—1,768 in 2001.

PASSED BALLS

Most passed balls, season (since 1900)
A.L. (14-club league)—267 in 1987.
A.L. (12-club league)—247 in 1969.
A.L. (10-club league)—211 in 1965.
A.L. (8-club league)—178 in 1914.
N.L. (12-club league)—217 in 1969.
N.L. (10-club league)—216 in 1962.
N.L. (8-club league)—202 in 1905.

Fewest passed balls, season
A.L. (8-club league)—53 in 1949.
A.L. (12-club league)—127 in 1976.
A.L. (14-club league)—128 in 1977.
N.L. (8-club league)—65 in 1936.
N.L. (12-club league)—122 in 1980.
N.L. (14-club league)—154 in 1997.
N.L. (16-club league)—170 in 2000.

DOUBLE PLAYS

Most double plays, season
N.L. (16-club league)—2,431 in 2000.
N.L. (14-club league)—2,075 in 1997.
N.L. (12-club league)—1,888 in 1971.
N.L. (10-club league)—1,596 in 1962.
N.L. (8-club league)—1,337 in 1951.
A.L. (14-club league)—2,368 in 1980.
A.L. (12-club league)—1,994 in 1973.
A.L. (10-club league)—1,585 in 1961.
A.L. (8-club league)—1,487 in 1949.

Fewest double plays, season (A.L. since 1912; N.L. since 1920)
A.L. (8-club league)—818 in 1912.
A.L. (12-club league)—1,388 in 1967, 1968.
A.L. (14-club league)—2,095 in 2001.
N.L. (8-club league)—1,007 in 1920.
N.L. (12-club league)—1,431 in 1963.
N.L. (14-club league)—2,028 in 1993.
N.L. (16-club league)—2,340 in 2001.

Most double plays, one day
N.L.—29—July 23, 1972.
A.L.—28—July 24, 1976.

Most unassisted double plays by first basemen, season
A.L.—38 in 1949.
N.L.—32 in 1953.

Most unassisted double plays by catchers, season
N.L.—5 in 1965.
A.L.—3 in 1914, 1969.

Most unassisted double plays by pitchers, season
N.L.—3 in 1935, 1940.
A.L.—2 in 1908, 1932.

TRIPLE PLAYS

Most triple plays, season
A.L. (14-club league)—10 in 1979.
A.L. (8-club league)—7 in 1922, 1936.
N.L.—7 in 1891, 1905, 1910, 1929.
A.A.—7 in 1890.
P.L.—7 in 1890.

Fewest triple plays, season
N.L.—0 in 1928, 1938, 1941, 1943, 1945, 1946, 1959, 1961, 1974, 1984, 1994, 2001.
A.L.—0 in 1904, 1933, 1942, 1956, 1961, 1962, 1974, 1975, 1987, 1993, 1998.

Fewest triple plays by both leagues, season
0 in 1961, 1974.

Most triple plays, one day
N.L.—2—May 29, 1897; August 30, 1921.
A.L.—2—July 17, 1990.

INDIVIDUAL MISCELLANEOUS

HISTORIC FIRSTS

First player with two clubs in one season
N.L.—Neal Phelps, New York, Philadelphia, 1876.
A.L.—Harry Lockhead, Detroit, Philadelphia, 1901.

First player with three clubs in one season
N.L.—Gus Krock, Chicago, Indianapolis, Washington, 1889.
A.L.—Pat Donahue, Boston, Cleveland, Philadelphia, 1910.
(See next entry: Frank Huelsman played with four clubs in 1904.)

First player with four clubs in one season
N.L.—Tom Dowse, Louisville, Cincinnati, Philadelphia, Washington, 63 games, 1892.
A.L.—Frank Huelsman, Chicago, Detroit, St. Louis, Washington, 112 games, 1904.

First pitcher with two clubs in one season
N.L.—Tom Healey, Providence, Indianapolis, 1878.
A.L.—Charles Baker, Cleveland, Philadelphia, 1901.

First pitcher with three clubs in one season
N.L.—Gus Krock, Chicago, Indianapolis, Washington, 1889.
A.L.—Bill James, Detroit, Boston, Chicago, 1919.

First player to enter military service in World War I
Hank Gowdy, Boston N.L., June 27, 1917.

First player to enter military service in World War II
Hugh Mulcahy, Philadelphia N.L., March 8, 1941.

First player to come to bat three times in one inning
N.L.—Tom Carey, Hartford, May 13, 1876, fourth inning.
A.L.—Ted Williams, Boston, July 4, 1948, seventh inning.

First player with seven at-bats in nine-inning game
N.L.—Jack Burdock, Hartford, May 13, 1876.
A.L.—Billy Gilbert, Milwaukee, May 5, 1901.

First player with eight at-bats in nine-inning game
N.L.—Ross Barnes, Chicago, July 22, 1876.

First player to score five runs in nine-inning game
N.L.—George Hall, Philadelphia, June 17, 1876.
A.L.—Mike Donlin, Baltimore, June 24, 1901.

First player to score six runs in nine-inning game
N.L.—Jim Whitney, Boston, June 9, 1883.
A.L.—Johnny Pesky, Boston, May 8, 1946.

First player with five hits in nine-inning game
N.L.—Joe Battin, St. Louis, May 13, 1876.
Jack Burdock, Hartford, May 13, 1876.
Tom Carey, Hartford, May 13, 1876.
A.L.—Irv Waldron, Milwaukee, April 28, 1901.

First player with six hits in nine-inning game
N.L.—Dave Force, Philadelphia, June 27, 1876 (six at-bats).
A.L.—Mike Donlin, Baltimore, June 24, 1901 (six at-bats).

First player with eight hits in a doubleheader
A.A.—Henry Simon, Syracuse, October 11, 1890. (See next entry: Fred Carroll had nine hits in doubleheader in 1886.)
N.L.—Joe Quinn, St. Louis, September 30, 1893. (See next entry: Wilbert Robinson had nine hits in doubleheader in 1892.)
A.L.—Charles Hickman, Washington, September 7, 1905.

First player with nine hits in a doubleheader
A.A.—Fred Carroll, Pittsburgh, July 5, 1886.
N.L.—Wilbert Robinson, Baltimore, June 10, 1892.
A.L.—Ray Morehart, Chicago, August 31, 1926.

First player with four long hits in nine-inning game
N.L.—George Hall, Philadelphia, June 14, 1876 (3 triples, 1 home run).
A.L.—Frank Dillon, Detroit, April 25, 1901 (4 doubles).

First player with five long hits in nine-inning game
A.A.—George Strief, Philadelphia, June 25, 1885 (4 triples, 1 double).

N.L.—George Gore, Chicago, July 9, 1885 (2 triples, 3 doubles).
A.L.—Lou Boudreau, Cleveland, July 14, 1946, first game (4 doubles, 1 home run).

First player with four doubles in nine-inning game
N.L.—John O'Rourke, Boston, September 15, 1880.
A.L.—Frank Dillon, Detroit, April 25, 1901.

First player with three triples in nine-inning game
N.L.—George Hall, Philadelphia, June 14, 1876.
Ezra Sutton, Philadelphia, June 14, 1876.
A.L.—Elmer Flick, Cleveland, July 6, 1902.

First player with four triples in nine-inning game
A.A.—George Strief, Philadelphia, June 25, 1885.
N.L.—Bill Joyce, New York, May 18, 1897.
A.L.—Never accomplished.

First player to hit home run
N.L.—Ross Barnes, Chicago, May 2, 1876.
Charley Jones, Cincinnati, May 2, 1876.
A.L.—Erve Beck, Cleveland, April 25, 1901.

First player to hit two homers in nine-inning game
N.L.—George Hall, Philadelphia, June 17, 1876.
A.L.—Buck Freeman, Boston, June 1, 1901.

First player to hit three homers in nine-inning game
N.L.—Ned Williamson, Chicago, May 30, 1884, p.m. game.
A.L.—Kenny Williams, St. Louis, April 22, 1922.

First player to hit four homers in nine-inning game
N.L.—Bobby Lowe, Boston, May 30, 1894, p.m. game.
A.L.—Lou Gehrig, New York, June 3, 1932.

First player to hit two homers in one inning
N.L.—Charley Jones, Boston, June 10, 1880, eighth inning.
A.L.—Kenny Williams, St. Louis, August 7, 1922, sixth inning.

First player to hit grand slam
N.L.—Roger Connor, Troy, September 10, 1881.
A.L.—Herm McFarland, Chicago, May 1, 1901.

First player to hit grand slam as pinch-hitter
N.L.—Mike O'Neill, St. Louis, June 3, 1902, ninth inning.
A.L.—Marty Kavanagh, Cleveland, September 24, 1916, fifth inning.

First player to hit home run in night game
N.L.—Babe Herman, Cincinnati, July 10, 1935.
A.L.—Frankie Hayes, Philadelphia, May 16, 1939.

First player to hit for cycle
N.L.—Curry Foley, Buffalo, May 25, 1882.
A.L.—Harry Davis, Philadelphia, July 10, 1901.

First player to receive five bases on balls in nine-inning game
A.A.—Henry Larkin, Philadelphia, May 2, 1887.
N.L.—Fred Carroll, Pittsburgh, July 4, 1889, a.m. game.
A.L.—Sammy Strang, Chicago, April 27, 1902.

First player to receive six bases on balls in nine-inning game
N.L.—Walt Wilmot, Chicago, August 22, 1891.
A.L.—Jimmie Foxx, Boston, June 16, 1938.

First player to receive two bases on balls in one inning
N.L.—Elmer Smith, Pittsburgh, April 22, 1892, first inning.
A.L.—Donie Bush, Detroit, August 27, 1909, fourth inning.

First player to strike out four times in nine-inning game
N.L.—George Derby, Detroit, August 6, 1881. (See next item: Oscar Walker had five strikeouts in game in 1879.)
A.L.—Emmett Heidrick, St. Louis, May 16, 1902.

First player to strike out five times in nine-inning game
N.L.—Oscar Walker, Buffalo, June 20, 1879.
A.L.—Lefty Grove, Philadelphia, June 10, 1933, first game.

First player to strike out twice in one inning
A.L.—Billy Purtell, Chicago, May 10, 1910, sixth inning.
N.L.—Edd Roush, Cincinnati, July 22, 1916, sixth inning.

First pinch-hitter
N.L.—Mickey Welch, New York, August 10, 1889 (struck out).
A.L.—Larry McLean, Boston, April 26, 1901 (doubled).

First hit by pinch-hitter
N.L.—Tom Daly, Brooklyn, May 14, 1892 (homered).
A.L.—Larry McLean, Boston, April 26, 1901 (doubled).

First pitcher to lose doubleheader (two complete games)
N.L.—Dave Anderson, Pittsburgh vs. Brooklyn, September 1, 1890; lost 3-2, 8-4 (pitched 2 games of tripleheader).

First player to be intentionally walked with bases filled
A.L.—Nap Lajoie, Philadelphia, May 23, 1901, ninth inning.

First manager ejected from two games in one day by umpires
N.L.—Mel Ott, New York vs. Pittsburgh, June 9, 1946, doubleheader.
A.L.—Jimmie Dykes, Baltimore vs. New York, June 6, 1954, doubleheader.

First lefthanded catcher
Bill Harbidge, Hartford N.L., May 6, 1876.

First lefthanded pitcher
Bobby Mitchell, Cincinnati N.L., 1878.

First pitcher to wear glasses
Will White, Boston N.L., 1877.

First infielder to wear glasses
George Toporcer, St. Louis N.L., 1921.

First catcher to wear glasses
Clint Courtney, New York A.L., 1951.

CLUB MISCELLANEOUS

HISTORIC FIRSTS

First shutout game
N.L.—April 25, 1876, Chicago 4, Louisville 0.
A.L.—May 15, 1901, Washington 4, Boston 0.

First 1-0 game
N.L.—May 5, 1876, St. Louis 1, Chicago 0.
A.L.—July 27, 1901, Detroit 1, Baltimore 0.

First tie game
N.L.—May 25, 1876, Philadelphia 2, Louisville 2, 14 innings (darkness).
A.L.—May 31, 1901, Washington 3, Milwaukee 3, 7 innings (darkness).

First extra-inning game
N.L.—April 29, 1876, Hartford 3, Boston 2, 10 innings.
A.L.—April 30, 1901, Boston 8, Philadelphia 6, 10 innings.

First extra-inning shutout game
N.L.—May 25, 1876, Boston 4, Cincinnati 0, 10 innings.
A.L.—August 11, 1902, Philadelphia 1, Detroit 0, 13 innings.

First extra-inning 1-0 game
N.L.—June 10, 1876, New York Mutuals 1, Cincinnati 0, 10 innings.
A.L.—August 11, 1902, Philadelphia 1, Detroit 0, 13 innings.

First extra-inning tie game
N.L.—May 25, 1876, Philadelphia 2, Louisville 2, 14 innings (darkness).
A.L.—August 27, 1901, Milwaukee 5, Baltimore 5, 11 innings (darkness).

First time two games played in one day
N.L.—September 9, 1876, Hartford 14, Cincinnati 6; Hartford 8, Cincinnati 3.
A.L.—May 30, 1901, Baltimore 10, Detroit 7; Detroit 4, Baltimore 1.
Chicago 8, Boston 3; Chicago 5, Boston 3.
Milwaukee 5, Washington 2; Milwaukee 14, Washington 3.
Philadelphia 3, Cleveland 1; Philadelphia 8, Cleveland 2, eight innings.

First doubleheader
N.L.—September 25, 1882, Worcester 4, Providence 3; Providence 8, Worcester 6.
A.L.—July 15, 1901, Washington 3, Baltimore 2; Baltimore 7, Washington 3.

First doubleheader shutout victory
N.L.—July 13, 1888, Pittsburgh 4, Boston 0; Pittsburgh 6, Boston 0.
A.L.—September 3, 1901, Cleveland 1, Boston 0; Cleveland 4, Boston 0.

First forfeited game
N.L.—August 21, 1876, St. Louis 7, Chicago 6; forfeited to St. Louis.
A.L.—May 2, 1901, Detroit 7, Chicago 5; forfeited to Detroit.

Last forfeited game
N.L.—August 10, 1995, St. Louis 2, Los Angeles 1, at Los Angeles; forfeited to St. Louis.
A.L.—July 12, 1979, second game, Detroit 9, Chicago 0, at Chicago; forfeited to Detroit.

First game played by
Boston N.L.—April 22, 1876—Boston 6, Philadelphia Athletics 5 (A).
Philadelphia Athletics N.L.—April 22, 1876—Boston 6, Philadelphia 5 (H).
New York Mutuals N.L.—April 25, 1876—Boston 7, New York Mutuals 6 (H).
Chicago N.L.—April 25, 1876—Chicago 4, Louisville 0 (A).
Cincinnati N.L.—April 25, 1876—Cincinnati 2, St. Louis 1 (H).
St. Louis N.L.—April 25, 1876—Cincinnati 2, St. Louis 1 (A).
Philadelphia N.L.—May 1, 1883—Providence 4, Philadelphia 3 (H).

New York N.L. (Original Club)—May 1, 1883—New York 7, Boston 5 (H).
Pittsburgh N.L.—April 30, 1887—Pittsburgh 6, Chicago 2 (H).
Brooklyn N.L.—April 19, 1890—Boston 15, Brooklyn 9 (A).
Chicago A.L.—April 24, 1901—Chicago 8, Cleveland 2 (H).
Cleveland A.L.—April 24, 1901—Chicago 8, Cleveland 2 (A).
Detroit A.L.—April 25, 1901—Detroit 14, Milwaukee 13 (H).
Baltimore A.L.—April 26, 1901—Baltimore 10, Boston 6 (H).
Boston A.L.—April 26, 1901—Baltimore 10, Boston 6 (A).
Philadelphia A.L.—April 26, 1901—Washington 5, Philadelphia 1 (H).
Washington A.L. (Original Club)—April 26, 1901—Washington 5, Philadelphia 1 (A).
Milwaukee A.L.—April 25, 1901—Detroit 14, Milwaukee 13 (A).
St. Louis A.L.—April 23, 1902—St. Louis 5, Cleveland 2 (H).
New York A.L.—April 22, 1903—Washington 3, New York 1 (A).
Milwaukee N.L. since 1900—April 13, 1953—Milwaukee 2, Cincinnati 0 (A).
Baltimore A.L. (Present Club)—April 13, 1954—Detroit 3, Baltimore 0 (A).
Kansas City A.L.—April 12, 1955—Kansas City 6, Detroit 2 (H).
Los Angeles N.L.—April 15, 1958—San Francisco 8, Los Angeles 0 (A).
San Francisco N.L.—April 15, 1958—San Francisco 8, Los Angeles 0 (H).
Los Angeles A.L.—April 11, 1961—Los Angeles 7, Baltimore 2 (A).
Minnesota A.L.—April 11, 1961—Minnesota 6, New York 0 (A).
Washington A.L. (Second Club)—April 10, 1961—Chicago 4, Washington 3 (H).
Houston N.L.—April 10, 1962—Houston 11, Chicago 2 (H).
New York N.L. (Present Club)—April 11, 1962—St. Louis 11, New York 4 (A).
Atlanta N.L.—April 12, 1966—Pittsburgh 3, Atlanta 2, 13 innings (H).
Oakland A.L.—April 10, 1968—Baltimore 3, Oakland 1 (A).
San Diego N.L.—April 8, 1969—San Diego 2, Houston 1 (H).
Seattle A.L. (Original Club)—April 8, 1969—Seattle 4, California 3 (A).
Montreal N.L.—April 8, 1969—Montreal 11, New York 10 (A).
Kansas City A.L. (Present Club)—April 8, 1969—Kansas City 4, Minnesota 3, 12 innings (H).
Milwaukee A.L. (Present Club)—April 7, 1970—California 12, Milwaukee 0 (H).
Texas A.L.—April 15, 1972—California 1, Texas 0 (A).
Seattle A.L. (Present Club)—April 6, 1977—California 7, Seattle 0 (H).
Toronto A.L.—April 7, 1977—Toronto 9, Chicago 5 (H).
Florida N.L.—April 5, 1993—Florida 6, Los Angeles 3 (H).
Colorado N.L.—April 5, 1993—New York 3, Colorado 0 (A).
Tampa Bay A.L.—March 31, 1998—Detroit 11, Tampa Bay 6 (H).
Arizona N.L.—March 31, 1998—Colorado 9, Arizona 2 (H).

First game played
At Sportsman's Park (later Busch Stadium), St. Louis—May 5, 1876—St. Louis N.L. 1, Chicago 0.
By St. Louis A.L.—April 23, 1902—St. Louis 5, Cleveland 2.
By St. Louis N.L. (since 1900)—July 1, 1920—Pittsburgh 6, St. Louis 2, 10 innings.
At Shibe Park (later Connie Mack Stadium), Philadelphia—April 12, 1909—Philadelphia A.L. 8, Boston 1.
At Shibe Park (later Connie Mack Stadium), Philadelphia—May 16, 1927—St. Louis N.L. 2, Philadelphia N.L. 1.
At Forbes Field, Pittsburgh—June 30, 1909—Chicago N.L. 3, Pittsburgh 2.
At Comiskey Park (old), Chicago—July 1, 1910—St. Louis A.L. 2, Chicago 0.
At League Park, Cleveland—April 21, 1910—Detroit A.L. 5, Cleveland 0.
At Griffith Stadium, Washington—April 12, 1911—Washington A.L. 8, Boston 5.
At Polo Grounds, New York (first game after fire)—June 28, 1911—New York N.L. 3, Boston 0.
Formal opening—April 19, 1912—New York N.L. 6, Brooklyn 2.
At Redland Field (later Crosley Field), Cincinnati—April 11, 1912—Cincinnati N.L. 10, Chicago 6.

At Navin Field (later Tiger Stadium), Detroit—April 20, 1912—Detroit A.L. 6, Cleveland 5, 11 innings.

At Fenway Park, Boston—April 20, 1912—Boston A.L. 7, New York 6 (11 innings).

Formal opening—May 17, 1912—Chicago A.L. 5, Boston 2.

At Ebbets Field, Brooklyn—April 9, 1913—Philadelphia N.L. 1, Brooklyn 0.

At Wrigley Field, Chicago—April 23, 1914—Chicago F.L. 9, Kansas City 1.

By Chicago N.L.—April 20, 1916—Chicago 7, Cincinnati 6, 11 innings.

At Braves Field, Boston—August 18, 1915—Boston N.L. 3, St. Louis 1.

At Yankee Stadium, New York—April 18, 1923, New York A.L. 4, Boston 1.

At Municipal Stadium, Cleveland—July 31, 1932, Philadelphia A.L. 1, Cleveland 0.

At Milwaukee County Stadium—April 14, 1953, Milwaukee N.L. 3, St. Louis 2, 10 innings.

At Memorial Stadium, Baltimore—April 15, 1954, Baltimore A.L. 3, Chicago 1.

At Municipal Stadium, Kansas City—April 12, 1955, Kansas City A.L. 6, Detroit 2.

At Roosevelt Stadium, Jersey City—April 19, 1956, Brooklyn N.L. 5, Philadelphia 4, 10 innings.

At Seals Stadium, San Francisco—April 15, 1958—San Francisco N.L. 8, Los Angeles 0.

At Memorial Coliseum, Los Angeles—April 18, 1958—Los Angeles N.L. 6, San Francisco 5.

At Candlestick Park, San Francisco—April 12, 1960—San Francisco N.L. 3, St. Louis 1.

At Metropolitan Stadium, Minnesota—April 21, 1961—Washington A.L. 5, Minnesota 3.

At Wrigley Field, Los Angeles—April 27, 1961—Minnesota A.L. 4, Los Angeles 2.

At Dodger Stadium, Los Angeles—April 10, 1962—Cincinnati N.L. 6, Los Angeles 3.

At Colt Stadium, Houston—April 10, 1962—Houston N.L. 11, Chicago 2.

At District of Columbia Stadium, Washington—April 9, 1962, Washington A.L. 4, Detroit 1.

At Shea Stadium, New York—April 17, 1964—Pittsburgh N.L. 4, New York 3.

At Astrodome, Houston—April 12, 1965—Philadelphia N.L. 2, Houston 0.

At Atlanta Stadium, Atlanta—April 12, 1966—Pittsburgh N.L. 3, Atlanta 2, 13 innings.

At Anaheim Stadium, California—April 19, 1966—Chicago A.L. 3, California 1.

At Busch Memorial Stadium, St. Louis—May 12, 1966—St. Louis N.L. 4, Atlanta 3, 12 innings.

At Oakland-Alameda County Coliseum—April 17, 1968—Baltimore A.L. 4, Oakland 1.

At San Diego Stadium—April 8, 1969—San Diego N.L. 2, Houston 1.

At Sicks' Stadium, Seattle—April 11, 1969—Seattle A.L. 7, Chicago 0.

At Jarry Park, Montreal—April 14, 1969—Montreal N.L. 8, St. Louis 7.

At Riverfront Stadium, Cincinnati—June 30, 1970—Atlanta N.L. 8, Cincinnati 2.

At Three Rivers Stadium, Pittsburgh—July 16, 1970—Cincinnati N.L. 3, Pittsburgh 2.

At Veterans Stadium, Philadelphia—April 10, 1971—Philadelphia N.L. 4, Montreal 1.

At Arlington Stadium, Texas—April 21, 1972—Texas A.L. 7, California 6.

At Royals Stadium, Kansas City—April 10, 1973—Kansas City A.L. 12, Texas 1.

At Kingdome, Seattle—April 6, 1977—California A.L. 7, Seattle 0.

At Exhibition Stadium, Toronto—April 7, 1977—Toronto A.L. 9, Chicago 5.

At Olympic Stadium, Montreal—April 15, 1977—Philadelphia N.L. 7, Montreal 2.

At Metrodome, Minnesota—April 6, 1982—Seattle A.L. 11, Minnesota 7.

At SkyDome, Toronto—June 5, 1989—Milwaukee A.L. 5, Toronto 3.

At Comiskey Park (new), Chicago—April 18, 1991—Detroit A.L. 16, Chicago 0.

At Oriole Park at Camden Yards, Baltimore—April 6, 1992—Baltimore A.L. 2, Cleveland 0.

At Joe Robbie Stadium, Florida—April 5, 1993—Florida N.L. 6, Los Angeles 3.

At Mile High Stadium, Colorado—April 9, 1993—Colorado N.L. 11, Montreal 4.

At Jacobs Field, Cleveland—April 4, 1994—Cleveland A.L. 4, Seattle 3 (11 innings).

At The Ballpark in Arlington, Texas—April 11, 1994—Milwaukee A.L. 4, Texas 3.

At Coors Field, Colorado—April 26, 1995—Colorado N.L. 11, New York 9 (11 innings).

At Cashman Field, Las Vegas—April 1, 1996—Toronto A.L. 9, Oakland 6.

At Monterrey Stadium, Mexico—August 16, 1996—San Diego N.L. 15, New York 10.

At Turner Field, Atlanta—April 4, 1997—Atlanta N.L. 5, Chicago 4.

At Aloha Stadium, Honolulu—April 19, 1997, first game, St. Louis N.L. 1, San Diego 0.

At Tropicana Field, Tampa Bay—March 31, 1998—Detroit A.L. 11, Tampa Bay 6.

At Bank One Ballpark, Arizona—March 31, 1998—Colorado N.L. 9, Arizona 2.

At Safeco Field, Seattle—July 15, 1999—San Diego N.L. 3, Seattle A.L. 2.

At Tokyo Dome, Japan—March 29, 2000—Chicago N.L. 5, New York N.L. 3.

At Enron Field, Houston—April 7, 2000—Philadelphia N.L. 4, Houston 1.

At Pacific Bell Park, San Francisco—April 11, 2000—Los Angeles N.L. 6, San Francisco 5.

At Comerica Park, Detroit—April 11, 2000—Detroit A.L. 5, Seattle 2.

At Hiram Bithorn Stadium, San Juan, Puerto Rico—April 1, 2001—Toronto A.L. 8, Texas 1.

At Miller Park, Milwaukee—April 6, 2001—Milwaukee N.L. 5, Cincinnati 4.

At PNC Park, Pittsburgh—April 9, 2001—Cincinnati N.L. 8, Pittsburgh 2.

First Sunday game

N.L.—At St. Louis—April 17, 1892, Cincinnati 5, St. Louis 1.

A.L.—At Detroit—April 28, 1901, Detroit 12, Milwaukee 11.
    At Chicago, A.L.—April 28, 1901, Chicago 13, Cleveland 1.

First night game

At Cincinnati—May 24, 1935, Cincinnati 2, Philadelphia 1.

By Pittsburgh (at Cincinnati)—May 31, 1935, Pittsburgh 4, Cincinnati 1.

By Chicago N.L. (at Cincinnati)—July 1, 1935, Chicago 8, Cincinnati 4.

By Brooklyn (at Cincinnati)—July 10, 1935, Cincinnati 15, Brooklyn 2.

By Boston N.L. (at Cincinnati)—July 24, 1935, Cincinnati 5, Boston 4.

By St. Louis N.L. (at Cincinnati)—July 31, 1935, Cincinnati 4, St. Louis 3, 10 innings.

At Brooklyn—June 15, 1938, Cincinnati 6, Brooklyn 0.

At Philadelphia A.L.—May 16, 1939, Cleveland 8, Philadelphia 3, 10 innings.

By Chicago A.L. (at Philadelphia)—May 24, 1939, Chicago 4, Philadelphia 1.

At Philadelphia N.L.—June 1, 1939, Pittsburgh 5, Philadelphia 2.

By St. Louis A.L. (at Philadelphia)—June 14, 1939, St. Louis 6, Philadelphia 0.

By Detroit (at Philadelphia)—June 20, 1939, Detroit 5, Philadelphia 0.

By New York A.L. (at Philadelphia)—June 26, 1939, Philadelphia 3, New York 2.

At Cleveland—June 27, 1939, Cleveland 5, Detroit 0.

By Washington (at Philadelphia)—July 6, 1939, Philadelphia 9, Washington 3.

At Chicago A.L.—August 14, 1939, Chicago 5, St. Louis 2.

By Boston A.L. (at Cleveland)—July 13, 1939, Boston 6, Cleveland 5, 10 innings.

At New York N.L.—May 24, 1940, New York 8, Boston 1.

By New York N.L.—May 24, 1940, New York 8, Boston 1.

At St. Louis A.L.—May 24, 1940, Cleveland 3, St. Louis 2.
At Pittsburgh—June 4, 1940, Pittsburgh 14, Boston 2.
At St. Louis N.L.—June 4, 1940, Brooklyn 10, St. Louis 1.
At Washington—May 28, 1941, New York 6, Washington 5.
At Boston N.L.—May 11, 1946, New York 5, Boston 1.
At New York A.L.—May 28, 1946, Washington 2, New York 1.
At Boston A.L.—June 13, 1947, Boston 5, Chicago 3.
At Detroit—June 15, 1948, Detroit 4, Philadelphia 1.
By Milwaukee N.L. (at St. Louis)—April 20, 1953, St. Louis 9, Milwaukee 4.
At Milwaukee N.L.—May 8, 1953, Milwaukee 2, Chicago 0.
At Baltimore—April 21, 1954, Cleveland 2, Baltimore 1.
At Kansas City—April 18, 1955, Cleveland 11, Kansas City 9.
At San Francisco—April 16, 1958, Los Angeles 13, San Francisco 1.
At Los Angeles N.L.—April 22, 1958, Los Angeles 4, Chicago 2.
By Minnesota—April 14, 1961, Minnesota 3, Baltimore 2.
At Minnesota—May 18, 1961, Kansas City 4, Minnesota 3.
At Los Angeles A.L.—April 28, 1961, Los Angeles 6, Minnesota 5, 12 innings.
At Houston—April 11, 1962, Houston 2, Chicago 0.
At Atlanta—April 12, 1966, Pittsburgh 3, Atlanta 2, 13 innings.
At Oakland—April 17, 1968, Baltimore 4, Oakland 1.
At San Diego—April 8, 1969, San Diego 2, Houston 1.
By Seattle—April 8, 1969, Seattle 4, California 3.
By Montreal—April 17, 1969, Montreal 7, Philadelphia 0.
At Seattle—April 12, 1969, Seattle 5, Chicago 1.
At Montreal—April 30, 1969, New York 2, Montreal 1.
By Milwaukee A.L.—April 13, 1970, Oakland 2, Milwaukee 1.
At Milwaukee A.L.—May 5, 1970, Boston 6, Milwaukee 0.
At Texas—April 21, 1972, Texas 7, California 6.
At Toronto—May 2, 1977, Milwaukee 3, Toronto 1.
At Chicago N.L.—August 9, 1988, Chicago 6, New York 4.
At Florida—April 6, 1993, Los Angeles 4, Florida 2.
At Colorado—April 13, 1993, New York 8, Colorado 4.
At Tampa Bay—March 31, 1998, Detroit 11, Tampa Bay 6.
At Arizona—March 31, 1998, Colorado 9, Arizona 2.

First night opening game
N.L.—At St. Louis—April 18, 1950, St. Louis 4, Pittsburgh 2.
A.L.—At Philadelphia—April 17, 1951, Washington 6, Philadelphia 1.

First ladies day
N.L.—At Cincinnati, 1876 season.
A.L.—At St. Louis, 1912 season.

First ladies night
N.L.—At New York, June 27, 1941, New York 7, Philadelphia 4.
A.L.—At Boston, August 17, 1950, Boston 10, Philadelphia 6.

First day games completed with lights
N.L.—At Boston, April 23, 1950, second game, Philadelphia 6, Boston 5.
A.L.—At New York, August 29, 1950, New York 6, Cleveland 5.

First time all games played at night
(8-club leagues)—August 9, 1946 (4 in N.L., 4 in A.L.).
(12-club leagues)—April 25, 1969 (6 in N.L., 6 in A.L.).

First time all games were twi-night doubleheaders
N.L.—August 25, 1953.

First time uniforms were numbered
N.L.—Cincinnati, 1883 season.
A.L.—New York, 1929 season, complete (Cleveland vs. Chicago at Cleveland, June 26, 1916 wore numbers on the sleeves of their uniforms).

First team with 1,000,000 home attendance
A.L.—New York, 1920 (1,289,422).
N.L.—Chicago, 1927 (1,159,168).

First team with 2,000,000 home attendance
A.L.—New York, 1946 (2,265,512).
N.L.—Milwaukee, 1954 (2,131,388).

First team with 3,000,000 home attendance
N.L.—Los Angeles, 1978 (3,347,845).
A.L.—Minnesota, 1988 (3,030,672).

First team with 4,000,000 home attendance
A.L.—Toronto, 1991 (4,001,527).
N.L.—Colorado, 1993 (4,483,350).

NIGHT GAMES AND POSTPONEMENTS

Most night games, season (includes twilight games)
A.L.—135—Texas, 1979 (won 68, lost 67).
N.L.—127—Florida, 1993 (won 49, lost 78).

Most games postponed at start of season
A.L.—5
Chicago, April 6 through 10, 1982.
New York, April 6 through 10, 1982.
N.L.—4—New York, April 12 through 15, 1933.

Most consecutive games postponed, season
N.L.—9—Philadelphia, August 10 through 19, 1903.
A.L.—7
Detroit, May 14 through 18, 1945.
Philadelphia, May 14 through 18, 1945.
Washington, April 23 through 29, 1952.

TIES AND ONE-RUN DECISIONS

Most tie games, season
A.L.—10—Detroit, 1904.
N.L.—9—St. Louis, 1911.

Fewest tie games, season
A.L.-N.L.—0—By all clubs in many seasons.
Last A.L. season—2000.
Last N.L. season—2001.

Most games decided by one run, season
A.L.—74—Chicago, 1968 (won 30, lost 44).
N.L.—75—Houston, 1971 (won 32, lost 43).

Fewest games decided by one run, season
A.L.—27—Cleveland, 1948 (won 9, lost 18).
N.L.—28—Brooklyn, 1949 (won 16, lost 12).

LENGTH OF GAMES
BY INNINGS

Longest game
N.L.—26 innings—Brooklyn 1, Boston 1, May 1, 1920, at Boston.
A.L.—25 innings—Chicago 7, Milwaukee 6, May 8, finished May 9, 1984, at Chicago.

For a complete list of games of 18 or more innings, see page 225.

Longest night game
N.L.—25 innings—St. Louis 4, New York 3, September 11, 1974, at New York.
A.L.—25 innings—Chicago 7, Milwaukee 6, May 8, finished May 9, 1984, at Chicago.

Longest opening game
A.L.—15 innings
Washington 1, Philadelphia 0, April 13, 1926 at Washington.
Detroit 4, Cleveland 2, April 19, 1960, at Cleveland.
N.L.—14 innings
Philadelphia 5, Brooklyn 5, April 17, 1923, at Brooklyn.
New York 1, Brooklyn 1, April 16, 1933, at Brooklyn (opener for New York only).
Pittsburgh 4, Milwaukee 3, April 15, 1958, at Milwaukee.
Pittsburgh 6, St. Louis 2, April 8, 1969, at St. Louis.
Cincinnati 2, Los Angeles 1, April 7, 1975, at Cincinnati.
New York 1, Philadelphia 0, March 31, 1998, at New York.

Longest 0-0 game
N.L.—19 innings—Brooklyn vs. Cincinnati, September 11, 1946, at Brooklyn.
A.L.—18 innings—Detroit vs. Washington, July 16, 1909, at Detroit.

Longest 0-0 night game
N.L.—18 innings—Philadelphia vs. New York, October 2, 1965, second game, at New York.
A.L.—None.

Longest 1-0 day game
N.L.—18 innings
  Providence 1, Detroit 0, August 17, 1882, at Providence.
  New York 1, St. Louis 0, July 2, 1933, first game, at New
  York.
A.L.—18 innings
  Washington 1, Chicago 0, May 15, 1918, at Washington.
  Washington 1, Chicago 0, June 8, 1947, first game, at
  Chicago.

Longest 1-0 night game
N.L.—24 innings—Houston 1, New York 0, April 15, 1968, at
  Houston.
A.L.—20 innings—Oakland 1, California 0, July 9, 1971, at
  Oakland.

Longest shutout game
N.L.—24 innings—Houston 1, New York 0, April 15, 1968, at
  Houston.
A.L.—20 innings—Oakland 1, California 0, July 9, 1971, at Oakland.

Longest tie game
N.L.—26 innings—Boston 1, Brooklyn 1, May 1, 1920, at
  Boston.
A.L.—24 innings—Detroit 1, Philadelphia 1, July 21, 1945, at
  Philadelphia.

Most innings, one day
N.L.—32—San Francisco at New York, May 31, 1964.
A.L.—29
  Boston at Philadelphia, July 4, 1905.
  Boston at New York, August 29, 1967,

Most extra-inning games, season
A.L.—31—Boston, 1943 (won 15, lost 14, tied 2).
N.L.—27
  Boston, 1943 (won 14, lost 13).
  Los Angeles, 1967 (won 10, lost 17).

Most consecutive extra-inning games, one club
A.L.—5—Detroit, September 9 through 13, 1908 (54 innings).
N.L.—4
  Pittsburgh, August 18 through 22, 1917 (59 innings).
  San Francisco, July 7 through 10, 1987 (49 innings).

Most consecutive extra-inning games between same clubs
A.L.—4
  Chicago and Detroit, September 9 through 12, 1908 (43
  innings).
  Cleveland and St. Louis, May 1, 2, 4, 5, 1910 (46 innings).
  Boston and St. Louis, May 31, first game, to June 2, second
  game, 1943 (45 innings).
N.L.—4—New York and Pittsburgh, May 24, 25, June 23, 24,
  1978 (44 innings; both clubs played other teams between
  these contests).
N.L.—3
  Brooklyn and Pittsburgh, August 20 through 22, 1917 (45
  innings).
  Chicago and Pittsburgh, August 18, 19, 20, 1961 (33
  innings).
  Cincinnati and New York, May 5, 6, 7, 1980 (36 innings).

Most innings, two consecutive extra-inning games
N.L.—45—Boston, May 1 (26), 3 (19), 1920.
A.L.—37—Minnesota vs. Milwaukee May 12 (22), May 13 (15),
  1972.

Most innings between same clubs, two consecutive extra-inning games
N.L.—40—Boston and Chicago, May 14 (18), May 17 (22), 1927.
A.L.—37—Minnesota and Milwaukee, May 12 (22), May 13
  (15), 1972.

Most innings, three consecutive extra-inning games
N.L.—58—Brooklyn, May 1 through 3, 1920.
A.L.—41
  Cleveland, April 16 through 21, 1935.
  Boston, April 8 through 11, 1969.

Most innings between same clubs, three consecutive extra-inning games
N.L.—45—Brooklyn and Pittsburgh, August 20 through 22, 1917.

A.L.—40
  Chicago and Washington, August 24 through 26, 1915.
  Detroit and Philadelphia, May 12 through 14, 1943.

Most innings, four consecutive extra-inning games
N.L.—59—Pittsburgh, August 18 through 22, 1917.
A.L.—51
  Chicago, August 23 through 26, 1915.
  Detroit, May 11, second game, through May 14, 1943.

Most innings between same clubs, four consecutive extra-inning games
A.L.—46—Cleveland and St. Louis, May 1, 2, 4, 5, 1910.
N.L.—No performance.

BY TIME

Longest nine-inning game
N.L.—4 hours, 27 minutes—Los Angeles 11, San Francisco 10,
  October 5, 2001.
A.L.—4 hours, 22 minutes—Baltimore 13, New York 9,
  September 5, 1997.

Longest extra-inning game
A.L.—8 hours, 6 minutes—Chicago 7, Milwaukee 6, May 8, finished May 9, 1984, 25 innings.
N.L.—7 hours, 23 minutes—San Francisco 8, New York 6, May
  31, 1964, second game, 23 innings.

Longest nine-inning 1-0 game
A.L.—3 hours, 20 minutes—Milwaukee 1, Oakland 0, May 7,
  1997.
Interleague—3 hours, 16 minutes—Anaheim A.L. 1, Los
  Angeles N.L. 0, June 8, 2001.
N.L.—3 hours, 7 minutes—New York 1, San Diego 0, May 17,
  1988.

Longest extra-inning 1-0 game
N.L.—6 hours, 14 minutes—Los Angeles 1, Montreal 0, August
  23, 1989, 22 innings.
A.L.—5 hours, 5 minutes—Oakland 1, California 0, July 9,
  1971, 20 innings.

Longest extra-inning 1-0 night game
N.L.—6 hours, 14 minutes—Los Angeles 1, Montreal 0, August
  23, 1989, 22 innings.
A.L.—5 hours, 5 minutes—Oakland 1, California 0, July 9,
  1971, 20 innings.

Longest nine-inning night game
N.L.—4 hours, 27 minutes—Los Angeles 11, San Francisco 10,
  October 5, 2001.
A.L.—4 hours, 22 minutes—Baltimore 13, New York 9,
  September 5, 1997.

Longest extra-inning night game
A.L.—8 hours, 6 minutes—Chicago 7, Milwaukee 6, at Chicago,
  May 8, finished May 9, 1984, 25 innings.
N.L.—7 hours, 14 minutes—Houston 5, Los Angeles 4, at
  Houston, June 3, 1989, 22 innings.

Longest doubleheader (18 innings)
A.L.—7 hours, 39 minutes—Texas at Chicago, May 24, 1995.
N.L.—6 hours, 46 minutes—Brooklyn at New York, August 7,
  1952.

Longest doubleheader (more than 18 innings)
N.L.—9 hours, 52 minutes—San Francisco at New York, May
  31, 1964, 32 innings.
A.L.—9 hours, 5 minutes—Kansas City at Detroit, June 17,
  1967, 28 innings.

Shortest nine-inning game
N.L.—51 minutes—New York 6, Philadelphia 1, September 28,
  first game, 1919.
A.L.—55 minutes—St. Louis 6, New York 2, September 26,
  second game, 1926.

Shortest nine-inning night game
N.L.—1 hour, 15 minutes—Boston 2, Cincinnati 0, August 10,
  1944.
A.L.—1 hour, 29 minutes—Chicago 1, Washington 0, May 21,
  1943.

Shortest 1-0 game
N.L.—57 minutes—New York 1, Brooklyn 0, August 30, 1918.
A.L.—1 hour, 13 minutes—Detroit 1, New York 0, August 8, 1920.

Shortest doubleheader (18 innings)
A.L.—2 hours, 7 minutes—New York at St. Louis, September 26, 1926.
N.L.—2 hours, 20 minutes—Chicago at Brooklyn, August 14, 1919.

GAMES WON

Most games won, league
N.L.—9,512—Chicago, 126 years, 1876 through 2001.
A.L.—8,674—New York, 99 years, 1903 through 2001.

For a complete list of franchise won-lost records, see page 220.

Most games won, season
N.L.—116—Chicago, 1906 (lost 36).
A.L.—116—Seattle, 2001 (lost 46).

For a complete list of clubs with 100 or more victories in a season, see page 222.

Fewest games won, season
N.L.—20—Cleveland, 1899 (lost 134).
N.L. since 1900—38—Boston, 1935 (lost 115).
A.L.—36—Philadelphia, 1916 (lost 117).

Most games won, two consecutive seasons
N.L.—223—Chicago, 1906, 1907 (lost 81).
A.L.—217—Baltimore, 1969, 1970 (lost 107).

Most games won, three consecutive seasons
N.L.—322—Chicago, 1906, 1907, 1908 (lost 130).
A.L.—318—Baltimore, 1969, 1970, 1971 (lost 164).

Most years winning 100 or more games
A.L.—15—New York, 1927, 1928, 1932, 1936, 1937, 1939, 1941, 1942, 1954, 1961, 1963, 1977, 1978, 1980, 1998.
N.L.—6
St. Louis, 1931, 1942, 1943, 1944, 1967, 1985.
Boston/Atlanta, 1892, 1898 in Boston, 1993, 1997, 1998, 1999 in Atlanta.

Most consecutive years winning 100 or more games
A.L.—3
Philadelphia, 1929, 1930, 1931.
Baltimore, 1969, 1970, 1971.
N.L.—3
St. Louis, 1942, 1943, 1944.
Atlanta, 1997, 1998, 1999.

Most games won at home, season
A.L.—65—New York, 1961 (lost 16).
N.L.—64—Cincinnati, 1975 (lost 17).

Most games won on road, season
N.L.—60—Chicago, 1906 (lost 15).
A.L.—59—Seattle, 2001 (lost 22).

Most games won from one club, season
N.L. (8-club league)—21
Chicago vs. Boston, 1909 (lost 1).
Pittsburgh vs. Cincinnati, 1937 (lost 1).
Chicago vs. Cincinnati, 1945 (lost 1).
N.L. (12-club league)—17
Atlanta vs. San Diego, 1974 (lost 1).
New York vs. Pittsburgh, 1986 (lost 1).
A.L. (8-club league)—21—New York vs. St. Louis, 1927 (lost 1).
A.L. (12-club league)—15—Baltimore vs. Milwaukee, 1973 (lost 3).

Most games won from one club at home
N.L.—16
Brooklyn vs. Pittsburgh, 1890 (lost 2).
Philadelphia vs. Pittsburgh, 1890 (lost 1).
N.L. since 1900—13—New York vs. Philadelphia, 1904 (lost 2).
A.L.—12—Chicago vs. St. Louis, 1915 (lost 0).

Most games won from one club on road
N.L. (8-club league)—11
Pittsburgh vs. St. Louis, 1908 (lost 0).
Chicago vs. Boston, 1909 (lost 0).
Brooklyn vs. Philadelphia, 1945 (lost 0).
A.L. (8-club league)—11
Chicago vs. Philadelphia, 1915 (lost 0).
New York vs. St. Louis, 1927 (lost 0).
New York vs. St. Louis, 1939 (lost 0).
Cleveland vs. Boston, 1954 (lost 0).

Most games won by one run, season
N.L.—42—San Francisco, 1978 (lost 26).
A.L.—40
Baltimore, 1970 (lost 15).
Baltimore, 1974 (lost 21).

Fewest games won by one run, season
A.L.—9—Cleveland, 1948 (lost 18).
N.L.—9—New York, 1953 (lost 24).

Most games won from league champions, season
N.L.—16—St. Louis vs. Chicago, 1945 (lost 6).
A.L.—14
Philadelphia vs. Detroit, 1909 (lost 8).
Minnesota vs. Oakland, 1973 (lost 4).

Most games won from one club, two consecutive seasons
N.L. (8-club league)—40—Pittsburgh vs. St. Louis, 1907, 1908.
A.L. (8-club league)—37
Philadelphia vs. St. Louis, 1910, 1911.
Chicago vs. Philadelphia, 1915, 1916.
New York vs. Philadelphia, 1919, 1920.
New York vs. St. Louis, 1926, 1927.

Fewest games won from one club, season (excludes interleague games)
A.L.—0
Kansas City vs. Baltimore, 1970 (lost 12; 12-club league).
Oakland vs. Baltimore, 1978 (lost 11; 14-club league).
Baltimore vs. Kansas City, 1988 (lost 12; 14-club league).
New York vs. Oakland, 1990 (lost 12; 14-club league).
Detroit vs. Cleveland, 1996 (lost 12; 14-club league).
Kansas City vs. New York, 1998 (lost 10; 14-club league).
Minnesota vs. Texas, 1999 (lost 12; 14-club league).
Kansas City vs. New York, 2001 (lost six; 14-club league).
N.L.—0
Philadelphia vs. Boston, 1883 (lost 14; 8-club league).
Buffalo vs. Chicago, 1885 (lost 16; 8-club league).
Baltimore vs. Boston, 1892 (lost 13; 12-club league).
Cleveland vs. Brooklyn, 1899 (lost 14; 12-club league).
Cleveland vs. Cincinnati, 1899 (lost 14; 12-club league).
Colorado vs. Atlanta, 1993 (lost 13; 14-club league).
San Diego vs. Montreal, 1994 (lost 12; 14-club league). (Note: San Diego and Montreal completed the schedule against each other. Los Angeles was 0-6 against Atlanta in 1994, but seven games were cancelled due to a strike.)
Florida vs. Cincinnati, 1998 (lost nine; 16-club league).
Florida vs. Milwaukee, 1998 (lost nine; 16-club league).
Florida vs. San Francisco, 1998 (lost nine; 16-club league).
San Diego vs. St. Louis, 2000 (lost nine; 16-club league).
Montreal vs. Houston, 2001 (lost six; 16-club league).
A.A.—1
Cleveland vs. St. Louis, 1887 (lost 18; 8-club league).
Louisville vs. Brooklyn, 1889 (lost 19; 8-club league).

Most times winning two games in one day, season
N.L.—20—Chicago, 1945 (lost 3).
A.L.—15—Chicago, 1961 (lost 7).

Most times winning two games in one day, from one club, season
A.L.—7—Chicago vs. Philadelphia, 1943 (lost 0).
N.L.—7—Chicago vs. Cincinnati, 1945 (lost 0).

Fewest games winning two games in one day, season
A.L.-N.L.—0—Held by many clubs.

Most games won, one month
N.L.—29—New York, September, 1916 (lost 5).
A.L.—28—New York, August, 1938 (lost 8).

Most games won, two consecutive days
N.L.—5—Baltimore, September 7 (3), September 8 (2), 1896.
A.L.—4—Made on many days.

Most consecutive games won, season
N.L.—26—New York, September 7 through 30, first game, 1916 (1 tie).
A.L.—19
Chicago, August 2 through 23, 1906 (1 tie).
New York, June 29, second game, through July 17, second game, 1947.

For a complete list of clubs with 13 or more consecutive victories in a season, see page 223.

Most consecutive games won with no tie games, season
N.L.—21
Chicago, June 2 through July 8, 1880.
Chicago, September 4 through 27, second game, 1935.
A.L.—19—New York, June 29, second game, through July 17, second game, 1947.

Most consecutive games won at start of season
U.A.—20—St. Louis, April 20 through May 22, 1884.
N.L.—13—Atlanta, April 6 through 21, 1982.
A.L.—13—Milwaukee, April 6 through 20, 1987.

For a complete list of clubs with eight or more consecutive victories at the start of a season, see page 225.

Most consecutive home games won, season
A.A.—27—St. Louis, April 26 through July 16, 1885.
N.L.—26—New York, September 7 through 30, first game, 1916 (1 tie).
A.L.—24—Boston, June 25 through August 13, 1988.

Most consecutive road games won, season
N.L.—17—New York, May 9 through 29, 1916.
A.L.—17—Detroit, April 3 through May 24, 1984 (start of season).

Most consecutive games won from one club, league
A.L. (12-club league)—23—Baltimore vs. Kansas City, May 10, 1969 through August 2, 1970 (last 11 in 1969, all 12 in 1970).
N.L. (8-club league)—22—Boston vs. Philadelphia, May 4, 1883 through June 3, 1884 (all 14 in 1883, first 8 in 1884).
N.L. since 1900 (8-club league)—20—Pittsburgh vs. Cincinnati, May 31, second game, 1937 through April 24, 1938 (last 17 in 1937, first 3 in 1938).
A.L. (8-club league)—22—Boston vs. Washington, August 31, 1903 through September 6, first game, 1904 (last 6 in 1903, first 16 in 1904).

Most consecutive games won from one club at home, league
N.L.—32—Baltimore vs. Louisville, June 7, 1894 through July 11, 1899 (last 6 in 1894, all 6 in 1895, 1896 and 1897, all 7 in 1898, first 1 in 1899).
N.L. since 1900—25—St. Louis vs. Cincinnati, April 27, 1929, second game through May 31, 1931, first game (last 9 in 1929, all 11 in 1930, first 5 in 1931).
A.L.—27—Cleveland vs. St. Louis/Baltimore, August 13, 1952, second game through August 15, 1954, second game (last 5 in 1952, all 11 in 1953 and 1954).

Most consecutive games won from one club on road, league
N.L.—18
Brooklyn vs. Philadelphia, May 5, first game, 1945 through August 10, 1946 (all 11 in 1945; first 7 in 1946).
St. Louis vs. Pittsburgh, May 7, 1964 through April 15, 1966 (last 8 in 1964, all 9 in 1965, first in 1966).
A.L.—18—Boston vs. New York, October 3, first game, 1911 through June 2, second game, 1913 (last 3 in 1911; all 10 in 1912; first 6, excluding one tie, in 1913).

Most consecutive doubleheaders won, season (no other games between)
A.L.—5—New York, August 30 through September 4, 1906.
N.L.—4
Brooklyn, September 1 through 4, 1924.
New York, September 10 through 14, 1928.

Most games lost, league
N.L.—9,572—Philadelphia, 119 years, 1883 through 2001.
A.L.—7,721—Chicago, 101 years, 1901 through 2001.

For a complete list of franchise won-lost records, see page 220.

Most games lost, season
N.L.—134—Cleveland, 1899 (won 20).
N.L. since 1900—120—New York, 1962 (won 40).
A.L.—117—Philadelphia, 1916 (won 36).

For a complete list of clubs with 100 or more games lost in a season, see page 222.

Most games lost, two consecutive seasons
N.L.—231—New York, 1962, 1963 (won 91).
A.L.—226—Philadelphia, 1915, 1916 (won 79).

Most games lost, three consecutive seasons
N.L.—340—New York, 1962 through 1964 (won 144).
A.L.—324—Philadelphia, 1915 through 1917 (won 134).

Most years losing 100 or more games
A.L.—15—Philadelphia/Kansas City, 1915, 1916, 1919, 1920, 1921, 1936, 1940, 1943, 1946, 1950, 1954 in Philadelphia, 1956, 1961, 1964, 1965 in Kansas City.
N.L.—14—Philadelphia, 1904, 1921, 1923, 1927, 1928, 1930, 1936, 1938, 1939, 1940, 1941, 1942, 1945, 1961.

Most consecutive years losing 100 or more games
N.L.—5—Philadelphia, 1938 through 1942.
A.L.—4—Washington, 1961 through 1964.

Most night games lost, season
A.L.—83—Seattle, 1980 (won 44).
N.L.—82—Atlanta, 1977 (won 43).

Most games lost at home, season
A.L.—59—St. Louis, 1939 (won 18).
N.L.—58—New York, 1962 (won 22).

Most games lost on road, season
N.L.—102—Cleveland, 1899 (won 11).
N.L. since 1900—65—Boston, 1935 (won 13).
A.L.—64—Philadelphia, 1916 (won 13).

Most games lost by one run, season
A.L.—44—Chicago, 1968 (won 30).
N.L.—43—Houston, 1971 (won 32).

Fewest games lost by one run, season
A.L.—10
Boston, 1986 (won 24).
New York, 1998 (won 21).
N.L.—12—Brooklyn, 1949 (won 16).

Most times losing two games in one day, season
N.L.—19—Chicago, 1950 (won 4).
A.L.—18—Philadelphia, 1943 (won 4).

Fewest times losing two games in one day, season
N.L.-A.L.—0—Held by many clubs.

Most games lost, one month
A.L.—29—Washington, July, 1909 (won 5).
N.L.—27
Pittsburgh, August, 1890 (won 1).
Cleveland, September, 1899 (won 1).
St. Louis, September, 1908 (won 7).
Brooklyn, September, 1908 (won 6).
Philadelphia, September, 1939 (won 6).

Most games lost, two consecutive days
N.L.—5—Louisville, September 7 (3), September 8 (2), 1896.
A.L.—4—Made on many days.

CONSECUTIVE

Most consecutive games lost, season
A.A.—26—Louisville, May 22 through June 22, second game, 1889.
N.L.—24—Cleveland, August 26 through September 16, 1899.
N.L. since 1900—23—Philadelphia, July 29 through August 20, first game, 1961.
A.L.—21—Baltimore, April 4 through 28, 1988.

For a complete list of clubs with 13 or more consecutive games lost in a season, see page 224.

Most consecutive games lost at start of season
A.L.—21—Baltimore, April 4 through 28, 1988.
N.L.—14—Chicago, April 1 through 20, first game, 1997.

For a complete list of clubs with eight or more consecutive games lost at the start of a season, see page 225.

Most consecutive home games lost, season
A.L.—20—St. Louis, June 3 through July 7, 1953.
N.L.—14—Boston, May 8 through 24, 1911.

Most consecutive road games lost, season
N.L.—41—Pittsburgh, July 18 through September 12, second game, 1890.
N.L. since 1900—22—New York, June 16, first game, through July 28, 1963.
A.L.—19—Philadelphia, July 25 through August 8, 1916.

Most consecutive games lost to one club, league
A.L. (12-club league)—23—Kansas City vs. Baltimore, May 9, 1969 through August 2, 1970; last 11 in 1969, all 12 in 1970.
A.L. (8-club league)—22—Washington vs. Boston, August 31, 1903 through September 6, first game, 1904; last 6 in 1903, first 16 in 1904.
N.L. (8-club league)—22—Philadelphia vs. Boston, May 4, 1883 through June 3, 1884; all 14 in 1883, first 8 in 1884.
N.L. since 1900 (8-club league)—20—Cincinnati vs. Pittsburgh, May 31, second game, 1937 through April 24, 1938; last 17 in 1937, first 3 in 1938.

Most consecutive doubleheaders lost, season (no other games between)
N.L.—5—Boston, September 8 through 14, 1928.
A.L.—4—Boston, June 29 through July 5, 1921.

WINNING PERCENTAGE
HIGHEST

Highest percentage games won, season
U.A.—.850—St. Louis, 1884 (won 91, lost 16).
N.L.—.798—Chicago, 1880 (won 67, lost 17).
N.L. since 1900—.763—Chicago, 1906 (won 116, lost 36).
A.L.—.721—Cleveland, 1954 (won 111, lost 43).

Highest percentage games won, season, for league champions since 1969
A.L.—.704—New York, 1998 (won 114, lost 48).
N.L.—.667
Cincinnati, 1975 (won 108, lost 54).
New York, 1986 (won 108, lost 54).

Highest percentage games won, season, for second-place team, through 1968
N.L.—.759—New York, 1885 (won 85, lost 27).
N.L. since 1900—.680—Chicago, 1909 (won 104, lost 49).
A.L.—.669—New York, 1954 (won 103, lost 51).

Highest percentage games won, season, for third-place team, through 1968
N.L.—.691—Hartford, 1876 (won 47, lost 21).
N.L. since 1900—.608—Pittsburgh, 1906 (won 93, lost 60).
A.L.—.617—New York, 1920 (won 95, lost 59).

Highest percentage games won, season, for fourth-place team, through 1968
N.L.—.623—Philadelphia, 1886 (won 71, lost 43).
N.L. since 1900 (10-club league)—.578—Pittsburgh, 1962 (won 93, lost 68).
N.L. since 1900 (8-club league)—.569—Pittsburgh, 1904 (won 87, lost 66).
A.L.—.597—Cleveland, 1950 (won 92, lost 62).

Highest percentage games won, season, for fifth-place team, through 1968
A.L. (10-club league)—.537—Cleveland, 1965 (won 87, lost 75).
A.L. (8-club league)—.536—Philadelphia, 1904 (won 81, lost 70).
N.L.—.571—Boston, 1890 (won 76, lost 57).
N.L. since 1900 (10-club league)—.543—Milwaukee, 1964 (won 88, lost 74).
N.L. since 1900 (8-club league)—.529—Chicago, 1924 (won 81, lost 72).

Highest percentage games won, season, for sixth-place team, through 1968
N.L. (10-club league)—.528—Philadelphia, 1965 (won 85, lost 76).
N.L. (8-club league)—.503—Brooklyn, 1928 (won 77, lost 76).
A.L.—.513—Detroit, 1962 (won 79, lost 75).

Highest percentage games won, season, for seventh-place team, through 1968
A.L.—.497—Washington, 1916 (won 76, lost 77).
N.L. (10-club league)—.506—Chicago, 1963 (won 82, lost 80).
N.L. (8-club league)—.464—Brooklyn, 1917 (won 70, lost 81).

Highest percentage games won, season, for eighth-place team, through 1968
A.L.—.475—Boston, 1962 (won 76, lost 84).
N.L.—.469
Chicago, 1964 (won 76, lost 86).
NOTE: Los Angeles and Philadelphia tied for seventh place in 1968 with .469 records (won 76, lost 86).

Highest percentage games won, season, for ninth-place team, through 1968
N.L.—.451—New York, 1968 (won 73, lost 89).
A.L.—.444
Kansas City, 1962 (won 72, lost 90).
Boston, 1966 (won 72, lost 90).
New York, 1967 (won 72, lost 90).

Highest percentage games won, season, for last-place team
N.L.—.454—New York, 1915 (won 69, lost 83).
A.L. (8-club league)—.431—Chicago, 1924 (won 66, lost 87).
A.L. (10-club league)—.440—New York, 1966 (won 70, lost 89).

Highest percentage games won, one month (15 or more games)
U.A.—.947—St. Louis, May, 1884 (won 18, lost 1).
N.L.—.944—Providence, August 1884 (won 17, lost 1).
N.L. since 1900—.897—Chicago, August 1906 (won 26, lost 3).
A.L.—.900—Detroit, April 1984 (won 18, lost 2).

LOWEST

Lowest percentage games won, season
N.L.—.130—Cleveland, 1899 (won 20, lost 134).
N.L. since 1900—.248—Boston, 1935 (won 38, lost 115).
A.L.—.235—Philadelphia, 1916 (won 36, lost 117).

Lowest percentage games won, pennant winner, through 1968
N.L.—.564—Los Angeles, 1959 (won 88, lost 68).
A.L.—.568—Boston, 1967 (won 92, lost 70).

Lowest percentage games won, league champion, since 1969
N.L.—.509—New York, 1973 (won 82, lost 79).
A.L.—.525—Minnesota, 1987 (won 85, lost 77).

Lowest percentage games won, second-place team, through 1968
A.L.—.532—Chicago, 1958 (won 82, lost 72).
N.L. (8-club league)—.543—Brooklyn, 1902 (won 75, lost 63).
N.L. (10-club league)—.543—San Francisco, 1968 (won 88, lost 74).

Lowest percentage games won, third-place team, through 1968
A.L.—.500—Chicago, 1941 (won 77, lost 77).
N.L.—.508—Chicago, 1889 (won 67, lost 65).

N.L. since 1900—.519
New York, 1955 (won 80, lost 74; 8-club league).
San Francisco, 1958 (won 80, lost 74; 8-club league).
Chicago, 1968 (won 84, lost 78; 10-club league).

Lowest percentage games won, fourth-place team, through 1968
A.L.—.448—Boston, 1954 (won 69, lost 85).
N.L.—.464—Philadelphia, 1906 (won 71, lost 82).

Lowest percentage games won, fifth-place team, through 1968
A.L.—.409—St. Louis, 1931 (won 63, lost 91).
N.L. since 1900—.434—Brooklyn, 1906 (won 66, lost 86).

Lowest percentage games won, sixth-place team, through 1968
N.L.—.250—Milwaukee, 1878 (won 15, lost 45, six-club league).
N.L. since 1900—.359—Brooklyn, 1909 (won 55, lost 98).
A.L.—.386—St. Louis, 1948 (won 59, lost 94).

Lowest percentage games won, seventh-place team, through 1968
N.L.—.237—Philadelphia, 1876 (won 14, lost 45).
N.L. since 1900—.327—Boston, 1928 (won 50, lost 103).
A.L.—.325—Chicago, 1932 (won 49, lost 102).

Lowest percentage games won, eighth-place team, through 1968
N.L.—.130—Cleveland, 1899 (won 20, lost 134, last in 12-club league).
N.L. since 1900 (8-club league)—.248—Boston, 1935 (won 38, lost 115).
N.L. since 1900 (10-club league)—.400—Houston, 1962 (won 64, lost 96).
A.L. (8-club league)—.235—Philadelphia, 1916 (won 36, lost 117).
A.L. (10-club league)—.414
California, 1968 (won 67, lost 95).
Chicago, 1968 (won 67, lost 95).

Lowest percentage games won, ninth-place team, through 1968
N.L.—.364—Chicago, 1962 (won 59, lost 103).
A.L.—.379
Kansas City, 1961 (won 61, lost 100).
Washington, 1961 (won 61, lost 100).

Lowest percentage games won, one month (15 or more games)
N.L.—.036
Pittsburgh, August 1890 (won 1, lost 27).
Cleveland, September 1899 (won 1, lost 27).
N.L. since 1900—.120—Philadelphia, May 1928 (won 3, lost 22).
A.L.—.043—Baltimore, April 1988 (won 1, lost 22).

CHAMPIONSHIPS AND FIRST-DIVISION FINISHES

Most championships won, club
A.L.—38—New York, 1921, 1922, 1923, 1926, 1927, 1928, 1932, 1936, 1937, 1938, 1939, 1941, 1942, 1943, 1947, 1949, 1950, 1951, 1952, 1953, 1955, 1956, 1957, 1958, 1960, 1961, 1962, 1963, 1964, 1976, 1977, 1978, 1981, 1996, 1998, 1999, 2000, 2001.
N.L.—21—Brooklyn/Los Angeles, 1890, 1899, 1900, 1916, 1920, 1941, 1947, 1949, 1952, 1953, 1955, 1956 in Brooklyn, 1959, 1963, 1965, 1966, 1974, 1977, 1978, 1981, 1988 in Los Angeles.
N.L. since 1900—19—Brooklyn/Los Angeles, 1900, 1916, 1920, 1941, 1947, 1949, 1952, 1953, 1955, 1956 in Brooklyn, 1959, 1963, 1965, 1966, 1974, 1977, 1978, 1981, 1988 in Los Angeles.

Most consecutive championships won, club
A.L.—5
New York, 1949, 1950, 1951, 1952, 1953.
New York, 1960, 1961, 1962, 1963, 1964.
A.A.—4—St. Louis, 1885, 1886, 1887, 1888.
N.L.—4—New York, 1921, 1922, 1923, 1924.

Most consecutive years without winning championship, league
N.L.—56—Chicago, 1946 through 2001.
A.L.—42
St. Louis, 1902 through 1943.
Chicago, 1960 through 2001.

Most consecutive years with first-division finishes
A.L.—39—New York, 1926 through 1964.

N.L.—14
Chicago, 1878 through 1891.
Pittsburgh, 1900 through 1913.
Chicago, 1926 through 1939.

LAST-PLACE AND SECOND-DIVISION FINISHES

Most times finished in last place, league
A.L.—26—Philadelphia/Kansas City/Oakland, 1915, 1916, 1917, 1918, 1919, 1920, 1921, 1935, 1936, 1938, 1940, 1941, 1942, 1943, 1945, 1946, 1950, 1954 in Philadelphia, 1956, 1960, 1961 (tied), 1964, 1965, 1967 in Kansas City, 1993, 1997 in Oakland.
N.L.—27—Philadelphia, 1883, 1904, 1919, 1920, 1921, 1923, 1926, 1927, 1928, 1930, 1936, 1938, 1939, 1940, 1941, 1942, 1944, 1945, 1947 (tied), 1958, 1959, 1960, 1961, 1972, 1996, 1997, 2000 (tied).

Most consecutive last-place finishes
A.L.—7—Philadelphia, 1915 through 1921.
N.L.—5—Philadelphia, 1938 through 1942.

Most consecutive times with lowest winning percentage, season
A.L.—7—Philadelphia, 1915 through 1921.
N.L.—5—Philadelphia, 1938 through 1942.

Most consecutive years with second-division finishes, through 1968
N.L.—20—Chicago, 1947 through 1966.
A.L.—16—Philadelphia/Kansas City/Oakland, 1953 through 1968.

Most consecutive years without lowest winning percentage, season
N.L.—86—Brooklyn/Los Angeles, 1906 through 1991.
A.L.—54—Cleveland, 1915 through 1968.

GAMES FINISHED AHEAD AND BEHIND

Best gain in games by pennant winner, one season
A.A.—64 games—Louisville, 1890 (won 88, lost 44, .667—in 1889, won 27, lost 111, .196; in eighth place, last).
N.L.—41.5 games—Brooklyn, *1899 (won 88, lost 42, .677—in 1898, won 54, lost 91, .372; in 10th place) (*some sources list 1899 record as 101-47, but N.L. president threw out 18 Brooklyn games from the records for illegally signing a player).
N.L. since 1900 (12-club league)—29 games—Atlanta, 1991 (won 94, lost 68, .580—in 1990, won 65, lost 97, .401; in sixth place).
N.L. since 1900 (8-club league)—27 games—New York, 1954 (won 97, lost 57, .630—in 1953, won 70, lost 84, .455; in fifth place).
A.L. (8-club league)—33 games—Boston, 1946 (won 104, lost 50, .675—in 1945, won 71 lost 83, .461; in seventh place).

Best gain in position from previous year, pennant winner, through 1968
N.L.—10th to first—Brooklyn, 1899 (won 88, lost 42, .677—in 1898 finished tenth in 12-club league, won 54 lost 91, .372; 41.5 games.)
N.L. since 1900 (8-club league)—Seventh to first—Los Angeles, 1959 (won 88, lost 68, .564—in 1958 finished seventh, won 71, lost 83, .461; 16 games.)
N.L. since 1900 (12-club league)—Ninth to first—New York, 1969 (won 100, lost 62, .617—in 1968, finished ninth in 10-club league, won 73, lost 89, .451; 27 games.).
A.A.—Eighth (last) to first—Louisville, 1890 (won 88, lost 44, .667—in 1889 finished eighth, won 27, lost 111, .196; 64 games.)
A.L. (8-club league)—Seventh to first
New York, 1926 (won 91, lost 63, .591—in 1925 finished seventh, won 69, lost 85, .448; 22 games.)
Boston, 1946, won 104, lost 50, .675—in 1945 finished seventh, won 71, lost 83, .461; 33 games.)
A.L. (10-club league)—Ninth to first—Boston, 1967 (won 92, lost 70, .568—in 1966 finished ninth in 10-club league, won 72, lost 90, .444; 20 games.)

Best gain in games by club from previous season
A.A.—64—Louisville, 1890 (won 88, lost 44, .667, first place—in 1889 won 27, lost 111, .196; in eighth place, last).

N.L.—41.5—Brooklyn, 1899 (won 88, lost 42, .677, first place—in 1898 won 54, lost 91, .372; in 10th place).

N.L. since 1900 (8-club league)—34.5—New York, 1903 (won 84, lost 55, .604, in second place—in 1902, won 48, lost 88, .353, in eighth place).

N.L. since 1900 (10-club league)—27.5—Chicago, 1967 (won 87, lost 74, .540, in third place—in 1966, won 59, lost 103, .364, in 10th place).

N.L. since 1900 (12-club league)—29—Atlanta, 1991 (won 94, lost 68, .580, in first place—in 1990, won 65, lost 97, .401, in sixth place).

N.L. since 1900 (14-club league)—31—San Francisco, 1993, won 103, lost 59, .636, in second place—in 1992, won 72, lost 90, .444, in fifth place).

N.L. since 1900 (16-club league)—35—Arizona, 1999, won 100, lost 62, .617, in first place—in 1998, won 65, lost 97, .401, in fifth place).

A.L.—33—Boston, 1946 (won 104, lost 50, .675, first place—in 1945, won 71, lost 83, .461; in seventh place).

Most games leading league or division at end of season
A.L.—30—Cleveland, 1995.
N.L.—27.5—Pittsburgh, 1902.

Fewest games leading league or division at end of season (before playoff)
N.L.—0
St. Louis and Brooklyn, 1946 (8-club league).
New York and Brooklyn, 1951 (8-club league).
Los Angeles and Milwaukee, 1959 (8-club league).
San Francisco and Los Angeles, 1962 (10-club league).
Houston and Los Angeles, 1980 (12-club league).
Houston and St. Louis, 2001 (16-club league).
A.L.—0
Cleveland and Boston, 1948 (8-club league).
New York and Boston, 1978 (14-club league).

Most games behind pennant winner, season, through 1968
N.L. (12-club league)—80—Cleveland, 1899.
N.L. since 1900 (8-club league)—66.5—Boston, 1906.
A.L. (8-club league)—64.5—St. Louis, 1939.

Fewest games behind pennant winner for last-place club, through 1968
N.L. (8-club league)—21—New York, 1915.
A.L. (8-club league)—25—Washington, 1944. (In shortened season of 1918, Philadelphia was 24 games behind.)

Fewest games behind Western Division leader, last-place club, since 1969
A.L.—10
California, 1987.
Texas, 1987.
N.L.—19.5—San Diego, 1980.

Fewest games behind Eastern Division leader, last-place club, since 1969
N.L.—11.5—Philadelphia, 1973.
A.L.—17
Toronto, 1982.
Cleveland, 1982.

Most games behind Western Division leader, last-place club, since 1969
N.L.—43.5—Houston, 1975.
A.L.—42—Chicago, 1970.

Most games behind Eastern Division leader, last-place club, since 1969
A.L.—50.5—Toronto, 1979.
N.L.—48—Montreal, 1969.

Largest lead (in games) for pennant winner on July 4, p.m., through 1968
N.L.—14.5—New York, 1912.
A.L.—12—New York, 1928.

Most games behind, eventual pennant winner, on July 4, p.m., through 1968
N.L.—15—Boston, 1914 (8th place).
A.L.—6.5—Detroit, 1907 (4th place).

PENNANT-CLINCHING DATES

Fewest games played before clinching pennant
A.L.—136—New York, September 4, 1941 (won 91, lost 45, .669).
N.L.—137—New York, September 22, 1904 (won 100, lost 37, .730).

Earliest date for pennant clinching, through 1968
A.L.—September 4, 1941—New York (won 91, lost 45, .669, 136th game).
N.L.—September 8, 1955—Brooklyn (won 92, lost 46, .667, 138th game).

Earliest date for Western Division pennant clinching, since 1969
A.L.—September 15, 1971, first game—Oakland (won 94, lost 55, .631, 148th game).
N.L.—September 7, 1975—Cincinnati (won 95, lost 47, .669, 142nd game).

Earliest date for Eastern Division pennant clinching, since 1969
A.L.—September 13, 1969—Baltimore (won 101, lost 45, .690, 146th game).
N.L.—September 17, 1986—New York (won 95, lost 50, .655, 145th game).

DAYS IN FIRST PLACE

Leading or tied for first place for entire season
A.L.—New York, April 12 through October 2, 1927.
Detroit, April 3 through September 30, 1984.
Baltimore, April 2 through September 28, 1997.
Cleveland, March 31 through September 27, 1998.
Seattle, April 2 through October 7, 2001.
N.L.—New York, April 17 through October 9, 1923.
Brooklyn Dodgers, April 13 through September 25, 1955.
Cincinnati Reds, April 9 through October 3, 1990.

Fewest days in first place, season, for pennant winner, through 1968
N.L.—3—New York, 1951 (before playoff).
A.L.—20—Boston, 1967 (6 days alone).

ATTENDANCE

Highest home attendance, season
N.L.—4,483,350—Colorado, 1993.
A.L.—4,057,947—Toronto, 1993.

For a complete list of clubs with 3,200,000 or higher home attendance, see page 226.

Highest road attendance, season
N.L.—3,016,074—Cincinnati, 2000.
A.L.—2,876,506—New York, 2000.

Largest crowd, day game
N.L.—80,227—Montreal at Colorado, April 9, 1993 (home opener).
A.L.—74,420—Detroit at Cleveland, April 7, 1973 (home opener).

Largest crowd, night game
A.L.—78,382—Chicago at Cleveland, August 20, 1948.
N.L.—72,208—San Francisco at Colorado, July 31, 1993.

Largest crowd, doubleheader
A.L.—84,587—New York at Cleveland, September 12, 1954.
N.L.—72,140—Cincinnati at Los Angeles, August 16, 1961.

Largest crowd, opening day
N.L.—80,227—Montreal at Colorado, April 9, 1993.
A.L.—74,420—Detroit at Cleveland, April 7, 1973.

LEAGUE MISCELLANEOUS

NIGHT GAMES

Most night games, season
A.L. (14-club league)—822 in 1982.
A.L. (12-club league)—661 in 1976.
A.L. (10-club league)—472 in 1965.
N.L. (12-club league)—799 in 1983.
N.L. (10-club league)—487 in 1968.
Note: N.L. had record of 864-876 in night games (including interleague games) in 1998.

Most night games in both leagues, season
1,675 in 1998 (16-club N.L.; 14-club A.L.; includes interleague games).
1,530 in 1993 (14-club leagues; 765 in A.L., 765 in N.L.).
1,432 in 1983 (14-club A.L.; 12-club N.L.; 633 in A.L., 799 in N.L.).
1,274 in 1975 (12-club leagues; 651 in A.L., 623 in N.L.).
960 in 1968 (10-club leagues; 487 in N.L., 473 in A.L.).

CANCELED AND POSTPONED GAMES

Most unplayed games, season (since 1900, except 1918)
A.L.—19 in 1901.
N.L.—14 in 1938.

Fewest unplayed scheduled games, season (since 1900)
N.L.-A.L.—0—Made in many years.

Fewest unplayed games in both leagues, season
0 in 1930, 1947, 1949, 1951, 1954, 1956, 1959, 1960, 1964, 1972, 1982, 1983, 1992, 1993 (14 years).

Most postponed games, season
A.L. (8-club league)—97 in 1935.
N.L.—49
   in 1956 (8-club league).
   in 1967 (10-club league).

Fewest postponed dates, season
A.L.—15 in 1987.
N.L.—12 in 1987.

Most postponed doubleheaders, season
A.L.—14 in 1945.
N.L.—5 in 1959.

Fewest postponed doubleheaders, season
A.L.—0 in 1914, 1957.
N.L.—0 in 1961, 1966, 1970.

TIE GAMES

Most tie games, season
A.L.—19 in 1910.
N.L.—16 in 1913.

Most tie games, one day
N.L.—3, April 6, 1897.
A.L.—2, made on many days.

Fewest tie games, season
N.L.—0 in 1925, 1954, 1958, 1970, 1976, 1977, 1978, 1982, 1984, 1986, 1987, 1990, 1991, 1992, 1995, 1996, 1997, 1999, 2001 (19 years).
A.L.—0 in 1930, 1963, 1965, 1971, 1972, 1973, 1975, 1976, 1977, 1978, 1979, 1987, 1988, 1989, 1990, 1991, 1992, 1993, 1994, 1997, 2000 (21 years).

Most 0-0 games, season
A.L.—6 in 1904.
N.L.—3 in 1917.

EXTRA-INNING GAMES

Most extra-inning games, season
A.L. (14-club league)—117 in 1991.
A.L. (12-club league)—116 in 1976.

A.L. (10-club league)—91 in 1965.
A.L. (8-club league)—91 in 1943.
N.L. (12-club league)—116 in 1986.
N.L. (10-club league)—93 in 1967.
N.L. (8-club league)—86 in 1916.
Note: N.L. had record of 126-121 in extra-inning games (including interleague games) in 1998.

Most extra-inning games, one day
N.L.—5—May 30, 1892, May 11, 1988.
A.L.—4—June 11, 1969, June 4, 1976.

Most extra-inning games in both leagues, one day
6 on August 22, 1951; 3 in N.L. (five games), 3 in A.L. (five games).
6 on May 12, 1963; 4 in N.L. (eight games), 2 in A.L. (seven games).
6 on May 11, 1988; 5 in N.L. (six games), 1 in A.L. (six games).

100- AND 90-WIN AND LOSS SEASONS

Most clubs winning 100 or more games, season
A.L. (14-club league)—2 in 1977, 1980, 2001
A.L. (12-club league)—2 in 1971.
A.L. (10-club league)—2 in 1961.
A.L. (8-club league)—2 in 1915, 1954.
N.L. (16-club league)—2 in 1998, 1999.
N.L. (14-club league)—2 in 1993.
N.L. (12-club league)—2 in 1976.
N.L. (10-club league)—2 in 1962.
N.L. (8-club league)—2 in 1909, 1942.

For a complete list of clubs with 100 or more victories in a season, see page 222.

Most clubs winning 90 or more games, season
N.L. (16-club league)—5 in 1999.
N.L. (14-club league)—4 in 1993.
N.L. (12-club league)—4 in 1969, 1976, 1980, 1987.
N.L. (10-club league)—4 in 1962, 1964.
N.L. (8-club league)—3 in many seasons.
A.L. (14-club league)—6 in 1977.
A.L. (12-club league)—4 in 1975.
A.L. (8-club league)—4 in 1950.

Most clubs losing 100 or more games, season
N.L. (14-club league)—2 in 1993.
N.L. (12-club league)—2 in 1969, 1985.
N.L. (10-club league)—2 in 1962.
N.L. (8-club league)—2 in 1898, 1905, 1908, 1923, 1938.
A.L. (14-club league)—2 in 1978, 1979.
A.L. (10-club league)—2 in 1961, 1964, 1965.
A.L. (8-club league)—2 in 1912, 1932, 1949, 1954.

For a complete list of clubs with 100 or more games lost in a season, see page 222.

HOME AND ROAD VICTORIES

Most games won by home clubs, season
N.L. (16-club league)—711 in 1998 (lost 586; includes interleague games).
N.L. (14-club league)—641 in 1996 (lost 493).
N.L. (12-club league)—556 in 1978 (lost 415), 1980 (lost 416).
N.L. (10-club league)—464 in 1967 (lost 345).
N.L. (8-club league)—358 in 1931 (lost 256), 1955 (lost 257).
A.L. (14-club league)—649 in 1978 (lost 482).
A.L. (12-club league)—540 in 1969 (lost 431).
A.L. (10-club league)—454 in 1961 (lost 353).
A.L. (8-club league)—360 in 1945 (lost 244), 1949 (lost 256).

Most games won by home clubs, one day
N.L.-A.L. (8-club leagues)—8—Made on many days.

Most games won by home clubs in both leagues, one day

14 on May 30, 1903 (A.L. won 8, lost 0; N.L. won 6, lost 2).

Most games won by visiting clubs, season

N.L. (16-club league)—622 in 1999 (lost 674; includes inter-league games).
N.L. (14-club league)—532 in 1993 (lost 602).
N.L. (12-club league)—473 in 1982 (lost 499).
N.L. (10-club league)—400 in 1968 (lost 410).
N.L. (8-club league)—307 in 1948 (lost 308).
A.L. (14-club league)—547 in 1980 (lost 582).
A.L. (12-club league)—469 in 1971 (lost 497).
A.L. (10-club league)—391 in 1968 (lost 418).
A.L. (8-club league)—312 in 1953 (lost 301).

Most games won by visiting clubs, one day

N.L.-A.L. (8-club league)—8—Made on many days.

Most games won by visiting clubs in both leagues, one day

(8-club leagues)—
12 on July 4, 1935 (N.L. won 7, lost 1; A.L. won 5, lost 3).
12 on August 5, 1951 (N.L. won 7, lost 0; A.L. won 5, lost 2).
12 on June 15, 1958 (A.L. won 8, lost 0; N.L. won 4, lost 1).

ONE-RUN DECISIONS

Most games won by one run, season

N.L. (16-club league)—413 in 1998 (includes interleague games).
N.L. (14-club league)—356 in 1993.
N.L. (12-club league)—346 in 1980.
N.L. (10-club league)—294 in 1968.
N.L. (8-club league)—223 in 1946.
A.L. (14-club league)—368 in 1978.
A.L. (12-club league)—332 in 1969.
A.L. (10-club league)—281 in 1967, 1968.
A.L. (8-club league)—217 in 1943.

Fewest games won by one run, season

A.L. (8-club league)—157 in 1938.
A.L. (12-club league)—279 in 1973.
A.L. (14-club league)—280 in 1998 (includes interleague games).
N.L. (8-club league)—170 in 1949.
N.L. (12-club league)—294 in 1970.
N.L. (14-club league)—351 in 1996.
N.L. (16-club league)—355 in 2001.

Most games won by one run, one day

A.L.—6—May 30, 1967 (10 games); August 22, 1967 (nine games).
N.L.—6—June 6, 1967 (seven games); June 8, 1969 (six games).

Most games won by one run both leagues, one day

10 on May 30, 1967, A.L. 6 (10 games), N.L. 4 (seven games).

ATTENDANCE

Highest attendance, season

N.L. (16-club league)—39,851,427 in 2000.
N.L. (14-club league)—36,923,856 in 1993.
N.L. (12-club league)—25,323,834 in 1989.
N.L. (10-club league)—15,015,471 in 1966.
N.L. (8-club league)—10,684,963 in 1960.
A.L. (14-club league)—33,332,603 in 1993.
A.L. (12-club league)—14,657,802 in 1976.
A.L. (10-club league)—11,336,923 in 1967.
A.L. (8-club league)—11,150,099 in 1948.

NON-PLAYING PERSONNEL

MANAGERS
INDIVIDUAL

Most years as manager
M.L.—53—Connie Mack, Pittsburgh N.L. (1894 through 1896), Philadelphia A.L. (1901 through 1950).
A.L.—50—Connie Mack, Philadelphia, 1901 through 1950.
N.L.—32—John McGraw, Baltimore, 1899; New York, 1902 through 1932.

Most clubs managed, career
M.L.—7—Frank Bancroft, Worcester N.L., Detroit N.L., Cleveland N.L., Providence N.L., Philadelphia A.A., Indianapolis N.L., Cincinnati N.L.
M.L. since 1900—6
 Jimmie Dykes, Chicago A.L., Philadelphia A.L., Baltimore A.L., Cincinnati N.L., Detroit A.L., Cleveland A.L.
 Dick Williams, Boston A.L., Oakland A.L., California A.L., Montreal N.L., San Diego N.L., Seattle A.L.
 John McNamara, Oakland A.L., San Diego N.L., Cincinnati N.L., California A.L., Boston A.L., Cleveland A.L.
N.L.—6—Frank Bancroft, Worcester, Detroit, Cleveland, Providence, Indianapolis, Cincinnati.
N.L. since 1900—4
 Bill McKechnie, Pittsburgh, St. Louis, Boston, Cincinnati.
 Rogers Hornsby, St. Louis, Chicago, Boston, Cincinnati.
 Leo Durocher, Brooklyn, New York, Chicago, Houston.
A.L.—5
 Jimmie Dykes, Chicago, Philadelphia, Baltimore, Detroit, Cleveland.
 Billy Martin, Minnesota, Detroit, Texas, New York, Oakland.

Most clubs managed in one season
U.A.—2—Ted Sullivan, St. Louis, Kansas City, 1884.
A.A.—2—Billy Barnie, Baltimore, Philadelphia, 1891.
N.L.—2
 Leo Durocher, Brooklyn, New York, 1948.
 Leo Durocher, Chicago, Houston, 1972.
A.L.—2
 Jimmie Dykes, Detroit, Cleveland, 1960.
 Joe Gordon, Cleveland, Detroit, 1960.
 Billy Martin, Detroit, Texas, 1973.
 Billy Martin, Texas, New York, 1975.
 Bob Lemon, Chicago, New York, 1978.
 Tony La Russa, Chicago, Oakland, 1986.

Most clubs managed in different major leagues, season
2—Joe Battin, 1884 (Pittsburgh A.A., Pittsburgh U.A.).
 Bill Watkins, 1888 (Detroit N.L., Kansas City A.A.).
 Gus Schmelz, 1890 (Cleveland N.L., Columbus A.A.).
 John McGraw, 1902 (Baltimore A.L., New York N.L.).
 Rogers Hornsby, 1952 (St. Louis A.L., Cincinnati N.L.).
 Bill Virdon, 1975 (New York A.L., Houston N.L.).
 Pat Corrales, 1983 (Philadelphia N.L., Cleveland A.L.).
 Buck Rodgers, 1991 (Montreal N.L., California A.L.).

Most different times as manager for one major league club
A.L.—5—Billy Martin, New York, 1975 (part) through 1978 (part), 1979 (part), 1983 (complete), 1985 (part), 1988 (part).
N.L.—4—Danny Murtaugh, Pittsburgh, 1957 (part) through 1964; 1967 (part), 1970 through 1971, 1973 (part) through 1976.

Most years managing championship club, league
N.L.—10—John McGraw, New York, 1904, 1905, 1911, 1912, 1913, 1917, 1921, 1922, 1923, 1924.
A.L.—10—Casey Stengel, New York, 1949, 1950, 1951, 1952, 1953, 1955, 1956, 1957, 1958, 1960.

Most consecutive years as championship manager
A.L.—5—Casey Stengel, New York, 1949 through 1953 (first five years as New York manager).
A.A.—4—Charlie Comiskey, St. Louis, 1885 through 1888.
N.L.—4—John McGraw, New York, 1921 through 1924.

Most years managed without winning championship, career
M.L.—26—Gene Mauch, Philadelphia N.L., 1960 to 1968; Montreal N.L., 1969 through 1975; Minnesota A.L., 1976 to 1980; California A.L., 1981 through 1982, 1985 through 1987.
A.L.—20—Jimmie Dykes, Chicago, 1934 through 1946, Philadelphia, 1951 through 1953, Baltimore, 1954, Detroit, 1959, 1960, Cleveland, 1960, 1961.
N.L.—16—Gene Mauch, Philadelphia, 1960 to 1968; Montreal, 1969 through 1975.

Most consecutive years managed without winning championship
M.L.—23—Gene Mauch, Philadelphia N.L., 1960 to 1968; Montreal N.L., 1969 through 1975; Minnesota A.L., 1976 to 1980; California A.L., 1981 through 1982.
A.L.—19—Connie Mack, Philadelphia, 1932 through 1950.
N.L.—16—Gene Mauch, Philadelphia, 1960 to 1968; Montreal, 1969 through 1975.

Youngest manager to start season
Lou Boudreau, Cleveland A.L., appointed November 25, 1941; 24 years, 4 months, 8 days when appointed.

Youngest manager to finish season
Roger Peckinpaugh, New York A.L., appointed September 16, 1914; 23 years, 7 months, 11 days.

Oldest to make debut as manager
Tom Sheehan, San Francisco N.L., appointed June 18, 1960; 66 years, 2 months, 18 days.

CLUB

Most managers on one club, season
A.A.—7—Louisville, 1889.
N.L.—4
 Washington, 1892, 1898.
 St. Louis, 1895, 1896, 1897, 1980.
 Chicago, 1961.
A.L.—4—Texas, 1977.

LEAGUE

Most managers, season (since 1900)
A.L. (14-club league)—19 in 1977, 1981, 1986 (Tony La Russa, Chicago, Oakland, counted as one), 1988.
A.L. (12-club league)—16 in 1969, 1975.
A.L. (10-club league)—15 in 1966.
A.L. (8-club league)—12 in 1933, 1946.
N.L. (12-club league)—16 in 1972, 1991 (Leo Durocher, Chicago, Houston, counted as one in 1972).
N.L. (14-club league)—16 in 1993.
N.L. (16-club league)—18 in 2001.
N.L. (8-club league)—12 in 1902, 1948 (Leo Durocher, Brooklyn, New York, counted as one in 1948).
N.L. (10-club league)—12 in 1965, 1966, 1967, 1968.

Most player/managers in both leagues, season
10 in 1934 (8-club leagues)—6 in N.L., 4 in A.L.

Most managerial changes, start of season
A.L.—6 in 1955.
N.L.—5 in 2001.

UMPIRES

Most years umpired
N.L.—37—Bill Klem, 1905 through 1941.
A.L.—31—Tommy Connolly, 1901 through 1931 (also umpired three years in the National League, 1898 through 1900).

Longest game, plate umpire by time
A.L.—8 hours, 6 minutes—Jim Evans, Milwaukee at Chicago, May 8, 1984, finished May 9 (Chicago won 7-6.)
N.L.—7 hours, 23 minutes—Ed Sudol, San Francisco at New York, May 31, 1964, second game, 23 innings (San Francisco won 8-6).

YEARLY LEADERS

PENNANT WINNERS
AMERICAN LEAGUE

Year	Club	Manager	W	L	Pct.	*GA
1901	Chicago	Clark Griffith	83	53	.610	4.0
1902	Philadelphia	Connie Mack	83	53	.610	5.0
1903	Boston	Jimmy Collins	91	47	.659	14.5
1904	Boston	Jimmy Collins	95	59	.617	1.5
1905	Philadelphia	Connie Mack	92	56	.622	2.0
1906	Chicago	Fielder Jones	93	58	.616	3.0
1907	Detroit	Hughey Jennings	92	58	.613	1.5
1908	Detroit	Hughey Jennings	90	63	.588	0.5
1909	Detroit	Hughey Jennings	98	54	.645	3.5
1910	Philadelphia	Connie Mack	102	48	.680	14.5
1911	Philadelphia	Connie Mack	101	50	.669	13.5
1912	Boston	Jake Stahl	105	47	.691	14.0
1913	Philadelphia	Connie Mack	96	57	.627	6.5
1914	Philadelphia	Connie Mack	99	53	.651	8.5
1915	Boston	Bill Carrigan	101	50	.669	2.5
1916	Boston	Bill Carrigan	91	63	.591	2.0
1917	Chicago	Pants Rowland	100	54	.649	9.0
1918	Boston	Ed Barrow	75	51	.595	1.5
1919	Chicago	Kid Gleason	88	52	.629	3.5
1920	Cleveland	Tris Speaker	98	56	.636	2.0
1921	New York	Miller Huggins	98	55	.641	4.5
1922	New York	Miller Huggins	94	60	.610	1.0
1923	New York	Miller Huggins	98	54	.645	16.0
1924	Washington	Bucky Harris	92	62	.597	2.0
1925	Washington	Bucky Harris	96	55	.636	8.5
1926	New York	Miller Huggins	91	63	.591	3.0
1927	New York	Miller Huggins	110	44	.714	19.0
1928	New York	Miller Huggins	101	53	.656	2.5
1929	Philadelphia	Connie Mack	104	46	.693	18.0
1930	Philadelphia	Connie Mack	102	52	.662	8.0
1931	Philadelphia	Connie Mack	107	45	.704	13.5
1932	New York	Joe McCarthy	107	47	.695	13.0
1933	Washington	Joe Cronin	99	53	.651	7.0
1934	Detroit	Mickey Cochrane	101	53	.656	7.0
1935	Detroit	Mickey Cochrane	93	58	.616	3.0
1936	New York	Joe McCarthy	102	51	.667	19.5
1937	New York	Joe McCarthy	102	52	.662	13.0
1938	New York	Joe McCarthy	99	53	.651	9.5
1939	New York	Joe McCarthy	106	45	.702	17.0
1940	Detroit	Del Baker	90	64	.584	1.0
1941	New York	Joe McCarthy	101	53	.656	17.0
1942	New York	Joe McCarthy	103	51	.669	9.0
1943	New York	Joe McCarthy	98	56	.636	13.5
1944	St. Louis	Luke Sewell	89	65	.578	1.0
1945	Detroit	Steve O'Neill	88	65	.575	1.5
1946	Boston	Joe Cronin	104	50	.675	12.0
1947	New York	Bucky Harris	97	57	.630	12.0
1948	Cleveland†	Lou Boudreau	97	58	.626	1.0
1949	New York	Casey Stengel	97	57	.630	1.0
1950	New York	Casey Stengel	98	56	.636	3.0
1951	New York	Casey Stengel	98	56	.636	5.0
1952	New York	Casey Stengel	95	59	.617	2.0
1953	New York	Casey Stengel	99	52	.656	8.5
1954	Cleveland	Al Lopez	111	43	.721	8.0
1955	New York	Casey Stengel	96	58	.623	3.0
1956	New York	Casey Stengel	97	57	.630	9.0
1957	New York	Casey Stengel	98	56	.636	8.0
1958	New York	Casey Stengel	92	62	.597	10.0
1959	Chicago	Al Lopez	94	60	.610	5.0
1960	New York	Casey Stengel	97	57	.630	8.0
1961	New York	Ralph Houk	109	53	.673	8.0
1962	New York	Ralph Houk	96	66	.593	5.0
1963	New York	Ralph Houk	104	57	.646	10.5
1964	New York	Yogi Berra	99	63	.611	1.0
1965	Minnesota	Sam Mele	102	60	.630	7.0
1966	Baltimore	Hank Bauer	97	63	.606	9.0
1967	Boston	Dick Williams	92	70	.568	1.0
1968	Detroit	Mayo Smith	103	59	.636	12.0
1969	Baltimore (E)	Earl Weaver	109	53	.673	19.0
1970	Baltimore (E)	Earl Weaver	108	54	.667	15.0

Year	Club	Manager	W	L	Pct.	*GA
1971	Baltimore (E)	Earl Weaver	101	57	.639	12.0
1972	Oakland (W)	Dick Williams	93	62	.600	5.5
1973	Oakland (W)	Dick Williams	94	68	.580	6.0
1974	Oakland (W)	Alvin Dark	90	72	.556	5.0
1975	Boston (E)	Darrell Johnson	95	65	.594	4.5
1976	New York (E)	Billy Martin	97	62	.610	10.5
1977	New York (E)	Billy Martin	100	62	.617	2.5
1978	New York (E)‡	Billy Martin, Bob Lemon	100	63	.613	1.0
1979	Baltimore (E)	Earl Weaver	102	57	.642	8.0
1980	Kansas City (W)	Jim Frey	97	65	.599	14.0
1981	New York (E)	Gene Michael, Bob Lemon	59	48	.551	§
1982	Milwaukee (E)	Buck Rodgers, Harvey Kuenn	95	67	.586	1.0
1983	Baltimore (E)	Joe Altobelli	98	64	.605	6.0
1984	Detroit (E)	Sparky Anderson	104	58	.642	15.0
1985	Kansas City (W)	Dick Howser	91	71	.562	1.0
1986	Boston (E)	John McNamara	95	66	.590	5.5
1987	Minnesota (W)	Tom Kelly	85	77	.525	2.0
1988	Oakland (W)	Tony La Russa	104	58	.642	13.0
1989	Oakland (W)	Tony La Russa	99	63	.611	7.0
1990	Oakland (W)	Tony La Russa	103	59	.636	9.0
1991	Minnesota (W)	Tom Kelly	95	67	.586	8.0
1992	Toronto (E)	Cito Gaston	96	66	.593	4.0
1993	Toronto (E)	Cito Gaston	95	67	.586	7.0
1994	No pennant winner.∞					
1995	Cleveland (C)	Mike Hargrove	100	44	.694	30.0
1996	New York (E)	Joe Torre	92	70	.568	4.0
1997	Cleveland (C)	Mike Hargrove	86	75	.534	6.0
1998	New York (E)	Joe Torre	114	48	.704	22.0
1999	New York (E)	Joe Torre	98	64	.605	4.0
2000	New York (E)	Joe Torre	87	74	.540	2.5
2001	New York (E)	Joe Torre	95	65	.594	13.5

*Games ahead of second-place club. †Defeated Boston in one-game playoff. ‡Defeated Boston in one-game playoff to win division. §First half 34-22; second 25-26. ∞New York finished the strike-shortened season with the league's best record (70-43; .619).

NATIONAL LEAGUE

Year	Club	Manager	W	L	Pct.	*GA
1876	Chicago	Al Spalding	52	14	.788	6.0
1877	Boston	Harry Wright	31	17	.646	3.0
1878	Boston	Harry Wright	41	19	.683	4.0
1879	Providence	George Wright	55	23	.705	6.0
1880	Chicago	Cap Anson	67	17	.798	15.0
1881	Chicago	Cap Anson	56	28	.667	9.0
1882	Chicago	Cap Anson	55	29	.655	3.0
1883	Boston	John Morrill	63	35	.643	4.0
1884	Providence	Frank Bancroft	84	28	.750	10.5
1885	Chicago	Cap Anson	87	25	.777	2.0
1886	Chicago	Cap Anson	90	34	.726	2.5
1887	Detroit	Bill Watkins	79	45	.637	3.5
1888	New York	Jim Mutrie	84	47	.641	9.0
1889	New York	Jim Mutrie	83	43	.659	1.0
1890	Brooklyn	Bill McGunnigle	86	43	.667	6.5
1891	Boston	Frank Selee	87	51	.630	3.5
1892	Boston	Frank Selee	102	48	.680	8.5
1893	Boston	Frank Selee	86	43	.667	5.0
1894	Baltimore	Ned Hanlon	89	39	.695	3.0
1895	Baltimore	Ned Hanlon	87	43	.669	3.0
1896	Baltimore	Ned Hanlon	90	39	.698	9.5
1897	Boston	Frank Selee	93	39	.705	2.0
1898	Boston	Frank Selee	102	47	.685	6.0
1899	Brooklyn	Ned Hanlon	88	42	.677	4.0
1900	Brooklyn	Ned Hanlon	82	54	.603	4.5
1901	Pittsburgh	Fred Clarke	90	49	.647	7.5
1902	Pittsburgh	Fred Clarke	103	36	.741	27.5
1903	Pittsburgh	Fred Clarke	91	49	.650	6.5
1904	New York	John McGraw	106	47	.693	13.0
1905	New York	John McGraw	105	48	.686	9.0
1906	Chicago	Frank Chance	116	36	.763	20.0
1907	Chicago	Frank Chance	107	45	.704	17.0
1908	Chicago	Frank Chance	99	55	.643	1.0
1909	Pittsburgh	Fred Clarke	110	42	.724	6.5
1910	Chicago	Frank Chance	104	50	.675	13.0
1911	New York	John McGraw	99	54	.647	7.5
1912	New York	John McGraw	103	48	.682	10.0
1913	New York	John McGraw	101	51	.664	12.5
1914	Boston	George Stallings	94	59	.614	10.5
1915	Philadelphia	Pat Moran	90	62	.592	7.0

Year	Club	Manager	W	L	Pct.	*GA
1916	Brooklyn	Wilbert Robinson	94	60	.610	2.5
1917	New York	John McGraw	98	56	.636	10.0
1918	Chicago	Fred Mitchell	84	45	.651	10.5
1919	Cincinnati	Pat Moran	96	44	.686	9.0
1920	Brooklyn	Wilbert Robinson	93	61	.604	7.0
1921	New York	John McGraw	94	59	.614	4.0
1922	New York	John McGraw	93	61	.604	7.0
1923	New York	John McGraw	95	58	.621	4.5
1924	New York	John McGraw	93	60	.608	1.5
1925	Pittsburgh	Bill McKechnie	95	58	.621	8.5
1926	St. Louis	Rogers Hornsby	89	65	.578	2.0
1927	Pittsburgh	Donie Bush	94	60	.610	1.5
1928	St. Louis	Bill McKechnie	95	59	.617	2.0
1929	Chicago	Joe McCarthy	98	54	.645	10.5
1930	St. Louis	Gabby Street	92	62	.597	2.0
1931	St. Louis	Gabby Street	101	53	.656	13.0
1932	Chicago	Charlie Grimm	90	64	.584	4.0
1933	New York	Bill Terry	91	61	.599	5.0
1934	St. Louis	Frankie Frisch	95	58	.621	2.0
1935	Chicago	Charlie Grimm	100	54	.649	4.0
1936	New York	Bill Terry	92	62	.597	5.0
1937	New York	Bill Terry	95	57	.625	3.0
1938	Chicago	Gabby Hartnett	89	63	.586	2.0
1939	Cincinnati	Bill McKechnie	97	57	.630	4.5
1940	Cincinnati	Bill McKechnie	100	53	.654	12.0
1941	Brooklyn	Leo Durocher	100	54	.649	2.5
1942	St. Louis	Billy Southworth	106	48	.688	2.0
1943	St. Louis	Billy Southworth	105	49	.682	18.0
1944	St. Louis	Billy Southworth	105	49	.682	14.5
1945	Chicago	Charlie Grimm	98	56	.636	3.0
1946	St. Louis†	Eddie Dyer	98	58	.628	2.0
1947	Brooklyn	Burt Shotton	94	60	.610	5.0
1948	Boston	Billy Southworth	91	62	.595	6.5
1949	Brooklyn	Burt Shotton	97	57	.630	1.0
1950	Philadelphia	Eddie Sawyer	91	63	.591	2.0
1951	New York‡	Leo Durocher	98	59	.624	1.0
1952	Brooklyn	Charlie Dressen	96	57	.627	4.5
1953	Brooklyn	Charlie Dressen	105	49	.682	13.0
1954	New York	Leo Durocher	97	57	.630	5.0
1955	Brooklyn	Walter Alston	98	55	.641	13.5
1956	Brooklyn	Walter Alston	93	61	.604	1.0
1957	Milwaukee	Fred Haney	95	59	.617	8.0
1958	Milwaukee	Fred Haney	92	62	.597	8.0
1959	Los Angeles§	Walter Alston	88	68	.564	2.0
1960	Pittsburgh	Danny Murtaugh	95	59	.617	7.0
1961	Cincinnati	Fred Hutchinson	93	61	.604	4.0
1962	San Francisco∞	Alvin Dark	103	62	.624	1.0
1963	Los Angeles	Walter Alston	99	63	.611	6.0
1964	St. Louis	Johnny Keane	93	69	.574	1.0
1965	Los Angeles	Walter Alston	97	65	.599	2.0
1966	Los Angeles	Walter Alston	95	67	.586	1.5
1967	St. Louis	Red Schoendienst	101	60	.627	10.5
1968	St. Louis	Red Schoendienst	97	65	.599	9.0
1969	New York (E)	Gil Hodges	100	62	.617	8.0
1970	Cincinnati (W)	Sparky Anderson	102	60	.630	14.5
1971	Pittsburgh (E)	Danny Murtaugh	97	65	.599	7.0
1972	Cincinnati (W)	Sparky Anderson	95	59	.617	10.5
1973	New York (E)	Yogi Berra	82	79	.509	1.5
1974	Los Angeles (W)	Walter Alston	102	60	.630	4.0
1975	Cincinnati (W)	Sparky Anderson	108	54	.667	20.0
1976	Cincinnati (W)	Sparky Anderson	102	60	.630	10.0
1977	Los Angeles (W)	Tommy Lasorda	98	64	.605	10.0
1978	Los Angeles (W)	Tommy Lasorda	95	67	.586	2.5
1979	Pittsburgh (E)	Chuck Tanner	98	64	.605	2.0
1980	Philadelphia (E)	Dallas Green	91	71	.562	1.0
1981	Los Angeles (W)	Tommy Lasorda	63	47	.573	▲
1982	St. Louis (E)	Whitey Herzog	92	70	.568	3.0
1983	Philadelphia (E)	Pat Corrales, Paul Owens	90	72	.556	6.0
1984	San Diego (W)	Dick Williams	92	70	.568	12.0
1985	St. Louis (E)	Whitey Herzog	101	61	.623	3.0
1986	New York (E)	Dave Johnson	108	54	.667	21.5
1987	St. Louis (E)	Whitey Herzog	95	67	.586	3.0
1988	Los Angeles (W)	Tommy Lasorda	94	67	.584	7.0
1989	San Francisco (W)	Roger Craig	92	70	.568	3.0
1990	Cincinnati (W)	Lou Piniella	91	71	.562	5.0
1991	Atlanta (W)	Bobby Cox	94	68	.580	1.0
1992	Atlanta (W)	Bobby Cox	98	64	.605	8.0
1993	Philadelphia (E)	Jim Fregosi	97	65	.599	3.0

Year	Club	Manager	W	L	Pct.	*GA
1994	No pennant winner.◆					
1995	Atlanta (E)	Bobby Cox	90	54	.625	21.0
1996	Atlanta (E)	Bobby Cox	96	66	.593	8.0
1997	Florida (E)	Jim Leyland	92	70	.568	■ 9.0
1998	San Diego (W)	Bruce Bochy	98	64	.605	9.5
1999	Atlanta (E)	Bobby Cox	103	59	.636	6.5
2000	New York (E)	Bobby Valentine	94	68	.580	■1.0
2001	Arizona (W)	Bob Brenly	92	70	.568	2.0

*Games ahead of second-place club. †Defeated Brooklyn, two games to none, in playoff for pennant. ‡Defeated Brooklyn, two games to one, in playoff for pennant. §Defeated Milwaukee, two games to none, in playoff for pennant. ∞Defeated Los Angeles, two games to one, in playoff for pennant. ▲First half 36-21; second half 27-26. ◆Montreal finished the strike-shortened season with the league's best record (74-40; .649). ■ Wild-card team (games behind; team did not finish in first place).

BATTING

BATTING AVERAGE

AMERICAN LEAGUE

Year	Player, Club	Avg.
1901	Nap Lajoie, Philadelphia	.422
1902	Ed Delahanty, Washington	.376
1903	Nap Lajoie, Cleveland	.355
1904	Nap Lajoie, Cleveland	.381
1905	Elmer Flick, Cleveland	.308
1906	George Stone, St. Louis	.358
1907	Ty Cobb, Detroit	.350
1908	Ty Cobb, Detroit	.324
1909	Ty Cobb, Detroit	.377
1910	Ty Cobb, Detroit	.385
1911	Ty Cobb, Detroit	.420
1912	Ty Cobb, Detroit	.410
1913	Ty Cobb, Detroit	.390
1914	Ty Cobb, Detroit	.368
1915	Ty Cobb, Detroit	.369
1916	Tris Speaker, Cleveland	.386
1917	Ty Cobb, Detroit	.383
1918	Ty Cobb, Detroit	.382
1919	Ty Cobb, Detroit	.384
1920	George Sisler, St. Louis	.407
1921	Harry Heilmann, Detroit	.394
1922	George Sisler, St. Louis	.420
1923	Harry Heilmann, Detroit	.403
1924	Babe Ruth, New York	.378
1925	Harry Heilmann, Detroit	.393
1926	Heinie Manush, Detroit	.378
1927	Harry Heilmann, Detroit	.398
1928	Goose Goslin, Washington	.379
1929	Lew Fonseca, Cleveland	.369
1930	Al Simmons, Philadelphia	.381
1931	Al Simmons, Philadelphia	.390
1932	Dale Alexander, Detroit/Boston	.367
1933	Jimmie Foxx, Philadelphia	.356
1934	Lou Gehrig, New York	.363
1935	Buddy Myer, Washington	.349
1936	Luke Appling, Chicago	.388
1937	Charlie Gehringer, Detroit	.371
1938	Jimmie Foxx, Boston	.349
1939	Joe DiMaggio, New York	.381
1940	Joe DiMaggio, New York	.352
1941	Ted Williams, Boston	.406
1942	Ted Williams, Boston	.356
1943	Luke Appling, Chicago	.328
1944	Lou Boudreau, Cleveland	.327
1945	George Stirnweiss, New York	.309
1946	Mickey Vernon, Washington	.353
1947	Ted Williams, Boston	.343
1948	Ted Williams, Boston	.369
1949	George Kell, Detroit	.343
1950	Billy Goodman, Boston	.354
1951	Ferris Fain, Philadelphia	.344
1952	Ferris Fain, Philadelphia	.327
1953	Mickey Vernon, Washington	.337
1954	Bobby Avila, Cleveland	.341
1955	Al Kaline, Detroit	.340
1956	Mickey Mantle, New York	.353

Year	Player, Club	Avg.
1957	Ted Williams, Boston	.388
1958	Ted Williams, Boston	.328
1959	Harvey Kuenn, Detroit	.353
1960	Pete Runnels, Boston	.320
1961	Norm Cash, Detroit	.361
1962	Pete Runnels, Boston	.326
1963	Carl Yastrzemski, Boston	.321
1964	Tony Oliva, Minnesota	.323
1965	Tony Oliva, Minnesota	.321
1966	Frank Robinson, Baltimore	.316
1967	Carl Yastrzemski, Boston	.326
1968	Carl Yastrzemski, Boston	.301
1969	Rod Carew, Minnesota	.332
1970	Alex Johnson, California	.329
1971	Tony Oliva, Minnesota	.337
1972	Rod Carew, Minnesota	.318
1973	Rod Carew, Minnesota	.350
1974	Rod Carew, Minnesota	.364
1975	Rod Carew, Minnesota	.359
1976	George Brett, Kansas City	.333
1977	Rod Carew, Minnesota	.388
1978	Rod Carew, Minnesota	.333
1979	Fred Lynn, Boston	.333
1980	George Brett, Kansas City	.390
1981	Carney Lansford, Boston	.336
1982	Willie Wilson, Kansas City	.332
1983	Wade Boggs, Boston	.361
1984	Don Mattingly, New York	.343
1985	Wade Boggs, Boston	.368
1986	Wade Boggs, Boston	.357
1987	Wade Boggs, Boston	.363
1988	Wade Boggs, Boston	.366
1989	Kirby Puckett, Minnesota	.339
1990	George Brett, Kansas City	.329
1991	Julio Franco, Texas	.341
1992	Edgar Martinez, Seattle	.343
1993	John Olerud, Toronto	.363
1994	Paul O'Neill, New York	.359
1995	Edgar Martinez, Seattle	.356
1996	Alex Rodriguez, Seattle	.358
1997	Frank Thomas, Chicago	.347
1998	Bernie Williams, New York	.339
1999	Nomar Garciaparra, Boston	.357
2000	Nomar Garciaparra, Boston	.372
2001	Ichiro Suzuki, Seattle	.350

NATIONAL LEAGUE

Year	Player, Club	Avg.
1876	Ross Barnes, Chicago	.404
1877	Deacon White, Boston	.385
1878	Abner Dalrymple, Milwaukee	.356
1879	Cap Anson, Chicago	.407
1880	George Gore, Chicago	.365
1881	Cap Anson, Chicago	.399
1882	Dan Brouthers, Buffalo	.367
1883	Dan Brouthers, Buffalo	.371
1884	Jim O'Rourke, Buffalo	.350
1885	Roger Connor, New York	.371
1886	King Kelly, Chicago	.388
1887	Cap Anson, Chicago	.421
1888	Cap Anson, Chicago	.343
1889	Dan Brouthers, Boston	.373

Year	Player, Club	Avg.
1890	Jack Glasscock, New York	.336
1891	Billy Hamilton, Philadelphia	.338
1892	Dan Brouthers, Brooklyn	.335
	Cupid Childs, Cleveland	.335
1893	Hugh Duffy, Boston	.378
1894	Hugh Duffy, Boston	.438
1895	Jesse Burkett, Cleveland	.423
1896	Jesse Burkett, Cleveland	.410
1897	Willie Keeler, Baltimore	.432
1898	Willie Keeler, Baltimore	.379
1899	Ed Delahanty, Philadelphia	.408
1900	Honus Wagner, Pittsburgh	.381
1901	Jesse Burkett, St. Louis	.382
1902	Ginger Beaumont, Pittsburgh	.357
1903	Honus Wagner, Pittsburgh	.355
1904	Honus Wagner, Pittsburgh	.349
1905	Cy Seymour, Cincinnati	.377
1906	Honus Wagner, Pittsburgh	.339
1907	Honus Wagner, Pittsburgh	.350
1908	Honus Wagner, Pittsburgh	.354
1909	Honus Wagner, Pittsburgh	.339
1910	Sherry Magee, Philadelphia	.331
1911	Honus Wagner, Pittsburgh	.334
1912	Heinie Zimmerman, Chicago	.372
1913	Jake Daubert, Brooklyn	.350
1914	Jake Daubert, Brooklyn	.329
1915	Larry Doyle, New York	.320
1916	Hal Chase, Cincinnati	.339
1917	Edd Roush, Cincinnati	.341
1918	Zack Wheat, Brooklyn	.335
1919	Edd Roush, Cincinnati	.321
1920	Rogers Hornsby, St. Louis	.370
1921	Rogers Hornsby, St. Louis	.397
1922	Rogers Hornsby, St. Louis	.401
1923	Rogers Hornsby, St. Louis	.384
1924	Rogers Hornsby, St. Louis	.424
1925	Rogers Hornsby, St. Louis	.403
1926	Bubbles Hargrave, Cincinnati	.353
1927	Paul Waner, Pittsburgh	.380
1928	Rogers Hornsby, Boston	.387
1929	Lefty O'Doul, Philadelphia	.398
1930	Bill Terry, New York	.401
1931	Chick Hafey, St. Louis	.349
1932	Lefty O'Doul, Brooklyn	.368
1933	Chuck Klein, Philadelphia	.368
1934	Paul Waner, Pittsburgh	.362
1935	Arky Vaughan, Pittsburgh	.385
1936	Paul Waner, Pittsburgh	.373
1937	Joe Medwick, St. Louis	.374
1938	Ernie Lombardi, Cincinnati	.342
1939	Johnny Mize, St. Louis	.349
1940	Debs Garms, Pittsburgh	.355
1941	Pete Reiser, Brooklyn	.343
1942	Ernie Lombardi, Boston	.330
1943	Stan Musial, St. Louis	.357
1944	Dixie Walker, Brooklyn	.357
1945	Phil Cavarretta, Chicago	.355
1946	Stan Musial, St. Louis	.365
1947	Harry Walker, St. Louis/Philadelphia	.363
1948	Stan Musial, St. Louis	.376
1949	Jackie Robinson, Brooklyn	.342
1950	Stan Musial, St. Louis	.346
1951	Stan Musial, St. Louis	.355
1952	Stan Musial, St. Louis	.336
1953	Carl Furillo, Brooklyn	.344
1954	Willie Mays, New York	.345
1955	Richie Ashburn, Philadelphia	.338
1956	Hank Aaron, Milwaukee	.328
1957	Stan Musial, St. Louis	.351
1958	Richie Ashburn, Philadelphia	.350
1959	Hank Aaron, Milwaukee	.355
1960	Dick Groat, Pittsburgh	.325
1961	Roberto Clemente, Pittsburgh	.351
1962	Tommy Davis, Los Angeles	.346
1963	Tommy Davis, Los Angeles	.326
1964	Roberto Clemente, Pittsburgh	.339
1965	Roberto Clemente, Pittsburgh	.329

Year	Player, Club	Avg.
1966	Matty Alou, Pittsburgh	.342
1967	Roberto Clemente, Pittsburgh	.357
1968	Pete Rose, Cincinnati	.335
1969	Pete Rose, Cincinnati	.348
1970	Rico Carty, Atlanta	.366
1971	Joe Torre, St. Louis	.363
1972	Billy Williams, Chicago	.333
1973	Pete Rose, Cincinnati	.338
1974	Ralph Garr, Atlanta	.353
1975	Bill Madlock, Chicago	.354
1976	Bill Madlock, Chicago	.339
1977	Dave Parker, Pittsburgh	.338
1978	Dave Parker, Pittsburgh	.334
1979	Keith Hernandez, St. Louis	.344
1980	Bill Buckner, Chicago	.324
1981	Bill Madlock, Pittsburgh	.341
1982	Al Oliver, Montreal	.331
1983	Bill Madlock, Pittsburgh	.323
1984	Tony Gwynn, San Diego	.351
1985	Willie McGee, St. Louis	.353
1986	Tim Raines Sr., Montreal	.334
1987	Tony Gwynn, San Diego	.370
1988	Tony Gwynn, San Diego	.313
1989	Tony Gwynn, San Diego	.336
1990	Willie McGee, St. Louis	*.335
1991	Terry Pendleton, Atlanta	.319
1992	Gary Sheffield, San Diego	.330
1993	Andres Galarraga, Colorado	.370
1994	Tony Gwynn, San Diego	.394
1995	Tony Gwynn, San Diego	.368
1996	Tony Gwynn, San Diego	†.353
1997	Tony Gwynn, San Diego	.372
1998	Larry Walker, Colorado	.363
1999	Larry Walker, Colorado	.379
2000	Todd Helton, Colorado	.372
2001	Larry Walker, Colorado	.350

Note—Bases on balls counted as hits in 1887.

*Eddie Murray of Los Angeles had the highest batting average in the majors in 1990 with a .330 mark. McGee won the N.L. title, but was traded to Oakland on August 29 and finished the season with a combined .324 average for both leagues.

†Gwynn's 498 plate appearances were four short of the qualifying mark. If, however, under Rule 10.23 (a), Gwynn were charged with four more at-bats, his subsequent batting average of .349 would still be higher than the next-highest mark of .344, achieved by Ellis Burks of Colorado.

SLUGGING AVERAGE

AMERICAN LEAGUE

Year	Player, Club	Slg. Avg.
1901	Nap Lajoie, Philadelphia	.635
1902	Ed Delahanty, Washington	.589
1903	Nap Lajoie, Cleveland	.533
1904	Nap Lajoie, Cleveland	.549
1905	Elmer Flick, Cleveland	.466
1906	George Stone, St. Louis	.496
1907	Ty Cobb, Detroit	.473
1908	Ty Cobb, Detroit	.475
1909	Ty Cobb, Detroit	.517
1910	Ty Cobb, Detroit	.554
1911	Ty Cobb, Detroit	.621
1912	Ty Cobb, Detroit	.586
1913	Joe Jackson, Cleveland	.551
1914	Ty Cobb, Detroit	.513
1915	Jack Fournier, Chicago	.491
1916	Tris Speaker, Cleveland	.502
1917	Ty Cobb, Detroit	.571
1918	Babe Ruth, Boston	.555
1919	Babe Ruth, Boston	.657
1920	Babe Ruth, New York	.847
1921	Babe Ruth, New York	.846
1922	Babe Ruth, New York	.672
1923	Babe Ruth, New York	.764
1924	Babe Ruth, New York	.739

Year	Player, Club	Slg. Avg.
1925	Ken Williams, St. Louis	.613
1926	Babe Ruth, New York	.737
1927	Babe Ruth, New York	.772
1928	Babe Ruth, New York	.709
1929	Babe Ruth, New York	.697
1930	Babe Ruth, New York	.732
1931	Babe Ruth, New York	.700
1932	Jimmie Foxx, Philadelphia	.749
1933	Jimmie Foxx, Philadelphia	.703
1934	Lou Gehrig, New York	.706
1935	Jimmie Foxx, Philadelphia	.636
1936	Lou Gehrig, New York	.696
1937	Joe DiMaggio, New York	.673
1938	Jimmie Foxx, Boston	.704
1939	Jimmie Foxx, Boston	.694
1940	Hank Greenberg, Detroit	.670
1941	Ted Williams, Boston	.735
1942	Ted Williams, Boston	.648
1943	Rudy York, Detroit	.527
1944	Bobby Doerr, Boston	.528
1945	George Stirnweiss, New York	.476
1946	Ted Williams, Boston	.667
1947	Ted Williams, Boston	.634
1948	Ted Williams, Boston	.615
1949	Ted Williams, Boston	.650
1950	Joe DiMaggio, New York	.585
1951	Ted Williams, Boston	.556
1952	Larry Doby, Cleveland	.541
1953	Al Rosen, Cleveland	.613
1954	Ted Williams, Boston	.635
1955	Mickey Mantle, New York	.611
1956	Mickey Mantle, New York	.705
1957	Ted Williams, Boston	.731
1958	Rocky Colavito, Cleveland	.620
1959	Al Kaline, Detroit	.530
1960	Roger Maris, New York	.581
1961	Mickey Mantle, New York	.687
1962	Mickey Mantle, New York	.605
1963	Harmon Killebrew, Minnesota	.555
1964	Boog Powell, Baltimore	.606
1965	Carl Yastrzemski, Boston	.536
1966	Frank Robinson, Baltimore	.637
1967	Carl Yastrzemski, Boston	.622
1968	Frank Howard, Washington	.552
1969	Reggie Jackson, Oakland	.608
1970	Carl Yastrzemski, Boston	.592
1971	Tony Oliva, Minnesota	.546
1972	Dick Allen, Chicago	.603
1973	Reggie Jackson, Oakland	.531
1974	Dick Allen, Chicago	.563
1975	Fred Lynn, Boston	.566
1976	Reggie Jackson, Baltimore	.502
1977	Jim Rice, Boston	.593
1978	Jim Rice, Boston	.600
1979	Fred Lynn, Boston	.637
1980	George Brett, Kansas City	.664
1981	Bobby Grich, California	.543
1982	Robin Yount, Milwaukee	.578
1983	George Brett, Kansas City	.563
1984	Harold Baines, Chicago	.541
1985	George Brett, Kansas City	.585
1986	Don Mattingly, New York	.573
1987	Mark McGwire, Oakland	.618
1988	Jose Canseco, Oakland	.569
1989	Ruben Sierra, Texas	.543
1990	Cecil Fielder, Detroit	.592
1991	Danny Tartabull, Kansas City	.593
1992	Mark McGwire, Oakland	.585
1993	Juan Gonzalez, Texas	.632
1994	Frank Thomas, Chicago	.729
1995	Albert Belle, Cleveland	.690
1996	Mark McGwire, Oakland	.730
1997	Ken Griffey Jr., Seattle	.646
1998	Albert Belle, Chicago	.655
1999	Manny Ramirez, Cleveland	.663
2000	Manny Ramirez, Cleveland	.697
2001	Jason Giambi, Oakland	.660

Year	Player, Club	Slg. Avg.
1900	Honus Wagner, Pittsburgh	.572
1901	Jimmy Sheckard, Brooklyn	.541
1902	Honus Wagner, Pittsburgh	.467
1903	Fred Clarke, Pittsburgh	.532
1904	Honus Wagner, Pittsburgh	.520
1905	Cy Seymour, Cincinnati	.559
1906	Harry Lumley, Brooklyn	.477
1907	Honus Wagner, Pittsburgh	.513
1908	Honus Wagner, Pittsburgh	.542
1909	Honus Wagner, Pittsburgh	.489
1910	Sherry Magee, Philadelphia	.507
1911	Frank Schulte, Chicago	.534
1912	Heinie Zimmerman, Chicago	.571
1913	Gavvy Cravath, Philadelphia	.568
1914	Sherry Magee, Philadelphia	.509
1915	Gavvy Cravath, Philadelphia	.510
1916	Zack Wheat, Brooklyn	.461
1917	Rogers Hornsby, St. Louis	.484
1918	Edd Roush, Cincinnati	.455
1919	Hy Myers, Brooklyn	.436
1920	Rogers Hornsby, St. Louis	.559
1921	Rogers Hornsby, St. Louis	.659
1922	Rogers Hornsby, St. Louis	.722
1923	Rogers Hornsby, St. Louis	.627
1924	Rogers Hornsby, St. Louis	.696
1925	Rogers Hornsby, St. Louis	.756
1926	Cy Williams, Philadelphia	.569
1927	Chick Hafey, St. Louis	.590
1928	Rogers Hornsby, Boston	.632
1929	Rogers Hornsby, Chicago	.679
1930	Hack Wilson, Chicago	.723
1931	Chuck Klein, Philadelphia	.584
1932	Chuck Klein, Philadelphia	.646
1933	Chuck Klein, Philadelphia	.602
1934	Rip Collins, St. Louis	.615
1935	Arky Vaughan, Pittsburgh	.607
1936	Mel Ott, New York	.588
1937	Joe Medwick, St. Louis	.641
1938	Johnny Mize, St. Louis	.614
1939	Johnny Mize, St. Louis	.626
1940	Johnny Mize, St. Louis	.636
1941	Pete Reiser, Brooklyn	.558
1942	Johnny Mize, New York	.521
1943	Stan Musial, St. Louis	.562
1944	Stan Musial, St. Louis	.549
1945	Tommy Holmes, Boston	.577
1946	Stan Musial, St. Louis	.587
1947	Ralph Kiner, Pittsburgh	.639
1948	Stan Musial, St. Louis	.702
1949	Ralph Kiner, Pittsburgh	.658
1950	Stan Musial, St. Louis	.596
1951	Ralph Kiner, Pittsburgh	.627
1952	Stan Musial, St. Louis	.538
1953	Duke Snider, Brooklyn	.627
1954	Willie Mays, New York	.667
1955	Willie Mays, New York	.659
1956	Duke Snider, Brooklyn	.598
1957	Willie Mays, New York	.626
1958	Ernie Banks, Chicago	.614
1959	Hank Aaron, Milwaukee	.636
1960	Frank Robinson, Cincinnati	.595
1961	Frank Robinson, Cincinnati	.611
1962	Frank Robinson, Cincinnati	.624
1963	Hank Aaron, Milwaukee	.586
1964	Willie Mays, San Francisco	.607
1965	Willie Mays, San Francisco	.645
1966	Dick Allen, Philadelphia	.632
1967	Hank Aaron, Atlanta	.573
1968	Willie McCovey, San Francisco	.545
1969	Willie McCovey, San Francisco	.656
1970	Willie McCovey, San Francisco	.612
1971	Hank Aaron, Atlanta	.669
1972	Billy Williams, Chicago	.606
1973	Willie Stargell, Pittsburgh	.646
1974	Mike Schmidt, Philadelphia	.546

Year	Player, Club	Slg. Avg.
1975	Dave Parker, Pittsburgh	.541
1976	Joe Morgan, Cincinnati	.576
1977	George Foster, Cincinnati	.631
1978	Dave Parker, Pittsburgh	.585
1979	Dave Kingman, Chicago	.613
1980	Mike Schmidt, Philadelphia	.624
1981	Mike Schmidt, Philadelphia	.644
1982	Mike Schmidt, Philadelphia	.547
1983	Dale Murphy, Atlanta	.540
1984	Dale Murphy, Atlanta	.547
1985	Pedro Guerrero, Los Angeles	.577
1986	Mike Schmidt, Philadelphia	.547
1987	Jack Clark, St. Louis	.597
1988	Darryl Strawberry, New York	.545
1989	Kevin Mitchell, San Francisco	.635
1990	Barry Bonds, Pittsburgh	.565
1991	Will Clark, San Francisco	.536
1992	Barry Bonds, Pittsburgh	.624
1993	Barry Bonds, San Francisco	.677
1994	Jeff Bagwell, Houston	.750
1995	Dante Bichette, Colorado	.620
1996	Ellis Burks, Colorado	.639
1997	Larry Walker, Colorado	.720
1998	Mark McGwire, St. Louis	.752
1999	Larry Walker, Colorado	.710
2000	Todd Helton, Colorado	.698
2001	Barry Bonds, San Francisco	.863

RUNS

AMERICAN LEAGUE

Year	Player, Club	No.
1901	Nap Lajoie, Philadelphia	145
1902	Dave Fultz, Philadelphia	110
1903	Patsy Dougherty, Boston	108
1904	Patsy Dougherty, Boston/New York	113
1905	Harry Davis, Philadelphia	92
1906	Elmer Flick, Cleveland	98
1907	Sam Crawford, Detroit	102
1908	Matty McIntyre, Detroit	105
1909	Ty Cobb, Detroit	116
1910	Ty Cobb, Detroit	106
1911	Ty Cobb, Detroit	147
1912	Eddie Collins, Philadelphia	137
1913	Eddie Collins, Philadelphia	125
1914	Eddie Collins, Philadelphia	122
1915	Ty Cobb, Detroit	144
1916	Ty Cobb, Detroit	113
1917	Donie Bush, Detroit	112
1918	Ray Chapman, Cleveland	84
1919	Babe Ruth, Boston	103
1920	Babe Ruth, New York	158
1921	Babe Ruth, New York	177
1922	George Sisler, St. Louis	134
1923	Babe Ruth, New York	151
1924	Babe Ruth, New York	143
1925	Johnny Mostil, Chicago	135
1926	Babe Ruth, New York	139
1927	Babe Ruth, New York	158
1928	Babe Ruth, New York	163
1929	Charlie Gehringer, Detroit	131
1930	Al Simmons, Philadelphia	152
1931	Lou Gehrig, New York	163
1932	Jimmie Foxx, Philadelphia	151
1933	Lou Gehrig, New York	138
1934	Charlie Gehringer, Detroit	134
1935	Lou Gehrig, New York	125
1936	Lou Gehrig, New York	167
1937	Joe DiMaggio, New York	151
1938	Hank Greenberg, Detroit	144
1939	Red Rolfe, New York	139
1940	Ted Williams, Boston	134
1941	Ted Williams, Boston	135
1942	Ted Williams, Boston	141
1943	George Case, Washington	102

Year	Player, Club	No.
1944	George Stirnweiss, New York	125
1945	George Stirnweiss, New York	107
1946	Ted Williams, Boston	142
1947	Ted Williams, Boston	125
1948	Tommy Henrich, New York	138
1949	Ted Williams, Boston	150
1950	Dom DiMaggio, Boston	131
1951	Dom DiMaggio, Boston	113
1952	Larry Doby, Cleveland	104
1953	Al Rosen, Cleveland	115
1954	Mickey Mantle, New York	129
1955	Al Smith, Cleveland	123
1956	Mickey Mantle, New York	132
1957	Mickey Mantle, New York	121
1958	Mickey Mantle, New York	127
1959	Eddie Yost, Detroit	115
1960	Mickey Mantle, New York	119
1961	Mickey Mantle, New York	132
	Roger Maris, New York	132
1962	Albie Pearson, Los Angeles	115
1963	Bob Allison, Minnesota	99
1964	Tony Oliva, Minnesota	109
1965	Zoilo Versalles, Minnesota	126
1966	Frank Robinson, Baltimore	122
1967	Carl Yastrzemski, Boston	112
1968	Dick McAuliffe, Detroit	95
1969	Reggie Jackson, Oakland	123
1970	Carl Yastrzemski, Boston	125
1971	Don Buford, Baltimore	99
1972	Bobby Murcer, New York	102
1973	Reggie Jackson, Oakland	99
1974	Carl Yastrzemski, Boston	93
1975	Fred Lynn, Boston	103
1976	Roy White, New York	104
1977	Rod Carew, Minnesota	128
1978	Ron LeFlore, Detroit	126
1979	Don Baylor, California	120
1980	Willie Wilson, Kansas City	133
1981	Rickey Henderson, Oakland	89
1982	Paul Molitor, Milwaukee	136
1983	Cal Ripken, Baltimore	121
1984	Dwight Evans, Boston	121
1985	Rickey Henderson, New York	146
1986	Rickey Henderson, New York	130
1987	Paul Molitor, Milwaukee	114
1988	Wade Boggs, Boston	128
1989	Wade Boggs, Boston	113
	Rickey Henderson, New York/Oakland	113
1990	Rickey Henderson, Oakland	119
1991	Paul Molitor, Milwaukee	133
1992	Tony Phillips, Detroit	114
1993	Rafael Palmeiro, Texas	124
1994	Frank Thomas, Chicago	106
1995	Albert Belle, Cleveland	121
	Edgar Martinez, Seattle	121
1996	Alex Rodriguez, Seattle	141
1997	Ken Griffey Jr., Seattle	125
1998	Derek Jeter, New York	127
1999	Roberto Alomar, Cleveland	138
2000	Johnny Damon, Kansas City	136
2001	Alex Rodriguez, Texas	133

NATIONAL LEAGUE

Year	Player, Club	No.
1900	Roy Thomas, Philadelphia	131
1901	Jesse Burkett, St. Louis	139
1902	Honus Wagner, Pittsburgh	105
1903	Ginger Beaumont, Pittsburgh	137
1904	George Browne, New York	99
1905	Mike Donlin, New York	124
1906	Honus Wagner, Pittsburgh	103
	Frank Chance, Chicago	103
1907	Spike Shannon, New York	104
1908	Fred Tenney, New York	101
1909	Tommy Leach, Pittsburgh	126
1910	Sherry Magee, Philadelphia	110
1911	Jimmy Sheckard, Chicago	121

Year	Player, Club	No.
1912	Bob Bescher, Cincinnati	120
1913	Tommy Leach, Chicago	99
	Max Carey, Pittsburgh	99
1914	George J. Burns, New York	100
1915	Gavvy Cravath, Philadelphia	89
1916	George J. Burns, New York	105
1917	George J. Burns, New York	103
1918	Heinie Groh, Cincinnati	88
1919	George J. Burns, New York	86
1920	George J. Burns, New York	115
1921	Rogers Hornsby, St. Louis	131
1922	Rogers Hornsby, St. Louis	141
1923	Ross Youngs, New York	121
1924	Frankie Frisch, New York	121
	Rogers Hornsby, St. Louis	121
1925	Kiki Cuyler, Pittsburgh	144
1926	Kiki Cuyler, Pittsburgh	113
1927	Lloyd Waner, Pittsburgh	133
	Rogers Hornsby, New York	133
1928	Paul Waner, Pittsburgh	142
1929	Rogers Hornsby, Chicago	156
1930	Chuck Klein, Philadelphia	158
1931	Bill Terry, New York	121
	Chuck Klein, Philadelphia	121
1932	Chuck Klein, Philadelphia	152
1933	Pepper Martin, St. Louis	122
1934	Paul Waner, Pittsburgh	122
1935	Augie Galan, Chicago	133
1936	Arky Vaughan, Pittsburgh	122
1937	Joe Medwick, St. Louis	111
1938	Mel Ott, New York	116
1939	Bill Werber, Cincinnati	115
1940	Arky Vaughan, Pittsburgh	113
1941	Pete Reiser, Brooklyn	117
1942	Mel Ott, New York	118
1943	Arky Vaughan, Brooklyn	112
1944	Bill Nicholson, Chicago	116
1945	Eddie Stanky, Brooklyn	128
1946	Stan Musial, St. Louis	124
1947	Johnny Mize, New York	137
1948	Stan Musial, St. Louis	135
1949	Pee Wee Reese, Brooklyn	132
1950	Earl Torgeson, Boston	120
1951	Stan Musial, St. Louis	124
	Ralph Kiner, Pittsburgh	124
1952	Stan Musial, St. Louis	105
	Solly Hemus, St. Louis	105
1953	Duke Snider, Brooklyn	132
1954	Stan Musial, St. Louis	120
	Duke Snider, Brooklyn	120
1955	Duke Snider, Brooklyn	126
1956	Frank Robinson, Cincinnati	122
1957	Hank Aaron, Milwaukee	118
1958	Willie Mays, San Francisco	121
1959	Vada Pinson, Cincinnati	131
1960	Billy Bruton, Milwaukee	112
1961	Willie Mays, San Francisco	129
1962	Frank Robinson, Cincinnati	134
1963	Hank Aaron, Milwaukee	121
1964	Dick Allen, Philadelphia	125
1965	Tommy Harper, Cincinnati	126
1966	Felipe Alou, Atlanta	122
1967	Hank Aaron, Atlanta	113
	Lou Brock, St. Louis	113
1968	Glenn Beckert, Chicago	98
1969	Bobby Bonds, San Francisco	120
	Pete Rose, Cincinnati	120
1970	Billy Williams, Chicago	137
1971	Lou Brock, St. Louis	126
1972	Joe Morgan, Cincinnati	122
1973	Bobby Bonds, San Francisco	131
1974	Pete Rose, Cincinnati	110
1975	Pete Rose, Cincinnati	112
1976	Pete Rose, Cincinnati	130
1977	George Foster, Cincinnati	124
1978	Ivan DeJesus, Chicago	104
1979	Keith Hernandez, St. Louis	116

Year	Player, Club	No.
1980	Keith Hernandez, St. Louis	111
1981	Mike Schmidt, Philadelphia	78
1982	Lonnie Smith, St. Louis	120
1983	Tim Raines Sr., Montreal	133
1984	Ryne Sandberg, Chicago	114
1985	Dale Murphy, Atlanta	118
1986	Tony Gwynn, San Diego	107
	Von Hayes, Philadelphia	107
1987	Tim Raines Sr., Montreal	123
1988	Brett Butler, San Francisco	109
1989	Will Clark, San Francisco	104
	Howard Johnson, New York	104
	Ryne Sandberg, Chicago	104
1990	Ryne Sandberg, Chicago	116
1991	Brett Butler, Los Angeles	112
1992	Barry Bonds, Pittsburgh	109
1993	Lenny Dykstra, Philadelphia	143
1994	Jeff Bagwell, Houston	104
1995	Craig Biggio, Houston	123
1996	Ellis Burks, Colorado	142
1997	Craig Biggio, Houston	146
1998	Sammy Sosa, Chicago	134
1999	Jeff Bagwell, Houston	143
2000	Jeff Bagwell, Houston	152
2001	Sammy Sosa, Chicago	146

HITS

AMERICAN LEAGUE

Year	Player, Club	No.
1901	Nap Lajoie, Philadelphia	229
1902	Charles Hickman, Boston/Cleveland	194
1903	Patsy Dougherty, Boston	195
1904	Nap Lajoie, Cleveland	211
1905	George Stone, St. Louis	187
1906	Nap Lajoie, Cleveland	214
1907	Ty Cobb, Detroit	212
1908	Ty Cobb, Detroit	188
1909	Ty Cobb, Detroit	216
1910	Nap Lajoie, Cleveland	227
1911	Ty Cobb, Detroit	248
1912	Ty Cobb, Detroit	227
1913	Joe Jackson, Cleveland	197
1914	Tris Speaker, Boston	193
1915	Ty Cobb, Detroit	208
1916	Tris Speaker, Cleveland	211
1917	Ty Cobb, Detroit	225
1918	George H. Burns, Philadelphia	178
1919	Ty Cobb, Detroit	191
	Bobby Veach, Detroit	191
1920	George Sisler, St. Louis	257
1921	Harry Heilmann, Detroit	237
1922	George Sisler, St. Louis	246
1923	Charlie Jamieson, Cleveland	222
1924	Sam Rice, Washington	216
1925	Al Simmons, Philadelphia	253
1926	George H. Burns, Cleveland	216
	Sam Rice, Washington	216
1927	Earle Combs, New York	231
1928	Heinie Manush, St. Louis	241
1929	Dale Alexander, Detroit	215
	Charlie Gehringer, Detroit	215
1930	Johnny Hodapp, Cleveland	225
1931	Lou Gehrig, New York	211
1932	Al Simmons, Philadelphia	216
1933	Heinie Manush, Washington	221
1934	Charlie Gehringer, Detroit	214
1935	Joe Vosmik, Cleveland	216
1936	Earl Averill Sr., Cleveland	232
1937	Beau Bell, St. Louis	218
1938	Joe Vosmik, Boston	201
1939	Red Rolfe, New York	213
1940	Rip Radcliff, St. Louis	200
	Barney McCosky, Detroit	200
	Doc Cramer, Boston	200
1941	Cecil Travis, Washington	218

Year	Player, Club	No.
1942	Johnny Pesky, Boston	205
1943	Dick Wakefield, Detroit	200
1944	George Stirnweiss, New York	205
1945	George Stirnweiss, New York	195
1946	Johnny Pesky, Boston	208
1947	Johnny Pesky, Boston	207
1948	Bob Dillinger, St. Louis	207
1949	Dale Mitchell, Cleveland	203
1950	George Kell, Detroit	218
1951	George Kell, Detroit	191
1952	Nellie Fox, Chicago	192
1953	Harvey Kuenn, Detroit	209
1954	Nellie Fox, Chicago	201
	Harvey Kuenn, Detroit	201
1955	Al Kaline, Detroit	200
1956	Harvey Kuenn, Detroit	196
1957	Nellie Fox, Chicago	196
1958	Nellie Fox, Chicago	187
1959	Harvey Kuenn, Detroit	198
1960	Minnie Minoso, Chicago	184
1961	Norm Cash, Detroit	193
1962	Bobby Richardson, New York	209
1963	Carl Yastrzemski, Boston	183
1964	Tony Oliva, Minnesota	217
1965	Tony Oliva, Minnesota	185
1966	Tony Oliva, Minnesota	191
1967	Carl Yastrzemski, Boston	189
1968	Bert Campaneris, Oakland	177
1969	Tony Oliva, Minnesota	197
1970	Tony Oliva, Minnesota	204
1971	Cesar Tovar, Minnesota	204
1972	Joe Rudi, Oakland	181
1973	Rod Carew, Minnesota	203
1974	Rod Carew, Minnesota	218
1975	George Brett, Kansas City	195
1976	George Brett, Kansas City	215
1977	Rod Carew, Minnesota	239
1978	Jim Rice, Boston	213
1979	George Brett, Kansas City	212
1980	Willie Wilson, Kansas City	230
1981	Rickey Henderson, Oakland	135
1982	Robin Yount, Milwaukee	210
1983	Cal Ripken, Baltimore	211
1984	Don Mattingly, New York	207
1985	Wade Boggs, Boston	240
1986	Don Mattingly, New York	238
1987	Kirby Puckett, Minnesota	207
	Kevin Seitzer, Kansas City	207
1988	Kirby Puckett, Minnesota	234
1989	Kirby Puckett, Minnesota	215
1990	Rafael Palmeiro, Texas	191
1991	Paul Molitor, Milwaukee	216
1992	Kirby Puckett, Minnesota	210
1993	Paul Molitor, Toronto	211
1994	Kenny Lofton, Cleveland	160
1995	Lance Johnson, Chicago	186
1996	Paul Molitor, Minnesota	225
1997	Nomar Garciaparra, Boston	209
1998	Alex Rodriguez, Seattle	213
1999	Derek Jeter, New York	219
2000	Darin Erstad, Anaheim	240
2001	Ichiro Suzuki, Seattle	242

NATIONAL LEAGUE

Year	Player, Club	No.
1900	Willie Keeler, Brooklyn	208
1901	Jesse Burkett, St. Louis	228
1902	Ginger Beaumont, Pittsburgh	194
1903	Ginger Beaumont, Pittsburgh	209
1904	Ginger Beaumont, Pittsburgh	185
1905	Cy Seymour, Cincinnati	219
1906	Harry Steinfeldt, Chicago	176
1907	Ginger Beaumont, Boston	187
1908	Honus Wagner, Pittsburgh	201
1909	Larry Doyle, New York	172
1910	Honus Wagner, Pittsburgh	178
	Bobby Byrne, Pittsburgh	178

Year	Player, Club	No.
1911	Doc Miller, Boston	192
1912	Heinie Zimmerman, Chicago	207
1913	Gavvy Cravath, Philadelphia	179
1914	Sherry Magee, Philadelphia	171
1915	Larry Doyle, New York	189
1916	Hal Chase, Cincinnati	184
1917	Heinie Groh, Cincinnati	182
1918	Charlie Hollocher, Chicago	161
1919	Ivy Olson, Brooklyn	164
1920	Rogers Hornsby, St. Louis	218
1921	Rogers Hornsby, St. Louis	235
1922	Rogers Hornsby, St. Louis	250
1923	Frankie Frisch, New York	223
1924	Rogers Hornsby, St. Louis	227
1925	Jim Bottomley, St. Louis	227
1926	Eddie Brown, Boston	201
1927	Paul Waner, Pittsburgh	237
1928	Fred Lindstrom, New York	231
1929	Lefty O'Doul, Philadelphia	254
1930	Bill Terry, New York	254
1931	Lloyd Waner, Pittsburgh	214
1932	Chuck Klein, Philadelphia	226
1933	Chuck Klein, Philadelphia	223
1934	Paul Waner, Pittsburgh	217
1935	Billy Herman, Chicago	227
1936	Joe Medwick, St. Louis	223
1937	Joe Medwick, St. Louis	237
1938	Frank McCormick, Cincinnati	209
1939	Frank McCormick, Cincinnati	209
1940	Stan Hack, Chicago	191
	Frank McCormick, Cincinnati	191
1941	Stan Hack, Chicago	186
1942	Enos Slaughter, St. Louis	188
1943	Stan Musial, St. Louis	220
1944	Stan Musial, St. Louis	197
	Phil Cavarretta, Chicago	197
1945	Tommy Holmes, Boston	224
1946	Stan Musial, St. Louis	228
1947	Tommy Holmes, Boston	191
1948	Stan Musial, St. Louis	230
1949	Stan Musial, St. Louis	207
1950	Duke Snider, Brooklyn	199
1951	Richie Ashburn, Philadelphia	221
1952	Stan Musial, St. Louis	194
1953	Richie Ashburn, Philadelphia	205
1954	Don Mueller, New York	212
1955	Ted Kluszewski, Cincinnati	192
1956	Hank Aaron, Milwaukee	200
1957	Red Schoendienst, New York/Milwaukee	200
1958	Richie Ashburn, Philadelphia	215
1959	Hank Aaron, Milwaukee	223
1960	Willie Mays, San Francisco	190
1961	Vada Pinson, Cincinnati	208
1962	Tommy Davis, Los Angeles	230
1963	Vada Pinson, Cincinnati	204
1964	Roberto Clemente, Pittsburgh	211
	Curt Flood, St. Louis	211
1965	Pete Rose, Cincinnati	209
1966	Felipe Alou, Atlanta	218
1967	Roberto Clemente, Pittsburgh	209
1968	Felipe Alou, Atlanta	210
	Pete Rose, Cincinnati	210
1969	Matty Alou, Pittsburgh	231
1970	Pete Rose, Cincinnati	205
	Billy Williams, Chicago	205
1971	Joe Torre, St. Louis	230
1972	Pete Rose, Cincinnati	198
1973	Pete Rose, Cincinnati	230
1974	Ralph Garr, Atlanta	214
1975	Dave Cash, Philadelphia	213
1976	Pete Rose, Cincinnati	215
1977	Dave Parker, Pittsburgh	215
1978	Steve Garvey, Los Angeles	202
1979	Garry Templeton, St. Louis	211
1980	Steve Garvey, Los Angeles	200
1981	Pete Rose, Philadelphia	140
1982	Al Oliver, Montreal	204

Year	Player, Club	No.
1983	Jose Cruz, Houston	189
	Andre Dawson, Montreal	189
1984	Tony Gwynn, San Diego	213
1985	Willie McGee, St. Louis	216
1986	Tony Gwynn, San Diego	211
1987	Tony Gwynn, San Diego	218
1988	Andres Galarraga, Montreal	184
1989	Tony Gwynn, San Diego	203
1990	Brett Butler, San Francisco	*192
	Lenny Dykstra, Philadelphia	*192
1991	Terry Pendleton, Atlanta	187
1992	Terry Pendleton, Atlanta	199
	Andy Van Slyke, Pittsburgh	199
1993	Lenny Dykstra, Philadelphia	194
1994	Tony Gwynn, San Diego	165
1995	Dante Bichette, Colorado	197
	Tony Gwynn, San Diego	197
1996	Lance Johnson, New York	227
1997	Tony Gwynn, San Diego	220
1998	Dante Bichette, Colorado	219
1999	Luis Gonzalez, Arizona	206
2000	Todd Helton, Colorado	216
2001	Rich Aurilia, San Francisco	206

*Willie McGee led the majors with 199 hits in 1990, collecting 168 with St. Louis (N.L.) and another 31 with Oakland (A.L.) following an August 29 trade.

SINGLES

AMERICAN LEAGUE

Year	Player, Club	No.
1901	Nap Lajoie, Philadelphia	154
1902	Fielder Jones, Chicago	148
1903	Patsy Dougherty, Boston	161
1904	Willie Keeler, New York	164
1905	Willie Keeler, New York	147
1906	Willie Keeler, New York	166
1907	Ty Cobb, Detroit	163
1908	Matty McIntyre, Detroit	131
	George Stone, St. Louis	131
1909	Ty Cobb, Detroit	164
1910	Nap Lajoie, Cleveland	165
1911	Ty Cobb, Detroit	169
1912	Ty Cobb, Detroit	167
1913	Eddie Collins, Philadelphia	145
1914	Stuffy McInnis, Philadelphia	160
1915	Ty Cobb, Detroit	161
1916	Tris Speaker, Cleveland	160
1917	Ty Cobb, Detroit	151
	Clyde Milan, Washington	151
1918	George H. Burns, Philadelphia	141
1919	Sam Rice, Washington	144
1920	George Sisler, St. Louis	171
1921	Jack Tobin, St. Louis	179
1922	George Sisler, St. Louis	178
1923	Charlie Jamieson, Cleveland	172
1924	Charlie Jamieson, Cleveland	168
1925	Sam Rice, Washington	182
1926	Sam Rice, Washington	167
1927	Earle Combs, New York	166
1928	Heinie Manush, St. Louis	161
1929	Earle Combs, New York	151
1930	Sam Rice, Washington	158
1931	Oscar Melillo, St. Louis	142
	John Stone, Detroit	142
1932	Heinie Manush, Washington	145
1933	Heinie Manush, Washington	167
1934	Doc Cramer, Philadelphia	158
1935	Doc Cramer, Philadelphia	170
1936	Rip Radcliff, Chicago	161
1937	Buddy Lewis, Washington	162
1938	Mel Almada, Washington/St. Louis	158
1939	Doc Cramer, Boston	147
1940	Doc Cramer, Boston	160
1941	Cecil Travis, Washington	153
1942	Johnny Pesky, Boston	165

Year	Player, Club	No.
1943	Doc Cramer, Detroit	159
1944	George Stirnweiss, New York	146
1945	Irv Hall, Philadelphia	139
1946	Johnny Pesky, Boston	159
1947	Johnny Pesky, Boston	172
1948	Dale Mitchell, Cleveland	162
1949	Dale Mitchell, Cleveland	161
1950	Phil Rizzuto, New York	150
1951	George Kell, Detroit	150
1952	Nellie Fox, Chicago	157
1953	Harvey Kuenn, Detroit	167
1954	Nellie Fox, Chicago	167
1955	Nellie Fox, Chicago	157
1956	Nellie Fox, Chicago	158
1957	Nellie Fox, Chicago	155
1958	Nellie Fox, Chicago	160
1959	Nellie Fox, Chicago	149
1960	Nellie Fox, Chicago	139
1961	Bobby Richardson, New York	148
1962	Bobby Richardson, New York	158
1963	Albie Pearson, Los Angeles	139
1964	Bobby Richardson, New York	148
1965	Don Buford, Chicago	129
1966	Luis Aparicio, Baltimore	143
1967	Horace Clarke, New York	140
1968	Bert Campaneris, Oakland	139
1969	Horace Clarke, New York	146
1970	Alex Johnson, California	156
1971	Cesar Tovar, Minnesota	171
1972	Rod Carew, Minnesota	143
1973	Rod Carew, Minnesota	156
1974	Rod Carew, Minnesota	180
1975	Thurman Munson, New York	151
1976	George Brett, Kansas City	160
1977	Rod Carew, Minnesota	171
1978	Ron LeFlore, Detroit	153
1979	Willie Wilson, Kansas City	148
1980	Willie Wilson, Kansas City	184
1981	Willie Wilson, Kansas City	115
1982	Willie Wilson, Kansas City	157
1983	Wade Boggs, Boston	154
1984	Wade Boggs, Boston	162
1985	Wade Boggs, Boston	187
1986	Tony Fernandez, Toronto	161
1987	Kevin Seitzer, Kansas City	151
1988	Kirby Puckett, Minnesota	163
1989	Steve Sax, New York	171
1990	Rafael Palmeiro, Texas	136
1991	Julio Franco, Texas	156
1992	Carlos Baerga, Cleveland	152
1993	Kenny Lofton, Cleveland	148
1994	Kenny Lofton, Cleveland	107
	Paul Molitor, Toronto	107
1995	Otis Nixon, Texas	151
1996	Paul Molitor, Minnesota	167
1997	Garret Anderson, Anaheim	142
	Derek Jeter, New York	142
1998	Derek Jeter, New York	151
1999	Randy Velarde, Anaheim/Oakland	152
2000	Darin Erstad, Anaheim	170
2001	Ichiro Suzuki, Seattle	192

NATIONAL LEAGUE

Year	Player, Club	No.
1900	Willie Keeler, Brooklyn	179
1901	Jesse Burkett, St. Louis	180
1902	Ginger Beaumont, Pittsburgh	167
1903	Ginger Beaumont, Pittsburgh	166
1904	Ginger Beaumont, Pittsburgh	158
1905	Mike Donlin, New York	162
1906	Miller Huggins, Cincinnati	141
	Spike Shannon, St. Louis/New York	141
1907	Ginger Beaumont, Pittsburgh	150
1908	Mike Donlin, New York	153
1909	Eddie Grant, Philadelphia	147
1910	Eddie Grant, Philadelphia	134

Year	Player, Club	No.	Year	Player, Club	No.
1911	Jake Daubert, Brooklyn	146	1984	Tony Gwynn, San Diego	177
	Doc Miller, Boston	146	1985	Willie McGee, St. Louis	162
1912	Bill Sweeney, Boston	159	1986	Tony Gwynn, San Diego	157
1913	Jake Daubert, Brooklyn	152		Steve Sax, Los Angeles	157
1914	Beals Becker, Philadelphia	128	1987	Tony Gwynn, San Diego	162
1915	Larry Doyle, New York	135	1988	Steve Sax, Los Angeles	147
1916	Dave Robertson, New York	142	1989	Tony Gwynn, San Diego	165
1917	Benny Kauff, New York	141	1990	Brett Butler, San Francisco	160
	Edd Roush, Cincinnati	141	1991	Brett Butler, Los Angeles	162
1918	Charlie Hollocher, Chicago	130	1992	Brett Butler, Los Angeles	143
1919	Ivy Olson, Brooklyn	140	1993	Brett Butler, Los Angeles	149
1920	Milt Stock, St. Louis	170	1994	Tony Gwynn, San Diego	117
1921	Carson Bigbee, Pittsburgh	161	1995	Tony Gwynn, San Diego	154
1922	Carson Bigbee, Pittsburgh	166	1996	Lance Johnson, New York	166
1923	Frankie Frisch, New York	169	1997	Tony Gwynn, San Diego	152
1924	Zack Wheat, Brooklyn	149	1998	Tony Womack, Pittsburgh	149
1925	Milt Stock, Brooklyn	164	1999	Doug Glanville, Philadelphia	149
1926	Eddie Brown, Boston	160	2000	Luis Castillo, Florida	158
1927	Lloyd Waner, Pittsburgh	198	2001	Juan Pierre, Colorado	163
1928	Lloyd Waner, Pittsburgh	180			
1929	Lefty O'Doul, Philadelphia	181			

DOUBLES

AMERICAN LEAGUE

Year	Player, Club	No.	Year	Player, Club	No.
	Lloyd Waner, Pittsburgh	181	1901	Nap Lajoie, Philadelphia	48
1930	Bill Terry, New York	177	1902	Harry Davis, Philadelphia	43
1931	Lloyd Waner, Pittsburgh	172	1903	Socks Seybold, Philadelphia	43
1932	Lefty O'Doul, Brooklyn	158	1904	Nap Lajoie, Cleveland	50
1933	Chick Fullis, Philadelphia	162	1905	Harry Davis, Philadelphia	47
1934	Bill Terry, New York	169	1906	Nap Lajoie, Cleveland	49
1935	Woody Jensen, Pittsburgh	160	1907	Harry Davis, Philadelphia	37
1936	Joe Moore, New York	160	1908	Ty Cobb, Detroit	36
1937	Paul Waner, Pittsburgh	178	1909	Sam Crawford, Detroit	35
1938	Frank McCormick, Cincinnati	160	1910	Nap Lajoie, Cleveland	53
1939	Buddy Hassett, Boston	162	1911	Ty Cobb, Detroit	47
1940	Burgess Whitehead, New York	141	1912	Tris Speaker, Boston	53
1941	Stan Hack, Chicago	141	1913	Joe Jackson, Cleveland	39
1942	Enos Slaughter, St. Louis	127	1914	Tris Speaker, Boston	46
1943	Mickey Witek, New York	172	1915	Bobby Veach, Detroit	40
1944	Phil Cavarretta, Chicago	142	1916	Jack Graney, Cleveland	41
1945	Stan Hack, Chicago	155		Tris Speaker, Cleveland	41
1946	Stan Musial, St. Louis	142	1917	Ty Cobb, Detroit	44
1947	Tommy Holmes, Boston	146	1918	Tris Speaker, Cleveland	33
1948	Stan Rojek, Pittsburgh	150	1919	Bobby Veach, Detroit	45
1949	Red Schoendienst, St. Louis	160	1920	Tris Speaker, Cleveland	50
1950	Eddie Waitkus, Philadelphia	143	1921	Tris Speaker, Cleveland	52
1951	Richie Ashburn, Philadelphia	181	1922	Tris Speaker, Cleveland	48
1952	Bobby Adams, Cincinnati	145	1923	Tris Speaker, Cleveland	59
1953	Richie Ashburn, Philadelphia	169	1924	Joe Sewell, Cleveland	45
1954	Don Mueller, New York	165		Harry Heilmann, Detroit	45
1955	Don Mueller, New York	152	1925	Marty McManus, St. Louis	44
1956	Johnny Temple, Cincinnati	157	1926	George H. Burns, Cleveland	64
1957	Richie Ashburn, Philadelphia	152	1927	Lou Gehrig, New York	52
1958	Richie Ashburn, Philadelphia	176	1928	Heinie Manush, St. Louis	47
1959	Don Blasingame, St. Louis	144		Lou Gehrig, New York	47
1960	Dick Groat, Pittsburgh	154	1929	Heinie Manush, St. Louis	45
1961	Vada Pinson, Cincinnati	150		Roy Johnson, Detroit	45
	Maury Wills, Los Angeles	150		Charlie Gehringer, Detroit	45
1962	Maury Wills, Los Angeles	179	1930	Johnny Hodapp, Cleveland	51
1963	Curt Flood, St. Louis	152	1931	Earl Webb, Boston	67
1964	Curt Flood, St. Louis	178	1932	Eric McNair, Philadelphia	47
1965	Maury Wills, Los Angeles	165	1933	Joe Cronin, Washington	45
1966	Sonny Jackson, Houston	160	1934	Hank Greenberg, Detroit	63
1967	Maury Wills, Pittsburgh	162	1935	Joe Vosmik, Cleveland	47
1968	Curt Flood, St. Louis	160	1936	Charlie Gehringer, Detroit	60
1969	Matty Alou, Pittsburgh	183	1937	Beau Bell, St. Louis	51
1970	Matty Alou, Pittsburgh	171	1938	Joe Cronin, Boston	51
1971	Ralph Garr, Atlanta	180	1939	Red Rolfe, New York	46
1972	Lou Brock, St. Louis	156	1940	Hank Greenberg, Detroit	50
1973	Pete Rose, Cincinnati	181	1941	Lou Boudreau, Cleveland	45
1974	Dave Cash, Philadelphia	167	1942	Don Kolloway, Chicago	40
1975	Dave Cash, Philadelphia	166	1943	Dick Wakefield, Detroit	38
1976	Willie Montanez, San Francisco/Atlanta	164	1944	Lou Boudreau, Cleveland	45
1977	Garry Templeton, St. Louis	155	1945	Wally Moses, Chicago	35
1978	Larry Bowa, Philadelphia	153	1946	Mickey Vernon, Washington	51
1979	Pete Rose, Philadelphia	159	1947	Lou Boudreau, Cleveland	45
1980	Gene Richards, San Diego	155			
1981	Pete Rose, Philadelphia	117			
1982	Bill Buckner, Chicago	147			
1983	Rafael Ramirez, Atlanta	160			

Year	Player, Club	No.
1948	Ted Williams, Boston	44
1949	Ted Williams, Boston	39
1950	George Kell, Detroit	56
1951	George Kell, Detroit	36
	Eddie Yost, Washington	36
	Sam Mele, Washington	36
1952	Ferris Fain, Philadelphia	43
1953	Mickey Vernon, Washington	43
1954	Mickey Vernon, Washington	33
1955	Harvey Kuenn, Detroit	38
1956	Jimmy Piersall, Boston	40
1957	Minnie Minoso, Chicago	36
	Billy Gardner, Baltimore	36
1958	Harvey Kuenn, Detroit	39
1959	Harvey Kuenn, Detroit	42
1960	Tito Francona, Cleveland	36
1961	Al Kaline, Detroit	41
1962	Floyd Robinson, Chicago	45
1963	Carl Yastrzemski, Boston	40
1964	Tony Oliva, Minnesota	43
1965	Zoilo Versalles, Minnesota	45
	Carl Yastrzemski, Boston	45
1966	Carl Yastrzemski, Boston	39
1967	Tony Oliva, Minnesota	34
1968	Reggie Smith, Boston	37
1969	Tony Oliva, Minnesota	39
1970	Tony Oliva, Minnesota	36
	Amos Otis, Kansas City	36
	Cesar Tovar, Minnesota	36
1971	Reggie Smith, Boston	33
1972	Lou Piniella, Kansas City	33
1973	Sal Bando, Oakland	32
	Pedro Garcia, Milwaukee	32
1974	Joe Rudi, Oakland	39
1975	Fred Lynn, Boston	47
1976	Amos Otis, Kansas City	40
1977	Hal McRae, Kansas City	54
1978	George Brett, Kansas City	45
1979	Chet Lemon, Chicago	44
	Cecil Cooper, Milwaukee	44
1980	Robin Yount, Milwaukee	49
1981	Cecil Cooper, Milwaukee	35
1982	Hal McRae, Kansas City	46
	Robin Yount, Milwaukee	46
1983	Cal Ripken, Baltimore	47
1984	Don Mattingly, New York	44
1985	Don Mattingly, New York	48
1986	Don Mattingly, New York	53
1987	Paul Molitor, Milwaukee	41
1988	Wade Boggs, Boston	45
1989	Wade Boggs, Boston	51
1990	George Brett, Kansas City	45
	Jody Reed, Boston	45
1991	Rafael Palmeiro, Texas	49
1992	Edgar Martinez, Seattle	46
	Frank Thomas, Chicago	46
1993	John Olerud, Toronto	54
1994	Chuck Knoblauch, Minnesota	45
1995	Albert Belle, Cleveland	52
	Edgar Martinez, Seattle	52
1996	Alex Rodriguez, Seattle	54
1997	John Valentin, Boston	47
1998	Juan Gonzalez, Texas	50
1999	Shawn Green, Toronto	45
2000	Carlos Delgado, Toronto	57
2001	Jason Giambi, Oakland	47

NATIONAL LEAGUE

Year	Player, Club	No.
1876	Ross Barnes, Chicago	23
1877	Cap Anson, Chicago	20
1878	Lew Brown, Providence	18
1879	Charlie Eden, Cleveland	31
1880	Fred Dunlap, Cleveland	27
1881	King Kelly, Chicago	28
1882	King Kelly, Chicago	36
1883	Ned Williamson, Chicago	50

Year	Player, Club	No.
1884	Paul Hines, Providence	34
1885	Cap Anson, Chicago	35
1886	Dan Brouthers, Detroit	41
1887	Dan Brouthers, Detroit	35
1888	Jimmy Ryan, Chicago	37
1889	Jack Glasscock, Indianapolis	39
1890	Sam Thompson, Philadelphia	38
1891	Mike Griffin, Brooklyn	36
1892	Dan Brouthers, Brooklyn	33
	Ed Delahanty, Philadelphia	33
1893	Patsy Tebeau, Cleveland	35
1894	Hugh Duffy, Boston	50
1895	Ed Delahanty, Philadelphia	47
1896	Ed Delahanty, Philadelphia	42
1897	Jake Stenzel, Baltimore	40
1898	Nap Lajoie, Philadelphia	40
1899	Ed Delahanty, Philadelphia	56
1900	Honus Wagner, Pittsburgh	45
1901	Honus Wagner, Pittsburgh	39
	Jake Beckley, Cincinnati	39
1902	Honus Wagner, Pittsburgh	33
1903	Fred Clarke, Pittsburgh	32
	Sam Mertes, New York	32
	Harry Steinfeldt, Cincinnati	32
1904	Honus Wagner, Pittsburgh	44
1905	Cy Seymour, Cincinnati	40
1906	Honus Wagner, Pittsburgh	38
1907	Honus Wagner, Pittsburgh	38
1908	Honus Wagner, Pittsburgh	39
1909	Honus Wagner, Pittsburgh	39
1910	Bobby Byrne, Pittsburgh	43
1911	Ed Konetchy, St. Louis	38
1912	Heinie Zimmerman, Chicago	41
1913	Red Smith, Brooklyn	40
1914	Sherry Magee, Philadelphia	39
1915	Larry Doyle, New York	40
1916	Bert Niehoff, Philadelphia	42
1917	Heinie Groh, Cincinnati	39
1918	Heinie Groh, Cincinnati	28
1919	Ross Youngs, New York	31
1920	Rogers Hornsby, St. Louis	44
1921	Rogers Hornsby, St. Louis	44
1922	Rogers Hornsby, St. Louis	46
1923	Edd Roush, Cincinnati	41
1924	Rogers Hornsby, St. Louis	43
1925	Jim Bottomley, St. Louis	44
1926	Jim Bottomley, St. Louis	40
1927	Riggs Stephenson, Chicago	46
1928	Paul Waner, Pittsburgh	50
1929	Johnny Frederick, Brooklyn	52
1930	Chuck Klein, Philadelphia	59
1931	Sparky Adams, St. Louis	46
1932	Paul Waner, Pittsburgh	62
1933	Chuck Klein, Philadelphia	44
1934	Kiki Cuyler, Chicago	42
	Ethan Allen, Philadelphia	42
1935	Billy Herman, Chicago	57
1936	Joe Medwick, St. Louis	64
1937	Joe Medwick, St. Louis	56
1938	Joe Medwick, St. Louis	47
1939	Enos Slaughter, St. Louis	52
1940	Frank McCormick, Cincinnati	44
1941	Pete Reiser, Brooklyn	39
	Johnny Mize, St. Louis	39
1942	Marty Marion, St. Louis	38
1943	Stan Musial, St. Louis	48
1944	Stan Musial, St. Louis	51
1945	Tommy Holmes, Boston	47
1946	Stan Musial, St. Louis	50
1947	Eddie Miller, Cincinnati	38
1948	Stan Musial, St. Louis	46
1949	Stan Musial, St. Louis	41
1950	Red Schoendienst, St. Louis	43
1951	Alvin Dark, New York	41
1952	Stan Musial, St. Louis	42
1953	Stan Musial, St. Louis	53
1954	Stan Musial, St. Louis	41

Year	Player, Club	No.
1955	Johnny Logan, Milwaukee	37
	Hank Aaron, Milwaukee	37
1956	Hank Aaron, Milwaukee	34
1957	Don Hoak, Cincinnati	39
1958	Orlando Cepeda, San Francisco	38
1959	Vada Pinson, Cincinnati	47
1960	Vada Pinson, Cincinnati	37
1961	Hank Aaron, Milwaukee	39
1962	Frank Robinson, Cincinnati	51
1963	Dick Groat, St. Louis	43
1964	Lee Maye, Milwaukee	44
1965	Hank Aaron, Milwaukee	40
1966	Johnny Callison, Philadelphia	40
1967	Rusty Staub, Houston	44
1968	Lou Brock, St. Louis	46
1969	Matty Alou, Pittsburgh	41
1970	Wes Parker, Los Angeles	47
1971	Cesar Cedeno, Houston	40
1972	Cesar Cedeno, Houston	39
	Willie Montanez, Philadelphia	39
1973	Willie Stargell, Pittsburgh	43
1974	Pete Rose, Cincinnati	45
1975	Pete Rose, Cincinnati	47
1976	Pete Rose, Cincinnati	42
1977	Dave Parker, Pittsburgh	44
1978	Pete Rose, Cincinnati	51
1979	Keith Hernandez, St. Louis	48
1980	Pete Rose, Philadelphia	42
1981	Bill Buckner, Chicago	35
1982	Al Oliver, Montreal	43
1983	Bill Buckner, Chicago	38
	Al Oliver, Montreal	38
	Johnny Ray, Pittsburgh	38
1984	Tim Raines Sr., Montreal	38
	Johnny Ray, Pittsburgh	38
1985	Dave Parker, Cincinnati	42
1986	Von Hayes, Philadelphia	46
1987	Tim Wallach, Montreal	42
1988	Andres Galarraga, Montreal	42
1989	Pedro Guerrero, St. Louis	42
	Tim Wallach, Montreal	42
1990	Gregg Jefferies, New York	40
1991	Bobby Bonilla, Pittsburgh	44
1992	Andy Van Slyke, Pittsburgh	45
1993	Charlie Hayes, Colorado	45
1994	Craig Biggio, Houston	44
	Larry Walker, Montreal	44
1995	Mark Grace, Chicago	51
1996	Jeff Bagwell, Houston	48
1997	Mark Grudzielanek, Montreal	54
1998	Craig Biggio, Houston	51
1999	Craig Biggio, Houston	56
2000	Todd Helton, Colorado	59
2001	Lance Berkman, Houston	55

TRIPLES

AMERICAN LEAGUE

Year	Player, Club	No.
1901	Jimmy Williams, Baltimore	22
1902	Jimmy Williams, Baltimore	23
1903	Sam Crawford, Detroit	25
1904	Chick Stahl, Boston	22
1905	Elmer Flick, Cleveland	19
1906	Elmer Flick, Cleveland	22
1907	Elmer Flick, Cleveland	18
1908	Ty Cobb, Detroit	20
1909	Home Run Baker, Philadelphia	19
1910	Sam Crawford, Detroit	19
1911	Ty Cobb, Detroit	24
1912	Joe Jackson, Cleveland	26
1913	Sam Crawford, Detroit	23
1914	Sam Crawford, Detroit	26
1915	Sam Crawford, Detroit	19
1916	Joe Jackson, Chicago	21
1917	Ty Cobb, Detroit	24

Year	Player, Club	No.
1918	Ty Cobb, Detroit	14
1919	Bobby Veach, Detroit	17
1920	Joe Jackson, Chicago	20
1921	Howard Shanks, Washington	19
1922	George Sisler, St. Louis	18
1923	Sam Rice, Washington	18
	Goose Goslin, Washington	18
1924	Wally Pipp, New York	19
1925	Goose Goslin, Washington	20
1926	Lou Gehrig, New York	20
1927	Earle Combs, New York	23
1928	Earle Combs, New York	21
1929	Charlie Gehringer, Detroit	19
1930	Earle Combs, New York	22
1931	Roy Johnson, Detroit	19
1932	Joe Cronin, Washington	18
1933	Heinie Manush, Washington	17
1934	Ben Chapman, New York	13
1935	Joe Vosmik, Cleveland	20
1936	Earl Averill Sr., Cleveland	15
	Joe DiMaggio, New York	15
	Red Rolfe, New York	15
1937	Dixie Walker, Chicago	16
	Mike Kreevich, Chicago	16
1938	Jeff Heath, Cleveland	18
1939	Buddy Lewis, Washington	16
1940	Barney McCosky, Detroit	19
1941	Jeff Heath, Cleveland	20
1942	Stan Spence, Washington	15
1943	Johnny Lindell, New York	12
	Wally Moses, Chicago	12
1944	Johnny Lindell, New York	16
	George Stirnweiss, New York	16
1945	George Stirnweiss, New York	22
1946	Hank Edwards, Cleveland	16
1947	Tommy Henrich, New York	13
1948	Tommy Henrich, New York	14
1949	Dale Mitchell, Cleveland	23
1950	Dom DiMaggio, Boston	11
	Bobby Doerr, Boston	11
	Hoot Evers, Detroit	11
1951	Minnie Minoso, Cleveland/Chicago	14
1952	Bobby Avila, Cleveland	11
1953	Jim Rivera, Chicago	16
1954	Minnie Minoso, Chicago	18
1955	Mickey Mantle, New York	11
	Andy Carey, New York	11
1956	Minnie Minoso, Chicago	11
	Jackie Jensen, Boston	11
	Harry Simpson, Kansas City	11
	Jim Lemon, Washington	11
1957	Gil McDougald, New York	9
	Hank Bauer, New York	9
	Harry Simpson, Kansas City	9
1958	Vic Power, Kansas City/Cleveland	10
1959	Bob Allison, Washington	9
1960	Nellie Fox, Chicago	10
1961	Jake Wood, Detroit	14
1962	Gino Cimoli, Kansas City	15
1963	Zoilo Versalles, Minnesota	13
1964	Rich Rollins, Minnesota	10
	Zoilo Versalles, Minnesota	10
1965	Bert Campaneris, Kansas City	12
	Zoilo Versalles, Minnesota	12
1966	Bobby Knoop, California	11
1967	Paul Blair, Baltimore	12
1968	Jim Fregosi, California	13
1969	Del Unser, Washington	8
1970	Cesar Tovar, Minnesota	13
1971	Fred Patek, Kansas City	11
1972	Carlton Fisk, Boston	9
	Joe Rudi, Oakland	9
1973	Al Bumbry, Baltimore	11
	Rod Carew, Minnesota	11
1974	Mickey Rivers, California	11
1975	George Brett, Kansas City	13
	Mickey Rivers, California	13

Year	Player, Club	No.
1976	George Brett, Kansas City	14
1977	Rod Carew, Minnesota	16
1978	Jim Rice, Boston	15
1979	George Brett, Kansas City	20
1980	Alfredo Griffin, Toronto	15
	Willie Wilson, Kansas City	15
1981	John Castino, Minnesota	9
1982	Willie Wilson, Kansas City	15
1983	Robin Yount, Milwaukee	10
1984	Dave Collins, Toronto	15
	Lloyd Moseby, Toronto	15
1985	Willie Wilson, Kansas City	21
1986	Brett Butler, Cleveland	14
1987	Willie Wilson, Kansas City	15
1988	Harold Reynolds, Seattle	11
	Willie Wilson, Kansas City	11
	Robin Yount, Milwaukee	11
1989	Ruben Sierra, Texas	14
1990	Tony Fernandez, Toronto	17
1991	Lance Johnson, Chicago	13
	Paul Molitor, Milwaukee	13
1992	Lance Johnson, Chicago	12
1993	Lance Johnson, Chicago	14
1994	Lance Johnson, Chicago	14
1995	Kenny Lofton, Cleveland	13
1996	Chuck Knoblauch, Minnesota	14
1997	Nomar Garciaparra, Boston	11
1998	Jose Offerman, Kansas City	13
1999	Jose Offerman, Boston	11
2000	Cristian Guzman, Minnesota	20
2001	Cristian Guzman, Minnesota	14

NATIONAL LEAGUE

Year	Player, Club	No.
1876	Ross Barnes, Chicago	14
1877	Deacon White, Boston	11
1878	Tom York, Providence	10
1879	Buttercup Dickerson, Cincinnati	14
1880	Harry Stovey, Worcester	14
1881	Jack Rowe, Buffalo	11
1882	Roger Connor, Troy	17
1883	Dan Brouthers, Buffalo	17
1884	Buck Ewing, New York	18
1885	Roger Connor, New York	15
	Jim O'Rourke, New York	15
1886	Roger Connor, New York	19
1887	Sam Thompson, Detroit	23
1888	Roger Connor, New York	17
	Dick Johnston, Boston	17
1889	Roger Connor, New York	17
	Jim Fogarty, Philadelphia	17
	Walt Wilmot, Washington	17
1890	Bid McPhee, Cincinnati	25
1891	Jake Beckley, Pittsburgh	20
1892	Dan Brouthers, Brooklyn	20
1893	Perry Werden, St. Louis	33
1894	Heinie Reitz, Baltimore	29
1895	Kip Selbach, Washington	22
	Sam Thompson, Philadelphia	22
1896	Tom McCreery, Louisville	21
	George Van Haltren, New York	21
1897	Harry Davis, Pittsburgh	28
1898	John Anderson, Brooklyn/Washington	19
1899	Jimmy Williams, Pittsburgh	27
1900	Honus Wagner, Pittsburgh	22
1901	Jimmy Sheckard, Brooklyn	21
1902	Sam Crawford, Cincinnati	23
1903	Honus Wagner, Pittsburgh	19
1904	Harry Lumley, Brooklyn	18
1905	Cy Seymour, Cincinnati	21
1906	Fred Clarke, Pittsburgh	13
	Frank Schulte, Chicago	13
1907	John Ganzel, Cincinnati	16
	Whitey Alperman, Brooklyn	16
1908	Honus Wagner, Pittsburgh	19
1909	Mike Mitchell, Cincinnati	17

Year	Player, Club	No.
1910	Mike Mitchell, Cincinnati	18
1911	Larry Doyle, New York	25
1912	Chief Wilson, Pittsburgh	36
1913	Vic Saier, Chicago	21
1914	Max Carey, Pittsburgh	17
1915	Tommy Long, St. Louis	25
1916	Bill Hinchman, Pittsburgh	16
1917	Rogers Hornsby, St. Louis	17
1918	Jake Daubert, Brooklyn	15
1919	Hy Myers, Brooklyn	14
	Billy Southworth, Pittsburgh	14
1920	Hy Myers, Brooklyn	22
1921	Rogers Hornsby, St. Louis	18
	Ray Powell, Boston	18
1922	Jake Daubert, Cincinnati	22
1923	Max Carey, Pittsburgh	19
	Pie Traynor, Pittsburgh	19
1924	Edd Roush, Cincinnati	21
1925	Kiki Cuyler, Pittsburgh	26
1926	Paul Waner, Pittsburgh	22
1927	Paul Waner, Pittsburgh	18
1928	Jim Bottomley, St. Louis	20
1929	Lloyd Waner, Pittsburgh	20
1930	Adam Comorosky, Pittsburgh	23
1931	Bill Terry, New York	20
1932	Babe Herman, Cincinnati	19
1933	Arky Vaughan, Pittsburgh	19
1934	Joe Medwick, St. Louis	18
1935	Ival Goodman, Cincinnati	18
1936	Ival Goodman, Cincinnati	14
1937	Arky Vaughan, Pittsburgh	17
1938	Johnny Mize, St. Louis	16
1939	Billy Herman, Chicago	18
1940	Arky Vaughan, Pittsburgh	15
1941	Pete Reiser, Brooklyn	17
1942	Enos Slaughter, St. Louis	17
1943	Stan Musial, St. Louis	20
1944	Johnny Barrett, Pittsburgh	19
1945	Luis Olmo, Brooklyn	13
1946	Stan Musial, St. Louis	20
1947	Harry Walker, St. Louis/Philadelphia	16
1948	Stan Musial, St. Louis	18
1949	Stan Musial, St. Louis	13
	Enos Slaughter, St. Louis	13
1950	Richie Ashburn, Philadelphia	14
1951	Stan Musial, St. Louis	12
	Gus Bell, Pittsburgh	12
1952	Bobby Thomson, New York	14
1953	Jim Gilliam, Brooklyn	17
1954	Willie Mays, New York	13
1955	Willie Mays, New York	13
	Dale Long, Pittsburgh	13
1956	Billy Bruton, Milwaukee	15
1957	Willie Mays, New York	20
1958	Richie Ashburn, Philadelphia	13
1959	Wally Moon, Los Angeles	11
	Charlie Neal, Los Angeles	11
1960	Billy Bruton, Milwaukee	13
1961	George Altman, Chicago	12
1962	Johnny Callison, Philadelphia	10
	Bill Virdon, Pittsburgh	10
	Willie Davis, Los Angeles	10
	Maury Wills, Los Angeles	10
1963	Vada Pinson, Cincinnati	14
1964	Dick Allen, Philadelphia	13
	Ron Santo, Chicago	13
1965	Johnny Callison, Philadelphia	16
1966	Tim McCarver, St. Louis	13
1967	Vada Pinson, Cincinnati	13
1968	Lou Brock, St. Louis	14
1969	Roberto Clemente, Pittsburgh	12
1970	Willie Davis, Los Angeles	16
1971	Joe Morgan, Houston	11
	Roger Metzger, Houston	11
1972	Larry Bowa, Philadelphia	13
1973	Roger Metzger, Houston	14

Year	Player, Club	No.
1974	Ralph Garr, Atlanta	17
1975	Ralph Garr, Atlanta	11
1976	Dave Cash, Philadelphia	12
1977	Garry Templeton, St. Louis	18
1978	Garry Templeton, St. Louis	13
1979	Garry Templeton, St. Louis	19
1980	Omar Moreno, Pittsburgh	13
	Rodney Scott, Montreal	13
1981	Craig Reynolds, Houston	12
	Gene Richards, San Diego	12
1982	Dickie Thon, Houston	10
1983	Brett Butler, Atlanta	13
1984	Juan Samuel, Philadelphia	19
	Ryne Sandberg, Chicago	19
1985	Willie McGee, St. Louis	18
1986	Mitch Webster, Montreal	13
1987	Juan Samuel, Philadelphia	15
1988	Andy Van Slyke, Pittsburgh	15
1989	Robby Thompson, San Francisco	11
1990	Mariano Duncan, Cincinnati	11
1991	Ray Lankford, St. Louis	15
1992	Deion Sanders, Atlanta	14
1993	Steve Finley, Houston	13
1994	Brett Butler, Los Angeles	9
	Darren Lewis, San Francisco	9
1995	Brett Butler, New York/Los Angeles	9
	Eric Young, Colorado	9
1996	Lance Johnson, New York	21
1997	Delino DeShields, St. Louis	14
1998	David Dellucci, Arizona	12
1999	Bobby Abreu, Philadelphia	11
	Neifi Perez, Colorado	11
2000	Tony Womack, Arizona	14
2001	Jimmy Rollins, Philadelphia	12

HOME RUNS

AMERICAN LEAGUE

Year	Player, Club	No.
1901	Nap Lajoie, Philadelphia	14
1902	Socks Seybold, Philadelphia	16
1903	Buck Freeman, Boston	13
1904	Harry Davis, Philadelphia	10
1905	Harry Davis, Philadelphia	8
1906	Harry Davis, Philadelphia	12
1907	Harry Davis, Philadelphia	8
1908	Sam Crawford, Detroit	7
1909	Ty Cobb, Detroit	9
1910	Jake Stahl, Boston	10
1911	Home Run Baker, Philadelphia	11
1912	Home Run Baker, Philadelphia	10
	Tris Speaker, Boston	10
1913	Home Run Baker, Philadelphia	12
1914	Home Run Baker, Philadelphia	9
1915	Braggo Roth, Chicago/Cleveland	7
1916	Wally Pipp, New York	12
1917	Wally Pipp, New York	9
1918	Babe Ruth, Boston	11
	Tilly Walker, Philadelphia	11
1919	Babe Ruth, Boston	29
1920	Babe Ruth, New York	54
1921	Babe Ruth, New York	59
1922	Ken Williams, St. Louis	39
1923	Babe Ruth, New York	41
1924	Babe Ruth, New York	46
1925	Bob Meusel, New York	33
1926	Babe Ruth, New York	47
1927	Babe Ruth, New York	60
1928	Babe Ruth, New York	54
1929	Babe Ruth, New York	46
1930	Babe Ruth, New York	49
1931	Babe Ruth, New York	46
	Lou Gehrig, New York	46
1932	Jimmie Foxx, Philadelphia	58
1933	Jimmie Foxx, Philadelphia	48
1934	Lou Gehrig, New York	49

Year	Player, Club	No.
1935	Jimmie Foxx, Philadelphia	36
	Hank Greenberg, Detroit	36
1936	Lou Gehrig, New York	49
1937	Joe DiMaggio, New York	46
1938	Hank Greenberg, Detroit	58
1939	Jimmie Foxx, Boston	35
1940	Hank Greenberg, Detroit	41
1941	Ted Williams, Boston	37
1942	Ted Williams, Boston	36
1943	Rudy York, Detroit	34
1944	Nick Etten, New York	22
1945	Vern Stephens, St. Louis	24
1946	Hank Greenberg, Detroit	44
1947	Ted Williams, Boston	32
1948	Joe DiMaggio, New York	39
1949	Ted Williams, Boston	43
1950	Al Rosen, Cleveland	37
1951	Gus Zernial, Chicago/Philadelphia	33
1952	Larry Doby, Cleveland	32
1953	Al Rosen, Cleveland	43
1954	Larry Doby, Cleveland	32
1955	Mickey Mantle, New York	37
1956	Mickey Mantle, New York	52
1957	Roy Sievers, Washington	42
1958	Mickey Mantle, New York	42
1959	Rocky Colavito, Cleveland	42
	Harmon Killebrew, Washington	42
1960	Mickey Mantle, New York	40
1961	Roger Maris, New York	61
1962	Harmon Killebrew, Minnesota	48
1963	Harmon Killebrew, Minnesota	45
1964	Harmon Killebrew, Minnesota	49
1965	Tony Conigliaro, Boston	32
1966	Frank Robinson, Baltimore	49
1967	Harmon Killebrew, Minnesota	44
	Carl Yastrzemski, Boston	44
1968	Frank Howard, Washington	44
1969	Harmon Killebrew, Minnesota	49
1970	Frank Howard, Washington	44
1971	Bill Melton, Chicago	33
1972	Dick Allen, Chicago	37
1973	Reggie Jackson, Oakland	32
1974	Dick Allen, Chicago	32
1975	Reggie Jackson, Oakland	36
	George Scott, Milwaukee	36
1976	Graig Nettles, New York	32
1977	Jim Rice, Boston	39
1978	Jim Rice, Boston	46
1979	Gorman Thomas, Milwaukee	45
1980	Reggie Jackson, New York	41
	Ben Oglivie, Milwaukee	41
1981	Tony Armas, Oakland	22
	Dwight Evans, Boston	22
	Bobby Grich, California	22
	Eddie Murray, Baltimore	22
1982	Reggie Jackson, California	39
	Gorman Thomas, Milwaukee	39
1983	Jim Rice, Boston	39
1984	Tony Armas, Boston	43
1985	Darrell Evans, Detroit	40
1986	Jesse Barfield, Toronto	40
1987	Mark McGwire, Oakland	49
1988	Jose Canseco, Oakland	42
1989	Fred McGriff, Toronto	36
1990	Cecil Fielder, Detroit	51
1991	Jose Canseco, Oakland	44
	Cecil Fielder, Detroit	44
1992	Juan Gonzalez, Texas	43
1993	Juan Gonzalez, Texas	46
1994	Ken Griffey Jr., Seattle	40
1995	Albert Belle, Cleveland	50
1996	Mark McGwire, Oakland	52
1997	Ken Griffey Jr., Seattle	56
1998	Ken Griffey Jr., Seattle	56
1999	Ken Griffey Jr., Seattle	48
2000	Troy Glaus, Anaheim	47
2001	Alex Rodriguez, Texas	52

NATIONAL LEAGUE

Year	Player, Club	No.
1876	George Hall, Philadelphia	5
1877	George Shaffer, Louisville	3
1878	Paul Hines, Providence	4
1879	Charley Jones, Boston	9
1880	Jim O'Rourke, Boston	6
	Harry Stovey, Worcester	6
1881	Dan Brouthers, Buffalo	8
1882	George Wood, Detroit	7
1883	Buck Ewing, New York	10
1884	Ned Williamson, Chicago	27
1885	Abner Dalrymple, Chicago	11
1886	Hardy Richardson, Detroit	11
1887	Roger Connor, New York	17
	Billy O'Brien, Washington	17
1888	Roger Connor, New York	14
1889	Sam Thompson, Philadelphia	20
1890	Walt Wilmot, Chicago	14
1891	Harry Stovey, Boston	16
	Mike Tiernan, New York	16
1892	Bug Holliday, Cincinnati	13
1893	Ed Delahanty, Philadelphia	19
1894	Hugh Duffy, Boston	18
	Bobby Lowe, Boston	18
1895	Bill Joyce, Washington	17
1896	Ed Delahanty, Philadelphia	13
	Sam Thompson, Philadelphia	13
1897	Hugh Duffy, Boston	11
1898	Jimmy Collins, Boston	15
1899	Buck Freeman, Washington	25
1900	Herman Long, Boston	12
1901	Sam Crawford, Cincinnati	16
1902	Tommy Leach, Pittsburgh	6
1903	Jimmy Sheckard, Brooklyn	9
1904	Harry Lumley, Brooklyn	9
1905	Fred Odwell, Cincinnati	9
1906	Tim Jordan, Brooklyn	12
1907	Dave Brain, Boston	10
1908	Tim Jordan, Brooklyn	12
1909	Red Murray, New York	7
1910	Fred Beck, Boston	10
	Frank Schulte, Chicago	10
1911	Frank Schulte, Chicago	21
1912	Heinie Zimmerman, Chicago	14
1913	Gavvy Cravath, Philadelphia	19
1914	Gavvy Cravath, Philadelphia	19
1915	Gavvy Cravath, Philadelphia	24
1916	Dave Robertson, New York	12
	Cy Williams, Chicago	12
1917	Dave Robertson, New York	12
	Gavvy Cravath, Philadelphia	12
1918	Gavvy Cravath, Philadelphia	8
1919	Gavvy Cravath, Philadelphia	12
1920	Cy Williams, Philadelphia	15
1921	George Kelly, New York	23
1922	Rogers Hornsby, St. Louis	42
1923	Cy Williams, Philadelphia	41
1924	Jack Fournier, Brooklyn	27
1925	Rogers Hornsby, St. Louis	39
1926	Hack Wilson, Chicago	21
1927	Hack Wilson, Chicago	30
	Cy Williams, Philadelphia	30
1928	Hack Wilson, Chicago	31
	Jim Bottomley, St. Louis	31
1929	Chuck Klein, Philadelphia	43
1930	Hack Wilson, Chicago	56
1931	Chuck Klein, Philadelphia	31
1932	Chuck Klein, Philadelphia	38
	Mel Ott, New York	38
1933	Chuck Klein, Philadelphia	28
1934	Rip Collins, St. Louis	35
	Mel Ott, New York	35
1935	Wally Berger, Boston	34
1936	Mel Ott, New York	33
1937	Mel Ott, New York	31
	Joe Medwick, St. Louis	31
1938	Mel Ott, New York	36
1939	Johnny Mize, St. Louis	28
1940	Johnny Mize, St. Louis	43
1941	Dolf Camilli, Brooklyn	34
1942	Mel Ott, New York	30
1943	Bill Nicholson, Chicago	29
1944	Bill Nicholson, Chicago	33
1945	Tommy Holmes, Boston	28
1946	Ralph Kiner, Pittsburgh	23
1947	Ralph Kiner, Pittsburgh	51
	Johnny Mize, New York	51
1948	Ralph Kiner, Pittsburgh	40
	Johnny Mize, New York	40
1949	Ralph Kiner, Pittsburgh	54
1950	Ralph Kiner, Pittsburgh	47
1951	Ralph Kiner, Pittsburgh	42
1952	Ralph Kiner, Pittsburgh	37
	Hank Sauer, Chicago	37
1953	Eddie Mathews, Milwaukee	47
1954	Ted Kluszewski, Cincinnati	49
1955	Willie Mays, New York	51
1956	Duke Snider, Brooklyn	43
1957	Hank Aaron, Milwaukee	44
1958	Ernie Banks, Chicago	47
1959	Eddie Mathews, Milwaukee	46
1960	Ernie Banks, Chicago	41
1961	Orlando Cepeda, San Francisco	46
1962	Willie Mays, San Francisco	49
1963	Hank Aaron, Milwaukee	44
	Willie McCovey, San Francisco	44
1964	Willie Mays, San Francisco	47
1965	Willie Mays, San Francisco	52
1966	Hank Aaron, Atlanta	44
1967	Hank Aaron, Atlanta	39
1968	Willie McCovey, San Francisco	36
1969	Willie McCovey, San Francisco	45
1970	Johnny Bench, Cincinnati	45
1971	Willie Stargell, Pittsburgh	48
1972	Johnny Bench, Cincinnati	40
1973	Willie Stargell, Pittsburgh	44
1974	Mike Schmidt, Philadelphia	36
1975	Mike Schmidt, Philadelphia	38
1976	Mike Schmidt, Philadelphia	38
1977	George Foster, Cincinnati	52
1978	George Foster, Cincinnati	40
1979	Dave Kingman, Chicago	48
1980	Mike Schmidt, Philadelphia	48
1981	Mike Schmidt, Philadelphia	31
1982	Dave Kingman, New York	37
1983	Mike Schmidt, Philadelphia	40
1984	Dale Murphy, Atlanta	36
	Mike Schmidt, Philadelphia	36
1985	Dale Murphy, Atlanta	37
1986	Mike Schmidt, Philadelphia	37
1987	Andre Dawson, Chicago	49
1988	Darryl Strawberry, New York	39
1989	Kevin Mitchell, San Francisco	47
1990	Ryne Sandberg, Chicago	40
1991	Howard Johnson, New York	38
1992	Fred McGriff, San Diego	35
1993	Barry Bonds, San Francisco	46
1994	Matt Williams, San Francisco	43
1995	Dante Bichette, Colorado	40
1996	Andres Galarraga, Colorado	47
1997	Larry Walker, Colorado	*49
1998	Mark McGwire, St. Louis	70
1999	Mark McGwire, St. Louis	65
2000	Sammy Sosa, Chicago	50
2001	Barry Bonds, San Francisco	73

*Mark McGwire led the majors with 58 home runs in 1997, hitting 34 with Oakland (A.L.) and another 24 with St. Louis (N.L.) following a July 31 trade.

TOTAL BASES

AMERICAN LEAGUE

Year	Player, Club	No.
1901	Nap Lajoie, Philadelphia	345
1902	Buck Freeman, Boston	287
1903	Buck Freeman, Boston	281
1904	Nap Lajoie, Cleveland	304
1905	George Stone, St. Louis	260
1906	George Stone, St. Louis	288
1907	Ty Cobb, Detroit	286
1908	Ty Cobb, Detroit	276
1909	Ty Cobb, Detroit	296
1910	Nap Lajoie, Cleveland	304
1911	Ty Cobb, Detroit	367
1912	Joe Jackson, Cleveland	331
1913	Sam Crawford, Detroit	298
1914	Tris Speaker, Boston	287
1915	Ty Cobb, Detroit	274
1916	Joe Jackson, Chicago	293
1917	Ty Cobb, Detroit	336
1918	George H. Burns, Philadelphia	236
1919	Babe Ruth, Boston	284
1920	George Sisler, St. Louis	399
1921	Babe Ruth, New York	457
1922	Ken Williams, St. Louis	367
1923	Babe Ruth, New York	399
1924	Babe Ruth, New York	391
1925	Al Simmons, Philadelphia	392
1926	Babe Ruth, New York	365
1927	Lou Gehrig, New York	447
1928	Babe Ruth, New York	380
1929	Al Simmons, Philadelphia	373
1930	Lou Gehrig, New York	419
1931	Lou Gehrig, New York	410
1932	Jimmie Foxx, Philadelphia	438
1933	Jimmie Foxx, Philadelphia	403
1934	Lou Gehrig, New York	409
1935	Hank Greenberg, Detroit	389
1936	Hal Trosky, Cleveland	405
1937	Joe DiMaggio, New York	418
1938	Jimmie Foxx, Boston	398
1939	Ted Williams, Boston	344
1940	Hank Greenberg, Detroit	384
1941	Joe DiMaggio, New York	348
1942	Ted Williams, Boston	338
1943	Rudy York, Detroit	301
1944	Johnny Lindell, New York	297
1945	George Stirnweiss, New York	301
1946	Ted Williams, Boston	343
1947	Ted Williams, Boston	335
1948	Joe DiMaggio, New York	355
1949	Ted Williams, Boston	368
1950	Walt Dropo, Boston	326
1951	Ted Williams, Boston	295
1952	Al Rosen, Cleveland	297
1953	Al Rosen, Cleveland	367
1954	Minnie Minoso, Chicago	304
1955	Al Kaline, Detroit	321
1956	Mickey Mantle, New York	376
1957	Roy Sievers, Washington	331
1958	Mickey Mantle, New York	307
1959	Rocky Colavito, Cleveland	301
1960	Mickey Mantle, New York	294
1961	Roger Maris, New York	366
1962	Rocky Colavito, Detroit	309
1963	Dick Stuart, Boston	319
1964	Tony Oliva, Minnesota	374
1965	Zoilo Versalles, Minnesota	308
1966	Frank Robinson, Baltimore	367
1967	Carl Yastrzemski, Boston	360
1968	Frank Howard, Washington	330
1969	Frank Howard, Washington	340
1970	Carl Yastrzemski, Boston	335
1971	Reggie Smith, Boston	302
1972	Bobby Murcer, New York	314

Year	Player, Club	No.
1973	Dave May, Milwaukee	295
	George Scott, Milwaukee	295
	Sal Bando, Oakland	295
1974	Joe Rudi, Oakland	287
1975	George Scott, Milwaukee	318
1976	George Brett, Kansas City	298
1977	Jim Rice, Boston	382
1978	Jim Rice, Boston	406
1979	Jim Rice, Boston	369
1980	Cecil Cooper, Milwaukee	335
1981	Dwight Evans, Boston	215
1982	Robin Yount, Milwaukee	367
1983	Jim Rice, Boston	344
1984	Tony Armas, Boston	339
1985	Don Mattingly, New York	370
1986	Don Mattingly, New York	388
1987	George Bell, Toronto	369
1988	Kirby Puckett, Minnesota	358
1989	Ruben Sierra, Texas	344
1990	Cecil Fielder, Detroit	339
1991	Cal Ripken, Baltimore	368
1992	Kirby Puckett, Minnesota	313
1993	Ken Griffey Jr., Seattle	359
1994	Albert Belle, Cleveland	294
1995	Albert Belle, Cleveland	377
1996	Alex Rodriguez, Seattle	379
1997	Ken Griffey Jr., Seattle	393
1998	Albert Belle, Chicago	399
1999	Shawn Green, Toronto	361
2000	Carlos Delgado, Toronto	378
2001	Alex Rodriguez, Texas	393

NATIONAL LEAGUE

Year	Player, Club	No.
1900	Elmer Flick, Philadelphia	305
1901	Jesse Burkett, St. Louis	313
1902	Sam Crawford, Cincinnati	256
1903	Ginger Beaumont, Pittsburgh	272
1904	Honus Wagner, Pittsburgh	255
1905	Cy Seymour, Cincinnati	325
1906	Honus Wagner, Pittsburgh	237
1907	Honus Wagner, Pittsburgh	264
1908	Honus Wagner, Pittsburgh	308
1909	Honus Wagner, Pittsburgh	242
1910	Sherry Magee, Philadelphia	263
1911	Frank Schulte, Chicago	308
1912	Heinie Zimmerman, Chicago	318
1913	Gavvy Cravath, Philadelphia	298
1914	Sherry Magee, Philadelphia	277
1915	Gavvy Cravath, Philadelphia	266
1916	Zack Wheat, Brooklyn	262
1917	Rogers Hornsby, St. Louis	253
1918	Charlie Hollocher, Chicago	202
1919	Hy Myers, Brooklyn	223
1920	Rogers Hornsby, St. Louis	329
1921	Rogers Hornsby, St. Louis	378
1922	Rogers Hornsby, St. Louis	450
1923	Frankie Frisch, New York	311
1924	Rogers Hornsby, St. Louis	373
1925	Rogers Hornsby, St. Louis	381
1926	Jim Bottomley, St. Louis	305
1927	Paul Waner, Pittsburgh	342
1928	Jim Bottomley, St. Louis	362
1929	Rogers Hornsby, Chicago	409
1930	Chuck Klein, Philadelphia	445
1931	Chuck Klein, Philadelphia	347
1932	Chuck Klein, Philadelphia	420
1933	Chuck Klein, Philadelphia	365
1934	Rip Collins, St. Louis	369
1935	Joe Medwick, St. Louis	365
1936	Joe Medwick, St. Louis	367
1937	Joe Medwick, St. Louis	406
1938	Johnny Mize, St. Louis	326
1939	Johnny Mize, St. Louis	353
1940	Johnny Mize, St. Louis	368
1941	Pete Reiser, Brooklyn	299

Year	Player, Club	No.
1942	Enos Slaughter, St. Louis	292
1943	Stan Musial, St. Louis	347
1944	Bill Nicholson, Chicago	317
1945	Tommy Holmes, Boston	367
1946	Stan Musial, St. Louis	366
1947	Ralph Kiner, Pittsburgh	361
1948	Stan Musial, St. Louis	429
1949	Stan Musial, St. Louis	382
1950	Duke Snider, Brooklyn	343
1951	Stan Musial, St. Louis	355
1952	Stan Musial, St. Louis	311
1953	Duke Snider, Brooklyn	370
1954	Duke Snider, Brooklyn	378
1955	Willie Mays, New York	382
1956	Hank Aaron, Milwaukee	340
1957	Hank Aaron, Milwaukee	369
1958	Ernie Banks, Chicago	379
1959	Hank Aaron, Milwaukee	400
1960	Hank Aaron, Milwaukee	334
1961	Hank Aaron, Milwaukee	358
1962	Willie Mays, San Francisco	382
1963	Hank Aaron, Milwaukee	370
1964	Dick Allen, Philadelphia	352
1965	Willie Mays, San Francisco	360
1966	Felipe Alou, Atlanta	355
1967	Hank Aaron, Atlanta	344
1968	Billy Williams, Chicago	321
1969	Hank Aaron, Atlanta	332
1970	Billy Williams, Chicago	373
1971	Joe Torre, St. Louis	352
1972	Billy Williams, Chicago	348
1973	Bobby Bonds, San Francisco	341
1974	Johnny Bench, Cincinnati	315
1975	Greg Luzinski, Philadelphia	322
1976	Mike Schmidt, Philadelphia	306
1977	George Foster, Cincinnati	388
1978	Dave Parker, Pittsburgh	340
1979	Dave Winfield, San Diego	333
1980	Mike Schmidt, Philadelphia	342
1981	Mike Schmidt, Philadelphia	228
1982	Al Oliver, Montreal	317
1983	Andre Dawson, Montreal	341
1984	Dale Murphy, Atlanta	332
1985	Dave Parker, Cincinnati	350
1986	Dave Parker, Cincinnati	304
1987	Andre Dawson, Chicago	353
1988	Andres Galarraga, Montreal	329
1989	Kevin Mitchell, San Francisco	345
1990	Ryne Sandberg, Chicago	344
1991	Will Clark, San Francisco	303
	Terry Pendleton, Atlanta	303
1992	Gary Sheffield, San Diego	323
1993	Barry Bonds, San Francisco	365
1994	Jeff Bagwell, Houston	300
1995	Dante Bichette, Colorado	359
1996	Ellis Burks, Colorado	392
1997	Larry Walker, Colorado	409
1998	Sammy Sosa, Chicago	416
1999	Sammy Sosa, Chicago	397
2000	Todd Helton, Colorado	405
2001	Sammy Sosa, Chicago	425

RUNS BATTED IN

AMERICAN LEAGUE

Year	Player, Club	No.
1907	Ty Cobb, Detroit	116
1908	Ty Cobb, Detroit	101
1909	Ty Cobb, Detroit	115
1910	Sam Crawford, Detroit	115
1911	Ty Cobb, Detroit	144
1912	Home Run Baker, Philadelphia	133
1913	Home Run Baker, Philadelphia	126
1914	Sam Crawford, Detroit	112
1915	Sam Crawford, Detroit	116
1916	Wally Pipp, New York	99

Year	Player, Club	No.
1917	Bobby Veach, Detroit	115
1918	George H. Burns, Philadelphia	74
	Bobby Veach, Detroit	74
1919	Babe Ruth, Boston	112
1920	Babe Ruth, New York	137
1921	Babe Ruth, New York	171
1922	Ken Williams, St. Louis	155
1923	Babe Ruth, New York	131
1924	Goose Goslin, Washington	129
1925	Bob Meusel, New York	138
1926	Babe Ruth, New York	145
1927	Lou Gehrig, New York	175
1928	Babe Ruth, New York	142
	Lou Gehrig, New York	142
1929	Al Simmons, Philadelphia	157
1930	Lou Gehrig, New York	174
1931	Lou Gehrig, New York	184
1932	Jimmie Foxx, Philadelphia	169
1933	Jimmie Foxx, Philadelphia	163
1934	Lou Gehrig, New York	165
1935	Hank Greenberg, Detroit	170
1936	Hal Trosky, Cleveland	162
1937	Hank Greenberg, Detroit	183
1938	Jimmie Foxx, Boston	175
1939	Ted Williams, Boston	145
1940	Hank Greenberg, Detroit	150
1941	Joe DiMaggio, New York	125
1942	Ted Williams, Boston	137
1943	Rudy York, Detroit	118
1944	Vern Stephens, St. Louis	109
1945	Nick Etten, New York	111
1946	Hank Greenberg, Detroit	127
1947	Ted Williams, Boston	114
1948	Joe DiMaggio, New York	155
1949	Ted Williams, Boston	159
	Vern Stephens, Boston	159
1950	Walt Dropo, Boston	144
	Vern Stephens, Boston	144
1951	Gus Zernial, Chicago-Philadelphia	129
1952	Al Rosen, Cleveland	105
1953	Al Rosen, Cleveland	145
1954	Larry Doby, Cleveland	126
1955	Ray Boone, Detroit	116
	Jackie Jensen, Boston	116
1956	Mickey Mantle, New York	130
1957	Roy Sievers, Washington	114
1958	Jackie Jensen, Boston	122
1959	Jackie Jensen, Boston	112
1960	Roger Maris, New York	112
1961	Roger Maris, New York	142
1962	Harmon Killebrew, Minnesota	126
1963	Dick Stuart, Boston	118
1964	Brooks Robinson, Baltimore	118
1965	Rocky Colavito, Cleveland	108
1966	Frank Robinson, Baltimore	122
1967	Carl Yastrzemski, Boston	121
1968	Ken Harrelson, Boston	109
1969	Harmon Killebrew, Minnesota	140
1970	Frank Howard, Washington	126
1971	Harmon Killebrew, Minnesota	119
1972	Dick Allen, Chicago	113
1973	Reggie Jackson, Oakland	117
1974	Jeff Burroughs, Texas	118
1975	George Scott, Milwaukee	109
1976	Lee May, Baltimore	109
1977	Larry Hisle, Minnesota	119
1978	Jim Rice, Boston	139
1979	Don Baylor, California	139
1980	Cecil Cooper, Milwaukee	122
1981	Eddie Murray, Baltimore	78
1982	Hal McRae, Kansas City	133
1983	Cecil Cooper, Milwaukee	126
	Jim Rice, Boston	126
1984	Tony Armas, Boston	123
1985	Don Mattingly, New York	145
1986	Joe Carter, Cleveland	121
1987	George Bell, Toronto	134

Year	Player, Club	No.
1988	Jose Canseco, Oakland	124
1989	Ruben Sierra, Texas	119
1990	Cecil Fielder, Detroit	132
1991	Cecil Fielder, Detroit	133
1992	Cecil Fielder, Detroit	124
1993	Albert Belle, Cleveland	129
1994	Kirby Puckett, Minnesota	112
1995	Albert Belle, Cleveland	126
	Mo Vaughn, Boston	126
1996	Albert Belle, Cleveland	148
1997	Ken Griffey Jr., Seattle	147
1998	Juan Gonzalez, Texas	157
1999	Manny Ramirez, Cleveland	165
2000	Edgar Martinez, Seattle	145
2001	Bret Boone, Seattle	141

NATIONAL LEAGUE

Year	Player, Club	No.
1907	Honus Wagner, Pittsburgh	91
1908	Honus Wagner, Pittsburgh	106
1909	Honus Wagner, Pittsburgh	102
1910	Sherry Magee, Philadelphia	116
1911	Frank Schulte, Chicago	121
1912	Heinie Zimmerman, Chicago	98
1913	Gavvy Cravath, Philadelphia	118
1914	Sherry Magee, Philadelphia	101
1915	Gavvy Cravath, Philadelphia	118
1916	Heinie Zimmerman, Chicago/New York	83
1917	Heinie Zimmerman, New York	100
1918	Fred Merkle, Chicago	71
1919	Hy Myers, Brooklyn	72
1920	George Kelly, New York	94
	Rogers Hornsby, St. Louis	94
1921	Rogers Hornsby, St. Louis	126
1922	Rogers Hornsby, St. Louis	152
1923	Irish Meusel, New York	125
1924	George Kelly, New York	136
1925	Rogers Hornsby, St. Louis	143
1926	Jim Bottomley, St. Louis	120
1927	Paul Waner, Pittsburgh	131
1928	Jim Bottomley, St. Louis	136
1929	Hack Wilson, Chicago	159
1930	Hack Wilson, Chicago	191
1931	Chuck Klein, Philadelphia	121
1932	Don Hurst, Philadelphia	143
1933	Chuck Klein, Philadelphia	120
1934	Mel Ott, New York	135
1935	Wally Berger, Boston	130
1936	Joe Medwick, St. Louis	138
1937	Joe Medwick, St. Louis	154
1938	Joe Medwick, St. Louis	122
1939	Frank McCormick, Cincinnati	128
1940	Johnny Mize, St. Louis	137
1941	Dolf Camilli, Brooklyn	120
1942	Johnny Mize, New York	110
1943	Bill Nicholson, Chicago	128
1944	Bill Nicholson, Chicago	122
1945	Dixie Walker, Brooklyn	124
1946	Enos Slaughter, St. Louis	130
1947	Johnny Mize, New York	138
1948	Stan Musial, St. Louis	131
1949	Ralph Kiner, Pittsburgh	127
1950	Del Ennis, Philadelphia	126
1951	Monte Irvin, New York	121
1952	Hank Sauer, Chicago	121
1953	Roy Campanella, Brooklyn	142
1954	Ted Kluszewski, Cincinnati	141
1955	Duke Snider, Brooklyn	136
1956	Stan Musial, St. Louis	109
1957	Hank Aaron, Milwaukee	132
1958	Ernie Banks, Chicago	129
1959	Ernie Banks, Chicago	143
1960	Hank Aaron, Milwaukee	126
1961	Orlando Cepeda, San Francisco	142
1962	Tommy Davis, Los Angeles	153
1963	Hank Aaron, Milwaukee	130
1964	Ken Boyer, St. Louis	119

Year	Player, Club	No.
1965	Deron Johnson, Cincinnati	130
1966	Hank Aaron, Atlanta	127
1967	Orlando Cepeda, St. Louis	111
1968	Willie McCovey, San Francisco	105
1969	Willie McCovey, San Francisco	126
1970	Johnny Bench, Cincinnati	148
1971	Joe Torre, St. Louis	137
1972	Johnny Bench, Cincinnati	125
1973	Willie Stargell, Pittsburgh	119
1974	Johnny Bench, Cincinnati	129
1975	Greg Luzinski, Philadelphia	120
1976	George Foster, Cincinnati	121
1977	George Foster, Cincinnati	149
1978	George Foster, Cincinnati	120
1979	Dave Winfield, San Diego	118
1980	Mike Schmidt, Philadelphia	121
1981	Mike Schmidt, Philadelphia	91
1982	Dale Murphy, Atlanta	109
	Al Oliver, Montreal	109
1983	Dale Murphy, Atlanta	121
1984	Gary Carter, Montreal	106
	Mike Schmidt, Philadelphia	106
1985	Dave Parker, Cincinnati	125
1986	Mike Schmidt, Philadelphia	119
1987	Andre Dawson, Chicago	137
1988	Will Clark, San Francisco	109
1989	Kevin Mitchell, San Francisco	125
1990	Matt Williams, San Francisco	122
1991	Howard Johnson, New York	117
1992	Darren Daulton, Philadelphia	109
1993	Barry Bonds, San Francisco	123
1994	Jeff Bagwell, Houston	116
1995	Dante Bichette, Colorado	128
1996	Andres Galarraga, Colorado	150
1997	Andres Galarraga, Colorado	140
1998	Sammy Sosa, Chicago	158
1999	Mark McGwire, St. Louis	147
2000	Todd Helton, Colorado	147
2001	Sammy Sosa, Chicago	160

Note—Not compiled prior to 1907; officially adopted in 1920.

BASES ON BALLS

AMERICAN LEAGUE

Year	Player, Club	No.
1913	Burt Shotton, St. Louis	102
1914	Donie Bush, Detroit	112
1915	Eddie Collins, Chicago	119
1916	Burt Shotton, St. Louis	110
1917	Jack Graney, Cleveland	94
1918	Ray Chapman, Cleveland	84
1919	Jack Graney, Cleveland	105
1920	Babe Ruth, New York	148
1921	Babe Ruth, New York	144
1922	Whitey Witt, New York	89
1923	Babe Ruth, New York	170
1924	Babe Ruth, New York	142
1925	Willie Kamm, Chicago	90
	Johnny Mostil, Chicago	90
1926	Babe Ruth, New York	144
1927	Babe Ruth, New York	138
1928	Babe Ruth, New York	135
1929	Max Bishop, Philadelphia	128
1930	Babe Ruth, New York	136
1931	Babe Ruth, New York	128
1932	Babe Ruth, New York	130
1933	Babe Ruth, New York	114
1934	Jimmie Foxx, Philadelphia	111
1935	Lou Gehrig, New York	132
1936	Lou Gehrig, New York	130
1937	Lou Gehrig, New York	127
1938	Jimmie Foxx, Boston	119
	Hank Greenberg, Detroit	119
1939	Harlond Clift, St. Louis	111
1940	Charlie Keller, New York	106
1941	Ted Williams, Boston	145

Year	Player, Club	No.
1942	Ted Williams, Boston	145
1943	Charlie Keller, New York	106
1944	Nick Etten, New York	97
1945	Roy Cullenbine, Cleveland/Detroit	112
1946	Ted Williams, Boston	156
1947	Ted Williams, Boston	162
1948	Ted Williams, Boston	126
1949	Ted Williams, Boston	162
1950	Eddie Yost, Washington	141
1951	Ted Williams, Boston	144
1952	Eddie Yost, Washington	129
1953	Eddie Yost, Washington	123
1954	Ted Williams, Boston	136
1955	Mickey Mantle, New York	113
1956	Eddie Yost, Washington	151
1957	Mickey Mantle, New York	146
1958	Mickey Mantle, New York	129
1959	Eddie Yost, Detroit	135
1960	Eddie Yost, Detroit	125
1961	Mickey Mantle, New York	126
1962	Mickey Mantle, New York	122
1963	Carl Yastrzemski, Boston	95
1964	Norm Siebern, Baltimore	106
1965	Rocky Colavito, Cleveland	93
1966	Harmon Killebrew, Minnesota	103
1967	Harmon Killebrew, Minnesota	131
1968	Carl Yastrzemski, Boston	119
1969	Harmon Killebrew, Minnesota	145
1970	Frank Howard, Washington	132
1971	Harmon Killebrew, Minnesota	114
1972	Dick Allen, Chicago	99
	Roy White, New York	99
1973	John Mayberry, Kansas City	122
1974	Gene Tenace, Oakland	110
1975	John Mayberry, Kansas City	119
1976	Mike Hargrove, Texas	97
1977	Toby Harrah, Texas	109
1978	Mike Hargrove, Texas	107
1979	Darrell Porter, Kansas City	121
1980	Willie Randolph, New York	119
1981	Dwight Evans, Boston	85
1982	Rickey Henderson, Oakland	116
1983	Rickey Henderson, Oakland	103
1984	Eddie Murray, Baltimore	107
1985	Dwight Evans, Boston	114
1986	Wade Boggs, Boston	105
1987	Brian Downing, California	106
	Dwight Evans	106
1988	Wade Boggs, Boston	125
1989	Rickey Henderson, New York/Oakland	126
1990	Mark McGwire, Oakland	110
1991	Frank Thomas, Chicago	138
1992	Mickey Tettleton, Detroit	122
	Frank Thomas, Chicago	122
1993	Tony Phillips, Detroit	132
1994	Frank Thomas, Chicago	109
1995	Frank Thomas, Chicago	136
1996	Tony Phillips, Chicago	125
1997	Jim Thome, Cleveland	120
1998	Rickey Henderson, Oakland	118
1999	Jim Thome, Cleveland	127
2000	Jason Giambi, Oakland	137
2001	Jason Giambi, Oakland	129

NATIONAL LEAGUE

Year	Player, Club	No.
1910	Miller Huggins, St. Louis	116
1911	Jimmy Sheckard, Chicago	147
1912	Jimmy Sheckard, Chicago	122
1913	Bob Bescher, Cincinnati	94
1914	Miller Huggins, St. Louis	105
1915	Gavvy Cravath, Philadelphia	86
1916	Heinie Groh, Cincinnati	84
1917	George J. Burns, New York	75
1918	Max Carey, Pittsburgh	62
1919	George J. Burns, New York	82
1920	George J. Burns, New York	76
1921	George J. Burns, New York	80
1922	Max Carey, Pittsburgh	80
1923	George J. Burns, New York	101
1924	Rogers Hornsby, St. Louis	89
1925	Jack Fournier, Brooklyn	86
1926	Hack Wilson, Chicago	69
1927	Rogers Hornsby, New York	86
1928	Rogers Hornsby, Boston	107
1929	Mel Ott, New York	113
1930	Hack Wilson, Chicago	105
1931	Mel Ott, New York	80
1932	Mel Ott, New York	100
1933	Mel Ott, New York	75
1934	Arky Vaughan, Pittsburgh	94
1935	Arky Vaughan, Pittsburgh	97
1936	Arky Vaughan, Pittsburgh	118
1937	Mel Ott, New York	102
1938	Dolf Camilli, Brooklyn	119
1939	Dolf Camilli, Brooklyn	110
1940	Elbie Fletcher, Pittsburgh	119
1941	Elbie Fletcher, Pittsburgh	118
1942	Mel Ott, New York	109
1943	Augie Galan, Brooklyn	103
1944	Augie Galan, Brooklyn	101
1945	Eddie Stanky, Brooklyn	148
1946	Eddie Stanky, Brooklyn	137
1947	Hank Greenberg, Pittsburgh	104
	Pee Wee Reese, Brooklyn	104
1948	Bob Elliott, Boston	131
1949	Ralph Kiner, Pittsburgh	117
1950	Eddie Stanky, New York	144
1951	Ralph Kiner, Pittsburgh	137
1952	Ralph Kiner, Pittsburgh	110
1953	Stan Musial, St. Louis	105
1954	Richie Ashburn, Philadelphia	125
1955	Eddie Mathews, Milwaukee	109
1956	Duke Snider, Brooklyn	99
1957	Richie Ashburn, Philadelphia	94
	Johnny Temple, Cincinnati	94
1958	Richie Ashburn, Philadelphia	97
1959	Jim Gilliam, Los Angeles	96
1960	Richie Ashburn, Chicago	116
1961	Eddie Mathews, Milwaukee	93
1962	Eddie Mathews, Milwaukee	101
1963	Eddie Mathews, Milwaukee	124
1964	Ron Santo, Chicago	86
1965	Joe Morgan, Houston	97
1966	Ron Santo, Chicago	95
1967	Ron Santo, Chicago	96
1968	Ron Santo, Chicago	96
1969	Jim Wynn, Houston	148
1970	Willie McCovey, San Francisco	137
1971	Willie Mays, San Francisco	112
1972	Joe Morgan, Cincinnati	115
1973	Darrell Evans, Atlanta	124
1974	Darrell Evans, Atlanta	126
1975	Joe Morgan, Cincinnati	132
1976	Jim Wynn, Atlanta	127
1977	Gene Tenace, San Diego	125
1978	Jeff Burroughs, Atlanta	117
1979	Mike Schmidt, Philadelphia	120
1980	Dan Driessen, Cincinnati	93
	Joe Morgan, Houston	93
1981	Mike Schmidt, Philadelphia	73
1982	Mike Schmidt, Philadelphia	107
1983	Mike Schmidt, Philadelphia	128
1984	Gary Matthews, Chicago	103
1985	Dale Murphy, Atlanta	90
1986	Keith Hernandez, New York	94
1987	Jack Clark, St. Louis	136
1988	Will Clark, San Francisco	100
1989	Jack Clark, San Diego	132
1990	Jack Clark, San Diego	104
1991	Brett Butler, Los Angeles	108
1992	Barry Bonds, Pittsburgh	127
1993	Lenny Dykstra, Philadelphia	129
1994	Barry Bonds, San Francisco	74

Year	Player, Club	No.
1995	Barry Bonds, San Francisco	120
1996	Barry Bonds, San Francisco	151
1997	Barry Bonds, San Francisco	145
1998	Mark McGwire, St. Louis	162
1999	Jeff Bagwell, Houston	149
2000	Barry Bonds, San Francisco	117
2001	Barry Bonds, San Francisco	177

Note—Not included in batting records in A.L. prior to 1913 and N.L. prior to 1910.

STRIKEOUTS

AMERICAN LEAGUE

Year	Player, Club	No.
1913	Danny Moeller, Washington	106
1914	Gus Williams, St. Louis	120
1915	Doc Lavan, St. Louis	83
1916	Wally Pipp, New York	82
1917	Braggo Roth, Cleveland	73
1918	Babe Ruth, Boston	58
1919	Red Shannon, Philadelphia/Boston	70
1920	Aaron Ward, New York	84
1921	Bob Meusel, New York	88
1922	Jimmie Dykes, Philadelphia	98
1923	Babe Ruth, New York	93
1924	Babe Ruth, New York	81
1925	Marty McManus, St. Louis	69
1926	Tony Lazzeri, New York	96
1927	Babe Ruth, New York	89
1928	Babe Ruth, New York	87
1929	Jimmie Foxx, Philadelphia	70
1930	Jimmie Foxx, Philadelphia	66
	Ed Morgan, Cleveland	66
1931	Jimmie Foxx, Philadelphia	84
1932	Bruce Campbell, Chicago/St. Louis	104
1933	Jimmie Foxx, Philadelphia	93
1934	Harlond Clift, St. Louis	100
1935	Jimmie Foxx, Philadelphia	99
1936	Jimmie Foxx, Boston	119
1937	Frank Crosetti, New York	105
1938	Frank Crosetti, New York	97
1939	Hank Greenberg, Detroit	95
1940	Sam Chapman, Philadelphia	96
1941	Jimmie Foxx, Boston	103
1942	Joe Gordon, New York	95
1943	Chet Laabs, St. Louis	105
1944	Pat Seerey, Cleveland	99
1945	Pat Seerey, Cleveland	97
1946	Charlie Keller, New York	101
	Pat Seerey, Cleveland	101
1947	Eddie Joost, Philadelphia	110
1948	Pat Seerey, Cleveland/Chicago	102
1949	Dick Kokos, St. Louis	91
1950	Gus Zernial, Chicago	110
1951	Gus Zernial, Chicago/Philadelphia	101
1952	Larry Doby, Cleveland	111
	Mickey Mantle, New York	111
1953	Larry Doby, Cleveland	121
1954	Mickey Mantle, New York	107
1955	Norm Zauchin, Boston	105
1956	Jim Lemon, Washington	138
1957	Jim Lemon, Washington	94
1958	Jim Lemon, Washington	120
	Mickey Mantle, New York	120
1959	Mickey Mantle, New York	126
1960	Mickey Mantle, New York	125
1961	Jake Wood, Detroit	141
1962	Harmon Killebrew, Minnesota	142
1963	Dave Nicholson, Chicago	175
1964	Nelson Mathews, Kansas City	143
1965	Zoilo Versalles, Minnesota	122
1966	George Scott, Boston	152
1967	Frank Howard, Washington	155
1968	Reggie Jackson, Oakland	171
1969	Reggie Jackson, Oakland	142
1970	Reggie Jackson, Oakland	135

Year	Player, Club	No.
1971	Reggie Jackson, Oakland	161
1972	Bobby Darwin, Minnesota	145
1973	Bobby Darwin, Minnesota	137
1974	Bobby Darwin, Minnesota	127
1975	Jeff Burroughs, Texas	155
1976	Jim Rice, Boston	123
1977	Butch Hobson, Boston	162
1978	Gary Alexander, Oakland/Cleveland	166
1979	Gorman Thomas, Milwaukee	175
1980	Gorman Thomas, Milwaukee	170
1981	Tony Armas, Oakland	115
1982	Reggie Jackson, California	156
1983	Ron Kittle, Chicago	150
1984	Tony Armas, Boston	156
1985	Steve Balboni, Kansas City	166
1986	Pete Incaviglia, Texas	185
1987	Rob Deer, Milwaukee	186
1988	Rob Deer, Milwaukee	153
	Pete Incaviglia, Texas	153
1989	Bo Jackson, Kansas City	172
1990	Cecil Fielder, Detroit	182
1991	Rob Deer, Detroit	175
1992	Dean Palmer, Texas	154
1993	Rob Deer, Detroit/Boston	169
1994	Travis Fryman, Detroit	128
1995	Mo Vaughn, Boston	150
1996	Jay Buhner, Seattle	159
1997	Jay Buhner, Seattle	175
1998	Jose Canseco, Toronto	159
1999	Jim Thome, Cleveland	171
2000	Mo Vaughn, Anaheim	181
2001	Jim Thome, Cleveland	185

NATIONAL LEAGUE

Year	Player, Club	No.
1910	John Hummel, Brooklyn	81
1911	Bob Coulson, Brooklyn	78
	Bob Bescher, Cincinnati	78
1912	Ed McDonald, Boston	91
1913	George J. Burns, New York	74
1914	Fred Merkle, New York	80
1915	Doug Baird, Pittsburgh	88
1916	Gavvy Cravath, Philadelphia	89
1917	Cy Williams, Chicago	78
1918	Ross Youngs, New York	49
	Dode Paskert, Chicago	49
1919	Ray Powell, Boston	79
1920	George Kelly, New York	92
1921	Ray Powell, Boston	85
1922	Frank Parkinson, Philadelphia	93
1923	George Grantham, Chicago	92
1924	George Grantham, Chicago	63
1925	Gabby Hartnett, Chicago	77
1926	Barney Friberg, Philadelphia	77
1927	Hack Wilson, Chicago	70
1928	Hack Wilson, Chicago	94
1929	Hack Wilson, Chicago	83
1930	Hack Wilson, Chicago	84
1931	Nick Cullop, Cincinnati	86
1932	Hack Wilson, Brooklyn	85
1933	Wally Berger, Boston	77
1934	Dolf Camilli, Chicago/Philadelphia	94
1935	Dolf Camilli, Philadelphia	113
1936	Bill Brubaker, Pittsburgh	96
1937	Vince DiMaggio, Boston	111
1938	Vince DiMaggio, Boston	134
1939	Dolf Camilli, Brooklyn	107
1940	Chet Ross, Boston	128
1941	Dolf Camilli, Brooklyn	115
1942	Vince DiMaggio, Pittsburgh	87
1943	Vince DiMaggio, Pittsburgh	126
1944	Vince DiMaggio, Pittsburgh	83
1945	Vince DiMaggio, Philadelphia	91
1946	Ralph Kiner, Pittsburgh	109
1947	Bill Nicholson, Chicago	83
1948	Hank Sauer, Cincinnati	85

Year	Player, Club	No.
1949	Duke Snider, Brooklyn	92
1950	Roy Smalley, Chicago	114
1951	Gil Hodges, Brooklyn	99
1952	Eddie Mathews, Boston	115
1953	Steve Bilko, St. Louis	125
1954	Duke Snider, Brooklyn	96
1955	Wally Post, Cincinnati	102
1956	Wally Post, Cincinnati	124
1957	Duke Snider, Brooklyn	104
1958	Harry Anderson, Philadelphia	95
1959	Wally Post, Philadelphia	101
1960	Frank Herrera, Philadelphia	136
1961	Dick Stuart, Pittsburgh	121
1962	Ken Hubbs, Chicago	129
1963	Donn Clendenon, Pittsburgh	136
1964	Dick Allen, Philadelphia	138
1965	Dick Allen, Philadelphia	150
1966	Byron Browne, Chicago	143
1967	Jim Wynn, Houston	137
1968	Donn Clendenon, Pittsburgh	163
1969	Bobby Bonds, San Francisco	187
1970	Bobby Bonds, San Francisco	189
1971	Willie Stargell, Pittsburgh	154
1972	Lee May, Houston	145
1973	Bobby Bonds, San Francisco	148
1974	Mike Schmidt, Philadelphia	138
1975	Mike Schmidt, Philadelphia	180
1976	Mike Schmidt, Philadelphia	149
1977	Greg Luzinski, Philadelphia	140
1978	Dale Murphy, Atlanta	145
1979	Dave Kingman, Chicago	131
1980	Dale Murphy, Atlanta	133
1981	Dave Kingman, New York	105
1982	Dave Kingman, New York	156
1983	Mike Schmidt, Philadelphia	148
1984	Juan Samuel, Philadelphia	168
1985	Dale Murphy, Atlanta	141
	Juan Samuel, Philadelphia	141
1986	Juan Samuel, Philadelphia	142
1987	Juan Samuel, Philadelphia	162
1988	Andres Galarraga, Montreal	153
1989	Andres Galarraga, Montreal	158
1990	Andres Galarraga, Montreal	169
1991	Delino DeShields, Montreal	151
1992	Ray Lankford, St. Louis	147
1993	Cory Snyder, Los Angeles	147
1994	Reggie Sanders, Cincinnati	114
1995	Andres Galarraga, Colorado	146
1996	Henry Rodriguez, Montreal	160
1997	Sammy Sosa, Chicago	174
1998	Sammy Sosa, Chicago	171
1999	Sammy Sosa, Chicago	171
2000	Preston Wilson, Florida	187
2001	Jose Hernandez, Milwaukee	185

Note—Not included in batting records in A.L. prior to 1913 and N.L. prior to 1910.

BASERUNNING
STOLEN BASES
AMERICAN LEAGUE

Year	Player, Club	No.
1901	Frank Isbell, Chicago	48
1902	Topsy Hartsel, Philadelphia	54
1903	Harry Bay, Cleveland	46
1904	Elmer Flick, Cleveland	42
	Harry Bay, Cleveland	42
1905	Danny Hoffman, Philadelphia	46
1906	Elmer Flick, Cleveland	39
	John Anderson, Washington	39
1907	Ty Cobb, Detroit	49
1908	Patsy Dougherty, Chicago	47
1909	Ty Cobb, Detroit	76
1910	Eddie Collins, Philadelphia	81
1911	Ty Cobb, Detroit	83

Year	Player, Club	No.
1912	Clyde Milan, Washington	88
1913	Clyde Milan, Washington	75
1914	Fritz Maisel, New York	74
1915	Ty Cobb, Detroit	96
1916	Ty Cobb, Detroit	68
1917	Ty Cobb, Detroit	55
1918	George Sisler, St. Louis	45
1919	Eddie Collins, Chicago	33
1920	Sam Rice, Washington	63
1921	George Sisler, St. Louis	35
1922	George Sisler, St. Louis	51
1923	Eddie Collins, Chicago	49
1924	Eddie Collins, Chicago	42
1925	Johnny Mostil, Chicago	43
1926	Johnny Mostil, Chicago	35
1927	George Sisler, St. Louis	27
1928	Buddy Myer, Boston	30
1929	Charlie Gehringer, Detroit	27
1930	Marty McManus, Detroit	23
1931	Ben Chapman, New York	61
1932	Ben Chapman, New York	38
1933	Ben Chapman, New York	27
1934	Bill Werber, Boston	40
1935	Bill Werber, Boston	29
1936	Lyn Lary, St. Louis	37
1937	Bill Werber, Philadelphia	35
	Ben Chapman, Washington/Boston	35
1938	Frank Crosetti, New York	27
1939	George Case, Washington	51
1940	George Case, Washington	35
1941	George Case, Washington	33
1942	George Case, Washington	44
1943	George Case, Washington	61
1944	George Stirnweiss, New York	55
1945	George Stirnweiss, New York	33
1946	George Case, Cleveland	28
1947	Bob Dillinger, St. Louis	34
1948	Bob Dillinger, St. Louis	28
1949	Bob Dillinger, St. Louis	20
1950	Dom DiMaggio, Boston	15
1951	Minnie Minoso, Cleveland/Chicago	31
1952	Minnie Minoso, Chicago	22
1953	Minnie Minoso, Chicago	25
1954	Jackie Jensen, Boston	22
1955	Jim Rivera, Chicago	25
1956	Luis Aparicio, Chicago	21
1957	Luis Aparicio, Chicago	28
1958	Luis Aparicio, Chicago	29
1959	Luis Aparicio, Chicago	56
1960	Luis Aparicio, Chicago	51
1961	Luis Aparicio, Chicago	53
1962	Luis Aparicio, Chicago	31
1963	Luis Aparicio, Baltimore	40
1964	Luis Aparicio, Baltimore	57
1965	Bert Campaneris, Kansas City	51
1966	Bert Campaneris, Kansas City	52
1967	Bert Campaneris, Kansas City	55
1968	Bert Campaneris, Oakland	62
1969	Tommy Harper, Seattle	73
1970	Bert Campaneris, Oakland	42
1971	Amos Otis, Kansas City	52
1972	Bert Campaneris, Oakland	52
1973	Tommy Harper, Boston	54
1974	Billy North, Oakland	54
1975	Mickey Rivers, California	70
1976	Billy North, Oakland	75
1977	Fred Patek, Kansas City	53
1978	Ron LeFlore, Detroit	68
1979	Willie Wilson, Kansas City	83
1980	Rickey Henderson, Oakland	100
1981	Rickey Henderson, Oakland	56
1982	Rickey Henderson, Oakland	130
1983	Rickey Henderson, Oakland	108
1984	Rickey Henderson, Oakland	66
1985	Rickey Henderson, New York	80
1986	Rickey Henderson, New York	87
1987	Harold Reynolds, Seattle	60

Year	Player, Club	No.
1988	Rickey Henderson, New York	93
1989	Rickey Henderson, New York/Oakland	77
1990	Rickey Henderson, Oakland	65
1991	Rickey Henderson, Oakland	58
1992	Kenny Lofton, Cleveland	66
1993	Kenny Lofton, Cleveland	70
1994	Kenny Lofton, Cleveland	60
1995	Kenny Lofton, Cleveland	54
1996	Kenny Lofton, Cleveland	75
1997	Brian L. Hunter, Detroit	74
1998	Rickey Henderson, Oakland	66
1999	Brian L. Hunter, Detroit/Seattle	44
2000	Johnny Damon, Kansas City	46
2001	Ichiro Suzuki, Seattle	56

NATIONAL LEAGUE

Year	Player, Club	No.
1886	Ed Andrews, Philadelphia	56
1887	Monte Ward, New York	111
1888	Dummy Hoy, Washington	82
1889	Jim Fogarty, Philadelphia	99
1890	Billy Hamilton, Philadelphia	102
1891	Billy Hamilton, Philadelphia	115
1892	Monte Ward, Brooklyn	94
1893	Monte Ward, New York	72
1894	Billy Hamilton, Philadelphia	99
1895	Billy Hamilton, Philadelphia	95
1896	Bill Lange, Chicago	100
1897	Bill Lange, Chicago	83
1898	Fred Clarke, Louisville	66
1899	Jimmy Sheckard, Baltimore	78
1900	Jimmy Barrett, Cincinnati	46
1901	Honus Wagner, Pittsburgh	48
1902	Honus Wagner, Pittsburgh	43
1903	Jimmy Sheckard, Brooklyn	67
	Frank Chance, Chicago	67
1904	Honus Wagner, Pittsburgh	53
1905	Billy Maloney, Chicago	59
	Art Devlin, New York	59
1906	Frank Chance, Chicago	57
1907	Honus Wagner, Pittsburgh	61
1908	Honus Wagner, Pittsburgh	53
1909	Bob Bescher, Cincinnati	54
1910	Bob Bescher, Cincinnati	70
1911	Bob Bescher, Cincinnati	81
1912	Bob Bescher, Cincinnati	67
1913	Max Carey, Pittsburgh	61
1914	George J. Burns, New York	62
1915	Max Carey, Pittsburgh	36
1916	Max Carey, Pittsburgh	63
1917	Max Carey, Pittsburgh	46
1918	Max Carey, Pittsburgh	58
1919	George J. Burns, New York	40
1920	Max Carey, Pittsburgh	52
1921	Frankie Frisch, New York	49
1922	Max Carey, Pittsburgh	51
1923	Max Carey, Pittsburgh	51
1924	Max Carey, Pittsburgh	49
1925	Max Carey, Pittsburgh	46
1926	Kiki Cuyler, Pittsburgh	35
1927	Frankie Frisch, St. Louis	48
1928	Kiki Cuyler, Chicago	37
1929	Kiki Cuyler, Chicago	43
1930	Kiki Cuyler, Chicago	37
1931	Frankie Frisch, St. Louis	28
1932	Chuck Klein, Philadelphia	20
1933	Pepper Martin, St. Louis	26
1934	Pepper Martin, St. Louis	23
1935	Augie Galan, Chicago	22
1936	Pepper Martin, St. Louis	23
1937	Augie Galan, Chicago	23
1938	Stan Hack, Chicago	16
1939	Stan Hack, Chicago	17
	Lee Handley, Pittsburgh	17
1940	Lonny Frey, Cincinnati	22
1941	Danny Murtaugh, Philadelphia	18
1942	Pete Reiser, Brooklyn	20

Year	Player, Club	No.
1943	Arky Vaughan, Brooklyn	20
1944	Johnny Barrett, Pittsburgh	28
1945	Red Schoendienst, St. Louis	26
1946	Pete Reiser, Brooklyn	34
1947	Jackie Robinson, Brooklyn	29
1948	Richie Ashburn, Philadelphia	32
1949	Jackie Robinson, Brooklyn	37
1950	Sam Jethroe, Boston	35
1951	Sam Jethroe, Boston	35
1952	Pee Wee Reese, Brooklyn	30
1953	Billy Bruton, Milwaukee	26
1954	Billy Bruton, Milwaukee	34
1955	Billy Bruton, Milwaukee	25
1956	Willie Mays, New York	40
1957	Willie Mays, New York	38
1958	Willie Mays, San Francisco	31
1959	Willie Mays, San Francisco	27
1960	Maury Wills, Los Angeles	50
1961	Maury Wills, Los Angeles	35
1962	Maury Wills, Los Angeles	104
1963	Maury Wills, Los Angeles	40
1964	Maury Wills, Los Angeles	53
1965	Maury Wills, Los Angeles	94
1966	Lou Brock, St. Louis	74
1967	Lou Brock, St. Louis	52
1968	Lou Brock, St. Louis	62
1969	Lou Brock, St. Louis	53
1970	Bobby Tolan, Cincinnati	57
1971	Lou Brock, St. Louis	64
1972	Lou Brock, St. Louis	63
1973	Lou Brock, St. Louis	70
1974	Lou Brock, St. Louis	118
1975	Dave Lopes, Los Angeles	77
1976	Dave Lopes, Los Angeles	63
1977	Frank Taveras, Pittsburgh	70
1978	Omar Moreno, Pittsburgh	71
1979	Omar Moreno, Pittsburgh	77
1980	Ron LeFlore, Montreal	97
1981	Tim Raines Sr., Montreal	71
1982	Tim Raines Sr., Montreal	78
1983	Tim Raines Sr., Montreal	90
1984	Tim Raines Sr., Montreal	75
1985	Vince Coleman, St. Louis	110
1986	Vince Coleman, St. Louis	107
1987	Vince Coleman, St. Louis	109
1988	Vince Coleman, St. Louis	81
1989	Vince Coleman, St. Louis	65
1990	Vince Coleman, St. Louis	77
1991	Marquis Grissom, Montreal	76
1992	Marquis Grissom, Montreal	78
1993	Chuck Carr, Florida	58
1994	Craig Biggio, Houston	39
1995	Quilvio Veras, Florida	56
1996	Eric Young, Colorado	53
1997	Tony Womack, Pittsburgh	60
1998	Tony Womack, Pittsburgh	58
1999	Tony Womack, Arizona	72
2000	Luis Castillo, Florida	62
2001	Juan Pierre, Colorado	46
	Jimmy Rollins, Philadelphia	46

PITCHING
WINNING PERCENTAGE
AMERICAN LEAGUE

Year	Pitcher, Club	W	L	Pct.
1901	Clark Griffith, Chicago	24	7	.774
1902	Bill Bernhard, Philadelphia/Cleveland	18	5	.783
1903	Cy Young, Boston	28	9	.757
1904	Jack Chesbro, New York	41	13	.759
1905	Jesse Tannehill, Boston	22	9	.710
1906	Eddie Plank, Philadelphia	19	6	.760
1907	Bill Donovan, Detroit	25	4	.862
1908	Ed Walsh Sr., Chicago	40	15	.727
1909	George Mullin, Detroit	29	8	.784

Year	Pitcher, Club	W	L	Pct.
1910	Chief Bender, Philadelphia	23	5	.821
1911	Chief Bender, Philadelphia	17	5	.773
1912	Joe Wood, Boston	34	5	.872
1913	Walter Johnson, Washington	36	7	.837
1914	Chief Bender, Philadelphia	17	3	.850
1915	Joe Wood, Boston	15	5	.750
1916	Ed Cicotte, Chicago	15	7	.682
1917	Reb Russell, Chicago	15	5	.750
1918	Sam Jones, Boston	16	5	.762
1919	Ed Cicotte, Chicago	29	7	.806
1920	Jim Bagby Sr., Cleveland	31	12	.721
1921	Carl Mays, New York	27	9	.750
1922	Joe Bush, New York	26	7	.788
1923	Herb Pennock, New York	19	6	.760
1924	Walter Johnson, Washington	23	7	.767
1925	Stan Coveleski, Washington	20	5	.800
1926	George Uhle, Cleveland	27	11	.711
1927	Waite Hoyt, New York	22	7	.759
1928	Alvin Crowder, St. Louis	21	5	.808
1929	Lefty Grove, Philadelphia	20	6	.769
1930	Lefty Grove, Philadelphia	28	5	.848
1931	Lefty Grove, Philadelphia	31	4	.886
1932	Johnny Allen, New York	17	4	.810
1933	Lefty Grove, Philadelphia	24	8	.750
1934	Lefty Gomez, New York	26	5	.839
1935	Eldon Auker, Detroit	18	7	.720
1936	Monte Pearson, New York	19	7	.731
1937	Johnny Allen, Cleveland	15	1	.938
1938	Red Ruffing, New York	21	7	.750
1939	Lefty Grove, Boston	15	4	.789
1940	Schoolboy Rowe, Detroit	16	3	.842
1941	Lefty Gomez, New York	15	5	.750
1942	Tiny Bonham, New York	21	5	.808
1943	Spud Chandler, New York	20	4	.833
1944	Tex Hughson, Boston	18	5	.783
1945	Hal Newhouser, Detroit	25	9	.735
1946	Boo Ferriss, Boston	25	6	.806
1947	Allie Reynolds, New York	19	8	.704
1948	Jack Kramer, Boston	18	5	.783
1949	Ellis Kinder, Boston	23	6	.793
1950	Vic Raschi, New York	21	8	.724
1951	Bob Feller, Cleveland	22	8	.733
1952	Bobby Shantz, Philadelphia	24	7	.774
1953	Eddie Lopat, New York	16	4	.800
1954	Sandy Consuegra, Chicago	16	3	.842
1955	Tommy Byrne, New York	16	5	.762
1956	Whitey Ford, New York	19	6	.760
1957	Dick Donovan, Chicago	16	6	.727
	Tom Sturdivant, New York	16	6	.727
1958	Bob Turley, New York	21	7	.750
1959	Bob Shaw, Chicago	18	6	.750
1960	Jim Perry, Cleveland	18	10	.643
1961	Whitey Ford, New York	25	4	.862
1962	Ray Herbert, Chicago	20	9	.690
1963	Whitey Ford, New York	24	7	.774
1964	Wally Bunker, Baltimore	19	5	.792
1965	Mudcat Grant, Minnesota	21	7	.750
1966	Sonny Siebert, Cleveland	16	8	.667
1967	Joe Horlen, Chicago	19	7	.731
1968	Denny McLain, Detroit	31	6	.838
1969	Jim Palmer, Baltimore	16	4	.800
1970	Mike Cuellar, Baltimore	24	8	.750
1971	Dave McNally, Baltimore	21	5	.808
1972	Catfish Hunter, Oakland	21	7	.750
1973	Catfish Hunter, Oakland	21	5	.808
1974	Mike Cuellar, Baltimore	22	10	.688
1975	Mike Torrez, Baltimore	20	9	.690
1976	Bill Campbell, Minnesota	17	5	.773
1977	Paul Splittorff, Kansas City	16	6	.727
1978	Ron Guidry, New York	25	3	.893
1979	Mike Caldwell, Milwaukee	16	6	.727
1980	Steve Stone, Baltimore	25	7	.781
1981	Pete Vuckovich, Milwaukee	14	4	.778
1982	Pete Vuckovich, Milwaukee	18	6	.750
1983	Rich Dotson, Chicago	22	7	.759
1984	Doyle Alexander, Toronto	17	6	.739
1985	Ron Guidry, New York	22	6	.786
1986	Roger Clemens, Boston	24	4	.857
1987	Roger Clemens, Boston	20	9	.690
1988	Frank Viola, Minnesota	24	7	.774
1989	Bret Saberhagen, Kansas City	23	6	.793
1990	Bob Welch, Oakland	27	6	.818
1991	Scott Erickson, Minnesota	20	8	.714
1992	Mike Mussina, Baltimore	18	5	.783
1993	Jimmy Key, New York	18	6	.750
1994	Jason Bere, Chicago	12	2	.857
1995	Randy Johnson, Seattle	18	2	.900
1996	Charles Nagy, Cleveland	17	5	.773
1997	Randy Johnson, Seattle	20	4	.833
1998	David Wells, New York	18	4	.818
1999	Pedro Martinez, Boston	23	4	.852
2000	Tim Hudson, Oakland	20	6	.769
2001	Roger Clemens, New York	20	3	.870

NATIONAL LEAGUE

Year	Pitcher, Club	W	L	Pct.
1876	Al Spalding, Chicago	47	13	.783
1877	Tommy Bond, Boston	31	17	.646
1878	Tommy Bond, Boston	40	19	.678
1879	Monte Ward, Providence	44	18	.710
1880	Fred Goldsmith, Chicago	22	3	.880
1881	Hoss Radbourn, Providence	25	11	.694
1882	Larry Corcoran, Chicago	27	13	.675
1883	Jim McCormick, Cleveland	27	13	.675
1884	Hoss Radbourn, Providence	60	12	.833
1885	Mickey Welch, New York	44	11	.800
1886	Jocko Flynn, Chicago	24	6	.800
1887	Charlie Getzien, Detroit	29	13	.690
1888	Tim Keefe, New York	35	12	.745
1889	John Clarkson, Boston	49	19	.721
1890	Tom Lovett, Brooklyn	32	11	.744
1891	John Ewing, New York	22	8	.733
1892	Cy Young, Cleveland	36	11	.766
1893	Frank Killen, Pittsburgh	34	10	.773
1894	Jouett Meekin, New York	34	9	.791
1895	Bill Hoffer, Baltimore	30	7	.811
1896	Bill Hoffer, Baltimore	26	7	.788
1897	Fred Klobedanz, Boston	26	7	.788
1898	Ted Lewis, Boston	26	8	.765
1899	Jim Hughes, Brooklyn	28	6	.824
1900	Joe McGinnity, Brooklyn	29	9	.763
1901	Jack Chesbro, Pittsburgh	21	9	.700
1902	Jack Chesbro, Pittsburgh	28	6	.824
1903	Sam Leever, Pittsburgh	25	7	.781
1904	Joe McGinnity, New York	35	8	.814
1905	Sam Leever, Pittsburgh	20	5	.800
1906	Ed Reulbach, Chicago	19	4	.826
1907	Ed Reulbach, Chicago	17	4	.810
1908	Ed Reulbach, Chicago	24	7	.774
1909	Christy Mathewson, New York	25	6	.806
	Howie Camnitz, Pittsburgh	25	6	.806
1910	King Cole, Chicago	20	4	.833
1911	Rube Marquard, New York	24	7	.774
1912	Claude Hendrix, Pittsburgh	24	9	.727
1913	Bert Humphries, Chicago	16	4	.800
1914	Bill James, Boston	26	7	.788
1915	Grover Alexander, Philadelphia	31	10	.756
1916	Tom Hughes, Boston	16	3	.842
1917	Ferdie Schupp, New York	21	7	.750
1918	Claude Hendrix, Chicago	20	7	.741
1919	Dutch Ruether, Cincinnati	19	6	.760
1920	Burleigh Grimes, Brooklyn	23	11	.676
1921	Bill Doak, St. Louis	15	6	.714
1922	Pete Donohue, Cincinnati	18	9	.667
1923	Dolf Luque, Cincinnati	27	8	.771
1924	Emil Yde, Pittsburgh	16	3	.842
1925	Willie Sherdel, St. Louis	15	6	.714
1926	Ray Kremer, Pittsburgh	20	6	.769
1927	Larry Benton, Boston/New York	17	7	.708
1928	Larry Benton, New York	25	9	.735
1929	Charlie Root, Chicago	19	6	.760
1930	Freddie Fitzsimmons, New York	19	7	.731

Year	Pitcher, Club	W	L	Pct.
1931	Paul Derringer, St. Louis	18	8	.692
1932	Lon Warneke, Chicago	22	6	.786
1933	Ben Cantwell, Boston	20	10	.667
1934	Dizzy Dean, St. Louis	30	7	.811
1935	Bill Lee, Chicago	20	6	.769
1936	Carl Hubbell, New York	26	6	.813
1937	Carl Hubbell, New York	22	8	.733
1938	Bill Lee, Chicago	22	9	.710
1939	Paul Derringer, Cincinnati	25	7	.781
1940	Freddie Fitzsimmons, Brooklyn	16	2	.889
1941	Elmer Riddle, Cincinnati	19	4	.826
1942	Larry French, Brooklyn	15	4	.789
1943	Mort Cooper, St. Louis	21	8	.724
1944	Ted Wilks, St. Louis	17	4	.810
1945	Harry Brecheen, St. Louis	15	4	.789
1946	Murry Dickson, St. Louis	15	6	.714
1947	Larry Jansen, New York	21	5	.808
1948	Harry Brecheen, St. Louis	20	7	.741
1949	Preacher Roe, Brooklyn	15	6	.714
1950	Sal Maglie, New York	18	4	.818
1951	Preacher Roe, Brooklyn	22	3	.880
1952	Hoyt Wilhelm, New York	15	3	.833
1953	Carl Erskine, Brooklyn	20	6	.769
1954	Johnny Antonelli, New York	21	7	.750
1955	Don Newcombe, Brooklyn	20	5	.800
1956	Don Newcombe, Brooklyn	27	7	.794
1957	Bob Buhl, Milwaukee	18	7	.720
1958	Warren Spahn, Milwaukee	22	11	.667
	Lew Burdette, Milwaukee	20	10	.667
1959	Roy Face, Pittsburgh	18	1	.947
1960	Ernie Broglio, St. Louis	21	9	.700
1961	Johnny Podres, Los Angeles	18	5	.783
1962	Bob Purkey, Cincinnati	23	5	.821
1963	Ron Perranoski, Los Angeles	16	3	.842
1964	Sandy Koufax, Los Angeles	19	5	.792
1965	Sandy Koufax, Los Angeles	26	8	.765
1966	Juan Marichal, San Francisco	25	6	.806
1967	Dick Hughes, St. Louis	16	6	.727
1968	Steve Blass, Pittsburgh	18	6	.750
1969	Tom Seaver, New York	25	7	.781
1970	Bob Gibson, St. Louis	23	7	.767
1971	Don Gullett, Cincinnati	16	6	.727
1972	Gary Nolan, Cincinnati	15	5	.750
1973	Tommy John, Los Angeles	16	7	.696
1974	Andy Messersmith, Los Angeles	20	6	.769
1975	Don Gullett, Cincinnati	15	4	.789
1976	Steve Carlton, Philadelphia	20	7	.741
1977	John Candelaria, Pittsburgh	20	5	.800
1978	Gaylord Perry, San Diego	21	6	.778
1979	Tom Seaver, Cincinnati	16	6	.727
1980	Jim Bibby, Pittsburgh	19	6	.760
1981	Tom Seaver, CIncinnati	14	2	.875
1982	Phil Niekro, Atlanta	17	4	.810
1983	John Denny, Philadelphia	19	6	.760
1984	Rick Sutcliffe, Chicago	16	1	.941
1985	Orel Hershiser, Los Angeles	19	3	.864
1986	Bob Ojeda, New York	18	5	.783
1987	Dwight Gooden, New York	15	7	.682
1988	David Cone, New York	20	3	.870
1989	Mike Bielecki, Chicago	18	7	.720
1990	Doug Drabek, Pittsburgh	22	6	.786
1991	John Smiley, Pittsburgh	20	8	.714
	Jose Rijo, Cincinnati	15	6	.714
1992	Bob Tewksbury, St. Louis	16	5	.762
1993	Mark Portugal, Houston	18	4	.818
1994	Marvin Freeman, Colorado	10	2	.833
1995	Greg Maddux, Atlanta	19	2	.905
1996	John Smoltz, Atlanta	24	8	.750
1997	Greg Maddux, Atlanta	19	4	.826
1998	John Smoltz, Atlanta	17	3	.850
1999	Mike Hampton, Houston	22	4	.846
2000	Randy Johnson, Arizona	19	7	.731
2001	Curt Schilling, Arizona	22	6	.786

Note—Based on 15 or more victories, except for 1981 and 1994 percentages, which are based on 10 or more victories.

EARNED-RUN AVERAGE

AMERICAN LEAGUE

Year	Pitcher, Club	G	IP	ERA
1913	Walter Johnson, Washington	48	346	1.14
1914	Dutch H. Leonard, Boston	35	225	1.00
1915	Joe Wood, Boston	25	157	1.49
1916	Babe Ruth, Boston	44	324	1.75
1917	Ed Cicotte, Chicago	49	346	1.53
1918	Walter Johnson, Washington	39	325	1.27
1919	Walter Johnson, Washington	39	290	1.49
1920	Bob Shawkey, New York	38	267	2.45
1921	Red Faber, Chicago	43	331	2.47
1922	Red Faber, Chicago	43	353	2.80
1923	Stan Coveleski, Cleveland	33	228	2.76
1924	Walter Johnson, Washington	38	278	2.72
1925	Stan Coveleski, Washington	32	241	2.84
1926	Lefty Grove, Philadelphia	45	258	2.51
1927	Wilcy Moore, New York	50	213	2.28
1928	Garland Braxton, Washington	38	218	2.52
1929	Lefty Grove, Philadelphia	42	275	2.81
1930	Lefty Grove, Philadelphia	50	291	2.54
1931	Lefty Grove, Philadelphia	41	289	2.06
1932	Lefty Grove, Philadelphia	44	292	2.84
1933	Monte Pearson, Cleveland	19	135	2.33
1934	Lefty Gomez, New York	38	282	2.33
1935	Lefty Grove, Boston	35	273	2.70
1936	Lefty Grove, Boston	35	253	2.81
1937	Lefty Gomez, New York	34	278	2.33
1938	Lefty Grove, Boston	24	164	3.07
1939	Lefty Grove, Boston	23	191	2.54
1940	Bob Feller, Cleveland	43	320	2.62
1941	Thornton Lee, Chicago	35	300	2.37
1942	Ted Lyons, Chicago	20	180	2.10
1943	Spud Chandler, New York	30	253	1.64
1944	Dizzy Trout, Detroit	49	352	2.12
1945	Hal Newhouser, Detroit	40	313	1.81
1946	Hal Newhouser, Detroit	37	293	1.94
1947	Spud Chandler, New York	17	128	2.46
1948	Gene Bearden, Cleveland	37	230	2.43
1949	Mel Parnell, Boston	39	295	2.78
1950	Early Wynn, Cleveland	32	214	3.20
1951	Saul Rogovin, Detroit/Chicago	27	217	2.78
1952	Allie Reynolds, New York	35	244	2.07
1953	Eddie Lopat, New York	25	178	2.43
1954	Mike Garcia, Cleveland	45	259	2.64
1955	Billy Pierce, Chicago	33	206	1.97
1956	Whitey Ford, New York	31	226	2.47
1957	Bobby Shantz, New York	30	173	2.45
1958	Whitey Ford, New York	30	219	2.01
1959	Hoyt Wilhelm, Baltimore	32	226	2.19
1960	Frank Baumann, Chicago	47	185	2.68
1961	Dick Donovan, Washington	23	169	2.40
1962	Hank Aguirre, Detroit	42	216	2.21
1963	Gary Peters, Chicago	41	243	2.33
1964	Dean Chance, Los Angeles	46	278	1.65
1965	Sam McDowell, Cleveland	42	273	2.18
1966	Gary Peters, Chicago	30	205	1.98
1967	Joe Horlen, Chicago	35	258	2.06
1968	Luis Tiant, Cleveland	34	258	1.60
1969	Dick Bosman, Washington	31	193	2.19
1970	Diego Segui, Oakland	47	162	2.56
1971	Vida Blue, Oakland	39	312	1.82
1972	Luis Tiant, Boston	43	179	1.91
1973	Jim Palmer, Baltimore	38	296	2.40
1974	Catfish Hunter, Oakland	41	318	2.49
1975	Jim Palmer, Baltimore	39	323	2.09
1976	Mark Fidrych, Detroit	31	250	2.34
1977	Frank Tanana, California	31	241	2.54
1978	Ron Guidry, New York	35	274	1.74
1979	Ron Guidry, New York	33	236	2.78
1980	Rudy May, New York	41	175	2.47
1981	Steve McCatty, Oakland	22	186	2.32
1982	Rick Sutcliffe, Cleveland	34	216	2.96
1983	Rick Honeycutt, Texas	25	174.2	2.42
1984	Mike Boddicker, Baltimore	34	261.1	2.79

Year	Pitcher, Club	G	IP	ERA
1985	Dave Stieb, Toronto	36	265.0	2.48
1986	Roger Clemens, Boston	33	254.0	2.48
1987	Jimmy Key, Toronto	36	261.0	2.76
1988	Allan Anderson, Minnesota	30	202.1	2.45
1989	Bret Saberhagen, Kansas City	36	262.1	2.16
1990	Roger Clemens, Boston	31	228.1	1.93
1991	Roger Clemens, Boston	35	271.1	2.62
1992	Roger Clemens, Boston	32	246.2	2.41
1993	Kevin Appier, Kansas City	34	238.2	2.56
1994	Steve Ontiveros, Oakland	27	115.1	2.65
1995	Randy Johnson, Seattle	30	214.1	2.48
1996	Juan Guzman, Toronto	27	187.2	2.93
1997	Roger Clemens, Toronto	34	264.0	2.05
1998	Roger Clemens, Toronto	33	234.2	2.65
1999	Pedro Martinez, Boston	31	213.1	2.07
2000	Pedro Martinez, Boston	29	217.0	1.74
2001	Freddy Garcia, Seattle	34	238.2	3.05

NATIONAL LEAGUE

Year	Pitcher, Club	G	IP	ERA
1912	Jeff Tesreau, New York	36	243	1.96
1913	Christy Mathewson, New York	40	306	2.06
1914	Bill Doak, St. Louis	36	256	1.72
1915	Grover Alexander, Philadelphia	49	376	1.22
1916	Grover Alexander, Philadelphia	48	390	1.55
1917	Grover Alexander, Philadelphia	45	388	1.83
1918	Hippo Vaughn, Chicago	35	290	1.74
1919	Grover Alexander, Chicago	30	235	1.72
1920	Grover Alexander, Chicago	46	363	1.91
1921	Bill Doak, St. Louis	32	209	2.58
1922	Rosy Ryan, New York	46	192	3.00
1923	Dolf Luque, Cincinnati	41	322	1.93
1924	Dazzy Vance, Brooklyn	35	309	2.16
1925	Dolf Luque, Cincinnati	36	291	2.63
1926	Ray Kremer, Pittsburgh	37	231	2.61
1927	Ray Kremer, Pittsburgh	35	226	2.47
1928	Dazzy Vance, Brooklyn	38	280	2.09
1929	Bill Walker, New York	29	178	3.08
1930	Dazzy Vance, Brooklyn	35	259	2.61
1931	Bill Walker, New York	37	239	2.26
1932	Lon Warneke, Chicago	35	277	2.37
1933	Carl Hubbell, New York	45	309	1.66
1934	Carl Hubbell, New York	49	313	2.30
1935	Cy Blanton, Pittsburgh	35	254	2.59
1936	Carl Hubbell, New York	42	304	2.31
1937	Jim Turner, Boston	33	257	2.38
1938	Bill Lee, Chicago	44	291	2.66
1939	Bucky Walters, Cincinnati	39	319	2.29
1940	Bucky Walters, Cincinnati	36	305	2.48
1941	Elmer Riddle, Cincinnati	33	217	2.24
1942	Mort Cooper, St. Louis	37	279	1.77
1943	Howie Pollet, St. Louis	16	118	1.75
1944	Ed Heusser, Cincinnati	30	193	2.38
1945	Hank Borowy, Chicago	15	122	2.14
1946	Howie Pollet, St. Louis	40	266	2.10
1947	Warren Spahn, Boston	40	290	2.33
1948	Harry Brecheen, St. Louis	33	233	2.24
1949	Dave Koslo, New York	38	212	2.50
1950	Jim Hearn, St. Louis/New York	22	134	2.49
1951	Chet Nichols, Boston	33	156	2.88
1952	Hoyt Wilhelm, New York	71	159	2.43
1953	Warren Spahn, Milwaukee	35	266	2.10
1954	Johnny Antonelli, New York	39	259	2.29
1955	Bob Friend, Pittsburgh	44	200	2.84
1956	Lew Burdette, Milwaukee	39	256	2.71
1957	Johnny Podres, Brooklyn	31	196	2.66
1958	Stu Miller, San Francisco	41	182	2.47
1959	Sam Jones, San Francisco	50	271	2.82
1960	Mike McCormick, San Francisco	40	253	2.70
1961	Warren Spahn, Milwaukee	38	263	3.01
1962	Sandy Koufax, Los Angeles	28	184	2.54
1963	Sandy Koufax, Los Angeles	40	311	1.88
1964	Sandy Koufax, Los Angeles	29	223	1.74
1965	Sandy Koufax, Los Angeles	43	336	2.04
1966	Sandy Koufax, Los Angeles	41	323	1.73
1967	Phil Niekro, Atlanta	46	207	1.87

Year	Pitcher, Club	G	IP	ERA
1968	Bob Gibson, St. Louis	34	305	1.12
1969	Juan Marichal, San Francisco	37	300	2.10
1970	Tom Seaver, New York	37	291	2.81
1971	Tom Seaver, New York	36	286	1.76
1972	Steve Carlton, Philadelphia	41	346	1.98
1973	Tom Seaver, New York	36	290	2.08
1974	Buzz Capra, Atlanta	39	217	2.28
1975	Randy Jones, San Diego	37	285	2.24
1976	John Denny, St. Louis	30	207	2.52
1977	John Candelaria, Pittsburgh	33	231	2.34
1978	Craig Swan, New York	29	207	2.43
1979	J.R. Richard, Houston	38	292	2.71
1980	Don Sutton, Los Angeles	32	212	2.21
1981	Nolan Ryan, Houston	21	149	1.69
1982	Steve Rogers, Montreal	35	277	2.40
1983	Atlee Hammaker, San Francisco	23	172.1	2.25
1984	Alejandro Pena, Los Angeles	28	199.1	2.48
1985	Dwight Gooden, New York	35	276.2	1.53
1986	Mike Scott, Houston	37	275.1	2.22
1987	Nolan Ryan, Houston	34	211.2	2.76
1988	Joe Magrane, St. Louis	24	165.1	2.18
1989	Scott Garrelts, San Francisco	30	193.1	2.28
1990	Danny Darwin, Houston	48	162.2	2.21
1991	Dennis Martinez, Montreal	31	222.0	2.39
1992	Bill Swift, San Francisco	30	164.2	2.08
1993	Greg Maddux, Atlanta	36	267.0	2.36
1994	Greg Maddux, Atlanta	25	202.0	1.56
1995	Greg Maddux, Atlanta	28	209.2	1.63
1996	Kevin Brown, Florida	32	233.0	1.89
1997	Pedro J. Martinez, Montreal	31	241.1	1.90
1998	Greg Maddux, Atlanta	34	251.0	2.22
1999	Randy Johnson, Arizona	35	271.2	2.48
2000	Kevin Brown, Los Angeles	33	230.0	2.58
2001	Randy Johnson, Arizona	35	249.2	2.49

Note—Based on 10 complete games through 1950, then 154 innings until 1961 in A.L. and 1962 in N.L., when it became 162 innings.
Note—ERA records not tabulated in N.L. prior to 1912 and A.L. prior to 1913.
Note—1981 ERA champion determined by taking leader who pitched as many innings as his team's total number of games played.
Note—Wilcy Moore pitched only six complete games—he started 12—in 1927, but was recognized as A.L. leader because of 213 innings pitched; Tiny Bonham, New York, had 1.91 ERA and 10 complete games in 1940, but appeared in only 12 games and 99 innings, and Bob Feller was recognized as the leader.

SHUTOUTS

AMERICAN LEAGUE

Year	Pitcher, Club	No.
1901	Clark Griffith, Chicago	5
	Cy Young, Boston	5
1902	Addie Joss, Cleveland	5
1903	Cy Young, Boston	7
1904	Cy Young, Boston	10
1905	Ed Killian, Detroit	8
1906	Ed Walsh Sr., Chicago	10
1907	Eddie Plank, Philadelphia	8
1908	Ed Walsh Sr., Chicago	12
1909	Ed Walsh Sr., Chicago	8
1910	Jack Coombs, Philadelphia	13
1911	Walter Johnson, Washington	6
	Eddie Plank, Philadelphia	6
1912	Joe Wood, Boston	10
1913	Walter Johnson, Washington	11
1914	Walter Johnson, Washington	9
1915	Walter Johnson, Washington	7
1916	Babe Ruth, Boston	9
1917	Stan Coveleski, Cleveland	9
1918	Walter Johnson, Washington	8
	Carl Mays, Boston	8
1919	Walter Johnson, Washington	7
1920	Carl Mays, New York	6
1921	Sam P. Jones, Boston	5
1922	George Uhle, Cleveland	5

Year	Pitcher, Club	No.
1923	Stan Coveleski, Cleveland	5
1924	Walter Johnson, Washington	6
1925	Ted Lyons, Chicago	5
1926	Ed Wells, Detroit	4
1927	Hod Lisenbee, Washington	4
1928	Herb Pennock, New York	5
1929	George Blaeholder, St. Louis	4
	Alvin Crowder, St. Louis	4
	Sam Gray, St. Louis	4
	Danny MacFayden, Boston	4
1930	Clint Brown, Cleveland	3
	George Earnshaw, Philadelphia	3
	George Pipgras, New York	3
1931	Lefty Grove, Philadelphia	4
	Vic Sorrell, Detroit	4
1932	Tommy Bridges, Detroit	4
	Lefty Grove, Philadelphia	4
1933	Oral Hildebrand, Cleveland	6
1934	Lefty Gomez, New York	6
	Mel Harder, Cleveland	6
1935	Schoolboy Rowe, Detroit	6
1936	Lefty Grove, Boston	6
1937	Lefty Gomez, New York	6
1938	Lefty Gomez, New York	4
1939	Red Ruffing, New York	5
1940	Bob Feller, Cleveland	4
	Ted Lyons, Chicago	4
	Al Milnar, Cleveland	4
1941	Bob Feller, Cleveland	6
1942	Tiny Bonham, New York	6
1943	Spud Chandler, New York	5
	Dizzy Trout, Detroit	5
1944	Dizzy Trout, Detroit	7
1945	Hal Newhouser, Detroit	8
1946	Bob Feller, Cleveland	10
1947	Bob Feller, Cleveland	5
1948	Bob Lemon, Cleveland	10
1949	Mike Garcia, Cleveland	6
	Ellis Kinder, Boston	6
	Virgil Trucks, Detroit	6
1950	Art Houtteman, Detroit	4
1951	Allie Reynolds, New York	7
1952	Mike Garcia, Cleveland	6
	Allie Reynolds, New York	6
1953	Bob Porterfield, Washington	9
1954	Mike Garcia, Cleveland	5
	Virgil Trucks, Chicago	5
1955	Billy Hoeft, Detroit	7
1956	Herb Score, Cleveland	5
1957	Jim Wilson, Chicago	5
1958	Whitey Ford, New York	7
1959	Camilo Pascual, Washington	6
1960	Whitey Ford, New York	4
	Jim Perry, Cleveland	4
	Early Wynn, Chicago	4
1961	Steve Barber, Baltimore	8
	Camilo Pascual, Minnesota	8
1962	Dick Donovan, Cleveland	5
	Jim Kaat, Minnesota	5
	Camilo Pascual, Minnesota	5
1963	Ray Herbert, Chicago	7
1964	Dean Chance, Los Angeles	11
1965	Mudcat Grant, Minnesota	6
1966	Tommy John, Chicago	5
	Sam McDowell, Cleveland	5
	Luis Tiant, Cleveland	5
1967	Steve Hargan, Cleveland	6
	Joe Horlen, Chicago	6
	Tommy John, Chicago	6
	Mickey Lolich, Detroit	6
	Jim McGlothlin, California	6
1968	Luis Tiant, Cleveland	9
1969	Denny McLain, Detroit	9
1970	Chuck Dobson, Oakland	5
	Jim Palmer, Baltimore	5
1971	Vida Blue, Oakland	8
1972	Nolan Ryan, California	9
1973	Bert Blyleven, Minnesota	9

Year	Pitcher, Club	No.
1974	Luis Tiant, Boston	7
1975	Jim Palmer, Baltimore	10
1976	Nolan Ryan, California	7
1977	Frank Tanana, California	7
1978	Ron Guidry, New York	9
1979	Nolan Ryan, California	5
	Mike Flanagan, Baltimore	5
	Dennis Leonard, Kansas City	5
1980	Tommy John, New York	6
1981	Rich Dotson, Chicago	4
	Ken Forsch, California	4
	Steve McCatty, Oakland	4
	Doc Medich, Texas	4
1982	Dave Stieb, Toronto	5
1983	Mike Boddicker, Baltimore	5
1984	Bob Ojeda, Boston	5
	Geoff Zahn, California	5
1985	Bert Blyleven, Cleveland/Minnesota	5
1986	Jack Morris, Detroit	6
1987	Roger Clemens, Boston	7
1988	Roger Clemens, Boston	8
1989	Bert Blyleven, California	5
1990	Roger Clemens, Boston	4
	Dave Stewart, Oakland	4
1991	Roger Clemens, Boston	4
1992	Roger Clemens, Boston	5
1993	Jack McDowell, Chicago	4
1994	Randy Johnson, Seattle	4
1995	Mike Mussina, Baltimore	4
1996	Pat Hentgen, Toronto	3
	Ken Hill, Texas	3
	Rich Robertson, Minnesota	3
1997	Roger Clemens, Toronto	3
	Pat Hentgen, Toronto	3
1998	David Wells, New York	5
1999	Scott Erickson, Baltimore	3
2000	Pedro Martinez, Boston	4
2001	Mark Mulder, Oakland	4

NATIONAL LEAGUE

Year	Pitcher, Club	No.
1900	Clark Griffith, Chicago	4
	Noodles Hahn, Cincinnati	4
	Kid Nichols, Boston	4
	Cy Young, St. Louis	4
1901	Jack Chesbro, Pittsburgh	6
	Al Orth, Philadelphia	6
	Vic Willis, Boston	6
1902	Jack Chesbro, Pittsburgh	8
	Christy Mathewson, New York	8
1903	Sam Leever, Pittsburgh	7
1904	Joe McGinnity, New York	9
1905	Christy Mathewson, New York	9
1906	Mordecai Brown, Chicago	9
1907	Orval Overall, Chicago	9
	Christy Mathewson, New York	9
1908	Christy Mathewson, New York	12
1909	Orval Overall, Chicago	9
1910	Earl Moore, Philadelphia	7
1911	Grover Alexander, Philadelphia	7
1912	Nap Rucker, Brooklyn	6
1913	Grover Alexander, Philadelphia	9
1914	Jeff Tesreau, New York	8
1915	Grover Alexander, Philadelphia	12
1916	Grover Alexander, Philadelphia	16
1917	Grover Alexander, Philadelphia	8
1918	Lefty Tyler, Chicago	8
	Hippo Vaughn, Chicago	8
1919	Grover Alexander, Chicago	9
1920	Babe Adams, Pittsburgh	8
1921	Grover Alexander, Chicago	3
	Phil Douglas, New York	3
	Dana Fillingim, Boston	3
	Dolf Luque, Cincinnati	3
	Clarence Mitchell, Brooklyn	3
	Johnny Morrison, Pittsburgh	3
	Joe Oeschger, Boston	3
	Jesse Haines, St. Louis	3

Year	Pitcher, Club	No.
1922	Dazzy Vance, Brooklyn	6
1923	Dolf Luque, Cincinnati	6
1924	Jesse Barnes, Boston	4
	Wilbur Cooper, Pittsburgh	4
	Ray Kremer, Pittsburgh	4
	Eppa Rixey, Cincinnati	4
	Allen Sothoron, St. Louis	4
	Emil Yde, Pittsburgh	4
1925	Hal Carlson, Philadelphia	4
	Dolf Luque, Cincinnati	4
	Dazzy Vance, Brooklyn	4
1926	Pete Donohue, Cincinnati	5
1927	Jesse Haines, St. Louis	6
1928	Sheriff Blake, Chicago	4
	Burleigh Grimes, Pittsburgh	4
	Red Lucas, Cincinnati	4
	Doug McWeeny, Brooklyn	4
	Dazzy Vance, Brooklyn	4
1929	Pat Malone, Chicago	5
1930	Charlie Root, Chicago	4
	Dazzy Vance, Brooklyn	4
1931	Bill Walker, New York	6
1932	Lon Warneke, Chicago	4
	Dizzy Dean, St. Louis	4
	Steve Swetonic, Pittsburgh	4
1933	Carl Hubbell, New York	10
1934	Dizzy Dean, St. Louis	7
1935	Cy Blanton, Pittsburgh	4
	Freddie Fitzsimmons, New York	4
	Larry French, Chicago	4
	Van Lingle Mungo, Brooklyn	4
	Jim Weaver, Pittsburgh	4
1936	Cy Blanton, Pittsburgh	4
	Tex Carleton, Chicago	4
	Larry French, Chicago	4
	Bill Lee, Chicago	4
	Al Smith, New York	4
	Bucky Walters, Philadelphia	4
	Lon Warneke, Chicago	4
1937	Lou Fette, Boston	5
	Lee Grissom, Cincinnati	5
	Jim Turner, Boston	5
1938	Bill Lee, Chicago	9
1939	Lou Fette, Boston	6
1940	Bill Lohrman, New York	5
	Manny Salvo, Boston	5
	Whitlow Wyatt, Brooklyn	5
1941	Whitlow Wyatt, Brooklyn	7
1942	Mort Cooper, St. Louis	10
1943	Hi Bithorn, Chicago	7
1944	Mort Cooper, St. Louis	7
1945	Claude Passeau, Chicago	5
1946	Ewell Blackwell, Cincinnati	6
1947	Warren Spahn, Boston	7
1948	Harry Brecheen, St. Louis	7
1949	Ken Heintzelman, Philadelphia	5
	Don Newcombe, Brooklyn	5
	Howie Pollet, St. Louis	5
	Ken Raffensberger, Cincinnati	5
1950	Jim Hearn, New York	5
	Larry Jansen, New York	5
	Sal Maglie, New York	5
	Robin Roberts, Philadelphia	5
1951	Warren Spahn, Boston	7
1952	Ken Raffensberger, Cincinnati	6
	Curt Simmons, Philadelphia	6
1953	Harvey Haddix, St. Louis	6
1954	Johnny Antonelli, New York	6
1955	Joe Nuxhall, Cincinnati	5
1956	Johnny Antonelli, New York	6
	Lew Burdette, Milwaukee	6
1957	Johnny Podres, Brooklyn	6
1958	Carl Willey, Milwaukee	4
1959	Johnny Antonelli, San Francisco	4
	Bob Buhl, Milwaukee	4
	Lew Burdette, Milwaukee	4
	Roger Craig, Los Angeles	4
	Don Drysdale, Los Angeles	4

Year	Pitcher, Club	No.
	Sam Jones, San Francisco	4
	Warren Spahn, Milwaukee	4
1960	Jack Sanford, San Francisco	6
1961	Joey Jay, Cincinnati	4
	Warren Spahn, Milwaukee	4
1962	Bob Friend, Pittsburgh	5
	Bob Gibson, St. Louis	5
1963	Sandy Koufax, Los Angeles	11
1964	Sandy Koufax, Los Angeles	7
1965	Juan Marichal, San Francisco	10
1966	Jim Bunning, Philadelphia	5
	Bob Gibson, St. Louis	5
	Larry Jackson, Philadelphia	5
	Larry Jaster, St. Louis	5
	Sandy Koufax, Los Angeles	5
	Jim Maloney, Cincinnati	5
1967	Jim Bunning, Philadelphia	6
1968	Bob Gibson, St. Louis	13
1969	Juan Marichal, San Francisco	8
1970	Gaylord Perry, San Francisco	5
1971	Steve Blass, Pittsburgh	5
	Al Downing, Los Angeles	5
	Bob Gibson, St. Louis	5
	Milt Pappas, Chicago	5
1972	Don Sutton, Los Angeles	9
1973	Jack Billingham, Cincinnati	7
1974	Jon Matlack, New York	7
1975	Andy Messersmith, Los Angeles	7
1976	Jon Matlack, New York	6
	John Montefusco, San Francisco	6
1977	Tom Seaver, New York/Cincinnati	7
1978	Bob Knepper, San Francisco	6
1979	Tom Seaver, Cincinnati	5
	Joe Niekro, Houston	5
	Steve Rogers, Montreal	5
1980	Jerry Reuss, Los Angeles	6
1981	Fernando Valenzuela, Los Angeles	8
1982	Steve Carlton, Philadelphia	6
1983	Steve Rogers, Montreal	5
1984	Joaquin Andujar, St. Louis	4
	Orel Hershiser, Los Angeles	4
	Alejandro Pena, Los Angeles	4
1985	John Tudor, St. Louis	10
1986	Bob Knepper, Houston	5
	Mike Scott, Houston	5
1987	Rick Reuschel, Pittsburgh/San Francisco	4
	Bob Welch, Los Angeles	4
1988	Orel Hershiser, Los Angeles	8
1989	Tim Belcher, Los Angeles	8
1990	Bruce Hurst, San Diego	4
	Mike Morgan, Los Angeles	4
1991	Dennis Martinez, Montreal	5
1992	David Cone, New York	5
	Tom Glavine, Atlanta	5
1993	Pete Harnisch, Houston	4
1994	Greg Maddux, Atlanta	3
	Ramon Martinez, Los Angeles	3
1995	Greg Maddux, Atlanta	3
	Hideo Nomo, Los Angeles	3
1996	Kevin Brown, Florida	3
1997	Carlos Perez, Montreal	5
1998	Greg Maddux, Atlanta	5
1999	Andy Ashby, San Diego	3
2000	Randy Johnson, Arizona	3
	Greg Maddux, Atlanta	3
2001	Greg Maddux, Atlanta	3
	Javier Vazquez, Montreal	3

SAVES

AMERICAN LEAGUE

Year	Pitcher, Club	No.
1969	Ron Perranoski, Minnesota	31
1970	Ron Perranoski, Minnesota	34
1971	Ken Sanders, Milwaukee	31
1972	Sparky Lyle, New York	35
1973	John Hiller, Detroit	38

Year	Pitcher, Club	No.
1974	Terry Forster, Chicago	24
1975	Rich Gossage, Chicago	26
1976	Sparky Lyle, New York	23
1977	Bill Campbell, Boston	31
1978	Rich Gossage, New York	27
1979	Mike Marshall, Minnesota	32
1980	Rich Gossage, New York	33
	Dan Quisenberry, Kansas City	33
1981	Rollie Fingers, Milwaukee	28
1982	Dan Quisenberry, Kansas City	35
1983	Dan Quisenberry, Kansas City	45
1984	Dan Quisenberry, Kansas City	44
1985	Dan Quisenberry, Kansas City	37
1986	Dave Righetti, New York	46
1987	Tom Henke, Toronto	34
1988	Dennis Eckersley, Oakland	45
1989	Jeff Russell, Texas	38
1990	Bobby Thigpen, Chicago	57
1991	Bryan Harvey, California	46
1992	Dennis Eckersley, Oakland	51
1993	Jeff Montgomery, Kansas City	45
	Duane Ward, Toronto	45
1994	Lee Smith, Baltimore	33
1995	Jose Mesa, Cleveland	46
1996	John Wetteland, New York	43
1997	Randy Myers, Baltimore	45
1998	Tom Gordon, Boston	46
1999	Mariano Rivera, New York	45
2000	Todd Jones, Detroit	42
	Derek Lowe, Boston	42
2001	Mariano Rivera, New York	50

NATIONAL LEAGUE

Year	Pitcher, Club	No.
1969	Fred Gladding, Houston	29
1970	Wayne Granger, Cincinnati	35
1971	Dave Giusti, Pittsburgh	30
1972	Clay Carroll, Cincinnati	37
1973	Mike Marshall, Montreal	31
1974	Mike Marshall, Los Angeles	21
1975	Rawly Eastwick, Cincinnati	22
	Al Hrabosky, St. Louis	22
1976	Rawly Eastwick, Cincinnati	26
1977	Rollie Fingers, San Diego	35
1978	Rollie Fingers, San Diego	37
1979	Bruce Sutter, Chicago	37
1980	Bruce Sutter, Chicago	28
1981	Bruce Sutter, St. Louis	25
1982	Bruce Sutter, St. Louis	36
1983	Lee Smith, Chicago	29
1984	Bruce Sutter, St. Louis	45
1985	Jeff Reardon, Montreal	41
1986	Todd Worrell, St. Louis	36
1987	Steve Bedrosian, Philadelphia	40
1988	John Franco, Cincinnati	39
1989	Mark Davis, San Diego	44
1990	John Franco, New York	33
1991	Lee Smith, St. Louis	47
1992	Lee Smith, St. Louis	43
1993	Randy Myers, Chicago	53
1994	John Franco, New York	30
1995	Randy Myers, Chicago	38
1996	Jeff Brantley, Cincinnati	44
	Todd Worrell, Los Angeles	44
1997	Jeff Shaw, Cincinnati	42
1998	Trevor Hoffman, San Diego	53
1999	Ugueth Urbina, Montreal	41
2000	Antonio Alfonseca, Florida	45
2001	Robb Nen, San Francisco	45

STRIKEOUTS

AMERICAN LEAGUE

Year	Pitcher, Club	No.
1901	Cy Young, Boston	158
1902	Rube Waddell, Philadelphia	210

Year	Pitcher, Club	No.
1903	Rube Waddell, Philadelphia	301
1904	Rube Waddell, Philadelphia	349
1905	Rube Waddell, Philadelphia	286
1906	Rube Waddell, Philadelphia	203
1907	Rube Waddell, Philadelphia	226
1908	Ed Walsh, Chicago	269
1909	Frank Smith, Chicago	177
1910	Walter Johnson, Washington	313
1911	Ed Walsh, Chicago	255
1912	Walter Johnson, Washington	303
1913	Walter Johnson, Washington	243
1914	Walter Johnson, Washington	225
1915	Walter Johnson, Washington	203
1916	Walter Johnson, Washington	228
1917	Walter Johnson, Washington	188
1918	Walter Johnson, Washington	162
1919	Walter Johnson, Washington	147
1920	Stan Coveleski, Cleveland	133
1921	Walter Johnson, Washington	143
1922	Urban Shocker, St. Louis	149
1923	Walter Johnson, Washington	130
1924	Walter Johnson, Washington	158
1925	Lefty Grove, Philadelphia	116
1926	Lefty Grove, Philadelphia	194
1927	Lefty Grove, Philadelphia	174
1928	Lefty Grove, Philadelphia	183
1929	Lefty Grove, Philadelphia	170
1930	Lefty Grove, Philadelphia	209
1931	Lefty Grove, Philadelphia	175
1932	Red Ruffing, New York	190
1933	Lefty Gomez, New York	163
1934	Lefty Gomez, New York	158
1935	Tommy Bridges, Detroit	163
1936	Tommy Bridges, Detroit	175
1937	Lefty Gomez, New York	194
1938	Bob Feller, Cleveland	240
1939	Bob Feller, Cleveland	246
1940	Bob Feller, Cleveland	261
1941	Bob Feller, Cleveland	260
1942	Bobo Newsom, Washington	113
	Tex Hughson, Boston	113
1943	Allie Reynolds, Cleveland	151
1944	Hal Newhouser, Detroit	187
1945	Hal Newhouser, Detroit	212
1946	Bob Feller, Cleveland	348
1947	Bob Feller, Cleveland	196
1948	Bob Feller, Cleveland	164
1949	Virgil Trucks, Detroit	153
1950	Bob Lemon, Cleveland	170
1951	Vic Raschi, New York	164
1952	Allie Reynolds, New York	160
1953	Billy Pierce, Chicago	186
1954	Bob Turley, Baltimore	185
1955	Herb Score, Cleveland	245
1956	Herb Score, Cleveland	263
1957	Early Wynn, Cleveland	184
1958	Early Wynn, Chicago	179
1959	Jim Bunning, Detroit	201
1960	Jim Bunning, Detroit	201
1961	Camilo Pascual, Minnesota	221
1962	Camilo Pascual, Minnesota	206
1963	Camilo Pascual, Minnesota	202
1964	Al Downing, New York	217
1965	Sam McDowell, Cleveland	325
1966	Sam McDowell, Cleveland	225
1967	Jim Lonborg, Boston	246
1968	Sam McDowell, Cleveland	283
1969	Sam McDowell, Cleveland	279
1970	Sam McDowell, Cleveland	304
1971	Mickey Lolich, Detroit	308
1972	Nolan Ryan, California	329
1973	Nolan Ryan, California	383
1974	Nolan Ryan, California	367
1975	Frank Tanana, California	269
1976	Nolan Ryan, California	327
1977	Nolan Ryan, California	341
1978	Nolan Ryan, California	260

Year	Pitcher, Club	No.
1979	Nolan Ryan, California	223
1980	Len Barker, Cleveland	187
1981	Len Barker, Cleveland	127
1982	Floyd Bannister, Seattle	209
1983	Jack Morris, Detroit	232
1984	Mark Langston, Seattle	204
1985	Bert Blyleven, Cleveland/Minnesota	206
1986	Mark Langston, Seattle	245
1987	Mark Langston, Seattle	262
1988	Roger Clemens, Boston	291
1989	Nolan Ryan, Texas	301
1990	Nolan Ryan, Texas	232
1991	Roger Clemens, Boston	241
1992	Randy Johnson, Seattle	241
1993	Randy Johnson, Seattle	308
1994	Randy Johnson, Seattle	204
1995	Randy Johnson, Seattle	294
1996	Roger Clemens, Boston	257
1997	Roger Clemens, Toronto	292
1998	Roger Clemens, Toronto	271
1999	Pedro Martinez, Boston	313
2000	Pedro Martinez, Boston	284
2001	Hideo Nomo, Boston	220

NATIONAL LEAGUE

Year	Pitcher, Club	No.
1900	Rube Waddell, Pittsburgh	133
1901	Noodles Hahn, Cincinnati	233
1902	Vic Willis, Boston	226
1903	Christy Mathewson, New York	267
1904	Christy Mathewson, New York	212
1905	Christy Mathewson, New York	206
1906	Fred Beebe, Chicago/St. Louis	171
1907	Christy Mathewson, New York	178
1908	Christy Mathewson, New York	259
1909	Orval Overall, Chicago	205
1910	Christy Mathewson, New York	190
1911	Rube Marquard, New York	237
1912	Grover Alexander, Philadelphia	195
1913	Tom Seaton, Philadelphia	168
1914	Grover Alexander, Philadelphia	214
1915	Grover Alexander, Philadelphia	241
1916	Grover Alexander, Philadelphia	167
1917	Grover Alexander, Philadelphia	200
1918	Hippo Vaughn, Chicago	148
1919	Hippo Vaughn, Chicago	141
1920	Grover Alexander, Chicago	173
1921	Burleigh Grimes, Brooklyn	136
1922	Dazzy Vance, Brooklyn	134
1923	Dazzy Vance, Brooklyn	197
1924	Dazzy Vance, Brooklyn	262
1925	Dazzy Vance, Brooklyn	221
1925	Dazzy Vance, Brooklyn	140
1927	Dazzy Vance, Brooklyn	184
1928	Dazzy Vance, Brooklyn	200
1929	Pat Malone, Chicago	166
1930	Bill Hallahan, St. Louis	177
1931	Bill Hallahan, St. Louis	159
1932	Dizzy Dean, St. Louis	191
1933	Dizzy Dean, St. Louis	199
1934	Dizzy Dean, St. Louis	195
1935	Dizzy Dean, St. Louis	182
1936	Van Lingle Mungo, Brooklyn	238
1937	Carl Hubbell, New York	159
1938	Clay Bryant, Chicago	135
1939	Claude Passeau, Philadelphia/Chicago	137
	Bucky Walters, Cincinnati	137
1940	Kirby Higbe, Philadelphia	137

Year	Pitcher, Club	No.
1941	Johnny Vander Meer, Cincinnati	202
1942	Johnny Vander Meer, Cincinnati	186
1943	Johnny Vander Meer, Cincinnati	174
1944	Bill Voiselle, New York	161
1945	Preacher Roe, Pittsburgh	148
1946	Johnny Schmitz, Chicago	135
1947	Ewell Blackwell, Cincinnati	193
1948	Harry Brecheen, St. Louis	149
1949	Warren Spahn, Boston	151
1950	Warren Spahn, Boston	191
1951	Warren Spahn, Boston	164
	Don Newcombe, Brooklyn	164
1952	Warren Spahn, Boston	183
1953	Robin Roberts, Philadelphia	198
1954	Robin Roberts, Philadelphia	185
1955	Sam Jones, Chicago	198
1956	Sam Jones, Chicago	176
1957	Jack Sanford, Philadelphia	188
1958	Sam Jones, St. Louis	225
1959	Don Drysdale, Los Angeles	242
1960	Don Drysdale, Los Angeles	246
1961	Sandy Koufax, Los Angeles	269
1962	Don Drysdale, Los Angeles	232
1963	Sandy Koufax, Los Angeles	306
1964	Bob Veale, Pittsburgh	250
1965	Sandy Koufax, Los Angeles	382
1966	Sandy Koufax, Los Angeles	317
1967	Jim Bunning, Philadelphia	253
1968	Bob Gibson, St. Louis	268
1969	Ferguson Jenkins, Chicago	273
1970	Tom Seaver, New York	283
1971	Tom Seaver, New York	289
1972	Steve Carlton, Philadelphia	310
1973	Tom Seaver, New York	251
1974	Steve Carlton, Philadelphia	240
1975	Tom Seaver, New York	243
1976	Tom Seaver, New York	235
1977	Phil Niekro, Atlanta	262
1978	J.R. Richard, Houston	303
1979	J.R. Richard, Houston	313
1980	Steve Carlton, Philadelphia	286
1981	Fernando Valenzuela, Los Angeles	180
1982	Steve Carlton, Philadelphia	286
1983	Steve Carlton, Philadelphia	275
1984	Dwight Gooden, New York	276
1985	Dwight Gooden, New York	268
1986	Mike Scott, Houston	306
1987	Nolan Ryan, Houston	270
1988	Nolan Ryan, Houston	228
1989	Jose DeLeon, St. Louis	201
1990	David Cone, New York	233
1991	David Cone, New York	241
1992	John Smoltz, Atlanta	*215
1993	Jose Rijo, Cincinnati	227
1994	Andy Benes, San Diego	189
1995	Hideo Nomo, Los Angeles	236
1996	John Smoltz, Atlanta	276
1997	Curt Schilling, Philadelphia	319
1998	Curt Schilling, Philadelphia	†300
1999	Randy Johnson, Arizona	364
2000	Randy Johnson, Arizona	347
2001	Randy Johnson, Arizona	372

*David Cone led the majors with 261 strikeouts in 1992, compiling 214 with New York (N.L.) and another 47 with Toronto (A.L.) following an August 27 trade.

†Randy Johnson led the majors with 329 strikeouts in 1998, compiling 213 with Seattle (A.L.) and another 116 with Houston (N.L.) following a July 31 trade.

CAREER MILESTONES

(Players active in the major leagues in 2000 are in boldface.)

SERVICE
20-YEAR PLAYERS

(Does not include pitchers)

	Player	Yrs.	Games
1.	Deacon McGuire	26	1,781
2.	Eddie Collins	25	2,826
	Bobby Wallace	25	2,369
4.	Pete Rose	24	3,562
	Ty Cobb	24	3,033
	Carlton Fisk	24	2,499
	Rick Dempsey	24	1,766
8.	Carl Yastrzemski	23	3,308
	Rabbit Maranville	23	2,670
	Rogers Hornsby	23	2,259
	Hank Aaron	23	3,298
	Rickey Henderson	**23**	**2,979**
	Rusty Staub	23	2,951
	Brooks Robinson	23	2,896
	Tony Perez	23	2,777
16.	Stan Musial	22	3,026
	Willie Mays	22	2,992
	Dave Winfield	22	2,973
	Al Kaline	22	2,834
	Harold Baines	**22**	**2,800**
	Tris Speaker	22	2,789
	Mel Ott	22	2,730
	Graig Nettles	22	2,700
	Joe Morgan	22	2,649
	Willie McCovey	22	2,588
	Bill Buckner	22	2,517
	Babe Ruth	22	2,503
	Harmon Killebrew	22	2,435
	Bill Dahlen	22	2,431
	Tim Raines Sr.	**22**	**2,404**
	Jimmie Dykes	22	2,282
	Cap Anson	22	2,253
	Phil Cavarretta	22	2,030
	Kid Gleason	22	1,942
	Harry H. Davis	22	1,746
36.	Eddie Murray	21	3,026
	Cal Ripken Jr.	**21**	**3,001**
	Reggie Jackson	21	2,820
	Frank Robinson	21	2,808
	Honus Wagner	21	2,785
	George Brett	21	2,707
	Darrell Evans	21	2,687
	Paul Molitor	21	2,683
	Andre Dawson	21	2,627
	Nap Lajoie	21	2,475
	Ted Simmons	21	2,456
	Ron Fairly	21	2,442
	Willie Stargell	21	2,360
	Lave Cross	21	2,259
	Fred Clarke	21	2,204
	Bob O'Farrell	21	1,492
	Tim McCarver	21	1,909
	Jack O'Connor	21	1,404
54.	Robin Yount	20	2,856
	Dwight Evans	20	2,606
	Paul Waner	20	2,549
	Gary Gaetti	20	2,507
	Max Carey	20	2,469
	Tony Gwynn	**20**	**2,440**
	Luke Appling	20	2,422
	Mickey Vernon	20	2,409
	Sam Rice	20	2,404
	Jake Beckley	20	2,373
	George Davis	20	2,370
	Brian Downing	20	2,344
	Jimmie Foxx	20	2,317
	Alan Trammell	20	2,293

Player	Yrs.	Games
Doc Cramer	20	2,239
Al Simmons	20	2,215
Joe Judge	20	2,170
Charlie Grimm	20	2,166
Joe Cronin	20	2,124
Gabby Hartnett	20	1,990
Elmer Valo	20	1,806
Jay Johnstone	20	1,748
Luke Sewell	20	1,630
Manny Mota	20	1,536
Johnny Cooney	20	1,172

Total number of players: 78

20-YEAR PITCHERS

	Pitcher	Yrs.	Games
1.	Nolan Ryan	27	807
2.	Tommy John	26	760
3.	Jim Kaat	25	898
	Charlie Hough	25	858
5.	Dennis Eckersley	24	1,071
	Phil Niekro	24	864
	Steve Carlton	24	741
8.	Don Sutton	23	774
	Dennis Martinez	23	692
	Early Wynn	23	691
11.	**Jesse Orosco**	**22**	**1,131**
	Rich Gossage	22	1,002
	Cy Young	22	906
	Gaylord Perry	22	777
	Joe Niekro	22	702
	Bert Blyleven	22	692
	Sam Jones	22	647
	Jerry Reuss	22	628
	Red Ruffing	22	624
	Herb Pennock	22	617
21.	Hoyt Wilhelm	21	1,070
	Lindy McDaniel	21	987
	Walter Johnson	21	802
	Rick Honeycutt	21	797
	Warren Spahn	21	750
	Danny Darwin	21	716
	Eppa Rixey	21	692
	Waite Hoyt	21	675
	Jack Quinn	21	665
	Frank Tanana	21	638
	Ted Lyons	21	594
	Mike Morgan	**21**	**568**
33.	Grover Alexander	20	696
	Red Faber	20	669
	Tom Seaver	20	656
	Dutch Leonard	20	640
	Bobo Newsom	20	600
	Mel Harder	20	582
	Curt Simmons	20	569
	Dolf Luque	20	550
	Clark Griffith	20	416

Total number of pitchers: 41

BATTING
2,400 GAMES

(Does not include pitchers)

	Player	No.
1.	Pete Rose	3,562
2.	Carl Yastrzemski	3,308
3.	Hank Aaron	3,298
4.	Ty Cobb	3,033
5.	Eddie Murray	3,026
	Stan Musial	3,026
7.	**Cal Ripken Jr.**	**3,001**

	Player	No.
8.	Willie Mays	2,992
9.	**Rickey Henderson**	**2,979**
10.	Dave Winfield	2,973
11.	Rusty Staub	2,951
12.	Brooks Robinson	2,896
13.	Robin Yount	2,856
14.	Al Kaline	2,834
15.	Eddie Collins	2,826
16.	Reggie Jackson	2,820
17.	Frank Robinson	2,808
18.	**Harold Baines**	**2,800**
19.	Tris Speaker	2,790
20.	Honus Wagner	2,785
21.	Tony Perez	2,777
22.	Mel Ott	2,730
23.	George Brett	2,707
24.	Graig Nettles	2,700
25.	Darrell Evans	2,687
26.	Paul Molitor	2,683
27.	Rabbit Maranville	2,670
28.	Joe Morgan	2,649
29.	Andre Dawson	2,627
30.	Lou Brock	2,616
31.	Dwight Evans	2,606
32.	Luis Aparicio	2,599
33.	Willie McCovey	2,588
34.	Ozzie Smith	2,573
35.	Paul Waner	2,549
36.	Ernie Banks	2,528
37.	Bill Buckner	2,517
38.	Gary Gaetti	2,507
39.	Sam Crawford	2,505
40.	Babe Ruth	2,503
41.	Carlton Fisk	2,499
42.	Billy Williams	2,488
	Dave Concepcion	2,488
44.	Nap Lajoie	2,475
45.	Max Carey	2,469
	Vada Pinson	2,469
	Rod Carew	2,469
48.	Dave Parker	2,466
49.	Ted Simmons	2,456
50.	Ron Fairly	2,442
51.	Wade Boggs	2,440
	Tony Gwynn	**2,440**
53.	Chili Davis	2,436
54.	Harmon Killebrew	2,435
	Roberto Clemente	2,433
56.	Bill Dahlen	2,431
57.	Willie Davis	2,429
58.	Luke Appling	2,422
59.	Mickey Vernon	2,409
60.	Zack Wheat	2,406
61.	Buddy Bell	2,405
62.	**Tim Raines Sr.**	**2,404**
	Sam Rice	2,404
	Mike Schmidt	2,404
65.	Mickey Mantle	2,401

Total number of players: 65

500 CONSECUTIVE GAMES

	Player	No.
1.	**Cal Ripken Jr.**	**2,632**
2.	Lou Gehrig	2,130
3.	Everett Scott	1,307
4.	Steve Garvey	1,207
5.	Billy Williams	1,117
6.	Joe Sewell	1,103
7.	Stan Musial	895
8.	Eddie Yost	829
9.	Gus Suhr	822

Player	No.
0. Nellie Fox	798
1. Pete Rose*	745
2. Dale Murphy	740
3. Richie Ashburn	730
4. Ernie Banks	717
5. Pete Rose*	678
6. Earl Averill	673
7. Frank McCormick	652
8. Sandy Alomar Sr.	648
9. Eddie Brown	618
0. Roy McMillan	585
1. George Pinckney	577
2. Steve Brodie	574
3. Aaron Ward	565
4. Candy LaChance	540
5. Buck Freeman	535
6. Fred Luderus	533
7. Charlie Gehringer*	511
Clyde Milan	511
9. Vada Pinson	508
0. Joe Carter	507
1. Tony Cuccinello	504
2. Charlie Gehringer*	504
3. Omar Moreno	503

*Only players with two streaks.
Total number of streaks: 33

BATTING .300, 10 TIMES

(50 or more games, season)

Player	Yrs.	Cons.
1. Ty Cobb	23	23
2. Tony Gwynn	18	17
Cap Anson	18	*11
Tris Speaker	18	10
5. Honus Wagner	17	*17
Stan Musial	†17	*16
Eddie Collins	17	9
Babe Ruth	17	8
Ted Williams	†16	*15
10. Rod Carew	15	15
Dennis Brouthers	15	14
Wade Boggs	15	*10
Nap Lajoie	15	10
Pete Rose	15	9
15. Rogers Hornsby	14	12
Paul Waner	14	*12
Luke Appling	14	9
Hank Aaron	14	5
Willie Keeler	13	13
Frankie Frisch	13	11
Al Simmons	13	*11
George Sisler	13	9
George Van Haltren	13	9
Roberto Clemente	13	8
Charlie Gehringer	13	8
Jim Ryan	13	7
Jake Beckley	13	6
Zack Wheat	13	6
Jim O'Rourke	13	5
Sam Rice	13	5
31. Ed Delahanty	12	12
Lou Gehrig	12	12
Billy Hamilton	12	12
Harry Heilmann	12	12
Edd Roush	12	11
Joe Medwick	12	*10
Arky Vaughan	12	*10
Riggs Stephenson	12	8
Roger Connor	12	6
Jimmie Foxx	12	5
Paul Molitor	12	4
42. Joe Kelley	11	11
Jesse Burkett	11	10
Hugh Duffy	11	10
Bill Terry	11	10
Al Oliver	11	9

Player	Yrs.	Cons.
Joe DiMaggio	11	7
Goose Goslin	11	7
Heinie Manush	11	7
Bill Dickey	11	6
George Brett	11	5
Fred Clarke	11	5
Stuffy McInnis	11	5
54. Buck Ewing	10	8
Pete Browning	10	7
Spud Davis	10	7
Edgar Martinez	10	7
Willie Mays	10	7
Kenny Williams	10	7
Jake Daubert	10	6
Patsy Donovan	10	6
Pie Traynor	10	6
Dixie Walker	10	6
Lloyd Waner	10	6
Ernie Lombardi	10	5
Mickey Mantle	10	5
Enos Slaughter	10	5
Sam Crawford	10	4
Kiki Cuyler	10	4
Mel Ott	10	3

*From start of career.
†Streak interrupted by military service.
Total number of players: 70

.300 LIFETIME AVERAGE

(1,500 or more hits)

Player	Hits	Avg.
1. Ty Cobb	4,191	.367
2. Rogers Hornsby	2,930	.358
3. Joe Jackson	1,772	.356
4. Pete Browning	1,719	.354
5. Dennis Brouthers	2,349	.349
6. Ed Delahanty	2,593	.346
7. Tris Speaker	3,515	.345
Willie Keeler	2,955	.345
9. Ted Williams	2,654	.344
Billy Hamilton	2,157	.344
11. Babe Ruth	2,873	.342
Jesse Burkett	2,872	.342
Harry Heilmann	2,660	.342
14. Bill Terry	2,193	.341
15. George Sisler	2,812	.340
Lou Gehrig	2,721	.340
17. Nap Lajoie	3,252	.339
Cap Anson	3,081	.339
19. Tony Gwynn	3,141	.338
20. Sam Thompson	2,016	.336
Riggs Stephenson	1,515	.336
22. Al Simmons	2,927	.334
23. Eddie Collins	3,309	.333
Paul Waner	3,152	.333
25. Stan Musial	3,630	.331
26. Heinie Manush	2,524	.330
Hugh Duffy	2,307	.330
28. Honus Wagner	3,430	.329
29. Rod Carew	3,053	.328
Wade Boggs	3,010	.328
31. Jimmie Foxx	2,646	.325
Roger Connor	2,535	.325
Joe DiMaggio	2,214	.325
Edd Roush	2,158	.325
Earle Combs	1,866	.325
Mike Piazza	1,507	.325
37. Joe Medwick	2,471	.324
Babe Herman	1,818	.324
39. Sam Rice	2,987	.322
40. George Van Haltren	2,573	.321
Kiki Cuyler	2,299	.321
Joe Kelley	2,245	.321
Harry Stovey	1,925	.321
44. Charlie Gehringer	2,839	.320
Pie Traynor	2,416	.320

Player	Hits	Avg.
Chuck Klein	2,076	.320
Mickey Cochrane	1,652	.320
48. Edgar Martinez	1,882	.319
Frank Thomas	1,770	.319
Kenny Williams	1,552	.319
51. Kirby Puckett	2,304	.318
Arky Vaughan	2,103	.318
Earl Averill	2,019	.318
54. Roberto Clemente	3,000	.317
Zack Wheat	2,884	.317
Mike Tiernan	1,875	.317
57. Frankie Frisch	2,880	.316
Goose Goslin	2,735	.316
Lloyd Waner	2,459	.316
60. Fred Clarke	2,703	.315
Elmer Flick	1,767	.315
Larry Walker	1,702	.315
Jack Tobin	1,579	.315
64. Jim Ryan	2,577	.314
Jim O'Rourke	2,314	.314
Cecil Travis	1,544	.314
Hughey Jennings	1,520	.314
68. Bill Dickey	1,969	.313
King Kelly	1,853	.313
Jack Fournier	1,631	.313
Hank Greenberg	1,628	.313
72. Joe Sewell	2,226	.312
Johnny Mize	2,011	.312
Ed Miller	1,937	.312
Cupid Childs	1,757	.312
76. Ginger Beaumont	1,754	.311
Fred Lindstrom	1,747	.311
Bill Jacobson	1,714	.311
Buck Ewing	1,663	.311
Jackie Robinson	1,518	.311
81. Luke Appling	2,749	.310
Jim Bottomley	2,313	.310
Ed McKean	2,139	.310
Bobby Veach	2,064	.310
Emil Meusel	1,521	.310
86. Sam Crawford	2,964	.309
Jake Beckley	2,930	.309
Bob Meusel	1,693	.309
Richie Ashburn	2,574	.308
Stuffy McInnis	2,406	.308
Steve Brodie	1,749	.308
George Gore	1,653	.308
93. Mark Grace	2,343	.307
Don Mattingly	2,153	.307
George Burns	2,018	.307
Home Run Baker	1,838	.307
Mike Griffin	1,830	.307
Joe Vosmik	1,682	.307
Chick Stahl	1,552	.307
Matty Alou	1,777	.307
101. Paul Molitor	3,319	.306
Roberto Alomar	2,389	.306
Dixie Walker	2,064	.306
George Kell	2,054	.306
Ernie Lombardi	1,792	.306
Deacon White	1,612	.306
Ralph Garr	1,562	.306
108. Hank Aaron	3,771	.305
George Brett	3,154	.305
Bill Madlock	2,008	.305
Bernie Williams	1,629	.305
112. Mel Ott	2,876	.304
Billy Herman	2,345	.304
Patsy Donovan	2,254	.304
Tony Oliva	1,917	.304
Paul Hines	1,884	.304
Cy Seymour	1,720	.304
Hardy Richardson	1,705	.304
Ivan Rodriguez	1,595	.304
120. Pete Rose	4,256	.303
Al Oliver	2,743	.303
Jake Daubert	2,326	.303

Player	Hits	Avg.
Will Clark	2,176	.303
Buddy Myer	2,131	.303
Harvey Kuenn	2,092	.303
Charlie Jamieson	1,990	.303
Jeff Bagwell	**1,803**	**.303**
128. Willie Mays	3,283	.302
Ben Chapman	1,958	.302
Jack Doyle	1,814	.302
Kenny Lofton	**1,642**	**.302**
Hal Trosky	1,561	.302
George Grantham	1,508	.302
Tommy Holmes	1,507	.302
135. Joe Cronin	2,285	.301
Julio Franco	**2,204**	**.301**
Stan Hack	2,193	.301
138. Enos Slaughter	2,383	.300
John Olerud	**1,768**	**.300**
Billy Goodman	1,691	.300
Pedro Guerrero	1,618	.300
Wally Berger	1,550	.300

Total number of players: 142

SLUGGING AVERAGE

(Players with 4,000 total bases)

Player	TB	Slg. Avg.
1. Babe Ruth	5,793	.690
2. Ted Williams	4,884	.634
3. Lou Gehrig	5,060	.632
4. Jimmie Foxx	4,956	.609
5. Barry Bonds	**4,639**	**.585**
6. Rogers Hornsby	4,712	.577
7. Stan Musial	6,134	.559
8. Willie Mays	6,066	.557
Mickey Mantle	4,511	.557
10. Hank Aaron	6,856	.555
11. Frank Robinson	5,373	.537
12. Al Simmons	4,685	.535
13. Mel Ott	5,041	.533
14. Willie Stargell	4,190	.529
15. Mike Schmidt	4,404	.527
16. Harry Heilmann	4,053	.520
17. Rafael Palmeiro	**4,386**	**.519**
18. Willie McCovey	4,219	.515
19. Fred McGriff	**4,045**	**.514**
20. Ty Cobb	5,862	.513
21. Eddie Mathews	4,349	.509
Harmon Killebrew	4,143	.509
23. Jim Rice	4,129	.502
24. Goose Goslin	4,325	.500
Tris Speaker	5,103	.500
Ernie Banks	4,706	.500
27. Billy Williams	4,599	.492
28. Reggie Jackson	4,834	.490
29. George Brett	5,044	.487
30. Andre Dawson	4,787	.482
31. Charlie Gehringer	4,257	.481
32. Al Kaline	4,852	.480
33. Eddie Murray	5,397	.476
34. Dave Winfield	5,221	.475
Roberto Clemente	4,492	.475
36. Paul Waner	4,478	.473
37. Dave Parker	4,405	.471
38. Dwight Evans	4,230	.470
39. Honus Wagner	4,888	.469
40. Nap Lajoie	4,478	.467
41. Harold Baines	**4,604**	**.465**
42. Tony Perez	4,532	.463
43. Carl Yastrzemski	5,539	.462
44. Tony Gwynn	**4,259**	**.459**
45. Cap Anson	4,145	.456
46. Sam Crawford	4,328	.452
47. Al Oliver	4,083	.451
48. Zack Wheat	4,100	450
49. Paul Molitor	4,854	.448
50. Cal Ripken Jr.	**5,168**	**.447**
51. Wade Boggs	4,064	.443

Player	TB	Slg. Avg.
52. Vada Pinson	4,264	.442
53. Jake Beckley	4,138	.437
54. Rusty Staub	4,185	.431
55. Robin Yount	4,730	.430
56. Eddie Collins	4,259	.428
57. Rickey Henderson	**4,503**	**.420**
58. Lou Brock	4,238	.410
59. Pete Rose	5,752	.409
60. Brooks Robinson	4,270	.401

Total number of players: 60

9,000 AT-BATS

Player	No.
1. Pete Rose	14,053
2. Hank Aaron	12,364
3. Carl Yastrzemski	11,988
4. Cal Ripken Jr.	**11,551**
5. Ty Cobb	11,429
6. Eddie Murray	11,336
7. Robin Yount	11,008
8. Dave Winfield	11,003
9. Stan Musial	10,972
10. Willie Mays	10,881
11. Paul Molitor	10,835
12. Rickey Henderson	**10,710**
13. Brooks Robinson	10,654
14. Honus Wagner	10,427
15. George Brett	10,349
16. Lou Brock	10,332
17. Luis Aparicio	10,230
18. Tris Speaker	10,196
19. Al Kaline	10,116
20. Rabbit Maranville	10,078
21. Frank Robinson	10,006
22. Eddie Collins	9,946
23. Andre Dawson	9,927
24. Harold Baines	**9,908**
25. Reggie Jackson	9,864
26. Tony Perez	9,778
27. Rusty Staub	9,720
28. Vada Pinson	9,645
29. Nap Lajoie	9,589
30. Sam Crawford	9,579
31. Jake Beckley	9,476
32. Paul Waner	9,459
33. Mel Ott	9,456
34. Roberto Clemente	9,454
35. Ernie Banks	9,421
36. Bill Buckner	9,397
37. Ozzie Smith	9,396
38. Max Carey	9,363
39. Dave Parker	9,358
40. Billy Williams	9,350
41. Rod Carew	9,315
42. Tony Gwynn	**9,288**
43. Joe Morgan	9,277
44. Sam Rice	9,269
45. Nellie Fox	9,232
46. Wade Boggs	9,180
47. Willie Davis	9,174
48. Roger Cramer	9,140
49. Frankie Frisch	9,112
50. Zack Wheat	9,106
51. Cap Anson	9,084
52. Lave Cross	9,065
53. Al Oliver	9,049
54. George Davis	9,027
55. Bill Dahlen	9,019

Total number of players: 55

1,500 RUNS

Player	No.
1. Rickey Henderson	2,248
2. Ty Cobb	2,245

Player	No.
3. Hank Aaron	2,174
Babe Ruth	2,174
5. Pete Rose	2,165
6. Willie Mays	2,062
7. Stan Musial	1,949
8. Lou Gehrig	1,888
9. Tris Speaker	1,881
10. Mel Ott	1,859
11. Frank Robinson	1,829
12. Eddie Collins	1,816
Carl Yastrzemski	1,816
14. Ted Williams	1,798
15. Paul Molitor	1,782
16. Charlie Gehringer	1,774
17. Jimmie Foxx	1,751
18. Honus Wagner	1,740
19. Willie Keeler	1,720
20. Barry Bonds	**1,713**
21. Cap Anson	1,712
22. Jesse Burkett	1,708
23. Billy Hamilton	1,690
24. Mickey Mantle	1,677
25. Bid McPhee	1,674
26. Dave Winfield	1,669
27. Joe Morgan	1,650
George Van Haltren	1,650
29. Cal Ripken Jr.	**1,647**
30. Jim Ryan	1,640
31. Robin Yount	1,632
32. Eddie Murray	1,627
Paul Waner	1,627
34. Al Kaline	1,622
35. Fred Clarke	1,620
36. Lou Brock	1,610
37. Roger Connor	1,607
38. Jake Beckley	1,601
39. Ed Delahanty	1,596
40. Bill Dahlen	1,594
41. George Brett	1,583
42. Rogers Hornsby	1,579
43. Tim Raines Sr.	**1,562**
44. Reggie Jackson	1,551
45. George Davis	1,546
46. Max Carey	1,545
Hugh Duffy	1,545
48. Frankie Frisch	1,532
49. Sam Rice	1,514
50. Wade Boggs	1,513
51. Eddie Mathews	1,509
52. Dennis Brouthers	1,507
Tom Brown	1,507
Al Simmons	1,507
55. Nap Lajoie	1,506
Mike Schmidt	1,506

Total number of players: 56

2,500 HITS

Player	No.
1. Pete Rose	4,256
2. Ty Cobb	4,191
3. Hank Aaron	3,771
4. Stan Musial	3,630
5. Tris Speaker	3,515
6. Honus Wagner	3,430
7. Carl Yastrzemski	3,419
8. Paul Molitor	3,319
9. Eddie Collins	3,309
10. Willie Mays	3,283
11. Eddie Murray	3,255
12. Nap Lajoie	3,252
13. Cal Ripken Jr.	**3,184**
14. George Brett	3,154
15. Paul Waner	3,152
16. Robin Yount	3,142
17. Tony Gwynn	**3,141**
18. Dave Winfield	3,110

Player	No.
19. Cap Anson	3,081
20. Rod Carew	3,053
21. Lou Brock	3,023
22. Wade Boggs	3,010
23. Al Kaline	3,007
24. Roberto Clemente	3,000
Rickey Henderson	**3,000**
26. Sam Rice	2,987
27. Sam Crawford	2,964
28. Willie Keeler	2,955
29. Frank Robinson	2,943
30. Jake Beckley	2,930
Rogers Hornsby	2,930
32. Al Simmons	2,927
33. Zack Wheat	2,884
34. Frankie Frisch	2,880
35. Mel Ott	2,876
36. Babe Ruth	2,873
37. Jesse Burkett	2,872
38. Harold Baines	**2,866**
39. Brooks Robinson	2,848
40. Charlie Gehringer	2,839
41. George Sisler	2,812
42. Andre Dawson	2,774
43. Vada Pinson	2,757
44. Luke Appling	2,749
45. Al Oliver	2,743
46. Goose Goslin	2,735
47. Tony Perez	2,732
48. Lou Gehrig	2,721
49. Rusty Staub	2,716
50. Bill Buckner	2,715
51. Dave Parker	2,712
52. Billy Williams	2,711
53. Roger Cramer	2,705
54. Fred Clarke	2,703
55. George Davis	2,683
56. Luis Aparicio	2,677
57. Max Carey	2,665
58. Nellie Fox	2,663
59. Harry Heilmann	2,660
60. Lave Cross	2,654
Ted Williams	2,654
62. Jimmie Foxx	2,646
63. Rabbit Maranville	2,605
64. Steve Garvey	2,599
65. Ed Delahanty	2,593
66. Tim Raines Sr.	**2,588**
67. Reggie Jackson	2,584
68. Ernie Banks	2,583
69. Jim Ryan	2,577
70. Richie Ashburn	2,574
71. George Van Haltren	2,573
72. Willie Davis	2,561
73. Roger Connor	2,535
74. Heinie Manush	2,524
75. Joe Morgan	2,517
76. Buddy Bell	2,514

Total number of players: 76

200-HIT SEASONS, 4 TIMES

Player	Yrs.
1. Pete Rose	10
2. Ty Cobb	9
3. Lou Gehrig	8
Willie Keeler	8
Paul Waner	8
6. Wade Boggs	7
Charlie Gehringer	7
Rogers Hornsby	7
9. Jesse Burkett	6
Steve Garvey	6
Stan Musial	6
Sam Rice	6
Al Simmons	6
George Sisler	6
Bill Terry	6
16. Tony Gwynn	**5**
Chuck Klein	5
Nap Lajoie	5
Kirby Puckett	5
20. Lou Brock	4
Rod Carew	4
Roberto Clemente	4
Harry Heilmann	4
Joe Jackson	4
Heinie Manush	4
Joe Medwick	4
Paul Molitor	4
Vada Pinson	4
Jim Rice	4
Tris Speaker	4
Jack Tobin	4
Lloyd Waner	4

Total number of players: 32

2,000 SINGLES

Player	No.
1. Pete Rose	3,215
2. Ty Cobb	3,052
3. Eddie Collins	2,639
4. Willie Keeler	2,534
5. Honus Wagner	2,426
6. Rod Carew	2,404
7. Tris Speaker	2,383
8. Tony Gwynn	**2,378**
9. Paul Molitor	2,366
10. Nap Lajoie	2,354
11. Cap Anson	2,330
12. Jesse Burkett	2,301
13. Hank Aaron	2,294
14. Sam Rice	2,272
15. Carl Yastrzemski	2,262
16. Wade Boggs	2,253
Stan Musial	2,253
18. Lou Brock	2,247
19. Paul Waner	2,243
Robin Yount	2,182
21. Frankie Frisch	2,171
22. Roger Cramer	2,163
23. Luke Appling	2,162
24. Nellie Fox	2,161
25. Eddie Murray	2,156
26. Roberto Clemente	2,154
27. Jake Beckley	2,142
Rickey Henderson	**2,142**
29. George Sisler	2,122
30. Richie Ashburn	2,119
31. Luis Aparicio	2,108
32. Cal Ripken	**2,106**
33. Zack Wheat	2,104
34. Sam Crawford	2,102
35. Lave Cross	2,077
36. Fred Clarke	2,061
37. George Brett	2,035
38. Al Kaline	2,035
39. Lloyd Waner	2,032
40. Brooks Robinson	2,030
41. Rabbit Maranville	2,020
42. Max Carey	2,018
43. Dave Winfield	2,017
44. George Van Haltren	2,008
45. George Davis	2,007

Total number of players: 45

450 DOUBLES

Player	No.
1. Tris Speaker	793
2. Pete Rose	746
3. Stan Musial	725
4. Ty Cobb	724
5. George Brett	665
6. Nap Lajoie	652
7. Honus Wagner	651
8. Carl Yastrzemski	646
9. Hank Aaron	624
10. Paul Molitor	605
Paul Waner	605
12. Cal Ripken Jr.	**603**
13. Robin Yount	583
14. Wade Boggs	578
15. Charlie Gehringer	574
16. Eddie Murray	560
17. Tony Gwynn	**543**
18. Harry Heilmann	542
19. Rogers Hornsby	541
20. Joe Medwick	540
Dave Winfield	540
22. Al Simmons	539
23. Lou Gehrig	534
24. Cap Anson	530
25. Al Oliver	529
26. Frank Robinson	528
27. Dave Parker	526
28. Ted Williams	525
29. Willie Mays	523
30. Joe Cronin	516
31. Ed Delahanty	508
32. Babe Ruth	506
33. Tony Perez	505
34. Andre Dawson	503
Rickey Henderson	**503**
36. Goose Goslin	500
37. Rusty Staub	499
38. Bill Buckner	498
Al Kaline	498
Sam Rice	498
41. Heinie Manush	491
42. Mickey Vernon	490
43. Harold Baines	**488**
Mel Ott	488
Rafael Palmeiro	**488**
46. Mark Grace	**487**
47. Lou Brock	486
Billy Herman	486
49. Vada Pinson	485
50. Hal McRae	484
51. Barry Bonds	**483**
Dwight Evans	483
Ted Simmons	483
54. Brooks Robinson	482
55. Zack Wheat	476
56. Frankie Frisch	466
57. Jim Bottomley	465
58. Reggie Jackson	463
59. Jimmie Foxx	458
60. Jake Beckley	455
Sam Crawford	455
62. Jimmie Dykes	453
63. Paul O'Neill	**451**

Total number of players: 63

150 TRIPLES

Player	No.
1. Sam Crawford	312
2. Ty Cobb	298
3. Honus Wagner	252
4. Jake Beckley	246
5. Roger Connor	227
6. Tris Speaker	223
7. Fred Clarke	219
8. Dennis Brouthers	212
9. Paul Waner	191
10. Joe Kelley	189
11. Eddie Collins	186
12. Jesse Burkett	185
Harry Stovey	185

Player	No.
14. Sam Rice	184
15. Ed Delahanty	182
16. Bid McPhee	180
17. Bill Ewing	179
18. Rabbit Maranville	177
Stan Musial	177
20. Goose Goslin	173
21. Zack Wheat	172
22. Elmer Flick	170
Tommy Leach	170
24. Rogers Hornsby	169
25. Joe Jackson	168
Edd Roush	168
27. George Davis	167
28. Roberto Clemente	166
Bill Dahlen	166
Sherry Magee	166
31. Jake Daubert	165
32. Nap Lajoie	164
George Sisler	164
Pie Traynor	164
35. Lou Gehrig	163
Ed Konetchy	163
37. Harry Hooper	160
Heinie Manush	160
39. Max Carey	159
Joe Judge	159
Mike Tiernan	159
George Van Haltren	159
43. Kiki Cuyler	157
44. Willie Keeler	155
45. Earle Combs	154
46. Jim Ryan	153
47. Ed McKean	152
48. Jim Bottomley	151
Tommy Corcoran	151
Harry Heilmann	151

Total number of players: 50

300 HOME RUNS

Player	No.
1. Hank Aaron	755
2. Babe Ruth	714
3. Willie Mays	660
4. Frank Robinson	586
5. **Mark McGwire**	**583**
6. Harmon Killebrew	573
7. **Barry Bonds**	**567**
8. Reggie Jackson	563
9. Mike Schmidt	548
10. Mickey Mantle	536
11. Jimmie Foxx	534
12. Willie McCovey	521
Ted Williams	521
14. Ernie Banks	512
Eddie Mathews	512
16. Mel Ott	511
17. Eddie Murray	504
18. Lou Gehrig	493
19. Stan Musial	475
Willie Stargell	475
21. Dave Winfield	465
22. **Jose Canseco**	**462**
23 **Ken Griffey Jr.**	**460**
24. Carl Yastrzemski	452
25. **Sammy Sosa**	**450**
26. **Fred McGriff**	**448**
27. **Rafael Palmeiro**	**447**
28. Dave Kingman	442
29. Andre Dawson	438
30. **Cal Ripken Jr.**	**431**
31. Billy Williams	426
32. Darrell Evans	414
33. Duke Snider	407
34. Al Kaline	399
35. Dale Murphy	398
36. **Juan Gonzalez**	**397**

Player	No.
37. Joe Carter	396
38. Graig Nettles	390
39. Johnny Bench	389
40. Dwight Evans	385
41. **Harold Baines**	**384**
42. Frank Howard	382
Jim Rice	382
44. Albert Belle	381
45. Orlando Cepeda	379
Tony Perez	379
47. Norm Cash	377
Andres Galarraga	**377**
49. Carlton Fisk	376
50. Rocky Colavito	374
51. Gil Hodges	370
52. Ralph Kiner	369
53. **Matt Williams**	**362**
54. Joe DiMaggio	361
55. Gary Gaetti	360
56. Johnny Mize	359
57. Yogi Berra	358
58. Lee May	354
59. Dick Allen	351
60. Chili Davis	350
61. **Jeff Bagwell**	**349**
62. George Foster	348
Frank Thomas	**348**
64. **Greg Vaughn**	**344**
65. Ron Santo	342
66. Jack Clark	340
67. Dave Parker	339
Boog Powell	339
69. Don Baylor	338
70. Joe Adcock	336
71. Darryl Strawberry	335
72. Bobby Bonds	332
73. Hank Greenberg	331
74. Willie Horton	325
75. Gary Carter	324
Lance Parrish	324
77. Cecil Fielder	319
78. Roy Sievers	318
79. George Brett	317
80. Ron Cey	316
81. **Gary Sheffield**	**315**
82. **Mike Piazza**	**314**
Reggie Smith	314
84. **Ellis Burks**	**313**
85. **Jay Buhner**	**310**
86. **Larry Walker**	**309**
87. Greg Luzinski	307
Al Simmons	307
89. Fred Lynn	306
90. **Ron Gant**	**302**
91. Rogers Hornsby	301
92. Chuck Klein	300

Total number of players: 92

10 PINCH HOME RUNS

Player	No.
1. Cliff Johnson	20
2. Jerry Lynch	18
3. **John Vander Wal**	**17**
4. Gates Brown	16
Smoky Burgess	16
Willie McCovey	16
7. George Crowe	14
8. **Dave Hansen**	**13**
Glenallen Hill	**13**
10. Joe Adcock	12
Bob Cerv	12
Jose Morales	12
Graig Nettles	12
14. Jeff Burroughs	11
Jay Johnstone	11
Candy Maldonado	11
Fred Whitfield	11

Player	No.
Cy Williams	11
19. Mark Carreon	10
Dave Clark	10
Jim Dwyer	10
Mike Lum	10
Ken McMullen	10
Orlando Merced	**10**
Don Mincher	10
Wally Post	10
Champ Summers	10
Jerry Turner	10
Gus Zernial	10

Total number of players: 29

25 MULTIPLE-HR GAMES

Player	No.
1. Babe Ruth	72
2. **Mark McGwire**	**67**
3. Willie Mays	63
4. Hank Aaron	62
5. **Barry Bonds**	**56**
6. Jimmie Foxx	55
7. Frank Robinson	54
Sammy Sosa	**54**
9. Eddie Mathews	49
Mel Ott	49
11. **Ken Griffey Jr.**	**46**
Harmon Killebrew	46
Mickey Mantle	46
14. Willie McCovey	44
Mike Schmidt	44
16. Lou Gehrig	43
Juan Gonzalez	**43**
Dave Kingman	43
19. Ernie Banks	42
Reggie Jackson	42
21. Ralph Kiner	39
22. Albert Belle	39
Andre Dawson	39
24. Stan Musial	37
Ted Williams	37
26. **Jose Canseco**	**36**
Fred McGriff	**36**
Willie Stargell	36
29. Joe DiMaggio	35
Hank Greenberg	35
Lee May	35
Jim Rice	35
33. Joe Carter	34
Cecil Fielder	34
Duke Snider	34
36. Dick Allen	32
Rocky Colavito	32
Dale Murphy	32
Gus Zernial	32
40. Eddie Murray	31
Hank Sauer	31
Billy Williams	31
43. **Andres Galarraga**	**30**
Gil Hodges	30
Willie Horton	30
Johnny Mize	30
Darryl Strawberry	30
Matt Williams	**30**
Dave Winfield	30
50. **Rafael Palmeiro**	**29**
Greg Vaughn	**29**
52. Joe Adcock	28
Gary Carter	28
Chili Davis	28
Chuck Klein	28
Mo Vaughn	28
57. **Carlos Delgado**	**27**
Graig Nettles	27
Mike Piazza	**27**
Manny Ramirez	**27**
Roy Sievers	27

Player	No.
Hack Wilson	27
Carl Yastrzemski	27
64. **Vinny Castilla**	**26**
Bob Horner	26
Frank Howard	26
Ron Santo	26
68. Norm Cash	25
Carlton Fisk	25
Roger Maris	25
Ryne Sandberg	25
Gary Sheffield	**25**
Hal Trosky	25
Larry Walker	**25**

Total number of players: 74

10 GRAND SLAMS

Player	No.
1. Lou Gehrig	23
2. Eddie Murray	19
3. Willie McCovey	18
4. Jimmie Foxx	17
Ted Williams	17
6. Hank Aaron	16
Dave Kingman	16
Babe Ruth	16
9. **Robin Ventura**	**15**
10. **Ken Griffey Jr.**	**14**
Gil Hodges	14
Mark McGwire	**14**
Manny Ramirez	**14**
14. **Harold Baines**	**13**
Albert Belle	13
Joe DiMaggio	13
George Foster	13
Ralph Kiner	13
19. Ernie Banks	12
Don Baylor	12
Rogers Hornsby	12
Mike Piazza	**12**
Joe Rudi	12
Rudy York	12
25. Johnny Bench	11
Gary Carter	11
Eric Davis	**11**
Cecil Fielder	11
Gary Gaetti	11
Hank Greenberg	11
Reggie Jackson	11
Harmon Killebrew	11
Lee May	11
Willie Stargell	11
Danny Tartabull	11
Devon White	**11**
Matt Williams	**11**
Dave Winfield	11
39. Joe Adcock	10
George Bell	10
Barry Bonds	**10**
Jay Buhner	**10**
Ellis Burks	**10**
Jeff Burroughs	10
Joe Carter	10
Darrell Evans	10
Andres Galarraga	**10**
John Milner	10
Roy Sievers	10
Al Simmons	10
Vern Stephens	10
Mo Vaughn	**10**
Vic Wertz	10

Total number of players: 53

4,000 TOTAL BASES

Player	No.
1. Hank Aaron	6,856
2. Stan Musial	6,134

Player	No.
3. Willie Mays	6,066
4. Ty Cobb	5,862
5. Babe Ruth	5,793
6. Pete Rose	5,752
7. Carl Yastrzemski	5,539
8. Eddie Murray	5,397
9. Frank Robinson	5,373
10. Dave Winfield	5,221
11. **Cal Ripken Jr.**	**5,168**
12. Tris Speaker	5,103
13. Lou Gehrig	5,060
14. George Brett	5,044
15. Mel Ott	5,041
16. Jimmie Foxx	4,956
17. Honus Wagner	4,888
18. Ted Williams	4,884
19. Paul Molitor	4,854
20. Al Kaline	4,852
21. Reggie Jackson	4,834
22. Andre Dawson	4,787
23. Robin Yount	4,730
24. Rogers Hornsby	4,712
25. Ernie Banks	4,706
26. Al Simmons	4,685
27. **Barry Bonds**	**4,639**
28. **Harold Baines**	**4,604**
29. Billy Williams	4,599
30. Tony Perez	4,532
31. Mickey Mantle	4,511
32. **Rickey Henderson**	**4,503**
33. Roberto Clemente	4,492
34. Nap Lajoie	4,478
Paul Waner	4,478
36. Dave Parker	4,405
37. Mike Schmidt	4,404
38. **Rafael Palmeiro**	**4,386**
39. Eddie Mathews	4,349
40. Sam Crawford	4,328
41. Goose Goslin	4,325
42. Brooks Robinson	4,270
43. Vada Pinson	4,264
44. Eddie Collins	4,259
Tony Gwynn	**4,259**
46. Charlie Gehringer	4,257
47. Lou Brock	4,238
48. Dwight Evans	4,230
49. Willie McCovey	4,219
50. Willie Stargell	4,190
51. Rusty Staub	4,185
52. Cap Anson	4,145
53. Harmon Killebrew	4,143
54. Jake Beckley	4,138
55. Jim Rice	4,129
56. Zack Wheat	4,100
57. Al Oliver	4,083
58. Wade Boggs	4,064
59. Harry Heilmann	4,053
60. **Fred McGriff**	**4,045**

Total number of players: 60

800 LONG HITS

Player	No.
1. Hank Aaron	1,477
2. Stan Musial	1,377
3. Babe Ruth	1,356
4. Willie Mays	1,323
5. Lou Gehrig	1,190
6. Frank Robinson	1,186
7. Carl Yastrzemski	1,157
8. Ty Cobb	1,139
9. Tris Speaker	1,132
10. **Barry Bonds**	**1,121**
11. George Brett	1,119
12. Jimmie Foxx	1,117
Ted Williams	1,117
14. Eddie Murray	1,099
15. Dave Winfield	1,093

Player	No.
16. **Cal Ripken Jr.**	**1,078**
17. Reggie Jackson	1,075
18. Mel Ott	1,071
19. Pete Rose	1,041
20. Andre Dawson	1,039
21. Mike Schmidt	1,015
22. Rogers Hornsby	1,011
23. Ernie Banks	1,009
24. Honus Wagner	1,004
25. Al Simmons	995
26. Al Kaline	972
27. **Rafael Palmeiro**	**971**
28. Tony Perez	963
29. Robin Yount	960
30. Paul Molitor	953
Willie Stargell	953
32. Mickey Mantle	952
33. Billy Williams	948
34. Dwight Evans	941
35. Dave Parker	940
36. Eddie Mathews	938
37. **Harold Baines**	**921**
Goose Goslin	921
39. Willie McCovey	920
40. Paul Waner	909
41. Charlie Gehringer	904
42. Nap Lajoie	898
43. Harmon Killebrew	887
44. Joe Carter	881
Joe DiMaggio	881
46. Harry Heilmann	876
47. Vada Pinson	868
48. **Fred McGriff**	**867**
49. Sam Crawford	862
50. **Rickey Henderson**	**858**
Joe Medwick	858
52. **Ken Griffey Jr.**	**857**
53. Duke Snider	850
54. Roberto Clemente	846
55. Carlton Fisk	844
56. Gary Gaetti	842
57. **Mark McGwire**	**841**
58. Rusty Staub	838
59. Jim Bottomley	835
60. Jim Rice	834
61. **Andres Galarraga**	**826**
62. Al Oliver	825
63. Orlando Cepeda	823
64. Brooks Robinson	818
65. Jose Canseco	816
66. Joe Morgan	813
67. Johnny Mize	809
68. Chili Davis	804
69. Joe Cronin	803

Total number of players: 69

1,500 EXTRA BASES

Player	No.
1. Hank Aaron	3,085
2. Babe Ruth	2,920
3. Willie Mays	2,783
4. Stan Musial	2,504
5. Frank Robinson	2,430
6. Lou Gehrig	2,339
7. **Barry Bonds**	**2,326**
8. Jimmie Foxx	2,310
9. Reggie Jackson	2,250
10. Ted Williams	2,230
11. Mike Schmidt	2,170
12. Mel Ott	2,165
13. Eddie Murray	2,142
14. Ernie Banks	2,123
15. Carl Yastrzemski	2,120
16. Dave Winfield	2,111
17. Mickey Mantle	2,096
18. Harmon Killebrew	2,057
19. Eddie Mathews	2,034

Player	No.
20. Andre Dawson	2,013
Mark McGwire	**2,013**
22. Willie McCovey	2,008
23. Cal Ripken Jr.	**1,984**
24. Willie Stargell	1,951
25. Rafael Palmeiro	**1,901**
26. George Brett	1,890
27. Billy Williams	1,888
28. Al Kaline	1,845
29. Ken Griffey Jr.	**1,812**
30. Tony Perez	1,800
31. Fred McGriff	**1,785**
32. Dwight Evans	1,784
33. Rogers Hornsby	1,782
34. Al Simmons	1,758
35. Jose Canseco	**1,754**
36. Duke Snider	1,749
37. Harold Baines	**1,738**
38. Joe DiMaggio	1,734
39. Joe Carter	1,726
40. Sammy Sosa	**1,710**
41. Dave Parker	1,693
42. Jim Rice	1,677
43. Ty Cobb	1,671
44. Darrell Evans	1,643
Carlton Fisk	1,643
46. Dale Murphy	1,622
47. Dave Kingman	1,616
48. Andres Galarraga	**1,612**
49. Johnny Mize	1,610
50. Orlando Cepeda	1,608
51. Gary Gaetti	1,601
52. Johnny Bench	1,596
53. Goose Goslin	1,590
54. Tris Speaker	1,588
Robin Yount	1,588
56. Juan Gonzalez	**1,581**
57. Albert Belle	1,574
58. Graig Nettles	1,554
59. Paul Molitor	1,535
60. Chili Davis	1,534
61. Dick Allen	1,531
62. Ron Santo	1,525
63. Hank Greenberg	1,514
64. Vada Pinson	1,507
65. Rickey Henderson	**1,503**
66. Gil Hodges	1,501
Total number of players: 66	

1,200 RUNS BATTED IN

Player	No.
1. Hank Aaron	2,297
2. Babe Ruth	2,204
3. Lou Gehrig	1,990
4. Ty Cobb	1,960
5. Stan Musial	1,951
6. Jimmie Foxx	1,921
7. Eddie Murray	1,917
8. Willie Mays	1,903
9. Mel Ott	1,861
10. Carl Yastrzemski	1,844
11. Ted Williams	1,839
12. Dave Winfield	1,833
13. Al Simmons	1,827
14. Frank Robinson	1,812
15. Reggie Jackson	1,702
16. Cal Ripken Jr.	**1,695**
17. Tony Perez	1,652
18. Ernie Banks	1,636
19. Harold Baines	**1,628**
20. Goose Goslin	1,609
21. George Brett	1,595
Mike Schmidt	1,595
23. Andre Dawson	1,591
24. Harmon Killebrew	1,584
25. Al Kaline	1,583
26. Rogers Hornsby	1,578

Player	No.
27. Tris Speaker	1,562
28. Willie McCovey	1,555
29. Harry Heilmann	1,551
30. Barry Bonds	**1,542**
31. Willie Stargell	1,540
32. Joe DiMaggio	1,537
33. Mickey Mantle	1,509
34. Dave Parker	1,493
35. Billy Williams	1,476
36. Rafael Palmeiro	**1,470**
37. Rusty Staub	1,466
38. Eddie Mathews	1,453
39. Jim Rice	1,451
40. Joe Carter	1,445
41. Yogi Berra	1,430
42. Charlie Gehringer	1,427
43. Joe Cronin	1,423
44. Jim Bottomley	1,422
45. Mark McGwire	**1,414**
46. Jose Canseco	**1,407**
47. Robin Yount	1,406
48. Fred McGriff	**1,400**
49. Ted Simmons	1,389
50. Dwight Evans	1,384
51. Joe Medwick	1,383
52. Johnny Bench	1,376
53. Chili Davis	1,372
54. Orlando Cepeda	1,365
55. Brooks Robinson	1,357
56. Darrell Evans	1,354
57. Gary Gaetti	1,341
Andres Galarraga	**1,341**
59. Johnny Mize	1,337
60. Ken Griffey Jr.	**1,335**
61. Duke Snider	1,333
62. Ron Santo	1,331
63. Carlton Fisk	1,330
64. Al Oliver	1,326
65. Graig Nettles	1,314
Pete Rose	1,314
67. Mickey Vernon	1,311
68. Paul Waner	1,309
69. Steve Garvey	1,308
70. Eddie Collins	1,307
Paul Molitor	1,307
72. Roberto Clemente	1,305
73. Enos Slaughter	1,304
74. Del Ennis	1,284
75. Bob Johnson	1,283
76. Juan Gonzalez	**1,282**
77. Don Baylor	1,276
Hank Greenberg	1,276
79. Gil Hodges	1,274
80. Pie Traynor	1,273
81. Paul O'Neill	**1,269**
82. Dale Murphy	1,266
83. Zack Wheat	1,265
84. Bobby Doerr	1,247
85. Lee May	1,244
86. Frankie Frisch	1,242
87. Albert Belle	1,239
George Foster	1,239
Sammy Sosa	**1,239**
90. Gary Carter	1,225
91. Jeff Bagwell	**1,223**
92. Dave Kingman	1,210
93. Bill Dickey	1,209
94. Bill Buckner	1,208
95. Will Clark	1,205
96. Chuck Klein	1,202
Total number of players: 96	

1,000 BASES ON BALLS

Player	No.
1. Rickey Henderson	**2,141**
2. Babe Ruth	2,062
3. Ted Williams	2,019

Player	No.
4. Joe Morgan	1,865
5. Carl Yastrzemski	1,845
6. Mickey Mantle	1,734
7. Barry Bonds	**1,724**
8. Mel Ott	1,708
9. Eddie Yost	1,614
10. Darrell Evans	1,605
11. Stan Musial	1,599
12. Pete Rose	1,566
13. Harmon Killebrew	1,559
14. Lou Gehrig	1,508
15. Mike Schmidt	1,507
16. Willie Mays	1,464
17. Jimmie Foxx	1,452
18. Eddie Mathews	1,444
19. Frank Robinson	1,420
20. Wade Boggs	1,412
21. Hank Aaron	1,402
22. Dwight Evans	1,391
23. Reggie Jackson	1,375
24. Willie McCovey	1,345
25. Eddie Murray	1,333
26. Tony Phillips	1,319
27. Mark McGwire	**1,317**
28. Tim Raines Sr.	**1,308**
29. Luke Appling	1,302
30. Al Kaline	1,277
31. Jack Clark	1,262
Ken Singleton	1,262
33. Rusty Staub	1,255
34. Willie Randolph	1,243
35. Jim Wynn	1,224
36. Dave Winfield	1,216
37. Eddie Collins	1,213
38. Pee Wee Reese	1,210
39. Fred McGriff	**1,202**
40. Richie Ashburn	1,198
Frank Thomas	**1,198**
42. Brian Downing	1,197
Lou Whitaker	1,197
44. Chili Davis	1,194
45. Charlie Gehringer	1,185
46. Max Bishop	1,153
Toby Harrah	1,153
48. Tris Speaker	1,146
49. Brett Butler	1,129
Cal Ripken Jr.	**1,129**
51. Ron Santo	1,108
52. Jeff Bagwell	**1,098**
53. George Brett	1,096
54. Paul Molitor	1,094
55. Lu Blue	1,092
Stan Hack	1,092
57. Paul Waner	1,091
58. Graig Nettles	1,088
59. Bobby Grich	1,087
60. Bob Johnson	1,073
61. Ozzie Smith	1,072
62. Harlond Clift	1,070
Keith Hernandez	1,070
64. Edgar Martinez	**1,066**
65. Harold Baines	**1,062**
66. Joe Cronin	1,059
67. Ron Fairly	1,052
68. Billy Williams	1,045
69. Norm Cash	1,043
70. Eddie Joost	1,041
71. Max Carey	1,040
72. Rogers Hornsby	1,038
73. Junior Gilliam	1,036
Rafael Palmeiro	**1,036**
75. Sal Bando	1,031
76. Rod Carew	1,018
Enos Slaughter	1,018
78. John Olerud	**1,016**
79. Mark Grace	**1,013**
80. Ron Cey	1,012

Player	No.
81. Ralph Kiner	1,011
82. Boog Powell	1,001

Total number of players: 82
Note—Does not include seasons in N.L. before 1910 and in A.L. prior to 1913.

1,200 STRIKEOUTS

Player	No.
1. Reggie Jackson	2,597
2. Jose Canseco	**1,942**
3. Willie Stargell	1,936
4. Mike Schmidt	1,883
5. Tony Perez	1,867
6. Andres Galarraga	**1,858**
7. Dave Kingman	1,816
8. Bobby Bonds	1,757
9. Dale Murphy	1,748
10. Lou Brock	1,730
11. Mickey Mantle	1,710
12. Harmon Killebrew	1,699
13. Chili Davis	1,698
Fred McGriff	1,698
15. Dwight Evans	1,697
16. Sammy Sosa	**1,690**
17. Dave Winfield	1,686
18. Rickey Henderson	**1,631**
19. Gary Gaetti	1,602
20. Mark McGwire	**1,596**
21. Lee May	1,570
22. Dick Allen	1,556
23. Willie McCovey	1,550
24. Dave Parker	1,537
25. Frank Robinson	1,532
26. Lance Parrish	1,527
27. Willie Mays	1,526
Devon White	1,526
29. Eddie Murray	1,516
30. Rick Monday	1,513
31. Andre Dawson	1,509
32. Tony Phillips	1,499
33. Greg Luzinski	1,495
34. Eddie Mathews	1,487
35. Frank Howard	1,460
36. Juan Samuel	1,442
37. Harold Baines	**1,441**
Jack Clark	1,441
39. Ray Lankford	**1,434**
40. Jim Wynn	1,427
41. Jim Rice	1,423
42. George Foster	1,419
43. George Scott	1,418
Greg Vaughn	**1,418**
45. Darrell Evans	1,410
46. Jay Buhner	**1,406**
47. Eric Davis	**1,398**
48. Jay Bell	**1,396**
49. Carl Yastrzemski	1,393
50. Joe Carter	1,387
51. Carlton Fisk	1,386
52. Hank Aaron	1,383
53. Rob Deer	1,379
54. Danny Tartabull	1,362
55. Larry Parrish	1,359
56. Darryl Strawberry	1,352
57. Robin Yount	1,350
58. Ron Gant	**1,343**
Ron Santo	1,343
60. Gorman Thomas	1,339
61. Babe Ruth	1,330
62. Deron Johnson	1,318
63. Cecil Fielder	1,316
64. Willie Horton	1,313
65. Jimmie Foxx	1,311
66. Tim Wallach	1,307
Mickey Tettleton	1,307
68. Cal Ripken Jr.	**1,305**

Player	No.
69. Dean Palmer	**1,299**
70. Matt Williams	**1,296**
71. Travis Fryman	**1,287**
72. Kirk Gibson	1,285
73. Barry Bonds	**1,282**
74. Johnny Bench	1,278
Bobby Grich	1,278
76. Pete Incaviglia	1,277
77. Claudell Washington	1,266
78. Mo Vaughn	1,262
79. Ryne Sandberg	1,260
80. Ken Singleton	1,246
81. Paul Molitor	1,244
82. Willie McGee	1,238
Jim Thome	**1,238**
84. Duke Snider	1,237
85. Ernie Banks	1,236
86. Ron Cey	1,235
87. Jesse Barfield	1,234
88. Roberto Clemente	1,230
89. Boog Powell	1,226
90. Graig Nettles	1,209
91. Bobby Bonilla	**1,204**
92. Tony Armas	1,201

Total number of players: 92

BASERUNNING
400 STOLEN BASES

Player	No.
1. Rickey Henderson	**1,395**
2. Lou Brock	938
3. Billy Hamilton	937
4. Ty Cobb	892
5. Tim Raines Sr.	**808**
6. Arlie Latham	791
7. Vince Coleman	752
8. Harry Stovey	744
9. Eddie Collins	743
10. Max Carey	738
11. Honus Wagner	720
12. Tom Brown	697
13. Joe Morgan	689
14. Willie Wilson	668
15. Bert Campaneris	649
16. George Davis	632
17. Otis Nixon	620
18. Dummy Hoy	605
Monte Ward	605
20. Bid McPhee	602
21. Hugh Duffy	597
22. Bill Dahlen	587
23. Maury Wills	586
24. Ozzie Smith	580
25. Jack Doyle	560
26. Brett Butler	558
27. Dave Lopes	557
28. Herman Long	554
29. Cesar Cedeno	550
30. Mike Griffin	549
31. George Van Haltren	537
32. Pat Donovan	531
33. Fred Clarke	527
34. Curt Welch	526
35. Willie Keeler	519
36. Luis Aparicio	506
Tom McCarthy	506
38. Paul Molitor	504
39. Clyde Milan	495
40. Omar Moreno	487
41. Barry Bonds	**484**
42. Kenny Lofton	**479**
43. Ed Delahanty	478
44. Jim Sheckard	475
45. Bobby Bonds	461
46. Joe Kelley	458

Player	No.
47. Ron LeFlore	455
48. Delino DeShields	**453**
Bill Lange	453
50. Mike Tiernan	449
51. Roberto Alomar	**446**
52. John McGraw	444
Steve Sax	444
54. Sherry Magee	441
55. Charlie Comiskey	440
56. Jim Ryan	434
57. Tris Speaker	433
58. Bob Bescher	428
59. Tommy Corcoran	420
60. Frankie Frisch	419
61. Marquis Grissom	**409**
62. Tommy Harper	408
63. Tom Daly	407
64. Donie Bush	405
Frank Chance	405

Total number of players: 65

10 STEALS OF HOME

Player	No.
1. Ty Cobb	50
2. Max Carey	33
3. George Burns	28
4. Honus Wagner	27
5. Sherry Magee	23
Frank Schulte	23
7. John Evers	21
8. George Sisler	20
9. Frankie Frisch	19
Jackie Robinson	19
11. Jim Sheckard	18
Tris Speaker	18
Joe Tinker	18
14. Rod Carew	17
Eddie Collins	17
Larry Doyle	17
17. Tommy Leach	16
18. Ben Chapman	15
Fred Clarke	15
Lou Gehrig	15
21. Bob Byrne	14
Fred Maisel	14
Fred Merkle	14
Vic Saier	14
25. Heinie Zimmerman	13
26. Donie Bush	12
Sam Rice	12
28. Shano Collins	11
Harry Hooper	11
George Moriarty	11
Bob Roth	11
32. Buck Herzog	10
Jim Johnston	10
Rabbit Maranville	10
Paul Molitor	10
Babe Ruth	10
Bill Werber	10
Ross Youngs	10

Total number of players: 38
Note—Steals of home are not recorded as official statistics and most are uncovered in newspaper accounts. Researchers are continually finding additional steals of home for many players, which explains the changes in this list each year.

PITCHING
700 GAMES

Pitcher	Yrs.	Games
1. Jesse Orosco	**22**	**1,131**
2. Dennis Eckersley	24	1,071

Pitcher	Yrs.	Games
3. Hoyt Wilhelm	21	1,070
4. Kent Tekulve	16	1,050
5. Lee Smith	18	1,022
6. Rich Gossage	22	1,002
7. John Franco	**18**	**998**
8. Lindy McDaniel	21	987
9. Dan Plesac	**16**	**946**
10. Rollie Fingers	17	944
11. Gene Garber	19	931
12. Cy Young	22	906
13. Mike Jackson	**15**	**902**
14. Sparky Lyle	16	899
15. Jim Kaat	25	898
16. Paul Assenmacher	14	884
17. Jeff Reardon	16	880
18. Don McMahon	18	874
19. Phil Niekro	24	864
20. Charlie Hough	25	858
21. Roy Face	16	848
22. Doug Jones	16	846
23. Tug McGraw	19	824
24. Nolan Ryan	27	807
25. Walter Johnson	21	802
26. Rick Honeycutt	21	797
27. Gaylord Perry	22	777
28. Don Sutton	23	774
29. Darold Knowles	16	765
30. Tommy John	26	760
31. Mike Stanton	**13**	**756**
32. Ron Reed	19	751
33. Warren Spahn	21	750
34. Tom Burgmeier	17	745
Gary Lavelle	13	745
36. Willie Hernandez	13	744
37. Steve Carlton	24	741
38. Ron Perranoski	13	737
39. Ron Kline	17	736
40. Rick Aguilera	16	732
41. Steve Bedrosian	14	732
42. Clay Carroll	15	731
43. Randy Myers	14	728
44. Mike G. Marshall	14	723
Roger McDowell	12	723
46. Dave Righetti	16	718
47. Danny Darwin	21	716
48. Eric Plunk	14	714
49. Johnny Klippstein	18	711
50. Greg Minton	16	710
51. Stu Miller	16	704
52. Greg A. Harris	15	703
53. Joe Niekro	22	702
54. Bill Campbell	15	700
Jeff Montgomery	13	700

Total number of pitchers: 55

500 GAMES STARTED

Pitcher	No.
1. Cy Young	818
2. Nolan Ryan	773
3. Don Sutton	756
4. Phil Niekro	716
5. Steve Carlton	709
6. Tommy John	700
7. Gaylord Perry	690
8. Bert Blyleven	685
9. Pud Galvin	682
10. Walter Johnson	666
11. Warren Spahn	665
12. Tom Seaver	647
13. Jim Kaat	625
14. Frank Tanana	616
15. Early Wynn	612
16. Robin Roberts	609
17. Grover Alexander	598
18. Ferguson Jenkins	594
19. Tim Keefe	593

Pitcher	No.
20. Dennis Martinez	562
21. Kid Nichols	561
22. Eppa Rixey	552
23. Christy Mathewson	551
24. Mickey Welch	549
25. Jerry Reuss	547
26. Roger Clemens	**544**
27. Red Ruffing	536
28. Rick Reuschel	529
29. Jerry Koosman	527
Jack Morris	527
31. Jim Palmer	521
32. Jim Bunning	519
33. John Clarkson	518
34. Jack Powell	517
35. Tony Mullane	505
36. Hoss Radbourn	503
Gus Weyhing	503
38. Greg Maddux	**501**

Total number of pitchers: 38

300 COMPLETE GAMES

Pitcher	No.
1. Cy Young	751
2. Pud Galvin	641
3. Tim Keefe	554
4. Walter Johnson	531
Kid Nichols	531
6. Mickey Welch	525
7. John Clarkson	487
8. Hoss Radbourn	479
9. Tony Mullane	464
10. Jim McCormick	462
11. Gus Weyhing	447
12. Grover Alexander	436
13. Christy Mathewson	434
14. Jack Powell	422
15. Will White	394
16. Amos Rusie	391
17. Vic Willis	388
18. Eddie Plank	387
19. Warren Spahn	382
20. Jim Whitney	373
21. William Terry	368
22. Ted Lyons	356
23. Charlie Buffinton	350
24. Chick Fraser	342
25. George Mullin	339
26. Clark Griffith	337
27. Red Ruffing	335
28. Charles King	327
29. Al Orth	323
30. Bill Hutchinson	321
31. Burleigh Grimes	314
Joe McGinnity	314
33. Red Donahue	312
34. Guy Hecker	310
35. Bill Dinneen	305
Robin Roberts	305
37. Gaylord Perry	303
38. Ted Breitenstein	300
Lefty Grove	300

Total number of pitchers: 39

3,500 INNINGS

Pitcher	No.
1. Cy Young	7,377.0
2. Pud Galvin	5,959.0
3. Walter Johnson	5,923.0
4. Phil Niekro	5,403.2
5. Nolan Ryan	5,387.0
6. Gaylord Perry	5,352.0
7. Don Sutton	5,281.2
8. Warren Spahn	5,246.0
9. Steve Carlton	5,216.1

Pitcher	No.
10. Grover Alexander	5,188.0
11. Kid Nichols	5,067.0
12. Tim Keefe	5,043.0
13. Bert Blyleven	4,970.1
14. Mickey Welch	4,784.0
15. Tom Seaver	4,782.0
16. Christy Mathewson	4,781.0
17. Tommy John	4,707.1
18. Robin Roberts	4,689.0
19. Early Wynn	4,566.0
20. Hoss Radbourn	4,543.0
21. John Clarkson	4,534.0
22. Jim Kaat	4,527.2
23. Tony Mullane	4,506.0
24. Ferguson Jenkins	4,498.2
25. Eppa Rixey	4,494.0
26. Jack Powell	4,390.0
27. Red Ruffing	4,342.0
28. Gus Weyhing	4,335.0
29. Jim McCormick	4,264.0
30. Eddie Plank	4,234.0
31. Frank Tanana	4,186.2
32. Burleigh Grimes	4,178.0
33. Ted Lyons	4,162.0
34. Urban Faber	4,087.0
35. Dennis Martinez	4,000.0
36. Vic Willis	3,994.0
37. Jim Palmer	3,947.1
38. Lefty Grove	3,940.0
39. Roger Clemens	**3,887.0**
40. Bob Gibson	3,885.0
41. Sam Jones	3,884.0
42. Jerry Koosman	3,839.1
43. Bob Feller	3,828.0
44. Jack Morris	3,824.2
45. Charlie Hough	3,800.1
46. Waite Hoyt	3,762.0
47. Jim Bunning	3,759.0
48. Bobo Newsom	3,758.0
49. Amos Rusie	3,750.0
50. Jerry Reuss	3,668.2
51. Paul Derringer	3,646.0
52. Mickey Lolich	3,640.0
53. Bob Friend	3,612.0
54. Carl Hubbell	3,591.0
55. Joe Niekro	3,584.2
56. Herb Pennock	3,572.0
57. Earl Whitehill	3,563.0
58. Greg Maddux	**3,551.0**
59. Rick Reuschel	3,549.2
60. Will White	3,543.0
61. William Terry	3,523.0
62. Juan Marichal	3,506.0

Total number of pitchers: 62

200 VICTORIES

Pitcher	W	L
1. Cy Young	511	313
2. Walter Johnson	417	279
3. Christy Mathewson	373	188
Grover Alexander	373	208
5. Warren Spahn	363	245
6. Kid Nichols	361	208
Pud Galvin	361	309
8. Tim Keefe	342	225
9. Steve Carlton	329	244
10. John Clarkson	327	176
11. Don Sutton	324	256
Nolan Ryan	324	292
13. Phil Niekro	318	274
14. Gaylord Perry	314	265
15. Tom Seaver	311	205
16. Hoss Radbourn	308	191
17. Mickey Welch	307	209
18. Eddie Plank	305	181
19. Lefty Grove	300	141
Early Wynn	300	244

	Pitcher	W	L
21.	Tommy John	288	231
22.	Bert Blyleven	287	250
23.	Robin Roberts	286	245
24.	Tony Mullane	285	213
25.	Ferguson Jenkins	284	226
26.	Jim Kaat	283	237
27.	**Roger Clemens**	**280**	**145**
28.	Red Ruffing	273	225
29.	Burleigh Grimes	270	212
30.	Jim Palmer	268	152
31.	Bob Feller	266	162
	Eppa Rixey	266	251
33.	Jim McCormick	265	215
34.	Gus Weyhing	262	226
35.	Ted Lyons	260	230
36.	**Greg Maddux**	**257**	**146**
37.	Jack Morris	254	186
	Urban Faber	254	212
39.	Carl Hubbell	253	154
40.	Bob Gibson	251	174
41.	Vic Willis	248	204
42.	Joe McGinnity	247	145
	Jack Powell	247	254
44.	Dennis Martinez	245	193
45.	Juan Marichal	243	142
46.	Amos Rusie	241	158
	Herb Pennock	241	162
48.	Clark Griffith	240	140
	Frank Tanana	240	236
50.	Waite Hoyt	237	182
51.	Whitey Ford	236	106
52.	Charlie Buffinton	231	153
53.	Luis Tiant	229	172
	Sam Jones	229	217
55.	Will White	227	167
56.	**Tom Glavine**	**224**	**132**
	Catfish Hunter	224	166
	Jim Bunning	224	184
59.	Hooks Dauss	223	182
	Mel Harder	223	186
	Paul Derringer	223	212
62.	Jerry Koosman	222	209
63.	Joe Niekro	221	204
64.	Jerry Reuss	220	191
65.	Earl Whitehill	218	186
66.	Bob Caruthers	217	101
	Fred Fitzsimmons	217	146
	Mickey Lolich	217	191
69.	Wilbur Cooper	216	178
	Charlie Hough	216	216
71.	Stan Coveleski	215	141
	Jim Perry	215	174
73.	Rick Reuschel	214	191
74.	George Mullin	212	181
	Jack Quinn	212	181
76.	Bob Welch	211	146
	Billy Pierce	211	169
	Bobo Newsom	211	222
79.	Jesse Haines	210	158
80.	Ed Cicotte	209	149
81.	Vida Blue	209	161
	Milt Pappas	209	164
	Don Drysdale	209	166
84.	Mordecai Brown	208	111
	Chief Bender	208	112
	Carl Mays	208	126
87.	Bob Lemon	207	128
	Hal Newhouser	207	150
89.	William Terry	205	197
90.	Orel Hershiser	204	150
	Charles King	204	152
92.	Jack Stivetts	203	132
	Lew Burdette	203	144
94.	Al Orth	202	182
95.	Charlie Root	201	160
	Rube Marquard	201	177
97.	**Randy Johnson**	**200**	**101**
98.	George Uhle	200	166

Total number of pitchers: 98

20 VICTORIES, 5 TIMES

	Pitcher	No.
1.	Cy Young	16
2.	Christy Mathewson	13
	Warren Spahn	13
4.	Walter Johnson	12
5.	Kid Nichols	11
6.	Pud Galvin	10
7.	Grover Alexander	9
	Hoss Radbourn	9
	Mickey Welch	9
10.	John Clarkson	8
	Lefty Grove	8
	Jim McCormick	8
	Joe McGinnity	8
	Tony Mullane	8
	Jim Palmer	8
	Amos Rusie	8
17.	Charlie Buffinton	7
	Clark Griffith	7
	Ferguson Jenkins	7
	Tim Keefe	7
	Bob Lemon	7
	Eddie Plank	7
	Gus Weyhing	7
	Vic Willis	7
25.	Mordecai Brown	6
	Steve Carlton	6
	Bob Caruthers	6
	Roger Clemens	**6**
	Bob Feller	6
	Wes Ferrell	6
	Juan Marichal	6
	Robin Roberts	6
	Jack Stivetts	6
	Jesse Tannehill	6
35.	Tommy Bond	5
	Jack Chesbro	5
	Larry Corcoran	5
	Stan Coveleski	5
	Bob Gibson	5
	Tom Glavine	**5**
	Burleigh Grimes	5
	Carl Hubbell	5
	Catfish Hunter	5
	Charles King	5
	Carl Mays	5
	John McMahon	5
	George Mullin	5
	Gaylord Perry	5
	Deacon Phillippe	5
	Tom Seaver	5
	Hippo Vaughn	5
	Will White	5
	Jim Whitney	5
	Early Wynn	5

Total number of pitchers: 54

30 VICTORIES, 2 TIMES

	Pitcher	Yrs.
1.	Kid Nichols	7
2.	John Clarkson	6
	Tim Keefe	6
4.	Tony Mullane	5
	Cy Young	5
6.	Tommy Bond	4
	Larry Corcoran	4
	Charles King	4
	Christy Mathewson	4
	Jim McCormick	4
	Mickey Welch	4
	Will White	4
13.	Grover Alexander	3
	Bob Caruthers	3
	Pud Galvin	3
	Bill Hutchison	3

	Pitcher	Yrs.
	Bobby Mathews	3
	Ed Morris	3
	Hoss Radbourn	3
	Amos Rusie	3
21.	Dave Foutz	2
	George Haddock	2
	Guy Hecker	2
	Walter Johnson	2
	Frank Killen	2
	Joe McGinnity	2
	John McMahon	2
	Tom Ramsey	2
	Jack Stivetts	2
	Monte Ward	2
	Gus Weyhing	2
	Jim Whitney	2

Total number of pitchers: 32

150 SAVES

(Since 1969)

	Pitcher	No.
1.	Lee Smith	478
2.	**John Franco**	**422**
3.	Dennis Eckersley	390
4.	Jeff Reardon	367
5.	Randy Myers	347
6.	Rollie Fingers	341
7.	John Wetteland	330
8.	Rick Aguilera	318
9.	**Trevor Hoffman**	**314**
10.	Tom Henke	311
11.	Rich Gossage	310
12.	Jeff Montgomery	304
13.	Doug Jones	303
14.	Bruce Sutter	300
15.	**Roberto Hernandez**	**294**
16.	**Robb Nen**	**271**
17.	**Rod Beck**	**266**
18.	Todd Worrell	256
19.	Dave Righetti	252
20.	Dan Quisenberry	244
21.	Sparky Lyle	222
22.	Gene Garber	218
23.	**Gregg Olson**	**217**
24.	Dave Smith	216
25.	**Mariano Rivera**	**215**
26.	**Troy Percival**	**210**
27.	**Jeff Shaw**	**203**
28.	Bobby Thigpen	201
29.	Mike Henneman	193
30.	Mitch Williams	192
31.	Jeff Russell	186
32.	Steve Bedrosian	184
	Kent Tekulve	184
34.	**Todd Jones**	**183**
35.	**Jose Mesa**	**180**
36.	Tug McGraw	179
37.	Mike Marshall	178
38.	Bryan Harvey	177
39.	**Jeff Brantley**	**172**
40.	Roger McDowell	159
41.	Jay Howell	155
	Dan Plesac	**155**
43.	Greg Minton	150

Total number of pitchers: 43

1,800 RUNS ALLOWED

	Pitcher	No.
1.	Pud Galvin	3,303
2.	Cy Young	3,168
3.	Gus Weyhing	2,770
4.	Mickey Welch	2,555
5.	Tony Mullane	2,520
6.	Kid Nichols	2,477
7.	Tim Keefe	2,461

Pitcher	No.
8. John Clarkson	2,396
9. Phil Niekro	2,337
10. Hoss Radbourn	2,300
11. Nolan Ryan	2,178
12. Steve Carlton	2,130
13. Jim McCormick	2,129
14. Gaylord Perry	2,128
15. Red Ruffing	2,117
16. Don Sutton	2,104
17. Jim Whitney	2,060
18. Ted Lyons	2,056
19. Burleigh Grimes	2,048
20. Jim Kaat	2,038
21. Early Wynn	2,037
22. Bert Blyleven	2,029
23. Earl Whitehill	2,018
24. Tommy John	2,017
25. Warren Spahn	2,016
26. Sam Jones	2,008
27. Eppa Rixey	1,986
28. Chick Fraser	1,984
29. Jack Powell	1,976
30. Robin Roberts	1,962
31. Frank Tanana	1,910
32. Bobo Newsom	1,908
Amos Rusie	1,908
34. Walter Johnson	1,902
35. Ferguson Jenkins	1,853
36. Grover Alexander	1,851
37. Dennis Martinez	1,835
38. Charles King	1,834
39. Jack Morris	1,815
40. Urban Faber	1,813
41. Jack Stivetts	1,809
42. Charlie Hough	1,807

Total number of pitchers: 42

3.50 OR UNDER ERA

(Pitchers with 3,000 or more innings; does not include any seasons in N.L. before 1912 and in A.L. prior to 1913)

Pitcher	IP	ERA
1. Walter Johnson*	4,195.0	2.37
2. Grover Alexander†	4,822.0	2.56
3. Whitey Ford	3,171.0	2.74
4. Greg Maddux	**3,551.0**	**2.84**
5. Tom Seaver	4,782.0	2.86
Jim Palmer	3,947.1	2.86
7. Stan Coveleski	3,071.0	2.88
8. Juan Marichal	3,506.0	2.89
Wilbur Cooper	3,482.0	2.89
10. Bob Gibson	3,885.0	2.91
11. Carl Mays	3,022.0	2.92
12. Don Drysdale	3,432.0	2.95
13. Carl Hubbell	3,591.0	2.98
14. Lefty Grove	3,940.0	3.06
15. Warren Spahn	5,246.0	3.08
16. Gaylord Perry	5,352.0	3.10
Roger Clemens	**3,887.0**	**3.10**
18. Eppa Rixey	4,494.0	3.15
Urban Faber	4,087.0	3.15
20. Nolan Ryan	5,387.0	3.19
21. Steve Carlton	5,216.1	3.22
22. Dolf Luque	3,221.0	3.24
23. Bob Feller	3,828.0	3.25
Dutch J. Leonard	3,220.0	3.25
25. Don Sutton	5,281.2	3.26
Catfish Hunter	3,449.0	3.26
Vida Blue	3,344.0	3.26
28. Jim Bunning	3,759.0	3.27
Billy Pierce	3,305.0	3.27
30. Luis Tiant	3,485.2	3.30
Bucky Walters	3,104.0	3.30
Claude Osteen	3,459.0	3.30
33. Bert Blyleven	4,970.1	3.31

Pitcher	IP	ERA
34. Hooks Dauss	3,374.0	3.32
35. Tommy John	4,707.1	3.34
Ferguson Jenkins	4,498.2	3.34
37. Phil Niekro	5,403.2	3.35
38. Jerry Koosman	3,839.1	3.36
39. Rick Reuschel	3,549.2	3.37
40. Lee Meadows	3,151.0	3.38
41. Robin Roberts	4,689.0	3.40
Larry Jackson	3,262.0	3.40
Milt Pappas	3,186.0	3.40
Tom Glavine	**3,120.0**	**3.40**
45. Mickey Lolich	3,640.0	3.44
Larry French	3,152.0	3.44
Jim Perry	3,287.0	3.44
48. Jim Kaat	4,527.2	3.46
Paul Derringer	3,646.0	3.46
50. Bob Welch	3,091.1	3.47
51. Orel Hershiser	3,130.1	3.48
52. Joe Bush	3,088.0	3.49
53. Dennis Eckersley	3,285.2	3.50

Total number of pitchers: 53

*Does not include 1,729 innings pitched 1907 through 1912; allowed 520 total runs in that period; earned-run total not available and if all the 520 runs were included in Johnson's earned-run total, his career earned-run average would be 2.47.

†Does not include 367 innings pitched in 1911; allowed 133 total runs in that year; earned-run total not available. If all the 133 runs were included in Alexander's earned-run total, his career ERA would be 2.61.

40 SHUTOUTS

Pitcher	No.
1. Walter Johnson	110
2. Grover Alexander	90
3. Christy Mathewson	83
4. Cy Young	76
5. Eddie Plank	64
6. Warren Spahn	63
7. Nolan Ryan	61
Tom Seaver	61
9. Bert Blyleven	60
10. Ed Walsh	58
Don Sutton	58
12. Pud Galvin	57
13. Bob Gibson	56
14. Steve Carlton	55
15. Jim Palmer	53
Gaylord Perry	53
17. Juan Marichal	52
18. Mordecai Brown	50
Rube Waddell	50
Vic Willis	50
21. Early Wynn	49
Don Drysdale	49
Luis Tiant	49
Ferguson Jenkins	49
25. Kid Nichols	48
26. Jack Powell	46
Guy White	46
Tommy John	46
29. Babe Adams	45
Roger Clemens	**45**
Addie Joss	45
Red Ruffing	45
Robin Roberts	45
Whitey Ford	45
Phil Niekro	45
36. Bob Feller	44
37. Milt Pappas	43
38. Bucky Walters	42
Catfish Hunter	42

Pitcher	No.
40. Chief Bender	41
Mickey Lolich	41
Hippo Vaughn	41
Mickey Welch	41
44. Larry French	40
Sandy Koufax	40
Jim Bunning	40
Mel Stottlemyre	40
Claude Osteen	40
Tim Keefe	40

Total number of pitchers: 49

10, 1-0 VICTORIES

(Complete Games)

Pitcher	No.
1. Walter Johnson	38
2. Grover Alexander	17
3. Bert Blyleven	15
4. Christy Mathewson	14
5. Eddie Plank	13
Ed Walsh	13
Doc White	13
Cy Young	13
Dean Chance	13
10. Stan Coveleski	12
Gaylord Perry	12
Steve Carlton	12
13. Nap Rucker	11
Kid Nichols	11
Ferguson Jenkins	11
Nolan Ryan	11
17. Joe Bush	10
Paul Derringer	10
Bill Doak	10
Addie Joss	10
Dick Rudolph	10
Hippo Vaughn	10
Lefty Tyler	10
Warren Spahn	10
Sandy Koufax	10

Total number of pitchers: 25

4,000 HITS ALLOWED

Pitcher	No.
1. Cy Young	7,078
2. Pud Galvin	*6,334
3. Phil Niekro	5,044
4. Gaylord Perry	4,938
5. Walter Johnson	4,920
6. Grover Alexander	4,868
7. Kid Nichols	4,854
8. Warren Spahn	4,830
9. Tommy John	4,783
10. Don Sutton	4,692
11. Steve Carlton	4,672
12. Gus Weyhing	*4,669
13. Mickey Welch	*4,646
14. Eppa Rixey	4,633
15. Bert Blyleven	4,632
16. Jim Kaat	4,620
17. Robin Roberts	4,582
18. Tim Keefe	*4,524
19. Hoss Radbourn	*4,500
20. Ted Lyons	4,489
21. Burleigh Grimes	4,406
22. John Clarkson	*4,376
23. Jack Powell	4,323
24. Red Ruffing	4,294
25. Early Wynn	4,291
26. Tony Mullane	*4,238
27. Christy Mathewson	4,203
28. Jim McCormick	*4,166
29. Ferguson Jenkins	4,142
30. Urban Faber	4,104

Pitcher	No.
31. Sam Jones	4,084
32. Frank Tanana	4,063
33. Waite Hoyt	4,037

Total number of pitchers: 33

*Includes 1887 bases on balls, scored as hits under rules in effect for that year.

7 GRAND SLAMS ALLOWED

Pitcher	No.
1. Nolan Ryan	10
2. Ned Garver	9
Jim Kaat	9
Milt Pappas	9
Jerry Reuss	9
Lee Smith	9
Frank Viola	9
8. **Willie Blair**	**8**
Bert Blyleven	8
Jim Brewer	8
Roy Face	8
Bob Feller	8
Alex Fernandez	8
Mike Jackson	**8**
Johnny Klippstein	8
Lindy McDaniel	8
Tug McGraw	8
Jesse Orosco	**8**
Frank Tanana	8
Early Wynn	8
21. Doug Bair	7
Steve Bedrosian	7
Tim Belcher	7
Ricky Bones	**7**
Larry French	7
Tom Gordon	**7**
Jimmy Haynes	**7**
Jim Hearn	7
Charlie Hough	7
Ramon Martinez	**7**
Terry Mulholland	**7**
Phil Niekro	7
Gaylord Perry	7
Dennis Rasmussen	7
Kenny Rogers	**7**
Ray Sadecki	7
Jack Sanford	7
Willie Sherdel	7
Don Sutton	7
Mike Torrez	7
Lon Warneke	7
Bobby Witt	**7**
Mike Witt	7
Matt Young	7

Total number of pitchers: 44

1,200 BASES ON BALLS

Pitcher	No.
1. Nolan Ryan	2,795
2. Steve Carlton	1,833
3. Phil Niekro	1,809
4. Early Wynn	1,775
5. Bob Feller	1,764
6. Bobo Newsom	1,732
7. Charlie Hough	1,665
8. Amos Rusie	1,637
9. Gus Weyhing	1,569
10. Red Ruffing	1,541
11. Bump Hadley	1,442
12. Warren Spahn	1,434
13. Earl Whitehill	1,431
14. Sam Jones	1,396
15. Jack Morris	1,390
Tom Seaver	1,390
17. Tony Mullane	1,379
Gaylord Perry	1,379
19. **Bobby Witt**	**1,375**
20. Mike Torrez	1,371
21. Walter Johnson	1,353
22. Don Sutton	1,343
23. Bob Gibson	1,336
24. Chick Fraser	1,332
25. Bert Blyleven	1,322
26. Sam McDowell	1,312
27. Jim Palmer	1,311
28. Mickey Welch	1,305
29. Burleigh Grimes	1,295
30. Mark Langston	1,289
31. Mark Baldwin	1,285
32. Joe Niekro	1,262
33. Allie Reynolds	1,261
34. Joe Bush	1,260
35. Tommy John	1,259
36. **Roger Clemens**	**1,258**
37. Frank Tanana	1,255
38. Bob Lemon	1,251
39. Hal Newhouser	1,249
40. Kid Nichols	1,245
41. Bill Terry	1,244
42. Tim Keefe	1,225
43. Urban Faber	1,213
44. Cy Young	1,209

Total number of pitchers: 44

2,000 STRIKEOUTS

Pitcher	No.
1. Nolan Ryan	5,714
2. Steve Carlton	4,136
3. **Roger Clemens**	**3,717**
4. Bert Blyleven	3,701
5. Tom Seaver	3,640
6. Don Sutton	3,574
7. Gaylord Perry	3,534
8. Walter Johnson	3,508
9. **Randy Johnson**	**3,412**
10. Phil Niekro	3,342
11. Ferguson Jenkins	3,192
12. Bob Gibson	3,117
13. Jim Bunning	2,855
14. Mickey Lolich	2,832
15. Cy Young	2,803
16. Frank Tanana	2,773
17. **David Cone**	**2,655**
18. Warren Spahn	2,583
19. Bob Feller	2,581
20. Jerry Koosman	2,556
21. Tim Keefe	2,538
22. **Greg Maddux**	**2,523**
23. Christy Mathewson	2,505
24. Don Drysdale	2,486
25. Jack Morris	2,478
26. Mark Langston	2,464
27. Jim Kaat	2,461
28. Sam McDowell	2,453
29. **Chuck Finley**	**2,436**
30. Luis Tiant	2,416
31. Dennis Eckersley	2,401
32. Sandy Koufax	2,396
33. Charlie Hough	2,362
34. Robin Roberts	2,357
35. Early Wynn	2,334
36. Rube Waddell	2,310
37. Juan Marichal	2,303
38. Dwight Gooden	2,293
39. Lefty Grove	2,266
40. Tommy John	2,245
41. Jim Palmer	2,212
42. Grover Alexander	2,198
43. Vida Blue	2,175
44. Camilo Pascual	2,167
45. **John Smoltz**	**2,155**
46. Dennis Martinez	2,149
47. Eddie Plank	2,112
48. John Smoltz	2,098
49. Bobo Newsom	2,082
50. Fernando Valenzuela	2,074
51. Dazzy Vance	2,045
52. **Curt Schilling**	**2,032**
53. **Kevin Brown**	**2,021**
54. Rick Reuschel	2,015
55. Orel Hershiser	2,014
56. Catfish Hunter	2,012

Total number of pitchers: 56

GENERAL REFERENCE

BATTING

TRIPLE CROWN HITTERS

AMERICAN LEAGUE

Year	Player, Club	Avg.	HR	RBI
1901	Napoleon Lajoie, Philadelphia	.422	14	*125
1909	Ty Cobb, Detroit	.377	9	*115
1933	Jimmie Foxx, Philadelphia	.356	48	163
1934	Lou Gehrig, New York	.363	49	165
1942	Ted Williams, Boston	.356	36	137
1947	Ted Williams, Boston	.343	32	114
1956	Mickey Mantle, New York	.353	52	130
1966	Frank Robinson, Baltimore	.316	49	122
1967	Carl Yastrzemski, Boston	.326	44	121

Total number of occurrences: 9

NATIONAL LEAGUE

Year	Player, Club	Avg.	HR	RBI
1912	Heinie Zimmerman, Chicago	.372	14	*98
1922	Rogers Hornsby, St. Louis	.401	42	152
1925	Rogers Hornsby, St. Louis	.403	39	143
1933	Chuck Klein, Philadelphia	.368	28	120
1937	Joe Medwick, St. Louis	.374	31	154

*RBIs not officially adopted until 1920.
Total number of occurrences: 5

.400 HITTERS

Year	Player, Club	Avg.
1887	Tip O'Neill, St. Louis A.A.†	.492
1887	Pete Browning, Louisville A.A.†	.471
1887	Denny Lyons, Philadelphia A.A.†	.469
1887	Bob Caruthers, St. Louis A.A.†	.459
1894	Hugh Duffy, Boston N.L.*	.438
1897	Willie Keeler, Baltimore N.L.*	.432
1887	Yank Robinson, St. Louis A.A.†	.426
1924	Rogers Hornsby, St. Louis N.L.*	.424
1894	George Turner, Philadelphia N.L.	.423
1895	Jesse Burkett, Cleveland N.L.*	.423
1901	Nap Lajoie, Philadelphia A.L.*	.422
1887	Cap Anson, Chicago N.L.†	.421
1884	Fred Dunlap, St. Louis U.A.	.420
1911	Ty Cobb, Detroit A.L.*	.420
1922	George Sisler, St. Louis A.L.*	.420
1887	Dennis Brouthers, Detroit N.L.†	.419
1887	Reddy Mack, Louisville A.A.†	.410
1896	Jesse Burkett, Cleveland N.L.*	.410
1912	Ty Cobb, Detroit A.L.*	.410
1893	Jacob Stenzel, Pittsburgh N.L.	.409
1884	Tom Esterbrook, New York A.A.*	.408
1899	Ed Delahanty, Philadelphia N.L.*	.408
1911	Joe Jackson, Cleveland A.L.*	.408
1879	Cap Anson, Chicago N.L.*	.407
1920	George Sisler, St. Louis A.L.*	.407
1887	Sam Thompson, Detroit N.L.†	.406
1897	Fred Clarke, Louisville N.L.*	.406
1941	Ted Williams, Boston A.L.*	.406
1876	Ross Barnes, Chicago N.L.*	.404
1884	Harry Stovey, Philadelphia A.A.*	.404
1887	Paul Radford, New York A.A.*	.404
1894	Sam Thompson, Philadelphia N.L.*	.404
1887	Dave Orr, New York A.A.†	.403
1923	Harry Heilmann, Detroit A.L.*	.403
1925	Rogers Hornsby, St. Louis N.L.*	.403
1887	Harry Stovey, Philadelphia A.A.†	.402
1899	Jesse Burkett, St. Louis N.L.*	.402
1887	Tom Burns, Baltimore A.A.†	.401
1922	Ty Cobb, Detroit A.L.*	.401
1922	Rogers Hornsby, St. Louis N.L.*	.401
1930	Bill Terry, New York N.L.*	.401
1894	Ed Delahanty, Philadelphia N.L.*	.400

*Qualify as .400 hitters under present rule 10.23 of Official Baseball Rules. †Bases on balls counted as hits in 1887.
Total number of occurrences: 42

200 HITS BY ROOKIES IN SEASON

AMERICAN LEAGUE

Year	Player, Club	G	H
2001	Ichiro Suzuki, Seattle	157	242
1964	Tony Oliva, Minnesota	161	217
1929	Dale Alexander, Detroit	155	215
1997	Nomar Garciaparra, Boston	153	209
1953	Harvey Kuenn, Detroit	155	209
1987	Kevin Seitzer, Kansas City	161	207
1936	Joe DiMaggio, New York	138	206
1934	Hal Trosky, Cleveland	154	206
1942	Johnny Pesky, Boston	147	205
1929	Roy Johnson, Detroit	148	201
1943	Dick Wakefield, Detroit	155	200

NATIONAL LEAGUE

Year	Player, Club	G	H
1927	Lloyd Waner, Pittsburgh	150	223
1899	Jimmy Williams, Pittsburgh	153	219
1929	Johnny Frederick, Brooklyn	148	206
1964	Dick Allen, Philadelphia	162	201

30-GAME BATTING STREAKS

Year	Player, Club	G
1941	Joe DiMaggio, New York A.L.	56
1897	Willie Keeler, Baltimore N.L.*	44
1978	Pete Rose, Cincinnati N.L.	44
1894	Bill Dahlen, Chicago N.L.	42
1922	George Sisler, St. Louis A.L.	41
1911	Ty Cobb, Detroit A.L.	40
1987	Paul Molitor, Milwaukee A.L.	39
1945	Tommy Holmes, Boston N.L.	37
1894	Billy Hamilton, Philadelphia N.L.	36
1895	Fred Clarke, Louisville N.L.	35
1917	Ty Cobb, Detroit A.L.	35
1925	George Sisler, St. Louis A.L.*	34
1938	George McQuinn, St. Louis A.L.	34
1949	Dom DiMaggio, Boston A.L.	34
1987	Benito Santiago, San Diego N.L.	34
1893	George Davis, New York N.L.	33
1907	Hal Chase, New York A.L.	33
1922	Rogers Hornsby, St. Louis N.L.	33
1933	Heinie Manush, Washington A.L.	33
1899	Ed Delahanty, Philadelphia N.L.	31
1906	Nap Lajoie, Cleveland A.L.	31
1924	Sam Rice, Washington A.L.	31
1969	Willie Davis, Los Angeles N.L.	31
1970	Rico Carty, Atlanta N.L.	31
1980	Ken Landreaux, Minnesota N.L.	31
1999	Vladimir Guerrero, Montreal N.L.	31
1876	Cal McVey, Chicago N.L.	30
1898	Elmer E. Smith, Cincinnati N.L.	30
1912	Tris Speaker, Boston A.L.	30
1934	Goose Goslin, Detroit A.L.	30
1950	Stan Musial, St. Louis N.L.	30
1976	Ron LeFlore, Detroit A.L.*	30
1980	George Brett, Kansas City A.L.	30
1989	Jerome Walton, Chicago N.L.	30
1997	Sandy Alomar Jr., Cleveland A.L.	30
1997	Nomar Garciaparra, Boston A.L.	30
1998	Eric Davis, Baltimore A.L.	30
1999	Luis Gonzalez, Arizona N.L.	30

*From start of season.
Total number of occurrences: 38

40 HOME RUNS IN SEASON

AMERICAN LEAGUE

Year	Player, Club	No.
1961	Roger Maris, New York	61
1927	Babe Ruth, New York	60
1921	Babe Ruth, New York	59

Year	Player, Club	No.
1932	Jimmie Foxx, Philadelphia	58
1938	Hank Greenberg, Detroit	58
1997	Ken Griffey Jr., Seattle	56
1998	Ken Griffey Jr., Seattle	56
1920	Babe Ruth, New York	54
1928	Babe Ruth, New York	54
1961	Mickey Mantle, New York	54
1956	Mickey Mantle, New York	52
1996	Mark McGwire, Oakland	52
2001	Alex Rodriguez, Texas	52
1990	Cecil Fielder, Detroit	51
1938	Jimmie Foxx, Boston	50
1995	Albert Belle, Cleveland	50
1996	Brady Anderson, Baltimore	50
1930	Babe Ruth, New York	49
1934	Lou Gehrig, New York	49
1936	Lou Gehrig, New York	49
1964	Harmon Killebrew, Minnesota	49
1966	Frank Robinson, Baltimore	49
1969	Harmon Killebrew, Minnesota	49
1987	Mark McGwire, Oakland	49
1996	Ken Griffey Jr., Seattle	49
1998	Albert Belle, Chicago	49
2001	Jim Thome, Cleveland	49
1933	Jimmie Foxx, Philadelphia	48
1962	Harmon Killebrew, Minnesota	48
1969	Frank Howard, Washington	48
1996	Albert Belle, Cleveland	48
1999	Ken Griffey Jr., Seattle	48
1926	Babe Ruth, New York	47
1927	Lou Gehrig, New York	47
1969	Reggie Jackson, Oakland	47
1987	George Bell, Toronto	47
1996	Juan Gonzalez, Texas	47
1999	Rafael Palmeiro, Texas	47
2000	Troy Glaus, Anaheim	47
2001	Rafael Palmeiro, Texas	47
1924	Babe Ruth, New York	46
1929	Babe Ruth, New York	46
1931	Lou Gehrig, New York	46
1931	Babe Ruth, New York	46
1937	Joe DiMaggio, New York	46
1961	Jim Gentile, Baltimore	46
1961	Harmon Killebrew, Minnesota	46
1978	Jim Rice, Boston	46
1993	Juan Gonzalez, Texas	46
1998	Jose Canseco, Toronto	46
1961	Rocky Colavito, Detroit	45
1963	Harmon Killebrew, Minnesota	45
1979	Gorman Thomas, Milwaukee	45
1993	Ken Griffey Jr., Seattle	45
1998	Juan Gonzalez, Texas	45
1998	Manny Ramirez, Cleveland	45
1934	Jimmie Foxx, Philadelphia	44
1946	Hank Greenberg, Detroit	44
1967	Harmon Killebrew, Minnesota	44
1967	Carl Yastrzemski, Boston	44
1968	Frank Howard, Washington	44
1970	Frank Howard, Washington	44
1991	Jose Canseco, Oakland	44
1991	Cecil Fielder, Detroit	44
1996	Jay Buhner, Seattle	44
1996	Mo Vaughn, Boston	44
1997	Tino Martinez, New York	44
1999	Carlos Delgado, Toronto	44
1999	Manny Ramirez, Cleveland	44
1949	Ted Williams, Boston	43
1953	Al Rosen, Cleveland	43
1984	Tony Armas, Boston	43
1992	Juan Gonzalez, Texas	43
1998	Rafael Palmeiro, Baltimore	43
2000	Jason Giambi, Oakland	43
2000	Frank Thomas, Chicago	43
1936	Hal Trosky, Cleveland	42
1953	Gus Zernial, Philadelphia	42
1957	Roy Sievers, Washington	42
1958	Mickey Mantle, New York	42
1959	Rocky Colavito, Cleveland	42
1959	Harmon Killebrew, Washington	42
1963	Dick Stuart, Boston	42
1988	Jose Canseco, Oakland	42
1992	Mark McGwire, Oakland	42
1997	Juan Gonzalez, Texas	42
1998	Alex Rodriguez, Seattle	42
1999	Shawn Green, Toronto	42
1999	Alex Rodriguez, Seattle	42
1923	Babe Ruth, New York	41
1930	Lou Gehrig, New York	41
1932	Babe Ruth, New York	41
1936	Jimmie Foxx, Boston	41
1940	Hank Greenberg, Detroit	41
1958	Rocky Colavito, Cleveland	41
1961	Norm Cash, Detroit	41
1970	Harmon Killebrew, Minnesota	41
1980	Reggie Jackson, New York	41
1980	Ben Oglivie, Milwaukee	41
1993	Frank Thomas, Chicago	41
2000	Tony Batista, Toronto	41
2000	Carlos Delgado, Toronto	41
2000	David Justice, Cleveland-New York	41
2000	Alex Rodriguez, Seattle	41
2001	Troy Glaus, Anaheim	41
2001	Manny Ramirez, Boston	41
1937	Hank Greenberg, Detroit	40
1960	Mickey Mantle, New York	40
1969	Rico Petrocelli, Boston	40
1969	Carl Yastrzemski, Boston	40
1970	Carl Yastrzemski, Boston	40
1985	Darrell Evans, Detroit	40
1986	Jesse Barfield, Toronto	40
1994	Ken Griffey Jr., Seattle	40
1995	Jay Buhner, Seattle	40
1995	Frank Thomas, Chicago	40
1996	Frank Thomas, Chicago	40
1997	Jay Buhner, Seattle	40
1997	Jim Thome, Cleveland	40
1998	Mo Vaughn, Boston	40

Total number of occurrences: 120

NATIONAL LEAGUE

Year	Player, Club	No.
2001	Barry Bonds, San Francisco	73
1998	Mark McGwire, St. Louis	70
1998	Sammy Sosa, Chicago	66
1999	Mark McGwire, St. Louis	65
2001	Sammy Sosa, Chicago	64
1999	Sammy Sosa, Chicago	63
2001	Luis Gonzalez, Arizona	57
1930	Hack Wilson, Chicago	56
1949	Ralph Kiner, Pittsburgh	54
1965	Willie Mays, San Francisco	52
1977	George Foster, Cincinnati	52
1947	Ralph Kiner, Pittsburgh	51
1947	Johnny Mize, New York	51
1955	Willie Mays, San Francisco	51
1998	Greg Vaughn, San Diego	50
2000	Sammy Sosa, Chicago	50
1954	Ted Kluszewski, Cincinnati	49
1962	Willie Mays, San Francisco	49
1987	Andre Dawson, Chicago	49
1997	Larry Walker, Colorado	49
2000	Barry Bonds, San Francisco	49
2001	Todd Helton, Colorado	49
2001	Shawn Green, Los Angeles	49
1971	Willie Stargell, Pittsburgh	48
1979	Dave Kingman, Chicago	48
1980	Mike Schmidt, Philadelphia	48
1950	Ralph Kiner, Pittsburgh	47
1953	Eddie Mathews, Milwaukee	47
1955	Ted Kluszewski, Cincinnati	47
1958	Ernie Banks, Chicago	47
1964	Willie Mays, San Francisco	47
1971	Hank Aaron, Atlanta	47
1989	Kevin Mitchell, San Francisco	47
1996	Andres Galarraga, Colorado	47
2000	Jeff Bagwell, Houston	47

Year	Player, Club	No.
1959	Eddie Mathews, Milwaukee	46
1961	Orlando Cepeda, San Francisco	46
1993	Barry Bonds, San Francisco	46
1998	Vinny Castilla, Colorado	46
1959	Ernie Banks, Chicago	45
1962	Hank Aaron, Milwaukee	45
1969	Willie McCovey, San Francisco	45
1970	Johnny Bench, Cincinnati	45
1979	Mike Schmidt, Philadelphia	45
1999	Chipper Jones, Atlanta	45
1999	Greg Vaughn, Cincinnati	45
2001	Richie Sexson, Milwaukee	45
1955	Ernie Banks, Chicago	44
1957	Hank Aaron, Milwaukee	44
1963	Hank Aaron, Milwaukee	44
1963	Willie McCovey, San Francisco	44
1966	Hank Aaron, Atlanta	44
1969	Hank Aaron, Atlanta	44
1973	Willie Stargell, Pittsburgh	44
1987	Dale Murphy, Atlanta	44
1998	Andres Galarraga, Atlanta	44
2000	Vladimir Guerrero, Montreal	44
2000	Richard Hidalgo, Houston	44
1929	Chuck Klein, Philadelphia	43
1940	Johnny Mize, St. Louis	43
1956	Duke Snider, Brooklyn	43
1957	Ernie Banks, Chicago	43
1973	Dave Johnson, Atlanta	43
1994	Matt Williams, San Francisco	43
1997	Jeff Bagwell, Houston	43
2000	Gary Sheffield, Los Angeles	43
1922	Rogers Hornsby, St. Louis	42
1929	Mel Ott, New York	42
1951	Ralph Kiner, Pittsburgh	42
1953	Duke Snider, Brooklyn	42
1954	Gil Hodges, Brooklyn	42
1955	Duke Snider, Brooklyn	42
1970	Billy Williams, Chicago	42
1996	Barry Bonds, San Francisco	42
1996	Gary Sheffield, Florida	42
1999	Jeff Bagwell, Houston	42
1999	Vladimir Guerrero, Montreal	42
2000	Jim Edmonds, St. Louis	42
2000	Todd Helton, Colorado	42
1923	Fred Williams, Philadelphia	41
1953	Roy Campanella, Brooklyn	41
1954	Hank Sauer, Chicago	41
1954	Willie Mays, New York	41
1955	Eddie Mathews, Milwaukee	41
1960	Ernie Banks, Chicago	41
1973	Darrell Evans, Atlanta	41
1977	Jeff Burroughs, Atlanta	41
1996	Todd Hundley, New York	41
1997	Andres Galarraga, Colorado	41
2001	Phil Nevin, San Diego	41
1930	Chuck Klein, Philadelphia	40
1948	Ralph Kiner, Pittsburgh	40
1948	Johnny Mize, New York	40
1951	Gil Hodges, Brooklyn	40
1953	Ted Kluszewski, Cincinnati	40
1954	Duke Snider, Brooklyn	40
1954	Eddie Mathews, Milwaukee	40
1955	Wally Post, Cincinnati	40
1957	Duke Snider, Brooklyn	40
1960	Hank Aaron, Milwaukee	40
1961	Willie Mays, San Francisco	40
1966	Dick Allen, Philadelphia	40
1970	Tony Perez, Cincinnati	40
1972	Johnny Bench, Cincinnati	40
1973	Hank Aaron, Atlanta	40
1978	George Foster, Cincinnati	40
1983	Mike Schmidt, Philadelphia	40
1990	Ryne Sandberg, Chicago	40
1993	David Justice, Atlanta	40
1995	Dante Bichette, Colorado	40
1996	Ellis Burks, Colorado	40
1996	Vinny Castilla, Colorado	40
1996	Ken Caminiti, San Diego	40

Year	Player, Club	No.
1996	Sammy Sosa, Chicago	40
1997	Barry Bonds, San Francisco	40
1997	Vinny Castilla, Colorado	40
1997	Mike Piazza, Los Angeles	40
1999	Mike Piazza, New York	40
2000	Ken Griffey Jr., Cincinnati	40

Total number of occurrences: 119

TWO LEAGUES IN SEASON

Year	Player, Club	No.
1997	Mark McGwire, Oakland A.L. (34), St. Louis, N.L. (24)	58
1996	Greg Vaughn, Milwaukee A.L. (31), San Diego N.L. (10)	41

Total number of occurrences: 2

PLAYERS WITH FOUR HOMERS IN GAME

NATIONAL LEAGUE

BOBBY LOWE, Boston, May 30, 1894, second game (H).
Ed Delahanty, Philadelphia, July 13, 1896 (A) (three consecutive).
Chuck Klein, Philadelphia, July 10, 1936, 10 innings (A) (three consecutive).
Gil Hodges, Brooklyn, August 31, 1950 (H).
Joe Adcock, Milwaukee, July 31, 1954 (A) (three consecutive).
Willie Mays, San Francisco, April 30, 1961 (A).
MIKE SCHMIDT, Philadelphia, April 17, 1976, 10 innings (A).
Bob Horner, Atlanta, July 6, 1986 (H).
Mark Whiten, St. Louis, September 7, 1993 (A) (three consecutive).
Note—Capitalized name denotes four consecutive homers (bases on balls excluded); parentheses denotes home or away games.
Total number of occurrences: 9

AMERICAN LEAGUE

LOU GEHRIG, New York, June 3, 1932 (A).
Pat Seerey, Chicago, July 18, 1948, first game, 11 innings (A) (three consecutive).
ROCKY COLAVITO, Cleveland, June 10, 1959 (A).
Note—Capitalized name denotes four consecutive homers (bases on balls excluded); parentheses denotes home or away games.
Total number of occurrences: 3

PLAYERS WITH THREE HOMERS IN GAME

AMERICAN ASSOCIATION

Guy Hecker, Louisville, August 15, 1886, second game (H).
Total number of occurrences: 1

AMERICAN LEAGUE

Kenny Williams, St. Louis, April 22, 1922 (H).
Joe Hauser, Philadelphia, August 2, 1924 (A).
Goose Goslin, Washington, June 19, 1925, 12 innings (A).
Ty Cobb, Detroit, May 5, 1925 (A).
Mickey Cochrane, Philadelphia, May 21, 1925 (A).
Tony Lazzeri, New York, June 8, 1927 (H).
Lou Gehrig, New York, June 23, 1927 (A).
Lou Gehrig, New York, May 4, 1929 (A).
Babe Ruth, New York, May 21, 1930, first game (A).
Lou Gehrig, New York, May 22, 1930, second game (A).
CARL REYNOLDS, Chicago, July 2, 1930, second game (A).
GOOSE GOSLIN, St. Louis, August 19, 1930 (A).
EARL AVERILL, Cleveland, September 17, 1930, first game (H).
Goose Goslin, St. Louis, June 23, 1932 (H).
Ben Chapman, New York, July 9, 1932, second game (H).
Jimmie Foxx, Philadelphia, July 10, 1932, 18 innings (A).
Al Simmons, Philadelphia, July 15, 1932 (H).
JIMMIE FOXX, Philadelphia, June 8, 1933 (H).
HAL TROSKY, Cleveland, May 30, 1934, second game (H).
ED COLEMAN, Philadelphia, August 17, 1934, first game (H).
FRANK HIGGINS, Philadelphia, June 27, 1935 (H).
MOOSE SOLTERS, St. Louis, July 7, 1935 (A).
Tony Lazzeri, New York, May 24, 1936 (A).
JOE DiMAGGIO, New York, June 13, 1937, second game, 11 innings (A).
Hal Trosky, Cleveland, July 5, 1937, first game (A).
MERV CONNORS, Chicago, September 17, 1938, second game (H).

KEN KELTNER, Cleveland, May 25, 1939 (A).
Jim Tabor, Boston, July 4, 1939, second game (A).
BILL DICKEY, New York, July 26, 1939 (H).
FRANK HIGGINS, Detroit, May 20, 1940 (H).
Charlie Keller, New York, July 28, 1940, first game (A).
Rudy York, Detroit, September 1, 1941, first game (H).
Pat Seerey, Cleveland, July 13, 1945 (A).
Ted Williams, Boston, July 14, 1946, first game (H).
Sam Chapman, Philadelphia, August 15, 1946 (H).
JOE DiMAGGIO, New York, May 23, 1948, first game (A).
Pat Mullin, Detroit, June 26, 1949, second game (A).
Bobby Doerr, Boston, June 8, 1950 (H).
LARRY DOBY, Cleveland, August 2, 1950 (H).
Joe DiMaggio, New York, September 10, 1950 (A).
JOHNNY MIZE, New York, September 15, 1950 (A).
Gus Zernial, Chicago, October 1, 1950, second game (H).
Bobby Avila, Cleveland, June 20, 1951 (A).
Clyde Vollmer, Boston, July 26, 1951 (H).
Al Rosen, Cleveland, April 29, 1952 (A).
BILL GLYNN, Cleveland, July 5, 1954, first game (A).
Al Kaline, Detroit, April 17, 1955 (H).
Mickey Mantle, New York, May 13, 1955 (H).
Norm Zauchin, Boston, May 27, 1955 (A).
JIM LEMON, Washington, August 31, 1956 (H).
Ted Williams, Boston, May 8, 1957 (A).
Ted Williams, Boston, June 13, 1957 (A).
Hector Lopez, Kansas City, June 26, 1958 (A).
PRESTON WARD, Kansas City, September 9, 1958 (H).
CHARLIE MAXWELL, Detroit, May 3, 1959, second game (H).
Bob Cerv, Kansas City, August 20, 1959 (H).
WILLIE KIRKLAND, Cleveland, July 9, 1961, second game (H).
Rocky Colavito, Detroit, August 27, 1961, second game (A).
Lee Thomas, Los Angeles, September 5, 1961, second game (A).
ROCKY COLAVITO, Detroit, July 5, 1962 (A).
Steve Boros, Detroit, August 6, 1962 (A).
DON LEPPERT, Washington, April 11, 1963 (H).
BOB ALLISON, Minnesota, May 17, 1963 (A).
BOOG POWELL, Baltimore, August 10, 1963 (A).
Harmon Killebrew, Minnesota, September 21, 1963, first game (A).
Jim King, Washington, June 8, 1964 (H).
Boog Powell, Baltimore, June 27, 1964 (A).
MANNY JIMENEZ, Kansas City, July 4, 1964 (A).
TOM TRESH, New York, June 6, 1965, second game (H).
Boog Powell, Baltimore, August 15, 1966 (A).
Tom McGraw, Chicago, May 24, 1967 (A).
Curt Blefary, Baltimore, June 6, 1967, first game (A).
KEN HARRELSON, Boston, June 14, 1968 (A).
Mike Epstein, Washington, May 16, 1969 (A).
Joe Lahoud, Boston, June 11, 1969 (A).
BILL MELTON, Chicago, June 24, 1969, second game (A).
Reggie Jackson, Oakland, July 2, 1969 (H).
Paul Blair, Baltimore, April 29, 1970 (A).
Tony Horton, Cleveland, May 24, 1970, second game (H).
Willie Horton, Detroit, June 9, 1970 (H).
BOBBY MURCER, New York, June 24, 1970, second game (H).
Bill Freehan, Detroit, August 9, 1971 (A).
GEORGE HENDRICK, Cleveland, June 19, 1973 (H).
Tony Oliva, Minnesota, July 3, 1973 (A).
Leroy Stanton, California, July 10, 1973, 10 innings (A).
Bobby Murcer, New York, July 13, 1973 (H).
BOBBY GRICH, Baltimore, June 18, 1974 (H).
Fred Lynn, Boston, June 18, 1975 (A).
John Mayberry, Kansas City, July 1, 1975 (A).
DON BAYLOR, Baltimore, July 2, 1975 (A).
TONY SOLAITA, Kansas City, September 7, 1975, 11 innings (A).
Carl Yastrzemski, Boston, May 19, 1976 (A).
Willie Horton, Texas, May 15, 1977 (A).
JOHN MAYBERRY, Kansas City, June 1, 1977 (A).
CLIFF JOHNSON, New York, June 30, 1977 (A).
Jim Rice, Boston, August 29, 1977 (A).
Al Oliver, Texas, May 23, 1979 (H).
Ben Oglivie, Milwaukee, July 8, 1979, first game (A).
Claudell Washington, Chicago, July 14, 1979 (H).
George Brett, Kansas City, July 22, 1979 (A).
Cecil Cooper, Milwaukee, July 27, 1979 (H).
EDDIE MURRAY, Baltimore, August 29, 1979, second game (A).
CARNEY LANSFORD, California, September 1, 1979 (A).
Otto Velez, Toronto, May 4, 1980, first game, 10 innings (H).
Fred Patek, California, June 20, 1980 (A).

AL OLIVER, Texas, August 17, 1980, second game (A).
Eddie Murray, Baltimore, September 14, 1980, 13 innings (A).
Jeff Burroughs, Seattle, August 14, 1981, second game (A).
Paul Molitor, Milwaukee, May 12, 1982 (A).
LARRY HERNDON, Detroit, May 18, 1982 (H).
BEN OGLIVIE, Milwaukee, June 20, 1982 (A).
HAROLD BAINES, Chicago, July 7, 1982 (H).
DOUG DeCINCES, California, August 3, 1982 (H).
Doug DeCinces, California, August 8, 1982 (A).
George Brett, Kansas City, April 20, 1983 (H).
Ben Oglivie, Milwaukee, May 14, 1983 (H).
Dan Ford, Baltimore, July 20, 1983 (H).
Jim Rice, Boston, August 29, 1983, second game (A).
DAVE KINGMAN, Oakland, April 16, 1984 (A).
Harold Baines, Chicago, September 17, 1984 (A).
GORMAN THOMAS, Seattle, April 11, 1985 (H).
LARRY PARRISH, Texas, April 29, 1985 (H).
Eddie Murray, Baltimore, August 26, 1985 (A).
Leon Lacy, Baltimore, June 8, 1986 (A).
JUAN BENIQUEZ, Baltimore, June 12, 1986 (H).
Joe Carter, Cleveland, August 29, 1986 (A).
Jim Presley, Seattle, September 1, 1986 (H).
Reggie Jackson, California, September 18, 1986 (H).
Cory Snyder, Cleveland, May 21, 1987 (H).
Joe Carter, Cleveland, May 28, 1987 (A).
Mark McGwire, Oakland, June 27, 1987 (A).
Bill Madlock, Detroit, June 28, 1987, 11 innings (A).
BROOK JACOBY, Cleveland, July 3, 1987 (H).
Dale Sveum, Milwaukee, July 17, 1987 (H).
Mike Brantley, Seattle, September 14, 1987 (H).
Ernie Whitt, Toronto, September 14, 1987 (H).
Wally Joyner, California, October 3, 1987 (H).
George Bell, Toronto, April 4, 1988 (A).
Jose Canseco, Oakland, July 3, 1988 (A).
JOE CARTER, Cleveland, June 24, 1989 (A).
Joe Carter, Cleveland, July 19, 1989 (A).
CECIL FIELDER, Detroit, May 6, 1990 (A).
CECIL FIELDER, Detroit, June 6, 1990 (A).
RANDY MILLIGAN, Baltimore, June 9, 1990 (H).
BO JACKSON, Kansas City, July 17, 1990 (A).
TOM BRUNANSKY, Boston, September 29, 1990 (H).
DAVE WINFIELD, California, April 13, 1991 (A).
Harold Baines, Oakland, May 7, 1991 (H).
Danny Tartabull, Kansas City, July 6, 1991 (H).
Jack Clark, Boston, July 31, 1991 (A).
DAVE HENDERSON, Oakland, August 3, 1991 (H).
Juan Gonzalez, Texas, June 7, 1992 (H).
Albert Belle, Cleveland, September 6, 1992 (H).
Carlos Baerga, Cleveland, June 17, 1993 (A).
Joe Carter, Toronto, August 23, 1993 (H).
Juan Gonzalez, Texas, August 28, 1993 (A).
Tim Raines Sr., Chicago, April 18, 1994 (A).
Jose Canseco, Texas, June 13, 1994 (H).
Darnell Coles, Toronto, July 5, 1994 (A).
JIM THOME, Cleveland, July 22, 1994 (H).
John Valentin, Boston, June 2, 1995 (H).
MARK McGWIRE, Oakland, June 11, 1995 (A).
MIKE STANLEY, New York, August 10, 1995, first game (H).
PAUL O'NEILL, New York, August 31, 1995 (H).
ALBERT BELLE, Cleveland, September 19, 1995 (A).
Dan Wilson, Seattle, April 11, 1996 (A).
CECIL FIELDER, Detroit, April 16, 1996 (A).
Ernie Young, Oakland, May 10, 1996 (H).
Geronimo Berroa, Oakland, May 22, 1996 (A).
KEN GRIFFEY JR., Seattle, May 24, 1996 (H).
Cal Ripken Jr., Baltimore, May 28, 1996 (A).
EDGAR MARTINEZ, Seattle, July 6, 1996 (A).
DARRYL STRAWBERRY, New York, August 6, 1996 (H).
Geronimo Berroa, Oakland, August 12, 1996 (A).
FRANK THOMAS, Chicago, September 15, 1996 (A).
MO VAUGHN, Boston, September 24, 1996 (H).
TINO MARTINEZ, New York, April 2, 1997 (A).
Matt Williams, Cleveland, April 25, 1997 (H).
Ken Griffey Jr., Seattle, April 25, 1997 (A).
ROBERTO ALOMAR, Baltimore, April 26, 1997 (H).
MO VAUGHN, Boston, May 30, 1997 (H).
BOB HIGGINSON, Detroit, June 30, 1997 (H).
IVAN RODRIGUEZ, Texas, September 11, 1997 (H).
Lee Stevens, Texas, April 13, 1998 (H).

CARLOS DELGADO, Toronto, August 4, 1998 (A).
MANNY RAMIREZ, Cleveland, September 15, 1998 (H).
Nomar Garciaparra, Boston, May 10, 1999 (H).
EDGAR MARTINEZ, Seattle, May 18, 1999 (H).
Miguel Tejada, Oakland, June 11, 1999 (H).
Trot Nixon, Boston, July 24, 1999 (A).
Albert Belle, Baltimore, July 25, 1999 (H).
Carlos Delgado, Toronto, August 6, 1999 (A).
Manny Ramirez, Cleveland, August 25, 1999 (A).
JUAN GONZALEZ, Texas, September 24, 1999 (H).
Alex Rodriguez, Seattle, April 16, 2000 (A).
BOBBY HIGGINSON, Detroit, June 24, 2000 (A).
Darrin Fletcher, Toronto, August 27, 2000 (A).
CARLOS DELGADO, Toronto, April 4, 2001 (A).
Carlos Delgado, Toronto, April 20, 2001 (A).
Jason Varitek, Boston, May 20, 2001 (A).
Ellis Burks, Cleveland, June 19, 2001 (H).
Miguel Tejada, Oakland, June 30, 2001 (A).
Jim Thome, Cleveland, July 6, 2001 (H).
Note—Capitalized name denotes three consecutive homers (bases on balls excluded); parentheses denotes home or away games.
Total number of occurrences: 203

NATIONAL LEAGUE

Ned Williamson, Chicago, May 30, 1884, second game (H).
CAP ANSON, Chicago, August 6, 1884 (H).
JACK MANNING, Philadelphia, October 9, 1884 (A).
Dennis Brouthers, Detroit, September 10, 1886 (A).
Roger Connor, New York, May 9, 1888 (A).
Frank Shugart, St. Louis, May 10, 1894 (A).
BILL JOYCE, Washington, August 20, 1894 (H).
Tom McCreery, Louisville, July 12, 1897 (A).
Jake Beckley, Cincinnati, September 26, 1897, first game (A).
Butch Henline, Philadelphia, September 15, 1922 (H).
Fred Williams, Philadelphia, May 11, 1923 (H).
GEORGE KELLY, New York, September 17, 1923 (A).
George Kelly, New York, June 14, 1924 (H).
Jack Fournier, Brooklyn, July 13, 1926 (A).
Les Bell, Boston, June 2, 1928 (H).
GEORGE HARPER, St. Louis, September 20, 1928, first game (A).
Hack Wilson, Chicago, July 26, 1930 (A).
MEL OTT, New York, August 31, 1930, second game (H).
ROGERS HORNSBY, Chicago, April 24, 1931 (A).
GEORGE WATKINS, St. Louis, June 24, 1931, second game (A).
Bill Terry, New York, August 13, 1932, first game (H).
Babe Herman, Chicago, July 20, 1933 (H).
Hal Lee, Boston, July 6, 1934 (H).
Babe Ruth, Boston, May 25, 1935 (A).
JOHNNY MOORE, Philadelphia, July 22, 1936 (H).
Alex Kampouris, Cincinnati, May 9, 1937 (A).
JOHNNY MIZE, St. Louis, July 13, 1938 (H).
Johnny Mize, St. Louis, July 20, 1938, second game (H).
HANK LEIBER, Chicago, July 4, 1939, first game (H).
Johnny Mize, St. Louis, May 13, 1940, 14 innings (A).
JOHNNY MIZE, St. Louis, September 8, 1940, first game (H).
JIM TOBIN, Boston, May 13, 1942 (H).
CLYDE McCULLOUGH, Chicago, July 26, 1942, first game (A).
BILL NICHOLSON, Chicago, July 23, 1944, first game (A).
JOHNNY MIZE, New York, April 24, 1947 (A).
WILLARD MARSHALL, New York, July 18, 1947 (H).
RALPH KINER, Pittsburgh, August 16, 1947 (H).
RALPH KINER, Pittsburgh, September 11, 1947, second game (H).
Ralph Kiner, Pittsburgh, July 5, 1948, first game (H).
GENE HERMANSKI, Brooklyn, August 5, 1948 (H).
Andy Seminick, Philadelphia, June 2, 1949 (H).
Walker Cooper, Cincinnati, July 6, 1949 (H).
BOB ELLIOTT, Boston, September 24, 1949 (A).
DUKE SNIDER, Brooklyn, May 30, 1950, second game (H).
Wes Westrum, New York, June 24, 1950 (H).
ANDY PAFKO, Chicago, August 2, 1950, second game (A).
ROY CAMPANELLA, Brooklyn, August 26, 1950 (A).
HANK SAUER, Chicago, August 28, 1950, first game (H).
TOMMY BROWN, Brooklyn, September 18, 1950 (H).
Ralph Kiner, Pittsburgh, July 18, 1951 (A).
DEL WILBER, Philadelphia, August 27, 1951, second game (H).
Don Mueller, New York, September 1, 1951 (H).
Hank Sauer, Chicago, June 11, 1952 (H).
EDDIE MATHEWS, Boston, September 27, 1952 (A).
DUSTY RHODES, New York, August 26, 1953 (H).

Jim Pendleton, Milwaukee, August 30, 1953, first game (A).
Stan Musial, St. Louis, May 2, 1954, first game (H).
HANK THOMPSON, New York, June 3, 1954 (A).
DUSTY RHODES, New York, July 28, 1954 (H).
Duke Snider, Brooklyn, June 1, 1955 (H).
GUS BELL, Cincinnati, July 21, 1955 (A).
Del Ennis, Philadelphia, July 23, 1955 (H).
Smoky Burgess, Cincinnati, July 29, 1955 (H).
Ernie Banks, Chicago, August 4, 1955 (H).
GUS BELL, Cincinnati, May 29, 1956 (A).
Ed Bailey, Cincinnati, June 24, 1956, first game (A).
Ted Kluszewski, Cincinnati, July 1, 1956, first game, 10 innings (A).
BOB THURMAN, Cincinnati, August 18, 1956 (H).
ERNIE BANKS, Chicago, September 14, 1957, second game (H).
Lee Walls, Chicago, April 24, 1958 (A).
Roman Mejias, Pittsburgh, May 4, 1958, first game (A).
Walt Moryn, Chicago, May 30, 1958, second game (H).
FRANK THOMAS, Pittsburgh, August 16, 1958 (A).
Don Demeter, Los Angeles, April 21, 1959, 11 innings (H).
Hank Aaron, Milwaukee, June 21, 1959 (A).
FRANK ROBINSON, Cincinnati, August 22, 1959 (H).
DICK STUART, Pittsburgh, June 30, 1960, second game (H).
Willie Mays, San Francisco, June 29, 1961, 10 innings (A).
BILL WHITE, St. Louis, July 5, 1961 (A).
Don Demeter, Philadelphia, September 12, 1961 (A).
ERNIE BANKS, Chicago, May 29, 1962 (H).
STAN MUSIAL, St. Louis, July 8, 1962 (A).
Willie Mays, San Francisco, June 2, 1963 (A).
Ernie Banks, Chicago, June 9, 1963 (H).
WILLIE McCOVEY, San Francisco, September 22, 1963, (H).
WILLIE McCOVEY, San Francisco, April 22, 1964 (A).
JOHNNY CALLISON, Philadelphia, September 27, 1964 (H).
Johnny Callison, Philadelphia, June 6, 1965, second game (A).
Willie Stargell, Pittsburgh, June 24, 1965 (A).
JIM HICKMAN, New York, September 3, 1965 (A).
Gene Oliver, Atlanta, July 30, 1966, second game (H).
ART SHAMSKY, Cincinnati, August 12, 1966, 13 innings (A).
Willie McCovey, San Francisco, September 17, 1966, 10 innings (H).
Roberto Clemente, Pittsburgh, May 15, 1967, 10 innings (A).
ADOLFO PHILLIPS, Chicago, June 11, 1967, second game (H).
JIM WYNN, Houston, June 15, 1967 (H).
Willie Stargell, Pittsburgh, May 22, 1968 (A).
Billy Williams, Chicago, September 10, 1968 (H).
DICK ALLEN, Philadelphia, September 29, 1968 (A).
BOB TILLMAN, Atlanta, July 30, 1969, first game (A).
ROBERTO CLEMENTE, Pittsburgh, August 13, 1969 (A).
Rico Carty, Atlanta, May 31, 1970 (H).
Mike Lum, Atlanta, July 3, 1970, first game (H).
JOHNNY BENCH, Cincinnati, July 26, 1970 (H).
ORLANDO CEPEDA, Atlanta, July 26, 1970, first game (A).
Willie Stargell, Pittsburgh, April 10, 1971, 12 innings (A).
WILLIE STARGELL, Pittsburgh, April 21, 1971 (H).
DERON JOHNSON, Philadelphia, July 11, 1971 (A).
RICK MONDAY, Chicago, May 16, 1972 (A).
Nate Colbert, San Diego, August 1, 1972, second game (A).
Johnny Bench, Cincinnati, May 9, 1973 (A).
Lee May, Houston, June 21, 1973 (A).
George Mitterwald, Chicago, April 17, 1974 (H).
Jim Wynn, Los Angeles, May 11, 1974 (A).
Dave Lopes, Los Angeles, August 20, 1974 (A).
Reggie Smith, St. Louis, May 22, 1976 (A).
Dave Kingman, New York, June 4, 1976 (A).
Bill Robinson, Pittsburgh, June 5, 1976, 15 innings (H).
Gary Matthews, San Francisco, September 25, 1976 (H).
GARY CARTER, Montreal, April 20, 1977 (H).
LARRY PARRISH, Montreal, May 29, 1977 (A).
GEORGE FOSTER, Cincinnati, July 14, 1977 (H).
Pete Rose, Cincinnati, April 29, 1978 (A).
Dave Kingman, Chicago, May 14, 1978 (A).
LARRY PARRISH, Montreal, July 30, 1978 (A).
Dave Kingman, Chicago, May 17, 1979 (H).
Dale Murphy, Atlanta, May 18, 1979 (H).
MIKE SCHMIDT, Philadelphia, July 7, 1979 (H).
DAVE KINGMAN, Chicago, July 28, 1979 (A).
Larry Parrish, Montreal, April 25, 1980 (A).
Johnny Bench, Cincinnati, May 29, 1980 (A).
Claudell Washington, New York, June 22, 1980 (A).
Darrell Evans, San Francisco, June 15, 1983 (H).

DARRYL STRAWBERRY, New York, August 5, 1985 (A).
GARY CARTER, New York, September 3, 1985 (A).
Andre Dawson, Montreal, September 24, 1985 (A).
Ken Griffey Sr., Atlanta, July 22, 1986, 11 innings (H).
Eric Davis, Cincinnati, September 10, 1986 (A).
ERIC DAVIS, Cincinnati, May 3, 1987 (A).
Tim Wallach, Montreal, May 4, 1987 (A).
MIKE SCHMIDT, Philadelphia, June 14, 1987 (A).
Andre Dawson, Chicago, August 1, 1987 (H).
GLENN DAVIS, Houston, September 30, 1987 (A).
Darnell Coles, Pittsburgh, September 30, 1987, second game (H).
Von Hayes, Philadelphia, August 29, 1989 (A).
KEVIN MITCHELL, San Francisco, May 25, 1990 (A).
Jeff Treadway, Atlanta, May 26, 1990 (A).
GLENN DAVIS, Houston, June 1, 1990 (A).
BARRY LARKIN, Cincinnati, June 28, 1991 (H).
Jeff Blauser, Atlanta, July 12, 1992, 10 innings (A).
KARL RHODES, Chicago, April 4, 1994 (H).
Cory Snyder, Los Angeles, April 17, 1994 (A).
JEFF BAGWELL, Houston, June 24, 1994 (H).
Barry Bonds, San Francisco, August 2, 1994 (H).
ANDRES GALARRAGA, Colorado, June 25, 1995 (A).
REGGIE SANDERS, Cincinnati, August 15, 1995 (H).
SAMMY SOSA, Chicago, June 5, 1996 (H).
Mike Piazza, Los Angeles, June 29, 1996 (A).
BENITO SANTIAGO, Philadelphia, September 15, 1996 (A).
Willie Greene, Cincinnati, September 24, 1996 (H).
LARRY WALKER, Colorado, April 5, 1997 (A).
Steve Finley, San Diego, May 19, 1997 (A).
Steve Finley, San Diego, June 23, 1997 (A).
Bobby Estalella, Philadelphia, September 4, 1997 (A).
JOSE VALENTIN, Milwaukee, April 3, 1998 (A).
MARK McGWIRE, St. Louis, April 14, 1998 (H).
Mark McGwire, St. Louis, May 19, 1998 (A).
Sammy Sosa, Chicago, June 15, 1998 (H).
Brant Brown, Chicago, June 18, 1998 (H).
Ken Caminiti, San Diego, July 12, 1998 (A).
BRET BOONE, Cincinnati, September 20, 1998 (A).
Mike Lansing, Colorado, September 22, 1998 (H).
Jeff Bagwell, Houston, April 21, 1999 (A).
Larry Walker, Colorado, April 28, 1999 (A).
Jeffrey Hammonds, Cincinnati, May 19, 1999 (A).
Vinny Castilla, Colorado, June 5, 1999 (H).
JEFF BAGWELL, Houston, June 9, 1999 (A).
Edgardo Alfonzo, New York, August 30, 1999 (A).
GREG VAUGHN, Cincinnati, September 7, 1999, second game (A).
STEVE FINLEY, Arizona, September 8, 1999 (A).
Kevin Elster, Los Angeles, April 11, 2000 (A).
Todd Helton, Colorado, May 1, 2000 (H).
Mark McGwire, St. Louis, May 18, 2000 (A).
BRET BOONE, San Diego, June 23, 2000 (A).
Jeff Cirillo, Colorado, June 28, 2000 (A).
TYLER HOUSTON, Milwaukee, July 9, 2000 (H).
ARAMIS RAMIREZ, Pittsburgh, April 8, 2001 (A).
TODD HOLLANDSWORTH, Colorado, April 15, 2001 (H).
GEOFF JENKINS, Milwaukee, April 28, 2001 (H).
Jeromy Burnitz, Milwaukee, May 10, 2001 (H).
Barry Bonds, San Francisco, May 19, 2001 (A).
Luis Gonzalez, Arizona, June 8, 2001 (A).
Vinny Castilla, Houston, July 28, 2001, first game (A).
SAMMY SOSA, Chicago, August 9, 2001 (H).
Shawn Green, Los Angeles, August 15, 2001 (H).
JOSE ORTIZ, Colorado, August 17, 2001 (H).
Sammy Sosa, Chicago, August 22, 2001 (H).
Barry Bonds, San Francisco, September 9, 2001 (A).
SAMMY SOSA, Chicago, September 23, 2001 (A).
RICHIE SEXSON, Milwaukee, September 25, 2001 (A).
JEROMY BURNITZ, Milwaukee, September 25, 2001 (A).
Phil Nevin, San Diego, October 6, 2001 (H).
Note—Capitalized name denotes three consecutive homers (bases on balls excluded); parentheses denotes home or away games.
Total number of occurrences: 202

SWITCH-HIT HOME RUNS IN GAME

(Players hitting home runs
from both sides of plate in game)

A.L.—Wally Schang, Philadelphia, September 8, 1916.
    Johnny Lucadello, St. Louis, September 16, 1940.

Mickey Mantle, New York, May 13, 1955 (1 righthanded, 2 lefthanded).
Mickey Mantle, New York, August 15, 1955, second game.
Mickey Mantle, New York, May 18, 1956.
Mickey Mantle, New York, July 1, 1956, second game.
Mickey Mantle, New York, June 12, 1957.
Mickey Mantle, New York, July 28, 1958.
Mickey Mantle, New York, September 15, 1959.
Mickey Mantle, New York, April 26, 1961.
Mickey Mantle, New York, May 6, 1962, second game.
Tom Tresh, New York, September 1, 1963.
Tom Tresh, New York, July 13, 1964.
Mickey Mantle, New York, August 12, 1964.
Tom Tresh, New York, June 6, 1965, second game (1 righthanded, 2 lefthanded).
Reggie Smith, Boston, August 20, 1967, first game.
Reggie Smith, Boston, August 11, 1968, second game.
Don Buford, Baltimore, April 9, 1970.
Roy White, New York, May 7, 1970.
Reggie Smith, Boston, July 2, 1972, first game.
Reggie Smith, Boston, April 16, 1973.
Roy White, New York, August 13, 1973.
Roy White, New York, April 23, 1975.
Ken Henderson, Chicago, August 29, 1975.
Roy White, New York, August 18, 1976.
Eddie Murray, Baltimore, August 3, 1977.
Roy White, New York, June 13, 1978.
Larry Milbourne, Seattle, July 15, 1978.
Willie Wilson, Kansas City, June 15, 1979.
Eddie Murray, Baltimore, August 29, 1979, second game (2 righthanded, 1 lefthanded).
U.L. Washington, Kansas City, September 21, 1979.
Eddie Murray, Baltimore, August 16, 1981.
Eddie Murray, Baltimore, April 24, 1982.
Ted Simmons, Milwaukee, May 2, 1982.
Eddie Murray, Baltimore, August 26, 1982.
Roy Smalley, New York, September 5, 1982.
Donnie Scott, Seattle, April 29, 1985.
Mike Young, Baltimore, August 13, 1985.
Eddie Murray, Baltimore, August 26, 1985 (1 righthanded, 2 lefthanded).
Nelson Simmons, Detroit, September 16, 1985.
Roy Smalley, Minnesota, May 30, 1986.
Tony Bernazard, Cleveland, July 1, 1986.
Ruben Sierra, Texas, September 13, 1986.
Eddie Murray, Baltimore, May 8, 1987.
Eddie Murray, Baltimore, May 9, 1987.
Devon White, California, June 23, 1987.
Dale Sveum, Milwaukee, July 17, 1987 (1 righthanded, 2 lefthanded).
Dale Sveum, Milwaukee, June 12, 1988.
Mickey Tettleton, Baltimore, June 13, 1988.
Chili Davis, California, July 30, 1988.
Ruben Sierra, Texas, August 27, 1988.
Ruben Sierra, Texas, June 8, 1989.
Chili Davis, California, July 1, 1989.
Devon White, California, June 29, 1990.
Roberto Alomar, Toronto, May 10, 1991.
Devon White, Toronto, June 1, 1991.
Chili Davis, Minnesota, October 2, 1992.
Carlos Baerga, Cleveland, April 8, 1993.
Mickey Tettleton, Detroit, May 7, 1993, 12 innings.
Tim Raines Sr., Chicago, August 31, 1993.
Chad Kreuter, Detroit, September 7, 1993.
Eddie Murray, Cleveland, April 21, 1994.
Chili Davis, California, May 11, 1994.
Bernie Williams, New York, June 6, 1994.
Ruben Sierra, Oakland, June 7, 1994.
Chili Davis, California, July 30, 1994.
Mickey Tettleton, Texas, April 28, 1995.
Roberto Alomar, Toronto, May 3, 1995, 10 innings.
Luis Alicea, Boston, July 28, 1995.
Raul Casanova, Detroit, June 6, 1996.
J.T. Snow, California, June 9, 1996, 13 innings.
Ruben Sierra, New York, June 22, 1996.
Melvin Nieves, Detroit, July 15, 1996.
Roberto Alomar, Baltimore, July 25, 1996.
Roberto Alomar, Baltimore, August 14, 1996.
Melvin Nieves, Detroit, August 20, 1996.
Chili Davis, California, August 21, 1996.

Bernie Williams, New York, September 12, 1996.
Tony Clark, Detroit, April 5, 1997.
Chili Davis, Kansas City, June 7, 1997.
Jose Cruz Jr., Toronto, August 24, 1997, 13 innings.
David Segui, Seattle, April 1, 1998.
Tony Clark, Detroit, June 17, 1998.
Tony Clark, Detroit, July 26, 1998.
Tony Clark, Detroit, August 1, 1998.
Jorge Posada, New York, August 23, 1998.
Bernie Williams, New York, September 4, 1998.
Brian Simmons, Chicago, September 26, 1998.
Bernie Williams, New York, May 4, 1999.
Jorge Posada, New York, July 10, 1999.
Tony Clark, Detroit, July 18, 1999.
Tony Clark, Detroit, July 25, 1999.
Carl Everett, Boston, April 11, 2000.
Bernie Williams, New York, April 23, 2000.
Jorge Posada, New York, April 23, 2000.
Bernie Williams, New York, May 17, 2000.
Carlos Beltran, Kansas City, June 29, 2000.
Carl Everett, Boston, August 29, 2000.
Jose Valentin, Chicago, September 30, 2000.
Ruben Sierra, Texas, June 13, 2001.
Bernie Williams, New York, June 30, 2001.
Roberto Alomar, Cleveland, July 16, 2001.
Total number of occurrences: 102

N.L.—Augie Galan, Chicago, June 25, 1937.
Jim Russell, Boston, June 7, 1948.
Jim Russell, Brooklyn, July 26, 1950.
Red Schoendienst, St. Louis, July 8, 1951, second game.
Maury Wills, Los Angeles, May 30, 1962, first game.
Ellis Burton, Chicago, August 1, 1963.
Ellis Burton, Chicago, September 7, 1964, first game.
Jim Lefebvre, Los Angeles, May 7, 1966.
Wes Parker, Los Angeles, June 5, 1966, first game.
Pete Rose, Cincinnati, August 30, 1966.
Pete Rose, Cincinnati, August 2, 1967.
Ted Simmons, St. Louis, April 17, 1975.
Reggie Smith, St. Louis, May 4, 1975.
Reggie Smith, St. Louis, May 22, 1976 (2 righthanded, 1 lefthanded).
Lee Mazzilli, New York, September 3, 1978.
Ted Simmons, St. Louis, June 11, 1979.
Alan Ashby, Houston, September 27, 1982.
Chili Davis, San Francisco, June 5, 1983.
Mark Bailey, Houston, September 16, 1984.
Chili Davis, San Francisco, June 27, 1987.
Bobby Bonilla, Pittsburgh, July 3, 1987.
Kevin Bass, Houston, August 3, 1987, 13 innings.
Kevin Bass, Houston, September 2, 1987.
Chili Davis, San Francisco, September 15, 1987.
Bobby Bonilla, Pittsburgh, April 6, 1988, 14 innings.
Tim Raines Sr., Montreal, July 16, 1988.
Steve Jeltz, Philadelphia, June 8, 1989.
Kevin Bass, Houston, August 20, 1989.
Eddie Murray, Los Angeles, April 18, 1990.
Eddie Murray, Los Angeles, June 9, 1990.
Bret Barberie, Montreal, August 2, 1991.
Howard Johnson, New York, August 31, 1991.
Kevin Bass, San Francisco, August 2, 1992, second game.
Bobby Bonilla, New York, April 23, 1993.
Bobby Bonilla, New York, June 10, 1993.
Todd Benzinger, San Francisco, August 30, 1993.
Mark Whiten, St. Louis, September 14, 1993.
Geronimo Pena, St. Louis, April 17, 1994.
Bobby Bonilla, New York, May 4, 1994.
Todd Hundley, New York, June 18, 1994.
Ken Caminiti, Houston, July 3, 1994.
Bobby Bonilla, New York, May 12, 1995.
Ken Caminiti, San Diego, September 16, 1995.
Ken Caminiti, San Diego, September 17, 1995.
Ken Caminiti, San Diego, September 19, 1995.
Todd Hundley, New York, May 18, 1996.
Todd Hundley, New York, June 10, 1996.
Ken Caminiti, San Diego, August 1, 1996.
Ken Caminiti, San Diego, August 21, 1996.
Ken Caminiti, San Diego, August 28, 1996, 12 innings.
Ken Caminiti, San Diego, September 11, 1996.

Carl Everett, New York, April 20, 1997, first game.
Todd Hundley, New York, May 5, 1997.
F.P. Santangelo, Montreal, June 7, 1997.
Todd Hundley, New York, July 20, 1997.
Carl Everett, Houston, April 24, 1998.
Ken Caminiti, San Diego, July 12, 1998.
Chipper Jones, Atlanta, May 1, 1999.
Jose Valentin, Milwaukee, July 1, 1999.
Chipper Jones, Atlanta, August 1, 1999.
Carl Everett, Houston, August 7, 1999.
Dale Sveum, Pittsburgh, August 18, 1999.
Ken Caminiti, Houston, August 20, 1999.
Chipper Jones, Atlanta, September 21, 1999.
Chipper Jones, Atlanta, May 14, 2000.
Jose Vidro, Montreal, July 3, 2000.
Chipper Jones, Atlanta, July 5, 2000.
Geoff Blum, Montreal, July 5, 2001.
Tomas Perez, Philadelphia, July 24, 2001.
Total number of occurrences: 69

40 STOLEN BASES AND 40 HOMERS IN SEASON

AMERICAN LEAGUE

Player, Club	Year	G	SB	HR
Jose Canseco, Oakland	1988	158	40	42
Alex Rodriguez, Seattle	1998	161	46	42

Total number of occurrences: 2

NATIONAL LEAGUE

Player, Club	Year	G	SB	HR
Barry Bonds, San Francisco	1996	158	40	42

Total number of occurrences: 1

30 STOLEN BASES AND 30 HOMERS IN SEASON

AMERICAN LEAGUE

Player, Club	Year	G	SB	HR
Kenny Williams, St. Louis	1922	153	37	39
Tommy Harper, Milwaukee	1970	154	38	31
Bobby Bonds, New York	1975	145	30	32
Bobby Bonds, California	1977	158	41	37
Bobby Bonds, Chicago/Texas	1978	156	43	31
Joe Carter, Cleveland	1987	149	31	32
Jose Canseco, Oakland	1988	158	40	42
Alex Rodriguez, Seattle	1998	161	46	42
Shawn Green, Toronto	1998	158	35	35
Jose Cruz Jr., Toronto	2001	146	32	34

Total number of occurrences: 10

NATIONAL LEAGUE

Player, Club	Year	G	SB	HR
Willie Mays, New York	1956	152	40	36
Willie Mays, New York	1957	152	38	35
Hank Aaron, Milwaukee	1963	161	31	44
Bobby Bonds, San Francisco	1969	158	45	32
Bobby Bonds, San Francisco	1973	160	43	39
Dale Murphy, Atlanta	1983	162	30	36
Eric Davis, Cincinnati	1987	129	50	37
Howard Johnson, New York	1987	157	32	36
Darryl Strawberry, New York	1987	154	36	39
Howard Johnson, New York	1989	153	41	36
Ron Gant, Atlanta	1990	152	33	32
Barry Bonds, Pittsburgh	1990	151	52	33
Ron Gant, Atlanta	1991	154	34	32
Howard Johnson, New York	1991	156	30	38
Barry Bonds, Pittsburgh	1992	140	39	34
Sammy Sosa, Chicago	1993	159	36	33
Sammy Sosa, Chicago	1995	144	34	36
Barry Bonds, San Francisco	1995	144	31	33
Dante Bichette, Colorado	1996	159	31	31
Barry Bonds, San Francisco	1996	158	40	42
Ellis Burks, Colorado	1996	156	32	40
Barry Larkin, Cincinnati	1996	152	36	33
Larry Walker, Colorado	1997	153	33	49
Jeff Bagwell, Houston	1997	162	31	43
Barry Bonds, San Francisco	1997	159	37	40
Raul Mondesi, Los Angeles	1997	159	32	30

Player, Club	Year	G	SB	HR
Jeff Bagwell, Houston	1999	162	30	42
Raul Mondesi, Los Angeles	1999	159	36	33
Preston Wilson, Florida	2000	161	36	31
Vladimir Guerrero, Montreal	2001	159	37	34
Bobby Abreu, Philadelphia	2001	162	36	31

Total number of occurrences: 31

20 STOLEN BASES AND 50 HOMERS IN SEASON

AMERICAN LEAGUE

Player, Club	Year	G	SB	HR
Brady Anderson, Baltimore	1996	149	21	50
Ken Griffey Jr., Seattle	1998	161	20	56

Total number of occurrences: 2

NATIONAL LEAGUE

Player, Club	Year	G	SB	HR
Willie Mays, New York	1955	152	24	51

Total number of occurrences: 1

50 STOLEN BASES AND 20 HOMERS IN SEASON

AMERICAN LEAGUE

Player, Club	Year	G	SB	HR
Rickey Henderson, New York	1985	143	80	24
Rickey Henderson, New York	1986	153	87	28
Rickey Henderson, Oakland	1990	136	65	28
Brady Anderson, Baltimore	1992	159	53	21
Rickey Henderson, Oak.-Tor.	1993	134	53	21

Total number of occurrences: 5

NATIONAL LEAGUE

Player, Club	Year	G	SB	HR
Lou Brock, St. Louis	1967	159	52	21
Cesar Cedeno, Houston	1972	139	55	22
Cesar Cedeno, Houston	1973	139	56	25
Joe Morgan, Cincinnati	1973	157	67	26
Cesar Cedeno, Houston	1974	160	57	26
Joe Morgan, Cincinnati	1974	149	58	22
Joe Morgan, Cincinnati	1976	141	60	27
Ryne Sandberg, Chicago	1985	153	54	26
Eric Davis, Cincinnati	1986	132	80	27
Eric Davis, Cincinnati	1987	129	50	37
Barry Bonds, Pittsburgh	1990	151	52	33
Craig Biggio, Houston	1998	160	50	20

Total number of occurrences: 12

400 TOTAL BASES IN SEASON

AMERICAN LEAGUE

Year	Player, Club	No.
1921	Babe Ruth, New York	457
1927	Lou Gehrig, New York	447
1932	Jimmie Foxx, Philadelphia	438
1930	Lou Gehrig, New York	419
1937	Joe DiMaggio, New York	418
1927	Babe Ruth, New York	417
1931	Lou Gehrig, New York	410
1934	Lou Gehrig, New York	409
1978	Jim Rice, Boston	406
1936	Hal Trosky, Cleveland	405
1936	Lou Gehrig, New York	403
1933	Jimmie Foxx, Philadelphia	403

Total number of occurrences: 12

NATIONAL LEAGUE

Year	Player, Club	No.
1922	Rogers Hornsby, St. Louis	450
1930	Chuck Klein, Philadelphia	445
1948	Stan Musial, St. Louis	429
2001	Sammy Sosa, Chicago	425
1930	Hack Wilson, Chicago	423
1932	Chuck Klein, Philadelphia	420
2001	Luis Gonzalez, Arizona	419
1930	Babe Herman, Brooklyn	416
1998	Sammy Sosa, Chicago	416

Year	Player, Club	No.
2001	Barry Bonds, San Francisco	411
1929	Rogers Hornsby, Chicago	409
1997	Larry Walker, Colorado	409
1937	Joe Medwick, St. Louis	406
1929	Chuck Klein, Philadelphia	405
2000	Todd Helton, Colorado	405
2001	Todd Helton, Colorado	402
1959	Hank Aaron, Milwaukee	400

Total number of occurrences: 17

100 LONG HITS IN SEASON

AMERICAN LEAGUE

Year	Player, Club	2B	3B	HR	EBH
1921	Babe Ruth, New York	44	16	59	119
1927	Lou Gehrig, New York	52	18	47	117
1937	Hank Greenberg, Detroit	49	14	40	103
1995	Albert Belle, Cleveland	52	1	50	103
1930	Lou Gehrig, New York	42	17	41	100
1932	Jimmie Foxx, Philadelphia	33	9	58	100

Total number of occurrences: 6

NATIONAL LEAGUE

Year	Player, Club	2B	3B	HR	EBH
1930	Chuck Klein, Philadelphia	59	8	40	107
2001	Barry Bonds, San Francisco	32	2	73	107
2001	Todd Helton, Colorado	54	2	49	105
1932	Chuck Klein, Philadelphia	50	15	38	103
1948	Stan Musial, St. Louis	46	18	39	103
2000	Todd Helton, Colorado	59	2	42	103
2001	Sammy Sosa, Chicago	34	5	64	103
1922	Rogers Hornsby, St. Louis	46	14	42	102
2001	Luis Gonzalez, Arizona	36	7	57	100

Total number of occurrences: 9

PLAYERS HITTING FOR CYCLE

(Single, double, triple and home run in game)

AMERICAN ASSOCIATION

Al Knight, Philadelphia, July 30, 1883.
John Reilly, Cincinnati, September 12, 1883.
John Reilly, Cincinnati, September 19, 1883.
Dave Orr, New York, June 12, 1885.
Henry Larkin, Philadelphia, June 16 ,1885.
Pete Browning, Louisville, August 8, 1886.
Jim McGarr, Philadelphia, September 23, 1886.
Tip O'Neill, St. Louis, April 30, 1887.
Tip O'Neill, St. Louis, May 7 ,1887.
Dave Orr, New York, August 10, 1887.
Bid McPhee, Cincinnati, August 26, 1887.
Harry Stovey, Philadelphia, May 15, 1888.
Sam Barkley, Kansas City, June 13, 1888.
Pete Browning, Louisville, June 7, 1889.
Bill Van Dyke, Toledo, July 5, 1890.
Jim Davis, Brooklyn, July 18, 1890.
Bill Weaver, Louisville, August 12, 1890.
Abner Dalrymple, Milwaukee, September 12, 1891.
Total number of occurrences: 18

PLAYERS LEAGUE

Roger Conner, New York, July 21, 1890.
Total number of occurrences: 1

AMERICAN LEAGUE

Harry Davis, Philadelphia, July 10, 1901.
Nap Lajoie, Philadelphia, July 30, 1901.
Patsy Dougherty, Boston, July 29, 1903.
Bill Bradley, Cleveland, September 24, 1903.
Otis Clymer, Washington, October 2, 1908.
Danny Murphy, Philadelphia, August 25, 1910.
Home Run Baker, Philadelphia, July 3, 1911, second game.
Tris Speaker, Boston, June 9, 1912.
Bert Daniels, New York, July 25, 1912.
George Sisler, St. Louis, August 8, 1920, second game.
Bobby Veach, Detroit, September 17, 1920, 12 innings.
Bob Meusel, New York, May 7, 1921.

George Sisler, St. Louis, August 13, 1921, 10 innings.
Ray Schalk, Chicago, June 27, 1922.
Bob Meusel, New York, July 3, 1922.
Bill Jacobson, St. Louis, April 17, 1924.
Goose Goslin, Washington, August 28, 1924.
Roy Carlyle, Boston, July 21, 1925, first game.
Bob Fothergill, Detroit, September 26, 1926, first game.
Bob Meusel, New York, July 26, 1928, first game, 12 innings.
Oscar Melillo, St. Louis, May 23, 1929, second game.
Joe Cronin, Washington, September 2, 1929, first game.
Tony Lazzeri, New York, June 3, 1932.
Mickey Cochrane, Philadelphia, July 22, 1932.
Mickey Cochrane, Philadelphia, August 2, 1933.
Pinky Higgins, Philadelphia, August 6, 1933.
Jimmie Foxx, Philadelphia, August 14, 1933.
Earl Averill, Cleveland, August 17, 1933.
Doc Cramer, Philadelphia, June 10, 1934.
Lou Gehrig, New York, June 25, 1934.
Moose Solters, Boston, August 19, 1934, first game.
Gee Walker, Detroit, April 20, 1937.
Joe DiMaggio, New York, July 9, 1937.
Lou Gehrig, New York, August 1, 1937.
Odell Hale, Cleveland, July 12, 1938.
Sam Chapman, Philadelphia, May 5, 1939.
Charlie Gehringer, Detroit, May 27, 1939.
Buddy Rosar, New York, July 19, 1940.
Joe Cronin, Boston, August 2, 1940.
Joe Gordon, New York, September 8, 1940.
George McQuinn, St. Louis, July 19, 1941, first game.
Leon Culberson, Boston, July 3, 1943.
Bobby Doerr, Boston, May 17, 1944, second game.
Bob Johnson, Boston, July 6, 1944.
Mickey Vernon, Washington, May 19, 1946, second game.
Ted Williams, Boston, July 21, 1946, second game.
Bobby Doerr, Boston, May 13, 1947.
Vic Wertz , Detroit, September 14, 1947, first game.
Joe DiMaggio, New York, May 20, 1948.
George Kell, Detroit, June 2, 1950, second game.
Elmer Valo, Philadelphia, August 2, 1950.
Hoot Evers, Detroit, September 7, 1950, 10 innings.
Larry Doby, Cleveland, June 4, 1952.
Mickey Mantle, New York, July 23. 1957.
Brooks Robinson, Baltimore, July 15, 1960.
Lu Clinton, Boston, July 13, 1962, 15 innings.
Jim King, Washington, May 26, 1964.
Jim Fregosi, Los Angeles, July 28, 1964.
Carl Yastrzemski, Boston, May 14, 1965, 10 innings.
Jim Fregosi, California, May 20, 1968, 11 innings.
Rod Carew, Minnesota, May 20, 1970.
Tony Horton, Cleveland, July 2, 1970.
Fred Patek, Kansas City, July 9, 1971.
Bobby Murcer, New York, August 29, 1972, first game, 11 innings.
Cesar Tovar, Minnesota, September 19, 1972.
Larry Hisle, Minnesota, June 4, 1976, 10 innings.
Lyman Bostock, Minnesota, July 24, 1976.
Mike Hegan, Milwaukee, September 3, 1976.
John Mayberry, Kansas City, August 5, 1977.
Jack Brohamer, Chicago, September 24, 1977.
Andre Thornton, Cleveland, April 22, 1978.
Mike Cubbage, Minnesota, July 27, 1978.
George Brett, Kansas City, May 28, 1979, 16 innings.
Dan Ford, California, August 10, 1979, 14 innings.
Bob Watson, Boston, September 15, 1979.
Frank White, Kansas City, September 26, 1979.
Fred Lynn, Boston, May 13, 1980.
Gary Ward, Minnesota, September 18, 1980, first game.
Charlie Moore, Milwaukee, October 1, 1980.
Frank White, Kansas City, August 3, 1982.
Cal Ripken, Baltimore, May 6, 1984.
Carlton Fisk, Chicago, May 16, 1984.
Dwight Evans, Boston, June 28, 1984, 11 innings.
Oddibe McDowell, Texas, July 23, 1985.
Rich Gedman, Boston, September 18, 1985.
Tony Phillips, Oakland, May 16, 1986.
Kirby Puckett, Minnesota, August 1, 1986.
Robin Yount, Milwaukee, June 12, 1988.
Mike Greenwell, Boston, September 14, 1988.
Kelly Gruber, Toronto, April 16, 1989.

George Brett, Kansas City, July 25, 1990.
Paul Molitor, Milwaukee, May 15, 1991.
Dave Winfield, California, June 24, 1991.
Jay Buhner, Seattle, June 23, 1993, 14 innings.
Travis Fryman, Detroit, July 28, 1993.
Scott Cooper, Boston, April 12, 1994.
Tony Fernandez, New York, September 3, 1995, 10 innings.
John Valentin, Boston, June 6, 1996.
Alex Rodriguez, Seattle, June 5, 1997.
Mike Blowers, Oakland, May 18, 1998.
Chris Singleton, Chicago, July 6, 1999, 10 innings.
Jose Valentin, Chicago, April 27, 2000.
Eric Chavez, Oakland, June 21, 2000.
Damion Easley, Detroit, June 8, 2001.
John Olerud, Seattle, June 16, 2001.
Jeff Frye, Toronto, August 17, 2001.
Miguel Tejada, Oakland, September 29, 2001.
Total number of occurrences: 107

NATIONAL LEAGUE

Charles Foley, Buffalo, May 25, 1882.
Jim O'Rourke, Buffalo, June 16, 1884.
George Wood, Detroit, June 13, 1885.
Bill McQuery, Detroit, September 28, 1885.
Fred Dunlap, St. Louis, May 24, 1886.
John Rowe, Detroit, August 21, 1886.
Fred Carroll, Pittsburgh, May 2, 1887.
Jimmy Ryan, Chicago, July 28, 1888.
Mike Tiernan, New York, August 25, 1888.
John Glasscock, Indianapolis, August 8, 1889.
Larry Twitchell, Cleveland, August 15, 1889.
Tom Burns, Brooklyn, August 1, 1890, second game.
John Reilly, Cincinnati, August 6, 1890.
Jimmy Ryan, Chicago, July 1, 1891.
Lave Cross, Philadelphia, April 24, 1894.
Bill Hassamaer, Washington, June 13, 1894.
Sam Thompson, Philadelphia, August 17, 1894.
Tom Parrett, Cincinnati, September 28, 1894.
Tom Dowd, St. Louis, August 16,1895.
Ed Cartwright, Washington, September 30, 1895, first game.
Herman Long, Boston, May 9, 1896.
Bill Joyce, Washington, May 30, 1896, first game.
Fred Clarke, Pittsburgh, July 23, 1901.
Fred Clarke, Pittsburgh, May 7, 1903.
Rich Cooley, Boston, June 20, 1904, second game.
Sam Mertes, New York, October 4, 1904, first game.
John Bates, Boston, April 26, 1907.
Chief Wilson, Pittsburgh, July 3, 1910.
Bill Collins, Boston, October 6, 1910.
Mike Mitchell, Cincinnati, August 19, 1911, second game.
Chief Meyers, New York, June 10, 1912.
Honus Wagner, Pittsburgh, August 22, 1912, second game.
Heinie Groh, Cincinnati, July 5, 1915, second game.
Cliff Heathcote, St. Louis, June 13, 1918, 19 innings.
George Burns, New York, September 17, 1920, 10 innings.
Dave Bancroft, New York, June 1, 1921, second game.
Dave Robertson, Pittsburgh, August 30, 1921.
Ross Youngs, New York, April 29, 1922.
Jimmy Johnston, Brooklyn, May 25, 1922, first game.
Pie Traynor, Pittsburgh, July 7, 1923.
Kiki Cuyler, Pittsburgh, June 4, 1925.
Max Carey, Pittsburgh, June 20, 1925.
Jim Bottomley, St. Louis, July 15, 1927.
Cy Williams, Philadelphia, August 5, 1927.
Bill Terry, New York, May 29, 1928.
Mel Ott, New York, May 16, 1929, second game.
Fred Lindstrom, New York, May 8, 1930.
Hack Wilson, Chicago, June 23, 1930.
Chick Hafey, St. Louis, August 21, 1930.
Babe Herman, Brooklyn, May 18, 1931.
Chuck Klein, Philadelphia, July 1, 1931.
Babe Herman, Brooklyn, July 24, 1931.
Pepper Martin, St. Louis, May 5, 1933.
Chuck Klein, Philadelphia, May 26, 1933, 14 innings.
Arky Vaughan, Pittsburgh, June 24, 1933.
Babe Herman, Chicago, September 30, 1933.
Joe Medwick, St. Louis, June 29, 1935.
Sam Leslie, New York, May 24, 1936.
Arky Vaughan, Pittsburgh, July 19, 1939.

Harry Craft, Cincinnati, June 8, 1940.
Harry Danning, New York, June 15, 1940.
Johnny Mize, St. Louis, July 13, 1940, first game.
Dixie Walker, Brooklyn, September 2, 1944.
Bob Elliott, Pittsburgh, July 15, 1945, second game.
Bill Salkeld, Pittsburgh, August 4, 1945.
Wally Westlake, Pittsburgh, July 30, 1948.
Jackie Robinson, Brooklyn, August 29, 1948, first game.
Wally Westlake, Pittsburgh, June 14, 1949.
Gil Hodges, Brooklyn, June 25, 1949.
Stan Musial, St. Louis, July 24, 1949.
Ralph Kiner, Pittsburgh, June 25, 1950.
Roy Smalley, Chicago, June 28, 1950.
Gus Bell, Pittsburgh, June 4, 1951.
Don Mueller, New York, July 11, 1954, first game.
Lee Walls, Chicago, July 2, 1957, 10 innings.
Frank Robinson, Cincinnati, May 2, 1959.
Bill White, St. Louis, August 14, 1960, first game.
Ken Boyer, St. Louis, September 14, 1961, second game, 11 innings.
Johnny Callison, Philadelphia, June 27, 1963.
Jim Hickman, New York, August 7, 1963.
Ken Boyer, St. Louis, June 16, 1964.
Willie Stargell, Pittsburgh, July 22, 1964.
Billy Williams, Chicago, July 17, 1966, second game.
Randy Hundley, Chicago, August 11, 1966, first game, 11 innings.
Wes Parker, Los Angeles, May 7, 1970, 10 innings.
Tommie Agee, New York, July 6, 1970.
Jim Hart, San Francisco, July 8, 1970.
Dave Kingman, San Francisco, April 16, 1972.
Cesar Cedeno, Houston, August 2, 1972.
Joe Torre, St. Louis, June 27, 1973.
Richie Zisk, Pittsburgh, June 9, 1974.
Lou Brock, St. Louis, May 27, 1975.
Tim Foli, Montreal, April 21, 1976, suspended game completed April 22.

Mike Phillips, New York, June 25, 1976.
Cesar Cedeno, Houston, August 9, 1976.
Bob Watson, Houston, June 24, 1977, 11 innings.
Chris Speier, Montreal, July 20, 1978.
Ivan DeJesus, Chicago, April 22, 1980.
Mike Easler, Pittsburgh, June 12, 1980.
Willie McGee, St. Louis, June 23, 1984, 11 innings.
Jeff Leonard, San Francisco, June 27, 1985.
Keith Hernandez, New York, July 4, 1985, 19 innings.
Andre Dawson, Chicago, April 29, 1987.
Candy Maldonado, San Francisco, May 4, 1987.
Tim Raines Sr., Montreal, August 16, 1987.
Albert Hall, Atlanta, September 23, 1987.
Chris Speier, San Francisco, July 9, 1988.
Eric Davis, Cincinnati, June 2, 1989.
Kevin McReynolds, New York, August 1, 1989.
Gary Redus, Pittsburgh, August 25, 1989.
Robby Thompson, San Francisco, April 22, 1991.
Ray Lankford, St. Louis, September 15, 1991.
Andujar Cedeno, Houston, August 25, 1992.
Mark Grace, Chicago, May 9, 1993.
Rondell White, Montreal, June 11, 1995, 13 innings.
Gregg Jefferies, Philadelphia, August 25, 1995.
John Mabry, St. Louis, May 18, 1996.
Alex Ochoa, New York, July 3, 1996.
John Olerud, New York, September 11, 1997.
Dante Bichette, Colorado, June 10, 1998.
Neifi Perez, Colorado, July 25, 1998.
Jeff Kent, San Francisco, May 3, 1999.
Todd Helton, Colorado, June 19, 1999.
Jason Kendall, Pittsburgh, May 19, 2000.
Mike Lansing, Colorado, June 18, 2000.
Luis Gonzalez, Arizona, July 5, 2000.
Jeff Bagwell, Houston, July 18, 2001.
Total number of occurrences: 127

SIX HITS IN ONE GAME
AMERICAN ASSOCIATION

Player	Club, Date	Place	AB	R	H	2B	3B	HR
Hick Carpenter	Cincinnati, September 12, 1883	H	7	5	6	0	0	0
John Reilly	Cincinnati, September 12, 1883	H	7	6	6	1	1	1
Oscar Walker	Brooklyn, May 31, 1884	H	6	2	6	1	1	0
Lon Knight	Philadelphia, July 30, 1884	H	6	5	6	0	1	0
Dave Orr	New York, June 12, 1885	H	6	4	6	2	1	1
Henry Larkin	Philadelphia, June 16, 1885	H	6	4	6	2	1	1
George Pinckney	Brooklyn, June 25, 1885	H	6	5	6	0	0	0
Arlie Latham	St. Louis, April 24, 1886	H	6	5	6	0	1	0
Guy Hecker	Louisville, August 15, 1886†	H	7	7	6	0	0	3
Denny Lyons	Philadelphia, April 26, 1887	H	6	4	6	2	1	0
Pete Hotaling	Cleveland, June 6, 1888	H	7	5	6	0	1	0
Jim McTamany	Kansas City, June 15, 1888	H	6	3	6	0	0	1
Darby O'Brien	Brooklyn, August 8, 1889	A	6	1	6	3	0	0
Farmer Weaver	Louisville, August 12, 1890	H	6	3	6	1	2	1
Frank Sheibeck	Toledo, September 27, 1890	H	6	4	6	1	1	0
Reddy Mack	Louisville, May 26, 1887	H	6	5	6	0	0	0

†Pitcher.
Total number of occurrences: 16

PLAYERS LEAGUE

Player	Club, Date	Place	AB	R	H	2B	3B	HR
Ed Delahanty	Cleveland, June 2, 1890	H	6	4	6	1	1	0
Bill Shindle	Philadelphia, August 26, 1890	H	6	3	6	2	1	0

Total number of occurrences: 2

AMERICAN LEAGUE

Player	Club, Date	Place	AB	R	H	2B	3B	HR
Mike Donlin	Baltimore, June 24, 1901	H	6	5	6	2	2	0
Doc Nance	Detroit, July 13, 1901	H	6	3	6	1	0	0
Erwin Harvey	Cleveland, April 25, 1902	A	6	3	6	0	0	0
Danny Murphy	Philadelphia, July 8, 1902	A	6	3	6	0	0	1
Jimmy Williams	Baltimore, August 25, 1902	H	6	1	6	1	1	0
Bobby Veach	Detroit, September 17, 1920, 12 innings	H	6	2	6	1	1	1
George Sisler	St. Louis, August 9, 1921, 19 innings	A	9	2	6	0	1	0
Frank Brower	Cleveland, August 7, 1923	A	6	3	6	1	0	0
George Burns	Cleveland, June 19, 1924, first game	A	6	2	6	3	1	0

Player	Club, Date	Place	AB	R	H	2B	3B	HR
Ty Cobb	Detroit, May 5, 1925	A	6	4	6	1	0	3
Jimmie Foxx	Philadelphia, May 30, 1930, first game, 13 innings	H	7	0	6	2	1	0
Roger Cramer	Philadelphia, June 20, 1932	A	6	3	6	0	0	0
Jimmie Foxx	Philadelphia, July 10, 1932, 18 innings	A	9	4	6	1	0	3
Johnny Burnett	Cleveland, July 10, 1932, 18 innings	H	11	4	9	2	0	0
Sam West	St. Louis, April 13, 1933, 11 innings	H	6	2	6	1	0	0
Myril Hoag	New York, June 6, 1934, first game	A	6	3	6	0	0	0
Bob Johnson	Philadelphia, June 16, 1934, second game, 11 innings	H	6	3	6	1	0	2
Roger Cramer	Philadelphia, July 13, 1935, first game	H	6	3	6	1	0	0
Bruce Campbell	Cleveland, July 2, 1936, first game	A	6	1	6	1	0	0
Ray Radcliff	Chicago, July 18, 1936, second game	A	7	4	6	2	0	0
Henry Steinbacher	Chicago, June 22, 1938	H	6	3	6	1	0	0
George Myatt	Washington, May 1, 1944	A	6	3	6	1	0	0
Stan Spence	Washington, June 1, 1944	A	6	2	6	0	0	1
George Kell	Detroit, September 20, 1946	A	7	4	6	1	0	0
Jim Fridley	Cleveland, April 29, 1952	A	6	4	6	0	0	0
Jimmy Piersall	Boston, July 10, 1953, first game	A	6	2	6	1	0	0
Joe DeMaestri	Kansas City, July 8, 1955, 11 innings	A	6	2	6	0	0	0
Jim Runnels	Boston, August 30, 1960, first game, 15 innings	H	7	1	6	1	0	0
Rocky Colavito	Detroit, June 24, 1962, 22 innings	H	10	1	7	0	1	0
Floyd Robinson	Chicago, July 22, 1962	H	6	1	6	0	0	0
Bob Oliver	Kansas City, May 4, 1969	A	6	2	6	1	0	1
Jim Northrup	Detroit, August 28, 1969, 13 innings	H	6	2	6	0	0	2
Cesar Gutierrez	Detroit, June 21, 1970, second game, 12 innings	A	7	3	7	1	0	0
John Briggs	Milwaukee, August 4, 1973	A	6	2	6	2	0	0
Jorge Orta	Cleveland, June 15, 1980	H	6	4	6	1	0	0
Jerry Remy	Boston, September 3, 1981, 20 innings	H	10	2	6	0	0	0
Kevin Seitzer	Kansas City, August 2, 1987	A	6	4	6	1	0	2
Kirby Puckett	Minnesota, August 30, 1987	A	6	4	6	2	0	2
Kirby Puckett	Minnesota, May 23, 1991, 11 innings	H	7	2	6	0	1	0
Carlos Baerga	Cleveland, April 11, 1992, 19 innings	A	9	1	6	0	0	0
Kevin Reimer	Milwaukee, August 24, 1993, second game	H	6	4	6	2	0	0
Lance Johnson	Chicago, September 23, 1995	A	6	4	6	0	3	0
Gerald Williams	New York, May 1, 1996, 15 innings	A	8	1	6	0	0	1
Garret Anderson	California, September 27, 1996, 15 innings	H	7	0	6	0	0	0
Cal Ripken Jr.	Baltimore, June 13, 1999	A	6	5	6	1	0	0
Damion Easley	Detroit, August 8, 2001	A	6	3	6	0	0	1

Total number of occurrences: 46

NATIONAL LEAGUE

Player	Club, Date	Place	AB	R	H	2B	3B	HR
David Force	Philadelphia, June 27, 1876	H	6	3	6	1	0	0
Cal McVey	Chicago, July 22, 1876	H	7	4	6	1	0	0
Cal McVey	Chicago, July 25, 1876	H	7	4	6	1	0	0
Ross Barnes	Chicago, July 27, 1876	H	6	3	6	1	1	0
Paul Hines	Providence, August 26, 1879, 10 innings	H	6	1	6	0	0	0
George Gore	Chicago, May 7, 1880	H	6	5	6	0	0	0
Lew Dickerson	Worcester, June 16, 1881	H	6	3	6	0	1	0
Sam Wise	Boston, June 20, 1883	H	7	5	6	1	1	0
Dennis Brouthers	Buffalo, July 19, 1883	H	6	3	6	2	0	0
Danny Richardson	New York, June 11, 1887	H	7	2	6	0	0	0
King Kelly	Boston, August 27, 1887	H	7	6	6	1	0	1
Jerry Denny	Indianapolis, May 4, 1889	H	6	3	6	1	0	1
Larry Twitchell	Cleveland, August 15, 1889	H	6	5	6	1	3	1
John Glasscock	New York, September 27, 1890	A	6	2	6	0	0	0
Bobby Lowe	Boston, June 11, 1891	H	6	4	6	1	0	1
Henry Larkin	Washington, June 7, 1892	H	7	3	6	0	1	0
Wilbert Robinson	Baltimore, June 10, 1892, first game	H	7	1	7	1	0	0
John Boyle	Philadelphia, July 6, 1893, 11 innings	A	6	1	6	1	0	0
Duff Cooley	St. Louis, September 30, 1893, second game	A	6	1	6	1	1	0
Ed Delahanty	Philadelphia, June 16, 1894	H	6	4	6	1	0	0
Steve Brodie	Baltimore, July 9, 1894	H	6	2	6	2	1	0
Chief Zimmer	Cleveland, July 11, 1894, 10 innings	H	6	3	6	2	0	0
Sam Thompson	Philadelphia, August 17, 1894	H	7	4	6	1	1	1
Roger Connor	St. Louis, June 1, 1895	A	6	4	6	2	1	0
George Davis	New York, August 15, 1895	A	6	3	6	2	0	0
Jacob Stenzel	Pittsburgh, May 14, 1896	H	6	3	6	0	0	0
Fred Tenney	Boston, May 31, 1897	H	8	3	6	1	0	0
Dick Harley	St. Louis, June 24, 1897, 12 innings	A	6	2	6	1	0	0
Barry McCormick	Chicago, June 29, 1897	H	8	5	6	0	1	1
Tommy Tucker	Washington, July 15, 1897	A	6	1	6	1	0	0
Willie Keeler	Baltimore, September 3, 1897	H	6	5	6	0	1	0
Jack Doyle	Baltimore, September 3, 1897	H	6	2	6	2	0	0
Chick Stahl	Boston, May 31, 1899	H	6	4	6	0	0	0
Ginger Beaumont	Pittsburgh, July 22, 1899	H	6	6	6	0	0	0
Kip Selbach	New York, June 9, 1901	A	7	4	6	2	0	0
George Cutshaw	Brooklyn, August 9, 1915	A	6	2	6	0	0	0
Carson Bigbee	Pittsburgh, August 22, 1917, 22 innings	A	11	0	6	0	0	0

Player	Club, Date	Place	AB	R	H	2B	3B	HR
Dave Bancroft	New York, June 28, 1920................A		6	2	6	0	0	0
Johnny Gooch	Pittsburgh, July 7, 1922, 18 innings ....H		8	1	6	1	0	0
Max Carey	Pittsburgh, July 7, 1922, 18 innings ....H		6	3	6	1	0	0
Jack Fournier	Brooklyn, June 29, 1923................A		6	1	6	2	0	1
Kiki Cuyler	Pittsburgh, August 9, 1924, first game........A		6	3	6	3	1	0
Frankie Frisch	New York, September 10, 1924, first game........H		7	3	6	0	0	1
Jim Bottomley	St. Louis, September 16, 1924 ....A		6	3	6	1	0	2
Paul Waner	Pittsburgh, August 26, 1926 ....H		6	1	6	2	1	0
Lloyd Waner	Pittsburgh, June 15, 1929, 14 innings ....H		8	2	6	1	1	0
Hank DeBerry	Brooklyn, June 23, 1929, 14 innings ....H		7	0	6	0	0	0
Wally Gilbert	Brooklyn, May 30, 1931, second game ....A		7	3	6	1	0	0
Jim Bottomley	St. Louis, August 5, 1931, second game ....A		6	2	6	1	0	0
Tony Cuccinello	Cincinnati, August 13, 1931, first game........A		6	4	6	2	1	0
Terry Moore	St. Louis, September 5, 1935................H		6	2	6	1	0	0
Ernie Lombardi	Cincinnati, May 9, 1937................A		6	3	6	1	0	0
Frank Demaree	Chicago, July 5, 1937, first game, 14 innings ....H		7	2	6	3	0	0
Cookie Lavagetto	Brooklyn, September 23, 1939, first game........H		6	4	6	1	1	0
Walker Cooper	Cincinnati, July 6, 1949................A		7	5	6	0	0	3
Johnny Hopp	Pittsburgh, May 14, 1950, second game ....A		6	3	6	0	0	2
Connie Ryan	Philadelphia, April 16, 1953................A		6	3	6	2	0	0
Dick Groat	Pittsburgh, May 13, 1960................A		6	2	6	3	0	0
Jesus Alou	San Francisco, July 10, 1964................A		6	1	6	0	0	1
Joe Morgan	Houston, July 8, 1965, 12 innings ....A		6	4	6	0	1	2
Felix Millan	Atlanta, July 6, 1970................H		6	2	6	1	1	0
Don Kessinger	Chicago, July 17, 1971, 10 innings ....H		6	3	6	1	0	0
Willie Davis	Los Angeles, May 24, 1973, 19 innings ....H		9	1	6	0	0	0
Bill Madlock	Chicago, July 26, 1975, 10 innings ....A		6	1	6	0	1	0
Rennie Stennett	Pittsburgh, September 16, 1975................A		7	5	7	2	1	0
Jose Cardenal	Chicago, May 2, 1976, first game, 14 innings ....A		7	2	6	1	0	1
Gene Richards	San Diego, July 26, 1977, second game, 15 innings ....H		7	1	6	1	0	0
Joe Lefebvre	San Diego, September 13, 1982, 16 innings ....A		8	1	6	1	0	1
Wally Backman	Pittsburgh, April 27, 1990 ....A		6	1	6	1	0	0
Sammy Sosa	Chicago, July 2, 1993 ....H		6	2	6	1	0	0
Tony Gwynn	San Diego, August 4, 1993, 12 innings ....H		7	2	6	2	0	0
Rondell White	Montreal, June 11, 1995, 13 innings ....A		7	5	6	2	1	1
Mike Benjamin	San Francisco, June 14, 1995, 13 innings ....A		7	0	6	1	0	0
Andres Galarraga	Colorado, July 3, 1995................H		6	4	6	1	0	2
Edgardo Alfonzo	New York, August 30, 1999................A		6	6	6	1	0	3
Paul LoDuca	Los Angeles, May 28, 2001, 11 innings ....H		6	3	6	0	0	1

Total number of occurrences: 76

BARRY BONDS' 73 HOME RUNS—2001

HR No.	Team game No.	Date		Opposing pitcher, Club	Place	Inning	On base
1.	1	April	2	Woody Williams (righthander), San Diego ....H		5	0
2.	9	April	12	Adam Eaton (righthander), San Diego ....A		4	0
3.	10	April	13	Jamey Wright (righthander), Milwaukee ....A		1	1
4.	11	April	14	Jimmy Haynes (righthander), Milwaukee ....A		5	2
5.	12	April	15	Dave Weathers (righthander), Milwaukee ....A		8	0
6.	13	April	17	Terry Adams (righthander), Los Angeles ....H		8	1
7.	14	April	18	Chan Ho Park (righthander), Los Angeles ....H		7	0
8.	16	April	20	Jimmy Haynes (righthander), Milwaukee ....H		4	1
9.	19	April	24	Jim Brower (righthander), Cincinnati........H		3	1
10.	21	April	26	Scott Sullivan (righthander), Cincinnati ....H		8	1
11.	24	April	29	Manny Aybar (righthander), Chicago N.L........H		4	0
12.	26	May	2	Todd Ritchie (righthander), Pittsburgh ....A		5	1
13.	27	May	3	Jimmy Anderson (righthander), Pittsburgh........A		1	1
14.	28	May	4	Bruce Chen (lefthander), Philadelphia ....H		6	1
15.	35	May	11	Steve Trachsel (righthander), New York N.L. ....H		4	0
16.	40	May	17	Chuck Smith (righthander), Florida........A		3	1
17.	41	May	18	Mike Remlinger (lefthander), Atlanta ....A		8	0
18.	42	May	19	Odalis Perez (lefthander), Atlanta ....A		3	0
19.	42	May	19	Jose Cabrera (righthander), Atlanta ....A		7	0
20.	42	May	19	Jason Marquis (righthander), Atlanta ....A		8	0
21.	43	May	20	John Burkett (righthander), Atlanta ....A		1	0
22.	43	May	20	Mike Remlinger (lefthander), Atlanta ....A		7	0
23.	44	May	21	Curt Schilling (righthander), Arizona ....A		4	0
24.	45	May	22	Russ Springer (righthander), Arizona ....A		9	1
25.	47	May	24	John Thomson (righthander), Colorado ....A		3	0
26.	50	May	27	Denny Neagle (lefthander), Colorado ....H		1	1
27.	53	May	30	Robert Ellis (righthander), Arizona ....H		2	0
28.	53	May	30	Robert Ellis (righthander), Arizona ....H		6	1
29.	54	June	1	Shawn Chacon (righthander), Colorado........A		3	1
30.	57	June	4	Bobby J. Jones (righthander), San Diego ....H		4	0
31.	58	June	5	Wascar Serrano (righthander), San Diego ....H		3	1
32.	60	June	7	Brian Lawrence (righthander), San Diego ....H		7	1
33.	64	June	12	Pat Rapp (righthander), Anaheim ....H		1	0

HR No.	Team game No.	Date		Opposing pitcher, Club	Place	Inning	On base
34.	66	June	14	Lou Pote (righthander), Anaheim	H	6	0
35.	67	June	15	Mark Mulder (lefthander), Oakland	H	1	0
36.	67	June	15	Mark Mulder (lefthander), Oakland	H	6	0
37.	70	June	19	Adam Eaton (righthander), San Diego	A	5	0
38.	71	June	20	Rodney Myers (righthander), San Diego	A	8	1
39.	74	June	23	Darryl Kile (righthander), St. Louis	A	1	1
40.	89	July	12	Paul Abbott (righthander), Seattle	A	1	0
41.	95	July	18	Mike Hampton (lefthander), Colorado	H	4	0
42.	95	July	18	Mike Hampton (lefthander), Colorado	H	5	1
43.	103	July	26	Curt Schilling (righthander), Arizona	A	4	0
44.	103	July	26	Curt Schilling (righthander), Arizona	A	5	3
45.	104	July	27	Brian Anderson (lefthander), Arizona	A	4	0
46.	108	Aug.	1	Joe Beimel (lefthander), Pittsburgh	H	1	0
47.	111	Aug.	4	Nelson Figueroa (righthander), Philadelphia	H	6	1
48.	113	Aug.	7	Danny Graves (righthander), Cincinnati	A	11	0
49.	115	Aug.	9	Scott Winchester (righthander), Cincinnati	A	3	0
50.	117	Aug.	11	Joe Borowski (righthander), Chicago N.L.	A	2	2
51.	119	Aug.	14	Ricky Bones (righthander), Florida	H	6	3
52.	121	Aug.	16	A.J. Burnett (righthander), Florida	H	4	0
53.	121	Aug.	16	Vic Darensbourg (lefthander), Florida	H	8	2
54.	123	Aug.	18	Jason Marquis (righthander), Atlanta	H	8	0
55.	127	Aug.	23	Graeme Lloyd (lefthander), Montreal	H	9	0
56.	131	Aug.	27	Kevin Appier (righthander), New York N.L.	A	5	0
57.	135	Aug.	31	John Thomson (righthander), Colorado	H	8	1
58.	138	Sept.	3	Jason Jennings (righthander), Colorado	H	4	0
59.	139	Sept.	4	Miguel Batista (righthander), Arizona	H	7	0
60.	141	Sept.	6	Albie Lopez (righthander), Arizona	H	2	0
61.	144	Sept.	9	Scott Elarton (righthander), Colorado	A	1	0
62.	144	Sept.	9	Scott Elarton (righthander), Colorado	A	5	0
63.	144	Sept.	9	Todd Belitz (lefthander), Colorado	A	11	2
64.	147	Sept.	20	Wade Miller (righthander), Houston	H	5	1
65.	150	Sept.	23	Jason Middlebrook (righthander), San Diego	A	2	0
66.	150	Sept.	23	Jason Middlebrook (righthander), San Diego	A	4	0
67.	151	Sept.	24	James Baldwin (righthander), Los Angeles	A	7	0
68.	154	Sept.	28	Jason Middlebrook (righthander), San Diego	H	2	0
69.	155	Sept.	29	Chuck McElroy (lefthander), San Diego	H	6	0
70.	159	Oct.	4	Wilfredo Rodriguez (lefthander), Houston	A	9	0
71.	160	Oct.	5	Chan Ho Park (righthander), Los Angeles	H	1	0
72.	160	Oct.	5	Chan Ho Park (righthander), Los Angeles	H	3	0
73.	162	Oct.	7	Dennis Springer (righthander), Los Angeles	H	1	0

Bonds played in 153 games.

MARK McGWIRE'S 70 HOME RUNS—1998

HR No.	Team game No.	Date		Opposing pitcher, Club	Place	Inning	On base
1.	1	March	31	Ramon Martinez (righthander), Los Angeles	H	5	3
2.	2	April	2	Frank Lankford (righthander), Los Angeles	H	12	2
3.	3	April	3	Mark Langston (lefthander), San Diego	H	5	1
4.	4	April	4	Don Wengert (righthander), San Diego	H	6	2
5.	13	April	14	Jeff Suppan (righthander), Arizona	H	3	1
6.	13	April	14	Jeff Suppan (righthander), Arizona	H	5	0
7.	13	April	14	Barry Manuel (righthander), Arizona	H	8	1
8.	16	April	17	Matt Whiteside (righthander), Philadelphia	H	4	1
9.	19	April	21	Trey Moore (lefthander), Montreal	A	3	1
10.	23	April	25	Jerry Spradlin (righthander), Philadelphia	A	7	1
11.	27	April	30	Marc Pisciotta (righthander), Chicago N.L.	A	8	1
12.	28	May	1	Rod Beck (righthander), Chicago N.L.	A	9	1
13.	34	May	8	Rick Reed (righthander), New York N.L.	A	3	1
14.	36	May	12	Paul Wagner (righthander), Milwaukee	H	5	2
15.	38	May	14	Kevin Millwood (righthander), Atlanta	H	4	0
16.	40	May	16	Livan Hernandez (righthander), Florida	H	4	1
17.	42	May	18	Jesus Sanchez (lefthander), Florida	H	4	0
18.	43	May	19	Tyler Green (righthander), Philadelphia	A	3	1
19.	43	May	19	Tyler Green (righthander), Philadelphia	A	5	1
20.	43	May	19	Wayne Gomes (righthander), Philadelphia	A	8	1
21.	46	May	22	Mark Gardner (righthander), San Francisco	H	6	1
22.	47	May	23	Rich Rodriguez (lefthander), San Francisco	H	4	0
23.	47	May	23	John Johnstone (righthander), San Francisco	H	5	2
24.	48	May	24	Robb Nen (righthander), San Francisco	H	12	1
25.	49	May	25	John Thomson (righthander), Colorado	H	1	0
26.	52	May	29	Dan Miceli (righthander), San Diego	A	9	1
27.	53	May	30	Andy Ashby (righthander), San Diego	A	1	0
28.	59	June	5	Orel Hershiser (righthander), San Francisco	H	1	1
29.	62	June	8	Jason Bere (righthander), Chicago A.L.	A	4	1
30.	64	June	10	Jim Parque (lefthander), Chicago A.L.	A	3	2
31.	65	June	12	Andy Benes (righthander), Arizona	A	3	3

HR No.	Team game No.	Date	Opposing pitcher, Club	Place	Inning	On base
32.	69	June 17	Jose Lima (righthander), Houston	A	3	0
33.	70	June 18	Shane Reynolds (righthander), Houston	A	5	0
34.	76	June 24	Jaret Wright (righthander), Cleveland	A	4	0
35.	77	June 25	Dave Burba (righthander), Cleveland	A	1	0
36.	79	June 27	Mike Trombley (righthander), Minnesota	A	7	1
37.	81	June 30	Glendon Rusch (lefthander), Kansas City	H	7	0
38.	89	July 11	Billy Wagner (lefthander), Houston	H	11	1
39.	90	July 12	Sean Bergman (righthander), Houston	H	1	0
40.	90	July 12	Scott Elarton (righthander), Houston	H	7	0
41.	95	July 17	Brian Bohanon (lefthander), Los Angeles	H	1	0
42.	95	July 17	Antonio Osuna (righthander), Los Angeles	H	8	0
43.	98	July 20	Brian Boehringer (righthander), San Diego	A	5	1
44.	104	July 26	John Thomson (righthander), Colorado	A	4	0
45.	105	July 28	Mike Myers (lefthander), Milwaukee	H	8	0
46.	115	Aug. 8	Mark Clark (righthander), Chicago N.L.	H	4	0
47.	118	Aug. 11	Bobby J. Jones (righthander), New York N.L.	H	4	0
48.	124	Aug. 19	Matt Karchner (righthander), Chicago N.L.	A	8	0
49.	124	Aug. 19	Terry Mulholland (lefthander), Chicago N.L.	A	10	0
50.	125	Aug. *20	Willie Blair (righthander), New York N.L.	A	7	0
51.	126	Aug. †20	Rick Reed (righthander), New York N.L.	A	1	0
52.	129	Aug. 22	Francisco Cordova (righthander), Pittsburgh	A	1	0
53.	130	Aug. 23	Ricardo Rincon (lefthander), Pittsburgh	A	8	0
54.	133	Aug. 26	Justin Speier (righthander), Florida	H	8	1
55.	137	Aug. 30	Dennis Martinez (righthander), Atlanta	H	7	2
56.	139	Sept. 1	Livan Hernandez (righthander), Florida	H	7	0
57.	139	Sept. 1	Donn Pall (righthander), Florida	A	9	0
58.	140	Sept. 2	Brian Edmondson (righthander), Florida	A	7	1
59.	140	Sept. 2	Rob Stanifer (righthander), Florida	A	8	1
60.	142	Sept. 5	Dennis Reyes (lefthander), Cincinnati	H	1	1
61.	144	Sept. 7	Mike Morgan (righthander), Chicago N.L.	H	1	0
62.	145	Sept. 8	Steve Trachsel (righthander), Chicago N.L.	H	4	0
63.	153	Sept. *15	Jason Christiansen (lefthander), Pittsburgh	H	9	0
64.	155	Sept. 18	Rafael Roque (lefthander), Milwaukee	A	4	1
65.	157	Sept. 20	Scott Karl (lefthander), Milwaukee	A	1	1
66.	161	Sept. 25	Shayne Bennett (righthander), Montreal	H	5	1
67.	162	Sept. 26	Dustin Hermanson (righthander), Montreal	H	4	0
68.	162	Sept. 26	Kirk Bullinger (righthander), Montreal	H	7	1
69.	163	Sept. 27	Mike Thurman (righthander), Montreal	H	3	0
70.	163	Sept. 27	Carl Pavano (righthander), Montreal	H	7	2

*First game of doubleheader. †Second game of doubleheader. St. Louis played 163 games in 1998 (one tie on August 24). McGwire did not play in this game. McGwire played in 155 games.

ROGER MARIS' 61 HOME RUNS—1961

HR No.	Team game No.	Date	Opposing pitcher, Club	Place	Inning	On base
1.	11	April 26	Paul Foytack (righthander), Detroit	A	5	0
2.	17	May 3	Pedro Ramos (righthander), Minnesota	A	7	2
3.	20	May 6	Eli Grba (righthander), Los Angeles	A	5	0
4.	29	May 17	Pete Burnside (lefthander), Washington	H	8	1
5.	30	May 19	Jim Perry (righthander), Cleveland	A	1	1
6.	31	May 20	Gary Bell (righthander), Cleveland	A	3	0
7.	32	May 21	Chuck Estrada (righthander), Baltimore	H	1	0
8.	35	May 24	Gene Conley (righthander), Boston	H	4	1
9.	38	May †28	Cal McLish (righthander), Chicago	H	2	1
10.	40	May 30	Gene Conley (righthander), Boston	A	3	0
11.	40	May 30	Mike Fornieles (righthander), Boston	A	8	2
12.	41	May 31	Billy Muffett (righthander), Boston	A	3	0
13.	43	June 2	Cal McLish (righthander), Chicago	A	3	2
14.	44	June 3	Bob Shaw (righthander), Chicago	A	8	2
15.	45	June 4	Russ Kemmerer (righthander), Chicago	A	3	0
16.	48	June 6	Ed Palmquist (righthander), Minnesota	H	6	2
17.	49	June 7	Pedro Ramos (righthander), Minnesota	H	3	2
18.	52	June 9	Ray Herbert (righthander), Kansas City	H	7	1
19.	55	June †11	Eli Grba (righthander), Los Angeles	H	3	0
20.	55	June †11	Johnny James (righthander), Los Angeles	H	7	0
21.	57	June 13	Jim Perry (righthander), Cleveland	A	6	0
22.	58	June 14	Gary Bell (righthander), Cleveland	A	4	1
23.	61	June 17	Don Mossi (lefthander), Detroit	A	4	0
24.	62	June 18	Jerry Casale (righthander), Detroit	A	8	1
25.	63	June 19	Jim Archer (lefthander), Kansas City	A	9	0
26.	64	June 20	Joe Nuxhall (lefthander), Kansas City	A	1	0
27.	66	June 22	Norm Bass (righthander), Kansas City	A	2	1
28.	74	July 1	Dave Sisler (righthander), Washington	H	9	1
29.	75	July 2	Pete Burnside (lefthander), Washington	H	3	2
30.	75	July 2	Johnny Klippstein (righthander), Washington	H	7	1
31.	77	July †4	Frank Lary (righthander), Detroit	H	8	1

HR No.	Team game No.	Date		Opposing pitcher, Club	Place	Inning	On base
32.	78	July	5	Frank Funk (righthander), Cleveland	H	7	0
33.	82	July	*9	Bill Monbouquette (righthander), Boston	H	7	0
34.	84	July	13	Early Wynn (righthander), Chicago	A	1	1
35.	86	July	15	Ray Herbert (righthander), Chicago	A	3	0
36.	92	July	21	Bill Monbouquette (righthander), Boston	A	1	0
37.	95	July	*25	Frank Baumann (lefthander), Chicago	H	4	1
38.	95	July	*25	Don Larsen (righthander), Chicago	H	8	0
39.	96	July	†25	Russ Kemmerer (righthander), Chicago	H	4	0
40.	96	July	†25	Warren Hacker (righthander), Chicago	H	6	2
41.	106	Aug.	4	Camilo Pascual (righthander), Minnesota	H	1	2
42.	114	Aug.	11	Pete Burnside (lefthander), Washington	A	5	0
43.	115	Aug.	12	Dick Donovan (righthander), Washington	A	4	0
44.	116	Aug.	*13	Bennie Daniels (righthander), Washington	A	4	0
45.	117	Aug.	†13	Marty Kutyna (righthander), Washington	A	1	1
46.	118	Aug.	15	Juan Pizarro (lefthander), Chicago	H	4	0
47.	119	Aug.	16	Billy Pierce (lefthander), Chicago	H	1	1
48.	119	Aug.	16	Billy Pierce (lefthander), Chicago	H	3	1
49.	124	Aug.	*20	Jim Perry (righthander), Cleveland	A	3	1
50.	125	Aug.	22	Ken McBride (righthander), Los Angeles	A	6	1
51.	129	Aug.	26	Jerry Walker (righthander), Kansas City	A	6	0
52.	135	Sept.	2	Frank Lary (righthander), Detroit	H	6	0
53.	135	Sept.	2	Hank Aguirre (lefthander), Detroit	H	8	1
54.	140	Sept.	6	Tom Cheney (righthander), Washington	H	4	0
55.	141	Sept.	7	Dick Stigman (lefthander), Cleveland	H	3	0
56.	143	Sept.	9	Mudcat Grant (righthander), Cleveland	H	7	0
57.	151	Sept.	16	Frank Lary (righthander), Detroit	A	3	1
58.	152	Sept.	17	Terry Fox (righthander), Detroit	A	12	1
59.	155	Sept.	20	Milt Pappas (righthander), Baltimore	A	3	0
60.	159	Sept.	26	Jack Fisher (righthander), Baltimore	H	3	0
61.	163	Oct.	1	Tracy Stallard (righthander), Boston	H	4	0

*First game of doubleheader .†Second game of doubleheader. New York played 163 games in 1961 (one tie on April 22). Maris did not hit a home run in this game. Maris played in 161 games.

BABE RUTH'S 60 HOME RUNS—1927

HR No.	Team game No.	Date		Opposing pitcher, Club	Place	Inning	On base
1.	4	April	15	Howard Ehmke (righthander), Philadelphia	H	1	0
2.	11	April	23	Rube Walberg (lefthander), Philadelphia	A	1	0
3.	12	April	24	Sloppy Thurston (righthander), Washington	A	6	0
4.	14	April	29	Slim Harriss (righthander), Boston	A	5	0
5.	16	May	1	Jack Quinn (righthander), Philadelphia	H	1	1
6.	16	May	1	Rube Walberg (lefthander), Philadelphia	H	8	0
7.	24	May	10	Milt Gaston (righthander), St. Louis	A	1	2
8.	25	May	11	Ernie Nevers (righthander), St. Louis	A	1	1
9.	29	May	17	Rip H. Collins (righthander), Detroit	A	8	0
10.	33	May	22	Benn Karr (righthander), Cleveland	A	6	1
11.	34	May	23	Sloppy Thurston (righthander), Washington	A	1	0
12.	37	May	*28	Sloppy Thurston (righthander), Washington	H	7	2
13.	39	May	29	Danny MacFayden (righthander), Boston	H	8	0
14.	41	May	‡30	Rube Walberg (lefthander), Philadelphia	A	11	0
15.	42	May	*31	Jack Quinn (righthander), Philadelphia	A	1	1
16.	43	May	†31	Howard Ehmke (righthander), Philadelphia	A	5	1
17.	47	June	5	Earl Whitehill (lefthander), Detroit	H	6	0
18.	48	June	7	Tommy Thomas (righthander), Chicago	H	4	0
19.	52	June	11	Garland Buckeye (lefthander), Cleveland	H	3	1
20.	52	June	11	Garland Buckeye (lefthander), Cleveland	H	5	0
21.	53	June	12	George Uhle (righthander), Cleveland	H	7	0
22.	55	June	16	Tom Zachary (lefthander), St. Louis	H	1	1
23.	60	June	*22	Hal Wiltse (lefthander), Boston	A	5	0
24.	60	June	*22	Hal Wiltse (lefthander), Boston	A	7	1
25.	70	June	30	Slim Harriss (righthander), Boston	H	4	1
26.	73	July	3	Hod Lisenbee (righthander), Washington	A	1	0
27.	78	July	†8	Don Hankins (righthander), Detroit	A	2	2
28.	79	July	*9	Ken Holloway (righthander), Detroit	A	1	1
29.	79	July	*9	Ken Holloway (righthander), Detroit	A	4	2
30.	83	July	12	Joe Shaute (lefthander), Cleveland	A	9	1
31.	94	July	24	Tommy Thomas (righthander), Chicago	A	3	0
32.	95	July	*26	Milt Gaston (righthander), St. Louis	H	1	1
33.	95	July	*26	Milt Gaston (righthander), St. Louis	H	6	0
34.	98	July	28	Lefty Stewart (lefthander), St. Louis	H	8	1
35.	106	Aug.	5	George S. Smith (righthander), Detroit	H	8	0
36.	110	Aug.	10	Tom Zachary (lefthander), Washington	A	3	2
37.	114	Aug.	16	Tommy Thomas (righthander), Chicago	A	5	0
38.	115	Aug.	17	Sarge Connally (righthander), Chicago	A	11	0
39.	118	Aug.	20	Jake Miller (lefthander), Cleveland	A	1	1
40.	120	Aug.	22	Joe Shaute (lefthander), Cleveland	A	6	0

HR No.	Team game No.	Date	Opposing pitcher, Club	Place	Inning	On base
1.	124	Aug. 27	Ernie Nevers (righthander), St. Louis	A	8	1
2.	125	Aug. 28	Ernie Wingard (lefthander), St. Louis	A	1	1
3.	127	Aug. 31	Tony Welzer (righthander), Boston	H	8	0
4.	128	Sept. 2	Rube Walberg (lefthander), Philadelphia	A	1	0
5.	132	Sept. *6	Tony Welzer (righthander), Boston	A	6	2
6.	132	Sept. *6	Tony Welzer (righthander), Boston	A	7	1
7.	133	Sept. †6	Jack Russell (righthander), Boston	A	9	0
8.	134	Sept. 7	Danny MacFayden (righthander), Boston	A	1	0
9.	134	Sept. 7	Slim Harriss (righthander), Boston	A	8	1
0.	138	Sept. 11	Milt Gaston (righthander), St. Louis	H	4	0
1.	139	Sept. *13	Willis Hudlin (righthander), Cleveland	H	7	1
2.	140	Sept. †13	Joe Shaute (lefthander), Cleveland	H	4	0
3.	143	Sept. 16	Ted Blankenship (righthander), Chicago	H	3	0
4.	147	Sept. †18	Ted Lyons (righthander), Chicago	H	5	1
5.	148	Sept. 21	Sam Gibson (righthander), Detroit	H	9	0
6.	149	Sept. 22	Ken Holloway (righthander), Detroit	H	9	1
7.	152	Sept. 27	Lefty Grove (lefthander), Philadelphia	H	6	3
8.	153	Sept. 29	Hod Lisenbee (righthander), Washington	H	1	0
9.	153	Sept. 29	Paul Hopkins (righthander), Washington	H	5	3
0.	154	Sept. 30	Tom Zachary (lefthander), Washington	H	8	1

*First game of doubleheader. †Second game of doubleheader. ‡Afternoon game of split doubleheader. New York A.L. played 155 games in 1927 (one tie on April 14), with Ruth participating in 151 games. (No home run for Ruth in game No. 155 on October 1.)

JOE DIMAGGIO'S 56-GAME HITTING STREAK—1941

Date		Opposing pitcher, Club	AB	R	H	2B	3B	HR	RBI
May	15	Eddie Smith, Chicago	4	0	1	0	0	0	1
	16	Thornton Lee, Chicago	4	2	2	1	1	1	1
	17	Johnny Rigney, Chicago	3	1	1	0	0	0	0
	18	Bob Harris (2), Johnny Niggeling (1), St. Louis	3	3	3	1	0	0	1
	19	Denny Galehouse, St. Louis	3	0	1	1	0	0	0
	20	Eldon Auker, St. Louis	5	1	1	0	0	0	1
	21	Schoolboy Rowe (1), Al Benton (1), Detroit	5	0	2	0	0	0	1
	22	Archie McKain, Detroit	4	0	1	0	0	0	1
	23	Dick Newsome, Boston	5	0	1	0	0	0	2
	24	Earl Johnson, Boston	4	2	1	0	0	0	1
	25	Lefty Grove, Boston	4	0	1	0	0	0	0
	27	Ken Chase (1), Red Anderson (2), Alex Carrasquel (1), Washington	5	3	4	0	0	1	3
	28	Sid Hudson, Washington	4	1	1	0	1	0	0
	29	Steve Sundra, Washington	3	1	1	0	0	0	0
	30	Earl Johnson, Boston	2	1	1	0	0	0	0
	30	Mickey Harris, Boston	3	0	1	1	0	0	0
June	1	Al Milnar, Cleveland	4	1	1	0	0	0	0
	1	Mel Harder, Cleveland	4	0	1	0	0	0	0
	2	Bob Feller, Cleveland	4	2	2	1	0	0	0
	3	Dizzy Trout, Detroit	4	1	1	0	0	1	1
	5	Hal Newhouser, Detroit	5	1	1	0	1	0	1
	7	Bob Muncrief (1), Johnny Allen (1), George Caster (1), St. Louis	5	2	3	0	0	0	1
	8	Eldon Auker, St. Louis	4	3	2	0	0	2	4
	8	George Caster (1), Jack Kramer (1), St. Louis	4	1	2	1	0	1	3
	10	Johnny Rigney, Chicago	5	1	1	0	0	0	0
	12	Thornton Lee, Chicago	4	1	2	0	0	1	1
	14	Bob Feller, Cleveland	2	0	1	0	0	0	1
	15	Jim Bagby, Cleveland	3	1	1	0	0	1	1
	16	Al Milnar, Cleveland	5	0	1	1	0	0	0
	17	Johnny Rigney, Chicago	4	1	1	0	0	0	0
	18	Thornton Lee, Chicago	3	0	1	0	0	0	0
	19	Eddie Smith (1), Buck Ross (2), Chicago	3	2	3	0	0	1	2
	20	Bobo Newsom (2), Archie McKain (2), Detroit	5	3	4	1	0	0	1
	21	Dizzy Trout, Detroit	4	0	1	0	0	0	1
	22	Hal Newhouser (1), Bobo Newsom (1), Detroit	5	1	2	1	0	1	2
	24	Bob Muncrief, St. Louis	4	1	1	0	0	0	0
	25	Denny Galehouse, St. Louis	4	1	1	0	0	1	3
	26	Eldon Auker, St. Louis	4	0	1	1	0	0	1
	27	Chubby Dean, Philadelphia	3	1	2	0	0	1	2
	28	Johnny Babich (1), Lum Harris (1), Philadelphia	5	1	2	1	0	0	1
	29	Dutch E. Leonard, Washington	4	1	1	0	0	0	0
	29	Red Anderson, Washington	5	1	1	0	0	0	1
July	1	Mickey Harris (1), Mike Ryba (1), Boston	4	0	2	0	0	0	1
	1	Jack Wilson, Boston	3	1	1	0	0	0	1
	2	Dick Newsome, Boston	5	1	1	0	0	1	3
	5	Phil Marchildon, Philadelphia	4	2	1	0	0	1	2
	6	Johnny Babich (1), Bump Hadley (3), Phi.	5	2	4	1	0	0	2
	6	Jack Knott, Philadelphia	4	0	2	0	1	0	2
	10	Johnny Niggeling, St. Louis	2	0	1	0	0	0	0

– 197 –

Date		Opposing pitcher, Club	AB	R	H	2B	3B	HR	RBI
July	11	Bob Harris (3), Jack Kramer (1), St. Louis	5	1	4	0	0	1	2
	12	Eldon Auker (1), Bob Muncrief (1), St. Louis	5	1	2	1	0	0	1
	13	Ted Lyons (2), Jack Hallett (1), Chicago	4	2	3	0	0	0	0
	13	Thornton Lee, Chicago	4	0	1	0	0	0	0
	14	Johnny Rigney, Chicago	3	0	1	0	0	0	0
	15	Eddie Smith, Chicago	4	1	2	1	0	0	2
	16	Al Milnar (2), Joe Krakauskas (1), Cleveland	4	3	3	1	0	0	0
Totals for 56 games			223	56	91	16	4	15	55

Note—Numbers in parentheses refer to hits off each pitcher. Streak stopped July 17 at Cleveland, New York won, 4-3. First inning, Al Smith pitching, thrown out by Ken Keltner; fourth inning, Smith pitching, received base on balls; seventh inning, Smith pitching, thrown out by Keltner; eighth inning, Jim Bagby Jr., pitching, grounded into double play.

HOME RUNS BY CLUBS, EACH YEAR

AMERICAN LEAGUE (1901-2001)

*Denotes leader or tie.

Year	Ana.	Bal.	Bos.	Chi.	Cle.	Det.	K.C.	Mil.	Min.	N.Y.	Oak.	Sea.	T.B.	Tex.	Tor.	Total
1901	..	..	*37	32	12	29	..	..	33	..	35	..	..	..	..	228
1902	..	29	42	14	33	22	..	..	*47	..	38	..	..	..	..	258
1903	..	12	*48	14	31	12	..	..	17	18	32	..	..	..	..	184
1904	..	10	26	14	27	11	..	..	10	27	*31	..	..	..	..	156
1905	..	16	*29	11	18	13	..	..	22	23	24	..	..	..	..	156
1906	..	20	13	7	12	10	..	..	26	17	*32	..	..	..	..	137
1907	..	10	18	5	11	11	..	..	12	15	*22	..	..	..	..	104
1908	..	*20	14	3	18	19	..	..	8	13	21	..	..	..	..	116
1909	..	10	*20	4	10	19	..	..	9	16	21	..	..	..	..	109
1910	..	12	*43	7	9	28	..	..	9	20	19	..	..	..	..	147
1911	..	17	*35	20	20	30	..	..	16	25	*35	..	..	..	..	198
1912	..	19	*29	17	12	19	..	..	20	18	22	..	..	..	..	156
1913	..	18	17	24	16	24	..	..	19	8	*33	..	..	..	..	159
1914	..	17	18	19	10	25	..	..	18	12	*29	..	..	..	..	148
1915	..	19	14	25	20	23	..	..	12	*31	16	..	..	..	..	160
1916	..	14	14	17	16	17	..	..	12	*35	19	..	..	..	..	144
1917	..	15	14	18	13	25	..	..	4	*27	17	..	..	..	..	133
1918	..	5	15	8	9	13	..	..	4	20	*22	..	..	..	..	96
1919	..	31	33	25	24	23	..	..	24	*45	35	..	..	..	..	240
1920	..	50	22	37	35	30	..	..	36	*115	44	..	..	..	..	369
1921	..	67	17	35	42	58	..	..	42	*134	82	..	..	..	..	477
1922	..	98	45	45	32	54	..	..	45	95	*111	..	..	..	..	525
1923	..	82	34	42	59	41	..	..	26	*105	53	..	..	..	..	442
1924	..	67	30	41	41	35	..	..	22	*98	63	..	..	..	..	397
1925	..	*110	41	38	52	50	..	..	56	*110	76	..	..	..	..	533
1926	..	72	32	32	27	36	..	..	43	*121	61	..	..	..	..	424
1927	..	55	28	36	26	51	..	..	29	*158	56	..	..	..	..	439
1928	..	63	38	24	34	62	..	..	40	*133	89	..	..	..	..	483
1929	..	46	28	37	62	110	..	..	48	*142	122	..	..	..	..	595
1930	..	75	47	63	72	82	..	..	57	*152	125	..	..	..	..	673
1931	..	76	37	27	71	43	..	..	49	*155	118	..	..	..	..	576
1932	..	67	53	36	78	80	..	..	61	160	*172	..	..	..	..	707
1933	..	64	50	43	50	57	..	..	60	*144	139	..	..	..	..	607
1934	..	62	51	71	100	74	..	..	51	135	*144	..	..	..	..	688
1935	..	73	69	74	93	106	..	..	32	104	*112	..	..	..	..	663
1936	..	79	86	60	123	94	..	..	62	*182	72	..	..	..	..	758
1937	..	71	100	67	103	150	..	..	47	*174	94	..	..	..	..	806
1938	..	92	98	67	113	137	..	..	85	*174	98	..	..	..	..	864
1939	..	91	124	64	85	124	..	..	44	*166	98	..	..	..	..	796
1940	..	118	145	73	101	134	..	..	52	*155	105	..	..	..	..	883
1941	..	91	124	47	103	81	..	..	52	*151	85	..	..	..	..	734
1942	..	98	103	25	50	76	..	..	40	*108	33	..	..	..	..	533
1943	..	78	57	33	55	77	..	..	47	*100	26	..	..	..	..	473
1944	..	72	69	23	70	60	..	..	33	*96	36	..	..	..	..	459
1945	..	63	50	22	65	77	..	..	27	*93	33	..	..	..	..	430
1946	..	84	109	37	79	108	..	..	60	*136	40	..	..	..	..	653
1947	..	90	103	53	112	103	..	..	42	*115	61	..	..	..	..	679
1948	..	63	121	55	*155	78	..	..	31	139	68	..	..	..	..	710
1949	..	117	*131	43	112	88	..	..	81	115	82	..	..	..	..	769
1950	..	106	161	93	*164	114	..	..	76	159	100	..	..	..	..	973
1951	..	86	127	86	*140	104	..	..	54	*140	102	..	..	..	..	839
1952	..	82	113	80	*148	103	..	..	50	129	89	..	..	..	..	794
1953	..	112	101	74	*160	108	..	..	69	139	116	..	..	..	..	879
1954	..	52	123	94	*156	90	..	..	81	133	94	..	..	..	..	823
1955	..	54	137	116	148	130	..	..	80	*175	121	..	..	..	..	961
1956	..	91	139	128	153	150	..	..	112	*190	112	..	..	..	..	1,075
1957	..	87	153	106	140	116	..	..	111	145	*166	..	..	..	..	1,024
1958	..	108	155	101	161	109	..	..	121	*164	138	..	..	..	..	1,057
1959	..	109	125	97	*167	160	..	..	163	153	117	..	..	..	..	1,091

Year	Ana.	Bal.	Bos.	Chi.	Cle.	Det.	K.C.	Mil.	Min.	N.Y.	Oak.	Sea.	T.B.	Tex.	Tor.	Total
1960	..	123	124	112	127	150	..	..	147	*193	110	..	..	..	..	1,086
1961	189	149	112	138	150	180	..	..	167	*240	90	..	..	119	..	1,534
1962	137	156	146	92	180	*209	..	..	185	199	116	..	..	132	..	1,552
1963	95	146	171	114	169	148	..	..	*225	188	95	..	..	138	..	1,489
1964	102	162	186	106	164	157	..	..	*221	162	166	..	..	125	..	1,551
1965	92	125	*165	125	156	162	..	..	150	149	110	..	..	136	..	1,370
1966	122	175	145	87	155	*179	..	..	144	162	70	..	..	126	..	1,365
1967	114	138	*158	89	131	152	..	..	131	100	69	..	..	115	..	1,197
1968	83	133	125	71	75	*185	..	..	105	109	94	..	..	124	..	1,104
1969	88	175	*197	112	119	182	98	†125	163	94	148	..	..	148	..	1,649
1970	114	179	*203	123	183	148	97	126	153	111	171	..	..	138	..	1,746
1971	96	158	161	138	109	*179	80	104	116	97	160	..	..	86	..	1,484
1972	78	100	124	108	91	122	78	88	93	103	*134	..	..	56	..	1,175
1973	93	119	147	111	*158	157	114	145	120	131	147	..	..	110	..	1,552
1974	95	116	109	*135	131	131	89	120	111	101	132	..	..	99	..	1,369
1975	55	124	134	94	*153	125	118	146	121	110	151	..	..	134	..	1,465
1976	63	119	*134	73	85	101	65	88	81	120	113	..	..	80	..	1,122
1977	131	148	*213	192	100	166	146	125	123	184	117	133	..	135	100	2,013
1978	108	154	172	106	106	129	98	*173	82	125	100	97	..	132	98	1,680
1979	164	181	*194	127	138	164	116	185	112	150	108	132	..	140	95	2,006
1980	106	156	162	91	89	143	115	*203	99	189	137	104	..	124	126	1,844
1981	97	88	90	76	39	65	61	96	47	100	*104	89	..	49	61	1,062
1982	186	179	136	136	109	177	132	*216	148	161	149	130	..	115	106	2,080
1983	154	*168	142	157	86	156	109	132	141	153	121	111	..	106	167	1,903
1984	150	160	181	172	123	*187	117	96	114	130	158	129	..	120	143	1,980
1985	153	*214	162	146	116	202	154	101	141	176	155	171	..	129	158	2,178
1986	167	169	144	121	157	*198	137	127	196	188	163	158	..	184	181	2,290
1987	172	211	174	173	187	*225	168	163	196	196	199	161	..	194	215	2,634
1988	124	137	124	132	134	143	121	113	151	148	156	148	..	112	*158	1,901
1989	*145	129	108	94	127	116	101	126	117	130	127	134	..	122	142	1,718
1990	147	132	106	106	110	*172	100	128	100	147	164	107	..	110	167	1,796
1991	115	170	126	139	79	*209	117	116	140	147	159	126	..	177	133	1,953
1992	88	148	84	110	127	*182	75	82	104	163	142	149	..	159	163	1,776
1993	114	157	114	162	141	178	125	125	121	178	158	161	..	*181	159	2,074
1994	120	139	120	121	*167	161	100	99	103	139	113	153	..	124	115	1,774
1995	186	173	175	146	*207	159	119	128	120	122	169	182	..	138	140	2,164
1996	192	*257	209	195	218	204	123	178	118	162	243	245	..	221	177	2,742
1997	161	196	185	158	220	176	158	135	132	161	197	*264	..	187	147	2,477
1998	147	214	205	198	198	165	134	..	115	207	149	*234	111	201	221	2,499
1999	158	203	176	162	209	212	151	...	105	193	235	*244	145	230	212	2,635
2000	236	184	167	216	221	177	150	...	116	205	239	198	162	173	*244	2,688
2001	158	136	198	214	212	139	152	...	164	203	199	169	121	*246	195	2,506
Totals	5,295	10,115	10,263	8,087	10,014	10,785	3,818	3,789	8,177	12,288	10,193	3,929	539	5,675	3,823	106,873

Note: Figures in Baltimore column 1902-1953 are for St. Louis (3,014); in Oakland column 1901-54 are for Philadelphia (3,502), Kansas City, 1955-67 (1,480); Minnesota column 1901-1960 are for old Washington club (2,786). Texas column represents second Washington club, 1961 through 1971. Second Milwaukee club totals include only those homers in American League. Figures in Totals column are all inclusive. (Baltimore had 24 in 1901 and 33 in 1902 and Milwaukee had 26 in 1901); these are included in League Totals but not in Club Totals. †Predecessor Seattle club. Anaheim column represents the Los Angeles Angels for 1961 through September 1, 1965 and California Angels through 1996.

NATIONAL LEAGUE (1900-2001)

*Denotes leader or tie.

Year	Ariz.	Atl.	Chi.	Cin.	Col.	Fla.	Hou.	L.A.	Mil.	Mon.	N.Y.	Phi.	Pit.	St.L.	S.D.	S.F.	Total
1900	..	*48	33	33	..	..	..	26	..	..	..	29	26	36	..	23	254
1901	..	28	18	38	..	..	..	32	..	..	..	24	29	*39	..	19	227
1902	..	14	6	18	..	..	..	*19	..	..	..	5	18	10	..	6	96
1903	..	25	9	28	..	..	..	15	..	..	..	12	*34	8	..	20	151
1904	..	24	22	21	..	..	..	15	..	..	..	23	15	24	..	*31	175
1905	..	17	12	27	..	..	..	29	..	..	..	16	22	20	..	*39	182
1906	..	16	20	16	..	..	..	*25	..	..	..	12	12	10	..	15	126
1907	..	22	13	15	..	..	..	18	..	..	..	12	19	18	..	*23	140
1908	..	17	19	14	..	..	..	*28	..	..	..	11	25	17	..	20	151
1909	..	14	20	22	..	..	..	16	..	..	..	12	25	15	..	*26	150
1910	..	31	*34	23	..	..	..	25	..	..	..	22	33	15	..	31	214
1911	..	37	54	21	..	..	..	28	..	..	..	*60	49	26	..	41	316
1912	..	35	42	21	..	..	..	32	..	..	..	43	39	27	..	*47	286
1913	..	32	59	27	..	..	..	39	..	..	..	*73	35	15	..	30	310
1914	..	35	42	16	..	..	..	31	..	..	..	*62	18	33	..	30	267
1915	..	17	53	15	..	..	..	14	..	..	..	*58	24	20	..	24	225
1916	..	22	*46	14	..	..	..	28	..	..	..	42	20	25	..	42	239
1917	..	22	17	26	..	..	..	25	..	..	..	38	9	26	..	*39	202
1918	..	13	21	15	..	..	..	10	..	..	..	25	15	*27	..	13	139
1919	..	24	21	20	..	..	..	25	..	..	..	*42	17	18	..	40	207
1920	..	23	34	18	..	..	..	28	..	..	..	*64	16	32	..	46	261
1921	..	61	37	20	..	..	..	59	..	..	..	*88	37	83	..	75	460
1922	..	32	42	45	..	..	..	56	..	..	..	*116	52	107	..	80	530
1923	..	32	90	45	..	..	..	62	..	..	..	*112	49	63	..	85	538
1924	..	25	66	36	..	..	..	72	..	..	..	94	44	67	..	*95	499
1925	..	41	86	44	..	..	..	64	..	..	..	100	78	109	..	*114	636

Year	Ariz.	Atl.	Chi.	Cin.	Col.	Fla.	Hou.	L.A.	Mil.	Mon.	N.Y.	Phi.	Pit.	St.L.	S.D.	S.F.	Total
1926	..	16	66	35	..	..	..	40	..	..	..	75	44	*90	..	73	439
1927	..	37	74	29	..	..	..	39	..	..	..	57	54	84	..	*109	483
1928	..	52	92	32	..	..	..	66	..	..	..	85	52	113	..	*118	610
1929	..	33	139	34	..	..	..	99	..	..	..	*153	60	100	..	136	754
1930	..	66	*171	74	..	..	..	122	..	..	..	126	86	104	..	143	892
1931	..	34	84	21	..	..	..	71	..	..	..	81	41	60	..	*101	493
1932	..	63	69	47	..	..	..	110	..	..	..	*122	48	76	..	116	651
1933	..	54	72	34	..	..	..	62	..	..	..	60	39	57	..	*82	460
1934	..	83	101	55	..	..	..	79	..	..	..	56	52	104	..	*126	656
1935	..	75	88	73	..	..	..	59	..	..	..	92	66	86	..	*123	662
1936	..	67	76	82	..	..	..	33	..	..	..	*103	60	88	..	97	606
1937	..	63	96	73	..	..	..	37	..	..	..	103	47	94	..	*111	624
1938	..	54	65	110	..	..	..	61	..	..	..	40	65	91	..	*125	611
1939	..	56	91	98	..	..	..	78	..	..	..	49	63	98	..	*116	649
1940	..	59	86	89	..	..	..	93	..	..	..	75	76	*119	..	91	688
1941	..	48	99	64	..	..	..	*101	..	..	..	64	56	70	..	95	597
1942	..	68	75	66	..	..	..	62	..	..	..	44	54	60	..	*109	538
1943	..	39	52	43	..	..	..	39	..	..	..	66	42	70	..	*81	432
1944	..	79	71	51	..	..	..	56	..	..	..	55	70	*100	..	93	575
1945	..	101	57	56	..	..	..	57	..	..	..	56	72	64	..	*114	577
1946	..	44	56	65	..	..	..	55	..	..	..	80	60	81	..	*121	562
1947	..	85	71	95	..	..	..	83	..	..	..	60	156	115	..	*221	886
1948	..	95	87	104	..	..	..	91	..	..	..	91	108	105	..	*164	655
1949	..	103	97	86	..	..	..	*152	..	..	..	122	126	102	..	147	935
1950	..	148	161	99	..	..	..	*194	..	..	..	125	138	102	..	133	1,100
1951	..	130	103	88	..	..	..	*184	..	..	..	108	137	95	..	179	1,024
1952	..	110	107	104	..	..	..	*153	..	..	..	93	92	97	..	151	907
1953	..	156	137	166	..	..	..	*208	..	..	..	115	99	140	..	176	1,197
1954	..	139	159	147	..	..	..	*186	..	..	..	102	76	119	..	*186	1,114
1955	..	182	164	181	..	..	..	*201	..	..	..	132	91	143	..	169	1,263
1956	..	177	142	*221	..	..	..	179	..	..	..	121	110	124	..	145	1,219
1957	..	*199	147	187	..	..	..	147	..	..	..	117	92	132	..	157	1,178
1958	..	167	*182	123	..	..	..	172	..	..	..	124	134	111	..	170	1,183
1959	..	*177	163	161	..	..	..	148	..	..	..	113	112	118	..	167	1,159
1960	..	*170	119	140	..	..	..	126	..	..	..	99	120	138	..	130	1,042
1961	..	*188	176	158	..	..	..	157	..	..	..	103	128	103	..	183	1,196
1962	..	181	126	167	..	..	105	140	..	..	139	142	108	137	..	*204	1,449
1963	..	139	127	122	..	..	62	110	..	..	96	126	108	128	..	*197	1,215
1964	..	159	145	130	..	..	70	79	..	..	103	130	121	109	..	*165	1,211
1965	..	*196	134	183	..	..	97	78	..	..	107	144	111	109	..	159	1,318
1966	..	*207	140	149	..	..	112	108	..	..	98	117	158	108	..	181	1,378
1967	..	*158	128	109	..	..	93	82	..	..	83	103	91	115	..	140	1,102
1968	..	80	*130	106	..	..	66	67	..	..	81	100	80	73	..	108	891
1969	..	141	142	*171	..	..	104	97	..	125	109	137	119	90	99	136	1,470
1970	..	160	179	*191	..	..	129	87	..	136	120	101	130	113	172	165	1,683
1971	..	153	128	138	..	..	71	95	..	88	98	123	*154	95	96	140	1,379
1972	..	144	133	124	..	..	134	98	..	91	105	98	110	70	102	*150	1,359
1973	..	*206	117	137	..	..	134	110	..	125	85	134	154	75	112	161	1,550
1974	..	120	110	135	..	..	110	*139	..	86	96	95	114	83	99	93	1,280
1975	..	107	95	124	..	..	84	118	..	98	101	125	*138	81	78	84	1,233
1976	..	82	105	*141	..	..	66	91	..	94	102	110	110	63	64	85	1,113
1977	..	139	111	181	..	..	114	*191	..	138	88	186	133	96	120	134	1,631
1978	..	123	72	136	..	..	70	*149	..	121	86	133	115	79	75	117	1,276
1979	..	126	135	132	..	..	49	*183	..	143	74	119	148	100	93	125	1,427
1980	..	144	107	113	..	..	75	*148	..	114	61	117	116	101	67	80	1,243
1981	..	64	57	64	..	..	45	*82	..	81	57	69	55	50	32	63	719
1982	..	*146	102	82	..	..	74	138	..	133	97	112	134	67	81	133	1,299
1983	..	130	140	107	..	..	97	*146	..	102	112	125	121	83	93	142	1,398
1984	..	111	136	106	..	..	79	102	..	96	107	*147	98	75	109	112	1,278
1985	..	126	*150	114	..	..	121	129	..	118	134	141	80	87	109	115	1,424
1986	..	138	*155	144	..	..	125	130	..	110	148	154	111	58	136	114	1,523
1987	..	152	*209	192	..	..	122	125	..	120	192	169	131	94	113	205	1,824
1988	..	96	113	122	..	..	96	99	..	107	*152	106	110	71	94	113	1,279
1989	..	128	124	128	..	..	97	89	..	100	*147	123	95	73	120	141	1,365
1990	..	162	136	125	..	..	94	129	..	114	*172	103	138	73	123	152	1,521
1991	..	141	159	*164	..	..	79	108	..	95	117	111	126	68	121	141	1,430
1992	..	*138	104	99	..	..	96	72	..	102	93	118	106	94	135	105	1,262
1993	..	*169	161	137	142	94	138	130	..	122	158	156	110	118	153	168	1,956
1994	..	*137	109	124	125	94	120	115	..	108	117	80	80	108	92	123	1,532
1995	..	168	158	161	*200	144	109	140	..	118	125	94	125	107	116	152	1,917
1996	..	197	175	191	*221	150	129	150	..	148	147	132	138	142	147	153	2,220
1997	..	174	127	142	*239	136	133	174	..	172	153	116	129	144	152	172	2,163
1998	159	215	212	138	183	114	166	159	152	147	136	126	107	*223	167	161	2,565
1999	216	197	189	209	*223	128	168	187	165	163	181	161	171	194	153	188	2,893
2000	179	179	183	200	161	160	249	211	177	178	198	144	168	235	157	226	3,005
2001	208	174	194	176	213	166	208	206	209	131	147	164	161	199	161	*235	2,952
Totals	762	10,031	10,168	9,543	1,707	1,186	4,290	9,612	703	3,924	4,722	9,453	8,498	8,631	3,741	11,550	98,521

Note: Figures in Atlanta column 1900-1952 are for Boston (2,569) and 1953-1965 for Milwaukee (2,230); in Los Angeles column 1900-1957 are for Brooklyn (4,018); San Francisco column 1900-1957 are for New York Giants (5,162); New York column represents the present Mets franchise. Figures in Totals columns are all inclusive. Milwaukee Brewers totals are as National League club.

CLUBS WITH FIVE HOME RUNS IN INNING

AMERICAN LEAGUE

Date	Inn.	Club (Players)
June 9, 1966	7	Minnesota (Rollins, Versalles, OLIVA, MINCHER, KILLEBREW).

Total number of clubs: 1

NATIONAL LEAGUE

Date	Inn.	Club (Players)
June 6, 1939	4	New York (Danning, Demaree, WHITEHEAD, SALVO, MOORE).
June 2, 1949	8	Philadelphia (Ennis, Seminick, Jones, Rowe, Seminick).
Aug. 23, 1961	9	San Francisco (Cepeda, F. Alou, Davenport, Mays, Orsino).

Note—Capitalized letters denote three or more consecutive homers.
Total number of clubs: 3

CLUBS WITH FOUR HOME RUNS IN INNING

AMERICAN LEAGUE

Date	Inn.	Club (Players)
Sept. 24, 1940*	6	Boston (WILLIAMS, FOXX, CRONIN, Tabor).
June 23, 1950	4	Detroit (Trout, Priddy, Wertz, Evers).
May 22, 1957	6	Boston (Mauch, Williams, Gernert, Malzone).
Aug. 26, 1957	7	Boston (Zauchin, Lepcio, Piersall, Malzone).
July 31, 1963†	6	Cleveland (HELD, RAMOS, FRANCONA, BROWN).
May 2, 1964	11	Minnesota (OLIVA, ALLISON, HALL, KILLEBREW).
May 17, 1967	7	Baltimore (Etchebarren, Bowens, Powell, D. Johnson).
July 29, 1974	1	Detroit (KALINE, FREEHAN, STANLEY, Brinkman).
June 17, 1977	1	Boston (Burleson, Lynn, Fisk, Scott).
July 4, 1977	8	Boston (LYNN, RICE, YASTRZEMSKI, Scott).
May 31, 1980	4	Boston (Stapleton, PEREZ, FISK, HOBSON).
May 16, 1983	9	Minnesota (Engle, Mitchell, Gaetti, Hatcher).
Sept. 10, 1986	4	Detroit (Lemon, Heath, Gibson, Coles).
May 2, 1992	5	Minnesota (Mack, Puckett, Hrbek, Bush).
Sept. 5, 1995	2	Baltimore (Hoiles, MANTO, SMITH, ANDERSON).
May 26, 1996	8	Chicago (THOMAS, BAINES, VENTURA, Kreuter).
Sept. 21, 1996	3	Seattle (RODRIGUEZ, GRIFFEY, MARTINEZ, Sorrento).
Aug. 21, 1997	3	Oakland (Giambi, Young, McDonald, Canseco).
July 18, 1998	4	Boston (Sadler, Lewis, Garciaparra, Vaughn).
Aug. 1, 1999	4	Oakland (Tejada, Chavez, Giambi, Jaha).
May 3, 2000	6	Chicago (Johnson, VALENTIN, THOMAS, KONERKO).
May 26, 2000	6	Kansas City (Dye, Quinn, Johnson, Febles).
May 28, 2000	5	Anaheim (Erstad, VAUGHN, SALMON, ANDERSON).
July 3, 2000	4	Boston (Everett, O'Leary, Varitek, Burkhart).
June 29, 2001	4	Kansas City (Sweeney, DYE, IBANEZ, BELTRAN).
Aug. 17, 2001	6	Toronto (Frye, Cruz, Stewart, Delgado).

Total number of clubs: 26

NATIONAL LEAGUE

Date	Inn.	Club (Players)
June 6, 1894	3	Pittsburgh (Stenzel, Lyons, Bierbauer, Stenzel).
May 12, 1930	7	Chicago (Heathcote, Wilson, Grimm, Beck).
Aug. 13, 1939*	4	New York (Bonura, KAMPOURIS, LOHRMAN, MOORE).
June 6, 1948*	6	St. Louis (Dusak, Schoendienst, Slaughter, Jones).
May 28, 1954	8	New York (Williams, Dark, Irvin, Gardner).
July 8, 1956*	4	New York (Mays, THOMPSON, SPENCER, WESTRUM).
June 8, 1961	7	Milwaukee (MATHEWS, AARON, ADCOCK, THOMAS).
June 8, 1965	10	Milwaukee (Torre, Mathews, Aaron, Oliver).
July 10, 1970	9	San Diego (Murrell, Spiezio, Campbell, Gaston).
June 21, 1971*	8	Atlanta (Lum, King, H. Aaron, Evans).
July 30, 1978	3	Montreal (Dawson, Parrish, Cash, Dawson).
Aug. 17, 1985	7	Philadelphia (SAMUEL, WILSON, SCHMIDT, Daulton).
Apr. 29, 1986	4	Montreal (Dawson, Brooks, Wallach, Fitzgerald).
Sept. 20, 1992	6	Atlanta (JUSTICE, HUNTER, GANT, Lemke).
June 19, 1994	1	Cincinnati (Morris, Mitchell, Branson, Taubensee).
Aug. 8, 1995	2	Pittsburgh (King, Merced, King, Cummings).
Aug. 17, 1996	8	Cincinnati (Taubensee, Sanders, Branson, Larkin).
June 22, 1997	3	Atlanta (Blauser, C. Jones, McGriff, Tucker).
Aug. 26, 1998	9	Florida (LEE, FLOYD, ORIE, Kotsay).
June 6, 1999	7	Colorado (Blanco, Perez, Bichette, Echevarria).
Apr. 27, 2000	1	Chicago (Young, Gutierrez, Rodriguez, Buford).
July 23, 2000	2	Houston (Spiers, Bagwell, Berkman, Hidalgo).
Aug. 8, 2000	4	Los Angeles (Elster, Dreifort, Sheffield, Green).
May 17, 2001	3	San Diego (Arias, Henderson, Klesko, Trammell).
May 20, 2001	7	Atlanta (A. Jones, Jordan, Lopez, Helms).

Note—Capitalized letters denote three or more consecutive homers.
*First game. †Second game.
Total number of clubs: 25

REGULAR SEASON *General reference*

PLAYERS LEAGUE

Date	Inn.	Club (Players)
May 31, 1890	8	New York (GORE, EWING, CONNOR).

Total number of clubs: 1

AMERICAN LEAGUE

Date	Inn.	Club (Players)
June 30, 1902*	6	Cleveland (LAJOIE, HICKMAN, BRADLEY).
May 2, 1922	4	Philadelphia (WALKER, PERKINS, MILLER).
Sept. 10, 1925*	4	New York (MEUSEL, RUTH, GEHRIG).
May 4, 1929	7	New York (RUTH, GEHRIG, MEUSEL).
June 18, 1930	5	Philadelphia (SIMMONS, FOXX, MILLER).
July 17, 1934	4	Philadelphia (JOHNSON, FOXX, HIGGINS).
June 25, 1939*	7	Cleveland (CHAPMAN, TROSKY, HEATH).
Sept. 24, 1940*‡	6	Boston (WILLIAMS, FOXX, CRONIN).
May 23, 1946	5	New York (DiMAGGIO, ETTEN, GORDON).
April 23, 1947	8	Detroit (CULLENBINE, WAKEFIELD, EVERS).
May 13, 1947	6	New York (KELLER, DiMAGGIO, LINDELL).
April 19, 1948*	2	Boston (SPENCE, STEPHENS, DOERR).
June 6, 1948†	6	Boston (WILLIAMS, SPENCE, STEPHENS).
July 28, 1950	3	Cleveland (DOBY, ROSEN, EASTER).
Sept. 2, 1951	1	Cleveland (SIMPSON, ROSEN, EASTER).
July 16, 1953†	5	St. Louis (COURTNEY, KRYHOSKI, DYCK).
July 7, 1956	7	Detroit (KUENN, TORGESON, MAXWELL).
Sept. 7, 1959	2	Boston (BUDDIN, CASALE, GREEN).
April 30, 1961†	7	Baltimore (GENTILE, TRIANDOS, HANSEN).
May 23, 1961	9	Detroit (CASH, BOROS, BROWN).
June 27, 1961	1	Washington (GREEN, TASBY, LONG).
June 17, 1962*	2	Cleveland (KINDALL, PHILLIPS, MAHONEY).
Aug. 19, 1962	7	Kansas City (CIMOLI, CAUSEY, BRYAN).
Aug. 28, 1962	4	Los Angeles (J. L. THOMAS, WAGNER, RODGERS).
July 31, 1963†‡	6	Cleveland (HELD, RAMOS, FRANCONA, BROWN).
May 2, 1964‡	11	Minnesota (OLIVA, ALLISON, HALL, KILLEBREW).
Sept. 10, 1965	8	Baltimore (ROBINSON, BLEFARY, ADAIR).
June 9, 1966‡	7	Minnesota (OLIVA, MINCHER, KILLEBREW).
June 29, 1966	3	New York (RICHARDSON, MANTLE, PEPITONE).
July 2, 1966	6	Washington (HOWARD, LOCK, McMULLEN).
June 22, 1969*	3	Oakland (KUBIAK, JACKSON, BANDO).
Aug. 10, 1969	6	New York (MURCER, MUNSON, MICHAEL).
Sept. 4, 1969	9	Baltimore (F. ROBINSON, POWELL, B. C. ROBINSON).
Aug. 22, 1970	6	Cleveland (SIMS, NETTLES, LEON).
April 17, 1971	7	Detroit (NORTHRUP, CASH, HORTON).
June 27, 1972	1	Detroit (RODRIGUEZ, KALINE, HORTON).
July 15, 1973	8	Minnesota (MITTERWALD, LIS, HOLT).
July 29, 1974‡	1	Detroit (KALINE, FREEHAN, STANLEY).
May 11, 1977	2	California (BONDS, BAYLOR, JACKSON).
July 4, 1977‡	8	Boston (LYNN, RICE, YASTRZEMSKI).
Aug. 13, 1977	6	Boston (SCOTT, HOBSON, EVANS).
May 8, 1979	6	Baltimore (MURRAY, MAY, ROENICKE).
June 19, 1979	4	Oakland (GROSS, REVERING, HEATH).
May 31, 1980‡	4	Boston (PEREZ, FISK, HOBSON).
June 3, 1980	9	Oakland (REVERING, PAGE, ARMAS).
May 28, 1982	6	Milwaukee (COOPER, MONEY, THOMAS).
June 5, 1982	7	Milwaukee (YOUNT, COOPER, OGLIVIE).
June 7, 1982	8	Minnesota (WASHINGTON, BRUNANSKY, HRBEK).
Sept. 12, 1982	3	Milwaukee (COOPER, SIMMONS, OGLIVIE).
Aug. 2, 1983	3	Seattle (S. HENDERSON, D. HENDERSON, RAMOS).
Sept. 9, 1983	1	Chicago (FISK, PACIOREK, LUZINSKI).
April 24, 1984	4	California (R.M. JACKSON, DOWNING, GRICH).
April 26, 1984	6	Toronto (UPSHAW, BELL, BARFIELD).
May 29, 1984	6	New York (MATTINGLY, BAYLOR, WINFIELD).
June 3, 1984	4	New York (GAMBLE, KEMP, HARRAH).
June 29, 1984	5	Cleveland (THORNTON, HALL, WILLARD).
Aug. 19, 1984	7	Kansas City (MOTLEY, WHITE, BALBONI).
Aug. 24, 1985	9	Chicago (LAW, LITTLE, BAINES).
Sept. 16, 1985	8	Baltimore (RIPKEN, MURRAY, LYNN).
July 8, 1986	4	Detroit (GIBSON, PARRISH, EVANS).
July 31, 1986	5	Detroit (TRAMMELL, GIBSON, GRUBB).
Sept. 28, 1986	4	Kansas City (BRETT, WHITE, QUIRK).
June 28, 1987	8	Detroit (GRUBB, NOKES, MADLOCK).
Sept. 12, 1987	8	Toronto (WHITT, BARFIELD, GRUBER).
July 9, 1988*	4	Chicago (PASQUA, WALKER, BOSTON).
May 16, 1990	4	Oakland (CANSECO, McGWIRE, HASSEY).
June 17, 1990	7	Cleveland (MALDONADO, JACOBY, SNYDER).
July 6, 1990†	3	Oakland (R. HENDERSON, LANSFORD, CANSECO).
Aug. 7, 1990	9	Detroit (TRAMMELL, FIELDER, WARD).
April 20, 1992	3	Detroit (TRAMMELL, FIELDER, TETTLETON).

Date		Inn.	Club (Players)
May 8,	1994	6	New York (TARTABULL, STANLEY, G. WILLIAMS).
May 28,	1995	4	Chicago (DURHAM, KARKOVICE, GREBECK).
Sept. 5,	1995‡	2	Baltimore (MANTO, SMITH, ANDERSON).
May 26,	1996‡	8	Chicago (THOMAS, BAINES, VENTURA).
Sept. 12,	1996	7	Cleveland (THOME, BELLE, FRANCO).
Sept. 21,	1996‡	3	Seattle (RODRIGUEZ, GRIFFEY, MARTINEZ).
Aug. 28,	1998	4	Texas (GONZALEZ, CLARK, RODRIGUEZ).
May 19,	1999	5	Texas (RODRIGUEZ, PALMEIRO, ZEILE).
May 28,	1999	1	Texas (GONZALEZ, PALMEIRO, RODRIGUEZ).
Apr. 9,	2000	6	Minnesota (COOMER, JONES, LeCROY).
Apr. 9,	2000	8	Kansas City (BELTRAN, DYE, SWEENEY).
Apr. 18,	2000	6	Toronto (GREBECK, MONDESI, DELGADO).
May 3,	2000	6	Chicago (VALENTIN, THOMAS, KONERKO).
May 28,	2000	5	Anaheim (VAUGHN, SALMON, ANDERSON).
June 16,	2000	8	Oakland (CHAVEZ, TEJADA, HERNANDEZ).
June 23,	2000	2	Oakland (VELARDE, JA. GIAMBI, GRIEVE).
June 24,	2000	2	Anaheim (ANDERSON, GLAUS, SPIEZIO).
June 24,	2001	2	Detroit (FICK, ENCARNACION, HALTER).
June 29,	2001	4	Kansas City (DYE, IBANEZ, BELTRAN).
July 12,	2001	3	Minnesota (MIENTKIEWICZ, KOSKIE, HUNTER).
July 26,	2001	1	Anaheim (GLAUS, ERSTAD, ANDERSON).
Aug. 21,	2001	6	Toronto (STEWART, DELGADO, MONDESI).

Total number of clubs: 92

NATIONAL LEAGUE

Date		Inn.	Club (Players)
May 10,	1894	7	St. Louis (SHUGART, MILLER, PEITZ).
Aug. 13,	1932*	4	New York (TERRY, OTT, LINDSTROM).
June 10,	1935	8	Pittsburgh (P. WANER, VAUGHAN, YOUNG).
July 9,	1938	3	Boston (CUCCINELLO, WEST, FLETCHER).
June 6,	1939‡	4	New York (WHITEHEAD, SALVO, MOORE).
Aug. 13,	1939*‡	4	New York (KAMPOURIS, LOHRMAN, MOORE).
Aug. 11,	1941	5	Chicago (CAVARRETTA, HACK, NICHOLSON).
June 11,	1944†	8	St. Louis (W. COOPER, KUROWSKI, LITWHILER).
Aug. 11,	1946*	8	Cincinnati (HATTON, WEST, MUELLER).
June 20,	1948†	8	New York (MIZE, MARSHALL, GORDON).
June 4,	1949	6	New York (LOCKMAN, GORDON, MARSHALL).
April 19,	1952	7	Brooklyn (CAMPANELLA, PAFKO, SNIDER).
Sept. 27,	1952	7	Pittsburgh (KINER, GARAGIOLA, BELL).
Sept. 4,	1953	4	New York (WESTRUM, CORWIN, LOCKMAN).
June 20,	1954	6	New York (HOFMAN, WESTRUM, RHODES).
Aug. 15,	1954	9	Cincinnati (BELL, KLUSZEWSKI, GREENGRASS).
April 16,	1955	2	Chicago (JACKSON, BANKS, FONDY).
July 6,	1955*	6	Pittsburgh (LYNCH, THOMAS, LONG).
May 30,	1956*	1	Milwaukee (MATHEWS, AARON, THOMSON).
May 31,	1956	9	Cincinnati (BELL, KLUSZEWSKI, ROBINSON).
June 29,	1956	9	Brooklyn (SNIDER, JACKSON, HODGES).
July 8,	1956*‡	4	New York (THOMPSON, SPENCER, WESTRUM).
April 21,	1957*	3	Pittsburgh (THOMAS, SMITH, GROAT).
June 26,	1957	5	Milwaukee (AARON, MATHEWS, COVINGTON).
May 7,	1958	5	Pittsburgh (SKINNER, KLUSZEWSKI, THOMAS).
May 31,	1958	1	Milwaukee (AARON, MATHEWS, COVINGTON).
June 8,	1961‡	7	Milwaukee (MATHEWS, AARON, ADCOCK, THOMAS).
June 18,	1961	3	Milwaukee (AARON, ADCOCK, THOMAS).
April 28,	1962	6	New York (THOMAS, NEAL, HODGES).
Aug. 27,	1963	3	San Francisco (MAYS, CEPEDA, F. ALOU).
July 18,	1964	8	St. Louis (BOYER, WHITE, McCARVER).
Aug. 5,	1969*	5	San Francisco (MARSHALL, HUNT, BONDS).
May 18,	1970	8	New York (MARSHALL, FOY, GROTE).
Aug. 1,	1970	7	Pittsburgh (ROBERTSON, STARGELL, PAGAN).
July 16,	1974	9	San Diego (COLBERT, McCOVEY, WINFIELD).
July 20,	1974	5	New York (THEODORE, STAUB, JONES).
May 17,	1977	5	Chicago (BIITTNER, MURCER, MORALES).
Sept. 30,	1977	2	Philadelphia (LUZINSKI, HEBNER, MADDOX).
Aug. 14,	1978	3	Atlanta (MATTHEWS, BURROUGHS, HORNER).
June 17,	1979	4	Montreal (PEREZ, CARTER, VALENTINE).
July 11,	1979	1	San Diego (TURNER, WINFIELD, TENACE).
May 27,	1980	3	Cincinnati (GRIFFEY, FOSTER, DRIESSEN).
Aug. 31,	1980†	2	Los Angeles (CEY, MONDAY, FERGUSON).
July 11,	1982	2	San Francisco (SMITH, MAY, SUMMERS).
June 24,	1984	5	Houston (CABELL, GARNER, CRUZ).
Aug. 17,	1985‡	7	Philadelphia (SAMUEL, WILSON, SCHMIDT).
July 27,	1986	3	New York (CARTER, STRAWBERRY, MITCHELL).
April 13,	1987	1	San Diego (WYNNE, GWYNN, KRUK).
July 26,	1987	8	Philadelphia (THOMPSON, HAYES, SCHMIDT).
May 1,	1988	5	New York (TEUFEL, HERNANDEZ, STRAWBERRY).
April 17,	1989	3	New York (STRAWBERRY, McREYNOLDS, HERNANDEZ).
June 16,	1990	5	Cincinnati (SABO, LARKIN, DAVIS).

Date	Inn.	Club (Players)
Sept. 14, 1991	4	Cincinnati (DUNCAN, MORRIS, O'NEILL).
Sept. 20, 1992‡	6	Atlanta (JUSTICE, HUNTER, GANT).
Sept. 6, 1993	6	Chicago (BUECHELE, WILSON, LAKE).
April 15, 1994	1	Atlanta (McGRIFF, PENDLETON, TARASCO).
April 18, 1994	1	Atlanta (KLESKO, McGRIFF, JUSTICE).
July 7, 1995	2	Colorado (WALKER, GALARRAGA, CASTILLA).
Aug. 8, 1995‡	2	Pittsburgh (MERCED, KING, CUMMINGS).
April 19, 1996	6	Chicago (McRAE, SANDBERG, GRACE).
June 30, 1996	3	Los Angeles (PIAZZA, KARROS, MONDESI).
July 23, 1996	1	Colorado (BICHETTE, GALARRAGA, CASTILLA).
April 1, 1997	6	San Diego (GOMEZ, HENDERSON, VERAS).
April 9, 1997	6	Cincinnati (LARKIN, GREENE, SANDERS).
May 29, 1997	6	Colorado (WALKER, GALARRAGA, BICHETTE).
June 1, 1997	4	Los Angeles (PIAZZA, KARROS, ZEILE).
June 7, 1997*	1	Colorado (WALKER, GALARRAGA, BICHETTE).
Aug. 23, 1997	9	Montreal (STANKIEWICZ, GRUDZIELANEK, LANSING).
Aug. 2, 1998	2	San Francisco (BURKS, BONDS, KENT).
Aug. 10, 1998	5	Chicago (SOSA, GRACE, RODRIGUEZ).
Aug. 26, 1998‡	9	Florida (LEE, FLOYD, ORIE).
April 28, 1999	1	Philadelphia (ROLEN, BROGNA, GANT).
June 18, 1999	8	Chicago (SOSA, GRACE, RODRIGUEZ).
Aug. 20, 1999	4	San Francisco (MARTINEZ, BONDS, BURKS).
Aug. 22, 1999	1	San Francisco (BONDS, KENT, BURKS).
Aug. 22, 1999	1	Arizona (GONZALEZ, WILLIAMS, DURAZO).
Sept. 17, 1999	4	St. Louis (McGWIRE, T. HOWARD, TATIS).
Apr. 6, 2000	3	St. Louis (TATIS, DREW, MATHENY).
May 13, 2000	8	Cincinnati (TUCKER, GRIFFEY, YOUNG).
June 14, 2000	8	Houston (ALOU, HIDALGO, EUSEBIO).
July 22, 2001	5	San Francisco (KENT, DAVIS, SANTIAGO).
Aug. 3, 2001	6	Cincinnati (YOUNG, LaRUE, REESE).
Sept. 29, 2001	1	Chicago (McGRIFF, WHITE, HUNDLEY).

*First game. †Second game. ‡Club had more than three homers in inning.
Total number of clubs: 83

PITCHING
NO-HIT GAMES
PERFECT GAMES OF NINE OR MORE INNINGS
AMERICAN LEAGUE

Year		Score
1904	Cy Young, Boston vs. Philadelphia, May 5	3-0
1908	Addie Joss, Cleveland vs. Chicago, October 2	1-0
1922	Charlie Robertson, Chicago at Detroit, April 30	2-0
1968	Catfish Hunter, Oakland vs. Minnesota, May 8	4-0
1981	Len Barker, Cleveland vs. Toronto, May 15	3-0
1984	Mike Witt, California at Texas, September 30	1-0
1994	Kenny Rogers, Texas vs. California, July 28	4-0
1998	David Wells, New York vs. Minnesota, May 17	4-0
1999	David Cone, New York vs. Montreal N.L., July 18	6-0

Note: Ernie Shore of Boston is often included in the list of perfect game pitchers. In the first game of a June 23, 1917 doubleheader at Boston, Babe Ruth, the starting Red Sox pitcher, was removed for arguing with umpire Brick Owens after giving a base on balls to Washington's Ray Morgan, the first batter. Shore, without warming up, took Ruth's place. Morgan was retired trying to steal second. From then on, Shore faced 26 batters, with none reaching base. Shore won the game, 4-0. He and Ruth are listed under the category "No-hit games of nine or more innings."

Note: Don Larsen of the New York Yankees pitched a perfect game in the World Series, defeating the Brooklyn Dodgers, 2-0, at Yankee Stadium on October 8, 1956.

Total number of games (excluding Shore's and Larsen's): 9

NATIONAL LEAGUE

Year		Score
1880	Lee Richmond, Worcester vs. Cleveland, June 12	1-0
	Monte Ward, Providence vs. Buffalo, June 17	5-0
1964	Jim Bunning, Philadelphia at New York, June 21, first game	6-0
1965	Sandy Koufax, Los Angeles vs. Chicago, September 9	1-0
1988	Tom Browning, Cincinnati vs. Los Angeles, September 16	1-0
1991	Dennis Martinez, Montreal at Los Angeles, July 28	2-0

Total number of games: 6

PERFECT GAMES FOR NINE INNINGS THAT WERE BROKEN UP IN EXTRA INNINGS
NATIONAL LEAGUE

Year		Score
1959	Harvey Haddix, Pittsburgh at Milwaukee, May 26 (Haddix pitched 12 perfect innings before Felix Mantilla, leading off the 13th, reached base on third baseman Don Hoak's throwing error. After Eddie Mathews sacrificed and Hank Aaron was walked intentionally, Joe Adcock doubled to score Mantilla, ending the game.)	0-1
1995	Pedro J. Martinez Montreal at San Diego, June 3 (Martinez pitched nine perfect innings before Bip Roberts doubled leading off the 10th. Mel Rojas then relieved and retired the game's final three batters.)	1-0

Total number of games: 2

PERFECT GAMES OF LESS THAN NINE INNINGS
AMERICAN LEAGUE

Year		Score
1907	Rube Vickers, Philadelphia at Washington, October 5, second game, five innings	4-0
1967	Dean Chance, Minnesota vs. Boston, August 6, five innings	2-0

Total number of games: 2

NATIONAL LEAGUE

Year		Score
1907	Ed Karger, St. Louis vs. Boston, August 11, second game, seven innings	4-0
1984	David Palmer, Montreal at St. Louis, April 21, second game, five innings	4-0

Total number of games: 2

NO-HIT GAMES OF NINE OR MORE INNINGS
AMERICAN ASSOCIATION

Year		Score
1882	Tony Mullane, Louisville at Cincinnati, September 11 (first no-hitter at 50-foot distance)	2-0
	Guy Hecker, Louisville at Pittsburgh, September 19	3-1
1884	Al Atkisson, Philadelphia vs. Pittsburgh, May 24	10-1
	Ed Morris, Columbus at Pittsburgh, May 29	5-0
	Frank Mountain, Columbus at Washington, June 5	12-0
	Sam Kimber, Brooklyn vs. Toledo, October 4, 10 innings	0-0
1886	Al Atkisson, Philadelphia vs. New York, May 1	3-2
	Adonis Terry, Brooklyn vs. St. Louis, July 24	1-0
	Matt Kilroy, Baltimore at Pittsburgh, October 6	6-0
1888	Adonis Terry, Brooklyn vs. Louisville, May 27	4-0
	Henry Porter, Kansas City at Baltimore, June 6	4-0
	Ed Seward, Philadelphia vs. Cincinnati, July 26	12-2
	Gus Weyhing, Philadelphia vs. Kansas City, July 31	4-0
1890	Cannonball Titcomb, Rochester vs. Syracuse, September 15	7-0
1891	Ted Breitenstein, St. Louis vs. Louisville, October 4, first game (first major league start)	8-0

Total number of games: 15

UNION ASSOCIATION

Year		Score
1884	Dick Burns, Cincinnati at Kansas City, August 26	3-1
1884	Ed Cushman, Milwaukee vs. Washington, September 28	5-0

Total number of games: 2

AMERICAN LEAGUE

Year		Score
1902	Nixey Callahan, Chicago vs. Detroit, September 20, first game	3-0
1904	Jesse Tannehill, Boston at Chicago, August 17	6-0
1905	Weldon Henley, Philadelphia at St. Louis, July 22, first game	6-0
	Frank E. Smith, Chicago at Detroit, September 6, second game	15-0
	Bill Dinneen, Boston vs. Chicago, September 27, first game	2-0
1908	Cy Young, Boston at New York, June 30	8-0
	Bob Rhoads, Cleveland vs. Boston, September 18	2-1
	Frank Smith, Chicago vs. Philadelphia, September 20	1-0
1910	Addie Joss, Cleveland at Chicago, April 20	1-0
	Chief Bender, Philadelphia vs. Cleveland, May 12	4-0
1911	Joe Wood, Boston vs. St. Louis, July 29, first game	5-0
	Ed Walsh Sr., Chicago vs. Boston, August 27	5-0
1912	George Mullin, Detroit vs. St. Louis, July 4, second game	7-0
	Earl Hamilton, St. Louis at Detroit, August 30	5-1
1914	Joe Benz, Chicago vs. Cleveland, May 31	6-1
1916	Rube Foster, Boston vs. New York, June 21	2-0
	Bullet Joe Bush, Philadelphia vs. Cleveland, August 26	5-0
	Dutch H. Leonard, Boston vs. St. Louis, August 30	4-0
1917	Eddie Cicotte, Chicago at St. Louis, April 14	11-0
	George Mogridge, New York at Boston, April 24	2-1
	Ernie Koob, St. Louis vs. Chicago, May 5	1-0
	Bob Groom, St. Louis vs. Chicago, May 6, second game	3-0
	Babe Ruth (0 innings) and Ernie Shore (9 innings), Boston vs. Washington, June 23, first game (see note under American League "perfect games of nine or more innings")	4-0
1918	Dutch H. Leonard, Boston at Detroit, June 3	5-0
1919	Ray Caldwell, Cleveland at New York, September 10, first game	3-0
1920	Walter Johnson, Washington at Boston, July 1	1-0
1923	Sad Sam Jones, New York at Philadelphia, September 4	2-0
	Howard Ehmke, Boston at Philadelphia, September 7	4-0
1926	Ted Lyons, Chicago at Boston, August 21	6-0
1931	Wes Ferrell, Cleveland vs. St. Louis, April 29	9-0
	Bobby Burke, Washington vs. Boston, August 8	5-0
1935	Vern Kennedy, Chicago vs. Cleveland, August 31	5-0
1937	Bill Dietrich, Chicago vs. St. Louis, June 1	8-0
1938	Monte Pearson, New York vs. Cleveland, August 27, second game	13-0
1940	Bob Feller, Cleveland at Chicago, April 16 (season opener for both clubs)	1-0
1945	Dick Fowler, Philadelphia vs. St. Louis, September 9, second game	1-0

Year		Score
1946	Bob Feller, Cleveland at New York, April 30	1-0
1947	Don Black, Cleveland vs. Philadelphia, July 10, first game	3-0
	Bill McCahan, Philadelphia vs. Washington, September 3	3-0
1948	Bob Lemon, Cleveland at Detroit, June 30	2-0
1951	Bob Feller, Cleveland vs. Detroit, July 1, first game	2-1
	Allie Reynolds, New York at Cleveland, July 12	1-0
	Allie Reynolds, New York vs. Boston, September 28, first game	8-0
1952	Virgil Trucks, Detroit vs. Washington, May 15	1-0
	Virgil Trucks, Detroit at New York, August 25	1-0
1953	Bobo Holloman, St. Louis vs. Philadelphia, May 6 (first major league start)	6-0
1956	Mel Parnell, Boston vs. Chicago, July 14	4-0
1957	Bob Keegan, Chicago vs. Washington, August 20, second game	6-0
1958	Jim Bunning, Detroit at Boston, July 20, first game	3-0
	Hoyt Wilhelm, Baltimore vs. New York, September 20	1-0
1962	Bo Belinsky, Los Angeles vs. Baltimore, May 5	2-0
	Earl Wilson, Boston vs. Los Angeles, June 26	2-0
	Bill Monbouquette, Boston at Chicago, August 1	1-0
	Jack Kralick, Minnesota vs. Kansas City, August 26	1-0
1965	Dave Morehead, Boston vs. Cleveland, September 16	2-0
1966	Sonny Siebert, Cleveland vs. Washington, June 10	2-0
1967	Steve Barber (8.2 innings) and Stu Miller (.1 inning), Baltimore vs. Detroit, April 30, first game	1-2
	Dean Chance, Minnesota at Cleveland, August 25, second game	2-1
	Joel Horlen, Chicago vs. Detroit, September 10, first game	6-0
1968	Tom Phoebus, Baltimore vs. Boston, April 27	6-0
1969	Jim Palmer, Baltimore vs. Oakland, August 13	8-0
1970	Clyde Wright, California vs. Oakland, July 3	4-0
	Vida Blue, Oakland vs. Minnesota, September 21	6-0
1973	Steve Busby, Kansas City at Detroit, April 27	3-0
	Nolan Ryan, California at Kansas City, May 15	3-0
	Nolan Ryan, California at Detroit, July 15	6-0
	Jim Bibby, Texas at Oakland, July 30	6-0
1974	Steve Busby, Kansas City at Milwaukee, June 19	2-0
	Dick Bosman, Cleveland vs. Oakland, July 19	4-0
	Nolan Ryan, California at Minnesota, September 28	4-0
1975	Nolan Ryan, California vs. Baltimore, June 1	1-0
	Vida Blue (five innings), Glenn Abbott (one inning), Paul Lindblad (one inning) and Rollie Fingers (two innings), Oakland vs. California, September 28	5-0
1976	Blue Moon Odom (five innings) and Francisco Barrios (four innings), Chicago at Oakland, July 28	2-1
1977	Jim Colborn, Kansas City vs. Texas, May 14	6-0
	Dennis Eckersley, Cleveland vs. California, May 30	1-0
	Bert Blyleven, Texas at California, September 22	6-0
1983	Dave Righetti, New York vs. Boston, July 4	4-0
	Mike Warren, Oakland vs. Chicago, September 29	3-0
1984	Jack Morris, Detroit at Chicago, April 7	4-0
1986	Joe Cowley, Chicago at California, September 19	7-1
1987	Juan Nieves, Milwaukee at Baltimore, April 15	7-0
1990	Mark Langston (seven innings) and Mike Witt (two innings), California vs. Seattle, April 11	1-0
	Randy Johnson, Seattle vs. Detroit, June 2	2-0
	Nolan Ryan, Texas at Oakland, June 11	5-0
	Dave Stewart, Oakland at Toronto, June 29	5-0
	Dave Stieb, Toronto at Cleveland, September 2	3-0
1991	Nolan Ryan, Texas vs. Toronto, May 1	3-0
	Bob Milacki (six innings), Mike Flanagan (one inning), Mark Williamson (one inning) and Gregg Olson (one inning), Baltimore at Oakland, July 13	2-0
	Wilson Alvarez, Chicago at Baltimore, August 11	7-0
	Bret Saberhagen, Kansas City vs. Chicago, August 26	7-0
1993	Chris Bosio, Seattle vs. Boston, April 22	2-0
	Jim Abbott, New York vs. Cleveland, September 4	4-0
1994	Scott Erickson, Minnesota vs. Milwaukee, April 27	6-0
1996	Dwight Gooden, New York vs. Seattle, May 14	2-0
1999	Eric Milton, Minnesota vs. Anaheim, September 11	7-0
2001	Hideo Nomo, Boston at Baltimore, April 4	3-0

Note—Andy Hawkins (1990) and Matt Young (1992), as visiting teams' pitchers, pitched all eight innings of nine-inning, no-hit losses. Both are listed under the category ``No-hit games of less than nine innings.''

Total number of games (excluding Hawkins' and M. Young's): 96

NATIONAL LEAGUE

Year		Score
1876	George Bradley, St. Louis vs. Hartford, July 15	2-0
1880	Larry Corcoran, Chicago vs. Boston, August 19	6-0
	Pud Galvin, Buffalo at Worcester, August 20	1-0
1882	Larry Corcoran, Chicago vs. Worcester, September 20	5-0
1883	Hoss Radbourn, Providence at Cleveland, July 25	8-0
	Hugh Daily, Cleveland at Philadelphia, September 13	1-0
1884	Larry Corcoran, Chicago vs. Providence, June 27	6-0
	Pud Galvin, Buffalo at Detroit, August 4	18-0
1885	John Clarkson, Chicago at Providence, July 27	4-0
	Charlie J. Ferguson, Philadelphia vs. Providence, August 29	1-0

Year		Score
1891	Tom Lovett, Brooklyn vs. New York, June 22	4-0
	Amos Rusie, New York vs. Brooklyn, July 31	6-0
1892	Jack Stivetts, Boston vs. Brooklyn, August 6	11-0
	Ben Sanders, Louisville vs. Baltimore, August 22	6-2
	Bumpus Jones, Cincinnati vs. Pittsburgh, October 15 (first major league game)	7-1
1893	Bill Hawke, Baltimore vs. Washington, August 16 (first no-hitter at 60-foot, 6-inch distance)	5-0
1897	Cy Young, Cleveland vs. Cincinnati, September 18, first game	6-0
1898	Ted Breitenstein, Cincinnati vs. Pittsburgh, April 22	11-0
	Jim J. Hughes, Baltimore vs. Boston, April 22	8-0
	Frank Donahue, Philadelphia vs. Boston, July 8	5-0
	Walter Thornton, Chicago vs. Brooklyn, August 21, second game	2-0
1899	Deacon Phillippe, Louisville vs. New York, May 25	7-0
	Vic Willis, Boston vs. Washington, August 7	7-1
1900	Noodles Hahn, Cincinnati vs. Philadelphia, July 12	4-0
1901	Christy Mathewson, New York at St. Louis, July 15	5-0
1903	Chick Fraser, Philadelphia at Chicago, September 18, second game	10-0
1905	Christy Mathewson, New York at Chicago, June 13	1-0
1906	Johnny Lush, Philadelphia at Brooklyn, May 1	6-0
	Mal Eason, Brooklyn at St. Louis, July 20	2-0
1907	Frank Pfeffer, Boston vs. Cincinnati, May 8	6-0
	Nick Maddox, Pittsburgh vs. Brooklyn, September 20	2-1
1908	Hooks Wiltse, New York vs. Philadelphia, July 4, first game, 10 innings	1-0
	Nap Rucker, Brooklyn vs. Boston, September 5, second game	6-0
1912	Jeff Tesreau, New York at Philadelphia, September 6, first game	3-0
1914	George A. Davis, Boston vs. Philadelphia, September 9, second game	7-0
1915	Rube Marquard, New York vs. Brooklyn, April 15	2-0
	Jimmy Lavender, Chicago at New York, August 31, first game	2-0
1916	Tom L. Hughes, Boston vs. Pittsburgh, June 16	2-0
1917	Fred Toney, Cincinnati at Chicago, May 2, 10 innings (Hippo Vaughn of Chicago pitched 9.1 hitless innings in the same game before his no-hitter was spoiled.)	1-0
1919	Hod Eller, Cincinnati vs. St. Louis, May 11	6-0
1922	Jesse Barnes, New York vs. Philadelphia, May 7	6-0
1924	Jesse Haines, St. Louis vs. Boston, July 17	5-0
1925	Dazzy Vance, Brooklyn vs. Philadelphia, September 13, first game	10-1
1929	Carl Hubbell, New York vs. Pittsburgh, May 8	11-0
1934	Paul Dean, St. Louis at Brooklyn, September 21, second game	3-0
1938	Johnny Vander Meer, Cincinnati vs. Boston, June 11	3-0
	Johnny Vander Meer, Cincinnati at Brooklyn, June 15 (His two no-hitters were consecutive.)	6-0
1940	Tex Carleton, Brooklyn at Cincinnati, April 30	3-0
1941	Lon Warneke, St. Louis at Cincinnati, August 30	2-0
1944	Jim Tobin, Boston vs. Brooklyn, April 27	2-0
	Clyde Shoun, Cincinnati vs. Boston, May 15	1-0
1946	Ed Head, Brooklyn vs. Boston, April 23	5-0
1947	Ewell Blackwell, Cincinnati vs. Boston, June 18	6-0
1948	Rex Barney, Brooklyn at New York, September 9	2-0
1950	Vern Bickford, Boston vs. Brooklyn, August 11	7-0
1951	Cliff Chambers, Pittsburgh at Boston, May 6, second game	3-0
1952	Carl Erskine, Brooklyn vs. Chicago, June 19	5-0
1954	Jim Wilson, Milwaukee vs. Philadelphia, June 12	2-0
1955	Sam Jones, Chicago vs. Pittsburgh, May 12	4-0
1956	Carl Erskine, Brooklyn vs. New York, May 12	3-0
	Sal Maglie, Brooklyn vs. Philadelphia, September 25	5-0
1960	Don Cardwell, Chicago vs. St. Louis, May 15, second game	4-0
	Lew Burdette, Milwaukee vs. Philadelphia, August 18	1-0
	Warren Spahn, Milwaukee vs. Philadelphia, September 16	4-0
1961	Warren Spahn, Milwaukee vs. San Francisco, April 28	1-0
1962	Sandy Koufax, Los Angeles vs. New York, June 30	5-0
1963	Sandy Koufax, Los Angeles vs. San Francisco, May 11	8-0
	Don Nottebart, Houston vs. Philadelphia, May 17	4-1
	Juan Marichal, San Francisco vs. Houston, June 15	1-0
1964	Ken Johnson, Houston vs. Cincinnati, April 23	0-1
	Sandy Koufax, Los Angeles at Philadelphia, June 4	3-0
1965	Jim Maloney, Cincinnati at Chicago, August 19, first game, 10 innings	1-0
1967	Don Wilson, Houston vs. Atlanta, June 18	2-0
1968	George Culver, Cincinnati at Philadelphia, July 29, second game	6-1
	Gaylord Perry, San Francisco vs. St. Louis, September 17	1-0
	Ray Washburn, St. Louis at San Francisco, September 18	2-0
1969	Bill Stoneman, Montreal at Philadelphia, April 17	7-0
	Jim Maloney, Cincinnati vs. Houston, April 30	10-0
	Don Wilson, Houston at Cincinnati, May 1	4-0
	Ken Holtzman, Chicago vs. Atlanta, August 19	3-0
	Bob Moose, Pittsburgh at New York, September 20	4-0
1970	Dock Ellis, Pittsburgh at San Diego, June 12, first game	2-0
	Bill Singer, Los Angeles vs. Philadelphia, July 20	5-0
1971	Ken Holtzman, Chicago at Cincinnati, June 3	1-0
	Rick Wise, Philadelphia at Cincinnati, June 23	4-0
	Bob Gibson, St. Louis at Pittsburgh, August 14	11-0
1972	Burt Hooton, Chicago vs. Philadelphia, April 16	4-0

Year		Score
1972	Milt Pappas, Chicago vs. San Diego, September 2	8-0
	Bill Stoneman, Montreal vs. New York, October 2, first game	7-0
1973	Phil Niekro, Atlanta vs. San Diego, August 5	9-0
1975	Ed Halicki, San Francisco vs. New York, August 24, second game	6-0
1976	Larry Dierker, Houston vs. Montreal, July 9	6-0
	John Candelaria, Pittsburgh vs. Los Angeles, August 9	2-0
	John Montefusco, San Francisco at Atlanta, September 29	9-0
1978	Bob Forsch, St. Louis vs. Philadelphia, April 16	5-0
	Tom Seaver, Cincinnati vs. St. Louis, June 16	4-0
1979	Ken Forsch, Houston vs. Atlanta, April 7	6-0
1980	Jerry Reuss, Los Angeles at San Francisco, June 27	8-0
1981	Charlie Lea, Montreal vs. San Francisco, May 10, second game	4-0
	Nolan Ryan, Houston vs. Los Angeles, September 26	5-0
1983	Bob Forsch, St. Louis vs. Montreal, September 26	3-0
1986	Mike Scott, Houston vs. San Francisco, September 25	2-0
1990	Fernando Valenzuela, Los Angeles vs. St. Louis, June 29	6-0
	Terry Mulholland, Philadelphia vs. San Francisco, August 15	6-0
1991	Tommy Greene, Philadelphia at Montreal, May 23	2-0
	Kent Mercker (six innings), Mark Wohlers (two innings) and Alejandro Pena (one inning), Atlanta vs. San Diego, September 11	1-0
1992	Kevin Gross, Los Angeles vs. San Francisco, August 17	2-0
1993	Darryl Kile, Houston vs. New York, September 8	7-1
1994	Kent Mercker, Atlanta vs. Los Angeles, April 8	6-0
1995	Ramon Martinez, Los Angeles vs. Florida, July 14	7-0
1996	Al Leiter, Florida vs. Colorado, May 11	11-0
	Hideo Nomo, Los Angeles at Colorado, September 17	9-0
1997	Kevin Brown, Florida at San Francisco, June 10	9-0
	Francisco Cordova (nine innings) and Ricardo Rincon (one inning), Pittsburgh vs. Houston, July 12, 10 innings	3-0
1999	Jose Jimenez, St. Louis at Arizona, June 25	1-0
2001	A.J. Burnett, Florida at San Diego, May 12	3-0
	Bud Smith, St. Louis at San Diego, September 3	4-0

Total number of games: 117

NO-HIT GAMES FOR NINE OR MORE INNINGS THAT WERE BROKEN UP IN EXTRA INNINGS
AMERICAN LEAGUE

Year		Score
1901	Earl Moore, Cleveland vs. Chicago, May 9 (Moore pitched nine hitless innings before Sam Mertes singled; lost on two hits in 10 innings.)	2-4
1910	Tom L. Hughes, New York vs. Cleveland, August 30, second game (Hughes pitched 9.1 hitless innings before Harry Niles singled; lost on seven hits in 11 innings.)	0-5
1914	Jim Scott, Chicago at Washington, May 14 (Scott pitched nine hitless innings before Chick Gandil singled; lost on two hits in 10 innings.)	0-1
1934	Bobo Newsom, St. Louis vs. Boston, September 18 (Newsom pitched 9.2 hitless innings before Roy Johnson singled; lost on one hit in 10 innings.)	1-2

Total number of games: 4

NATIONAL LEAGUE

Year		Score
1904	Bob Wicker, Chicago at New York, June 11 (pitched 9.1 hitless innings before Sam Mertes singled; won on one hit in 12 innings.)	1-0
1906	Harry McIntire, Brooklyn vs. Pittsburgh, August 1. (pitched 10.2 hitless innings before Claude Ritchey singled; lost on four hits in 13 innings.)	0-1
1909	Red Ames, New York vs. Brooklyn, April 15 (pitched 9.1 hitless innings before Whitey Alperman singled; lost on seven hits in 13 innings. The game was both teams' season opener.)	0-3
1917	Hippo Vaughn, Chicago vs. Cincinnati, May 2 (pitched 9.1 hitless innings before Larry Kopf singled; lost on two hits in 10 innings. Fred Toney of Cincinnati pitched 10 no-hit innings in the same game.)	0-1
1956	Johnny Klippstein (seven innings), Hershell Freeman (one inning) and Joe Black (three innings), Cincinnati at Milwaukee, May 26 (Jack Dittmer doubled for the first hit with two outs in the 10th inning and Black lost on three hits in 11 innings.)	1-2
1965	Jim Maloney, Cincinnati vs. New York, June 14 (pitched 10 hitless innings before Johnny Lewis homered; lost on two hits in 11 innings.)	0-1
1991	Mark Gardner (nine innings) and Jeff Fassero (no innings), Montreal at Los Angeles, July 26 (Lenny Harris singled off Gardner in the 10th inning; Gardner allowed another hit and Fassero allowed one hit; Gardner lost the game in the 10th inning.)	0-1

Total number of games: 7

NO-HIT GAMES OF LESS THAN NINE INNINGS
AMERICAN ASSOCIATION

Year		Score
1884	Larry McKeon, Indianapolis at Cincinnati, May 6, six innings	0-0
1889	Matt Kilroy, Baltimore vs. St. Louis, July 29, second game, seven innings	0-0
1890	George Nicol, St. Louis vs. Philadelphia, September 23, seven innings	21-2
	Hank Gastright, Columbus vs. Toledo, October 12, eight innings	6-0

Total number of games: 4

PLAYERS LEAGUE

Year		Score
1890	Charles King, Chicago vs. Brooklyn, June 21, eight innings	0-1

Total number of games: 1

UNION ASSOCIATION

Year		Score
1884	Charlie Geggus, Washington vs. Wilmington, August 21, eight innings	12-1
	Charlie Sweeney (two innings) and Henry Boyle (three innings), St. Louis vs. St. Paul, October 5, five innings	0-1

Total number of games: 2

AMERICAN LEAGUE

Year		Score
1905	Rube Waddell, Philadelphia vs. St. Louis, August 15, five innings	2-0
1907	Ed Walsh Sr., Chicago vs. New York, May 26, five innings	8-1
1912	Jay Cashion, Washington vs. Cleveland, August 20, second game, six innings	2-0
1924	Walter Johnson, Washington vs. St. Louis, August 25, seven innings	2-0
1940	John Whitehead, St. Louis vs. Detroit, August 5, second game, six innings	4-0
1990	Andy Hawkins, New York at Chicago, July 1 (As a visiting team's pitcher, he pitched all eight innings of a nine-inning, no-hit loss.)	0-4
	Melido Perez, Chicago at New York, July 12, six innings	8-0
1992	Matt Young, Boston at Cleveland, April 12 (As a visiting team's pitcher, he pitched all eight innings of a nine-inning, no-hit loss.)	1-2

Total number of games: 8

NATIONAL LEAGUE

Year		Score
1884	Charlie Getzien, Detroit vs. Philadelphia, October 1, six innings	1-0
1885	Fred Shaw, Providence at Buffalo, October 7, first game, five innings	4-0
1888	George Van Haltren, Chicago vs. Pittsburgh, June 21, six innings	1-0
	Cannonball Crane, New York vs. Washington, September 27, seven innings	3-0
1892	Jack Stivetts, Boston at Washington, October 15, second game, five innings	4-0
1893	Elton Chamberlain, Cincinnati vs. Boston, September 23, second game, seven innings	6-0
1894	Ed Stein, Brooklyn vs. Chicago, June 2, six innings	1-0
1903	Red Ames, New York at St. Louis, September 14, second game, five innings (first major league game)	5-0
1906	Jake Weimer, Cincinnati vs. Brooklyn, August 24, second game, seven innings	1-0
	Stoney McGlynn, St. Louis at Brooklyn, September 24, second game, seven innings	1-1
	Lefty Leifield, Pittsburgh at Philadelphia, September 26, second game, six innings	8-0
1907	Howie Camnitz, Pittsburgh at New York, August 23, second game, five innings	1-0
1908	Johnny Lush, St. Louis at Brooklyn, September 6, six innings	2-0
1910	King Cole, Chicago at St. Louis, July 31, second game, seven innings	4-0
1937	Fred Frankhouse, Brooklyn vs. Cincinnati, August 27, eight innings	5-0
1944	Jim Tobin, Boston vs. Philadelphia, June 22, second game, five innings	7-0
1959	Mike McCormick, San Francisco at Philadelphia, June 12, five innings (McCormick allowed a single to Richie Ashburn in the sixth inning, but the game was halted because of rain before completion of the inning. The hit was erased because, under existing rules, records reverted to the last completed inning.)	3-0
	Sam Jones, San Francisco at St. Louis, September 26, seven innings	4-0
1988	Pascual Perez, Montreal at Philadelphia, September 24, five innings	1-0

Total number of games: 19

PLAYERS LEAGUE

		Scores	
July 26, 1890	Henry Gruber, Cleveland	6-1	8-7
Aug. 20, 1890	Bert Cunningham, Buffalo	6-2	7-0
Sept. 27, 1890	Ed Crane, New York	9-8	8-3

Total number of occurrences: 3

AMERICAN ASSOCIATION

		Scores	
July 4, 1883	Tim Keefe, New York	9-1	3-0
July 4, 1884	Guy Hecker, Louisville	5-4	8-2
July 26, 1887	Matt Kilroy, Baltimore	‡8-0	9-1
Oct. 1, 1887	Matt Kilroy, Baltimore	5-2	‡8-1
Sept. 20, 1888	Tony Mullane, Cincinnati	1-0	2-1

Total number of occurrences: 5

AMERICAN LEAGUE

		Scores	
July 1, 1905	Frank Owen, Chicago	3-2	2-0
Sept. 26, 1905	Ed Walsh, Chicago	10-5	§3-1
Sept. 22, 1906	George Mullin, Detroit	5-3	4-3
Sept. 25, 1908	Ed Summers, Detroit	7-2	∞1-0
Sept. 29, 1908	Ed Walsh, Chicago	5-1	2-0
Sept. 22, 1914	Ray Collins, Boston	5-3	§5-0
July 29, 1916	Dave Davenport, St. Louis	3-1	3-2
Aug. 30, 1918	Carl Mays, Boston	12-0	4-1
Sept. 6, 1924	Urban Shocker, St. Louis	6-2	6-2
Aug. 28, 1926	Dutch Levsen, Cleveland	6-1	5-1

Total number of occurrences: 10

NATIONAL LEAGUE

		Scores	
Sept. 19, 1876	Candy Cummings, Hartford	14-4	8-4
Aug. 9, 1878	Monte Ward, Providence	12-6	8-5
July 12, 1879	Pud Galvin, Buffalo	4-3	◆5-4
July 4, 1881	Mickey Welch, Troy	8-0	12-3
July 4, 1882	Pud Galvin, Buffalo	9-5	18-8
May 30, 1884	Hoss Radbourn, Providence	12-9	9-2
Oct. 7, 1885	Fred Shaw, Providence	*4-0	*6-1
Oct. 10, 1885	Fred Shaw, Providence	†3-0	*7-3
Oct. 9, 1886	Charlie Ferguson, Philadelphia	5-1	†6-1
Aug. 20, 1887	Jim Whitney, Washington	3-1	4-3
Sept. 12, 1889	John Clarkson, Boston	3-2	5-0
May 30, 1890	Bill Hutchinson, Chicago	6-4	11-7
Oct. 4, 1890	Cy Young, Cleveland	5-1	7-3
Sept. 12, 1891	Mark Baldwin, Pittsburgh	13-3	8-4
Sept. 28, 1891	Amos Rusie, New York	10-4	†13-5
May 30, 1892	Mark Baldwin, Pittsburgh	11-1	4-3
Sept. 5, 1892	Jack Stivetts, Boston	▲2-1	5-2
Oct. 4, 1892	Amos Rusie, New York	6-4	9-5
May 30, 1893	William Kennedy, Brooklyn	3-0	6-2
June 3, 1897	Cy Seymour, New York	6-1	‡10-6
Oct. 13, 1898	Al Orth, Philadelphia	5-1	*9-6
Aug. 1, 1903	Joe McGinnity, New York	4-1	5-2
Aug. 8, 1903	Joe McGinnity, New York	6-1	4-3
Aug. 31, 1903	Joe McGinnity, New York	4-1	9-2
Oct. 3, 1905	Doc Scanlan, Brooklyn	4-0	3-2
Sept. 26, 1908	Ed Reulbach, Chicago	5-0	3-0
Sept. 9, 1916	Pol Perritt, New York	3-1	3-0
Sept. 20, 1916	Al Demaree, Philadelphia	7-0	3-2
Sept. 23, 1916	Grover Alexander, Philadelphia	7-3	4-0
July 1, 1917	Fred Toney, Cincinnati	4-1	5-1

		Scores	
Sept. 3, 1917	Grover Alexander, Philadelphia	5-0	9-3
Sept. 18, 1917	Bill Doak, St. Louis	2-0	12-4
Aug. 13, 1921	Mule Watson, Boston	4-3	8-0
July 10, 1923	Johnny Stuart, St. Louis	11-1	6-3
July 19, 1924	Herman Bell, St. Louis	6-1	2-1

*5 innings. †6 innings. ‡7 innings. §8 innings. ∞10 innings.
▲11 innings. ◆12 innings.

Total number of occurrences: (35)

PITCHERS WITH 12 STRAIGHT VICTORIES IN SEASON

AMERICAN ASSOCIATION

Year	Pitcher	Won
1890	Scott Stratton, Louisville	15
1884	John Lynch, New York	14
1882	Will White, Cincinnati	12

Total number of occurrences: 3

UNION ASSOCIATION

Year	Pitcher	Won
1884	Jim McCormick, Cincinnati	14

Total number of occurrences: 1

AMERICAN LEAGUE

Year	Pitcher	Won
1912	Walter Johnson, Washington	16
1912	Joe Wood, Boston	16
1931	Lefty Grove, Philadelphia	16
1934	Schoolboy Rowe, Detroit	16
2001	Roger Clemens, New York	16
1932	Alvin Crowder, Washington	15
1937	Johnny Allen, Cleveland	15
1969	Dave McNally, Baltimore	15
1974	Gaylord Perry, Cleveland	15
1998	Roger Clemens, Toronto	15
1904	Jack Chesbro, New York	14
1913	Walter Johnson, Washington	14
1914	Chief Bender, Philadelphia	14
1928	Lefty Grove, Philadelphia	14
1961	Whitey Ford, New York	14
1980	Steve Stone, Baltimore	14
1986	Roger Clemens, Boston	14
1924	Walter Johnson, Washington	13
1925	Stan Coveleski, Washington	13
1930	Wes Ferrell, Cleveland	13
1940	Bobo Newsom, Detroit	13
1949	Ellis Kinder, Boston	13
1971	Dave McNally, Baltimore	13
1973	Catfish Hunter, Oakland	13
1978	Ron Guidry, New York	13
1983	LaMarr Hoyt, Chicago	13
1901	Cy Young, Boston	12
1910	Russ Ford, New York	12
1914	Dutch H. Leonard, Boston	12
1929	Tom Zachary, New York	12
1931	George Earnshaw, Philadelphia	12
1938	Johnny Allen, Cleveland	12
1939	Atley Donald, New York	12
1946	Dave Ferriss, Boston	12
1961	Luis Arroyo, New York	12
1963	Whitey Ford, New York	12
1968	Dave McNally, Baltimore	12
1971	Pat Dobson, Baltimore	12
1985	Ron Guidry, New York	12
1990	Bobby Witt, Texas	12
1991	Scott Erickson, Minnesota	12
1997	Brad Radke, Minnesota	12

Total number of occurrences: 42

NATIONAL LEAGUE

Year	Pitcher	Won
1888	Tim Keefe, New York	19
1912	Rube Marquard, New York	19
1884	Hoss Radbourn, Providence	18
1885	Mickey Welch, New York	17
1890	Pat Luby, Chicago	17
1959	Elroy Face, Pittsburgh	17

Year	Pitcher	Won
1886	Jim McCormick, Chicago	16
1936	Carl Hubbell, New York	16
1947	Ewell Blackwell, Cincinnati	16
1962	Jack Sanford, San Francisco	16
1924	Dazzy Vance, Brooklyn	15
1968	Bob Gibson, St. Louis	15
1972	Steve Carlton, Philadelphia	15
1885	Jim McCormick, Chicago	14
1886	John Flynn, Chicago	14
1904	Joe McGinnity, New York	14
1909	Ed Reulbach, Chicago	14
1984	Rick Sutcliffe, Chicago	14
1985	Dwight Gooden, New York	14
1996	John Smoltz, Atlanta	14
1880	Larry Corcoran, Chicago	13
1884	Charlie Buffinton, Boston	13
1885	John Clarkson, Chicago	13
1892	Cy Young, Cleveland	13
1893	Frank Killen, Pittsburgh	13
1896	Frank Dwyer, Cincinnati	13
1897	Fred Klobedanz, Boston	13
1898	Ted Lewis, Boston	13
1909	Christy Mathewson, New York	13
1910	Deacon Phillippe, Pittsburgh	13
1927	Burleigh Grimes, New York	13
1956	Brooks Lawrence, Cincinnati	13
1966	Phil Regan, Los Angeles	13
1971	Dock Ellis, Pittsburgh	13
1992	Tom Glavine, Atlanta	13
1886	Charlie Ferguson, Philadelphia	12
1902	Jack Chesbro, Pittsburgh	12
1904	George Wiltse, New York	12
1906	Ed Reulbach, Chicago	12
1975	Burt Hooton, Los Angeles	12
1993	Mark Portugal, Houston	12

Total number of occurrences: 41

PITCHERS WITH 12 STRAIGHT LOSSES IN SEASON

AMERICAN ASSOCIATION

Year	Pitcher	Lost
1882	Fred Nichols, Baltimore	12
1887	Billy Crowell, Cleveland	12

Total number of occurrences: 2

AMERICAN LEAGUE

Year	Pitcher	Lost
1916	John Nabors, Philadelphia	19
1980	Mike Parrott, Seattle	16
1909	Bob Groom, Washington	15
1906	Joe Harris, Boston	14
1949	Howard Judson, Chicago	14
1949	Paul Calvert, Washington	14
1979	Matt Keough, Oakland	14
1914	Guy Morton, Cleveland	13
1920	Roy Moore, Philadelphia	13
1930	Frank Henry, Chicago	13
1943	Luman Harris, Philadelphia	13
1982	Terry Felton, Minnesota	13
1901	Bill Carrick, Washington	12
1929	Red Ruffing, Boston	12
1940	Walt Masterson, Washington	12
1945	Bobo Newsom, Philadelphia	12
1945	Steve Gerkin, Philadelphia	12
1953	Charlie Bishop, Philadelphia	12

Total number of occurrences: 18

NATIONAL LEAGUE

Year	Pitcher	Lost
1910	Cliff Curtis, Boston	18
1963	Roger Craig, New York	18
1876	Dory Dean, Cincinnati	16
1899	Jim Hughey, Cleveland	16
1962	Craig Anderson, New York	16
1887	Frank Gilmore, Washington	14
1899	Fred Bates, Cleveland	14
1908	Jim Pastorius, Brooklyn	14

Year	Pitcher	Lost
1911	Buster Brown, Boston	14
1992	Anthony Young, New York	14
1884	Sam Moffett, Cleveland	13
1917	Burleigh Grimes, Pittsburgh	13
1922	Joe Oeschger, Boston	13
1935	Ben Cantwell, Boston	13
1948	Bob McCall, Chicago	13
1993	Anthony Young, New York	13
2000	Jose Lima, Houston	13
1880	William Purcell, Cincinnati	12
1883	John Coleman, Philadelphia	12
1897	Bill Hart, St. Louis	12
1902	Henry Thielman, Cincinnati	12
1905	Mal Eason, Brooklyn	12
1914	Rube Marquard, New York	12
1914	Pete Schneider, Cincinnati	12
1928	Russ Miller, Philadelphia	12
1933	Silas Johnson, Cincinnati	12
1939	Max Butcher, Philadelphia-Pittsburgh	12
1940	Hugh Mulcahy, Philadelphia	12
1962	Bob Miller, New York	12
1972	Ken Reynolds, Philadelphia	12

Total number of occurrences: 30

20-GAME WINNERS

(Numbers in parentheses after club denote
position of team at close of season)

AMERICAN ASSOCIATION

1882 (5)	W	L
Will White, Cincinnati (1)	40	12
Tony Mullane, Louisville (2)	30	24
Sam Weaver, Philadelphia (3)	26	15
George McGinnis, St. Louis (5)	25	21
Harry Salisbury, Pittsburgh (5)	20	19
1883 (8)		
Will White, Cincinnati (3)	43	22
Tim Keefe, New York (4)	41	27
Tony Mullane, St. Louis (2)	35	15
Bobby Mathews, Philadelphia (1)	30	14
George McGinnis, St. Louis (2)	29	15
Guy Hecker, Louisville (5)	28	25
Frank Mountain, Columbus (6)	26	33
Sam Weaver, Louisville (5)	24	20
1884 (12)		
Guy Hecker, Louisville (3)	52	20
Jack Lynch, New York (1)	37	15
Tim Keefe, New York (1)	37	17
Ed Morris, Columbus (2)	35	13
Tony Mullane, Toledo (8)	35	25
Will White, Cincinnati (5)	34	18
Bob Emslie, Baltimore (6)	32	18
Bobby Mathews, Philadelphia (7)	30	18
Hardie Henderson, Baltimore (6)	27	22
George McGinnis, St. Louis (4)	24	16
Frank Mountain, Columbus (2)	24	17
Billy Mountjoy, Cincinnati (5)	20	12
1885 (9)		
Bob Caruthers, St. Louis (1)	40	13
Ed Morris, Pittsburgh (3)	39	24
Dave Foutz, St. Louis (1)	33	14
Henry Porter, Brooklyn (5T)	33	21
Bobby Mathews, Philadelphia (4)	30	17
Guy Hecker, Louisville (5T)	30	24
Hardie Henderson, Baltimore (8)	26	35
Jack Lynch, New York (7)	23	21
Larry McKeon, Cincinnati (2)	20	15
1886 (11)		
Dave Foutz, St. Louis (1)	41	16
Ed Morris, Pittsburgh (2)	41	20
Tom Ramsey, Louisville (4)	37	27
Tony Mullane, Cincinnati (5)	31	27
Bob Caruthers, St. Louis (1)	30	14
Pud Galvin, Pittsburgh (2)	29	21
Matt Kilroy, Baltimore (8)	29	34
Henry Porter, Brooklyn (3)	28	20
Guy Hecker, Louisville (4)	27	23

	W	L
Al Atkinson, Philadelphia (6)	25	17
Jack Lynch, New York (7)	20	20
1887 (10)		
Matt Kilroy, Baltimore (3)	46	20
Tom Ramsey, Louisville (4)	39	27
Charles King, St. Louis (1)	34	11
Elmer Smith, Cincinnati (2)	33	18
Tony Mullane, Cincinnati (2)	31	17
Bob Caruthers, St. Louis (1)	29	9
John Smith, Baltimore (3)	29	29
Gus Weyhing, Philadelphia (5)	26	25
Ed Seward, Philadelphia (5)	25	24
Dave Foutz, St. Louis (1)	24	12
1888 (12)		
Charles King, St. Louis (1)	45	21
Ed Seward, Philadelphia (3)	34	19
Bob Caruthers, Brooklyn (2)	29	15
Gus Weyhing, Philadelphia (3)	29	19
Lee Viau, Cincinnati (4)	27	14
Tony Mullane, Cincinnati (4)	26	16
Nat Hudson, St. Louis (1)	25	11
Elton Chamberlain, 9-8 Louisville (7),		
16-4 St. Louis (1)	25	12
Mickey Hughes, Brooklyn (2)	25	13
Ed Bakely, Cleveland (6)	25	33
Elmer Smith, Cincinnati (4)	22	17
Bert Cunningham, Baltimore (5)	22	29
1889 (11)		
Bob Caruthers, Brooklyn (1)	40	12
Elton Chamberlain, St. Louis (2)	35	15
Charles King, St. Louis (2)	33	17
Jesse Duryea, Cincinnati (4)	32	21
Gus Weyhing, Philadelphia (3)	28	19
Matt Kilroy, Baltimore (5)	28	25
Mark Baldwin, Columbus (6)	26	24
Frank Foreman, Baltimore (5)	25	21
William Terry, Brooklyn (1)	21	16
Ed Seward, Philadelphia (3)	21	16
Lee Viau, Cincinnati (4)	21	19
1890 (8)		
John McMahon, 29-19 Philadelphia (8),		
7-2 Baltimore (6)	36	21
Scott Stratton, Louisville (1)	34	13
Hank Gastright, Columbus (2)	29	13
Bob Barr, Rochester (5)	28	25
Jack Stivetts, St. Louis (3)	27	21
Tom Ramsey, St. Louis (3)	26	16
Red Ehret, Louisville (1)	25	14
John Healy, Toledo (4)	22	23
1891 (8)		
John McMahon, Baltimore (3)	35	24
George Haddock, Boston (1)	34	11
Jack Stivetts, St. Louis (2)	33	22
Gus Weyhing, Philadelphia (4)	31	20
Charlie Buffinton, Boston (1)	29	9
Phil Knell, Columbus (5)	27	26
Elton Chamberlain, Philadelphia (4)	23	23
Willie McGill, 2-5 Cincinnati (5),		
19-10 St. Louis (2)	21	15

PLAYERS LEAGUE

1890 (9)	W	L
Mark Baldwin, Chicago (4)	32	24
Gus Weyhing, Brooklyn (2)	30	16
Charles King, Chicago (4)	30	22
Hoss Radbourn, Boston (1)	27	12
Adison Gumbert, Boston (1)	23	12
Hank O'Day, New York (3)	22	13
Henry Gruber, Cleveland (7)	22	23
Phil Knell, Philadelphia (5)	21	10
Harry Staley, Pittsburgh (6)	21	23

UNION ASSOCIATION

1884 (9)	W	L
Bill Sweeney, Baltimore (3)	40	21
Hugh Daily, 22-25 Chicago (6), 1-1 Washington (5),		
5-4 Pittsburgh (8)	28	30
Billy Taylor, St. Louis (1)	25	4

	W	L
Dick Burns, Cincinnati (2)	25	15
Charlie Sweeney, St. Louis (1)	24	8
Bill Wise, Washington (5)	23	20
Jim McCormick, Cincinnati (2)	22	4
Fred Shaw, Boston (4)	22	15
George Bradley, Cincinnati (2)	21	13

AMERICAN LEAGUE

1901 (5)

	W	L
Cy Young, Boston (2)	33	10
Joe McGinnity, Baltimore (5)	26	21
Clark Griffith, Chicago (1)	24	7
Roscoe Miller, Detroit (3)	23	13
Chick Fraser, Philadelphia (4)	20	15

1902 (7)

	W	L
Cy Young, Boston (3)	32	11
Rube Waddell, Philadelphia (1)	23	7
Frank Donahue, St. Louis (2)	22	11
Jack Powell, St. Louis (2)	22	17
Bill Dinneen, Boston (3)	21	21
Roy Patterson, Chicago (4)	20	12
Eddie Plank, Philadelphia (1)	20	15

1903 (7)

	W	L
Cy Young, Boston (1)	28	9
Eddie Plank, Philadelphia (2)	23	16
Bill Dinneen, Boston (3)	21	13
Willie Sudhoff, St. Louis (6)	21	15
Jack Chesbro, New York (4)	21	15
Rube Waddell, Philadelphia (2)	21	16
Tom Hughes, Boston (1)	20	7

1904 (9)

	W	L
Jack Chesbro, New York (2)	41	13
Cy Young, Boston (1)	26	16
Eddie Plank, Philadelphia (5)	26	17
Rube Waddell, Philadelphia (5)	25	19
Bill Bernhard, Cleveland (4)	23	13
Bill Dinneen, Boston (1)	23	14
Jack Powell, New York (2)	23	19
Jesse Tannehill, Boston (1)	21	11
Frank Owen, Chicago (3)	21	15

1905 (9)

	W	L
Rube Waddell, Philadelphia (1)	26	11
Eddie Plank, Philadelphia (1)	25	12
Nick Altrock, Chicago (2)	24	12
Ed Killian, Detroit (3)	23	13
Jesse Tannehill, Boston (4)	22	9
Frank Owen, Chicago (2)	21	13
George Mullin, Detroit (3)	21	20
Addie Joss, Cleveland (5)	20	11
Frank Smith, Chicago (2)	20	14

1906 (8)

	W	L
Al Orth, New York (2)	27	17
Jack Chesbro, New York (2)	24	16
Bob Rhoads, Cleveland (3)	22	10
Frank Owen, Chicago (1)	22	13
Addie Joss, Cleveland (3)	21	9
George Mullin, Detroit (6)	21	18
Nick Altrock, Chicago (1)	20	13
Otto Hess, Cleveland (3)	20	17

1907 (10)

	W	L
Addie Joss, Cleveland (4)	27	10
Guy White, Chicago (3)	27	13
Bill Donovan, Detroit (1)	25	4
Ed Killian, Detroit (1)	25	13
Eddie Plank, Philadelphia (2)	24	16
Ed Walsh, Chicago (3)	24	18
Frank Smith, Chicago (3)	22	11
Cy Young, Boston (7)	22	15
Jimmy Dygert, Philadelphia (2)	20	9
George Mullin, Detroit (1)	20	20

1908 (4)

	W	L
Ed Walsh, Chicago (3)	40	15
Addie Joss, Cleveland (2)	24	11
Ed Summers, Detroit (2)	24	12
Cy Young, Boston (5)	21	11

1909 (3)

	W	L
George Mullin, Detroit (1)	29	8
Frank Smith, Chicago (4)	25	17
Ed Willett, Detroit (1)	22	9

1910 (5)

	W	L
Jack Coombs, Philadelphia (1)	31	9
Russ Ford, New York (2)	26	6
Walter Johnson, Washington (7)	25	17
Chief Bender, Philadelphia (1)	23	5
George Mullin, Detroit (3)	21	12

1911 (7)

	W	L
Jack Coombs, Philadelphia (1)	28	12
Ed Walsh, Chicago (4)	27	18
Walter Johnson, Washington (7)	25	13
Vean Gregg, Cleveland (3)	23	7
Joe Wood, Boston (5)	23	17
Eddie Plank, Philadelphia (1)	22	8
Russ Ford, New York (6)	22	11

1912 (9)

	W	L
Joe Wood, Boston (1)	34	5
Walter Johnson, Washington (2)	33	12
Ed Walsh, Chicago (4)	27	17
Eddie Plank, Philadelphia (3)	26	6
Bob Groom, Washington (2)	24	13
Jack Coombs, Philadelphia (1)	21	10
Hugh Bedient, Boston (1)	20	9
Vean Gregg, Cleveland (5)	20	13
Tom O'Brien, Boston (1)	20	13

1913 (6)

	W	L
Walter Johnson, Washington (2)	36	7
Fred Falkenberg, Cleveland (3)	23	10
Ewell Russell, Chicago (5)	22	16
Chief Bender, Philadelphia (1)	21	10
Vean Gregg, Cleveland (3)	20	13
Jim Scott, Chicago (5)	20	20

1914 (3)

	W	L
Walter Johnson, Washington (3)	28	18
Harry Coveleski, Detroit (4)	22	12
Ray Collins, Boston (2)	20	13

1915 (5)

	W	L
Walter Johnson, Washington (4)	27	13
Jim Scott, Chicago (3)	24	11
Hooks Dauss, Detroit (2)	24	13
Red Faber, Chicago (3)	24	14
Harry Coveleski, Detroit (2)	22	13

1916 (4)

	W	L
Walter Johnson, Washington (7)	25	20
Bob Shawkey, New York (4)	24	14
Babe Ruth, Boston (1)	23	12
Harry Coveleski, Detroit (3)	21	11

1917 (5)

	W	L
Ed Cicotte, Chicago (1)	28	12
Babe Ruth, Boston (2)	24	13
Jim Bagby, Cleveland (3)	23	13
Walter Johnson, Washington (5)	23	16
Carl Mays, Boston (2)	22	9

1918 (4)

	W	L
Walter Johnson, Washington (3)	23	13
Stan Coveleski, Cleveland (2)	22	13
Carl Mays, Boston (1)	21	13
Scott Perry, Philadelphia (8)	20	19

1919 (7)

	W	L
Ed Cicotte, Chicago (1)	29	7
Lefty Williams, Chicago (1)	23	11
Stan Coveleski, Cleveland (2)	23	12
Hooks Dauss, Detroit (4)	21	9
Allen Sothoron, St. Louis (5)	21	11
Bob Shawkey, New York (3)	20	13
Walter Johnson, Washington (7)	20	14

1920 (10)

	W	L
Jim Bagby, Cleveland (1)	31	12
Carl Mays, New York (3)	26	11
Stan Coveleski, Cleveland (1)	24	14
Red Faber, Chicago (2)	23	13
Lefty Williams, Chicago (2)	22	14
Dickie Kerr, Chicago (2)	21	9
Ed Cicotte, Chicago (2)	21	10
Ray Caldwell, Cleveland (1)	20	10
Urban Shocker, St. Louis (4)	20	10
Bob Shawkey, New York (3)	20	13

1921 (5)

	W	L
Carl Mays, New York (1)	27	9
Urban Shocker, St. Louis (3)	27	12
Red Faber, Chicago (7)	25	15

	W	L
Stan Coveleski, Cleveland (2)	23	13
Sam Jones, Boston (5)	23	16
1922 (6)		
Eddie Rommel, Philadelphia (7)	27	13
Joe Bush, New York (1)	26	7
Urban Shocker, St. Louis (2)	24	17
George Uhle, Cleveland (4)	22	16
Red Faber, Chicago (5)	21	17
Bob Shawkey, New York (1)	20	12
1923 (5)		
George Uhle, Cleveland (3)	26	16
Sam Jones, New York (1)	21	8
Hooks Dauss, Detroit (2)	21	13
Urban Shocker, St. Louis (5)	20	12
Howard Ehmke, Boston (8)	20	17
1924 (4)		
Walter Johnson, Washington (1)	23	7
Herb Pennock, New York (2)	21	9
Sloppy Thurston, Chicago (8)	20	14
Joe Shaute, Cleveland (6)	20	17
1925 (4)		
Eddie Rommel, Philadelphia (2)	21	10
Ted Lyons, Chicago (5)	21	11
Stan Coveleski, Washington (1)	20	5
Walter Johnson, Washington (1)	20	7
1926 (2)		
George Uhle, Cleveland (2)	27	11
Herb Pennock, New York (1)	23	11
1927 (3)		
Waite Hoyt, New York (1)	22	7
Ted Lyons, Chicago (5)	22	14
Lefty Grove, Philadelphia (2)	20	13
1928 (5)		
Lefty Grove, Philadelphia (2)	24	8
George Pipgras, New York (1)	24	13
Waite Hoyt, New York (1)	23	7
Alvin Crowder, St. Louis (3)	21	5
Sam Gray, St. Louis (3)	20	12
1929 (3)		
George Earnshaw, Philadelphia (1)	24	8
Wes Ferrell, Cleveland (3)	21	10
Lefty Grove, Philadelphia (1)	20	6
1930 (5)		
Lefty Grove, Philadelphia (1)	28	5
Wes Ferrell, Cleveland (4)	25	13
George Earnshaw, Philadelphia (1)	22	13
Ted Lyons, Chicago (7)	22	15
Walter Stewart, St. Louis (6)	20	12
1931 (5)		
Lefty Grove, Philadelphia (1)	31	4
Wes Ferrell, Cleveland (4)	22	12
George Earnshaw, Philadelphia (1)	21	7
Lefty Gomez, New York (2)	21	9
Rube Walberg, Philadelphia (1)	20	12
1932 (5)		
Alvin Crowder, Washington (3)	26	13
Lefty Grove, Philadelphia (2)	25	10
Lefty Gomez, New York (1)	24	7
Wes Ferrell, Cleveland (4)	23	13
Monte Weaver, Washington (3)	22	10
1933 (3)		
Lefty Grove, Philadelphia (3)	24	8
Alvin Crowder, Washington (1)	24	15
Earl Whitehill, Washington (1)	22	8
1934 (4)		
Lefty Gomez, New York (2)	26	5
Schoolboy Rowe, Detroit (1)	24	8
Tommy Bridges, Detroit (1)	22	11
Mel Harder, Cleveland (3)	20	12
1935 (4)		
Wes Ferrell, Boston (4)	25	14
Mel Harder, Cleveland (3)	22	11
Tommy Bridges, Detroit (1)	21	10
Lefty Grove, Boston (4)	20	12
1936 (5)		
Tommy Bridges, Detroit (2)	23	11
Vern Kennedy, Chicago (3)	21	9
Johnny Allen, Cleveland (5)	20	10

	W	L
Red Ruffing, New York (1)	20	12
Wes Ferrell, Boston (6)	20	15
1937 (2)		
Lefty Gomez, New York (1)	21	11
Red Ruffing, New York (1)	20	7
1938 (2)		
Red Ruffing, New York (1)	21	7
Bobo Newsom, St. Louis (7)	20	16
1939 (4)		
Bob Feller, Cleveland (3)	24	9
Red Ruffing, New York (1)	21	7
Dutch E. Leonard, Washington (6)	20	8
Bobo Newsom, 3-1 St. Louis (8)		
17-10 Detroit (5)	20	11
1940 (2)		
Bob Feller, Cleveland (2)	27	11
Bobo Newsom, Detroit (1)	21	5
1941 (2)		
Bob Feller, Cleveland (4T)	25	13
Thornton Lee, Chicago (3)	22	11
1942 (2)		
Cecil Hughson, Boston (2)	22	6
Ernie Bonham, New York (1)	21	5
1943 (2)		
Spud Chandler, New York (1)	20	4
Dizzy Trout, Detroit (5)	20	12
1944 (2)		
Hal Newhouser, Detroit (2)	29	9
Dizzy Trout, Detroit (2)	27	14
1945 (3)		
Hal Newhouser, Detroit (1)	25	9
Dave Ferriss, Boston (7)	21	10
Roger Wolff, Washington (2)	20	10
1946 (5)		
Hal Newhouser, Detroit (2)	26	9
Bob Feller, Cleveland (6)	26	15
Dave Ferriss, Boston (1)	25	6
Spud Chandler, New York (3)	20	8
Cecil Hughson, Boston (1)	20	11
1947 (1)		
Bob Feller, Cleveland (4)	20	11
1948 (3)		
Hal Newhouser, Detroit (5)	21	12
Gene Bearden, Cleveland (1)	20	7
Bob Lemon, Cleveland (1)	20	14
1949 (5)		
Mel Parnell, Boston (2)	25	7
Ellis Kinder, Boston (2)	23	6
Bob Lemon, Cleveland (3)	22	10
Vic Raschi, New York (1)	21	10
Alex Kellner, Philadelphia (5)	20	12
1950 (2)		
Bob Lemon, Cleveland (4)	23	11
Vic Raschi, New York (1)	21	8
1951 (6)		
Bob Feller, Cleveland (2)	22	8
Eddie Lopat, New York (1)	21	9
Vic Raschi, New York (1)	21	10
Ned Garver, St. Louis (8)	20	12
Mike Garcia, Cleveland (2)	20	13
Early Wynn, Cleveland (2)	20	13
1952 (5)		
Bobby Shantz, Philadelphia (4)	24	7
Early Wynn, Cleveland (2)	23	12
Mike Garcia, Cleveland (2)	22	11
Bob Lemon, Cleveland (2)	22	11
Allie Reynolds, New York (1)	20	8
1953 (4)		
Bob Porterfield, Washington (5)	22	10
Mel Parnell, Boston (4)	21	8
Bob Lemon, Cleveland (2)	21	15
Virgil Trucks, 5-4 St. Louis (8)		
15-6 Chicago (3)	20	10
1954 (3)		
Bob Lemon, Cleveland (1)	23	7
Early Wynn, Cleveland (1)	23	11
Bob Grim, New York (2)	20	6
1955 (0)		

1956 (6)		W	L

	W	L
1956 (6)		
Frank Lary, Detroit (5)	21	13
Herb Score, Cleveland (2)	20	9
Early Wynn, Cleveland (2)	20	9
Billy Pierce, Chicago (3)	20	9
Bob Lemon, Cleveland (2)	20	14
Billy Hoeft, Detroit (5)	20	14
1957 (2)		
Jim Bunning, Detroit (4)	20	8
Billy Pierce, Chicago (2)	20	12
1958 (1)		
Bob Turley, New York (1)	21	7
1959 (1)		
Early Wynn, Chicago (1)	22	10
1960 (0)		
1961 (2)		
Whitey Ford, New York (1)	25	4
Frank Lary, Detroit (2)	23	9
1962 (4)		
Ralph Terry, New York (1)	23	12
Ray Herbert, Chicago (5)	20	9
Dick Donovan, Cleveland (6)	20	10
Camilo Pascual, Minnesota (2)	20	11
1963 (5)		
Whitey Ford, New York (1)	24	7
Jim Bouton, New York (1)	21	7
Camilo Pascual, Minnesota (3)	21	9
Bill Monbouquette, Boston (7)	20	10
Steve Barber, Baltimore (4)	20	13
1964 (2)		
Dean Chance, Los Angeles (5)	20	9
Gary Peters, Chicago (2)	20	8
1965 (2)		
Mudcat Grant, Minnesota (1)	21	7
Mel Stottlemyre, New York (6)	20	9
1966 (2)		
Jim Kaat, Minnesota (2)	25	13
Denny McLain, Detroit (3)	20	14
1967 (3)		
Jim Lonborg, Boston (1)	22	9
Earl Wilson, Detroit (2T)	22	11
Dean Chance, Minnesota (2T)	20	14
1968 (4)		
Denny McLain, Detroit (1)	31	6
Dave McNally, Baltimore (2)	22	10
Luis Tiant, Cleveland (3)	21	9
Mel Stottlemyre, New York (5)	21	12
1969 (6)		
Denny McLain, Detroit (2E)	24	9
Mike Cuellar, Baltimore (1E)	23	11
Jim Perry, Minnesota (1W)	20	6
Dave McNally, Baltimore (1E)	20	7
Dave Boswell, Minnesota (1W)	20	12
Mel Stottlemyre, New York (5E)	20	14
1970 (7)		
Mike Cuellar, Baltimore (1E)	24	8
Dave McNally, Baltimore (1E)	24	9
Jim Perry, Minnesota (1W)	24	12
Clyde Wright, California (3W)	22	12
Jim Palmer, Baltimore (1E)	20	10
Fritz Peterson, New York (2E)	20	11
Sam McDowell, Cleveland (5E)	20	12
1971 (10)		
Mickey Lolich, Detroit (2E)	25	14
Vida Blue, Oakland (1W)	24	8
Wilbur Wood, Chicago (3W)	22	13
Dave McNally, Baltimore (1E)	21	5
Catfish Hunter, Oakland (1W)	21	11
Pat Dobson, Baltimore (1E)	20	8
Jim Palmer, Baltimore (1E)	20	9
Mike Cuellar, Baltimore (1E)	20	9
Joe Coleman, Detroit (2E)	20	9
Andy Messersmith, California (4W)	20	13
1972 (6)		
Gaylord Perry, Cleveland (5W)	24	16
Wilbur Wood, Chicago (2W)	24	17
Mickey Lolich, Detroit (1E)	22	14
Catfish Hunter, Oakland (1W)	21	7
Jim Palmer, Baltimore (3E)	21	10
Stan Bahnsen, Chicago (2W)	21	16
1973 (12)		
Wilbur Wood, Chicago (5W)	24	20
Joe Coleman, Detroit (3E)	23	15
Jim Palmer, Baltimore (1E)	22	9
Catfish Hunter, Oakland (1W)	21	5
Ken Holtzman, Oakland (1W)	21	13
Nolan Ryan, California (4W)	21	16
Vida Blue, Oakland (1W)	20	9
Paul Splittorff, Kansas City (2W)	20	11
Jim Colborn, Milwaukee (5E)	20	12
Luis Tiant, Boston (2E)	20	13
Bill Singer, California (4W)	20	14
Bert Blyleven, Minnesota (3W)	20	17
1974 (9)		
Catfish Hunter, Oakland (1W)	25	12
Ferguson Jenkins, Texas (2W)	25	12
Mike Cuellar, Baltimore (1E)	22	10
Luis Tiant, Boston (3E)	22	13
Steve Busby, Kansas City (5W)	22	14
Nolan Ryan, California (6W)	22	16
Jim Kaat, Chicago (4W)	21	13
Gaylord Perry, Cleveland (4E)	21	13
Wilbur Wood, Chicago (4W)	20	19
1975 (5)		
Jim Palmer, Baltimore (2E)	23	11
Catfish Hunter, New York (3E)	23	14
Vida Blue, Oakland (1W)	22	11
Mike Torrez, Baltimore (2E)	20	9
Jim Kaat, Chicago (5W)	20	14
1976 (3)		
Jim Palmer, Baltimore (2E)	22	13
Luis Tiant, Boston (3E)	21	12
Wayne Garland, Baltimore (2E)	20	7
1977 (3)		
Jim Palmer, Baltimore (2TE)	20	11
Dave Goltz, Minnesota (4W)	20	11
Dennis Leonard, Kansas City (1W)	20	12
1978 (6)		
Ron Guidry, New York (1E)	25	3
Mike Caldwell, Milwaukee (3E)	22	9
Jim Palmer, Baltimore (4E)	21	12
Dennis Leonard, Kansas City (1W)	21	17
Dennis Eckersley, Boston (2E)	20	8
Ed Figueroa, New York (1E)	20	9
1979 (3)		
Mike Flanagan, Baltimore (1E)	23	9
Tommy John, New York (4E)	21	9
Jerry Koosman, Minnesota (4W)	20	13
1980 (5)		
Steve Stone, Baltimore (2E)	25	7
Tommy John, New York (1E)	22	9
Mike Norris, Oakland (2W)	22	9
Scott McGregor, Baltimore (2E)	20	8
Dennis Leonard, Kansas City (1W)	20	11
1981 (0)		
1982 (0)		
1983 (4)		
LaMarr Hoyt, Chicago (1W)	24	10
Rich Dotson, Chicago (1W)	22	7
Ron Guidry, New York (3E)	21	9
Jack Morris, Detroit (2E)	20	13
1984 (1)		
Mike Boddicker, Baltimore (5E)	20	11
1985 (2)		
Ron Guidry, New York (2E)	22	6
Bret Saberhagen, Kansas City (1W)	20	6
1986 (3)		
Roger Clemens, Boston (1E)	24	4
Jack Morris, Detroit (3E)	21	8
Ted Higuera, Milwaukee (6E)	20	11
1987 (2)		
Roger Clemens, Boston (5E)	20	9
Dave Stewart, Oakland (3W)	20	13
1988 (3)		
Frank Viola, Minnesota (2W)	24	7
Dave Stewart, Oakland (1W)	21	12
Mark Gubicza, Kansas City (3W)	20	8
1989 (2)		
Bret Saberhagen, Kansas City (2W)	23	6
Dave Stewart, Oakland (1W)	21	9

1990 (3)	W	L
Bob Welch, Oakland (1W)	27	6
Dave Stewart, Oakland (1W)	22	11
Roger Clemens, Boston (1E)	21	6

1991 (2)	W	L
Scott Erickson, Minnesota (1W)	20	8
Bill Gullickson, Detroit (2TE)	20	9

1992 (3)	W	L
Jack Morris, Toronto (1E)	21	6
Kevin Brown, Texas (4W)	21	11
Jack McDowell, Chicago (3W)	20	10

1993 (1)	W	L
Jack McDowell, Chicago (1W)	22	10

1994 (0)

1995 (0)

1996 (2)	W	L
Andy Pettitte, New York (1E)	21	8
Pat Hentgen, Toronto (4E)	20	10

1997 (3)	W	L
Roger Clemens, Toronto (5E)	21	7
Randy Johnson, Seattle (1W)	20	4
Brad Radke, Minnesota (4C)	20	10

1998 (3)	W	L
Roger Clemens, Toronto (3E)	20	6
David Cone, New York (1E)	20	7
Rick Helling, Texas (1W)	20	7

1999 (1)	W	L
Pedro Martinez, Boston (2E)	23	4

2000 (2)	W	L
Tim Hudson, Oakland (1W)	20	6
David Wells, Toronto (3E)	20	8

2001 (3)	W	L
Mark Mulder, Oakland (2W)	21	8
Roger Clemens, New York (1E)	20	3
Jamie Moyer, Seattle (1W)	20	6

NATIONAL LEAGUE

1876 (5)	W	L
Al Spalding, Chicago (1)	47	13
George Bradley, St. Louis (2)	45	19
Tommy Bond, Hartford (3)	32	13
Jim Devlin, Louisville (5)	30	34
Bobby Mathews, New York (6)	21	34

1877 (3)	W	L
Tommy Bond, Boston (1)	31	17
Jim Devlin, Louisville (2)	28	20
Terry Larkin, Hartford (3)	22	21

1878 (4)	W	L
Tommy Bond, Boston (1)	40	19
Will White, Cincinnati (2)	29	21
Terry Larkin, Chicago (4)	29	26
Monte Ward, Providence (3)	22	13

1879 (6)	W	L
Monte Ward, Providence (1)	44	18
Tommy Bond, Boston (2)	43	19
Will White, Cincinnati (5)	43	31
Pud Galvin, Buffalo (3T)	37	27
Terry Larkin, Chicago (3T)	30	23
Jim McCormick, Cleveland (6)	20	40

1880 (8)	W	L
Jim McCormick, Cleveland (3)	45	28
Larry Corcoran, Chicago (1)	43	14
Monte Ward, Providence (2)	40	23
Mickey Welch, Troy (4)	34	30
Lee Richmond, Worcester (5)	31	33
Tommy Bond, Boston (6)	26	29
Fred Goldsmith, Chicago (1)	22	3
Pud Galvin, Buffalo (7)	20	37

1881 (9)	W	L
Larry Corcoran, Chicago (1)	31	14
Jim Whitney, Boston (6)	31	33
Pud Galvin, Buffalo (3)	29	24
George Derby, Detroit (4)	29	26
Jim McCormick, Cleveland (7)	26	30
Hoss Radbourn, Providence (2)	25	11
Fred Goldsmith, Chicago (1)	25	13
Lee Richmond, Worcester (8)	25	27
Mickey Welch, Troy (5)	21	18

1882 (7)	W	L
Jim McCormick, Cleveland (5)	36	29
Hoss Radbourn, Providence (2)	31	19

	W	L
Pud Galvin, Buffalo (3T)	28	22
Fred Goldsmith, Chicago (1)	28	16
Larry Corcoran, Chicago (1)	27	13
George Weidman, Detroit (6)	26	20
Jim Whitney, Boston (3T)	24	22

1883 (9)	W	L
Hoss Radbourn, Providence (3)	49	25
Pud Galvin, Buffalo (5)	46	29
Jim Whitney, Boston (1)	37	21
Larry Corcoran, Chicago (2)	31	21
Fred Goldsmith, Chicago (2)	28	18
Jim McCormick, Cleveland (4)	27	13
Charlie Buffinton, Boston (1)	25	14
Mickey Welch, New York (6)	25	23
Hugh Daily, Cleveland (4)	24	18

1884 (7)	W	L
Hoss Radbourn, Providence (1)	60	12
Charlie Buffinton, Boston (2)	48	16
Pud Galvin, Buffalo (3)	46	22
Mickey Welch, New York (4T)	39	21
Larry Corcoran, Chicago (4T)	35	23
Jim Whitney, Boston (2)	23	14
Charlie Ferguson, Philadelphia (6)	21	24

1885 (9)	W	L
John Clarkson, Chicago (1)	53	16
Mickey Welch, New York (2)	44	11
Tim Keefe, New York (2)	32	13
Charlie Ferguson, Philadelphia (3)	26	19
Hoss Radbourn, Providence (4)	26	20
Ed Daily, Philadelphia (3)	26	22
Fred Shaw, Providence (4)	23	26
Charlie Buffinton, Boston (5)	22	27
Jim McCormick, 1-3 Providence (4) 20-4 Chicago (1)	21	7

1886 (11)	W	L
Charles Baldwin, Detroit (2)	42	13
Tim Keefe, New York (3)	42	20
John Clarkson, Chicago (1)	35	17
Mickey Welch, New York (3)	33	22
Charlie Ferguson, Philadelphia (4)	32	9
Charlie Getzien, Detroit (2)	31	11
Jim McCormick, Chicago (1)	31	11
Hoss Radbourn, Boston (5)	27	30
Dan Casey, Philadelphia (4)	25	19
John Flynn, Chicago (1)	24	6
Bill Stemmeyer, Boston (5)	22	18

1887 (11)	W	L
John Clarkson, Chicago (3)	38	21
Tim Keefe, New York (4)	35	19
Charlie Getzien, Detroit (1)	29	13
Dan Casey, Philadelphia (2)	28	13
Pud Galvin, Pittsburgh (6)	28	21
Jim Whitney, Washington (7)	24	21
Hoss Radbourn, Boston (5)	24	23
Mickey Welch, New York (4)	22	15
Michael Madden, Boston (5)	22	14
Charlie Ferguson, Philadelphia (2)	21	10
Charlie Buffinton, Philadelphia (2)	21	17

1888 (8)	W	L
Tim Keefe, New York (1)	35	12
John Clarkson, Boston (4)	33	20
Pete Conway, Detroit (5)	30	14
Ed Morris, Pittsburgh (6)	29	23
Charlie Buffinton, Philadelphia (3)	28	17
Mickey Welch, New York (1)	26	19
Gus Krock, Chicago (2)	25	14
Pud Galvin, Pittsburgh (6)	23	25

1889 (10)	W	L
John Clarkson, Boston (2)	49	19
Tim Keefe, New York (1)	28	13
Mickey Welch, New York (1)	27	12
Charlie Buffinton, Philadelphia (4)	26	17
Pud Galvin, Pittsburgh (5)	23	16
John O'Brien, Cleveland (6)	22	17
Harry Staley, Pittsburgh (5)	21	26
Hoss Radbourn, Boston (2)	20	11
Ed Beatin, Cleveland (6)	20	14
Henry Boyle, Indianapolis (7)	20	23

1890 (13)

	W	L
Bill Hutchison, Chicago (2)	42	25
Kid Gleason, Philadelphia (3)	38	16
Tom Lovett, Brooklyn (1)	32	11
Amos Rusie, New York (6)	29	30
Billy Rhines, Cincinnati (4)	28	17
Kid Nichols, Boston (5)	27	19
John Clarkson, Boston (5)	26	18
William Terry, Brooklyn (1)	25	16
Bob Caruthers, Brooklyn (1)	23	11
Charlie Getzien, Boston (5)	23	17
Tom Vickery, Philadelphia (3)	22	23
Ed Beatin, Cleveland (7)	22	31
Pat Luby, Chicago (2)	21	9

1891 (12)

	W	L
Bill Hutchison, Chicago (2)	43	19
John Clarkson, Boston (1)	33	19
Amos Rusie, New York (3)	32	19
Kid Nichols, Boston (1)	30	17
Cy Young, Cleveland (5)	27	20
Harry Staley, 4-5 Pittsburgh (8) 20-8 Boston (1)	24	13
Kid Gleason, Philadelphia (4)	24	19
Tony Mullane, Cincinnati (7)	24	25
John Ewing, New York (3)	22	8
Tom Lovett, Brooklyn (6)	21	20
Mark Baldwin, Pittsburgh (8)	21	27
Charles Esper, Philadelphia (4)	20	14

1892 (22)

	W	L
Bill Hutchison, Chicago (7)	37	34
Cy Young, Cleveland (2)	36	11
Kid Nichols, Boston (1)	35	16
Jack Stivetts, Boston (1)	35	16
George Haddock, Brooklyn (3)	31	13
Amos Rusie, New York (8)	31	28
Frank Killen, Washington (10)	30	23
George Cuppy, Cleveland (2)	28	12
Gus Weyhing, Philadelphia (4)	28	18
Mark Baldwin, Pittsburgh (6)	27	20
Ed Stein, Brooklyn (3)	26	16
John Clarkson, 8-6 Boston (1) 17-10 Cleveland (2)	25	16
Ad Gumbert, Chicago (7)	23	21
Harry Staley, Boston (1)	22	10
Charles King, New York (8)	22	24
Tony Mullane, Cincinnati (5)	21	10
William Terry 2-4, Baltimore (12) 19-6 Pittsburgh (6)	21	10
Frank Dwyer 3-11, St. Louis (11) 18-8 Cincinnati (7)	21	19
Scott Stratton, Louisville (9)	21	19
Elton Chamberlain, Cincinnati (5)	20	22
Kid Gleason, St. Louis (11)	20	24
John McMahon, Baltimore (12)	20	25

1893 (8)

	W	L
Frank Killen, Pittsburgh (2)	36	14
Kid Nichols, Boston (1)	34	14
Cy Young, Cleveland (3)	32	16
Amos Rusie, New York (5)	29	18
William Kennedy, Brooklyn (6T)	26	19
John McMahon, Baltimore (8)	24	16
Gus Weyhing, Philadelphia (4)	24	16
Jack Stivetts, Boston (1)	20	12

1894 (13)

	W	L
Amos Rusie, New York (2)	36	13
Jouett Meekin, New York (2)	34	9
Kid Nichols, Boston (3)	32	13
Ted Breitenstein, St. Louis (9)	27	22
Jack Stivetts, Boston (3)	26	14
John McMahon, Baltimore (1)	25	8
Ed Stein, Brooklyn (5)	25	15
Cy Young, Cleveland (6)	25	22
George Cuppy, Cleveland (6)	23	17
John B. Taylor, Philadelphia (4)	22	11
William Kennedy, Brooklyn (5)	22	20
Clark Griffith, Chicago (8)	21	11
Frank Dwyer, Cincinnati (10)	20	18

1895 (13)

	W	L
Cy Young, Cleveland (2)	35	10
Emerson Hawley, Pittsburgh (7)	32	21
Bill Hoffer, Baltimore (1)	30	7
John B. Taylor, Philadelphia (3)	26	13
Kid Carsey, Philadelphia (3)	26	15
Kid Nichols, Boston (5T)	26	16
Clark Griffith, Chicago (4)	25	13
George Cuppy, Cleveland (2)	25	15
William Terry, Chicago (4)	23	13
Amos Rusie, New York (9)	22	21
George Hemming, Baltimore (1)	20	10
Billy Rhines, Cincinnati (8)	20	10
Ted Breitenstein, St. Louis (11)	20	29

1896 (12)

	W	L
Kid Nichols, Boston (4)	30	14
Frank Killen, Pittsburgh (6)	29	15
Cy Young, Cleveland (2)	29	16
Bill Hoffer, Baltimore (1)	26	7
Jouett Meekin, New York (7)	26	13
Frank Dwyer, Cincinnati (3)	25	10
George Cuppy, Cleveland (2)	25	15
George Mercer, Washington (9T)	25	19
Clark Griffith, Chicago (5)	22	13
Jack Stivetts, Boston (4)	22	14
John B. Taylor, Philadelphia (8)	21	20
Emerson Hawley, Pittsburgh (6)	21	21

1897 (13)

	W	L
Kid Nichols, Boston (1)	31	11
Amos Rusie, New York (3)	29	8
Fred Klobedanz, Boston (1)	26	7
Joe Corbett, Baltimore (2)	24	8
George Mercer, Washington (6T)	24	21
Ted Breitenstein, Cincinnati (4)	23	12
Bill Hoffer, Baltimore (2)	22	10
Ed Lewis, Boston (1)	21	12
Cy Young, Cleveland (5)	21	18
Clark Griffith, Chicago (9)	21	19
Jerry Nops, Baltimore (2)	20	7
Jouett Meekin, New York (3)	20	11
Cy Seymour, New York (3)	20	14

1898 (17)

	W	L
Kid Nichols, Boston (1)	31	12
Bert Cunningham, Louisville (9)	28	15
James McJames, Baltimore (2)	27	14
Ed Lewis, Boston (1)	26	8
Clark Griffith, Chicago (4)	26	10
Emerson Hawley, Cincinnati (3)	26	12
Vic Willis, Boston (1)	25	13
Cy Young, Cleveland (5)	25	14
Cy Seymour, New York (7)	25	17
Wiley Piatt, Philadelphia (6)	24	14
Jesse Tannehill, Pittsburgh (8)	24	14
Jack Powell, Cleveland (5)	24	15
Jim Hughes, Baltimore (2)	21	11
Ted Breitenstein, Cincinnati (3)	21	14
Al Maul, Baltimore (2)	20	7
Amos Rusie, New York (7)	20	10
Jim Callahan, Chicago (4)	20	11

1899 (17)

	W	L
Jim Hughes, Brooklyn (1)	28	6
Joe McGinnity, Baltimore (4)	28	17
Vic Willis, Boston (2)	27	8
Cy Young, St. Louis (5)	26	15
Frank Hahn, Cincinnati (6)	23	7
Jim Callahan, Chicago (8)	23	12
Jesse Tannehill, Pittsburgh (7)	23	14
Wiley Piatt, Philadelphia (3)	23	15
Jack Powell, St. Louis (5)	23	21
Frank Donahue, Philadelphia (3)	22	7
Clark Griffith, Chicago (8)	22	13
Jack Dunn, Brooklyn (1)	21	13
Charles Fraser, Philadelphia (3)	21	13
Kid Nichols, Boston (2)	21	19
Frank Kitson, Baltimore (4)	20	16
Deacon Phillippe, Louisville (9)	20	17
Sam Leever, Pittsburgh (7)	20	23

1900 (5)

	W	L
Joe McGinnity, Brooklyn (1)	29	9
William Kennedy, Brooklyn (1)	22	15
Bill Dinneen, Boston (4)	21	16
Jesse Tannehill, Pittsburgh (2)	20	7
Cy Young, St. Louis (5T)	20	18

1901 (9)	W	L
Bill Donovan, Brooklyn (3)	25	15
Deacon Phillippe, Pittsburgh (1)	22	12
Frank Hahn, Cincinnati (8)	22	19
Jack Chesbro, Pittsburgh (1)	21	9
Al Orth, Philadelphia (2)	20	12
Jack Harper, St. Louis (4)	20	12
Frank Donahue, Philadelphia (2)	20	13
Christy Mathewson, New York (7)	20	17
Vic Willis, Boston (5)	20	17

1902 (7)		
Jack Chesbro, Pittsburgh (1)	28	6
Charlie Pittinger, Boston (3)	27	16
Vic Willis, Boston (3)	27	20
John W. Taylor, Chicago (5)	22	10
Frank Hahn, Cincinnati (4)	22	12
Jesse Tannehill, Pittsburgh (1)	20	6
Deacon Phillippe, Pittsburgh (1)	20	9

1903 (9)		
Joe McGinnity, New York (2)	31	20
Christy Mathewson, New York (2)	30	13
Sam Leever, Pittsburgh (1)	25	7
Deacon Phillippe, Pittsburgh (1)	25	9
Frank Hahn, Cincinnati (4)	22	12
Henry Schmidt, Brooklyn (5)	22	13
John W. Taylor, Chicago (3)	21	14
Jacob Weimer, Chicago (3)	20	8
Bob Wicker, 0-0 St. Louis (8) 20-9 Chicago (3)	20	9

1904 (7)		
Joe McGinnity, New York (1)	35	8
Christy Mathewson, New York (1)	33	12
Jack Harper, Cincinnati (3)	23	9
Kid Nichols, St. Louis (5)	21	13
Luther Taylor, New York (1)	21	15
Jacob Weimer, Chicago (2)	20	14
John W. Taylor, St. Louis (5)	20	19

1905 (8)		
Christy Mathewson, New York(1)	31	9
Charlie Pittinger, Philadelphia (4)	23	14
Leon Ames, New York (1)	22	8
Joe McGinnity, New York (1)	21	15
Sam Leever, Pittsburgh (2)	20	5
Bob Ewing, Cincinnati (5)	20	11
Deacon Phillippe, Pittsburgh (2)	20	13
Irv Young, Boston (7)	20	21

1906 (8)		
Joe McGinnity, New York (2)	27	12
Mordecai Brown, Chicago (1)	26	6
Vic Willis, Pittsburgh (3)	23	13
Sam Leever, Pittsburgh (3)	22	7
Christy Mathewson, New York (2)	22	12
Jack Pfiester, Chicago (1)	20	8
John W. Taylor, 8-9 St. Louis (7), 12-3 Chicago (1)	20	12
Jacob Weimer, Cincinnati (6)	20	14

1907 (6)		
Christy Mathewson, New York (4)	24	12
Orval Overall, Chicago (1)	23	8
Frank Sparks, Philadelphia (3)	22	8
Vic Willis, Pittsburgh (2)	21	11
Mordecai Brown, Chicago (1)	20	6
Lefty Leifield, Pittsburgh (2)	20	16

1908 (7)		
Christy Mathewson, New York (2T)	37	11
Mordecai Brown, Chicago (1)	29	9
Ed Reulbach, Chicago (1)	24	7
Nick Maddox, Pittsburgh (2T)	23	8
Vic Willis, Pittsburgh (2T)	23	11
George Wiltse, New York (2T)	23	14
George McQuillan, Philadelphia (4)	23	17

1909 (6)		
Mordecai Brown, Chicago (2)	27	9
Howie Camnitz, Pittsburgh (1)	25	6
Christy Mathewson, New York (3)	25	6
Vic Willis, Pittsburgh (1)	22	11
George Wiltse, New York (3)	20	11
Orval Overall, Chicago (2)	20	11

1910 (5)		
Christy Mathewson, New York (2)	27	9
Mordecai Brown, Chicago (1)	25	14

	W	L
Earl Moore, Philadelphia (4)	22	15
Leonard Cole, Chicago (1)	20	4
George Suggs, Cincinnati (5)	20	12

1911 (8)		
Grover Alexander, Philadelphia (4)	28	13
Christy Mathewson, New York (1)	26	13
Rube Marquard, New York (1)	24	7
Bob Harmon, St. Louis (5)	23	16
Babe Adams, Pittsburgh (3)	22	12
George Rucker, Brooklyn (7)	22	18
Mordecai Brown, Chicago (2)	21	11
Howie Camnitz, Pittsburgh (3)	20	15

1912 (5)		
Larry Cheney, Chicago (3)	26	10
Rube Marquard, New York (1)	26	11
Claude Hendrix, Pittsburgh (2)	24	9
Christy Mathewson, New York (1)	23	12
Howie Camnitz, Pittsburgh (2)	22	12

1913 (7)		
Tom Seaton, Philadelphia (2)	27	12
Christy Mathewson, New York (1)	25	11
Rube Marquard, New York (1)	23	10
Grover Alexander, Philadelphia (2)	22	8
Jeff Tesreau, New York (1)	22	13
Babe Adams, Pittsburgh (4)	21	10
Larry Cheney, Chicago (3)	21	14

1914 (9)		
Grover Alexander, Philadelphia (6)	27	15
Dick Rudolph, Boston (1)	26	10
Bill James, Boston (1)	26	7
Jeff Tesreau, New York (2)	26	10
Christy Mathewson, New York (2)	24	13
Jeff Pfeffer, Brooklyn (5)	23	12
Hippo Vaughn, Chicago (4)	21	13
Erskine Mayer, Philadelphia (6)	21	19
Larry Cheney, Chicago (4)	20	18

1915 (5)		
Grover Alexander, Philadelphia (1)	31	10
Dick Rudolph, Boston (2)	22	19
Al Mamaux, Pittsburgh (5)	21	8
Erskine Mayer, Philadelphia (1)	21	15
Hippo Vaughn, Chicago (4)	20	12

1916 (4)		
Grover Alexander, Philadelphia (2)	33	12
Jeff Pfeffer, Brooklyn (1)	25	11
Eppa Rixey, Philadelphia (2)	22	10
Al Mamaux, Pittsburgh (6)	21	15

1917 (5)		
Grover Alexander, Philadelphia (2)	30	13
Fred Toney, Cincinnati (4)	24	16
Hippo Vaughn, Chicago (5)	23	13
Ferdie Schupp, New York (1)	21	7
Pete Schneider, Cincinnati (4)	20	19

1918 (2)		
Hippo Vaughn, Chicago (1)	22	10
Claude Hendrix, Chicago (1)	20	7

1919 (3)		
Jesse Barnes, New York (2)	25	9
Harry Sallee, Cincinnati (1)	21	7
Hippo Vaughn, Chicago (3)	21	14

1920 (7)		
Grover Alexander, Chicago (5T)	27	14
Wilbur Cooper, Pittsburgh (4)	24	15
Burleigh Grimes, Brooklyn (1)	23	11
Fred Toney, New York (2)	21	11
Art Nehf, New York (2)	21	12
Bill Doak, St. Louis (5T)	20	12
Jesse Barnes, New York (2)	20	15

1921 (4)		
Burleigh Grimes, Brooklyn (5)	22	13
Wilbur Cooper, Pittsburgh (2)	22	14
Art Nehf, New York (1)	20	10
Joe Oeschger, Boston (4)	20	14

1922 (3)		
Eppa Rixey, Cincinnati (2)	25	13
Wilbur Cooper, Pittsburgh (3T)	23	14
Walt Ruether, Brooklyn (6)	21	12

1923 (7)		
Dolf Luque, Cincinnati (2)	27	8
Johnny Morrison, Pittsburgh (3)	25	13

	W	L
Grover Alexander, Chicago (4)	22	12
Pete Donohue, Cincinnati (2)	21	15
Burleigh Grimes, Brooklyn (6)	21	18
Jesse Haines, St. Louis (5)	20	13
Eppa Rixey, Cincinnati (2)	20	15
1924 (4)		
Dazzy Vance, Brooklyn (2)	28	6
Burleigh Grimes, Brooklyn (2)	22	13
Carl Mays, Cincinnati (4)	20	9
Wilbur Cooper, Pittsburgh (3)	20	14
1925 (3)		
Dazzy Vance, Brooklyn (6T)	22	9
Eppa Rixey, Cincinnati (3)	21	11
Pete Donohue, Cincinnati (3)	21	14
1926 (4)		
Remy Kremer, Pittsburgh (3)	20	6
Flint Rhem, St. Louis (1)	20	7
Lee Meadows, Pittsburgh (3)	20	9
Pete Donohue, Cincinnati (2)	20	14
1927 (4)		
Charlie Root, Chicago (4)	26	15
Jesse Haines, St. Louis (2)	24	10
Carmen Hill, Pittsburgh (1)	22	11
Grover Alexander, St. Louis (2)	21	10
1928 (6)		
Larry Benton, New York (2)	25	9
Burleigh Grimes, Pittsbrugh (4)	25	14
Dazzy Vance, Brooklyn (6)	22	10
Bill Sherdel, St. Louis (1)	21	10
Jesse Haines, St. Louis (1)	20	8
Fred Fitzsimmons, New York (2)	20	9
1929 (1)		
Pat Malone, Chicago (1)	22	10
1930 (2)		
Pat Malone, Chicago (2)	20	9
Remy Kremer, Pittsburgh (5)	20	12
1931 (0)		
1932 (2)		
Lon Warneke, Chicago (1)	22	6
Watty Clark, Brooklyn (3)	20	12
1933 (4)		
Carl Hubbell, New York (1)	23	12
Ben Cantwell, Boston (4)	20	10
Guy Bush, Chicago (3)	20	12
Dizzy Dean, St. Louis (5)	20	18
1934 (4)		
Dizzy Dean, St. Louis (1)	30	7
Hal Schumacher, New York (2)	23	10
Lon Warneke, Chicago (3)	22	10
Carl Hubbell, New York (2)	21	12
1935 (5)		
Dizzy Dean, St. Louis (2)	28	12
Carl Hubbell, New York (3)	23	12
Paul Derringer, Cincinnati (6)	22	13
Bill Lee, Chicago (1)	20	6
Lon Warneke, Chicago (1)	20	13
1936 (2)		
Carl Hubbell, New York (1)	26	6
Dizzy Dean, St. Louis (2T)	24	13
1937 (4)		
Carl Hubbell, New York (1)	22	8
Cliff Melton, New York (1)	20	9
Lou Fette, Boston (5)	20	10
Jim Turner, Boston (5)	20	11
1938 (2)		
Bill Lee, Chicago (1)	22	9
Paul Derringer, Cincinnati (4)	21	14
1939 (4)		
Bucky Walters, Cincinnati (1)	27	11
Paul Derringer, Cincinnati (1)	25	7
Curt Davis, St. Louis (2)	22	16
Luke Hamlin, Brooklyn (3)	20	13
1940 (3)		
Bucky Walters, Cincinnati (1)	22	10
Paul Derringer, Cincinnati (1)	20	12
Claude Passeau, Chicago (5)	20	13
1941 (2)		
Kirby Higbe, Brooklyn (1)	22	9
Whit Wyatt, Brooklyn (1)	22	10

	W	L
1942 (2)		
Mort Cooper, St. Louis (1)	22	7
Johnny Beazley, St. Louis (1)	21	6
1943 (3)		
Mort Cooper, St. Louis (1)	21	8
Rip Sewell, Pittsburgh (4)	21	9
Elmer Riddle, Cincinnati (2)	21	11
1944 (4)		
Bucky Walters, Cincinnati (3)	23	8
Mort Cooper, St. Louis (1)	22	7
Rip Sewell, Pittsburgh (2)	21	12
Bill Voiselle, New York (5)	21	16
1945 (2)		
Red Barrett, 2-3 Boston (6)		
21-9 St. Louis (2)	23	12
Hank Wyse, Chicago (1)	22	10
1946 (2)		
Howie Pollet, St. Louis (1)	21	10
Johnny Sain, Boston (4)	20	14
1947 (5)		
Ewell Blackwell, Cincinnati (5)	22	8
Larry Jansen, New York (4)	21	5
Warren Spahn, Boston (3)	21	10
Ralph Branca, Brooklyn (1)	21	12
Johnny Sain, Boston (4)	21	12
1948 (2)		
Johnny Sain, Boston (1)	24	15
Harry Brecheen, St. Louis (2)	20	7
1949 (2)		
Warren Spahn, Boston (4)	21	14
Howie Pollet, St. Louis (2)	20	9
1950 (3)		
Warren Spahn, Boston (4)	21	17
Robin Roberts, Philadelphia (1)	20	11
Johnny Sain, Boston (4)	20	13
1951 (7)		
Sal Maglie, New York (1)	23	6
Larry Jansen, New York (1)	23	11
Preacher Roe, Brooklyn (2)	22	3
Warren Spahn, Boston (4)	22	14
Robin Roberts, Philadelphia (5)	21	15
Don Newcombe, Brooklyn (2)	20	9
Murry Dickson, Pittsburgh (7)	20	16
1952 (1)		
Robin Roberts, Philadelphia (4)	28	7
1953 (4)		
Warren Spahn, Milwaukee (2)	23	7
Robin Roberts, Philadelphia (3T)	23	16
Carl Erskine, Brooklyn (1)	20	6
Harvey Haddix, St. Louis (3T)	20	9
1954 (3)		
Robin Roberts, Philadelphia (4)	23	15
Johnny Antonelli, New York (1)	21	7
Warren Spahn, Milwaukee (3)	21	12
1955 (2)		
Robin Roberts, Philadelphia (4)	23	14
Don Newcombe, Brooklyn (1)	20	5
1956 (3)		
Don Newcombe, Brooklyn (1)	27	7
Warren Spahn, Milwaukee (2)	20	11
Johnny Antonelli, New York (6)	20	13
1957 (1)		
Warren Spahn, Milwaukee (1)	21	11
1958 (3)		
Warren Spahn, Milwaukee (1)	22	11
Bob Friend, Pittsburgh (2)	22	14
Lew Burdette, Milwaukee (1)	20	10
1959 (3)		
Lew Burdette, Milwaukee (2)	21	15
Warren Spahn, Milwaukee (2)	21	15
Sam Jones, San Francisco (3)	21	15
1960 (3)		
Ernie Broglio, St. Louis (3)	21	9
Warren Spahn, Milwaukee (2)	21	10
Vernon Law, Pittsburgh (1)	20	9
1961 (2)		
Joey Jay, Cincinnati (1)	21	10
Warren Spahn, Milwaukee (4)	21	13
1962 (4)		
Don Drysdale, Los Angeles (2)	25	9
Jack Sanford, San Francisco (1)	24	7

	W	L
Bob Purkey, Cincinnati (3)	23	5
Joey Jay, Cincinnati (3)	21	14

1963 (5)

	W	L
Sandy Koufax, Los Angeles (1)	25	5
Juan Marichal, San Francisco (3)	25	8
Jim Maloney, Cincinnati (5)	23	7
Warren Spahn, Milwaukee (6)	23	7
Dick Ellsworth, Chicago (7)	22	10

1964 (3)

	W	L
Larry Jackson, Chicago (8)	24	11
Juan Marichal, San Francisco (4)	21	8
Ray Sadecki, St. Louis (1)	20	11

1965 (7)

	W	L
Sandy Koufax, Los Angeles (1)	26	8
Tony Cloninger, Milwaukee (5)	24	11
Don Drysdale, Los Angeles (1)	23	12
Sammy Ellis, Cincinnati (4)	22	10
Juan Marichal, San Francisco (2)	22	13
Jim Maloney, Cincinnati (4)	20	9
Bob Gibson, St. Louis (7)	20	12

1966 (5)

	W	L
Sandy Koufax, Los Angeles (1)	27	9
Juan Marichal, San Francisco (2)	25	6
Gaylord Perry, San Francisco (2)	21	8
Bob Gibson, St. Louis (6)	21	12
Chris Short, Philadelphia (4)	20	10

1967 (2)

	W	L
Mike McCormick, San Francisco (2)	22	10
Ferguson Jenkins, Chicago (3)	20	13

1968 (3)

	W	L
Juan Marichal, San Francisco (2)	26	9
Bob Gibson, St. Louis (1)	22	9
Ferguson Jenkins, Chicago (3)	20	15

1969 (9)

	W	L
Tom Seaver, New York (1E)	25	7
Phil Niekro, Atlanta (1W)	23	13
Juan Marichal, San Francisco (2W)	21	11
Ferguson Jenkins, Chicago (2E)	21	15
Bill Singer, Los Angeles (4W)	20	12
Larry Dierker, Houston (5W)	20	13
Bob Gibson, St. Louis (4E)	20	13
Bill Hands, Chicago (2E)	20	14
Claude Osteen, Los Angeles (4W)	20	15

1970 (4)

	W	L
Bob Gibson, St. Louis (4E)	23	7
Gaylord Perry, San Francisco (3W)	23	13
Ferguson Jenkins, Chicago (2E)	22	16
Jim Merritt, Cincinnati (1W)	20	12

1971 (4)

	W	L
Ferguson Jenkins, Chicago (3ET)	24	13
Al Downing, Los Angeles (2W)	20	9
Steve Carlton, St. Louis (2E)	20	9
Tom Seaver, New York (3ET)	20	10

1972 (4)

	W	L
Steve Carlton, Philadelphia (6E)	27	10
Tom Seaver, New York (3E)	21	12
Claude Osteen, Los Angeles (3W)	20	11
Ferguson Jenkins, Chicago (2E)	20	12

1973 (1)

	W	L
Ron Bryant, San Francisco (3W)	24	12

1974 (2)

	W	L
Andy Messersmith, Los Angeles (1W)	20	6
Phil Niekro, Atlanta (3W)	20	13

1975 (2)

	W	L
Tom Seaver, New York (3ET)	22	9
Randy Jones, San Diego (4W)	20	12

1976 (5)

	W	L
Randy Jones, San Diego (5W)	22	14
Jerry Koosman, New York (3E)	21	10
Don Sutton, Los Angeles (2W)	21	10
Steve Carlton, Philadelphia (1E)	20	7
J.R. Richard, Houston (3W)	20	15

1977 (6)

	W	L
Steve Carlton, Philadelphia (1E)	23	10
Tom Seaver, 7-3, New York (6E), 14-3, Cincinnati (2W)	21	6
John Candelaria, Pittsburgh (2E)	20	5
Bob Forsch, St. Louis (3E)	20	7

	W	L
Tommy John, Los Angeles (1W)	20	7
Rick Reuschel, Chicago (4E)	20	10

1978 (2)

	W	L
Gaylord Perry, San Diego (3W)	21	6
Ross Grimsley, Montreal (4E)	20	11

1979 (2)

	W	L
Joe Niekro, Houston (2W)	21	11
Phil Niekro, Atlanta (6W)	21	20

1980 (2)

	W	L
Steve Carlton, Philadelphia (1E)	24	9
Joe Niekro, Houston (1W)	20	12

1981 (0)

1982 (1)

	W	L
Steve Carlton, Philadelphia (2E)	23	11

1983 (0)

1984 (1)

	W	L
Joaquin Andujar, St. Louis (3E)	20	14

1985 (4)

	W	L
Dwight Gooden, New York (2E)	24	4
John Tudor, St. Louis (1E)	21	8
Joaquin Andujar, St. Louis (1E)	21	12
Tom Browning, Cincinnati (2W)	20	9

1986 (2)

	W	L
Fernando Valenzuela, Los Angeles (5W)	21	11
Mike Krukow, San Francisco (3W)	20	9

1987 (0)

1988 (3)

	W	L
Orel Hershiser, Los Angeles (1W)	23	8
Danny Jackson, Cincinnati (2W)	23	8
David Cone, New York (1E)	20	3

1989 (1)

	W	L
Mike Scott, Houston (3W)	20	10

1990 (3)

	W	L
Doug Drabek, Pittsburgh (1E)	22	6
Ramon Martinez, Los Angeles (2W)	20	6
Frank Viola, New York (2E)	20	12

1991 (2)

	W	L
John Smiley, Pittsburgh (1E)	20	8
Tom Glavine, Atlanta (1W)	20	11

1992 (2)

	W	L
Tom Glavine, Atlanta (1W)	20	8
Greg Maddux, Chicago (4E)	20	11

1993 (4)

	W	L
Tom Glavine, Atlanta (1W)	22	6
John Burkett, San Francisco (2W)	22	7
Bill Swift, San Francisco (2W)	21	8
Greg Maddux, Atlanta (1W)	20	10

1994 (0)

1995 (0)

1996 (1)

	W	L
John Smoltz, Atlanta (1E)	24	8

1997 (1)

	W	L
Denny Neagle, Atlanta (1E)	20	5

1998 (1)

	W	L
Tom Glavine, Atlanta (1E)	20	6

1999 (2)

	W	L
Mike Hampton, Houston (1C)	22	4
Jose Lima, Houston (1C)	21	10

2000 (2)

	W	L
Tom Glavine, Atlanta (1E)	21	9
Darryl Kile, St. Louis (1C)	20	9

2001 (4)

	W	L
Curt Schilling, Arizona (1W)	22	6
Matt Morris, St. Louis (2C)	22	8
Randy Johnson, Arizona (1W)	21	6
Jon Lieber, Chicago (3C)	20	6

TWO LEAGUES IN SEASON

1884 (4)

	W	L
Billy Taylor, 25-4 St. Louis U.A. (1), 18-12 Philadelphia A.A. (7)	43	16
Charlie Sweeney, 17-7 Providence N.L. (1), 24-8 St. Louis U.A. (1)	41	15
Jim McCormick, 19-22 Cleveland N.L. (7), 22-4 Cincinnati U.A. (2)	41	26
Fred Shaw, 8-18 Detroit N.L. (8), 22-15 Boston U.A. (4)	30	33

1902 (1)	W	L	1945 (1)	W	L
Joe McGinnity, 13-10 Baltimore A.L. (8),			Hank Borowy, 10-5 New York A.L. (4),		
8-8 New York N.L. (8) 21		18	11-2 Chicago N.L. (1)............21		7
1904 (1)			**1984 (1)**		
Patsy Flaherty, 2-2 Chicago A.L. (3),			Rick Sutcliffe, 4-5 Cleveland A.L. (6E),		
19-9 Pittsburgh N.L. (4)............21		11	16-1 Chicago N.L. (1E)............20		6

FIELDING
UNASSISTED TRIPLE PLAYS

Neal Ball, shortstop, Cleveland A.L. vs. Boston at Cleveland, July 19, 1909, first game, second inning. Ball caught McConnell's liner, touched second, retiring Wagner, who was on his way to third base, and then tagged Stahl as he came up to second.

George H. Burns, first baseman, Boston A.L. vs. Cleveland at Boston, September 14, 1923, second inning. Burns caught Brower's liner, tagged Lutzke off first and then ran to second and reached that bag before Stephenson could return from third base.

Ernie Padgett, shortstop, Boston N.L. vs. Philadelphia at Boston, October 6, 1923, second game, fourth inning. Padgett caught Holke's liner, ran to second to retire Tierney, then tagged Lee before he could return to first.

Glenn Wright, shortstop, Pittsburgh N.L. vs. St. Louis at Pittsburgh, May 7, 1925, ninth inning. Wright caught Bottomley's liner, ran to second to retire Cooney and then tagged Hornsby, who was on his way to second.

Jimmy E. Cooney, shortstop, Chicago N.L. vs. Pittsburgh at Pittsburgh, May 30, 1927, a.m. game, fourth inning. Cooney caught Paul Waner's liner, stepped on second to retire Lloyd Waner, then tagged Barnhart off first.

Johnny Neun, first baseman, Detroit A.L. vs. Cleveland at Detroit, May 31, 1927, ninth inning. Neun caught Summa's liner, ran over and tagged Jamieson between first and second and then touched second base before Myatt could return.

Ron Hansen, shortstop, Washington A.L. vs. Cleveland at Cleveland, July 30, 1968, first inning. With the count 3-and-2 on Azcue, Nelson broke for third base. Hansen caught Azcue's liner, stepped on second to double Nelson and then tagged Snyder going into second.

Mickey Morandini, second baseman, Philadelphia N.L. vs. Pittsburgh at Pittsburgh, September 20, 1992, sixth inning. Morandini caught King's liner, stepped on second to retire Van Slyke, then tagged Bonds coming from first.

John Valentin, shortstop, Boston A.L. vs. Seattle at Boston, July 8, 1994, sixth inning. Valentin caught Newfield's line drive, stepped on second to retire Blowers, then tagged Mitchell coming from first.

Randy Velarde, second baseman, Oakland A.L. vs. New York at New York, May 29, 2000, sixth inning. Velarde caught Spencer's line drive, tagged Posada off first, then stepped on second to retire Martinez.

(Note: All above unassisted triple plays made with runners on first and second bases only. In addition to the nine regular-season unassisted triple plays, Bill Wambsganss turned one in the 1920 World Series. For details see World Series General Reference section.)

Total number of occurrences (excluding Wambsganss'): 10

CLUB MISCELLANEOUS
LIFETIME FRANCHISE WON-LOST RECORDS
CURRENT AMERICAN LEAGUE CLUBS (1901 THROUGH 2001)

Present franchise	Years	Total Games	Won	Lost	Tied	Pct.
Anaheim*	1961-2001	6,515	3,144	3,368	3	.483
Baltimore............	1954-2001	7,576	3,990	3,575	11	.527
Boston............	1901-2001	15,678	7,977	7,617	84	.512
Chicago	1901-2001	15,685	7,861	7,721	103	.504
Cleveland	1901-2001	15,691	7,987	7,613	91	.512
Detroit............	1901-2001	15,718	7,980	7,644	94	.511
Kansas City............	1969-2001	5,209	2,613	2,594	2	.502
Minnesota............	1961-2001	6,510	3,206	3,296	8	.493
New York............	1903-2001	15,390	8,674	6,629	87	.567
Oakland	1968-2001	5,379	2,777	2,601	1	.516
Seattle	1977-2001	3,927	1,831	2,094	2	.466
Tampa Bay............	1998-2001	647	263	384	0	.406
Texas	1972-2001	4,728	2,285	2,438	5	.484
Toronto............	1977-2001	3,928	1,947	1,979	2	.496
Present Totals		122,581	62,535	59,553	493	.512

*Known as Los Angeles 1961-65, California 1966-96.

EXTINCT AMERICAN LEAGUE CLUBS (1901 THROUGH 1997)

Extinct franchise	Years	Total Games	Won	Lost	Tied	Pct.
Baltimore............	1901-02	276	118	153	5	.437
Kansas City............	1955-67	2,060	829	1,224	7	.404
Milwaukee (original club)	1901	139	48	89	2	.353
Milwaukee (second club)	1970-97	4,407	2,136	2,269	2	.485
Philadelphia............	1901-54	8,213	3,886	4,248	79	.478
St. Louis............	1902-53	7,974	3,414	4,465	95	.434
Seattle............	1969	163	64	98	1	.396
Washington (original club)............	1901-60	9,188	4,223	4,864	101	.465
Washington (second club)	1961-71	1,773	740	1,032	1	.418
Extinct totals............		34,193	15,458	18,442	293	.456
American League totals		156,774	77,993	77,995	786	.500

CURRENT NATIONAL LEAGUE CLUBS (1876 THROUGH 2001)

Present franchise	Years	Total Games	Won	Lost	Tied	Pct.
Arizona	1998-2001	648	342	306	0	.528
Atlanta	1966-2001	5,698	2,881	2,810	7	.506
Chicago	1876-2001	18,627	9,512	8,961	154	.515
Cincinnati	1890-2001	17,256	8,675	8,456	125	.506
Colorado	1993-2001	1,395	667	728	0	.478
Florida	1993-2001	1,391	627	764	0	.451
Houston	1962-2001	6,356	3,145	3,207	4	.495
Los Angeles	1958-2001	6,978	3,741	3,231	6	.537
Milwaukee	1998-2001	648	289	358	1	.447
Montreal	1969-2001	5,216	2,522	2,690	4	.484
New York	1962-2001	6,350	3,016	3,326	8	.476
Philadelphia	1883-2001	18,024	8,339	9,572	113	.466
Pittsburgh	1887-2001	17,636	8,967	8,540	129	.512
St. Louis	1892-2001	16,983	8,514	8,340	129	.505
San Diego	1969-2001	5,221	2,394	2,825	2	.459
San Francisco	1958-2001	6,979	3,609	3,365	5	.517
Present Totals		135,406	67,240	67,479	687	.499

NOTE: For purposes of these charts, totals for the current Milwaukee Brewers franchise include only their National League totals in the Current National League Clubs chart and their American League totals in the Extinct American League Clubs chart.

EXTINCT NATIONAL LEAGUE CLUBS (1876 THROUGH 1965)

Extinct franchise	Years	Total Games	Won	Lost	Tied	Pct.
Baltimore	1892-99	1,117	644	447	26	.588
Boston	1876-52	10,852	5,118	5,598	136	.478
Brooklyn	1890-57	10,253	5,214	4,926	113	.514
Buffalo	1879-85	656	314	333	9	.486
Cincinnati	1876-80	348	125	217	6	.368
Cleveland	1879-84	549	242	299	8	.448
Cleveland	1889-99	1,534	738	764	32	.492
Detroit	1881-88	879	426	437	16	.494
Hartford	1876-77	129	78	48	3	.619
Indianapolis	1878	63	24	36	3	.405
Indianapolis	1887-89	398	146	249	3	.371
Kansas City	1886	126	30	91	5	.258
Louisville	1876-77	130	65	61	4	.515
Louisville	1892-99	1,121	419	683	19	.382
Milwaukee	1878	61	15	45	1	.254
Milwaukee	1953-65	2,044	1,146	890	8	.563
New York	1876	57	21	35	1	.377
New York	1883-57	11,116	6,067	4,898	151	.553
Philadelphia	1876	60	14	45	1	.242
Providence	1878-85	725	438	278	9	.610
St. Louis	1876-77	124	73	51	0	.589
St. Louis	1885-86	236	79	151	6	.347
Syracuse	1879	71	22	48	1	.317
Troy	1879-82	330	134	191	5	.414
Washington	1886-89	514	163	337	14	.331
Washington	1892-99	1,125	410	697	18	.372
Worcester	1880-82	252	90	159	3	.363
Extinct totals		44,870	22,255	22,014	601	.503
National League totals		180,276	89,495	89,493	1,288	.500

AMERICAN ASSOCIATION CLUBS (1882 THROUGH 1891)

Extinct franchise	Years	Total Games	Won	Lost	Tied	Pct.
Baltimore	1882-89	944	403	519	22	.439
Baltimore	1890-91	174	87	81	6	.517
Boston	1891	139	93	42	4	.684
Brooklyn	1884-89	783	410	354	19	.536
Brooklyn	1890	101	26	74	1	.262
Cincinnati	1882-89	957	549	396	12	.580
Cincinnati	1891	102	43	57	2	.431
Cleveland	1887-88	268	89	174	5	.341
Columbus	1883-84	207	101	104	2	.493
Columbus	1889-91	418	200	209	9	.489
Indianapolis	1884	110	29	78	3	.277
Kansas City	1888-89	271	98	171	2	.365
Louisville	1882-91	1,233	575	638	20	.475
Milwaukee	1891	36	21	15	0	.583
New York	1883-87	592	270	309	13	.467
Philadelphia	1882-91	1,223	633	564	26	.528
Pittsburgh	1882-86	538	236	296	6	.444
Richmond	1884	46	12	30	4	.304
Rochester	1890	133	63	63	7	.500

Extinct franchise	Years	Total Games	Won	Lost	Tied	Pct.
St. Louis	1882-91	1,235	782	433	20	.641
Syracuse	1890	128	55	72	1	.434
Toledo	1884	110	46	58	6	.446
Toledo	1890	134	68	64	2	.515
Washington	1884	63	12	51	0	.191
Washington	1891	139	43	92	4	.324
American Association totals		10,084	4,944	4,944	196	.500

CLUBS WITH 100 VICTORIES IN SEASON

AMERICAN LEAGUE

Year	Club	Won	Lost	Pct.
2001	Seattle	116	46	.716
1998	New York	114	48	.704
1954	Cleveland	111	43	.721
1927	New York	110	44	.714
1961	New York	109	53	.673
1969	Baltimore	109	53	.673
1970	Baltimore	108	54	.667
1931	Philadelphia	107	45	.704
1932	New York	107	47	.695
1939	New York	106	45	.702
1912	Boston	105	47	.691
1929	Philadelphia	104	46	.693
1946	Boston	104	50	.675
1963	New York	104	57	.646
1984	Detroit	104	58	.642
1988	Oakland	104	58	.642
1942	New York	103	51	.669
1954	New York	103	51	.669
1968	Detroit	103	59	.636
1980	New York	103	59	.636
1990	Oakland	103	59	.636
1910	Philadelphia	102	48	.680
1936	New York	102	51	.667
1930	Philadelphia	102	52	.662
1937	New York	102	52	.662
1979	Baltimore	102	57	.642
1965	Minnesota	102	60	.630
1977	Kansas City	102	60	.630
2001	Oakland	102	60	.630
1911	Philadelphia	101	50	.669
1915	Boston	101	50	.669
1928	New York	101	53	.656
1934	Detroit	101	53	.656
1941	New York	101	53	.656
1971	Baltimore	101	57	.639
1971	Oakland	101	60	.627
1961	Detroit	101	61	.623
1995	Cleveland	100	44	.694
1915	Detroit	100	54	.649
1917	Chicago	100	54	.649
1977	New York	100	62	.617
1980	Baltimore	100	62	.617
1978	New York	100	63	.613

NATIONAL LEAGUE

Year	Club	Won	Lost	Pct.
1906	Chicago	116	36	.763
1909	Pittsburgh	110	42	.724
1975	Cincinnati	108	54	.667
1986	New York	108	54	.667
1907	Chicago	107	45	.704
1904	New York	106	47	.693
1942	St. Louis	106	48	.688
1998	Atlanta	106	56	.654
1905	New York	105	48	.686
1943	St. Louis	105	49	.682
1944	St. Louis	105	49	.682
1953	Brooklyn	105	49	.682
1909	Chicago	104	49	.680
1910	Chicago	104	50	.675
1942	Brooklyn	104	50	.675
1993	Atlanta	104	58	.642
1902	Pittsburgh	103	36	.741
1912	New York	103	48	.682
1993	San Francisco	103	59	.636
1999	Atlanta	103	59	.636
1962	San Francisco	103	62	.624
1898	Boston	102	47	.685
1892	Boston	102	48	.680
1970	Cincinnati	102	60	.630
1998	Houston	102	60	.630
1974	Los Angeles	102	60	.630
1976	Cincinnati	102	60	.630
1962	Los Angeles	102	63	.618
1899	Brooklyn	101	47	.682
1913	New York	101	51	.664
1931	St. Louis	101	53	.656
1967	St. Louis	101	60	.627
1976	Philadelphia	101	61	.623
1977	Philadelphia	101	61	.623
1985	St. Louis	101	61	.623
1997	Atlanta	101	61	.623
1940	Cincinnati	100	53	.654
1935	Chicago	100	54	.649
1941	Brooklyn	100	54	.649
1988	New York	100	60	.625
1969	New York	100	62	.617
1999	Arizona	100	62	.617

CLUBS WITH 100 LOSSES IN SEASON

AMERICAN ASSOCIATION

Year	Club	Won	Lost	Pct.
1890	Pittsburgh	23	113	.169
1889	Louisville	27	111	.196

AMERICAN LEAGUE

Year	Club	Won	Lost	Pct.
1916	Philadelphia	36	117	.235
1904	Washington	38	113	.251
1932	Boston	43	111	.279
1939	St. Louis	43	111	.279
1909	Washington	42	110	.276
1915	Philadelphia	43	109	.283
1996	Detroit	53	109	.327
1979	Toronto	53	109	.327
1937	St. Louis	46	108	.299
1979	Oakland	54	108	.333
1911	St. Louis	45	107	.296
1926	Boston	46	107	.301
1910	St. Louis	47	107	.305
1988	Baltimore	54	107	.335
1977	Toronto	54	107	.335
1920	Philadelphia	48	106	.312
1970	Chicago	56	106	.346
1963	Washington	56	106	.346
1925	Boston	47	105	.309
1906	Boston	49	105	.318
1943	Philadelphia	49	105	.318
1946	Philadelphia	49	105	.318
1991	Cleveland	57	105	.352
1964	Kansas City	57	105	.352
1973	Texas	57	105	.352
1919	Philadelphia	36	104	.257
1952	Detroit	50	104	.325
1949	Washington	50	104	.325
1978	Seattle	56	104	.350
1927	Boston	51	103	.331
1908	New York	51	103	.331
1954	Philadelphia	51	103	.331
1989	Detroit	59	103	.364

Year	Club	Won	Lost	Pct.
1965	Kansas City	59	103	.364
1980	Seattle	59	103	.364
1932	Chicago	49	102	.325
1907	Washington	49	102	.325
1912	New York	50	102	.329
1914	Cleveland	51	102	.333
1930	Boston	52	102	.338
1956	Kansas City	52	102	.338
1950	Philadelphia	52	102	.338
1951	St. Louis	52	102	.338
1975	Detroit	57	102	.358
1978	Toronto	59	102	.366
1971	Cleveland	60	102	.370
1985	Cleveland	60	102	.370
1982	Minnesota	60	102	.370
1983	Seattle	60	102	.370
1948	Chicago	51	101	.336
1912	St. Louis	53	101	.344
1949	St. Louis	53	101	.344
1955	Washington	53	101	.344
1962	Washington	60	101	.373
1987	Cleveland	61	101	.377
1921	Philadelphia	53	100	.346
1936	Philadelphia	53	100	.346
1954	Baltimore	54	100	.351
1940	Philadelphia	54	100	.351
1953	St. Louis	54	100	.351
1972	Texas	54	100	.351
1961	Kansas City	61	100	.379
1961	Washington	61	100	.379
1965	Boston	62	100	.383
1964	Washington	62	100	.383
2001	Tampa Bay	62	100	.383

Year	Club	Won	Lost	Pct.
1898	Washington	51	101	.336
1912	Boston	52	101	.340
1907	St. Louis	52	101	.340
1908	Brooklyn	53	101	.344
1954	Pittsburgh	53	101	.344
1977	Atlanta	61	101	.377
1982	Cincinnati	61	101	.377
1967	New York	61	101	.377
1993	San Diego	61	101	.377
1904	Philadelphia	52	100	.342
1910	Boston	53	100	.346
1922	Boston	53	100	.346
1924	Boston	53	100	.346
1923	Boston	54	100	.351
1936	Philadelphia	54	100	.351
1971	San Diego	61	100	.379
1985	San Francisco	62	100	.383
2001	Pittsburgh	62	100	.383

NATIONAL LEAGUE

Year	Club	Won	Lost	Pct.
1899	Cleveland	20	134	.130
1962	New York	40	120	.250
1935	Boston	38	115	.248
1952	Pittsburgh	42	112	.273
1965	New York	50	112	.309
1898	St. Louis	39	111	.260
1941	Philadelphia	43	111	.279
1963	New York	51	111	.315
1969	Montreal	52	110	.321
1969	San Diego	52	110	.321
1942	Philadelphia	42	109	.278
1928	Philadelphia	43	109	.283
1964	New York	53	109	.327
1909	Boston	45	108	.294
1945	Philadelphia	46	108	.299
1998	Florida	54	108	.333
1911	Boston	44	107	.291
1961	Philadelphia	47	107	.305
1976	Montreal	55	107	.340
1939	Philadelphia	45	106	.298
1988	Atlanta	54	106	.338
1938	Philadelphia	45	105	.300
1908	St. Louis	49	105	.318
1905	Brooklyn	48	104	.316
1923	Philadelphia	50	104	.325
1953	Pittsburgh	50	104	.325
1985	Pittsburgh	57	104	.354
1928	Boston	50	103	.327
1940	Philadelphia	50	103	.327
1905	Boston	51	103	.331
1921	Philadelphia	51	103	.331
1927	Philadelphia	51	103	.331
1917	Pittsburgh	51	103	.331
1962	Chicago	59	103	.364
1966	Chicago	59	103	.364
1993	New York	59	103	.364
1897	St. Louis	29	102	.221
1906	Boston	49	102	.325
1930	Philadelphia	52	102	.338
1973	San Diego	60	102	.370
1974	San Diego	60	102	.370
1892	Baltimore	46	101	.313

CLUBS WITH 13 STRAIGHT VICTORIES IN SEASON

AMERICAN ASSOCIATION

Year	Club	G	Home	Away
1885	St. Louis	17	14	3
1887	St. Louis	15	15	0
1889	Philadelphia (1 tie)	14	13	1

UNION ASSOCIATION

Year	Club	G	Home	Away
1884	St. Louis	20	16	4
1884	Baltimore	16	7	9

AMERICAN LEAGUE

Year	Club	G	Home	Away
1906	Chicago (1 tie)	19	11	8
1947	New York	19	6	13
1953	New York	18	3	15
1912	Washington	17	1	16
1931	Philadelphia	17	5	12
1926	New York	16	12	4
1977	Kansas City	16	9	7
1906	New York	15	12	3
1913	Philadelphia	15	13	2
1946	Boston	15	11	4
1960	New York	15	9	6
1991	Minnesota	15	10	5
2001	Seattle	15	10	5
1909	Detroit	14	14	0
1916	St. Louis	14	13	1
1934	Detroit	14	9	5
1941	New York	14	6	8
1951	Chicago	14	3	11
1973	Baltimore	14	10	4
1988	Oakland	14	5	9
1991	Texas	14	7	7
1994	Kansas City	14	12	2
1908	Chicago	13	12	1
1910	Philadelphia (1 tie)	13	12	1
1927	Detroit (1 tie)	13	13	0
1931	Philadelphia	13	13	0
1933	Washington	13	1	12
1942	Cleveland	13	4	9
1948	Boston	13	12	1
1951	Cleveland	13	7	6
1954	New York	13	8	5
1961	New York	13	12	1
1978	Baltimore	13	3	10
1987	Milwaukee	13	6	7
1999	Baltimore	13	5	8

NATIONAL LEAGUE

Year	Club	G	Home	Away
1916	New York (1 tie)	26	26	0
1880	Chicago (1 tie)	21	11	10
1935	Chicago	21	18	3
1884	Providence	20	16	4
1885	Chicago	18	14	4

Year	Club	G	Home	Away
1891	Boston (1 tie)	18	16	2
1894	Baltimore	18	13	5
1904	New York	18	13	5
1897	Boston	17	16	1
1907	New York	17	14	3
1916	New York	17	0	17
1887	Philadelphia (1 tie)	16	5	11
1890	Philadelphia	16	14	2
1892	Philadelphia	16	11	5
1909	Pittsburgh	16	12	4
1912	New York	16	11	5
1951	New York	16	13	3
1886	Detroit	15	12	3
1903	Pittsburgh	15	11	4
1924	Brooklyn	15	3	12
1936	Chicago	15	11	4
1936	New York	15	7	8
2000	Atlanta	15	9	6
1886	Chicago	14	13	1
1895	Baltimore	14	13	1
1899	Cincinnati	14	10	4
1903	Pittsburgh (1 tie)	14	7	7
1906	Chicago	14	14	0
1909	Pittsburgh	14	12	2
1913	New York	14	6	8
1932	Chicago	14	14	0
1935	St. Louis	14	12	2
1965	San Francisco	14	6	8
1999	San Diego	14	10	4
1880	Chicago	13	9	4
1890	Cincinnati	13	13	0
1892	Chicago	13	11	2
1905	New York	13	8	5
1911	Pittsburgh	13	9	4
1922	Pittsburgh	13	2	11
1928	Chicago	13	13	0
1938	Pittsburgh	13	5	8
1947	Brooklyn	13	2	11
1953	Brooklyn	13	7	6
1962	Los Angeles	13	8	5
1965	Los Angeles	13	7	6
1977	Philadelphia	13	8	5
1982	Atlanta	13	5	8
1991	Philadelphia	13	9	4
1992	Atlanta	13	3	10

CLUBS WITH 13 STRAIGHT LOSSES IN SEASON

AMERICAN ASSOCIATION

Year	Club	G	Home	Away
1889	Louisville	26	5	21
1890	Philadelphia	22	6	16
1882	Baltimore	15	0	15
1884	Washington	15	0	15
1891	Louisville	15	0	15
1889	Louisville	14	14	0
1886	Louisville	13	0	13
1890	Brooklyn	13	0	13

UNION ASSOCIATION

Year	Club	G	Home	Away
1884	Kansas City (1 tie)	15	3	12
1884	Kansas City	14	0	14

AMERICAN LEAGUE

Year	Club	G	Home	Away
1988	Baltimore	21	8	13
1906	Boston	20	19	1
1916	Philadelphia	20	1	19
1943	Philadelphia	20	3	17
1975	Detroit	19	9	10
1920	Philadelphia	18	0	18
1948	Washington	18	8	10
1959	Washington	18	3	15
1926	Boston	17	14	3
1907	Boston (2 ties)	16	9	7

Year	Club	G	Home	Away
1927	Boston	15	10	5
1937	Philadelphia (1 tie)	15	10	5
1972	Texas	15	5	10
1911	St. Louis	14	6	8
1930	Boston	14	3	11
1940	St. Louis	14	0	14
1945	Philadelphia	14	0	14
1953	St. Louis	14	14	0
1954	Baltimore	14	7	7
1961	Washington	14	11	3
1970	Washington	14	4	10
1977	Oakland	14	9	5
1982	Minnesota	14	6	8
1992	Seattle	14	4	10
1994	Milwaukee	14	6	8
1904	Washington (1 tie)	13	7	6
1913	New York	13	7	6
1920	Detroit	13	5	8
1924	Chicago	13	2	11
1935	Philadelphia	13	10	3
1936	St. Louis	13	2	11
1953	Detroit (2 ties)	13	12	1
1958	Washington	13	4	9
1959	Kansas City	13	4	9
1961	Minnesota	13	0	13
1962	Washington	13	7	6

NATIONAL LEAGUE

Year	Club	G	Home	Away
1899	Cleveland	24	5	19
1890	Pittsburgh	23	1	22
1961	Philadelphia	23	6	17
1894	Louisville	20	0	20
1969	Montreal	20	12	8
1906	Boston	19	3	16
1914	Cincinnati	19	6	13
1876	Cincinnati	18	9	9
1894	Louisville	18	0	18
1897	St. Louis	18	4	14
1894	Washington	17	4	13
1962	New York	17	7	10
1977	Atlanta	17	8	9
1882	Troy (1 tie)	16	5	11
1885	Buffalo	16	12	4
1888	Detroit	16	5	11
1899	Cleveland	16	0	16
1907	Boston	16	5	11
1911	Boston	16	8	8
1944	Brooklyn	16	0	16
1895	Louisville	15	10	5
1909	Boston	15	0	15
1909	St. Louis	15	11	4
1927	Boston	15	0	15
1935	Boston	15	0	15
1963	New York	15	8	7
1982	New York	15	6	9
1878	Milwaukee	14	9	5
1882	Worcester	14	2	12
1883	Philadelphia	14	4	10
1896	St. Louis (1 tie)	14	9	5
1898	Washington	14	3	11
1899	Cleveland	14	1	13
1905	St. Louis	14	9	5
1911	Boston	14	14	0
1916	St. Louis	14	0	14
1927	Philadelphia	14	1	13
1935	Boston	14	4	10
1936	Philadelphia	14	10	4
1937	Brooklyn	14	0	14
1937	Cincinnati	14	10	4
1997	Chicago	14	6	8
1876	Cincinnati	13	6	7
1877	Cincinnati	13	3	10
1884	Cleveland	13	1	12
1885	Detroit	13	1	12
1885	Providence	13	2	11
1886	Washington	13	13	0

Year	Club	G	Home	Away
1886	Kansas City (2 ties)	13	0	13
1888	Indianapolis	13	0	13
1890	Pittsburgh	13	2	11
1892	Baltimore	13	2	11
1899	Cleveland	13	3	10
1902	New York	13	4	9
1909	Boston	13	13	0
1910	St. Louis	13	5	8
1919	Philadelphia	13	0	13
1919	Philadelphia	13	7	6
1930	Cincinnati	13	1	12
1942	Philadelphia	13	4	9
1944	Chicago	13	7	6
1944	New York	13	0	13
1945	Cincinnati	13	2	11
1955	Philadelphia	13	9	4
1962	New York	13	9	4
1976	Atlanta	13	6	7
1980	New York	13	3	10
1982	Chicago	13	7	6
1985	Chicago	13	4	9
1993	Colorado	13	7	6
1994	San Diego	13	4	9

CLUBS WINNING FIRST EIGHT GAMES OF SEASON

AMERICAN ASSOCIATION

Never accomplished

UNION ASSOCIATION

Year	Club	G	Home	Away
1884	St. Louis	20	16	4

AMERICAN LEAGUE

Year	Club	G	Home	Away
1987	Milwaukee	13	6	7
1981	Oakland	11	3	8
1966	Cleveland	10	8	2
1944	St. Louis	9	5	4
1984	Detroit	9	3	6
1982	Chicago	8	3	5

NATIONAL LEAGUE

Year	Club	G	Home	Away
1982	Atlanta	13	5	8
1884	New York	12	12	0
1955	Brooklyn	10	3	7
1962	Pittsburgh	10	3	7
1888	Boston	9	0	9
1918	New York	9	6	3
1940	Brooklyn	9	3	6
1990	Cincinnati	9	3	6
1881	Worcester	8	3	5
1915	Philadelphia	8	2	6
1980	Cincinnati	8	1	7

CLUBS LOSING FIRST EIGHT GAMES OF SEASON

AMERICAN ASSOCIATION

Year	Club	G	Home	Away
1884	Toledo	8	0	8
1887	New York	10	0	10

UNION ASSOCIATION

Year	Club	G	Home	Away
1884	Altoona	11	4	7

AMERICAN LEAGUE

Year	Club	G	Home	Away
1988	Baltimore	21	8	13
1904	Washington (1 tie)	13	7	6
1920	Detroit	13	5	8
1968	Chicago	10	4	6
1914	Cleveland	8	1	7
1945	Boston	8	3	5
1952	Detroit	8	3	5

NATIONAL LEAGUE

Year	Club	G	Home	Away
1997	Chicago	14	6	8
1884	Detroit	11	0	11
1988	Atlanta	10	8	2
1918	Brooklyn	9	3	6
1919	Boston	9	5	4
1962	New York	9	6	3
1983	Houston	9	6	3
1883	Philadelphia	8	6	2
1889	Washington	8	4	4
1955	Pittsburgh	8	4	4
1963	New York	8	2	6

GAMES OF 18 OR MORE INNINGS

AMERICAN LEAGUE

25 Innings—(1)
Chicago 7 vs. Milwaukee 6, May 8, finished May 9, 1984.
24 Innings—(2)
Philadelphia 4 at Boston 1, September 1, 1906.
Detroit 1 at Philadelphia 1 (tie), July 21, 1945.
22 Innings—(4)
New York 9 at Detroit 7, June 24, 1962.
Washington 6 vs. Chicago 5, June 12, 1967.
Milwaukee 4 at Minnesota 3, May 12, finished May 13, 1972.
Minnesota 5 vs. Cleveland 4, August 31, 1993.
21 innings—(3)
Detroit 6 at Chicago 5, May 24, 1929.
Oakland 5 at Washington 3, June 4, 1971.
Chicago 6 vs. Cleveland 3, May 26, finished May 28, 1973.
20 Innings—(8)
Philadelphia 4 at Boston 2, July 4, 1905, p.m. game.
Washington 9 at Minnesota 7, August 9, 1967.
New York 4 vs. Boston 3, August 29, 1967, second game.
Boston 5 at Seattle 3, July 27, 1969.
Oakland 1 vs. California 0, July 9, 1971.
Washington 8 at Cleveland 6, September 14, second game, finished
    September 20, 1971 (game completed at Washington).
Seattle 8 at Boston 7, September 3, finished September 4, 1981.
California 4 vs. Seattle 3, April 13, finished April 14, 1982.
19 Innings—(15)
Washington 5 at Philadelphia 4, September 27, 1912.
Chicago 5 at Cleveland 4, June 24, 1915.
Cleveland 3 at New York 2, May 24, 1918.
St. Louis 8 at Washington 6, August 9, 1921.
Chicago 5 vs. Boston 4, July 13, 1951.
Cleveland 4 vs. St. Louis 3, July 1, 1952.
Cleveland 3 vs. Washington 2, June 14, 1963, second game.
Baltimore 7 vs. Washington 5, June 4, 1967.
Kansas City 6 at Detroit 5, June 17, 1967, second game.
Detroit 3 at New York 3 (tie), August 23, 1968, second game.
Oakland 5 vs. Chicago 3, August 10, finished August 11, 1972.
New York 5 vs. Minnesota 4, August 25, 1976.
Cleveland 8 at Detroit 4, April 27, 1984.
Milwaukee 10 vs. Chicago 9, May 1, 1991.
Boston 7 at Cleveland 5, April 11, 1992.
Seattle 5 vs. Boston 4, August 1, 2000.
18 Innings—(23)
Chicago 6 vs. New York 6 (tie), June 25, 1903.
Washington 0 at Detroit 0 (tie), July 16, 1909.
Washington 1 vs. Chicago 0, May 15, 1918.
Detroit 7 vs. Washington 6, August 4, 1918.
Boston 12 vs. New York 11, September 5, 1927, first game.
Philadelphia 18 at Cleveland 17, July 10, 1932.
New York 3 at Chicago 3 (tie), August 21, 1933.
Washington 1 at Chicago 0, June 8, 1947, first game.
Washington 5 at St. Louis 5 (tie), June 20, 1952.
Chicago 1 at Baltimore 1 (tie), August 6, 1959.
New York 7 vs. Boston 6, April 16, 1967.
Minnesota 3 at New York 2, July 26, 1967, second game.
Baltimore 3 vs. Boston 2, August 25, 1968.
Minnesota 11 at Seattle 7, July 19, finished July 20, 1969.
Oakland 9 vs. Baltimore 8, August 24, 1969, second game.
Minnesota 8 at Oakland 6, September 6, 1969.
Washington 2 vs. New York 1, April 22, 1970.
Texas 4 at Kansas City 3, May 17, 1972.
Detroit 4 vs. Cleveland 3, June 9, finished September 24, 1982.

New York 5 vs. Detroit 4, September 11, 1988.
Kansas City 4 vs. Texas 3, June 6, 1991.
Boston 4 vs. Detroit 3, June 5, 2001.
Texas 8 vs. Boston 7, August 25, 2001.

NATIONAL LEAGUE

26 Innings—(1)
Brooklyn 1 at Boston 1 (tie), May 1, 1920.
25 Innings—(1)
St. Louis 4 at New York 3, September 11, 1974.
24 Innings—(1)
Houston 1 vs. New York 0, April 15, 1968.
23 Innings—(2)
Brooklyn 2 at Boston 2 (tie), June 27, 1939.
San Francisco 8 at New York 6, May 31, 1964, second game.
22 Innings—(4)
Brooklyn 6 vs. Pittsburgh 5, August 22, 1917.
Chicago 4 at Boston 3, May 17, 1927.
Houston 5 vs. Los Angeles 4, June 3, 1989.
Los Angeles 1 at Montreal 0, August 23, 1989.
21 Innings—(7)
New York 3 at Pittsburgh 1, July 17, 1914.
Chicago 2 vs. Philadelphia 1, July 17, 1918.
Pittsburgh 2 at Boston 0, August 1, 1918.
San Francisco 1 at Cincinnati 0, September 1, 1967.
Houston 2 at San Diego 1, September 24, 1971, first game.
San Diego 11 at Montreal 8, May 21, 1977.
Los Angeles 2 at Chicago 1, August 17, finished August 18, 1982.
20 Innings—(9)
Chicago 7 at Cincinnati 7 (tie), June 30, 1892.
Chicago 2 at Philadelphia 1, August 24, 1905.
Brooklyn 9 at Philadelphia 9 (tie), April 30, 1919.
St. Louis 8 at Chicago 7, August 28, 1930.
Brooklyn 6 at Boston 2, July 5, 1940.
Philadelphia 5 vs. Atlanta 4, May 4, 1973.
Pittsburgh 5 vs. Chicago 4, July 6, 1980.
Houston 3 at San Diego 1, August 15, 1980.
Philadelphia 7 vs. Los Angeles 6, July 7, 1993.
19 Innings—(16)
Chicago 3 vs. Pittsburgh 2, June 22, 1902.
Pittsburgh 7 at Boston 6, July 31, 1912.
Chicago 4 vs. Brooklyn 3, June 17, 1915.
St. Louis 8 at Philadelphia 8 (tie), June 13, 1918.
Boston 2 vs. Brooklyn 1, May 3, 1920.
Chicago 3 vs. Boston 2, August 17, 1932.
Brooklyn 9 at Chicago 9 (tie), May 17, 1939.
Cincinnati 0 at Brooklyn 0 (tie), September 11, 1946.
Philadelphia 8 vs. Cincinnati 7, September 15, 1950, second game.
Pittsburgh 4 vs. Milwaukee 3, July 19, 1955.
Cincinnati 2 vs. Los Angeles 1, August 8, 1972.
New York 7 at Los Angeles 3, May 24, 1973.
Pittsburgh 4 at San Diego 3, August 25, 1979.
New York 16 at Atlanta 13, July 4, 1985.
Montreal 6 at Houston 3, July 7, 1985.
Atlanta 7 at St. Louis 5, May 14, 1988.
18 Innings—(33)
Providence 1 vs. Detroit 0, August 17, 1882.
Brooklyn 7 at St. Louis 7 (tie), August 17, 1902.
Chicago 2 at St. Louis 1, June 24, 1905.
Pittsburgh 3 at Chicago 2, June 28, 1916, second game.
Philadelphia 10 at Brooklyn 9, June 1, 1919.
New York 9 at Pittsburgh 8, July 7, 1922.
Chicago 7 at Boston 2, May 14, 1927.
New York 1 vs. St. Louis 0, July 2, 1933, first game.
St. Louis 8 at Cincinnati 6, July 1, 1934, first game.
Chicago 10 at Cincinnati 8, August 9, 1942, first game.
Philadelphia 4 vs. Pittsburgh 3, June 9, 1949.
Cincinnati 7 vs. Chicago 6, September 7, 1951.
Philadelphia 0 at New York 0 (tie), October 2, 1965, second game.
Cincinnati 3 at Chicago 2, July 19, 1966.
Philadelphia 2 vs. Cincinnati 1, May 21, 1967.
Pittsburgh 1 at San Diego 0, June 7, 1972, second game.
New York 3 vs. Philadelphia 2, August 1, 1972, first game.
Montreal 5 at Chicago 4, June 27, 1973, finished June 28, 1973.
Chicago 8 at Montreal 7, June 28, 1974, first game.
New York 4 vs. Montreal 3, September 16, 1975.
Pittsburgh 2 vs. Chicago 1, August 10, 1977.

Chicago 9 vs. Cincinnati 8, May 10, finished July 23.
Houston 3 vs. New York 2, June 18, 1979.
San Diego 8 at New York 6, August 26, 1980.
St. Louis 3 at Houston 1, May 27, 1983.
Pittsburgh 4 vs. San Francisco 3, July 13, 1984, second game.
Atlanta 3 at Los Angeles 2, September 6, 1984.
New York 5 vs. Pittsburgh 4, April 28, 1985.
San Francisco 5 at Atlanta 4, June 11, 1985.
Houston 8 at Chicago 7, September 2, finished September 3, 1986.
Pittsburgh 5 vs. Chicago 4, August 6, 1989.
Atlanta 5 at Los Angeles 3, August 3, 1996.
Arizona 1 at San Francisco 0, May 29, 2001.

CLUBS WITH 3,200,000 HOME ATTENDANCE

AMERICAN LEAGUE

Year	Club	Attendance
1993	Toronto Blue Jays	4,057,947
1992	Toronto Blue Jays	4,028,318
1991	Toronto Blue Jays	4,001,527
1990	Toronto Blue Jays	3,885,284
1997	Baltimore Orioles	3,711,132
1998	Baltimore Orioles	3,685,194
1996	Baltimore Orioles	3,646,950
1993	Baltimore Orioles	3,644,965
1992	Baltimore Orioles	3,567,819
2001	Seattle Mariners	3,507,975
1999	Cleveland Indians	3,468,456
1998	Cleveland Indians	3,467,299
2000	Cleveland Indians	3,456,278
1999	Baltimore Orioles	3,433,150
1997	Cleveland Indians	3,404,750
1989	Toronto Blue Jays	3,375,883
1996	Cleveland Indians	3,318,174
2000	Baltimore Orioles	3,295,128
1999	New York Yankees	3,292,736
2001	New York Yankees	3,264,777
2000	New York Yankees	3,227,657

NATIONAL LEAGUE

Year	Club	Attendance
1993	Colorado Rockies	4,483,350
1996	Colorado Rockies	3,891,014
1997	Colorado Rockies	3,888,453
1993	Atlanta Braves	3,884,725
1998	Colorado Rockies	3,789,347
1982	Los Angeles Dodgers	3,608,881
1998	Arizona Diamondbacks	3,600,412
1983	Los Angeles Dodgers	3,510,313
1999	Colorado Rockies	3,481,065
1997	Atlanta Braves	3,464,488
1995	Colorado Rockies	3,390,037
1998	Atlanta Braves	3,361,350
1991	Los Angeles Dodgers	3,348,170
1978	Los Angeles Dodgers	3,347,845
2000	St. Louis Cardinals	3,336,493
1997	Los Angeles Dodgers	3,319,504
2000	San Francisco Giants	3,315,330
2000	Colorado Rockies	3,285,710
1999	Atlanta Braves	3,284,897
1994	Colorado Rockies	3,281,511
2001	San Francisco Giants	3,277,244
1985	Los Angeles Dodgers	3,264,593
1980	Los Angeles Dodgers	3,249,287
2000	Atlanta Braves	3,234,301
1999	St. Louis Cardinals	3,225,334

NON-PLAYING PERSONNEL
COMMISSIONERS

Kenesaw Landis, January 12, 1921 to November 25, 1944.
Happy Chandler, April 24, 1945 to July 15, 1951.
Ford Frick, October 8, 1951 through December 14, 1965.
William Eckert, December 15, 1965 to February 4, 1969.

owie Kuhn, February 4, 1969 through September 30, 1984.
eter Ueberroth, October 1, 1984 through March 31, 1989.
art Giamatti, April 1 through September 1, 1989.
ay Vincent, September 2, 1989 through September 7, 1992.
ud Selig, July 9, 1998 to present (acting commissioner since September 9, 1992).

PRESIDENTS
NATIONAL LEAGUE

lorgan Bulkeley, 1876.
/illiam Hulbert, 1876 to 1882.
rthur Soden, 1882.
. G. Mills, 1882 to 1884.
licholas Young, 1884 to 1902.
arry Pulliam, 1902 to July 29, 1909.
ohn Heydler, July 30, 1909 to December 15, 1909.

Thomas Lynch, December 15, 1909 to December 9, 1913.
John Tener, December 9, 1913 to August 6, 1918.
John Heydler, December 10, 1918 to December 11, 1934.
Ford Frick, December 11, 1934 to October 8, 1951.
Warren Giles, October 8, 1951 through December 31, 1969.
Chub Feeney, January 1, 1970 to December 11, 1986.
Bart Giamatti, December 11, 1986 through March 31, 1989.
Bill White, April 1, 1989 through February 28, 1994.
Leonard Coleman Jr., March 1, 1994 through October 31, 1999.

AMERICAN LEAGUE

Byron Bancroft Johnson, 1901 to October 17, 1927.
Ernest Barnard, October 31, 1927 to March 27, 1931.
Will Harridge, May 27, 1931 through January 31, 1959.
Joe Cronin, February 1, 1959 through 1973.
Lee MacPhail Jr., January 1, 1974 through 1983.
Bobby Brown, 1984 through July 31, 1994.
Gene Budig, August 1, 1994 through December 31, 1999.

REGULAR SEASON *General reference*

AMERICAN LEAGUE TEAM RECORDS

ANAHEIM ANGELS
YEARLY FINISHES

(Known as Los Angeles Angels through September 1, 1965 and California Angels through 1996)

Year	Position	W	L	Pct.	*GB	Manager	Attendance
1961	8th	70	91	.435	38.5	Bill Rigney	603,510
1962	3rd	86	76	.531	10.0	Bill Rigney	1,144,063
1963	9th	70	91	.435	34.0	Bill Rigney	821,015
1964	5th	82	80	.506	17.0	Bill Rigney	760,439
1965	7th	75	87	.463	27.0	Bill Rigney	566,727
1966	6th	80	82	.494	18.0	Bill Rigney	1,400,321
1967	5th	84	77	.522	7.5	Bill Rigney	1,317,713
1968	8th	67	95	.414	36.0	Bill Rigney	1,025,956

WEST DIVISION

Year	Position	W	L	Pct.	*GB	Manager	Attendance
1969	3rd	71	91	.438	26.0	Bill Rigney, Lefty Phillips	758,388
1970	3rd	86	76	.531	12.0	Lefty Phillips	1,077,741
1971	4th	76	86	.469	25.5	Lefty Phillips	926,373
1972	5th	75	80	.484	18.0	Del Rice	744,190
1973	4th	79	83	.488	15.0	Bobby Winkles	1,058,206
1974	6th	68	94	.420	22.0	Bobby Winkles, Dick Williams	917,269
1975	6th	72	89	.447	25.5	Dick Williams	1,058,163
1976	4th (tied)	76	86	.469	14.0	Dick Williams, Norm Sherry	1,006,774
1977	5th	74	88	.457	28.0	Norm Sherry, Dave Garcia	1,432,633
1978	2nd (tied)	87	75	.537	5.0	Dave Garcia, Jim Fregosi	1,755,386
1979	1st†	88	74	.543	+3.0	Jim Fregosi	2,523,575
1980	6th	65	95	.406	31.0	Jim Fregosi	2,297,327
1981	4th/7th	51	59	.464	‡	Jim Fregosi, Gene Mauch	1,441,545
1982	1st†	93	69	.574	+3.0	Gene Mauch	2,807,360
1983	5th (tied)	70	92	.432	29.0	John McNamara	2,555,016
1984	2nd (tied)	81	81	.500	3.0	John McNamara	2,402,997
1985	2nd	90	72	.556	1.0	Gene Mauch	2,567,427
1986	1st†	92	70	.568	+5.0	Gene Mauch	2,655,872
1987	6th (tied)	75	87	.463	10.0	Gene Mauch	2,696,299
1988	4th	75	87	.463	29.0	Cookie Rojas	2,340,925
1989	3rd	91	71	.562	8.0	Doug Rader	2,647,291
1990	4th	80	82	.494	23.0	Doug Rader	2,555,688
1991	7th	81	81	.500	14.0	Doug Rader, Buck Rodgers	2,416,236
1992	5th (tied)	72	90	.444	24.0	Buck Rodgers	2,065,444
1993	5th (tied)	71	91	.438	23.0	Buck Rodgers	2,057,460
1994	4th	47	68	.409	5.5	Buck Rodgers, Marcel Lachemann	1,512,622
1995	2nd§	78	67	.538	1.0	Marcel Lachemann	1,748,680
1996	4th	70	91	.435	19.5	Marcel Lachemann, John McNamara, Joe Maddon	1,820,521
1997	2nd	84	78	.519	6.0	Terry Collins	1,767,330
1998	2nd	85	77	.525	3.0	Terry Collins	2,519,210
1999	4th	70	92	.432	25.0	Terry Collins, Joe Maddon	2,253,123
2000	3rd	82	80	.506	9.5	Mike Scioscia	2,066,977
2001	3rd	75	87	.463	41.0	Mike Scioscia	2,000,917

*Games behind winner. †Lost championship series. ‡First half 31-29; second 20-30. §Lost division playoff.

INDIVIDUAL RECORDS (1961 TO DATE)

SERVICE

Most years by non-pitcher
13—Brian Downing

Most years by pitcher
14—Chuck Finley

BATTING

Most games
162— Bobby Knoop, 1964
Jim Fregosi, 1966
Sandy Alomar, 1970, 1971
Don Baylor, 1979

Most games, career
1,661—Brian Downing

Most at-bats
689—Sandy Alomar, 162 games, 1971

Most at-bats, career
5,854—Brian Downing

Most runs
121—Darin Erstad, 157 games, 2000

Most runs, career
889—Brian Downing

Most hits
240—Darin Erstad, 157 games, 2000

Most hits, career
1,588—Brian Downing

Most singles
170—Darin Erstad, 157 games, 2000

Most singles, career
1,062—Brian Downing

Most doubles
42— Doug DeCinces, 153 games, 1982
Johnny Ray, 153 games, 1988
Jim Edmonds, 154 games, 1998

Most doubles, career
282—Brian Downing

Most triples
13— Jim Fregosi, 159 games, 1968
Mickey Rivers, 155 games, 1975
Devon White, 156 games, 1989

Most triples, career
70—Jim Fregosi

Most homers by righthander
47—Troy Glaus, 159 games, 2000

Most homers by lefthander
39—Reggie Jackson, 153 games, 1982

Most homers by switch-hitter
28—Chili Davis, 145 games, 1996

Most homers by rookie
31—Tim Salmon, 142 games, 1993

Most homers at home
24—Troy Glaus, 2000

Most homers on road
24—Leon Wagner, 1962, 1963

Most homers, month
3—Tim Salmon, June, 1996
    Mo Vaughn, May, 2000

Most homers by righthander, career
47—Tim Salmon

Most homers by lefthander, career
23—Reggie Jackson

Most homers by switch-hitter, career
56—Chili Davis

Most grand slams
—Joe Rudi, 133 games, 1978
    Joe Rudi, 90 games, 1979

Most grand slams, career
—Joe Rudi

Most total bases
66—Darin Erstad, 157 games, 2000

Most total bases, career
,580—Brian Downing

Most long hits
5—Troy Glaus, 159 games, 2000

Most long hits, career
26—Brian Downing

Most extra bases on long hits
80—Troy Glaus, 159 games, 2000

Most extra bases on long hits, career
,027—Tim Salmon

Most sacrifice hits
26—Tim Foli, 150 games, 1982

Most sacrifice flies
3—Danny Ford, 142 games, 1979

Most bases on balls
13—Tony Phillips, 139 games, 1995

Most bases on balls, career
366—Brian Downing

Most strikeouts
81—Mo Vaughn, 161 games, 2000

Most strikeouts, career
,080—Tim Salmon

Fewest strikeouts
29—Gary DiSarcina, 154 games, 1997

Most hit by pitch
21—David Eckstein, 153 games, 2001

Longest batting streak
28 games—Garret Anderson, 1998

Most runs batted in
139—Don Baylor, 162 games, 1979

Most runs batted in, career
846—Brian Downing

Most game-winning RBIs
21—Don Baylor, 157 games, 1982

Highest batting average
355—Darin Erstad, 157 games, 2000

Highest batting average, career
314—Rod Carew

Highest slugging average
604—Troy Glaus, 159 games, 2000

Highest slugging average, career
511—Tim Salmon

Most grounded into double play
26—Lyman Bostock, 147 games, 1978

Fewest grounded into double play
5—Leon Wagner, 160 games, 1962
    Albie Pearson, 154 games, 1963
    Dick Schofield, 155 games, 1988

BASERUNNING

Most stolen bases
70—Mickey Rivers, 155 games, 1975

Most stolen bases, career
186—Gary Pettis

Most caught stealing
24— Chad Curtis, 152 games, 1993
    Luis Polonia, 152 games, 1993

PITCHING

Most games
72—Minnie Rojas, 1967

Most games, career
436—Chuck Finley

Most games started
41—Nolan Ryan, 1974

Most games started, career
379—Chuck Finley

Most complete games
26—Nolan Ryan, 1973, 1974

Most complete games, career
156—Nolan Ryan

Most games finished
63—Bryan Harvey, 1991

Most innings
333—Nolan Ryan, 1974

Most innings, career
2,675.0—Chuck Finley

Most games won
22— Clyde Wright, 1970
    Nolan Ryan, 1974

Most games won, career
165—Chuck Finley

Highest winning percentage
.773—Bert Blyleven (17-5), 1989

Longest winning streak
10 games— Ken McBride, 1962
    Bert Blyleven, 1989
    Chuck Finley, 1997

Longest losing streak
11 games—Andy Hassler, 1975
    Jim Abbott, 1996

Most saves
46—Bryan Harvey, 1991

Most 20-victory seasons
2—Nolan Ryan

Most games lost
19— George Brunet, 1967
    Clyde Wright, 1973
    Frank Tanana, 1974
    Kirk McCaskill, 1991

Most games lost, career
140—Chuck Finley

Most bases on balls
204—Nolan Ryan, 1977

Most bases on balls, career
1,302—Nolan Ryan

Most strikeouts
383—Nolan Ryan, 1973

Most strikeouts, career
2,416—Nolan Ryan

Most strikeouts, game
19— Nolan Ryan, August 12, 1974
    Nolan Ryan, June 14, 1974, pitched
        first 13 innings of 15-inning
        game
    Nolan Ryan, August 20, 1974, 11
        innings
    Nolan Ryan, June 8, 1977, pitched
        first 10 innings of 13-inning
        game

Most shutouts
11—Dean Chance, 1964

Most shutouts, career
40—Nolan Ryan

Most 1-0 shutouts won
5—Dean Chance, 1964

Most runs
130—Mike Witt, 1988

Most earned runs
118—Jim Abbott, 1996

Most hits
280—Bill Singer, 1973

Most hit batsmen
21—Tom Murphy, 1969

Most wild pitches
21—Nolan Ryan, 1977

Most home runs
40—Shawn Boskie, 1996

Most sacrifice hits
22—Nolan Ryan, 1977

Most sacrifice flies
14—Nolan Ryan, 1978

Lowest ERA
1.65—Dean Chance, 278 innings, 1964

CLUB RECORDS

Most players
53 in 1996

Fewest players
33 in 1963

Most games
163 in 1969, 1974

Most at-bats
5,686 in 1996

Most runs
866 in 1979

Fewest runs
498 in 1968

Most opponents' runs
943 in 1996

Most hits
1,574 in 2000

Fewest hits
1,209 in 1968

Most singles
1,114 in 1979

Most doubles
314 in 1998

Most triples
54 in 1966

Most homers
236 in 2000

Fewest homers
55 in 1975

Most homers at Wrigley Field, home
    and opponents
248 in 1961

Most homers at Chavez Ravine, home
    and opponents
102 in 1964

Most homers at Anaheim Stadium/
    Edison Field, home and opponents
243 in 2000

Most grand slams
8 in 1979, 1983

Most pinch home runs
9 in 1987

Most total bases
2,659 in 2000

Most long hits
579 in 2000

Most extra bases on long hits
1,085 in 2000

Most sacrifice hits
114 in 1982

Most sacrifice flies
61 in 1986

Most stolen bases
220 in 1975

Most caught stealing
108 in 1975

Most bases on balls
681 in 1961

Most strikeouts
1,080 in 1968

Fewest strikeouts
682 in 1978

Most hit by pitch
77 in 2001

Fewest hit by pitch
22 in 1965

Most runs batted in
837 in 2000

Most game-winning RBIs
85 in 1982

Highest batting average
.282 in 1979

Lowest batting average
.227 in 1968

Highest slugging average
.472 in 2000

Lowest slugging average
.318 in 1968, 1976

Most grounded into double play
148 in 1996

Fewest grounded into double play
98 in 1975

Most left on bases
1,209 in 1996

Fewest left on bases
975 in 1992

Most .300 hitters
2 in 1963, 1964, 1979, 1982, 1995, 1998

Most putouts
4,443 in 1971

Fewest putouts
4,133 in 1972

Most assists
2,077 in 1983

Fewest assists
1,576 in 1980

Most chances accepted
6,499 in 1983

Fewest chances accepted
5,740 in 1972

Most errors
192 in 1961

Fewest errors
96 in 1989

Most errorless games
91 in 1989

Most consecutive errorless games
14 in 1991

Most double plays
202 in 1985

Fewest double plays
135 in 1967, 1972, 1978

Most passed balls
30 in 1969

Fewest passed balls
4 in 1982, 1984

Highest fielding average
.985 in 1989

Lowest fielding average
.969 in 1961

Highest home attendance
2,807,360 in 1982

Highest road attendance
2,491,562 in 2001

Most games won
93 in 1982

Most games lost
95 in 1968, 1980

Most games won, month
22 in June 1998

Most games lost, month
22 in June 1961, May 1964, August 1968

Games won, league
3,144 in 41 years

Games lost, league
3,368 in 41 years

Highest percentage games won
.574 in 1982 (won 93, lost 69)

Lowest percentage games won
.406 in 1980 (won 65, lost 95)

Most shutouts won
28 in 1964

Most shutouts lost
23 in 1971

Most 1-0 games won
10 in 1964

Most 1-0 games lost
5 in 1968

Most consecutive games won
11 in 1964

Most consecutive games lost
12 in 1988

Number of times league champions
0

Number of last-place finishes
2

Most runs, game
24 vs. Toronto, August 25, 1979

Most runs by opponent, game
21 by Seattle, September 30, 2000

Most hits, game
26 vs. Toronto, August 25, 1979
vs. Boston, June 20, 1980

Most home runs, game
6 vs. Boston, June 20, 1980
vs. Oakland, April 23, 1985
vs. Chicago, June 28, 1987
vs. Tampa Bay, April 21, 2000

Most runs, shutout game
17 vs. Washington, August 23, 1963
vs. Minnesota, April 23, 1980

Most runs by opponent, shutout game
14 by Seattle, August 7, 1987

Most runs, doubleheader shutout
7 vs. Kansas City, June 26, 1964

Most runs, inning
13 vs. Texas, September 14, 1978, ninth inning
vs. Chicago, May 12, 1997, seventh inning

Longest 1-0 game won
15 innings vs. Chicago, April 13, 1963

Longest 1-0 game lost
20 innings vs. Oakland, July 9, 1971

Longest shutout game won
16 innings, 3-0 vs. Chicago, September 22, 1975

Most consecutive games with one or more homers
18 (30 homers), 1982

Most total bases, game
52 vs. Boston, June 20, 1980

Largest crowd, day game
63,132 vs. Kansas City, July 4, 1983

Largest crowd, doubleheader
43,461 vs. Chicago, August 5, 1988

Largest crowd, night game
63,073 vs. Baltimore, April 23, 1983

Largest crowd, home opener
51,145 vs. Detroit, April 26, 1995

BALTIMORE ORIOLES
YEARLY FINISHES

Year	Position	W	L	Pct.	*GB	Manager	Attendance
1954	7th	54	100	.351	57.0	Jimmie Dykes	1,060,910
1955	7th	57	97	.370	39.0	Paul Richards	852,039
1956	6th	69	85	.448	28.0	Paul Richards	901,201
1957	5th	76	76	.500	21.0	Paul Richards	1,029,581
1958	6th	74	79	.484	17.5	Paul Richards	829,991
1959	6th	74	80	.481	20.0	Paul Richards	891,926
1960	2nd	89	65	.578	8.0	Paul Richards	1,187,849
1961	3rd	95	67	.586	14.0	Paul Richards, Luman Harris	951,089
1962	7th	77	85	.475	19.0	Billy Hitchcock	790,254
1963	4th	86	76	.531	18.5	Billy Hitchcock	774,343
1964	3rd	97	65	.599	2.0	Hank Bauer	1,116,215
1965	3rd	94	68	.580	8.0	Hank Bauer	781,649
1966	1st	97	63	.606	+9.0	Hank Bauer	1,203,366
1967	6th (tied)	76	85	.472	15.5	Hank Bauer	955,053
1968	2nd	91	71	.562	12.0	Hank Bauer, Earl Weaver	943,977

EAST DIVISION

Year	Position	W	L	Pct.	*GB	Manager	Attendance
1969	1st†	109	53	.673	+19.0	Earl Weaver	1,058,168
1970	1st†	108	54	.667	+15.0	Earl Weaver	1,057,069
1971	1st†	101	57	.639	+12.0	Earl Weaver	1,023,037
1972	3rd	80	74	.519	5.0	Earl Weaver	899,950
1973	1st‡	97	65	.599	+8.0	Earl Weaver	958,667
1974	1st‡	91	71	.562	+2.0	Earl Weaver	962,572
1975	2nd	90	69	.566	4.5	Earl Weaver	1,002,157
1976	2nd	88	74	.543	10.5	Earl Weaver	1,058,609
1977	2nd (tied)	97	64	.602	2.5	Earl Weaver	1,195,769
1978	4th	90	71	.559	9.0	Earl Weaver	1,051,724
1979	1st†	102	57	.642	+8.0	Earl Weaver	1,681,009
1980	2nd	100	62	.617	3.0	Earl Weaver	1,797,438
1981	2nd/4th	59	46	.562	§	Earl Weaver	1,024,652
1982	2nd	94	68	.580	1.0	Earl Weaver	1,613,031
1983	1st†	98	64	.605	+6.0	Joe Altobelli	2,042,071
1984	5th	85	77	.525	19.0	Joe Altobelli	2,045,784
1985	4th	83	78	.516	16.0	Joe Altobelli, Earl Weaver	2,132,387
1986	7th	73	89	.451	22.5	Earl Weaver	1,973,176
1987	6th	67	95	.414	31.0	Cal Ripken Sr.	1,835,692
1988	7th	54	107	.335	34.5	Cal Ripken Sr., Frank Robinson	1,660,738
1989	2nd	87	75	.537	2.0	Frank Robinson	2,535,208
1990	5th	76	85	.472	11.5	Frank Robinson	2,415,189
1991	6th	67	95	.414	24.0	Frank Robinson, Johnny Oates	2,552,753
1992	3rd	89	73	.549	7.0	Johnny Oates	3,567,819
1993	3rd (tied)	85	77	.525	10.0	Johnny Oates	3,644,965
1994	2nd	63	49	.563	6.5	Johnny Oates	2,535,359
1995	3rd	71	73	.493	15.0	Phil Regan	3,098,475
1996	2nd∞‡	88	74	.543	4.0	Dave Johnson	3,646,950
1997	1st∞‡	98	64	.605	+2.0	Dave Johnson	3,711,132
1998	4th	79	83	.488	35.0	Ray Miller	3,685,194
1999	4th	78	84	.481	20.0	Ray Miller	3,433,150
2000	4th	74	88	.457	13.5	Mike Hargrove	3,295,128
2001	4th	63	98	.391	32.5	Mike Hargrove	3,094,841

*Games behind winner. †Won championship series. ‡Lost championship series. §First half 31-23; second 28-23. ∞Won division series.

INDIVIDUAL RECORDS (1954 TO DATE)

SERVICE

Most years by non-pitcher
23—Brooks Robinson

Most years by pitcher
19—Jim Palmer

BATTING

Most games
163—Brooks Robinson, 1961, 1964
Cal Ripken Jr., 1996

Most games, career
3,001—Cal Ripken Jr.

Most at-bats
673—B.J. Surhoff, 162 games, 1999

Most at-bats, career
11,551—Cal Ripken Jr.

Most runs
132—Roberto Alomar, 153 games, 1996.

Most runs, career
1,647—Cal Ripken Jr.

Most hits
211—Cal Ripken Jr., 162 games, 1983

Most hits, career
3,184—Cal Ripken Jr.

Most singles
158—Al Bumbry, 160 games, 1980

Most singles, career
2,106—Cal Ripken Jr.

Most doubles
47—Cal Ripken Jr., 162 games, 1983

Most doubles, career
603—Cal Ripken Jr.

Most triples
12—Paul Blair, 151 games, 1967

Most triples, career
68—Brooks Robinson

Most homers by lefthander
50—Brady Anderson, 149 games, 1996

Most homers by righthander
49—Frank Robinson, 155 games, 1966

Most homers by switch-hitter
35—Ken Singleton, 159 games, 1979

Most homers by rookie
28—Cal Ripken Jr., 160 games, 1982

Most homers at home
27—Frank Robinson, 1966

Most homers on road
31—Brady Anderson, 1996

Most homers, month
15—Jim Gentile, August, 1961

Most homers by righthander, career
431—Cal Ripken Jr.

Most homers by lefthander, career
303—Boog Powell

Most homers by switch-hitter, career
343—Eddie Murray

Most grand slams
5—Jim Gentile, 148 games, 1961

Most grand slams, career
16—Eddie Murray

Most total bases
369—Brady Anderson, 149 games, 1996

Most total bases, career
5,168—Cal Ripken Jr.

Most long hits
92—Brady Anderson, 149 games, 1996

Most long hits, career
1,078—Cal Ripken Jr.

Most extra bases on long hits
197—Brady Anderson, Baltimore, 149 games, 1996

Most extra bases on long hits, career
1,984—Cal Ripken Jr.

Most sacrifice hits
23—Mark Belanger, 152 games, 1975

Most sacrifice flies
17—Bobby Bonilla, 159 games, 1996

Most bases on balls
118—Ken Singleton, 155 games, 1975

Most bases on balls, career
1,129—Cal Ripken Jr.

Most strikeouts
160—Mickey Tettleton, 135 games, 1990

Most strikeouts, career
1,305—Cal Ripken Jr.

Fewest strikeouts
19—Rich Dauer, 152 games, 1980

Most hit by pitch
24—Brady Anderson, 150 games, 1999

Most runs batted in
142—Rafael Palmeiro, 162 games, 1996

Most runs batted in, career
1,695—Cal Ripken Jr.

Most game-winning RBIs
20—Eddie Murray, 151 games, 1982

Highest batting average
.328—Ken Singleton, 152 games, 1977
Roberto Alomar, 153 games, 1996

Highest batting average, career
.303—Bob Nieman

Highest slugging average
.646—Jim Gentile, 148 games, 1961

Highest slugging average, career
.545—Rafael Palmeiro

Longest batting streak
30 games—Eric Davis, 1998

Most grounded into double play
32—Cal Ripken Jr., 161 games, 1985

Fewest grounded into double play
1—Brady Anderson, 151 games, 1997

BASERUNNING

Most stolen bases
57—Luis Aparicio, 146 games, 1964

Most stolen bases, career
295—Brady Anderson

Most caught stealing
18—Don Buford, 144 games, 1969

PITCHING

Most games
76—Tippy Martinez, 1982

Most games, career
558—Jim Palmer

Most games started
40— Dave McNally, 1969
Mike Cuellar, 1970
Dave McNally, 1970
Jim Palmer, 1976
Mike Flanagan, 1978

Most games started, career
521—Jim Palmer

Most complete games
25—Jim Palmer, 1975

Most complete games, career
211—Jim Palmer

Most games finished
62—Gregg Olson, 1991

Most innings
323—Jim Palmer, 1975

Most innings, career
3,947.1—Jim Palmer

Most games won
25—Steve Stone, 1980

Most games won, career
268—Jim Palmer

Most 20-victory seasons
8—Jim Palmer

Most games, lost
21—Don Larsen, 1954

Most games lost, career
152—Jim Palmer

Highest winning percentage
.808—Dave McNally (21-5), 1971

Longest winning streak
15 games—Dave McNally, 1969

Longest winning streak over two seasons
17 games—Dave McNally, 1968 (2),
1969 (15)

Longest losing streak
10—Jay Tibbs, 1988

Longest losing streak over two seasons
13—Mike Boddicker, 1987 (5), 1988 (8)

Most saves
45—Randy Myers, 1997

Most bases on balls
181—Bob Turley, 1954

Most bases on balls, career
1,311—Jim Palmer

Most strikeouts
218—Mike Mussina, 1997

Most strikeouts, career
2,212—Jim Palmer

Most strikeouts, game
15— Mike Mussina, August 1, 2000
Mike Mussina, September 24, 2000

Most shutouts
10—Jim Palmer, 1975

Most shutouts, career
53—Jim Palmer

Most 1-0 shutouts won
3—Mike Cuellar, 1974
Ross Grimsley, 1974
Jim Palmer, 1975, 1978

Most runs
137—Scott Erickson, 1996
Mike Mussina, 1996

Most earned runs
130—Mike Mussina, 1996

Most hits
284—Scott Erickson, 1998

Most wild pitches
14—Milt Pappas, 1959

Most hits batsmen
15—Chuck Estrada, 1960

Most home runs
35— Robin Roberts, 1963
Scott McGregor, 1986
Sidney Ponson, 1999

Most sacrifice hits
20—Mike Cuellar, 1975

Most sacrifice flies
14—Jim Palmer, 1976
David Wells, 1996

Lowest ERA
1.95—Dave McNally, 273 innings, 1968

CLUB RECORDS

Most players
54 in 1955

Fewest players
30 in 1969

Most games
163 in 1961, 1964, 1982, 1996

Most at-bats
5,689 in 1996

Most runs
949 in 1996

Fewest runs
483 in 1954

Most opponents' runs
913 in 2000

Most hits
1,572 in 1999

Fewest hits
1,187 in 1968

Most singles
1,080 in 1980

Most doubles
310 in 2000

Most triples
49 in 1954

Most homers
257 in 1996

Fewest homers
52 in 1954

Most homers at Memorial Stadium, home and opponents
235 in 1987

Most homers at Oriole Park at Camden Yards, home and opponents
229 in 1996

Most grand slams
11 in 1996

Most pinch home runs
11 in 1982

Most long hits
585 in 1996

Most extra bases on long hits
1,128 in 1996

Most total bases
2,685 in 1996

Most sacrifice hits
110 in 1957

Most sacrifice flies
67 in 1996

Most stolen bases
150 in 1976

Most caught stealing
65 in 2000

Most bases on balls
717 in 1970

Most strikeouts
1,019 in 1964, 1968

Fewest strikeouts
634 in 1954

Most hit by pitch
77 in 2001

Fewest hit by pitch
19 in 1955, 1985

Most runs batted in
914 in 1996

Most game-winning RBIs
95 in 1980, 1983

Highest batting average
.279 in 1999

Lowest batting average
.225 in 1968

Highest slugging average
.472 in 1996

Lowest slugging average
.320 in 1955

Most grounded into double play
159 in 1986

Fewest grounded into double play
102 in 1968

Most left on bases
1,262 in 1970

Fewest left on bases
1,043 in 1972

Most .300 hitters
3 in 1980

Most putouts
4,436 in 1970

Fewest putouts
4,082 in 1956

Most assists
1,974 in 1975

Fewest assists
1,516 in 1958

Most chances accepted
6,344 in 1974

Fewest chances accepted
5,625 in 1958

Most errors
167 in 1955

Fewest errors
81 in 1998

Most errorless games
104 in 1998

Most consecutive errorless games
13 in 1991

Most double plays
191 in 1999

Fewest double plays
131 in 1968

Most passed balls
49 in 1959

Fewest passed balls
4 in 1985

Highest fielding average
.987 in 1998

Lowest fielding average
.972 in 1955

Highest home attendance
3,711,132 in 1997

Highest road attendance
2,333,664 in 2001

Most games won
109 in 1969

Most games lost
107 in 1988

Most games won, month
25 in June 1966

Most games lost, month
25 in August 1954

Highest percentage games won
.673 in 1969 (won 109, lost 53)

Lowest percentage games won
.335 in 1988 (won 54, lost 107)

Games won, league
3,990 in 48 years

Games lost, league
3,575 in 48 years

Most shutouts won
21 in 1961

Most shutouts lost
22 in 1955

Most 1-0 games won
8 in 1974

Most 1-0 games lost
5 in 1973

Most consecutive games won
14 in 1973

Most consecutive games lost
21 in 1988

Number of times league champions
6

Number of last-place finishes
1

Most runs, game
23 vs. Toronto, September 28, 2000

Most runs by opponent, game
26 by Texas, April 19, 1996

Most runs, shutout game
17 vs. Chicago, July 27, 1969

Most runs by opponent, shutout game
16 by New York, April 30, 1960

Most runs doubleheader shutout
13 vs. Washington, July 9, 1959

Most runs, inning
10 vs. New York, July 8, 1969, first
 game, fourth inning
 vs. Oakland, April 29, 1979, seventh
 inning
 vs. Seattle, August 21, 1985, third
 inning

 vs. Texas, May 23, 1999, first inning
 vs. Toronto, September 28, 2000,
 fourth inning
 vs. New York, September 29, 2000,
 second inning

Longest 1-0 game won
17 innings vs. Milwaukee, September 27,
 1974

Longest 1-0 game lost
15 innings vs. Cleveland, May 14, 1961,
 first game

Most hits, game
26 vs. California, August 28, 1980

Most home runs, game
7 vs. Boston, May 17, 1967
 vs. California, August 26, 1985

**Most consecutive games with one or
 more homers**
20 (38 homers), 1998

Most total bases, game
44 vs. Atlanta N.L., June 13, 1999

Largest crowd, day game
52,395 vs. Milwaukee, April 4, 1988

Largest crowd, doubleheader
51,883 vs. Milwaukee, October 1, 1982

Largest crowd, night game
52,159 vs. Boston, June 27, 1986

Largest crowd, home opener
52,395 vs. Milwaukee, April 4, 1988

BOSTON RED SOX
YEARLY FINISHES

Year	Position	W	L	Pct.	*GB	Manager	Attendance
1901	2nd	79	57	.581	4.0	Jimmy Collins	289,448
1902	3rd	77	60	.562	6.5	Jimmy Collins	348,567
1903	1st	91	47	.659	+14.5	Jimmy Collins	379,338
1904	1st	95	59	.617	+1.5	Jimmy Collins	623,295
1905	4th	78	74	.513	16.0	Jimmy Collins	468,828
1906	8th	49	105	.318	45.5	Jimmy Collins, Chick Stahl	410,209
1907	7th	59	90	.396	32.5	George Huff, Bob Unglaub, Deacon McGuire	436,777
1908	5th	75	79	.487	15.5	Deacon McGuire, Fred Lake	473,048
1909	3rd	88	63	.583	9.5	Fred Lake	668,965
1910	4th	81	72	.529	22.5	Patsy Donovan	584,619
1911	5th	78	75	.510	24.0	Patsy Donovan	503,961
1912	1st	105	47	.691	+14.0	Jake Stahl	597,096
1913	4th	79	71	.527	15.5	Jake Stahl, Bill Carrigan	437,194
1914	2nd	91	62	.595	8.5	Bill Carrigan	481,359
1915	1st	101	50	.669	+2.5	Bill Carrigan	539,885
1916	1st	91	63	.591	+2.0	Bill Carrigan	496,397
1917	2nd	90	62	.592	9.0	Jack Barry	387,856
1918	1st	75	51	.595	+2.5	Ed Barrow	249,513
1919	6th	66	71	.482	20.5	Ed Barrow	417,291
1920	5th	72	81	.471	25.5	Ed Barrow	402,445
1921	5th	75	79	.487	23.5	Hugh Duffy	279,273
1922	8th	61	93	.396	33.0	Hugh Duffy	259,184
1923	8th	61	91	.401	37.0	Frank Chance	229,668
1924	7th	67	87	.435	25.0	Lee Fohl	448,556
1925	8th	47	105	.309	49.5	Lee Fohl	267,782
1926	8th	46	107	.301	44.5	Lee Fohl	285,155
1927	8th	51	103	.331	59.0	Bill Carrigan	305,275
1928	8th	57	96	.373	43.5	Bill Carrigan	396,920
1929	8th	58	96	.377	48.0	Bill Carrigan	394,620
1930	8th	52	102	.338	50.0	Heinie Wagner	444,045
1931	6th	62	90	.408	45.0	Shano Collins	350,975
1932	8th	43	111	.279	64.0	Shano Collins, Marty McManus	182,150
1933	7th	63	86	.423	34.5	Marty McManus	268,715
1934	4th	76	76	.500	24.0	Bucky Harris	610,640
1935	4th	78	75	.510	16.0	Joseph Cronin	558,568
1936	6th	74	80	.481	28.5	Joe Cronin	626,895
1937	5th	80	72	.526	21.0	Joe Cronin	559,659

Year	Position	W	L	Pct.	*GB	Manager	Attendance
1938	2nd	88	61	.591	9.5	Joe Cronin	646,459
1939	2nd	89	62	.589	17.0	Joe Cronin	573,070
1940	4th (tied)	82	72	.532	8.0	Joe Cronin	716,234
1941	2nd	84	70	.545	17.0	Joe Cronin	718,497
1942	2nd	93	59	.612	9.0	Joe Cronin	730,340
1943	7th	68	84	.447	29.0	Joe Cronin	358,275
1944	4th	77	77	.500	12.0	Joe Cronin	506,975
1945	7th	71	83	.461	17.5	Joe Cronin	603,794
1946	1st	104	50	.675	+12.0	Joe Cronin	1,416,944
1947	3rd	83	71	.539	14.0	Joe Cronin	1,427,315
1948	2nd†	96	59	.619	1.0	Joe McCarthy	1,558,798
1949	2nd	96	58	.623	1.0	Joe McCarthy	1,596,650
1950	3rd	94	60	.610	4.0	Joe McCarthy, Steve O'Neill	1,344,080
1951	3rd	87	67	.565	11.0	Steve O'Neill	1,312,282
1952	6th	76	78	.494	19.0	Lou Boudreau	1,115,750
1953	4th	84	69	.549	16.0	Lou Boudreau	1,026,133
1954	4th	69	85	.448	42.0	Lou Boudreau	931,127
1955	4th	84	70	.545	12.0	Pinky Higgins	1,203,200
1956	4th	84	70	.545	13.0	Pinky Higgins	1,137,158
1957	3rd	82	72	.532	16.0	Pinky Higgins	1,181,087
1958	3rd	79	75	.513	13.0	Pinky Higgins	1,077,047
1959	5th	75	79	.487	19.0	Pinky Higgins, Billy Jurges	984,102
1960	7th	65	89	.422	32.0	Billy Jurges, Pinky Higgins	1,129,866
1961	6th	76	86	.469	33.0	Pinky Higgins	850,589
1962	8th	76	84	.475	19.0	Pinky Higgins	733,080
1963	7th	76	85	.472	28.0	Johnny Pesky	942,642
1964	8th	72	90	.444	27.0	Johnny Pesky, Billy Herman	883,276
1965	9th	62	100	.383	40.0	Billy Herman	652,201
1966	9th	72	90	.444	26.0	Billy Herman, Pete Runnels	811,172
1967	1st	92	70	.568	+1.0	Dick Williams	1,727,832
1968	4th	86	76	.531	17.0	Dick Williams	1,940,788

EAST DIVISION

Year	Position	W	L	Pct.	*GB	Manager	Attendance
1969	3rd	87	75	.537	22.0	Dick Williams, Eddie Popowski	1,833,246
1970	3rd	87	75	.537	21.0	Eddie Kasko	1,595,278
1971	3rd	85	77	.525	18.0	Eddie Kasko	1,678,732
1972	2nd	85	70	.548	0.5	Eddie Kasko	1,441,718
1973	2nd	89	73	.549	8.0	Eddie Kasko	1,481,002
1974	3rd	84	78	.519	7.0	Darrell Johnson	1,556,411
1975	1st‡	95	65	.594	+4.5	Darrell Johnson	1,748,587
1976	3rd	83	79	.512	15.5	Darrell Johnson, Don Zimmer	1,895,846
1977	2nd (tied)	97	64	.602	2.5	Don Zimmer	2,074,549
1978	2nd§	99	64	.607	1.0	Don Zimmer	2,320,643
1979	3rd	91	69	.569	11.5	Don Zimmer	2,353,114
1980	4th	83	77	.519	19.0	Don Zimmer, Johnny Pesky	1,956,092
1981	5th/2nd (tied)	59	49	.546	∞	Ralph Houk	1,060,379
1982	3rd	89	73	.549	6.0	Ralph Houk	1,950,124
1983	6th	78	84	.481	20.0	Ralph Houk	1,782,285
1984	4th	86	76	.531	18.0	Ralph Houk	1,661,618
1985	5th	81	81	.500	18.5	John McNamara	1,786,633
1986	1st‡	95	66	.590	+5.5	John McNamara	2,147,641
1987	5th	78	84	.481	20.0	John McNamara	2,231,551
1988	1st▲	89	73	.549	+1.0	John McNamara, Joe Morgan	2,464,851
1989	3rd	83	79	.512	6.0	Joe Morgan	2,510,012
1990	1st▲	88	74	.543	+2.0	Joe Morgan	2,528,986
1991	2nd (tied)	84	78	.519	7.0	Joe Morgan	2,562,435
1992	7th	73	89	.451	23.0	Butch Hobson	2,468,574
1993	5th	80	82	.494	15.0	Butch Hobson	2,422,021
1994	4th	54	61	.470	17.0	Butch Hobson	1,775,818
1995	1st◆	86	58	.597	+7.0	Kevin Kennedy	2,164,410
1996	3rd	85	77	.525	7.0	Kevin Kennedy	2,315,231
1997	4th	78	84	.481	20.0	Jimy Williams	2,226,136
1998	2nd◆	92	70	.568	22.0	Jimy Williams	2,343,947
1999	2nd■▲	94	68	.580	4.0	Jimy Williams	2,446,162
2000	2nd	85	77	.525	2.5	Jimy Williams	2,586,032
2001	2nd	82	79	.509	13.5	Jimy Williams, Joe Kerrigan	2,625,333

*Games behind winner. †Lost pennant playoff. ‡Won championship series. §Lost division playoff. ∞First half 30-26; second 29-23. ▲Lost championship series. ◆Lost division series. ■Won division series.

INDIVIDUAL RECORDS (1901 TO DATE)

SERVICE

Most years by non-pitcher
23—Carl Yastrzemski

Most years by pitcher
13—Bob Stanley
Roger Clemens

BATTING

Most games
163—Jim Rice, 1978

Most games, career
3,308—Carl Yastrzemski

Most at-bats
684—Nomar Garciaparra, 153 games, 1997

Most at-bats, career
11,988—Carl Yastrzemski

Most runs
150—Ted Williams, 155 games, 1949

Most runs, career
1,816—Carl Yastrzemski

Most hits
240—Wade Boggs, 161 games, 1985

Most hits, career
3,419—Carl Yastrzemski

Most singles
187—Wade Boggs, 161 games, 1985

Most singles, career
2,262—Carl Yastrzemski

Most doubles
67—Earl Webb, 151 games, 1931

Most doubles, career
646—Carl Yastrzemski

Most triples
22— Chick Stahl, 157 games, 1904
    Tris Speaker, 141 games, 1913

Most triples, career
130—Harry Hooper

Most homers by righthander
50—Jimmie Foxx, 149 games, 1938

Most homers by lefthander
44—Carl Yastrzemski, 161 games, 1967
    Mo Vaughn, 161 games, 1996

Most homers by switch-hitter
34—Carl Everett, 137 games, 2000

Most homers by rookie
34—Walt Dropo, 136 games, 1950

Most homers at home
35—Jimmie Foxx, 1938

Most homers on road
26—Ted Williams, 1957

Most homers, month
14—Jackie Jensen, June, 1958

Most homers by righthander, career
382—Jim Rice

Most homers by lefthander, career
521—Ted Williams

Most homers by switch-hitter, career
149—Reggie Smith

Most grand slams
4—Babe Ruth, 130 games, 1919

Most grand slams, career
17—Ted Williams

Most total bases
406—Jim Rice, 163 games, 1978

Most total bases, career
5,539—Carl Yastrzemski

Most long hits
92—Jimmie Foxx, 149 games, 1938

Most long hits, career
1,157—Carl Yastrzemski

Most extra bases on long hits
201—Jimmie Foxx, 149 games, 1938

Most extra bases on long hits, career
2,230—Ted Williams

Most sacrifices (sacrifice hits and sacrifice flies)
54—Jack Barry, 116 games, 1917

Most sacrifice hits
35—Freddy Parent, 153 games, 1905

Most sacrifice flies
12— Jackie Jensen, 152 games, 1955
    Jimmy Piersall, 155 games, 1956
    Jackie Jensen, 148 games, 1959

Most bases on balls
162—Ted Williams, 156 games, 1947
    Ted Williams, 155 games, 1949

Most bases on balls, career
2,019—Ted Williams

Most strikeouts
162—Butch Hobson, 159 games, 1977

Most strikeouts, career
1,423—Jim Rice

Fewest strikeouts
9—Stuffy McInnis, 152 games, 1921

Most hit by pitch
35—Don Baylor, 1986

Most runs batted in
175—Jimmie Foxx, 149 games, 1938

Most runs batted in, career
1,844—Carl Yastrzemski

Most game-winning RBIs
23—Mike Greenwell, 158 games, 1988

Most consecutive games with RBI
12—Ted Williams (18 RBIs), 1942
    Joe Cronin (19 RBIs), 1939

Highest batting average
.406—Ted Williams, 143 games, 1941

Highest batting average, career
.344—Ted Williams

Highest slugging average
.735—Ted Williams, 143 games, 1941

Highest slugging average, career
.634—Ted Williams

Longest batting streak
34 games—Dom DiMaggio, 1949

Most grounded into double play
36—Jim Rice, 159 games, 1984

Fewest grounded into double play
3—Tony Lupien, 154 games, 1943

BASERUNNING

Most stolen bases
54—Tommy Harper, 147 games, 1973

Most stolen bases, career
300—Harry Hooper

Most caught stealing
19—Mike Menosky, 141 games, 1920

PITCHING

Most games
80—Greg Harris, 1993

Most games, career
637—Bob Stanley

Most games started
43—Cy Young, 1902

Most games started, career
382—Roger Clemens

Most complete games
41—Cy Young, 1902

Most complete games, career
275—Cy Young

Most games finished
69—Tom Gordon, 1998

Most innings
386—Cy Young, 1902

Most innings, career
2,776—Roger Clemens

Most games won
34—Smokey Joe Wood, 1912

Most games won, career
192—Cy Young
    Roger Clemens

Most 20-victory seasons
6—Cy Young

Most games lost
25—Red Ruffing, 1928

Most games lost, career
112—Cy Young

Highest winning percentage
.882—Bob Stanley (15-2), 1978

Longest winning streak
16 games—Smokey Joe Wood, 1912

Longest losing streak
14 games—Joe W. Harris, 1906

Most saves
46—Tom Gordon, 1998

Most bases on balls
134—Mel Parnell, 1949

Most bases on balls, career
856—Roger Clemens

Most strikeouts
313—Pedro Martinez, 1999

Most strikeouts, career
2,590—Roger Clemens

Most strikeouts, game
20—Roger Clemens, April 29, 1986
    Roger Clemens, September 18, 1996

Most shutouts
10— Cy Young, 1904
    Smokey Joe Wood, 1912

Most shutouts, career
38—Cy Young
    Roger Clemens

Most 1-0 shutouts won
5—Joe Bush, 1918

Most runs
162—Red Ruffing, 1929
    Jack Russell, 1930

Most earned runs
139—Jack Russell, 1930

Most hits
337—Cy Young, 1902

Most hit batsmen
20—Howard Ehmke, 1923

Most wild pitches
21—Earl Wilson, 1963

Most home runs
38—Tim Wakefield, 1996

Most sacrifice hits
24—Tex Hughson, 1943

Most sacrifice flies
14—Dave Morehead, 1964

Lowest ERA
1.00—H. Dutch Leonard, 225 innings, 1914

CLUB RECORDS

Most players
55 in 1996

Fewest players
18 in 1904

Most games
163 in 1961, 1978, 1985

Most at-bats
5,781 in 1997

Most runs
1,027 in 1950

Fewest runs
463 in 1906

Most opponents' runs
922 in 1925

Most hits
1,684 in 1997

Fewest hits
1,175 in 1905

Most singles
1,156 in 1950

Most doubles
373 in 1997

Most triples
112 in 1903

Most homers
213 in 1977

Fewest homers (154 or 162-game schedule)
12 in 1906

Most homers at Fenway Park, home and opponents
219 in 1977

Most grand slams
9 in 1941, 1950, 1987, 2001

Most pinch home runs
6 in 1953

Most long hits
590 in 1997

Most extra bases on long hits
1,023 in 1998

Most total bases
2,676 in 1997

Most sacrifices (sacrifice hits and sacrifice flies)
310 in 1917

Most sacrifice hits
142 in 1906

Most sacrifice flies
59 in 1976, 1977, 1979

Most stolen bases
215 in 1909

Most caught stealing
111 in 1920

Most bases on balls
835 in 1949

Most strikeouts
1,131 in 2001

Fewest strikeouts
329 in 1921

Most hit by pitch
70 in 1998, 2001

Fewest hit by pitch
11 in 1934

Most runs batted in
974 in 1950

Most game-winning RBIs
84 in 1982, 1986

Highest batting average
.302 in 1950

Lowest batting average
.234 in 1905, 1907

Highest slugging average
.465 in 1977

Lowest slugging average
.318 in 1916, 1917

Most grounded into double play
174 in 1990

Fewest grounded into double play
94 in 1942

Most left on bases
1,308 in 1989

Fewest left on bases
1,015 in 1929

Most .300 hitters
9 in 1950

Most putouts
4,418 in 1978

Fewest putouts
3,949 in 1938

Most assists
2,195 in 1907

Fewest assists
1,542 in 1988

Most chances accepted
6,425 in 1907

Fewest chances accepted
5,667 in 1938

Most errors
373 in 1901

Fewest errors
93 in 1988

Most errorless games
92 in 1988, 1998

Most consecutive errorless games
10 in 1986

Most double plays
207 in 1949

Fewest double plays
74 in 1913

Most passed balls
36 in 1997

Fewest passed balls
3 in 1933, 1975

Highest fielding average
.984 in 1988

Lowest fielding average
.943 in 1901

Highest home attendance
2,625,333 in 2001

Highest road attendance
2,695,389 in 2001

Most games won
105 in 1912

Most games lost
111 in 1932

Most games won, month
25 in July 1948

Most games lost, month
24 in July 1925, June 1927, July 1928

Highest percentage games won
.691 in 1912 (won 105, lost 47)

Lowest percentage games won
.279 in 1932 (won 43, lost 111)

Games won, league
7,977 in 101 years

Games lost, league
7,617 in 101 years

Most shutouts won
26 in 1918

Most shutouts lost
28 in 1906

Most 1-0 games won
8 in 1918

Most 1-0 games lost
7 in 1909, 1914

Most consecutive games won
15 in 1946

Most consecutive games lost
20 in 1906

Number of times league champions
10

Number of last-place finishes
10

Most runs, game
29 vs. St. Louis, June 8, 1950

Most runs by opponent, game
27 by Cleveland, July 7, 1923, first game

Most runs, shutout game
19 vs. Philadelphia, April 30, 1950, first game

Most runs by opponent, shutout game
19 by Cleveland, May 18, 1955

Most runs, doubleheader shutout
16 vs. Cleveland, August 21, 1920

Most runs, inning
17 vs. Detroit, June 18, 1953, seventh inning

Longest 1-0 game won
15 innings vs. Detroit, May 11, 1904

Longest 1-0 game lost
15 innings vs. Washington, July 3, 1915

Most hits, game
28 vs. St. Louis, June 8, 1950

Most home runs, game
8 vs. Toronto, July 4, 1977

Most consecutive games with one or more homers
19 (30 homers), 1996

Most total bases, game
60 vs. St. Louis, June 8, 1950

Largest crowd, day game
36,388 vs. Cleveland, April 22, 1978

Largest crowd, doubleheader
47,627 vs. New York, September 22, 1935

Largest crowd, night game
36,228 vs. New York, June 28, 1949

Largest crowd, home opener
35,343 vs. Baltimore, April 14, 1969

CHICAGO WHITE SOX
YEARLY FINISHES

Year	Position	W	L	Pct.	*GB	Manager	Attendance
1901	1st	83	53	.610	+4.0	Clark Griffith	354,350
1902	4th	74	60	.552	8.0	Clark Griffith	337,898
1903	7th	60	77	.438	30.5	Nixey Callahan	286,183
1904	3rd	89	65	.578	6.0	Nixey Callahan, Fielder Jones	557,123
1905	2nd	92	60	.605	2.0	Fielder Jones	687,419
1906	1st	93	58	.616	+3.0	Fielder Jones	585,202
1907	3rd	87	64	.576	5.5	Fielder Jones	666,307

Year	Position	W	L	Pct.	*GB	Manager	Attendance
908	3rd	88	64	.579	1.5	Fielder Jones	636,096
909	4th	78	74	.513	20.0	Billy Sullivan	478,400
910	6th	68	85	.444	35.5	Hugh Duffy	552,084
911	4th	77	74	.510	24.0	Hugh Duffy	583,208
912	4th	78	76	.506	28.0	Nixey Callahan	602,241
913	5th	78	74	.513	17.5	Nixey Callahan	644,501
914	6th (tied)	70	84	.455	30.0	Nixey Callahan	469,290
915	3rd	93	61	.604	9.5	Pants Rowland	539,461
916	2nd	89	65	.578	2.0	Pants Rowland	679,923
917	1st	100	54	.649	+9.0	Pants Rowland	684,521
918	6th	57	67	.460	17.0	Pants Rowland	195,081
919	1st	88	52	.629	+3.5	Kid Gleason	627,186
920	2nd	96	58	.623	2.0	Kid Gleason	833,492
921	7th	62	92	.403	36.5	Kid Gleason	543,650
922	5th	77	77	.500	17.0	Kid Gleason	602,860
923	7th	69	85	.448	30.0	Kid Gleason	573,778
924	8th	66	87	.431	25.5	Johnny Evers	606,658
925	5th	79	75	.513	18.5	Eddie Collins	832,231
926	5th	81	72	.529	9.5	Eddie Collins	710,339
1927	5th	70	83	.458	29.5	Ray Schalk	614,423
1928	5th	72	82	.468	29.0	Ray Schalk, Lena Blackburne	494,152
929	7th	59	93	.388	46.0	Lena Blackburne	426,795
1930	7th	62	92	.403	40.0	Donie Bush	406,123
1931	8th	56	97	.366	51.0	Donie Bush	403,550
1932	7th	49	102	.325	56.5	Lew Fonseca	233,198
1933	6th	67	83	.447	31.0	Lew Fonseca	397,789
1934	8th	53	99	.349	47.0	Lew Fonseca, Jimmie Dykes	236,559
1935	5th	74	78	.487	19.5	Jimmie Dykes	470,281
1936	3rd	81	70	.536	20.0	Jimmie Dykes	440,810
1937	3rd	86	68	.558	16.0	Jimmie Dykes	589,245
1938	6th	65	83	.439	32.0	Jimmie Dykes	338,278
1939	4th	85	69	.552	22.5	Jimmie Dykes	594,104
1940	4th (tied)	82	72	.532	8.0	Jimmie Dykes	660,336
1941	3rd	77	77	.500	24.0	Jimmie Dykes	677,077
1942	6th	66	82	.446	34.0	Jimmie Dykes	425,734
1943	4th	82	72	.532	16.0	Jimmie Dykes	508,962
1944	7th	71	83	.461	18.0	Jimmie Dykes	563,539
1945	6th	71	78	.477	15.0	Jimmie Dykes	657,981
1946	5th	74	80	.481	30.0	Jimmie Dykes, Ted Lyons	983,403
1947	6th	70	84	.455	27.0	Ted Lyons	876,948
1948	8th	51	101	.336	44.5	Ted Lyons	777,844
1949	6th	63	91	.409	34.0	Jack Onslow	937,151
1950	6th	60	94	.390	38.0	Jack Onslow, Red Corriden	781,330
1951	4th	81	73	.526	17.0	Paul Richards	1,328,234
1952	3rd	81	73	.526	14.0	Paul Richards	1,231,675
1953	3rd	89	65	.578	11.5	Paul Richards	1,191,353
1954	3rd	94	60	.610	17.0	Paul Richards, Marty Marion	1,231,629
1955	3rd	91	63	.591	5.0	Marty Marion	1,175,684
1956	3rd	85	69	.552	12.0	Marty Marion	1,000,090
1957	2nd	90	64	.584	8.0	Al Lopez	1,135,668
1958	2nd	82	72	.532	10.0	Al Lopez	797,451
1959	1st	94	60	.610	+5.0	Al Lopez	1,423,144
1960	3rd	87	67	.565	10.0	Al Lopez	1,644,460
1961	4th	86	76	.531	23.0	Al Lopez	1,146,019
1962	5th	85	77	.525	11.0	Al Lopez	1,131,562
1963	2nd	94	68	.580	10.5	Al Lopez	1,158,848
1964	2nd	98	64	.605	1.0	Al Lopez	1,250,053
1965	2nd	95	67	.586	7.0	Al Lopez	1,130,519
1966	4th	83	79	.512	15.0	Eddie Stanky	990,016
1967	4th	89	73	.549	3.0	Eddie Stanky	985,634
1968	8th (tied)	67	95	.414	36.0	Eddie Stanky, Al Lopez	803,775

WEST DIVISION

Year	Position	W	L	Pct.	*GB	Manager	Attendance
1969	5th	68	94	.420	29.0	Al Lopez, Don Gutteridge	589,546
1970	6th	56	106	.346	42.0	Don Gutteridge, Chuck Tanner	495,355
1971	3rd	79	83	.488	22.5	Chuck Tanner	833,891
1972	2nd	87	67	.565	5.5	Chuck Tanner	1,177,318
1973	5th	77	85	.475	17.0	Chuck Tanner	1,302,527
1974	4th	80	80	.500	9.0	Chuck Tanner	1,149,596
1975	5th	75	86	.466	22.5	Chuck Tanner	750,802
1976	6th	64	97	.398	25.5	Paul Richards	914,945
1977	3rd	90	72	.556	12.0	Bob Lemon	1,657,135
1978	5th	71	90	.441	20.5	Bob Lemon, Larry Doby	1,491,100
1979	5th	73	87	.456	14.0	Don Kessinger, Tony La Russa	1,280,702
1980	5th	70	90	.438	26.0	Tony La Russa	1,200,365
1981	3rd/6th	54	52	.509	†	Tony La Russa	946,651
1982	3rd	87	75	.537	6.0	Tony La Russa	1,567,787

Year	Position	W	L	Pct.	*GB	Manager	Attendance
1983	1st‡	99	63	.611	+20.0	Tony La Russa	2,132,821
1984	5th (tied)	74	88	.457	10.0	Tony La Russa	2,136,988
1985	3rd	85	77	.525	6.0	Tony La Russa	1,669,888
1986	5th	72	90	.444	20.0	Tony La Russa, Jim Fregosi	1,424,313
1987	5th	77	85	.475	8.0	Jim Fregosi	1,208,060
1988	5th	71	90	.441	32.5	Jim Fregosi	1,115,749
1989	7th	69	92	.429	29.5	Jeff Torborg	1,045,651
1990	2nd	94	68	.580	9.0	Jeff Torborg	2,002,357
1991	2nd	87	75	.537	8.0	Jeff Torborg	2,934,154
1992	3rd	86	76	.531	10.0	Gene Lamont	2,681,156
1993	1st‡	94	68	.580	+8.0	Gene Lamont	2,581,091

CENTRAL DIVISION

Year	Position	W	L	Pct.	*GB	Manager	Attendance
1994	1st	67	46	.593	+1.0	Gene Lamont	1,697,398
1995	3rd	68	76	.472	32.0	Gene Lamont, Terry Bevington	1,609,773
1996	2nd	85	77	.525	14.5	Terry Bevington	1,676,403
1997	2nd	80	81	.497	6.0	Terry Bevington	1,864,782
1998	2nd	80	82	.494	9.0	Jerry Manuel	1,391,146
1999	2nd	75	86	.466	21.5	Jerry Manuel	1,338,851
2000	1st§	95	67	.586	+5.0	Jerry Manuel	1,947,799
2001	3rd	83	79	.512	8.0	Jerry Manuel	1,766,172

*Games behind winner. †First half 31-22; second 23-30. ‡Lost championship series. §Lost division series.

INDIVIDUAL RECORDS (1901 TO DATE)

SERVICE

Most years by non-pitcher
20—Luke Appling

Most years by pitcher
21—Ted Lyons

BATTING

Most games
163— Don Buford, 1966
Greg Walker, 1985
Albert Belle, 1998

Most games, career
2,422—Luke Appling

Most at-bats
649—Nellie Fox, 154 games, 1956

Most at-bats, career
8,857—Luke Appling

Most runs
135—Johnny Mostil, 153 games, 1925

Most runs, career
1,319—Luke Appling

Most hits
222—Eddie Collins, 153 games, 1920

Most hits, career
2,749—Luke Appling

Most singles
169—Eddie Collins, 153 games, 1920

Most singles, career
2,162—Luke Appling

Most doubles
48—Albert Belle, 163 games, 1998

Most doubles, career
440—Luke Appling

Most triples
21—Joe Jackson, 153 games, 1916

Most triples, career
104— Shano Collins
Nellie Fox

Most homers by righthander
49—Albert Belle, 163 games, 1998

Most homers by lefthander
34—Robin Ventura, 158 games, 1996

Most homers by switch-hitter
28—Jose Valentin, 124 games, 2001

Most homers by rookie
35—Ron Kittle, 145 games, 1983

Most homers at home
30—Frank Thomas, 2000

Most homers on road
25—Frank Thomas, 1995

Most homers, month
16—Albert Belle, July, 1998

Most homers by righthander, career
348—Frank Thomas

Most homers by lefthander, career
221—Harold Baines

Most homers by switch-hitter, career
97—Ray Durham

Most grand slams
4—Albert Belle, 161 games, 1997

Most grand slams, career
10—Robin Ventura

Most total bases
399—Albert Belle, 163 games, 1998

Most total bases, career
3,528—Luke Appling

Most long hits
99—Albert Belle, 163 games, 1998

Most long hits, career
722—Frank Thomas

Most extra bases on long hits
199—Albert Belle, 163 games, 1998

Most extra bases on long hits, career
1,428—Frank Thomas

Most sacrifices (sacrifice hits and sacrifice flies)
44—Buck Weaver, 151 games, 1916

Most sacrifice hits
40—George Davis, 151 games, 1905

Most sacrifice flies
15—Albert Belle, 163 games, 1998
Magglio Ordonez, 153 games, 2000

Most bases on balls
138—Frank Thomas, 158 games, 1991

Most bases on balls, career
1,302—Luke Appling

Most strikeouts
175—Dave Nicholson, 126 games, 1963

Most strikeouts, career
918—Harold Baines

Fewest strikeouts
11—Nellie Fox, 155 games, 1958

Most hit by pitch
23—Minnie Minoso, 151 games, 1956

Most runs batted in
152—Albert Belle, 163 games, 1998

Most runs batted in, career
1,193—Frank Thomas

Most game-winning RBIs
22—Harold Baines, 156 games, 1983

Most consecutive games with RBI
13—Taft Wright (22 RBIs), 1941

Highest batting average
.388—Luke Appling, 138 games, 1936

Highest batting average, career
.340—Joe Jackson

Highest slugging average
.655—Albert Belle, 163 games, 1998

Highest slugging average, career
.577—Frank Thomas

Longest batting streak
27 games—Luke Appling, 1936
Albert Belle, 1997

Most grounded into double play
29—George Bell, 155 games, 1992

Fewest grounded into double play
3—Tony Lupien, 154 games, 1948
Don Buford, 163 games, 1966
Don Buford, 156 games, 1967

BASERUNNING

Most stolen bases
77—Rudy Law, 141 games, 1983

Most stolen bases, career
368—Eddie Collins

Most caught stealing
29—Eddie Collins, 145 games, 1923

PITCHING

Most games
88—Wilbur Wood, 1968

Most games, career
669—Red Faber

Most games started
49— Ed A. Walsh, 1908
Wilbur Wood, 1972

Most games started, career
484— Red Faber
Ted Lyons

– 238 –

Most complete games
42—Ed A. Walsh, 1908

Most complete games, career
356—Ted Lyons

Most games finished
73—Bobby Thigpen, 1990

Most innings
465—Ed A. Walsh, 1908

Most innings, career
4,162—Ted Lyons

Most games won
40—Ed A. Walsh, 1908

Most games won, career
260—Ted Lyons

Most 20-victory seasons
4—Ed A. Walsh
    Red Faber
    Wilbur Wood

Most games lost
25—Patrick Flaherty, 1903

Most games lost, career
230—Ted Lyons

Highest winning percentage
.842—Sandy Consuegra (16-3), 1954

Longest winning streak
13 games—LaMarr Hoyt, 1983

Longest winning streak, two seasons
15 games—LaMarr Hoyt, 1983 (13),
           1984 (2)
        Wilson Alvarez, 1993 (7),
           1994 (8)

Longest losing streak
14 games—Howard Judson, 1949

Most saves
57—Bobby Thigpen, 1990

Most bases on balls
147—Vern Kennedy, 1936

Most bases on balls, career
1,213—Red Faber

Most strikeouts
269—Ed A. Walsh, 1908

Most strikeouts, career
1,796—Billy Pierce

Most strikeouts, game
16—Jack Harshman, July 25, 1954, first
    game

Most shutouts
12—Ed A. Walsh, 1908

Most shutouts, career
58—Ed A. Walsh

Most 1-0 shutouts won
5—Reb Russell, 1913

Most runs
182—Dick Kerr, 1921

Most earned runs
162—Dick Kerr, 1921

Most hits
381—Wilbur Wood, 1973

Most hit batsmen
16—Jim Scott, 1909

Most wild pitches
18—Jaime Navarro, 1998

Most home runs
38—Floyd Bannister, 1987

Most sacrifice hits
21—Wilbur Wood, 1972

Most sacrifice flies
16—Charlie Hough, 1991

Lowest ERA
1.53—Ed Cicotte, 346 innings, 1917

Most players
50 in 1932

Fewest players
19 in 1905

Most games
163 in 1961, 1966, 1974, 1985, 1998

Most at-bats
5,646 in 2000

Most runs
978 in 2000

Fewest runs
447 in 1910

Most opponents' runs
946 in 1934

Most hits
1,615 in 2000

Fewest hits
1,061 in 1910

Most singles
1,199 in 1936

Most doubles
325 in 2000

Most triples
102 in 1915

Most homers
216 in 2000

Fewest homers (154 or 162-game schedule)
3 in 1908

Most homers at old Comiskey Park, home and opponents
175 in 1970

Most homers at new Comiskey Park, home and opponents
229 in 2000

Most grand slams
8 in 1996

Most pinch home runs
9 in 1984

Most total bases
2,654 in 2000

Most long hits
574 in 2000

Most extra bases on long hits
1,039 in 2000

Most sacrifices (sacrifice hits and sacrifice flies)
270 in 1915

Most sacrifice hits
207 in 1906

Most sacrifice flies
69 in 1992

Most stolen bases
275 in 1901

Most caught stealing
119 in 1923

Most bases on balls
702 in 1949

Most strikeouts
998 in 2001

Fewest strikeouts
355 in 1920

Most hit by pitch
75 in 1956

Fewest hit by pitch
10 in 1940

Highest batting average
.295 in 1920

Lowest batting average
.212 in 1910

Most runs batted in
926 in 2000

Most game-winning RBIs
95 in 1983

Highest slugging average
.470 in 2000

Lowest slugging average
.261 in 1910

Most grounded into double play
156 in 1950, 1974

Fewest grounded into double play
94 in 1966

Most left on bases
1,279 in 1936

Fewest left on bases
1,009 in 1985

Most .300 hitters
8 in 1924

Most putouts
4,471 in 1967

Fewest putouts
3,943 in 1942

Most assists
2,446 in 1907

Fewest assists
1,439 in 1997

Most chances accepted
6,655 in 1907

Fewest chances accepted
5,670 in 1942

Most errors
358 in 1901

Fewest errors
107 in 1957

Most errorless games
89 in 1962

Most consecutive errorless games
9 in 1955, 1964, 1995

Most double plays
190 in 2000

Fewest double plays
94 in 1915

Most passed balls
45 in 1965

Fewest passed balls
3 in 1922

Highest fielding average
.982 in 1954, 1957, 1960, 1962, 1985,
      1991, 1993, 1996

Lowest fielding average
.938 in 1901

Highest home attendance
2,934,154 in 1991

Highest road attendance
2,571,969 in 1993

Most games won
100 in 1917

Most games lost
106 in 1970

Most games won, month
23 in September 1905

Most games lost, month
24 in June 1934, August 1968

Highest percentage games won
.649 in 1917 (won 100, lost 54)

Lowest percentage games won
.325 in 1932 (won 49, lost 102)

Games won, league
7,861 in 101 years

Games lost, league
7,721 in 101 years

Most shutouts won
30 in 1906

Most shutouts lost
24 in 1910

Most 1-0 games won
9 in 1909, 1967

Most 1-0 games lost
9 in 1968

Most consecutive games won
19 in 1906

Most consecutive games lost
13 in 1924

Number of times league champion
5

Number of last-place finishes
6

Most runs, game
29 vs. Kansas City, April 23, 1955

Most runs by opponent, game
22 by New York, July 26, 1931, second game

Most runs, shutout game
17 vs. Washington, September 19, 1925, second game
vs. Cleveland, July 5, 1987

Most runs by opponent, shutout game
17 by Baltimore, July 27, 1969

Most runs, doubleheader shutout
17 vs. Detroit, September 6, 1905

Most runs, inning
13 vs. Washington, September 26, 1943, first game, fourth inning

Most hits, game
29 vs. Kansas City, April 23, 1955

Most home runs, game
7 vs. Kansas City, April 23, 1955

Longest 1-0 game won
17 innings vs. Cleveland, September 13, 1967, night game

Longest 1-0 game lost
18 innings vs. Washington, May 15, 1918
vs. Washington, June 8, 1947, first game

Most consecutive games with one or more homers
17 (28 homers), 2000

Most total bases, game
55 vs. Kansas City, April 23, 1955

Largest crowd, day game
51,560 vs. Milwaukee, April 14, 1981

Largest crowd, doubleheader
55,555 vs. Minnesota, May 20, 1973

Largest crowd, night game
53,940 vs. New York, June 8, 1951

Largest crowd, home opener
51,560 vs. Milwaukee, April 14, 1981

CLEVELAND INDIANS
YEARLY FINISHES

Year	Position	W	L	Pct.	*GB	Manager	Attendance
1901	7th	54	82	.397	29.0	James McAleer	131,380
1902	5th	69	67	.507	14.0	Bill Armour	275,395
1903	3rd	77	63	.550	15.0	Bill Armour	311,280
1904	4th	86	65	.570	7.5	Bill Armour	264,749
1905	5th	76	78	.494	19.0	Nap Lajoie	316,306
1906	3rd	89	64	.582	5.0	Nap Lajoie	325,733
1907	4th	85	67	.559	8.0	Nap Lajoie	382,046
1908	2nd	90	64	.584	0.5	Nap Lajoie	422,242
1909	6th	71	82	.464	27.5	Nap Lajoie, Deacon McGuire	354,627
1910	5th	71	81	.467	32.0	Deacon McGuire	293,456
1911	3rd	80	73	.523	22.0	Deacon McGuire, George Stovall	406,296
1912	5th	75	78	.490	30.5	Harry Davis, J.L. Birmingham	336,844
1913	3rd	86	66	.566	9.5	J.L. Birmingham	541,000
1914	8th	51	102	.333	48.5	J.L. Birmingham	185,997
1915	7th	57	95	.375	44.5	J.L. Birmingham, Lee Fohl	159,285
1916	6th	77	77	.500	14.0	Lee Fohl	492,106
1917	3rd	88	66	.571	12.0	Lee Fohl	477,298
1918	2nd	73	54	.575	2.5	Lee Fohl	295,515
1919	2nd	84	55	.604	3.5	Lee Fohl, Tris Speaker	538,135
1920	1st	98	56	.636	+2.0	Tris Speaker	912,832
1921	2nd	94	60	.610	4.5	Tris Speaker	748,705
1922	4th	78	76	.507	16.0	Tris Speaker	528,145
1923	3rd	82	71	.536	16.5	Tris Speaker	558,856
1924	6th	67	86	.438	24.5	Tris Speaker	481,905
1925	6th	70	84	.455	27.5	Tris Speaker	419,005
1926	2nd	88	66	.571	3.0	Tris Speaker	627,426
1927	6th	66	87	.431	43.5	Jack McAllister	373,138
1928	7th	62	92	.403	39.0	Roger Peckinpaugh	375,907
1929	3rd	81	71	.533	24.0	Roger Peckinpaugh	536,210
1930	4th	81	73	.536	21.0	Roger Peckinpaugh	528,657
1931	4th	78	76	.506	30.0	Roger Peckinpaugh	483,027
1932	4th	87	65	.572	19.0	Roger Peckinpaugh	468,953
1933	4th	75	76	.497	23.5	Roger Peckinpaugh, Walter Johnson	387,936
1934	3rd	85	69	.552	16.0	Walter Johnson	391,338
1935	3rd	82	71	.536	12.0	Walter Johnson, Steve O'Neill	397,615
1936	5th	80	74	.519	22.5	Steve O'Neill	500,391
1937	4th	83	71	.539	19.0	Steve O'Neill	564,849
1938	3rd	86	66	.566	13.0	Ossie Vitt	652,006
1939	3rd	87	67	.565	20.5	Ossie Vitt	563,926
1940	2nd	89	65	.578	1.0	Ossie Vitt	902,576
1941	4th (tied)	75	79	.487	26.0	Roger Peckinpaugh	745,948
1942	4th	75	79	.487	28.0	Lou Boudreau	459,447
1943	3rd	82	71	.536	15.5	Lou Boudreau	438,894
1944	5th (tied)	72	82	.468	17.0	Lou Boudreau	475,272
1945	5th	73	72	.503	11.0	Lou Boudreau	558,182
1946	6th	68	86	.442	36.0	Lou Boudreau	1,057,289
1947	4th	80	74	.519	17.0	Lou Boudreau	1,521,978
1948	1st†	97	58	.626	+1.0	Lou Boudreau	2,620,627
1949	3rd	89	65	.578	8.0	Lou Boudreau	2,233,771
1950	4th	92	62	.597	6.0	Lou Boudreau	1,727,464
1951	2nd	93	61	.604	5.0	Al Lopez	1,704,984

Year	Position	W	L	Pct.	*GB	Manager	Attendance
1952	2nd	93	61	.604	2.0	Al Lopez	1,444,607
1953	2nd	92	62	.597	8.5	Al Lopez	1,069,176
1954	1st	111	43	.721	+8.0	Al Lopez	1,335,472
1955	2nd	93	61	.604	3.0	Al Lopez	1,221,780
1956	2nd	88	66	.571	9.0	Al Lopez	865,467
1957	6th	76	77	.497	21.5	Kerby Farrell	722,256
1958	4th	77	76	.503	14.5	Bobby Bragan, Joe Gordon	663,805
1959	2nd	89	65	.578	5.0	Joe Gordon	1,497,976
1960	4th	76	78	.494	21.0	Joe Gordon, Jimmie Dykes	950,985
1961	5th	78	83	.484	30.5	Jimmie Dykes	725,547
1962	6th	80	82	.494	16.0	Mel McGaha	716,076
1963	5th (tied)	79	83	.488	25.5	Birdie Tebbetts	562,507
1964	6th (tied)	79	83	.488	20.0	Birdie Tebbetts	653,293
1965	5th	87	75	.537	15.0	Birdie Tebbetts	934,786
1966	5th	81	81	.500	17.0	Birdie Tebbetts, George Strickland	903,359
1967	8th	75	87	.463	17.0	Joe Adcock	662,980
1968	3rd	86	75	.534	16.5	Alvin Dark	857,994

EAST DIVISION

Year	Position	W	L	Pct.	*GB	Manager	Attendance
1969	6th	62	99	.385	46.5	Alvin Dark	619,970
1970	5th	76	86	.469	32.0	Alvin Dark	729,752
1971	6th	60	102	.370	43.0	Alvin Dark, John Lipon	591,361
1972	5th	72	84	.462	14.0	Ken Aspromonte	626,354
1973	6th	71	91	.438	26.0	Ken Aspromonte	615,107
1974	4th	77	85	.475	14.0	Ken Aspromonte	1,114,262
1975	4th	79	80	.497	15.5	Frank Robinson	977,039
1976	4th	81	78	.509	16.0	Frank Robinson	948,776
1977	5th	71	90	.441	28.5	Frank Robinson, Jeff Torborg	900,365
1978	6th	69	90	.434	29.0	Jeff Torborg	800,584
1979	6th	81	80	.503	22.0	Jeff Torborg, Dave Garcia	1,011,644
1980	6th	79	81	.494	23.0	Dave Garcia	1,033,827
1981	6th/5th	52	51	.504	‡	Dave Garcia	661,395
1982	6th (tied)	78	84	.481	17.0	Dave Garcia	1,044,021
1983	7th	70	92	.432	28.0	Mike Ferraro, Pat Corrales	768,941
1984	6th	75	87	.463	29.0	Pat Corrales	734,079
1985	7th	60	102	.370	39.5	Pat Corrales	655,181
1986	5th	84	78	.519	11.5	Pat Corrales	1,471,805
1987	7th	61	101	.377	37.0	Pat Corrales, Doc Edwards	1,077,898
1988	6th	78	84	.481	11.0	Doc Edwards	1,411,610
1989	6th	73	89	.451	16.0	Doc Edwards, John Hart	1,285,542
1990	4th	77	85	.475	11.0	John McNamara	1,225,240
1991	7th	57	105	.352	34.0	John McNamara, Mike Hargrove	1,051,863
1992	4th (tied)	76	86	.469	20.0	Mike Hargrove	1,224,274
1993	6th	76	86	.469	19.0	Mike Hargrove	2,177,908

CENTRAL DIVISION

Year	Position	W	L	Pct.	*GB	Manager	Attendance
1994	2nd	66	47	.584	1.0	Mike Hargrove	1,995,174
1995	1st§∞	100	44	.694	+30.0	Mike Hargrove	2,842,745
1996	1st▲	99	62	.615	+14.5	Mike Hargrove	3,318,174
1997	1st§∞	86	75	.534	+6.0	Mike Hargrove	3,404,750
1998	1st§◆	89	73	.549	+9.0	Mike Hargrove	3,467,299
1999	1st▲	97	65	.599	+21.5	Mike Hargrove	3,468,456
2000	2nd	90	72	.556	5.0	Charlie Manuel	3,456,278
2001	1st▲	91	71	.562	+6.0	Charlie Manuel	3,175,523

*Games behind winner. †Won pennant playoff. ‡First half 26-24; second 26-27. §Won division series. ∞Won championship series. ▲Lost division series. ◆Lost championship series.

INDIVIDUAL RECORDS (1901 TO DATE)

SERVICE

Most years by non-pitcher
15—Terry Turner

Most years by pitcher
20—Mel Harder

BATTING

Most games
163—Leon Wagner, 1964

Most games, career
1,619—Terry Turner

Most at-bats
663—Joe Carter, 162 games, 1986

Most at-bats, career
6,037—Nap Lajoie

Most runs
140—Earl Averill, 155 games, 1931

Most runs, career
1,154—Earl Averill

Most hits
233—Joe Jackson, 147 games, 1911

Most hits career
2,051—Nap Lajoie

Most singles
172—Charles Jamieson, 152 games, 1923

Most singles, career
1,516—Nap Lajoie

Most doubles
64—George Burns, 151 games, 1926

Most doubles, career
486—Tris Speaker

Most triples
26—Joe Jackson, 152 games, 1912

Most triples, career
121—Earl Averill

Most homers by righthander
50—Albert Belle, 143 games, 1995

Most homers by lefthander
49—Jim Thome, 156 games, 2001

Most homers by switch-hitter
24—Roberto Alomar, 159 games, 1999

Most homers by rookie
37—Al Rosen, 155 games, 1950

Most homers at home
30—Hal Trosky, 1936
Jim Thome, 2001

Most homers on road
26—Albert Belle, 1996

Most homers, month
17—Albert Belle, September 1995

Most homers by righthander, career
242—Albert Belle

Most homers by lefthander, career
282—Jim Thome

Most homers by switch-hitter, career
104—Carlos Baerga

Most grand slams
4—Al Rosen, 154 games, 1951

Most grand slams, career
13—Manny Ramirez

Most total bases
405—Hal Trosky, 151 games, 1936

Most total bases, career
3,201—Earl Averill

Most long hits
103—Albert Belle, 143 games, 1995

Most long hits, career
724—Earl Averill

Most extra bases on long hits
204—Albert Belle, 143 games, 1995

Most extra bases on long hits, career
1,904—Earl Averill

Most sacrifices (sacrifice hits and sacrifice flies)
67—Ray Chapman, 156 games, 1917

Most sacrifice hits
46—Bill Bradley, 139 games, 1907

Most sacrifice flies
16—Juan Gonzalez, 140 games, 2001

Most bases on balls
127—Jim Thome, 146 games, 1999

Most bases on balls, career
726—Earl Averill

Most strikeouts
185—Jim Thome, 156 games, 2001

Most strikeouts, career
1,238—Jim Thome

Fewest strikeouts
4—Joe Sewell, 155 games, 1925
Joe Sewell, 152 games, 1929

Most hit by pitch
17—Minnie Minoso, 148 games, 1959

Most runs batted in
165—Manny Ramirez, 147 games, 1999

Most runs batted in, career
1,085—Earl Averill

Most game-winning RBIs
15—Andre Thornton, 161 games, 1982

Most consecutive games with RBI
9—Al Rosen (18 RBI), 1954

Highest batting average
.408—Joe Jackson, 147 games, 1911

Highest batting average, career
.375—Joe Jackson

Highest slugging average
.697—Manny Ramirez, 118 games, 2000

Highest slugging average, career
.592—Manny Ramirez

Longest batting streak
31 games—Nap Lajoie, 1906

Most grounded into double play
28—Julio Franco, 149 games, 1986

Fewest grounded into double play
3—Jose Cardenal, 157 games, 1968
Cory Snyder, 157 games, 1987

BASERUNNING

Most stolen bases
75—Kenny Lofton, 154 games, 1996

Most stolen bases, career
450—Kenny Lofton

Most caught stealing
23—Bobby Bonds, 146 games, 1979

PITCHING

Most games
76—Sid Monge, 1979

Most games, career
582—Mel Harder

Most games started
44—George Uhle, 1923

Most games started, career
484—Bob Feller

Most complete games
36—Bob Feller, 1946

Most complete games, career
279—Bob Feller

Most games finished
65—Mike Jackson, 1999

Most innings
371—Bob Feller, 1946

Most innings, career
3,828—Bob Feller

Most games won
31—Jim Bagby Sr., 1920

Most games won, career
266—Bob Feller

Most 20-victory seasons
7—Bob Lemon

Most games lost
22—Peter Dowling, 1901

Most games lost, career
186—Mel Harder

Highest winning precentage
.938—Johnny Allen (15-1), 1937

Longest winning streak
15— Johnny Allen, 1937
Gaylord Perry, 1974

Longest winning streak over two seasons
17—Johnny Allen, 1936 (2), 1937 (15)

Longest losing streak
13—Guy Morton, 1914

Most saves, season
46—Jose Mesa, 1995

Most bases on balls
208—Bob Feller, 1938

Most bases on balls, career
1,764—Bob Feller

Most strikeouts
348—Bob Feller, 1946

Most strikeouts, game
19—Luis Tiant, July 3, 1968, 10 innings
18—Bob Feller, October 2, 1938, first game

Most strikeouts, career
2,581—Bob Feller

Most shutouts
10— Bob Feller, 1946
Bob Lemon, 1948

Most shutouts, career
45—Adrian Joss

Most 1-0 shutouts won
3—Adrian Joss, 1908
Stan Coveleski, 1917
James Bagby Jr., 1943
Bob Feller, 1946

Most runs
167—George Uhle, 1923

Most earned runs
150—George Uhle, 1923

Most hits
378—George Uhle, 1923

Most hit batsmen
20—Otto Hess, 1906

Most wild pitches
18—Sam McDowell, 1967

Most home runs
37—Luis Tiant, 1969

Most sacrifice hits
20—Early Wynn, 1951

Most sacrifice flies
12— Early Wynn, 1956
Gaylord Perry, 1974
Ken Schrom, 1986

Lowest ERA
1.60—Luis Tiant, 258 innings, 1968

CLUB RECORDS

Most players
55 in 2000

Fewest players
24 in 1904

Most games
164 in 1964

Most at-bats
5,702 in 1986

Most runs
1,009 in 1999

Fewest runs
493 in 1909

Most opponents' runs
957 in 1987

Most hits
1,715 in 1936

Fewest hits
1,210 in 1915

Most singles
1,218 in 1925

Most doubles
358 in 1930

Most triples
95 in 1920

Most homers
221 in 2000

Fewest homers (154 or 162-game schedule)
8 in 1910

Most homers at Municipal Stadium, home and opponents
236 in 1970

Most homers at Jacobs Field, home and opponents
219 in 1999

Most grand slams
12 in 1999

Most pinch home runs
9 in 1965, 1970

Most total bases
2,700 in 1996

Most long hits
576 in 1996

Most extra bases on long hits
1,035 in 1996

Most sacrifices (sacrifice hits and sacrifice flies)
262 in 1917

Most sacrifice hits
195 in 1906

Most sacrifice flies
74 in 1980

Most stolen bases
210 in 1917

Most caught stealing
92 in 1920

Most bases on balls
743 in 1999

Most strikeouts
1,099 in 1999

Fewest strikeouts
331 in 1922, 1926

Most hit by pitch
69 in 2001

Fewest hit by pitch
11 in 1943, 1976

Most runs batted in
960 in 1999

Most game-winning RBIs
80 in 1986

Highest batting average
.308 in 1921

Lowest batting average
.234 in 1968, 1972

Highest slugging average
.475 in 1996

Lowest slugging average
.305 in 1910

Most grounded into double play
165 in 1980

Fewest grounded into double play
94 in 1941

Most left on bases
1,260 in 2000

Fewest left on bases
995 in 1959

Most .300 hitters
9 in 1921

Most putouts
4,463 in 1964

Fewest putouts
3,907 in 1945

Most assists
2,206 in 1907

Fewest assists
1,468 in 1968

Most chances accepted
6,563 in 1910

Fewest chances accepted
5,470 in 1945

Most errors
329 in 1901

Fewest errors
72 in 2000

Most errorless games
99 in 2000

Most consecutive errorless games
11 in 1967

Most double plays
197 in 1953

Fewest double plays
77 in 1915

Most passed balls
35 in 1958

Fewest passed balls
3 in 1943

Highest fielding average
.988 in 2000

Lowest fielding average
.941 in 1901

Highest home attendance
3,468,456 in 1999

Highest road attendance
2,449,537 in 1999

Most games won
111 in 1954

Most games lost
105 in 1991

Most games won, month
26 in August 1954

Most games lost, month
24 in July 1914

Highest percentage games won
.721 in 1954 (won 111, lost 43)

Lowest percentage games won
.333 in 1914 (won 51, lost 102)

Games won, league
7,987 in 101 years

Games lost, league
7,613 in 101 years

Most shutouts won, season
27 in 1906

Most shutouts lost, season
24 in 1914

Most 1-0 games won
7 in 1989

Most 1-0 games lost
7 in 1918, 1955

Most consecutive games won
13 in 1942, 1951

Most consecutive games lost
12 in 1931

Number of times league champions
5

Number of last-place finishes
6

Most runs, game
27 vs. Boston, July 7, 1923, first game

Most runs by opponent, game
24 by Boston, August 21, 1986

Most runs, shutout game
19 vs. Boston, May 18, 1955

Most runs by opponent, shutout game
21 by Detroit, September 15, 1901, eight innings

Most runs, doubleheader shutout
23 vs. Boston, June 23, 1931

Longest 1-0 game won
15 innings vs. Baltimore, May 14, 1961, first game

Longest 1-0 game lost
17 innings vs. Chicago, September 13, 1967

Most runs, inning
14 vs. Philadelphia, June 18, 1950, second game, first inning

Most hits, game
29 vs. St. Louis, August 12, 1948, second game

Most home runs, game
8 vs. Milwaukee, April 25, 1997

Most consecutive games with one or more homers
19 (40 homers), 2000

Most total bases, game
45 vs. Philadelphia, July 10, 1932, 18 innings
43 vs. Boston, May 25, 1934
    vs. Detroit, July 17, 1966, second game
    vs. Minnesota, July 13, 1996

Largest crowd, day game
74,420 vs. Detroit, April 7, 1973

Largest crowd, doubleheader
84,587 vs. New York, September 12, 1954

Largest crowd, night game
78,382 vs. Chicago, August 20, 1948

Largest crowd, home opener
74,420 vs. Detroit, April 7, 1973

DETROIT TIGERS
YEARLY FINISHES

Year	Position	W	L	Pct.	*GB	Manager	Attendance
1901	3rd	74	61	.548	8.5	George Stallings	259,430
1902	7th	52	83	.385	30.5	Frank Dwyer	189,469
1903	5th	65	71	.478	25.0	Ed Barrow	224,523
1904	7th	62	90	.408	32.0	Ed Barrow, Bobby Lowe	177,796
1905	3rd	79	74	.516	15.5	Bill Armour	193,384
1906	6th	71	78	.477	21.0	Bill Armour	174,043
1907	1st	92	58	.613	+1.5	Hughey Jennings	297,079
1908	1st	90	63	.588	+.5	Hughey Jennings	436,199
1909	1st	98	54	.645	+3.5	Hughey Jennings	490,490
1910	3rd	86	68	.558	18.0	Hughey Jennings	391,288
1911	2nd	89	65	.578	13.5	Hughey Jennings	484,988
1912	6th	69	84	.451	36.5	Hughey Jennings	402,870
1913	6th	66	87	.431	30.0	Hughey Jennings	398,502

Year	Position	W	L	Pct.	*GB	Manager	Attendance
1914	4th	80	73	.523	19.5	Hughey Jennings	416,225
1915	2nd	100	54	.649	2.5	Hughey Jennings	476,105
1916	3rd	87	67	.565	4.0	Hughey Jennings	616,772
1917	4th	78	75	.510	21.5	Hughey Jennings	457,289
1918	7th	55	71	.437	20.0	Hughey Jennings	203,719
1919	4th	80	60	.571	8.0	Hughey Jennings	643,805
1920	7th	61	93	.396	37.0	Hughey Jennings	579,650
1921	6th	71	82	.464	27.0	Ty Cobb	661,527
1922	3rd	79	75	.513	15.0	Ty Cobb	861,206
1923	2nd	83	71	.539	16.0	Ty Cobb	911,377
1924	3rd	86	68	.558	6.0	Ty Cobb	1,015,136
1925	4th	81	73	.526	16.5	Ty Cobb	820,766
1926	6th	79	75	.513	12.0	Ty Cobb	711,914
1927	4th	82	71	.536	27.5	George Moriarty	773,716
1928	6th	68	86	.442	33.0	George Moriarty	474,323
1929	6th	70	84	.455	36.0	Bucky Harris	869,318
1930	5th	75	79	.487	27.0	Bucky Harris	649,450
1931	7th	61	93	.396	47.0	Bucky Harris	434,056
1932	5th	76	75	.503	29.5	Bucky Harris	397,157
1933	5th	75	79	.487	25.0	Del Baker	320,972
1934	1st	101	53	.656	+7.0	Mickey Cochrane	919,161
1935	1st	93	58	.616	+3.0	Mickey Cochrane	1,034,929
1936	2nd	83	71	.539	19.5	Mickey Cochrane	875,948
1937	2nd	89	65	.578	13.0	Mickey Cochrane	1,072,276
1938	4th	84	70	.545	16.0	Mickey Cochrane, Del Baker	799,557
1939	5th	81	73	.526	26.5	Del Baker	836,279
1940	1st	90	64	.584	+1.0	Del Baker	1,112,693
1941	4th (tied)	75	79	.487	26.0	Del Baker	684,915
1942	5th	73	81	.474	30.0	Del Baker	580,087
1943	5th	78	76	.506	20.0	Steve O'Neill	606,287
1944	2nd	88	66	.571	1.0	Steve O'Neill	923,176
1945	1st	88	65	.575	+1.5	Steve O'Neill	1,280,341
1946	2nd	92	62	.597	12.0	Steve O'Neill	1,722,590
1947	2nd	85	69	.552	12.0	Steve O'Neill	1,398,093
1948	5th	78	76	.506	18.5	Steve O'Neill	1,743,035
1949	4th	87	67	.565	10.0	Red Rolfe	1,821,204
1950	2nd	95	59	.617	3.0	Red Rolfe	1,951,474
1951	5th	73	81	.474	25.0	Red Rolfe	1,132,641
1952	8th	50	104	.325	45.0	Red Rolfe, Fred Hutchinson	1,026,846
1953	6th	60	94	.390	40.5	Fred Hutchinson	884,658
1954	5th	68	86	.442	43.0	Fred Hutchinson	1,079,847
1955	5th	79	75	.513	17.0	Bucky Harris	1,181,838
1956	5th	82	72	.532	15.0	Bucky Harris	1,051,182
1957	4th	78	76	.506	20.0	Jack Tighe	1,272,346
1958	5th	77	77	.500	15.0	Jack Tighe, Bill Norman	1,098,924
1959	4th	76	78	.494	18.0	Bill Norman, Jimmie Dykes	1,221,221
1960	6th	71	83	.461	26.0	Jimmie Dykes, Billy Hitchcock, Joe Gordon	1,167,669
1961	2nd	101	61	.623	8.0	Bob Scheffing	1,600,710
1962	4th	85	76	.528	10.5	Bob Scheffing	1,207,881
1963	5th (tied)	79	83	.488	25.5	Bob Scheffing, Charlie Dressen	821,952
1964	4th	85	77	.525	14.0	Charlie Dressen	816,139
1965	4th	89	73	.549	13.0	Charlie Dressen, Bob Swift	1,029,645
1966	3rd	88	74	.543	10.0	Charlie Dressen, Bob Swift, Frank Skaff	1,124,293
1967	2nd (tied)	91	71	.562	1.0	Mayo Smith	1,447,143
1968	1st	103	59	.636	+12.0	Mayo Smith	2,031,847

EAST DIVISION

Year	Position	W	L	Pct.	*GB	Manager	Attendance
1969	2nd	90	72	.556	19.0	Mayo Smith	1,577,481
1970	4th	79	83	.488	29.0	Mayo Smith	1,501,293
1971	2nd	91	71	.562	12.0	Billy Martin	1,591,073
1972	1st†	86	70	.551	+0.5	Billy Martin	1,892,386
1973	3rd	85	77	.525	12.0	Billy Martin, Joe Schultz	1,724,146
1974	6th	72	90	.444	19.0	Ralph Houk	1,243,080
1975	6th	57	102	.358	37.5	Ralph Houk	1,058,836
1976	5th	74	87	.460	24.0	Ralph Houk	1,467,020
1977	4th	74	88	.457	26.0	Ralph Houk	1,359,856
1978	5th	86	76	.531	13.5	Ralph Houk	1,714,893
1979	5th	85	76	.528	18.0	Les Moss, Dick Tracewski, Sparky Anderson	1,630,929
1980	5th	84	78	.519	19.0	Sparky Anderson	1,785,293
1981	4th/2nd (tied)	60	49	.550	‡	Sparky Anderson	1,149,144
1982	4th	83	79	.512	12.0	Sparky Anderson	1,636,058
1983	2nd	92	70	.568	6.0	Sparky Anderson	1,829,636
1984	1st§	104	58	.642	+15.0	Sparky Anderson	2,704,794
1985	3rd	84	77	.522	15.0	Sparky Anderson	2,286,609
1986	3rd	87	75	.537	8.5	Sparky Anderson	1,899,437
1987	1st†	98	64	.605	+2.0	Sparky Anderson	2,061,830
1988	2nd	88	74	.543	1.0	Sparky Anderson	2,081,162

Year	Position	W	L	Pct.	*GB	Manager	Attendance
1989	7th	59	103	.364	30.0	Sparky Anderson	1,543,656
1990	3rd	79	83	.488	9.0	Sparky Anderson	1,495,785
1991	2nd	84	78	.519	7.0	Sparky Anderson	1,641,661
1992	6th	75	87	.463	21.0	Sparky Anderson	1,423,963
1993	3rd (tied)	85	77	.525	10.0	Sparky Anderson	1,971,421
1994	5th	53	62	.461	18.0	Sparky Anderson	1,184,783
1995	4th	60	84	.417	26.0	Sparky Anderson	1,180,979
1996	5th	53	109	.327	39.0	Buddy Bell	1,168,610
1997	3rd	79	83	.488	19.0	Buddy Bell	1,365,157

CENTRAL DIVISION

Year	Position	W	L	Pct.	*GB	Manager	Attendance
1998	5th	65	97	.401	24.0	Buddy Bell, Larry Parrish	1,409,391
1999	3rd	69	92	.429	27.5	Larry Parrish	2,026,441
2000	3rd	79	83	.488	16.0	Phil Garner	2,533,752
2001	4th	66	96	.407	25.0	Phil Garner	1,921,305

*Games behind winner. †Lost championship series. ‡First half 31-26; second 29-23. §Won championship series.

INDIVIDUAL RECORDS (1901 TO DATE)

SERVICE

Most years by non-pitcher
22—Ty Cobb
Al Kaline

Most years by pitcher
16—Tommy Bridges

BATTING

Most games
163—Rocky Colavito, 1961

Most games, career
2,834—Al. Kaline

Most at-bats
679—Harvey Kuenn, 155 games, 1953

Most at-bats, career
10,586—Ty Cobb

Most singles
169—Ty Cobb, 146 games, 1911

Most singles, career
2,839—Ty Cobb

Most runs
147—Ty Cobb, 146 games, 1911

Most runs, career
2,086—Ty Cobb

Most hits
248—Ty Cobb, 146 games, 1911

Most hits, career
3,902—Ty Cobb

Most doubles
63—Hank Greenberg, 153 games, 1934

Most doubles, career
664—Ty Cobb

Most triples
26—Sam Crawford, 157 games, 1914

Most triples, career
287—Ty Cobb

Most homers by righthander
58—Hank Greenberg, 155 games, 1938

Most homers by lefthander
41—Norm Cash, 159 games, 1961

Most homers by switch-hitter
34—Tony Clark, 157 games, 1998

Most homers by rookie
35—Rudy York, 104 games, 1937

Most homers at home
39—Hank Greenberg, 1938

Most homers on road
27—Rocky Colavito, 1961

Most homers, month
18—Rudy York, August, 1937

Most homers by righthander, career
399—Al Kaline

Most homers by lefthander, career
373—Norm Cash

Most homers by switch-hitter, career
156—Tony Clark

Most grand slams
4—Rudy York, 135 games, 1938
Jim Northrup, 155 games, 1968

Most grand slams, career
10— Rudy York
Hank Greenberg
Cecil Fielder

Most total bases
397—Hank Greenberg, 154 games, 1937

Most total bases, career
5,474—Ty Cobb

Most long hits
103—Hank Greenberg, 154 games, 1937

Most long hits, career
1,063—Ty Cobb

Most extra bases on long hits
205—Hank Greenberg, 155 games, 1938

Most extra bases on long hits, career
1,845—Al Kaline

Most sacrifices (sacrifice hits and sacrifice flies)
52—Donie Bush, 157 games, 1909

Most sacrifice hits
36—Bill Coughlin, 147 games, 1906

Most sacrifice flies
16—Sam Crawford, 157 games, 1914

Most bases on balls
137—Roy Cullenbine, 142 games, 1947

Most bases on balls, career
1,277—Al Kaline

Most strikeouts
182—Cecil Fielder, 159 games, 1990

Most strikeouts, career
1,081—Norm Cash

Fewest strikeouts
13— Charlie Gehringer, 154 games, 1936
Harvey Kuenn, 155 games, 1954

Most hit by pitch
24—Bill Freehan, 155 games, 1968

Most runs batted in
183—Hank Greenberg, 154 games, 1937

Most runs batted in, career
1,826—Ty Cobb

Most game-winning RBIs
17—Kirk Gibson, 149 games, 1984

Most consecutive games with RBI
10—Willie Horton (17 RBIs), 1976

Highest batting average
.420—Ty Cobb, 146 games, 1911

Highest batting average, career
.368—Ty Cobb

Highest slugging average
.683—Hank Greenberg, 155 games, 1938

Highest slugging average, career
.616—Hank Greenberg

Longest batting streak
40 games—Ty Cobb, 1911

Most grounded into double play
29—Jimmy Bloodworth, 129 games, 1943

Fewest grounded into double play
0—Dick McAuliffe, 151 games, 1968

BASERUNNING

Most stolen bases
96—Ty Cobb, 156 games, 1915

Most stolen bases, career
865—Ty Cobb

Most caught stealing
38—Ty Cobb, 156 games, 1915

PITCHING

Most games
88—Mike Myers, 1997
Sean Runyan, 1998

Most games, career
545—John Hiller

Most games started
45—Mickey Lolich, 1971

Most games started, career
459—Mickey Lolich

Most complete games
42—George Mullin, 1904

Most complete games, career
336—George Mullin

Most games finished
68—Willie Hernandez, 1984

Most innings
382—George Mullin 1904

Most innings, career
3,398—George Mullin

Most games won
31—Denny McLain, 1968

Most games won, career
223—Hooks Dauss

Most games lost, career
182—Hooks Dauss

Most 20-victory seasons
5—George Mullin

Most games lost
23—George Mullin, 1904

Highest winning percentage
.862—Bill Donovan (25-4), 1907

Longest winning streak
16 games—Schoolboy Rowe, 1934

Longest winning streak, two seasons
16 games—Bill Donovan, 1907 (8), 1908 (8)

Longest losing streak
10 games—Mickey Lolich, 1967
Mike Moore, 1995

Most saves
42—Todd Jones, 2000

Most bases on balls
158—Joe Coleman Jr., 1974

Most bases on balls, career
1,227—Hal Newhouser

Most strikeouts
308—Mickey Lolich, 1971

Most strikeouts, career
2,679—Mickey Lolich

Most strikeouts, game
16—Mickey Lolich, May 23, 1969
Mickey Lolich, June 9, 1969, first nine innings of 10-inning game

Most shutouts
9—Denny McLain, 1969

Most shutouts, career
39—Mickey Lolich

Most 1-0 shutouts won
4—Ed Summers, 1908

Most runs
160—Joe Coleman Jr., 1974

Most earned runs
142—Mickey Lolich, 1974

Most hits
336—Mickey Lolich, 1971

Most hit batsmen
23—Howard Ehmke, 1922

Most wild pitches
24—Jack Morris, 1987

Most home runs
42—Denny McLain, 1966

Most sacrifice hits
28—Earl Whitehill, 1931

Most sacrifice flies
13—Jack Morris, 1980

Lowest ERA
1.81—Hal Newhouser, 313 innings, 1945

CLUB RECORDS

Most players
53 in 1912, 1996

Fewest players
24 in 1906, 1907

Most games
164 in 1968

Most at-bats
5,664 in 1998

Most runs
958 in 1934

Fewest runs
499 in 1904

Most opponents' runs
1,103 in 1996

Most hits
1,724 in 1921

Fewest hits
1,204 in 1905

Most singles
1,298 in 1921

Most doubles
349 in 1934

Most triples
102 in 1913

Most homers
225 in 1987

Fewest homers (154 or 162-game schedule)
9 in 1906

Most homers at Tiger Stadium, home and opponents
235 in 1999

Most homers at Comerica Park, home and opponents
137 in 2000

Most grand slams
10 in 1938

Most pinch home runs
8 in 1971

Most total bases
2,548 in 1987

Most long hits
546 in 1929

Most extra bases on long hits
1,013 in 1987

Most sacrifices (sacrifice hits and sacrifice flies)
256 in 1923

Most sacrifice hits
182 in 1906

Most sacrifice flies
59 in 1983

Most stolen bases
281 in 1909

Most caught stealing
92 in 1921

Most bases on balls
765 in 1993

Most strikeouts
1,268 in 1996

Fewest strikeouts
376 in 1921

Most hit by pitch
82 in 1999

Fewest hit by pitch
9 in 1945

Most runs batted in
873 in 1937

Most game-winning RBIs
97 in 1984

Highest batting average
.316 in 1921

Lowest batting average
.230 in 1904

Highest slugging average
.453 in 1929

Lowest slugging average
.321 in 1918

Most grounded into double play
164 in 1949

Fewest grounded into double play
81 in 1985

Most left on base
1,312 in 1993

Fewest left on base
1,025 in 1972

Most .300 hitters
8 in 1922, 1924, 1934

Most putouts
4,469 in 1968

Fewest putouts
4,006 in 1906

Most assists
2,272 in 1914

Fewest assists, season
1,443 in 1962

Most chances accepted
6,504 in 1914

Fewest chances accepted
5,594 in 1959

Most errors
425 in 1901

Fewest errors
92 in 1997

Most errorless games
92 in 1997

Most consecutive errorless games
12 in 1963

Most double plays
194 in 1950

Fewest double plays
94 in 1912, 1917

Most passed balls
30 in 2001

Fewest passed balls
4 in 1924

Highest fielding average
.985 in 1997

Lowest fielding average
.922 in 1901

Highest home attendance
2,704,794 in 1984

Highest road attendance
2,396,528 in 1991

Most games won
104 in 1984

Most games lost
109 in 1996

Most games won, month
23 in July 1908, August 1915, August 1934, August 1935

Most games lost, month
24 in June 1975

Highest percentage games won
.656 in 1934 (won 101, lost 53)

Lowest percentage games won
.325 in 1952 (won 50, lost 104)

Games won, league
7,980 in 101 years

Games lost, league
7,644 in 101 years

Most shutouts won
20 in 1917, 1944, 1969

Most shutouts lost
22 in 1904

Most 1-0 games won
9 in 1908

Most 1-0 games lost
7 in 1903, 1943

Most consecutive games won
14 in 1909, 1934

Most consecutive games lost
19 in 1975

Number of times league champions

Number of last-place finishes

Most runs, game
21 vs. Cleveland, September 15, 1901,
   eight innings
vs. Philadelphia, July 17, 1908
vs. St. Louis, July 25, 1920
vs. Chicago, July 1, 1936

Most runs by opponent, game
24 by Philadelphia, May 18, 1912
by Minnesota, April 24, 1996

Most runs, shutout game
21 vs. Cleveland, September 15, 1901,
   eight innings

Most runs by opponent, shutout game
16 by St. Louis, September 9, 1922

Most runs, doubleheader shutout
26 vs. St. Louis, September 22, 1936

Most runs, inning
13 vs. New York, June 17, 1925, sixth
   inning
vs. Texas, August 8, 2001, ninth
   inning

Longest 1-0 game won
12 innings vs. St. Louis, September 8,
   1917
vs. Cleveland, June 26, 1919
vs. Chicago, September 10,
   1950, first game

Longest 1-0 game lost
16 innings vs. Chicago, August 14, 1954

Most hits, game
28 vs. New York, September 29, 1928

Most home runs, game
8 vs. Toronto, June 20, 2000

**Most consecutive games with one or
   more homers**
25 (46 homers), 1994

Most total bases, game
47 vs. Toronto, June 20, 2000

Largest crowd, day game
57,888 vs. Cleveland, September 26,
   1948

Largest crowd, doubleheader
58,369 vs. New York, July 20, 1947

Largest crowd, night game
56,586 vs. Cleveland, August 9, 1948

Largest crowd, home opener
54,089 vs. Cleveland, April 6, 1971

KANSAS CITY A'S
YEARLY FINISHES

Year	Position	W	L	Pct.	*GB	Manager	Attendance
1955	6th	63	91	.409	33.0	Lou Boudreau	1,393,054
1956	8th	52	102	.338	45.0	Lou Boudreau	1,015,154
1957	7th	59	94	.386	38.5	Lou Boudreau, Harry Craft	901,067
1958	7th	73	81	.474	19.0	Harry Craft	925,090
1959	7th	66	88	.429	28.0	Harry Craft	963,683
1960	8th	58	96	.377	39.0	Bob Elliot	774,944
1961	9th (tied)	61	100	.379	47.5	Joe Gordon, Hank Bauer	683,817
1962	9th	72	90	.444	24.0	Hank Bauer	635,675
1963	8th	73	89	.451	31.5	Ed Lopat	762,364
1964	10th	57	105	.352	42.0	Ed Lopat, Mel McGaha	642,478
1965	10th	59	103	.364	43.0	Mel McGaha, Haywood Sullivan	528,344
1966	7th	74	86	.463	23.0	Alvin Dark	773,929
1967	10th	62	99	.385	29.5	Alvin Dark, Luke Appling	726,639

*Games behind winner.

INDIVIDUAL RECORDS (1955 TO 1967)

SERVICE

Most years by non-pitcher
6—Ed Charles, Billy Bryan, Wayne
   Causey

Most years by pitcher
6—John Wyatt

BATTING

Most games
162—Norm Siebern, 1962

Most games, career
726—Ed Charles

Most at-bats
641—Jerry Lumpe, 156 games, 1962

Most at-bats, career
2,782—Jerry Lumpe

Most runs
114—Norm Siebern, 162 games, 1962

Most runs, career
361—Jerry Lumpe

Most hits
193—Jerry Lumpe, 156 games, 1962

Most hits, career
775—Jerry Lumpe

Most doubles
36—Norm Siebern, 153 games, 1961

Most doubles, career
119—Jerry Lumpe

Most triples
15—Gino Cimoli, 152 games, 1962

Most triples, career
34—Jerry Lumpe

Most homers by righthander
38—Bob Cerv, 141 games, 1958

Most homers by lefthander
28—Jim Gentile, 136 games, 1964

Most homers by switch-hitter
3—Jerry Walker, 36 games, 1962

Most homers by rookie
20—Woodie Held, 92 games, 1957

Most homers at home
22—Rocky Colavito, 1964

Most homers on road
17—Bob Cerv, 1958

Most homers, month
10—Rocky Colavito, May, 1964

Most homers, lefthander, career
78—Norm Siebern

Most homers, righthander, career
75—Bob Cerv

Most homers, switch-hitter, career
3—Jerry Walker

Most grand slams
2—Roger Maris, 99 games, 1958
   Marv Throneberry, 104 games, 1960

Most grand slams, career
3—Roger Maris, Marv Throneberry

Most pinch homers, career
4—George Alusik, Bob Cerv

Most total bases
305—Bob Cerv, 141 games, 1958

Most total bases, career
1,065—Ed Charles

Most long hits
67—Rocky Colavito, 160 games, 1964

Most extra bases on long hits
148—Bob Cerv, 141 games, 1958

Most sacrifice hits
11—Dick Williams, 130 games, 1959

Most sacrifice flies
12—Leo Posada, 116 games, 1961

Most bases on balls
110—Norm Siebern, 162 games, 1962

Most bases on balls, career
343—Norm Siebern

Most strikeouts
143—Nelson Mathews, 157 games,
   1964

Fewest strikeouts
38—Dick Howser, 158 games, 1961
   Jerry Lumpe, 156 games, 1962

Most strikeouts, career
379—Ed Charles

Most hit by pitch
13—Bobby Del Greco, 132 games, 1962

Most runs batted in
117—Norm Siebern, 162 games, 1962

Most runs batted in, career
367—Norm Siebern

Highest batting average
.319—Vic Power, 147 games, 1955

Highest batting average, career
.289—Norm Siebern

Highest slugging average
.592—Bob Cerv, 148 games, 1958

– 247 –

Highest slugging average
.463—Norm Siebern

Longest batting streak
22 games—Hector Lopez, 1957
      Vic Power, 1958

Most grounded into double play
23—Hector Lopez, 151 games, 1958

Fewest grounded into double play
4—Norm Siebern, 153 games, 1961

BASERUNNING

Most stolen bases
55—Bert Campaneris, 147 games, 1967

Most stolen bases, career
168—Bert Campaneris

Most caught stealing
19—Bert Campaneris, 144 games, 1965

PITCHING

Most games
81—John Wyatt, 1964

Most games, career
292—John Wyatt

Most games started
35— Bud Daley, 1960
     Ed Rakow, 1962
     Diego Segui, 1964
     Catfish Hunter, 1967

Most games started, career
98—Ray Herbert

Most complete games
14—Art Ditmar, 1956
     Ray Herbert, 1960

Most complete games, career
32—Ray Herbert

Most games finished
57—John Wyatt, 1964
     Jack Aker, 1966

Most innings
260—Catfish Hunter, 1967

Most innings, career
784—Ray Herbert

Most games won
16—Bud Daley, 1959, 1960

Most games won, career
39—Bud Daley

Most games lost
22—Art Ditmar, 1956

Most games lost, career
48—Ray Herbert

Highest winning percentage
.552—Bud Daley (16-13), 1959

Longest winning streak
9 games—Bud Daley, 1960

Longest losing streak
11 games—Troy Herriage, 1956

Most bases on balls
108—Art Ditmar, 1956

Most bases on balls, career
280—Diego Segui

Most strikeouts
196—Catfish Hunter, 1967

Most strikeouts, game
12—Jim Nash, July 13, 1967
     Jim Nash, July 23, 1967, second
     game
     Catfish Hunter, September 12, 1967

Most strikeouts, career
513—Diego Segui

Most shutouts
5—Catfish Hunter, 1967

Most shutouts, career
8—Ned Garver

Most 1-0 shutouts won
2—Alex Kellner, 1955
     Catfish Hunter, 1967

Most runs
141—Art Ditmar, 1956

Most earned runs
125—Art Ditmar, 1956

Most hits
256—Ray Herbert, 1960

Most hit batsmen
12—Johnny Kucks, 1959

Most wild pitches
13—John Wyatt, 1965

Most home runs
40—Orlando Pena, 1964

Lowest ERA
2.80—Catfish Hunter, 260 innings, 1967

CLUB RECORDS

Most players
52 in 1955, 1961

Fewest players
38 in 1957

Most games
163 in 1964

Most at-bats
5,576 in 1962

Most runs
745 in 1962

Most opponents' runs
911 in 1955

Most hits
1,467 in 1962

Most singles
1,073 in 1962

Most doubles
231 in 1959

Most triples
59 in 1965

Most homers
166 in 1957, 1964

Fewest homers
69 in 1967

Most homers at Municipal Stadium, home and opponents
239 in 1964

Most grand slams
4 in 1958, 1959, 1960

Most pinch home runs
7 in 1964

Most total bases
2,151 in 1962

Most long hits
411 in 1964

Most extra bases on long hits
773 in 1957

Most sacrifice hits
89 in 1961

Most sacrifice flies
50 in 1962

Fewest sacrifice flies
25 in 1964

Most stolen bases
132 in 1966, 1967

Most caught stealing
59 in 1967

Fewest caught stealing
11 in 1960

Most bases on balls
580 in 1961

Most strikeouts
1,104 in 1964

Most hit by pitch
42 in 1962, 1964, 1967

Fewest hit by pitch
12 in 1960

Most runs batted in
691 in 1962

Highest batting average
.263 in 1959, 1962

Lowest batting average
.233 in 1967

Highest slugging average
.394 in 1957

Lowest slugging average
.330 in 1967

Most grounded into double play
154 in 1960

Fewest grounded into double play
79 in 1967

Most left on bases
1,224 in 1962

Fewest left on bases
925 in 1957

Most .300 hitters
4 in 1955

Most putouts
4,374 in 1963

Most assists
1,782 in 1956

Fewest assists
1,532 in 1967

Most chances accepted
6,103 in 1963

Fewest chances accepted
5,750 in 1959

Most errors
175 in 1961

Most errorless games
78 in 1963

Fewest errors
125 in 1957, 1958

Most consecutive errorless games
8 in 1960, 1964

Most double plays
187 in 1956

Most passed balls
34 in 1958

Highest fielding average
.980 in 1963

Lowest fielding average
.972 in 1961

Highest home attendance
1,393,054 in 1955

Highest road attendance
938,214 in 1967

Most games won
74 in 1966

Most games lost
105 in 1964

Most games won, month
19, July 1959

Most games lost, month
26, August 1961

Highest percentage games won
.474 in 1958 (won 73, lost 81)

Lowest percentage games won
.338 in 1956 (won 52, lost 102)

Games won, league
429 in 13 years
Games lost, league
1,224 in 13 years
Most shutouts won
41 in 1963, 1966
Most shutouts lost
49 in 1967
Most 1-0 games won
4 in 1966
Most 1-0 games lost
5 in 1967
Most consecutive games won
11 in 1959
Most consecutive games lost
13 in 1959
Number of times league champions
0
Number of last-place finishes
6 (tied in 1961)
Most runs, game
20 vs. Minnesota, April 25, 1961
Most runs by opponent, game
29 by Chicago, April 23, 1955

Most runs, shutout game
16 vs. Chicago, May 23, 1959
Most runs by opponent, shutout game
16 by Detroit, April 17, 1955
   by Boston, August 26, 1957
Most runs, doubleheader shutout
9 vs. Detroit, July 9, 1959
Most runs, inning
13 vs. Chicago, April 21, 1956, second
   inning
Longest 1-0 game won
11 innings vs. Cleveland, September 15,
   1966
Longest 1-0 game lost
None over nine innings
Most hits, nine-inning game
21 vs. Washington, June 13, 1956
   vs. Chicago, May 23, 1959
   vs. Cleveland, May 5, 1962, first
   game
Most hits, extra-inning game
26 vs. New York, July 27, 1956, 14
   innings

Most home runs, game
5 vs. Cleveland, April 18, 1955
   vs. Cleveland, April 24, 1957
   vs. Baltimore, September 9, 1958
Most consecutive games with one or
   more homer
11 (13 homers), 1964
Most total bases, game
36 vs. New York, July 27, 1956, 14
   innings
   vs. Washington, June 13, 1956
   vs. Chicago, May 23, 1959
   vs. Cleveland, May 5, 1962, first
   game
Largest crowd, day game
34,065 vs. New York, August 27, 1961
Largest crowd, doubleheader
35,147 vs. New York, August 18, 1962
Largest crowd, night game
33,471 vs. New York, April 29, 1955
Largest crowd, home opener
32,147 vs. Detroit, April 12, 1955

KANSAS CITY ROYALS
YEARLY FINISHES
WEST DIVISION

Year	Position	W	L	Pct.	*GB	Manager	Attendance
1969	4th	69	93	.429	28	Joe Gordon	902,414
1970	4th (tied)	65	97	.401	33	Charlie Metro, Bob Lemon	693,047
1971	2nd	85	76	.528	16	Bob Lemon	910,784
1972	4th	76	78	.494	16.5	Bob Lemon	707,656
1973	2nd	88	74	.543	6	Jack McKeon	1,345,341
1974	5th	77	85	.475	13	Jack McKeon	1,173,292
1975	2nd	91	71	.562	7	Jack McKeon, Whitey Herzog	1,151,836
1976	1st†	90	72	.556	+2.5	Whitey Herzog	1,680,265
1977	1st†	102	60	.630	+8	Whitey Herzog	1,852,603
1978	1st†	92	70	.568	+5	Whitey Herzog	2,255,493
1979	2nd	85	77	.525	3	Whitey Herzog	2,261,845
1980	1st‡	97	65	.599	+14	Jim Frey	2,288,714
1981	5th/1st∞	50	53	.485	§	Jim Frey, Dick Howser	1,279,403
1982	2nd	90	72	.556	3	Dick Howser	2,284,464
1983	2nd	79	83	.488	20	Dick Howser	1,963,875
1984	1st†	84	78	.519	+3	Dick Howser	1,810,018
1985	1st‡	91	71	.562	+1	Dick Howser	2,162,717
1986	3rd (tied)	76	86	.469	16	Dick Howser, Mike Ferraro	2,320,794
1987	2nd	83	79	.512	2	Billy Gardner, John Wathan	2,392,471
1988	3rd	84	77	.522	19.5	John Wathan	2,350,181
1989	2nd	92	70	.568	7	John Wathan	2,477,700
1990	6th	75	86	.466	27.5	John Wathan	2,244,956
1991	6th	82	80	.506	13	John Wathan, Hal McRae	2,161,537
1992	5th (tied)	72	90	.444	24	Hal McRae	1,867,689
1993	3rd	84	78	.519	10	Hal McRae	1,934,578

CENTRAL DIVISION

Year	Position	W	L	Pct.	*GB	Manager	Attendance
1994	3rd	64	51	.557	4	Hal McRae	1,400,494
1995	2nd	70	74	.486	30	Bob Boone	1,233,530
1996	5th	75	86	.466	24	Bob Boone	1,435,997
1997	5th	67	94	.416	19	Bob Boone, Tony Muser	1,517,638
1998	3rd	72	89	.447	16.5	Tony Muser	1,494,875
1999	4th	64	97	.398	32.5	Tony Muser	1,506,068
2000	4th	77	85	.475	18.0	Tony Muser	1,677,915
2001	5th	65	97	.401	26.0	Tony Muser	1,536,371

*Games behind winner. †Lost championship series. ‡Won championship series. §First half 20-30; second 30-23. ∞Lost division series.

INDIVIDUAL RECORDS (1969 TO DATE)

SERVICE

Most years by non-pitcher
21—George Brett

Most years by pitcher
15—Paul Splittorff

BATTING

Most games
162— Al Cowens, 1977
   Hal McRae, 1977

– 249 –

Most games, career
2,707—George Brett

Most at-bats
705—Willie Wilson, 161 games, 1980

Most at-bats, career
10,349—George Brett

Most runs
136—Johnny Damon, 159 games, 2000

Most runs, career
1,583—George Brett

Most hits
230—Willie Wilson, 161 games, 1980

Most hits, career
3,154—George Brett

Most singles
184—Willie Wilson, 161 games, 1980

Most singles, career
2,035—George Brett

Most doubles
54—Hal McRae, 162 games, 1977

Most doubles, career
665—George Brett

Most triples
21—Willie Wilson, 141 games, 1985

Most triples, career
137—George Brett

Most homers by lefthander
34—John Mayberry, 156 games, 1975

Most homers by righthander
36—Steve Balboni, 160 games, 1985

Most homers by switch-hitter
30—Chili Davis, 140 games, 1997

Most homers by rookie
24—Bob Hamelin, 101 games, 1994

Most homers, month
12—John Mayberry, July, 1975
    Chili Davis, August, 1997

Most homers at home
21—Chili Davis, 1997
    Dean Palmer, 1998

Most homers on road
23—John Mayberry, 1975

Most homers by lefthander, career
317—George Brett

Most homers by righthander, career
193—Amos Otis

Most homers by switch-hitter, career
53—Carlos Beltran

Most grand slams
3—Danny Tartabull, 1988

Most grand slams, career
6—Frank White

Most total bases
363—George Brett, 154 games, 1979

Most total bases, career
5,044—George Brett

Most long hits
86—Hal McRae, 162 games, 1977

Most long hits, career
1,119—George Brett

Most extra bases on long hits
151—George Brett, 154 games, 1979

Most extra bases on long hits, career
1,890—George Brett

Most sacrifice hits
21—Tom Goodwin, 143 games, 1996

Most sacrifice flies
13—Darrell Porter, 157 games, 1979
    Dean Palmer, 152 games, 1998
    Mike Sweeney, 159 games, 2000

Most bases on balls
122—John Mayberry, 152 games, 1973

Most bases on balls, career
1,096—George Brett

Most strikeouts
172—Bo Jackson, 135 games, 1989

Most strikeouts, career
1,035—Frank White

Fewest strikeouts
22—George Brett, 117 games, 1980

Most hit by pitch
18—Mike Macfarlane, 92 games, 1994

Most runs batted in
144—Mike Sweeney, 159 games, 2000

Most runs batted in, career
1,595—George Brett

Most game-winning RBIs
21—Danny Tartabull, 158 games, 1987

Longest batting streak
30 games—George Brett, 1980

Highest batting average
.390—George Brett, 117 games, 1980

Highest batting average, career
.305—George Brett

Highest slugging average
.664—George Brett, 117 games, 1980

Highest slugging average, career
.518—Danny Tartabull

Most grounded into double play
26—John Wathan, 121 games, 1982

Fewest grounded into double play
1—Willie Wilson, 154 games, 1979

BASERUNNING

Most stolen bases
83—Willie Wilson, 154 games, 1979

Most stolen bases, career
612—Willie Wilson

Most caught stealing
22—Tom Goodwin, 143 games, 1996

PITCHING

Most games
84—Dan Quisenberry, 1985

Most games, career
686—Jeff Montgomery

Most games started
40—Dennis Leonard, 1978

Most games started, career
392—Paul Splittorff

Most complete games
21—Dennis Leonard, 1977

Most complete games, career
103—Dennis Leonard

Most games finished
76—Dan Quisenberry, 1985

Most innings
295—Dennis Leonard, 1978

Most innings, career
2,555—Paul Splittorff

Most games won
23—Bret Saberhagen, 1989

Most games won, career
166—Paul Splittorff

Most games lost
19—Paul Splittorff, 1974

Most games lost, career
143—Paul Splittorff

Most 20-victory seasons
3—Dennis Leonard

Highest winning percentage
.800—Larry Gura (16-4), 1978

Longest winning streak
11 games—Rich Gale, 1980

Longest winning streak, two seasons
11 games—Paul Splittorff, 1977-78

Longest losing streak
8 games—Dick Drago, 1970
    Wally Bunker, 1970
    Bill Butler, 1970

Most saves
45—Dan Quisenberry, 1983
    Jeff Montgomery, 1993

Most bases on balls
120—Mark Gubicza, 1987

Most bases on balls, career
783—Mark Gubicza

Most strikeouts
244—Dennis Leonard, 1977

Most strikeouts, career
1,451—Kevin Appier

Most strikeouts, game
14—Mark Gubicza, August 27, 1988

Most shutouts won
6—Roger Nelson, 1972

Most 1-0 shutouts won
2—Dick Drago, 1971
    Roger Nelson, 1972
    Al Fitzmorris, 1974
    Dennis Leonard, 1979
    Larry Gura, 1982

Most shutouts, career
23—Dennis Leonard

Most runs
137—Larry Gura, 1979
    Paul Splittorff, 1979

Most earned runs
119—Chris Haney, 1996
    Tim Belcher, 1997
    Jeff Suppan, 2000

Most hits
284—Steve Busby, 1974

Most wild pitches
18—Dan Reichert, 2000

Most hit batsmen
13—Jim Colborn, 1977
    Mike Boddicker, 1991

Most home runs
37—Tim Belcher, 1998

Most sacrifice hits
18—Larry Gura, 1978

Most sacrifice flies
17—Larry Gura, 1983

Lowest ERA
2.08—Roger Nelson, 173 innings, 1972

CLUB RECORDS

Most players
53 in 1997

Fewest players
32 in 1975

Most games
163 in 1969, 1983

Most at-bats
5,714 in 1980

Most runs
879 in 2000

Fewest runs
586 in 1969

Most opponents' runs
930 in 2000

Most hits
1,644 in 2000

Fewest hits
1,311 in 1969

Most singles
1,193 in 1980

Most doubles
316 in 1990

Most triples
79 in 1979

Most homers
168 in 1987

Fewest homers
65 in 1976

Most homers at Municipal Stadium, home and opponents
102 in 1969

Most homers at Royals Stadium, home and opponents
201 in 2000

Most grand slams
7 in 1991

Most pinch home runs
6 in 1995

Most total bases
2,440 in 1977

Most long hits
522 in 1977

Most extra bases on long hits
891 in 1977

Most sacrifice hits
72 in 1972

Most sacrifice flies
76 in 1979

Most stolen bases
218 in 1976

Most caught stealing
87 in 1977

Most bases on balls
641 in 1970

Most strikeouts
1,061 in 1997

Fewest strikeouts
644 in 1978

Most hit by pitch
64 in 1999

Fewest hit by pitch
23 in 1983

Most runs batted in
831 in 2000

Most game-winning RBIs
92 in 1980

Highest batting average
.288 in 2000

Lowest batting average
.240 in 1969

Highest slugging average
.436 in 1977

Lowest slugging average
.338 in 1969

Most grounded into double play
156 in 1999

Fewest grounded into double play
95 in 1978

Most left on bases
1,209 in 1980

Fewest left on bases
1,057 in 1985

Most .300 hitters
4 in 2000

Most putouts
4,417 in 1976

Fewest putouts
4,144 in 1972

Most assists
1,912 in 1973

Fewest assists
1,598 in 1990

Most chances accepted
6,290 in 1974, 1985

Fewest chances accepted
5,860 in 1990

Most errors
167 in 1973

Fewest errors
91 in 1997

Most errorless games
95 in 1993

Most consecutive errorless games
11 in 1997

Most double plays
204 in 2001

Fewest double plays
114 in 1969

Most passed balls
29 in 1974

Fewest passed balls
3 in 1984

Highest fielding average
.985 in 1997

Lowest fielding average
.974 in 1973, 1983

Highest home attendance
2,477,700 in 1989

Highest road attendance
2,378,624 in 1993

Most games won
102 in 1977

Most games lost
97 in 1970, 1999, 2001

Most games won, month
25 in September 1977

Most games lost, month
21 in August 1999

Highest percentage games won
.630 in 1977 (won 102, lost 60)

Lowest percentage games won
.398 in 1999 (won 64, lost 97)

Games won, league
2,613 in 33 years

Games lost, league
2,594 in 33 years

Most shutouts won
16 in 1972

Most shutouts lost
18 in 1971, 1989

Most 1-0 shutouts won
5 in 1972

Most 1-0 shutouts lost
4 in 1971, 1989, 1992

Most consecutive games won
16 in 1977

Most consecutive games lost
12 in 1997

Number of times league champions
2

Number of last-place finishes
0

Most runs, game
23 vs. Minnesota, April 6, 1974

Most runs by opponent, game
22 by Boston, April 12, 1994

Most runs, shutout game
16 vs. Oakland, June 25, 1984

Most runs by opponent, shutout game
17 by Detroit, July 19, 1991

Most runs, doubleheader shutout
No performance

Most runs, inning
11 vs. Toronto, August 6, 1979, seventh inning
vs. Boston, August 2, 1986, seventh inning
vs. Milwaukee, August 21, 1995, second game, fourth inning

Longest 1-0 game won
15 innings vs. Minnesota, May 23, 1981

Longest 1-0 game lost
14 innings vs. Cleveland, July 23, 1992

Most hits, game
24 vs. Detroit, June 15, 1976

Most home runs, game
6 vs. Detroit, July 14, 1991

Most consecutive games with one or more homers
12 (19 homers), 1985

Most total bases, game
37 vs. Chicago, July 18, 2000

Largest crowd, day game
41,329 vs. Oakland, September 21, 1980

Largest crowd, doubleheader
42,039 vs. Milwaukee, August 8, 1983

Largest crowd, night game
41,860 vs. New York, July 26, 1980

Largest crowd, home opener
41,086 vs. Toronto, April 8, 1985

MINNESOTA TWINS
YEARLY FINISHES

Year	Position	W	L	Pct.	*GB	Manager	Attendance
1961	7th	70	90	.438	38.0	Cookie Lavagetto, Sam Mele	1,256,723
1962	2nd	91	71	.562	5.0	Sam Mele	1,433,116
1963	3rd	91	70	.565	13.0	Sam Mele	1,406,652
1964	6th (tied)	79	83	.488	20.0	Sam Mele	1,207,514
1965	1st	102	60	.630	+7.0	Sam Mele	1,463,258

Year	Position	W	L	Pct.	*GB	Manager	Attendance
1966	2nd	89	73	.549	9.0	Sam Mele	1,259,374
1967	2nd (tied)	91	71	.562	1.0	Sam Mele, Cal Ermer	1,483,547
1968	7th	79	83	.488	24.0	Cal Ermer	1,143,257

WEST DIVISION

Year	Position	W	L	Pct.	*GB	Manager	Attendance
1969	1st†	97	65	.599	+9.0	Billy Martin	1,349,328
1970	1st†	98	64	.605	+9.0	Bill Rigney	1,261,887
1971	5th	74	86	.463	26.5	Bill Rigney	940,858
1972	3rd	77	77	.500	15.5	Bill Rigney, Frank Quilici	797,901
1973	3rd	81	81	.500	13.0	Frank Quilici	907,499
1974	3rd	82	80	.506	8.0	Frank Quilici	662,401
1975	4th	76	83	.478	20.5	Frank Quilici	737,156
1976	3rd	85	77	.525	5.0	Gene Mauch	715,394
1977	4th	84	77	.522	17.5	Gene Mauch	1,162,727
1978	4th	73	89	.451	19.0	Gene Mauch	787,878
1979	4th	82	80	.506	6.0	Gene Mauch	1,070,521
1980	3rd	77	84	.478	19.5	Gene Mauch, Johnny Goryl	769,206
1981	7th/4th	41	68	.376	‡	Johnny Goryl, Billy Gardner	469,090
1982	7th	60	102	.370	33.0	Billy Gardner	921,186
1983	5th (tied)	70	92	.432	29.0	Billy Gardner	858,939
1984	2nd (tied)	81	81	.500	3.0	Billy Gardner	1,598,422
1985	4th (tied)	77	85	.475	14.0	Billy Gardner, Ray Miller	1,651,814
1986	6th	71	91	.438	21.0	Ray Miller, Tom Kelly	1,255,453
1987	1st§	85	77	.525	+2.0	Tom Kelly	2,081,976
1988	2nd	91	71	.562	13.0	Tom Kelly	3,030,672
1989	5th	80	82	.494	19.0	Tom Kelly	2,277,438
1990	7th	74	88	.457	29.0	Tom Kelly	1,751,584
1991	1st§	95	67	.586	+8.0	Tom Kelly	2,293,842
1992	2nd	90	72	.556	6.0	Tom Kelly	2,482,428
1993	5th (tied)	71	91	.438	23.0	Tom Kelly	2,048,673

CENTRAL DIVISION

Year	Position	W	L	Pct.	*GB	Manager	Attendance
1994	4th	53	60	.469	14.0	Tom Kelly	1,398,565
1995	5th	56	88	.389	44.0	Tom Kelly	1,057,667
1996	4th	78	84	.481	21.5	Tom Kelly	1,437,352
1997	4th	68	94	.420	18.5	Tom Kelly	1,411,064
1998	4th	70	92	.432	19.0	Tom Kelly	1,165,980
1999	5th	63	97	.397	33.0	Tom Kelly	1,202,829
2000	5th	69	93	.426	26.0	Tom Kelly	1,059,715
2001	2nd	85	77	.525	6.0	Tom Kelly	1,782,926

*Games behind winner. †Lost championship series. ‡First half 17-39; second 24-29. §Won championship series.

INDIVIDUAL RECORDS (1961 TO DATE)

SERVICE

Most years by non-pitcher
15—Tony Oliva

Most years by pitcher
13—Jim Kaat

BATTING

Most games
164—Cesar Tovar, 1967

Most games, career
1,939—Harmon Killebrew

Most at-bats
691—Kirby Puckett, 161 games, 1985

Most at-bats, career
7,244—Kirby Puckett

Most runs
140—Chuck Knoblauch, 153 games, 1996

Most runs, career
1,071—Kirby Puckett

Most hits
239—Rod Carew, 155 games, 1977

Most hits, career
2,304—Kirby Puckett

Most singles
180—Rod Carew, 153 games, 1974

Most singles, career
1,626—Kirby Puckett

Most doubles
46—Marty Cordova, 145 games, 1996

Most doubles, career
414—Kirby Puckett

Most triples
20—Christian Guzman, 156 games, 2000

Most triples, career
90—Rod Carew

Most homers by righthander
49—Harmon Killebrew, 158 games, 1964
Harmon Killebrew, 162 games, 1969

Most homers by lefthander
34—Kent Hrbek, 143 games, 1987

Most homers by switch-hitter
29—Chili Davis, 153 games, 1991

Most homers by rookie
33—Jimmie Hall, 156 games, 1963

Most homers at home
29—Harmon Killebrew, 1961

Most homers on road
28—Harmon Killebrew, 1962

Most homers, month
14—Harmon Killebrew, June, 1964

Most homers by righthander, career
475—Harmon Killebrew

Most homers by lefthander, career
293—Kent Hrbek

Most homers by switch-hitter, career
110—Roy Smalley

Most grand slams
3— Bob Allison, 159 games, 1961
Rod Carew, 156 games, 1976
Kent Hrbek, 158 games, 1985
Kirby Puckett, 160 games, 1992

Most grand slams, career
10—Harmon Killebrew

Most total bases
374—Tony Oliva, 161 games, 1964

Most total bases, career
3,453—Kirby Puckett

Most long hits
84—Tony Oliva, 161 games, 1964

Most long hits, career
728—Harmon Killebrew

Most extra bases on long hits
172—Harmon Killebrew, 150 games, 1961

Most extra bases on long hits, career
1,699—Harmon Killebrew

Most sacrifice hits
25—Rob Wilfong, 140 games, 1979

Most sacrifice flies
13—Gary Gaetti, 145 games, 1982
Tom Brunansky, 157 games, 1985

Most bases on balls
145—Harmon Killebrew, 162 games, 1969

Most bases on balls, career
1,321—Harmon Killebrew

Most strikeouts
145—Bob Darwin, 145 games, 1972

Fewest strikeouts
24—Vic Power, 138 games, 1963

Most strikeouts, career
1,314—Harmon Killebrew

Most hit by pitch
19—Chuck Knoblauch, 153 games, 1996

Most runs batted in
140—Harmon Killebrew, 162 games, 1969

Most runs batted in, career
1,325—Harmon Killebrew

Most game-winning RBIs
15—Tom Brunansky, 151 games, 1983

Most consecutive games with RBI
11—Kirby Puckett (15 RBIs), 1988

Highest batting average
.388—Rod Carew, 155 games, 1977

Highest batting average, career
.334—Rod Carew

Highest slugging percentage
.606—Harmon Killebrew, 150 games, 1961

Highest slugging average, career
.518—Harmon Killebrew

Longest batting streak
31 games—Ken Landreaux, 1980

Most grounded into double play
28—Harmon Killebrew, 157 games, 1970

Fewest grounded into double play
2—Cesar Tovar, 157 games, 1968

BASERUNNING

Most stolen bases
62—Chuck Knoblauch, 156 games, 1997

Most stolen bases, career
276—Chuck Knoblauch

Most caught stealing
22—Rod Carew, 156 games, 1976

PITCHING

Most games
90—Mike Marshall, 1979

Most games, career
490—Rick Aguilera

Most games started
42—Jim Kaat, 1965

Most games started, career
422—Jim Kaat

Most complete games
25—Bert Blyleven, 1973

Most complete games, career
133—Jim Kaat

Most games finished
84—Mike Marshall, 1979

Most innings
325—Bert Blyleven, 1973

Most innings pitched, career
2,958—Jim Kaat

Most games won
25—Jim Kaat, 1966

Most games won, career
189—Jim Kaat

Most games lost, season
20—Pedro Ramos, 1961

Most games lost, career
152—Jim Kaat

Highest winning percentage
.774—Frank Viola (24-7), 1988

Longest winning streak
12 games—Scott Erickson, 1991
    Brad Radke, 1997

Longest losing streak
13 games—Terry Felton, 1982

Most saves
42—Jeff Reardon, 1988
    Rick Aguilera, 1991

Most 20-victory seasons
2—Camilo Pascual, Jim Perry

Most bases on balls
127—Jim Hughes, 1975

Most bases on balls, career
694—Jim Kaat

Most strikeouts
258—Bert Blyleven, 1973

Most strikeouts, career
2,035—Bert Blyleven

Most strikeouts, game
15— Camilo Pascual, July 19, 1961, first game
    Joe Decker, June 26, 1973
    Jerry Koosman, June 23, 1980
    Bert Blyleven, August 1, 1986

Most shutouts
9—Bert Blyleven, 1973

Most shutouts, career
29—Bert Blyleven

Most 1-0 shutouts won
3—Bert Blyleven, 1971

Most runs
141—Frank Viola, 1983

Most earned runs
129—LaTroy Hawkins, 1999

Most hits
296—Bert Blyleven, 1973

Most hit batsmen
18—Jim Kaat, 1962

Most wild pitches
15—Dave Goltz, 1976
    Mike Smithson, 1986
    Jack Morris, 1991

Most home runs
50—Bert Blyleven, 1986

Most sacrifice hits
17—Dean Chance, 1968
    Jerry Koosman, 1980

Most sacrifice flies
13—Bert Blyleven, 1973
    Scott Erickson, 1993

Lowest ERA
2.45—Allan Anderson, 202.1 innings, 1988

CLUB RECORDS

Most players
46 in 1995

Fewest players
31 in 1976

Most games
164 in 1967

Most at-bats
5,677 in 1969

Most runs
877 in 1996

Fewest runs
562 in 1968

Most opponents' runs
900 in 1996

Most hits
1,633 in 1996

Fewest hits
1,274 in 1968

Most singles
1,192 in 1974

Most doubles
332 in 1996

Most triples
60 in 1977

Most homers
225 in 1963

Fewest homers
81 in 1976

Most homers at Metropolitan Stadium, home and opponents
211 in 1963

Most homers at Metrodome, home and opponents
223 in 1986

Most grand slams
8 in 1961

Most pinch home runs
7 in 1964, 1967

Most total bases
2,413 in 1996

Most long hits
530 in 2001

Most extra bases on long hits
982 in 1964

Most sacrifice hits
142 in 1979

Most sacrifice flies
63 in 1996

Most stolen bases
151 in 1997

Most caught stealing
75 in 1976

Most bases on balls
649 in 1962

Most strikeouts
1,121 in 1997

Fewest strikeouts
684 in 1978

Most hit by pitch
65 in 1996

Fewest hit by pitch
21 in 1980

Most runs batted in
812 in 1996

Most game-winning RBIs
86 in 1988

Highest batting average
.288 in 1996

Lowest batting average
.237 in 1968

Highest slugging average
.433 in 2001

Lowest slugging average
.350 in 1968

Most grounded into double play
172 in 1996

Fewest grounded into double play
93 in 1965

Most left on bases
1,263 in 1974

Fewest left on bases
1,041 in 1987

Most .300 hitters
3 in 1969, 1970, 1977, 1988, 1992, 1996

Most putouts
4,493 in 1969

Fewest putouts
4,198 in 1972

Most assists
2,007 in 1979

Fewest assists
1,500 in 1988

Most chances accepted
6,349 in 1969

Fewest chances accepted
5,795 in 1988

Most errors
174 in 1961

Fewest errors
84 in 1988

Most errorless games
96 in 1988

Most consecutive errorless games
10 in 1987, 2001

Most double plays
203 in 1979

Fewest double plays
117 in 1968

Most passed balls
21 in 1987, 1993

Fewest passed balls
4 in 1984, 2001

Highest fielding average
.986 in 1988

Lowest fielding average
.972 in 1961

Highest home attendance
3,030,672 in 1988

Highest road attendance
2,332,786 in 2000

Most games won
102 in 1965

Most games lost
102 in 1982

Most games won, month
23 in July 1969

Most games lost, month
26 in May 1981, May 1982

Highest percentage games won
.630, in 1965 (won 102, lost 60)

Lowest percentage games won
.370, in 1982 (won 60, lost 102)

Games won, league
3,206 in 41 years

Games lost, league
3,296 in 41 years

Most shutouts won
18 in 1967, 1973

Most shutouts lost
14 in 1964, 1972, 1990

Most 1-0 games won
5 in 1966

Most 1-0 games lost
5 in 1974

Most consecutive games won
15 in 1991

Most consecutive games lost
14 in 1982

Number of times league champions
3

Number of last-place finishes
4 (tied in 1995)

Most runs, game
24 vs. Detroit, April 24, 1996

Most runs by opponent, game
23 by Kansas City, April 6, 1974

Most runs, shutout game
16 vs. Boston, May 25, 1990

Most runs by opponent, shutout game
17 by California, April 23, 1980

Most runs, doubleheader shutout
16 vs. Oakland, June 26, 1988

Most runs, inning
11 vs. Cleveland, July 18, 1962, first inning
vs. Oakland, June 21, 1969, 10th inning
vs. Cleveland, August 5, 1977, fourth inning
vs. Boston, May 20, 1994, fifth inning

Longest 1-0 game won
13 innings vs. Texas, September 22, 1992

Longest 1-0 game lost
15 innings vs. Kansas City, May 23, 1981

Most hits, game
24 vs. Boston, May 25, 1977
vs. Seattle, September 20, 1989, 11 innings
vs. Detroit, June 4, 1994

Most home runs, game
8 vs. Washington, August 29, 1963, first game

Most consecutive games with one or more homers
16 (28 homers), 1979

Most total bases, game
47 vs. Washington, August 29, 1963, first game

Largest crowd, day game
53,106 vs. Kansas City, September 27, 1987

Largest crowd, doubleheader
51,017 vs. Oakland, July 28, 1990

Largest crowd, night game
53,067 vs. Toronto, April 8, 1988

Largest crowd, home opener
53,067 vs. Toronto, April 8, 1988

NEW YORK YANKEES
YEARLY FINISHES

(Baltimore Orioles, 1901 to 1902)

Year	Position	W	L	Pct.	*GB	Manager	Attendance
1901	5th	68	65	.511	13.5	John McGraw	141,952
1902	8th	50	88	.362	34.0	John McGraw, Wilbert Robinson	174,606
1903	4th	72	62	.537	17.0	Clark Griffith	211,808
1904	2nd	92	59	.609	1.5	Clark Griffith	438,919
1905	6th	71	78	.477	21.5	Clark Griffith	309,100
1906	2nd	90	61	.596	3.0	Clark Griffith	434,709
1907	5th	70	78	.473	21.0	Clark Griffith	350,020
1908	8th	51	103	.331	39.5	Clark Griffith, Kid Elberfeld	305,500
1909	5th	74	77	.490	23.5	George Stallings	501,000
1910	2nd	88	63	.583	14.5	George Stallings, Hal Chase	355,857
1911	6th	76	76	.500	25.5	Hal Chase	302,444
1912	8th	50	102	.329	55.0	Harry Wolverton	242,194
1913	7th	57	94	.377	38.0	Frank Chance	357,551
1914	6th (tied)	70	84	.455	30.0	Frank Chance, Roger Peckinpaugh	359,477
1915	5th	69	83	.454	32.5	Bill Donovan	256,035
1916	4th	80	74	.519	11.0	Bill Donovan	469,211
1917	6th	71	82	.464	28.5	Bill Donovan	330,294
1918	4th	60	63	.488	13.5	Miller Huggins	282,047
1919	3rd	80	59	.576	7.5	Miller Huggins	619,164
1920	3rd	95	59	.617	3.0	Miller Huggins	1,289,422
1921	1st	98	55	.641	+4.5	Miller Huggins	1,230,696
1922	1st	94	60	.610	+1.0	Miller Huggins	1,026,134
1923	1st	98	54	.645	+16.0	Miller Huggins	1,007,066
1924	2nd	89	63	.586	2.0	Miller Huggins	1,053,533
1925	7th	69	85	.448	30.0	Miller Huggins	697,267
1926	1st	91	63	.591	+3.0	Miller Huggins	1,027,095
1927	1st	110	44	.714	+19.0	Miller Huggins	1,164,015
1928	1st	101	53	.656	+2.5	Miller Huggins	1,072,132

Year	Position	W	L	Pct.	*GB	Manager	Attendance
1929	2nd	88	66	.571	18.0	Miller Huggins, Art Fletcher	960,148
1930	3rd	86	68	.558	16.0	Bob Shawkey	1,169,230
1931	2nd	94	59	.614	13.5	Joe McCarthy	912,437
1932	1st	107	47	.695	+13.0	Joe McCarthy	962,320
1933	2nd	91	59	.607	7.0	Joe McCarthy	728,014
1934	2nd	94	60	.610	7.0	Joe McCarthy	854,682
1935	2nd	89	60	.597	3.0	Joe McCarthy	657,508
1936	1st	102	51	.667	+19.5	Joe McCarthy	976,913
1937	1st	102	52	.662	+13.0	Joe McCarthy	998,148
1938	1st	99	53	.651	+9.5	Joe McCarthy	970,916
1939	1st	106	45	.702	+17.0	Joe McCarthy	859,785
1940	3rd	88	66	.571	2.0	Joe McCarthy	988,975
1941	1st	101	53	.656	+17.0	Joe McCarthy	964,722
1942	1st	103	51	.669	+9.0	Joe McCarthy	988,251
1943	1st	98	56	.636	+13.5	Joe McCarthy	645,006
1944	3rd	83	71	.539	6.0	Joe McCarthy	822,864
1945	4th	81	71	.533	6.5	Joe McCarthy	881,846
1946	3rd	87	67	.565	17.0	Joe McCarthy, Bill Dickey, Johnny Neun	2,265,512
1947	1st	97	57	.630	+12.0	Bucky Harris	2,178,937
1948	3rd	94	60	.610	2.5	Bucky Harris	2,373,901
1949	1st	97	57	.630	+1.0	Casey Stengel	2,281,676
1950	1st	98	56	.636	+3.0	Casey Stengel	2,081,380
1951	1st	98	56	.636	+5.0	Casey Stengel	1,950,107
1952	1st	95	59	.617	+2.0	Casey Stengel	1,629,665
1953	1st	99	52	.656	+8.5	Casey Stengel	1,537,811
1954	2nd	103	51	.669	8.0	Casey Stengel	1,475,171
1955	1st	96	58	.623	+3.0	Casey Stengel	1,490,138
1956	1st	97	57	.630	+9.0	Casey Stengel	1,491,784
1957	1st	98	56	.636	+8.0	Casey Stengel	1,497,134
1958	1st	92	62	.597	+10.0	Casey Stengel	1,428,438
1959	3rd	79	75	.513	15.0	Casey Stengel	1,552,030
1960	1st	97	57	.630	+8.0	Casey Stengel	1,627,349
1961	1st	109	53	.673	+8.0	Ralph Houk	1,747,725
1962	1st	96	66	.593	+5.0	Ralph Houk	1,493,574
1963	1st	104	57	.646	+10.5	Ralph Houk	1,308,920
1964	1st	99	63	.611	+1.0	Yogi Berra	1,305,638
1965	6th	77	85	.475	25.0	Johnny Keane	1,213,552
1966	10th	70	89	.440	26.5	Johnny Keane, Ralph Houk	1,124,648
1967	9th	72	90	.444	20.0	Ralph Houk	1,259,514
1968	5th	83	79	.512	20.0	Ralph Houk	1,185,666

EAST DIVISION

Year	Position	W	L	Pct.	*GB	Manager	Attendance
1969	5th	80	81	.497	28.5	Ralph Houk	1,067,996
1970	2nd	93	69	.574	15.0	Ralph Houk	1,136,879
1971	4th	82	80	.506	21.0	Ralph Houk	1,070,771
1972	4th	79	76	.510	6.5	Ralph Houk	966,328
1973	4th	80	82	.494	17.0	Ralph Houk	1,262,103
1974	2nd	89	73	.549	2.0	Bill Virdon	1,273,075
1975	3rd	83	77	.519	12.0	Bill Virdon, Billy Martin	1,288,048
1976	1st†	97	62	.610	+10.5	Billy Martin	2,012,434
1977	1st†	100	62	.617	+2.5	Billy Martin	2,103,092
1978	1st‡†	100	63	.613	+1.0	Billy Martin, Bob Lemon	2,335,871
1979	4th	89	71	.556	13.5	Bob Lemon, Billy Martin	2,537,765
1980	1st§	103	59	.636	+3.0	Dick Howser	2,627,417
1981	1st/6th▲†	59	48	.551	∞	Gene Michael, Bob Lemon	1,614,533
1982	5th	79	83	.488	16.0	Bob Lemon, Gene Michael, Clyde King	2,041,219
1983	3rd	91	71	.562	7.0	Billy Martin	2,257,976
1984	3rd	87	75	.537	17.0	Yogi Berra	1,821,815
1985	2nd	97	64	.602	2.0	Yogi Berra, Billy Martin	2,214,587
1986	2nd	90	72	.556	5.5	Lou Piniella	2,268,030
1987	4th	89	73	.549	9.0	Lou Piniella	2,427,672
1988	5th	85	76	.528	3.5	Billy Martin, Lou Piniella	2,633,701
1989	5th	74	87	.460	14.5	Dallas Green, Bucky Dent	2,170,485
1990	7th	67	95	.414	21.0	Bucky Dent, Stump Merrill	2,006,436
1991	5th	71	91	.438	20.0	Stump Merrill	1,863,733
1992	4th (tied)	76	86	.469	20.0	Buck Showalter	1,748,733
1993	2nd	88	74	.543	7.0	Buck Showalter	2,416,965
1994	1st	70	43	.619	+6.5	Buck Showalter	1,675,556
1995	2nd◆	79	65	.549	7.0	Buck Showalter	1,705,263
1996	1st▲†	92	70	.568	+4.0	Joe Torre	2,250,877
1997	2nd◆	96	66	.593	2.0	Joe Torre	2,580,325
1998	1st▲†	114	48	.704	+22.0	Joe Torre	2,949,734
1999	1st▲†	98	64	.605	+4.0	Joe Torre	3,292,736
2000	1st▲†	87	74	.540	+2.5	Joe Torre	3,227,657
2001	1st▲†	95	65	.594	+13.5	Joe Torre	3,264,777

*Games behind winner. †Won championship series. ‡Won division playoff. §Lost championship series. ∞First half 34-22; second 25-26. ▲Won division series. ◆Lost division series.

INDIVIDUAL RECORDS (1903 TO DATE)

SERVICE

Most years by non-pitcher
18—Yogi Berra
Mickey Mantle

Most years by pitcher
16—Whitey Ford

BATTING

Most games
162—Bobby Richardson, 1961
Roy White, 1970
Chris Chambliss, 1978
Don Mattingly, 1986
Roberto Kelly, 1990

Most games, career
2,401—Mickey Mantle

Most at-bats
692—Bobby Richardson, 161 games, 1962

Most at-bats, career
8,102—Mickey Mantle

Most runs
177—Babe Ruth, 152 games, 1921

Most runs, career
1,959—Babe Ruth

Most hits
238—Don Mattingly, 162 games, 1986

Most hits, career
2,721—Lou Gehrig

Most singles
171—Steve Sax, 158 games, 1989

Most singles, career
1,531—Lou Gehrig

Most doubles
53—Don Mattingly, 162 games, 1986

Most doubles, career
535—Lou Gehrig

Most triples
23—Earle Combs, 152 games, 1927

Most triples, career
162—Lou Gehrig

Most homers by righthander
46—Joe DiMaggio, 151 games, 1937

Most homers by lefthander
61—Roger Maris, 161 games, 1961

Most homers by switch-hitter
54—Mickey Mantle, 153 games, 1961

Most homers by rookie
29—Joe DiMaggio, 138 games, 1936

Most grand slams
6—Don Mattingly, 141 games, 1987

Most grand slams, career
23—Lou Gehrig

Most homers at home
32—Babe Ruth, 1921 (Polo Grounds)
30—Lou Gehrig, 1934 (Yankee Stadium)
Roger Maris, 1961 (Yankee Stadium)

Most homers on road
32—Babe Ruth, 1927

Most homers, month
17—Babe Ruth, September, 1927

Most homers by lefthander, career
659—Babe Ruth

Most homers by righthander, career
361—Joe DiMaggio

Most homers by switch-hitter, career
536—Mickey Mantle

Most total bases
457—Babe Ruth, 152 games, 1921

Most total bases, career
5,131—Babe Ruth

Most long hits
119—Babe Ruth, 152 games, 1921

Most long hits, career
1,190—Lou Gehrig

Most extra bases on long hits
253—Babe Ruth, 152 games, 1921

Most extra bases on long hits, career
2,613—Babe Ruth

Most sacrifice hits
42—Willie Keeler, 149 games, 1905

Most sacrifice flies
17—Roy White, 147 games, 1971

Most bases on balls
170—Babe Ruth, 152 games, 1923

Most bases on balls, career
1,847—Babe Ruth

Most strikeouts, season
156—Danny Tartabull, 138 games, 1993

Most strikeouts, career
1,710—Mickey Mantle

Fewest strikeouts
3—Joe Sewell, 124 games, 1932

Most hit by pitch
24—Don Baylor, 142 games, 1985

Most runs batted in
184—Lou Gehrig, 155 games, 1931

Most runs batted in, career
1,990—Lou Gehrig

Most game-winning RBIs
21—Dave Winfield, 152 games, 1983
Don Mattingly, 159 games, 1985

Most consecutive games with RBI
11—Babe Ruth (18 RBIs), 1931

Highest batting average
.393—Babe Ruth, 152 games, 1923

Highest batting average, career
.349—Babe Ruth

Highest slugging average
.847—Babe Ruth, 142 games, 1920

Highest slugging average, career
.711—Babe Ruth

Longest batting streak
56 games—Joe DiMaggio, 1941

Most grounded into double play
30—Dave Winfield, 152 games, 1983

Fewest grounded into double play
2—Mickey Mantle, 153 games, 1961

BASERUNNING

Most stolen bases
93—Rickey Henderson, 140 games, 1988

Most stolen bases, career
326—Rickey Henderson

Most caught stealing
23—Ben Chapman, 149 games, 1931

PITCHING

Most games
77—Jeff Nelson, 1997

Most games, career
522—Dave Righetti

Most games started
51—Jack Chesbro, 1904

Most games started, career
438—Whitey Ford

Most complete games
48—Jack Chesbro, 1904

Most complete games, career
262—Red Ruffing

Most games finished
68—Dave Righetti, 1986

Most innings
454—Jack Chesbro, 1904

Most innings, career
3,171—Whitey Ford

Most games won
41—Jack Chesbro, 1904

Most games won, career
236—Whitey Ford

Most 20-victory seasons
4—Bob Shawkey, Lefty Gomez, Red Ruffing

Most games lost
21—Al Orth, 1907
Sam Jones, 1925
Joe Lake, 1908
Russ Ford, 1912

Most games lost, career
139—Mel Stottlemyre Sr.

Highest winning percentage
.893—Ron Guidry (25-3), 1978

Longest winning streak
16 games—Roger Clemens, 2001

Longest losing streak
11 games—George Mogridge, 1916

Most saves
50—Mariano Rivera, 2001

Most bases on balls
179—Tommy Byrne, 1949

Most bases on balls, career
1,090—Lefty Gomez

Most strikeouts
248—Ron Guidry, 1978

Most strikeouts, career
1,956—Whitey Ford

Most strikeouts, game
18—Ron Guidry, June 17, 1978

Most shutouts
9—Ron Guidry, 1978

Most shutouts, career
45—Whitey Ford

Most 1-0 shutouts won
2—Held by many pitchers

Most runs
165—Russ Ford, 1912

Most earned runs
127—Sam Jones, 1925

Most hits
337—Jack Chesbro, 1904

Most hit batsmen
26—Jack Warhop, 1909

Most wild pitches
23—Tim Leary, 1990

Most home runs
40—Ralph Terry, 1962

Most sacrifice hits
22—Lefty Gomez, 1935

Most sacrifice flies
15—Doc Medich, 1975

Lowest ERA
1.64—Spud Chandler, 253 innings, 1943

CLUB RECORDS

Most players
18 in 1987, 1996

Fewest players
25 in 1923, 1927

Most games
164 in 1964, 1968

Most at-bats
5,710 in 1997

Most runs
1,067 in 1931

Fewest runs
459 in 1908

Most opponents' runs
898 in 1930

Most hits
1,683 in 1930

Fewest hits
1,137 in 1968

Most singles
1,157 in 1931

Most doubles
325 in 1997

Most triples
110 in 1930

Most homers
240 in 1961

Fewest homers (154 or 162-game schedule)
8 in 1913

Most homers at Yankee Stadium, home and opponents
209 in 2000

Most pinch home runs
10 in 1961

Most grand slams
10 in 1987

Most long hits
580 in 1936

Most extra bases on long hits
1,027 in 1936

Most total bases
2,703 in 1936

Most sacrifices (sacrifice hits and sacrifice flies)
218 in 1922, 1926

Most sacrifice hits
178 in 1906

Most sacrifice flies
72 in 1974, 1996

Most stolen bases
289 in 1910

Most caught stealing
82 in 1920

Most bases on balls
766 in 1932

Most strikeouts
1,043 in 1967

Fewest strikeouts
420 in 1924

Most hit by pitch
64 in 2001

Fewest hit by pitch
14 in 1969

Most runs batted in
995 in 1936

Most game-winning RBIs
96 in 1980

Highest batting average
.309 in 1930

Lowest batting average
.214 in 1968

Highest slugging average
.489 in 1927

Lowest slugging average
.287 in 1914

Most grounded into double play
153 in 1996

Fewest grounded into double play
91 in 1963

Most left on bases
1,276 in 1997

Fewest left on bases
1,010 in 1920

Most .300 hitters
9 in 1930

Most putouts
4,520 in 1964

Fewest putouts
3,993 in 1935

Most assists
2,086 in 1904

Fewest assists
1,487 in 2000

Most chances accepted
6,377 in 1968

Fewest chances accepted
5,551 in 1935

Most errors
386 in 1912

Fewest errors
91 in 1996

Most errorless games
94 in 1996

Most consecutive errorless games
10 in 1977, 1993, 1995

Most double plays
214 in 1956

Fewest double plays
81 in 1912

Most passed balls
32 in 1913

Fewest passed balls
0 in 1931

Highest fielding average
.985 in 1996

Lowest fielding average
.939 in 1912

Highest home attendance
3,292,736 in 1999

Highest road attendance
2,876,506 in 2000

Most games won
114 in 1998

Most games lost
103 in 1908

Most games won, month
28 in August 1938

Most games lost, month
24 in July 1908

Highest percentage games won
.714 in 1927 (won 110, lost 44)

Lowest percentage games won
.329 in 1912 (won 50, lost 102)

Games won, league
8,674 in 99 years

Games lost, league
6,629 in 99 years

Most shutouts won
24 in 1951

Most shutouts lost
27 in 1914

Most 1-0 games won
6 in 1908, 1968

Most 1-0 games lost
9 in 1914

Most consecutive games won
19 in 1947

Most consecutive games lost
13 in 1913

Number of times league champions
38

Number of last-place finishes
5

Most runs, game
25 vs. Philadelphia, May 24, 1936

Most runs by opponent, game
24 by Cleveland, July 29, 1928

Most runs, shutout game
21 vs. Philadelphia, August 13, 1939, second game, eight innings

Most runs by opponent, shutout game
15 by Chicago, July 15, 1907
by Chicago, May 4, 1950

Most runs, doubleheader shutout
24 vs. Philadelphia, September 4, 1944

Most runs, inning
14 vs. Washington, July 6, 1920, fifth inning

Longest 1-0 game won
15 innings vs. Philadelphia, July 4, 1925, first game

Longest 1-0 game lost
14 innings vs. Boston, September 24, 1969

Most hits, game
30 vs. Boston, September 28, 1923

Most home runs, game
8 vs. Philadelphia, June 28, 1939, first game

Most consecutive games with one or more homers
25 (40 homers), 1941

Most total bases, game
53 vs. Philadelphia, June 28, 1939, first game

Largest crowd, day game
73,205 vs. Philadelphia, April 19, 1931

Largest crowd, doubleheader
81,841 vs. Boston, May 30, 1938

Largest crowd, night game
74,747 vs. Boston, May 26, 1947

Largest crowd, home opener
56,717 vs. Oakland, April 10, 1998

OAKLAND A'S
YEARLY FINISHES

Year	Position	W	L	Pct.	*GB	Manager	Attendance
1968	6th	82	80	.506	21.0	Bob Kennedy	837,466

WEST DIVISION

Year	Position	W	L	Pct.	*GB	Manager	Attendance
1969	2nd	88	74	.543	9.0	Hank Bauer, John McNamara	778,232
1970	2nd	89	73	.549	9.0	John McNamara	778,355
1971	1st†	101	60	.627	+16.0	Dick Williams	914,993
1972	1st‡	93	62	.600	+5.5	Dick Williams	921,323
1973	1st‡	94	68	.580	+6.0	Dick Williams	1,000,763
1974	1st‡	90	72	.556	+5.0	Alvin Dark	845,693
1975	1st†	98	64	.605	+7.0	Alvin Dark	1,075,518
1976	2nd	87	74	.540	2.5	Chuck Tanner	780,593
1977	7th	63	98	.391	38.5	Jack McKeon, Bobby Winkles	495,599
1978	6th	69	93	.426	23.0	Bobby Winkles, Jack McKeon	526,999
1979	7th	54	108	.333	34.0	Jim Marshall	306,763
1980	2nd	83	79	.512	14.0	Billy Martin	842,259
1981	1st/2nd∞†	64	45	.587	§	Billy Martin	1,304,054
1982	5th	68	94	.420	25.0	Billy Martin	1,735,489
1983	4th	74	88	.457	25.0	Steve Boros	1,294,941
1984	4th	77	85	.475	7.0	Steve Boros, Jackie Moore	1,353,281
1985	4th (tied)	77	85	.475	14.0	Jackie Moore	1,334,599
1986	3rd (tied)	76	86	.469	16.0	Jackie Moore, Tony La Russa	1,314,646
1987	3rd	81	81	.500	4.0	Tony La Russa	1,678,921
1988	1st‡	104	58	.642	+13.0	Tony La Russa	2,287,335
1989	1st‡	99	63	.611	+7.0	Tony La Russa	2,667,225
1990	1st‡	103	59	.636	+9.0	Tony La Russa	2,900,217
1991	4th	84	78	.519	11.0	Tony La Russa	2,713,493
1992	1st†	96	66	.593	+6.0	Tony La Russa	2,494,160
1993	7th	68	94	.420	26.0	Tony La Russa	2,035,025
1994	2nd	51	63	.447	1.0	Tony La Russa	1,242,692
1995	4th	67	77	.465	11.5	Tony La Russa	1,174,310
1996	3rd	78	84	.481	12.0	Art Howe	1,148,380
1997	4th	65	97	.401	25.0	Art Howe	1,264,218
1998	4th	74	88	.457	14.0	Art Howe	1,232,339
1999	2nd	87	75	.537	8.0	Art Howe	1,434,610
2000	1st▲	91	70	.565	+0.5	Art Howe	1,728,888
2001	2nd▲	102	60	.630	14.0	Art Howe	2,133,277

*Games behind winner. †Lost championship series. ‡Won championship series. §First half 37-23; second 27-22. ∞Won division series. ▲Lost division series.

INDIVIDUAL RECORDS (1968 TO DATE)

SERVICE

Most years by non-pitcher
14—Rickey Henderson
Most years by pitcher
11—Mike Norris

BATTING

Most games
162—Sal Bando, 1968, 1969, 1973
Alfredo Griffin, 1985, 1986
Terrence Long, 2001
Miguel Tejada, 2001
Most games, career
1,704—Rickey Henderson
Most at-bats
644—Johnny Damon, 155 games, 2001
Most at-bats, career
6,140—Rickey Henderson
Most runs
123—Reggie Jackson, 152 games, 1969
Most runs, career
1,270—Rickey Henderson
Most hits
187—Jose Canseco, 158 games, 1988
Most hits, career
1,768—Rickey Henderson
Most singles
153—Carney Lansford, 148 games, 1989

Most singles, career
1,271—Rickey Henderson
Most doubles
47—Jason Giambi, 154 games, 2001
Most doubles, career
289—Rickey Henderson
Most triples
12—Phil Garner, 159 games, 1976
Most triples, career
41—Rickey Henderson
Most homers by righthander
52—Mark McGwire, 130 games, 1996
Most homers by lefthander
47—Reggie Jackson, 152 games, 1969
Most homers by switch-hitter
23—Ruben Sierra, 110 games, 1994
Most homers by rookie
49—Mark McGwire, 151 games, 1987
Most homers at home
27—Jason Giambi, 2001
Most homers on road
28— Mark McGwire, 1987, 1996
Jose Canseco, 1991
Most homers by righthander, career
363—Mark McGwire
Most homers by lefthander, career
268—Reggie Jackson

Most homers by switch-hitter, career
60—Ruben Sierra
Most grand slams
4—Jason Giambi, 152 games, 2000
Most grand slams, career
9—Mark McGwire
Most homers, month
15—Mark McGwire, May 1987
Most total bases
347—Jose Canseco, 158 games, 1988
Most total bases, career
2,640—Reggie Jackson
Most long hits
87—Jason Giambi, 154 games, 2001
Most long hits, career
563—Mark McGwire
Most extra bases on long hits
183—Reggie Jackson, 152 games, 1969
Mark McGwire, 151 games, 1987
Most extra bases on long hits, career
1,294—Mark McGwire
Most sacrifice hits
22—Dwayne Murphy, 159 games, 1980
Most sacrifice flies
14—Dave Kingman, 147 games, 1984
Most bases on balls
137—Jason Giambi, 152 games, 2000

Most bases on balls, career
,227—Rickey Henderson

Most strikeouts
75—Jose Canseco, 157 games, 1986

Most strikeouts, career
,180—Reggie Jackson

Fewest strikeouts
1—Felipe Alou, 154 games, 1970

Most hit by pitch
0—Don Baylor, 157 games,1976

Most runs batted in
37—Jason Giambi, 152 games, 2000

Most runs batted in, career
41—Mark McGwire

Most game-winning RBIs
0—Mark McGwire, 155 games, 1988

Highest batting average
342—Jason Giambi, 154 games, 2001

Highest batting average, career
308—Jason Giambi

Highest slugging average
730—Mark McGwire, 130 games, 1996

Highest slugging average, career
551—Mark McGwire

Most consecutive games with RBI
0—Rick Monday (18 RBIs), 1969

Longest batting streak
5 games—Jason Giambi, 1997

Most grounded into double play
2—Ben Grieve, 158 games, 2000

Fewest grounded into double play
—Reggie Jackson, 154 games, 1968

BASERUNNING

Most stolen bases
30—Rickey Henderson, 149 games,
1982

Most stolen bases, career
67—Rickey Henderson

Most caught stealing
2—Rickey Henderson, 149 games,
1982

PITCHING

Most games
8—Buddy Groom, 1997

Most games, career
25—Dennis Eckersley

Most games started
1—Catfish Hunter, 1974

Most games started, career
70—Catfish Hunter

Most complete games
8—Rick Langford, 1980

Most complete games, career
6—Catfish Hunter

Most games finished
5—Dennis Eckersley, 1992

Most innings
18—Catfish Hunter, 1974

Most innings, career
,946—Vida Blue

Most games won
27—Bob Welch, 1990

Most games won, career
31—Catfish Hunter

Most 20-victory seasons
—Catfish Hunter, Dave Stewart

Most games lost
20—Brian Kingman, 1980

Most games lost, career
105—Rick Langford

Longest winning streak
13 games—Catfish Hunter, 1973

Longest losing streak
14 games—Matt Keough, 1979

Highest winning percentage
.818—Bob Welch (27-6), 1990

Most saves
51—Dennis Eckersley, 1992

Most bases on balls
112—John Odom, 1969

Most bases on balls, career
655—Dave Stewart

Most strikeouts
301—Vida Blue, 1971

Most strikeouts, career
1,315—Vida Blue

Most strikeouts, game
17—Vida Blue, July 9, 1971, first 11
innings of 20-inning game
16—Jose Rijo, April 19, 1986, first eight
innings of nine-inning game

Most shutouts won
8—Vida Blue, 1971

Most shutouts won, career
28—Vida Blue

Most 1-0 shutouts won
2—Vida Blue, 1971
Catfish Hunter, 1971

Most runs
144—Matt Keough, 1982

Most earned runs
133—Matt Keough, 1982

Most hits
284—Vida Blue, 1977

Most hit batsmen
13—Barry Zito, 2001

Most wild pitches
22—Mike Moore, 1992

Most home runs
39—Catfish Hunter, 1973

Most sacrifice hits
17—Bob Lacey, 1977

Most sacrifice flies
15—Dave Stewart, 1991

Lowest ERA
1.82—Vida Blue, 312 innings, 1971

CLUB RECORDS

Most players
49 in 1997

Fewest players
34 in 1968, 1980

Most games
163 in 1968

Most at-bats
5,630 in 1996

Most runs
947 in 2000

Fewest runs
532 in 1978

Most opponents' runs
946 in 1997

Most hits
1,501 in 2000

Fewest hits
1,276 in 1979

Most singles
1,061 in 1983

Most doubles
334 in 2001

Most triples
40 in 1968

Most homers
243 in 1996

Fewest homers
94 in 1968

Most homers at Oakland Coliseum,
home and opponents
215 in 1996

Most grand slams
14 in 2000

Most pinch home runs
8 in 1970

Most long hits
555 in 2001

Most extra bases on long hits
1,054 in 1996

Most total bases
2,546 in 1996

Most sacrifice hits
108 in 1978

Most sacrifice flies
77 in 1984

Most stolen bases
341 in 1976

Most caught stealing
123 in 1976

Most bases on balls
770 in 1999

Most strikeouts
1,181 in 1997

Fewest strikeouts
751 in 1979

Most hit by pitch
88 in 2001

Fewest hit by pitch
16 in 1985

Most runs batted in
908 in 2000

Most game-winning RBIs
99 in 1988

Highest batting average
.270 in 2000

Lowest batting average
.236 in 1982

Highest slugging average
.458 in 2000

Lowest slugging average
.343 in 1968

Most grounded into double play
163 in 1989

Fewest grounded into double play
87 in 1968

Most left on bases
1,246 in 1999

Fewest left on bases
1,030 in 1979

Most .300 hitters
2 in 1988

Most putouts
4,468 in 1988

Fewest putouts
4,288 in 1979

Most assists
1,821 in 1976

Fewest assists
1,508 in 1984

Most chances accepted
6,230 in 1969

Fewest chances accepted
5,798 in 1984

Most errors
190 in 1977

Fewest errors
87 in 1990

Most errorless games
95 in 1990

Most consecutive errorless games
11 in 1999

Most double plays
195 in 1997

Fewest double plays
115 in 1980

Most passed balls
26 in 1969

Fewest passed balls
4 in 2001

Highest fielding average
.986 in 1990

Lowest fielding average
.970 in 1977

Highest home attendance
2,900,217 in 1990

Highest road attendance
2,636,157 in 1991

Most games won
104 in 1988

Most games lost
108 in 1979

Most games won, month
23 in August 1971

Most games lost, month
24 in June 1979

Games won, league
2,777 in 34 years

Games lost, league
2,601 in 34 years

Highest percentage games won
.642 in 1988 (won 104, lost 58)

Lowest percentage games won
.333 in 1979 (won 54, lost 108)

Most shutouts won
23 in 1972

Most shutouts lost
19 in 1978

Most 1-0 games won
5 in 1971

Most 1-0 games lost
5 in 1971, 1978

Most consecutive games won
14 in 1988

Most consecutive games lost
14 in 1977

Number of times, league champions
6

Number of last-place finishes
2

Most runs, game
23 vs. Texas, September 30, 2000

Most runs by opponents, game
20 by Minnesota, April 27, 1980
by Cleveland, May 4, 1991
by Detroit, April 13, 1993

Most runs, shutout game
15 vs. Baltimore, August 30, 2001

Most runs by opponents, shutout game
16 by Kansas City, June 25, 1984

Most runs, doubleheader shutout
10 vs. Kansas City, September 9, 1974

Most runs, inning
13 vs. California, July 5, 1996, first inning

Longest 1-0 game won
20 innings vs. California, July 9, 1971

Longest 1-0 game lost
13 innings vs. Detroit, May 25, 1973

Most hits, nine-inning game
25 vs. Boston, June 14, 1969

Most hits, extra-inning game
29 vs. Texas, July 1, 1979, 15 innings

Most home runs, game
8 vs. California, June 27, 1996

Most consecutive games with one or more homers
23 (50 homers), 1996

Most total bases, game
44 vs. California, June 27, 1996

Largest crowd, day game
51,263 vs. San Francisco N.L., July 17, 1999

Largest crowd, doubleheader
48,592 vs. New York, May 3, 1981

Largest crowd, night game
54,268 vs. Arizona N.L., July 8, 2000

Largest crowd, home opener
53,498 vs. Detroit, April 3, 2000

PHILADELPHIA A'S
YEARLY FINISHES

Year	Position	W	L	Pct.	*GB	Manager	Attendance
1901	4th	74	62	.544	9.0	Connie Mack	206,329
1902	1st	83	53	.610	+5.0	Connie Mack	442,473
1903	2nd	75	60	.556	14.5	Connie Mack	420,078
1904	5th	81	70	.536	12.5	Connie Mack	512,294
1905	1st	92	56	.622	+2.0	Connie Mack	554,576
1906	4th	78	67	.538	12.0	Connie Mack	489,129
1907	2nd	88	57	.607	1.5	Connie Mack	625,581
1908	6th	68	85	.444	22.0	Connie Mack	455,062
1909	2nd	95	58	.621	3.5	Connie Mack	674,915
1910	1st	102	48	.680	+14.5	Connie Mack	588,905
1911	1st	101	50	.669	+13.5	Connie Mack	605,749
1912	3rd	90	62	.592	15.0	Connie Mack	517,653
1913	1st	96	57	.627	+6.5	Connie Mack	571,896
1914	1st	99	53	.651	+8.5	Connie Mack	346,641
1915	8th	43	109	.283	58.5	Connie Mack	146,223
1916	8th	36	117	.235	54.5	Connie Mack	184,471
1917	8th	55	98	.359	44.5	Connie Mack	221,432
1918	8th	52	76	.406	24.0	Connie Mack	177,926
1919	8th	36	104	.257	52.0	Connie Mack	225,209
1920	8th	48	106	.312	50.0	Connie Mack	287,888
1921	8th	53	100	.346	45.0	Connie Mack	344,430
1922	7th	65	89	.422	29.0	Connie Mack	425,356
1923	6th	69	83	.454	29.0	Connie Mack	534,122
1924	5th	71	81	.467	20.0	Connie Mack	531,992
1925	2nd	88	64	.579	8.5	Connie Mack	869,703
1926	3rd	83	67	.553	6.0	Connie Mack	714,308
1927	2nd	91	63	.591	19.0	Connie Mack	605,529
1928	2nd	98	55	.641	2.5	Connie Mack	689,756
1929	1st	104	46	.693	+18.0	Connie Mack	839,176
1930	1st	102	52	.662	+8.0	Connie Mack	721,663
1931	1st	107	45	.704	+13.5	Connie Mack	627,464
1932	2nd	94	60	.610	13.0	Connie Mack	405,500
1933	3rd	79	72	.523	19.5	Connie Mack	297,138
1934	5th	68	82	.453	31.0	Connie Mack	305,847
1935	8th	58	91	.389	34.0	Connie Mack	233,173

Year	Position	W	L	Pct.	*GB	Manager	Attendance
1936	8th	53	100	.346	49.0	Connie Mack	285,173
1937	7th	54	97	.358	46.5	Connie Mack	430,733
1938	8th	53	99	.349	46.0	Connie Mack	385,357
1939	7th	55	97	.362	51.5	Connie Mack	395,022
1940	8th	54	100	.351	36.0	Connie Mack	432,145
1941	8th	64	90	.416	37.0	Connie Mack	528,894
1942	8th	55	99	.357	48.0	Connie Mack	423,487
1943	8th	49	105	.318	49.0	Connie Mack	376,735
1944	5th (tied)	72	82	.468	17.0	Connie Mack	505,322
1945	8th	52	98	.347	34.5	Connie Mack	462,631
1946	8th	49	105	.318	55.0	Connie Mack	621,793
1947	5th	78	76	.506	19.0	Connie Mack	911,566
1948	4th	84	70	.545	12.5	Connie Mack	945,076
1949	5th	81	73	.526	16.0	Connie Mack	816,514
1950	8th	52	102	.338	46.0	Connie Mack	309,805
1951	6th	70	84	.455	28.0	Jimmie Dykes	465,469
1952	4th	79	75	.513	16.0	Jimmie Dykes	627,100
1953	7th	59	95	.383	41.5	Jimmie Dykes	362,113
1954	8th	51	103	.331	60.0	Ed Joost	304,666

*Games behind winner.

INDIVIDUAL RECORDS (1901 TO 1954)

SERVICE

Most years by non-pitcher
16—Harry Davis

Most years by pitcher
14—Eddie Plank

BATTING

Most games
157—Dave Philley, 1953

Most games, career
1,702—Jimmie Dykes

Most at-bats
670—Al Simmons, 154 games, 1932

Most at-bats, career
7,023—Jimmie Dykes

Most runs
152—Al Simmons, 138 games, 1930

Most runs, career
997—Bob Johnson

Most hits
253—Al Simmons, 153 games, 1925

Most hits, career
1,827—Al Simmons

Most singles
174—Al Simmons, 153 games, 1925

Most doubles
53—Al Simmons, 147 games, 1926

Most doubles, career
365—Jimmie Dykes

Most triples
21—Home Run Baker, 149 games, 1912

Most triples, career
104—Danny Murphy

Most homers by righthander
58—Jimmie Foxx, 154 games, 1932

Most homers by lefthander
27—Joe Hauser, 149 games, 1924

Most homers by switch-hitter
4—Dave Philley, 157 games, 1953

Most homers by rookie
21—Bob Johnson, 142 games, 1933

Most homers at home
31—Jimmie Foxx, 1932

Most homers on road
27—Jimmie Foxx, 1932

Most homers, month
15—Bob Johnson, June, 1934

Most homers, righthander, career
302—Jimmie Foxx

Most homers, lefthander, career
108—Mickey Cochrane

Most homers, switch-hitter, career
23—Dave Philley

Most grand slams
3—Jimmie Foxx, 154 games, 1932
Jimmie Foxx, 150 games, 1934
Bob Johnson, 152 games, 1938
Gus Zernial, 145 games, 1952

Most grand slams, career
9—Jimmie Foxx, Sam Chapman

Most total bases
438—Jimmie Foxx, 154 games, 1932

Most total bases, career
2,998—Al Simmons

Most long hits
100—Jimmie Foxx, 154 games, 1932

Most extra bases on long hits
225—Jimmie Foxx, 154 games, 1932

Most sacrifices (sacrifice hits and sacrifice flies)
43—Roy Grover, 141 games, 1917

Most sacrifice hits
34—Simon Nicholls, 124 games, 1907

Most sacrifice flies
7—Joe DeMaestri, 146 games, 1954

Most bases on balls
149—Ed Joost, 144 games, 1949

Most strikeouts
110—Ed Joost, 151 games, 1947

Fewest strikeouts
17—Dick Siebert, 153 games, 1942

Most hit by pitch
12—Joe Hauser, 146 games, 1923

Most runs batted in
169—Jimmie Foxx, 154 games, 1932

Most runs batted in, career
1,178—Al Simmons

Most consecutive games with RBI
11—Al Simmons (20 RBIs), 1931

Highest batting average
.422—Nap Lajoie, 131 games, 1901

Highest batting average, career
.356—Al Simmons

Highest slugging average
.749—Jimmie Foxx, 154 games, 1932

Highest slugging average, career
.640—Jimmie Foxx

Longest batting streak
29 games—Bill Lamar, 1925

Most grounded into double play
30—Billy Hitchcock, 115 games, 1950

Fewest grounded into double play
5—Ed Joost, 151 games, 1947

BASERUNNING

Most stolen bases
81—Eddie Collins, 153 games, 1910

Most stolen bases, career
375—Eddie Collins

Most caught stealing
15— Whitey Witt, 154 games, 1921
Al Simmons, 152 games, 1924
Bill Werber, 134 games, 1938

PITCHING

Most games
58—Morrie Martin, 1953

Most games, career
524—Eddie Plank

Most games started
46—Rube Waddell, 1904

Most complete games
36—Rube Waddell, 1904

Most games finished
47—Joe Berry, 1944

Most innings
384—Rube Waddell, 1904

Most games won, season
31— Jack Coombs, 1910
Lefty Grove, 1931

Most games won, career
283—Eddie Plank

Most 20-victory seasons
7—Eddie Plank, Lefty Grove

Most games lost
25—Scott Perry, 1920

Most games lost, career
158—Eddie Plank

Highest winning percentage
.886—Lefty Grove (31-4), 1931

Longest winning streak
16 games—Lefty Grove, 1931

Longest losing streak
19 games—Jack Nabors, 1916

Most bases on balls
168—Elmer Myers, 1916

Most bases on balls, career
879—Eddie Plank

Most strikeouts
349—Rube Waddell, 1904

Most strikeouts, career
1,998—Eddie Plank

Most strikeouts, nine-inning game
14—Rube Waddell, July 14, 1903
Rube Waddell, September 6, 1904, first game
Rube Waddell, August 2, 1905

Most strikeouts, extra-inning game
18—Jack Coombs, September 1, 1906, 24 innings
Jack Coombs, August 4, 1910, 16 innings

Most shutouts
13—Jack Coombs, 1910

Most shutouts, career
60—Eddie Plank

Most 1-0 shutouts won
4—Harry Krause, 1909

Most runs
169—Elmer Myers, 1916

Most earned runs
146—George Earnshaw, 1930

Most hits
360—Jack Coombs, 1911

Most hit batsmen
31—Chick Fraser, 1901

Most wild pitches
16—Stu Flythe, 1936

Most home runs
28—Alex Kellner, 1950

Lowest ERA
1.98—Scott Perry, 332 innings, 1918

CLUB RECORDS

Most players
56 in 1915

Fewest players
19 in 1905

Most games
158 in 1914

Most at-bats
5,537 in 1932

Most runs
981 in 1932

Fewest runs
447 in 1916

Most hits
1,659 in 1925

Fewest hits
1,132 in 1908

Most singles
1,206 in 1925

Most doubles
323 in 1928

Most triples
108 in 1912

Most homers
173 in 1932

Fewest homers (154 or 162-game schedule)
16 in 1915, 1917

Most home runs at Shibe Park, home and opponents
189 in 1932

Most pinch home runs
6 in 1952

Most grand slams
8 in 1932

Most long hits
527 in 1932

Most extra bases on long hits
924 in 1932

Most total bases
2,530 in 1932

Most sacrifices (sacrifice hits and sacrifice flies)
239 in 1926

Most sacrifice hits
147 in 1906

Most sacrifice flies
31 in 1954

Most stolen bases
259 in 1912

Most bases on balls
783 in 1949

Most strikeouts
667 in 1954

Fewest strikeouts
326 in 1927

Most hit by pitch
46 in 1920

Fewest hit by pitch
5 in 1937

Most runs batted in
923 in 1932

Highest batting average
.307 in 1925

Lowest batting average
.223 in 1908

Highest slugging average
.457 in 1932

Lowest slugging average
.308 in 1918

Most grounded into double play
170 in 1950

Fewest grounded into double play
105 in 1945

Most left on bases
1,235 in 1949

Fewest left on bases
999 in 1924

Most .300 hitters
11 in 1927

Most putouts
4,231 in 1910

Fewest putouts
3,953 in 1906

Most assists
2,172 in 1920

Fewest assists
1,591 in 1906

Most chances accepted
6,297 in 1920

Fewest chances accepted
5,610 in 1938

Most errors
317 in 1901

Fewest errors
113 in 1948

Most consecutive errorless games
7 in 1951

Most double plays
217 in 1949

Fewest double plays
102 in 1917

Most passed balls
25 in 1914

Fewest passed balls
5 in 1947

Highest fielding average
.981 in 1948

Lowest fielding average
.936 in 1901

Highest home attendance
945,076 in 1948

Highest road attendance
1,562,360 in 1948

Most games won
107 in 1931

Most games lost
117 in 1916

Most games won, month
26—July 1931

Most games lost, month
28—July 1916

Highest percentage games won
.704 in 1931 (won 107, lost 45)

Lowest percentage games won
.235 in 1916 (won 36, lost 117)

Games won, league
3,886 in 54 years

Games lost, league
4,248 in 54 years

Most shutouts won
27 in 1909 (also 1 tie), 26 in 1908

Most shutouts lost
24 in 1943

Most 1-0 games won
9 in 1909

Most 1-0 games lost
7 in 1908, 1909

Most consecutive games won
17 in 1931

Most consecutive games lost
20 in 1916, 1943

Number of times league champions
9

Number of last-place finishes
18

Most runs, game
24 vs. Detroit, May 18, 1912
vs. Boston, May 1, 1929

Most runs by opponent, game
25 by Cleveland, May 11, 1930
by New York, May 24, 1936

Most runs, shutout game
16 vs. Chicago, July 25, 1928, first game
vs. Chicago, August 29, 1937, first game

Most runs by opponent, shutout game
21 by New York, August 13, 1939, second game, eight innings

Most runs, doubleheader shutout
17 vs. Detroit, August 13, 1902

Most runs, inning
13 vs. Cleveland, June 15, 1925, eighth inning

Most hits, game
29 vs. Boston, May 1, 1929

Longest 1-0 game won
13 innings vs. Detroit, August 11, 1902
vs. Boston, September 10, 1904
vs. Chicago, May 16, 1909
vs. Cleveland, May 14, 1914

Longest 1-0 game, lost	Most total bases, game	Largest crowd, night game
16 innings vs. St. Louis, June 5, 1942	44 vs. Boston, May 1, 1929	37,383 vs. New York, June 27, 1947

Most home runs, game
7 vs. Detroit, June 3, 1921

Most consecutive games with one or more homers
12 (20 homers), 1951

Largest crowd, day game
37,534 vs. New York, May 16, 1937

Largest crowd, doubleheader
38,800 vs. New York, July 13, 1931

Largest crowd, home opener
32,825 vs. New York, April 20, 1927

ST. LOUIS BROWNS
YEARLY FINISHES

(Milwaukee Brewers, 1901)

Year	Position	W	L	Pct.	*GB	Manager	Attendance
1901	8th	48	89	.350	35.5	Hugh Duffy	139,034
1902	2nd	78	58	.574	5.0	Jimmy McAleer	272,283
1903	6th	65	74	.468	26.5	Jimmy McAleer	380,405
1904	6th	65	87	.428	29.0	Jimmy McAleer	318,108
1905	8th	54	99	.354	40.5	Jimmy McAleer	339,112
1906	5th	76	73	.510	16.0	Jimmy McAleer	389,157
1907	6th	69	83	.454	24.0	Jimmy McAleer	419,025
1908	4th	83	69	.546	6.5	Jimmy McAleer	618,947
1909	7th	61	89	.407	36.0	Jimmy McAleer	366,274
1910	8th	47	107	.305	57.0	John O'Connor	249,889
1911	8th	45	107	.296	56.5	Bobby Wallace	207,984
1912	7th	53	101	.344	53.0	Bobby Wallace, George Stovall	214,070
1913	8th	57	96	.373	39.0	George Stovall, Branch Rickey	250,330
1914	5th	71	82	.464	28.5	Branch Rickey	244,714
1915	6th	63	91	.409	39.5	Branch Rickey	150,358
1916	5th	79	75	.513	12.0	Fielder Jones	335,740
1917	7th	57	97	.370	43.0	Fielder Jones	210,486
1918	5th	58	64	.475	15.0	Fielder Jones, Jimmy Austin, Jimmy Burke	122,076
1919	5th	67	72	.482	20.5	Jimmy Burke	349,350
1920	4th	76	77	.497	21.5	Jimmy Burke	419,311
1921	3rd	81	73	.526	17.5	Lee Fohl	355,978
1922	2nd	93	61	.604	1.0	Lee Fohl	712,918
1923	5th	74	78	.487	24.0	Lee Fohl, Jimmy Austin	430,296
1924	4th	74	78	.487	17.0	George Sisler	533,349
1925	3rd	82	71	.536	15.0	George Sisler	462,898
1926	7th	62	92	.403	29.0	George Sisler	283,986
1927	7th	59	94	.336	50.5	Dan Howley	247,879
1928	3rd	82	72	.532	19.0	Dan Howley	339,497
1929	4th	79	73	.520	26.0	Dan Howley	280,697
1930	6th	64	90	.416	38.0	Bill Killefer	152,088
1931	5th	63	91	.409	45.0	Bill Killefer	179,126
1932	6th	63	91	.409	44.0	Bill Killefer	112,558
1933	8th	55	96	.364	43.5	Bill Killefer, Allen Sothoron, Rogers Hornsby	88,113
1934	6th	67	85	.441	33.0	Rogers Hornsby	115,305
1935	7th	65	87	.428	28.5	Rogers Hornsby	80,922
1936	7th	57	95	.375	44.5	Rogers Hornsby	93,267
1937	8th	46	108	.299	56.0	Rogers Hornsby, Jim Bottomley	123,121
1938	7th	55	97	.362	44.0	Gabby Street	130,417
1939	8th	43	111	.279	64.5	Fred Haney	109,159
1940	6th	67	87	.435	23.0	Fred Haney	239,591
1941	6th (tied)	70	84	.455	31.0	Fred Haney, Luke Sewell	176,240
1942	3rd	82	69	.543	19.5	Luke Sewell	255,617
1943	6th	72	80	.474	25.0	Luke Sewell	214,392
1944	1st	89	65	.578	+1.0	Luke Sewell	508,644
1945	3rd	81	70	.536	6.0	Luke Sewell	482,986
1946	7th	66	88	.429	38.0	Luke Sewell, Zack Taylor	526,435
1947	8th	59	95	.383	38.0	Muddy Ruel	320,474
1948	6th	59	94	.386	37.0	Zack Taylor	335,546
1949	7th	53	101	.344	44.0	Zack Taylor	270,936
1950	7th	58	96	.377	40.0	Zack Taylor	247,131
1951	8th	52	102	.338	46.0	Zack Taylor	293,790
1952	7th	64	90	.416	31.0	Rogers Hornsby, Marty Marion	518,796
1953	8th	54	100	.351	46.5	Marty Marion	297,238

*Games behind winner.

INDIVIDUAL RECORDS (1902 TO 1953)

SERVICE

Most years by non-pitcher
16—Jimmy Austin

Most years by pitcher
10— George Blaeholder
      Barney Pelty
      Jack Powell

BATTING

Most games
159—Del Pratt, 1915

Most games, career
1,647—George Sisler

Most at-bats
671—Jack Tobin, 150 games, 1921

Most at-bats, career
6,667—George Sisler

Most runs
145—Harlond Clift, 152 games, 1936

Most runs, career
1,091—George Sisler

Most hits
257—George Sisler, 154 games, 1920

Most hits, career
2,295—George Sisler

Most singles
179—Jack Tobin, 150 games, 1921

Most doubles
51—Beau Bell, 156 games, 1937

Most doubles, career
343—George Sisler

Most triples
20—Heinie Manush, 154 games, 1928

Most triples, career
145—George Sisler

Most homers by righthander
34—Harlond Clift, 149 games, 1938

Most homers by lefthander
39—Ken Williams, 153 games, 1922

Most homers by switch-hitter
14—Lu Blue, 154 games, 1928

Most homers by rookie
24—Walt Judnich, 137 games, 1940

Most homers at home
32—Ken Williams, 1922

Most homers, month
15—Harlond Clift, August, 1938

Most homers, lefthander, career
185—Ken Williams

Most homers, righthander, career
170—Harlond Clift

Most homers, switch-hitter, career
24—Lu Blue

Most grand slams
2—Held by many players

Most grand slams, career
5—Ken Williams
  Harlond Clift
  Vern Stephens

Most total bases
399—George Sisler, 154 games, 1920

Most total bases, career
3,201—George Sisler

Most long hits
86—George Sisler, 154 games, 1920

Most extra bases on long hits
173—Ken Williams, 153 games, 1922

Most sacrifices (sacrifice hits and sacrifice flies)
48—Joe Gedeon, 153 games, 1920

Most sacrifice hits
40—Tom Jones, 144 games, 1906

Most bases on balls
126—Lu Blue, 151 games, 1929

Most strikeouts
120—Gus Williams, 143 games, 1914

Fewest strikeouts
13—Jack Tobin, 151 games, 1923

Most hit by pitch
12—Frank O'Rourke, 140 games, 1927

Most runs batted in
155—Ken Williams, 153 games, 1922

Most runs batted in, career
964—George Sisler

Highest batting average
.420—George Sisler, 142 games, 1922

Highest batting average, career
.344—George Sisler

Highest slugging average
.632—George Sisler, 154 games, 1920

Highest slugging average, career
.558—Ken Williams

Longest batting streak
41 games—George Sisler, 1922

Most grounding into double play
21—Glenn McQuillen, 100 games, 1942

Fewest grounding into double play
7—Vern Stephens, 150 games, 1947

BASERUNNING

Most stolen bases
51—George Sisler, 142 games, 1922

Most stolen bases, career
351—George Sisler

Most caught stealing
19—George Sisler, 142 games, 1922
  Ken Williams, 153 games, 1922

PITCHING

Most games
60—Marlin Stuart, 1953

Most games, career
323—Elam Vangilder

Most games started
40—Bobo Newsom, 1938

Most complete games
36—Jack Powell, 1902

Most games finished
35—Satchel Paige, 1952

Most innings
348—Urban Shocker, 1922

Most games won
27—Urban Shocker, 1922

Most games won, career
126—Urban J. Shocker

Most 20-victory seasons
4—Urban J. Shocker

Most games lost
25—Fred Glade, 1905

Most games lost, career
142—Jack Powell

Highest winning percentage
.808—General Crowder (21-5), 1928

Longest winning streak
10 games—Alvin Crowder, 1928

Longest winning streak, two seasons
10 games—Bill Dinneen, 1907 (1), 1908 (9)

Longest losing streak
9 games—Walter Leverenz, 1913, 1914
  Earl Hamilton, 1917

Longest losing streak, two seasons
12 games—Earl Hamilton, 1916 (3), 1917 (9)

Most bases on balls
192—Bobo Newsom, 1938

Most bases on balls, career
640—Dixie Davis

Most strikeouts
232—Rube Waddell, 1908

Most strikeouts, career
884—Jack Powell

Most strikeouts, game
17—Rube Waddell, September 20, 1908, 10 innings
16—Rube Waddell, July 29, 1908

Most shutouts
6—Fred Glade, 1904
  Harry Howell, 1906

Most shutouts, career
27—Jack Powell

Most 1-0 shutouts won
3—Fred Glade, 1904

Most runs
205—Bobo Newsom, 1938

Most earned runs
186—Bobo Newsom, 1938

Most hits
365—Urban Shocker, 1922

Most hits batsmen
19—Barney Pelty, 1907

Most wild pitches
11—Carl Weilman, 1914
  Dave Davenport, 1917
  Jack Knott, 1936

Most home runs
21—Urban Shocker, 1921

Lowest ERA
2.12—Carl Weilman, 307 innings, 1914

CLUB RECORDS

Most players
52 in 1951

Fewest players
19 in 1906

Most games
159 in 1914, 1915

Most at-bats
5,510 in 1937

Most runs
897 in 1925

Fewest runs
441 in 1909

Most hits
1,693 in 1922

Fewest hits
1,092 in 1910

Most singles
1,239 in 1920

Most doubles
327 in 1937

Most triples
106 in 1921

Most homers
118 in 1940

Fewest homers (154 or 162-game schedule)
9 in 1906

Most homers at Sportsman's Park, home and opponents
135 in 1940

Most grand slams
5 in 1950

Most home runs by pinch-hitters
4 in 1951

Most total bases
2,463 in 1922

Most long hits
482 in 1922, 1925

Most extra bases on long hits
770 in 1922, 1925

Most sacrifices (sacrifice hits and sacrifice flies)
214 in 1928

Most sacrifices hits
163 in 1906

Most stolen bases
234 in 1916

Most bases on balls
775 in 1941

Most strikeouts
863 in 1914

Fewest strikeouts
339 in 1920

Most hit by pitch
43 in 1927

Fewest hit by pitch
12 in 1931

Most runs batted in
761 in 1936

Highest batting average
.313 in 1922

Lowest batting average
.216 in 1910

Highest slugging average
.455 in 1922

Lowest slugging average
.273 in 1910

Most grounded into double play
151 in 1951

Fewest grounded into double play
93 in 1944

Most left on bases
1,334 in 1941

Fewest left on bases
1,055 in 1951

Most .300 hitters
8 in 1922

Most putouts
4,328 in 1916

Fewest putouts
3,993 in 1911

Most assists
2,189 in 1910

Fewest assists
1,584 in 1938

Most chances accepted
6,516 in 1916

Fewest chances accepted
5,618 in 1938

Most errors
378 in 1910

Fewest errors
134 in 1947

Most consecutive errorless games
8 in 1928

Most double plays
190 in 1948

Fewest double plays
116 in 1914

Most passed balls
30 in 1914, 1915

Fewest passed balls
4 in 1930, 1933

Highest fielding average
.977 in 1947

Lowest fielding average
.943 in 1910

Highest home attendance
712,918 in 1922

Highest road attendance
1,170,349 in 1948

Most games won
93 in 1922

Most games lost
111 in 1939

Most games won, month
23—August 1945

Most games lost, month
24—September 1939
July 1952

Highest percentage games won
.604 in 1922 (won 93, lost 61)

Lowest percentage games won
.279 in 1939 (won 43, lost 111)

Games won, league
3,416 in 52 years

Games lost, league
4,465 in 52 years

Most shutouts won
21 in 1909

Most shutouts lost
25 in 1904, 1906, 1910

Most 1-0 games won
6 in 1909

Most 1-0 games lost
7 in 1907

Most consecutive games won
14 in 1916

Most consecutive games lost
14 in 1911, 1953

Number of times league champions
1

Number of last-place finishes
10

Most runs, game
20 vs. Detroit, August 18, 1951

Most runs by opponent, game
29 by Boston, June 8, 1950

Most runs, shutout game
16 vs. Detroit, September 9, 1922

Most runs by opponent, shutout game
18 by Detroit, April 29, 1935

Most runs, doubleheader shutout
5 vs. Philadelphia, September 23, 1906

Most runs, inning
11 vs. Philadelphia, July 21, 1949, first
game, sixth inning
vs. Detroit, August 18, 1951, seventh
inning

Longest 1-0 game won
16 innings vs. Philadelphia, June 5, 1942

Longest 1-0 game lost
15 innings vs. Washington, August 14,
1903, first game
vs. Washington, July 25, 1918

Most hits, game
24 vs. Philadelphia, September 17, 1920
vs. Washington, June 14, 1932

Most home runs, game
5 vs. New York, September 16, 1940

Most consecutive games with one or
more homers
11 (20 homers), 1922

Most total bases, game
40 vs. Chicago, May 31, 1925

Largest crowd, day game
34,625 vs. New York, October 1, 1944

Largest crowd, night game
22,847 vs. Cleveland, May 24, 1940

Largest crowd, home opener
19,561 vs. Detroit, April 18, 1923

SEATTLE MARINERS
YEARLY FINISHES
WEST DIVISION

Year	Position	W	L	Pct.	*GB	Manager	Attendance
1977	6th	64	98	.395	38.0	Darrell Johnson	1,338,511
1978	7th	56	104	.350	35.0	Darrell Johnson	877,440
1979	6th	67	95	.414	21.0	Darrell Johnson	844,447
1980	7th	59	103	.364	38.0	Darrell Johnson, Maury Wills	836,204
1981	6th/5th	44	65	.404	†	Maury Wills, Rene Lachemann	636,276
1982	4th	76	86	.469	17.0	Rene Lachemann	1,070,404
1983	7th	60	102	.370	39.0	Rene Lachemann, Del Crandall	813,537
1984	5th (tied)	74	88	.457	10.0	Del Crandall, Chuck Cottier	870,372
1985	6th	74	88	.457	17.0	Chuck Cottier	1,128,696
1986	7th	67	95	.414	25.0	Chuck Cottier, Marty Martinez, Dick Williams	1,029,045
1987	4th	78	84	.481	7.0	Dick Williams	1,134,255
1988	7th	68	93	.422	35.5	Dick Williams, Jim Snyder	1,022,398
1989	6th	73	89	.451	26.0	Jim Lefebvre	1,298,443
1990	5th	77	85	.475	26.0	Jim Lefebvre	1,509,727
1991	5th	83	79	.512	12.0	Jim Lefebvre	2,147,905
1992	7th	64	98	.395	32.0	Bill Plummer	1,651,398
1993	4th	82	80	.506	12.0	Lou Piniella	2,051,853
1994	3rd	49	63	.438	2.0	Lou Piniella	1,104,206
1995	1st‡§∞	79	66	.545	+1.0	Lou Piniella	1,643,203

Year	Position	W	L	Pct.	*GB	Manager	Attendance
1996	2nd.......................85	76		.528	4.5	Lou Piniella	2,723,850
1997	1st▲.....................90	72		.556	+6.0	Lou Piniella	3,192,237
1998	3rd 76	85		.472	11.5	Lou Piniella	2,644,166
1999	3rd 79	83		.488	16.0	Lou Piniella	2,916,346
2000	2nd§∞..................91	71		.562	0.5	Lou Piniella	3,148,317
2001	1st§∞..................116	46		.716	+14.0	Lou Piniella	3,507,975

*Games behind winner. †First half 21-36; second 23-29. ‡Won division playoff. §Won division series. ∞Lost championship series. ▲Lost division series.

INDIVIDUAL RECORDS (1977 TO DATE)

SERVICE

Most years by non-pitcher
15—Edgar Martinez

Most years by pitcher
10—Randy Johnson

BATTING

Most games
162—Ruppert Jones, 1979
    Willie Horton, 1979

Most games, career
1,672—Edgar Martinez

Most at-bats
692—Ichiro Suzuki, 157 games, 2001

Most at-bats, career
5,902—Edgar Martinez

Most runs
141—Alex Rodriguez, 146 games, 1996

Most runs, career
1,063—Ken Griffey Jr.

Most hits
242—Ichiro Suzuki, 157 games, 2001

Most hits, career
1,882—Edgar Martinez

Most singles
192—Ichiro Suzuki, 157 games, 2001

Most singles, career
1,166—Edgar Martinez

Most doubles
54—Alex Rodriguez, 146 games, 1996

Most doubles, career
443—Edgar Martinez

Most triples
11—Harold Reynolds, 158 games, 1988

Most triples, career
48—Harold Reynolds

Most homers by lefthander
56—Ken Griffey Jr., 157 games, 1997
    Ken Griffey Jr., 161 games, 1998

Most homers by righthander
44—Jay Buhner, 150 games, 1996

Most homers by switch-hitter
19—David Segui, 143 games, 1998

Most homers by rookie
27—Alvin Davis, 152 games, 1984

Most homers at home
30—Ken Griffey Jr., 1998

Most homers on road
29—Ken Griffey Jr., 1997

Most homers, month
15—Ken Griffey Jr., May 1994

Most homers by lefthander, career
398—Ken Griffey Jr.

Most homers by righthander, career
307—Jay Buhner

Most homers by switch-hitter, career
28—David Segui

Most grand slams
4—Edgar Martinez, 153 games, 2000

Most grand slams, career
12—Ken Griffey Jr.

Most total bases
393—Ken Griffey Jr., 157 games, 1997

Most total bases, career
3,316—Ken Griffey Jr.

Most long hits
93—Ken Griffey Jr., 157 games, 1997

Most long hits, career
748—Ken Griffey Jr.

Most extra bases on long hits
208—Ken Griffey Jr., 157 games, 1997

Most extra bases on long hits, career
1,574—Ken Griffey Jr.

Most sacrifice hits
15—Craig Reynolds, 135 games, 1977
    Larry Milbourne, 106 games, 1980

Most sacrifice flies
13—Bret Boone, 158 games, 2001
    Mike Cameron, 150 games, 2001

Most bases on balls
123—Edgar Martinez, 139 games, 1996

Most bases on balls, career
1,066—Edgar Martinez

Most strikeouts
175—Jay Buhner, 157 games, 1997

Most strikeouts, career
1,375—Jay Buhner

Fewest strikeouts
34—Harold Reynolds, 160 games, 1987

Most hit by pitch
17—Dave Valle, 135 games, 1993

Most runs batted in
147—Ken Griffey Jr., 157 games, 1997

Most runs batted in, career
1,152—Ken Griffey Jr.

Most game-winning RBIs
13— Tom Paciorek, 104 games, 1981
    Alvin Davis, 152 games, 1984
    Jim Presley, 155 games, 1986

Highest batting average
.358—Alex Rodriguez, 146 games, 1996

Highest batting average, career
.319—Edgar Martinez

Highest slugging average
.646—Ken Griffey Jr., 157 games, 1997

Highest slugging average, career
.569—Ken Griffey Jr.

Longest batting streak
24 games—Joey Cora, 1997

Most grounded into double play
29—Jim Presley, 155 games, 1985

Fewest grounded into double play
3—Ichiro Suzuki, 157 games, 2001

BASERUNNING

Most stolen bases
60—Harold Reynolds, 160 games, 1987

Most stolen bases, career
290—Julio Cruz

Most caught stealing
29—Harold Reynolds, 158 games, 1988

PITCHING

Most games
78—Ed Vande Berg, 1982

Most games, career
335—Mike Jackson

Most games started
37—Mike Moore, 1986

Most games started, career
266—Randy Johnson

Most complete games
14—Mike Moore, 1985
    Mark Langston, 1987

Most complete games, career
56—Mike Moore

Most games finished
64—Bill Caudill, 1982

Most innings
272—Mark Langston, 1987

Most innings, career
1,838.1—Randy Johnson

Most games won
20—Randy Johnson, 1997
    Jamie Moyer, 2001

Most games won, career
130—Randy Johnson

Most games lost
19—Matt Young, 1985
    Mike Moore, 1987

Most games lost, career
96—Mike Moore

Highest winning percentage
.900—Randy Johnson (18-2), 1995

Longest winning streak
10 games—Paul Abbott, 2001
    Jamie Moyer, 2001

Longest winning streak, two seasons
12 games—Randy Johnson, 1995 (7), 1996 (5)

Longest winning streak, three seasons
16 games—Randy Johnson, 1995 (7), 1996 (5), 1997 (4)

Longest losing streak
16 games—Mike Parrott, 1980

Most saves
45—Kazuhiro Sasaki, 2001

Most bases on balls
152—Randy Johnson, 1991

Most bases on balls, career
884—Randy Johnson

Most strikeouts
308—Randy Johnson, 1993

Most strikeouts, career
2,162—Randy Johnson

Most strikeouts, game
19—Randy Johnson, June 24, 1997
    Randy Johnson, August 8, 1997

Most shutouts won
—Dave Fleming, 1992
   Randy Johnson, 1994

Most shutouts won, career
9—Randy Johnson

Most 1-0 shutouts won
—Held by many pitchers

Most runs
45—Mike Moore, 1987

Most earned runs
29—Mark Langston, 1986

Most hits
279—Mike Moore, 1986

Most hit batsmen
18—Randy Johnson, 1992

Most wild pitches
16—Matt Young, 1990

Most home runs allowed
35—Scott Bankhead, 1987

Most sacrifice hits
15—Shane Rawley, 1980

Most sacrifice flies
14—Rich DeLucia, 1991

Lowest ERA
2.28—Randy Johnson, 213 innings,
   1997

CLUB RECORDS

Most players
51 in 1999

Fewest players
34 in 1978, 1980

Most games
163 in 1980

Most at-bats
5,680 in 2001

Most runs
993 in 1996

Fewest runs
558 in 1983

Most opponents' runs
905 in 1999

Most hits
1,637 in 2001

Fewest hits
1,280 in 1983

Most singles
1,120 in 2001

Most doubles
343 in 1996

Most triples
52 in 1979

Most homers
264 in 1997

Fewest homers
97 in 1978

Most homers at Kingdome, home and
   opponents
237 in 1996

Most homers at Safeco Field, home and
   opponents
164 in 2000

Most grand slams
11 in 1996, 2000

Most pinch home runs
5 in 1994, 1996

Most total bases
2,741 in 1996

Most long hits
607 in 1996

Most extra bases on long hits
1,146 in 1997

Most sacrifice hits
106 in 1980

Most sacrifice flies
70 in 2001

Most stolen bases
174 in 1987, 2001

Most caught stealing
82 in 1982

Most bases on balls
775 in 2000

Most strikeouts
1,148 in 1986

Fewest strikeouts
702 in 1978

Most hit by pitch
75 in 1996

Fewest hit by pitch
19 in 1980

Most runs batted in
954 in 1996

Most game-winning RBIs
73 in 1987

Highest batting average
.288 in 2001

Lowest batting average
.240 in 1983

Highest slugging average
.485 in 1997

Lowest slugging average
.356 in 1980

Most grounded into double play
158 in 1979

Fewest grounded into double play
101 in 1984

Most left on bases
1,257 in 2001

Fewest left on bases
1,034 in 1983

Most .300 hitters
4 in 1997, 2001

Most putouts
4,429 in 1982

Fewest putouts
4,255 in 1983

Most assists
1,930 in 1980

Fewest assists
1,534 in 2001

Most chances accepted
6,302 in 1980

Fewest chances accepted
5,837 in 1996

Most errors
156 in 1986

Most errorless games
99 in 2001

Most consecutive errorless games
11 in 1993

Fewest errors
83 in 2001

Most double plays
191 in 1986

Fewest double plays
137 in 2001

Most passed balls
24 in 1991

Fewest passed balls
3 in 1997

Highest fielding average
.986 in 2001

Lowest fielding average
.975 in 1986

Highest home attendance
3,507,975 in 2001

Highest road attendance
2,572,882 in 2001

Most games won
116 in 2001

Most games lost
104 in 1978

Most games won, month
20 in June 1997, April 2001, May 2001,
   August 2001

Most games lost, month
22 in August 1977

Games won, league
1,831 in 25 years

Games lost, league
2,094 in 25 years

Highest percentage games won
.716 in 2001 (won 116, lost 46)

Lowest percentage games won
.350 in 1978 (won 56, lost 104)

Most shutouts won
14 in 2001

Most shutouts lost
15 in 1978, 1983, 1990

Most 1-0 games won
3 in 1979

Most 1-0 games lost
4 in 1980, 1989, 1990

Most consecutive games won
15 in 2001

Most consecutive games lost
14 in 1992

Number of times league champions
0

Number of last-place finishes
5

Most runs, game
22 vs. Detroit, April 29, 1999

Most runs by opponent, game
20 by Detroit, April 17, 1993

Most runs, shutout game
14 vs. California, August 7, 1987
   vs. Minnesota, May 15, 2000
   vs. Baltimore, September 16, 2000

Most runs by opponent, shutout game
15 by Minnesota, July 10, 1977

Most runs, inning
11 vs. Detroit, April 29, 1999, fifth inning

Longest 1-0 game won
None over nine innings

Longest 1-0 game lost
12 innings vs. Texas, June 29, 1988

Most hits, game
24 vs. Boston, September 3, 1981, 20
   innings
   vs. Minnesota, June 11, 1996

Most home runs, game
7 vs. Oakland, April 11, 1985
   vs. Milwaukee, July 31, 1996
   vs. Anaheim, July 5, 1999

Most consecutive games with one or
   more homers
19 (29 homers), 1999

Most total bases, game
44, vs. Toronto, April 16, 2000

Largest crowd, day game
57,822 vs. Cleveland, March 31, 1998

Largest crowd, night game
57,806 vs. Minnesota, April 11, 1994

Largest crowd, home opener
57,822 vs. Cleveland, March 31, 1998

Largest crowd, doubleheader
32,597 vs. California, August 12, 1985

SEATTLE PILOTS
YEARLY FINISHES
WEST DIVISION

Year	Position	W	L	Pct.	*GB	Manager	Attendance
1969	6th	64	98	.395	33	Joe Schultz	677,944

*Games behind winner.

INDIVIDUAL RECORDS (1969)

BATTING

Most games
148—Tommy Harper, 1969

Most at-bats
537—Tommy Harper, 148 games, 1969

Most runs
88—Wayne Comer, 147 games, 1969

Most hits
126—Tommy Harper, 148 games, 1969

Most singles
105—Tommy Harper, 148 games, 1969

Most doubles
29—Tommy Davis, 123 games, 1969

Most triples
6—Mike Hegan, 95 games, 1969

Most homers by lefthander
25—Don Mincher, 140 games, 1969

Most homers by righthander
15—Wayne Comer, 147 games, 1969

Most homers by switch-hitter
Never accomplished

Most homers by rookie
3—Steve Hovley, 91 games, 1969
Danny Walton, 23 games, 1969

Most homers, month
8—Don Mincher, July 1969

Most homers at home
13—Don Mincher, 1969

Most homers on road
12—Don Mincher, 1969

Most grand slams
1—Don Mincher, 140 games, 1969
Rich Rollins, 58 games, 1969
Fred Talbot, 27 games, 1969

Most total bases
194—Don Mincher, 140 games, 1969

Most long hits
39—Don Mincher, 140 games, 1969

Most extra bases on long hits
89—Don Mincher, 140 games, 1969

Most sacrifice hits
9—Jerry McNertney, 128 games, 1969

Most sacrifice flies
5—Tommy Davis, 123 games, 1969

Most bases on balls
95—Tommy Harper, 148 games, 1969

Most strikeouts
90—Tommy Harper, 148 games, 1969

Fewest strikeouts
46—Tommy Davis, 123 games, 1969

Most hit by pitch
5—Don Mincher, 140 games, 1969
Rich Rollins, 58 games, 1969

Most runs batted in
80—Tommy Davis, 123 games, 1969

Highest batting average
.271—Tommy Davis, 123 games, 1969

Highest slugging average
.454—Don Mincher, 140 games, 1969

Longest batting streak
18 games—Tommy Davis, 1969

Most grounded into double play
17—Tommy Davis, 123 games, 1969

Fewest grounded into double play
8—Tommy Harper, 148 games, 1969

BASERUNNING

Most stolen bases
73—Tommy Harper, 148 games, 1969

Most caught stealing
18—Tommy Harper, 148 games, 1969

PITCHING

Most games
66—Diego Segui, 1969

Most games started
29—Gene Brabender, 1969

Most complete games
7—Gene Brabender, 1969

Most games finished
38—Diego Segui, 1969

Most innings
202—Gene Brabender, 1969

Most games won
13—Gene Brabender, 1969

Most games lost
14—Gene Brabender, 1969

Highest winning percentage
.667—Diego Segui (12-6), 1969

Longest winning streak
5 games—Diego Segui, 1969

Longest losing streak
9 games—John Gelnar, 1969

Most saves
12—Diego Segui, 1969

Most bases on balls
103—Gene Brabender, 1969

Most strikeouts
139—Gene Brabender, 1969

Most strikeouts, game
11—Marty Pattin, April 29, 1969

Most shutouts won
1—held by 5 pitchers

Most 1-0 shutouts won
1—Gene Brabender
Marty Pattin

Most runs
111—Gene Brabender, 1969

Most earned runs
99—Marty Pattin, 1969

Most hits
193—Gene Brabender, 1969

Most wild pitches
8—Jim Bouton, 1969

Most hit batsmen
13—Gene Brabender, 1969

Most home runs
29—Marty Pattin, 1969

Most sacrifice hits
10—Diego Segui, 1969

Most sacrifice flies
6—Gene Brabender, 1969

Lowest ERA
3.36—Diego Segui, 142 innings, 1969

CLUB RECORDS

Most players
53 in 1969

Most games
163 in 1969

Most at-bats
5,444 in 1969

Most runs
639 in 1969

Most opponents' runs
799 in 1969

Most hits
1,276 in 1969

Most singles
945 in 1969

Most doubles
179 in 1969

Most triples
27 in 1969

Most homers
125 in 1969

Fewest homers
125 in 1969

Most homers at Sick's Stadium, home and opponents
167 in 1969

Most grand slams
3 in 1969

Most pinch home runs
3 in 1969

Most total bases
1,884 in 1969

Most long hits
331 in 1969

Most extra bases on long hits
608 in 1969

Most sacrifice hits
72 in 1969
Most sacrifice flies
29 in 1969
Most stolen bases
167 in 1969
Most caught stealing
59 in 1969
Most bases on balls
626 in 1969
Most strikeouts
1,015 in 1969
Most hit by pitch
34 in 1969
Most runs batted in
583 in 1969
Highest batting average
.234 in 1969
Highest slugging average
.346 in 1969
Most grounded into double play
111 in 1969
Most left on bases
1,130 in 1969
Most putouts
4,391 in 1969
Most assists
1,763 in 1969
Most chances accepted
6,154 in 1969
Most errors
167 in 1969
Most errorless games
65 in 1969
Most consecutive errorless games
4 in 1969

Most double plays
149 in 1969
Most passed balls
21 in 1969
Highest fielding average
.974 in 1969
Highest home attendance
677,944 in 1969
Highest road attendance
889,578 in 1969
Most games won
64 in 1969
Most games lost
98 in 1969
Most games won, month
14—June 1969, September 1969
Most games lost, month
22—August 1969
Highest percentage games won
.395 in 1969 (won 64, lost 98)
Most consecutive games won
5 in 1969
Most consecutive games lost
10 in 1969
Most shutouts won
6 in 1969
Most shutouts lost
6 in 1969
Most 1-0 games won
2 in 1969
Most 1-0 games lost
0 in 1969
Number of times league champions
0
Number of last-place finishes
0

Most runs, inning
6 vs. Boston, May 16, 1969, 11th inning
Most runs, game
16 vs. Washington, May 10, 1969
Most runs by opponent, game
15 by Baltimore, August 16, 1969
Most runs, shutout game
8 vs. California, July 9, 1969, first game
Most runs by opponent, shutout game
10 by Baltimore, June 7, 1969
Most runs, doubleheader shutout
No performance
Longest 1-0 game won
None over 9 innings
Longest 1-0 game lost
None
Most hits, game
16 vs. Oakland, September 10, 1969
Most hits, extra-inning game
20 vs. Minnesota, July 19, 1969, 18 innings
Most home runs, game
4 vs. Boston, May 16, 1969, 11 innings
Most consecutive games with one or more homers
5 (8 homers), 1969
Most total bases, game
31 vs. Boston, May 16, 1969, 11 innings
Largest crowd, day game
23,657 vs. New York, August 3, 1969
Largest crowd, doubleheader
18,413 vs. Kansas City, June 20, 1969
Largest crowd, night game
20,490 vs. Baltimore, May 28, 1969
Largest crowd, home opener
14,993 vs. Chicago, April 11, 1969

TAMPA BAY DEVIL RAYS
YEARLY FINISHES
EAST DIVISION

Year	Position	W	L	Pct.	*GB	Manager	Attendance
1998	5th	63	99	.389	51.0	Larry Rothschild	2,506,023
1999	5th	69	93	.426	29.0	Larry Rothschild	1,562,827
2000	5th	69	92	.429	18.0	Larry Rothschild	1,549,052
2001	5th	62	100	.383	34.0	Larry Rothschild, Hal McRae	1,227,673

*Games behind winner.

INDIVIDUAL RECORDS (1998 TO DATE)

SERVICE

Most years by non-pitcher
4—Held by many players
Most years by pitcher
4—Albie Lopez
  Bryan Rekar
  Esteban Yan

BATTING

Most games
158—Fred McGriff, 2000
Most games, career
550—Fred McGriff
Most at-bats
632—Gerald Williams, 146 games, 2000
Most at-bats, career
2,002—Fred McGriff
Most runs
87—Gerald Williams, 146 games, 2000

Most runs, career
270—Fred McGriff
Most hits
179—Quinton McCracken, 155 games, 1998
Most hits, career
590—Fred McGriff
Most singles
127—Quinton McCracken, 155 games, 1998
Most singles, career
393—Fred McGriff
Most doubles
38—Quinton McCracken, 155 games, 1998
Most doubles, career
99—Fred McGriff
Most triples
9—Randy Winn, 109 games, 1998

Most triples, career
19—Randy Winn
Most homers by lefthander
32—Fred McGriff, 144 games, 1999
Most homers by righthander
34—Jose Canseco, 113 games, 1999
Most homers by switch-hitter
7—Quinton McCracken, 155 games, 1998
Most homers by rookie
12—Bubba Trammell, 59 games, 1998
Most homers at home
18—Fred McGriff, 1999
Most homers on road
22—Jose Canseco, 1999
Most homers, month
10—Jose Canseco, April 1999
Most homers by lefthander, career
97—Fred McGriff

Most homers by righthander, career
52—Greg Vaughn

Most homers by switch-hitter, career
10—Randy Winn

Most grand slams
2—Paul Sorrento, 137 games, 1998
Fred McGriff, 158 games, 2000
Ben Grieve, 154 games, 2001
Greg Vaughn, 136 games, 2001

Most grand slams, career
2—Paul Sorrento
Fred McGriff
Ben Grieve
Greg Vaughn

Most total bases
292—Fred McGriff, 144 games, 1999

Most total bases, career
982—Fred McGriff

Most long hits
63—Fred McGriff, 144 games, 1999

Most long hits, career
197—Fred McGriff

Most extra bases on long hits
128—Fred McGriff, 144 games, 1999

Most extra bases on long hits, career
392—Fred McGriff

Most sacrifice hits
12—Felix Martinez, 106 games, 2000

Most sacrifice flies
10—John Flaherty, 117 games, 1999

Most bases on balls
91—Fred McGriff, 158 games, 2000

Most bases on balls, career
296—Fred McGriff

Most strikeouts
159—Ben Grieve, 154 games, 2001

Most strikeouts, career
414—Fred McGriff

Fewest strikeouts
44—Miguel Cairo, 150 games, 1998

Most hit by pitch
13—Jose Guillen, 105 games, 2000

Most runs batted in
106—Fred McGriff, 158 games, 2000

Most runs batted in, career
352—Fred McGriff

Highest batting average
.310—Fred McGriff, 144 games, 1999

Highest batting average, career
.295—Fred McGriff

Highest slugging average
.563—Jose Canseco, 113 games, 1999

Highest slugging average, career
.491—Fred McGriff

Longest batting streak
18 games—Quinton McCracken, 1998

Most grounded into double play
18—Aubrey Huff, 111 games, 2001

Fewest grounded into double play
9—Miguel Cairo, 150 games, 1998

BASERUNNING

Most stolen bases
31—Jason Tyner, 105 games, 2001

Most stolen bases, career
69—Miguel Cairo

Most caught stealing
12—Randy Winn, 109 games, 1998
Gerald Williams, 146 games, 2000

PITCHING

Most games
72—Roberto Hernandez, 1999

Most games, career
211—Esteban Yan

Most games started
32—Rolando Arrojo, 1998
Bobby Witt, 1999

Most games started, career
79—Bryan Rekar

Most complete games
4—Albie Lopez, 2000

Most complete games, career
5—Albie Lopez

Most games finished
66—Roberto Hernandez, 1999

Most innings
202.0—Rolando Arrojo, 1998

Most innings, career
495.1—Bryan Rekar

Most games won
14—Rolando Arrojo, 1998

Most games won, career
26—Albie Lopez

Most games lost
15—Tony Saunders, 1998
Bobby Witt, 1999

Most games lost, career
37—Bryan Rekar

Most 20-victory seasons
Never occurred

Highest winning percentage
No qualifying pitchers

Longest winning streak
5 games—Wilson Alvarez, 1999
Jim Mecir, 2000
Ryan Rupe, 2000
Victor Zambrano, 2001

Longest losing streak
10 games—Albie Lopez, 2001

Most saves
43—Roberto Hernandez, 1999

Most bases on balls
111—Tony Saunders, 1998

Most bases on balls, career
177—Albie Lopez

Most strikeouts
172—Tony Saunders, 1998

Most strikeouts, career
298—Esteban Yan

Most strikeouts, game
12—Dan Wheeler, September 12, 1999

Most shutouts
2—Rolando Arrojo, 1998
Bobby Witt, 1999

Most shutouts, career
2—Rolando Arrojo
Bobby Witt
Albie Lopez

Most 1-0 shutouts won
1—Steve Trachsel, 2000

Most runs
130—Bobby Witt, 1999

Most earned runs
117—Bobby Witt, 1999

Most hits
213—Bobby Witt, 1999

Most wild pitches
11—Tanyon Sturtze, 2001

Most hit batsmen
19—Rolando Arrojo, 1998

Most home runs
30—Ryan Rupe, 2001

Most sacrifice hits
7—Bobby Witt, 1999
Roberto Hernandez, 2000

Most sacrifice flies
12—Paul Wilson, 2001

Lowest ERA
3.56—Rolando Arrojo, 202 innings, 1998

CLUB RECORDS

Most players
51 in 2000

Fewest players
42 in 1998

Most games
162 in 1998, 1999, 2001

Most at-bats
5,586 in 1999

Most runs
772 in 1999

Fewest runs
620 in 1998

Most opponents' runs
913 in 1999

Most hits
1,531 in 1999

Fewest hits
1,414 in 2000

Most singles
1,085 in 1999

Most doubles
311 in 2001

Most triples
43 in 1998

Most homers
162 in 2000

Most homers at Tropicana Field, home and opponents
185 in 2000

Fewest homers
111 in 1998

Most grand slams
4 in 2000, 2001

Most pinch home runs
3 in 1998, 2000

Most total bases
2,296 in 1999

Most long hits
453 in 2001

Most extra bases on long hits
765 in 1999

Most sacrifice hits
53 in 1998

Most sacrifice flies
48 in 1999

Most stolen bases
120 in 1998

Most caught stealing
73 in 1998

Most bases on balls
558 in 2000

Most strikeouts
1,116 in 2001

Fewest strikeouts
1,022 in 2000

Most hit by pitch
64 in 1999

Fewest hit by pitch
37 in 1998

Most runs batted in
728 in 1999

Highest batting average
.274 in 1999

Lowest batting average
.257 in 2000

Highest slugging average
.411 in 1999

Lowest slugging average
.385 in 1998

Most grounded into double play
157 in 1999

Fewest grounded into double play
126 in 2000

Most left on bases
1,169 in 1999

Fewest left on bases
1,104 in 2000

Most .300 hitters
1 in 1999

Most putouts
4,329 in 1998

Fewest putouts
4,271 in 2001

Most assists
1,814 in 2000

Fewest assists
1,531 in 2001

Most chances accepted
6,108 in 2000

Fewest chances accepted
5,802 in 2001

Most errors
139 in 2001

Fewest errors
94 in 1998

Most errorless games
90 in 1998

Most consecutive errorless games
7 in 1998

Most double plays
198 in 1999

Fewest double plays
144 in 2001

Most passed balls
19 in 1998

Fewest passed balls
8 in 2001

Highest fielding average
.985 in 1998

Lowest fielding average
.977 in 2001

Highest home attendance
2,261,158 in 1998

Highest road attendance
2,289,235 in 2001

Most games won
69 in 1999, 2000

Most games lost
100 in 2001

Most games won, month
16—August 1999

Most games lost, month
20—August 1998, May 2001

Games won, league
263 in 4 years

Games lost, league
384 in 4 years

Highest percentage games won
.429 in 2000 (won 69, lost 92)

Lowest percentage games won
.383 in 2001 (won 62, lost 100)

Most consecutive games won
6 in 1999, 2000 (twice)

Most consecutive games lost
11 in 1998

Most shutouts won
8 in 2000

Most shutouts lost
17 in 1998

Most 1-0 games won
3 in 2000

Most 1-0 games lost
1 in 2000, 2001

Number of times league champions
0

Number of last-place finishes
2

Most runs, game
15 vs. Seattle, May 30, 1999
   vs. Texas, September 19, 1999
   vs. New York N.L., June 4, 2000

Most runs by opponent, game
20 by Cleveland, May 7, 1999

Most runs, shutout game
10 vs. Seattle, September 8, 1998
   vs. Montreal N.L., July 12, 2001

Most runs by opponent, shutout game
11 by Detroit, July 4, 2000
   by Toronto, April 5, 2001
   by Florida N.L., June 16, 2001

Most runs, doubleheader shutout
Never accomplished

Most runs, inning
11 vs. Seattle, May 28, 2000, eighth
   inning

Longest 1-0 game won
None over nine innings

Longest 1-0 game lost
None over nine innings

Most hits, game
20 vs. Seattle, May 28, 2000
   vs. Baltimore, August 22, 2001

Most home runs, game
5 vs. Anaheim, April 22, 2000, 10 innings
4 vs. Minnesota, April 13, 1998, 14
   innings
   vs. Kansas City, May 5, 1999
   vs. Texas, May 17, 1999
   vs. Seattle, May 30, 1999
   vs. New York, September 28, 2000
   vs. Baltimore, April 15, 2001
   vs. Detroit, May 20, 2001
   vs. Boston, June 25, 2001

Most consecutive games with one or more homers
10 (17 homers), 2000

Most total bases, game
36 vs. Seattle, May 30, 1999

Largest crowd, day game
43,373 vs. New York, July 12, 1998

Largest crowd, night game
45,369 vs. Detroit, March 31, 1998

Largest crowd, doubleheader
No occurrence

Largest crowd, home opener
45,369 vs. Detroit, March 31, 1998

TEXAS RANGERS
YEARLY FINISHES
WEST DIVISION

Year	Position	W	L	Pct.	*GB	Manager	Attendance
1972	6th	54	100	.351	38.5	Ted Williams	662,974
1973	6th	57	105	.352	37.0	Whitey Herzog, Del Wilber, Billy Martin	686,085
1974	2nd	84	76	.525	5.0	Billy Martin	1,193,902
1975	3rd	79	83	.488	19.0	Billy Martin, Frank Lucchesi	1,127,924
1976	4th (tied)	76	86	.469	14.0	Frank Lucchesi	1,164,982
1977	2nd	94	68	.580	8.0	Frank Lucchesi, Eddie Stanky, Connie Ryan, Billy Hunter	1,250,722
1978	2nd (tied)	87	75	.537	5.0	Billy Hunter, Pat Corrales	1,447,963
1979	3rd	83	79	.512	5.0	Pat Corrales	1,519,671
1980	4th	76	85	.472	20.5	Pat Corrales	1,198,175
1981	2nd/3rd	57	48	.543	†	Don Zimmer	850,076
1982	6th	64	98	.395	29.0	Don Zimmer, Darrell Johnson	1,154,432
1983	3rd	77	85	.475	22.0	Doug Rader	1,363,469
1984	7th	69	92	.429	14.5	Doug Rader	1,102,471
1985	7th	62	99	.385	28.5	Doug Rader, Bobby Valentine	1,112,497
1986	2nd	87	75	.537	5.0	Bobby Valentine	1,692,002
1987	6th (tied)	75	87	.463	10.0	Bobby Valentine	1,763,053
1988	6th	70	91	.435	33.5	Bobby Valentine	1,581,901

Year	Position	W	L	Pct.	*GB	Manager	Attendance
1989	4th	83	79	.512	16.0	Bobby Valentine	2,043,993
1990	3rd	83	79	.512	20.0	Bobby Valentine	2,057,911
1991	3rd	85	77	.525	10.0	Bobby Valentine	2,297,720
1992	4th	77	85	.475	19.0	Bobby Valentine, Toby Harrah	2,198,231
1993	2nd	86	76	.531	8.0	Kevin Kennedy	2,244,616
1994	1st	52	62	.456	+1.0	Kevin Kennedy	2,503,198
1995	3rd	74	70	.514	4.5	Johnny Oates	1,985,910
1996	1st‡	90	72	.556	+4.5	Johnny Oates	2,889,020
1997	3rd	77	85	.475	13.0	Johnny Oates	2,945,228
1998	1st‡	88	74	.543	+3.0	Johnny Oates	2,927,409
1999	1st‡	95	67	.586	+8.0	Johnny Oates	2,771,469
2000	4th	71	91	.438	20.5	Johnny Oates	2,800,147
2001	4th	73	89	.451	43.0	Johnny Oates, Jerry Narron	2,831,111

*Games behind winner. †First half 33-22; second 24-26. ‡Lost division series.

INDIVIDUAL RECORDS (1972 TO DATE)

SERVICE

Most years by non-pitcher
12—Jim Sundberg

Most years by pitcher
11—Charlie Hough

BATTING

Most games
163—Al Oliver, 1980

Most games, career
1,512—Jim Sundberg

Most at-bats
670—Buddy Bell, 162 games, 1979

Most at-bats, career
5,248—Ivan Rodriguez

Most runs
133—Alex Rodriguez, 162 games, 2001

Most runs, career
791—Juan Gonzalez

Most hits
210—Mickey Rivers, 147 games, 1980

Most hits, career
1,595—Ivan Rodriguez

Most singles
165—Mickey Rivers, 147 games, 1980

Most singles, career
1,061—Ivan Rodriguez

Most doubles
50—Juan Gonzalez, 154 games, 1998

Most doubles, career
312—Ivan Rodriguez

Most triples
14—Ruben Sierra, 162 games, 1989

Most triples, career
44—Ruben Sierra

Most homers by righthander
52—Alex Rodriguez, 162 games, 2001

Most homers by lefthander
47—Rafael Palmeiro, 158 games, 1999
Rafael Palmeiro, 160 games, 2001

Most homers by switch-hitter
32—Mickey Tettleton, 134 games, 1995

Most homers by rookie
30—Pete Incaviglia, 153 games, 1986

Most homers at home
28—Rafael Palmeiro, 1999

Most homers on road
26—Alex Rodriguez, 2001

Most homers, month
15—Juan Gonzalez, July 1996
Rafael Palmeiro, August 1999

Most homers by righthander, career
340—Juan Gonzalez

Most homers by lefthander, career
240—Rafael Palmeiro

Most homers by switch-hitter, career
177—Ruben Sierra

Most grand slams
3—Jeff Burroughs, 151 games, 1973
Larry Parrish, 128 games, 1982
Rafael Palmeiro, 158 games, 1999

Most grand slams, career
7—Juan Gonzalez

Most total bases
393—Alex Rodriguez, 162 games, 2001

Most total bases, career
2,761—Juan Gonzalez

Most long hits
97—Juan Gonzalez, 154 games, 1998

Most long hits, career
641—Juan Gonzalez

Most extra bases on long hits
192—Alex Rodriguez, 162 games, 2001

Most extra bases on long hits, career
1,340—Juan Gonzalez

Most sacrifice hits
40—Bert Campaneris, 150 games, 1977

Most sacrifice flies
12— Jeff Burroughs, 152 games, 1974
Ruben Sierra, 158 games, 1987
Juan Gonzalez, 144 games, 1999

Most bases on balls
113—Toby Harrah, 126 games, 1985

Most bases on balls, career
668—Toby Harrah

Most strikeouts
185—Pete Incaviglia, 153 games, 1986

Most strikeouts, career
947—Juan Gonzalez

Fewest strikeouts
43—Lenny Randle, 151 games, 1974

Most hit by pitch
16—Alex Rodriguez, 162 games, 2001

Most runs batted in
157—Juan Gonzalez, 154 games, 1998

Most runs batted in, career
1,075—Juan Gonzalez

Most game-winning RBIs
17—Larry Parrish, 145 games, 1983

Highest batting average
.341—Julio Franco, 146 games, 1991

Highest batting average, career
.319—Al Oliver

Highest slugging average
.643—Juan Gonzalez, 134 games, 1996

Highest slugging average, career
.572—Juan Gonzalez

Longest batting streak
28 games—Gabe Kapler, 2000

Most grounded into double play
31—Ivan Rodriguez, 144 games, 1999

Fewest grounded into double play
2—Tom Goodwin, 154 games, 1998

BASERUNNING

Most stolen bases
52—Bump Wills, 157 games, 1978

Most stolen bases, career
161—Bump Wills

Most caught stealing
21—Otis Nixon, 139 games, 1995

PITCHING

Most games
85—Mitch Williams, 1987

Most games, career
445—Jeff Russell

Most games started
41— Jim Bibby, 1974
Ferguson Jenkins, 1974

Most games started, career
313—Charlie Hough

Most complete games
29—Ferguson Jenkins, 1974

Most complete games, career
98—Charlie Hough

Most games finished
66—Jeff Russell, 1989

Most innings
328—Ferguson Jenkins, 1974

Most innings, career
2,307.2—Charlie Hough

Most games won
25—Ferguson Jenkins, 1974

Most games won, career
139—Charlie Hough

Most games lost
19—Jim Bibby, 1974

Most games lost, career
123—Charlie Hough

Most 20-victory seasons
1—Ferguson Jenkins
Kevin Brown
Rick Helling

Highest winning percentage
.741—Rick Helling (20-7), 1998

Longest winning streak
12 games—Bobby Witt, 1990

Longest losing streak
9 games—David Clyde, 1974

Most saves
43—John Wetteland, 1999

Most bases on balls
143—Bobby Witt, 1986

Most bases on balls, career
1,001—Bobby Witt

Most strikeouts
301—Nolan Ryan, 1989

Most strikeouts, career
1,452—Charlie Hough

Most strikeouts, game
16—Nolan Ryan, April 26, 1990
  Nolan Ryan, May 1, 1991

Most shutouts
6—Ferguson Jenkins, 1974
  Bert Blyleven, 1976

Most shutouts, career
17—Ferguson Jenkins

Most 1-0 shutouts won
4—Ferguson Jenkins, 1974
  Bert Blyleven, 1976

Most runs
159—Charlie Hough, 1987

Most earned runs
139—Jim Bibby, 1974

Most hits
286—Ferguson Jenkins, 1974

Most hit batsmen
19—Charlie Hough, 1987

Most wild pitches
22—Bobby Witt, 1986

Most home runs
41—Rick Helling, 1999

Most sacrifice hits
16—Jim Umbarger, 1976

Most sacrifice flies
14—Charlie Hough, 1987

Lowest ERA
2.17—Mike Paul, 162 innings, 1972

CLUB RECORDS

Most players
52 in 1992

Fewest players
35 in 1984

Most games
163 in 1980, 1983, 1996

Most at-bats
5,703 in 1991

Most runs
945 in 1999

Fewest runs
590 in 1982

Most opponents' runs
974 in 2000

Most hits
1,653 in 1999

Fewest hits
1,353 in 1978

Most singles
1,202 in 1980

Most doubles
330 in 2000

Most triples
46 in 1989

Most homers
246 in 2001

Fewest homers
80 in 1976

Most homers at Arlington Stadium,
  home and opponents
204 in 1987

Most homers at The Ballpark in Arlington,
  home and opponents
233 in 2001

Most grand slams
8 in 1999

Most pinch home runs
7 in 1980

Most long hits
595 in 2001

Most extra bases on long hits
1,110 in 2001

Most total bases
2,705 in 1999

Most sacrifice hits
116 in 1977

Most sacrifice flies
69 in 1979

Most stolen bases
196 in 1978

Most caught stealing
91 in 1978

Most bases on balls
660 in 1996

Most strikeouts
1,116 in 1997

Fewest strikeouts
589 in 1980

Most hit by pitch
75 in 2001

Fewest hit by pitch
20 in 1984

Most runs batted in
897 in 1999

Most game-winning RBIs
80 in 1986

Highest batting average
.293 in 1999

Highest slugging average
.479 in 1999

Most grounded into double play
161 in 2000

Most grounded into double play
111 in 1988, 1993

Most left on bases
1,253 in 1996

Fewest left on bases
1,034 in 1993

Most .300 hitters
4 in 1998, 1999

Most putouts
4,437 in 1991

Fewest putouts
4,235 in 1985

Most assists
1,980 in 1975

Fewest assists
1,580 in 1998

Most chances accepted
6,377 in 1975

Fewest chances accepted
5,881 in 2000

Most errors
191 in 1975

Fewest errors
87 in 1996

Most errorless games
95 in 1996

Most consecutive errorless games
15 in 1996

Most double plays
173 in 1975

Fewest double plays
137 in 1989

Most passed balls
73 in 1987

Fewest passed balls
2 in 1999, 2001

Highest fielding average
.986 in 1996

Lowest fielding average
.971 in 1975

Highest home attendance
2,945,228 in 1997

Highest road attendance
2,406,986 in 2000

Most games won
95 in 1999

Most games lost
105 in 1973

Most games won, month
21 in September 1978

Most games lost, month
24 in August 1973

Highest percentage games won
.586 in 1999 (won 95, lost 67)

Lowest percentage games won
.351 in 1972 (won 54, lost 100)

Games won, league
2,285 in 30 years

Games lost, league
2,438 in 30 years

Most shutouts won
17 in 1977

Most shutouts lost
27 in 1972

Most 1-0 games won
5 in 1974, 1975, 1976, 1990

Most 1-0 games lost
7 in 1976

Most consecutive games won
14 in 1991

Most consecutive games lost
15 in 1972

Number of times league champions
0

Number of last-place finishes
2

Most runs, game
26 vs. Baltimore, April 19, 1996

Most runs by opponent, game
23 by Oakland, September 30, 2000

Most runs, shutout game
14 vs. Oakland, July 26, 1977

Most runs by opponent, shutout game
14 by Chicago, April 18, 1972
  by Chicago, September 4, 1973

Most runs, doubleheader shutout
No performance

Most runs, inning
16 vs. Baltimore, April 19, 1996, eighth
  inning

Longest 1-0 game won
14 innings vs. Boston, April 17, 1983

Longest 1-0 games lost
13 innings vs. Minnesota, September 22,
  1992

Most hits, game
23 vs. Chicago, April 2, 1998

Most home runs, game
7 vs. Minnesota, September 13, 1986

Most consecutive games with one or more homers
14 (31 homers), 2001

Most total bases, game
43 vs. Minnesota, September 13, 1986

Largest crowd, day game
49,512 vs. Anaheim, April 3, 2001

Largest crowd, doubleheader
42,163 vs. Detroit, July 10, 1982

Largest crowd, night game
49,603 vs. Houston N.L., June 9, 2001

Largest crowd, home opener
49,512 vs. Anaheim, April 3, 2001

TORONTO BLUE JAYS
YEARLY FINISHES
EAST DIVISION

Year	Position	W	L	Pct.	*GB	Manager	Attendance
1977	7th	54	107	.335	45.5	Roy Hartsfield	1,701,052
1978	7th	59	102	.366	40.0	Roy Hartsfield	1,562,585
1979	7th	53	109	.327	50.5	Roy Hartsfield	1,431,651
1980	7th	67	95	.414	36.0	Bobby Mattick	1,400,327
1981	7th/7th	37	69	.349	†	Bobby Mattick	755,083
1982	6th (tied)	78	84	.481	17.0	Bobby Cox	1,275,978
1983	4th	89	73	.549	9.0	Bobby Cox	1,930,415
1984	2nd	89	73	.549	15.0	Bobby Cox	2,110,009
1985	1st‡	99	62	.615	+2.0	Bobby Cox	2,468,925
1986	4th	86	76	.531	9.5	Jimy Williams	2,455,477
1987	2nd	96	66	.593	2.0	Jimy Williams	2,778,429
1988	3rd (tied)	87	75	.537	2.0	Jimy Williams	2,595,175
1989	1st‡	89	73	.549	+2.0	Jimy Williams, Cito Gaston	3,375,883
1990	2nd	86	76	.531	2.0	Cito Gaston	3,885,284
1991	1st‡	91	71	.562	+7.0	Cito Gaston	4,001,527
1992	1st§	96	66	.593	+4.0	Cito Gaston	4,028,318
1993	1st§	95	67	.586	+7.0	Cito Gaston	4,057,947
1994	3rd	55	60	.478	16.0	Cito Gaston	2,907,933
1995	5th	56	88	.389	30.0	Cito Gaston	2,826,483
1996	4th	74	88	.457	18.0	Cito Gaston	2,559,573
1997	5th	76	86	.469	22.0	Cito Gaston, Mel Queen	2,589,297
1998	3rd	88	74	.543	26.0	Tim Johnson	2,454,183
1999	3rd	84	78	.519	14.0	Jim Fregosi	2,163,464
2000	3rd	83	79	.512	4.5	Jim Fregosi	1,819,886
2001	3rd	80	82	.494	16.0	Buck Martinez	1,915,438

*Games behind winner. †First half 16-42; second 21-27. ‡Lost championship series. §Won championship series.

INDIVIDUAL RECORDS (1977 TO DATE)

SERVICE

Most years by non-pitcher
12—Ernie Whitt
Tony Fernandez

Most years by pitcher
15—Dave Stieb

BATTING

Most games
163—Tony Fernandez, 1986

Most games, career
1,450—Tony Fernandez

Most at-bats
687—Tony Fernandez, 163 games, 1986

Most at-bats, career
5,335—Tony Fernandez

Most runs
134—Shawn Green, 153 games, 1999

Most runs, career
768—Lloyd Moseby

Most hits
213—Tony Fernandez, 163 games, 1986

Most hits, career
1,583—Tony Fernandez

Most singles
161—Tony Fernandez, 163 games, 1986

Most singles, career
1,160—Tony Fernandez

Most doubles
57—Carlos Delgado, 162 games, 2000

Most doubles, career
291—Tony Fernandez

Most triples
17—Tony Fernandez, 161 games, 1990

Most triples, career
72—Tony Fernandez

Most homers by righthander
47—George Bell, 156 games, 1987

Most homers by lefthander
44—Carlos Delgado, 152 games, 1999

Most homers by switch-hitter
34—Jose Cruz Jr., 146 games, 2001

Most homers by rookie
20—Fred McGriff, 107 games, 1987

Most homers, month
12—Carlos Delgado, August 1999
Jose Cruz Jr., August 2001

Most homers at home
30—Carlos Delgado, 2000

Most homers on road
28—George Bell, 1987

Most homers by righthander, career
203—Joe Carter

Most homers by lefthander, career
229—Carlos Delgado

Most homers by switch-hitter, career
72—Devon White

Most grand slams
3—Carlos Delgado, 1997
Darrin Fletcher, 2000

Most grand slams, career
7—George Bell
Carlos Delgado

Most total bases
378—Carlos Delgado, 162 games, 2000

Most total bases, career
2,201—George Bell

Most long hits
99—Carlos Delgado, 162 games, 2000

Most long hits, career
482—Carlos Delgado

Most extra bases on long hits
182—Carlos Delgado, 162 games, 2000

Most extra bases on long hits, career
948—Carlos Delgado

Most sacrifice hits
19—Luis Gomez, 153 games, 1978

Most sacrifice flies
14—George Bell, 153 games, 1989

Most bases on balls
123—Carlos Delgado, 162 games, 2000

Most bases on balls, career
547—Lloyd Moseby
Carlos Delgado

Most strikeouts
159—Jose Canseco, 151 games, 1998

Most strikeouts, career
1,015—Lloyd Moseby

Fewest strikeouts
21—Bob Bailor, 154 games, 1978

Most hit by pitch
17—Charlie O'Brien, 109 games, 1996

Most runs batted in
137—Carlos Delgado, 162 games, 2000

Most runs batted in, career
740—George Bell

Most game-winning RBIs
17—George Bell, 156 games, 1988

Highest batting average
.363—John Olerud, 158 games, 1993

Highest batting average, career
.307—Roberto Alomar

Highest slugging average
.664—Carlos Delgado, 162 games, 2000

Highest slugging average, career
.554—Carlos Delgado

Longest batting streak
28 games—Shawn Green, 1999

Most grounded into double play
23—Ed Sprague, 150 games, 1993

Fewest grounded into double play
5—Alfredo Griffin, 162 games, 1983
    Willie Upshaw, 155 games, 1986
    Roberto Alomar, 161 games, 1991

BASERUNNING

Most stolen bases
60—Dave Collins, 128 games, 1984

Most stolen bases, career
255—Lloyd Moseby

Most caught stealing
23—Alfredo Griffin, 155 games, 1980

PITCHING

Most games
89—Mark Eichhorn, 1987

Most games, career
452—Duane Ward

Most games started
40—Jim Clancy, 1982

Most games started, career
408—Dave Stieb

Most complete games
19—Dave Stieb, 1982

Most complete games, career
103—Dave Stieb

Most games finished
70—Duane Ward, 1993

Most innings
288.1—Dave Stieb, 1982

Most innings, career
2,873—Dave Stieb

Most games won
21—Jack Morris, 1992
    Roger Clemens, 1997

Most games won, career
175—Dave Stieb

Most 20-victory seasons
2—Roger Clemens

Most games lost
18—Jerry Garvin, 1977
    Phil Huffman, 1979

Most games lost, career
140—Jim Clancy

Longest winning streak
15 games—Roger Clemens, 1998

Longest losing streak
10 games—Jerry Garvin, 1977, 1978
    Paul Mirabella, 1980

Highest winning percentage
.778—Jack Morris (21-6), 1992

Most saves
45—Duane Ward, 1993

Most bases on balls
128—Jim Clancy, 1980

Most bases on balls, career
1,020—Dave Stieb

Most strikeouts
292—Roger Clemens, 1997

Most strikeouts, career
1,658—Dave Stieb

Most strikeouts, game
18—Roger Clemens, August 25, 1998

Most shutouts
5—Dave Stieb, 1982

Most shutouts, career
30—Dave Stieb

Most 1-0 shutouts won
2—Jim Clancy, 1980
    Jimmy Key, 1988

Most runs
143—Dave Lemanczyk, 1977
    Erik Hanson, 1996

Most earned runs
129—Erik Hanson, 1996

Most hits
278—Dave Lemanczyk, 1977

Most hit batsmen
16—Chris Carpenter, 2001

Most wild pitches
26—Juan Guzman, 1993

Most home runs
36—Woody Williams, 1998

Most sacrifice hits
16—Jerry Garvin, 1977

Most sacrifice flies
12—Jim Clancy, 1983

Lowest ERA
2.05—Roger Clemens, 264 innings, 1997

CLUB RECORDS

Most players
53 in 1999

Fewest players
33 in 1983

Most games
163 in 1984, 1986, 1998

Most at-bats
5,716 in 1986

Most runs
883 in 1999

Fewest runs
590 in 1978

Most opponent's runs
908 in 2000

Most hits
1,580 in 1999

Fewest hits
1,333 in 1997

Most singles
1,069 in 1984

Most doubles
337 in 1999

Most triples
68 in 1984

Most homers
244 in 2000

Fewest homers
95 in 1979

Most homers at Exhibition Stadium, home and opponents
185 in 1983

Most homers at SkyDome, home and opponents
226 in 2000

Most grand slams
9 in 2000

Most pinch home runs
6 in 1984

Most total bases
2,664 in 2000

Most long hits
593 in 2000

Most extra bases on long hits
1,102 in 2000

Most sacrifice hits
81 in 1977

Most sacrifice flies
65 in 1991

Most stolen bases
193 in 1984

Most caught stealing
81 in 1982, 1998

Most bases on balls
588 in 1993

Most strikeouts
1,138 in 1997

Fewest strikeouts
645 in 1978

Most hit by pitch
92 in 1996

Fewest hit by pitch
23 in 1977, 1978

Most runs batted in
856 in 1999

Most game-winning RBIs
90 in 1985, 1987

Highest batting average
.280 in 1999

Lowest batting average
.244 in 1997

Highest slugging average
.469 in 2000

Lowest slugging average
.359 in 1978

Most grounded into double play
156 in 1979

Fewest grounded into double play
91 in 1984

Most left on bases
1,187 in 1993

Fewest left on bases
1,064 in 1979

Most .300 hitters
4 in 1999

Most putouts
4,428 in 1986

Fewest putouts
4,251 in 1979

Most assists
1,939 in 1980

Fewest assists
1,532 in 1998

Most chances accepted
6,337 in 1980

Fewest chances accepted
5,864 in 1997

Most errors
164 in 1977

Fewest errors
86 in 1990

Most errorless games
103 in 1990

Most consecutive errorless games
11 in 1986

Most double plays
206 in 1980

Fewest double plays
109 in 1992

Most passed balls
31 in 1995

Fewest passed balls
3 in 1985

Highest fielding average
.986 in 1990

Lowest fielding average
.974 in 1977

Highest home attendance
4,057,947 in 1993

Highest road attendance
2,549,898 in 1993

Most games won
99 in 1985

Most games lost
109 in 1979

Most games won, month
20 in September 1988, August 1989

Most games lost, month
23 in May 1979

Highest percentage games won
.615 in 1985 (won 99, lost 62)

Lowest percentage games won
.327 in 1979 (won 53, lost 109)

Games won, league
1,947 in 25 years

Games lost, league
1,979 in 25 years

Most shutouts won
17 in 1988

Most shutouts lost
20 in 1981

Most 1-0 games won
5 in 1980

Most 1-0 games lost
3 in 1979, 1992

Most consecutive games won
11 in 1987, 1998

Most consecutive games lost
12 in 1981

Number of times league champions
2

Number of last-place finishes
4 (tied in 1995)

Most runs, game
24 vs. Baltimore, June 26, 1978

Most runs by opponent, game
24 by California, August 25, 1979

Most runs, shutout game
15 vs. Detroit, July 6, 1996

Most runs by opponent, shutout game
15 by New York, September 25, 1977, first game

Most runs, inning
11 vs. Seattle, July 20, 1984, ninth inning

Longest 1-0 game won
12 innings vs. Boston, September 26, 1986

Longest 1-0 game lost
15 innings vs. Oakland, July 27, 1986

Most hits, game
25 vs. Texas, August 9, 1999

Most home runs, game
10 vs. Baltimore, September 14, 1987

Most consecutive games with one or more home runs
23 (44 homers), 2000

Most total bases, game
53 vs. Baltimore, September 14, 1987

Largest crowd, day game
50,533 vs. Cleveland, April 9, 1993

Largest crowd, doubleheader
48,641 vs. California, July 17, 1989

Largest crowd, night game
50,532 vs. Boston, September 22, 1993

Largest crowd, home opener
50,533 vs. Cleveland, April 9, 1993

WASHINGTON SENATORS (ORIGINAL CLUB)
YEARLY FINISHES

Year	Position	W	L	Pct.	*GB	Manager	Attendance
1901	6th	61	72	.459	20.5	Jimmy Manning	161,661
1902	6th	61	75	.449	22.0	Tom Loftus	188,158
1903	8th	43	94	.314	47.5	Tom Loftus	128,878
1904	8th	38	113	.251	55.5	Patsy Donovan	131,744
1905	7th	64	87	.421	29.5	Jake Stahl	252,027
1906	7th	55	95	.367	37.5	Jake Stahl	129,903
1907	8th	49	102	.325	43.5	Joe Cantillon	221,929
1908	7th	67	85	.441	22.5	Joe Cantillon	264,252
1909	8th	42	110	.276	56.0	Joe Cantillon	205,199
1910	7th	66	85	.437	36.5	Jimmy McAleer	254,591
1911	7th	64	90	.416	38.5	Jimmy McAleer	244,884
1912	2nd	91	61	.599	14.0	Clark Griffith	350,663
1913	2nd	90	64	.584	6.5	Clark Griffith	325,831
1914	3rd	81	73	.526	19.0	Clark Griffith	243,888
1915	4th	85	68	.556	17.0	Clark Griffith	167,332
1916	7th	76	77	.497	14.5	Clark Griffith	177,265
1917	5th	74	79	.484	25.5	Clark Griffith	89,682
1918	3rd	72	56	.563	4.0	Clark Griffith	182,122
1919	7th	56	84	.400	32.0	Clark Griffith	234,096
1920	6th	68	84	.447	29.0	Clark Griffith	359,260
1921	4th	80	73	.523	18.0	George McBride	456,069
1922	6th	69	85	.448	25.0	Clyde Milan	458,552
1923	4th	75	78	.490	23.5	Donie Bush	357,406
1924	1st	92	62	.597	+2.0	Bucky Harris	534,310
1925	1st	96	55	.636	+8.5	Bucky Harris	817,199
1926	4th	81	69	.540	8.0	Bucky Harris	551,580
1927	3rd	85	69	.552	25.0	Bucky Harris	528,976
1928	4th	75	79	.487	26.0	Bucky Harris	378,501
1929	5th	71	81	.467	34.0	Walter Johnson	355,506
1930	2nd	94	60	.610	8.0	Walter Johnson	614,474
1931	3rd	92	62	.597	16.0	Walter Johnson	492,657
1932	3rd	93	61	.604	14.0	Walter Johnson	371,396
1933	1st	99	53	.651	+7.0	Joe Cronin	437,533
1934	7th	66	86	.434	34.0	Joe Cronin	330,074
1935	6th	67	86	.438	27.0	Bucky Harris	255,011
1936	4th	82	71	.536	20.0	Bucky Harris	379,525
1937	6th	73	80	.477	28.5	Bucky Harris	397,799
1938	5th	75	76	.497	23.5	Bucky Harris	522,694
1939	6th	65	87	.428	41.5	Bucky Harris	339,257

Year	Position	W	L	Pct.	*GB	Manager	Attendance
1940	7th	64	90	.416	26.0	Bucky Harris	381,241
1941	6th (tied)	70	84	.455	31.0	Bucky Harris	415,663
1942	7th	62	89	.411	39.5	Bucky Harris	403,493
1943	2nd	84	69	.549	13.5	Ossie Bluege	574,694
1944	8th	64	90	.416	25.0	Ossie Bluege	525,235
1945	2nd	87	67	.565	1.5	Ossie Bluege	652,660
1946	4th	76	78	.494	28.0	Ossie Bluege	1,027,216
1947	7th	64	90	.416	33.0	Ossie Bluege	850,758
1948	7th	56	97	.366	40.0	Joe Kuhel	795,254
1949	8th	50	104	.325	47.0	Joe Kuhel	770,745
1950	5th	67	87	.435	31.0	Bucky Harris	699,697
1951	7th	62	92	.403	36.0	Bucky Harris	695,167
1952	5th	78	76	.506	17.0	Bucky Harris	699,457
1953	5th	76	76	.500	23.5	Bucky Harris	595,594
1954	6th	66	88	.429	45.0	Bucky Harris	503,542
1955	8th	53	101	.344	43.0	Chuck Dressen	425,238
1956	7th	59	95	.383	38.0	Chuck Dressen	431,647
1957	8th	55	99	.357	43.0	Chuck Dressen, Cookie Lavagetto	457,079
1958	8th	61	93	.396	31.0	Cookie Lavagetto	475,288
1959	8th	63	91	.409	31.0	Cookie Lavagetto	615,372
1960	5th	73	81	.474	24.0	Cookie Lavagetto	743,404

*Games behind winner.

INDIVIDUAL RECORDS (1901 TO 1960)

SERVICE

Most years, non-pitcher
19—Sam Rice

Most years played by pitcher
21—Walter Johnson

BATTING

Most games
158—Eddie Foster, 1916

Most games, career
2,307—Sam Rice

Most at-bats
668—Buddy Lewis, 156 games, 1937

Most at-bats, career
8,934—Sam Rice

Most runs
127—Joe Cronin, 154 games, 1930

Most runs, career
1,467—Sam Rice

Most hits
227—Sam Rice, 152 games, 1925

Most hits, career
2,889—Sam Rice

Most singles
182—Sam Rice, 152 games, 1925

Most doubles
51—Mickey Vernon, 148 games, 1946

Most doubles, career
478—Sam Rice

Most triples
20—Goose Goslin, 150 games, 1925

Most triples, career
183—Sam Rice

Most homers by righthander
42— Roy Sievers, 152 games, 1957
Harmon Killebrew, 153 games, 1959

Most homers by lefthander
20—Mickey Vernon, 151 games, 1954

Most homers by switch-hitter
6—Danny Moeller, 132 games, 1912

Most homers by rookie
30—Bob Allison, 150 games, 1959

Most homers at home
26—Roy Sievers, 1957

Most homers on road
21—Roy Sievers, 1958

Most homers, month
15—Harmon Killebrew, May, 1959

Most homers, righthander, career
180—Roy Sievers

Most homers, lefthander, career
127—Goose Goslin

Most homers, righthander, career
15—Danny Moeller

Most grand slams
2—held by many players—last player, Roy Sievers, 152 games, 1957

Most grand slams, career
4—Roy Sievers

Most total bases
331—Roy Sievers, 152 games, 1957

Most total bases, career
3,832—Sam Rice

Most long hits
76—Stan Spence, 152 games, 1946

Most extra bases on long hits
159—Roy Sievers, 152 games, 1957

Most sacrifice (sacrifice hits and sacrifice flies)
52—Bob Ganley, 150 games, 1908

Most sacrifice hits
36—Hunter Hill, 103 games, 1905

Most sacrifice flies
16—Chick Gandil, 145 games, 1914

Most bases on balls
151—Eddie Yost, 152 games, 1956

Most strikeouts
138—Jim Lemon, 146 games, 1956

Fewest strikeouts
9—Sam Rice, 150 games, 1929

Most hit by pitch
24—Kid Elberfeld, 127 games, 1911

Most runs batted in
129—Goose Goslin, 154 games, 1924

Most runs batted in, career
1,044—Sam Rice

Highest batting average
.379—Goose Goslin, 135 games, 1923

Highest batting average, career
.328—Heinie Manush

Highest slugging average
.614—Goose Goslin, 135 games, 1928

Highest slugging average, career
.502—Goose Goslin

Longest batting streak
33 games—Heinie Manush, 1933

Most grounded into double play
25—Sam Dente, 155 games, 1950

Fewest grounded into double play
5—George Case, 154 games, 1940
George Case, 153 games, 1941
Stan Spence, 153 games, 1944
Eddie Yost, 155 games, 1954

BASERUNNING

Most stolen bases
88—Clyde Milan, 154 games, 1912

Most stolen bases, career
494—Clyde Milan

Most caught stealing
30—Sam Rice, 153 games, 1920

PITCHING

Most games
64—Firpo Marberry, 1926

Most games, career
802—Walter Johnson

Most games started
42—Walter Johnson, 1910

Most games started, career
666—Walter Johnson

Most complete games
38—Walter Johnson, 1910

Most complete games, career
531—Walter Johnson

Most games finished
47—Firpo Marberry, 1926

Most innings
374—Walter Johnson, 1910

Most innings, career
5,923—Walter Johnson

Most games won
36—Walter Johnson, 1913

Most games won, career
417—Walter Johnson

Most 20-victory seasons
12—Walter Johnson

– 277 –

Highest winning percentage
.837—Walter Johnson (36-7), 1913
Longest winning streak
16 games—Walter Johnson, 1912
Longest winning streak, two seasons
16 games—Alvin Crowder, 1932 (15), 1933 (1)
Longest losing streak
15 games—Bob Groom, 1909
Most games lost
26—Jack Townsend, 1904
Bob Groom, 1909
Most games lost, career
279—Walter Johnson
Most bases on balls
146—Bobo Newsom, 1936
Most bases on balls, career
1,353—Walter Johnson
Most strikeouts
313—Walter Johnson, 1910
Most strikeouts, career
3,508—Walter Johnson
Most strikeouts, game
15—Camilo Pascual, April 18, 1960
Most shutouts
12—Walter Johnson, 1913
Most 1-0 shutouts won
5—Walter Johnson, 1913 and 1919
Most shutouts, career
110—Walter Johnson
Most runs
172—Al Orth, 1903
Most earned runs
144—Jimmie DeShong, 1937
Most hits
328—Dutch Leonard, 1940
Most hit batsmen
20—Walter Johnson, 1923
Most wild pitches
21—Walter Johnson, 1910
Most home runs
43—Pedro Ramos, 1957
Lowest ERA
1.14—Walter Johnson, 346 innings, 1913

CLUB RECORDS

Most players
44 in 1909
Fewest players
25 in 1908, 1917
Most games
159 in 1916
Most at-bats
5,592 in 1935
Most runs
892 in 1930
Fewest runs
380 in 1909
Most hits
1,620 in 1930
Fewest hits
1,112 in 1909
Most singles
1,209 in 1935
Most doubles
308 in 1931
Most triples
100 in 1932

Most homers
163 in 1959
Fewest homers (154 or 162-game schedule)
4 in 1917
Most homers at Griffith Stadium, home and opponents
158 in 1956
Most grand slams
8 in 1938
Most pinch home runs
4 in 1955, 1960
Most total bases
2,287 in 1930
Most long hits
464 in 1932
Most extra bases on long hits
732 in 1960
Most sacrifices (sacrifice hits and sacrifice flies)
232 in 1923, 1924
Most sacrifice hits
135 in 1906
Most sacrifice flies
42 in 1954
Most stolen bases
291 in 1913
Most bases on balls
690 in 1956
Most strikeouts
883 in 1960
Fewest strikeouts
359 in 1927
Most hit by pitch
80 in 1911
Fewest hit by pitch
8 in 1947
Most runs batted in
822 in 1936
Highest batting average
.303 in 1925
Lowest batting average
.223 in 1909
Highest slugging average
.426 in 1930
Lowest slugging average
.287 in 1910
Most grounded into double play
145 in 1951
Fewest grounded into double play
94 in 1943
Most left on bases
1,305 in 1935
Fewest left on bases
998 in 1959
Most .300 hitters
9 in 1925
Most putouts
4,291 in 1916
Fewest putouts
3,944 in 1906
Most assists
2,232 in 1911
Fewest assists
1,587 in 1951
Most chances accepted
6,363 in 1910
Fewest chances accepted
5,672 in 1953
Most errors
325 in 1901

Fewest errors
118 in 1958
Most consecutive errorless games
9 in 1952
Most double plays
186 in 1935
Fewest double plays
93 in 1912
Most passed balls
40 in 1945
Fewest passed balls
3 in 1927
Highest fielding average
.980 in 1958
Lowest fielding average
.936 in 1902
Highest home attendance
1,027,216 in 1946
Highest road attendance
1,055,171 in 1948
Most games won
99 in 1933
Most games lost
113 in 1904
Most games won, month
24—August 1945
Most games lost, month
29—July 1909
Highest percentage games won
.651 in 1933 (won 99, lost 53)
Lowest percentage games won
.252 in 1904 (won 38, lost 113)
Games won, league
4,223 in 60 years
Games lost, league
4,864 in 60 years
Most shutouts won
25 in 1914
Most shutouts lost
29 in 1909
Most 1-0 games won
11 in 1914
Most 1-0 games lost
7 in 1915
Most consecutive games won
17 in 1912
Most consecutive games lost
18 in 1948, 1959
Number of times league champions
3
Number of last-place finishes
10
Most runs, game
21 vs. Detroit, August 5, 1929
Most runs by opponent, game
24 by Boston, September 27, 1940
Most runs, shutout game
14 vs. Boston, September 11, 1905, second game, seven innings
vs. Chicago, September 3, 1942, second game
Most runs by opponent, shutout game
17 by New York, April 24, 1909
by New York, July 6, 1920
by Chicago, September 19, 1925, second game
Most runs, doubleheader shutout
13 vs. Cleveland, August 20, 1945
Most runs, inning
12 vs. St. Louis, July 10, 1926, eighth inning

Longest 1-0 game won
18 innings vs. Chicago, May 15, 1918
vs. Chicago, June 8, 1947,
first game

Longest 1-0 game lost
13 innings vs. Boston, August 15, 1916
vs. Chicago, July 29, 1918

Most hits, game
24 vs. Detroit, July 9, 1903
vs. Cleveland, July 18, 1925

Most home runs, nine-inning game
5 vs. Detroit, May 2, 1959

Most home runs, extra-inning game
7 vs. Chicago, May 3, 1949, 10 innings

Most consecutive games with one or more homers
8 (14 homers), 1959

Most total bases, game
41 vs. Detroit, July 9, 1904

Largest crowd, day game
31,728 vs. New York, April 19, 1948

Largest crowd, doubleheader
35,563 vs. New York, July 4, 1936

Largest crowd, night game
30,701 vs. Cleveland, June 17, 1947

Largest crowd, home opener
31,728 vs. New York, April 19, 1948

WASHINGTON SENATORS (SECOND CLUB)
YEARLY FINISHES

Year	Position	W	L	Pct.	*GB	Manager	Attendance
1961	9th (tied)	61	100	.379	47.5	Mickey Vernon	597,287
1962	10th	60	101	.373	35.5	Mickey Vernon	729,775
1963	10th	56	106	.346	48.5	Mickey Vernon, Gil Hodges	535,604
1964	9th	62	100	.383	37.0	Gil Hodges	600,106
1965	8th	70	92	.432	32.0	Gil Hodges	560,083
1966	8th	71	88	.447	25.5	Gil Hodges	576,260
1967	6th (tied)	76	85	.472	15.5	Gil Hodges	770,863
1968	10th	65	96	.404	37.5	Jim Lemon	546,661

EAST DIVISION

Year	Position	W	L	Pct.	*GB	Manager	Attendance
1969	4th	86	76	.531	23.0	Ted Williams	918,106
1970	6th	70	92	.432	38.0	Ted Williams	824,789
1971	5th	63	96	.396	38.5	Ted Williams	655,156

*Games behind winner.

INDIVIDUAL RECORDS (1961 TO 1971)

SERVICE

Most years played by non-pitcher
10—Eddie Brinkman

Most years played by pitcher
9—Jim Hannan

BATTING

Most games
161—Frank Howard, 1969, 1970

Most games, career
1,142—Eddie Brinkman

Most at-bats
635—Del Unser, 156 games, 1968

Most at-bats, career
3,845—Eddie Brinkman

Most runs
111—Frank Howard, 161 games, 1969

Most runs, career
516—Frank Howard

Most hits
175—Frank Howard, 161 games, 1969

Most hits, career
1,071—Frank Howard

Most singles
144—Eddie Brinkman, 158 games, 1970

Most singles, career
685—Eddie Brinkman

Most doubles
31—Aurelio Rodriguez, 142 games, 1970

Most triples
12—Chuck Hinton, 150 games, 1963

Most homers by righthander
48—Frank Howard, 161 games, 1969

Most homers by lefthander
30—Mike Epstein, 131 games, 1969

Most homers by switch-hitter
16—Fred Valentine, 146 games, 1966

Most homers by rookie
12—Don Lock, 71 games, 1962

Most homers at home
27—Frank Howard, 1969

Most homers on road
26—Frank Howard, 1968

Most homers, month
15—Frank Howard, May 1968

Most homers, righthander, career
237—Frank Howard

Most homers, lefthander, career
89—Jim King

Most homers, switch-hitter, career
34—Fred Valentine

Most grand slams
2—Don Zimmer, 121 games, 1964

Most grand slams, career
3—Mike Epstein

Most total bases
340—Frank Howard, 161 games, 1969

Most total bases, career
1,968—Frank Howard

Most long hits
75—Frank Howard, 158 games, 1968

Most long hits, career
403—Frank Howard

Most extra bases on long hits
166—Frank Howard, 158 games, 1968

Most extra bases on long hits, career
897—Frank Howard

Most sacrifice hits
15—Danny O'Connell, 138 games, 1961

Most sacrifice flies
8—Ken McMullen, 158 games, 1959

Most bases on balls
132—Frank Howard, 161 games, 1970

Most strikeouts
155—Frank Howard, 149 games, 1967

Fewest strikeouts
41—Eddie Brinkman, 158 games, 1970

Most hit by pitch
13—Mike Epstein, 123 games, 1968

Most runs batted in
126—Frank Howard, 161 games, 1970

Most runs batted in, career
670—Frank Howard

Highest batting average
.310—Chuck Hinton, 151 games, 1962

Highest batting average
.280—Chuck Hinton

Highest slugging average
.574—Frank Howard, 161 games, 1969

Highest slugging average, career
.513—Frank Howard

Longest batting streak
19 games—Ken McMullen, 1967

Most grounding into double play
29— Frank Howard, 161 games, 1969
Frank Howard, 153 games, 1971

Fewest grounding into double play
4—Del Unser, 153 games, 1971

BASERUNNING

Most stolen bases
29—Ed Stroud, 129 games, 1970

Most caught stealing
10— Willie Tasby, 141 games, 1961
Chuck Hinton, 150 games, 1962
Fred Valentine, 146 games, 1966
Del Unser, 153 games, 1969

PITCHING

Most games
74—Ron Kline, 1965

Most games started
36— Claude Osteen, 1964
Joe H. Coleman, 1969

Most complete games
13—Claude Osteen, 1964

Most games finished
58—Ron Kline, 1965

Most innings
257—Claude Osteen, 1964

Most games won
16—Dick Bosman, 1970

Most games won, career
49—Dick Bosman

Most games lost
22—Denny McLain, 1971

Most games lost, career
60—Bennie Daniels

Highest winning percentage
.737—Dick Bosman (14-5), 1969

Longest winning streak
8 games—Dick Bosman, 1969

Longest losing streak
10 games—Bennie Daniels, 1962

Most saves
27—Darold Knowles, 1970

Most bases on balls
100—Joe H. Coleman, 1969

Most strikeouts
195—Pete Richert, 1966

Most strikeouts, nine-inning game
13—Jim Duckworth, September 25, 1965, second game

Most strikeouts, extra-inning game
21—Tom Cheney, September 12, 1962, 16 innings

Most shutouts
4—Tom Cheney, 1963
Frank Bertaina, 1967
Camilo Pascual, 1968
Joe H. Coleman, 1969

Most shutouts, career
7—Tom Cheney

Most 1-0 games won
2—Dick Donovan, 1961
Dave Stenhouse, 1962

Most runs
115—Denny McLain, 1971

Most earned runs
103—Denny McLain, 1971

Most hits
256—Claude Osteen, 1964

Most hit batsmen
12—Joe H. Coleman, 1968

Most wild pitches
17—Frank Bertaina, 1968

Most home runs
36—Pete Richert, 1966

Most sacrifice hits
20—Buster Narum, 1965

Most sacrifice flies
12—Held by four pitchers

Lowest ERA
2.19—Dick Bosman, 193 innings, 1969

CLUB RECORDS

Most players
43 in 1963

Fewest players
36 in 1969

Most games
162 in 1962, 1963, 1964, 1966, 1969, 1970

Fewest games
159 in 1966, 1971

Most at-bats
5,484 in 1962

Most runs
694 in 1969

Fewest runs
524 in 1968

Most opponents' runs
812 in 1963

Most hits
1,370 in 1962

Most singles
1,006 in 1969

Most doubles
217 in 1961

Most triples
44 in 1961

Most homers
148 in 1969

Fewest homers
86 in 1971

Most homers at Griffith Stadium, home and opponents
87 in 1961

Most homers at Robert F. Kennedy Mem. Stadium, home and opponents
166 in 1964

Most grand slams
4 in 1961, 1963, 1967

Most pinch home runs
8 in 1965, 1966

Most total bases
2,060 in 1969

Most long hits
380 in 1961

Most extra bases on long hits
695 in 1969

Most sacrifice hits
84 in 1966

Most sacrifice flies
44 in 1961

Most stolen bases
99 in 1962

Most caught stealing
53 in 1962

Most bases on balls
635 in 1970

Most strikeouts
1,125 in 1965

Fewest strikeouts
789 in 1962

Most hit by pitch
46 in 1970

Fewest hit by pitch
15 in 1962

Most runs batted in
640 in 1969

Highest batting average
.251 in 1969

Lowest batting average
.223 in 1967

Highest slugging average
.378 in 1969

Lowest slugging average
.326 in 1967, 1971

Most grounding into double plays
158 in 1969

Fewest grounding into double plays
111 in 1963

Most left on bases
1,196 in 1970

Fewest left on bases
1,054 in 1966

Most .300 hitters
1 in 1961, 1962

Most putouts
4,420 in 1967

Fewest putouts
4,256 in 1971

Most assists
1,946 in 1970

Fewest assists
1,647 in 1965

Most chances accepted
6,319 in 1970

Fewest chances accepted
5,954 in 1965

Most errors
182 in 1963

Fewest errors
116 in 1970

Most errorless games
83 in 1964

Most consecutive errorless games
6 in 1970

Most double plays
173 in 1970

Fewest double plays
139 in 1966

Most passed balls
23 in 1961, 1971

Fewest passed balls
12 in 1970

Highest fielding average
.982 in 1970

Lowest fielding average
.971 in 1963

Highest home attendance
918,106 in 1969

Highest road attendance
1,042,638 in 1968

Most games won
86 in 1969

Most games lost
106 in 1963

Most games won, month
19—July 1967

Most games lost, month
24—August 1961

Games won in franchise history
740 in 11 years

Games lost in franchise history
1,032 in 11 years

Highest percentage games won
.531 in 1969 (won 86, lost 76)

Lowest percentage games won
.346 in 1963 (won 56, lost 106)

Most shutouts won
14 in 1967

Most shutouts lost
22 in 1964

Most 1-0 games won
4 in 1962, 1967, 1968

Most 1-0 games lost
5 in 1963, 1971

Most consecutive games won
8 in 1967

Most consecutive games lost
14 in 1961, 1970

Number of times league champions

Number of last-place finishes
(tied in 1961)

Most runs, game
15 vs. Detroit, May 18, 1965
    vs. Cleveland, July 5, 1971

Most runs by opponent, game
18 by Baltimore, April 22, 1965

Most runs, shutout game
13 vs. Los Angeles, June 2, first game,
    1965

Most runs by opponent, shutout game
17 by Los Angeles, August 23, 1963

Most runs, doubleheader shutout
No performance

Most runs, inning
11 vs. Baltimore, May 11, 1962, sixth
    inning

Longest 1-0 game won
10 innings vs. Chicago, June 9, first
        game, 1961
    vs. Chicago, September 19,
        1964

Longest 1-0 game lost
10 innings by Chicago, September 9,
    1966

Most hits, game
20 vs. Boston, July 27, 1962, second
    game

Most home runs, game
5 vs. Detroit, May 20, 1965
    vs. Chicago, May 16, 1969
    vs. Chicago, June 13, 1970

**Most consecutive games with one or
    more homers**
10 (16 homers), 1970

Most total bases, game
32 vs. Boston, July 27, 1962, second
        game
    vs. Chicago, June 13, 1970

Largest crowd, day game
45,125 vs. New York, April 7, 1969

Largest crowd, doubleheader
40,359 vs. Minnesota, June 14, 1964

Largest crowd, night game
30,421 vs. New York, July 31, 1962

Largest crowd, home opener
45,125 vs. New York, April 7, 1969

NATIONAL LEAGUE TEAM RECORDS

ARIZONA DIAMONDBACKS
YEARLY FINISHES
WEST DIVISION

Year	Position	W	L	Pct.	*GB	Manager	Attendance
1998	5th	65	97	.401	33.0	Buck Showalter	3,600,412
1999	1st†	100	62	.617	+14.0	Buck Showalter	3,019,654
2000	3rd	85	77	.525	12.0	Buck Showalter	2,942,516
2001	1st‡§	92	70	.556	2.0	Bob Brenly	2,740,554

*Games behind winner. †Lost division series. ‡Won division series. §Won championship series.

INDIVIDUAL RECORDS (1998 TO DATE)

SERVICE

Most years by non-pitcher
4—Held by many players

Most years by pitcher
4—Brian Anderson

BATTING

Most games
162—Luis Gonzalez, 2000, 2001

Most games, career
584—Jay Bell

Most at-bats
627—Matt Williams, 154 games, 1999

Most at-bats, career
2,131—Jay Bell

Most runs
132—Jay Bell, 151 games, 1999

Most runs, career
357—Jay Bell

Most hits
206—Luis Gonzalez, 153 games, 1999

Most hits, career
596—Luis Gonzalez

Most singles
131—Luis Gonzalez, 153 games, 1999
Tony Womack, 144 games, 1999

Most singles, career
343—Jay Bell

Most doubles
47—Luis Gonzalez, 162 games, 2000

Most doubles, career
128—Luis Gonzalez

Most triples
14—Tony Womack, 146 games, 2000

Most triples, career
29—Tony Womack

Most homers by lefthander
57—Luis Gonzalez, 162 games, 2001

Most homers by righthander
38—Jay Bell, 151 games, 1999

Most homers by switch-hitter
22—Devon White, 146 games, 1998

Most homers by rookie
22—Travis Lee, 146 games, 1998

Most homers at home
26—Luis Gonzalez, 2001

Most homers on road
31—Luis Gonzalez, 2001

Most homers, month
13—Luis Gonzalez, April 2001

Most homers by righthander, career
89—Jay Bell

Most homers by lefthander, career
114—Luis Gonzalez

Most homers by switch-hitter, career
22—Devon White

Most grand slams
2—Matt Williams, 135 games, 1998
Travis Lee, 120 games, 1999
Matt Williams, 154 games, 1999
Luis Gonzalez, 162 games, 2001

Most grand slams, career
6—Matt Williams

Most total bases
419—Luis Gonzalez, 162 games, 2001

Most total bases, career
1,092—Luis Gonzalez

Most long hits
100—Luis Gonzalez, 162 games, 2001

Most long hits, career
255—Luis Gonzalez

Most extra bases on long hits
221—Luis Gonzalez, 162 games, 2001

Most extra bases on long hits, career
496—Luis Gonzalez

Most sacrifice hits
14—Curt Schilling, 35 games, 2001

Most sacrifice flies
12—Luis Gonzalez, 162 games, 2000

Most bases on balls
100—Luis Gonzalez, 162 games, 2001

Most bases on balls, career
298—Jay Bell

Most strikeouts
132—Jay Bell, 151 games, 1999

Most strikeouts, career
428—Jay Bell

Fewest strikeouts
63—Luis Gonzalez, 153 games, 1999

Most hit by pitch
18—Andy Fox, 139 games, 1998

Most runs batted in
142—Matt Williams, 154 games, 1999
Luis Gonzalez, 162 games, 2001

Most runs batted in, career
367—Luis Gonzalez

Highest batting average
.336—Luis Gonzalez, 153 games, 1999

Highest batting average, career
.324—Luis Gonzalez

Highest slugging average
.688—Luis Gonzalez, 162 games, 2001

Highest slugging average, career
.593—Luis Gonzalez

Longest batting streak
30 games—Luis Gonzalez, 1999

Most grounded into double play
19—Matt Williams, 135 games, 1998

Fewest grounded into double play
4—Steve Finley, 156 games, 1999

BASERUNNING

Most stolen bases
72—Tony Womack, 144 games, 1999

Most stolen bases, career
145—Tony Womack

Most caught stealing
13—Tony Womack, 144 games, 1999

PITCHING

Most games
78—Byung-Hyun Kim, 2001

Most games, career
191—Greg Swindell

Most games started
35—Randy Johnson, 1999
Randy Johnson, 2000
Curt Schilling, 2001

Most games started, career
105—Brian Anderson

Most complete games
12—Randy Johnson, 1999

Most complete games, career
23—Randy Johnson

Most games finished
49—Gregg Olson, 1998

Most innings
271.2—Randy Johnson, 1999

Most innings, career
770.0—Randy Johnson

Most games won
22—Curt Schilling, 2001

Most games won, career
57—Randy Johnson

Most 20-victory seasons
1—Randy Johnson
Curt Schilling

Most games lost
15—Willie Blair, 1998

Most games lost, career
31—Omar Daal
Brian Anderson

Highest winning percentage
.786—Curt Schilling (22-6), 2001

Longest winning streak
8 games—Randy Johnson, 2001

Longest losing streak
7 games—Willie Blair, 1998

Most saves
30—Gregg Olson, 1998

Most bases on balls
82—Andy Benes, 1999

Most bases on balls, career
217—Randy Johnson

Most strikeouts
364—Randy Johnson, 1999

Most strikeouts, career
1,083—Randy Johnson

Most strikeouts, game
20—Randy Johnson, May 8, 2001
  (pitched first nine innings of 11-
  inning game)
17—Randy Johnson, June 30, 1999

Most shutouts
3—Randy Johnson, 2000

Most shutouts, career
7—Randy Johnson

Most 1-0 shutouts won
1—Brian Anderson, 1998
  Randy Johnson, 2000

Most runs
117—Andy Benes, 1999

Most earned runs
106—Andy Benes, 1999

Most hits
237—Curt Schilling, 2001

Most wild pitches
10—Andy Benes, 1999

Most hit batsmen
18—Randy Johnson, 2001

Most home runs
39—Brian Anderson, 1998

Most sacrifice hits
14—Randy Johnson, 2000

Most sacrifice flies
8—Andy Benes, 1998

Lowest ERA
2.48—Randy Johnson, 271.2 innings,
  1999

CLUB RECORDS

Most players
47 in 2001

Fewest players
41 in 2000

Most games
162 in 1998, 1999, 2000, 2001

Most at-bats
5,658 in 1999

Most runs
908 in 1999

Fewest runs
665 in 1998

Most opponents' runs
812 in 1998

Most hits
1,566 in 1999

Fewest hits
1,353 in 1998

Most singles
1,015 in 1999

Most doubles
289 in 1999

Most triples
46 in 1998, 1999

Most homers
216 in 1999

**Most homers at Bank One Ballpark,
  home and opponents**
228 in 2001

Fewest homers
159 in 1998

Most grand slams
9 in 2001

Most pinch home runs
14 in 2001

Most total bases
2,595 in 1999

Most long hits
551 in 1999

Most extra bases on long hits
1,029 in 1999

Most sacrifice hits
71 in 2001

Most sacrifice flies
60 in 1999

Most stolen bases
137 in 1999

Most caught stealing
44 in 2000

Most bases on balls
588 in 1999

Most strikeouts
1,239 in 1998

Fewest strikeouts
975 in 2000

Most hit by pitch
64 in 1998

Fewest hit by pitch
48 in 1999

Most runs batted in
865 in 1999

Highest batting average
.277 in 1999

Lowest batting average
.246 in 1998

Highest slugging average
.459 in 1999

Lowest slugging average
.393 in 1998

Most grounded into double play
125 in 1998

Fewest grounded into double play
94 in 1999

Most left on bases
1,183 in 2001

Fewest left on bases
1,104 in 1998

Most .300 hitters
2 in 1999

Most putouts
4,402 in 1999

Fewest putouts
4,297 in 1998

Most assists
1,721 in 1998

Fewest assists
1,541 in 2000

Most chances accepted
6,018 in 1998

Fewest chances accepted
5,872 in 2000

Most errors
107 in 2000

Fewest errors
84 in 2001

Most errorless games
94 in 2001

Most consecutive errorless games
9 in 1999

Most double plays
148 in 2001

Fewest double plays
125 in 1998

Most passed balls
17 in 1999

Fewest passed balls
4 in 2000

Highest fielding average
.986 in 2001

Lowest fielding average
.982 in 2000

Highest home attendance
3,600,412 in 1998

Highest road attendance
2,566,082 in 2001

Most games won
100 in 1999

Most games lost
97 in 1998

Most games won, month
20—August 1999

Most games lost, month
19—April 1998, May 1998

Games won, league
342 in 4 years

Games lost, league
306 in 4 years

Highest percentage games won
.617 in 1999 (won 100, lost 62)

Lowest percentage games won
.401 in 1998 (won 65, lost 97)

Most consecutive games won
9 in 2000, 2001 (twice)

Most consecutive games lost
8 in 1998

Most shutouts won
13 in 2001

Most shutouts lost
16 in 1998

Most 1-0 games won
1 in 1998, 2000, 2001

Most 1-0 games lost
3 in 1998, 2001

Number of times league champions
1

Number of last-place finishes
0

Most runs, game
17 vs. St. Louis, July 4, 1999
  vs. St. Louis, July 27, 2000
  vs. St. Louis, April 17, 2001

Most runs by opponent, game
19 by Colorado, June 18, 2000

Most runs, shutout game
11 vs. San Diego, July 24, 2001

Most runs by opponent, shutout game
11 by Houston, April 27, 1999

Most runs, doubleheader shutout
Never accomplished

Most runs, inning
8 vs. Florida, August 26, 1999, ninth
  inning
  vs. Chicago, August 19, 2000, third
  inning
  vs. Kansas City A.L., June 10, 2001,
  fourth inning

Longest 1-0 game won
18 innings vs. San Francisco, May 29,
  2001

Longest 1-0 game lost
13 innings by San Diego, September 2, 2001

Most hits, game
21 vs. Los Angeles, April 13, 1999, 16 innings
20 vs. Montreal, June 2, 1999
vs. Los Angeles, May 8, 2000

Most home runs, game
5 vs. Seattle A.L., June 26, 1998
vs. Colorado, September 22, 1998

vs. Houston, July 7, 1999
vs. San Francisco, August 4, 1999
vs. San Diego, April 10, 2000
vs. St. Louis, April 17, 2001
vs. Atlanta, April 26, 2001

Most consecutive games with one or more homers
13 (21 homers), 1999

Most total bases, game
40 vs. St. Louis, April 17, 2001

Largest crowd, day game
48,682 vs. Los Angeles, May 24, 1998

Largest crowd, night game
49,645 vs. Los Angeles, May 22, 1998

Largest crowd, doubleheader
No occurrence

Largest crowd, home opener
47,484 vs. Colorado, March 31, 1998

ATLANTA BRAVES
YEARLY FINISHES

Year	Position	W	L	Pct.	*GB	Manager	Attendance
1966	5th	85	77	.525	10.0	Bobby Bragan, Billy Hitchcock	1,539,801
1967	7th	77	85	.475	24.5	Billy Hitchcock, Ken Silvestri	1,389,222
1968	5th	81	81	.500	16.0	Lum Harris	1,126,540

WEST DIVISION

Year	Position	W	L	Pct.	*GB	Manager	Attendance
1969	1st†	93	69	.574	+3.0	Lum Harris	1,458,320
1970	5th	76	86	.469	26.0	Lum Harris	1,078,848
1971	3rd	82	80	.506	8.0	Lum Harris	1,006,320
1972	4th	70	84	.455	25.0	Lum Harris, Eddie Mathews	752,973
1973	5th	76	85	.472	22.5	Eddie Mathews	800,655
1974	3rd	88	74	.543	14.0	Eddie Mathews, Clyde King	981,085
1975	5th	67	94	.416	40.5	Clyde King, Connie Ryan	534,672
1976	6th	70	92	.432	32.0	Dave Bristol	818,179
1977	6th	61	101	.377	37.0	Dave Bristol, Ted Turner	872,464
1978	6th	69	93	.426	26.0	Bobby Cox	904,494
1979	6th	66	94	.413	23.5	Bobby Cox	769,465
1980	4th	81	80	.503	11.0	Bobby Cox	1,048,411
1981	4th/5th	50	56	.472	‡	Bobby Cox	535,418
1982	1st†	89	73	.549	+1.0	Joe Torre	1,801,985
1983	2nd	88	74	.543	3.0	Joe Torre	2,119,935
1984	2nd (tied)	80	82	.494	12.0	Joe Torre	1,724,892
1985	5th	66	96	.407	29.0	Eddie Haas, Bobby Wine	1,350,137
1986	6th	72	89	.447	23.5	Chuck Tanner	1,387,181
1987	5th	69	92	.429	20.5	Chuck Tanner	1,217,402
1988	6th	54	106	.338	39.5	Chuck Tanner, Russ Nixon	848,089
1989	6th	63	97	.394	28.0	Russ Nixon	984,930
1990	6th	65	97	.401	26.0	Russ Nixon, Bobby Cox	980,129
1991	1st§	94	68	.580	+1.0	Bobby Cox	2,140,217
1992	1st§	98	64	.605	+8.0	Bobby Cox	3,077,400
1993	1st†	104	58	.642	+1.0	Bobby Cox	3,884,725

EAST DIVISION

Year	Position	W	L	Pct.	*GB	Manager	Attendance
1994	2nd	68	46	.596	6.0	Bobby Cox	2,539,240
1995	1st∞§	90	54	.625	+21.0	Bobby Cox	2,561,831
1996	1st∞§	96	66	.593	+8.0	Bobby Cox	2,901,242
1997	1st∞†	101	61	.623	+9.0	Bobby Cox	3,464,488
1998	1st∞†	106	56	.654	+18.0	Bobby Cox	3,361,350
1999	1st∞§	103	59	.636	+6.5	Bobby Cox	3,284,897
2000	1st◆	95	67	.586	+1.0	Bobby Cox	3,234,301
2001	1st◆	88	74	.543	+2.0	Bobby Cox	2,823,494

*Games behind winner. †Lost championship series. ‡First half 25-29; second 25-27. §Won championship series. ∞Won division series. ◆Lost division series.

INDIVIDUAL RECORDS (1966 TO DATE)

SERVICE

Most years by non-pitcher
15—Dale Murphy

Most years by pitcher
19—Phil Niekro

BATTING

Most games
162— Felix Millan, 1969
Dale Murphy, 1982, 1983, 1984, 1985
Andruw Jones, 1999

Most games, career
1,926—Dale Murphy

Most at-bats
671—Marquis Grissom, 158 games, 1996

Most at-bats, career
7,098—Dale Murphy

Most runs
131—Dale Murphy, 162 games, 1983

Most runs, career
1,103—Dale Murphy

Most hits
219—Ralph Garr, 154 games, 1971

Most hits, career
1,901—Dale Murphy

Most singles
180—Ralph Garr, 154 games, 1971

Most singles, career
1,187—Dale Murphy

Most doubles
41—Chipper Jones, 157 games, 1997
Chipper Jones, 157 games, 1999

Most doubles, career
306—Dale Murphy

Most triples
17—Ralph Garr, 143 games, 1974

Most triples, career
40—Ralph Garr

Most homers by righthander
47—Hank Aaron, 139 games, 1971

Most homers by lefthander
41—Darrell Evans, 161 games, 1973

Most homers by switch-hitter
45—Chipper Jones, 157 games, 1999

Most homers by rookie
33—Earl Williams, 145 games, 1971

Most homers at home
31—Hank Aaron, 1971

Most homers on road
28—Andres Galarraga, 1998

Most homers, month
14—Bob Horner, July 1980

Most homers by righthander, career
371—Dale Murphy

Most homers by lefthander, career
160—David Justice

Most homers by switch-hitter, career
227—Chipper Jones

Most grand slams
3—Chipper Jones, 157 games, 1997

Most grand slams, career
7—Hank Aaron

Most total bases
359—Chipper Jones, 157 games, 1999

Most total bases, career
3,394—Dale Murphy

Most long hits
87—Chipper Jones, 157 games, 1999

Most long hits, career
714—Dale Murphy

Most extra bases on long hits
178—Chipper Jones, 157 games, 1999

Most extra bases on long hits, career
1,493—Dale Murphy

Most sacrifice hits
20— Rod Gilbreath, 116 games, 1976
    Glenn Hubbard, 145 games, 1982

Most sacrifice flies
10— Bob Horner, 141 games, 1986
    Gerald Perry, 141 games, 1988
    Chipper Jones, 156 games, 2000

Most bases on balls
127—Jimmy Wynn, 148 games, 1976

Most bases on balls, career
912—Dale Murphy

Most strikeouts
146—Andres Galarraga, 153 games, 1998

Most strikeouts, career
1,581—Dale Murphy

Fewest strikeouts
35—Felix Millan, 162 games, 1969

Most hit by pitch
25—Andres Galarraga, 153 games, 1998

Most runs batted in
122—Hank Aaron, 158 games, 1966

Most runs batted in, career
1,143—Dale Murphy

Most game-winning RBIs
14—Dale Murphy, 162 games, 1982, 1983, 1985
    Claudell Washington, 150 games, 1982

Highest batting average
.366—Rico Carty, 136 games, 1970

Highest batting average, career
.317—Ralph Garr

Highest slugging average
.669—Hank Aaron, 139 games, 1971

Highest slugging average, career
.567—Hank Aaron

Longest batting streak
31 games—Rico Carty, 1970

Most grounded into double play
24—Dale Murphy, 156 games, 1988

Fewest grounded into double play
5—Brett Butler, 151 games, 1983

BASERUNNING

Most stolen bases
72—Otis Nixon, 124 games, 1991

Most stolen bases, career
174—Jerry Royster

Most caught stealing
23—Brett Butler, 151 games, 1983

PITCHING

Most games
81—Brad Clontz, 1996

Most games, career
689—Phil Niekro

Most games started
44—Phil Niekro, 1979

Most games started, career
594—Phil Niekro

Most complete games
23—Phil Niekro, 1979

Most complete games, career
226—Phil Niekro

Most games finished
64—Mark Wohlers, 1996

Most innings
342—Phil Niekro, 1979

Most innings, career
4,532—Phil Niekro

Most games won
24—John Smoltz, 1996

Most games won, career
266—Phil Niekro

Most 20-victory seasons
5—Tom Glavine

Most games lost
20—Phil Niekro, 1977, 1979

Most games lost, career
227—Phil Niekro

Highest winning percentage
.905—Greg Maddux (19-2), 1995

Longest winning streak
14 games—John Smoltz, 1996

Longest losing streak
9 games—Tommy Boggs, 1981
    Marty Clary, 1990

Longest losing streak over two seasons
11 games—Jim Acker, 1986 (6), 1987 (5)

Most saves
39—Mark Wohlers, 1996

Most bases on balls
164—Phil Niekro, 1977

Most bases on balls, career
1,425—Phil Niekro

Most strikeouts
276—John Smoltz, 1996

Most strikeouts, career
2,855—Phil Niekro

Most strikeouts, game
15—John Smoltz, May 24, 1992

Most shutouts won
6—Phil Niekro, 1974

Most shutouts, career
43—Phil Niekro

Most 1-0 shutouts won
2—Phil Niekro, 1969
    Greg Maddux, 1995

Most runs
166—Phil Niekro, 1977

Most earned runs
148—Phil Niekro, 1977

Most hits
315—Phil Niekro, 1977

Most hit batsmen
13—Phil Niekro, 1978

Most wild pitches
27—Tony Cloninger, 1966

Most home runs
41—Phil Niekro, 1979

Most sacrifice hits
22—Tom Glavine, 1999

Most sacrifice flies
12— Tony Cloninger, 1966
    Carl Morton, 1974

Lowest ERA
1.56—Greg Maddux, 202 innings, 1994

CLUB RECORDS

Most players
47 in 2000, 2001

Fewest players
32 in 1980

Most games
163 in 1966, 1968, 1974

Most at-bats
5,631 in 1973

Most runs
840 in 1999

Fewest runs
514 in 1968

Most opponents' runs
895 in 1977

Most hits
1,514 in 1996

Fewest hits
1,281 in 1989

Most singles
1,109 in 1968

Most doubles
309 in 1999

Most triples
48 in 1992

Most homers
215 in 1998

Fewest homers
80 in 1968

Most homers at Atlanta Stadium, home and opponents
211 in 1970

Most homers at Turner Field, home and opponents
166 in 2000

Most grand slams
12 in 1997

Most pinch home runs
9 in 1992

Most total bases
2,483 in 1998

Most long hits
538 in 1998

Most extra bases on long hits
994 in 1998

Most sacrifice hits
109 in 1974

Most sacrifice flies
52 in 1997, 2001

Most stolen bases
165 in 1991

Most caught stealing
88 in 1983

Most bases on balls
641 in 1987

Most strikeouts
1,160 in 1997

Fewest strikeouts
665 in 1969

Most hit by pitch
61 in 1998

Fewest hit by pitch
17 in 1977, 1983

Most runs batted in
794 in 1998

Most game-winning RBIs
82 in 1982, 1983

Highest batting average
.272 in 1983, 1998

Lowest batting average
.234 in 1989

Highest slugging average
.453 in 1998

Lowest slugging average
.334 in 1976

Most grounded into double play
154 in 1985

Fewest grounded into double play
82 in 1992

Most left on bases
1,213 in 1974

Fewest left on bases
1,038 in 1988

Most .300 hitters
3 in 1966, 1970, 2000

Most putouts
4,424 in 1971

Fewest putouts
4,223 in 1979

Most assists
2,028 in 1985

Fewest assists
1,635 in 1969

Most chances accepted
6,400 in 1985

Fewest chances accepted
5,970 in 1969

Most errors
183 in 1979

Fewest errors
91 in 1998

Most errorless games
97 in 1998

Most consecutive errorless games
10 in 2001

Most double plays
197 in 1985

Fewest double plays
114 in 1969

Most passed balls
42 in 1967

Fewest passed balls
6 in 1983

Highest fielding average
.985 in 1998

Lowest fielding average
.970 in 1979

Highest home attendance
3,884,725 in 1993

Highest road attendance
2,944,157 in 1993

Most games won
106 in 1998

Most games lost
106 in 1988

Most games won, month
21 in May 1998
21 in August 1999

Most games lost, month
21 in May 1976

Games won, league
2,881 in 36 years

Games lost, league
2,810 in 36 years

Highest percentage games won
.654 in 1998 (won 106, lost 56)

Lowest percentage games won
.338 in 1988 (won 54, lost 106)

Most shutouts won
24 in 1992

Most shutouts lost
24 in 1978

Most 1-0 shutouts won
7 in 1974

Most 1-0 shutouts lost
4 in 1988, 1989

Most consecutive games won
15 in 2000

Most consecutive games lost
17 in 1977

Number of times league champions
5

Number of last-place finishes
5

Most runs, game
20 vs. Colorado, April 18, 1999
  vs. Florida, October 5, 2001

Most runs by opponent, game
23 by Cincinnati, April 25, 1977
  by San Francisco, June 8, 1990

Most runs, shutout game
18 vs. Florida, October 3, 1999

Most runs by opponent, shutout game
19 by Montreal, July 30, 1978

Most runs, doubleheader shutout
No performance

Most runs, inning
13 vs. Houston, September 20, 1972,
second inning

Longest 1-0 game won
13 innings vs. St. Louis, May 16, 1997

Longest 1-0 game lost
13 innings vs. Los Angeles, May 18,
1974
13 innings vs. St. Louis, May 20, 1989

Most hits, game
25 vs. Cincinnati, May 1, 1985

Most home runs, game
7 vs. Chicago, August 3, 1967

**Most consecutive games with one or
more homers**
25 (45 homers), 1998

Most total bases, game
46 vs. Chicago, April 15, 1994

Largest crowd, day game
51,275 vs. Los Angeles, June 26, 1966

Largest crowd, doubleheader
50,597 vs. Chicago, July 4, 1972

Largest crowd, night game
53,775 vs. Los Angeles, April 8, 1974

Largest crowd, home opener
53,775 vs. Los Angeles, April 8, 1974

BOSTON BRAVES
YEARLY FINISHES

Year	Position	W	L	Pct.	*GB	Manager	Attendance
1901	5th	69	69	.500	20.5	Frank Selee	146,502
1902	3rd	73	64	.533	29.0	Al Buckenberger	116,960
1903	6th	58	80	.420	32.0	Al Buckenberger	143,155
1904	7th	55	98	.359	51.0	Al Buckenberger	140,694
1905	7th	51	103	.331	54.5	Fred Tenney	150,003
1906	8th	49	102	.325	66.5	Fred Tenney	143,280
1907	7th	58	90	.392	47.0	Fred Tenney	203,221
1908	6th	63	91	.409	36.0	Joe Kelley	253,750
1909	8th	45	108	.294	65.5	Frank Bowerman, Harry Smith	195,188
1910	8th	53	100	.346	50.5	Fred Lake	149,027
1911	8th	44	107	.291	54.0	Fred Tenney	116,000
1912	8th	52	101	.340	52.0	Johnny Kling	121,000
1913	5th	69	82	.457	31.5	George Stallings	208,000
1914	1st	94	59	.614	+10.5	George Stallings	382,913

Year	Position	W	L	Pct.	*GB	Manager	Attendance
1915	2nd	83	69	.546	7.0	George Stallings	376,283
1916	3rd	89	63	.586	4.0	George Stallings	313,495
1917	6th	72	81	.471	25.5	George Stallings	174,253
1918	7th	53	71	.427	28.5	George Stallings	84,938
1919	6th	57	82	.410	38.5	George Stallings	167,401
1920	7th	62	90	.408	30.0	George Stallings	162,483
1921	4th	79	74	.516	15.0	Fred Mitchell	318,627
1922	8th	53	100	.346	39.5	Fred Mitchell	167,965
1923	7th	54	100	.351	41.5	Fred Mitchell	227,802
1924	8th	53	100	.346	40.0	Dave Bancroft	117,478
1925	5th	70	83	.458	25.0	Dave Bancroft	313,528
1926	7th	66	86	.434	22.0	Dave Bancroft	303,598
1927	7th	60	94	.390	34.0	Dave Bancroft	288,685
1928	7th	50	103	.327	44.5	Jack Slattery, Rogers Hornsby	227,001
1929	8th	56	98	.364	43.0	Emil Fuchs	372,351
1930	6th	70	84	.455	22.0	Bill McKechnie	464,835
1931	7th	64	90	.416	37.0	Bill McKechnie	515,005
1932	5th	77	77	.500	13.0	Bill McKechnie	507,606
1933	4th	83	71	.539	9.0	Bill McKechnie	517,803
1934	4th	78	73	.517	16.0	Bill McKechnie	303,205
1935	8th	38	115	.248	61.5	Bill McKechnie	232,754
1936	6th	71	83	.461	21.0	Bill McKechnie	340,585
1937	5th	79	73	.520	16.0	Bill McKechnie	385,339
1938	5th	77	75	.507	12.0	Casey Stengel	341,149
1939	7th	63	88	.417	32.5	Casey Stengel	285,994
1940	7th	65	87	.428	34.5	Casey Stengel	241,616
1941	7th	62	92	.403	38.0	Casey Stengel	263,680
1942	7th	59	89	.399	44.0	Casey Stengel	285,332
1943	6th	68	85	.444	36.5	Casey Stengel	271,289
1944	6th	65	89	.422	40.0	Bob Coleman	208,691
1945	6th	67	85	.441	30.0	Bob Coleman, Del Bissonette	374,178
1946	4th	81	72	.529	15.5	Billy Southworth	969,673
1947	3rd	86	68	.558	8.0	Billy Southworth	1,277,361
1948	1st	91	62	.595	+6.5	Billy Southworth	1,455,439
1949	4th	75	79	.487	22.0	Billy Southworth	1,081,795
1950	4th	83	71	.539	8.0	Billy Southworth	944,391
1951	4th	76	78	.494	20.5	Billy Southworth, Tommy Holmes	487,475
1952	7th	64	89	.418	32.0	Tommy Holmes, Charlie Grimm	281,278

INDIVIDUAL RECORDS (1876 TO 1952)

SERVICE

Most years, non-pitcher
15—Fred Tenney
    Rabbit Maranville
    Johnny Cooney

Most years played by pitcher
12—Kid Nichols

Most years played by pitcher (since 1900)
11—Dick Rudolph

BATTING

Most games
158—Ed Konetchy, 1916

Most games, career
1,795—Rabbit Maranville

Most at-bats
647—Herman Long, 151 games, 1892

Most at-bats, career
6,764—Herman Long

Most at-bats (since 1900)
637—Gene Moore, 151 games, 1936

Most at-bats, career (since 1900)
6,724—Rabbit Maranville

Most runs
160—Hugh Duffy, 124 games, 1894

Most runs (since 1900)
125—Tommy Holmes, 154 games, 1945

Most runs, career
1,294—Herman Long

Most hits
236—Hugh Duffy, 124 games, 1894

Most hits, career
2,002—Fred Tenney

Most hits (since 1900)
224—Tommy Holmes, 154 games, 1945

Most singles
166—Lance Richbourg, 148 games, 1928

Most doubles
50—Hugh Duffy, 124 games, 1894

Most doubles (since 1900)
47—Tommy Holmes, 154 games, 1945

Most doubles, career
291—Tommy Holmes

Most triples
20—Dick Johnston, 124 games, 1887

Most triples (since 1900)
18—Ray Powell, 149 games, 1921

Most triples, career
103—Rabbit Maranville

Most homers by righthander
38—Wally Berger, 151 games, 1930

Most homers by lefthander
28—Tommy Holmes, 154 games, 1945

Most homers by switch-hitter
18—Sam Jethroe, 141 games, 1950
    Sam Jethroe, 148 games, 1951

Most homers, rookie
38—Wally Berger, 151 games, 1930

Most homers at home
19—Chuck Workman, 1945

Most homers on road
22—Sid Gordon, 1950

Most home runs, month
11—Wally Berger, May, 1930

Most homers, righthander, career
199—Wally Berger

Most homers, lefthander, career
88—Tommy Holmes

Most homers, switch-hitter, career
49—Sam Jethroe

Most grand slams
4—Sid Gordon, 134 games, 1950

Most grand slams, career
6—Wally Berger

Most total bases
372—Hugh Duffy, 124 games, 1894

Most total bases (since 1900)
367—Tommy Holmes, 154 games, 1945

Most total bases, career
2,629—Herman Long

Most long hits
81— Hugh Duffy, 124 games, 1894
    Tommy Holmes, 154 games, 1945

Most extra bases on long hits
169—Wally Berger, 151 games, 1930

Most sacrifices (sacrifice hits and sacrifice flies)
37—Stuffy McInnis, 154 games, 1923

Most sacrifice hits
31—Freddie Maguire, 148 games, 1931

Most bases on balls
131—Bob Elliott, 151 games, 1948

Most strikeouts
134—Vince DiMaggio, 150 games, 1938

Fewest strikeouts
9—Tommy Holmes, 154 games, 1945

Most hit by pitch
11—Sam Jethroe, 148 games, 1951

Most runs batted in
130—Wally Berger, 150 games, 1935

Most runs batted in, career
746—Wally Berger

Highest batting average
.438—Hugh Duffy, 124 games, 1894

Highest batting average (since 1900)
.387—Rogers Hornsby, 140 games, 1928

Highest batting average, career
.338—Billy Hamilton

Highest batting average, career (since 1900)
.304—Wally Berger

Highest slugging average
.694—Hugh Duffy, 125 games, 1894

Highest slugging average (since 1900)
.632—Rogers Hornsby, 140 games, 1928

Highest slugging average, career
.533—Wally Berger

Longest batting streak
37 games—Tommy Holmes, 1945

Most grounded into double play
28—Sid Gordon, 150 games, 1951

Fewest grounded into double play
4—Vince DiMaggio, 150 games, 1938

BASERUNNING

Most stolen bases
93—Billy Hamilton, 131 games, 1896

Most stolen bases (since 1900)
57—Hap Myers, 140 games, 1913

Most stolen bases, career
446—Herman Long

Most caught stealing
20—Billy Southworth, 141 games, 1921

PITCHING

Most games
57—Johnny Hutchings, 1945

Most games, career
556—Kid Nichols

Most games started
46—Vic Willis, 1902

Most complete games
45—Vic Willis, 1902

Most games finished
29—Nels Potter, 1949

Most innings
411—Vic Willis, 1902

Most games won
27— Togie Pittinger, 1902
Vic Willis, 1902

Most games won, career
329—Kid Nichols

Most games won, career (since 1900)
122—Warren Spahn

Most 20-victory seasons
4—Johnny Sain, Warren Spahn

Most games lost
29—Vic Willis, 1905

Highest winning percentage
.842—Tom Hughes (16-3), 1916

Longest winning streak
13 games—Charlie Buffinton, 1884
Fred Klobedanz, 1897
Ted Lewis, 1898

Longest winning streak, since 1900
11 games—Dick Rudolph, 1914

Longest winning streak, two seasons
13 games—Charlie Buffinton, 1883 (5), 1884 (8)
Harry Staley, 1891 (5), 1892 (8)
Bill James, 1914 (10), 1915 (3)

Longest losing streak
18 games—Cliff Curtis, 1910

Most bases on balls
149—Chick Fraser, 1905

Most bases on balls, career
1,118—Kid Nichols

Most bases on balls, career
678—Lefty Tyler

Most strikeouts
226—Vic Willis, 1902

Most strikeouts, career
1,649—Kid Nichols

Most strikeouts, career (since 1900)
1,000—Warren Spahn

Most strikeouts, game
18—Warren Spahn, June 14, 1952, 15 innings
13—Vic Willis, May 28, 1902
Warren Spahn, September 13, 1952

Most shutouts
7—Togie Pittinger, 1902
Irv Young, 1905
Warren Spahn, 1947, 1951

Most shutouts league
29—Dick Rudolph

Most 1-0 shutouts won
4—Dick Rudolph, 1916
Joe Oeschger, 1920

Most runs
196—Togie Pittinger, 1903

Most earned runs
130—Johnny Sain, 1949

Most hits
394—Togie Pittinger, 1903

Most hit batsmen
16—Jeff Pfeffer, 1906

Most wild pitches
14—Togie Pittinger, 1903

Most home runs
34—Johnny Sain, 1950

Lowest ERA
1.90—Bill James, 332 innings, 1914

CLUB RECORDS

Most players
48 in 1946

Fewest players
23 in 1905

Most games
158 in 1914, 1916

Most at-bats
5,506 in 1932

Most runs
1,220 in 1894

Most runs (since 1900)
785 in 1950

Fewest runs
408 in 1906

Most hits
1,567 in 1925

Fewest hits
1,115 in 1906

Most singles
1196 in 1925

Most doubles
272 in 1948

Most triples
100 in 1921

Most home runs
148 in 1950

Fewest homers (154 or 162-game schedule)
15 in 1909

Most homers at Braves Field, home and opponents
131 in 1945

Most grand slams
7 in 1950

Most total bases
2,173 in 1950

Most long hits
430 in 1950

Most extra bases on long hits
762 in 1950

Most sacrifices (sacrifice hits and sacrifice flies)
221 in 1914

Most sacrifice hits
140 in 1948

Most stolen bases
189 in 1902

Most bases on balls
684 in 1949

Most strikeouts
711 in 1952

Fewest strikeouts
348 in 1926

Most hit by pitch
45 in 1917

Fewest hit by pitch
13 in 1941

Most runs batted in
726 in 1950

Highest batting average
.292 in 1925

Lowest batting average
.223 in 1909

Highest slugging average
.405 in 1950

Lowest slugging average
.274 in 1909

Most grounded into double play
146 in 1936

Fewest grounded into double play
93 in 1944

Most left on bases
1,255 in 1948

Fewest left on bases
1,003 in 1933

Most .300 hitters
8 in 1931

Most putouts
4,262 in 1914

Fewest putouts
3,975 in 1906

Most assists
2,225 in 1908

Fewest assists
1,665 in 1946

Most chances accepted
6,424 in 1914

Fewest chances accepted
5,750 in 1935

Most errors
353 in 1904

Fewest errors
138 in 1933

Most consecutive errorless games
5 in 1933 (twice)

Most double plays
178 in 1939

Fewest double plays
101 in 1935

Most passed balls
167 in 1883

Most passed balls (since 1900)
42 in 1905

Fewest passed balls
2 in 1943

Highest fielding average
.978 in 1933

Lowest fielding average
.945 in 1904

Highest home attendance
1,455,439 in 1948

Highest road attendance
1,308,175 in 1947

Most games won
102 in 1892, 1898

Most games won (since 1900)
94 in 1914

Most games lost
115 in 1935

Most games won, month
26—September 1914

Most games lost, month
25— September 1928
        September 1935

Highest percentage games won
.705 in 1897 (won 93, lost 39)

Highest percentage games won (since 1900)
.614 in 1914 (won 94, lost 59)

Lowest percentage games won
.248 in 1935 (won 38, lost 115)

Games won, league
5,118 in 77 years

Games lost, league
5,598 in 77 years

Most shutouts won
21 in 1916

Most shutouts lost
28 in 1906

Most 1-0 games won
9 in 1916

Most 1-0 games lost
6 in 1906, 1933

Most consecutive games won
18 in 1891

Most consecutive games won (since 1900)
9 in 1902, 1914 (twice), 1945

Most consecutive games lost
19 in 1906

Number of times league champions
10

Number of last-place finishes
9

Most runs, game
30 vs. Detroit, June 9, 1883

Most runs, game (since 1900)
20 vs. Philadelphia, June 25, 1900
     vs. Philadelphia, October 6, 1910
     vs. St. Louis, September 18, 1915,
        first game
     vs. St. Louis, August 25, 1936, first
        game

Most runs by opponent, game
27 by Pittsburgh, June 6, 1894

Most runs by opponent, game (since 1900)
26 by Cincinnati, June 4, 1911

Most runs, shutout game
18 vs. Buffalo, October 3, 1885

Most runs, shutout game (since 1900)
16 vs. Brooklyn, May 7, 1918
     vs. Pittsburgh, September 12, 1952,
        second game

Most runs by opponent, shutout game
17 by Chicago, September 16, 1884

Most runs by opponent, shutout game (since 1900)
15 by New York, April 15, 1905
     by Cincinnati, May 19, 1906

     by Philadelphia, July 3, 1928
     by New York, May 29, 1936
     by New York, July 4, 1934, second
        game
     by St. Louis, August 18, 1934
     by St. Louis, May 7, 1950

Most runs, doubleheader shutout
8 vs. Cincinnati, August 7, 1916
     vs. Brooklyn, June 30, 1937
     vs. Cincinnati, August 3, 1941

Most runs, inning
16 vs. Baltimore, June 18, 1894, a.m.
     game, first inning

Most runs, inning (since 1900)
13 vs. St. Louis, July 25, 1900, first
     inning

Longest 1-0 game won
13 innings, six times; last time vs.
     Brooklyn, May 4, 1923

Longest 1-0 game lost
17 innings vs. Chicago, September 21,
     1901

Most hits, game
32 vs. St. Louis, September 3, 1896, first
     game

Most hits, game (since 1900)
25 vs. St. Louis, August 25, 1936, first
     game

Most home runs, game
5 vs. Cincinnati, May 30, 1894, p.m.
     game
     vs. Chicago, May 13, 1942
     vs. Cincinnati, May 6, 1950

Most total bases, game
46 vs. Detroit, June 9, 1883
     vs. Cleveland, July 5, 1894

Most total bases, game (since 1900)
37 vs. Philadelphia, July 6, 1934
     vs. Cincinnati, May 6, 1950

Largest crowd, day game
41,527 vs. Chicago, August 8, 1948

Largest crowd, doubleheader
47,123 vs. Philadelphia, May 22, 1932

Largest crowd, night game
39,549 vs. Brooklyn, August 5, 1946

Largest crowd, home opener
25,000 vs. New York, April 16, 1935

BROOKLYN DODGERS
YEARLY FINISHES

Year	Position	W	L	Pct.	*GB	Manager	Attendance
1901	3rd	79	57	.581	9.5	Ned Hanlon	189,200
1902	2nd	75	63	.543	27.5	Ned Hanlon	199,868
1903	5th	70	66	.515	19.0	Ned Hanlon	224,670
1904	6th	56	97	.366	50.0	Ned Hanlon	214,600
1905	8th	48	104	.316	56.5	Ned Hanlon	227,924
1906	5th	66	86	.434	50.0	Patsy Donovan	227,400
1907	5th	65	83	.439	40.0	Patsy Donovan	312,500
1908	7th	53	101	.344	46.0	Patsy Donovan	275,600
1909	6th	55	98	.359	55.5	Harry Lumley	321,300
1910	6th	64	90	.416	40.0	Bill Dahlen	279,321
1911	7th	64	86	.427	33.5	Bill Dahlen	269,000
1912	7th	58	95	.379	46.0	Bill Dahlen	243,000
1913	6th	65	84	.436	34.5	Bill Dahlen	347,000
1914	5th	75	79	.487	19.5	Wilbert Robinson	122,671
1915	3rd	80	72	.526	10.0	Wilbert Robinson	297,766
1916	1st	94	60	.610	+2.5	Wilbert Robinson	447,747
1917	7th	70	81	.464	26.5	Wilbert Robinson	221,619
1918	5th	57	69	.452	25.5	Wilbert Robinson	83,831
1919	5th	69	71	.493	27.0	Wilbert Robinson	360,721

Year	Position	W	L	Pct.	*GB	Manager	Attendance
1920	1st	93	61	.604	+7.0	Wilbert Robinson	808,722
1921	5th	77	75	.507	16.5	Wilbert Robinson	613,245
1922	6th	76	78	.494	17.0	Wilbert Robinson	498,856
1923	6th	76	78	.494	19.5	Wilbert Robinson	564,666
1924	2nd	92	62	.597	1.5	Wilbert Robinson	818,883
1925	6th (tied)	68	85	.444	27.0	Wilbert Robinson	659,435
1926	6th	71	82	.464	17.5	Wilbert Robinson	650,819
1927	6th	65	88	.425	28.5	Wilbert Robinson	637,230
1928	6th	77	76	.503	17.5	Wilbert Robinson	664,863
1929	6th	70	83	.458	28.5	Wilbert Robinson	731,886
1930	4th	86	68	.558	6.0	Wilbert Robinson	1,097,339
1931	4th	79	73	.520	21.0	Wilbert Robinson	753,133
1932	3rd	81	73	.526	9.0	Max Carey	681,827
1933	6th	65	88	.425	26.5	Max Carey	526,815
1934	6th	71	81	.467	23.5	Casey Stengel	434,188
1935	5th	70	83	.458	29.5	Casey Stengel	470,517
1936	7th	67	87	.435	25.0	Casey Stengel	489,618
1937	6th	62	91	.405	33.5	Burleigh Grimes	482,481
1938	7th	69	80	.463	18.5	Burleigh Grimes	663,087
1939	3rd	84	69	.549	12.5	Leo Durocher	955,668
1940	2nd	88	65	.575	12.0	Leo Durocher	975,978
1941	1st	100	54	.649	+2.5	Leo Durocher	1,214,910
1942	2nd	104	50	.675	2.0	Leo Durocher	1,037,765
1943	3rd	81	72	.529	23.5	Leo Durocher	661,739
1944	7th	63	91	.409	42.0	Leo Durocher	605,905
1945	3rd	87	67	.565	11.0	Leo Durocher	1,059,220
1946	2nd†	96	60	.615	2.0	Leo Durocher	1,796,824
1947	1st	94	60	.610	+5.0	Clyde Sukeforth, Burt Shotton	1,807,526
1948	3rd	84	70	.545	7.5	Leo Durocher, Burt Shotton	1,398,967
1949	1st	97	57	.630	+1.0	Burt Shotton	1,633,747
1950	2nd	89	65	.578	2.0	Burt Shotton	1,185,896
1951	2nd†	97	60	.618	1.0	Chuck Dressen	1,282,628
1952	1st	96	57	.627	+4.5	Chuck Dressen	1,088,704
1953	1st	105	49	.682	+13.0	Chuck Dressen	1,163,419
1954	2nd	92	62	.597	5.0	Walter Alston	1,020,531
1955	1st	98	55	.641	+13.5	Walter Alston	1,033,589
1956	1st	93	61	.604	+1.0	Walter Alston	1,213,562
1957	3rd	84	70	.545	11.0	Walter Alston	1,028,258

*Games behind winner. †Lost pennant playoff.

INDIVIDUAL RECORDS (1890 TO 1957)

SERVICE

Most years by non-pitcher
18—Zack Wheat

Most years by pitcher
12—Dazzy Vance

BATTING

Most games
158— Carl Furillo, 1951
Gil Hodges, 1951

Most games, career
2,318—Zack Wheat

Most at-bats
667—Carl Furillo, 158 games, 1951

Most at-bats, career
8,859—Zack Wheat

Most runs
143— Hub Collins, 129 games, 1890
Babe Herman, 153 games, 1930

Most runs, career
1,317—Pee Wee Reese

Most hits
241—Babe Herman, 153 games, 1930

Most hits, career
2,804—Zack Wheat

Most singles
179—Willie Keeler, 137 games, 1900

Most singles, career
2,038—Zack Wheat

Most doubles
52—Johnny Frederick, 148 games, 1929

Most doubles, career
464—Zack Wheat

Most triples
27—George Treadway, 122 games, 1894

Most triples, career
171—Zack Wheat

Most triples (since 1900)
22—Hy Myers, 154 games, 1920

Most homers by righthander
42—Gil Hodges, 154 games, 1954

Most homers by lefthander
43—Duke Snider, 151 games, 1956

Most homers by switch-hitter
13—Jim Gilliam, 146 games, 1954

Most homers by rookie
25—Del Bissonette, 155 games, 1928

Most homers, month
15—Duke Snider, August, 1953

Most homers at home
25— Duke Snider (includes 2 at Jersey
City), 1956
Gil Hodges, 1954

Most homers on road
24—Gil Hodges, 1951

Most homers by righthander, career
298—Gil Hodges

Most homers by lefthander, career
316—Duke Snider

Most homers by switch-hitter, career
44—Tom Daly

Most grand slams
2—Held by many players

Most grand slams, career
13—Gil Hodges

Most total bases
416—Babe Herman, 153 games, 1930

Most total bases, career
4,003—Zack Wheat

Most long hits
94—Babe Herman, 153 games, 1930

Most long hits, career
766—Zack Wheat

Most extra bases on long hits
179—Duke Snider, 149 games, 1954

Most extra bases on long hits, career
1,368—Duke Snider

**Most sacrifices (sacrifice hits and sacri-
fice flies)**
39—Jake Daubert, 150 games, 1915

Most sacrifice hits
32—Doc Casey, 138 games, 1907

Most sacrifice flies
19—Gil Hodges, 154 games, 1954

Most bases on balls
148—Eddie Stanky, 153 games, 1945

Most strikeouts
115—Dolf Camilli, 149 games, 1941

Fewest strikeouts
15—Jimmy Johnston, 151 games, 1923

Most hit by pitch
14—Jackie Robinson, 149 games, 1952

Most runs batted in
42—Roy Campanella, 144 games, 1953

Most runs batted in, career
,227—Zack Wheat

Highest batting average
393—Babe Herman, 153 games, 1930

Highest batting average, career
352—Willie Keeler

Highest batting average, career (since 1900)
339—Babe Herman

Highest slugging average
678—Babe Herman, 153 games, 1930

Highest slugging average, career
660—Duke Snider

Longest batting streak
9 games—Zack Wheat, 1916

Most grounded into double play
7—Carl Furillo, 149 games, 1956

Fewest grounded into double play
—Jackie Robinson, 151 games, 1947
Pee Wee Reese, 155 games, 1949
Jim Gilliam, 153 games, 1956

BASERUNNING

Most stolen bases
4—Monte Ward, 148 games, 1892

Most stolen bases (since 1900)
67—Jimmy Sheckard, 139 games, 1903

Most stolen bases, career
31—Pee Wee Reese

Most caught stealing
6—Jimmy Johnston, 152 games, 1921

PITCHING (SINCE 1900)

Most games
62—Clem Labine, 1956

Most games, career
78—Dazzy Vance

Most games started
41—Oscar Jones, 1904

Most complete games
8—Oscar Jones, 1904

Most games finished
7—Clem Labine, 1956

Most innings
78—Oscar Jones, 1904

Most games won
29—Joe McGinnity, 1900

Most games won, career
90—Dazzy Vance

Most 20-victory seasons
—Burleigh Grimes

Most games lost
7—George Bell, 1910

Highest winning percentage
889—Freddie Fitzsimmons (16-2), 1940

Longest winning streak
5 games—Dazzy Vance, 1924

Longest losing streak
4 games—Jim Pastorius, 1908

Most bases on balls
151—Bill Donovan, 1901

Most bases on balls, career
764—Dazzy Vance

Most strikeouts
62—Dazzy Vance, 1924

Most strikeouts, career
,915—Dazzy Vance

Most strikeouts, game
17—Dazzy Vance, July 20, 1925, 10 innings
16—Nap Rucker, July 24, 1909

Most shutouts
7—Burleigh Grimes, 1918
Whit Wyatt, 1941

Most shutouts, career
38—Nap Rucker

Most 1-0 shutouts won
3—Nap Rucker, 1911

Most runs
188—Harry McIntire, 1905

Most earned runs
138—Burleigh Grimes, 1925

Most hits
364—Joe McGinnity, 1900

Most hit batsmen
41—Joe McGinnity, 1900

Most wild pitches
15—Larry Cheney, 1916

Most home runs
35—Don Newcombe, 1955

Lowest ERA
1.58—Rube Marquard, 205 innings, 1916

CLUB RECORDS

Most players
53 in 1944

Fewest players
23 in 1905

Most games
158 in 1951

Most at-bats
5,574 in 1936

Most runs
955 in 1953

Fewest runs
375 in 1908

Most hits
1,654 in 1930

Fewest hits
1,044 in 1908

Most singles
1,223 in 1925

Most doubles
303 in 1930

Most triples
99 in 1920

Most homers
208 in 1953

Fewest homers (154 or 162-game schedule)
14 in 1915

Most homers at Ebbets Field, home and opponents
207 in 1950

Most grand slams
8 in 1952

Most pinch home runs
7 in 1932

Most long hits
541 in 1953

Most extra bases on long hits
1,016 in 1953

Most total bases
2,545 in 1953

Most sacrifices (sacrifice hits and sacrifice flies)
203 in 1916

Most sacrifice hits
197 in 1907

Most sacrifice flies
59 in 1954

Most stolen bases
205 in 1904

Most caught stealing
73 in 1921

Most bases on balls
732 in 1947

Most strikeouts
848 in 1957

Fewest strikeouts
318 in 1922

Most hit by pitch
44 in 1951

Fewest hit by pitch
14 in 1942, 1944

Most runs batted in
887 in 1953

Fewest runs batted in
499 in 1927

Highest batting average
.304 in 1930

Lowest batting average
.213 in 1908

Highest slugging average
.474 in 1953

Lowest slugging average
.277 in 1908

Most grounded into double play
151 in 1952

Fewest grounded into double play
86 in 1947

Most left on bases
1,278 in 1947

Fewest left on bases
1,012 in 1921

Most .300 hitters
6 in 1900, 1922, 1925, 1930, 1943, 1953

Most putouts
4,295 in 1940

Fewest putouts
3,911 in 1909

Most assists
2,132 in 1921

Fewest assists
1,574 in 1944

Most chances accepted
6,334 in 1920

Fewest chances accepted
5,672 in 1944

Most errors
408 in 1905

Fewest errors
106 in 1952

Most consecutive errorless games
10 in 1942

Most double plays
192 in 1951

Fewest double plays
95 in 1926

Most passed balls
21 in 1905

Fewest passed balls
4 in 1933, 1951, 1953, 1954

Highest fielding average
.982 in 1952

Lowest fielding average
.937 in 1905

Highest home attendance
1,807,526 in 1947

Highest road attendance
1,863,542 in 1947

Most games won
105 in 1953

Most games lost
104 in 1905

Most games won, month
25—July 1947
    August 1953

Most games lost, month
27—September 1908

Highest percentage games won
.682 in 1953 (won 105, lost 49)

Lowest percentage games won
.316 in 1905 (won 48, lost 104)

Games won, league
5,214 in 68 years

Games lost, league
4,926 in 68 years

Most shutouts won
22 in 1906, 1916

Most shutouts lost
26 in 1907

Most 1-0 games won
7 in 1907, 1909

Most 1-0 games lost
9 in 1910, 1913

Most consecutive games won
15 in 1924

Most consecutive games lost
16 in 1944

Number of times league champions
12

Number of last-place finishes
1

Most runs, game
25 vs. Pittsburgh, May 20, 1896
    vs. Cincinnati, September 23, 1901

Most runs by opponent, game
28 by Chicago, August 25, 1891

Most runs by opponent, game (since 1900)
26 by New York, April 30, 1944, first game

Most runs, shutout game
15 vs. Philadelphia, August 16, 1952, 6 innings

Most runs by opponent, shutout game
17 by St. Louis, August 24, 1924, second game

Most runs, doubleheader shutout
18 vs. Philadelphia, September 3, 1906

Most runs, inning
15 vs. Cincinnati, May 21, 1952, first inning

Longest 1-0 game won
13 innings vs. St. Louis, August 21, 1909
    vs. Boston, May 29, 1938

Longest 1-0 game lost
15 innings vs. Cincinnati, June 11, 1915

Most hits, game
28 vs. Pittsburgh, June 23, 1930

Most home runs, game
6 vs. Milwaukee, June 1, 1955

Most consecutive games with one or more homers
24 (39 homers), 1953

Most total bases, game
46 vs. Philadelphia, September 23, 1939, first game

Largest crowd, day game
37,512 vs. New York, August 30, 1947

Largest crowd, doubleheader
41,209 vs. New York, May 30, 1934

Largest crowd, night game
35,583 vs. Philadelphia, September 24, 1949

Largest crowd, home opener
34,530 vs. New York, April 19, 1949

CHICAGO CUBS
YEARLY FINISHES

Year	Position	W	L	Pct.	*GB	Manager	Attendance
1901	6th	53	86	.381	37.0	Tom Loftus	205,071
1902	5th	68	69	.496	34.0	Frank Selee	263,700
1903	3rd	82	56	.594	8.0	Frank Selee	386,205
1904	2nd	93	60	.608	13.0	Frank Selee	439,100
1905	3rd	92	61	.601	13.0	Frank Selee, Frank Chance	509,900
1906	1st	116	36	.763	+20.0	Frank Chance	654,300
1907	1st	107	45	.704	+17.0	Frank Chance	422,550
1908	1st	99	55	.643	+1.0	Frank Chance	665,325
1909	2nd	104	49	.680	6.5	Frank Chance	633,480
1910	1st	104	50	.675	+13.0	Frank Chance	526,152
1911	2nd	92	62	.597	7.5	Frank Chance	576,000
1912	3rd	91	59	.607	11.5	Frank Chance	514,000
1913	3rd	88	65	.575	13.5	Johnny Evers	419,000
1914	4th	78	76	.506	16.5	Hank O'Day	202,516
1915	4th	73	80	.477	17.5	Roger Bresnahan	217,058
1916	5th	67	86	.438	26.5	Joe Tinker	453,685
1917	5th	74	80	.481	24.0	Fred Mitchell	360,218
1918	1st	84	45	.651	+10.5	Fred Mitchell	337,256
1919	3rd	75	65	.536	21.0	Fred Mitchell	424,430
1920	5th (tied)	75	79	.487	18.0	Fred Mitchell	480,783
1921	7th	64	89	.418	30.0	Johnny Evers, Bill Killefer	410,107
1922	5th	80	74	.519	13.0	Bill Killefer	542,283
1923	4th	83	71	.539	12.5	Bill Killefer	703,705
1924	5th	81	72	.529	12.0	Bill Killefer	716,922
1925	8th	68	86	.442	27.5	Bill Killefer, Rabbit Maranville, George Gibson	622,610
1926	4th	82	72	.532	7.0	Joe McCarthy	885,063
1927	4th	85	68	.556	8.5	Joe McCarthy	1,159,168
1928	3rd	91	63	.591	4.0	Joe McCarthy	1,143,740
1929	1st	98	54	.645	+10.5	Joe McCarthy	1,485,166
1930	2nd	90	64	.584	2.0	Joe McCarthy, Rogers Hornsby	1,463,624
1931	3rd	84	70	.545	17.0	Rogers Hornsby	1,086,422
1932	1st	90	64	.584	+4.0	Rogers Hornsby, Charlie Grimm	974,688
1933	3rd	86	68	.558	6.0	Charlie Grimm	594,112
1934	3rd	86	65	.570	8.0	Charlie Grimm	707,525
1935	1st	100	54	.649	+4.0	Charlie Grimm	692,604
1936	2nd (tied)	87	67	.565	5.0	Charlie Grimm	699,370
1937	2nd	93	61	.604	3.0	Charlie Grimm	895,020
1938	1st	89	63	.586	+2.0	Charlie Grimm, Gabby Hartnett	951,640
1939	4th	84	70	.545	13.0	Gabby Hartnett	726,663
1940	5th	75	79	.487	25.5	Gabby Hartnett	534,878

Year	Position	W	L	Pct.	*GB	Manager	Attendance
1941	6th	70	84	.455	30.0	Jimmy Wilson	545,159
1942	6th	68	86	.442	38.0	Jimmy Wilson	590,872
1943	5th	74	79	.484	30.5	Jimmy Wilson	508,247
1944	4th	75	79	.487	30.0	Jimmy Wilson, Charlie Grimm	640,110
1945	1st	98	56	.636	+3.0	Charlie Grimm	1,036,386
1946	3rd	82	71	.536	14.5	Charlie Grimm	1,342,970
1947	6th	69	85	.448	25.0	Charlie Grimm	1,364,039
1948	8th	64	90	.416	27.5	Charlie Grimm	1,237,792
1949	8th	61	93	.396	36.0	Charlie Grimm, Frankie Frisch	1,143,139
1950	7th	64	89	.418	26.5	Frankie Frisch	1,165,944
1951	8th	62	92	.403	34.5	Frankie Frisch, Phil Cavarretta	894,415
1952	5th	77	77	.500	19.5	Phil Cavarretta	1,024,826
1953	7th	65	89	.422	40.0	Phil Cavarretta	763,658
1954	7th	64	90	.416	33.0	Stan Hack	748,183
1955	6th	72	81	.471	26.0	Stan Hack	875,800
1956	8th	60	94	.390	33.0	Stan Hack	720,118
1957	7th (tied)	62	92	.403	33.0	Bob Scheffing	670,629
1958	5th (tied)	72	82	.468	20.0	Bob Scheffing	979,904
1959	5th (tied)	74	80	.481	13.0	Bob Scheffing	858,255
1960	7th	60	94	.390	35.0	Charlie Grimm, Lou Boudreau	809,770
1961	7th	64	90	.416	29.0	Vedie Himsl, Harry Craft, Elvin Tappe, Lou Klein	673,057
1962	9th	59	103	.364	42.5	Charlie Metro, Elvin Tappe, Lou Klein	609,802
1963	7th	82	80	.506	17.0	Bob Kennedy	979,551
1964	8th	76	86	.469	17.0	Bob Kennedy	751,647
1965	8th	72	90	.444	25.0	Bob Kennedy, Lou Klein	641,361
1966	10th	59	103	.364	36.0	Leo Durocher	635,891
1967	3rd	87	74	.540	14.0	Leo Durocher	977,226
1968	3rd	84	78	.519	13.0	Leo Durocher	1,043,409

EAST DIVISION

Year	Position	W	L	Pct.	*GB	Manager	Attendance
1969	2nd	92	70	.568	8.0	Leo Durocher	1,674,993
1970	2nd	84	78	.519	5.0	Leo Durocher	1,642,705
1971	3rd (tied)	83	79	.512	14.0	Leo Durocher	1,653,007
1972	2nd	85	70	.548	11.0	Leo Durocher, Whitey Lockman	1,299,163
1973	5th	77	84	.478	5.0	Whitey Lockman	1,351,705
1974	6th	66	96	.407	22.0	Whitey Lockman, Jim Marshall	1,015,378
1975	5th (tied)	75	87	.463	17.5	Jim Marshall	1,034,819
1976	4th	75	87	.463	26.0	Jim Marshall	1,026,217
1977	4th	81	81	.500	20.0	Herman Franks	1,439,834
1978	3rd	79	83	.488	11.0	Herman Franks	1,525,311
1979	5th	80	82	.494	18.0	Herman Franks, Joe Amalfitano	1,648,587
1980	6th	64	98	.395	27.0	Preston Gomez, Joe Amalfitano	1,206,776
1981	6th/5th	38	65	.369	†	Joe Amalfitano	565,637
1982	5th	73	89	.451	19.0	Lee Elia	1,249,278
1983	5th	71	91	.438	19.0	Lee Elia, Charlie Fox	1,479,717
1984	1st‡	96	65	.596	+6.5	Jim Frey	2,104,219
1985	4th	77	84	.478	23.5	Jim Frey	2,161,534
1986	5th	70	90	.438	37.0	Jim Frey, John Vukovich, Gene Michael	1,859,102
1987	6th	76	85	.472	18.5	Gene Michael, Frank Lucchesi	2,035,130
1988	4th	77	85	.475	24.0	Don Zimmer	2,089,034
1989	1st‡	93	69	.574	+6.0	Don Zimmer	2,491,942
1990	4th	77	85	.475	18.0	Don Zimmer	2,243,791
1991	4th	77	83	.481	20.0	Don Zimmer, Joe Altobelli, Jim Essian	2,314,250
1992	4th	78	84	.481	18.0	Jim Lefebvre	2,126,720
1993	4th	84	78	.519	13.0	Jim Lefebvre	2,653,763

CENTRAL DIVISION

Year	Position	W	L	Pct.	*GB	Manager	Attendance
1994	5th	49	64	.434	16.5	Tom Trebelhorn	1,845,208
1995	3rd	73	71	.507	12.0	Jim Riggleman	1,918,265
1996	4th	76	86	.469	12.0	Jim Riggleman	2,219,110
1997	5th	68	94	.420	16.0	Jim Riggleman	2,190,308
1998	2nd§∞	90	73	.552	12.5	Jim Riggleman	2,623,000
1999	6th	67	95	.414	30.0	Jim Riggleman	2,813,854
2000	6th	65	97	.401	30.0	Don Baylor	2,789,511
2001	3rd	88	74	.543	5.0	Don Baylor	2,779,456

*Games behind winner. †First half 15-37; second 23-28. ‡Lost championship series. §Won wild-card playoff. ∞Lost division series.

INDIVIDUAL RECORDS (1876 TO DATE)

SERVICE

Most years by non-pitcher
22—Cap Anson

Most years (since 1900)
20—Phil Cavarretta

Most years by pitcher
16—Charlie Root

BATTING

Most games
164— Ron Santo, 1965
Billy Williams, 1965

Most games, career
2,528—Ernie Banks

Most at-bats
666—Billy Herman, 154 games, 1935

Most at-bats, career
9,421—Ernie Banks

Most runs
156—Rogers Hornsby, 156 games, 1929

Most runs, career
1,712—Cap Anson

Most runs, career (since 1900)
1,306—Billy Williams

Most hits
229—Rogers Hornsby, 156 games, 1929

Most hits, career
3,081—Cap Anson

Most hits, career (since 1900)
2,583—Ernie Banks

Most singles
165—Sparky Adams, 146 games, 1927

Most singles, career
2,330—Cap Anson

Most singles, career (since 1900)
1,692—Stan Hack

Most doubles
57— Billy Herman, 154 games, 1935
Billy Herman, 153 games, 1936

Most doubles, career
530—Cap Anson

Most doubles, career (since 1900)
407—Ernie Banks

Most triples
21— Wildfire Schulte, 154 games, 1911
Vic Saier, 149 games, 1913

Most triples, career
137—Jimmy Ryan

Most triples, career (since 1900)
117—Wildfire Schulte

Most homers by righthander
66—Sammy Sosa, 159 games, 1998

Most homers by lefthander
42—Billy Williams, 161 games, 1970

Most homers by switch-hitter
18—Augie Galan, 147 games, 1937

Most homers at home
35—Sammy Sosa, 1998

Most homers on road
31—Sammy Sosa, 1998

Most homers, rookie
25—Billy Williams, 146 games, 1961

Most homers, month
20—Sammy Sosa, June 1998

Most homers by righthander, career
512—Ernie Banks

Most homers by lefthander, career
392—Billy Williams

Most homers by switch-hitter, career
59—Augie Galan

Most grand slams
5—Ernie Banks, 154 games, 1955

Most grand slams, career
12—Ernie Banks

Most total bases
425—Sammy Sosa, 160 games, 2001

Most total bases, career
4,706—Ernie Banks

Most long hits
103—Sammy Sosa, 160 games, 2001

Most long hits, career
1,009—Ernie Banks

Most extra bases on long hits
236—Sammy Sosa, 160 games, 2001

Most extra bases on long hits, career
2,123—Ernie Banks

Most sacrifices (sacrifice hits and sacrifice flies)
46—Jimmy Sheckard, 148 games, 1909

Most sacrifice hits
40—Jimmy Sheckard, 149 games, 1906

Most sacrifice flies
14—Ron Santo, 1969

Most bases on balls
147—Jimmy Sheckard, 156 games, 1911

Most bases on balls, career
1,092—Stan Hack

Most strikeouts
174—Sammy Sosa, 162 games, 1997

Most strikeouts, career
1,271—Ron Santo

Fewest strikeouts
5—Charlie Hollocher, 152 games, 1922

Most hit by pitch
14—Scott Servais, 129 games, 1996

Most runs batted in
191—Hack Wilson, 155 games, 1930

Most runs batted in, career
1,636—Ernie Banks

Most game-winning RBIs
19—Gary Matthews, 147 games, 1984

Most consecutive games with RBI
17—Ray Grimes (22 RBIs), 1922

Highest batting average
.388—King Kelly, 118 games, 1886
Bill Lange, 122 games, 1895

Highest batting average (since 1900)
.380—Rogers Hornsby, 156 games, 1929

Highest batting average, career
.339—Cap Anson

Highest batting average, career (since 1900)
.336—Riggs Stephenson

Highest slugging average
.737—Sammy Sosa, 160 games, 2001

Highest slugging average, career
.590—Hack Wilson

Longest batting streak
42 games—Bill Dahlen, 1894

Longest batting streak (since 1900)
30 games—Jerome Walton, 1989

Most grounded into double play
27—Ron Santo, 149 games, 1973

Fewest grounded into double play
0—Augie Galan, 154 games, 1935

BASERUNNING

Most stolen bases
100—Bill Lange, 123 games, 1896

Most stolen bases (since 1900)
67—Frank Chance, 123 games, 1903

Most stolen bases, career
404—Frank Chance

Most caught stealing
29—Charlie Hollocher, 152 games, 1922

PITCHING (SINCE 1900)

Most games
84—Ted Abernathy, 1965
Dick Tidrow, 1980

Most games, career
605—Charlie Root

Most games started
42—Ferguson Jenkins, 1969

Most games started, career
347—Ferguson Jenkins

Most complete games
33—Jack Taylor, 1903
Grover Alexander, 1920

Most complete games, career
205—Mordecai Brown

Most games finished
70—Rod Beck, 1998

Most innings
363—Grover Alexander, 1920

Most innings, career
3,138—Charlie Root

Most games won
29—Mordecai Brown, 1908

Most games won, career
201—Charlie Root

Most 20-victory seasons
6—Mordecai Brown, Ferguson Jenkins

Most games lost
22— Tom Hughes, 1901
Dick Ellsworth, 1966
Bill Bonham, 1974

Most games lost, career
156—Charlie Root

Highest winning percentage
.941—Rick Sutcliffe (16-1), 1984

Longest winning streak
14 games—Ed Reulbach, 1909
Rick Sutcliffe, 1984

Longest winning streak, two seasons
16 games—Rick Sutcliffe, 1984-85

Longest losing streak
13 games—Dutch McCall, 1948

Most saves
53—Randy Myers, 1993

Most bases on balls
185—Sam Jones, 1955

Most bases on balls, career
871—Charlie Root

Most strikeouts
274—Ferguson Jenkins, 1970

Most strikeouts, game
20—Kerry Wood vs. Houston, May 6, 1998

Most strikeouts, career
2,036—Ferguson Jenkins

Most shutouts
9—Mordecai Brown, 1906, 1908
Orval Overall, 1907, 1909
Grover Alexander, 1919
Bill Lee, 1938

Most shutouts, career
48—Mordecai Brown

Most 1-0 shutouts won
3—held by many pitchers

Most runs
174—Guy Bush, 1930

Most earned runs
155—Guy Bush, 1930

Most hits
335—Grover Alexander, 1920

Most hit batsmen
20—Nixey Callahan, 1900

Most wild pitches
26—Larry Cheney, 1914

Most home runs
38—Warren Hacker, 1955

Most sacrifice hits
3—Bill Bonham, 1974

Most sacrifice flies
4—Rick Reuschel, 1980
   Steve Trachsel, 1999

Lowest ERA
1.72—Grover Alexander, 235 innings,
   1919

CLUB RECORDS

Most players
51 in 2000

Fewest players
20 in 1905

Most games
164 in 1965

Most at-bats
5,675 in 1988

Most runs
998 in 1930

Most opponents' runs
920 in 1999

Fewest runs
530 in 1906

Most hits
1,722 in 1930

Fewest hits
1,224 in 1907

Most singles
1,226 in 1921

Most doubles
340 in 1931

Most triples
101 in 1911

Most homers
212 in 1998

**Fewest homers (154 or 162-game
   schedule)**
12 in 1905

**Most homers at Wrigley Field, home
   and opponents**
222 in 1999

Most grand slams
9 in 1929

Most pinch home runs
10 in 1998

Most total bases
2,684 in 1930

Most long hits
548 in 1930

Most extra bases on long hits
962 in 1930

**Most sacrifices (sacrifice hits and sacri-
   fice flies)**
270 in 1908

Most sacrifice hits
231 in 1906

Most sacrifice flies
66 in 1975

Most stolen bases
283 in 1906

Most caught stealing
149 in 1924

Most bases on balls
650 in 1975

Most strikeouts
1,223 in 1998

Fewest strikeouts
374 in 1921

Most hit by pitch
66 in 2001

Fewest hit by pitch
13 in 1956

Most runs batted in
940 in 1930

Most game-winning RBIs
86 in 1984

Highest batting average
.309 in 1930

Lowest batting average
.238 in 1963, 1965

Highest slugging average
.481 in 1930

Lowest slugging average
.311 in 1907

Most grounded into double play
157 in 1938

Fewest grounded into double play
87 in 1991

Most left on bases
1,262 in 1975

Fewest left on bases
964 in 1924

Most .300 hitters
8 in 1921

Most putouts
4,437 in 1980

Fewest putouts
4,024 in 1909

Most assists
2,155 in 1916

Fewest assists
1,493 in 2001

Most chances accepted
6,508 in 1977

Fewest chances accepted
5,706 in 1953

Most errors
310 in 1914

Fewest errors
100 in 2000

Most errorless games
96 in 2000

Most consecutive errorless games
10 in 1998

Most double plays
176 in 1928

Fewest double plays
107 in 1998

Most passed balls
35 in 1961

Fewest passed balls
4 in 1967

Highest fielding average
.984 in 1998

Lowest fielding average
.951 in 1914

Highest home attendance
2,813,854 in 1999

Highest road attendance
2,900,959 in 1998

Most games won
116 in 1906

Most games lost
103 in 1962, 1966

Most games won, month
26 in August 1906, July 1935, July 1945

Most games lost, month
24 in July 1957
24 in August 1999

Highest percentage games won
.798 in 1880 (won 67, lost 17)

**Highest percentage games won (since
   1900)**
.763 in 1906 (won 116, lost 36)

Lowest percentage games won
.364 in 1962, 1966 (won 59, lost 103)

Games won, league
9,512 in 126 years

Games lost, league
8,961 in 126 years

Most shutouts won
32 in 1907, 1909

Most shutouts lost
22 in 1915, 1968

Most 1-0 games won
9 in 1906

Most 1-0 games lost
10 in 1916

Most consecutive games won
21 in 1880, 1935

Most consecutive games lost
14 in 1997

Number of times league champions
16

Number of last-place finishes
14 (tied in 1997, 2000)

Most runs, game
36 vs. Louisville, June 29, 1897

Most runs, game (since 1900)
26 vs. Philadelphia, August 25, 1922
   vs. Colorado, August 18, 1995

**Most runs by opponent, game (since
   1900)**
23 by Philadelphia, August 25, 1922
   by Cincinnati, July 6, 1949
   by Philadelphia, May 17, 1979, 10
      innings
   by New York, August 16, 1987

Most runs, shutout game
20 vs. Washington, May 28, 1886

Most runs, shutout game (since 1900)
19 vs. New York, June 7, 1906
   vs. San Diego, May 13, 1969

Most runs by opponent, shutout game
22 by Pittsburgh, September 16, 1975

Most runs, doubleheader shutout
12 vs. St. Louis, July 11, 1965

Most runs, inning
18 vs. Detroit, September 6, 1883, seventh inning

Most runs, inning (since 1900)
14 vs. Philadelphia, August 25, 1922,
   fourth inning

Longest 1-0 game won
17 innings vs. Boston, September 21,
   1901

Longest 1-0 game lost
17 innings vs. Houston, August 23, 1980

Most hits, game
32 vs. Buffalo, July 3, 1883
   vs. Louisville, June 29, 1897

Most hits, game (since 1900)
28 vs. Boston, July 3, 1945

Most home runs, game
7 vs. New York, June 11, 1967, second
   game
   vs. San Diego, August 19, 1970
   vs. San Diego, May 17, 1977

Most consecutive games with one or more homers
17 (28 homers), 1998

Most consecutive games with one or more homers, two seasons
15 (3 games, last 2 games); (28 homers), 1954 (first 13 games)

Most total bases, game
54 vs. Brooklyn, August 25, 1891

Most total bases, game (since 1900)
49 vs. Philadelphia, May 17, 1979, 10 innings
45 vs. New York, June 11, 1967, second game
vs. Colorado, August 18, 1995

Largest crowd, day game
46,572 vs. Brooklyn, May 18, 1947

Largest crowd, doubleheader
46,965 vs. Pittsburgh, May 31, 1948

Largest crowd, night game
40,657 vs. Milwaukee, August 20, 2001

Largest crowd, home opener
45,777 vs. Pittsburgh, April 14, 1978
(Cubs drew 55,000 to their 2000 "home opener" in Tokyo, Japan, March 30.)

CINCINNATI REDS
YEARLY FINISHES

Year	Position	W	L	Pct.	*GB	Manager	Attendance
1901	8th	52	87	.374	38.0	Bid McPhee	205,728
1902	4th	70	70	.500	33.5	Bid McPhee, Frank Bancroft, Joe Kelley	217,300
1903	4th	74	65	.532	16.5	Joe Kelley	351,680
1904	3rd	88	65	.575	18.0	Joe Kelley	391,915
1905	5th	79	74	.516	26.0	Joe Kelley	313,927
1906	6th	64	87	.424	51.5	Ned Hanlon	330,056
1907	6th	66	87	.431	41.5	Ned Hanlon	317,500
1908	5th	73	81	.474	26.0	John Ganzel	399,200
1909	4th	77	76	.503	33.5	Clark Griffith	424,643
1910	5th	75	79	.487	29.0	Clark Griffith	380,622
1911	6th	70	83	.458	29.0	Clark Griffith	300,000
1912	4th	75	78	.490	29.0	Hank O'Day	344,000
1913	7th	64	89	.418	37.5	Joe Tinker	258,000
1914	8th	60	94	.390	34.5	Buck Herzog	100,791
1915	7th	71	83	.461	20.0	Buck Herzog	218,878
1916	7th (tied)	60	93	.392	33.5	Buck Herzog, Christy Mathewson	255,846
1917	4th	78	76	.506	20.0	Christy Mathewson	269,056
1918	3rd	68	60	.531	15.5	Christy Mathewson, Heinie Groh	163,009
1919	1st	96	44	.686	+9.0	Pat Moran	532,501
1920	3rd	82	71	.536	10.5	Pat Moran	568,107
1921	6th	70	83	.458	24.0	Pat Moran	311,227
1922	2nd	86	68	.558	7.0	Pat Moran	493,754
1923	2nd	91	63	.591	4.5	Pat Moran	575,063
1924	4th	83	70	.542	10.0	Jack Hendricks	437,707
1925	3rd	80	73	.523	15.0	Jack Hendricks	464,920
1926	2nd	87	67	.565	2.0	Jack Hendricks	672,987
1927	5th	75	78	.490	18.5	Jack Hendricks	442,164
1928	5th	78	74	.513	16.0	Jack Hendricks	490,490
1929	7th	66	88	.429	33.0	Jack Hendricks	295,040
1930	7th	59	95	.383	33.0	Dan Howley	386,727
1931	8th	58	96	.377	43.0	Dan Howley	263,316
1932	8th	60	94	.390	30.0	Dan Howley	356,950
1933	8th	58	94	.382	33.0	Donie Bush	218,281
1934	8th	52	99	.344	42.0	Bob O'Farrell, Chuck Dressen	206,773
1935	6th	68	85	.444	31.5	Chuck Dressen	448,247
1936	5th	74	80	.481	18.0	Chuck Dressen	466,245
1937	8th	56	98	.364	40.0	Chuck Dressen, Bobby Wallace	411,221
1938	4th	82	68	.547	6.0	Bill McKechnie	706,756
1939	1st	97	57	.630	+4.5	Bill McKechnie	981,443
1940	1st	100	53	.654	+12.0	Bill McKechnie	850,180
1941	3rd	88	66	.571	12.0	Bill McKechnie	643,513
1942	4th	76	76	.500	29.0	Bill McKechnie	427,031
1943	2nd	87	67	.565	18.0	Bill McKechnie	379,122
1944	3rd	89	65	.578	16.0	Bill McKechnie	409,567
1945	7th	61	93	.396	37.0	Bill McKechnie	290,070
1946	6th	67	87	.435	30.0	Bill McKechnie	715,751
1947	5th	73	81	.474	21.0	Johnny Neun	899,975
1948	7th	64	89	.418	27.0	Johnny Neun, Bucky Walters	823,386
1949	7th	62	92	.403	35.0	Bucky Walters	707,782
1950	6th	66	87	.431	24.5	Luke Sewell	538,794
1951	6th	68	86	.442	28.5	Luke Sewell	588,268
1952	6th	69	85	.448	27.5	Luke Sewell, Rogers Hornsby	604,197
1953	6th	68	86	.442	37.0	Rogers Hornsby, Buster Mills	548,086
1954	5th	74	80	.481	23.0	Birdie Tebbetts	704,167
1955	5th	75	79	.487	23.5	Birdie Tebbetts	693,662
1956	3rd	91	63	.591	2.0	Birdie Tebbetts	1,125,928
1957	4th	80	74	.519	15.0	Birdie Tebbetts	1,070,850
1958	4th	76	78	.494	16.0	Birdie Tebbetts, Jimmie Dykes	788,582
1959	5th (tied)	74	80	.481	13.0	Mayo Smith, Fred Hutchinson	801,289
1960	6th	67	87	.435	28.0	Fred Hutchinson	663,486
1961	1st	93	61	.604	+4.0	Fred Hutchinson	1,117,603
1962	3rd	98	64	.605	3.5	Fred Hutchinson	982,085
1963	5th	86	76	.531	13.0	Fred Hutchinson	858,805

Year	Position	W	L	Pct.	*GB	Manager	Attendance
1964	2nd (tied)	92	70	.549	1.0	Fred Hutchinson, Dick Sisler	862,466
1965	4th	89	73	.549	8.0	Dick Sisler	1,047,824
1966	7th	76	84	.475	18.0	Don Heffner, Dave Bristol	742,958
1967	4th	87	75	.537	14.5	Dave Bristol	958,300
1968	4th	83	79	.512	14.0	Dave Bristol	733,354

WEST DIVISION

Year	Position	W	L	Pct.	*GB	Manager	Attendance
1969	3rd	89	73	.549	4.0	Dave Bristol	987,991
1970	1st†	102	60	.630	+14.5	Sparky Anderson	1,803,568
1971	4th (tied)	79	83	.488	11.0	Sparky Anderson	1,501,122
1972	1st†	95	59	.617	+10.5	Sparky Anderson	1,611,459
1973	1st‡	99	63	.611	+3.5	Sparky Anderson	2,017,601
1974	2nd	98	64	.605	4.0	Sparky Anderson	2,164,307
1975	1st†	108	54	.667	+20.0	Sparky Anderson	2,315,603
1976	1st†	102	60	.630	+10.0	Sparky Anderson	2,629,708
1977	2nd	88	74	.543	10.0	Sparky Anderson	2,519,670
1978	2nd	92	69	.571	2.5	Sparky Anderson	2,532,497
1979	1st‡	90	71	.559	+1.5	John McNamara	2,356,933
1980	3rd	89	73	.549	3.5	John McNamara	2,022,450
1981	2nd/2nd	66	42	.611	§	John McNamara	1,093,730
1982	6th	61	101	.377	28.0	John McNamara, Russ Nixon	1,326,528
1983	6th	74	88	.457	17.0	Russ Nixon	1,190,419
1984	5th	70	92	.432	22.0	Vern Rapp, Pete Rose	1,275,887
1985	2nd	89	72	.553	5.5	Pete Rose	1,834,619
1986	2nd	86	76	.531	10.0	Pete Rose	1,692,432
1987	2nd	84	78	.519	6.0	Pete Rose	2,185,205
1988	2nd	87	74	.540	7.0	Pete Rose	2,072,528
1989	5th	75	87	.463	17.0	Pete Rose, Tommy Helms	1,979,320
1990	1st†	91	71	.562	+5.0	Lou Piniella	2,400,892
1991	5th	74	88	.457	20.0	Lou Piniella	2,372,377
1992	2nd	90	72	.556	8.0	Lou Piniella	2,315,946
1993	5th	73	89	.451	31.0	Tony Perez, Dave Johnson	2,453,232

CENTRAL DIVISION

Year	Position	W	L	Pct.	*GB	Manager	Attendance
1994	1st	66	48	.579	+0.5	Dave Johnson	1,897,681
1995	1st∞‡	85	59	.590	+9.0	Dave Johnson	1,837,649
1996	3rd	81	81	.500	7.0	Ray Knight	1,861,428
1997	3rd	76	86	.469	8.0	Ray Knight, Jack McKeon	1,785,788
1998	4th	77	85	.475	25.0	Jack McKeon	1,793,679
1999	2nd▲	96	67	.589	1.5	Jack McKeon	2,061,222
2000	2nd	85	77	.525	10.0	Jack McKeon	2,577,351
2001	5th	66	96	.407	27.0	Bob Boone	1,882,732

*Games behind winner. †Won championship series. ‡Lost championship series. §First half 35-21; second 31-21. ∞Won division series.
▲Lost wild-card playoff.

INDIVIDUAL RECORDS (1890 TO DATE)

SERVICE

Most years by non-pitcher
19—Pete Rose
    Dave Concepcion

Most years by pitcher
15—Joe Nuxhall

BATTING

Most games
163— Leo Cardenas, 1964
    Pete Rose, 1974

Most games, career
2,722—Pete Rose

Most at-bats
680—Pete Rose, 160 games, 1973

Most at-bats, career
10,934—Pete Rose

Most runs
134—Frank Robinson, 162 games, 1962

Most runs, career
1,741—Pete Rose

Most hits
230—Pete Rose, 160 games, 1973

Most hits, career
3,358—Pete Rose

Most singles
181—Pete Rose, 160 games, 1973

Most singles, career
2,490—Pete Rose

Most doubles
51— Frank Robinson, 162 games, 1962
    Pete Rose, 159 games, 1978

Most doubles, career
601—Pete Rose

Most triples
25—Bid McPhee, 132 games, 1890

Most triples (since 1900)
23—Sam Crawford, 140 games, 1902

Most triples, career
153—Edd Roush

Most homers by righthander
52—George Foster, 158 games, 1977

Most homers by lefthander
49—Ted Kluszewski, 149 games, 1954

Most homers by switch-hitter
21—Dmitri Young, 142 games, 2001

Most homers by rookie
38—Frank Robinson, 152 games, 1956

Most homers, month
14—Frank Robinson, August 1962
    Greg Vaughn, September 1999

Most homers at home
34—Ted Kluszewski, 1954

Most homers on road
31—George Foster, 1977

Most homers by righthander, career
389—Johnny Bench

Most homers by lefthander, career
251—Ted Kluszewski

Most homers by switch-hitter, career
152—Pete Rose

Most grand slams
3—Frank Robinson, 162 games, 1962
    Lee May, 153 games, 1970
    Ray Knight, 162 games, 1980
    Eric Davis, 129 games, 1987
    Chris Sabo, 148 games, 1993

Most grand slams, career
11—Johnny Bench

Most total bases
388—George Foster, 158 games, 1977

Most total bases, career
4,645—Pete Rose

Most long hits
92—Frank Robinson, 162 games, 1962

Most long hits, career
868—Pete Rose

Most extra bases on long hits
191—George Foster, 158 games, 1977

Most extra bases on long hits, career
1,596—Johnny Bench

Most sacrifices (sacrifice hits and sacrifice flies)
39—Jake Daubert, 140 games, 1919

Most sacrifice hits
31—Roy McMillan, 154 games, 1954

Most sacrifice flies
13—Johnny Temple, 149 games, 1959

Most bases on balls
132—Joe Morgan, 146 games, 1975

Most bases on balls, career
1,210—Pete Rose

Most strikeouts
145—Mike Cameron, 146 games, 1999

Most strikeouts, career
1,306—Tony Perez

Fewest strikeouts
13—Frank McCormick, 154 games, 1941

Most hit by pitch
20—Frank Robinson, 152 games, 1956

Most runs batted in
149—George Foster, 158 games, 1977

Most runs batted in, career
1,376—Johnny Bench

Most game-winning RBIs
21—Eric Davis, 135 games, 1988

Highest batting average
.383—Bug Holliday, 122 games, 1894

Highest batting average (since 1900)
.377—Cy Seymour, 149 games, 1905

Highest batting average, career
.332—Cy Seymour

Highest slugging average
.642—Ted Kluszewski, 149 games, 1954

Highest slugging average, career
.554—Frank Robinson

Longest batting streak
44 games—Pete Rose, 1978

Most grounded into double play
30—Ernie Lombardi, 129 games, 1938

Fewest grounded into double play
3—Billy Myers, 151 games, 1939

BASERUNNING

Most stolen bases
93—Arlie Latham, 135 games, 1891

Most stolen bases (since 1900)
81—Bob Bescher, 153 games, 1911

Most stolen bases, career
406—Joe Morgan

Most caught stealing
28—Pat Duncan, 151 games, 1922

PITCHING (SINCE 1900)

Most games
90—Wayne Granger, 1969

Most games, career
531—Pedro Borbon

Most games started
42—Noodles Hahn, 1901

Most games started, career
356—Eppa Rixey

Most complete games
41—Noodles Hahn, 1901

Most complete games, career
195—Bucky Walters

Most games finished
62—Tom Hume, 1980
    Jeff Shaw, 1997

Most innings
375—Noodles Hahn, 1901

Most innings, career
2,890—Eppa Rixey

Most games won
27— Dolf Luque, 1923
    Bucky Walters, 1939

Most games won, career
179—Eppa Rixey

Most 20-victory seasons
4—Paul Derringer

Most games lost
25—Paul Derringer, 1933

Most games lost, career
150—Paul Derringer

Highest winning percentage
.826—Elmer Riddle (19-4), 1941

Longest winning streak
16 games—Ewell Blackwell, 1947

Longest losing streak
12 games—Henry Thielman, 1902
    Pete Schneider, 1914
    Si Johnson, 1933

Most saves
44—Jeff Brantley, 1996

Most bases on balls
162—Johnny Vander Meer, 1943

Most bases on balls, career
1,072—Johnny Vander Meer

Most strikeouts
274—Mario Soto, 1982

Most strikeouts, game
18—Jim Maloney, June 14, 1965, 11
    innings
16—Noodles Hahn, May 22, 1901
    Jim Maloney, May 21, 1963
    Ron Villone, September 29, 2000

Most strikeouts, career
1,592—Jim Maloney

Most shutouts
7—Jake Weimer, 1906
    Fred Toney, 1917
    Hod Eller, 1919
    Jack Billingham, 1973

Most shutouts, career
32—Bucky Walters

Most 1-0 shutouts won
4—Jake Weimer, 1906

Most runs
158—Noodles Hahn, 1901

Most earned runs
145—Herm Wehmeier, 1950

Most hits
368—Noodles Hahn, 1901

Most hits batsmen
23—Jake Weimer, 1907

Most wild pitches
21—Scott Williamson, 2000

Most home runs
36—Tom Browning, 1988

Most sacrifice hits
17—Joey Jay, 1962
    Bruce Berenyi, 1982
    John Smiley, 1995

Most sacrifice flies
13—Bill Gullickson, 1986

Lowest ERA
1.57—Fred Toney, 223 innings, 1915

Most players
51 in 1993, 1997

Fewest players
21 in 1904

Most games
163 in 1964, 1968, 1969, 1974, 1980,
    1999, 2000

Most at-bats
5,767 in 1968

Most runs
865 in 1999

Fewest runs
488 in 1908

Most opponents' runs
857 in 1930

Most hits
1,599 in 1976

Fewest hits
1,108 in 1908

Most singles
1,191 in 1922

Most doubles
312 in 1999

Most triples
120 in 1926

Most homers
221 in 1956

Fewest homers (154 or 162-game schedule)
14 in 1908, 1916

Most homers at Crosley Field, home and opponents
219 in 1957

Most homers at Riverfront Stadium, home and opponents
213 in 1999

Most grand slams
7 in 1974, 1980, 1987

Most pinch home runs
12 in 1957

Most long hits
558 in 1999

Most extra bases on long hits
1,013 in 1999

Most total bases
2,549 in 1999

Most sacrifices (sacrifice hits and sacrifice flies)
239 in 1926

Most sacrifice hits
195 in 1907

Most sacrifice flies
66 in 1993

Most stolen bases
310 in 1910

Most caught stealing
136 in 1922

Most bases on balls
693 in 1974

Most strikeouts
1,172 in 2001

Fewest strikeouts
308 in 1921

Most hit by pitch
65 in 2001

Fewest hit by pitch
11 in 1951

Most runs batted in
320 in 1999

Most game-winning RBIs
34 in 1980, 1985

Highest batting average
.296 in 1922

Lowest batting average
.227 in 1908

Highest slugging average
.451 in 1999

Lowest slugging average
.304 in 1906

Most grounded into double play
143 in 1982

Fewest grounded into double play
93 in 1935

Most left on bases
1,328 in 1976

Fewest left on bases
997 in 1921

Most .300 hitters
8 in 1926

Most putouts
4,471 in 1968

Fewest putouts
4,006 in 1930

Most assists
2,151 in 1905

Fewest assists
1,534 in 1966

Most chances accepted
6,399 in 1915

Fewest chances accepted
5,655 in 1950

Most errors
314 in 1914

Fewest errors
95 in 1977

Most errorless games
99 in 1992

Most consecutive errorless games
15 in 1975

Most double plays
194 in 1928, 1931, 1954

Fewest double plays
108 in 1989

Most passed balls
39 in 1914

Fewest passed balls
3 in 1975

Highest fielding average
.984 in 1971, 1975, 1976, 1977, 1992

Lowest fielding average
.952 in 1914

Highest home attendance
2,629,708 in 1976

Highest road attendance
3,016,074 in 2000

Most games won
108 in 1975

Most games lost
101 in 1982

Most games won, month
24 in August 1918, July 1973

Most games lost, month
26 in September 1914

Highest percentage games won
.686 in 1919 (won 96, lost 44)

Lowest percentage games won
.344 in 1934 (won 52, lost 99)

Games won, league (since 1890)
8,675 in 112 years

Games lost, league (since 1890)
8,456 in 112 years

Most shutouts won
23 in 1919

Most shutouts lost
24 in 1908

Most 1-0 games won
7 in 1910, 1943, 1963

Most 1-0 games lost
7 in 1907, 1916

Most consecutive games won
14 in 1899

Most consecutive games won (since 1900)
12 in 1939, 1957

Most consecutive games lost
19 in 1914

Number of times league champions
9

Number of last-place finishes
11 (tied in 1916)

Most runs, game
30 vs. Louisville, June 18, 1893

Most runs, game (since 1900)
26 vs. Boston, June 4, 1911

Most runs by opponent, game
26 by Philadelphia, July 26, 1892

Most runs by opponent, game (since 1900)
25 by New York, June 9, 1901
by Brooklyn, September 23, 1901

Most runs, shutout game
18 vs. Los Angeles, August 8, 1965

Most runs by opponent, shutout game
18 by Philadelphia, August 10, 1930, first game
by Philadelphia, July 14, 1934, first game
by St. Louis, June 10, 1944

Most runs, doubleheader shutout
14 vs. St. Louis, September 1, 1924
vs. Los Angeles, August 16, 1961

Most runs, inning
14 vs. Louisville, June 18, 1893, first inning
vs. Houston, August 3, 1989, first inning

Longest 1-0 game won
15 innings vs. New York, July 16, 1933, first game
vs. Brooklyn, June 11, 1915

Longest 1-0 game lost
21 innings vs. San Francisco, September 1, 1967

Most hits, game
32 vs. Louisville, June 18, 1893

Most hits, game (since 1900)
28 vs. Philadelphia, May 13, 1902
vs. Colorado, May 19, 1999

Most home runs, game
9 vs. Philadelphia, September 4, 1999

Most consecutive games with one or more homers
21 (41 homers), 1956

Most total bases, game
55 vs. Louisville, June 18, 1893

Most total bases, game (since 1900)
55 vs. Colorado, May 19, 1999

Largest crowd, day game
55,596 vs. Milwaukee, April 3, 2000

Largest crowd, doubleheader
53,328 vs. Pittsburgh, July 9, 1976

Largest crowd, night game
54,621 vs. New York, October 4, 1999

Largest crowd, home opener
55,596 vs. Milwaukee, April 3, 2000

COLORADO ROCKIES
YEARLY FINISHES
WEST DIVISION

Year	Position	W	L	Pct.	*GB	Manager	Attendance
1993	6th	67	95	.414	37.0	Don Baylor	4,483,350
1994	3rd	53	64	.453	6.5	Don Baylor	3,281,511
1995	2nd†	77	67	.535	1.0	Don Baylor	3,390,037
1996	3rd	83	79	.512	8.0	Don Baylor	3,891,014
1997	3rd	83	79	.512	7.0	Don Baylor	3,888,453
1998	4th	77	85	.475	21.0	Don Baylor	3,789,347
1999	5th	72	90	.444	28.0	Jim Leyland	3,481,065
2000	4th	82	80	.506	15.0	Buddy Bell	3,285,710
2001	5th	73	89	.451	19.0	Buddy Bell	3,159,385

*Games behind winner. †Lost division series.

SERVICE

Most years by non-pitcher
7—Dante Bichette
  Vinny Castilla
  Larry Walker

Most years by pitcher
7—Curtis Leskanic

BATTING

Most games
162—Vinny Castilla, 1998
  Neifi Perez, 1998, 2000

Most games, career
1,018—Dante Bichette

Most at-bats
690—Neifi Perez, 157 games, 1999

Most at-bats, career
4,050—Dante Bichette

Most runs
143—Larry Walker, 153 games, 1997

Most runs, career
689—Larry Walker

Most hits
219—Dante Bichette, 161 games, 1998

Most hits, career
1,278—Dante Bichette

Most singles
163—Juan Pierre, 156 games, 2001

Most singles, career
789—Dante Bichette

Most doubles
59—Todd Helton, 160 games, 2000

Most doubles, career
270—Dante Bichette

Most triples
11—Neifi Perez, 157 games, 1999
  Neifi Perez, 162 games, 2000
  Juan Pierre, 156 games, 2001
  Juan Uribe, 72 games, 2001

Most triples, career
49—Neifi Perez

Most homers by righthander
47—Andres Galarraga, 159 games, 1996

Most homers by lefthander
49—Larry Walker, 153 games, 1997
  Todd Helton, 159 games, 2001

Most homers by switch-hitter
13—Greg Norton, 117 games, 2001

Most homers by rookie
25—Todd Helton, 152 games, 1998

Most homers at home
32—Andres Galarraga, 1996

Most homers on road
29—Larry Walker, 1997

Most homers, month
12—Dante Bichette, August 1995
  Vinny Castilla, June 1996
  Andres Galarraga, August 1996
  Vinny Castilla, July 1998

Most homers by righthander, career
203—Vinny Castilla

Most homers by lefthander, career
210—Larry Walker

Most homers by switch-hitter, career
43—Neifi Perez

Most grand slams
2—Dante Bichette, 1994
  Andres Galarraga, 1994, 1995, 1997
  Vinny Castilla, 1996
  Larry Walker, 1998
  Tom Goodwin, 2000

Most grand slams, career
6—Andres Galarraga
  Dante Bichette

Most total bases
409—Larry Walker, 153 games, 1997

Most total bases, career
2,187—Dante Bichette

Most long hits
105—Todd Helton, 159 games, 2001

Most long hits, career
489—Dante Bichette

Most extra bases on long hits
205—Todd Helton, 159 games, 2001

Most extra bases on long hits, career
913—Larry Walker

Most sacrifice hits
22—Neifi Perez, 162 games, 1998

Most sacrifice flies
12—Jeff Cirillo, 157 games, 2000

Most bases on balls
103—Todd Helton, 160 games, 2000

Most bases on balls, career
396—Larry Walker

Most strikeouts
157—Andres Galarraga, 159 games, 1996

Most strikeouts, career
620—Dante Bichette

Fewest strikeouts
29—Juan Pierre, 156 games, 2001

Most hit by pitch
21—Eric Young, 141 games, 1996

Most runs batted in
150—Andres Galarraga, 159 games, 1996

Most runs batted in, career
826—Dante Bichette

Highest batting average
.379—Larry Walker, 127 games, 1999

Highest batting average, career
.341—Larry Walker

Highest slugging average
.720—Larry Walker, 153 games, 1997

Highest slugging average, career
.642—Larry Walker

Longest batting streak
23—Dante Bichette, 1995

Most grounded into double play
25—Charlie Hayes, 157 games, 1993

Fewest grounded into double play
4—Neifi Perez, 157 games, 1999

BASERUNNING

Most stolen bases
53—Eric Young, 141 games, 1996

Most stolen bases, career
180—Eric Young

Most caught stealing
19—Eric Young, 144 games, 1993
  Eric Young, 141 games, 1996

PITCHING

Most games
78—Chuck McElroy, 1998
  Mike Myers, 2000

Most games, career
356—Curtis Leskanic

Most games started
35—Kevin Ritz, 1996
  Darryl Kile, 1998

Most games started, career
129—Pedro Astacio

Most complete games
7—Pedro Astacio, 1999

Most complete games, career
14—Pedro Astacio

Most games finished
63—Dave Veres, 1999

Most innings
232.0—Pedro Astacio, 1999

Most innings, career
827.1—Pedro Astacio

Most games won
17—Kevin Ritz, 1996
  Pedro Astasio, 1999

Most games won, career
53—Pedro Astacio

Most games lost
17—Darryl Kile, 1998

Most games lost, career
48—Pedro Astacio

Highest winning percentage
.607—Kevin Ritz (17-11), 1996
  Pedro Astacio (17-11), 1999

Longest winning streak
9 games—Julian Tavarez, 2000

Longest losing streak
8 games—Greg Harris, 1994
  Darryl Kile, 1998

Most saves
31—Dave Veres, 1999

Most bases on balls
109—Darryl Kile, 1999

Most bases on balls, career
290—Pedro Astacio

Most strikeouts
210—Pedro Astacio, 1999

Most strikeouts, career
749—Pedro Astacio

Most strikeouts, game
14—Darryl Kile, August 20, 1998

Most shutouts won
2—Roger Bailey, 1997

Most shutouts won, career
2—Roger Bailey
  Brian Bohanon
  John Thomson

Most 1-0 shutouts won
Never occurred

Most runs
160—Pedro Astacio, 1998

Most earned runs
145—Pedro Astacio, 1998

Most hits
258—Pedro Astacio, 1999

Most hit batsmen
17—Pedro Astacio, 1998

Most wild pitches
3—Marvin Freeman, 1996
  Darryl Kile, 1999

Most home runs allowed
49—Pedro Astacio, 1998

Most sacrifice hits
18—Brian Bohanon, 1999

Most sacrifice flies
10—Pedro Astacio, 1999

Lowest ERA
4.00—Armando Reynoso, 1993

CLUB RECORDS

Most players
53 in 2001

Fewest players
42 in 1998

Most games
162 in 1993, 1996, 1997, 1998, 1999,
  2000, 2001

Most at-bats
5,717 in 1999

Most runs
968 in 2000

Fewest runs
758 in 1993

Most opponents' runs
1,028 in 1999

Most hits
1,664 in 2000

Fewest hits
1,507 in 1993

Most singles
1,130 in 2000

Most doubles
333 in 1998

Most triples
61 in 2001

Most homers
239 in 1997

Fewest homers
142 in 1993

**Most homers at Mile High Stadium,
  home and opponents**
184 in 1993

**Most homers at Coors Field, home and
  opponents**
303 in 1999

Most grand slams
5 in 1994, 1998, 2000

Most pinch home runs
11 in 1995

Most total bases
2,748 in 2001

Most long hits
598 in 2001

Most extra bases on long hits
1,085 in 2001

Most sacrifice hits
98 in 1998

Most sacrifice flies
75 in 2000

Most stolen bases
201 in 1996

Most caught stealing
90 in 1993

Most bases on balls
601 in 2000

Most strikeouts
1,108 in 1996

Fewest strikeouts
863 in 1999

Most hit by pitch
82 in 1996

Fewest hit by pitch
37 in 1998

Most runs batted in
909 in 1996

Highest batting average
.294 in 2000

Lowest batting average
.273 in 1993

Highest slugging average
.483 in 2001

Lowest slugging average
.422 in 1993

Most grounded into double play
148 in 1998

Fewest grounded into double play
116 in 2001

Most left on bases
1,198 in 2000

Fewest left on bases
978 in 1993

Most .300 hitters
5 in 1996

Most putouts
4,298 in 1997, 1998

Fewest putouts
4,268 in 1996

Most assists
1,946 in 1997

Fewest assists
1,694 in 2001

Most chances accepted
6,244 in 1997

Fewest chances accepted
5,984 in 2001

Most errors
167 in 1993

Most errorless games
93 in 2001

Most consecutive errorless games
13 in 1998

Fewest errors
94 in 2000

Most double plays
202 in 1997

Fewest double plays
149 in 1993

Most passed balls
19 in 1996

Fewest passed balls
5 in 1997

Highest fielding average
.985 in 2000

Lowest fielding average
.973 in 1993

Highest home attendance
4,483,350 in 1993

Highest road attendance
2,695,071 in 1993

Most games won
83 in 1996, 1997

Most games lost
95 in 1993

Most games won, month
18 in August 2000

Most games lost, month
22 in July 2000

Games won, league
667 in 9 years

Games lost, league
728 in 9 years

Highest percentage games won
.512 in 1996, 1997 (won 83, lost 79)

Most shutouts won
8 in 2001

Most shutouts lost
13 in 1993

Most 1-0 games won
2 in 1994, 1998

Most 1-0 games lost
1 in 1993, 2001

Most consecutive games won
9 in 1997

Most consecutive games lost
13 in 1993

Number of times league champions
0

Number of last-place finishes
0

Most runs, game
19 vs. Atlanta, June 7, 1996
  vs. Arizona, June 18, 2000

Most runs by opponent, game
26 by Chicago, August 18, 1995

Most runs, shutout game
11 vs. Florida, August 6, 1996
  vs. San Diego, September 13, 2000

Most runs by opponent, shutout game
17 by Florida, September 17, 1995

Most runs, inning
11 vs. San Diego, July 12, 1996, seventh
  inning

Longest 1-0 game won
11 innings vs. San Diego, September 20,
  1998

Longest 1-0 game lost
9 innings by Chicago, July 15, 1993
  by Florida, May 19, 2001

Most hits, game
24 vs. Montreal, May 3, 2000

Most home runs, game
7 vs. Montreal, April 5, 1997

**Most consecutive games with one or
  more homers**
17 (24 home runs), 1993
  (36 home runs), 1996

Most total bases, game
42 vs. Arizona, June 18, 2000

Largest crowd, day game
80,227 vs. Montreal, April 9, 1993

Largest crowd, doubleheader
60,613 vs. New York, August 21, 1993

Largest crowd, night game
73,957 vs. San Francisco, June 24, 1994

Largest crowd, home opener
80,227 vs. Montreal, April 9, 1993

FLORIDA MARLINS
YEARLY FINISHES
EAST DIVISION

Year	Position	W	L	Pct.	*GB	Manager	Attendance
1993	6th	64	98	.395	33.0	Rene Lachemann	3,064,847
1994	5th	51	64	.443	23.5	Rene Lachemann	1,937,467
1995	4th	67	76	.469	22.5	Rene Lachemann	1,700,466
1996	3rd	80	82	.494	16.0	Rene Lachemann, John Boles	1,746,767
1997	2nd†‡	92	70	.568	9.0	Jim Leyland	2,364,387
1998	5th	54	108	.333	52.0	Jim Leyland	1,750,395
1999	5th	64	98	.395	39.0	John Boles	1,369,421
2000	3rd	79	82	.491	15.5	John Boles	1,218,326
2001	4th	76	86	.469	12.0	John Boles, Tony Perez	1,261,220

*Games behind winner. †Won division series. ‡Won championship series.

INDIVIDUAL RECORDS (1993 TO DATE)

SERVICE

Most years by non-pitcher
6—Gary Sheffield
Luis Castillo
Charles Johnson

Most years by pitcher
5—Chris Hammond
Robb Nen
Pat Rapp
Antonio Alfonseca

BATTING

Most games
162—Jeff Conine, 1993

Most games, career
718—Jeff Conine

Most at-bats
617—Edgar Renteria, 154 games, 1997

Most at-bats, career
2,531—Jeff Conine

Most runs
123—Cliff Floyd, 149 games, 2001

Most runs, career
365—Gary Sheffield

Most hits
180—Luis Castillo, 136 games, 2000

Most hits, career
737—Jeff Conine

Most singles
158—Luis Castillo, 136 games, 2000

Most singles, career
503—Jeff Conine

Most doubles
45—Cliff Floyd, 153 games, 1998

Most doubles, career
147—Cliff Floyd

Most triples
10—Luis Castillo, 134 games, 2001

Most triples, career
22—Mark Kotsay

Most homers by righthander
42—Gary Sheffield, 161 games, 1996

Most homers by lefthander
31—Cliff Floyd, 149 games, 2001

Most homers by switch-hitter
20—Orestes Destrade, 153 games, 1993

Most homers by rookie
26—Preston Wilson, 149 games, 1999

Most homers at home
19—Gary Sheffield, 1996

Most homers on road
23—Gary Sheffield, 1996

Most homers, month
11—Gary Sheffield, April 1996

Most homers by righthander, career
122—Gary Sheffield

Most homers by lefthander, career
92—Cliff Floyd

Most homers by switch-hitter, career
25—Orestes Destrade

Most grand slams
3—Bobby Bonilla, 153 games, 1997

Most grand slams, career
3—Kurt Abbott
Bobby Bonilla
Jeff Conine
Gary Sheffield
Devon White
Derrek Lee
Mike Lowell

Most total bases
324—Gary Sheffield, 161 games, 1996

Most total bases, career
1,181—Jeff Conine

Most long hits
79—Cliff Floyd, 149 games, 2001

Most long hits, career
248—Cliff Floyd

Most extra bases on long hits
161—Gary Sheffield, 161 games, 1996

Most extra bases on long hits, career
478—Gary Sheffield

Most sacrifice hits
19—Edgar Renteria, 154 games, 1997

Most sacrifice flies
12—Jeff Conine, 133 games, 1995

Most bases on balls
142—Gary Sheffield, 161 games, 1996

Most bases on balls, career
424—Gary Sheffield

Most strikeouts
187—Preston Wilson, 161 games, 2000

Most strikeouts, career
531—Jeff Conine

Fewest strikeouts
46—Mark Kotsay, 152 games, 2000

Most hit by pitch
15—Gary Sheffield, 135 games, 1997

Most runs batted in
121—Preston Wilson, 161 games, 2000

Most runs batted in, career
422—Jeff Conine

Highest batting average
.334—Luis Castillo, 136 games, 2000

Highest batting average, career
.295—Cliff Floyd

Highest slugging average
.624—Gary Sheffield, 161 games, 1996

Highest slugging average
.543—Gary Sheffield

Longest batting streak
22 games—Edgar Renteria, 1996
Luis Castillo, 1999

Most grounded into double play
22—Greg Colbrunn, 141 games, 1996

Fewest grounded into double play
3—Luis Castillo, 128 games, 1999

BASERUNNING

Most stolen bases
62—Luis Castillo, 136 games, 2000

Most stolen bases, career
181—Luis Castillo

Most caught stealing
22—Chuck Carr, 142 games, 1993
Edgar Renteria, 133 games, 1998
Luis Castillo, 136 games, 2000

PITCHING

Most games
75—Robb Nen, 1996

Most games, career
274—Antonio Alfonseca

Most games started
34—Charlie Hough, 1993
Ryan Dempster, 2001

Most games started, career
115—Pat Rapp

Most complete games
9—Livan Hernandez, 1998

Most complete games, career
11—Kevin Brown
Livan Hernandez

Most games finished
66—Robb Nen, 1996

Most innings
237.1—Kevin Brown, 1997

Most innings, career
665.2—Pat Rapp

Most games won
17—Kevin Brown, 1996
Alex Fernandez, 1997

Most games won, career
37—Pat Rapp
Ryan Dempster

Most games lost
17—Jack Armstrong, 1993

Most games lost, career
43—Pat Rapp

Highest winning percentage
.667—Kevin Brown (16-8), 1997

Longest winning streak
9—Pat Rapp, 1995
Livan Hernandez, 1997

Longest losing streak
8—Reid Cornelius, 2000
Brad Penny, 2001

Most saves
45—Bryan Harvey, 1993
Antonio Alfonseca, 2000

Most bases on balls
119—Al Leiter, 1996

Most bases on balls, career
340—Ryan Dempster

Most strikeouts
209—Ryan Dempster, 2000

Most strikeouts, career
541—Ryan Dempster

Most strikeouts, game
13—Brad Penny, June 26, 2001

Most shutouts won
3—Kevin Brown, 1996

Most shutouts won, career
5—Kevin Brown

Most 1-0 shutouts won
1—Alex Fernandez, 1997

Most runs
133—Livan Hernandez, 1998

Most earned runs
123—Livan Hernandez, 1998

Most hits
265—Livan Hernandez, 1998

Most hit batsmen
16—Kevin Brown, 1996

Most wild pitches
15—Matt Clement, 2001

Most home runs allowed
37—Livan Hernandez, 1998

Most sacrifice hits
16—Brian Meadows, 1999

Most sacrifice flies
12—Jesus Sanchez, 2000

Lowest ERA
1.89—Kevin Brown, 233 innings, 1996

CLUB RECORDS

Most players
49 in 1998

Fewest players
40 in 2000

Most games
162 in 1993, 1996, 1997, 1998, 1999,
2001

Most at-bats
5,578 in 1999

Most runs
742 in 2001

Fewest runs
581 in 1993

Most opponents' runs
923 in 1998

Most hits
1,465 in 1999

Fewest hits
1,356 in 1993

Most singles
1,034 in 1993

Most doubles
325 in 2001

Most triples
44 in 1999

Most homers
166 in 2001

Fewest homers
94 in 1993

**Most homers at Pro Player Stadium,
home and opponents**
153 in 2001

Most grand slams
9 in 1997

Most pinch home runs
8 in 1999

Most total bases
2,344 in 2001

Most long hits
521 in 2001

Most extra bases on long hits
883 in 2001

Most sacrifice hits
71 in 1997

Most sacrifice flies
56 in 1999

Most stolen bases
168 in 2000

Most caught stealing
58 in 1997

Most bases on balls
686 in 1997

Most strikeouts
1,184 in 2000

Fewest strikeouts
1,054 in 1993

Most hit by pitch
67 in 2001

Most runs batted in
713 in 2001

Highest batting average
.264 in 2001

Lowest batting average
.248 in 1993, 1998

Highest slugging average
.423 in 2001

Lowest slugging average
.346 in 1993

Most grounded into double play
138 in 1996

Fewest grounded into double play
100 in 2000

Most left on bases
1,248 in 1997

Fewest left on bases
1,117 in 2001

Most .300 hitters
1 in 1995, 1996, 1999, 2000, 2001

Most putouts
4,349 in 1998

Fewest putouts
4,289 in 2000

Most assists
1,797 in 1996

Fewest assists
1,650 in 1997

Most chances accepted
6,125 in 1996

Fewest chances accepted
5,981 in 2001

Most errors
129 in 1998

Most errorless games
84 in 1999

Most consecutive errorless games
8 in 1994, 1999

Fewest errors
103 in 2001

Most double plays
187 in 1996

Fewest double plays
130 in 1993

Most passed balls
29 in 1993

Fewest passed balls
7 in 1997

Highest fielding average
.983 in 2001

Lowest fielding average
.979 in 1998, 1999

Highest home attendance
3,064,847 in 1993

Highest road attendance
2,701,068 in 1993

Most games won
92 in 1997

Most games lost
108 in 1998

Most games won, month
19 in August 1997

Most games lost, month
20 in May 1995, May 1998, August
1998, August 2001

Games won, league
627 in 9 years

Games lost, league
764 in 9 years

Highest percentage games won
.568 in 1997 (won 92, lost 70)

Lowest percentage games won
.333 in 1998 (won 54, lost 108)

Most shutouts won
13 in 1996

Most shutouts lost
14 in 1993, 1996

Most 1-0 games won
3 in 2001

Most 1-0 games lost
4 in 1993

Most consecutive games won
9 in 1996

Most consecutive games lost
11 in 1998

Number of times league champions
1

Number of last-place finishes
2

Most runs, game
17 vs. Colorado, September 17, 1995

Most runs by opponent, game
22 by Cincinnati, August 31, 1996

Most runs, shutout game
17 vs. Colorado, September 17, 1995

Most runs by opponent, shutout game
18 by Atlanta, October 3, 1999

Most runs, inning
8 vs. Colorado, April 25, 1993, fourth
    inning
  vs. San Diego, April 9, 1994, seventh
    inning
  vs. Philadelphia, July 13, 1997, fourth
    inning
  vs. Tampa Bay A.L., June 5, 1999,
    sixth inning
  vs. Montreal, September 17, 2001,
    sixth inning

Longest 1-0 game won
13 innings vs. Philadelphia, September
    26, 1998

Longest 1-0 game lost
None over nine innings

Most hits, game
24 vs. Houston, July 15, 1996

Most home runs, game
4 vs. San Francisco, April 30, 1995
  vs. Montreal, June 30, 1995
  vs. Colorado, September 16, 1995
  vs. Colorado, September 17, 1995
  vs. St. Louis, August 29, 1996
  vs. Philadelphia, September 17, 1996
  vs. Chicago, August 26, 1997
  vs. Los Angeles, September 8, 1997
  vs. Colorado, September 16, 1997
  vs. Arizona, April 26, 1998
  vs. San Francisco, May 6, 1998
  vs. St. Louis, August 26, 1998, 10
    innings
  vs. Milwaukee, May 14, 1999
  vs. Chicago, May 24, 1999
  vs. St. Louis, May 25, 2000
  vs. Chicago, June 24, 2000
  vs. Atlanta, April 8, 2001
  vs. Houston, April 29, 2001

**Most consecutive games with one or
    more homers**
11 in 1995 (18 homers)

Most total bases, game
39 vs. Colorado, September 17, 1995

Largest crowd, day game
45,900 vs. New York, October 3, 1993

Largest crowd, doubleheader
37,007 vs. Philadelphia, September 27,
    1998

Largest crowd, night game
45,796 vs. San Francisco, August 27,
    1993

Largest crowd, home opener
43,290 vs. Houston, April 12, 1994

HOUSTON ASTROS
YEARLY FINISHES

(Known as Houston Colt .45s through 1964)

Year	Position	W	L	Pct.	*GB	Manager	Attendance
1962	8th	64	96	.400	36.5	Harry Craft	924,456
1963	9th	66	96	.407	33.0	Harry Craft	719,502
1964	9th	66	96	.407	27.0	Harry Craft, Luman Harris	725,773
1965	9th	65	97	.401	32.0	Luman Harris	2,151,470
1966	8th	72	90	.444	23.0	Grady Hatton	1,872,108
1967	9th	69	93	.426	32.5	Grady Hatton	1,348,303
1968	10th	72	90	.444	25.0	Grady Hatton, Harry Walker	1,312,887

WEST DIVISION

Year	Position	W	L	Pct.	*GB	Manager	Attendance
1969	5th	81	81	.500	12.0	Harry Walker	1,442,995
1970	4th	79	83	.488	23.0	Harry Walker	1,253,444
1971	4th (tied)	79	83	.488	11.0	Harry Walker	1,261,589
1972	2nd	84	69	.549	10.5	Harry Walker, Salty Parker, Leo Durocher	1,469,247
1973	4th	82	80	.506	17.0	Leo Durocher, Preston Gomez	1,394,004
1974	4th	81	81	.500	21.0	Preston Gomez	1,090,728
1975	6th	64	97	.398	43.5	Preston Gomez, Bill Virdon	858,002
1976	3rd	80	82	.494	22.0	Bill Virdon	886,146
1977	3rd	81	81	.500	17.0	Bill Virdon	1,109,560
1978	5th	74	88	.457	21.0	Bill Virdon	1,126,145
1979	2nd	89	73	.549	1.5	Bill Virdon	1,900,312
1980	1st†‡	93	70	.571	+1.0	Bill Virdon	2,278,217
1981	3rd/1st∞	61	49	.555	§	Bill Virdon	1,321,282
1982	5th	77	85	.475	12.0	Bill Virdon, Bob Lillis	1,558,555
1983	3rd	85	77	.525	6.0	Bob Lillis	1,351,962
1984	2nd (tied)	80	82	.494	12.0	Bob Lillis	1,229,862
1985	3rd (tied)	83	79	.512	12.0	Bob Lillis	1,184,314
1986	1st‡	96	66	.593	+10.0	Hal Lanier	1,734,276
1987	3rd	76	86	.469	14.0	Hal Lanier	1,909,902
1988	5th	82	80	.506	12.5	Hal Lanier	1,933,505
1989	3rd	86	76	.531	6.0	Art Howe	1,834,908
1990	4th (tied)	75	87	.463	16.0	Art Howe	1,310,927
1991	6th	65	97	.401	29.0	Art Howe	1,196,152
1992	4th	81	81	.500	17.0	Art Howe	1,211,412
1993	3rd	85	77	.525	19.0	Art Howe	2,084,546

CENTRAL DIVISION

Year	Position	W	L	Pct.	*GB	Manager	Attendance
1994	2nd	66	49	.574	0.5	Terry Collins	1,561,136
1995	2nd	76	68	.528	9.0	Terry Collins	1,363,801
1996	2nd	82	80	.506	6.0	Terry Collins	1,975,888
1997	1st∞	84	78	.519	+5.0	Larry Dierker	2,046,781
1998	1st∞	102	60	.630	+12.5	Larry Dierker	2,450,451
1999	1st∞	97	65	.599	+1.5	Larry Dierker	2,706,017
2000	4th	72	90	.444	23.0	Larry Dierker	3,056,139
2001	1st (tied)∞	93	69	.574	0.0	Larry Dierker	2,904,280

*Games behind winner. †Won division playoff. ‡Lost championship series. §First half 28-29; second 33-20. ∞Lost division series.

SERVICE

Most years by non-pitcher
14—Bob Watson
Terry Puhl
Craig Biggio
Most years by pitcher
13—Larry Dierker

BATTING

Most games
162—Enos Cabell, 1978
Bill Doran, 1987
Jeff Bagwell, 1992, 1996, 1997, 1999
Craig Biggio, 1992, 1996, 1997
Steve Finley, 1992
Most games, career
1,955—Craig Biggio
Most at-bats
660—Enos Cabell, 162 games, 1978
Most at-bats, career
7,383—Craig Biggio
Most runs
152—Jeff Bagwell, 159 games, 2000
Most runs, career
1,305—Craig Biggio
Most hits
210—Craig Biggio, 160 games, 1998
Most hits, career
2,149—Craig Biggio
Most singles
160—Sonny Jackson, 150 games, 1966
Most singles, career
1,486—Craig Biggio
Most doubles
56—Craig Biggio, 160 games, 1999
Most doubles, career
437—Craig Biggio
Most triples
14—Roger Metzger, 154 games, 1973
Most triples, career
80—Jose Cruz
Most homers by righthander
47—Jeff Bagwell, 159 games, 2000
Most homers by lefthander
23—Franklin Stubbs, 146 games, 1990
Most homers by switch-hitter
34—Lance Berkman, 156 games, 2001
Most homers by rookie
20—Glenn Davis, 100 games, 1985
Most homers at home
28—Jeff Bagwell, 2000
Most homers on road
30, Jeff Bagwell, 1999
Most homers, month
13—Jeff Bagwell, June 1994
Most homers by righthander, career
349—Jeff Bagwell
Most homers by lefthander, career
138—Jose Cruz
Most homers by switch-hitter, career
103—Ken Caminiti
Most grand slams
2—Held by many players
Most grand slams, career
6—Bob Aspromonte
Most total bases
363—Jeff Bagwell, 159 games, 2000

Most total bases, career
3,296—Jeff Bagwell
Most long hits
94—Lance Berkman, 156 games, 2001
Most long hits, career
769—Jeff Bagwell
Most extra bases on long hits
180—Jeff Bagwell, 159 games, 2000
Richard Hidalgo, 153 games, 2000
Most extra bases on long hits, career
1,493—Jeff Bagwell
Most sacrifice hits
34—Craig Reynolds, 146 games, 1979
Most sacrifice flies
13—Ray Knight, 158 games, 1982
Jeff Bagwell, 162 games, 1992
Most bases on balls
149—Jeff Bagwell, 162 games, 1999
Most bases on balls, career
1,098—Jeff Bagwell
Most strikeouts
145—Lee May, 148 games, 1972
Most strikeouts, career
1,146—Craig Biggio
Fewest strikeouts
39—Greg Gross, 156 games, 1974
Most hit by pitch
34—Craig Biggio, 162 games, 1997
Most runs batted in
135—Jeff Bagwell, 162 games, 1997
Most runs batted in, career
1,223—Jeff Bagwell
Most game-winning RBIs
18—Dickie Thon, 154 games, 1983
Highest batting average
.355—Moises Alou, 126 games, 2000
Highest batting average, career
.303—Jeff Bagwell
Highest slugging average
.636—Richard Hidalgo, 153 games, 2000
Highest slugging average, career
.554—Jeff Bagwell
Longest batting streak
24 games—Tony Eusebio, 2000
Most grounded into double play
23—Doug Rader, 156 games, 1970
Fewest grounded into double play
0—Craig Biggio, 162 games, 1997

BASERUNNING

Most stolen bases
65—Gerald Young, 149 games, 1988
Most stolen bases, career
487—Cesar Cedeno
Most caught stealing
27—Gerald Young, 149 games, 1988

PITCHING

Most games
82—Juan Agosto, 1990
Most games, career
563—Dave Smith
Most games started
40—Jerry Reuss, 1973
Most games started, career
320—Larry Dierker

Most complete games
20—Larry Dierker, 1969
Most complete games, career
106—Larry Dierker
Most games finished
70—Doug Jones, 1992
Most innings
305—Larry Dierker, 1969
Most innings, career
2,296—Larry Dierker
Most games won
22—Mike Hampton, 1999
Most games won, career
144—Joe Niekro
Most 20-victory seasons
2—Joe Niekro
Most games lost, season
20—Dick Farrell, 1962
Most games lost, career
117—Larry Dierker
Highest winning percentage
.846—Mike Hampton (22-4), 1999
Longest winning streak
12 games—Mark Portugal, 1993
Longest losing streak
13 games—Jose Lima, 2000
Most saves
39—Billy Wagner, 1999, 2001
Most bases on balls
151—J.R. Richard, 1976
Most bases on balls, career
818—Joe Niekro
Most strikeouts
313—J.R. Richard, 1979
Most strikeouts, career
1,866—Nolan Ryan
Most strikeouts, game
18—Don Wilson, July 14, 1968, second game
Most shutouts
6—Dave A. Roberts, 1973
Most shutouts won, career
25—Larry Dierker
Most 1-0 shutouts won
3—Bob Bruce, 1964
Bob Knepper, 1981
Most runs
152—Jose Lima, 2000
Most earned runs
145—Jose Lima, 2000
Jerry Reuss, 1973
Most hits
271—Jerry Reuss, 1973
Most hit batsmen
16—Jack Billingham, 1971
Darryl Kile, 1996
Most wild pitches
21—Joe Niekro, 1985
Most home runs
48—Jose Lima, 2000
Most sacrifice hits
22—Bob Knepper, 1986
Most sacrifice flies
13—Mark Lemongello, 1978
Jim Deshaies, 1988
Lowest ERA
2.21—Danny Darwin, 162.2 innings, 1990

REGULAR SEASON N.L.—Houston Astros

CLUB RECORDS

Most players
48 in 1965

Fewest players
32 in 1972

Most games
163 in 1966, 1980

Most at-bats
5,641 in 1998

Most runs
938 in 2000

Fewest runs
464 in 1963

Most opponents' runs
944 in 2000

Most hits
1,578 in 1998

Fewest hits
1,184 in 1963

Most singles
1,097 in 1984

Most doubles
326 in 1998

Most triples
67 in 1980, 1984

Most homers
249 in 2000

Fewest homers
49 in 1979

Most homers at Colt Stadium, home and opponents
85 in 1962

Most homers at Astrodome, home and opponents
153 in 1998

Most homers at Enron Field, home and opponents
266 in 2000

Most grand slams
7 in 2001

Most pinch home runs
10 in 1995

Most total bases
2,655 in 2000

Most long hits
574 in 2000

Most extra bases on long hits
1,108 in 2000

Most sacrifice hits
109 in 1979

Most sacrifice flies
61 in 2000

Most stolen bases
198 in 1988

Most caught stealing
95 in 1979, 1983

Most bases on balls
728 in 1999

Most strikeouts
1,138 in 1999

Fewest strikeouts
719 in 1976

Most hit by pitch
100 in 1997

Fewest hit by pitch
13 in 1980

Most runs batted in
900 in 2000

Most game-winning RBIs
90 in 1986

Highest batting average
.280 in 1998

Lowest batting average
.220 in 1963

Most .300 hitters
4 in 1998

Highest slugging average
.477 in 2000

Lowest slugging average
.301 in 1963

Most grounded into double play
154 in 2000

Fewest grounded into double play
76 in 1983

Most left on bases
1,252 in 1999

Fewest left on bases
1,040 in 1964

Most putouts
4,448 in 1980

Fewest putouts
4,284 in 1964

Most assists
1,880 in 1975

Fewest assists
1,561 in 2000

Most chances accepted
6,255 in 1975

Fewest chances accepted
5,827 in 1972

Most errors
174 in 1966

Fewest errors
106 in 1971, 1999

Most errorless games
87 in 2001

Most consecutive errorless games
11 in 1973, 1994

Most double plays
175 in 1999

Fewest double plays
100 in 1963

Most passed balls
38 in 1984

Fewest passed balls
4 in 2001

Highest fielding average
.983 in 1971, 1998, 1999

Lowest fielding average
.972 in 1966

Highest home attendance
3,056,139 in 2000

Highest road attendance
2,446,596 in 2000

Most games won
102 in 1998

Most games lost
97 in 1965, 1975, 1991

Most games won, month
22 in August 1998

Most games lost, month
24 in July 1962

Highest percentage games won
.630 in 1998 (won 102, lost 60)

Lowest percentage games won
.398 in 1975 (won 64, lost 97)

Games won, league
3,145 in 40 years

Games lost, league
3,207 in 40 years

Most shutouts won
19 in 1979, 1981, 1986

Most shutouts lost
23 in 1963

Most 1-0 games won
9 in 1976

Most 1-0 games lost
6 in 1964, 1969

Most consecutive games won
12 in 1999

Most consecutive games lost
11 in 1995

Number of times league champions
0

Number of last-place finishes
3

Longest 1-0 game won
24 innings vs. New York, April 15, 1968

Longest 1-0 game lost
13 innings vs. Cincinnati, August 6, 1962

Most runs, inning
12 vs. Philadelphia, May 31, 1975, eighth inning

Most runs, game
19 vs. Chicago, June 25, 1995
vs. Pittsburgh, May 11, 1999

Most runs by opponent, game
22 by Chicago, June 3, 1987

Most runs, shutout game
15 vs. Montreal, April 26, 1998

Most runs by opponent, shutout game
16 by Philadelphia, September 10, 1963

Most runs, doubleheader shutout
No performance

Most hits, game
25 vs. Atlanta, May 30, 1976, second game
vs. Cincinnati, July 2, 1976, first game, 14 innings

Most home runs, game
7 vs. Chicago, September 9, 2000

Most consecutive games with one or more homers
18 (33 homers), 2000

Most total bases, game
44 vs. Chicago, September 9, 2000

Largest crowd, day game
52,199 vs. Chicago, August 16, 1998

Largest crowd, doubleheader
45,115 vs. Atlanta, August 4, 1979

Largest crowd, night game
54,037 vs. Cincinnati, September 28, 1999

Largest crowd, home opener
51,668 vs. Chicago, April 6, 1999

LOS ANGELES DODGERS
YEARLY FINISHES

Year	Position	W	L	Pct.	*GB	Manager	Attendance
1958	7th	71	83	.461	21.0	Walter Alston	1,845,556
1959	1st†	88	68	.564	+2.0	Walter Alston	2,071,045
1960	4th	82	72	.532	13.0	Walter Alston	2,253,887
1961	2nd	89	65	.578	4.0	Walter Alston	1,804,250
1962	2nd‡	102	63	.618	1.0	Walter Alston	2,755,184
1963	1st	99	63	.611	+6.0	Walter Alston	2,538,602
1964	6th (tied)	80	82	.494	13.0	Walter Alston	2,228,751
1965	1st	97	65	.599	+2.0	Walter Alston	2,553,577
1966	1st	95	67	.586	+1.5	Walter Alston	2,617,029
1967	8th	73	89	.451	28.5	Walter Alston	1,664,362
1968	7th	76	86	.469	21.0	Walter Alston	1,581,093

WEST DIVISION

Year	Position	W	L	Pct.	*GB	Manager	Attendance
1969	4th	85	77	.525	8.0	Walter Alston	1,784,527
1970	2nd	87	74	.540	14.5	Walter Alston	1,697,142
1971	2nd	89	73	.549	1.0	Walter Alston	2,064,594
1972	3rd	85	70	.548	10.5	Walter Alston	1,860,858
1973	2nd	95	66	.590	3.5	Walter Alston	2,136,192
1974	1st§	102	60	.630	+4.0	Walter Alston	2,632,474
1975	2nd	88	74	.543	20.0	Walter Alston	2,539,349
1976	2nd	92	70	.568	10.0	Walter Alston, Tommy Lasorda	2,386,301
1977	1st§	98	64	.605	+10.0	Tommy Lasorda	2,955,087
1978	1st§	95	67	.586	+2.5	Tommy Lasorda	3,347,845
1979	3rd	79	83	.488	11.5	Tommy Lasorda	2,860,954
1980	2nd∞	92	71	.564	1.0	Tommy Lasorda	3,249,287
1981	1st/4th◆§	63	47	.573	▲	Tommy Lasorda	2,381,292
1982	2nd	88	74	.543	1.0	Tommy Lasorda	3,608,881
1983	1st■	91	71	.652	+3.0	Tommy Lasorda	3,510,313
1984	4th	79	83	.488	13.0	Tommy Lasorda	3,134,824
1985	1st■	95	67	.586	+5.5	Tommy Lasorda	3,264,593
1986	5th	73	89	.451	23.0	Tommy Lasorda	3,023,208
1987	4th	73	89	.451	17.0	Tommy Lasorda	2,797,409
1988	1st§	94	67	.584	+7.0	Tommy Lasorda	2,980,262
1989	4th	77	83	.481	14.0	Tommy Lasorda	2,944,653
1990	2nd	86	76	.531	5.0	Tommy Lasorda	3,002,396
1991	2nd	93	69	.574	1.0	Tommy Lasorda	3,348,170
1992	6th	63	99	.389	35.0	Tommy Lasorda	2,473,266
1993	4th	81	81	.500	23.0	Tommy Lasorda	3,170,392
1994	1st	58	56	.509	+3.5	Tommy Lasorda	2,279,355
1995	1st▼	78	66	.542	+1.0	Tommy Lasorda	2,766,251
1996	2nd▼	90	72	.556	1.0	Tommy Lasorda, Bill Russell	3,188,454
1997	2nd	88	74	.543	2.0	Bill Russell	3,319,504
1998	3rd	83	79	.512	15.0	Bill Russell, Glenn Hoffman	3,089,201
1999	3rd	77	85	.475	23.0	Dave Johnson	3,095,346
2000	2nd	86	76	.531	11.0	Dave Johnson	3,010,819
2001	3rd	86	76	.531	6.0	Jim Tracy	3,017,502

*Games behind winner. †Won pennant playoff. ‡Lost pennant playoff. §Won championship series. ∞Lost division playoff. ▲First half 36-21; second half 27-26. ◆Won division series. ■Lost championship series. ▼Lost division series.

INDIVIDUAL RECORDS (1958 TO DATE)

SERVICE

Most years by non-pitcher
18—Bill Russell

Most years by pitcher
16—Don Sutton

BATTING

Most games
165—Maury Wills, 1962

Most games, career
2,181—Bill Russell

Most at-bats
695—Maury Wills, 165 games, 1962

Most at-bats, career
7,495—Willie Davis

Most runs
130—Maury Wills, 165 games, 1962

Most runs, career
1,004—Willie Davis

Most hits
230—Tommy Davis, 163 games, 1962

Most hits, career
2,091—Willie Davis

Most singles
179—Maury Wills, 165 games, 1962

Most singles, career
1,530—Bill Russell

Most doubles
47—Wes Parker, 161 games, 1970

Most doubles, career
333—Steve Garvey

Most triples
16—Willie Davis, 146 games, 1970

Most triples, career
110—Willie Davis

Most homers by righthander
43—Gary Sheffield, 141 games, 2000

Most homers by lefthander
49—Shawn Green, 161 games, 2001

Most homers by switch-hitter
32—Reggie Smith, 148 games, 1977

Most homers by rookie
35—Mike Piazza, 149 games, 1993

Most homers, month
15—Pedro Guerrero, June, 1985

Most homers by righthander, career
257—Eric Karros

Most homers by lefthander, career
154—Willie Davis

Most homers by switch-hitter, career
97—Reggie Smith

Most homers at home
23—Gary Sheffield, 2000

Most homers on road
30—Shawn Green, 2001

Most grand slams
3—Kal Daniels, 130 games, 1990
Mike Piazza, 37 games, 1998

Most grand slams, career
8—Mike Piazza

Most total bases
370—Shawn Green, 161 games, 2001

Most total bases, career
3,094—Willie Davis

Most long hits
84—Shawn Green, 161 games, 2001

Most long hits, career
585—Willie Davis

Most extra bases on long hits
186—Shawn Green, 161 games, 2001

Most extra bases on long hits, career
1,065—Eric Karros

Most sacrifice hits
25—Jose Offerman, 158 games, 1993

Most sacrifice flies
13—Reggie Smith, 128 games, 1978

Most bases on balls
110—Jimmy Wynn, 130 games, 1975

Most bases on balls, career
765—Ron Cey

Most strikeouts
149—Bill Grabarkewitz, 156 games, 1970

Most strikeouts, career
1,031—Eric Karros

Fewest strikeouts
28—Jim Gilliam, 151 games, 1960

Most hit by pitch
16—Lou Johnson, 131 games, 1965

Most runs batted in
153—Tommy Davis, 163 games, 1962

Most runs batted in, career
992—Steve Garvey

Most game-winning RBIs
18—Pedro Guerrero, 150 games, 1982

Highest batting average
.362—Mike Piazza, 152 games, 1997

Highest batting average, career
.331—Mike Piazza

Highest slugging average
.643—Gary Sheffield, 141 games, 2000

Highest slugging average, career
.573—Gary Sheffield

Longest batting streak
31 games—Willie Davis, 1969

Most grounded into double play
27—Eric Karros, 154 games, 1996

Fewest grounded into double play
3—Willie Davis, 160 games, 1968
Davey Lopes, 134 games, 1977
Brett Butler, 161 games, 1991
Raul Mondesi, 159 games, 1999

BASERUNNING

Most stolen bases
104—Maury Wills, 165 games, 1962

Most stolen bases, career
490—Maury Wills

Most caught stealing
31—Maury Wills, 158 games, 1965

PITCHING

Most games
106—Mike G. Marshall, 1974

Most games, career
550—Don Sutton

Most games started
42—Don Drysdale, 1963, 1965

Most games started, career
533—Don Sutton

Most complete games
27—Sandy Koufax, 1965, 1966

Most complete games, career
156—Don Drysdale, Don Sutton

Most games finished
83—Mike G. Marshall, 1974

Most innings
336—Sandy Koufax, 1965

Most innings, career
3,815.1—Don Sutton

Most games won
27—Sandy Koufax, 1966

Most games won, career
233—Don Sutton

Most 20-victory seasons
3—Sandy Koufax

Most games lost
18—Claude Osteen, 1968

Most games lost, career
181—Don Sutton

Highest winning percentage
.864—Orel Hershiser (19-3), 1985

Longest winning streak
13 games—Phil Regan, 1966

Longest winning streak, two seasons
15 games—Phil Regan, 1966 (13), 1967 (2)

Longest losing streak
11 games—Rick Honeycutt, 1987

Most saves
44—Todd Worrell, 1996

Most bases on balls
124—Fernando Valenzuela, 1987
Chan Ho Park, 2000

Most bases on balls, career
996—Don Sutton

Most strikeouts
382—Sandy Koufax, 1965

Most strikeouts, game
18— Sandy Koufax, August 31, 1959
Sandy Koufax, April 24, 1962
Ramon Martinez, June 4, 1990

Most strikeouts, career
2,696—Don Sutton

Most shutouts
11—Sandy Koufax, 1963

Most shutouts, career
52—Don Sutton

Most 1-0 shutouts won
4—Don Drysdale, 1968

Most hits
298—Claude Osteen, 1967

Most runs
127—Don Sutton, 1970

Most earned runs
118—Don Sutton, 1970

Most home runs
38—Don Sutton, 1970

Most hit batsmen
20—Don Drysdale, 1961
Chan Ho Park, 2001

Most wild pitches
19—Hideo Nomo, 1995

Most sacrifice hits
27—Fernando Valenzuela, 1983

Most sacrifice flies
11—Burt Hooton, 1979

Lowest ERA
1.73—Sandy Koufax, 323 innings, 1966

CLUB RECORDS

Most players
53 in 1998

Fewest players
30 in 1962

Most games
165 in 1962

Most at-bats
5,642 in 1982

Most runs
842 in 1962

Fewest runs
470 in 1968

Most opponents' runs
787 in 1999

Most hits
1,515 in 1970

Fewest hits
1,234 in 1968

Most singles
1,128 in 1970

Most doubles
265 in 2000

Most triples
67 in 1970

Most homers
211 in 2000

Fewest homers
67 in 1968

Most homers at Los Angeles Coliseum, home and opponents
193 in 1958

Most homers at Dodger Stadium, home and opponents
194 in 1999

Most grand slams
9 in 2000

Most pinch home runs
12 in 2000

Most long hits
504 in 2000

Most extra bases on long hits
954 in 2000

Most total bases
2,362 in 2000

Most sacrifice hits
120 in 1964

Most sacrifice flies
64 in 1974

Most stolen bases
198 in 1962

Most caught stealing
78 in 1992

Most bases on balls
668 in 2000

Most strikeouts
1,190 in 1996

Fewest strikeouts
744 in 1976

Most hit by pitch
56 in 2001

Fewest hit by pitch
14 in 1984

Most runs batted in
781 in 1962

Most game-winning RBIs
90 in 1988

Highest batting average
.272 in 1974

Lowest batting average
.230 in 1968

Highest slugging average
.431 in 2000

Lowest slugging average
.319 in 1968

Most grounded into double play
145 in 1979

Fewest grounded into double play
79 in 1965

Most left on bases
1,223 in 1982

Fewest left on bases
1,012 in 1958

Most .300 hitters
4 in 1970

Most putouts
4,473 in 1973

Fewest putouts
4,105 in 1958

Most assists
1,946 in 1982

Fewest assists
1,563 in 1997

Most errors
193 in 1962

Fewest errors
114 in 1959

Most errorless games
90 in 1979

Most consecutive errorless games
11 in 1979

Most chances accepted
6,411 in 1982

Fewest chances accepted
5,708 in 1961

Most double plays
198 in 1958

Fewest double plays
104 in 1997

Most passed balls
24 in 1973

Fewest passed balls
6 in 1958

Highest fielding average
.981 in 1959, 1973, 1977, 1979, 1980,
        1989, 1997, 2001

Lowest fielding average
.970 in 1962

Highest home attendance
3,608,881 in 1982

Highest road attendance
2,678,742 in 2000

Most games won
102 in 1962, 1974

Most games lost
99 in 1992

Most games won, month
21 in May 1962, July 1963, June 1973

Most games lost, month
20 in July 1968, June 1979

Highest percentage games won
.630 in 1974 (won 102, lost 60)

Lowest percentage games won
.389 in 1992 (won 63, lost 99)

Games won, league
3,741 in 44 years

Games lost, league
3,231 in 44 years

Most shutouts won
24 in 1963, 1988

Most shutouts lost
23 in 1968

Most 1-0 games won
7 in 1963, 1984

Most 1-0 games lost
7 in 1989

Most consecutive games won
13 in 1962, 1965

Most consecutive games lost
10 in 1961, 1992

Number of times league champions
9

Number of last-place finishes
1

Most runs, game
22 vs. Colorado, July 21, 2001

Most runs by opponent, game
20 by Chicago, May 20, 1967
        by Chicago, May 5, 2001

Most runs, shutout game
19 vs. San Diego, June 28, 1969

Most runs by opponent, shutout game
18 by Cincinnati, August 8, 1965

Most runs, doubleheader shutout
16 vs. Atlanta, September 19, 1971

Most runs, inning
10 vs. San Diego, June 28, 1969, third
        inning
        vs. San Francisco, July 4, 1971,
        eighth inning
        vs. San Diego, September 13, 1977,
        second innings

Longest 1-0 game won
22 innings vs. Montreal, August 23, 1989

Longest 1-0 game lost
16 innings vs. Houston, April 21, 1976

Most hits, game
24 vs. Chicago, August 20, 1974

Most home runs, game
7 vs. Chicago, May 5, 1976
        vs. Cincinnati, May 25, 1979

**Most consecutive games with one or
        more homers**
15 (23 homers), 1977

Most total bases, game
48 vs. Chicago, August 20, 1974

Largest crowd, day game
78,672 vs. San Francisco, April 18, 1958

Largest crowd, doubleheader
72,140 vs. Cincinnati, August 16, 1961

Largest crowd, night game
67,550 vs. Chicago, April 12, 1960

Largest crowd, home opener
78,672 vs. San Francisco, April 18, 1958

MILWAUKEE BRAVES
YEARLY FINISHES

Year	Position	W	L	Pct.	*GB	Manager	Attendance
1953	2nd	92	62	.597	13.0	Charlie Grimm	1,826,397
1954	3rd	89	65	.578	8.0	Charlie Grimm	2,131,388
1955	2nd	85	69	.552	13.5	Charlie Grimm	2,005,836
1956	2nd	92	62	.597	1.0	Charlie Grimm, Fred Haney	2,046,331
1957	1st	95	59	.617	+8.0	Fred Haney	2,215,404
1958	1st	92	62	.597	+8.0	Fred Haney	1,971,101
1959	2nd†	86	70	.551	2.0	Fred Haney	1,749,112
1960	2nd	88	66	.571	7.0	Chuck Dressen	1,497,799
1961	4th	83	71	.539	10.0	Chuck Dressen, Birdie Tebbetts	1,101,441
1962	5th	86	76	.531	15.5	Birdie Tebbetts	766,921
1963	6th	84	78	.519	15.0	Bobby Bragan	773,018
1964	5th	88	74	.543	5.0	Bobby Bragan	910,911
1965	5th	86	76	.531	11.0	Bobby Bragan	555,584

*Games behind winner. †Lost pennant playoff.

INDIVIDUAL RECORDS (1953 TO 1965)

SERVICE

Most years by non-pitcher
13—Eddie Mathews

Most years by pitcher
12—Warren Spahn

BATTING

Most games
161—Hank Aaron, 1963

Most games, career
1944—Eddie Mathews

Most at-bats
636—Bill Bruton, 149 games, 1955

Most at-bats, career
7,080—Hank Aaron

Most runs
127—Hank Aaron, 156 games, 1962

Most runs, career
1,300—Eddie Mathews

Most hits
223—Hank Aaron, 154 games, 1959

Most hits, career
2,266—Hank Aaron

Most singles
132—Joe Torre, 154 games, 1964

Most doubles
46—Hank Aaron, 154 games, 1959

Most doubles, career
391—Hank Aaron

Most triples
15—Bill Bruton, 147 games, 1956

Most triples, career
80—Hank Aaron

Most homers by lefthander
47—Eddie Mathews, 157 games, 1953

Most homers by righthander
45—Hank Aaron, 156 games, 1962

Most homers by switch-hitter
6—Red Schoendienst, 93 games, 1957

Most homers by rookie
22—Rico Carty, 133 games, 1964

Most homers, month
15—Joe Adcock, July, 1956

Most homers at home
23—Joe Adcock, 1956
Eddie Mathews, 1960

Most homers on road
30—Eddie Mathews, 1953

Most homers, lefthander, career
452—Eddie Mathews

Most homers, righthander, career
398—Hank Aaron

Most homers, switch-hitter, career
8—Red Schoendienst

Most grand slams
3—Del Crandall, 133 games, 1955
Hank Aaron, 156 games, 1962

Most grand slams, career
9—Hank Aaron

Most total bases
400—Hank Aaron, 154 games, 1959

Most total bases, career
4,011—Hank Aaron

Most long hits
92—Hank Aaron, 154 games, 1959

Most extra bases on long hits
188—Eddie Mathews, 157 games, 1953

Most sacrifice hits
31—Johnny Logan, 148 games, 1956

Most sacrifice flies
12—Hank Aaron, 153 games, 1960
Del Crandall, 142 games, 1960

Most base on balls
124—Eddie Mathews, 158 games, 1963

Most strikeouts
122—Mack Jones, 122 games, 1965

Fewest strikeouts
33—Johnny Logan, 150 games, 1953

Most hit by pitch
9—Frank Torre, 129 games, 1957
Mack Jones, 122 games, 1965

Most runs batted in
135—Eddie Mathews, 157 games, 1953

Most runs batted in, career
1,305—Hank Aaron

Highest batting average
.355—Hank Aaron, 154 games, 1959

Highest batting average, career
.320—Hank Aaron

Highest slugging average
.636—Hank Aaron, 154 games, 1959

Highest slugging average, career
.567—Hank Aaron

Longest batting streak
25 games—Hank Aaron, 1956
Hank Aaron, 1962

Most grounded into double play
26—Joe Torre, 154 games, 1964

Fewest grounded into double play
4—Eddie Mathews, 151 games, 1956
Bill Bruton, 151 games, 1960

BASERUNNING

Most stolen bases
34—Bill Bruton, 142 games, 1954

Most caught stealing
13—Bill Bruton, 142 games, 1954

PITCHING

Most games
62—Billy O'Dell, 1965

Most games, started
39—Lew Burdette, 1959

Most complete games
24—Warren Spahn, 1953

Most games finished
49—Don McMahon, 1959

Most innings
292—Warren Spahn, 1959

Most games won
24—Tony Cloninger, 1965

Most games won, career
234—Warren Spahn

Most 20-victory seasons
9—Warren Spahn

Most games lost
15—Lew Burdette, Warren Spahn, 1959

Most games lost, career
138—Warren Spahn

Highest winning percentage
.767—Warren Spahn (23-7), 1953, 1963

Longest winning streak
11 games—Warren Spahn, 1954

Most bases on balls
121—Bob Buhl, 1957

Most strikeouts
211—Tony Cloninger, 1965

Most strikeouts, game
15—Warren Spahn, September 16, 1960

Most shutouts
7—Warren Spahn, 1963

Most shutouts, career
36—Warren Spahn

Most runs
144—Lew Burdette, 1959

Most earned runs
131—Lew Burdette, 1959

Most hits
312—Lew Burdette, 1959

Most hit batsmen
12—Bob Shaw, 1962

Most wild pitches
22—Tony Cloninger, 1965

Most home runs
38—Lew Burdette, 1959

Lowest ERA
2.10—Warren Spahn, 266 innings, 1953

CLUB RECORDS

Most players
42 in 1964

Fewest players
31 in 1953, 1954

Most games
163 in 1963

Most at-bats
5,591 in 1964

Most runs
803 in 1964

Fewest runs
670 in 1954

Most opponents' runs
744 in 1964

Fewest opponents' runs
541 in 1968

Most hits
1,522 in 1964

Most singles
1,057 in 1964

Most doubles
274 in 1964

Most triples
62 in 1957

Most homers
199 in 1957

Fewest homers
139 in 1954

Most homers at County Stadium, home and opponents
173 in 1965

Most grand slams
8 in 1962

Most pinch home runs
7 in 1965

Most total bases
2,411 in 1957

Most long hits
482 in 1957

Most extra bases on long hits
942 in 1957

Most sacrifice hits
142 in 1956

Most sacrifice flies
60 in 1960

Most stolen bases
75 in 1963

Most caught stealing
52 in 1963

Most bases on balls
581 in 1962

Most strikeouts
976 in 1965

Fewest strikeouts
619 in 1954

Most hit by pitcher
38 in 1964

Most runs batted in
755 in 1964

Highest batting average
.272 in 1964

Highest slugging average
.442 in 1957

Most grounded into double play
134 in 1964

Fewest grounded into double play
99 in 1956

Most left on bases
1,138 in 1962, 1963

Most .300 hitters
5 in 1964

Most putouts
4,416 in 1963

Most assists
1,848 in 1961, 1963

Most chances accepted
6,264 in 1963

Most errors
152 in 1955

Fewest errors
111 in 1961

Most consecutive errorless games
7 in 1954, 1956, 1964

Most double plays
173 in 1957

Most passed balls
28 in 1965

Fewest passed balls
5 in 1956, 1959

Highest fielding average
.982 in 1961

Highest home attendance
2,215,404 in 1957

Highest road attendance
1,633,569 in 1959

Most games won
95 in 1957

Most games lost
78 in 1963

Most games won, month
23 in August 1953, August 1958

Most games lost, month
18 in June 1954

Highest percentage games won
.617 in 1957 (won 95, lost 59)

Lowest percentage games won
.519 in 1963 (won 84, lost 78)

Games won, league
1,146 in 13 years

Games lost, league
890 in 13 years

Most shutouts won
18 in 1959, 1963

Most shutouts lost
13 in 1963

Most 1-0 games won
4 in 1963

Most consecutive games won
11 in 1956

Most consecutive games lost
8 in 1961

Number of times league champions
2

Number of last-place finishes
0

Most runs, game
23 vs. Chicago, September 2, 1957, first game

Most runs, shutout game
15 vs. Cincinnati, May 13, 1956, first game

Most runs by opponent, shutout game
10 by Philadelphia, July 21, 1953, first game

Most runs, doubleheader shutout
No performance

Most runs, inning
10 vs. Pittsburgh, June 12, 1953, second game, first inning

Longest 1-0 game won
13 innings vs. Pittsburgh, May 26, 1959

Longest 1-0 game lost
16 innings vs. San Francisco, July 2, 1963

Most hits, game
26 vs. Chicago, September 2, 1957, first game

Most home runs, game
8 vs. Pittsburgh, August 30, 1953, first game

Most consecutive games with one or more homers
22 (39 homers), 1956

Most total bases, game
47 vs. Pittsburgh, August 30, 1953, first game

Largest crowd, day game
48,642 vs. Philadelphia, September 27, 1959

Largest crowd, doubleheader
47,604 vs. Cincinnati, September 3, 1956

Largest crowd, night game
46,944 vs. New York, August 27, 1954

Largest crowd, home opener
43,640 vs. Cincinnati, April 12, 1955

MILWAUKEE BREWERS
YEARLY FINISHES

AMERICAN LEAGUE WEST DIVISION

Year	Position	W	L	Pct.	*GB	Manager	Attendance
1970	4th	65	97	.401	33.0	Dave Bristol	933,690
1971	6th	69	92	.429	32.0	Dave Bristol	731,531

AMERICAN LEAGUE EAST DIVISION

Year	Position	W	L	Pct.	*GB	Manager	Attendance
1972	6th	65	91	.417	21.0	Dave Bristol, Del Crandall	600,440
1973	5th	74	88	.457	23.0	Del Crandall	1,092,158
1974	5th	76	86	.469	15.0	Del Crandall	955,741
1975	5th	68	94	.420	28.0	Del Crandall	1,213,357
1976	6th	66	95	.410	32.0	Alex Grammas	1,012,164
1977	6th	67	95	.414	33.0	Alex Grammas	1,114,938
1978	3rd	93	69	.574	6.5	George Bamberger	1,601,406
1979	2nd	95	66	.590	8.0	George Bamberger	1,918,343
1980	3rd	86	76	.531	17.0	George Bamberger, Buck Rodgers	1,857,408
1981	3rd/1st‡	62	47	.569	†	Buck Rodgers	878,432
1982	1st§	95	67	.586	+1.0	Buck Rodgers, Harvey Kuenn	1,978,896
1983	5th	87	75	.537	11.0	Harvey Kuenn	2,397,131
1984	7th	67	94	.416	36.5	Rene Lachemann	1,608,509
1985	6th	71	90	.441	28.0	George Bamberger	1,360,265
1986	6th	77	84	.478	18.0	George Bamberger, Tom Trebelhorn	1,265,041
1987	3rd	91	71	.562	7.0	Tom Trebelhorn	1,909,244
1988	3rd (tied)	87	75	.537	2.0	Tom Trebelhorn	1,923,238
1989	4th	81	81	.500	8.0	Tom Trebelhorn	1,970,735
1990	6th	74	88	.457	14.0	Tom Trebelhorn	1,752,900
1991	4th	83	79	.512	8.0	Tom Trebelhorn	1,478,729
1992	2nd	92	70	.568	4.0	Phil Garner	1,857,314
1993	7th	69	93	.426	26.0	Phil Garner	1,688,080

AMERICAN LEAGUE CENTRAL DIVISION

Year	Position	W	L	Pct.	*GB	Manager	Attendance
1994	5th	53	62	.461	15.0	Phil Garner	1,268,399
1995	4th	65	79	.451	35.0	Phil Garner	1,087,560
1996	3rd	80	82	.494	19.5	Phil Garner	1,327,155
1997	3rd	78	83	.484	8.0	Phil Garner	1,444,027

NATIONAL LEAGUE CENTRAL DIVISION

Year	Position	W	L	Pct.	*GB	Manager	Attendance
1998	5th	74	88	.457	28.0	Phil Garner	1,811,548
1999	5th	74	87	.460	22.5	Phil Garner, Jim Lefebvre	1,701,796
2000	3rd	73	89	.451	22.0	Davey Lopes	1,573,621
2001	4th	68	94	.420	25.0	Davey Lopes	2,811,041

*Games behind winner. †First half 31-25; second 31-22. ‡Lost division series. §Won championship series.

INDIVIDUAL RECORDS (1970 TO DATE)

Note: All records prior to 1998 are as an American League club.

SERVICE

Most years by non-pitcher
20—Robin Yount

Most years by pitcher
12—Jim Slaton

BATTING

Most games
162— Gorman Thomas, 1980
Robin Yount, 1988

Most games, career
2,856—Robin Yount

Most at-bats
666—Paul Molitor, 160 games, 1982

Most at-bats, career
11,008—Robin Yount

Most runs
136—Paul Molitor, 160 games, 1982

Most runs, career
1,632—Robin Yount

Most hits
219—Cecil Cooper, 153 games, 1980

Most hits, career
3,142—Robin Yount

Most singles
157—Cecil Cooper, 153 games, 1980

Most singles, career
2,182—Robin Yount

Most doubles
49—Robin Yount, 143 games, 1980

Most doubles, career
583—Robin Yount

Most triples
16—Paul Molitor, 140 games, 1979

Most triples, career
126—Robin Yount

Most homers by righthander
45—Gorman Thomas, 156 games, 1979
Richie Sexson, 158 games, 2001

Most homers by lefthander
41—Ben Oglivie, 156 games, 1980

Most homers by switch-hitter
25—Dale Sveum, 153 games, 1987

Most homers by rookie
17—Greg Vaughn, 120 games, 1990

Most homers at home
28—Richie Sexson, 2001

Most homers on road
26—Ben Oglivie, 1980

Most homers, month
12—Gorman Thomas, August 1979
Greg Vaughn, June 1996
Jeromy Burnitz, June 1999

Most homers by righthander, career
251—Robin Yount

Most homers by lefthander, career
201—Cecil Cooper

Most homers by switch-hitter, career
66—Ted Simmons

Most grand slams
3—John Jaha, 88 games, 1995
Devon White, 126 games, 2001

Most grand slams, career
5—Cecil Cooper
John Jaha
Jeromy Burnitz

Most total bases
367—Robin Yount, 156 games, 1982

Most total bases, career
4,730—Robin Yount

Most long hits
87—Robin Yount, 156 games, 1982

Most long hits, career
960—Robin Yount

Most extra bases on long hits
165—Richie Sexson, 158 games, 2001

Most extra bases on long hits, career
1,588—Robin Yount

Most sacrifice hits
19—Ron Theobald, 126 games, 1971

Most sacrifice flies
14—Dave Parker, 157 games, 1990

Most bases on balls
99—Jeromy Burnitz, 161 games, 2000

Most bases on balls, career
966—Robin Yount

Most strikeouts
186—Rob Deer, 134 games, 1987

Most strikeouts, career
1,350—Robin Yount

Fewest strikeouts
42—Cecil Cooper, 153 games, 1980

Most hit by pitch
25—Fernando Vina, 159 games, 1998

Longest batting streak
39 games—Paul Molitor, 1987

Most runs batted in
126—Cecil Cooper, 160 games, 1983

Most runs batted in, career
1,406—Robin Yount

Most game-winning RBIs
17—Cecil Cooper, 160 games, 1983
Ted Simmons, 153 games, 1983
Robin Yount, 158 games, 1987

Highest batting average
.353—Paul Molitor, 118 games, 1987

Highest batting average, career
.307—Jeff Cirillo

Highest slugging average
.588—Geoff Jenkins, 135 games, 2000

Highest slugging average, career
.508—Jeromy Burnitz

Most grounded into double play
26—George Scott, 158 games, 1975
Jeff Cirillo, 156 games, 1998

Fewest grounded into double play
2—Jose Valentin, 151 games, 1998

BASERUNNING

Most stolen bases
54—Pat Listach, 149 games, 1992

Most stolen bases, career
412—Paul Molitor

Most caught stealing
18—Pat Listach, 149 games, 1992

PITCHING

Most games
83—Ken Sanders, 1971

Most games, career
365—Dan Plesac

Most games started
38—Jim Slaton, 1973, 1976

Most games started, career
268—Jim Slaton

Most complete games
23—Mike Caldwell, 1978

Most complete games, career
81—Mike Caldwell

Most games finished
77—Ken Sanders, 1971

Most innings
314—Jim Colborn, 1973

Most innings, career
2,025—Jim Slaton

Most games won
22—Mike Caldwell, 1978

Most games won, career
117—Jim Slaton

Most games lost
20—Clyde Wright, 1974

Most games lost, career
121—Jim Slaton

Highest winning percentage
.750—Pete Vuckovich (18-6), 1982

Most 20-victory seasons
1—Jim Colborn, Mike Caldwell, Teddy Higuera

Longest winning streak
10 games—Chris Bosio, 1992
Cal Eldred, 1992

Longest losing streak
10 games—Danny Darwin, 1985

Most saves, season
37—Bob Wickman, 1999

Most bases on balls
106—Pete Broberg, 1975

Most bases on balls, career
760—Jim Slaton

Most strikeouts
240—Teddy Higuera, 1987

Most strikeouts, career
1,081—Teddy Higuera

Most strikeouts, game
14—Moose Haas, April 12, 1978

Most shutouts won
6—Mike Caldwell, 1978

Most shutouts, career
19—Jim Slaton

Most 1-0 shutouts won
1—Held by many pitchers

Most runs
135—Jaime Navarro, 1993

Most earned runs
127—Jaime Navarro, 1993

Most hits
297—Jim Colborn, 1973

Most hit batsmen
20—Jamey Wright, 2001

Most wild pitches
14—Jim Slaton, 1974
    Chris Bosio, 1987

Most home runs allowed
35—Mike Caldwell, 1983

Most sacrifice hits
15—Jim Slaton, 1976

Most sacrifice flies
17—Jaime Navarro, 1993

Lowest ERA
2.37—Mike Caldwell, 293 innings, 1978

CLUB RECORDS

Most players
49 in 1996

Fewest players
31 in 1979

Most games
163 in 1970, 1982, 2000

Most at-bats
5,733 in 1982

Most runs
894 in 1996

Fewest runs
534 in 1971

Most opponents' runs
899 in 1996

Most hits
1,599 in 1982

Fewest hits
1,188 in 1971

Most singles
1,107 in 1991

Most doubles
304 in 1996

Most triples
57 in 1983

Most homers
216 in 1982

Fewest homers
82 in 1992

Most homers at County Stadium, home and opponents
187 in 1999

Most homers at Miller Park, home and opponents
222 in 2001

Most grand slams
10 in 1995

Most pinch home runs
7 in 1998

Most long hits
537 in 1980

Most extra bases on long hits
1,007 in 1982

Most total bases
2,606 in 1982

Most sacrifice hits
115 in 1970

Most sacrifice flies
72 in 1992

Most stolen bases
256 in 1992

Most caught stealing
115 in 1992

Most bases on balls
658 in 1999

Most strikeouts
1,399 in 2001

Fewest strikeouts
673 in 1984

Most hit by pitch
72 in 2001

Fewest hit by pitch
18 in 1982

Most runs batted in
845 in 1996

Most game-winning RBIs
87 in 1982

Highest batting average
.280 in 1979

Lowest batting average
.229 in 1971

Most .300 batters
3 in 1979, 1980, 1982, 1983, 1996

Highest slugging average
.455 in 1982

Lowest slugging average
.329 in 1971

Most grounded into double play
152 in 1984

Fewest grounded into double play
94 in 1978

Most left on bases
1,276 in 1999

Fewest left on bases
1,031 in 1972

Most putouts
4,402 in 1982

Fewest putouts
4,175 in 1972

Most assists
1,976 in 1978

Fewest assists
1,606 in 1987

Most chances accepted
6,284 in 1978

Fewest chances accepted
5,784 in 1972

Most errors
180 in 1975

Fewest errors
89 in 1992

Most errorless games
90 in 1992

Most consecutive errorless games
10 in 1970, 1979

Most double plays
192 in 1998

Fewest double plays
142 in 1970

Most passed balls
34 in 1995

Fewest passed balls
4 in 1978

Highest fielding average
.986 in 1992

Lowest fielding average
.971 in 1975

Highest home attendance
2,811,041 in 2001

Highest road attendance
2,331,670 in 1998

Most games won
95 in 1979, 1982

Most games lost
97 in 1970

Most games won, month
21 in June 1978

Most games lost, month
23 in August 1977

Games won, league
2,425 in 32 years (289 in 4 years in N.L.)

Games lost, league
2,627 in 32 years (358 in 4 years in N.L.)

Highest percentage games won
.590 in 1979 (won 95, lost 66)

Lowest percentage games won
.401 in 1970 (won 65, lost 97)

Most shutouts won
23 in 1971

Most shutouts lost
20 in 1972

Most 1-0 games won
5 in 1971

Most 1-0 games lost
5 in 2001

Most consecutive games won
13 in 1987

Most consecutive games lost
14 in 1994

Number of times league champion
1

Number of last-place finishes
1

Most runs, game
22 vs. Toronto, August 28, 1992

Most runs by opponent, game
20 by Boston, September 6, 1975
    by Chicago, May 15, 1996

Most runs, shutout game
18 vs. Boston, April 16, 1990

Most runs by opponent, shutout game
17 by Cincinnati, August 7, 1998

Most runs, doubleheader shutout
No performance

Most runs, inning
13 vs. California, July 8, 1990, fifth
    inning

Longest 1-0 game won
14 innings vs. California, August 24,
    1983

Longest 1-0 game lost
17 innings vs. Baltimore, September 27,
    1974

Most hits, game
31 vs. Toronto, August 28, 1992

Most home runs, game
7 vs. Cleveland, April 29, 1980

Most consecutive games with one or more homers
19 (35 homers), 1996

Most total bases, game
40 vs. Philadelphia, May 15, 2001, 10 innings
38 vs. Toronto, August 28, 1992
  vs. New York, April 26, 2001

Largest crowd, day game
56,354 vs. Cincinnati, September 28, 2000

Largest crowd doubleheader
54,630 vs. Detroit, July 6, 1979

Largest crowd, night game
55,716 vs. Boston, July 3, 1982

Largest crowd, home opener
55,887 vs. New York, April 15, 1988

MONTREAL EXPOS
YEARLY FINISHES
EAST DIVISION

Year	Position	W	L	Pct.	*GB	Manager	Attendance
1969	6th	52	110	.321	48.0	Gene Mauch	1,212,608
1970	6th	73	89	.451	16.0	Gene Mauch	1,424,683
1971	5th	71	90	.441	25.5	Gene Mauch	1,290,963
1972	5th	70	86	.449	26.5	Gene Mauch	1,142,145
1973	4th	79	83	.488	3.5	Gene Mauch	1,246,863
1974	4th	79	82	.491	8.5	Gene Mauch	1,019,134
1975	5th (tied)	75	87	.463	17.5	Gene Mauch	908,292
1976	6th	55	107	.340	46.0	Karl Kuehl, Charlie Fox	646,704
1977	5th	75	87	.463	26.0	Dick Williams	1,433,757
1978	4th	76	86	.469	14.0	Dick Williams	1,427,007
1979	2nd	95	65	.594	2.0	Dick Williams	2,102,173
1980	2nd	90	72	.556	1.0	Dick Williams	2,208,175
1981	3rd/1st‡§	60	48	.556	†	Dick Williams, Jim Fanning	1,534,564
1982	3rd	86	76	.531	6.0	Jim Fanning	2,318,292
1983	3rd	82	80	.506	8.0	Bill Virdon	2,320,651
1984	5th	78	83	.484	18.0	Bill Virdon, Jim Fanning	1,606,531
1985	3rd	84	77	.522	16.5	Buck Rodgers	1,502,494
1986	4th	78	83	.484	29.5	Buck Rodgers	1,128,981
1987	3rd	91	71	.562	4.0	Buck Rodgers	1,850,324
1988	3rd	81	81	.500	20.0	Buck Rodgers	1,478,659
1989	4th	81	81	.500	12.0	Buck Rodgers	1,783,533
1990	3rd	85	77	.525	10.0	Buck Rodgers	1,373,087
1991	6th	71	90	.441	26.5	Buck Rodgers, Tom Runnells	934,742
1992	2nd	87	75	.537	9.0	Tom Runnells, Felipe Alou	1,669,077
1993	2nd	94	68	.580	3.0	Felipe Alou	1,641,437
1994	1st	74	40	.649	+6.0	Felipe Alou	1,276,250
1995	5th	66	78	.458	24.0	Felipe Alou	1,309,618
1996	2nd	88	74	.543	8.0	Felipe Alou	1,616,709
1997	4th	78	84	.481	23.0	Felipe Alou	1,497,609
1998	4th	65	97	.401	41.0	Felipe Alou	914,717
1999	4th	68	94	.420	35.0	Felipe Alou	773,277
2000	4th	67	95	.414	28.0	Felipe Alou	926,263
2001	5th	68	94	.420	20.0	Felipe Alou, Jeff Torborg	609,473

*Games behind winner. †First half 30-25; second 30-23. ‡Won division series. §Lost championship series.

INDIVIDUAL RECORDS (1969 TO DATE)

SERVICE

Most years by non-pitcher
13—Tim Wallach
  Tim Raines

Most years by pitcher
13—Steve Rogers

BATTING

Most games
162—Rusty Staub, 1971
  Ken Singleton, 1973
  Warren Cromartie, 1980
  Orlando Cabrera, 2001

Most games, career
1,767—Tim Wallach

Most at-bats
659—Warren Cromartie, 158 games, 1979

Most at-bats, career
6,529—Tim Wallach

Most runs
133—Tim Raines Sr., 156 games, 1983

Most runs, career
947—Tim Raines Sr.

Most hits
204—Al Oliver, 160 games, 1982

Most hits, career
1,694—Tim Wallach

Most singles
157—Mark Grudzielanek, 153 games, 1996

Most singles, career
1,148—Tim Raines Sr.

Most doubles
54—Mark Grudzielanek, 156 games, 1997

Most doubles, career
360—Tim Wallach

Most triples
13—Rodney Scott, 154 games, 1980
  Tim Raines Sr., 150 games, 1985
  Mitch Webster, 151 games, 1986

Most triples, career
82—Tim Raines Sr.

Most homers by righthander
44—Vladimir Guerrero, 154 games, 2000

Most homers by lefthander
36—Henry Rodriguez, 145 games, 1996

Most homers by switch-hitter
24—Jose Vidro, 153 games, 2000

Most homers by rookie
19—Andre Dawson, 139 games, 1977
  Larry Walker, 133 games, 1990

Most homers, month
13—Vladimir Guerrero, September 2000

Most homers at home
25—Vladimir Guerrero, 2000

Most homers on road
22—Andre Dawson, 1983

Most homers by righthander, career
225—Andre Dawson

Most homers by lefthander, career
99—Larry Walker

Most homers by switch-hitter, career
96—Tim Raines Sr.

Most grand slams
2—Held by many players

Most grand slams, career
7—Gary Carter

Most total bases
379—Vladimir Guerrero, 154 games, 2000

Most total bases, career
2,728—Tim Wallach

Most long hits
84—Vladimir Guerrero, 160 games, 1999

Most long hits, career
595—Tim Wallach

Most extra bases on long hits
182—Vladimir Guerrero, 154 games, 2000

Most extra bases on long hits, career
1,104—Andre Dawson

Most sacrifice hits
23—Larry Lintz, 113 games, 1974

Most sacrifice flies
18—Andre Dawson, 159 games, 1983

Most bases on balls
123—Ken Singleton, 162 games, 1973

Most bases on balls, career
793—Tim Raines Sr.

Most strikeouts
169—Andres Galarraga, 155 games, 1990

Most strikeouts, career
1,009—Tim Wallach

Fewest strikeouts
29—Dave Cash, 159 games, 1978

Most hit by pitch
50—Ron Hunt, 152 games, 1971

Most runs batted in
131—Vladimir Guerrero, 160 games, 1999

Most runs batted in, career
905—Tim Wallach

Most game-winning RBIs
17—Andre Dawson, 151 games, 1980

Highest batting average
.345—Vladimir Guerrero, 154 games, 2000

Highest batting average, career
.319—Vladimir Guerrero

Highest slugging average
.664—Vladimir Guerrero, 154 games, 2000

Highest slugging average, career
.587—Vladimir Guerrero

Longest batting streak
31 games—Vladimir Guerrero, 1999

Most grounded into double play
27—John Bateman, 139 games, 1971
Ken Singleton, 162 games, 1973

Fewest grounded into double play
1—Ron Hunt, 152 games, 1971

BASERUNNING

Most stolen bases
97—Ron LeFlore, 139 games, 1980

Most stolen bases, career
635—Tim Raines Sr.

Most caught stealing
23—Delino DeShields, 151 games, 1991

PITCHING

Most games
92—Mike Marshall, 1973

Most games, career
425—Tim Burke

Most games started
40—Steve Rogers, 1977

Most games started, career
393—Steve Rogers

Most complete games
20—Bill Stoneman, 1971

Most complete games, career
129—Steve Rogers

Most games finished
73—Mike Marshall, 1973

Most innings
302—Steve Rogers, 1977

Most innings, career
2,839.1—Steve Rogers

Most games won
20—Ross Grimsley, 1978

Most games won, career
158—Steve Rogers

Most 20-victory seasons
1—Ross Grimsley

Most games lost
22—Steve Rogers, 1974

Most games lost, career
152—Steve Rogers

Highest winning percentage
.783—Bryn Smith (18-5), 1985

Longest winning streak
11 games—Dennis Martinez, 1989

Longest losing streak
10 games—Steve Renko, 1972

Most saves
43—John Wetteland, 1993

Most bases on balls
146—Bill Stoneman, 1971

Most bases on balls, career
876—Steve Rogers

Most strikeouts
305—Pedro Martinez, 1997

Most strikeouts, career
1,621—Steve Rogers

Most strikeouts, game
18—Bill Gullickson, September 10, 1980

Most shutouts won
5—Bill Stoneman, 1969
Steve Rogers, 1979, 1983
Dennis Martinez, 1991
Carlos Perez, 1997

Most shutouts won, career
37—Steve Rogers

Most 1-0 shutouts won
2—Carl Morton, 1970
Bill Stoneman, 1972
Scott Sanderson, 1980
Pascual Perez, 1988
Carlos Perez, 1997

Most runs
139—Steve Rogers, 1974

Most earned runs
126—Steve Rogers, 1974

Most hits
281—Carl Morton, 1970

Most wild pitches
19—Steve Renko, 1974

Most hit batsmen
14—Bill Stoneman, 1970

Most home runs
31—Javier Vazquez, 1998

Most sacrifice hits
21—Steve Rogers, 1979

Most sacrifice flies
11—Woodie Fryman, 1976
Miguel Batista, 1999

Lowest ERA
1.90—Pedro Martinez, 241.1 innings, 1997

CLUB RECORDS

Most players
49 in 2000

Fewest players
30 in 1972

Most games
163 in 1983, 1988, 1993

Most at-bats
5,675 in 1977

Most runs
741 in 1987, 1996

Fewest runs
536 in 1976

Most opponents' runs
902 in 2000

Most hits
1,482 in 1983

Fewest hits
1,275 in 1976

Most singles
1,042 in 1983

Most doubles
339 in 1997

Most triples
61 in 1980

Most homers
178 in 2000

Fewest homers
86 in 1974

Most homers at Jarry Park, home and opponents
168 in 1970

Most homers at Olympic Stadium, home and opponents
190 in 2000

Most grand slams
9 in 1996

Most pinch home runs
9 in 1973

Most total bases
2,389 in 2000

Most long hits
545 in 1997

Most extra bases on long hits
923 in 1997

Most sacrifice hits
115 in 1973

Most sacrifice flies
57 in 1983

Most stolen bases
237 in 1980

Most caught stealing
100 in 1991

Most bases on balls
695 in 1973

Most strikeouts
1,084 in 1997

Fewest strikeouts
733 in 1983

Most hit by pitch
78 in 1971

Fewest hit by pitch
16 in 1976

Most runs batted in
705 in 2000

Most game-winning RBIs
83 in 1980

Highest batting average
.266 in 2000

Lowest batting average
.235 in 1976

Highest slugging average
.432 in 2000

Lowest slugging average
.340 in 1976

Most grounded into double play
151 in 2001

Fewest grounded into double play
95 in 1993, 1997

Most left on bases
1,232 in 1973

Fewest left on bases
1,024 in 2001

Most .300 hitters
3 in 1999

Most putouts
4,448 in 1988

Fewest putouts
4,204 in 1972

Most assists
1,956 in 1976

Fewest assists
1,618 in 1999

Most chances accepted
6,393 in 1975

Fewest chances accepted
5,915 in 2001

Most errors
184 in 1969

Fewest errors
108 in 2001

Most errorless games
87 in 1990

Most consecutive errorless games
10 in 1977

Most double plays
193 in 1970

Fewest double plays
113 in 1992

Most passed balls
24 in 1973

Fewest passed balls
3 in 1978

Highest fielding average
.982 in 1990, 2001

Lowest fielding average
.971 in 1969

Highest home attendance
2,320,651 in 1983

Highest road attendance
2,620,064 in 1993

Most games won
95 in 1979

Most games lost
110 in 1969

Most games won, month
23 in September 1979

Most games lost, month
23 in August 1969, September 1976

Highest percentage games won
.594 in 1979 (won 95, lost 65)

Lowest percentage games won
.321 in 1969 (won 52, lost 110)

Games won, league
2,522 in 33 years

Games lost, league
2,690 in 33 years

Most shutouts won
18 in 1979

Most shutouts lost
20 in 1972

Most 1-0 shutouts won
4 in 1972, 1991

Most 1-0 shutouts lost
5 in 1982, 1986

Most consecutive games won
10 in 1979, 1980, 1997

Most consecutive games lost
20 in 1969

Number of times league champions
0

Number of last-place finishes
2 (tied in 1969)

Most runs, inning
13 vs. San Francisco, May 7, 1997, sixth inning

Most runs, game
21 vs. Colorado, April 28, 1996

Most runs by opponent, game
20 by San Diego, May 19, 2001

Most runs, shutout game
19 vs. Atlanta, July 30, 1978

Most runs by opponent, shutout game
18 by San Francisco, May 24, 2000

Most runs, doubleheader shutout
14 vs. New York, August 5, 1975

Longest 1-0 game won
17 innings vs. Philadelphia, September 21, 1981

Longest 1-0 game lost
22 innings vs. Los Angeles, August 23, 1989

Most hits, game
28 vs. Atlanta, July 30, 1978

Most home runs, game
8 vs. Atlanta, July 30, 1978

Most consecutive games with one or more homers
16 (29 homers), 1999

Most total bases, game
58 vs. Atlanta, July 30, 1978

Largest crowd, day game
57,694 vs. Philadelphia, August 15, 1982

Largest crowd, doubleheader
59,282 vs. St. Louis, September 16, 1979

Largest crowd, night game
57,121 vs. Philadelphia, October 3, 1980

Largest crowd, home opener
57,592 vs. Philadelphia, April 15, 1977

NEW YORK GIANTS
YEARLY FINISHES

Year	Position	W	L	Pct.	*GB	Manager	Attendance
1901	7th	52	85	.380	37.0	George Davis	297,650
1902	8th	48	88	.353	53.5	Horace Fogel, Heinie Smith, John McGraw	302,875
1903	2nd	84	55	.604	6.5	John McGraw	579,530
1904	1st	106	47	.693	+13.0	John McGraw	609,826
1905	1st	105	48	.686	+9.0	John McGraw	552,700
1906	2nd	96	56	.632	20.0	John McGraw	402,850
1907	4th	82	71	.536	25.5	John McGraw	538,350
1908	2nd (tied)	98	56	.636	1.0	John McGraw	910,000
1909	3rd	92	61	.601	18.5	John McGraw	783,700
1910	2nd	91	63	.591	13.0	John McGraw	511,785
1911	1st	99	54	.647	+7.5	John McGraw	675,000
1912	1st	103	48	.682	+10.0	John McGraw	638,000
1913	1st	101	51	.664	+12.5	John McGraw	630,000
1914	2nd	84	70	.545	10.5	John McGraw	364,313
1915	8th	69	83	.454	21.0	John McGraw	391,850
1916	4th	86	66	.566	7.0	John McGraw	552,056
1917	1st	98	56	.636	+10.0	John McGraw	500,264
1918	2nd	71	53	.573	10.5	John McGraw	256,618
1919	2nd	87	53	.621	9.0	John McGraw	708,857
1920	2nd	86	68	.558	7.0	John McGraw	929,609
1921	1st	94	59	.614	+4.0	John McGraw	773,477
1922	1st	93	61	.604	+7.0	John McGraw	945,809
1923	1st	95	58	.621	+4.5	John McGraw	820,780
1924	1st	93	60	.608	+1.5	John McGraw	844,068
1925	2nd	86	66	.566	8.5	John McGraw	778,993
1926	5th	74	77	.490	13.5	John McGraw	700,362
1927	3rd	92	62	.597	2.0	John McGraw	858,190
1928	2nd	93	61	.604	2.0	John McGraw	916,191

Year	Position	W	L	Pct.	*GB	Manager	Attendance
1929	3rd	84	67	.556	13.5	John McGraw	868,806
1930	3rd	87	67	.565	5.0	John McGraw	868,714
1931	2nd	87	65	.572	13.0	John McGraw	812,163
1932	6th (tied)	72	82	.468	18.0	John McGraw, Bill Terry	484,868
1933	1st	91	61	.599	+5.0	Bill Terry	604,471
1934	2nd	93	60	.608	2.0	Bill Terry	730,851
1935	3rd	91	62	.595	8.5	Bill Terry	748,748
1936	1st	92	62	.597	+5.0	Bill Terry	837,952
1937	1st	95	57	.625	+3.0	Bill Terry	926,887
1938	3rd	83	67	.553	5.0	Bill Terry	799,633
1939	5th	77	74	.510	18.5	Bill Terry	702,457
1940	6th	72	80	.474	27.5	Bill Terry	747,852
1941	5th	74	79	.484	25.5	Bill Terry	763,098
1942	3rd	85	67	.559	20.0	Mel Ott	779,621
1943	8th	55	98	.359	49.5	Mel Ott	466,095
1944	5th	67	87	.435	38.0	Mel Ott	674,083
1945	5th	78	74	.513	19.0	Mel Ott	1,016,468
1946	8th	61	93	.396	36.0	Mel Ott	1,219,873
1947	4th	81	73	.526	13.0	Mel Ott	1,600,793
1948	5th	78	76	.506	13.5	Mel Ott, Leo Durocher	1,459,269
1949	5th	73	81	.474	24.0	Leo Durocher	1,218,446
1950	3rd	86	68	.558	5.0	Leo Durocher	1,008,876
1951	1st†	98	59	.624	+1.0	Leo Durocher	1,059,539
1952	2nd	92	62	.597	4.5	Leo Durocher	984,940
1953	5th	70	84	.455	35.0	Leo Durocher	811,518
1954	1st	97	57	.630	+5.0	Leo Durocher	1,155,067
1955	3rd	80	74	.519	18.5	Leo Durocher	824,112
1956	6th	67	87	.435	26.0	Bill Rigney	629,179
1957	6th	69	85	.448	26.0	Bill Rigney	653,923

*Games behind winner. †Won pennant playoff.

INDIVIDUAL RECORDS (1883 TO 1957)

SERVICE

Most years by non-pitcher
22—Mel Ott

Most years by pitcher
17—Christy Mathewson

BATTING

Most games
157—Art Devlin, 1908

Most games, career
2,730—Mel Ott

Most at-bats
681—Joe Moore, 155 games, 1935

Most at-bats, career
9,456—Mel Ott

Most runs
146—Mike Tiernan, 122 games, 1889

Most runs, career
1,859—Mel Ott

Most runs (since 1900)
139—Bill Terry, 154 games, 1930

Most hits
254—Bill Terry, 154 games, 1930

Most hits, career
2,876—Mel Ott

Most singles
177—Bill Terry, 154 games, 1930

Most singles, career
1,805—Mel Ott

Most doubles
43—Bill Terry, 153 games, 1931

Most doubles, career
488—Mel Ott

Most triples
26—George Davis, 133 games, 1893

Most triples (since 1900)
25—Larry Doyle, 141 games, 1911

Most triples, career
159—Mike Tiernan

Most triples, career (since 1900)
117—Larry Doyle

Most homers by lefthander
51—Johnny Mize, 154 games, 1947

Most homers by righthander
51—Willie Mays, 152 games, 1955

Most homers by switch-hitter
12—Frank Frisch, 151 games, 1923

Most homers by rookie
29—Bobby Thomson, 138 games, 1947

Most homers, month
13—Walker Cooper, June, 1947
Johnny Mize, August, 1947
Willie Mays, July, 1955

Most homers at home
29—Johnny Mize, 1947

Most homers on road
29—Willie Mays, 1955

Most homers by lefthander, career
511—Mel Ott

Most homers by righthander, career
187—Willie Mays

Most homers by switch-hitter, career
54—Frank Frisch

Most grand slams
3—George Kelly, 149 games, 1921
Sid Gordon, 142 games, 1948
Wes Westrum, 124 games, 1951

Most grand slams, career
7—George Kelly
Mel Ott

Most total bases
392—Bill Terry, 154 games, 1930

Most total bases, career
5,041—Mel Ott

Most long hits
87—Willie Mays, 151 games, 1954

Most long hits, career
1,071—Mel Ott

Most extra bases on long hits
197—Willie Mays, 152 games, 1955

Most extra bases on long hits, career
2,165—Mel Ott

Most sacrifice hits
36—Art Devlin, 143 games, 1907

Most sacrifice flies
8—Don Mueller, 153 games, 1954
Hank Thompson, 135 games, 1955

Most bases on balls
144—Eddie Stanky, 152 games, 1950

Most strikeouts
93—Wes Westrum, 124 games, 1951

Fewest strikeouts
12—Frankie Frisch, 151 games, 1923

Most hit by pitch
19—Art Fletcher, 151 games, 1917

Most runs batted in
151—Mel Ott, 150 games, 1929

Most runs batted in, career
1,860—Mel Ott

Most consecutive games with RBI
11—Mel Ott (27 RBIs), 1929

Highest batting average
.401—Bill Terry, 154 games, 1930

Highest batting average, career
.341—Bill Terry

Highest slugging average
.667—Willie Mays, 151 games, 1954

Highest slugging average, career
.593—Willie Mays

Longest batting streak
33 games—George Davis, 1893

Longest batting streak (since 1900)
24 games—Freddie Lindstrom, 1930
Don Mueller, 1955

Most grounded into double play
26—Bill Jurges, 138 games, 1939
Sid Gordon, 131 games, 1943

Fewest grounded into double play
3—Joe Moore, 152 games, 1936

BASERUNNING

Most stolen bases
111—Monte Ward, 129 games, 1887

Most stolen bases (since 1900)
62—George J. Burns, 154 games, 1914

Most stolen bases, career
334—George J. Burns

Most caught stealing
22—George J. Burns, 154 games, 1920

PITCHING (SINCE 1900)

Most games
71—Hoyt Wilhelm, 1952

Most games, career
634—Christy Mathewson

Most games started
48—Joe McGinnity, 1903

Most complete games
44—Joe McGinnity, 1903

Most games finished
52—Ace Adams, 1943

Most innings
434—Joe McGinnity, 1903

Most games won
37—Christy Mathewson, 1908

Most games won, career
372—Christy Mathewson

Most 20-victory seasons
13—Christy Mathewson

Most games lost
27—Dummy Taylor, 1901

Most games lost, career
188—Christy Mathewson

Highest winning percentage
.833—Hoyt Wilhelm (15-3), 1952

Longest winning streak
19 games—Rube Marquard, 1912

Longest winning streak over two seasons
24 games—Carl Hubbell, 1936 (16), 1937 (8)

Longest losing streak
12 games—Rube Marquard, 1914

Most bases on balls
128—Jeff Tesreau, 1914

Most bases on balls, career
902—Hal Schumacher

Most strikeouts
267—Christy Mathewson, 1903

Most strikeouts, game
16—Christy Mathewson, October 3, 1904

Most strikeouts, career
2,502—Christy Mathewson

Most shutouts
12—Christy Mathewson, 1908

Most shutouts, career
83—Christy Mathewson

Most 1-0 shutouts won
5—Carl Hubbell, 1933

Most runs
224—Bill Carrick, 1900

Most earned runs
117—Freddie Fitzsimmons, 1932

Most hits
415—Bill Carrick, 1900

Most hit batsmen
36—Ed Doheny, 1899

Most wild pitches
30—Red Ames, 1905

Most home runs
36—Larry Jansen, 1949

Lowest ERA
1.66—Carl Hubbell, 309 innings, 1933

CLUB RECORDS

Most players
49 in 1946

Fewest players
21 in 1905

Most games
158 in 1904, 1909, 1917

Most at-bats
5,623 in 1935

Most runs
959 in 1930

Fewest runs
540 in 1956

Most opponents runs
814 in 1930

Most hits
1,769 in 1930

Fewest hits
1,217 in 1906

Most singles
1,279 in 1930

Most doubles
276 in 1928

Most triples
105 in 1911

Most homers
221 in 1947

Fewest homers (154 or 162-game schedule)
15 in 1906

Most grand slams
7 in 1951, 1954

Most pinch home runs
10 in 1954

Most total bases
2,628 in 1930

Most long hits
490 in 1930

Most extra bases on long hits
979 in 1947

Most sacrifices (sacrifice hits and sacrifice flies)
250 in 1908

Most sacrifice hits
166 in 1904

Most sacrifice flies
52 in 1954

Most stolen bases
347 in 1911

Most caught stealing
114 in 1921

Most bases on balls
671 in 1951

Most strikeouts
672 in 1952

Fewest strikeouts
376 in 1928

Most hit by pitch
52 in 1917

Fewest hit by pitch
15 in 1933

Most runs batted in
880 in 1930

Highest batting average
.319 in 1930

Lowest batting average
.243 in 1909

Highest slugging average
.473 in 1930

Lowest slugging average
.302 in 1906

Most grounded into double play
153 in 1939

Fewest grounded into double play
96 in 1952

Most left on bases
1,214 in 1935

Fewest left on bases
975 in 1926

Most .300 hitters
8 in 1921, 1922, 1924, 1930, 1931

Most putouts
4,306 in 1909

Fewest putouts
3,964 in 1939

Most assists
2,240 in 1920

Fewest assists
1,660 in 1956

Most chances accepted
6,472 in 1920

Fewest chances accepted
5,794 in 1956

Most errors
307 in 1909

Fewest errors
137 in 1950

Most consecutive errorless games
8 in 1950

Most double plays
181 in 1950

Fewest double plays
112 in 1945

Most passed balls
26 in 1906

Fewest passed balls
4 in 1928

Highest fielding average
.977 in 1940, 1942, 1950

Lowest fielding average
.954 in 1909

Highest home attendance
1,600,793 in 1947

Highest road attendance
1,228,330 in 1949

Most games won
106 in 1904

Most games lost
98 in 1943

Most games won, month
29—September 1916

Most games lost, month
25—August 1953

Highest percentage games won
.759 in 1885 (won 85, lost 27)

Highest percentage games won (since 1900)
.693 in 1904 (won 106, lost 47)

Lowest percentage games won
.353 in 1902 (won 48, lost 88)

Games won, league
6,067 in 75 years

Games lost, league
4,898 in 75 years

Most shutouts won
25 in 1908

Most shutouts lost
20 in 1915

Most 1-0 games won
6 in 1907, 1933

Most 1-0 games lost
8 in 1907

Most consecutive games won
26 in 1916

Most consecutive games lost
13 in 1902, 1944

Number of times league champions
17

Number of last-place finishes
5

Most runs, game
29 vs. Philadelphia, June 15, 1887

Most runs, game (since 1900)
26 vs. Brooklyn, April 30, 1944, first game

Most runs by opponent, game
28 by Hartford, May 13, 1876

Most runs by opponent, game (since 1900)
21 by St. Louis, August 2, 1948

Most runs, shutout game
24 vs. Buffalo, May 27, 1885

Most runs, shutout game (since 1900)
16 vs. Brooklyn, July 3, 1949

Most runs by opponent, shutout game
19 by Chicago, June 7, 1906

Most runs, doubleheader shutout
19 vs. Cincinnati, July 31, 1949

Most runs, inning
13 vs. Philadelphia, September 8, 1883, third inning
vs. Cleveland, July 19, 1890, first game, second inning
vs. St. Louis, May 13, 1911, first inning

Longest 1-0 game won
18 innings vs. St. Louis, July 2, 1933, first game

Longest 1-0 game lost
15 innings vs. Cincinnati, July 16, 1933, first game

Most hits, game
31 vs. Cincinnati, June 9, 1901

Most home runs, game
7 vs. Indianapolis, May 9, 1888
vs. Cincinnati, June 6, 1939
vs. Philadelphia, August 13, 1939, first game
vs. Cincinnati, June 24, 1950
vs. Pittsburgh, July 8, 1956, first game

Most consecutive games with one or more homers
19 (33 homers), 1947

Most total bases, game
47 vs. Philadelphia, July 11, 1931, first game

Largest crowd, day game
54,922 vs. Brooklyn, April 20, 1941

Largest crowd, doubleheader
60,747 vs. Brooklyn, May 31, 1937

Largest crowd, night game
51,790 vs. Brooklyn, May 27, 1947

Largest crowd, home opener
54,392 vs. Brooklyn, April 14, 1936

NEW YORK METS
YEARLY FINISHES

Year	Position	W	L	Pct.	*GB	Manager	Attendance
1962	10th	40	120	.250	60.5	Casey Stengel	922,530
1963	10th	51	111	.315	48.0	Casey Stengel	1,080,108
1964	10th	53	109	.327	40.0	Casey Stengel	1,732,597
1965	10th	50	112	.309	47.0	Casey Stengel, Wes Westrum	1,768,389
1966	9th	66	95	.410	28.5	Wes Westrum	1,932,693
1967	10th	61	101	.377	40.5	Wes Westrum, Salty Parker	1,565,492
1968	9th	73	89	.451	24.0	Gil Hodges	1,781,657

EAST DIVISION

Year	Position	W	L	Pct.	*GB	Manager	Attendance
1969	1st†	100	62	.617	+8.0	Gil Hodges	2,175,373
1970	3rd	83	79	.512	6.0	Gil Hodges	2,697,479
1971	3rd (tied)	83	79	.512	14.0	Gil Hodges	2,266,680
1972	3rd	83	73	.532	13.5	Yogi Berra	2,134,185
1973	1st†	82	79	.509	+1.5	Yogi Berra	1,912,390
1974	5th	71	91	.438	17.0	Yogi Berra	1,722,209
1975	3rd (tied)	82	80	.506	10.5	Yogi Berra, Roy McMillan	1,730,566
1976	3rd	86	76	.531	15.0	Joe Frazier	1,468,754
1977	6th	64	98	.395	37.0	Joe Frazier, Joe Torre	1,066,825
1978	6th	66	96	.407	24.0	Joe Torre	1,007,328
1979	6th	63	99	.389	35.0	Joe Torre	788,905
1980	5th	67	95	.414	24.0	Joe Torre	1,192,073
1981	5th/4th	41	62	.398	‡	Joe Torre	704,244
1982	6th	65	97	.401	27.0	George Bamberger	1,323,036
1983	6th	68	94	.420	22.0	George Bamberger, Frank Howard	1,112,774
1984	2nd	90	72	.556	6.5	Dave Johnson	1,842,695
1985	2nd	98	64	.605	3.0	Dave Johnson	2,761,601
1986	1st†	108	54	.667	+21.5	Dave Johnson	2,767,601
1987	2nd	92	70	.568	3.0	Dave Johnson	3,034,129
1988	1st§	100	60	.625	+15.0	Dave Johnson	3,055,445
1989	2nd	87	75	.537	6.0	Dave Johnson	2,918,710
1990	2nd	91	71	.562	4.0	Dave Johnson, Bud Harrelson	2,732,745
1991	5th	77	84	.478	20.5	Bud Harrelson, Mike Cubbage	2,284,484
1992	5th	72	90	.444	24.0	Jeff Torborg	1,779,534
1993	7th	59	103	.364	38.0	Jeff Torborg, Dallas Green	1,873,183
1994	3rd	55	58	.487	18.5	Dallas Green	1,151,471
1995	2nd (tied)	69	75	.479	21.0	Dallas Green	1,273,183
1996	4th	71	91	.438	25.0	Dallas Green, Bobby Valentine	1,588,323
1997	3rd	88	74	.543	13.0	Bobby Valentine	1,766,174
1998	2nd	88	74	.543	18.0	Bobby Valentine	2,287,942
1999	2nd∞	97	66	.595	6.5	Bobby Valentine	2,725,668
2000	2nd▲†	94	68	.580	1.0	Bobby Valentine	2,800,221
2001	3rd	82	80	.506	6.0	Bobby Valentine	2,658,279

*Games behind winner. †Won championship series. ‡First half 17-34; second 24-28. §Lost championship series. ∞Won wild-card playoff. ▲Won division series.

SERVICE

Most years by non-pitcher
18—Ed Kranepool

Most years by pitcher
12—Jerry Koosman
    Tom Seaver
    Craig Swan
    John Franco

BATTING

Most games
162—Felix Millan, 1975
    John Olerud, 1999

Most games, career
1,853—Ed Kranepool

Most at-bats
682—Lance Johnson, 160 games, 1996

Most at-bats, career
5,436—Ed Kranepool

Most runs
123—Edgardo Alfonzo, 158 games, 1999

Most runs, career
662—Darryl Strawberry

Most hits
227—Lance Johnson, 160 games, 1996

Most hits, career
1,418—Ed Kranepool

Most singles
166—Lance Johnson, 160 games, 1996

Most singles, career
1,050—Ed Kranepool

Most doubles
44—Bernard Gilkey, 153 games, 1996

Most doubles, career
225—Ed Kranepool

Most triples
21—Lance Johnson, 160 games, 1996

Most triples, career
62—Mookie Wilson

Most homers by righthander
40—Mike Piazza, 141 games, 1999

Most homers by lefthander
39—Darryl Strawberry, 154 games, 1987
    Darryl Strawberry, 153 games, 1988

Most homers by switch-hitter
41—Todd Hundley, 153 games, 1996

Most homers by rookie
26—Darryl Strawberry, 122 games, 1983

Most homers, month
13—Dave Kingman, July, 1975
    Gary Carter, September, 1985

Most homers at home
24—Darryl Strawberry, 1990

Most homers on road
23—Howard Johnson, 1987

Most homers by lefthander, career
252—Darryl Strawberry

Most homers by righthander, career
154—Dave Kingman

Most homers by switch-hitter, career
192—Howard Johnson

Most grand slams
3—John Milner, 127 games, 1976
   Robin Ventura, 161 games, 1999
   Mike Piazza, 136 games, 2000

Most grand slams, career
5—John Milner
   Howard Johnson

Kevin McReynolds
Darryl Strawberry
Robin Ventura

Most total bases
327—Lance Johnson, 160 games, 1996

Most total bases, career
2,047—Ed Kranepool

Most long hits
80—Howard Johnson, 153 games, 1989

Most long hits, career
469—Darryl Strawberry

Most extra bases on long hits
159—Darryl Strawberry, 154 games,
    1987

Most extra bases on long hits, career
1,003—Darryl Strawberry

Most sacrifice hits
24—Felix Millan, 136 games, 1974

Most sacrifice flies
15—Gary Carter, 132 games, 1986
    Howard Johnson, 156 games, 1991

Most bases on balls
125—John Olerud, 162 games, 1999

Most bases on balls, career
580—Darryl Strawberry

Most strikeouts
156—Tommie Agee, 153 games, 1970
    Dave Kingman, 149 games, 1982

Fewest strikeouts
14—Felix Millan, 136 games, 1974

Most strikeouts, career
960—Darryl Strawberry

Most hit by pitch
13—Ron Hunt, 143 games, 1963
    John Olerud, 154 games, 1997

Most runs batted in
124—Mike Piazza, 141 games, 1999

Most runs batted in, career
733—Darryl Strawberry

Most game-winning RBIs
24—Keith Hernandez, 158 games, 1985

Most consecutive games with RBI
9—Bobby Bonilla (13 RBIs), 1995

Highest batting average
.354—John Olerud, 160 games, 1998

Highest batting average, career
.317—Mike Piazza

Highest slugging average
.614—Mike Piazza, 136 games, 2000

Highest slugging average, career
.591—Mike Piazza

Longest batting streak
24 games—Hubie Brooks, 1984
    Mike Piazza, 1999

Most grounded into double play
27—Mike Piazza, 141 games, 1999

Fewest grounded into double play
4—Lee Mazzilli, 159 games, 1977
   Darryl Strawberry, 154 games, 1987
   Howard Johnson, 153 games, 1989
   Howard Johnson, 156 games, 1991
   Edgardo Alfonzo, 151 games, 1997

BASERUNNING

Most stolen bases
66—Roger Cedeno, 155 games, 1999

Most stolen bases, career
281—Mookie Wilson

Most caught stealing
21—Lenny Randle, 136 games, 1977

PITCHING

Most games
80—Turk Wendell, 1999

Most games, career
605—John Franco

Most complete games
21—Tom Seaver, 1971

Most complete games, career
171—Tom Seaver

Most games started
36—Jack Fisher, 1965
    Tom Seaver, 1970, 1973, 1975

Most games started, career
395—Tom Seaver

Most games finished
68—Armando Benitez, 2000

Most innings
291—Tom Seaver, 1970

Most innings, career
3,045—Tom Seaver

Most games won
25—Tom Seaver, 1969

Most games, won, career
198—Tom Seaver

Most 20-victory seasons
4—Tom Seaver

Most games lost
24—Roger Craig, 1962
    Jack Fisher, 1965

Most games lost, career
137—Jerry Koosman

Highest winning percentage
.870—David Cone (20-3), 1988

Most saves
43—Armando Benitez, 2001

Longest winning streak
14 games—Dwight Gooden, 1985

Longest losing streak
18 games—Roger Craig, 1963

Longest losing streak, two seasons
27 games—Anthony Young, 1992 (14),
    1993 (13)

Most bases on balls
116—Nolan Ryan, 1971

Most bases on balls, career
847—Tom Seaver

Most strikeouts
289—Tom Seaver, 1971

Most strikeouts, career
2,541—Tom Seaver

Most strikeouts, game
19—Tom Seaver, April 22, 1970
    David Cone, October 6, 1991

Most shutouts
8—Dwight Gooden, 1985

Most shutouts, career
44—Tom Seaver

Most 1-0 shutouts won
3—Bob Ojeda, 1988

Most runs
137—Jay Hook, 1962

Most earned runs
117—Roger Craig, 1962

Most hits
261—Roger Craig, 1962

Most hit batsmen
5—Nolan Ryan, 1971
   Kevin Appier, 2001

Most wild pitches
18—Jack Hamilton, 1966

Most home runs
35—Roger Craig, 1962

Most sacrifice hits
21—Mike Scott, 1982

Most sacrifice flies
13—Ron Darling, 1989

Lowest ERA
1.53—Dwight Gooden, 276.2 innings, 1985

CLUB RECORDS

Most players
54 in 1967

Fewest players
32 in 1988

Most games
164 in 1965

Most at-bats
5,618 in 1996

Most runs
853 in 1999

Fewest runs
473 in 1968

Most opponents' runs
948 in 1962

Most hits
1,553 in 1999

Fewest hits
1,168 in 1963

Most singles
1,087 in 1980

Most doubles
297 in 1999

Most triples
47 in 1978, 1996

Most homers
198 in 2000

Fewest homers
61 in 1980

Most homers at Polo Grounds, home and opponents
213 in 1962

Most homers at Shea Stadium, home and opponents
262 in 2000 (An additional three home runs were hit at Tokyo Stadium, Japan when the Mets played a "home" game there on April 29.)

Most grand slams
8 in 1999, 2000

Most pinch home runs
12 in 1983

Most total bases
2,430 in 1987

Most long hits
513 in 1987

Most extra bases on long hits
831 in 1987

Most sacrifice hits
108 in 1973

Most sacrifice flies
69 in 1997

Most stolen bases
159 in 1987

Most caught stealing
99 in 1980

Most bases on balls
717 in 1999

Most strikeouts
1,203 in 1968

Fewest strikeouts
735 in 1974

Most hit by pitch
65 in 2001

Fewest hit by pitch
20 in 1984, 1985

Most runs batted in
814 in 1999

Most game-winning RBIs
102 in 1986

Highest batting average
.279 in 1999

Lowest batting average
.219 in 1963

Highest slugging average
.434 in 1987, 1999

Lowest slugging average
.315 in 1963, 1968

Most grounded into double play
149 in 1999

Fewest grounded into double play
87 in 1989

Most left on bases
1,267 in 1999

Fewest left on bases
1,011 in 1993

Most .300 hitters
5 in 1999

Most putouts
4,464 in 1985

Fewest putouts
4,244 in 1972

Most assists
1,995 in 1966

Fewest assists
1,462 in 1989

Most chances accepted
6,309 in 1965

Fewest chances accepted
5,783 in 1972

Most errors
210 in 1962, 1963

Fewest errors
68 in 1999

Most errorless games
104 in 1999

Most consecutive errorless games
12 in 1999

Most double plays
171 in 1966, 1983

Fewest double plays
107 in 1990

Most passed balls
32 in 1964

Fewest passed balls
2 in 1980

Highest fielding average
.989 in 1999

Lowest fielding average
.967 in 1962, 1963

Highest home attendance
3,055,445 in 1988

Highest road attendance
2,660,426 in 1993

Most games won
108 in 1986

Most games lost
120 in 1962

Most games won, month
23 in September 1969

Most games lost, month
26 in August 1962

Games won, league
3,016 in 40 years

Games lost, league
3,326 in 40 years

Highest percentage games won
.667 in 1986 (won 108, lost 54)

Lowest percentage games won
.250 in 1962 (won 40, lost 120)

Most shutouts won
28 in 1969

Most shutouts lost
30 in 1963

Most 1-0 games won
9 in 1969

Most 1-0 games lost
8 in 1963

Most consecutive games won
11 in 1969, 1972, 1986, 1990

Most consecutive games lost
17 in 1962

Number of times league champions
4

Number of last-place finishes
9

Most runs, game
23 vs. Chicago, August 16, 1987

Most runs by opponent, game
26 by Philadelphia, June 11, 1985

Most runs, shutout game
14 vs. Chicago, July 29, 1965, first game
   vs. Cincinnati, April 19, 1998

Most runs by opponent, shutout game
16 by Atlanta, July 2, 1999

Most runs, doubleheader shutout
2 vs. Pittsburgh, September 12, 1969

Most runs, inning
10 vs. Cincinnati, June 12, 1979, sixth inning
   vs. Atlanta, June 30, 2000, eighth inning

Longest 1-0 game won
15 innings vs. Los Angeles, July 4, 1969

Longest 1-0 game lost
24 innings vs. Houston, April 15, 1968

Most hits, extra-inning game
28 vs. Atlanta, July 4, 1985, 19 innings

Most hits, nine-inning game
23 vs. Chicago, May 26, 1964
   vs. Colorado, April 29, 2000

Most home runs, game
6 vs. Montreal, April 4, 1988
   vs. Cincinnati, June 15, 1999

Most consecutive games with one or more homers
21 (29 homers), 1996

Most total bases, game
38 vs. Atlanta, July 4, 1985, 19 innings
   vs. Houston, August 30, 1999

Largest crowd, day game
56,738 vs. Los Angeles, June 23, 1968

Largest crowd, doubleheader	Largest crowd, night game	Largest crowd, home opener
57,175 vs. Los Angeles, June 13, 1965	56,658 vs. San Francisco, May 13, 1966	53,640 vs. Atlanta, April 9, 2001
		(Mets drew 55,000 to their 2000 "home opener" in Tokyo, Japan, March 29.)

PHILADELPHIA PHILLIES
YEARLY FINISHES

Year	Position	W	L	Pct.	*GB	Manager	Attendance
1901	2nd	83	57	.593	7.5	Bill Shettsline	234,937
1902	7th	56	81	.409	46.0	Bill Shettsline	112,066
1903	7th	49	86	.363	39.5	Chief Zimmer	151,729
1904	8th	52	100	.342	53.5	Hugh Duffy	140,771
1905	4th	83	69	.546	21.5	Hugh Duffy	317,932
1906	4th	71	82	.464	45.5	Hugh Duffy	294,680
1907	3rd	83	64	.565	21.5	Bill Murray	341,216
1908	4th	83	71	.539	16.0	Bill Murray	420,660
1909	5th	74	79	.484	36.5	Bill Murray	303,177
1910	4th	78	75	.510	25.5	Red Dooin	296,597
1911	4th	79	73	.520	19.5	Red Dooin	416,000
1912	5th	73	79	.480	30.5	Red Dooin	250,000
1913	2nd	88	63	.583	12.5	Red Dooin	470,000
1914	6th	74	80	.481	20.5	Red Dooin	138,474
1915	1st	90	62	.592	+7.0	Pat Moran	449,898
1916	2nd	91	62	.595	2.5	Pat Moran	515,365
1917	2nd	87	65	.572	10.0	Pat Moran	354,428
1918	6th	55	68	.447	26.0	Pat Moran	122,266
1919	8th	47	90	.343	47.5	Jack Coombs, Gavvy Cravath	240,424
1920	8th	62	91	.405	30.5	Gavvy Cravath	330,998
1921	8th	51	103	.331	43.5	Bill Donovan, Kaiser Wilhelm	273,961
1922	7th	57	96	.373	35.5	Kaiser Wilhelm	232,471
1923	8th	50	104	.325	45.5	Art Fletcher	228,168
1924	7th	55	96	.364	37.0	Art Fletcher	299,818
1925	6th (tied)	68	85	.444	27.0	Art Fletcher	304,905
1926	8th	58	93	.384	29.5	Art Fletcher	240,600
1927	8th	51	103	.331	43.0	Stuffy McInnis	305,420
1928	8th	43	109	.283	51.0	Burt Shotton	182,168
1929	5th	71	82	.464	27.5	Burt Shotton	281,200
1930	8th	52	102	.338	40.0	Burt Shotton	299,007
1931	6th	66	88	.429	35.0	Burt Shotton	284,849
1932	4th	78	76	.506	12.0	Burt Shotton	268,914
1933	7th	60	92	.395	31.0	Burt Shotton	156,421
1934	7th	56	93	.376	37.0	Jimmy Wilson	169,885
1935	7th	64	89	.418	35.5	Jimmy Wilson	205,470
1936	8th	54	100	.351	38.0	Jimmy Wilson	249,219
1937	7th	61	92	.399	34.5	Jimmy Wilson	212,790
1938	8th	45	105	.300	43.0	Jimmy Wilson, Hans Lobert	166,111
1939	8th	45	106	.298	50.5	Doc Prothro	277,973
1940	8th	50	103	.327	50.0	Doc Prothro	207,177
1941	8th	43	111	.279	57.0	Doc Prothro	231,401
1942	8th	42	109	.278	62.5	Hans Lobert	230,183
1943	7th	64	90	.416	41.0	Bucky Harris, Fred Fitzsimmons	466,975
1944	8th	61	92	.399	43.5	Fred Fitzsimmons	369,586
1945	8th	46	108	.299	52.0	Fred Fitzsimmons, Ben Chapman	285,057
1946	5th	69	85	.448	28.0	Ben Chapman	1,045,247
1947	7th (tied)	62	92	.403	32.0	Ben Chapman	907,332
1948	6th	66	88	.429	25.5	Ben Chapman, Dusty Cooke, Eddie Sawyer	767,429
1949	3rd	81	73	.526	16.0	Eddie Sawyer	819,698
1950	1st	91	63	.591	+2.0	Eddie Sawyer	1,217,035
1951	5th	73	81	.474	23.5	Eddie Sawyer	937,658
1952	4th	87	67	.565	9.5	Eddie Sawyer, Steve O'Neill	775,417
1953	3rd (tied)	83	71	.539	22.0	Steve O'Neill	853,644
1954	4th	75	79	.487	22.0	Steve O'Neill, Terry Moore	738,991
1955	4th	77	77	.500	21.5	Mayo Smith	922,886
1956	5th	71	83	.461	22.0	Mayo Smith	934,798
1957	5th	77	77	.500	19.0	Mayo Smith	1,146,230
1958	8th	69	85	.448	23.0	Mayo Smith, Eddie Sawyer	931,110
1959	8th	64	90	.416	23.0	Eddie Sawyer	802,815
1960	8th	59	95	.383	36.0	Eddie Sawyer, Andy Cohen, Gene Mauch	862,205
1961	8th	47	107	.305	46.0	Gene Mauch	590,039
1962	7th	81	80	.503	20.0	Gene Mauch	762,034
1963	4th	87	75	.537	12.0	Gene Mauch	907,141
1964	2nd (tied)	92	70	.568	1.0	Gene Mauch	1,425,891
1965	6th	85	76	.528	11.5	Gene Mauch	1,166,376
1966	4th	87	75	.537	8.0	Gene Mauch	1,108,201
1967	5th	82	80	.506	19.5	Gene Mauch	828,888
1968	7th (tied)	76	86	.469	21.0	Gene Mauch, George Myatt, Bob Skinner	664,546

EAST DIVISION

Year	Position	W	L	Pct.	*GB	Manager	Attendance
1969	5th	63	99	.389	37.0	Bob Skinner, George Myatt	519,414
1970	5th	73	88	.453	15.5	Frank Lucchesi	708,247
1971	6th	67	95	.414	30.0	Frank Lucchesi	1,511,223
1972	6th	59	97	.378	37.5	Frank Lucchesi, Paul Owens	1,343,329
1973	6th	71	91	.438	11.5	Danny Ozark	1,475,934
1974	3rd	80	82	.494	8.0	Danny Ozark	1,808,648
1975	2nd	86	76	.531	6.5	Danny Ozark	1,909,233
1976	1st†	101	61	.623	+9.0	Danny Ozark	2,480,150
1977	1st†	101	61	.623	+5.0	Danny Ozark	2,700,070
1978	1st†	90	72	.556	+1.5	Danny Ozark	2,583,389
1979	4th	84	78	.519	14.0	Danny Ozark, Dallas Green	2,775,011
1980	1st‡	91	71	.562	+1.0	Dallas Green	2,651,650
1981	1st/3rd∞	59	48	.551	§	Dallas Green	1,638,752
1982	2nd	89	73	.549	3.0	Pat Corrales	2,376,394
1983	1st‡	90	72	.556	+6.0	Pat Corrales, Paul Owens	2,128,339
1984	4th	81	81	.500	15.5	Paul Owens	2,062,693
1985	5th	75	87	.463	26.0	John Felske	1,830,350
1986	2nd	86	75	.534	21.5	John Felske	1,933,335
1987	4th (tied)	80	82	.494	15.0	John Felske, Lee Elia	2,100,110
1988	6th	65	96	.404	35.5	Lee Elia, John Vukovich	1,990,041
1989	6th	67	95	.414	26.0	Nick Leyva	1,861,985
1990	4th (tied)	77	85	.475	18.0	Nick Leyva	1,992,484
1991	3rd	78	84	.481	20.0	Nick Leyva, Jim Fregosi	2,050,012
1992	6th	70	92	.432	26.0	Jim Fregosi	1,927,448
1993	1st‡	97	65	.599	+3.0	Jim Fregosi	3,137,674
1994	4th	54	61	.470	20.5	Jim Fregosi	2,290,971
1995	2nd (tied)	69	75	.479	21.0	Jim Fregosi	2,043,598
1996	5th	67	95	.414	29.0	Jim Fregosi	1,801,677
1997	5th	68	94	.420	33.0	Terry Francona	1,490,638
1998	3rd	75	87	.463	31.0	Terry Francona	1,715,702
1999	3rd	77	85	.475	26.0	Terry Francona	1,825,337
2000	5th	65	97	.401	30.0	Terry Francona	1,612,769
2001	2nd	86	76	.531	2.0	Larry Bowa	1,782,460

*Games behind winner. †Lost championship series. ‡Won championship series. §First half 34-21; second 25-27. ∞Lost division series.

INDIVIDUAL RECORDS (1883 TO DATE)

SERVICE

Most years by non-pitcher
18—Mike Schmidt

Most years by pitcher
15—Steve Carlton

BATTING

Most games
163—Pete Rose, 1979

Most games, career
2,404—Mike Schmidt

Most at-bats
701—Juan Samuel, 160 games, 1984

Most at-bats, career
8,352—Mike Schmidt

Most runs
196—Billy Hamilton, 131 games, 1894

Most runs (since 1900)
158—Chuck Klein, 156 games, 1930

Most runs, career
1,506—Mike Schmidt

Most hits
254—Lefty O'Doul, 154 games, 1929

Most hits, career
2,234—Mike Schmidt

Most singles
181—Lefty O'Doul, 154 games, 1929
Richie Ashburn, 154 games, 1951

Most singles, career
1,811—Richie Ashburn

Most doubles
59—Chuck Klein, 156 games, 1930

Most doubles, career
432—Ed Delahanty

Most doubles, career (since 1900)
408—Mike Schmidt

Most triples
26—Sam Thompson, 102 games, 1894

Most triples (since 1900)
19—Juan Samuel, 160 games, 1984

Most triples, career
151—Ed Delahanty

Most triples, career (since 1900)
127—Sherry Magee

Most homers by righthander
48—Mike Schmidt, 150 games, 1980

Most homers by lefthander
43—Chuck Klein, 149 games, 1929

Most homers by switch-hitter
27—Dave Hollins, 156 games, 1992

Most homers by rookie
30—Willie Montanez, 158 games, 1971

Most homers, month
15—Cy Williams, May, 1923

Most homers at home
29—Chuck Klein, 1932

Most homers on road
29—Mike Schmidt, 1979

Most homers by righthander, career
548—Mike Schmidt

Most homers by lefthander, career
243—Chuck Klein

Most homers by switch-hitter, career
67—Dave Hollins

Most grand slams
4—Vince DiMaggio, 127 games, 1945

Most grand slams, career
7—Mike Schmidt

Most total bases
445—Chuck Klein, 156 games, 1930

Most total bases, career
4,404—Mike Schmidt

Most long hits
107—Chuck Klein, 156 games, 1930

Most long hits, career
1,015—Mike Schmidt

Most extra bases on long hits
195—Chuck Klein, 156 games, 1930

Most extra bases on long hits, career
2,170—Mike Schmidt

Most sacrifice hits
43—Kid Gleason, 155 games, 1905

Most sacrifice flies
13—Willie Montanez, 158 games, 1971
Mike Schmidt, 150 games, 1980

Most bases on balls
129—Lenny Dykstra, 161 games, 1993

Most bases on balls, career
1,507—Mike Schmidt

Most strikeouts
180—Mike Schmidt, 158 games, 1975

Fewest strikeouts
8—Emil Verban, 155 games, 1947

Most strikeouts, career
1,883—Mike Schmidt

Most hit by pitch
19—Dave Hollins, 156 games, 1992

Most runs batted in
170—Chuck Klein, 154 games, 1930

Most runs batted in, career
1,595—Mike Schmidt

Most game-winning RBIs
17—Mike Schmidt, 150 games, 1980
Gary Matthews, 162 games, 1982

Highest batting average
.408—Ed Delahanty, 145 games, 1899

Highest batting average (since 1900)
.398—Lefty O'Doul, 154 games, 1929

Highest batting average, career
.362—Billy Hamilton

Highest batting average, career (since 1900)
.326—Chuck Klein

Highest slugging average
.687—Chuck Klein, 156 games, 1930

Highest slugging average, career
.553—Chuck Klein

Longest batting streak
36 games—Billy Hamilton, 1894

Longest batting streak (since 1900)
26 games—Chuck Klein, 1930 (twice)

Most grounded into double play
25—Del Ennis, 153 games, 1950
Ted Sizemore, 152 games, 1977

Fewest grounded into double play
3—Chuck Klein, 152 games, 1933
Richie Ashburn, 156 games, 1953
Richie Ashburn, 153 games, 1954

BASERUNNING

Most stolen bases
115—Billy Hamilton, 133 games, 1891

Most stolen bases (since 1900)
72—Juan Samuel, 160 games, 1984

Most stolen bases, career
437—Ed Delahanty

Most stolen bases, career (since 1900)
387—Sherry Magee

Most caught stealing
19—Juan Samuel, 161 games, 1985

PITCHING (SINCE 1900)

Most games
90—Kent Tekulve, 1987

Most games, career
529—Robin Roberts

Most games started
45—Grover Alexander, 1916

Most games started, career
499—Steve Carlton

Most complete games
38—Grover Alexander, 1916

Most complete games, career
272—Robin Roberts

Most games finished
62—Jim Konstanty, 1950

Most innings
389—Grover Alexander, 1916

Most innings, career
3,740—Robin Roberts

Most games won
33—Grover Alexander, 1916

Most games won, career
241—Steve Carlton

Most 20-victory seasons
6—Grover Alexander
Robin Roberts

Most games lost
24—Chick Fraser, 1904

Most games lost, career
199—Robin Roberts

Highest winning percentage
.800—Robin Roberts (28-7), 1952
Tommy Greene (16-4), 1993

Longest winning streak
15 games—Steve Carlton, 1972

Longest losing streak
12 games—Russ Miller, 1928
Hugh Mulcahy, 1940
Ken Reynolds, 1972

Most saves, season
43—Mitch Williams, 1993

Most bases on balls
164—Earl Moore, 1911

Most bases on balls, career
1,252—Steve Carlton

Most strikeouts
319—Curt Schilling, 1997

Most strikeouts, game
18—Chris Short, October 2, 1965, second game, first 15 innings of 18-inning game
17—Art Mahaffey, April 23, 1961, second game

Most strikeouts, career
3,031—Steve Carlton

Most shutouts
16—Grover Alexander, 1916

Most shutouts, career
61—Grover Alexander

Most 1-0 shutouts won
4—Grover Alexander, 1916

Most runs
178—Ray Benge, 1930

Most earned runs
147—Robin Roberts, 1956

Most hits
348—Claude Passeau, 1937

Most hit batsmen
19—Fred Mitchell, 1903
Jim Bunning, 1966

Most wild pitches
22—Jack Hamilton, 1962

Most home runs
46—Robin Roberts, 1956

Most sacrifice hits
21—Curt Simmons, 1954
Dennis Bennett, 1964
Jim Bunning, 1965
Wayne Twitchell, 1973

Most sacrifice flies
15—Randy Lerch, 1979

Lowest ERA
1.22—Grover Alexander, 376 innings, 1915

CLUB RECORDS

Most players
54 in 1996

Fewest players
23 in 1915

Most games
163 in 1979, 1983, 1989

Most at-bats
5,685 in 1993

Most runs
944 in 1930

Fewest runs
394 in 1942

Most opponents' runs
1,199 in 1930

Most hits
1,783 in 1930

Fewest hits
1,113 in 1907

Most singles
1,338 in 1894

Most singles (since 1900)
1,268 in 1930

Most doubles
345 in 1930

Most triples
148 in 1894

Most triples (since 1900)
82 in 1905

Most homers
186 in 1977

Fewest homers (154 or 162-game schedule)
11 in 1908

Most homers at Baker Bowl, home and opponents
160 in 1929

Most homers at Shibe Park, home and opponents
154 in 1955

Most homers at Veterans Stadium, home and opponents
185 in 1999

Most pinch home runs
11 in 1958

Most grand slams
8 in 1993

Most total bases
2,594 in 1930

Most long hits
519 in 1932

Most extra bases on long hits
936 in 1977

Most sacrifices (sacrifice hits and sacrifice flies)
239 in 1909

Most sacrifice hits
174 in 1905

Most sacrifice flies
74 in 1977

Most stolen bases
200 in 1908

Most caught stealing
80 in 1921

Most bases on balls
665 in 1993

Most strikeouts
1,154 in 1986

Fewest strikeouts
452 in 1924

Most hit by pitch
53 in 1962

Fewest hit by pitch
9 in 1939

Most runs batted in
884 in 1930

Most game-winning RBIs
86 in 1980

Highest batting average
.343 in 1894

Highest batting average (since 1900)
.315 in 1930

Lowest batting average
.232 in 1942

Highest slugging average
.467 in 1929

west slugging average
05 in 1907

ost grounded into double play
4 in 1950

west grounded into double play
| in 1935, 1973

ost left on bases
281 in 1993

ewest left on bases
1 in 1920

ost .300 hitters
| in 1925

ost putouts
440 in 1980

ewest putouts
887 in 1907

ost assists
176 in 1921

ewest assists
437 in 1957

ost chances accepted
440 in 1913

ewest chances accepted
545 in 1955

ost errors
03 in 1904

ewest errors
4 in 2001

ost errorless games
3 in 2001

ost consecutive errorless games
1 in 1967, 1998

ost double plays
79 in 1961, 1973

ewest double plays
1 in 1991

ost passed balls
7 in 1947, 1971

ewest passed balls
in 1952, 1956

ighest fielding average
85 in 2001

owest fielding average
36 in 1904

ighest home attendance
,137,674 in 1993

ighest road attendance
,666,219 in 1993

ost games won
01 in 1976, 1977

Most games lost
111 in 1941

Most games won, month
22 in September 1916, July 1950, July 1952, May 1976, August 1977, September 1983

Most games lost, month
27 in September 1939

Highest percentage games won
.623 in 1886 (won 71, lost 43)
in 1976 and 1977 (won 101, lost 61)

Lowest percentage games won
.173 in 1883 (won 17, lost 81)

Lowest percentage games won (since 1900)
.279 in 1941 (won 43, lost 111)

Games won, league
8,339 in 119 years

Games lost, league
9,572 in 119 years

Most shutouts won
24 in 1916

Most shutouts lost
23 in 1908, 1909

Most 1-0 games won
7 in 1913

Most 1-0 games lost
10 in 1967

Most consecutive games won
16 in 1887, 1890, 1892

Most consecutive games won (since 1900)
13 in 1977, 1991

Most consecutive games lost
23 in 1961

Number of times league champions
5

Number of last-place finishes
27 (tied in 1947, 1997, 2000)

Most runs, game
29 vs. Louisville, August 17, 1894

Most runs, game (since 1900)
26 vs. New York, June 11, 1985

Most runs by opponent, game
29 by Boston, June 20, 1883
by New York, June 15, 1887

Most runs by opponent, game (since 1900)
28 by St. Louis, July 6, 1929, second game

Most runs, shutout game
24 vs. Indianapolis, June 28, 1887

Most runs, shutout game (since 1900)
18 vs. Pittsburgh, July 11, 1910
vs. Cincinnati, August 10, 1930, first game
vs. Cincinnati, July 14, 1934, first game

Most runs by opponent, shutout game
28 by Providence, August 21, 1883

Most runs by opponent, shutout game (since 1900)
16 by Chicago, May 4, 1929, first game

Most runs doubleheader shutout
18 vs. Brooklyn, September 26, 1912

Most runs, inning
12 vs. New York, October 2, 1897, second inning
vs. Chicago, July 21, 1923, first game, sixth inning

Longest 1-0 game won
16 innings vs. Chicago, May 17, 1991

Longest 1-0 game lost
17 innings vs. Montreal, September 21, 1981

Most hits, game
36 vs. Louisville, August 17, 1894

Most hits, game (since 1900)
27 vs. New York, June 11, 1985

Most home runs, game
7 vs. New York, September 8, 1998

Most consecutive games with one or more homers
13 (16 homers), 1964

Most total bases, game
49 vs. Louisville, August 17, 1894
48 vs. Pittsburgh, July 23, 1930, second game, 13 innings
vs. Chicago, May 17, 1979, 10 innings
47 vs. New York, June 11, 1985

Largest crowd, day game
60,985 vs. Chicago, April 9, 1993

Largest crowd, doubleheader
63,346 vs. Pittsburgh, August 10, 1979

Largest crowd, night game
63,816 vs. Cincinnati, July 3, 1984

Largest crowd, home opener
60,985 vs. Chicago, April 9, 1993

PITTSBURGH PIRATES
YEARLY FINISHES

ear	Position	W	L	Pct.	*GB	Manager	Attendance
901	1st	90	49	.647	+7.5	Fred Clarke	251,955
902	1st	103	36	.741	+27.5	Fred Clarke	243,826
903	1st	91	49	.650	+6.5	Fred Clarke	326,855
904	4th	87	66	.569	19.0	Fred Clarke	340,615
905	2nd	96	57	.627	9.0	Fred Clarke	369,124
906	3rd	93	60	.608	23.5	Fred Clarke	394,877
907	2nd	91	63	.591	17.0	Fred Clarke	319,506
908	2nd	98	56	.636	1.0	Fred Clarke	382,444
909	1st	110	42	.724	+6.5	Fred Clarke	534,950
910	3rd	86	67	.562	17.5	Fred Clarke	436,586
911	3rd	85	69	.552	14.5	Fred Clarke	432,000
912	2nd	93	58	.616	10.0	Fred Clarke	384,000
913	4th	78	71	.523	21.5	Fred Clarke	296,000
914	7th	69	85	.448	25.5	Fred Clarke	139,620
915	5th	73	81	.474	18.0	Fred Clarke	225,743
916	6th	65	89	.422	29.0	Jimmy Callahan	289,132

Year	Position	W	L	Pct.	*GB	Manager	Attendance
1917	8th	51	103	.331	47.0	Jimmy Callahan, Honus Wagner, Hugo Bezdek	192,807
1918	4th	65	60	.520	17.0	Hugo Bezdek	213,610
1919	4th	71	68	.511	24.5	Hugo Bezdek	276,810
1920	4th	79	75	.513	14.0	George Gibson	429,037
1921	2nd	90	63	.588	4.0	George Gibson	701,567
1922	3rd (tied)	85	69	.552	8.0	George Gibson, Bill McKechnie	523,675
1923	3rd	87	67	.565	8.5	Bill McKechnie	611,082
1924	3rd	90	63	.588	3.0	Bill McKechnie	736,883
1925	1st	95	58	.621	+8.5	Bill McKechnie	804,354
1926	3rd	84	69	.549	4.5	Bill McKechnie	798,542
1927	1st	94	60	.610	+1.5	Donie Bush	869,720
1928	4th	85	67	.559	9.0	Donie Bush	495,070
1929	2nd	88	65	.575	10.5	Donie Bush, Jewel Ens	491,377
1930	5th	80	74	.519	12.0	Jewel Ens	357,795
1931	5th	75	79	.487	26.0	Jewel Ens	260,392
1932	2nd	86	68	.558	4.0	George Gibson	287,262
1933	2nd	87	67	.565	5.0	George Gibson	288,747
1934	5th	74	76	.493	19.5	George Gibson, Pie Traynor	322,622
1935	4th	86	67	.562	13.5	Pie Traynor	352,885
1936	4th	84	70	.545	8.0	Pie Traynor	372,524
1937	3rd	86	68	.558	10.0	Pie Traynor	459,679
1938	2nd	86	64	.573	2.0	Pie Traynor	641,033
1939	6th	68	85	.444	28.5	Pie Traynor	376,734
1940	4th	78	76	.506	22.5	Frankie Frisch	507,934
1941	4th	81	73	.526	19.0	Frankie Frisch	482,241
1942	5th	66	81	.449	36.5	Frankie Frisch	448,897
1943	4th	80	74	.519	25.0	Frankie Frisch	604,278
1944	2nd	90	63	.588	14.5	Frankie Frisch	498,740
1945	4th	82	72	.532	16.0	Frankie Frisch	604,694
1946	7th	63	91	.409	34.0	Frankie Frisch, Spud Davis	749,962
1947	7th (tied)	62	92	.403	32.0	Billy Herman, Bill Burwell	1,283,531
1948	4th	83	71	.539	8.5	Billy Meyer	1,517,021
1949	6th	71	83	.461	26.0	Billy Meyer	1,499,435
1950	8th	57	96	.373	33.5	Billy Meyer	1,166,267
1951	7th	64	90	.416	32.5	Billy Meyer	980,590
1952	8th	42	112	.273	54.5	Billy Meyer	686,673
1953	8th	50	104	.325	55.0	Fred Haney	572,757
1954	8th	53	101	.344	44.0	Fred Haney	475,494
1955	8th	60	94	.390	38.5	Fred Haney	469,397
1956	7th	66	88	.429	27.0	Bobby Bragan	949,878
1957	7th (tied)	62	92	.403	33.0	Bobby Bragan, Danny Murtaugh	850,732
1958	2nd	84	70	.545	8.0	Danny Murtaugh	1,311,988
1959	4th	78	76	.506	9.0	Danny Murtaugh	1,359,917
1960	1st	95	59	.617	+7.0	Danny Murtaugh	1,705,828
1961	6th	75	79	.487	18.0	Danny Murtaugh	1,199,128
1962	4th	93	68	.578	8.0	Danny Murtaugh	1,090,648
1963	8th	74	88	.457	25.0	Danny Murtaugh	783,648
1964	6th (tied)	80	82	.494	13.0	Danny Murtaugh	759,496
1965	3rd	90	72	.556	7.0	Harry Walker	909,279
1966	3rd	92	70	.568	3.0	Harry Walker	1,196,618
1967	6th	81	81	.500	20.5	Harry Walker, Danny Murtaugh	907,012
1968	6th	80	82	.494	17.0	Larry Shepard	693,485

EAST DIVISION

Year	Position	W	L	Pct.	*GB	Manager	Attendance
1969	3rd	88	74	.543	12.0	Larry Shepard, Alex Grammas	769,369
1970	1st†	89	73	.549	+5.0	Danny Murtaugh	1,341,947
1971	1st‡	97	65	.599	+7.0	Danny Murtaugh	1,501,132
1972	1st†	96	59	.619	+11.0	Bill Virdon	1,427,460
1973	3rd	80	82	.494	2.5	Bill Virdon, Danny Murtaugh	1,319,913
1974	1st†	88	74	.543	+1.5	Danny Murtaugh	1,110,552
1975	1st†	92	69	.571	+6.5	Danny Murtaugh	1,270,018
1976	2nd	92	70	.568	9.0	Danny Murtaugh	1,025,945
1977	2nd	96	66	.593	5.0	Chuck Tanner	1,237,349
1978	2nd	88	73	.547	1.5	Chuck Tanner	964,106
1979	1st‡	98	64	.605	+2.0	Chuck Tanner	1,435,454
1980	3rd	83	79	.512	8.0	Chuck Tanner	1,646,757
1981	4th/6th	46	56	.451	§.0	Chuck Tanner	541,789
1982	4th	84	78	.519	8.0	Chuck Tanner	1,024,106
1983	2nd	84	78	.519	6.0	Chuck Tanner	1,225,916
1984	6th	75	87	.463	21.5	Chuck Tanner	773,500
1985	6th	57	104	.354	43.5	Chuck Tanner	735,900
1986	6th	64	98	.395	44.0	Jim Leyland	1,000,917
1987	4th (tied)	80	82	.494	15.0	Jim Leyland	1,161,193
1988	2nd	85	75	.531	15.0	Jim Leyland	1,866,713
1989	5th	74	88	.457	19.0	Jim Leyland	1,374,141
1990	1st†	95	67	.586	+4.0	Jim Leyland	2,049,908
1991	1st†	98	64	.605	+14.0	Jim Leyland	2,065,302

Year	Position	W	L	Pct.	*GB	Manager	Attendance
1992	1st†	96	66	.593	+9.0	Jim Leyland	1,829,395
1993	5th	75	87	.463	22.0	Jim Leyland	1,650,593

CENTRAL DIVISION

Year	Position	W	L	Pct.	*GB	Manager	Attendance
1994	3rd (tied)	53	61	.465	13.0	Jim Leyland	1,222,520
1995	5th	58	86	.403	27.0	Jim Leyland	905,517
1996	5th	73	89	.451	15.0	Jim Leyland	1,332,150
1997	2nd	79	83	.488	5.0	Gene Lamont	1,657,022
1998	6th	69	93	.426	33.0	Gene Lamont	1,560,950
1999	3rd	78	83	.484	18.5	Gene Lamont	1,638,023
2000	5th	69	93	.426	26.0	Gene Lamont	1,748,908
2001	6th	62	100	.383	31.0	Lloyd McClendon	2,436,126

*Games behind winner. †Lost championship series. ‡Won championship series. §First half 25-23; second half 21-33.

INDIVIDUAL RECORDS (1887 TO DATE)

SERVICE

Most years by non-pitcher
21—Willie Stargell

Most years by pitcher
18—Babe Adams

BATTING

Most games
163— Bill Mazeroski, 1967
Bobby Bonilla, 1989

Most games, career
2,433—Roberto Clemente

Most at-bats
698—Matty Alou, 162 games, 1969

Most at-bats, career
9,454—Roberto Clemente

Most runs
148—Jake Stenzel, 131 games, 1894

Most runs (since 1900)
144—Kiki Cuyler, 153 games, 1925

Most runs, career
1,520—Honus Wagner

Most hits
237—Paul Waner, 155 games, 1927

Most hits, career
3,000—Roberto Clemente

Most singles
198—Lloyd Waner, 150 games, 1927

Most singles, career
2,154—Roberto Clemente

Most doubles
62—Paul Waner, 154 games, 1932

Most doubles, career
556—Honus Wagner, Paul Waner

Most triples
36—Owen Wilson, 152 games, 1912

Most triples, career
231—Honus Wagner

Most homers by righthander
54—Ralph Kiner, 152 games, 1949

Most homers by lefthander
48—Willie Stargell, 141 games, 1971

Most homers by switch-hitter
32—Bobby Bonilla, 160 games, 1990

Most homers by rookie
23— Johnny Rizzo, 143 games, 1938
Ralph Kiner, 144 games, 1946

Most homers, month
16—Ralph Kiner, September, 1949

Most homers at home
31—Ralph Kiner, 1948

Most homers on road
27—Willie Stargell, 1971

Most homers by lefthander, career
475—Willie Stargell

Most homers by righthander, career
301—Ralph Kiner

Most homers by switch-hitter, career
114—Bobby Bonilla

Most grand slams
4—Ralph Kiner, 152 games, 1949

Most grand slams, career
11—Ralph Kiner
Willie Stargell

Most total bases
366—Kiki Cuyler, 153 games, 1925

Most total bases, career
4,492—Roberto Clemente

Most long hits, career
953—Willie Stargell

Most long hits
90—Willie Stargell, 148 games, 1973

Most extra bases on long hits
191—Ralph Kiner, 152 games, 1949

Most extra bases on long hits, career
1,958—Willie Stargell

Most sacrifice hits
39—Jay Bell, 159 games, 1990

Most sacrifice flies
15—Bobby Bonilla, 160 games, 1990

Most bases on balls
137—Ralph Kiner, 151 games, 1951

Most bases on balls, career
937—Willie Stargell

Most strikeouts
163—Donn Clendenon, 158 games, 1968

Most strikeouts, career
1,936—Willie Stargell

Fewest strikeouts
13—Carson Bigbee, 150 games, 1922
Lloyd Waner, 152 games, 1928

Most hit by pitch
31—Jason Kendall, 144 games, 1997
Jason Kendall, 149 games, 1998

Most runs batted in
131—Paul Waner, 155 games, 1927

Most runs batted in, career
1,540—Willie Stargell

Most game-winning RBIs
16—Andy Van Slyke, 154 games, 1988

Most consecutive games with RBI
12—Paul Waner (23 RBIs), 1927

Highest batting average
.385—Arky Vaughan, 137 games, 1935

Highest batting average, career
.340—Paul Waner

Highest slugging average
.658—Ralph Kiner, 152 games, 1949

Highest slugging average, career
.567—Ralph Kiner

Longest batting streak
27 games—Jimmy Williams, 1899

Longest batting streak (since 1900)
26 games—Danny O'Connell, 1953

Longest batting streak, two seasons
30 games—Charlie Grimm, 1922 (5), 1923 (25)

Most grounded into double play
25—Al Todd, 133 games, 1938

Fewest grounded into double play
4—Omar Moreno, 150 games, 1977
Frank Taveras, 157 games, 1978
Barry Bonds, 150 games, 1987
Bobby Bonilla, 159 games, 1988
Tony Womack, 159 games, 1998

BASERUNNING

Most stolen bases
96—Omar Moreno, 162 games, 1980

Most stolen bases, career
688—Max Carey

Most caught stealing
33—Omar Moreno, 162 games, 1980

PITCHING (SINCE 1900)

Most games
94—Kent Tekulve, 1979

Most games, career
802—Roy Face

Most games, started
42—Bob Friend, 1956

Most games, started, career
477—Bob Friend

Most complete games
32—Vic Willis, 1906

Most complete games, career
263—Wilbur Cooper

Most games finished
67—Kent Tekulve, 1979

Most innings
331—Burleigh Grimes, 1928

Most innings, career
3,481—Bob Friend

Most games won
28—Jack Chesbro, 1902

Most games won, career
202—Wilbur Cooper

– 327 –

Most 20-victory seasons
4—Deacon Phillippe
   Vic Willis
   Wilbur Cooper
   Jesse Tannehill

Most games lost
21—Murry Dickson, 1952

Most games lost, career
218—Bob Friend

Highest winning percentage
.947—Roy Face (18-1), 1959

Longest winning streak
17 games, Roy Face, 1959

Longest winning streak, two seasons
22 games, Roy Face, 1958 (5), 1959 (17)

Longest losing streak
13 games—Burleigh Grimes, 1917

Most saves, season
34—Jim Gott, 1988

Most bases on balls
159—Marty O'Toole, 1912

Most bases on balls, career
869—Bob Friend

Most strikeouts
276—Bob Veale, 1965

Most strikeouts, game
16—Bob Veale, June 1, 1965

Most strikeouts, career
1,682—Bob Friend

Most shutouts
8—Jack Chesbro, 1902
   Lefty Leifield, 1906
   Al Mamaux, 1915
   Babe Adams, 1920

Most shutouts, career
45—Babe Adams

Most 1-0 shutouts won
3—Vic Willis, 1908
   Claude Hendrix, 1912
   Wilbur Cooper, 1917
   Ed Brandt, 1937

Most runs
181—Ray Kremer, 1930

Most earned runs
154—Ray Kremer, 1930

Most hits
366—Ray Kremer, 1930

Most hit batsmen
21—Jack Chesbro, 1902

Most wild pitches
18—Bob Veale, 1964

Most home runs
32—Murry Dickson, 1951

Most sacrifice hits
20—Max Surkont, 1954
   Jerry Reuss, 1974

Most sacrifice flies
12—Vern Law, 1954
   John Candelaria, 1974

Lowest ERA
1.87—Wilbur Cooper, 246 innings, 1916

CLUB RECORDS

Most players
49 in 1987, 2001

Fewest players
25 in 1938

Most games
164 in 1989

Most at-bats
5,724 in 1967

Most runs
912 in 1925

Fewest runs
464 in 1917

Most opponents' runs
928 in 1930

Most hits
1,698 in 1922

Fewest hits
1,197 in 1914

Most singles
1,297 in 1922

Most doubles
320 in 2000

Most triples
129 in 1912

Most homers
171 in 1999

Fewest homers (154 or 162-game schedule)
9 in 1917

Most homers at Forbes Field, home and opponents
182 in 1947

Most homers at Three Rivers Stadium, home and opponents
172 in 2000

Most homers at PNC Park, home and opponents
150 in 2001

Most grand slams
7 in 1978, 1996

Most pinch home runs
10 in 1996, 2001

Most total bases
2,430 in 1966

Most long hits
519 in 2000

Most extra bases on long hits
886 in 2000

Most sacrifices (sacrifice hits and sacrifice flies)
214 in 1927

Most sacrifice hits
190 in 1906

Most sacrifice flies
67 in 1982

Most stolen bases
264 in 1907

Most caught stealing
120 in 1977

Most bases on balls
620 in 1991

Most strikeouts
1,197 in 1999

Fewest strikeouts
326 in 1922

Most hit by pitch
92 in 1997

Fewest hit by pitch
11 in 1937

Most runs batted in
844 in 1930

Most game-winning RBIs
80 in 1980, 1982

Highest batting average
.309 in 1928

Lowest batting average
.231 in 1952

Highest slugging average
.449 in 1930

Lowest slugging average
.298 in 1917

Most grounded into double play
142 in 1950

Fewest grounded into double play
95 in 1978

Most left on bases
1,241 in 1936

Fewest left on bases
992 in 1924

Most .300 hitters
9 in 1928

Most putouts
4,480 in 1979

Fewest putouts
3,983 in 1934

Most assists
2,089 in 1905

Fewest assists
1,584 in 1934

Most chances accepted
6,462 in 1968

Fewest chances accepted
5,567 in 1934

Most errors
291 in 1904

Fewest errors
101 in 1992

Most errorless games
87 in 1992

Most consecutive errorless games
10 in 2001

Most double plays
215 in 1966

Fewest double plays
94 in 1935

Most passed balls
32 in 1953

Fewest passed balls
3 in 1941, 1943

Highest fielding average
.984 in 1992

Lowest fielding average
.955 in 1904

Highest home attendance
2,436,126 in 2001

Highest road attendance
2,507,346 in 1993

Most games won
110 in 1909

Most games lost
113 in 1890

Most games lost (since 1900)
112 in 1952

Most games won, month
25 in September 1901, September 1908, July 1932

Most games lost, month
24 in September 1916

Highest percentage games won
.741 in 1902 (won 103, lost 36)

Lowest percentage games won
.169 in 1890 (won 23, lost 113)

Lowest percentage games won (since 1900)
.273 in 1952 (won 42, lost 112)

Games won, league
8,967 in 115 years

Games lost, league
8,540 in 115 years

Most shutouts won
26 in 1906

Most shutouts lost
27 in 1916

Most 1-0 games won
10 in 1908

Most 1-0 games lost
10 in 1914

Most consecutive games won
16 in 1909

Most consecutive games lost
23 in 1890

Most consecutive games lost (since 1900)
12 in 1939

Number of times league champions
9

Number of last-place finishes
14 (tied in 1947, 1957)

Most runs, game
27 vs. Boston, June 6, 1894

Most runs, game (since 1900)
24 vs. St. Louis, June 22, 1925

Most runs by opponent, game
28 by Boston, August 27, 1887

Most runs by opponent, game (since 1900)
23 by Philadelphia, July 13, 1900, eight innings
by Brooklyn, July 10, 1943

Most runs, shutout game
22 vs. Chicago, September 16, 1975

Most runs by opponent, shutout game
18 by Philadelphia, July 11, 1910

Most runs, doubleheader shutout
15 vs. Philadelphia, August 7, 1915

Most runs, inning
12 vs. St. Louis, April 22, 1892, first inning
vs. Boston, June 6, 1894, third inning

Most runs, inning (since 1900)
11 vs. St. Louis, September 7, 1942, first game, sixth inning
vs. Cincinnati, May 4, 1992, sixth inning

Longest 1-0 game won
18 innings vs. San Diego, June 7, 1972, second game

Longest 1-0 game lost
14 innings vs. Cincinnati, June 18, 1943

Most hits, game
27 vs. Philadelphia, August 8, 1922, first game

Most home runs, game
7 vs. Boston, June 8, 1894
vs. St. Louis, August 16, 1947

Most consecutive games with one or more homers
13 (21 homers), 1994

Most total bases, game
47 vs. Atlanta, August 1, 1970

Largest crowd, day game
55,351 vs. Chicago, October 1, 2000

Largest crowd, doubleheader
49,886 vs. New York, July 27, 1972

Largest crowd, night game
54,274 vs. Montreal, April 8, 1991

Largest crowd, home opener
54,274 vs. Montreal, April 8, 1991

ST. LOUIS CARDINALS
YEARLY FINISHES

Year	Position	W	L	Pct.	*GB	Manager	Attendance
1901	4th	76	64	.543	14.5	Patsy Donovan	379,988
1902	6th	56	78	.418	44.5	Patsy Donovan	226,417
1903	8th	43	94	.314	46.5	Patsy Donovan	226,538
1904	5th	75	79	.487	31.5	Kid Nichols	386,750
1905	6th	58	96	.377	47.5	Kid Nichols, Jimmy Burke, Matt Robison	292,800
1906	7th	52	98	.347	63.0	John McCloskey	283,770
1907	8th	52	101	.340	55.5	John McCloskey	185,377
1908	8th	49	105	.318	50.0	John McCloskey	205,129
1909	7th	54	98	.355	56.0	Roger Bresnahan	299,982
1910	7th	63	90	.412	40.5	Roger Bresnahan	355,668
1911	5th	75	74	.503	22.0	Roger Bresnahan	447,768
1912	6th	63	90	.412	41.0	Roger Bresnahan	241,759
1913	8th	51	99	.340	49.0	Miller Huggins	203,531
1914	3rd	81	72	.529	13.0	Miller Huggins	256,099
1915	6th	72	81	.471	18.5	Miller Huggins	252,666
1916	7th (tied)	60	93	.392	33.5	Miller Huggins	224,308
1917	3rd	82	70	.539	15.0	Miller Huggins	288,491
1918	8th	51	78	.395	33.0	Jack Hendricks	110,599
1919	7th	54	83	.394	40.5	Branch Rickey	167,059
1920	5th (tied)	75	79	.487	18.0	Branch Rickey	326,836
1921	3rd	87	66	.569	7.0	Branch Rickey	384,773
1922	3rd (tied)	85	69	.552	8.0	Branch Rickey	536,998
1923	5th	79	74	.516	16.0	Branch Rickey	338,551
1924	6th	65	89	.422	28.5	Branch Rickey	272,885
1925	4th	77	76	.503	18.0	Branch Rickey, Rogers Hornsby	404,959
1926	1st	89	65	.578	+2.0	Rogers Hornsby	668,428
1927	2nd	92	61	.601	1.5	Bob O'Farrell	749,340
1928	1st	95	59	.617	+2.0	Bill McKechnie	761,574
1929	4th	78	74	.513	20.0	Bill McKechnie, Billy Southworth	399,887
1930	1st	92	62	.597	+2.0	Gabby Street	508,501
1931	1st	101	53	.656	+13.0	Gabby Street	608,535
1932	6th (tied)	72	82	.468	18.0	Gabby Street	279,219
1933	5th	82	71	.536	9.5	Gabby Street, Frankie Frisch	256,171
1934	1st	95	58	.621	+2.0	Frankie Frisch	325,056
1935	2nd	96	58	.623	4.0	Frankie Frisch	506,084
1936	2nd (tied)	87	67	.565	5.0	Frankie Frisch	448,078
1937	4th	81	73	.526	15.0	Frankie Frisch	430,811
1938	6th	71	80	.470	17.5	Frankie Frisch, Mike Gonzalez	291,418
1939	2nd	92	61	.601	4.5	Ray Blades	400,245
1940	3rd	84	69	.549	16.0	Ray Blades, Mike Gonzalez, Billy Southworth	324,078
1941	2nd	97	56	.634	2.5	Billy Southworth	633,645
1942	1st	106	48	.688	+2.0	Billy Southworth	553,552
1943	1st	105	49	.682	+18.0	Billy Southworth	517,135
1944	1st	105	49	.682	+14.5	Billy Southworth	461,968
1945	2nd	95	59	.617	3.0	Billy Southworth	594,630

Year	Position	W	L	Pct.	*GB	Manager	Attendance
1946	1st†	98	58	.628	+2.0	Eddie Dyer	1,061,807
1947	2nd	89	65	.578	5.0	Eddie Dyer	1,247,913
1948	2nd	85	69	.552	6.5	Eddie Dyer	1,111,440
1949	2nd	96	58	.623	1.0	Eddie Dyer	1,430,676
1950	5th	78	75	.510	12.5	Eddie Dyer	1,093,411
1951	3rd	81	73	.526	15.5	Marty Marion	1,013,429
1952	3rd	88	66	.571	8.5	Eddie Stanky	913,113
1953	3rd (tied)	83	71	.539	22.0	Eddie Stanky	880,242
1954	6th	72	82	.468	25.0	Eddie Stanky	1,039,698
1955	7th	68	86	.442	30.5	Eddie Stanky, Harry Walker	849,130
1956	4th	76	78	.494	17.0	Fred Hutchinson	1,029,773
1957	2nd	87	67	.565	8.0	Fred Hutchinson	1,183,575
1958	5th (tied)	72	82	.468	20.0	Fred Hutchinson, Stan Hack	1,063,730
1959	7th	71	83	.461	16.0	Solly Hemus	929,953
1960	3rd	86	68	.558	9.0	Solly Hemus	1,096,632
1961	5th	80	74	.519	13.0	Solly Hemus, Johnny Keane	855,305
1962	6th	84	78	.519	17.5	Johnny Keane	953,895
1963	2nd	93	69	.574	6.0	Johnny Keane	1,170,546
1964	1st	93	69	.574	+1.0	Johnny Keane	1,143,294
1965	7th	80	81	.497	16.5	Red Schoendienst	1,241,201
1966	6th	83	79	.512	12.0	Red Schoendienst	1,712,980
1967	1st	101	60	.627	+10.5	Red Schoendienst	2,090,145
1968	1st	97	65	.599	+9.0	Red Schoendienst	2,011,167

EAST DIVISION

Year	Position	W	L	Pct.	*GB	Manager	Attendance
1969	4th	87	75	.537	13.0	Red Schoendienst	1,682,783
1970	4th	76	86	.469	13.0	Red Schoendienst	1,629,736
1971	2nd	90	72	.556	7.0	Red Schoendienst	1,604,671
1972	4th	75	81	.481	21.5	Red Schoendienst	1,196,894
1973	2nd	81	81	.500	1.5	Red Schoendienst	1,574,046
1974	2nd	86	75	.534	1.5	Red Schoendienst	1,838,413
1975	3rd (tied)	82	80	.506	10.5	Red Schoendienst	1,695,270
1976	5th	72	90	.444	29.0	Red Schoendienst	1,207,079
1977	3rd	83	79	.512	18.0	Vern Rapp	1,659,287
1978	5th	69	93	.426	21.0	Vern Rapp, Jack Krol, Ken Boyer	1,278,215
1979	3rd	86	76	.531	12.0	Ken Boyer	1,627,256
1980	4th	74	88	.457	17.0	Ken Boyer, Jack Krol, Whitey Herzog, Red Schoendienst	1,385,147
1981	2nd/2nd	59	43	.578	‡	Whitey Herzog	1,010,247
1982	1st§	92	70	.568	+3.0	Whitey Herzog	2,111,906
1983	4th	79	83	.488	11.0	Whitey Herzog	2,317,914
1984	3rd	84	78	.519	12.5	Whitey Herzog	2,037,448
1985	1st§	101	61	.623	+3.0	Whitey Herzog	2,637,563
1986	3rd	79	82	.491	28.5	Whitey Herzog	2,471,974
1987	1st§	95	67	.586	+3.0	Whitey Herzog	3,072,122
1988	5th	76	86	.469	25.0	Whitey Herzog	2,892,799
1989	3rd	86	76	.531	7.0	Whitey Herzog	3,080,980
1990	6th	70	92	.432	25.0	Whitey Herzog, Red Schoendienst, Joe Torre	2,573,225
1991	2nd	84	78	.519	14.0	Joe Torre	2,448,699
1992	3rd	83	79	.512	13.0	Joe Torre	2,418,483
1993	3rd	87	75	.537	10.0	Joe Torre	2,844,328

CENTRAL DIVISION

Year	Position	W	L	Pct.	*GB	Manager	Attendance
1994	3rd (tied)	53	61	.465	13.0	Joe Torre	1,866,544
1995	4th	62	81	.434	22.5	Joe Torre, Mike Jorgensen	1,756,727
1996	1st∞▲	88	74	.543	+6.0	Tony La Russa	2,654,718
1997	4th	73	89	.451	11.0	Tony La Russa	2,634,014
1998	3rd	83	79	.512	19.0	Tony La Russa	3,194,092
1999	4th	75	86	.466	21.5	Tony La Russa	3,225,334
2000	1st∞▲	95	67	.586	+10.0	Tony La Russa	3,336,493
2001	1st (tied)◆	93	69	.574	0.0	Tony La Rusa	3,113,091

*Games behind winner. †Won pennant playoff. ‡First half 30-20; second 29-23. §Won championship series. ∞Won division series. ▲Lost championship series. ◆Lost division series.

INDIVIDUAL RECORDS (1892 TO DATE)

SERVICE

Most years by non-pitcher
22—Stan Musial

Most years by pitcher
18—Jesse Haines

BATTING

Most games, season
163—Jose Oquendo, 1989

Most games, career
3,026—Stan Musial

Most at-bats
689—Lou Brock, 159 games, 1967

Most at-bats, career
10,972—Stan Musial

Most runs
141—Rogers Hornsby, 154 games, 1922

Most runs, career
1,949—Stan Musial

Most hits
250—Rogers Hornsby, 154 games, 1922

Most hits, career
3,630—Stan Musial

Most singles
180—Jesse Burkett, 142 games, 1901

Most singles, career
,253—Stan Musial

Most doubles
4—Joe Medwick, 155 games, 1936

Most doubles, career
25—Stan Musial

Most triples
3—Perry Werden, 124 games, 1893

Most triples (since 1900)
5—Tommy Long, 140 games, 1915

Most triples, career
77—Stan Musial

Most homers by righthander
0—Mark McGwire, 155 games, 1998

Most homers by lefthander
3—Johnny Mize, 155 games, 1940

Most homers by switch-hitter
5—Rip Collins, 154 games, 1934

Most homers by rookie
37—Albert Pujols, 161 games, 2001

Most homers, month
6—Mark McGwire, May 1998
Mark McGwire, July 1999

Most homers at home
8—Mark McGwire, 1998

Most homers on road
2—Mark McGwire, 1998

Most homers by lefthander, career
475—Stan Musial

Most homers by righthander, career
255—Ken Boyer

Most homers by switch-hitter, career
72—Ted Simmons

Most grand slams
3—Jim Bottomley, 153 games, 1925
Keith Hernandez, 161 games, 1977
Fernando Tatis, 149 games, 1999

Most grand slams, career
9—Stan Musial

Most total bases
450—Rogers Hornsby, 154 games, 1922

Most total bases, career
6,134—Stan Musial

Most long hits
103—Stan Musial, 155 games, 1948

Most long hits, career
1,377—Stan Musial

Most extra bases on long hits
231—Mark McGwire, 155 games, 1998

Most extra bases on long hits, career
2,504—Stan Musial

Most sacrifices (sacrifice hits and sacrifice flies)
37—Taylor Douthit, 139 games, 1926

Most sacrifice hits
36—Harry Walker, 148 games, 1943

Most sacrifice flies
14—George Hendrick, 136 games, 1982

Most bases on balls
162—Mark McGwire, 155 games, 1998

Most bases on balls, career
1,599—Stan Musial

Most intentional bases on balls
28—Mark McGwire, 155 games, 1998

Most strikeouts
167—Jim Edmonds, 152 games, 2000

Most strikeouts, career
1,469—Lou Brock

Fewest strikeouts
10—Frankie Frisch, 153 games, 1927

Most hit by pitch
31—Steve Evans, 151 games, 1910

Most runs batted in
154—Joe Medwick, 156 games, 1937

Most runs batted in, career
1,951—Stan Musial

Most game-winning RBIs
21—Keith Hernandez, 160 games, 1982

Most consecutive games with RBI
10—Bill White (15 RBIs), 1961

Highest batting average
.424—Rogers Hornsby, 143 games, 1924

Highest batting average, career
.359—Rogers Hornsby

Highest slugging average
.756—Rogers Hornsby, 138 games, 1925

Highest slugging average, career
.683—Mark McGwire

Longest batting streak
33 games—Rogers Hornsby, 1922

Most grounded into double play
29—Ted Simmons, 161 games, 1973

Fewest grounded into double play
2—Lou Brock, 155 games, 1965

BASERUNNING

Most stolen bases
118—Lou Brock, 153 games, 1974

Most stolen bases, career
888—Lou Brock

Most caught stealing
36—Miller Huggins, 148 games, 1914

PITCHING (SINCE 1900)

Most games
89—Steve Kline, 2001

Most games, career
554—Jesse Haines

Most games started
41—Bob Harmon, 1911

Most games started, career
482—Bob Gibson

Most complete games
39—Jack W. Taylor, 1904

Most complete games, career
255—Bob Gibson

Most games finished
63—Bruce Sutter, 1984

Most innings
352—Stoney McGlynn, 1907

Most innings, career
3,885—Bob Gibson

Most games won
30—Dizzy Dean, 1934

Most games won, career
251—Bob Gibson

Most 20-victory seasons
5—Bob Gibson

Most games lost
25—Stoney McGlynn, 1907
Bugs Raymond, 1908

Most games lost, career
174—Bob Gibson

Highest winning percentage
.811—Dizzy Dean (30-7), 1934

Longest winning streak
15 games—Bob Gibson, 1968

Longest losing streak
12 games—Bill Hart, 1897

Longest losing streak (since 1900)
9 games—Bill McGee, 1938
Tom Poholsky, 1951
Bob Forsch, 1978
Danny Jackson, 1995

Most saves
47—Lee Smith, 1991

Most bases on balls
181—Bob Harmon, 1911

Most bases on balls, career
1,336—Bob Gibson

Most strikeouts
274—Bob Gibson, 1970

Most strikeouts, game
19—Steve Carlton, September 15, 1969

Most strikeouts, career
3,117—Bob Gibson

Most shutouts
13—Bob Gibson, 1968

Most shutouts, career
56—Bob Gibson

Most 1-0 shutouts won
4—Bob Gibson, 1968

Most runs
162—Stoney McGlynn, 1907

Most earned runs
129—Bill Sherdel, 1929

Most hits
337—Cy Young, 1900

Most hits batsmen
17—Gerry Staley, 1953

Most wild pitches
15— Fred Beebe, 1907, 1909
Dave LaPoint, 1984

Most home runs
39—Murry Dickson, 1948

Most sacrifice hits
17—Dave LaPoint, 1983
Larry McWilliams, 1988

Most sacrifice flies
13—Bob Forsch, 1979

Lowest ERA
1.12—Bob Gibson, 305 innings, 1968

CLUB RECORDS

Most players
52 in 1997

Fewest players
25 in 1904

Most games
164 in 1989

Most at-bats
5,734 in 1979

Most runs
1,004 in 1930

Fewest runs
372 in 1908

Most opponents' runs
838 in 1999

Most hits
1,732 in 1930

Fewest hits
1,105 in 1908

Most singles
1,223 in 1920

Most doubles
373 in 1939

Most triples
96 in 1920

Most homers
235 in 2000

Fewest homers (154 or 162-game schedule)
10 in 1906

Most homers at Sportsman's Park, home and opponents
176 in 1955

Most homers at Busch Memorial Stadium, home and opponents
229 in 2000

Most grand slams
12 in 2000

Most pinch home runs
10 in 1998

Most total bases
2,595 in 1930

Most long hits
566 in 1930

Most extra bases on long hits
1,021 in 1998

Most sacrifices (sacrifice hits and sacrifice flies)
212 in 1926

Most sacrifice hits
172 in 1943

Most sacrifice flies
66 in 1954

Most stolen bases
314 in 1985

Most caught stealing
118 in 1992

Most bases on balls
676 in 1998

Most strikeouts
1,253 in 2000

Fewest strikeouts
414 in 1925

Most hit by pitch
84 in 2000

Fewest hit by pitch
15 in 1925

Most runs batted in
942 in 1930

Most game-winning RBIs
94 in 1985

Highest batting average
.314 in 1930

Lowest batting average
.223 in 1908

Highest slugging average
.471 in 1930

Lowest slugging average
.288 in 1908

Most grounded into double play
166 in 1958

Fewest grounded into double play
75 in 1945

Most left on bases
1,251 in 1939

Fewest left on bases
968 in 1924

Most .300 hitters
11 in 1930

Most putouts
4,460 in 1979

Fewest putouts
3,952 in 1906

Most assists
2,293 in 1917

Fewest assists
1,524 in 2000

Most chances accepted
6,459 in 1917

Fewest chances accepted
5,752 in 1935

Most errors
348 in 1908

Fewest errors
94 in 1992

Most errorless games
100 in 1992

Most consecutive errorless games
16 in 1992

Most double plays
192 in 1974

Fewest double plays
114 in 1990

Most passed balls
38 in 1906

Fewest passed balls
4 in 1925

Highest fielding average
.985 in 1992

Lowest fielding average
.946 in 1908

Highest home attendance
3,336,493 in 2000

Highest road attendance
2,820,564 in 1999

Most games won
106 in 1942

Most games lost
111 in 1898

Most games lost (since 1900)
105 in 1908

Most games won, month
26 in July 1944

Most games lost, month
27 in September 1908

Highest percentage games won
.688 in 1942 (won 106, lost 48)

Lowest percentage games won
.221 in 1897 (won 29, lost 102)

Lowest percentage games won (since 1900)
.314 in 1903 (won 43, lost 94)

Games won, league
8,514 in 110 years

Games lost, league
8,340 in 110 years

Most shutouts won
30 in 1968

Most shutouts lost
33 in 1908

Most 1-0 games won
8 in 1907, 1968

Most 1-0 games lost
8 in 1918

Most consecutive games won
14 in 1935

Most consecutive games lost
18 in 1897

Most consecutive games lost (since 1900)
15 in 1909

Number of times league champions
15

Number of last-place finishes
10 (tied in 1916)

Most runs, game
28 vs. Philadelphia, July 6, 1929, second game

Most runs by opponent, game
28 by Boston, September 3, 1896, first game

Most runs by opponent, game (since 1900)
24 by Pittsburgh, June 22, 1925

Most runs, inning
12 vs. Philadelphia, September 16, 1926 first game, third inning

Most runs, shutout game
18 vs. Cincinnati, June 10, 1944

Most runs by opponent, shutout game
19 by Pittsburgh, August 3, 1961

Most runs, doubleheader shutout
16 vs. Brooklyn, September 21, 1934

Most hits, game
30 vs. New York, June 1, 1895

Longest 1-0 game won
14 innings vs. Boston, June 15, 1939

Longest 1-0 game lost
18 innings vs. New York, July 2, 1933, first game

Most hits, game (since 1900)
28 vs. Philadelphia, July 6, 1929, second game

Most home runs, game
7 vs. Brooklyn, May 7, 1940
  vs. Chicago, July 12, 1996

Most consecutive games with one or more homers
18 (43 homers), 1998

Most total bases, game
49 vs. Brooklyn, May 7, 1940

Largest crowd, day game
52,876 vs. Cincinnati, September 28, 1996

Largest crowd, night game
53,415 vs. Chicago, July 30, 1994

Largest crowd, doubleheader
52,657 vs. Atlanta, July 22, 1994

Largest crowd, home opener
52,841 vs. Montreal, April 8, 1996

SAN DIEGO PADRES
YEARLY FINISHES
WEST DIVISION

Year	Position	W	L	Pct.	*GB	Manager	Attendance
1969	6th	52	110	.321	41.0	Preston Gomez	512,970
1970	6th	63	99	.389	39.0	Preston Gomez	643,679
1971	6th	61	100	.379	28.5	Preston Gomez	557,513
1972	6th	58	95	.379	36.5	Preston Gomez, Don Zimmer	644,273
1973	6th	60	102	.370	39.0	Don Zimmer	611,826
1974	6th	60	102	.370	42.0	John McNamara	1,075,399
1975	4th	71	91	.438	37.0	John McNamara	1,281,747
1976	5th	73	89	.451	29.0	John McNamara	1,458,478
1977	5th	69	93	.426	29.0	John McNamara, Bob Skinner, Alvin Dark	1,376,269
1978	4th	84	78	.519	11.0	Roger Craig	1,670,107
1979	5th	68	93	.422	22.0	Roger Craig	1,456,967
1980	6th	73	89	.451	19.5	Jerry Coleman	1,139,026
1981	6th/6th	41	69	.373	†	Frank Howard	519,161
1982	4th	81	81	.500	8.0	Dick Williams	1,607,516
1983	4th	81	81	.500	10.0	Dick Williams	1,539,815
1984	1st‡	92	70	.568	+12.0	Dick Williams	1,983,904
1985	3rd (tied)	83	79	.512	12.0	Dick Williams	2,210,352
1986	4th	74	88	.457	22.0	Steve Boros	1,805,716
1987	6th	65	97	.401	25.0	Larry Bowa	1,454,061
1988	3rd	83	78	.516	11.0	Larry Bowa, Jack McKeon	1,506,896
1989	2nd	89	73	.549	3.0	Jack McKeon	2,009,031
1990	4th (tied)	75	87	.463	16.0	Jack McKeon, Greg Riddoch	1,856,396
1991	3rd	84	78	.519	10.0	Greg Riddoch	1,804,289
1992	3rd	82	80	.506	16.0	Greg Riddoch, Jim Riggleman	1,722,102
1993	7th	61	101	.377	43.0	Jim Riggleman	1,375,432
1994	4th	47	70	.402	12.5	Jim Riggleman	953,857
1995	3rd	70	74	.486	8.0	Bruce Bochy	1,041,805
1996	1st§	91	71	.562	+1.0	Bruce Bochy	2,187,886
1997	4th	76	86	.469	14.0	Bruce Bochy	2,089,333
1998	1st∞‡	98	64	.605	+9.5	Bruce Bochy	2,555,901
1999	4th	74	88	.457	26.0	Bruce Bochy	2,523,538
2000	5th	76	86	.469	21.0	Bruce Bochy	2,423,149
2001	4th	79	83	.488	13.0	Bruce Bochy	2,377,969

*Games behind winner. †First half 23-33; second 18-36. ‡Won championship series. §Lost division series. ∞Won division series.

INDIVIDUAL RECORDS (1969 TO DATE)

SERVICE

Most years by non-pitcher
20—Tony Gwynn

Most years by pitcher
10—Eric Show

BATTING

Most games
162—Dave Winfield, 1980
Steve Garvey, 1985
Joe Carter, 1990

Most games, career
2,440—Tony Gwynn

Most at-bats
655—Steve Finley, 161 games, 1996

Most at-bats, career
9,288—Tony Gwynn

Most runs
126—Steve Finley, 161 games, 1996

Most runs, career
1,383—Tony Gwynn

Most hits
220—Tony Gwynn, 149 games, 1997

Most hits, career
3,141—Tony Gwynn

Most singles
177—Tony Gwynn, 158 games, 1984

Most singles, career
2,378—Tony Gwynn

Most doubles
49—Tony Gwynn, 149 games, 1997

Most doubles, career
543—Tony Gwynn

Most triples
13—Tony Gwynn, 157 games, 1987

Most triples, career
85—Tony Gwynn

Most homers by righthander
50—Greg Vaughn, 158 games, 1998

Most homers by lefthander
35—Fred McGriff, 152 games, 1992

Most homers by switch-hitter
40—Ken Caminiti, 146 games, 1996

Most homers by rookie
18—Benito Santiago, 146 games, 1987

Most homers, month
14—Ken Caminiti, August 1996

Most homers at home
23—Greg Vaughn, 1998

Most homers on road
27—Greg Vaughn, 1998

Most homers by righthander, career
163—Nate Colbert

Most homers by lefthander, career
135—Tony Gwynn

Most homers by switch-hitter, career
121—Ken Caminiti

Most grand slams
4—Phil Nevin, 149 games, 2001

Most grand slams, career
5—Nate Colbert
Phil Nevin

Most total bases
348—Steve Finley, 161 games, 1996

Most total bases, career
4,259—Tony Gwynn

Most long hits
84—Steve Finley, 161 games, 1996

Most long hits, career
763—Tony Gwynn

Most extra bases on long hits
186—Greg Vaughn, 158 games, 1998

Most extra bases on long hits, career
1,118—Tony Gwynn

Most sacrifice hits
28—Ozzie Smith, 159 games, 1978

Most sacrifice flies
12—Tony Gwynn, 149 games, 1997

Most bases on balls
132—Jack Clark, 142 games, 1989

Most bases on balls, career
790—Tony Gwynn

Most strikeouts
150—Nate Colbert, 156 games, 1970

Most strikeouts, career
773—Nate Colbert

Fewest strikeouts
23—Tony Gwynn, 158 games, 1984

Most hit by pitch
13—Gene Tenace, 147 games, 1977

Most runs batted in
130—Ken Caminiti, 146 games, 1996

Most runs batted in, career
1,138—Tony Gwynn

Most game-winning RBIs
15—Terry Kennedy, 153 games, 1982
Steve Garvey, 161 games, 1984

Highest batting average
.372—Tony Gwynn, 149 games, 1997

Highest batting average, career
.338—Tony Gwynn

Highest slugging average
.621—Ken Caminiti, 146 games, 1996

Highest slugging average, career
.540—Ken Caminiti

Longest batting streak
34 games—Benito Santiago, 1987

Most grounded into double play
25—Steve Garvey, 161 games, 1984
Steve Garvey, 162 games, 1985

Fewest grounded into double play
2—Alan Wiggins, 158 games, 1984

BASERUNNING

Most stolen bases
70—Alan Wiggins, 158 games, 1984

Most stolen bases, career
319—Tony Gwynn

Most caught stealing
21—Alan Wiggins, 158 games, 1984

PITCHING

Most games
83—Craig Lefferts, 1986

Most games, career
481—Trevor Hoffman

Most games started
40—Randy Jones, 1976

Most games started, career
253—Randy Jones

Most complete games
25—Randy Jones, 1976

Most complete games, career
71—Randy Jones

Most games finished
69—Rollie Fingers, 1977

Most innings
315—Randy Jones, 1976

Most innings, career
1,765—Randy Jones

Most games won
22—Randy Jones, 1976

Most games won, career
100—Eric Show

Most 20-victory seasons
2—Randy Jones

Most games lost
22—Randy Jones, 1974

Most games lost, career
105—Randy Jones

Highest winning percentage
.778—Gaylord Perry (21-6), 1978

Most saves
53—Trevor Hoffman, 1998

Longest winning streak
11 games—Andy Hawkins, 1985
LaMarr Hoyt, 1985
Kevin Brown, 1998

Longest losing streak
11 games—Gary Ross, 1969

Most bases on balls
125—Matt Clement, 2000

Most bases on balls, career
593—Eric Show

Most strikeouts
257—Kevin Brown, 1998

Most strikeouts, career
1,036—Andy Benes

Most strikeouts, game
15—Fred Norman, September 15, 1972
Sterling Hitchcock, August 29, 1998

Most shutouts won
6—Fred Norman, 1972
Randy Jones, 1975

Most shutouts won, career
18—Randy Jones

Most 1-0 shutouts won
2—Joe Niekro, 1969
Randy Jones, 1978
Greg W. Harris, 1991

Most runs, allowed
137—Bobby J. Jones, 2001

Most earned runs
117—Bill Greif, 1974
Matt Clement, 2000

Most hits
274—Randy Jones, 1976

Most wild pitches
23—Matt Clement, 2000

Most hit batsmen
16—Matt Clement, 2000

Most homers
37—Kevin Jarvis, 2001
Bobby J. Jones, 2001

Most sacrifice hits
23—Randy Jones, 1979

Most sacrifice flies
12—David Roberts, 1971
Andy Hawkins, 1985

Lowest ERA
2.10—David Roberts, 270 innings, 1971

CLUB RECORDS

Most players
56 in 2000

Fewest players
31 in 1984

Most games
163 in 1980, 1983

Most at-bats
5,655 in 1996

Most runs
795 in 1997

Fewest runs
468 in 1969

Most opponents' runs
891 in 1997

Most hits
1,519 in 1997

Fewest hits
1,203 in 1969

Most singles
1,105 in 1980

Most doubles
292 in 1998

Most triples
53 in 1979

Most homers
172 in 1970

Fewest homers
64 in 1976

Most homers at San Diego Stadium, home and opponents
178 in 2001

Most grand slams
10 in 2001

Most pinch home runs
10 in 1995

Most total bases
2,282 in 1997

Most long hits
489 in 1998

Most extra bases on long hits
853 in 1998

Most sacrifice hits
133 in 1975

Most sacrifice flies
58 in 1997

Most stolen bases
239 in 1980

Most caught stealing
91 in 1987

Most bases on balls
678 in 2001

Most strikeouts
1,273 in 2001

Fewest strikeouts
716 in 1976

Most hit by pitch
59 in 1993

Fewest hit by pitch
9 in 1989

Most runs batted in
761 in 1997

Most game-winning RBIs
83 in 1984

Most .300 hitters
3 in 1987

Highest batting average
.271 in 1997

Lowest batting average
.225 in 1969

Highest slugging average
.409 in 1998

Lowest slugging average
.329 in 1969

Most grounded into double play
146 in 1996

Fewest grounded into double play
81 in 1978

Most left on bases
1,239 in 1980

Fewest left on bases
1,006 in 1972

Most putouts
4,467 in 1996

Fewest putouts
4,211 in 1972

Most assists
2,012 in 1980

Fewest assists
1,607 in 2001

Most chances accepted
6,411 in 1980

Fewest chances accepted
5,832 in 1972

Most errors
189 in 1977

Fewest errors
104 in 1998

Most errorless games
84 in 1998

Most consecutive errorless games
9 in 1979

Most double plays
171 in 1978

Fewest double plays
126 in 1974

Most passed balls
22 in 1987

Fewest passed balls
2 in 1992

Highest fielding average
.983 in 1998

Lowest fielding average
.971 in 1975, 1977

Highest home attendance
2,555,901 in 1998

Highest road attendance
2,534,072 in 1993

Most games won
98 in 1998

Most games lost
110 in 1969

Most games won, month
19 in June 1984, July 1984, September 1989

Most games lost, month
22 in June 1969, August 1969, May 1974

Games won, league
2,394 in 33 years

Games lost, league
2,825 in 33 years

Highest percentage games won
.605 in 1998 (won 98, lost 64)

Lowest percentage games won
.321 in 1969 (won 52, lost 110)

Most shutouts won
19 in 1985

Most shutouts lost
23 in 1969, 1976

Most 1-0 shutouts won
6 in 1985

Most 1-0 shutouts lost
5 in 1976, 1996

Most consecutive games won
14 in 1999

Most consecutive games lost
13 in 1994

Number of times league champions
2

Number of last-place finishes
7 (tied in 1969)

Most runs, inning
13 vs. St. Louis, August 24, 1993, first inning
vs. Pittsburgh, May 31, 1994, second inning

Most runs, game
20 vs. Florida, July 27, 1996
vs. Montreal, May 19, 2001

Most runs by opponent, game
23 by Chicago, May 17, 1977

Most runs, shutout game
13 vs. Cincinnati, August 11, 1991

Most runs by opponent, shutout game
19 by Chicago, May 13, 1969
by Los Angeles, June 28, 1969

Most runs, doubleheader shutout
No performance

Longest 1-0 game won
14 innings vs. Cincinnati, August 4, 1974, second game

Longest 1-0 game lost
18 innings vs. Pittsburgh, June 7, 1972, second game

Most hits, game
24 vs. San Francisco, April 19, 1982

Most home runs, game
6 vs. Cincinnati, July 17, 1998

Most consecutive games with one or more homers
14 (23 homers), 1998

Most total bases, game
39 vs. San Francisco, May 23, 1970, 15 innings
38 vs. Philadelphia, August 10, 2000

Largest crowd, day game
61,277 vs. San Francisco, April 10, 2001

Largest crowd, doubleheader
43,473 vs. Philadelphia, June 13, 1976

Largest crowd, night game
61,674 vs. Arizona, April 24, 1999

Largest crowd, home opener
61,277 vs. San Francisco, April 10, 2001

SAN FRANCISCO GIANTS
YEARLY FINISHES

Year	Position	W	L	Pct.	*GB	Manager	Attendance
1958	3rd	80	74	.519	12.0	Bill Rigney	1,272,625
1959	3rd	83	71	.539	4.0	Bill Rigney	1,422,130
1960	5th	79	75	.513	16.0	Bill Rigney, Tom Sheehan	1,795,356
1961	3rd	85	69	.552	8.0	Alvin Dark	1,390,679
1962	1st†	103	62	.624	+1.0	Alvin Dark	1,592,594
1963	3rd	88	74	.543	11.0	Alvin Dark	1,571,306
1964	4th	90	72	.556	3.0	Alvin Dark	1,504,364
1965	2nd	95	67	.586	2.0	Herman Franks	1,546,075
1966	2nd	93	68	.578	1.5	Herman Franks	1,657,192
1967	2nd	91	71	.562	10.5	Herman Franks	1,242,480
1968	2nd	88	74	.543	9.0	Herman Franks	837,220

WEST DIVISION

Year	Position	W	L	Pct.	*GB	Manager	Attendance
1969	2nd	90	72	.556	3.0	Clyde King	873,603
1970	3rd	86	76	.531	16.0	Clyde King, Charlie Fox	740,720
1971	1st‡	90	72	.556	+1.0	Charlie Fox	1,106,043
1972	5th	69	86	.445	26.5	Charlie Fox	647,744
1973	3rd	88	74	.543	11.0	Charlie Fox	834,193
1974	5th	72	90	.444	30.0	Charlie Fox, Wes Westrum	519,987
1975	3rd	80	81	.497	27.5	Wes Westrum	522,919
1976	4th	74	88	.457	28.0	Bill Rigney	626,868
1977	4th	75	87	.463	23.0	Joe Altobelli	700,056
1978	3rd	89	73	.549	6.0	Joe Altobelli	1,740,477
1979	4th	71	91	.438	19.5	Joe Altobelli, Dave Bristol	1,456,402
1980	5th	75	86	.466	17.0	Dave Bristol	1,096,115
1981	5th/3rd	56	55	.505	§	Frank Robinson	632,274
1982	3rd	87	75	.537	2.0	Frank Robinson	1,200,948
1983	5th	79	83	.488	12.0	Frank Robinson	1,251,530
1984	6th	66	96	.407	26.0	Frank Robinson, Danny Ozark	1,001,545
1985	6th	62	100	.383	33.0	Jim Davenport, Roger Craig	818,697
1986	3rd	83	79	.512	13.0	Roger Craig	1,528,748
1987	1st‡	90	72	.556	+6.0	Roger Craig	1,917,168
1988	4th	83	79	.512	11.5	Roger Craig	1,785,297
1989	1st∞	92	70	.568	+3.0	Roger Craig	2,059,701
1990	3rd	85	77	.525	6.0	Roger Craig	1,975,528

Year	Position	W	L	Pct.	*GB	Manager	Attendance
1991	4th	75	87	.463	19.0	Roger Craig	1,737,478
1992	5th	72	90	.444	26.0	Roger Craig	1,561,987
1993	2nd	103	59	.636	1.0	Dusty Baker	2,606,354
1994	2nd	55	60	.478	3.5	Dusty Baker	1,704,608
1995	4th	67	77	.465	11.0	Dusty Baker	1,241,500
1996	4th	68	94	.420	23.0	Dusty Baker	1,413,922
1997	1st▲	90	72	.556	+2.0	Dusty Baker	1,690,869
1998	2nd◆	89	74	.546	9.5	Dusty Baker	1,925,634
1999	2nd	86	76	.531	14.0	Dusty Baker	2,078,399
2000	1st▲	97	65	.599	+11.0	Dusty Baker	3,315,330
2001	2nd	90	72	.556	2.0	Dusty Baker	3,277,244

*Games behind winner. †Won pennant playoff. ‡Lost championship series. §First half 27-32; second half 29-23. ∞Won championship series. ▲Lost division series. ◆Lost wild-card playoff.

INDIVIDUAL RECORDS (1958 TO DATE)

SERVICE

Most years by non-pitcher
19—Willie McCovey

Most years by pitcher
14—Juan Marichal

BATTING

Most games
164—Jose Pagan, 1962

Most games, career
2,256—Willie McCovey

Most at-bats
663—Bobby Bonds, 157 games, 1970

Most at-bats, career
7,578—Willie Mays

Most runs
134—Bobby Bonds, 157 games, 1970

Most runs, career
1,480—Willie Mays

Most hits
208—Willie Mays, 152 games, 1958

Most hits, career
2,284—Willie Mays

Most singles
146—Tito Fuentes, 160 games, 1973

Most singles, career
1,373—Willie Mays

Most doubles
49—Jeff Kent, 159 games, 2001

Most doubles, career
376—Willie Mays

Most triples
12—Willie Mays, 153 games, 1960

Most triples, career
76—Willie Mays

Most homers by righthander
52—Willie Mays, 157 games, 1965

Most homers by lefthander
73—Barry Bonds, 153 games, 2001

Most homers by switch-hitter
28—J.T. Snow, 157 games, 1997

Most homers by rookie
31—Jim Hart, 153 games, 1964

Most homers, month
17—Willie Mays, August, 1965
Barry Bonds, May 2001

Most homers at home
37—Barry Bonds, 2001

Most homers on road
36—Barry Bonds, 2001

Most homers by lefthander, career
469—Willie McCovey

Most homers by righthander, career
459—Willie Mays

Most homers by switch-hitter, career
101—Chili Davis

Most grand slams
3—Willie McCovey, 135 games, 1967
Jeff Kent, 155 games, 1997

Most grand slams, career
16—Willie McCovey

Most total bases
411—Barry Bonds, 153 games, 2001

Most total bases, career
4,189—Willie Mays

Most long hits
107—Barry Bonds, 153 games, 2001

Most long hits, career
911—Willie Mays

Most extra bases on long hits
255—Barry Bonds, 153 games, 2001

Most extra bases on long hits, career
1,905—Willie Mays

Most sacrifice hits
19—Rick Reuschel, 36 games, 1988

Most sacrifice flies
14—J.T. Snow, 155 games, 2000

Most bases on balls
177—Barry Bonds, 153 games, 2001

Most intentional bases on balls
45—Willie McCovey, 149 games, 1969

Most bases on balls, career
1,168—Willie McCovey

Most strikeouts
189—Bobby Bonds, 157 games, 1970

Most strikeouts, career
1,351—Willie McCovey

Fewest strikeouts
48—Ken Reitz, 155 games, 1976

Most hit by pitch
26—Ron Hunt, 117 games, 1970

Most runs batted in
142—Orlando Cepeda, 152 games, 1961

Most runs batted in, career
1,388—Willie McCovey

Most game-winning RBIs
21—Jack Clark, 157 games, 1982

Highest batting average
.347—Willie Mays, 152 games, 1958

Highest batting average, career
.308—Orlando Cepeda

Highest slugging average
.863—Barry Bonds, 153 games, 2001

Highest slugging average, career
.652—Barry Bonds

Longest batting streak
26 games—Jack Clark, 1978

Most grounded into double play, season
25—Bill Madlock, 140 games, 1977

Fewest grounded into double play
2—Jose Uribe, 157 games, 1986
Will Clark, 150 games, 1987
Brett Butler, 157 games, 1988

BASERUNNING

Most stolen bases
58—Bill North, 142 games, 1979

Most stolen bases, career
263—Bobby Bonds

Most caught stealing
24—Bill North, 142 games, 1979

PITCHING

Most games
89—Julian Tavarez, 1997

Most games, career
647—Gary Lavelle

Most games started
42—Jack Sanford, 1963

Most games started, career
446, Juan Marichal

Most complete games
30—Juan Marichal, 1968

Most complete games, career
244—Juan Marichal

Most games finished
71—Rod Beck, 1993
Robb Nen, 2001

Most innings
329—Gaylord Perry, 1970

Most innings, career
3,443—Juan Marichal

Most games won, season
26—Juan Marichal, 1968

Most games won, career
238—Juan Marichal

Most games lost, career
140—Juan Marichal

Most 20-victory season
6—Juan Marichal

Most games lost, season
18—Ray Sadecki, 1968

Highest winning percentage
.806—Juan Marichal (25-6), 1966

Longest winning streak
16—Jack Sanford, 1962

Longest losing streak
9—Mark Davis, 1984
Terry Mulholland, 1995
Rod Beck, 1996

Most saves
48—Rod Beck, 1993
     Robb Nen, 1998

Most bases on balls
125—Russ Ortiz, 1999

Most bases on balls, career
690—Juan Marichal

Most strikeouts
248—Juan Marichal, 1963

Most strikeouts, career
2,281—Juan Marichal

Most strikeouts, game
15—Gaylord Perry, July 22, 1966

Most shutouts, season
10—Juan Marichal, 1965

Most 1-0 shutouts won
2—Held by many pitchers

Most shutouts, career
52—Juan Marichal

Most runs
143—Vida Blue, 1979
     Livan Hernandez, 2001

Most earned runs
132—Vida Blue, 1979
     Livan Hernandez, 2001

Most hits
295—Juan Marichal, 1968

Most hit batsmen
17—Mark Leiter, 1995

Most wild pitches
18—Rich Robertson, 1970

Most home runs
34—Juan Marichal, 1962

Most sacrifice hits
19—Kirk Rueter, 2000

Most sacrifice flies
14—Rick Reuschel, 1988

Lowest ERA
1.98—Bobby Bolin, 177 innings, 1968

CLUB RECORDS

Most players
51 in 1990

Fewest players
31 in 1968

Most games
165 in 1962

Most at-bats
5,650 in 1984

Most runs
925 in 2000

Fewest runs
556 in 1985

Most opponents' runs
862 in 1996

Most hits
1,552 in 1962

Fewest hits
1,263 in 1985

Most singles
1,132 in 1984

Most doubles
307 in 1999

Most triples
62 in 1960

Most homers
235 in 2001

Fewest homers
80 in 1980

Most homers at Seals Stadium, home and opponents
173 in 1958

Most homers at Candlestick Park, home and opponents
190 in 1987

Most homers at Pacific Bell Park, home and opponents
171 in 2000

Most grand slams
7 in 1970, 1998, 2000

Most pinch home runs
14 in 2001

Most long hits
579 in 2001

Most extra bases on long hits
1,089 in 2001

Most total bases
2,605 in 2000

Most sacrifice hits
127 in 1978

Most sacrifice flies
66 in 2000

Most stolen bases
148 in 1986

Most caught stealing
97 in 1987

Most bases on balls
729 in 1970

Most strikeouts
1,189 in 1996

Fewest strikeouts
764 in 1961

Most hit by pitch
66 in 1969

Fewest hit by pitch
14 in 1980

Most runs batted in
889 in 2000

Most game-winning RBIs
83 in 1987

Highest batting average
.278 in 1962, 2000

Lowest batting average
.233 in 1985

Highest slugging average
.472 in 2000

Lowest slugging average
.341 in 1968

Most left on bases
1,280 in 1969

Fewest left on bases
983 in 1961

Most grounded into double play
149 in 1965

Fewest grounded into double play
83 in 1986, 1990

Most .300 hitters
4 in 1962

Most putouts
4,431 in 1998

Fewest putouts
4,129 in 1959

Most assists
1,940 in 1976

Fewest assists
1,513 in 1961

Most chances accepted
6,349 in 1969

Fewest chances accepted
5,677 in 1961

Most errors
186 in 1976

Fewest errors
93 in 2000

Most errorless games
96 in 2000

Most consecutive errorless games
11 in 1999, 2000

Most double plays
183 in 1987

Fewest double plays
109 in 1983

Most passed balls
30 in 1970

Fewest passed balls
6 in 1978

Highest fielding average
.985 in 2000

Lowest fielding average
.971 in 1976

Highest home attendance
3,315,330 in 2000

Highest road attendance
2,856,363 in 2001

Most games won
103 in 1962, 1993

Most games lost
100 in 1985

Most games won, month
21 in September 1965, August 1968

Most games lost, month
21 in May 1972

Highest percentage games won
.636 in 1993 (won 103, lost 59)

Lowest percentage games won
.383 in 1985 (won 62, lost 100)

Games won, league
3,609 in 44 years

Games lost, league
3,365 in 44 years

Most shutouts won
20 in 1968

Most shutouts lost
18 in 1992

Most 1-0 games won
6 in 1968

Most 1-0 games lost
4 in 1972, 1978, 1985, 1989, 1996

Most consecutive games won
14 in 1965

Most consecutive games lost
10 in 1985, 1996

Number of times league champions
2

Number of last-place finishes
1

Most runs, inning
13 vs. St. Louis, May 7, 1966, third inning
     vs. San Diego, July 15, 1997, seventh inning

Most runs, game
23 vs. Atlanta, June 8, 1990

Most runs by opponent, game
20 by Chicago, August 13, 1959

Most runs, shutout game
18 vs. Montreal, May 24, 2000

Most runs by opponent, shutout game
15 by Chicago, August 22, 1970

Most runs, doubleheader shutout
13 vs. Chicago, April 29, 1962

Longest 1-0 game won
21 innings vs. Cincinnati, September 1, 1967

Longest 1-0 game lost
18 innings vs. Arizona, May 29, 2001

Most hits, game
27 vs. Atlanta, June 8, 1990

Most home runs, game
8 vs. Milwaukee, April 30, 1961

Most consecutive games with one or more homers
16 (22 homers), 1962
   (30 homers), 1963

Most total bases, game
50 vs. Los Angeles, May 13, 1958

Largest crowd, day game
61,389 vs. Los Angeles, September 30, 1999

Largest crowd, doubleheader
53,178 vs. Los Angeles, July 31, 1983

Largest crowd, night game
55,920 vs. Cincinnati, June 20, 1978

Largest crowd, home opener
58,077 vs. Pittsburgh, April 4, 1994

DIVISION SERIES

Service (Individual, Club)

Batting (Individual, Club)

Baserunning (Individual, Club)

Pitching (Individual, Club)

Fielding (Individual, Club)

Miscellaneous

Non-Playing Personnel

General Reference

INDIVIDUAL SERVICE

ALL PLAYERS
SERIES AND CLUBS

Most series played
A.L.—7
  Tino Martinez, Seattle, 1995; New York, 1996 through 2001.
  Paul O'Neill, New York, 1995 through 2001.
  Bernie Williams, New York, 1995 through 2001.
N.L.—7
  Tom Glavine, Atlanta, 1995 through 2001.
  Chipper Jones, Atlanta, 1995 through 2001.
  Greg Maddux, Atlanta, 1995 through 2001.

Most clubs, career
Both leagues—4
  Bobby Bonilla, Baltimore A.L., 1996; Florida N.L., 1997; New
    York N.L., 1999; Atlanta N.L. 2000.
  Rickey Henderson, Oakland A.L., 1981; San Diego N.L., 1996;
    New York N.L., 1999; Seattle A.L., 2000.
  Jose Vizcaino, Cleveland A.L., 1996; San Francisco N.L.,
    1997; New York A.L., 1998; Houston N.L., 2001.
A.L.—3
  Harold Baines, Baltimore, 1997; Cleveland, 1999; Chicago,
    2000.
  Mike Stanton, Boston, 1995; Texas, 1996; New York, 1997,
    2001.
N.L.—3
  Bobby Bonilla, Florida, 1997; New York, 1999; Atlanta, 2000.
  Ken Caminiti, San Diego, 1996, 1998; Houston, 1999; Atlanta,
    2001.
  Reggie Sanders, Cincinnati, 1995; Atlanta, 2000; Arizona,
    2001.

BY POSITION (EXCEPT PITCHERS)

Most series by first baseman
A.L.—7—Tino Martinez, Seattle, 1995; New York, 1996 through
  2001; 30 games.
N.L.—4—Jeff Bagwell, Houston, 1997 through 1999, 2001, 14
  games.

Most series by second baseman
N.L.—5—Keith Lockhart, Atlanta, 1997 through 2001; 10 games.
A.L.—4
  Mark McLemore, Texas, 1996, 1998, 1999; Seattle, 2000; 13
    games.
  Roberto Alomar, Baltimore, 1996, 1997; Cleveland, 1999,
    2001; 18 games.

Most series by third baseman
N.L.—7—Chipper Jones, Atlanta, 1995 through 2001; 23 games.
A.L.—4—Scott Brosius, New York, 1998 through 2001; 16 games.

Most series by shortstop
A.L.—6
  Omar Vizquel, Cleveland, 1995 through 1999, 2001; 26 games.
  Derek Jeter, New York, 1996 through 2001; 25 games.
N.L.—4—Walt Weiss, Colorado, 1995; Atlanta, 1998 through
  2000; 11 games.

Most series by outfielder
A.L.—7
  Paul O'Neill, New York, 1995 through 2001; 25 games.
  Bernie Williams, New York, 1995 through 2001; 30 games.
N.L.—6—Andruw Jones, Atlanta, 1996 through 2001; 19
  games.

Most series by catcher
Both leagues—5
  Joe Girardi, Colorado N.L., 1995; New York A.L., 1996, 1997,
    1998, 1999; 17 games.
A.L.—5
  Sandy Alomar Jr., Cleveland, 1995 through 1999; 21 games.
  Jorge Posada, New York, 1997 through 2001; 14 games.
N.L.—5
  Javy Lopez, Atlanta, 1995 through 1998, 2000; 12 games.

YOUNGEST AND OLDEST NON-PITCHERS

Youngest division series non-pitcher
N.L.—19 years, 5 months, 9 days—Andruw Jones, Atlanta,
  October 2, 1996.
A.L.—20 years, 2 months, 11 days—Alex Rodriguez, Seattle,
  October 8, 1995.

Oldest division series non-pitcher
N.L.—41 years, 9 months, 10 days—Ozzie Smith, St. Louis,
  October 5, 1996.
A.L.—40 years, 7 months, 11 days—Eddie Murray, Baltimore,
  October 5, 1996.

YEARS BETWEEN SERIES (INCLUDES PITCHERS)

Most years between first and second series
Both Leagues—15—Rickey Henderson, Oakland A.L., 1981;
  San Diego N.L., 1996.
N.L.—15—Fernando Valenzuela, Los Angeles, 1981; San Diego,
  1996.
A.L.—6—Held by many players.

Most years between first and last series
A.L.—19—Rickey Henderson, Oakland, 1981; New York, 2000.
N.L.—15—Fernando Valenzuela, Los Angeles, 1981; San Diego,
  1996.

POSITIONS

Most positions played, career
A.L.-N.L.—3—Held by many players.

Most positions played, series
A.L.—3
  Randy Velarde, New York, 1995 (second base, third base, left
    field).
  Jeff Kent, Cleveland, 1996 (second base, first base, third base).
N.L.—3—Craig Paquette, St. Louis, 2001 (right field, left field,
  third base).

PITCHERS
SERIES

Most series pitched
A.L.—7
  Jeff Nelson, Seattle, 1995, 2001; New York, 1996 through
    2000; 19 games.
  Andy Pettitte, New York, 1995 through 2001; nine games.
  Mariano Rivera, New York, 1995 through 2001; 18 games.
N.L.—7
  Tom Glavine, Atlanta, 1995 through 2001; seven games.
  Greg Maddux, Atlanta, 1995 through 2001; nine games.

Most series pitched by relief pitcher
A.L.—7
  Jeff Nelson, Seattle, 1995, 2001; New York, 1996 through
    2000; 19 games.
  Mariano Rivera, New York, 1995 through 2001; 18 games.
N.L.—4
  Doug Henry, San Francisco, 1997, 2000; Houston, 1998,
    1999; eight games.
  Billy Wagner, Houston, 1997, 1998, 1999, 2001; five games.

YOUNGEST AND OLDEST PITCHERS

Youngest division series pitcher
N.L.—20 years, 11 months, 5 days—Fernando Valenzuela, Los
  Angeles, October 6, 1981.
A.L.—21 years, 2 months, 22 days—C.C. Sabathia, Cleveland,
  October 13, 2001.

Oldest division series pitcher
A.L.—43 years, 11 months, 29 days—Dennis Eckersley,
  Boston, October 2, 1998.
N.L.—42 years, 3 months, 6 days—Rick Honeycutt, St. Louis,
  October 5, 1996.

CLUB SERVICE

PLAYERS USED

Most players, series
A.L.-N.L.—25—Held by many clubs.

For a list of players and pitchers used each series, see page 391.

Most players used by both clubs, series
A.L.—50—Boston 25, Cleveland 25, 1999 (5-game series).
N.L.—49—San Francisco 25, New York 24, 2000 (4-game series).

Fewest players, series
A.L.—16—Kansas City vs. Oakland, 1981 (3-game series).
N.L.—18
  Cincinnati vs. Los Angeles, 1995 (3-game series).
  Atlanta vs. Houston, 1997 (3-game series).

Fewest players used by both clubs, series
A.L.—36
  Oakland 20, Kansas City 16, 1981 (3-game series).
  New York 19, Texas 17, 1998 (3-game series).
N.L.—40
  Los Angeles 22, Cincinnati 18, 1995 (3-game series).
  San Francisco 21, Florida 19, 1997 (3-game series).

Most times one club using only nine players in game, series
N.L.—1—Arizona vs. St. Louis, 2001 (5-game series).
A.L.—Never occurred.

Most players, nine-inning game
N.L.—20—Colorado vs. Atlanta, October 3, 1995.
A.L.—20—Texas vs. New York, October 5, 1996.

Most players, extra-inning game
A.L.—20—New York vs. Texas, October 2, 1996, 12 innings.
N.L.—20—Atlanta vs. Houston, October 8, 1999, 12 innings.

Most players used by both clubs, nine-inning game
A.L.—39—Texas 20, New York 19, October 5, 1996.
N.L.—37—Colorado 20, Atlanta 17, October 3, 1995.

Most players used by both clubs, extra-inning game
N.L.—38—San Francisco 19, New York 19, October 7, 2000, 10 innings.
A.L.—Less than nine-inning record.

PINCH-HITTERS

Most pinch-hitters, series
N.L.—12—Atlanta vs. Colorado, 1995 (4-game series).
A.L.—10—Oakland vs. New York, 2001 (5-game series).

Most pinch-hitters used by both clubs, series
N.L.—22—Atlanta 12, Colorado 10, 1995 (4-game series).
A.L.—12—Oakland 10, New York 2, 2001 (5-game series).

Fewest pinch-hitters, series
A.L.—0
  Kansas City vs. Oakland, 1981 (3-game series).
  Cleveland vs. New York, 1997 (5-game series).
  Texas vs. New York, 1999 (3-game series).
N.L.—1—Atlanta vs. Houston, 1997 (3-game series).

Fewest pinch-hitters used by both clubs, series
A.L.—1—Oakland 1, Kansas City 0, 1981 (3-game series).
N.L.—8—Houston 7, Atlanta 1, 1997 (3-game series).

Most pinch-hitters, game
N.L.—4
  Atlanta vs. Colorado, October 4, 1995.
  Atlanta vs. Colorado, October 6, 1995, 10 innings.
  New York vs. Arizona, October 6, 1999.
  Atlanta vs. Houston, October 8, 1999, 12 innings.
  Atlanta vs. St. Louis, October 3, 2000.
  San Francisco vs. New York, October 5, 2000, 10 innings.
  Arizona vs. St. Louis, October 10, 2001.

A.L.—4
  Seattle vs. Cleveland, October 13, 2001.
  Oakland vs. New York, October 14, 2001.

Most pinch-hitters used by both clubs, game
N.L.—7
  Atlanta 4, Colorado 3, October 4, 1995.
  Atlanta 4, Houston 3, October 8, 1999, 12 innings.
A.L.—5
  Seattle 4, Cleveland 1, October 13, 2001.
  Oakland 4, New York 1, October 14, 2001.

Most pinch-hitters, inning
N.L.—4—Arizona vs. St. Louis, October 10, 2001, eighth inning.
A.L.—2—Held by many clubs.

PINCH-RUNNERS

Most pinch-runners, series
A.L.—7—Baltimore vs. Cleveland, 1996 (4-game series).
N.L.—3
  San Diego vs. Houston, 1998 (4-game series).
  New York vs. San Francisco, 2000 (4-game series).
  Arizona vs. St. Louis, 2001 (5-game series).

Most pinch-runners used by both clubs, series
A.L.—9—Baltimore 7, Cleveland 2, 1996 (4-game series).
N.L.—3
  Philadelphia 2, Montreal 1, 1981 (5-game series).
  San Diego 3, Houston 0, 1998 (4-game series).
  Arizona 3, St. Louis 0, 2001 (5-game series).

Fewest pinch-runners used, series
A.L.-N.L.—0—Held by many clubs.

Fewest pinch-runners used by both clubs, series
N.L.—0
  Houston 0, Atlanta 0, 1997 (3-game series).
  Atlanta 0, Chicago 0, 1998 (3-game series).
  Atlanta 0, Houston 0, 2001 (3-game series).
A.L.—1
  Cleveland 1, Boston 0, 1995 (3-game series).
  Baltimore 1, Seattle 0, 1997 (4-game series).
  New York 1, Texas 0, 1998 (3-game series).
  New York 1, Oakland 0, 2001 (5-game series).
  Seattle 1, Cleveland 0, 2001 (5-game series).

Most pinch-runners, game
A.L.—3—Baltimore vs. Cleveland, October 2, 1996.
N.L.—2—Arizona vs. St. Louis, October 14, 2001.

Most pinch-runners used by both clubs, game
A.L.—4—Baltimore 3, Cleveland 1, October 2, 1996.
N.L.—2—Arizona 2, St. Louis 0, October 14, 2001.

Most pinch-runners, inning
A.L.—3—Baltimore vs. Cleveland, October 2, 1996, eighth inning.
N.L.—2—Arizona vs. St. Louis, October 14, 2001, ninth inning.

NUMBER OF PLAYERS USED BY POSITION
FIRST BASEMEN

Most first basemen, series
A.L.—3—Cleveland vs. Baltimore, 1996 (4-game series).
N.L.—2—Held by many clubs.

Most first basemen used by both clubs, series
A.L.—4
  Kansas City 2, Oakland 2, 1981 (3-game series).
  Cleveland 3, Baltimore 1, 1996 (4-game series).
  Baltimore 2, Seattle 2, 1997 (4-game series).
  Boston 2, Cleveland 2, 1998 (4-game series).
  Boston 2, Cleveland 2, 1999 (5-game series).
N.L.—4
  New York 2, San Francisco 2, 2000 (4-game series).
  Arizona 2, St. Louis 2, 2001 (5-game series).

Most first basemen, game
A.L.-N.L.—2—Made in many games.

Most first basemen used by both clubs, game
A.L.-N.L.—3—Made in many games.

SECOND BASEMEN

Most second basemen, series
A.L.—3
  Milwaukee vs. New York, 1981 (5-game series).
  New York vs. Cleveland, 1997 (5-game series).
N.L.—2—Held by many clubs.

Most second basemen used by both clubs, series
A.L.—5—New York 3, Cleveland 2, 1997 (5-game series).
N.L.—4—Florida 2, San Francisco 2, 1997 (3-game series).

Most second basemen, game
A.L.—3—New York vs. Cleveland, October 6, 1997.
N.L.—2—Held by many clubs.

Most second basemen used by both clubs, game
A.L.—4
  New York 2, Seattle 2, October 4, 1995, 15 innings.
  New York 3, Cleveland 1, October 6, 1997.
N.L.—3—Made in many games.

THIRD BASEMEN

Most third basemen, series
A.L.—3—Seattle vs. Baltimore, 1997 (4-game series).
N.L.—2—Held by many clubs.

Most third basemen used by both clubs, series
A.L.—4
  New York 2, Seattle 2, 1995 (5-game series).
  Seattle 3, Baltimore 1, 1997 (4-game series).
N.L.—3—Held by many clubs.

Most third basemen, game
A.L.-N.L.—2—Held by many clubs.

Most third basemen used by both clubs, game
A.L.-N.L.—3—Made in many games.

SHORTSTOPS

Most shortstops, series
A.L.—3—Seattle vs. New York, 1995 (5-game series).
N.L.—3
  Houston vs. Los Angeles, 1981 (5-game series).
  Atlanta vs. Colorado, 1995 (3-game series).

Most shortstops used by both clubs, series
A.L.—4—Seattle 3, New York 1, 1995 (5-game series).
N.L.—4
  Houston 3, Los Angeles 1, 1981 (5-game series).
  Atlanta 3, Colorado 1, 1995 (4-game series).
  Atlanta 2, Houston 2, 1999 (4-game series).
  San Francisco 2, New York 2, 2000 (4-game series).
  Atlanta 2, Houston 2, 2001 (5-game series).

Most shortstops, nine-inning game
A.L.-N.L.—2—Held by many clubs.

Most shortstops, extra-inning game
N.L.—3—Atlanta vs. Colorado, October 6, 1995, 10 innings.
A.L.—2—Held by many clubs.

Most shortstops used by both clubs, game
N.L.—4
  Atlanta 3, Colorado 1, October 6, 1995, 10 innings.
  New York 2, San Francisco 2, October 7, 2000, 13 innings.
  Atlanta 2, Houston 2, October 9, 2001.
A.L.—3—Made in many games.

LEFT FIELDERS

Most left fielders, series
A.L.—4—Cleveland vs. Seattle, 2001 (5-game series).

N.L.—4
  Houston vs. Atlanta, 1999 (4-game series).
  St. Louis vs. Arizona, 2001 (5-game series).

Most left fielders used by both clubs, series
A.L.—7—Cleveland 4, Seattle 3, 2001 (5-game series).
N.L.—6—Houston 4, Atlanta 2, 1999 (4-game series).

Most left fielders, game
A.L.—3
  New York vs. Seattle, October 4, 1995, 15 innings.
  Seattle vs. Chicago, October 4, 2000.
N.L.—3
  Houston vs. Atlanta, October 8, 1999, 12 innings.
  New York vs. San Francisco, October 4, 2000.
  New York vs. San Francisco, October 5, 2000, 10 innings.
  St. Louis vs. Arizona, October 10, 2001.

Most left fielders used by both clubs, nine-inning game
A.L.—4—Seattle 3, Chicago 1, October 4, 2000.
N.L.—4—Made in many games.

Most left fielders used by both clubs, extra-inning game
A.L.—5—New York 3, Seattle 2, October 4, 1995, 15 innings.
N.L.—5—Houston 3, Atlanta 2, October 8, 1999, 12 innings.

CENTER FIELDERS

Most center fielders, series
N.L.—4—New York vs. Arizona, 1999 (4-game series).
A.L.—3—Boston vs. Cleveland, 1995 (3-game series).

Most center fielders used by both clubs, series
N.L.—5—New York 4, Arizona 1, 1999 (4-game series).
A.L.—3
  Boston 3, Cleveland 1, 1995 (3-game series).
  Boston 2, Cleveland 2, 1999 (5-game series).

Most center fielders, game
N.L.—3—New York vs. Arizona, October 5, 1999.
A.L.—2—Held by many clubs.

Most center fielders used by both clubs, game
N.L.—4—New York 3, Arizona 1, October 5, 1999.
A.L.—3—Made in many games.

RIGHT FIELDERS

Most right fielders, series
A.L.—5—Oakland vs. New York, 2000 (5-game series).
N.L.—3
  Philadelphia vs. Montreal, 1981 (5-game series).
  Houston vs. Atlanta, 1999 (4-game series).

Most right fielders used by both clubs, series
N.L.—6—Philadelphia 4, Montreal 2, 1981 (5-game series).
A.L.—6—Oakland 5, New York 1, 2000 (5-game series).

Most right fielders, game
A.L.—3
  Baltimore vs. Seattle, October 2, 1997.
  Oakland vs. New York, October 7, 2000.
N.L.—2—Held by many clubs.

Most right fielders used by both clubs, game
N.L.—4
  Montreal 2, Philadelphia 2, October 10, 1981, 10 innings.
  Montreal 2, Philadelphia 2, October 11, 1981.
A.L.—4
  Baltimore 3, Seattle 1, October 2, 1997.
  Oakland 3, New York 1, October 7, 2000.
  New York 2, Oakland 2, October 14, 2001.

CATCHERS

Most catchers, series
A.L.—3—Houston vs. Atlanta, 1997 (3-game series).
N.L.—3—Chicago vs. Atlanta, 1998 (3-game series).

Most catchers used by both clubs, series
N.L.—5
  Houston 3, Atlanta 2, 1997 (3-game series).
  Chicago 3, Atlanta 2, 1998 (3-game series).
A.L.—4—Made in many games.

Most catchers, game
A.L.-N.L.—2—Held by many clubs.
Most catchers used by both clubs, game
A.L.-N.L.—4—Made in many games.

PITCHERS

Most pitchers, series
3-game series
  A.L.—10—Boston vs. Cleveland, 1995.
      Chicago vs. Seattle, 2000.
  N.L.—10—Los Angeles vs. Atlanta, 1996.
4-game series
  N.L.—11—Colorado vs. Atlanta, 1995.
      New York vs. Arizona, 1999.
      San Francisco vs. New York, 2000.
  A.L.—11—Texas vs. New York, 1996.
      Cleveland vs. Boston, 1998.
5-game series
  A.L.—11—Boston vs. Cleveland, 1999.
      Cleveland vs. Boston, 1999.
      Oakland vs. New York, 2001.
  N.L.—10—St. Louis vs. Arizona, 2001.

For a list of players and pitchers used each series, see page 391.

Most pitchers used by both clubs, series
3-game series
  A.L.—19—Boston 10, Cleveland 9, 1995.
  N.L.—18—St. Louis 9, Atlanta 9, 2000.
4-game series
  N.L.—21—Colorado 11, Atlanta 10, 1995.
      New York 11, Arizona 10, 1999.
      San Francisco 11, New York 10, 2000.
  A.L.—21—Texas 11, New York 10, 1996.
      Cleveland 11, Boston 10, 1998.
5-game series
  A.L.—22—Boston 11, Cleveland 11, 1999.
  N.L.—18—St. Louis 10, Arizona 8, 2001.

Fewest pitchers, series
N.L.—5—Atlanta vs. Houston, 1997 (3-game series).
A.L.—5
  Kansas City vs. Oakland, 1981 (3-game series).
  Oakland vs. Kansas City, 1981 (3-game series).
  Texas vs. New York, 1998 (3-game series).
  New York vs. Texas, 1999 (3-game series).

Fewest pitchers used by both clubs, series
A.L.—10—Kansas City 5, Oakland 5, 1981 (3-game series).
N.L.—14
  Los Angeles 8, Cincinnati 6, 1995 (3-game series).
  Houston 9, Atlanta 5, 1997 (3-game series).
  San Francisco 8, Florida 6, 1997 (3-game series).

Most pitchers, nine-inning game
A.L.—8—Texas vs. New York, October 5, 1996.
N.L.—6
  Colorado vs. Atlanta, October 3, 1995.
  Colorado vs. Atlanta, October 4, 1995.
  Los Angeles vs. Cincinnati, October 6, 1995.
  Los Angeles vs. Atlanta, October 5, 1996.
  Atlanta vs. St. Louis, October 5, 2000.

Most pitchers, extra-inning game
N.L.—7—Colorado vs. Atlanta, October 6, 1995, 10 innings.
      Atlanta vs. Houston, October 8, 1999, 12 innings.
A.L.—Less than nine-inning record.

Most pitchers used by winning club, nine-inning game
A.L.—6
  Seattle vs. New York, October 7, 1995.
  Cleveland vs. Baltimore, October 4, 1996.
  Cleveland vs. Boston, October 3, 1998.
  Boston vs. Cleveland, October 10, 1999.
N.L.—5
  St. Louis vs. San Diego, October 5, 1996.
  St. Louis vs. Atlanta, October 3, 2000.
  St. Louis vs. Atlanta, October 7, 2000.

Most pitchers used by winning club, extra-inning game
N.L.—7
  Colorado vs. Atlanta, October 6, 1995, 10 innings.
  Atlanta vs. Houston, October 8, 1999, 12 innings.
A.L.—7
  Cleveland vs. Boston, October 3, 1995, 13 innings.
  New York vs. Texas, October 2, 1996, 12 innings.

Most pitchers used by losing club, game
A.L.—8—Texas vs. New York, October 5, 1996.
N.L.—6—Held by many clubs.

Most pitchers used by both clubs, nine-inning game
A.L.—13—Texas 8, New York 5, October 5, 1996.
N.L.—10—Made in many games.

Most pitchers used by both clubs, extra-inning game
A.L.—14—Boston 7, Cleveland 7, October 3, 1995, 13 innings.
N.L.—13—Colorado 7, Atlanta 6, October 6, 1995, 10 innings.

Most pitchers, inning
N.L.—4
  Los Angeles vs. Cincinnati, October 6, 1995, sixth inning.
  Colorado vs. Atlanta, October 6, 1995, seventh inning.
  Atlanta vs. Houston, October 9, 1999, eighth inning.
A.L.—4
  New York vs. Texas, October 2, 1996, 12th inning.
  Boston vs. Cleveland, October 10, 1999, fifth inning.

SERIES

Most series played
A.L.—8—New York, 1981, 1995 through 2001; won six, lost two.
N.L.—7—Atlanta, 1995 through 2001; won six, lost one.

For a complete list of results and a complete list of series won and lost by teams, see page 387.

INDIVIDUAL BATTING

GAMES

Most games, career
A.L.—30
Tino Martinez, Seattle, 1995; New York, 1996 through 2001; seven series.
Bernie Williams, New York, 1995 through 2001; seven series.
N.L.—23—Chipper Jones, Atlanta, 1995 through 2001; seven series.

Most games with one club, career
A.L.—30—Bernie Williams, New York, 1995 through 2001; seven series.
N.L.—23—Chipper Jones, Atlanta, 1995 through 2001; seven series.

Most games by pinch-hitter, career
N.L.—7—John Vander Wal, Colorado, 1995; San Diego, 1998 (seven plate appearances, seven at-bats).
A.L.—4—Olmedo Saenz, Oakland, 2000, 2001 (four plate appearances, four at-bats).

Most games by pinch-hitter, series
N.L.—4
George Vukovich, Philadelphia, 1981 (5-game series).
John Vander Wal, Colorado, 1995 (4-game series).
Dwight Smith, Atlanta, 1995 (4-game series).
Felipe Crespo, San Francisco, 2000 (4-game series).
A.L.—3
Roy Howell, Milwaukee, 1981 (5-game series).
Midre Cummings, Boston, 1998 (4-game series).
Olmedo Saenz, Oakland, 2001 (5-game series).

Most games by pinch-runner, career
A.L.—4
Andy Fox, New York, 1996, 1997; two series.
Damon Buford, Texas, 1996; Boston, 1998; two series.
N.L.—3—Joe McEwing, New York, 2000; one series.

Most games by pinch-runner, series
A.L.—3
Pat Kelly, New York, 1995 (5-game series).
Manny Alexander, Baltimore, 1996 (4-game series).
Mike Devereaux, Baltimore, 1996 (4-game series).
N.L.—3—Joe McEwing, New York, 2000 (4-game series).

BATTING AVERAGE

Highest batting average, career (50 or more at-bats)
A.L.—.400—Mike Stanley, New York, 1995, 1997; Boston, 1998, 1999; four series, 15 games, 55 at-bats, 22 hits.
N.L.—.353—Brian Jordan, St. Louis, 1996; Atlanta, 1999 through 2001; four series, 13 games, 51 at-bats, 18 hits.

> **For a list of batting leaders each series and a complete list of .450 hitters, see page 388.**

Highest batting average, series (10 or more at-bats)
3-game series
A.L.—.600—Luis Alicea, Boston, 1995.
N.L.—.571—Jim Edmonds, St. Louis, 2000.
4-game series
N.L.—.588—Dante Bichette, Colorado, 1995.
A.L.—.467—Bernie Williams, New York, 1996.
John Valentin, Boston, 1998.
5-game series
A.L.—.600—Ichiro Suzuki, Seattle, 2001.
N.L.—.462—Keith Moreland, Philadelphia, 1981.

SLUGGING AVERAGE

Highest slugging average, career (50 or more at-bats)
A.L.—.781—Edgar Martinez, Seattle, 1995, 1997, 2000, 2001; four series, 17 games, 64 at-bats, 24 hits, five doubles, seven home runs, 50 total bases.

N.L.—.595—Chipper Jones, Atlanta, 1995 through 2001; seven series, 23 games, 79 at-bats, 26 hits, three doubles, six home runs, 47 total bases.
(Ken Caminiti, San Diego, 1996, 1998; Houston, 1999; Atlanta, 2001; had a .721 slugging percentage in 43 at-bats. If under rule 10.23 (a) Caminiti were charged with another seven at-bats to give him enough to qualify, he would have a slugging percentage of .620.)

Highest slugging average, series (10 or more at-bats)
3-game series
N.L.—1.286—Jim Edmonds, St. Louis, 2000.
A.L.—1.000—Luis Alicea, Boston, 1995.
4-game series
A.L.—1.375—Juan Gonzalez, Texas, 1996.
N.L.—1.300—Jim Leyritz, San Diego, 1998.
5-game series
A.L.—1.083—Nomar Garciaparra, Boston, 1999.
(Oscar Gamble, New York, 1981, had a 1.333 slugging percentage in nine at-bats. If under rule 10.23 (a) he were charged with another at-bat to give him enough to qualify, his slugging average would be 1.200.)
N.L.—.895—Gary Carter, Montreal, 1981.

AT-BATS AND PLATE APPEARANCES

Most at-bats, career
A.L.—114—Tino Martinez, Seattle, 1995; New York, 1996 through 2001; seven series, 30 games.
N.L.—79—Chipper Jones, Atlanta, 1995 through 2001; seven series, 23 games.

Most at-bats by pinch-hitter, career
N.L.—7—John Vander Wal, Colorado, 1995; San Diego, 1998; two series, seven games.
A.L.—4—Olmedo Saenz, Oakland, 2000, 2001; two series, four games.

Most plate appearances by pinch-hitter, career
N.L.—7—John Vander Wal, Colorado, 1995; San Diego, 1998; two series, seven games.
A.L.—4—Olmedo Saenz, Oakland, 2000, 2001; two series, four games.

Most consecutive hitless times at bat, career
A.L.—19—Joey Cora, Seattle, 1997 (last nine times at bat); Cleveland, 1998 (all 10 times at bat).
N.L.—17—Tim Wallach, Los Angeles, 1995 (last six times at bat), 1996 (all 11 times at bat).

Most at-bats, series
3-game series
A.L.—15—Mike Greenwell, Boston, 1995.
N.L.—15—Brett Butler, Los Angeles, 1995.
4-game series
N.L.—21—Marquis Grissom, Atlanta, 1995.
A.L.—19—Darryl Hamilton, Texas, 1996.
Dean Palmer, Texas, 1996.
Todd Zeile, Baltimore, 1996.
5-game series
A.L.—24—Jay Buhner, Seattle, 1995.
Don Mattingly, New York, 1995.
N.L.—22—Warren Cromartie, Montreal, 1981.

Most at-bats by pinch-hitter, series
N.L.—4
George Vukovich, Philadelphia, 1981 (5-game series).
John Vander Wal, Colorado, 1995 (4-game series).
Felipe Crespo, San Francisco, 2000 (4-game series).
A.L.—3
Midre Cummings, Boston, 1998 (4-game series).
Olmedo Saenz, Oakland, 2001 (5-game series).

Most at-bats by player with no hits, career
A.L.—13—Jose Canseco, Boston, 1995.
N.L.—8
Jerry Reuss, Los Angeles, 1981.
Al Leiter, Florida, 1997; New York, 2000.
Julio Lugo, Houston, 2001.

Most at-bats, nine-inning game
N.L.—6—Marquis Grissom, Atlanta, October 4, 1995.
A.L.—6

Brian Daubach, Boston, October 10, 1999.
Mike Stanley, Boston, October 10, 1999.
Juan Gonzalez, Cleveland, October 13, 2001.
Jim Thome, Cleveland, October 13, 2001.
Omar Vizquel, Cleveland, October 13, 2001.

Most at-bats, extra-inning game
A.L.—7

Luis Sojo, Seattle, October 4, 1995, 15 innings.
Tino Martinez, Seattle, October 4, 1995, 15 innings.
Ruben Sierra, New York, October 4, 1995, 15 innings.
N.L.—6—Held by many players.

Most at-bats by player with no hits, game
A.L.—6—Brian Daubach, Boston, October 10, 1999.
N.L.—5—Held by many players.

Most at-bats, inning
A.L.—2

Mike Stanley, Boston, October 10, 1999, second inning.
Chuck Knoblauch, New York, October 8, 2000, first inning.
Juan Gonzalez, Cleveland, October 13, 2001, third inning.
N.L.—2

Brian Jordan, Atlanta, October 9, 1999, sixth inning.
Fernando Vina, St. Louis, October 3, 2000, first inning.

Most times faced pitcher, inning
A.L.—2

Lou Merloni, Boston, October 9, 1999, seventh inning.
Jason Varitek, Boston, October 9, 1999, seventh inning.
Mike Stanley, Boston, October 10, 1999, second inning.
Roberto Alomar, Cleveland, October 10, 1999, fifth inning.
Chuck Knoblauch, New York, October 8, 2000, first inning.
Derek Jeter, New York, October 8, 2000, first inning.
Juan Gonzalez, Cleveland, October 13, 2001, third inning.
N.L.—2

Todd Pratt, New York, October 8, 1999, sixth inning.
Brian Jordan, Atlanta, October 9, 1999, sixth inning.
Fernando Vina, St. Louis, October 3, 2000, first inning.

RUNS

Most runs, career
A.L.—25—Bernie Williams, New York, 1995 through 2001;
seven series, 30 games.
N.L.—17—Chipper Jones, Atlanta, 1995 through 2001; seven series,
23 games.

Most runs by pinch-hitter, career
A.L.-N.L.—1—Held by many players.

Most runs by pinch-runner, career
A.L.—2—Pat Kelly, New York, 1995; one series, three games.
N.L.—1—Held by many players.

Most runs, series
3-game series
N.L.—5—Hal Morris, Cincinnati, 1995.
Charles Johnson, Florida, 1997.
Jim Edmonds, St. Louis, 2000.
Edgar Renteria, St. Louis, 2000.
A.L.—4—Dwayne Murphy, Oakland, 1995.
4-game series
N.L.—6—Dante Bichette, Colorado, 1995.
Edgardo Alfonzo, New York, 1999.
A.L.—5—Bernie Williams, New York, 1996.
Juan Gonzalez, Texas, 1996.
Kenny Lofton, Cleveland, 1998.
John Valentin, Boston, 1998.
5-game series
A.L.—9—Ken Griffey Jr., Seattle, 1995.
N.L.—4—Steve Garvey, Los Angeles, 1981.
Chris Speier, Montreal, 1981.

Most runs by pinch-hitter, series
A.L.-N.L.—1—Held by many players.

Most runs by pinch-runner, series
A.L.—2—Pat Kelly, New York, 1995 (5-game series).
N.L.—1—Held by many players.

Most runs, game
A.L.—5—Jason Varitek, Boston, October 10, 1999.
N.L.—3—Held by many players.

Most runs, inning
A.L.-N.L.—1—Held by many players.

HITS
CAREER AND SERIES

Most hits, career
A.L.—32

Derek Jeter, New York, 1996 through 2001; six series, 25
games.
Tino Martinez, Seattle, 1995; New York, 1996 through 2001;
seven series, 30 games.
Omar Vizquel, Cleveland, 1995 through 1999, 2001; six
series, 26 games.
N.L.—26—Chipper Jones, Atlanta, 1995 through 2001; seven
series, 23 games.

Most hits by pinch-hitter, career
N.L.—3

George Vukovich, Philadelphia, 1981; one series, four games.
Greg Colbrunn, Atlanta, 1997, 1998; Arizona, 2001; three
series, six games.
A.L.—1—Held by many players.

Most hits, series
3-game series
N.L.—8—Jim Edmonds, St. Louis, 2000.
A.L.—6—Tony Armas, Oakland, 1981.
Dwayne Murphy, Oakland, 1981.
Luis Alicea, Boston, 1995.
4-game series
N.L.—11—Marquis Grissom, Atlanta, 1995.
A.L.—8—Cal Ripken, Baltimore, 1996.
5-game series
A.L.—12—Edgar Martinez, Seattle, 1995.
Ichiro Suzuki, Seattle, 2001.
N.L.—8—Gary Carter, Montreal, 1981.
Gary Matthews, Philadelphia, 1981.
Steve Finley, Arizona, 2001.

Most hits by pinch-hitter, series
N.L.—3—George Vukovich, Philadelphia, 1981; four games.
A.L.—1—Held by many players.

Most hits, two consecutive series
A.L.—16—Bernie Williams, New York, 1995 (9), 1996 (7).
N.L.—13—Steve Finley, Arizona, 1999 (5), 2001 (8).

Most series with one or more hits
A.L.—7

Tino Martinez, Seattle, 1995; New York, 1996 through 2001.
Paul O'Neill, New York, 1995 through 2001.
N.L.—7—Chipper Jones, Atlanta, 1995 through 2001.

Most consecutive hits, career
A.L.—5

Tony Armas, Oakland, October 7 (4), 9 (1), 1981.
Jason Varitek, Boston, October 9 (1), 10 (4), 1999 (one hit by
pitcher during streak).
N.L.—5

Marquis Grissom, Atlanta, October 7 (5), 1995.
Chad Fonville, Los Angeles, October 3 (1), 4 (4), 1995 (one
sacrifice hit during streak).
Andruw Jones, Atlanta, October 9 (2), 10 (3), 2001.

Most consecutive hits by pinch-hitter, career
N.L.—2

George Vukovich, Philadelphia, October 9, 10, 1981.
Chris Gwynn, San Diego, October 1, 3, 1996.
Darryl Hamilton, New York, October 5, 7, 2000.
Greg Colbrunn, Arizona, October 10, 12, 2001.
A.L.—No batter with more than one hit.

Most consecutive hits, series

A.L.—5

Tony Armas, Oakland, October 7 (4), 9 (1), 1981.
Jason Varitek, Boston, October 9 (1), 10 (4), 1999 (one hit by pitcher during streak).

N.L.—5

Marquis Grissom, Atlanta, October 7 (5), 1995.
Chad Fonville, Los Angeles, October 3 (1), 4 (4), 1995 (one sacrifice hit during streak).
Andruw Jones, Atlanta, October 9 (2), 10 (3), 2001.

GAME AND INNING

Most hits, game

N.L.—5—Marquis Grissom, Atlanta, October 7, 1995.
A.L.—5—Mike Stanley, Boston, October 10, 1999.

Most times reached base safely, game (batting 1.000)

N.L.—5—Marquis Grissom, Atlanta, October 7, 1995 (four singles, one double).
A.L.—5—Johnny Damon, Oakland, October 10, 2001 (four singles, one base on balls).

Most hits accounting for all club's hits, game

A.L.—2—Ivan Rodriguez, Texas, October 5, 1999.
N.L.—1

Ken Caminiti, Houston, October 6, 1999.
Jeff Kent, San Francisco, October 8, 2000.

Most consecutive games with one or more hits, career

N.L.—7

Fred McGriff, Atlanta, 1995 (all four), 1996 (all three).
Brian Jordan, St. Louis, 1995 (last one); Atlanta, 1999 (all four); 2000 (first two).

A.L.—6

Tino Martinez, Seattle, 1995 (all five); New York, 1996 (first one).
Omar Vizquel, Cleveland, 1999 (last one), 2001 (all five).

Most hits in two consecutive games, series (18 innings)

A.L.—6

John Valentin, Boston, October 9 (2), 10 (4), 1999.
Johnny Damon, Oakland, October 10 (4), 11 (2), 2001.
Juan Gonzalez, Cleveland, October 13 (4), 14 (2), 2001.
Omar Vizquel, Cleveland, October 13 (4), 14 (2), 2001.
Ichiro Suzuki, Seattle, October 14 (3), 15 (3), 2001.

N.L.—6—Jim Edmonds, St. Louis, October 3 (3), 5 (3), 2000.

Most hits in two consecutive games, series (more than 18 innings)

N.L.—7

Marquis Grissom, Atlanta, October 6, 10 innings (2), October 7 (5), 1995.

A.L.—6

Edgar Martinez, Seattle, October 3 (3), October 4, 15 innings (3), 1995.
Edgar Martinez, Seattle, October 7 (3), October 8, 11 innings (3), 1995.
Jay Buhner, Seattle, October 7 (3), October 8, 11 innings (3), 1995.

Most hits, inning

A.L.—2—Chuck Knoblauch, New York, October 8, 2000, first inning.
N.L.—1—Held by many players.

SINGLES

Most singles, career

A.L.—26—Omar Vizquel, Cleveland, 1995 through 1999, 2001; six series, 26 games.
N.L.—17—Chipper Jones, Atlanta, 1995 through 2001; seven series, 23 games.

Most singles by pinch-hitter, career

N.L.—3—Greg Colbrunn, Atlanta, 1997, 1998; Arizona, 2001; three series, six games.
A.L.—1—Held by many players.

Most singles, series

3-game series

N.L.—6—Chad Fonville, Los Angeles, 1995.
A.L.—4—Held by many players.

4-game series

A.L.—6—Derek Jeter, New York, 1996.
        John Valentin, Boston, 1998.
N.L.—6—Dante Bichette, Colorado, 1995.
        Marquis Grissom, Atlanta, 1995.
        Ryan Klesko, Atlanta, 1995.

5-game series

A.L.—11—Ichiro Suzuki, Seattle, 2001.
N.L.—7—Steve Finley, Arizona, 2001.

Most singles by pinch-hitter, series

N.L.—2

George Vukovich, Philadelphia, 1981 (5-game series).
Dave Hansen, Los Angeles, 1995 (3-game series).
Chris Gwynn, San Diego, 1996 (3-game series).
Greg Colbrunn, Arizona, 2001 (5-game series).

A.L.—1—Held by many players.

Most singles, game

N.L.—4

Chad Fonville, Los Angeles, October 4, 1995.
Marquis Grissom, Atlanta, October 7, 1995.

A.L.—4

Johnny Damon, Oakland, October 10, 2001.
Jason Giambi, Oakland, October 15, 2001.

Most singles, inning

A.L.—2—Chuck Knoblauch, New York, October 8, 2000, first inning.
N.L.—1—Held by many players.

DOUBLES

Most doubles, career

A.L.—10—Bernie Williams, New York, 1995 through 2001; seven series, 30 games.
N.L.—5—Jim Edmonds, St. Louis, 2000, 2001; two series, eight games.

Most doubles by pinch-hitter, career

N.L.-A.L.—1—Held by many players.

Most doubles, series

3-game series

N.L.—4—Jim Edmonds, St. Louis, 2000.
A.L.—2—Held by many players.

4-game series

A.L.—4—David Justice, Cleveland, 1998.
N.L.—3—Dante Bichette, Colorado, 1995.

5-game series

A.L.—4—Don Mattingly, New York, 1995.
        Roberto Alomar, Cleveland, 1999.
N.L.—3—Gary Carter, Montreal, 1981.

Most doubles, game

N.L.—3—Jim Edmonds, St. Louis, October 5, 2000.
A.L.—2—Held by many players.

Most doubles, inning

A.L.-N.L.—1—Held by many players.

TRIPLES

Most triples, career

A.L.—2—Omar Vizquel, Cleveland, 1995 through 1999, 2001; six series, 26 games.
N.L.—1—Held by many players.

Most triples by pinch-hitter, career

N.L.—1—John Vander Wal, Colorado, 1995; San Diego, 1998; two series, seven games.
A.L.—Never accomplished.

Most triples, series and game

A.L.-N.L.—1—Held by many players.

Most bases-loaded triples, game

A.L.-N.L.—Never accomplished.

HOME RUNS
CAREER AND SERIES

Most home runs, career
A.L.—8
  Juan Gonzalez, Texas, 1996, 1998, 1999; Cleveland, 2001; four series, 15 games.
  Jim Thome, Cleveland, 1995 through 1999, 2001; six series, 25 games.
N.L.—6
  Ken Caminiti, San Diego, 1996, 1998; Houston, 1999; Atlanta, 2001; four series, 13 games.
  Chipper Jones, Atlanta, 1995 through 2001; seven series, 23 games.

For a list of all home runs each series, and a complete list of players with four or more career home runs, see page 389.

Most home runs, series
3-game series
  N.L.—3—Ken Caminiti, San Diego, 1996.
  A.L.—2—Shane Spencer, New York, 1998.
4-game series
  A.L.—5—Juan Gonzalez, Texas, 1995.
  N.L.—3—Marquis Grissom, Atlanta, 1995.
      Vinny Castilla, Colorado, 1995.
      Jim Leyritz, San Diego, 1998.
      Ken Caminiti, Houston, 1999.
      Edgardo Alfonzo, New York, 1999.
5-game series
  A.L.—5—Ken Griffey Jr., Seattle, 1995.
  N.L.—2—Steve Garvey, Los Angeles, 1981.
      Gary Carter, Montreal, 1981.
      Jim Edmonds, St. Louis, 2001.

Most series with one or more home runs
N.L.—4—Chipper Jones, Atlanta, 1995 (2), 1996 (1), 1997 (1), 2001 (2).
A.L.—4
  Jim Thome, Cleveland, 1995 (1), 1998 (2), 1999 (4), 2001 (1).
  David Justice, Cleveland, 1997 (1), 1998 (1); New York, 2000 (1), 2001 (1).
  Edgar Martinez, Seattle, 1995 (2), 1997 (2), 2000 (1), 2001 (2).

Most series with two or more home runs
A.L.—3—Edgar Martinez, Seattle, 1995 (2), 1997 (2), 2001 (2).
N.L.—2
  Ken Caminiti, San Diego, 1996 (3); Houston, 1999 (3).
  Jim Edmonds, St. Louis, 2000 (2), 2001 (2).
  Chipper Jones, Atlanta, 1995 (2), 2001 (2).

GAME AND INNING

Most home runs, game
N.L.—2
  Chipper Jones, Atlanta, October 3, 1995.
  Eric Karros, Los Angeles, October 4, 1995.
  Marquis Grissom, Atlanta, October 4, 1995.
  Fred McGriff, Atlanta, October 7, 1995.
  Ken Caminiti, San Diego, October 5, 1996.
  Jeff Kent, San Francisco, October 3, 1997.
  Edgardo Alfonzo, New York, October 5, 1999.
A.L.—2
  Ken Griffey Jr., Seattle, October 3, 1995.
  Bernie Williams, New York, October 6, 1995.
  Edgar Martinez, Seattle, October 7, 1995.
  B.J. Surhoff, Baltimore, October 1, 1996.
  Juan Gonzalez, Texas, October 2, 1996.
  Bernie Williams, New York, October 5, 1996.
  Mo Vaughn, Boston, September 29, 1998.
  Manny Ramirez, Cleveland, October 2, 1998.
  John Valentin, Boston, October 10, 1999.
  Jim Thome, Cleveland, October 11, 1999.
  Troy O'Leary, Boston, October 11, 1999.
  Terrence Long, Oakland, October 10, 2001.

Most grand slams, game
A.L.—1
  Edgar Martinez, Seattle, October 7, 1995, eighth inning.
  Bobby Bonilla, Baltimore, October 1, 1996, sixth inning.
  Albert Belle, Cleveland, October 4, 1996, seventh inning.
  Paul O'Neill, New York, October 4, 1997, fourth inning.
  Jim Thome, Cleveland, October 7, 1999, fourth inning.
  Troy O'Leary, Boston, October 11, 1999, third inning.
N.L.—1
  Mark Lewis, Cincinnati, October 6, 1995, sixth inning.
  Devon White, Florida, October 3, 1997, sixth inning.
  Ryan Klesko, Atlanta, September 30, 1998, seventh inning.
  Eddie Perez, Atlanta, October 3, 1998, eighth inning.
  Edgardo Alfonzo, New York, October 5, 1999, ninth inning.

Inside-the-park home runs
A.L.-N.L.—Never accomplished.

Most home runs by pinch-hitter, game
N.L.—1
  George Vukovich, Philadelphia, October 10, 1981, 10th inning.
  Mark Lewis, Cincinnati, October 6, 1995, sixth inning.
  Jim Leyritz, San Diego, October 1, 1998, ninth inning.
  Turner Ward, Arizona, October 8, 1999, fifth inning.
  Mark McGwire, St. Louis, October 5, 2000, eighth inning.
  J.T. Snow, San Francisco, October 5, 2000, ninth inning.
  Daryle Ward, Houston, October 12, 2001, seventh inning.
A.L.—1—David Justice, New York, October 15, 2001, sixth inning.

Home runs by leadoff batter, start of game
N.L.—Marquis Grissom, Atlanta, October 4, 1995 (at Colorado).
    Fernando Vina, St. Louis, October 7, 2000 (at Atlanta).
A.L.—Brady Anderson, Baltimore, October 1, 1996 (at Baltimore).

Home runs winning 1-0 games
A.L.—Jorge Posada, New York, October 13, 2001, fifth inning.
N.L.—Never occurred.

Most home runs by pitcher, game
A.L.-N.L.—Never occurred.

Most home runs by rookie, game
N.L.—2—Chipper Jones, Atlanta, October 3, 1995.

Hitting home runs from both sides of plate, game
A.L.—Bernie Williams, New York, October 6, 1995.
    Bernie Williams, New York, October 5, 1996.
N.L.—Never accomplished.

Most consecutive games hitting one or more home runs, series
A.L.—4—Juan Gonzalez, Texas, October 1, 2 (2), 4, 5, 1996, second game 12 innings.
N.L.—3—Jim Leyritz, San Diego, October 1, 3, 4, 1998.

Most home runs in two consecutive games, series (homering each game)
A.L.—3
  Juan Gonzalez, Texas, October 1 (1), 2 (2), 1996, second game 12 innings.
  Juan Gonzalez, Texas, October 2 (2), 4 (1), 1996, first game 12 innings.
  Bernie Williams, New York, October 4 (1), 5 (2), 1996.
N.L.—3—Ken Caminiti, San Diego, October 3 (1), 5 (2), 1996.

Most home runs in three consecutive games, series (homering each game)
A.L.—4—Juan Gonzalez, Texas, October 1 (1), 2 (2), 4 (1), 1996, second game 12 innings.
N.L.—3—Jim Leyritz, San Diego, October 1, 3, 4, 1998.

Most home runs in four consecutive games, series (homering each game)
A.L.—5—Juan Gonzalez, Texas, October 1 (1), 2 (2), 4 (1), 5 (1), 1996, second game 12 innings.
N.L.—Never accomplished.

Hitting home run in first division series at-bat (*not first plate appearance)
N.L.—Keith Moreland, Philadelphia, October 7, 1981, second inning.
    Benito Santiago, Cincinnati, October 3, 1995, first inning.
    Edgardo Alfonzo, New York, October 5, 1999, first inning.
    Mark McGwire, St. Louis, October 5, 2000, eighth inning*.

A.L.—Brady Anderson, Baltimore, October 1, 1996, first inning.
Harold Baines, Baltimore, October 2, 1997, second inning.
Shane Spencer, New York, September 30, 1998, second inning.

Hitting home runs in first two division series at-bats
A.L.-N.L.—Never accomplished.

Most home runs, inning
A.L.-N.L.—1—Held by many players.

Most home runs, two consecutive innings
A.L.—2—Juan Gonzalez, Texas, October 2, 1996, second and third innings.
N.L.—Never accomplished.

TOTAL BASES

Most total bases, career
A.L.—59—Bernie Williams, New York, 1995 through 2001; seven series, 30 games.
N.L.—47—Chipper Jones, Atlanta, 1995 through 2001; seven series, 23 games.

Most total bases by pinch-hitter, career
N.L.—6—George Vukovich, Philadelphia, 1981; one series, four games.
A.L.—4—David Justice, New York, 2001; one series, one game.

Most total bases, series
3-game series
N.L.—18—Jim Edmonds, St. Louis, 2000.
A.L.—10—Dwayne Murphy, Oakland, 1981.
Luis Alicea, Boston, 1995.
Eddie Murray, Cleveland, 1995.
4-game series
A.L.—22—Juan Gonzalez, Texas, 1996.
N.L.—22—Marquis Grissom, Atlanta, 1995.
5-game series
A.L.—24—Ken Griffey Jr., Seattle, 1995.
N.L.—17—Gary Carter, Montreal, 1981.

Most total bases by pinch-hitter, series
N.L.—6—George Vukovich, Philadelphia, 1981; four games.
A.L.—4—David Justice, New York, 2001; one game.

Most total bases, game
A.L.—11—John Valentin, Boston, October 10, 1999 (one single, one double, two home runs).
N.L.—10—Eric Karros, Los Angeles, October 4, 1995 (one double, two home runs).

Most total bases, inning
A.L.-N.L.—4—Held by many players.

LONG HITS

Most long hits, career
A.L.—16—Bernie Williams, New York, 1995 through 2001; seven series, 30 games.
N.L.—9
Jim Edmonds, St. Louis, 2000, 2001; two series, eight games.
Chipper Jones, Atlanta, 1995 through 2001; seven series, 23 games.

Most long hits, series
3-game series
N.L.—6—Jim Edmonds, St. Louis, 2000.
A.L.—3—Paul O'Neill, New York, 1998.
4-game series
A.L.—5—Juan Gonzalez, Texas, 1996.
David Justice, Cleveland, 1998.
N.L.—5—Marquis Grissom, Atlanta, 1995.
5-game series
A.L.—5—Ken Griffey Jr., Seattle, 1995.
Edgar Martinez, Seattle, 1995.
Don Mattingly, New York, 1995.
John Valentin, Boston, 1999.
Juan Gonzalez, Cleveland, 2001.
Terrence Long, Oakland, 2001.
N.L.—5—Gary Carter, Montreal, 1981.

Most long hits, game
N.L.—3
Eric Karros, Los Angeles, October 4, 1995 (one double, two home runs).
Jim Edmonds, St. Louis, October 5, 2000 (three doubles).
A.L.—3
Mo Vaughn, Boston, September 29, 1998 (one double, two home runs).
John Valentin, Boston, October 10, 1999 (one double, two home runs).
Jason Varitek, Boston, October 10, 1999 (two doubles, one home run).
Juan Gonzalez, Cleveland, October 13, 2001 (two doubles, one home run).

Most long hits in two consecutive games, series
A.L.—5
John Valentin, Boston, October 9 (double and home run), October 10 (double and two home runs), 1999.
Juan Gonzalez, Cleveland, October 13 (two doubles and one home run), October 14 (double and home run), 2001.
N.L.—5—Jim Edmonds, St. Louis, October 5 (three doubles), October 7 (double and home run), 2000.

Most long hits, inning
A.L.-N.L.—1—Held by many players.

RUNS BATTED IN

Most runs batted in, career
A.L.—23—Bernie Williams, New York, 1995 through 2001; seven series, 30 games.
N.L.—16
Chipper Jones, Atlanta, 1995 through 2001; seven series, 23 games.
Brian Jordan, St. Louis, 1996; Atlanta, 1999 through 2001; four series, 13 games.

Most runs batted in by pinch-hitter, career
N.L.—5—Mark Lewis, Cincinnati, 1995; one series, two games.
A.L.—2—B.J. Surhoff, Baltimore, 1996, 1997; two series, two games.

Most runs batted in, series
3-game series
N.L.—7—Jim Edmonds, St. Louis, 2000.
A.L.—6—Bernie Williams, New York, 1999.
4-game series
A.L.—9—Juan Gonzalez, Texas, 1996.
N.L.—8—Ken Caminiti, Houston, 1999.
5-game series
A.L.—12—John Valentin, Boston, 1999.
N.L.—6—Gary Carter, Montreal, 1981.

Most runs batted in by pinch-hitter, series
N.L.—5—Mark Lewis, Cincinnati, 1995; two games.
A.L.—2—B.J.Surhoff, Baltimore, 1997; one game.

Most runs batted in, game
A.L.—7
Edgar Martinez, Seattle, October 7, 1995.
Mo Vaughn, Boston, September 29, 1998.
John Valentin, Boston, October 10, 1999.
Troy O'Leary, Boston, October 11, 1999.
N.L.—5
Fred McGriff, Atlanta, October 7, 1995.
Edgardo Alfonzo, New York, October 5, 1999.
Steve Finley, Arizona, October 6, 1999.
Brian Jordan, Atlanta, October 8, 1999, 12 innings.

Most runs batted in by pinch-hitter, game
N.L.—4—Mark Lewis, Cincinnati, October 6, 1995.
A.L.—2—B.J. Surhoff, Baltimore, October 1, 1997.

Most consecutive games with one or more runs batted in, career
A.L.—5—Nomar Garciaparra, Boston, September 29, 1998 through October 6, 1999.
N.L.—4
Gary Carter, Montreal, October 7 through 10, 1981.
Ken Caminiti, Houston, October 5 through 9, 1999.

Most runs batted in accounting for all club's runs, game
L.—5—Brian Jordan, October 8, 1999, 12 innings.
.L.—4—Juan Gonzalez, Texas, October 2, 1996, 12 innings.

Most runs batted in, inning
.L.—4
Edgar Martinez, Seattle, October 7, 1995, eighth inning.
Bobby Bonilla, Baltimore, October 1, 1996, sixth inning.
Albert Belle, Cleveland, October 4, 1996, seventh inning.
Paul O'Neill, New York, October 4, 1997, fourth inning.
Jim Thome, Cleveland, October 7, 1999, fourth inning.
Troy O'Leary, Boston, October 11, 1999, third inning.
.L.—4
Mark Lewis, Cincinnati, October 6, 1995, sixth inning.
Devon White, Florida, October 3, 1997, sixth inning.
Ryan Klesko, Atlanta, September 30, 1998, seventh inning.
Eddie Perez, Atlanta, October 3, 1998, eighth inning.
Edgardo Alfonzo, New York, October 5, 1999, ninth inning.

Most game-winning RBIs, career (1980-88)
.L.—2—Tony Armas, Oakland, 1981 (2).
.L.—2—Chris Speier, Montreal, 1981 (2).

Most game-winning RBIs, series (1980-88)
.L.—2—Tony Armas, Oakland, 1981 (2).
.L.—2—Chris Speier, Montreal, 1981 (2).

BASES ON BALLS

Most bases on balls, career
.L.—21—Chipper Jones, Atlanta, 1995 through 2001; seven series, 23 games.
.L.—19—Bernie Williams, New York, 1995 through 2001; seven series, 30 games.

Most bases on balls, series
-game series
N.L.—5—Gary Sheffield, Florida, 1997.
Jeff Bagwell, Houston, 2001.
A.L.—4—Albert Belle, Cleveland, 1995.
Frank Thomas, Chicago, 2000.
-game series
A.L.—5—Mickey Tettleton, Texas, 1996.
N.L.—5—David Justice, Atlanta, 1995.
Luis Gonzalez, Arizona, 1999.
Jeff Bagwell, Houston, 1999.
Chipper Jones, Atlanta, 1999.
-game series
A.L.—7—Bernie Williams, New York, 1995.
Jose Offerman, Boston, 1999.
Jason Giambi, Oakland, 2000.
N.L.—4—Mike Schmidt, Philadelphia, 1981.
Chris Speier, Montreal, 1981.
Manny Trillo, Philadelphia, 1981.
Tim Wallach, Montreal, 1981.
Matt Williams, Arizona, 2001.

Most consecutive bases on balls, series
.L.—4—Edgar Martinez, Seattle, October 6, 1995 (3), October 7 (1), 1995.
.L.—3
Chris Speier, Montreal, October 7, 1981.
Chipper Jones, Atlanta, October 1, 1997.
Jeff Bagwell, Houston, October 8, 1999, 12 innings.
Richard Hidalgo, Houston, October 9, 2001.

Most bases on balls, nine-inning game
.L.—3
Chris Speier, Montreal, October 7, 1981.
Chipper Jones, Atlanta, October 1, 1997.
Andruw Jones, Atlanta, October 3, 1998.
Andruw Jones, Atlanta, October 3, 2000.
Richard Hidalgo, Houston, October 9, 2001.
.L.—3
Willie Aikens, Kansas City, October 7, 1981.
Edgar Martinez, Seattle, October 6, 1995.
Randy Velarde, New York, October 7, 1995.
Travis Fryman, Cleveland, October 7, 1999.
Jason Giambi, Oakland, October 7, 2000.

Most bases on balls, extra-inning game
A.L.—4—Bernie Williams, New York, October 8, 1995, 11 innings.
N.L.—3
Bill Russell, Los Angeles, October 7, 1981, 11 innings.
Jeff Bagwell, Houston, October 8, 1999, 12 innings.

Most bases on balls with bases filled, game
A.L.-N.L.—1—Held by many players.

Bases on balls with bases filled by pinch-hitters, game
A.L.—Jim Leyritz, New York, October 7, 1999, eighth inning.
N.L.—Never accomplished.

Most bases on balls, two consecutive games
A.L.—5
Jason Giambi, Oakland, October 6 (2), 7 (3), 2000.
Bernie Williams, New York, October 7 (1), 8 (4), 1995, second game 11 innings.
N.L.—4
Chris Speier, Montreal, October 7 (3), 8 (1), 1981.
Jeff Bagwell, Houston, October 8 (3), 9 (1), 1999, first game 12 innings.
Andruw Jones, Atlanta, October 3 (3), 5 (1), 2000.
Jeff Bagwell, Houston, October 10 (2), 12 (2), 2001.

Most bases on balls, inning
A.L.-N.L.—1—Held by many players.

STRIKEOUTS

Most strikeouts, career
A.L.—34—Jim Thome, Cleveland, 1995 through 1999, 2001; six series, 25 games.
N.L.—18—Chipper Jones, Atlanta, 1995 through 2001; seven series, 23 games.

Most strikeouts, series
3-game series
N.L.—9—Reggie Sanders, Cincinnati, 1995.
A.L.—7—Mo Vaughn, Boston, 1995.
4-game series
A.L.—9—Dan Wilson, Seattle, 1997.
N.L.—8—Carl Everett, Houston, 1999.
5-game series
A.L.—11—Bret Boone, Seattle, 2001.
N.L.—9—Warren Cromartie, Montreal, 1981.

Most strikeouts by pinch-hitter, series
N.L.—2
John Vander Wal, Colorado, 1995; four games.
Dave Clark, Los Angeles, 1996; two games.
Billy Ashley, Los Angeles, 1996; two games.
Bob Abreu, Houston, 1997; two games.
A.L.—1—Held by many players.

Most consecutive strikeouts, series (consecutive at-bats)
N.L.—8—Jerry Reuss, Los Angeles, October 7 (4), October 11 (4), 1981, first game 11 innings.
A.L.—6—Dan Wilson, Seattle, October 1 (1), October 2 (4), October 4 (1), 1997.

Most consecutive strikeouts, series (consecutive plate appearances)
N.L.—8—Jerry Reuss, Los Angeles, October 7 (4), October 11 (4), 1981, first game 11 innings.
A.L.—6—Dan Wilson, Seattle, October 1 (1), October 2 (4), October 4 (1), 1997.

Most strikeouts, nine-inning game
N.L.—5—Reggie Sanders, Cincinnati, October 6, 1995.
A.L.—4
Dan Wilson, Seattle, October 2, 1997.
Brady Anderson, Baltimore, October 5, 1997.
Ben Grieve, Oakland, October 8, 2000.
Bret Boone, Seattle, October 13, 2001.

Most strikeouts, extra-inning game
A.L.—4
Rafael Palmeiro, Baltimore, October 5, 1996, 12 innings.
Bobby Bonilla, Baltimore, October 5, 1996, 12 innings.
Pete Incaviglia, Baltimore, October 5, 1996, 12 innings.
N.L.—Less than nine-inning record.

Most strikeouts, inning
A.L.-N.L.—1—Held by many players.

SACRIFICE HITS

Most sacrifice hits, career
A.L.—3
Joey Cora, Seattle, 1995, 1997; two series, nine games.
Omar Vizquel, Cleveland, 1995 through 1999, 2001; six series, 26 games.
Scott Brosius, New York, 1998 through 2001; four series, 16 games.
Stan Javier, Seattle, 2000, 2001; two series, seven games.
N.L.—3—Placido Polanco, St. Louis, 2000, 2001; two series, eight games.

Most sacrifice hits, series
A.L.—3—Joey Cora, Seattle, 1995; five games.
N.L.—3—Placido Polanco, St. Louis, 2001; five games.

Most sacrifice hits, game
N.L.—3—Placido Polanco, St. Louis, October 13, 2001.
A.L.—2—Stan Javier, Seattle, October 15, 2001.

SACRIFICE FLIES

Most sacrifice flies, career
A.L.—3—Luis Sojo, Seattle, 1995; New York, 1996, 2000; three series, 12 games.
N.L.—2—Held by many players.

Most sacrifice flies, series
A.L.—2
Cecil Cooper, Milwaukee, 1981; five games.
Luis Sojo, Seattle, 1995; five games.
Nomar Garciaparra, Boston, 1998; four games.
Trot Nixon, Boston, 1999; five games.
N.L.—1—Held by many players.

Most sacrifice flies, game
A.L.-N.L.—1—Held by many players.

HIT BY PITCH

Most hit by pitch, career
A.L.—3—Tino Martinez, Seattle, 1995; New York, 1996 through 2001; seven series, 30 games.

N.L.—2
Jeff Bagwell, Houston, 1997, 1998, 1999; three series, 11 games.
Mike Bordick, New York, 2000; one series, four games.

Most hit by pitch, series
A.L.—2—Tino Martinez, New York, 2001; five games.
N.L.—1—Held by many players.

Most hit by pitch, game
A.L.-N.L.—1—Held by many players.

GROUNDING INTO DOUBLE PLAYS

Most grounding into double plays, career
Both leagues—5—Joe Girardi, Colorado N.L., 1995; New York A.L., 1996, 1997, 1998, 1999 (2 in N.L., 3 in A.L.); five series, 17 games.
A.L.—5—Bernie Williams, New York, 1995 through 2001; seven series, 30 games.
N.L.—3
Chipper Jones, Atlanta, 1995 through 2001; seven series, 23 games.
Ken Caminiti, San Diego, 1996, 1998; Houston, 1999, Atlanta, 2001; four series, 13 games.

Most grounding into double plays, series
A.L.—3—Joe Girardi, New York, 1997 (5-game series).
N.L.—2
Chipper Jones, Atlanta, 1995 (4-game series).
Joe Girardi, Colorado, 1995 (4-game series).
Ken Caminiti, Houston, 1999 (4-game series).
Lance Berkman, Houston, 2001 (3-game series).

Most grounding into double plays, game
N.L.—2
Chipper Jones, Atlanta, October 3, 1995.
Lance Berkman, Houston, October 10, 2001.
A.L.—2
Paul O'Neill, New York, October 4, 1996.
Sandy Alomar Jr., Cleveland, September 30, 1998.

REACHING BASE ON INTERFERENCE

Most times awarded first base on catcher's interference, game
A.L.-N.L.—Never occurred.

CLUB BATTING

GAMES

Most games played, total series
A.L.—35—New York; eight series, won 22, lost 13.
N.L.—23—Atlanta; seven series, won 18, lost five.

For complete lists of results, and series, games, and home and road games played by all teams, see page 387. For a yearly list of batting statistics by teams, see page 390.

BATTING AVERAGE

Highest batting average, series
3-game series
  N.L.—.303—Atlanta vs. Houston, 2001.
  A.L.—.283—Seattle vs. Chicago, 2000.
4-game series
  N.L.—.331—Atlanta vs. Colorado, 1995.
  A.L.—.289—Baltimore vs. Cleveland, 1996.
             Baltimore vs. Seattle, 1997.
5-game series
  A.L.—.318—Boston vs. Cleveland, 1999.
  N.L.—.265—Philadelphia vs. Montreal, 1981.

Highest batting average by both clubs, series
3-game series
  N.L.—.279—Cincinnati .279, Los Angeles .279, 1995.
  A.L.—.236—Seattle .283, Chicago .185, 2000.
4-game series
  N.L.—.310—Atlanta .331, Colorado .287, 1995.
  A.L.—.267—Baltimore .289, Cleveland .245, 1996.
5-game series
  A.L.—.288—Seattle .315, New York .259, 1995.
  N.L.—.260—Philadelphia .265, Montreal .255, 1981.

Highest batting average by losing club, series
N.L.—.287—Colorado vs. Atlanta, 1995 (4-game series).
A.L.—.263—Oakland vs. New York, 2000 (5-game series).

Lowest batting average, series
3-game series
  A.L.—.141—Texas vs. New York, 1998.
  N.L.—.147—Los Angeles vs. Atlanta, 1996.
4-game series
  N.L.—.182—Houston vs. San Diego, 1998.
  A.L.—.206—Cleveland vs. Boston, 1998.
5-game series
  N.L.—.179—Houston vs. Los Angeles, 1981.
  A.L.—.222—Milwaukee vs. New York, 1981.

Lowest batting average by both clubs, series
3-game series
  N.L.—.163—Atlanta .180, Los Angeles .147, 1996.
  A.L.—.195—New York .235, Texas .152, 1999.
4-game series
  N.L.—.199—San Diego .216, Houston .182, 1998.
  A.L.—.230—Boston .252, Cleveland .206, 1998.
5-game series
  N.L.—.188—Los Angeles .198, Houston .179, 1981.
  A.L.—.244—Oakland .247, New York .241, 2001.

Lowest batting average by winning club, series
N.L.—.180—Atlanta vs. Los Angeles, 1996 (3-game series).
A.L.—.206—Cleveland vs. Boston, 1998 (4-game series).

SLUGGING AVERAGE

Highest slugging average, series
3-game series
  N.L.—.545—Atlanta vs. Houston, 2001.
  A.L.—.451—New York vs. Texas, 1998.

4-game series
  N.L.—.519—Atlanta vs. Colorado, 1995.
  A.L.—.510—Baltimore vs. Cleveland, 1996.
5-game series
  A.L.—.597—Boston vs. Cleveland, 1999.
  N.L.—.392—Philadelphia vs. Montreal, 1981.

Highest slugging average by both clubs, series
3-game series
  N.L.—.432—Atlanta .545, Houston .316, 2001.
  A.L.—.377—Seattle .424, Chicago .326, 2000.
4-game series
  N.L.—.492—Atlanta .519, Colorado .462, 1995.
  A.L.—.448—Baltimore .504, Seattle .391, 1997.
5-game series
  A.L.—.510—Boston .597, Cleveland .417, 1999.
  N.L.—.379—Philadelphia .392, Montreal .366, 1981.

Lowest slugging average, series
3-game series
  A.L.—.174—Texas vs. New York, 1998.
  N.L.—.208—Houston vs. Atlanta, 1997.
4-game series
  N.L.—.248—Houston vs. San Diego, 1998.
  A.L.—.373—Texas vs. New York, 1996.
5-game series
  N.L.—.235—Houston vs. Los Angeles, 1981.
  A.L.—.327—Milwaukee vs. New York, 1981.

Lowest slugging average by both clubs, series
3-game series
  N.L.—.282—Atlanta .359, Houston .208, 1997.
  A.L.—.295—New York .378, Texas .207, 1999.
4-game series
  A.L.—.311—New York .322, San Francisco .301, 2000.
  N.L.—.317—San Diego .384, Houston .248, 1998.
5-game series
  N.L.—.269—Los Angeles .302, Houston .235, 1981.
  A.L.—.343—Oakland .353, New York .333, 2000.

AT-BATS AND PLATE APPEARANCES

Most at-bats, total series
A.L.—1,193—New York; eight series, 35 games.
N.L.—778—Atlanta; seven series, 23 games.

Most at-bats, series
3-game series
  A.L.—114—Boston vs. Cleveland, 1995.
             Cleveland vs. Boston, 1995.
  N.L.—111—Los Angeles vs. Cincinnati, 1995.
4-game series
  N.L.—154—Atlanta vs. Colorado, 1995.
  A.L.—149—Baltimore vs. Cleveland, 1996.
5-game series
  A.L.—200—Seattle vs. New York, 1995.
  N.L.—166—Philadelphia vs. Montreal, 1981.

Most at-bats by both clubs, series
3-game series
  A.L.—228—Boston 114, Cleveland 114, 1995.
  N.L.—215—Los Angeles 111, Cincinnati 104, 1995.
4-game series
  N.L.—297—Atlanta 154, Colorado 143, 1995.
  A.L.—292—Baltimore 149, Cleveland 143, 1996.
5-game series
  A.L.—393—Seattle 200, New York 193, 1995.
  N.L.—327—Philadelphia 166, Montreal 161, 1981.

Most at-bats by pinch-hitters, series
N.L.—11—Atlanta vs. Colorado, 1995 (4-game series).
A.L.—9—Oakland vs. New York, 2001 (5-game series).

Most at-bats by pinch-hitters on both clubs, series
N.L.—20—Atlanta 11, Colorado 9, 1995 (4-game series).
A.L.—11—Oakland 9, New York 2, 2001 (5-game series).

Most plate appearances by pinch-hitters, series
N.L.—11—Atlanta vs. Colorado, 1995 (4-game series).
A.L.—9—Oakland vs. New York, 2001 (5-game series).

Most plate appearances by pinch-hitters on both clubs, series
N.L.—21—Atlanta 11, Colorado 10, 1995 (4-game series).
A.L.—11—Oakland 9, New York 2, 2001 (5-game series).

Fewest at-bats, series
3-game series
  N.L.—89—Atlanta vs. Los Angeles, 1996.
  A.L.—91—New York vs. Texas, 1998.
4-game series
  N.L.—121—Houston vs. San Diego, 1998.
  A.L.—126—Cleveland vs. Boston, 1998.
5-game series
  N.L.—152—St. Louis vs. Arizona, 2001.
  A.L.—158—Seattle vs. Cleveland, 2001.

Fewest at-bats by both clubs, series
3-game series
  A.L.—183—Texas 92, New York 91, 1998.
  N.L.—184—Los Angeles 95, Atlanta 89, 1996.
4-game series
  N.L.—246—San Diego 125, Houston 121, 1998.
  A.L.—261—Boston 135, Cleveland 126, 1998.
5-game series
  N.L.—308—Arizona 156, St. Louis 152, 2001.
  A.L.—331—Cleveland 173, Seattle 158, 2001.

Most at-bats by club, nine-inning game
A.L.—48—Boston vs. Cleveland, October 10, 1999.
N.L.—41—Atlanta vs. Colorado, October 4, 1995.

Most at-bats by club, extra-inning game
A.L.—56—Seattle vs. New York, October 4, 1995, 15 innings.
N.L.—49—San Francisco vs. New York, October 7, 2000, 13 innings.

Most at-bats by both clubs, nine-inning game
A.L.—79—Boston 48, Cleveland 31, October 10, 1999.
N.L.—77—Atlanta 41, Colorado 36, October 4, 1995.

Most at-bats by both clubs, extra-inning game
A.L.—107—Seattle 56, New York 51, October 4, 1995, 15 innings.
N.L.—92—San Francisco 49, New York 43, October 7, 2000, 13 innings.

Most at-bats by pinch-hitters, game
N.L.—4
  Atlanta vs. Colorado, October 4, 1995.
  San Diego vs. Houston, October 1, 1998.
  New York vs. Arizona, October 6, 1999.
  Atlanta vs. Houston, October 8, 1999, 12 innings.
  Atlanta vs. St. Louis, October 3, 2000.
A.L.—4—Seattle vs. Cleveland, October 13, 2001.

Most at-bats by pinch-hitters on both clubs, game
N.L.—7—Atlanta 4, Colorado 3, October 4, 1995.
A.L.—5—Seattle 4, Cleveland 1, October 13, 2001.

Most plate appearances by pinch-hitters, game
N.L.—4
  Atlanta vs. Colorado, October 4, 1995.
  San Diego vs. Houston, October 1, 1998.
  New York vs. Arizona, October 6, 1999.
  Atlanta vs. Houston, October 8, 1999, 12 innings.
  Atlanta vs. St. Louis, October 3, 2000.
  San Francisco vs. New York, October 5, 2000, 10 innings.
A.L.—4—Seattle vs. Cleveland, October 13, 2001.

Most plate appearances by pinch-hitters on both clubs, game
N.L.—7—Atlanta 4, Colorado 3, October 4, 1995.
A.L.—5—Seattle 4, Cleveland 1, October 13, 2001.

Fewest at-bats, game
N.L.—24—San Diego vs. Houston, October 3, 1998 (batted eight innings).

A.L.—25
  New York vs. Texas, September 29, 1998 (batted eight innings).
  Chicago vs. Seattle, October 6, 2000.

Fewest at-bats by both clubs, game
N.L.—52—Houston 28, San Diego 24, October 3, 1998 (San Diego batted eight innings).
A.L.—53—Seattle 28, Chicago 25, October 6, 2000.

Most at-bats, inning
A.L.—10—Boston vs. Cleveland, October 10, 1999, second inning.
N.L.—9—Atlanta vs. Houston, October 9, 1999, sixth inning.

Most at-bats by both clubs, inning
A.L.—13—New York 7, Milwaukee 6, October 9, 1981, seventh inning.
N.L.—13
  Atlanta 7, Colorado 6, October 7, 1995, third inning.
  Atlanta 7, Chicago 6, October 3, 1998, eighth inning.

Most batters facing pitcher, inning
A.L.—11
  Boston vs. Cleveland, October 9, 1999, seventh inning.
  New York vs. Oakland, October 8, 2000, first inning.
N.L.—10
  Atlanta vs. Houston, October 9, 1999, sixth inning.
  St. Louis vs. Atlanta, October 3, 2000, first inning.

Most batters facing pitcher by both clubs, inning
A.L.—17
  Boston 11, Cleveland 6, October 9, 1999, seventh inning.
  Cleveland 10, Boston 7, October 10, 1999, fifth inning.
N.L.—16—Atlanta 9, Chicago 7, October 3, 1998, eighth inning.

RUNS
SERIES AND GAMES

Most runs, total series
A.L.—152—New York; eight series, 35 games.
N.L.—113—Atlanta; seven series, 23 games.

Most runs, series
3-game series
  N.L.—24—St. Louis vs. Atlanta, 2000.
  A.L.—20—Boston vs. Cleveland, 1998.
4-game series
  N.L.—27—Atlanta vs. Colorado, 1995.
  A.L.—25—Baltimore vs. Cleveland, 1996.
5-game series
  A.L.—47—Boston vs. Cleveland, 1999.
  N.L.—16—Montreal vs. Philadelphia, 1981.

Most runs by both clubs, series
3-game series
  N.L.—34—St. Louis 24, Atlanta 10, 2000.
  A.L.—23—Cleveland 17, Boston 6, 1995.
4-game series
  N.L.—46—Atlanta 27, Colorado 19, 1995.
  A.L.—45—Baltimore 25, Cleveland 20, 1996.
5-game series
  A.L.—79—Boston 47, Cleveland 32, 1999.
  N.L.—30—Montreal 16, Philadelphia 14, 1981.

Most runs by losing club, series
A.L.—33—New York vs. Seattle, 1995 (5-game series).
N.L.—19—Colorado vs. Atlanta, 1995 (4-game series).

Fewest runs, series
3-game series
  A.L.—1—Texas vs. New York, 1998.
        Texas vs. New York, 1999.
  N.L.—4—Chicago vs. Atlanta, 1998.
4-game series
  N.L.—8—Houston vs. San Diego, 1998.
  A.L.—11—Seattle vs. Baltimore, 1997.
5-game series
  N.L.—6—Houston vs. Los Angeles, 1981.
  A.L.—12—Oakland vs. New York, 2001.

ewest runs by both clubs, series

-game series
A.L.—10—New York 9, Texas 1, 1998.
N.L.—15—Atlanta 10, Los Angeles 5, 1996.

-game series
N.L.—22—San Diego 14, Houston 8, 1998.
A.L.—32—New York 16, Texas 16, 1996.

-game series
N.L.—19—Los Angeles 13, Houston 6, 1981.
A.L.—30—New York 18, Oakland 12, 2001.

Most runs, game
A.L.—23—Boston vs. Cleveland, October 10, 1999.
N.L.—13—Atlanta vs. Houston, October 1, 1997.

Most earned runs, game
A.L.—23—Boston vs. Cleveland, October 10, 1999.
N.L.—10
Cincinnati vs. Los Angeles, October 6, 1995.
St. Louis vs. Atlanta, October 5, 2000.

Most runs by both clubs, game
A.L.—30—Boston 23, Cleveland 7, October 10, 1999.
N.L.—14
Atlanta 10, Colorado 4, October 7, 1995.
St. Louis 10, Atlanta 4, October 5, 2000.

Largest score, shutout game
A.L.—New York 8, Texas 0, October 5, 1999.
N.L.—Los Angeles 4, Houston 0, October 11, 1981.
New York 4, San Francisco 0, October 8, 2000.

Most players scoring one or more runs, game
A.L.—10—Cleveland vs. Seattle, October 13, 2001.
N.L.—7
Atlanta vs. Colorado, October 7, 1995.
Atlanta vs. Houston, October 9, 1999.

Most players from both clubs scoring one or more runs, game
A.L.—15—Boston 9, Cleveland 6, October 10, 1999.
N.L.—11
Atlanta 7, Colorado 4, October 7, 1995.
Atlanta 7, Houston 4, October 9, 1999.

INNING

Most runs, inning
A.L.—6
Cleveland vs. Boston, October 7, 1999, third inning.
Boston vs. Cleveland, October 9, 1999, seventh inning.
New York vs. Oakland, October 8, 2000, first inning.
N.L.—6
New York vs. Arizona, October 8, 1999, sixth inning.
St. Louis vs. Atlanta, October 3, 2000, first inning.

Most runs by both clubs, inning
N.L.—7
Atlanta 4, Colorado 3, October 7, 1995, third inning.
Atlanta 5, Chicago 2, October 3, 1998, eighth inning.
A.L.—7
Cleveland 6, Boston 1, October 7, 1999, third inning.
Boston 6, Cleveland 1, October 9, 1999, seventh inning.
Cleveland 4, Boston 3, October 10, 1999, fifth inning.

Most runs, extra inning
A.L.—3—Seattle vs. Chicago, October 3, 2000, 10th inning.
N.L.—2
Colorado vs. Atlanta, October 6, 1995, 10th inning.
Atlanta vs. Houston, October 8, 1999, 12th inning.

Most runs by both clubs, extra inning
A.L.—3
Seattle 2, New York 1, October 8, 1995, 11th inning.
Seattle 3, Chicago 0, October 3, 2000, 10th inning.
N.L.—2
Colorado 2, Atlanta 0, October 6, 1995, 10th inning.
Atlanta 2, Houston 0, October 8, 1999, 12th inning.

Most innings scored, game
A.L.—7—Boston vs. Cleveland, October 10, 1999.
N.L.—6
San Francisco vs. Florida, October 1, 1997.
St. Louis vs. Atlanta, October 5, 2000.

Most innings scored by both clubs, game
N.L.—11—San Francisco 6, Florida 5, October 1, 1997.
A.L.—11—Boston 7, Cleveland 4, October 10, 1999.

Most runs, first inning
A.L.—6—New York vs. Oakland, October 8, 2000.
N.L.—6—St. Louis vs. Atlanta, October 3, 2000.

Most runs, second inning
A.L.—5
Cleveland vs. Boston, September 30, 1998.
Boston vs. Cleveland, October 10, 1999.
N.L.—2
Philadelphia vs. Montreal, October 9, 1981.
San Diego vs. St. Louis, October 5, 1996.
Atlanta vs. Chicago, September 30, 1998.
New York vs. San Francisco, October 5, 2000.
Atlanta vs. Houston, October 10, 2001.

Most runs, third inning
A.L.—6—Cleveland vs. Boston, October 7, 1999.
N.L.—4
Atlanta vs. Colorado, October 7, 1995.
Atlanta vs. St. Louis, October 3, 2000.
San Francisco vs. New York, October 4, 2000.

Most runs, fourth inning
A.L.—5
Texas vs. New York, October 1, 1996.
Cleveland vs. New York, October 2, 1997.
Cleveland vs. Boston, October 7, 1999.
Boston vs. Cleveland, October 10, 1999.
N.L.—4—Atlanta vs. Los Angeles, October 5, 1996.

Most runs, fifth inning
A.L.—4
Baltimore vs. Seattle, October 1, 1997.
Cleveland vs. Boston, October 10, 1999.
N.L.—3
Cincinnati vs. Los Angeles, October 3, 1995.
St. Louis vs. San Diego, October 3, 1996.

Most runs, sixth inning
N.L.—6—New York vs. Arizona, October 8, 1999.
A.L.—5
Cleveland vs. Boston, October 6, 1995.
Baltimore vs. Cleveland, October 1, 1996.
New York vs. Cleveland, September 30, 1997.

Most runs, seventh inning
A.L.—6—Boston vs. Cleveland, October 9, 1999.
N.L.—4
Atlanta vs. Chicago, September 30, 1998.
Arizona vs. St. Louis, October 12, 2001.

Most runs, eighth inning
A.L.—5
Seattle vs. New York, October 7, 1995.
Cleveland vs. Seattle, October 13, 2001.
N.L.—5—Atlanta vs. Chicago, October 3, 1998.

Most runs, ninth inning
N.L.—4
Atlanta vs. Colorado, October 4, 1995.
New York vs. Arizona, October 5, 1999.
Houston vs. Atlanta, October 5, 1999.
A.L.—4—Oakland vs. New York, October 7, 2000.

Most runs, 10th inning
A.L.—3—Seattle vs. Chicago, October 3, 2000.
N.L.—2—Colorado vs. Atlanta, October 6, 1995.

Most runs, 11th inning
A.L.—2—Seattle vs. New York, October 8, 1995.
N.L.—Never accomplished.

Most runs, 12th inning
N.L.—2—Atlanta vs. Houston, October 8, 1999.
A.L.—1
New York vs. Seattle, October 4, 1995.
Seattle vs. New York, October 4, 1995.
New York vs. Texas, October 2, 1996.
Baltimore vs. Cleveland, October 5, 1996.

Most runs, 13th inning
A.L.—1—Cleveland vs. Boston, October 3, 1995.
N.L.—1—New York vs. San Francisco, October 7, 2000.

Most runs, 15th inning
A.L.—2—New York vs. Seattle, October 4, 1995.
N.L.—Never accomplished.

GAMES BEING SHUT OUT

Most times being shut out, total series
A.L.—4—Texas; three series, 10 games.
N.L.—2—Houston; five series, 19 games.

Most consecutive games without being shut out, total series
A.L.—31—New York, October 7, 1981 through October 10, 2001.
N.L.—23—Atlanta, October 3, 1995 through October 12, 2001.

HITS
SERIES

Most hits, total series
A.L.—303—New York; eight series, 35 games.
N.L.—203—Atlanta; seven series, 23 games.

Most hits, series
3-game series
  N.L.—31—Los Angeles vs. Cincinnati, 1995.
  A.L.—28—Seattle vs. Chicago, 2000.
4-game series
  N.L.—51—Atlanta vs. Colorado, 1995.
  A.L.—43—Baltimore vs. Cleveland, 1996.
5-game series
  A.L.—63—Seattle vs. New York, 1995.
  N.L.—44—Philadelphia vs. Montreal, 1981.

Most hits by both clubs, series
3-game series
  N.L.—60—Los Angeles 31, Cincinnati 29, 1995.
  A.L.—46—Cleveland 25, Boston 21, 1995.
4-game series
  N.L.—92—Atlanta 51, Colorado 41, 1995.
  A.L.—78—Baltimore 43, Cleveland 35, 1996.
5-game series
  A.L.—113—Seattle 63, New York 50, 1995.
  N.L.—85—Philadelphia 44, Montreal 41, 1981.

Fewest hits, series
3-game series
  A.L.—13—Texas vs. New York, 1998.
  N.L.—14—Los Angeles vs. Atlanta, 1996.
4-game series
  N.L.—22—Houston vs. San Diego, 1998.
  A.L.—26—Cleveland vs. Boston, 1998.
5-game series
  N.L.—29—Houston vs. Los Angeles, 1981.
        St. Louis vs. Arizona, 2001.
  A.L.—36—Milwaukee vs. New York, 1981.

Fewest hits by both clubs, series
3-game series
  N.L.—30—Atlanta 16, Los Angeles 14, 1996.
  A.L.—37—New York 23, Texas 14, 1999.
4-game series
  N.L.—49—San Diego 27, Houston 22, 1998.
  A.L.—60—Boston 34, Cleveland 26, 1998.
5-game series
  N.L.—61—Los Angeles 32, Houston 29, 1981.
  A.L.—82—New York 46, Milwaukee 36, 1981.

Most hits by pinch-hitters, series
N.L.—5—Atlanta vs. Colorado, 1995 (4-game series).
A.L.—1—Held by many clubs.

Most hits by pinch-hitters on both clubs, series
N.L.—6—Atlanta 5, Colorado 1, 1995 (4-game series).

A.L.—2
  Baltimore 1, Seattle 1, 1997 (4-game series).
  Boston 1, Cleveland 1, 1999 (5-game series).
  New York 1, Oakland 1, 2000 (5-game series).
  Oakland 1, New York 1, 2001 (5-game series).

GAME AND INNING

Most hits, game
A.L.—24—Boston vs. Cleveland, October 10, 1999.
N.L.—15
  Atlanta vs. Colorado, October 7, 1995.
  Atlanta vs. Houston, October 9, 1999.

Most hits by both clubs, game
A.L.—32—Boston 24, Cleveland 8, October 10, 1999.
N.L.—26—Atlanta 15, Colorado 11, October 7, 1995.

Most hits by pinch-hitters, game
N.L.—2
  Montreal vs. Philadelphia, October 10, 1981, 10 innings.
  Atlanta vs. Colorado, October 4, 1995.
  Atlanta vs. Colorado, October 6, 1995, 10 innings.
  Houston vs. Atlanta, October 8, 1999, 12 innings.
  San Francisco vs. New York, October 5, 2000, 10 innings.
  Arizona vs. St. Louis, October 10, 2001.
  St. Louis vs. Arizona, October 12, 2001.
A.L.—1—Held by many clubs.

Most hits by pinch-hitters on both clubs, game
N.L.—3
  Montreal 2, Philadelphia 1, October 10, 1981, 10 innings.
  Atlanta 2, Colorado 1, October 4, 1995.
  San Francisco 2, New York 1, October 5, 2000, 10 innings.
A.L.—1—Occurred in many games.

Fewest hits, game
N.L.—1
  Houston vs. Atlanta, October 6, 1999.
  San Francisco vs. New York, October 8, 2000.
A.L.—2
  Seattle vs. Baltimore, October 5, 1997.
  Texas vs. New York, October 5, 1999.
  New York vs. Oakland, October 13, 2001.

Fewest hits by both clubs, game
A.L.—7—Cleveland 4, Boston 3, October 4, 1995.
N.L.—7
  Houston 4, San Diego 3, October 3, 1998.
  New York 6, San Francisco 1, October 8, 2000.

Most players with one or more hits, game
N.L.—10—Atlanta vs. Colorado, October 4, 1995.
A.L.—9
  Baltimore vs. Cleveland, October 5, 1996, 12 innings.
  New York vs. Texas, October 5, 1996.
  Baltimore vs. Seattle, October 1, 1997.
  Boston vs. Cleveland, October 10, 1999.
  Seattle vs. Chicago, October 3, 2000, 10 innings.

Most players with one or more hits by both clubs, game
A.L.—16
  New York 8, Seattle 8, October 7, 1995.
  Baltimore 8, Seattle 8, October 2, 1997.
  Seattle 9, Chicago 7, October 3, 2000, 10 innings.
N.L.—16—Atlanta 10, Colorado 6, October 4, 1995.

Most hits, inning
N.L.—7—Atlanta vs. Houston, October 9, 1999, sixth inning.
A.L.—6
  Boston vs. Cleveland, October 10, 1999, second inning.
  New York vs. Oakland, October 8, 2000, first inning.

Most hits by pinch-hitters, inning
N.L.—2
  Montreal vs. Philadelphia, October 10, 1981, sixth inning.
  Houston vs. Atlanta, October 8, 1999, seventh inning.
  Arizona vs. St. Louis, October 10, 2001, eighth inning.
A.L.—1—Held by many clubs.

Most hits by both clubs, inning
N.L.—8—Atlanta 4, Chicago 4, October 3, 1998, eighth inning.

.L.—8
Milwaukee 4, New York 4, October 9, 1981, seventh inning.
New York 6, Oakland 2, October 8, 2000, first inning.

Most consecutive hits, inning (consecutive at-bats)
.L.—6—Boston vs. Cleveland, October 10, 1999, second inning.
.L.—6—Atlanta vs. Houston, October 9, 1999, sixth inning (one sacrifice hit during streak).

Most consecutive hits, inning (consecutive plate appearances)
.L.—6—Boston vs. Cleveland, October 10, 1999, second inning.
.L.—5—Atlanta vs. Houston, October 9, 1999, sixth inning.

SINGLES

Most singles, total series
.L.—201—New York; eight series, 35 games.
.L.—143—Atlanta; seven series, 23 games.

Most singles, series
-game series
    N.L.—26—Los Angeles vs. Cincinnati, 1995.
    A.L.—22—Seattle vs. Chicago, 2000.
-game series
    N.L.—36—Atlanta vs. Colorado, 1995.
    A.L.—29—New York vs. Texas, 1996.
-game series
    A.L.—45—Seattle vs. New York, 1995.
    N.L.—33—Philadelphia vs. Montreal, 1981.

Most singles by both clubs, series
-game series
    N.L.—44—Los Angeles 26, Cincinnati 18, 1995.
    A.L.—36—Kansas City 19, Oakland 17, 1981.
-game series
    N.L.—64—Atlanta 36, Colorado 28, 1995.
    A.L.—52—Baltimore 28, Cleveland 24, 1996.
-game series
    A.L.—72—Seattle 45, New York 27, 1995.
    N.L.—61—Philadelphia 33, Montreal 28, 1981.

Fewest singles, series
-game series
    N.L.—7—Los Angeles vs. Atlanta, 1996.
    A.L.—8—Chicago vs. Seattle, 2000.
-game series
    A.L.—7—Cleveland vs. Boston, 1998.
    N.L.—16—Houston vs. San Diego, 1998.
-game series
    N.L.—20—St. Louis vs. Arizona, 2001.
    A.L.—23—Cleveland vs. Boston, 1999.

Fewest singles by both clubs, series
-game series
    N.L.—15—Atlanta 8, Los Angeles 7, 1996.
    A.L.—23—New York 13, Texas 10, 1998.
-game series
    A.L.—30—Boston 23, Cleveland 7, 1998.
    N.L.—33—San Diego 17, Houston 16, 1998.
-game series
    N.L.—46—Houston 24, Los Angeles 22, 1981.
    A.L.—51—Boston 28, Cleveland 23, 1999.

Most singles by pinch-hitters, series
.L.—3
    Atlanta vs. Colorado, 1995 (4-game series).
    San Diego vs. St. Louis, 1996 (3-game series).
    Arizona vs. St. Louis, 2001 (5-game series).
A.L.—1—Held by many clubs.

Most singles by pinch-hitters on both clubs, series
.L.—5—Arizona 3, St. Louis 2, 2001 (5-game series).
A.L.—1—Occurred many times.

Most singles, game
.L.—13—Atlanta vs. Houston, October 9, 1999.

A.L.—12
    Seattle vs. New York, October 7, 1995.
    Boston vs. Cleveland, October 10, 1999.

Most singles by both clubs, game
A.L.—21—Seattle 12, New York 9, October 7, 1995.
N.L.—19—Atlanta 10, Colorado 9, October 7, 1995.

Fewest singles, game
N.L.—0
    Atlanta vs. Houston, September 30, 1997.
    Houston vs. Atlanta, October 6, 1999.
    San Francisco vs. New York, October 8, 2000.
A.L.—0—New York vs. Oakland, October 13, 2001.

Fewest singles by both clubs, game
N.L.—2—New York 2, San Francisco 0, October 8, 2000.
A.L.—4
    Boston 3, Cleveland 1, October 4, 1995.
    Boston 2, Cleveland 2, October 3, 1998.
    Boston 3, Cleveland 1, October 11, 1999.
    Oakland 4, New York 0, October 13, 2001.

Most singles, inning
N.L.—7—Atlanta vs. Houston, October 9, 1999, sixth inning.
A.L.—5—New York vs. Oakland, October 8, 2000, first inning.

Most singles by both clubs, inning
A.L.—7
    New York 4, Milwaukee 3, October 9, 1981, seventh inning.
    New York 5, Oakland 2, October 8, 2000, first inning.
N.L.—7—Atlanta 7, Houston 0, October 9, 1999, sixth inning.

DOUBLES

Most doubles, total series
A.L.—63—New York; eight series, 35 games.
N.L.—33—Atlanta; seven series, 23 games.

Most doubles, series
3-game series
    N.L.—7—Los Angeles vs. Atlanta, 1996.
    A.L.—6—New York vs. Texas, 1998.
                New York vs. Texas, 1999.
                Chicago vs. Seattle, 2000.
4-game series
    A.L.—12—Boston vs. Cleveland, 1998.
    N.L.—8—Atlanta vs. Colorado, 1995.
5-game series
    A.L.—17—Boston vs. Cleveland, 1999.
    N.L.—10—Montreal vs. Philadelphia, 1981.

Most doubles by both clubs, series
3-game series
    N.L.—10—Los Angeles 7, Atlanta 3, 1996.
                St. Louis 5, Atlanta 5, 2000.
    A.L.—9—New York 6, Texas 3, 1998.
4-game series
    A.L.—18—Cleveland 12, Boston 6, 1998.
    N.L.—15—Atlanta 8, Colorado 7, 1995.
5-game series
    A.L.—24—Boston 17, Cleveland 7, 1999.
    N.L.—16—Montreal 10, Philadelphia 6, 1981.

Fewest doubles, series
3-game series
    A.L.—1—Kansas City vs. Oakland, 1981.
    N.L.—1—Houston vs. Atlanta, 1997.
4-game series
    N.L.—2—Houston vs. Atlanta, 1999.
    A.L.—4—New York vs. Texas, 1996.
                Texas vs. New York, 1996.
5-game series
    N.L.—3—Houston vs. Los Angeles, 1981.
                St. Louis vs. Arizona, 2001.
    A.L.—6—Milwaukee vs. New York, 1981.
                Seattle vs. New York, 1995.
                Cleveland vs. New York, 1997.

Fewest doubles by both clubs, series
3-game series
   N.L.—4—Atlanta 2, Chicago 2, 1998.
   A.L.—6—Oakland 5, Kansas City 1, 1981.
      Cleveland 4, Boston 2, 1995.
4-game series
   N.L.—7—Atlanta 5, Houston 2, 1999.
   A.L.—8—New York 4, Texas 4, 1996.
5-game series
   N.L.—8—Arizona 5, St. Louis 3, 2001.
   A.L.—13—New York 7, Cleveland 6, 1997.

Most doubles by pinch-hitters, series
N.L.—2—Atlanta vs. Colorado, 1995 (4-game series).
A.L.—1
   Baltimore vs. Seattle, 1997 (4-game series).
   Boston vs. Cleveland, 1999 (5-game series).
   Oakland vs. New York, 2000 (5-game series).

Most doubles by pinch-hitters on both clubs, series
N.L.—2—Atlanta 2, Colorado 0, 1995 (4-game series).
A.L.—1
   Baltimore 1, Seattle 0, 1997 (4-game series).
   Boston 1, Cleveland 0, 1999 (5-game series).
   Oakland 1, New York 0, 2000 (5-game series).

Most doubles, game
A.L.—7—Boston vs. Cleveland, October 10, 1999.
N.L.—5—Cincinnati vs. Los Angeles, October 3, 1995.

Most doubles by both clubs, game
A.L.—9—Cleveland 5, Seattle 4, October 13, 2001.
N.L.—7—Los Angeles 4, Atlanta 3, October 5, 1996.

Most doubles, inning
N.L.—3—Cincinnati vs. Los Angeles, October 3, 1995, fifth inning.
A.L.—3—Cleveland vs. Seattle, October 13, 2001, eighth inning.

TRIPLES

Most triples, total series
A.L.—4—Cleveland; six series, 26 games.
N.L.—1—Held by many clubs.

Most triples, series
A.L.—2—Chicago vs. Seattle, 2000 (3-game series).
N.L.—1—Held by many clubs.

Most triples by both clubs, series
3-game series
   A.L.—2—Chicago 2, Seattle 0, 2000.
   N.L.—1—St. Louis 1, San Diego 0, 1996.
4-game series
   N.L.—1—San Diego 1, Houston 0, 1998.
      San Francisco 1, New York 0, 2000.
   A.L.—Never accomplished.
5-game series
   N.L.—2—Montreal 1, Philadelphia 1, 1981.
   A.L.—2—Boston 1, Cleveland 1, 1999.
      Oakland 1, New York 1, 2001.

Fewest triples, series
A.L.-N.L.—0—Held by many clubs.

Fewest triples by both clubs, series
A.L.-N.L.—0—Occurred in many series.

Most triples by pinch-hitters, series
N.L.—1—San Diego vs. Houston, 1998 (4-game series).
A.L.—Never accomplished.

Most triples, nine-inning game
A.L.-N.L.—1—Held by many clubs.

Most triples, extra-inning game
A.L.—2—Chicago vs. Seattle, October 3, 2000, 10 innings.
N.L.—1—Held by many clubs.

Most triples by both clubs, nine-inning
N.L.—2—Montreal 1, Philadelphia 1, October 7, 1981.
A.L.—1—Made in many games.

Most triples by both clubs, extra-inning
A.L.—2—Chicago 2, Seattle 0, October 3, 2000, 10 innings.
N.L.—Less than nine-inning record.

Most triples, inning
A.L.-N.L.—1—Held by many clubs.

HOME RUNS
SERIES

Most home runs, total series
A.L.—37—New York; eight series, 35 games.
N.L.—27—Atlanta; seven series, 23 games.

Most grand slams, total series
N.L.—2—Atlanta; seven series, 23 games.
A.L.—2—Cleveland; six series, 26 games.

Most home runs, series
3-game series
   N.L.—6—St. Louis vs. Atlanta, 2000.
      Atlanta vs. Houston, 2001.
   A.L.—4—Cleveland vs. Boston, 1995.
      New York vs. Texas, 1998.
      Seattle vs. Chicago, 2000.
4-game series
   A.L.—9—Baltimore vs. Cleveland, 1996.
   N.L.—7—Atlanta vs. Colorado, 1995.
5-game series
   A.L.—11—New York vs. Seattle, 1995.
      Seattle vs. New York, 1995.
   N.L.—6—St. Louis vs. Arizona, 2001.

Most home runs by both clubs, series
3-game series
   N.L.—9—Atlanta 6, Houston 3, 2001.
   A.L.—7—Cleveland 4, Boston 3, 1995.
4-game series
   A.L.—13—Baltimore 9, Cleveland 4, 1996.
   N.L.—13—Atlanta 7, Colorado 6, 1995.
5-game series
   A.L.—22—New York 11, Seattle 11, 1995.
   N.L.—9—St. Louis 6, Arizona 3, 2001.

Fewest home runs, series
3-game series
   A.L.—0—Kansas City vs. Oakland, 1981.
      Texas vs. New York, 1998.
   N.L.—0—Los Angeles vs. Atlanta, 1996.
4-game series
   N.L.—1—Houston vs. San Diego, 1998.
   A.L.—4—Cleveland vs. Baltimore, 1996.
      New York vs. Texas, 1996.
5-game series
   A.L.—1—New York vs. Oakland, 2000.
   N.L.—2—Houston vs. Los Angeles, 1981.
      Montreal vs. Philadelphia, 1981.

Fewest home runs by both clubs, series
3-game series
   A.L.—3—Oakland 3, Kansas City 0, 1981.
      New York 2, Texas 1, 1999.
   N.L.—5—Atlanta 5, Los Angeles 0, 1996.
      Atlanta 4, Chicago 1, 1998.
4-game series
   N.L.—5—New York 3, San Francisco 2, 2000.
   A.L.—10—Texas 6, New York 4, 1996.
5-game series
   A.L.—3—Oakland 2, New York 1, 2000.
   N.L.—5—Los Angeles 3, Houston 2, 1981.

Most grand slams, series
N.L.—2—Atlanta vs. Chicago, 1998.
A.L.—1—Held by many clubs.

Most home runs by pinch-hitters, series
A.L.—1—New York vs. Oakland, 2001 (5-game series).

N.L.—1
Philadelphia vs. Montreal, 1981 (5-game series).
Cincinnati vs. Los Angeles, 1995 (3-game series).
San Diego vs. Houston, 1998 (4-game series).
Arizona vs. New York, 1999 (4-game series).
St. Louis vs. Atlanta, 2000 (3-game series).
San Francisco vs. New York, 2000 (4-game series).
Houston vs. Atlanta, 2001 (3-game series).

GAME AND INNING

Most home runs, game
A.L.—4
New York vs. Seattle, October 4, 1995, 15 innings.
Seattle vs. New York, October 7, 1995.
Baltimore vs. Cleveland, October 1, 1996.
New York vs. Cleveland, September 30, 1997.
Cleveland vs. Boston, October 2, 1998.
Boston vs. Cleveland, October 10, 1999.
N.L.—3
Philadelphia vs. Montreal, October 10, 1981, 10 innings.
Atlanta vs. Colorado, October 3, 1995.
Cincinnati vs. Los Angeles, October 6, 1995.
Atlanta vs. Los Angeles, October 3, 1996.
New York vs. Arizona, October 5, 1999.
St. Louis vs. Atlanta, October 5, 2000.
Atlanta vs. Houston, October 9, 2001.
Atlanta vs. Houston, October 12, 2001.

Most home runs by both clubs, nine-inning game
A.L.—5
Seattle 4, New York 1, October 7, 1995.
Baltimore 4, Cleveland 1, October 1, 1996.
New York 4, Cleveland 1, September 30, 1997.
Cleveland 4, Boston 1, October 2, 1998.
Boston 4, Cleveland 1, October 10, 1999.
N.L.—5
New York 3, Arizona 2, October 5, 1999.
Atlanta 3, Houston 2, October 9, 2001.

Most home runs by both clubs, extra-inning game
A.L.—6—New York 4, Seattle 2, October 4, 1995, 15 innings.
N.L.—Less than nine-inning record.

Most consecutive games with one or more home runs, total series
N.L.—10
Atlanta, last game vs. Colorado, 1995 (two home runs), all three games vs. Los Angeles, 1996 (five home runs), all three games vs. Houston, 1997 (three home runs), all three games vs. Chicago, 1998 (four home runs).
A.L.—6
New York, last game vs. Milwaukee, 1981 (three home runs), all five games vs. Seattle, 1995 (11 home runs).
Cleveland, all three games vs. Boston, 1995 (four home runs), first three games vs. Baltimore, 1996 (four home runs).
New York, last three games vs. Texas, 1996 (four home runs), first three games vs. Cleveland, 1997 (six home runs).

Most consecutive games with one or more home runs, series
A.L.—5
New York vs. Seattle, October 3, 4, 6, 7, 8, 1995 (11 home runs).
Seattle vs. New York, October 3, 4, 6, 7, 8, 1995 (11 home runs).
N.L.—4
Colorado vs. Atlanta, October 3, 4, 6, 7, 1995 (six home runs).
San Diego vs. Houston, September 29, October 1, 3, 4, 1998 (five home runs).
St. Louis vs. Arizona, October 10, 12, 13, 14, 2001 (six home runs).

Most home runs, inning
A.L.—3—New York vs. Cleveland, September 30, 1997, sixth inning (consecutive).
N.L.—2—Atlanta vs. Los Angeles, October 3, 1996, seventh inning.

Most home runs by both clubs, inning
A.L.—3—New York 3, Cleveland 0, September 30, 1997, sixth inning.
N.L.—2
Cincinnati 1, Los Angeles 1, October 4, 1995, fourth inning.
Colorado 1, Atlanta 1, October 7, 1995, third inning.
Atlanta 2, Los Angeles 0, October 3, 1996, seventh inning.
Atlanta 1, Houston 1, October 9, 2001, ninth inning.
Arizona 1, St. Louis 1, October 12, 2001, seventh inning.

Most consecutive home runs, inning
A.L.—3—New York (Raines Sr., Jeter and O'Neill) vs. Cleveland, September 30, 1997, sixth inning.
N.L.—No club has had consecutive home runs.

TOTAL BASES

Most total bases, total series
A.L.—481—New York; eight series, 35 games.
N.L.—317—Atlanta; seven series, 23 games.

Most total bases, series
3-game series
　N.L.—54—Atlanta vs. Houston, 2001.
　A.L.—43—Cleveland vs. Boston, 1995.
4-game series
　N.L.—80—Atlanta vs. Colorado, 1995.
　A.L.—76—Baltimore vs. Cleveland, 1996.
5-game series
　A.L.—105—Boston vs. Cleveland, 1999.
　N.L.—64—Philadelphia vs. Montreal, 1981.

Most total bases by both clubs, series
3-game series
　N.L.—92—Cincinnati 50, Los Angeles 42, 1995.
　A.L.—75—Cleveland 43, Boston 32, 1995.
4-game series
　N.L.—146—Atlanta 80, Colorado 66, 1995.
　A.L.—130—Baltimore 76, Cleveland 54, 1996.
5-game series
　A.L.—199—Seattle 104, New York 95, 1995.
　N.L.—123—Philadelphia 64, Montreal 59, 1981.

Fewest total bases, series
3-game series
　A.L.—16—Texas vs. New York, 1998.
　N.L.—20—Houston vs. Atlanta, 1997.
4-game series
　N.L.—30—Houston vs. San Diego, 1998.
　A.L.—30—Chicago vs. Seattle, 2000.
5-game series
　N.L.—38—Houston vs. Los Angeles, 1981.
　A.L.—53—Milwaukee vs. New York, 1981.

Fewest total bases by both clubs, series
3-game series
　N.L.—53—Atlanta 33, Houston 20, 1997.
　A.L.—56—New York 37, Texas 19, 1999.
4-game series
　A.L.—72—Seattle 42, Chicago 30, 2000.
　N.L.—78—San Diego 48, Houston 30, 1998.
5-game series
　N.L.—87—Los Angeles 49, Houston 38, 1981.
　A.L.—115—Oakland 59, New York 56, 2000.

Most total bases, game
A.L.—45—Boston vs. Cleveland, October 10, 1999.
N.L.—24
Atlanta vs. Colorado, October 7, 1995.
Atlanta vs. Houston, October 9, 2001.

Most total bases by both clubs, game
A.L.—57—Boston 45, Cleveland 12, October 10, 1999.
N.L.—41
Atlanta 22, Colorado 19, October 3, 1995.
Atlanta 24, Colorado 17, October 7, 1995.

Fewest total bases, game
N.L.—2—San Francisco vs. New York, October 8, 2000.

A.L.—3
   Boston vs. Cleveland, October 4, 1995.
   Texas vs. New York, October 2, 1998.
   Texas vs. New York, October 5, 1999.

Fewest total bases by both clubs, game
N.L.—10—San Diego 6, Houston 4, October 3, 1998.
A.L.—10—Seattle 6, Chicago 4, October 6, 2000.

Most total bases, inning
A.L.—14—New York vs. Cleveland, September 30, 1997, sixth inning.
N.L.—9—St. Louis vs. San Diego, October 5, 1996, sixth inning.

Most total bases by both clubs, inning
A.L.—15—Cleveland 8, Boston 7, October 11, 1999, third inning.
N.L.—14—Atlanta 8, Colorado 6, October 7, 1995, third inning.

LONG HITS

Most long hits, total series
A.L.—102—New York; eight series, 35 games.
N.L.—60—Atlanta; seven series, 23 games.

Most long hits, series
3-game series
   N.L.—12—Atlanta vs. Houston, 2001.
   A.L.—10—New York vs. Texas, 1998.
4-game series
   A.L.—19—Cleveland vs. Boston, 1998.
   N.L.—15—Atlanta vs. Colorado, 1995.
5-game series
   A.L.—28—Boston vs. Cleveland, 1999.
   N.L.—13—Montreal vs. Philadelphia, 1981.

Most long hits by both clubs, series
3-game series
   N.L.—17—Florida 9, San Francisco 8, 1997.
      St. Louis 11, Atlanta 6, 2000.
      Atlanta 12, Houston 5, 2001.
   A.L.—14—Cleveland 9, Boston 5, 1995.
4-game series
   N.L.—28—Atlanta 15, Colorado 13, 1995.
   A.L.—30—Cleveland 19, Boston 11, 1998.
      Oakland 18, New York 12, 2001.
5-game series
   A.L.—43—Boston 28, Cleveland 15, 1999.
   N.L.—24—Montreal 13, Philadelphia 11, 1981.

Fewest long hits, series
3-game series
   A.L.—1—Kansas City vs. Oakland, 1981.
   N.L.—2—Houston vs. Atlanta, 1997.
4-game series
   N.L.—6—Houston vs. San Diego, 1998.
      Atlanta vs. Houston, 1999.
   A.L.—8—New York vs. Texas, 1996.
5-game series
   N.L.—5—Houston vs. Los Angeles, 1981.
   A.L.—10—Milwaukee vs. New York, 1981.

Fewest long hits by both clubs, series
3-game series
   A.L.—9—Oakland 8, Kansas City 1, 1981.
   N.L.—9—Atlanta 7, Houston 2, 1997.
      Atlanta 6, Chicago 3, 1998.
4-game series
   N.L.—13—Houston 7, Atlanta 6, 1999.
   A.L.—18—Texas 10, New York 8, 1996.
5-game series
   N.L.—15—Los Angeles 10, Houston 5, 1981.
   A.L.—24—New York 14, Milwaukee 10, 1981.
      New York 13, Cleveland 11, 1997.
      New York 13, Oakland 11, 2000.

Most long hits, game
A.L.—12—Boston vs. Cleveland, October 10, 1999 (seven doubles, one triple, four home runs).

N.L.—7—St. Louis vs. Atlanta, October 5, 2000 (four doubles, three home runs).

Most long hits by both clubs, game
A.L.—14—Boston 12 (seven doubles, one triple, four home runs), Cleveland 2 (one double, one home run), October 10, 1999.
N.L.—10—St. Louis 7 (four doubles, three home runs), Atlanta 3 (two doubles, one home run), October 5, 2000.

EXTRA BASES ON LONG HITS

Most extra bases on long hits, total series
A.L.—178—New York; eight series, 35 games; 63 on doubles, four on triples, 111 on home runs.
N.L.—114—Atlanta; seven series, 23 games; 33 on doubles, 81 on home runs.

Most extra bases on long hits, series
3-game series
   N.L.—24—Atlanta vs. Houston, 2001.
   A.L.—18—Cleveland vs. Boston, 1995.
      New York vs. Texas, 1998.
4-game series
   A.L.—33—Baltimore vs. Cleveland, 1996.
      Cleveland vs. Boston, 1998.
   N.L.—29—Atlanta vs. Colorado, 1995.
5-game series
   A.L.—49—Boston vs. Cleveland, 1999.
   N.L.—21—Philadelphia vs. Montreal, 1981.
      St. Louis vs. Arizona, 2001.

Most extra bases on long hits by both clubs, series
3-game series
   N.L.—35—Atlanta 24, Houston 11, 2001.
   A.L.—29—Cleveland 18, Boston 11, 1995.
4-game series
   N.L.—54—Atlanta 29, Colorado 25, 1995.
   A.L.—54—Cleveland 33, Boston 21, 1998.
5-game series
   A.L.—86—New York 45, Seattle 41, 1995.
   N.L.—39—Philadelphia 21, Montreal 18, 1981.

Fewest extra bases on long hits, series
3-game series
   A.L.—1—Kansas City vs. Oakland, 1981.
   N.L.—4—Houston vs. Atlanta, 1997.
4-game series
   N.L.—8—Atlanta vs. Houston, 1999.
   A.L.—16—New York vs. Texas, 1996.
5-game series
   N.L.—9—Houston vs. Los Angeles, 1981.
   A.L.—15—New York vs. Oakland, 2000.
      Oakland vs. New York, 2000.

Fewest extra bases on long hits by both clubs, series
3-game series
   A.L.—15—Oakland 14, Kansas City 1, 1981.
   N.L.—17—Atlanta 13, Houston 4, 1997.
4-game series
   N.L.—25—Houston 17, Atlanta 8, 1999.
   A.L.—38—Texas 22, New York 16, 1996.
5-game series
   N.L.—26—Los Angeles 17, Houston 9, 1981.
   A.L.—30—New York 15, Oakland 15, 2000.

RUNS BATTED IN

Most runs batted in, total series
A.L.—144—New York; eight series, 35 games.
N.L.—103—Atlanta; seven series, 23 games.

Most runs batted in, series
3-game series
   N.L.—23—St. Louis vs. Atlanta, 2000.
   A.L.—17—Cleveland vs. Boston, 1995.

4-game series
    N.L.—24—Atlanta vs. Colorado, 1995.
    A.L.—23—Baltimore vs. Cleveland, 1996.
            Baltimore vs. Seattle, 1997.
5-game series
    A.L.—47—Boston vs. Cleveland, 1999.
    N.L.—16—Montreal vs. Philadelphia, 1981.

Most runs batted in by both clubs, series
3-game series
    N.L.—32—St. Louis 23, Atlanta 9, 2000.
    A.L.—23—Cleveland 17, Boston 6, 1995.
4-game series
    A.L.—43—Baltimore 23, Cleveland 20, 1996.
    N.L.—42—Atlanta 24, Colorado 18, 1995.
5-game series
    A.L.—78—Boston 47, Cleveland 31, 1999.
    N.L.—28—Montreal 16, Philadelphia 12, 1981.

Fewest runs batted in, series
3-game series
    A.L.—1—Texas vs. New York, 1998.
           Texas vs. New York, 1999.
    N.L.—4—Chicago vs. Atlanta, 1998.
4-game series
    N.L.—7—Houston vs. San Diego, 1998.
    A.L.—15—New York vs. Texas, 1996.
5-game series
    N.L.—6—Houston vs. Los Angeles, 1981.
    A.L.—13—Milwaukee vs. New York, 1995.

Fewest runs batted in by both clubs, series
3-game series
    A.L.—9—New York 8, Texas 1, 1998.
    N.L.—15—Atlanta 10, Los Angeles 5, 1996.
4-game series
    N.L.—20—San Diego 13, Houston 7, 1998.
    A.L.—31—Texas 16, New York 15, 1996.
5-game series
    N.L.—18—Los Angeles 12, Houston 6, 1981.
    A.L.—31—New York 18, Milwaukee 13, 1981.

Most runs batted in by pinch-hitters, series
N.L.—5—Cincinnati vs. Los Angeles, 1995 (3-game series).
A.L.—2—Baltimore vs. Seattle, 1997 (4-game series).

Most runs batted in by pinch-hitters on both clubs, series
N.L.—5—Cincinnati 5, Los Angeles 0, 1995 (3-game series).
A.L.—3—Baltimore 2, Seattle 1, 1997 (4-game series).

Most runs batted in, game
A.L.—23—Boston vs. Cleveland, October 10, 1999.
N.L.—10
Cincinnati vs. Los Angeles, October 6, 1995.
Atlanta vs. Houston, October 1, 1997.
St. Louis vs. Atlanta, October 5, 2000.

Most runs batted in by both clubs, game
A.L.—30—Boston 23, Cleveland 7, October 10, 1999.
N.L.—14—St. Louis 10, Atlanta 4, October 5, 2000.

Fewest runs batted in by both clubs, game
N.L.—0—Atlanta 0, Houston 0, October 10, 2001.
A.L.—1
New York 1, Texas 0, September 29, 1998.
Oakland 1, New York 0, October 11, 2001.
New York 1, Oakland 0, October 13, 2001.

Most runs batted in, inning
A.L.—6
Cleveland vs. Boston, October 7, 1999, third inning.
Boston vs. Cleveland, October 9, 1999, seventh inning.
New York vs. Oakland, October 8, 2000, first inning.
N.L.—6—New York vs. Arizona, October 8, 1999, sixth inning.

Most runs batted in by both clubs, inning
N.L.—7—Atlanta 4, Colorado 3, October 7, 1995, third inning.
A.L.—7
Cleveland 6, Boston 1, October 7, 1999, third inning.
Cleveland 4, Boston 3, October 10, 1999, fifth inning.

Most runs batted in by pinch-hitters, inning
N.L.—4—Cincinnati vs. Los Angeles, October 6, 1995, sixth inning.
A.L.—2—Baltimore vs. Seattle, October 1, 1997, sixth inning.

BASES ON BALLS

Most bases on balls, total series
A.L.—118—New York; eight series, 35 games.
N.L.—84—Atlanta; seven series, 23 games.

Most bases on balls, series
3-game series
    N.L.—19—Florida vs. San Francisco, 1997.
    A.L.—15—Chicago vs. Seattle, 2000.
4-game series
    N.L.—21—New York vs. Arizona, 1999.
    A.L.—20—Texas vs. New York, 1996.
5-game series
    A.L.—32—New York vs. Seattle, 1995.
    N.L.—18—Montreal vs. Philadelphia, 1981.
           Arizona vs. St. Louis, 2001.

Most bases on balls by both clubs, series
3-game series
    N.L.—25—Florida 19, San Francisco 6, 1997.
    A.L.—27—Chicago 15, Seattle 12, 2000.
4-game series
    N.L.—36—New York 20, San Francisco 16, 2000.
    A.L.—33—Texas 20, New York 13, 1996.
5-game series
    A.L.—57—New York 32, Seattle 25, 1995.
    N.L.—31—Montreal 18, Philadelphia 13, 1995.

Fewest bases on balls, series
3-game series
    N.L.—4—San Diego vs. St. Louis, 1996.
           Atlanta vs. Houston, 2001.
    A.L.—4—Texas vs. New York, 1998.
4-game series
    A.L.—7—Seattle vs. Baltimore, 1997.
    N.L.—9—Colorado vs. Atlanta, 1995.
           San Diego vs. Houston, 1998.
5-game series
    A.L.—9—New York vs. Milwaukee, 1981.
    N.L.—12—St. Louis vs. Arizona, 2001.

Fewest bases on balls by both clubs, series
3-game series
    A.L.—11—New York 7, Texas 4, 1998.
    N.L.—12—Houston 8, Atlanta 4, 2001.
4-game series
    N.L.—20—Houston 11, San Diego 9, 1998.
    A.L.—29—Cleveland 15, Boston 14, 1998.
5-game series
    A.L.—22—Milwaukee 13, New York 9, 1995.
    N.L.—26—Los Angeles 13, Houston 13, 1995.

Most bases on balls by pinch-hitters, series
N.L.—3—Houston vs. Atlanta, 1999 (4-game series).
A.L.—2
Milwaukee vs. New York, 1981 (5-game series).
Seattle vs. New York, 1995 (5-game series).

Most bases on balls by pinch-hitters on both clubs, series
A.L.—3—Milwaukee 2, New York 1, 1981 (5-game series).
N.L.—3
Houston 2, San Diego 1, 1998 (4-game series).
New York 2, Arizona 1, 1999 (4-game series).
Houston 3, Atlanta 0, 1999 (4-game series).

Most bases on balls, nine-inning game
N.L.—10—Atlanta vs. Houston, October 1, 1997.
A.L.—8—New York vs. Seattle, October 7, 1995.

Most bases on balls, extra-inning game
A.L.—10—New York vs. Seattle, October 8, 1995, 11 innings.
N.L.—Less than nine-inning record.

Most bases on balls by both clubs, game
N.L.—16—Atlanta 10, Houston 6, October 1, 1997.
A.L.—14
New York 10, Seattle 4, October 8, 1995, 11 innings.
Cleveland 9, Boston 5, October 10, 1999.

Fewest bases on balls, game
A.L.-N.L.—0—Held by many clubs.

Fewest bases on balls by both clubs, game
N.L.—1—Atlanta 1, Los Angeles 0, October 3, 1996.
A.L.—1—New York 1, Texas 0, September 30, 1998.

Most bases on balls by pinch-hitters, nine-inning game
A.L.-N.L.—1—Held by many clubs.

Most bases on balls by pinch-hitters, extra-inning game
A.L.—2—Seattle vs. New York, October 8, 1995, 11 innings.
N.L.—1—Held by many clubs.

Most bases on balls by pinch-hitters on both clubs, nine-inning game
N.L.—2—San Diego 1, Houston 1, October 3, 1998.
A.L.—1—Occurred in many games.

Most bases on balls by pinch-hitters on both clubs, extra-inning game
A.L.—2—Seattle 2, New York 0, October 8, 1995, 11 innings.
N.L.—Less than nine-inning record.

Most bases on balls, inning
N.L.—5—Florida vs. San Francisco, October 1, 1997, fourth inning.
A.L.—5—Cleveland vs. Boston, October 10, 1999, fifth inning.

Most bases on balls by both clubs, inning
N.L.—6—Florida 5, San Francisco 1, October 1, 1997, fourth inning.
A.L.—5
Baltimore 4, Cleveland 1, October 2, 1996, eighth inning.
Cleveland 3, Baltimore 2, October 4, 1996, seventh inning.
Cleveland 5, Boston 0, October 10, 1999, fifth inning.

Most bases on balls by pinch-hitters, inning
A.L.—2—Seattle vs. New York, October 8, 1995, eighth inning.
N.L.—1—Held by many clubs.

STRIKEOUTS

Most strikeouts, total series
A.L.—218—New York; eight series, 35 games.
N.L.—164—Atlanta; seven series, 23 games.

Most strikeouts, series
3-game series
N.L.—29—Los Angeles vs. Atlanta, 1996.
A.L.—27—Texas vs. New York, 1998.
4-game series
N.L.—49—Houston vs. San Diego, 1998.
A.L.—42—Seattle vs. Baltimore, 1997.
5-game series
A.L.—48—Seattle vs. Cleveland, 2001.
N.L.—38—St. Louis vs. Arizona, 2001.

Most strikeouts by both clubs, series
3-game series
N.L.—53—Los Angeles 29, Atlanta 24, 1996.
A.L.—51—Texas 27, New York 24, 1998.
4-game series
N.L.—81—Houston 49, San Diego 32, 1998.
A.L.—72—Baltimore 40, Cleveland 32, 1996.
5-game series
A.L.—91—Seattle 48, Cleveland 43, 2001.
N.L.—67—St. Louis 38, Arizona 29, 2001.

Fewest strikeouts, series
3-game series
A.L.—10—Oakland vs. Kansas City, 1981.
N.L.—16—Florida vs. San Francisco, 1997.
Houston vs. Atlanta, 2001.

4-game series
A.L.—20—New York vs. Texas, 1996.
N.L.—22—Arizona vs. New York, 1999.
5-game series
N.L.—19—Philadelphia vs. Montreal, 1981.
A.L.—22—New York vs. Milwaukee, 1981.
Cleveland vs. New York, 1997.

Fewest strikeouts by both clubs, series
3-game series
A.L.—21—Kansas City 11, Oakland 10, 1981.
N.L.—34—Atlanta 18, Houston 16, 2001.
4-game series
A.L.—50—Texas 30, New York 20, 1996.
N.L.—50—New York 28, Arizona 22, 1999.
5-game series
A.L.—48—New York 26, Cleveland 22, 1997.
N.L.—55—Montreal 36, Philadelphia 19, 1981.

Most strikeouts by pinch-hitters, series
N.L.—4
Los Angeles vs. Atlanta, 1996 (3-game series).
Houston vs. Atlanta, 1997 (3-game series).
A.L.—3
New York vs. Seattle, 1995 (5-game series).
Seattle vs. Baltimore, 1997 (4-game series).

Most strikeouts by pinch-hitters on both clubs, series
N.L.—6—Los Angeles 4, Atlanta 2, 1996 (3-game series).
A.L.—4—New York 3, Seattle 1, 1995 (5-game series).

Most strikeouts, nine-inning game
N.L.—17—Houston vs. San Diego, September 29, 1998.
A.L.—14—Milwaukee vs. New York, October 8, 1981.

Most strikeouts, extra-inning game
A.L.—23—Baltimore vs. Cleveland, October 5, 1996, 12 innings.
N.L.—18—Atlanta vs. Houston, October 8, 1999, 12 innings.

Most strikeouts by pinch-hitters, game
N.L.—3—Houston vs. Atlanta, October 3, 1997.
A.L.—1—Held by many clubs.

Most strikeouts by both clubs, nine-inning game
N.L.—28—Houston 17, San Diego 11, September 29, 1998.
A.L.—25—Cleveland 13, Seattle 12, October 9, 2001.

Most strikeouts by both clubs, extra-inning game
A.L.—33—Baltimore 23, Cleveland 10, October 5, 1996, 12 innings.
N.L.—30—Atlanta 18, Houston 12, October 8, 1999, 12 innings.

Fewest strikeouts, game
N.L.—1—Los Angeles vs. Houston, October 10, 1981.
A.L.—1
Milwaukee vs. New York, October 9, 1981.
New York vs. Milwaukee, October 11, 1981.
Cleveland vs. New York, October 4, 1997.

Fewest strikeouts by both clubs, game
A.L.—3—New York 2, Cleveland 1, October 4, 1997.
N.L.—5—Houston 4, Los Angeles 1, October 10, 1981.

Most consecutive strikeouts, game
A.L.—5
Seattle vs. New York, October 8, 1995 (three in sixth inning, two in seventh inning).
Chicago vs. Seattle, October 4, 2000 (two in eighth inning, three in ninth inning).
N.L.—5—Arizona vs. St. Louis, October 12, 2001 (two in first inning, three in second inning).

Most strikeouts, inning
A.L.-N.L.—3—Held by many clubs.

Most strikeouts by both clubs, inning
A.L.—6—Seattle 3, Chicago 3, October 4, 2000, ninth inning.
N.L.—5—Atlanta 3, Houston 2, October 3, 1997, second inning.

Most strikeouts by pinch-hitters, inning
N.L.—2—Houston vs. Atlanta, October 3, 1997, eighth inning.
A.L.—1—Held by many clubs.

SACRIFICE HITS

Most sacrifice hits, total series
A.L.—12—New York; eight series 35 games.
N.L.—12—St. Louis; three series, 11 games.

Most sacrifice hits, series
N.L.—8—St. Louis vs. Arizona, 2001 (5-game series).
A.L.—4
Seattle vs. New York, 1995 (5-game series).
Texas vs. New York, 1996 (4-game series).
Cleveland vs. New York, 1997 (5-game series).
Seattle vs. Chicago, 2000 (3-game series).

Most sacrifice hits by both clubs, series
N.L.—14—St. Louis 8, Arizona 6, 2001 (5-game series).
A.L.—7—Texas 4, New York 3, 1996 (4-game series).

Fewest sacrifice hits, series
A.L.-N.L.—0—Held by many clubs.

Fewest sacrifice hits by both clubs, series
N.L.—0—Atlanta 0, Houston 0, 1997 (3-game series).
A.L.—1
Boston 1, Cleveland 0, 1998 (4-game series).
New York 1, Texas 0, 1999 (3-game series).
Cleveland 1, Boston 0, 1999 (5-game series).

Most sacrifice hits, game
A.L.—3
Oakland vs. Kansas City, October 7, 1981.
Seattle vs. Chicago, October 6, 2000.
N.L.—3
Chicago vs. Atlanta, October 1, 1998, 10 innings.
St. Louis vs. Arizona, October 13, 2001.

Most sacrifice hits by both clubs, nine-inning game
A.L.—4—Seattle 3, Chicago 1, October 6, 2000.
N.L.—3
Los Angeles 2, Houston 1, October 10, 1981.
Atlanta 2, Houston 1, October 9, 1999.
St. Louis 2, Arizona 1, October 12, 2001.
Arizona 2, St. Louis 1, October 12, 2001.
St. Louis 3, Arizona 0, October 13, 2001.
Arizona 2, St. Louis 1, October 14, 2001.

Most sacrifice hits by both clubs, extra-inning game
N.L.—5—Chicago 3, Atlanta 2, October 1, 1998, 10 innings.
A.L.—4—Texas 2, New York 2, October 2, 1996, 12 innings.

Most sacrifice hits, inning
A.L.-N.L.—1—Held by many clubs.

SACRIFICE FLIES

Most sacrifice flies, total series
A.L.—12—New York; eight series, 35 games.
N.L.—8—Atlanta; seven series, 23 games.

Most sacrifice flies, series
A.L.—4—Cleveland vs. Boston, 1999 (5-game series).
N.L.—3—Atlanta vs. Houston, 1999 (4-game series).

Most sacrifice flies by both clubs, series
A.L.—7—Cleveland 4, Boston 3, 1999 (5-game series).
N.L.—4—Atlanta 3, Houston 1, 1999 (4-game series).

Most sacrifice flies, game
A.L.—2
Cleveland vs. Boston, October 10, 1999.
New York vs. Oakland, October 8, 2000.
Oakland vs. New York, October 8, 2000.
Oakland vs. New York, October 10, 2001.
N.L.—2—Atlanta vs. Houston, October 6, 1999.

Most sacrifice flies by both clubs, game
A.L.—4—New York 2, Oakland 2, October 8, 2000.
N.L.—2—Atlanta 2, Houston 0, October 6, 1999.

Most sacrifice flies, inning
A.L.—2
New York vs. Oakland, October 8, 2000, first inning.
Oakland vs. New York, October 8, 2000, fourth inning.
N.L.—1—Held by many clubs.

HIT BY PITCH

Most hit by pitch, total series
A.L.—14—New York; eight series, 35 games.
N.L.—6—Houston; five series, 19 games.

Most hit by pitch, series
A.L.—4
Cleveland vs. Boston, 1995 (3-game series).
Baltimore vs. Cleveland, 1996 (4-game series).
New York vs. Oakland, 2001 (5-game series).
N.L.—4—Houston vs. San Diego, 1998 (4-game series).

Most hit by pitch by both clubs, series
A.L.—7—New York 4, Oakland 3, 2001 (5-game series).
N.L.—6—Houston 4, San Diego 2, 1998 (4-game series).

Most hit by pitch, game
A.L.-N.L.—2—Held by many clubs.

Most hit by pitch by both clubs, game
A.L.—3
Baltimore 2, Cleveland 1, October 1, 1996.
New York 2, Oakand 1, October 15, 2001.
N.L.—2—Occurred in many games.

Most hit by pitch, inning
A.L.-N.L.—1—Held by many clubs.

INDIVIDUAL BASERUNNING

STOLEN BASES

Most stolen bases, career
A.L.—10—Omar Vizquel, Cleveland, 1995 through 1999, 2001; six series, 26 games.
N.L.—6—Rickey Henderson, San Diego, 1996; New York, 1999; two series, seven games.

Most stolen bases, series
3-game series
  N.L.—4—Barry Larkin, Cincinnati, 1995.
  A.L.—3—Jose Valentin, Chicago, 2000.
4-game series
  N.L.—6—Rickey Henderson, New York, 1999.
  A.L.—5—Kenny Lofton, Cleveland, 1996.
5-game series
  N.L.—3—Jerry White, Montreal, 1981.
  A.L.—2—Ken Griffey Jr., Seattle, 1997.
        Johnny Damon, Oakland, 2001.

Most stolen bases, game
A.L.—3—Kenny Lofton, Cleveland, October 4, 1995.
N.L.—3—Rickey Henderson, New York, October 6, 1999.

Most stolen bases by pinch-runner, game
A.L.-N.L.—Never occurred.

Most times stealing home, game
A.L.-N.L.—Never accomplished.

Most stolen bases, inning
A.L.—2—Kenny Lofton, Cleveland, October 2, 1996, sixth inning.
N.L.—2
  Barry Larkin, Cincinnati, October 3, 1995, ninth inning.
  Reggie Sanders, Cincinnati, October 4, 1995, ninth inning.
  Barry Larkin, Cincinnati, October 6, 1995, first inning.

CAUGHT STEALING

Most caught stealing, career
N.L.—2
  Cesar Cedeno, Houston, 1981; one series, four games.
  Sammy Sosa, Chicago, 1998; one series, three games.
  Javy Lopez, Atlanta, 1995 through 1998, 2000; five series, 12 games.
  Brian Jordan, St. Louis, 1996; Atlanta, 1999 through 2001; four series, 13 games.
A.L.—3—Bernie Williams, New York, 1995 through 2001; seven series, 30 games.

Most caught stealing by pinch-runner, career
A.L.-N.L.—Never occurred.

Most caught stealing, series
N.L.—2
  Cesar Cedeno, Houston, 1981; two stolen bases (5-game series).
  Sammy Sosa, Chicago, 1998; no stolen bases (3-game series).
A.L.—2
  Omar Vizquel, Cleveland, 1996; four stolen bases (4-game series).
  Ichiro Suzuki, Seattle, 2001; one stolen base (5-game series).

Most caught stealing by pinch-runner, series
A.L-N.L.—Never occurred.

Most caught stealing, game
A.L.-N.L.—1—Held by many players.

Most caught stealing by pinch-runner, game
A.L.-N.L.—Never occurred.

Most caught stealing, inning
A.L.-N.L.—1—Held by many players.

CLUB BASERUNNING

STOLEN BASES

Most stolen bases, total series
A.L.—27—Cleveland; six series, 26 games.
N.L.—18—Atlanta, seven series, 23 games.

Most stolen bases, series
3-game series
 N.L.—9—Cincinnati vs. Los Angeles, 1995.
 A.L.—4—Chicago vs. Seattle, 2000.
4-game series
 A.L.—11—Cleveland vs. Baltimore, 1996.
 N.L.—8—New York vs. Arizona, 1999.
5-game series
 N.L.—7—Montreal vs. Philadelphia, 1981.
 A.L.—6—Cleveland vs. New York, 1997.

Most stolen bases by both clubs, series
3-game series
 N.L.—9—Cincinnati 9, Los Angeles 0, 1995.
 A.L.—6—Chicago 4, Seattle 2, 2000.
4-game series
 A.L.—12—Cleveland 11, Baltimore 1, 1996.
 N.L.—8—New York 8, Arizona 0, 1999.
5-game series
 A.L.—9—Cleveland 6, New York 3, 1997.
 N.L.—7—Montreal 7, Philadelphia 0, 1981.
     St. Louis 6, Atlanta 1, 2000.

Fewest stolen bases, series
A.L.-N.L.—0—Held by many clubs.

Fewest stolen bases by both clubs, series
3-game series
 A.L.—1—Texas 1, New York 0, 1999.
 N.L.—1—Atlanta 1, Houston 0, 2001.
4-game series
 N.L.—1—Houston 1, San Diego 0, 1998.
 A.L.—2—New York 1, Texas 1, 1996.
5-game series
 A.L.—2—Milwaukee 1, New York 1, 1981.
 N.L.—4—St. Louis 3, Arizona 1, 2001.

Most stolen bases, game
A.L.—5—Cleveland vs. Baltimore, October 4, 1996.
N.L.—4
 Montreal vs. Philadelphia, October 7, 1981.
 Cincinnati vs. Los Angeles, October 4, 1995.
 New York vs. Arizona, October 6, 1999.

Most stolen bases by both clubs, game
A.L.—6—Cleveland 5, Baltimore 1, October 4, 1996.
N.L.—5—St. Louis 3, San Diego 2, October 1, 1996.

Longest game with no stolen bases
A.L.—15 innings
 New York vs. Seattle, October 4, 1995.
 Seattle vs. New York, October 4, 1995.
N.L.—13 innings—San Francisco vs. New York, October 7, 2000.

Longest game with no stolen bases by either club
A.L.—15 innings—New York 0, Seattle 0, October 4, 1995.
N.L.—10 innings—Arizona 0, New York 0, October 9, 1999.

Most stolen bases, inning
N.L.—3—Cincinnati vs. Los Angeles, October 4, 1995, ninth inning.
A.L.—2
 Seattle vs. New York, October 6, 1995, seventh inning.
 Cleveland vs. Baltimore, October 2, 1996, sixth inning.
 Cleveland vs. Baltimore, October 4, 1996, first inning.
 Cleveland vs. Baltimore, October 4, 1996, eighth inning.
 Chicago vs. Seattle, October 4, 2000, third inning.

CAUGHT STEALING

Most caught stealing, series
3-game series
 N.L.—3—Atlanta vs. Los Angeles, 1996.
     San Francisco vs. Florida, 1997.
     Chicago vs. Atlanta, 1998.
     Atlanta vs. St. Louis, 2000.
     Atlanta vs. Houston, 2001.
 A.L.—2—Oakland vs. Kansas City, 1981.
     New York vs. Texas, 1998.
4-game series
 A.L.—3—Cleveland vs. Baltimore, 1996.
     New York vs. Texas, 1996.
 N.L.—2—Atlanta vs. Colorado, 1995.
     New York vs. San Francisco, 2000.
5-game series
 N.L.—5—Montreal vs. Philadelphia, 1981.
 A.L.—4—New York vs. Oakland, 2001.

Most caught stealing by both clubs, series
3-game series
 N.L.—4—Atlanta 3, Los Angeles 1, 1996.
     Atlanta 3, St. Louis 1, 2000.
     Atlanta 3, Houston 1, 2001.
 A.L.—3—New York 2, Texas 1, 1998.
4-game series
 A.L.—4—Cleveland 3, Baltimore 1, 1996.
     New York 3, Texas 1, 1996.
 N.L.—2—Atlanta 2, Colorado 0, 1995.
     Arizona 1, Houston 1, 1999.
     New York 2, San Francisco 0, 2000.
5-game series
 N.L.—8—Montreal 5, Philadelphia 3, 1995.
 A.L.—4—Milwaukee 2, New York 2, 1981.
     New York 4, Oakland 0, 2001.

Fewest caught stealing, series
A.L.-N.L.—0—Held by many clubs.

Fewest caught stealing by both clubs, series
3-game series
 N.L.—0—Cincinnati 0, Los Angeles 0, 1995.
 A.L.—0—New York 0, Texas 0, 1999.
4-game series
 N.L.—1—Arizona 1, New York 0, 1999.
 A.L.—4—Cleveland 3, Baltimore 1, 1996.
     New York 3, Texas 1, 1996.
5-game series
 A.L.—1—Boston 1, Cleveland 0, 1999.
 N.L.—2—Arizona 2, St. Louis 0, 2001.

Most caught stealing, nine-inning game
A.L.—3—New York vs. Texas, October 4, 1996.
N.L.—2
 Montreal vs. Philadelphia, October 6, 1981.
 Montreal vs. Philadelphia, October 7, 1981.
 Atlanta vs. St. Louis, October 3, 2000.
 Atlanta vs. Houston, October 9, 2001.

Most caught stealing, extra-inning game
N.L.—3—Atlanta vs. Los Angeles, October 2, 1996, 10 innings.
A.L.—Less than nine-inning record.

Most caught stealing by both clubs, nine-inning game
N.L.—3—Montreal 2, Philadelphia 1, October 6, 1981.
A.L.—3—New York 3, Texas 0, October 4, 1996.

Most caught stealing by both clubs, extra-inning game
N.L.—4—Atlanta 3, Los Angeles 1, October 2, 1996, 10 innings.
A.L.—Less than nine-inning record.

Most caught stealing, inning
A.L.—2
 Oakland vs. Kansas City, October 9, 1981, third inning.
 New York vs. Texas, October 4, 1996, fourth inning.
N.L.—1—Held by many clubs.

LEFT ON BASE

Most left on base, total series
A.L.—251—New York; eight series, 35 games.
N.L.—153—Atlanta; seven series, 23 games.

Most left on base, series
3-game series
   N.L.—30—Los Angeles vs. Cincinnati, 1995.
   A.L.—28—Boston vs. Cleveland, 1995.
4-game series
   A.L.—36—Baltimore vs. Cleveland, 1996.
   N.L.—36—New York vs. San Francisco, 2000.
5-game series
   A.L.—49—Seattle vs. New York, 1981.
   N.L.—40—Arizona vs. St. Louis, 2001.

Most left on base by both clubs, series
3-game series
   A.L.—55—Boston 28, Cleveland 27, 1995.
   N.L.—49—Los Angeles 30, Cincinnati 19, 1995.
4-game series
   N.L.—69—New York 36, San Francisco 33, 2000.
   A.L.—65—Baltimore 36, Cleveland 29, 1996.
5-game series
   A.L.—94—Seattle 49, New York 45, 1981.
   N.L.—70—Philadelphia 35, Montreal 35, 1981.
      Arizona 40, St. Louis 30, 2001.

Fewest left on base, series
3-game series
   N.L.—14—Atlanta vs. Los Angeles, 1996.
      Los Angeles vs. Atlanta, 1996.
      Atlanta vs. Houston, 1997.
      Atlanta vs. Houston, 2001.
   A.L.—15—Texas vs. New York, 1998.
4-game series
   A.L.—21—Seattle vs. Baltimore, 1997.
   N.L.—23—San Diego vs. Houston, 1998.
5-game series
   A.L.—25—Boston vs. Cleveland, 1999.
   N.L.—30—St. Louis vs. Arizona, 2001.

Fewest left on base by both clubs, series
3-game series
   N.L.—28—Atlanta 14, Los Angeles 14, 1996.
   N.L.—31—New York 16, Texas 15, 1998.
4-game series
   A.L.—46—Baltimore 25, Seattle 21, 1997.
   N.L.—48—Houston 25, San Diego 23, 1998.
5-game series
   A.L.—61—Cleveland 36, Boston 25, 1999.
   N.L.—67—Los Angeles 35, Houston 32, 1981.

Most left on bases, nine-inning game
N.L.—12—Atlanta vs. Colorado, October 4, 1995.
A.L.—12—New York vs. Seattle, October 7, 1995.

Most left on base, extra-inning game
N.L.—16—San Francisco vs. New York, October 7, 2000, 13 innings.
A.L.—13
   Seattle vs. New York, October 8, 1995, 11 innings.
   Baltimore vs. Cleveland, October 5, 1996, 12 innings.

Most left on base by both clubs, nine-inning game
A.L.—22
   Boston 12, Cleveland 10, October 6, 1995.
   New York 12, Seattle 10, October 7, 1995.
N.L.—22—Atlanta 11, St. Louis 11, October 3, 2000.

Most left on base by both clubs, extra-inning game
N.L.—26—San Francisco 16, New York 10, October 7, 2000, 13 innings.
A.L.—23—Seattle 13, New York 10, October 8, 1995, 11 innings.

Fewest left on base, game
N.L.—1
   Los Angeles vs. Houston, October 6, 1981.
   Los Angeles vs. Atlanta, October 3, 1996.
   Houston vs. Atlanta, October 6, 1999.
A.L.—2
   Milwaukee vs. New York, October 10, 1981.
   Seattle vs. Cleveland, October 11, 2001.

Fewest left on base by both clubs, game
N.L.—3—Atlanta 2, Los Angeles 1, October 3, 1996.
A.L.—6—Cleveland 3, Boston 3, October 2, 1998.

Most left on base, nine-inning shutout defeat
A.L.—11—Milwaukee vs. New York, October 8, 1981 (lost 3-0).
N.L.—9—Houston vs. Los Angeles, October 11, 1981 (lost 4-0).

Most left on base, extra-inning shutout defeat
N.L.—13—Los Angeles vs. Houston, October 7, 1981, 11 innings (lost 1-0).
A.L.—Less than nine-inning record.

Most left on base, two consecutive games (18 innings)
N.L.—22—Los Angeles vs. Cincinnati, October 4 (11), October 6 (11), 1995.
A.L.—19—Cleveland vs. Boston, October 9 (10), October 10 (9), 1999.

Most left on base, two consecutive games (more than 18 innings)
A.L.—23—Seattle vs. New York, October 7 (10), October 8 (13), 1995, second game 11 innings.
N.L.—22—Los Angeles vs. Houston, October 7 (13), October 9 (9), 1981, first game 11 innings.

INDIVIDUAL PITCHING

GAMES

Most games pitched, career
A.L.—19—Jeff Nelson, Seattle, 1995, 2001; New York, 1996 through 2000; seven series.
N.L.—9—Greg Maddux, Atlanta, 1995 through 2001; seven series.

Most games pitched, series
3-game series
  A.L.-N.L.—3—Held by many pitchers.
4-game series
  A.L.—4—Jesse Orosco, Baltimore, 1996.
  N.L.—4—Mike Munoz, Colorado, 1995.
      Bruce Ruffin, Colorado, 1995.
      Trevor Hoffman, San Diego, 1998.
5-game series
  N.L.—4—Ron Reed, Philadelphia, 1981.
      Steve Kline, St. Louis, 2001.
  A.L.—4—Jim Slaton, Milwaukee, 1981.
      Norm Charlton, Seattle, 1995.
      Bill Risley, Seattle, 1995.
      Paul Assenmacher, Cleveland, 1997.
      Mike Jackson, Cleveland, 1997.
      Jeff Nelson, New York, 1997.

Most consecutive games pitched, series
N.L.—4
  Mike Munoz, Colorado, October 3, 4, 6, 7, 1995.
  Bruce Ruffin, Colorado, October 3, 4, 6, 7, 1995.
  Trevor Hoffman, San Diego, September 29, October 1, 3, 4, 1998.
  Steve Kline, St. Louis, October 10, 12, 13, 14, 2001.
A.L.—4
  Bill Risley, Seattle, October 3, 4, 6, 7, 1995.
  Norm Charlton, Seattle, October 4, 6, 7, 8, 1995.
  Jesse Orosco, Baltimore, October 1, 2, 4, 5, 1996.

GAMES STARTED

Most games started, career
A.L.—9—Andy Pettitte, New York, 1995 through 2001; seven series, nine games.
N.L.—8—Greg Maddux, Atlanta, 1995 through 2001; seven series, nine games.

Most opening games started, career
N.L.—5—Greg Maddux, Atlanta, 1995, 1997, 1999, 2000, 2001.
A.L.—3
  David Cone, New York, 1995, 1996, 1997.
  Roger Clemens, Boston, 1995; New York, 2000, 2001.

Most games started, series
A.L.-N.L.—2—Held by many pitchers.

GAMES RELIEVED AND FINISHED

Most games by relief pitcher, career
A.L.—19—Jeff Nelson, Seattle, 1995, 2001; New York, 1996 through 2000; seven series.
N.L.—8—Doug Henry, San Francisco, 1997, 2000; Houston, 1998, 1999; four series.

Most games by relief pitcher, series
A.L.-N.L.—4—Held by many pitchers.

Most games finished, career
A.L.—11—Mariano Rivera, New York, 1995 through 2001; seven series, 18 games.
N.L.—6
  Mark Wohlers, Atlanta, 1995, 1996, 1997; three series, seven games.
  Trevor Hoffman, San Diego, 1996, 1998; two series, six games.

Most games finished, series
N.L.—4
  Trevor Hoffman, San Diego, 1998 (4-game series).
  Steve Kline, St. Louis, 2001 (5-game series).
A.L.—3—Held by many pitchers.

COMPLETE GAMES

Most complete games pitched, career
N.L.—2—Curt Schilling, Arizona, 2001; one series, two games.
A.L.—1—Held by many pitchers.

Most complete games, series
N.L.—2—Curt Schilling, Arizona, 2001 (5-game series).
A.L.—1—Held by many pitchers.

INNINGS

Most innings pitched, career
A.L.—57.0—Andy Pettitte, New York, 1995 through 2001; seven series, nine games.
N.L.—54.0—Greg Maddux, Atlanta, 1995 through 2001; seven series, nine games.

Most innings pitched, series
3-game series
  A.L.—9.0—Steve McCatty, Oakland, 1981.
      Mike Norris, Oakland, 1981.
  N.L.—9.0—John Smoltz, Atlanta, 1996, 1997.
      Greg Maddux, Atlanta, 1997.
4-game series
  N.L.—14.2—Kevin Brown, San Diego, 1998.
  A.L.—14.0—Mike Mussina, Baltimore, 1997.
5-game series
  N.L.—18.0—Jerry Reuss, Los Angeles, 1981.
      Curt Schilling, Arizona, 2001.
  A.L.—15.2—David Cone, New York, 1995.

Most innings pitched, game
A.L.-N.L.—9.0—Held by many pitchers.

GAMES WON

Most games won, career
Both leagues—4—David Wells, Cincinnati N.L., 1995; Baltimore A.L., 1996; New York A.L., 1997, 1998 (1 in N.L., 3 in A.L.); four series, five games.
N.L.—4
  Greg Maddux, Atlanta, 1995 through 2001; seven series, nine games.
  John Smoltz, Atlanta, 1995 through 1999, 2001; six series, eight games.
A.L.—3
  David Wells, Baltimore, 1996; New York, 1997, 1998; three series, four games.
  Charles Nagy, Cleveland, 1995 through 1999; five series, seven games.
  Andy Pettitte, New York 1995 through 2001; seven series, nine games.
  Mike Mussina, Baltimore, 1996, 1997; New York, 2001; three series, four games.

For a complete list of pitchers with three or more victories, see page 389.

Most games won by undefeated pitcher, career
Both leagues—4—David Wells, Cincinnati N.L., 1995; Baltimore A.L., 1996; New York A.L., 1997, 1998 (1 in N.L., 3 in A.L.); four series, five games.
N.L.—4—John Smoltz, Atlanta, 1995 through 1999, 2001; six series, eight games.

DIVISION SERIES *Individual pitching*

A.L.—3

David Wells, Baltimore, 1996; New York, 1997, 1998; three series, four games.

Mike Mussina, Baltimore, 1996, 1997; New York, 2001; three series, four games.

Most opening games won, career

A.L.—2—David Wells, Baltimore, 1996; New York, 1998.

N.L.—2—John Smoltz, Atlanta, 1996, 1998.

Most consecutive games won, career

Both leagues—4—David Wells, Cincinnati N.L., October 6, 1995; Baltimore A.L., October 1, 1996; New York A.L., October 4, 1997; September 29, 1998.

N.L.—4

Greg Maddux, Atlanta, October 7, 1995; October 3, 1996; September 30, 1997; October 3, 1998.

John Smoltz, Atlanta, October 2, 1996; October 3, 1997; September 30, 1998; October 9, 1999.

A.L.—3—David Wells, Baltimore, October 1, 1996; New York, October 4, 1997; September 29, 1998.

Most consecutive complete games won, career

N.L.—2—Curt Schilling, Arizona, October 9, 14, 2001.

A.L.—No pitcher with more than one complete game.

Most games won, series

A.L.—2

Dave Righetti, New York, 1981 (5-game series).
Randy Johnson, Seattle, 1995 (5-game series).
Armando Benitez, Baltimore, 1996 (4-game series).
Mike Mussina, Baltimore, 1997 (5-game series).
Jaret Wright, Cleveland, 1997 (5-game series).
Jamie Moyer, Seattle, 2001 (5-game series).

N.L.—2

Steve Rogers, Montreal, 1981 (5-game series).
Alejandro Pena, Atlanta, 1995 (4-game series).
Curt Schilling, Arizona, 2001 (5-game series).

Most games won by relief pitcher, series

N.L.—2—Alejandro Pena, Atlanta, 1995 (4-game series).

A.L.—2—Armando Benitez, Baltimore, 1996 (4-game series).

SAVES

Most saves, career

A.L.—10—Mariano Rivera, New York, 1995 through 2001; seven series, 18 games.

N.L.—5—Mark Wohlers, Atlanta, 1995, 1996, 1997; three series, seven games.

Most saves, series

3-game series

N.L.—3—Dennis Eckersley, St. Louis, 1996.
Mark Wohlers, Atlanta, 1996.

A.L.—2—Mariano Rivera, New York, 1998.
Kazuhiro Sasaki, Seattle, 2000.

4-game series

A.L.—3—Mike Jackson, Cleveland, 1998.

N.L.—2—Mark Wohlers, Atlanta, 1995.
Trevor Hoffman, San Diego, 1998.

5-game series

A.L.—3—Rich Gossage, New York, 1981.
Mariano Rivera, New York, 2000.

N.L.—2—Jeff Reardon, Montreal, 1981.
John Smoltz, Atlanta, 2001.
Steve Kline, St. Louis, 2001.

GAMES LOST

Most games lost, career

Both leagues—6—Randy Johnson, Seattle A.L., 1995, 1997; Houston N.L., 1998; Arizona N.L., 1999, 2001 (2 in A.L., 4 in N.L.); five series, eight games.

A.L.—3

Andy Pettitte, New York, 1995 through 2001; seven series, nine games.

Roger Clemens, Boston, 1995; New York, 1999 through 2001; four series, six games.

Aaron Sele, Texas, 1998, 1999; Seattle, 2000, 2001; four series, four games.

N.L.—2—Held by many pitchers.

Most games lost by winless pitcher, career

Both leagues—3—Bret Saberhagen, Colorado N.L., 1995; Boston, 1998, 1999 (2 in A.L., 1 in N.L.); three series, four games.

A.L.—3—Aaron Sele, Texas, 1998, 1999; Seattle, 2000, 2001; four series, four games.

N.L.—2—Held by many pitchers.

Most consecutive games lost, career

Both leagues—6—Randy Johnson, Seattle A.L., October 1, 5, 1997; Houston N.L., September 29, October 5; Arizona N.L., October 5, 2000, October 10, 2001.

A.L.—3

Roger Clemens, New York, October 3, 7, 2000, October 10, 2001.

Aaron Sele, Texas, October 2, 1998, October 5, 1999; Seattle, October 13, 2001.

N.L.—2—Held by many pitchers.

Most games lost, series

N.L.—2

Dave Stewart, Los Angeles, 1981 (5-game series).
Steve Carlton, Philadelphia, 1981 (5-game series).
Randy Johnson, Houston, 1998 (4-game series).

A.L.—2

Moose Haas, Milwaukee, 1981 (5-game series).
Jack McDowell, New York, 1995 (5-game series).
Randy Johnson, Seattle, 1997 (4-game series).
Andy Pettitte, New York, 1997 (5-game series).
Roger Clemens, New York, 2000 (5-game series).
Chuck Finley, Cleveland, 2001 (5-game series).

RUNS

Most runs allowed, career

A.L.—27—Andy Pettitte, New York, 1995 through 2001; seven series, nine games.

N.L.—24—Greg Maddux, Atlanta, 1995 through 2001; seven series, nine games.

Most runs allowed, series

3-game series

A.L.—7—Tim Wakefield, Boston, 1995.

N.L.—7—Ramon Martinez, Los Angeles, 1995.
Tom Glavine, Atlanta, 2000.
Greg Maddux, Atlanta, 2000.

4-game series

A.L.—9—Charles Nagy, Cleveland, 1996.

N.L.—7—Greg Maddux, Atlanta, 1995.
Kevin Ritz, Colorado, 1995.
Randy Johnson, Arizona, 1999.

5-game series

A.L.—11—Andy Pettitte, New York, 1997.
Bret Saberhagen, Boston, 1999.

N.L.—6—Steve Carlton, Philadelphia, 1981.

Most runs allowed, game

A.L.—8

Steve Reed, Cleveland, October 10, 1999.
Charles Nagy, Cleveland, October 11, 1999.
Paul Abbott, Seattle, October 13, 2001.

N.L.—7

Ramon Martinez, Los Angeles, October 3, 1995.
Randy Johnson, Arizona, October 5, 1999.
Greg Maddux, Atlanta, October 3, 2000.
Tom Glavine, Atlanta, October 5, 2000.

Most runs allowed, inning

A.L.—6

Bret Saberhagen, Boston, October 7, 1999, third inning.
Gil Heredia, Oakland, October 8, 2000, first inning.

N.L.—6—Greg Maddux, Atlanta, October 3, 2000, first inning.

EARNED RUNS

Most earned runs allowed, career
A.L.—27—Andy Pettitte, New York, 1995 through 2001; seven series, nine games.
N.L.—19—Greg Maddux, Atlanta, 1995 through 2001; seven series, nine games.

Most earned runs allowed, series
3-game series
A.L.—7—Tim Wakefield, Boston, 1995.
N.L.—7—Ramon Martinez, Los Angeles, 1995.
  Tom Glavine, Atlanta, 2000.
4-game series
A.L.—9—Charles Nagy, Cleveland, 1996.
N.L.—7—Greg Maddux, Atlanta, 1995.
  Randy Johnson, Arizona, 1999.
5-game series
A.L.—11—Andy Pettitte, New York, 1997.
  Bret Saberhagen, Boston, 1999.
N.L.—6—Steve Carlton, Philadelphia, 1981.

Most earned runs allowed, game
A.L.—8
Steve Reed, Cleveland, October 10, 1999.
Paul Abbott, Seattle, October 13, 2001.
N.L.—7
Ramon Martinez, Los Angeles, October 3, 1995.
Randy Johnson, Arizona, October 5, 1999.
Tom Glavine, Atlanta, October 5, 2000.

Most earned runs allowed, inning
A.L.—6
Bret Saberhagen, Boston, October 7, 1999, third inning.
Gil Heredia, Oakland, October 8, 2000, first inning.
N.L.—5—Greg Maddux, Atlanta, October 3, 2000, first inning.

SHUTOUTS AND SCORELESS INNINGS

Most shutouts, series
A.L.—1—Mike Norris, Oakland, 1981.
N.L.—1
Jerry Reuss, Los Angeles, 1981.
Steve Rogers, Montreal, 1981.
Bobby J. Jones, New York, 2000.
Curt Schilling, Arizona, 2001.

For a complete list of shutouts, see page 388.

Most consecutive scoreless innings, career
N.L.—18—Jerry Reuss, Los Angeles, October 7 (nine innings), October 11 (nine innings), 1981.
A.L.—9—Mike Norris, Oakland, October 6 (nine innings), 1981.

Most consecutive scoreless innings, series
N.L.—18—Jerry Reuss, Los Angeles, October 7 (nine innings), October 11 (nine innings), 1981.
A.L.—9—Mike Norris, Oakland, October 6 (nine innings), 1981.

HITS

Most hits allowed, career
A.L.—60—Andy Pettitte, New York, 1995 through 2001; seven series, nine games.
N.L.—59—Greg Maddux, Atlanta, 1995 through 2001; seven series, nine games.

Most consecutive hitless innings, career
A.L.—8—Mike Mussina, Baltimore, October 5, 1997 (five innings), October 13, 2001 (three innings).
N.L.—7—Kevin Millwood, Atlanta, October 6, 1999.

Most hits allowed, series
3-game series
A.L.—10—Rick Langford, Oakland, 1981.
N.L.—10—Ramon Martinez, Los Angeles, 1995.

4-game series
N.L.—19—Greg Maddux, Atlanta, 1995.
A.L.—15—David Wells, Baltimore, 1996.
  Charles Nagy, Cleveland, 1996.
5-game series
N.L.—16—Steve Rogers, Montreal, 1981.
A.L.—15—David Cone, New York, 1995.
  Andy Pettitte, New York, 1997.
  Andy Pettitte, New York, 2000.

Most hits allowed, game
A.L.—10
Rick Langford, Oakland, October 9, 1981.
John Burkett, Texas, October 1, 1996.
Andy Pettitte, New York, October 8, 2000.
N.L.—10
Steve Rogers, Montreal, October 7, 1981.
Ramon Martinez, Los Angeles, October 3, 1995.
Greg Maddux, Atlanta, October 7, 1995.
Greg Maddux, Atlanta, October 5, 1999.

Most consecutive hitless innings, game
N.L.—7—Kevin Millwood, Atlanta, October 6, 1999 (third through ninth innings).
A.L.—5—Mike Mussina, Baltimore, October 5, 1997 (third through seventh innings).

Fewest hits allowed, nine-inning game
N.L.—1
Kevin Millwood, Atlanta, October 6, 1999.
Bobby J. Jones, New York, October 8, 2000.
A.L.—4
Mike Norris, Oakland, October 6, 1981.
Erik Hanson, Boston, October 4, 1995.

Most hits allowed, inning
A.L.—5
Andy Pettitte, New York, October 2, 1997, fourth inning.
Bartolo Colon, Cleveland, October 10, 1999, second inning.
Paul Assenmacher, Cleveland, October 10, 1999, seventh inning.
Freddy Garcia, Seattle, October 9, 2001, fourth inning.
Paul Abbott, Seattle, October 13, 2001, third inning.
N.L.—5—Greg Maddux, Atlanta, October 3, 2000, first inning.

Most consecutive hits allowed, inning (consecutive at-bats)
A.L.—5
Bartolo Colon, Cleveland, October 10, 1999, second inning.
Freddy Garcia, Seattle, October 9, 2001, fourth inning.
N.L.—4
Bret Saberhagen, Colorado, October 7, 1995, third inning.
Greg Maddux, Atlanta, October 3, 2000, first inning.

Most consecutive hits allowed, inning (consecutive plate appearances)
A.L.—5—Bartolo Colon, Cleveland, October 10, 1999, second inning.
N.L.—4
Bret Saberhagen, Colorado, October 7, 1995, third inning.
Greg Maddux, Atlanta, October 3, 2000, first inning.

DOUBLES, TRIPLES AND HOME RUNS

Most doubles allowed, game
N.L.—4
Steve Carlton, Philadelphia, October 7, 1981.
Ramon Martinez, Los Angeles, October 3, 1995.
A.L.—4—Andy Pettitte, New York, October 11, 2001.

Most triples allowed, game
A.L.—2—Freddie Garcia, Seattle, October 3, 2000; pitched 3.1 innings of 10-inning game.
N.L.—1—Held by many pitchers.

Most home runs allowed, career
Both leagues—9—Randy Johnson, Seattle A.L., 1995, 1997; Houston N.L., 1998; Arizona N.L., 1999, 2001 (4 in A.L., 5 in N.L.); five series, eight games.
A.L.—7—David Cone, New York, 1995, 1996, 1997, 1998; four series, five games.

N.L.—7—John Smoltz, Atlanta, 1995 through 1999, 2001; six series, eight games.

Most home runs allowed, series

3-game series
N.L.—3—Ismael Valdes, Los Angeles, 1996.
A.L.—2—Held by many pitchers.
4-game series
A.L.—4—Charles Nagy, Cleveland, 1996.
N.L.—3—Kevin Ritz, Colorado, 1995.
    Greg Maddux, Atlanta, 1995.
5-game series
A.L.—4—David Cone, New York, 1995.
N.L.—2—Albie Lopez, Arizona, 2001.

Most home runs allowed, game

N.L.—3—Ismael Valdes, Los Angeles, October 3, 1996.
A.L.—3
Bret Saberhagen, Boston, October 2, 1998.
Chuck Finley, Cleveland, October 11, 2001.
Paul Abbott, Seattle, October 13, 2001.

Most grand slams allowed, game

N.L.—1
Mark Guthrie, Los Angeles, October 6, 1995, sixth inning.
Wilson Alvarez, San Francisco, October 3, 1997, sixth inning.
Matt Karchner, Chicago, September 30, 1998, seventh inning.
Rod Beck, Chicago, October 3, 1998, eighth inning.
Bobby Chouinard, Arizona, October 5, 1999, ninth inning.
A.L.—1
John Wetteland, New York, October 7, 1995, eighth inning.
Paul Shuey, Cleveland, October 1, 1996, sixth inning.
Armando Benitez, Baltimore, October 4, 1996, seventh inning.
Chad Ogea, Cleveland, October 4, 1997, fourth inning.
John Wasdin, Boston, October 7, 1999, fourth inning.
Charles Nagy, Cleveland, October 11, 1999, third inning.

Most home runs allowed, inning

N.L.—2—Ismael Valdes, Los Angeles, October 3, 1996, seventh inning.
A.L.—2
Moose Haas, Milwaukee, October 11, 1981; fourth inning (consecutive).
Andy Benes, Seattle, October 4, 1995, sixth inning (consecutive).
Bill Risley, Seattle, October 6, 1995, eighth inning (consecutive).
David Cone, New York, October 1, 1996, fourth inning.
Charles Nagy, Cleveland, October 5, 1996, second inning (consecutive).
Eric Plunk, Cleveland, September 30, 1997, sixth inning (consecutive).
Terry Mathews, Baltimore, October 4, 1997, ninth inning (consecutive).
Keith Foulke, Chicago, October 3, 2000, 10th inning (consecutive).
Chuck Finley, Cleveland, October 11, 2001, first inning.

Most consecutive home runs allowed, inning

A.L.—2
Moose Haas, Milwaukee, October 11, 1981; fourth inning.
Andy Benes, Seattle, October 4, 1995, sixth inning.
Bill Risley, Seattle, October 6, 1995, eighth inning.
Charles Nagy, Cleveland, October 5, 1996, second inning.
Eric Plunk, Cleveland, September 30, 1997, sixth inning.
Terry Mathews, Baltimore, October 4, 1997, ninth inning.
Keith Foulke, Chicago, October 3, 2000, 10th inning.
N.L.—1—Held by many pitchers.

TOTAL BASES

Most total bases allowed, game

A.L.—19—Paul Abbott, Seattle, October 13, 2001.
N.L.—17—Ramon Martinez, Los Angeles, October 3, 1995.

BASES ON BALLS

Most bases on balls, career

Both leagues—19—Randy Johnson, Seattle A.L., 1995, 1997; Houston N.L., 1998; Arizona, 1999, 2001 (12 in A.L., 7 in N.L.); five series, eight games.

A.L.—18—Charles Nagy, Cleveland, 1995, 1996, 1997, 1998, 1999; five series, seven games.
N.L.—16—Tom Glavine, Atlanta, 1995 through 2001; seven series, seven games.

Most bases on balls, series

3-game series
N.L.—8—Mike Hampton, Houston, 1997.
A.L.—6—Orlando Hernandez, New York, 1999.
4-game series
N.L.—7—Kevin Brown, San Diego, 1998.
A.L.—6—Andy Pettitte, New York, 1996.
    Randy Johnson, Seattle, 1997.
5-game series
A.L.—9—Andy Benes, Seattle, 1995.
    David Cone, New York, 1995.
N.L.—8—Steve Carlton, Philadelphia, 1981.

Most bases on balls, game

N.L.—8—Mike Hampton, Houston, October 1, 1997.
A.L.—6
David Cone, New York, October 3, 1995.
Andy Benes, Seattle, October 8, 1995.
Andy Pettitte, New York, October 2, 1996.
Orlando Hernandez, New York, October 5, 1999.

Most bases on balls, inning

A.L.—4—Andy Benes, Seattle, October 8, 1995, sixth inning.
N.L.—4
Mike Hampton, Houston, October 1, 1997, fifth inning (consecutive).
Rick Ankiel, St. Louis, October 3, 2000, third inning.

Most consecutive bases on balls, inning

N.L.—4—Mike Hampton, Houston, October 1, 1997, fifth inning.
A.L.—3
Tim Wakefield, Boston, October 6, 1995, third inning.
Andy Benes, Seattle, October 8, 1995, sixth inning.

STRIKEOUTS

Most strikeouts, career

Both leagues—69—Randy Johnson, Seattle A.L., 1995, 1997; Houston N.L., 1998; Arizona, 1999, 2001 (32 in A.L., 37 in N.L.); five series, eight games.
N.L.—36
Greg Maddux, Atlanta, 1995 through 2001; seven series, nine games.
John Smoltz, Atlanta, 1995 through 1999, 2001; six series, eight games.
A.L.—32
Randy Johnson, Seattle, 1995, 1997; two series, four games.
Andy Pettitte, New York, 1995 through 2001; seven series, nine games.

Most strikeouts, series

3-game series
N.L.—11—John Smoltz, Atlanta, 1997.
A.L.—9—Rick Helling, Texas, 1998.
    David Wells, New York, 1998.
4-game series
N.L.—21—Kevin Brown, San Diego, 1998.
A.L.—16—Randy Johnson, Seattle, 1997.
    Mike Mussina, Baltimore, 1997.
5-game series
N.L.—18—Curt Schilling, Arizona, 2001.
A.L.—16—Randy Johnson, Seattle, 1995.

Most strikeouts, game

N.L.—16—Kevin Brown, San Diego, September 29, 1998.
A.L.—13—Randy Johnson, Seattle, October 5, 1997.

For a complete list of pitchers with 10 or more strikeouts in a game, see page 390.

Most strikeouts, game, relief pitcher

A.L.—8—Pedro Martinez, Boston, October 11, 1999; pitched six innings.

DIVISION SERIES *Individual pitching*

N.L.—6—Jose Cabrera, Houston, October 8, 1999; pitched two innings.

Most consecutive strikeouts, game
A.L.—5—David Cone, New York, October 8, 1995 (three in sixth inning, two in seventh inning).
N.L.—5—Darryl Kile, St. Louis, October 12, 2001 (two in first inning, three in second inning).

Most consecutive strikeouts from start of game
N.L.—3—Steve Carlton, Philadelphia, October 11, 1981.
A.L.—2
  Dave Righetti, New York, October 8, 1981.
  Andy Benes, Seattle, October 8, 1995.

Most strikeouts, inning
A.L.-N.L.—3—Held by many pitchers.

HIT BATSMEN, WILD PITCHES AND BALKS

Most hit batsmen, career
Both leagues—4—Steve Reed, Colorado N.L., 1995; Cleveland, 1998, 1999; Atlanta, 2001; four series, eight games.
A.L.—3—Steve Reed, Cleveland, 1998, 1999; two series, four games.
N.L.—3—Kevin Brown, Florida, 1997; San Diego, 1998; two series, three games.

Most hit batsmen, series
N.L.—3—Kevin Brown, San Diego, 1998.
A.L.—2
  Steve Reed, Cleveland, 1999 (5-game series).
  Dwight Gooden, New York, 2000 (5-game series).
  Roger Clemens, New York, 2001 (5-game series).
  Barry Zito, Oakland, 2001 (5-game series).
  Mark Mulder, Oakland, 2001 (5-game series).

Most hit batsmen, game
N.L.—2—Kevin Brown, San Diego, October 3, 1998.

A.L.—2
  Steve Reed, Cleveland, October 10, 1999.
  Dwight Gooden, New York, October 7, 2000.
  Barry Zito, Oakland, October 13, 2001.
  Mark Mulder, Oakland, October 15, 2001.

Most hit batsmen, inning
A.L.-N.L.—1—Held by many pitchers.

Most wild pitches, career
N.L.—5—Rick Ankiel, St. Louis, 2000; one series, one game.
A.L.—3—David Cone, New York, 1995, 1996, 1997, 1998; four series, five games.

Most wild pitches, series
N.L.—5—Rick Ankiel, St. Louis, 2000 (3-game series).
A.L.—2
  David Cone, New York, 1995 (5-game series).
  Steve Karsay, Cleveland, 1999 (5-game series).

Most wild pitches, game
N.L.—5—Rick Ankiel, St. Louis, October 3, 2000, pitched 2.2 innings.
A.L.—2
  David Cone, New York, October 8, 1995, pitched 7.2 innings of 11-inning game.
  Steve Karsay, Cleveland, October 10, 1999, pitched two innings.

Most wild pitches, inning
N.L.—5—Rick Ankiel, St. Louis, October 3, 2000, third inning.
A.L.—1—Held by many pitchers.

Most balks, game
N.L.—1
  Kevin Tapani, Chicago, October 1, 1998, pitched nine innings of 10-inning game.
  Kevin Millwood, Atlanta, October 7, 2000.
A.L.—Never occurred.

CLUB PITCHING

APPEARANCES

Most appearances by pitchers, series
3-game series
  N.L.—16—Los Angeles vs. Cincinnati, 1995.
               Atlanta vs. St. Louis, 2000.
  A.L.—15—Chicago vs. Seattle, 2000.
4-game series
  N.L.—24—Colorado vs. Atlanta, 1995.
  A.L.—21—Cleveland vs. Baltimore, 1996.
5-game series
  A.L.—22—Seattle vs. New York, 1995.
  N.L.—16—Philadelphia vs. Montreal, 1981.
               St. Louis vs. Arizona, 2001.

Most appearances by pitchers of both clubs, series
3-game series
  N.L.—30—Atlanta 16, St. Louis 14, 2000.
  A.L.—28—Chicago 15, Seattle 13, 2000.
4-game series
  A.L.—40—Cleveland 21, Baltimore 19, 1996.
  N.L.—40—Colorado 24, Atlanta 16, 1995.
5-game series
  A.L.—41—Seattle 22, New York 19, 1995.
               Boston 21, Cleveland 20, 1999.
  N.L.—30—St. Louis 16, Arizona 14, 2001.

COMPLETE GAMES

Most complete games, series
A.L.—2—Oakland vs. Kansas City, 1981 (3-game series).
N.L.—2—Houston vs. Los Angeles, 1981 (5-game series).
      Los Angeles vs. Houston, 1981 (5-game series).
      Atlanta vs. Houston, 1997 (3-game series).
      Arizona vs. St. Louis, 2001 (5-game series).

Most complete games by both clubs, series
N.L.—4—Houston 2, Los Angeles 2, 1981 (5-game series).
A.L.—2—Oakland 2, Kansas City 0, 1981 (3-game series).

SAVES

Most saves, series
3-game series
  N.L.—3—St. Louis vs. San Diego, 1996.
          Atlanta vs. Los Angeles, 1996.
  A.L.—2—New York vs. Texas, 1998.
          New York vs. Texas, 1999.
          Seattle vs. Chicago, 2000.
4-game series
  A.L.—3—Cleveland vs. Boston, 1998.
  N.L.—2—Atlanta vs. Colorado, 1995.
          San Diego vs. Houston, 1998.
          Atlanta vs. Houston, 1999.
5-game series
  A.L.—3—New York vs. Milwaukee, 1981.
          New York vs. Oakland, 2000.
  N.L.—2—Montreal vs. Philadelphia, 1981.
          St. Louis vs. Arizona, 2001.

Most saves by both clubs, series
3-game series
  N.L.—3—St. Louis 3, San Diego 0, 1996.
          Atlanta 3, Los Angeles 0, 1996.
  A.L.—2—New York 2, Texas 0, 1998.
          New York 2, Texas 0, 1999.
          Seattle 2, Chicago 0, 2000.
4-game series
  N.L.—3—Atlanta 2, Colorado 1, 1995.
  A.L.—3—Cleveland 3, Boston 0, 1998.
5-game series
  A.L.—4—New York 3, Milwaukee 1, 1981.
          New York 3, Oakland 1, 2000.
          Oakland 2, New York 2, 2001.

N.L.—3—St. Louis 2, Arizona 1, 2001.

Fewest saves by one and both clubs, series
A.L.-N.L.—0—Held by many clubs.

RUNS AND SHUTOUTS

Most runs allowed, total series
A.L.—138—Cleveland; six series, 26 games.
N.L.—78
  Atlanta; seven series, 23 games.
  Houston; five series, 19 games.

Most shutouts won, total series
A.L.—7—New York; eight series, 35 games.
N.L.—1—Held by many clubs.

For a complete list of shutouts, see page 388.

Most shutouts won, series
A.L.—2
  New York vs. Texas, 1998 (3-game series).
  New York vs. Texas, 1999 (3-game series).
N.L.—1—Held by many clubs.

Most consecutive shutouts won, series
A.L.-N.L.—1—Held by many clubs.

Most shutouts by both clubs, series
N.L.—2—Houston 1, Los Angeles 1, 1981 (5-game series).
A.L.—2
  New York 2, Texas 0, 1998 (3-game series).
  New York 2, Texas 0, 1999 (3-game series).
  Oakland 1, New York 1, 2001 (5-game series).

Largest score, shutout game
A.L.—8-0—New York 8, Texas 0, October 5, 1999.
N.L.—4-0
  Los Angeles 4, Houston 0, October 11, 1981.
  New York 4, San Francisco 0, October 8, 2000.

Longest shutout game
N.L.—11 innings—Houston 1, Los Angeles 0, October 7, 1981.
A.L.—9 innings—Held by many clubs.

Most consecutive innings shutting out opponent, total series
A.L.—25—New York vs. Texas, September 30 (sixth inning),
  1998 through October 7 (third inning), 1999.
N.L.—18—New York vs. San Francisco, October 7 (fifth inning
  of 13-inning game) through October 8 (ninth inning), 2000.

Most consecutive innings shutting out opponent, series
A.L.—19—New York vs. Milwaukee, October 7 (sixth inning)
  through October 9 (sixth inning), 1981.
N.L.—18—New York vs. San Francisco, October 7 (fifth inning
  of 13-inning game) through October 8 (ninth inning), 2000.

WILD PITCHES AND BALKS

Most wild pitches, series
N.L.—5—St. Louis vs. Atlanta, 2000 (3-game series).
A.L.—3—New York vs. Seattle, 1995 (5-game series).

Most wild pitches by both clubs, series
N.L.—6—St. Louis 5, Atlanta 1, 2000 (3-game series).
A.L.—4—New York 3, Seattle 1, 1995 (5-game series).

Most balks, series
N.L.—1
  Chicago vs. Atlanta, 1998 (3-game series).
  Atlanta vs. St. Louis, 2000 (3-game series).
A.L.—Never occurred.

INDIVIDUAL FIELDING

FIRST BASEMEN
GAMES

Most games played, career
A.L.—30—Tino Martinez, Seattle, 1995; New York, 1996 through 2001; seven series.
N.L.—14—Jeff Bagwell, Houston, 1997, 1998, 1999, 2001; four series.

PUTOUTS, ASSISTS AND CHANCES ACCEPTED

Most putouts, career
A.L.—268—Tino Martinez, Seattle, 1995; New York, 1996 through 2001; seven series, 30 games.
N.L.—105—Jeff Bagwell, Houston, 1997, 1998, 1999, 2001; four series, 14 games.

Most putouts, series
3-game series
    A.L.—29—Tino Martinez, New York, 1999.
    N.L.—28—Eric Karros, Los Angeles, 1996.
4-game series
    N.L.—41—Andres Galarraga, Colorado, 1995.
    A.L.—35—Will Clark, Texas, 1996.
           Rafael Palmeiro, Texas, 1996.
5-game series
    A.L.—53—Jason Giambi, Oakland, 2001.
    N.L.—49—Steve Garvey, Los Angeles, 1981.

Most putouts, nine-inning game
A.L.—16—Tino Martinez, New York, October 4, 2000.
N.L.—14
    Fred McGriff, Atlanta, October 3, 1995.
    Jeff Bagwell, Houston, October 5, 1999.

Most putouts, extra-inning game
N.L.—15—Steve Garvey, Los Angeles, October 7, 1981, 11 innings.
A.L.—Less than nine-inning record.

Fewest putouts, nine-inning game
A.L.—2—Mike Stanley, Boston, October 7, 1999.
N.L.—3
    Pete Rose, Philadelphia, October 9, 1981.
    Eric Karros, Los Angeles, October 6, 1995.
    J.T. Snow, San Francisco, September 30, 1997.
    Andres Galarraga, Atlanta, October 1, 1998, 10 innings.

Most putouts, inning
A.L.-N.L.—3—Held by many first basemen.

Most assists, career
A.L.—25—Tino Martinez, Seattle, 1995; New York, 1996 through 2001; seven series, 30 games.
N.L.—15—Jeff Bagwell, Houston, 1997, 1998, 1999, 2001; four series, 14 games.

Most assists, series
3-game series
    N.L.—6—Jeff Bagwell, Houston, 1997.
    A.L.—5—Paul Sorrento, Cleveland, 1995.
4-game series
    A.L.—4—Will Clark, Texas, 1996.
           Paul Sorrento, Seattle, 1997.
    N.L.—4—Jeff Bagwell, Houston, 1998.
           John Olerud, New York, 1999.
           Todd Zeile, New York, 2000.
5-game series
    N.L.—8—Pete Rose, Philadelphia, 1981.
    A.L.—7—Jim Thome, Cleveland, 1999.

Most assists, game
N.L.—4—Pete Rose, Philadelphia, October, 7, 1981.
A.L.—4—Jim Thome, Cleveland, October 7, 1999.

Most assists, inning
A.L.-N.L.—2—Held by many first basemen.

Most chances accepted, career
A.L.—293—Tino Martinez, Seattle, 1995; New York, 1996 through 2001; seven series, 30 games.
N.L.—120—Jeff Bagwell, Houston, 1997, 1998, 1999, 2001; four series, 14 games.

Most chances accepted, series
3-game series
    A.L.—34—Mo Vaughn, Boston, 1998.
    N.L.—30—Eric Karros, Los Angeles, 1996.
           Fred McGriff, Atlanta, 1997.
4-game series
    N.L.—43—Andres Galarraga, Colorado, 1995.
    A.L.—39—Will Clark, Texas, 1996.
5-game series
    A.L.—55—Jason Giambi, Oakland, 2001.
    N.L.—54—Steve Garvey, Los Angeles, 1981.

Most chances accepted, nine-inning game
A.L.—17—Tino Martinez, New York, October 4, 2000 (16 putouts, one assist).
N.L.—15
    Fred McGriff, Atlanta, October 3, 1995 (14 putouts, one assist).
    Jeff Bagwell, Houston, October 5, 1999 (14 putouts, one assist).

Most chances accepted, extra-inning game
N.L.—16—Steve Garvey, Los Angeles, October 7, 1981, 11 innings (15 putouts, one assist).
A.L.—Less than nine-inning record.

Fewest chances offered, nine-inning game
N.L.—3
    Eric Karros, Los Angeles, October 6, 1995 (three putouts).
    J.T. Snow, San Francisco, September 30, 1997 (three putouts).
A.L.—3
    Bob Watson, New York, October 7, 1981 (three putouts).
    Mike Stanley, Boston, October 7, 1999 (two putouts, one assist).

Most chances accepted, inning
A.L.-N.L.—3—Held by many first basemen.

ERRORS AND DOUBLE PLAYS

Most errors, career
A.L.—3—Paul Sorrento, Cleveland, 1995; Seattle, 1997; two series, seven games.
N.L.—2—Jeff Bagwell, Houston, 1997, 1998, 1999, 2001; four series, 14 games.

Most consecutive errorless games, career
A.L.—18—Tino Martinez, Seattle, New York, October 3, 1995 through October 5, 1999.
N.L.—11—Jeff Bagwell, Houston, September 29, 1998 through October 12, 2001.

Most errors, series
A.L.—2—Paul Sorrento, Cleveland, 1995 (3-game series).
N.L.—2—Jeff Bagwell, Houston, 1997 (3-game series).

Most chances accepted, errorless series
N.L.—54—Steve Garvey, Los Angeles, 1981 (5-game series).
A.L.—54—Tino Martinez, New York, 1997 (5-game series).

Most errors, game
A.L.-N.L.—1—Held by many first basemen.

Most double plays, career
A.L.—25—Tino Martinez, Seattle, 1995; New York, 1996 through 2001; seven series, 30 games.
N.L.—12—Jeff Bagwell, Houston, 1997, 1998, 1999, 2001; four series, 14 games.

Most double plays, series
A.L.—6
    Jim Thome, Cleveland, 1997 (5-game series).
    Tino Martinez, New York, 2000 (5-game series).

N.L.—5
  Fred McGriff, Atlanta, 1995 (4-game series).
  Jeff Bagwell, Houston, 2001 (3-game series).
  Julio Franco, Atlanta, 2001 (3-game series).

Most double plays started, series
A.L.—3—Tino Martinez, New York, 2001 (5-game series).
N.L.—1—Held by many first basemen.

Most double plays, game
N.L.—4—Fred McGriff, Atlanta, October 3, 1995.
A.L.—3—Held by many first basemen.

Most double plays started, game
A.L.-N.L.—1—Held by many first basemen.

Most unassisted double plays, game
A.L.—1
  Tino Martinez, New York, October 5, 1999, sixth inning.
  Tino Martinez, New York, October 10, 2001, seventh inning.
N.L.—Never accomplished.

SECOND BASEMEN
GAMES

Most games played, career
A.L.—18—Roberto Alomar, Baltimore, 1996, 1997; Cleveland, 1999, 2001; four series.
N.L.—14—Craig Biggio, Houston, 1997, 1998, 1999, 2001; four series.

PUTOUTS, ASSISTS AND CHANCES ACCEPTED

Most putouts, career
A.L.—35—Roberto Alomar, Baltimore, 1996, 1997; Cleveland, 1999, 2001; four series, 18 games.
N.L.—33—Craig Biggio, Houston, 1997, 1998, 1999, 2001; four series, 14 games.

Most putouts, series
3-game series
  A.L.—10—Ray Durham, Chicago, 2000.
  N.L.—9—Keith Lockhart, Atlanta, 1998.
4-game series
  N.L.—14—Craig Biggio, Houston, 1999.
  A.L.—10—Roberto Alomar, Baltimore, 1996.
            Mark McLemore, Texas, 1996.
5-game series
  A.L.—15—Rey Sanchez, New York, 1997.
  N.L.—14—Fernando Vina, St. Louis, 2001.

Most putouts, nine-inning game
A.L.—8—Rey Sanchez, New York, October 4, 1997.
N.L.—6—Craig Biggio, Houston, October 3, 1998.

Most putouts, extra-inning game
A.L.—6—Randy Velarde, New York, October 4, 1995, 15 innings.
N.L.—Less than nine-inning record.

Most putouts, inning
A.L.-N.L.—2—Held by many second basemen.

Most assists, career
A.L.—46—Mark McLemore, Texas, 1996, 1998, 1999; Seattle, 2000; four series, 13 games.
N.L.—35—Craig Biggio, Houston, 1997, 1998, 1999, 2001; four series, 14 games.

Most assists, series
3-games series
  N.L.—13—Fernando Vina, St. Louis, 2000.
  A.L.—12—Mark McLemore, Texas, 1998.
4-game series
  A.L.—16—Mark McLemore, Texas, 1996.
  N.L.—16—Mark Lemke, Atlanta, 1995.
5-game series
  N.L.—18—Jerry Manuel, Montreal, 1981.
  A.L.—22—Luis Sojo, New York, 2000.

Most assists, game
N.L.—8
  Jerry Manuel, Montreal, October 7, 1981.
  Mark Lemke, Atlanta, October 3, 1995.
A.L.—6
  Luis Alicea, Boston, October 3, 1995, 13 innings.
  Mike Benjamin, Boston, September 30, 1998.
  Joey Cora, Cleveland, October 2, 1998.
  Mark McLemore, Texas, October 9, 1999.
  Frank Menechino, Oakland, October 10, 2001.

Most assists, inning
A.L.-N.L.—2—Held by many second basemen.

Most chances accepted, career
A.L.—70—Roberto Alomar, Baltimore, 1996, 1997; Cleveland, 1999, 2001; four series, 18 games.
N.L.—68—Craig Biggio, Houston, 1997, 1998, 1999, 2001; four series, 14 games.

Most chances accepted, series
3-game series
  N.L.—20—Fernando Vina, St. Louis, 2000.
  A.L.—17—Luis Alicea, Boston, 1995.
4-game series
  A.L.—26—Mark McLemore, Texas, 1996.
  N.L.—26—Bret Boone, Atlanta, 1999.
5-game series
  N.L.—31—Jerry Manuel, Montreal, 1981.
  A.L.—31—Luis Sojo, New York, 2000.

Most chances accepted, game
N.L.—11—Mark Lemke, Atlanta, October 3, 1981 (three putouts, eight assists).
A.L.—11
  Luis Sojo, New York, October 7, 2000 (four putouts, seven assists).
  Randy Velarde, New York, October 4, 1995, 15 innings (six putouts, five assists).

Fewest chances offered, game
A.L.—0—Mark McLemore, Texas, October 7, 1999.
N.L.—1
  Phil Garner, Houston, October 7, 1981, 11 innings.
  Fernando Vina, St. Louis, October 9, 2001.
  Marcus Giles, Atlanta, October 12, 2001.

Most chances accepted, inning
A.L.-N.L.—3—Held by many second basemen.

ERRORS AND DOUBLE PLAYS

Most errors, career
N.L.—3
  Jerry Manuel, Montreal, 1981; one series, five games.
  Eric Young, Colorado, 1995; one series, four games.
A.L.—2
  Jim Gantner, Milwaukee, 1981; one series, four games.
  Chuck Knoblauch, New York, 1998, 1999; two series, six games.
  Randy Velarde, New York, 1995; Oakland, 2000; two series, nine games.

Most consecutive errorless games, career
A.L.—13—Mark McLemore, Texas, Seattle, October 1, 1996 through October 6, 2000.
N.L.—9—Craig Biggio, Houston, October 3, 1998 through October 12, 2001.

Most errors, series
N.L.—3
  Jerry Manuel, Montreal, 1981 (5-game series).
  Eric Young, Colorado, 1995 (4-game series).
A.L.—2
  Jim Gantner, Milwaukee, 1981 (5-game series).
  Randy Velarde, Oakland, 2000 (5-game series).

Most chances accepted, errorless series
A.L.—29—Rey Sanchez, New York, 1997 (5-game series).
N.L.—24
  Manny Trillo, Philadelphia, 1981 (5-game series).
  Mark Lemke, Atlanta, 1995 (4-game series).

Most errors, game
N.L.—2—Eric Young, Colorado, October 4, 1995.
A.L.—1—Held by many second basemen.

Most errors, inning
A.L.-N.L.—1—Held by many second basemen.

Most double plays, career
A.L.—11—Mark McLemore, Texas, 1996, 1998, 1999; New York, 2000; four series, 13 games.
N.L.—9—Craig Biggio, Houston, 1997, 1998, 1999, 2001; four series, 14 games.

Most double plays, series
A.L.—6—Luis Sojo, New York, 2000 (5-game series).
N.L.—5
Jerry Manuel, Montreal, 1981 (5-game series).
Quilvio Veras, San Diego, 1998 (4-game series).
Edgardo Alfonzo, New York, 1999 (4-game series).

Most double plays started, series
N.L.—4—Quilvio Veras, San Diego, 1998 (4-game series).
A.L.—3
Mark McLemore, Seattle, 2000 (3-game series).
Luis Sojo, New York, 2000 (5-game series).

Most double plays, game
N.L.—3—Mark Lemke, Atlanta, October 3, 1981.
A.L.—3—Bip Roberts, Cleveland, September 30, 1997.

Most double plays started, game
N.L.—2
Mark Lemke, Atlanta, October 3, 1995.
Quilvio Veras, San Diego, October 3, 1998.
Bret Boone, Atlanta, October 8, 1999, 12 innings.
A.L.—2
Ray Durham, Chicago, October 3, 2000, 10 innings.
Mark McLemore, Seattle, October 6, 2000.

Most unassisted double plays, game
A.L.-N.L.—Never accomplished.

THIRD BASEMEN
GAMES

Most games played, career
N.L.—23—Chipper Jones, Atlanta, 1995 through 2001; seven series.
A.L.—16—Scott Brosius, New York, 1998 through 2001; four series.

PUTOUTS, ASSISTS AND CHANCES ACCEPTED

Most putouts, career
N.L.—14—Chipper Jones, Atlanta, 1995 through 2001; seven series, 23 games.
A.L.—14—Scott Brosius, New York, 1998 through 2001; four series, 16 games.

Most putouts, series
3-game series
A.L.—6—Jim Thome, Cleveland, 1995.
N.L.—5—Vinny Castilla, Houston, 2001.
4-game series
N.L.—7—Robin Ventura, New York, 2000.
A.L.—5—John Valentin, Boston, 1998.
T. Fryman, Cleveland, 1998.
5-game series
N.L.—8—Larry Parrish, Montreal, 1981.
A.L.—7—Graig Nettles, New York, 1981.

Most putouts, nine-inning game
N.L.—4—Vinny Castilla, Houston, October 10, 2001.
A.L.—3
Todd Zeile, Baltimore, October 1, 1996.
Herbert Perry, Chicago, October 6, 2000.
Scott Brosius, New York, October 3, 2000.

Most putouts, extra-inning game
N.L.—5—Robin Ventura, New York, October 5, 2000, 10 innings.
A.L.—Less than nine-inning record.

Most putouts, inning
A.L.-N.L.—2—Held by many third basemen.

Most assists, career
Both leagues—34—Matt Williams, Cleveland A.L., 1997; Arizona N.L., 1999, 2001 (10 in A.L., 24 in N.L.); three series, 14 games.
A.L.—27—Scott Brosius, New York, 1998 through 2001; four series, 16 games.
N.L.—26—Chipper Jones, Atlanta, 1995 through 2001; seven series, 23 games.

Most assists, series
3-game series
N.L.—9—Bill Mueller, San Francisco, 1997.
A.L.—7—Herbert Perry, Chicago, 2000.
4-game series
N.L.—13—Vinny Castilla, Colorado, 1995.
A.L.—10—Dean Palmer, Texas, 1996.
John Valentin, Boston, 1998.
5-game series
N.L.—15—Pedro Guerrero, Los Angeles, 1981.
Placido Polanco, St. Louis, 2001.
Matt Williams, Arizona, 2001.
A.L.—11—John Valentin, Boston, 1999.
Eric Chavez, Oakland, 2001.

Most assists, nine-inning game
N.L.—7—Matt Williams, Arizona, October 12, 2001.
A.L.—5—Scott Brosius, New York, October 4, 2000.

Most assists, extra-inning game
A.L.—6—Todd Zeile, Baltimore, October 5, 1996, 12 innings.
N.L.—Less than nine-inning record.

Most assists, inning
N.L.—3—Vinny Castilla, Colorado, October 4, 1995, fourth inning.
A.L.—3—Travis Fryman, Cleveland, October 11, 2001, third inning.

Most chances accepted, career
Both leagues—41—Matt Williams, Cleveland, 1997; Arizona, 1999, 2001 (12 in A.L., 29 in N.L.); three series, 14 games.
A.L.—41—Scott Brosius, New York, 1998 through 2001; four series, 16 games.
N.L.—40—Chipper Jones, Atlanta, 1995 through 2001; seven series, 23 games.

Most chances accepted, series
3-game series
A.L.—12—Jim Thome, Cleveland, 1995.
Herbert Perry, Chicago, 2000.
N.L.—12—Vinny Castilla, Houston, 2001.
4-game series
N.L.—16—Vinny Castilla, Colorado, 1995.
A.L.—15—John Valentin, Boston, 1998.
5-game series
N.L.—18—Pedro Guerrero, Los Angeles, 1981.
A.L.—15—Scott Brosius, New York, 2001.
Eric Chavez, Oakland, 2001.

Most chances accepted, nine-inning game
N.L.—9—Vinny Castilla, Houston, October 10, 2001 (four putouts, five assists).
A.L.—6
Todd Zeile, Baltimore, October 1, 1996 (three putouts, three assists).
Scott Brosius, New York, September 30, 1998 (two putouts, four assists).
John Valentin, Boston, October 9, 1999 (two putouts, four assists).

Most chances accepted, extra-inning game
A.L.—7—Todd Zeile, Baltimore, October 5, 1996 (one putout, six assists).
N.L.—Less than nine-inning record.

Fewest chances offered, game
A.L.-N.L.—0—Held by many third basemen.

Most chances accepted, inning
A.L.-N.L.—3—Held by many third basemen.

ERRORS AND DOUBLE PLAYS

Most errors, career
A.L.—4—Todd Zeile, Texas, 1996, 1998, 1999; three series, 10 games.
N.L.—4
Ken Caminiti, San Diego, 1996, 1998, 1999; three series, 11 games.
Chipper Jones, Atlanta, 1995 through 2001; seven series, 23 games.

Most consecutive errorless games, career
A.L.—14—Travis Fryman, Cleveland, September 29, 1998 through October 15, 2001.
N.L.—9—Chipper Jones, Atlanta, October 3, 1995 through October 1, 1997.

Most errors, series
N.L.—3—Ken Caminiti, San Diego, 1996 (3-game series).
A.L.—3
Charlie Hayes, New York, 1997 (5-game series).
Scott Brosius, New York, 2001 (5-game series).

Most chances accepted, errorless series
A.L.—15—John Valentin, Boston, 1998 (4-game series).
N.L.—14—Larry Parrish, Montreal, 1981 (5-game series).

Most errors, game
N.L.—2—Ken Caminiti, San Diego, October 5, 1996.
A.L.—1—By many third basemen.

Most errors, inning
A.L.-N.L.—1—Held by many third basemen.

Most double plays, career
A.L.—5—John Valentin, Boston, 1998, 1999; two series, nine games.
N.L.—3
Vinny Castilla, Colorado, 1995; Houston, 2001; two series, seven games.
Matt Williams, Arizona, 1999, 2001; two series, nine games.

Most double plays, series
A.L.—3
John Valentin, Boston, 1998 (4-game series).
Scott Brosius, New York, 2000 (5-game series).
N.L.—3
Vinny Castilla, Houston, 2001 (3-game series).
Matt Williams, Arizona, 2001 (5-game series).

Most double plays started, series
A.L.—3
John Valentin, Boston, 1998 (4-game series).
Scott Brosius, New York, 2000 (5-game series).
N.L.—3
Vinny Castilla, Houston, 2001 (3-game series).
Matt Williams, Arizona, 2001 (5-game series).

Most double plays, game
N.L.—3—Vinny Castilla, Houston, October 10, 2001.
A.L.—2
Wayne Gross, Oakland, October 6, 1981.
Scott Brosius, New York, October 4, 2000.

Most double plays started, game
N.L.—3—Vinny Castilla, Houston, October 10, 2001.
A.L.—2
Wayne Gross, Oakland, October 6, 1981.
Scott Brosius, New York, October 4, 2000.

Most unassisted double plays, game
A.L.—1—Scott Brosius, New York, October 3, 2000.
N.L.—Never accomplished.

SHORTSTOPS
GAMES

Most games played, career
A.L.—26—Omar Vizquel, Cleveland, 1995 through 1999, 2001; six series.
N.L.—11
Walt Weiss, Colorado, 1995; Atlanta, 1998 through 2000; four series.
Edgar Renteria, Florida, 1997; St. Louis, 2000, 2001; three series.

PUTOUTS, ASSISTS AND CHANCES ACCEPTED

Most putouts, career
A.L.—44—Derek Jeter, New York, 1996 through 2001; six series, 25 games.
N.L.—22—Edgar Renteria, Florida, 1997; St. Louis, 2000, 2001; three series, 11 games.

Most putouts, series
3-game series
A.L.—10—Jose Valentin, Chicago, 2000.
N.L.—9—Edgar Renteria, Florida, 1997.
4-game series
N.L.—10—Rich Aurilia, San Francisco, 2000.
A.L.—8—Derek Jeter, New York, 1996.
5-game series
N.L.—17—Chris Speier, Montreal, 1981.
A.L.—12—Derek Jeter, New York, 1997.
Omar Vizquel, Cleveland, 1997.

Most putouts, game
N.L.—7—Larry Bowa, Philadelphia, October 7, 1981.
A.L.—5
Fred Stanley, Oakland, October 9, 1981.
Tony Fernandez, New York, October 11, 1995, 11 innings.
Alex Rodriguez, Seattle, October 2, 1997.
Omar Vizquel, Cleveland, October 6, 1997.
Jose Valentin, Chicago, October 3, 2000, 10 innings.

Most putouts, inning
A.L.-N.L.—2—Held by many shortstops.

Most assists, career
A.L.—81—Omar Vizquel, Cleveland, 1995, 1996, 1997, 1998, 1999, 2001; six series, 26 games.
N.L.—34—Ricky Gutierrez, Houston, 1997, 1998, 1999; three series, 10 games.

Most assists, series
3-game series
A.L.—17—Jose Valentin, Chicago, 2000.
N.L.—11—Edgar Renteria, Florida, 1997.
4-game series
A.L.—16—Omar Vizquel, Cleveland, 1998.
N.L.—16—Ricky Gutierrez, Houston, 1999.
5-game series
A.L.—23—Robin Yount, Milwaukee, 1981.
N.L.—15—Chris Speier, Montreal, 1981.

Most assists, nine-inning game
A.L.—7
Robin Yount, Milwaukee, October 8, 1995.
Cal Ripken, Baltimore, October 4, 1996.
Jose Valentin, Chicago, October 4, 2000.
N.L.—7—Ricky Gutierrez, Houston, October 3, 1998.

Most assists, extra-inning game
A.L.—8—Luis Sojo, Seattle, October 4, 1995, 15 innings.
N.L.—Less than nine-inning record.

Most assists, inning
N.L.—3—Jeff Blauser, Atlanta, October 4, 1995, seventh inning.
A.L.—2—Held by many shortstops.

Most chances accepted, career
A.L.—120—Omar Vizquel, Cleveland, 1995, 1996, 1997, 1998, 1999, 2001; six series, 26 games.

N.L.—51—Edgar Renteria, Florida, 1997; St. Louis, 2000, 2001; three series, 11 games.

Most chances accepted, series
3-game series
  A.L.—27—Jose Valentin, Chicago, 2000.
  N.L.—20—Edgar Renteria, Florida, 1997.
4-game series
  A.L.—22—Cal Ripken, Baltimore, 1996.
  N.L.—21—Rich Aurilia, San Francisco, 2000.
5-game series
  N.L.—32—Chris Speier, Montreal, 1981.
  A.L.—30—Robin Yount, Milwaukee, 1981.

Most chances accepted, game
A.L.—11
  Luis Sojo, Seattle, October 4, 1995, 15 innings (three putouts, eight assists).
  Jose Valentin, Chicago, October 3, 2000, 10 innings (five putouts, six assists).
  Jose Valentin, Chicago, October 4, 2000 (four putouts, seven assists).
N.L.—9
  Dickie Thon, Houston, October 7, 1981, 11 innings (three putouts, six assists).
  Ricky Gutierrez, Houston, October 3, 1998 (two putouts, seven assists).
  Rey Sanchez, Atlanta, October 10, 2001 (six putouts, three assists).

Fewest chances offered, game
N.L.—0
  Chris Gomez, San Diego, October 3, 1996.
  Jose Vizcaino, San Francisco, September 30, 1997.
  Hanley Frias, Arizona, October 5, 1999.
A.L.—1
  Alex Rodriguez, Seattle, October 5, 1997.
  Derek Jeter, New York, September 30, 1998.
  Nomar Garciaparra, Boston, October 6, 1999.

Most chances accepted, inning
A.L.-N.L.—3—Held by many shortstops.

ERRORS AND DOUBLE PLAYS

Most errors, career
N.L.—4—Edgar Renteria, Florida, 1997; St. Louis, 2000, 2001; three series, 11 games.
A.L.—1—Held by many shortstops.

Most consecutive errorless games, career
A.L.—24—Omar Vizquel, Cleveland, October 3, 1995 through October 13, 2001.
N.L.—11—Walt Weiss, Colorado, Atlanta, October 3, 1995 through October 3, 2000.

Most errors, series
N.L.—3—Julio Lugo, Houston, 2001 (3-game series).
A.L.—1—Held by many shortstops.

Most chances accepted, errorless series
N.L.—32—Chris Speier, Montreal, 1981 (5-game series).
A.L.—27—Derek Jeter, New York, 1997 (5-game series).

Most errors, game
N.L.—2
  Edgar Renteria, Florida, October 3, 1997.
  Julio Lugo, Houston, October 10, 2001.
A.L.—1—Held by many shortstops.

Most errors, inning
A.L.-N.L.—1—Held by many shortstops.

Most double plays, career
A.L.—14—Derek Jeter, New York, 1996 through 2001; six series, 25 games.
N.L.—7
  Chris Gomez, San Diego, 1996, 1998; two series, seven games.
  Edgar Renteria, Florida, 1997; St. Louis, 2000, 2001; three series, 11 games.

Most double plays, series
A.L.—5—Jose Valentin, Chicago, 2000 (3-game series).
N.L.—5—Rey Sanchez, Atlanta, 2001 (3-game series).

Most double plays started, series
N.L.—3—Rey Sanchez, Atlanta, 2001 (3-game series).
A.L.—3—Mark McLemore, Seattle, 2001 (5-game series).

Most double plays, game
N.L.—3
  Jeff Blauser, Atlanta, October 3, 1995.
  Rey Sanchez, Atlanta, October 10, 2001.
A.L.—3
  Kevin Elster, Texas, October 4, 1996.
  Jose Valentin, Chicago, October 4, 2000.

Most double plays started, game
A.L.—2—Tony Fernandez, New York, October 6, 1995.
N.L.—2—Rey Sanchez, Atlanta, October 9, 2001.

Most unassisted double plays, game
A.L.-N.L.—Never occurred.

OUTFIELDERS
GAMES

Most games played, career
A.L.—30—Bernie Williams, New York, 1995 through 2001; seven series.
N.L.—19—Andruw Jones, Atlanta, 1996 through 2001; six series.

PUTOUTS, ASSISTS AND CHANCES ACCEPTED

Most putouts, career
A.L.—76—Bernie Williams, New York, 1995 through 2001; seven series, 30 games.
N.L.—47—Andruw Jones, Atlanta, 1996 through 2001; six series, 19 games.

Most putouts, series
3-game series
  A.L.—15—Bernie Williams, New York, 1999.
  N.L.—13—Luis Gonzalez, Houston, 1997.
4-game series
  A.L.—15—Darryl Hamilton, Texas, 1996.
  N.L.—12—Andruw Jones, Atlanta, 1999.
        Brian Jordan, Atlanta, 1999.
5-game series
  N.L.—16—Ken Landreaux, Los Angeles, 1981.
  A.L.—15—Jerry Mumphrey, New York, 1981.
        Ken Griffey Jr., Seattle, 1995.

Most putouts by left fielder, nine-inning game
N.L.—6—Luis Gonzalez, Houston, September 30, 1997.
A.L.—5—Dave Winfield, New York, October 11, 1981.
       Albert Belle, Cleveland, October 4, 1995.

Most putouts by left fielder, extra-inning game
A.L.—6—Vince Coleman, Seattle, October 8, 1995, 11 innings.
N.L.—Less than nine-inning record.

Most putouts by center fielder, game
A.L.—7
  Dwayne Murphy, Oakland, October 6, 1981.
  Amos Otis, Kansas City, October 7, 1981.
  Bernie Williams, New York, October 5, 1999.
  Johnny Damon, Oakland, October 13, 2001.
N.L.—6
  Willie McGee, St. Louis, October 1, 1996.
  Andruw Jones, Atlanta, October 9, 1999.

Most putouts by right fielder, game
N.L.—6
  Stan Javier, San Francisco, September 30, 1997.
  Andruw Jones, Atlanta, October 1, 1997.
A.L.—6
  Paul O'Neill, New York, October 2, 1996, 12 innings.
  Ichiro Suzuki, Seattle, October 11, 2001.

Most consecutive putouts, game

A.L.—3—Johnny Damon, Oakland, October 13, 2001; two in fifth inning, one in sixth inning.

N.L.—2—Held by many outfielders.

Most putouts, inning

N.L.—3—Jerry White, Montreal, October 8, 1981, second inning (right fielder).

A.L.—3

Bernie Williams, New York, October 5, 1999, third inning (center fielder).

Adam Piatt, Oakland, October 4, 2000, first inning (right fielder).

Mike Cameron, Seattle, October 6, 2000, second inning (center fielder).

Johnny Damon, Oakland, October 13, 2001, fifth inning (center fielder).

Most assists, career

A.L.—3

Manny Ramirez, Cleveland, 1995, 1996, 1997, 1998, 1999; five series, 21 games.

David Justice, Cleveland, 1998, 1999; New York, 2000, 2001; four series, 12 games.

Jay Buhner, Seattle, 1995, 1997, 2000, 2001; four series, 13 games.

N.L.—1—Held by many outfielders.

Most games played with no assists, career

A.L.—30—Bernie Williams, New York, 1995 through 2001; seven series.

N.L.—19—Andruw Jones, Atlanta, 1996 through 2001; six series.

Most assists, series

A.L.—2

Manny Ramirez, Cleveland, 1996 (4-game series).

David Justice, Cleveland, 1999 (5-game series).

N.L.—1—Held by many outfielders.

Most assists, game

A.L.-N.L.—1—Held by many outfielders.

Most chances accepted, career

A.L.—76—Bernie Williams, New York, 1995 through 2001; seven series, 30 games.

N.L.—47—Andruw Jones, Atlanta, 1996 through 2001; six series, 19 games.

Most chances accepted, series

3-game series

A.L.—15—Bernie Williams, New York, 1999.

N.L.—14—Luis Gonzalez, Houston, 1997.

4-game series

A.L.—16—Darryl Hamilton, Texas, 1996.

N.L.—13—Brian Jordan, Atlanta, 1999.

5-game series

N.L.—16—Ken Landreaux, Los Angeles, 1981.

A.L.—16—Jerry Mumphrey, New York, 1981.

Ken Griffey Jr., Seattle, 1995.

Most chances accepted by left fielder, nine-inning game

N.L.—6—Luis Gonzalez, Houston, September 30, 1997 (six putouts).

A.L.—5

Dave Winfield, New York, October 11, 1981 (five putouts).

Albert Belle, Cleveland, October 4, 1995 (five putouts).

Most chances accepted by left fielder, extra-inning game

A.L.—6—Vince Coleman, Seattle, October 8, 1995, 11 innings (six putouts).

N.L.—Less than nine-inning record.

Most chances accepted by center fielder, game

A.L.—7

Dwayne Murphy, Oakland, October 6, 1981 (seven putouts).

Amos Otis, Kansas City, October 7, 1981 (seven putouts).

Darryl Hamilton, Texas, October 2, 1996, 12 innings (six putouts, one assist).

Bernie Williams, New York, October 5, 1999 (seven putouts).

Johnny Damon, Oakland, October 13, 2001 (seven putouts).

N.L.—6

Willie McGee, St. Louis, October 1, 1996 (six putouts).

Andruw Jones, Atlanta, October 9, 1999 (six putouts).

Most chances accepted by right fielder, game

N.L.—6

George Vukovich, Philadelphia, October 11, 1981 (five putouts, one assist).

Stan Javier, San Francisco, September 30, 1997 (six putouts).

Andruw Jones, Atlanta, October 1, 1997 (six putouts).

A.L.—6

Paul O'Neill, New York, October 2, 1996, 12 innings (six putouts).

Ichiro Suzuki, Seattle, October 11, 2001 (six putouts).

Longest game with no chances offered to outfielder

A.L.—13 innings—Albert Belle, Cleveland, October 3, 1995.

N.L.—12 innings—Carl Everett, Houston, October 8, 1999.

Most chances accepted, inning

A.L.-N.L.—3—Held by many outfielders.

ERRORS AND DOUBLE PLAYS

Most errors, career

A.L.—3—Kenny Lofton, Cleveland, 1995, 1996, 1998, 1999, 2001; five series, 21 games.

N.L.—2

Ryan Klesko, Atlanta, 1995, 1996, 1997, 1998; four series, 13 games.

Tony Womack, Arizona, 1999; one series, four games.

Most consecutive errorless games, career

A.L.—30—Bernie Williams, New York, October 3, 1995 through October 15, 2001.

N.L.—19—Andruw Jones, Atlanta, October 2, 1996 through October 12, 2001.

Most errors, series

A.L.—2—Kenny Lofton, Cleveland, 1995 (3-game series).

N.L.—2—Tony Womack, Arizona, 1999 (4-game series).

Most chances accepted, errorless series

N.L.—16—Ken Landreaux, Los Angeles, 1981 (5-game series).

A.L.—16

Jerry Mumphrey, New York, 1981 (5-game series).

Ken Griffey Jr., Seattle, 1995 (5-game series).

Darryl Hamilton, Texas, 1996 (4-game series).

Most errors, game

A.L.-N.L.—1—Held by many outfielders.

Most errors, inning

A.L.-N.L.—1—Held by many outfielders.

Most double plays, career

A.L.-N.L.—1—Held by many outfielders.

Most double plays, game

A.L.-N.L.—1—Held by many outfielders.

Most double plays started, game

A.L.-N.L.—1—Held by many outfielders.

Most unassisted double plays, game

A.L.-N.L.—Never accomplished.

CATCHERS
GAMES

Most games caught, career

A.L.—21—Sandy Alomar Jr., Cleveland, 1995, 1996, 1997, 1998, 1999; five series.

N.L.—12

Javy Lopez, Atlanta, 1995, 1996, 1997, 1998, 2000; five series.

Mike Piazza, Los Angeles, 1995, 1996; New York, 1999, 2000; four series.

PUTOUTS, ASSISTS AND CHANCES ACCEPTED

Most putouts, career
A.L.—149—Sandy Alomar Jr., Cleveland, 1995 through 1999;
five series, 21 games.
N.L.—101—Mike Piazza, Los Angeles, 1995, 1996; New York,
1999, 2000; four series, 12 games.

Most putouts, series
3-game series
  N.L.—31—Mike Piazza, Los Angeles, 1995.
  A.L.—27—Ivan Rodriguez, Texas, 1998.
4-game series
  A.L.—40—Sandy Alomar Jr., Cleveland, 1995.
  N.L.—35—Eddie Perez, Atlanta, 1999.
5-game series
  A.L.—42—Rick Cerone, New York, 1981.
  N.L.—39—Damian Miller, Arizona, 2001.

Most putouts, nine-inning game
A.L.—15—Rick Cerone, New York, October 8, 1981.
N.L.—15—Carlos Hernandez, San Diego, September 29, 1998.

Most putouts, extra-inning game
A.L.—22—Sandy Alomar Jr., Cleveland, October 5, 1996, 12
innings.
N.L.—16—Tony Eusebio, Houston, October 8, 1999, 12 innings.

Fewest putouts, game
A.L.—1
  Rick Cerone, New York, October 9, 1981.
  Joe Girardi, New York, October 4, 1997.
N.L.—2—Carlos Hernandez, San Diego, October 4, 1998.

Most putouts, inning
A.L.-N.L.—3—Held by many catchers.

Most assists, career
N.L.—10
  Javy Lopez, Atlanta, 1995 through 1998, 2000; five series, 12
  games.
  Carlos Hernandez, San Diego, 1998; St. Louis, 2000; two
  series, seven games.
A.L.—7—Sandy Alomar Jr., Cleveland, 1995, 1996, 1997, 1998,
1999; five series, 21 games.

Most assists, series
3-game series
  N.L.—4—Mike Piazza, Los Angeles, 1996.
          Carlos Hernandez, St. Louis, 2000.
  A.L.—3—John Wathan, Kansas City, 1981.
          Ivan Rodriguez, Texas, 1998.
4-game series
  N.L.—6—Carlos Hernandez, San Diego, 1998.
  A.L.—4—Sandy Alomar, Cleveland, 1996.
5-game series
  N.L.—4—Gary Carter, Montreal, 1981.
          Mike Scioscia, Los Angeles, 1981.
  A.L.—4—Greg Myers, Oakland, 2001.
          Einar Diaz, Cleveland, 2001.

Most assists, game
N.L.—3
  Mike Piazza, Los Angeles, October 2, 1996, 10 innings.
  Carlos Hernandez, San Diego, October 1, 1998.
A.L.—2—Held by many catchers.

Most assists, inning
A.L.-N.L.—1—Held by many catchers.

Most chances accepted, career
A.L.—156—Sandy Alomar Jr., Cleveland, 1995, 1996, 1997,
1998, 1999; five series, 21 games.
N.L.—107—Mike Piazza, Los Angeles, 1995, 1996; New York,
1999, 2000; four series, 12 games.

Most chances accepted, series
3-game series
  N.L.—31—Mike Piazza, Los Angeles, 1995.
  A.L.—30—Ivan Rodriguez, Texas, 1998.

4-game series
  A.L.—44—Sandy Alomar Jr., Cleveland, 1996.
  N.L.—40—Carlos Hernandez, San Diego, 1998.
5-game series
  A.L.—43—Rick Cerone, New York, 1981.
  N.L.—42—Damian Miller, Arizona, 2001.

Most chances accepted, nine-inning game
N.L.—17—Carlos Hernandez, San Diego, September 29, 1998
(15 putouts, two assists).
A.L.—15—Rick Cerone, New York, October 8, 1981 (15 putouts).

Most chances accepted, extra-inning game
A.L.—24—Sandy Alomar Jr., Cleveland, October 5, 1996, 12
innings (22 putouts, two assists).
N.L.—18—Tony Eusebio, Houston, October 8, 1999, 12
innings.

Fewest chances offered, game
A.L.—1
  Rick Cerone, New York, October 9, 1981.
  Joe Girardi, New York, October 4, 1997.
N.L.—2—Eli Marrero, St. Louis, October 13, 2001.

Most chances accepted, inning
A.L.-N.L.—3—Held by many catchers.

ERRORS AND PASSED BALLS

Most errors, career
A.L.—4—Sandy Alomar Jr., Cleveland, 1995, 1996, 1997, 1998,
1999; five series, 21 games.
N.L.—1—Held by many catchers.

Most consecutive errorless games, career
A.L.—14—Jorge Posada, New York, October 2, 1997 through
October 15, 2001.
N.L.—12—Mike Piazza, Los Angeles, New York, October 3,
1995 through October 8, 2000.

Most errors, series
A.L.—2—Mike Macfarlane, Boston, 1995 (3-game series).
N.L.—1—Held by many catchers.

Most chances accepted, errorless series
N.L.—42—Damian Miller, Arizona, 2001 (5-game series).
A.L.—41—Dan Wilson, Seattle, 2001 (5-game series).

Most errors, game
A.L.-N.L.—1—Held by many catchers.

Most errors, inning
A.L.-N.L.—1—Held by many catchers.

Most passed balls, career
A.L.—5—Jason Varitek, Boston, 1998, 1999; two series, six games.
N.L.—2—Carlos Hernandez, San Diego, 1998; St. Louis, 2000; two
series, seven games.

Most passed balls, series
A.L.—3—Jason Varitek, Boston, 1999 (5-game series).
N.L.—2—Carlos Hernandez, San Diego, 1998 (4-game series).

Most passed balls, game
N.L.—2—Carlos Hernandez, San Diego, September 29, 1998.
A.L.—2
  Jason Varitek, Boston, September 30, 1998.
  Jason Varitek, Boston, October 10, 1999.

Most passed balls, inning
N.L.—2—Carlos Hernandez, San Diego, September 29, 1998, third
inning.
A.L.—2—Jason Varitek, Boston, September 30, 1998, first inning.

DOUBLE PLAYS AND RUNNERS CAUGHT STEALING

Most double plays, career
Both leagues—3—Joe Girardi, Colorado N.L., 1995; New York
  A.L., 1996, 1997, 1998, 1999; five series, 17 games (2 in
  A.L., 1 in N.L.).

N.L.—3—Javy Lopez, Atlanta, 1995 through 1998, 2000; five
series, 12 games.
A.L.—2—Ivan Rodriguez, Texas, 1996, 1998, 1999; three
series, 10 games.

Most double plays, series
N.L.—2
Brian Johnson, San Diego, 1996 (3-game series).
Mike Piazza, Los Angeles, 1996 (3-game series).
Javy Lopez, Atlanta, 1998 (3-game series).
Bobby Estalella, San Francisco, 2000 (4-game series).
A.L.—1—Held by many catchers.

Most double plays started, series
N.L.—2
Mike Piazza, Los Angeles, 1996 (3-game series).
Javy Lopez, Atlanta, 1998 (3-game series).
Bobby Estalella, San Francisco, 2000 (4-game series).
A.L.—1—Held by many catchers.

Most double plays, game
N.L.—2
Mike Piazza, Los Angeles, October 5, 1996.
Javy Lopez, Atlanta, October 1, 1998, 10 innings.
A.L.—1—Held by many catchers.

Most double plays started, game
N.L.—2
Mike Piazza, Los Angeles, October 5, 1996.
Javy Lopez, Atlanta, October 1, 1998, 10 innings.
A.L.—1—Held by many catchers.

Most unassisted double plays, game
A.L.-N.L.—Never accomplished.

Most runners caught stealing, career
N.L.—5—Javy Lopez, Atlanta, 1995 through 1998, 2000; five
series, 12 games.
A.L.—3
Ivan Rodriguez, Texas, 1996, 1998, 1999; three series, 10
games.
Ramon Hernandez, Oakland, 2000, 2001; two series, 10
games.

Most runners caught stealing, series
A.L.—3—Chris Hoiles, Baltimore, 1996 (4-game series).
N.L.—3
Mike Piazza, Los Angeles, 1996 (3-game series).
Javy Lopez, Atlanta, 1998 (3-game series).
Carlos Hernandez, St. Louis, 2000 (3-game series).

Most runners caught stealing, nine-inning game
A.L.—2
John Wathan, Kansas City, October 9, 1981.
Ivan Rodriguez, Texas, September 29, 1998.
N.L.—2
Carlos Hernandez, St. Louis, October 3, 2000.
Brad Ausmus, Houston, October 9, 2001.

Most runners caught stealing, extra-inning game
N.L.—3—Mike Piazza, Los Angeles, October 2, 1996, 10 innings.
A.L.—2—Chris Hoiles, Baltimore, October 5, 1996, 12 innings.

Most runners caught stealing, inning
A.L.—2—John Wathan, Kansas City, October 9, 1981, third
inning.
N.L.—1—Held by many catchers.

PITCHERS
GAMES

Most games pitched, career
A.L.—19—Jeff Nelson, Seattle, 1995, 2001; New York, 1996
through 2000; seven series.
N.L.—9—Greg Maddux, Atlanta, 1995 through 2001; seven
series.

Most games pitched, series
3-game series
A.L.-N.L.—3—Held by many pitchers.

4-game series
A.L.—4—Jesse Orosco, Baltimore, 1996.
N.L.—4—Mike Munoz, Colorado, 1995.
Bruce Ruffin, Colorado, 1995.
Trevor Hoffman, San Diego, 1998.
5-game series
N.L.—4—Ron Reed, Philadelphia, 1981.
Steve Kline, St. Louis, 2001.
A.L.—4—Jim Slaton, Milwaukee, 1981.
Norm Charlton, Seattle, 1995.
Bill Risley, Seattle, 1995.
Paul Assenmacher, Cleveland, 1997.
Mike Jackson, Cleveland, 1997.
Jeff Nelson, New York, 1997.

PUTOUTS, ASSISTS AND CHANCES ACCEPTED

Most putouts, career
N.L.—6—Mike Hampton, Houston, 1997 through 1999; New
York, 2000; four series, four games.
A.L.—5—Charles Nagy, Cleveland, 1995, 1996, 1997, 1998,
1999; five series, seven games.

Most putouts, series
3-game series
N.L.—3—Mike Hampton, Houston, 1997.
A.L.—2—Moose Haas, Milwaukee, 1981.
Rick Langford, Oakland, 1981.
Mike Norris, Oakland, 1981.
Charles Nagy, Cleveland, 1995.
4-game series
A.L.—2—Mike Mussina, Baltimore, 1997.
Pete Schourek, Boston, 1998.
N.L.—2—Jay Powell, Houston, 1998.
Rick Reed, New York, 1999.
5-game series
A.L.—3—Charles Nagy, Cleveland, 1999.
N.L.—3—Mike Hampton, New York, 2000.

Most putouts, game
N.L.—3
Mike Hampton, Houston, October 1, 1997.
Mike Hampton, New York, October 4, 2000.
A.L.—3—Charles Nagy, Cleveland, October 7, 1999.

Most putouts, inning
A.L.—2
Rick Langford, Oakland, October 9, 1981, first inning.
Moose Haas, Milwaukee, October 11, 1981, first inning.
Charles Nagy, Cleveland, October 6, 1995, fourth inning.
N.L.—2—Jay Powell, Houston, October 1, 1998, eighth inning.

Most assists, career
N.L.—13—Greg Maddux, Atlanta, 1995 through 2001; seven
series, nine games.
A.L.—13—Andy Pettitte, New York, 1995 through 2001; seven
series, nine games.

Most assists, series
3-game series
A.L.—4—Steve McCatty, Oakland, 1981.
N.L.—3—Tom Glavine, Atlanta, 2001.
Shane Reynolds, Houston, 2001.
4-game series
N.L.—5—Greg Maddux, Atlanta, 1995.
A.L.—4—Charles Nagy, Cleveland, 1996.
Jeff Fassero, Seattle, 1997.
Mike Mussina, Baltimore, 1997.
5-game series
N.L.—5—Fernando Valenzuela, Los Angeles, 1981.
A.L.—5—Andy Pettitte, New York, 1997.

Most assists, game
A.L.—4
Steve McCatty, Oakland, October 7, 1981.
Charles Nagy, Cleveland, October 1, 1996.
Jeff Fassero, Seattle, October 4, 1997.
Andy Pettitte, New York, October 6, 1997.

N.L.—4

Nolan Ryan, Houston, October 6, 1981.
Greg Maddux, Atlanta, October 3, 1995.
Kevin Millwood, Atlanta, October 6, 1999.

Most assists, inning

A.L.—2

Ken Hill, Cleveland, October 3, 1995, 13th inning.
Steve McCatty, Oakland, October 7, 1981, first inning.
Tommy John, New York, October 9, 1981, seventh inning.
Jeff Fassero, Seattle, October 4, 1997, first inning.
Mike Mussina, Baltimore, October 5, 1997, seventh inning.
Roger Clemens, New York, October 7, 2000, fourth inning.

N.L.—2—Kevin Millwood, Atlanta, October 6, 1999, third inning.

Most chances accepted, career

N.L.—18—Greg Maddux, Atlanta, 1995 through 2001; seven series, nine games.

A.L.—14—Andy Pettitte, New York, 1995 through 2001; seven series, nine games.

Most chances accepted, series

3-game series
    A.L.—4—Steve McCatty, Oakland, 1981.
              Erik Hanson, Boston, 1995.
              Roger Clemens, New York, 1999.
    N.L.—4—Greg Maddux, Atlanta, 1996.
              Tom Glavine, Atlanta, 2001.

4-game series
    N.L.—6—Greg Maddux, Atlanta, 1995.
    A.L.—6—Mike Mussina, Baltimore, 1997.

5-game series
    A.L.—6—Andy Pettitte, New York, 1997.
    N.L.—5—Held by many pitchers.

Most chances accepted, game

N.L.—5

Vern Ruhle, Houston, October 10, 1981.
Greg Maddux, Atlanta, October 3, 1995.
Kevin Millwood, Atlanta, October 6, 1999.

A.L.—5

Jeff Fassero, Seattle, October 4, 1997.
Andy Pettitte, New York, October 6, 1997.

Most chances accepted, inning

A.L.-N.L.—2—Held by many pitchers.

ERRORS AND DOUBLE PLAYS

Most errors, career

A.L.-N.L.—1—Held by many pitchers.

Most consecutive errorless games, career

A.L.—19—Jeff Nelson, Seattle, New York, October 3, 1995 through October 15, 2001.

N.L.—9—Greg Maddux, Atlanta, October 3, 1995 through October 9, 2001.

Most errors, series

A.L.-N.L.—1—Held by many pitchers.

Most chances accepted, errorless series

N.L.—6—Greg Maddux, Atlanta, 1995 (4-game series).

A.L.—6

Mike Mussina, Baltimore, 1997 (4-game series).
Andy Pettitte, New York, 1997 (5-game series).

Most errors, game

A.L.-N.L.—1—Held by many pitchers.

Most double plays, career

A.L.-N.L.—1—Held by many pitchers.

Most double plays, series

A.L.-N.L.—1—Held by many pitchers.

Most double plays started, series

A.L.-N.L.—1—Held by many pitchers.

Most double plays, game

A.L.-N.L.—1—Held by many pitchers.

Most double plays started, career

A.L.-N.L.—1—Held by many pitchers.

Most unassisted double plays, game

A.L.-N.L.—Never accomplished.

CLUB FIELDING

AVERAGE

Highest fielding average, series
3-game series
 N.L.—1.000—San Francisco vs. Florida, 1997.
  Atlanta vs. Chicago, 1998.
 A.L.—.991—New York vs. Texas, 1998.
  Texas vs. New York, 1998.
  Seattle vs. Chicago, 2000.
4-game series
 A.L.—1.000—Baltimore vs. Seattle, 1997.
  Boston vs. Cleveland, 1998.
 N.L.—1.000—New York vs. Arizona, 1999.
  New York vs. San Francisco, 2000.
5-game series
 A.L.—.990—Seattle vs. New York, 1995.
 N.L.—.985—Los Angeles vs. Houston, 1981.

For a list of fielding statistics by teams each series, see page 391.

Highest fielding average by both clubs, series
3-game series
 N.L.—.983—Los Angeles .991, Atlanta .974, 1996.
 A.L.—.991—New York .991, Texas .991, 1998.
4-game series
 A.L.—.997—Baltimore 1.000, Seattle .993, 1997.
  Boston 1.000, Cleveland .993, 1998.
 N.L.—.997—New York 1.000, San Francisco, .994, 2000.
5-game series
 A.L.—.988—Seattle .990, New York .985, 1995.
 N.L.—.981—St. Louis .984, Arizona .979, 2001.

Lowest fielding average, series
3-game series
 N.L.—.954—Atlanta vs. St. Louis, 2000.
 A.L.—.955—Cleveland vs. Boston, 1995.
4-game series
 N.L.—.958—Colorado vs. Atlanta, 1995.
 A.L.—.975—Baltimore vs. Cleveland, 1996.
5-game series
 N.L.—.969—Montreal vs. Philadelphia, 1981.
 A.L.—.970—Oakland vs. New York, 2001.

Lowest fielding average by both clubs, series
3-game series
 A.L.—.961—Boston .967, Cleveland .955, 1995.
 N.L.—.969—Atlanta .974, Houston .962, 1997.
4-game series
 N.L.—.972—Atlanta .988, Colorado .958, 1995.
 A.L.—.977—Cleveland .980, Baltimore .975, 1996.
5-game series
 A.L.—.974—New York .978, Oakland .970, 2001.
 N.L.—.976—Philadelphia .984, Montreal .969, 1981.

PUTOUTS

Most putouts, total series
A.L.—961—New York; eight series, 35 games.
N.L.—633—Atlanta; seven series, 23 games.

Most putouts, series
3-game series
 A.L.—93—Cleveland vs. Boston, 1995.
 N.L.—84—Atlanta vs. Los Angeles, 1996.
  Atlanta vs. Chicago, 1998.
4-game series
 N.L.—120—New York vs. San Francisco, 2000.
 A.L.—117—New York vs. Texas, 1996.
5-game series
 A.L.—154—Seattle vs. New York, 1995.
 N.L.—139—Los Angeles vs. Houston, 1981.

Most putouts by both clubs, series
3-game series
 A.L.—182—Cleveland 93, Boston 89, 1995.
 N.L.—165—Atlanta 84, Los Angeles 81, 1996.
4-game series
 N.L.—238—New York 120, San Francisco 118, 2000.
 A.L.—231—New York 117, Texas 114, 1996.
5-game series
 A.L.—304—Seattle 154, New York 150, 1995.
 N.L.—271—Los Angeles 139, Houston 132, 1981.

Fewest putouts, series
3-game series
 N.L.—75—San Diego vs. St. Louis, 1996.
  Houston vs. Atlanta, 1997.
  Atlanta vs. St. Louis, 2000.
 A.L.—75—Texas vs. New York, 1998.
  Texas vs. New York, 1999.
4-game series
 N.L.—102—Houston vs. San Diego, 1998.
 A.L.—105—Seattle vs. Baltimore, 1997.
  Boston vs. Cleveland, 1998.
5-game series
 A.L.—129—Cleveland vs. Boston, 1999.
  Cleveland vs. Seattle, 2001.
 N.L.—131—St. Louis vs. Arizona, 2001.

Fewest putouts by both clubs, series
3-game series
 N.L.—156—St. Louis 81, San Diego 75, 1996.
  Atlanta 81, Houston 75, 1997.
  St. Louis 81, Atlanta 75, 2000.
 A.L.—156—New York 81, Texas 75, 1998.
  New York 81, Texas 75, 1999.
4-game series
 N.L.—208—San Diego 106, Houston 102, 1998.
 A.L.—213—Baltimore 108, Seattle 105, 1997.
  Cleveland 108, Boston 105, 1998.
5-game series
 A.L.—259—Boston 130, Cleveland 129, 1999.
 N.L.—263—Arizona 132, St. Louis 131, 2001.

Most players with one or more putouts, game
N.L.—12—New York vs. Arizona, October 5, 1999.
A.L.—11—Seattle vs. New York, October 4, 1995, 15 innings.
 Baltimore vs. Seattle, October 1, 1997.
 Boston vs. Cleveland, October 10, 1999.
 Cleveland vs. Boston, October 10, 1999.
 Oakland vs. New York, October 7, 2000.

Most players with one or more putouts by both clubs, nine-inning game
A.L.—22—Boston 11, Cleveland 11, October 10, 1999.
N.L.—19
 Los Angeles 10, Houston 9, October 9, 1981.
 Colorado 10, Atlanta 9, October 6, 1995, 10 innings.

Most putouts by outfield, nine-inning game
A.L.—13—New York vs. Texas, October 5, 1999.
N.L.—12—San Francisco vs. Florida, September 30, 1997.

Most putouts by outfield, extra-inning game
N.L.—13—New York vs. San Francisco, October 7, 2000, 13 innings.
A.L.—Less than nine-inning record.

Most putouts by outfield of both clubs, nine-inning game
A.L.—22—New York 12, Seattle 10, October 3, 1995.
N.L.—19
 Philadelphia 11, Montreal 8, October 9, 1981.
 Cincinnati 11, Los Angeles 8, October 4, 1995.

Most putouts by outfield of both clubs, extra-inning game
N.L.—24—San Francisco 13, New York 11, October 7, 2000, 13 innings.
A.L.—Less than nine-inning record.

Fewest putouts by outfield, nine-inning game
N.L.—0—Philadelphia vs. Montreal, October 8, 1981 (fielded
eight innings).
A.L.—2
Baltimore vs. Seattle, October 2, 1997.
Boston vs. Cleveland, October 11, 1999.
Cleveland vs. Seattle, October 9, 2001.
Cleveland vs. Seattle, October 15, 2001 (fielded eight innings).
Oakland vs. New York, October 11, 2001.

Fewest putouts by outfield, extra-inning game
N.L.—4—Colorado vs. Atlanta, October 6, 1981, 10 innings.
A.L.—6—New York vs. Seattle, October 8, 1995, 11 innings.

Fewest putouts by outfield of both clubs, nine-inning game
N.L.—6—Montreal 4, Philadelphia 2, October 7, 1981 (Montreal
fielded eight innings).
A.L.—5—Seattle 3, Cleveland 2, October 15, 2001 (Cleveland
fielded eight innings).

Fewest putouts by outfield of both clubs, extra-inning game
N.L.—9—Atlanta 5, Colorado 4, October 6, 1981, 10 innings.
A.L.—15—Seattle 9, New York 6, October 8, 1995, 11 innings.

Most putouts by outfield, inning
A.L.-N.L.—3—Held by many clubs.

Most putouts by outfield of both clubs, inning
A.L.-N.L.—5—Occurred many times.

Most putouts by catchers of both clubs, inning
A.L.—6—Chicago 3, Seattle 3, October 4, 2000, ninth inning.
N.L.—5—Houston 3, Atlanta 2, October 3, 1997, second inning.

ASSISTS

Most assists, total series
A.L.—339—New York; eight series, 35 games.
N.L.—241—Atlanta; seven series, 23 games.

Most assists, series
3-game series
A.L.—38—Chicago vs. Seattle, 2000.
N.L.—33—Florida vs. San Francisco, 1997.
Atlanta vs. Houston, 1997.
4-game series
N.L.—50—Colorado vs. Atlanta, 1995.
Houston vs. Atlanta, 1999.
A.L.—47—Texas vs. New York, 1996.
5-game series
A.L.—60—Oakland vs. New York, 2001.
N.L.—57—Los Angeles vs. Houston, 1981.

Most assists by both clubs, series
3-game series
A.L.—66—Chicago 38, Seattle 28, 2000.
N.L.—64—Florida 33, San Francisco 31, 1997.
4-game series
N.L.—99—Colorado 50, Atlanta 49, 1995.
A.L.—85—Texas 47, New York 38, 1996.
5-game series
A.L.—113—Cleveland 58, New York 55, 1997.
N.L.—106—Montreal 55, Philadelphia 51, 1981.

Fewest assists, series
3-game series
N.L.—18—St. Louis vs. San Diego, 1996.
A.L.—27—Texas vs. New York, 1999.
4-game series
A.L.—33—Boston vs. Cleveland, 1998.
N.L.—33—New York vs. San Francisco, 2000.
5-game series
A.L.—42—New York vs. Milwaukee, 1981.
Oakland vs. New York, 2000.
New York vs. Oakland, 2001.
N.L.—46—Houston vs. Los Angeles, 1981.

Fewest assists by both clubs, series
3-game series
N.L.—45—Atlanta 25, Chicago 20, 1998.
A.L.—56—New York 29, Texas 27, 1999.

4-game series
N.L.—73—San Francisco 40, New York 33, 2000.
A.L.—76—Cleveland 43, Boston 33, 1998.
5-game series
A.L.—93—Cleveland 48, Boston 45, 1999.
N.L.—103—Los Angeles 57, Houston 46, 1981.

Most assists, nine-inning game
N.L.—21—Atlanta vs. Colorado, October 3, 1995.
A.L.—18—New York vs. Milwaukee, October 9, 1981.

Most assists, extra-inning game
A.L.—21—New York vs. Seattle, October 4, 1995, 15 innings.
N.L.—Less than nine-inning game.

Most assists by both clubs, nine-inning game
N.L.—35—Atlanta 21, Colorado 14, October 3, 1995.
A.L.—32—New York 17, Cleveland 15, October 6, 1997.

Most assists by both clubs, extra-inning game
A.L.—38—New York 21, Seattle 17, October 4, 1995, 15 innings.
N.L.—Less than nine-inning record.

Most players with one or more assists, game
A.L.—9—Cleveland vs. Baltimore, October 2, 1996.
N.L.—8
Colorado vs. Atlanta, October 3, 1995.
St. Louis vs. Arizona, October 12, 2001.

Most players with one or more assists by both clubs, nine-inning game
N.L.—14—Colorado 8, Atlanta 6, October 3, 1995.
A.L.—13—New York 7, Oakland 6, October 15, 2001.

Most players with one or more assists by both clubs, extra-inning game
A.L.—16—New York 8, Seattle 8, October 4, 1995, 15 innings.
N.L.—Less than nine-inning record.

Fewest assists, game
A.L.—4
New York vs. Milwaukee, October 7, 1981.
New York vs. Milwaukee, October 11, 1981.
Cleveland vs. Baltimore, October 5, 1996, 12 innings.
Boston vs. Cleveland, October 2, 1998, fielded eight innings.
N.L.—4
Houston vs. Los Angeles, October 11, 1981, fielded eight
innings.
Los Angeles vs. Cincinnati, October 6, 1995, fielded eight
innings.
Houston vs. Atlanta, September 30, 1997, fielded eight innings.
San Francisco vs. New York, October 4, 2000, fielded eight
innings.

Fewest assists by both clubs, game
N.L.—12
St. Louis 6, San Diego 6, October 3, 1996, San Diego fielded
eight innings.
Atlanta 7, Chicago 5, September 30, 1998, Chicago fielded
eight innings.
A.L.—10— New York 5, Seattle 5, October 8, 1995, 11 innings.

Most assists by outfield, game
A.L.—2
Seattle vs. New York, October 4, 1995, 15 innings.
Cleveland vs. Baltimore, October 2, 1996.
Seattle vs. Baltimore, October 2, 1997.
N.L.—1—Held by many clubs.

Most assists by outfield of both clubs, game
A.L.—3
Seattle 2, New York 1, October 4, 1995, 15 innings.
Seattle 2, Baltimore 1, October 2, 1997.
N.L.—1—Occurred in many games.

Most assists by outfield, inning
A.L.-N.L.—1—Held by many clubs.

CHANCES OFFERED

Fewest chances offered to outfield, nine-inning game
N.L.—0—Philadelphia vs. Montreal, October 8, 1981 (fielded
eight innings).
A.L.—2—Boston vs. Cleveland, October 11, 1999.

Fewest chances offered to outfield, extra-inning game
N.L.—4—Colorado vs. Atlanta, October 6, 1981, 10 innings.
A.L.—6—New York vs. Seattle, October 8, 1995, 11 innings.

Fewest chances offered to outfield of both clubs, nine-inning game
N.L.—6—Montreal 4, Philadelphia 2, October 7, 1981 (Montreal fielded eight innings).
A.L.—7—Boston 4, Cleveland 3, September 30, 1998 (Boston fielded eight innings).

Fewest chances offered to outfield of both clubs, extra-inning game
N.L.—9—Atlanta 5, Colorado 4, October 6, 1981, 10 innings.
A.L.—15—Seattle 9, New York 6, October 8, 1995, 11 innings.

ERRORS

Most errors, total series
A.L.—21—New York; eight series, 35 games.
N.L.—18—Houston; five series, 19 games.

Most errors, series
3-game series
A.L.—6—Cleveland vs. Boston, 1995.
N.L.—5—Atlanta vs. St. Louis, 2000.
4-game series
N.L.—7—Colorado vs. Atlanta, 1995.
A.L.—4—Baltimore vs. Cleveland, 1996.
5-game series
N.L.—6—Montreal vs. Philadelphia, 1981.
A.L.—6—Oakland vs. New York, 2001.

Most errors by both clubs, series
3-game series
A.L.—10—Cleveland 6, Boston 4, 1995.
N.L.—7—Houston 4, Atlanta 3, 1997.
4-game series
N.L.—9—Colorado 7, Atlanta 2, 1995.
A.L.—7—Baltimore 4, Cleveland 3, 1996.
5-game series
A.L.—10—Oakland 6, New York 4, 2001.
N.L.—9—Montreal 6, Philadelphia 3, 1981.

Fewest errors, series
3-game series
N.L.—0—San Francisco vs. Florida, 1997.
Atlanta vs. Chicago, 1998.
A.L.—0—Boston vs. Cleveland, 1998.
4-game series
A.L.—0—Baltimore vs. Seattle, 1997.
N.L.—0—New York vs. Arizona, 1999.
New York vs. San Francisco, 2000.
5-game series
A.L.—2—Seattle vs. New York, 1995.
New York vs. Oakland, 2000.
N.L.—3—Los Angeles vs. Houston, 1981.
Philadelphia vs. Montreal, 1981.
St. Louis vs. Arizona, 2001.

Fewest errors by both clubs, series
3-game series
A.L.—1—Cleveland 1, Boston 0, 1998.
N.L.—4—Atlanta 3, Los Angeles 1, 1996.
Florida 4, San Francisco 0, 1997.
Chicago 4, Atlanta 0, 1998.
Houston 3, Atlanta 1, 2001.
4-game series
A.L.—1—Seattle 1, Baltimore 0, 1997.
N.L.—1—San Francisco 1, New York 0, 2000.
5-game series
A.L.—5—New York 3, Seattle 2, 1995.
N.L.—7—Arizona 4, St. Louis 3, 2001.

Most errors, game
N.L.—4
Montreal vs. Philadelphia, October 9, 1981.
Colorado vs. Atlanta, October 3, 1995.

A.L.—3
Milwaukee vs. New York, October 7, 1981.
Kansas City vs. Oakland, October 9, 1981.
Seattle vs. Cleveland, October 13, 2001.
Oakland vs. New York, October 15, 2001.

Most errors by both clubs, game
N.L.—5—Colorado 4, Atlanta 1, October 3, 1995.
A.L.—4
Milwaukee 3, New York 1, October 7, 1981.
Boston 2, Cleveland 2, October 3, 1995, 13 innings.
Oakland 3, New York 1, October 15, 2001.

Most errors by infield, game
N.L.—3—Houston vs. Los Angeles, October 11, 1981.
A.L.—2—Held by many clubs.

Most errors by infields of both clubs, game
N.L.—5—Houston 3, Los Angeles 2, October 11, 1981.
A.L.—2—Occurred many times.

Most errors by outfield, game
N.L.—2—Atlanta vs. Los Angeles, October 3, 1996.
A.L.—1—Held by many clubs.

Most errors by outfields of both clubs, game
N.L.—2
Atlanta 1, Colorado 1, October 3, 1995.
Cincinnati 1, Los Angeles 1, October 6, 1995.
Atlanta 2, Los Angeles 0, October 3, 1996.
A.L.—1—Occurred many times.

Longest errorless game
A.L.—15 innings—New York vs. Seattle, October 4, 1995.
N.L.—13 innings
New York vs. San Francisco, October 7, 2000.
San Francisco vs. New York, October 7, 2000.

Longest errorless game by both clubs
A.L.—11 innings—New York 0, Seattle 0, October 8, 1995.
N.L.—13 innings—New York 0, San Francisco 0, October 7, 2000.

Most errors, inning
A.L.—3—Kansas City vs. Oakland, October 9, 1981, third inning.
N.L.—2
Montreal vs. Philadelphia, October 9, 1981, eighth inning.
Colorado vs. Atlanta, October 3, 1995, sixth inning.
Atlanta vs. St. Louis, October 3, 2000, first inning.

PASSED BALLS

Most passed balls, total series
A.L.—7—Boston; three series, 12 games.
N.L.—2—San Diego; two series, seven games.

Most passed balls, series
A.L.—3—Boston vs. Cleveland, 1999 (5-game series).
N.L.—2—San Diego vs. Houston, 1998 (4-game series).

Most passed balls by both clubs, series
A.L.—3—Boston 3, Cleveland 0, 1999 (5-game series).
N.L.—2—San Diego 2, Houston 0, 1998 (4-game series).

Most passed balls, game
N.L.—2—San Diego vs. Houston, September 29, 1998.
A.L.—2
Boston vs. Cleveland, September 30, 1998.
Boston vs. Cleveland, October 10, 1999.

DOUBLE AND TRIPLE PLAYS

Most double plays, total series
A.L.—28—New York; eight series, 35 games.
N.L.—19—Atlanta; seven series, 23 games.

Most double plays, series
3-game series
N.L.—7—Houston vs. Atlanta, 2001.
A.L.—5—New York vs. Texas, 1999.
Seattle vs. Chicago, 2000.
Chicago vs. Seattle, 2000.

-game series
  A.L.—6—Cleveland vs. New York, 1997.
  N.L.—5—Atlanta vs. Colorado, 1995.
      Colorado vs. Atlanta, 1995.
      San Diego vs. Houston, 1998.
      New York vs. Arizona, 1999.
-game series
  A.L.—7—New York vs. Oakland, 2000.
  N.L.—5—Montreal vs. Philadelphia, 1981.

lost double plays by both clubs, series

-game series
  N.L.—12—Houston 7, Atlanta 5, 2001.
  A.L.—10—Seattle 5, Chicago 5, 2000.
-game series
  N.L.—10—Atlanta 5, Colorado 5, 1995.
  A.L.—8—Texas 5, New York 3, 1996.
      Cleveland 6, New York 2, 1997.
-game series
  A.L.—10—New York 7, Oakland 3, 2000.
  N.L.—8—Arizona 4, St. Louis 4, 2001.

ewest double plays, series

-game series
  A.L.—0—Boston vs. Cleveland, 1995.
  N.L.—0—St. Louis vs. San Diego, 1996.
      Atlanta vs. St. Louis, 2000.
-game series
  A.L.—1—Cleveland vs. Baltimore, 1996.
  N.L.—1—Houston vs. San Diego, 1998.
      New York vs. San Francisco, 2000.
-game series
  A.L.—1—New York vs. Milwaukee, 1981.
      Baltimore vs. Seattle, 1997.
  N.L.—1—Houston vs. Los Angeles, 1981.

Fewest double plays by both clubs, series

3-game series
  A.L.—1—Cleveland 1, Boston 0, 1995.
  N.L.—2—St. Louis 2, Atlanta 0, 2000.
4-game series
  A.L.—3—Baltimore 2, Cleveland 1, 1996.
  N.L.—5—San Francisco 4, New York 1, 2000.
5-game series
  A.L.—4—Seattle 3, Baltimore 1, 1997.
  N.L.—7—Montreal 5, Philadelphia 2, 1981.

Most double plays, game

N.L.—4
  Atlanta vs. Colorado, October 3, 1995.
  Houston vs. Atlanta, October 10, 2001.
A.L.—3
  Milwaukee vs. New York, October 11, 1981.
  Texas vs. New York, October 4, 1996.
  Cleveland vs. New York, September 30, 1997.
  Chicago vs. Seattle, October 4, 2000.
  Seattle vs. Chicago, October 6, 2000.

Most double plays by both clubs, game

N.L.—7—Houston 4, Atlanta 3, October 10, 2001.
A.L.—4
  Cleveland 3, New York 1, September 30, 1997.
  New York 2, Texas 2, October 2, 1998.
  Chicago 3, Seattle 1, October 4, 2000.

Most triple plays, series

A.L.-N.L.—Never accomplished.

MISCELLANEOUS

CLUB AND DIVISION
ONE-RUN DECISIONS

Most one-run games won, series
A.L.—2
New York vs. Texas, 1996 (4-game series).
Cleveland vs. New York, 1997 (5-game series).
Cleveland vs. Boston, 1998 (4-game series).
N.L.—2
Atlanta vs. Los Angeles, 1996 (3-game series).
Florida vs. San Francisco, 1997 (3-game series).
San Diego vs. Houston, 1998 (4-game series).
New York vs. San Francisco, 2000 (4-game series).
Arizona vs. St. Louis, 2001 (5-game series).

Most one-run games by both clubs, series
N.L.—3—San Diego (won two) vs. Houston (won one), 1998
(4-game series).
A.L.—2
New York (won two) vs. Texas, 1996 (4-game series).
Cleveland (won two) vs. New York, 1997 (5-game series).
Cleveland (won two) vs. Boston, 1998 (4-game series).

LENGTH OF GAMES
BY INNINGS

Longest game
A.L.—15 innings—New York 7, Seattle 5, October 4, 1995 (at
Seattle).
N.L.—13 innings—New York 3, San Francisco 2, October 7,
2000 (at New York).

**For a complete list of extra-inning games,
see page 388.**

Most extra-inning games, total series
N.L.—4—Atlanta; seven series, 23 games; won three, lost one.
A.L.—3—New York; eight series, 35 games; won two, lost one.
Seattle; four series, 17 games; won two, lost one.

Most extra-inning games won, total series
N.L.—3—Atlanta; seven series, 23 games; lost one.
New York; two series, 15 games; lost none.
A.L.—2—New York; eight series, 35 games; lost none.
Seattle; four series, 17 games; lost one.

Most extra-inning games lost, total series
N.L.—2—Los Angeles; three series, 11 games; won none.
San Francisco; two series, seven games; won none.
A.L.—1—Held by many clubs.

Most extra-inning games, series
A.L.—2—New York vs. Seattle, 1995 (5-game series).
N.L.—1—Occurred often.

BY TIME

Longest nine-inning game
A.L.—4 hours, 13 minutes—New York 9, Oakland 2 October 14,
2001 (at Oakland).
N.L.—3 hours, 36 minutes—Arizona 5, St. Louis 3, October 12,
2001 (at St. Louis).

Longest extra-inning game
N.L.—5 hours, 22 minutes—New York 3, San Francisco 2,
October 7, 2000, 13 innings (at New York).
A.L.—5 hours, 13 minutes—New York 7, Seattle 5, October 4,
1995, 15 innings (at New York).

Shortest game
N.L.—2 hours, 0 minutes—Los Angeles 2, Houston 1, October
10, 1981 (at Los Angeles).
A.L.—2 hours, 27 minutes—Cleveland 4, Boston 3, October 2,
1998 (at Boston).

SERIES STARTING AND FINISHING DATES

Earliest date for series game
N.L.—September 29, 1998—San Diego at Houston.
A.L.—September 29, 1998—Texas at New York.
September 29, 1998—Boston at Cleveland.

Earliest date for series final game
A.L.—October 2, 1998—New York at Texas (3-game series).
N.L.—October 3, 1997—Florida at San Francisco (3-game series).
October 3, 1997—Atlanta at Houston (3-game series).
October 3, 1998—Atlanta at Chicago (3-game series).

Latest date for series start
A.L.—October 10, 2001—Oakland at New York.
N.L.—October 9, 2001—Atlanta at Houston.
October 9, 2001—St. Louis at Arizona.

Latest date for series finish
A.L.—October 15, 2001—Oakland at New York (5-game series).
October 15, 2001—Cleveland at Seattle (5-game series).
N.L.—October 14, 2001—St. Louis at Arizona (5-game series).

SERIES AND GAMES WON

Most series won
N.L.—6—Atlanta, 1995, 1996, 1997, 1998, 1999, 2001 (lost one).
A.L.—6—New York, 1981, 1996, 1998, 1999, 2000, 2001 (lost
two).

**For complete lists of results, and series
played by all teams, see page 387.**

Most times winning series in three consecutive games
N.L.—4—Atlanta, 1996, 1997, 1998, 2001.
A.L.—2—New York, 1998, 1999.

Winning series after winning first game
N.L.—Accomplished 13 times.
A.L—Accomplished eight times.

Winning series after losing first game
A.L.—Accomplished eight times.
N.L.—Accomplished three times.

Winning series after trailing two games to one
N.L.—Los Angeles vs. Houston, 1981 (5-game series).
A.L.—Seattle vs. New York, 1995 (5-game series).
Cleveland vs. New York, 1997 (5-game series).
Boston vs. Cleveland, 1999 (5-game series).
New York vs. Oakland, 2001 (5-game series).
Seattle vs. Cleveland, 2001 (5-game series).

Winning series after losing first two games
N.L.—Los Angeles vs. Houston, 1981 (5-game series).
A.L.—Seattle vs. New York, 1995 (5-game series).
Boston vs. Cleveland, 1999 (5-game series).
New York vs. Oakland, 2001 (5-game series).

Most games won, total series
A.L.—22—New York; eight series; won 22, lost 13.
N.L.—18—Atlanta; seven series; won 18, lost 5.

**For complete lists of results, and games
played by all teams, see page 387.**

Most consecutive games won, total series
N.L.—10—Atlanta, 1995 (last one), 1996 (all three), 1997 (all
three), 1998 (all three).
A.L.—6—New York, 1998 (all three), 1999 (all three).

SERIES AND GAMES LOST

Most series lost
N.L.—5—Houston, 1981, 1997, 1998, 1999, 2001 (won none).
A.L.—3
Texas, 1996, 1998, 1999 (won none).
Cleveland, 1996, 1999, 2001 (won three).

For complete lists of results, and games played by all teams, see page 387.

Most games lost, total series
N.L.—15—Houston, five series; won 4, lost 15.
A.L.—13—New York; eight series; won 22, lost 13.

Most consecutive games lost, total series
A.L.—9—Texas, 1996 (last three), 1998 (all three), 1999 (all three).
N.L.—7—Houston, 1981 (last three), 1997 (all three), 1998 (first one).

ATTENDANCE

Largest attendance, series
3-game series
A.L.—164,853—New York vs. Texas, 1999.
N.L.—164,844—St. Louis vs. San Diego, 1996.
4-game series
N.L.—225,763—San Diego vs. Houston, 1998.
A.L.—216,791—Baltimore vs. Seattle, 1997.
5-game series
A.L.—286,839—New York vs. Seattle, 1995.
N.L.—246,016—Houston vs. Los Angeles, 1981.

For a list of attendance each series, see page 388.

Smallest attendance, series
3-game series
N.L.—111,180—Atlanta vs. Houston, 2001.
A.L.—120,868—Kansas City vs. Oakland, 1981.
4-game series
A.L.—157,065—Cleveland vs. Boston, 1998.
N.L.—178,210—Atlanta vs. Houston, 1999.
5-game series
A.L.—202,917—Boston vs. Cleveland, 1999.
N.L.—203,260—Montreal vs. Philadelphia, 1981.

Largest attendance, game
N.L.—65,235—At San Diego, October 3, 1998 (San Diego 2, Houston 1).
A.L.—59,579—At Seattle, October 1, 1997 (Baltimore 9, Seattle 3).

Smallest attendance, game
A.L.—26,395—At Milwaukee, October 8, 1981 (New York 3, Milwaukee 0).
N.L.—34,327—At Montreal, October 7, 1981 (Montreal 3, Philadelphia 1).

Largest attendance by each club, game

AMERICAN LEAGUE

Club	Attendance	Date
Baltimore	49,137	Oct. 4, 1997
Boston	34,211	Oct. 6, 1995
Chicago	45,383	Oct. 4, 2000
Cleveland	45,274	Oct. 4, 1997
Kansas City	40,592	Oct. 6, 1981
Milwaukee	35,064	Oct. 7, 1981
New York	57,485	Oct. 7, 1999
Oakland	55,861	Oct. 13, 2001
Seattle	59,579	Oct. 1, 1997
Texas	50,860	Oct. 4, 1996

NATIONAL LEAGUE

Club	Attendance	Date
Arizona	49,584	Oct. 5, 1999
Atlanta	52,529	Oct. 5, 1996
Chicago	39,597	Oct. 3, 1998
Cincinnati	53,276	Oct. 6, 1995
Colorado	50,063	Oct. 4, 1995
Florida	42,167	Sept. 30, 1997
Houston	53,688	Oct. 3, 1997
Los Angeles	55,983	Oct. 10, 1981
Montreal	45,896	Oct. 8, 1981
New York	56,270	Oct. 7, 2000
Philadelphia	47,384	Oct. 11, 1981
St. Louis	56,752	Oct. 3, 1996
San Diego	65,235	Oct. 3, 1998
San Francisco	57,188	Oct. 3, 1997

Smallest attendance by each club, game

AMERICAN LEAGUE

Club	Attendance	Date
Baltimore	47,644	Oct. 1, 1996
Boston	33,114	Oct. 2, 1998
Chicago	45,290	Oct. 3, 2000
Cleveland	44,218	Oct. 3, 1995
Kansas City	40,274	Oct. 7, 1981
Milwaukee	26,395	Oct. 8, 1981
New York	47,505	Oct. 11, 1981
Oakland	40,002	Oct. 9, 1981
Seattle	47,867	Oct. 15, 2001
Texas	49,950	Oct. 2, 1998

NATIONAL LEAGUE

Club	Attendance	Date
Arizona	41,793	Oct. 10, 2001
Atlanta	39,119	Oct. 5, 1999
Chicago	39,597	Oct. 3, 1998
Cincinnati	53,276	Oct. 6, 1995
Colorado	50,040	Oct. 3, 1995
Florida	41,283	Oct. 1, 1997
Houston	35,553	Oct. 9, 2001
Los Angeles	44,199	Oct. 3, 1995
Montreal	34,327	Oct. 7, 1981
New York	52,888	Oct. 8, 2000
Philadelphia	36,835	Oct. 9, 1981
St. Louis	52,378	Oct. 3, 2000
San Diego	53,899	Oct. 5, 1996
San Francisco	40,430	Oct. 4, 2000
		Oct. 5, 2000

NON-PLAYING PERSONNEL

MANAGERS

Most series by manager
N.L.—7—Bobby Cox, Atlanta, 1995 through 2001; won six, lost one.
A.L.—6—Joe Torre, New York, 1996 through 2001; won five, lost one.

For a complete list of managers and their records, see page 392.

Most division series winners managed
N.L.—6—Bobby Cox, Atlanta, 1995, 1996, 1997, 1998, 1999, 2001; lost one.
A.L.—5—Joe Torre, New York, 1996, 1998, 1999, 2000, 2001; lost one.

Most division series losers managed
N.L.—4—Larry Dierker, Houston, 1997, 1998, 1999, 2001; won none.
A.L.—3—Johnny Oates, Texas, 1996, 1998, 1999; won none.

Most different clubs managed, major leagues
2—
Dave Johnson, Cincinnati N.L., 1995; Baltimore A.L., 1996, 1997.
Buck Showalter, New York A.L., 1995; Arizona N.L., 1999.

Most different clubs managed, league
A.L.-N.L.—1—Held by many managers.

UMPIRES

Most series umpired
N.L.—6—Bruce Froemming, 1981, 1995, 1996, 1998, 1999, 2001; 24 games.
A.L.—4
Joe Brinkman, 1981, 1995, 1998, 1999; 15 games.
Mike Reilly, 1981, 1995, 1999, 2000; 17 games.
Rocky Roe, 1995, 1997, 1999, 2000; 18 games.
Tim Welke, 1995, 1996, 1999, 2000; 17 games.

Most games umpired
N.L.—24—Bruce Froemming, six series.
A.L.—18—Rocky Roe, four series.

DIVISION SERIES *Non-playing personnel*

GENERAL REFERENCE

RESULTS
YEAR BY YEAR

*Wild-card team.

AMERICAN LEAGUE

Year	Winner	Loser	Games
1981	New York (East)	Milwaukee (East)	3-2
	Oakland (West)	Kansas City (West)	3-0
1995	Cleveland (Central)	Boston (East)	3-0
	Seattle (West)	New York* (East)	3-2
1996	Baltimore* (East)	Cleveland (Central)	3-1
	New York (East)	Texas (West)	3-1
1997	Baltimore (East)	Seattle (West)	3-1
	Cleveland (Central)	New York* (East)	3-2
1998	Cleveland (Central)	Boston* (East)	3-1
	New York (East)	Texas (West)	3-0
1999	Boston* (East)	Cleveland (Central)	3-2
	New York (East)	Texas (West)	3-0
2000	Seattle* (West)	Chicago (Central)	3-0
	New York (East)	Oakland (West)	3-2
2001	Seattle (West)	Cleveland (Central)	3-2
	New York (East)	Oakland (West)*	3-2

NATIONAL LEAGUE

Year	Winner	Loser	Games
1981	Montreal (East)	Philadelphia (East)	3-2
	Los Angeles (West)	Houston (West)	3-2
1995	Atlanta (East)	Colorado* (West)	3-1
	Cincinnati (Central)	Los Angeles (West)	3-0
1996	Atlanta (East)	Los Angeles* (West)	3-0
	St. Louis (Central)	San Diego (West)	3-0
1997	Atlanta (East)	Houston (Central)	3-0
	Florida* (East)	San Francisco (West)	3-0
1998	San Diego (West)	Houston (Central)	3-1
	Atlanta (East)	Chicago* (Central)	3-0
1999	Atlanta (East)	Houston (Central)	3-1
	New York* (East)	Arizona (West)	3-1
2000	St. Louis (Central)	Atlanta (East)	3-0
	New York* (East)	San Francisco (West)	3-1
2001	Arizona (West)	St. Louis (Central)*	3-2
	Atlanta (East)	Houston (Central)	3-0

SERIES WON AND LOST BY TEAMS
AMERICAN LEAGUE

	W	L	Pct.
Baltimore	2	0	1.000
New York	6	2	.750
Seattle	3	1	.750
Cleveland	3	3	.500
Boston	1	2	.333
Oakland	1	2	.333
Chicago	0	1	.000
Kansas City	0	1	.000
Milwaukee	0	1	.000
Texas	0	3	.000
Totals	16	16	.500

NATIONAL LEAGUE

	W	L	Pct.
New York	2	0	1.000
Cincinnati	1	0	1.000
Florida	1	0	1.000
Montreal	1	0	1.000
Atlanta	6	1	.857
St. Louis	2	1	.667
Arizona	1	1	.500
San Diego	1	1	.500
Los Angeles	1	2	.333
Chicago	0	1	.000
Colorado	0	1	.000

	W	L	Pct.
Philadelphia	0	1	.000
San Francisco	0	2	.000
Houston	0	5	.000
Totals	16	16	.500

GAMES WON AND LOST BY TEAMS
AMERICAN LEAGUE

	W	L	Pct.
Baltimore	6	2	.750
New York	22	13	.629
Seattle	10	7	.588
Cleveland	14	12	.538
Oakland	7	6	.538
Milwaukee	2	3	.400
Boston	4	8	.333
Texas	1	9	.100
Chicago	0	3	.000
Kansas City	0	3	.000
Totals	66	66	.500

NATIONAL LEAGUE

	W	L	Pct.
Cincinnati	3	0	1.000
Florida	3	0	1.000
Atlanta	18	5	.783
New York	6	2	.750
St. Louis	8	3	.727
Montreal	3	2	.600
Arizona	4	5	.444
San Diego	3	4	.429
Philadelphia	2	3	.400
Los Angeles	3	8	.273
Colorado	1	3	.250
Houston	4	15	.211
San Francisco	1	6	.143
Chicago	0	3	.000
Totals	59	59	.500

HOME AND ROAD GAMES BY TEAMS
AMERICAN LEAGUE

	Years	Games	Home	Away
New York	8	35	18	17
Cleveland	6	26	14	12
Seattle	4	17	9	8
Oakland	3	13	6	7
Boston	3	12	5	7
Texas	3	10	4	6
Baltimore	2	8	4	4
Milwaukee	1	5	2	3
Chicago	1	3	2	1
Kansas City	1	3	2	1
Totals	7	132	66	66

NATIONAL LEAGUE

	Years	Games	Home	Away
Atlanta	7	23	11	12
Houston	5	19	9	10
Los Angeles	3	11	7	4
St. Louis	3	11	6	5
Arizona	2	9	5	4
New York	2	8	4	4
San Diego	2	7	3	4
San Francisco	2	7	3	4
Philadelphia	1	5	3	2
Montreal	1	5	2	3
Colorado	1	4	2	2
Chicago	1	3	1	2
Cincinnati	1	3	1	2
Florida	1	3	2	1
Totals	7	118	59	59

SHUTOUTS

AMERICAN LEAGUE

Oct. 6, 1981	Mike Norris, Oakland 4, Kansas City 0 (four hits).
Oct. 8, 1981	Dave Righetti, Ron Davis and Rich Gossage, New York 3, Milwaukee 0 (seven hits).
Oct. 4, 1995	Orel Hershiser, Julian Tavarez, Paul Assenmacher and Jose Mesa, Cleveland 4, Boston 0 (three hits).
Sept. 29, 1998	David Wells and Mariano Rivera, New York 2, Texas 0 (five hits).
Oct. 2, 1998	David Cone, Graeme Lloyd, Jeff Nelson and Mariano Rivera, New York 4, Texas 0 (three hits).
Oct. 5, 1999	Orlando Hernandez and Jeff Nelson, New York 8, Texas 0 (two hits).
Oct. 9, 1999	Roger Clemens, Jeff Nelson and Mariano Rivera, New York 3, Texas 0 (five hits).
Oct. 4, 2000	Andy Pettitte and Mariano Rivera, New York 4, Oakland 0 (six hits).
Oct. 9, 2001	Bartolo Colon and Bob Wickman, Cleveland 5, Seattle 0 (six hits).
Oct. 11, 2001	Tim Hudson and Jason Isringhausen, Oakland 2, New York 0 (seven hits).
Oct. 13, 2001	Mike Mussina and Mariano Rivera, New York 1, Oakland 0 (six hits).

Total number of shutouts: 11

NATIONAL LEAGUE

Oct. 7, 1981	Joe Niekro, Dave Smith and Joe Sambito, Houston 1, Los Angeles 0, 11 innings (nine hits).
Oct. 11, 1981	Jerry Reuss, Los Angeles 4, Houston 0 (five hits).
Oct. 11, 1981	Steve Rogers, Montreal 3, Philadelphia 0 (six hits).
Oct. 8, 2000	Bobby J. Jones, New York 4, San Francisco 0 (one hit).
Oct. 9, 2001	Curt Schilling, Arizona 1, St. Louis 0 (three hits).
Oct. 10, 2001	Tom Glavine and John Smoltz, Atlanta 1, Houston 0 (seven hits).

Total number of shutouts: 6

EXTRA-INNING GAMES

AMERICAN LEAGUE

Oct. 3, 1995	13 innings, Cleveland 5, Boston 4.
Oct. 4, 1995	15 innings, New York 7, Seattle 5.
Oct. 8, 1995	11 innings, Seattle 6, New York 5.
Oct. 2, 1996	12 innings, New York 5, Texas 4.
Oct. 5, 1996	12 innings, Baltimore 4, Cleveland 3.
Oct. 3, 2000	10 innings, Seattle 7, Chicago 4

Total number of extra-inning games: 6

NATIONAL LEAGUE

Oct. 7, 1981	11 innings, Houston 1, Los Angeles 0.
Oct. 10, 1981	10 innings, Philadelphia 6, Montreal 5.
Oct. 6, 1995	10 innings, Colorado 7, Atlanta 5.
Oct. 2, 1996	10 innings, Atlanta 2, Los Angeles 1.
Oct. 1, 1998	10 innings, Atlanta 2, Chicago 1.
Oct. 8, 1999	12 innings, Atlanta 5, Houston 3.
Oct. 9, 1999	10 innings, New York 4, Arizona 3.
Oct. 5, 2000	10 innings, New York 5, San Francisco 4.
Oct. 7, 2000	13 innings, New York 3, San Francisco 2.

Total number of extra-inning games: 9

ATTENDANCE

AMERICAN LEAGUE

Year	Series	Games	Total	Series	Games	Total
1981	N.Y.-Mil.	5	215,212	Oak.-K.C.	3	120,868
1995	Cle.-Bos.	3	122,693	Sea.-N.Y.	5	286,839
1996	Bal.-Cle.	4	185,144	N.Y.-Tex.	4	215,287
1997	Bal.-Sea.	4	216,791	Cle.-N.Y.	5	250,466
1998	Cle.-Bos.	4	157,065	N.Y.-Tex.	3	164,672
1999	Bos.-Cle.	5	202,917	N.Y.-Tex.	3	164,853
2000	Sea.-Chi.	3	138,683	N.Y.-Oak.	5	249,911
2001	Sea.-Cle.	5	234,046	N.Y.-Oak.	5	269,565

NATIONAL LEAGUE

Year	Series	Games	Total	Series	Games	Total
1981	L.A.-Hou.	5	246,016	Mon.-Phi.	5	203,260
1995	Cin.-L.A.	3	143,526	Atl.-Col.	4	201,430
1996	Atl.-L.A.	3	151,873	St.L.-S.D.	3	164,844
1997	Fla.-S.F.	3	140,638	Atl.-Hou.	3	149,355
1998	S.D.-Hou.	4	225,763	Atl.-Chi.	3	136,908
1999	N.Y.-Ari.	4	211,269	Atl.-Hou.	4	178,210
2000	N.Y.-S.F.	4	190,018	St.L.-Atl.	3	154,665
2001	Atl.-Hou.	3	111,180	Ari.-St.L.	5	231,321

INDIVIDUAL BATTING

LEADING BATTERS

(Playing in all games, each series, with four or more hits)

AMERICAN LEAGUE

Year	Player, Club	AB	H	TB	Avg.
1981	Oscar Gamble, New York	9	5	12	.556
1995	Luis Alicea, Boston	10	6	10	.600
1996	Bernie Williams, New York	15	7	16	.467
1997	Omar Vizquel, Cleveland	18	9	9	.500
1998	John Valentin, Boston	15	7	8	.467
1999	Mike Stanley, Boston	20	10	14	.500
2000	Herbert Perry, Chicago	9	4	5	.444
2001	Ichiro Suzuki, Seattle	20	12	13	.600

NATIONAL LEAGUE

Year	Player, Club	AB	H	TB	Avg.
1981	Keith Moreland, Philadelphia	13	6	9	.462
1995	Dante Bichette, Colorado	17	10	16	.588
1996	Ron Gant, St. Louis	10	4	8	.400
1997	Gary Sheffield, Florida	9	5	9	.556
1998	Carlos Hernandez, San Diego	12	5	5	.417
1999	Bret Boone, Atlanta	19	9	10	.474
2000	Jim Edmonds, St. Louis	14	8	18	.571
2001	Andruw Jones, Atlanta	12	6	9	.500

.450 HITTERS

(Playing in all games and having nine or more at-bats)

AMERICAN LEAGUE

Player, Club	Year	AB	H	TB	Avg.
Ichiro Suzuki, Seattle	2001	20	12	13	.600
Luis Alicea, Boston	1995	10	6	10	.600
Edgar Martinez, Seattle	1995	21	12	21	.571
Oscar Gamble, New York	1981	9	5	12	.556
Tony Armas, Oakland	1981	11	6	8	.545
Dwayne Murphy, Oakland	1981	11	6	10	.545
Omar Vizquel, Cleveland	1997	18	9	9	.500
Bernie Williams, New York	1996	15	7	16	.467
John Valentin, Boston	1998	15	7	8	.467
Jay Buhner, Seattle	1995	24	11	15	.458
Derek Jeter, New York	1999	11	5	8	.455

Total number of occurrences: 11

NATIONAL LEAGUE

Player, Club	Year	AB	H	TB	Avg.
Dante Bichette, Colorado	1995	17	10	16	.588
Jim Edmonds, St. Louis	2000	14	8	18	.571
Gary Sheffield, Florida	1997	9	5	9	.556
Marquis Grissom, Atlanta	1995	21	11	22	.524
Mike Stanley, Boston	1999	20	10	14	.500
Chad Fonville, Los Angeles	1995	12	6	6	.500
Eric Karros, Los Angeles	1995	12	6	13	.500
Andruw Jones, Atlanta	2001	12	6	9	.500
Hal Morris, Cincinnati	1995	10	5	6	.500
Bret Boone, Atlanta	1999	19	9	10	.474
Ken Caminiti, Houston	1999	17	8	17	.471
Brian Jordan, Atlanta	1999	17	8	12	.471
Vinny Castilla, Colorado	1995	15	7	17	.467
Ryan Klesko, Atlanta	1995	15	7	8	.467
Keith Moreland, Philadelphia	1981	13	6	9	.462

Total number of occurrences: 14

AMERICAN LEAGUE

1981—6—New York (East), Oscar Gamble 2, Reggie Jackson 2, Rick Cerone, Lou Piniella.
3—Milwaukee (East), Paul Molitor, Ted Simmons, Gorman Thomas.
3—Oakland (West), Wayne Gross, Dave McKay, Dwayne Murphy.
0—Kansas City (West), None.
1995—11—Seattle (West), Ken Griffey Jr. 5, Edgar Martinez 2, Jay Buhner, Vince Coleman, Joey Cora, Tino Martinez.
11—New York (East), Paul O'Neill 3, Ruben Sierra 2, Bernie Williams 2, Wade Boggs, Jim Leyritz, Don Mattingly, Mike Stanley.
4—Cleveland (Central), Albert Belle, Eddie Murray, Tony Pena, Jim Thome.
3—Boston (East), Luis Alicea, Tim Naehring, John Valentin.
1996—9—Baltimore (East), B.J. Surhoff 3, Brady Anderson 2, Bobby Bonilla 2, Roberto Alomar, Rafael Palmeiro.
4—Cleveland (Central), Albert Belle 2, Manny Ramirez 2.
6—Texas (West), Juan Gonzalez 5, Dean Palmer.
4—New York (East), Bernie Williams 3, Cecil Fielder.
1997—4—Cleveland (Central), Sandy Alomar 2, David Justice, Matt Williams.
6—New York (East), Derek Jeter 2, Paul O'Neill 2, Tino Martinez, Tim Raines Sr.
6—Baltimore (East), German Berroa 2, Brady Anderson, Harold Baines, Chris Hoiles, Jeff Reboulet.
6—Seattle (West), Jay Buhner 2, Edgar Martinez 2, Alex Rodriguez, Paul Sorrento.
1998—4—New York (East), Shane Spencer 2, Scott Brosius, Paul O'Neill.
0—Texas (West), None.
7—Cleveland (Central), Kenny Lofton 2, Manny Ramirez 2, Jim Thome 2, David Justice.
5—Boston (East), Nomar Garciaparra 3, Mo Vaughn 2.
1999—2—New York (East), Darryl Strawberry, Bernie Williams.
1—Texas (West), Juan Gonzalez.
10—Boston (East), John Valentin 3, Nomar Garciaparra 2, Troy O'Leary 2, Brian Daubach, Jose Offerman, Jason Varitek.
7—Cleveland (Central), Jim Thome 4, Harold Baines, Wil Cordero, Travis Fryman.
2000—1—New York (East), David Justice.
2—Oakland (West), Terrence Long, Olmedo Saenz.
4—Seattle (West), Jay Buhner, Edgar Martinez, John Olerud, Joe Oliver.
1—Chicago (Central), Ray Durham.
2001—4—Seattle (West), Edgar Martinez 2, David Bell, Mike Cameron.
5—Cleveland (Central), Juan Gonzalez 2, Ellis Burks, Kenny Lofton, Jim Thome.
3—New York (East), David Justice, Tino Martinez, Jorge Posada.
4—Oakland (West), Terrence Long 2, Ron Gant, Jason Giambi.
Total number of home runs: 146

NATIONAL LEAGUE

1981—4—Philadelphia (East), Gary Matthews, Keith Moreland, Mike Schmidt, George Vukovich.
2—Montreal (East), Gary Carter 2.
3—Los Angeles (West), Steve Garvey 2, Pedro Guerrero.
2—Houston (West), Alan Ashby, Art Howe.
1995—7—Atlanta (East), Marquis Grissom 3, Chipper Jones 2, Fred McGriff 2.
6—Colorado (West), Vinny Castilla 3, Dante Bichette, Larry Walker, Eric Young.
5—Cincinnati (Central), Bret Boone, Ron Gant, Mark Lewis, Reggie Sanders, Benito Santiago.
3—Los Angeles (West), Eric Karros 2, Mike Piazza.
1996—5—Atlanta (East), Jermaine Dye, Chipper Jones, Ryan Klesko, Javy Lopez, Fred McGriff.
0—Los Angeles (West), None.

4—San Diego (West), Ken Caminiti 3, Rickey Henderson.
3—St. Louis (Central), Gary Gaetti, Ron Gant, Brian Jordan.
1997—3—Atlanta (East), Jeff Blauser, Chipper Jones, Ryan Klesko.
1—Houston (Central), Chuck Carr.
4—Florida (East), Bobby Bonilla, Charles Johnson, Gary Sheffield, Devon White.
4—San Francisco (West), Jeff Kent 2, Brian Johnson, Bill Mueller.
1998—5—San Diego (West), Jim Leyritz 3, Wally Joyner, Greg Vaughn.
1—Houston (Central), Derek Bell.
4—Atlanta (East), Ryan Klesko, Javy Lopez, Eddie Perez, Michael Tucker.
1—Chicago (Central), Tyler Houston.
1999—1—Atlanta (East), Brian Jordan.
5—Houston (Central), Ken Caminiti 3, Tony Eusebio, Daryle Ward.
5—New York (East), Edgardo Alfonzo 3, John Olerud, Todd Pratt.
4—Arizona (West), Greg Colbrunn, Erubiel Durazo, Luis Gonzalez, Turner Ward.
2000—3—New York (East), Benny Agbayani, Edgardo Alfonzo, Robin Ventura.
2—San Francisco (West), Ellis Burks, J.T. Snow.
6—St. Louis (Central), Jim Edmonds 2, Will Clark, Carlos Hernandez, Mark McGwire, Fernando Vina.
1—Atlanta (East), Andruw Jones.
Total number of home runs: 112

BOTH LEAGUES

Player	Series	No.
Jim Leyritz	4	4

Total number of players: 1

AMERICAN LEAGUE

Player	Series	No.
Juan Gonzalez	4	8
Jim Thome	6	8
Edgar Martinez	4	7
Paul O'Neill	7	6
Bernie Williams	7	6
Nomar Garciaparra	2	5
Ken Griffey Jr.	2	5
David Justice	4	5
John Valentin	3	4
Jay Buhner	4	4
Manny Ramirez	5	4

Total number of players: 11

NATIONAL LEAGUE

Player	Series	No.
Ken Caminiti	4	6
Chipper Jones	7	6
Edgardo Alfonzo	2	4
Vinny Castilla	2	4
Jim Edmonds	2	4

Total number of players: 5

BOTH LEAGUES

Pitcher, Club	Yrs.	W	L
David Wells, Cincinnati N.L., Baltimore A.L., New York A.L.	4	4	0
Armando Benitez, Baltimore A.L., New York N.L.	4	3	0

Total number of pitchers: 2

AMERICAN LEAGUE

Pitcher, Club	Yrs.	W	L
David Wells, Baltimore, New York	3	3	0
Charles Nagy, Cleveland	5	3	2
Andy Pettitte, New York	7	3	3

Total number of pitchers: 3

NATIONAL LEAGUE

Pitcher, Club	Yrs.	W	L
John Smoltz, Atlanta	6	4	0
Greg Maddux, Atlanta	7	4	2
Tom Glavine, Atlanta	7	3	1

Total number of pitchers: 3

Date	Pitcher, Club	No.
Oct. 5, 1996	Charles Nagy, Cle. vs. Bal.	12
Oct. 5, 1997	Randy Johnson, Sea. vs. Bal.	13
Oct. 6, 1999	Bartolo Colon, Cle. vs. Bos.	11
Oct. 9, 2001	Bartolo Colon, Cle. vs. Sea.	10

Total number of occurrences: 6

10-STRIKEOUT GAMES BY PITCHERS

AMERICAN LEAGUE

Date	Pitcher, Club	No.
Oct. 8, 1981	Dave Righetti, N.Y. vs. Mil.	10
Oct. 6, 1995	Randy Johnson, Sea. vs. N.Y.	10

NATIONAL LEAGUE

Date	Pitcher, Club	No.
Sept.29, 1998	Kevin Brown, S.D. vs. Hou.	16
Oct. 4, 1998	Sterling Hitchcock, S.D. vs. Hou.	11
Oct. 5, 1999	Randy Johnson, Ari. vs. N.Y.	11

Total number of occurrences: 3

CLUB BATTING

AMERICAN LEAGUE

Year	Team, Division	G	AB	R	H	TB	2B	3B	HR	SH	SF	SB	BB	SO	RBI	Avg.	LOB
1981	New York, East	5	171	19	46	72	8	0	6	0	1	1	9	22	18	.269	30
	Milwaukee, East	5	162	13	36	53	6	1	3	2	3	1	13	39	13	.222	32
	Oakland, West	3	99	10	25	39	5	0	3	0	0	2	6	10	9	.253	20
	Kansas City, West	3	98	2	20	21	1	0	0	0	0	0	7	11	2	.204	23
1995	Boston, East	3	114	6	21	32	2	0	3	1	1	2	11	26	6	.184	28
	Cleveland, Central	3	114	17	25	43	4	1	4	2	0	1	13	22	17	.219	27
	New York, East*	5	193	33	50	95	12	0	11	2	3	1	32	43	32	.259	45
	Seattle, West	5	200	35	63	104	6	1	11	4	3	3	25	41	33	.315	49
1996	Baltimore, East*	4	149	25	43	76	6	0	9	0	2	1	17	40	23	.289	36
	Cleveland, Central	4	143	20	35	54	7	0	4	2	2	11	15	32	20	.245	29
	New York, East	4	140	16	37	53	4	0	4	3	2	1	13	20	15	.264	30
	Texas, West	4	142	16	31	53	4	0	6	4	0	1	20	30	16	.218	33
1997	Baltimore, East*	4	135	23	39	68	11	0	6	2	0	2	16	27	23	.289	25
	Seattle, West	4	133	11	29	52	5	0	6	0	0	2	7	42	11	.218	21
	Cleveland, Central	5	167	21	43	63	6	1	4	4	1	6	10	22	20	.257	32
	New York, East*	5	166	24	43	68	7	0	6	2	2	3	20	26	23	.259	37
1998	Cleveland, Central	4	126	18	26	59	12	0	7	0	1	3	15	26	17	.206	22
	Boston, East*	4	135	20	34	55	6	0	5	1	2	1	14	28	19	.252	26
	New York, East	3	91	9	23	41	6	0	4	1	0	2	7	24	8	.253	16
	Texas, West	3	92	1	13	16	3	0	0	1	0	0	4	27	1	.141	15
1999	Boston, East*	5	176	47	56	105	17	1	10	0	3	1	19	35	47	.318	25
	Cleveland, Central	5	163	32	38	68	7	1	7	1	4	5	28	43	31	.233	34
	New York, East	3	98	14	23	37	6	1	2	1	0	0	10	19	13	.235	21
	Texas, West	3	92	1	14	19	2	0	1	0	0	1	9	17	1	.152	19
2000	New York, East	5	168	19	41	56	12	0	1	1	3	1	16	35	19	.244	38
	Oakland, West	5	167	23	44	59	9	0	2	1	2	3	19	31	22	.263	36
	Seattle, West*	3	99	14	28	42	2	0	4	4	1	2	12	13	14	.283	22
	Chicago, Central	3	92	7	17	30	6	2	1	2	2	4	15	16	6	.185	21
2001	New York, East	5	166	18	40	59	8	1	3	2	1	4	11	29	16	.241	34
	Oakland, West*	5	174	12	43	70	13	1	4	0	2	3	11	31	11	.247	43
	Seattle, West	5	158	16	39	59	8	0	4	2	1	3	18	48	16	.247	35
	Cleveland, Central	5	173	26	45	71	9	1	5	0	1	1	13	43	25	.260	30

*Wild-card team.

NATIONAL LEAGUE

Year	Team, Division	G	AB	R	H	TB	2B	3B	HR	SH	SF	SB	BB	SO	RBI	Avg.	LOB
1981	Los Angeles, West	5	162	13	32	49	6	1	3	4	1	2	13	34	12	.198	35
	Houston, West	5	162	6	29	38	3	0	2	2	0	4	13	24	6	.179	32
	Philadelphia, East	5	166	14	44	65	6	1	4	2	0	0	13	19	12	.265	35
	Montreal, East	5	161	16	41	59	10	1	2	2	2	7	18	36	16	.255	35
1995	Cincinnati, Central	3	104	22	29	50	6	0	5	1	1	9	13	28	22	.279	19
	Los Angeles, West	3	111	7	31	42	2	0	3	1	0	0	5	17	7	.279	30
	Atlanta, East	4	154	27	51	80	8	0	7	0	1	3	12	27	24	.331	33
	Colorado, West*	4	143	19	41	66	7	0	6	3	1	3	9	29	18	.287	24
1996	Atlanta, East	3	89	10	16	34	3	0	5	2	1	5	12	24	10	.180	14
	Los Angeles, West*	3	95	5	14	21	7	0	0	0	1	0	7	29	5	.147	14
	St. Louis, Central	3	94	15	24	38	3	1	3	2	0	3	13	23	14	.255	20
	San Diego, West	3	105	10	25	40	3	0	4	2	0	2	4	28	9	.238	21
1997	Florida, East*	3	99	15	27	44	5	0	4	1	0	1	19	16	14	.273	24
	San Fran., West	3	98	9	22	38	4	0	4	2	1	2	6	21	8	.224	17
	Atlanta, East	3	92	19	20	33	4	0	3	0	1	1	15	20	15	.217	14
	Houston, Central	3	96	5	16	20	1	0	1	0	0	2	8	24	5	.167	18

ear	Team, Division	G	AB	R	H	TB	2B	3B	HR	SH	SF	SB	BB	SO	RBI	Avg.	LOB
998	San Diego, West.....4		125	14	27	48	4	1	5	2	1	0	9	32	13	.216	23
	Houston, Central 4		121	8	22	30	5	0	1	2	0	1	11	49	7	.182	25
	Atlanta, East 3		101	15	23	37	2	0	4	2	1	3	14	20	14	.228	24
	Chicago, Central* ...3		94	4	17	22	2	0	1	3	1	1	5	24	4	.181	15
999	New York, East* 4		134	22	34	54	5	0	5	4	1	8	21	28	22	.254	32
	Arizona, West........4		126	16	26	47	7	1	4	0	1	0	14	22	16	.206	20
	Atlanta, East 4		148	18	45	53	5	0	1	3	3	4	11	35	18	.304	33
	Houston, Central 4		141	15	31	48	2	0	5	2	1	3	17	33	15	.220	31
000	New York, East* 4		143	13	30	46	7	0	3	0	1	3	20	30	13	.210	36
	San Fran., West.....4		146	11	30	44	6	1	2	2	0	2	16	36	11	.205	33
	St. Louis, Central ...3		102	24	28	51	5	0	6	2	1	6	14	19	23	.275	22
	Atlanta, East 3		95	10	18	26	5	0	1	0	0	1	16	20	9	.189	21
001	Atlanta, East 3		99	14	30	54	6	0	6	1	1	1	4	18	13	.303	14
	Houston, Central ...3		95	6	19	30	2	0	3	0	0	0	8	16	6	.200	16
	Arizona, West........5		156	10	37	51	5	0	3	6	0	1	18	29	10	.237	40
	St. Louis, Central* .5		152	12	29	50	3	0	6	8	1	3	12	38	12	.191	30

CLUB FIELDING AND PLAYERS USED
AMERICAN LEAGUE

ear	Team, Division	G	PO	A	E	DP	PB	Fielding Avg.	Players Used	Pitchers Used
981	New York, East 5		135	42	3	1	0	.983	21	7
	Milwaukee, East..5		132	59	5	6	0	.974	23	9
	Oakland, West...3		81	29	3	3	0	.973	20	5
	Kansas City, West 3		78	28	4	1	0	.964	16	5
995	Boston, East 3		89	29	4	0	2	.967	23	10
	Cleveland, Central...3		93	34	6	1	0	.955	22	9
	New York, East* 5		150	49	3	4	0	.985	24	9
	Seattle, West...5		154	47	2	5	0	.990	24	9
996	Baltimore, East* 4		114	43	4	2	0	.975	21	8
	Cleveland, Central...4		111	34	3	1	0	.980	24	10
	New York, East 4		117	38	2	3	0	.987	25	10
	Texas, West 4		114	47	2	5	0	.988	23	11
997	Baltimore, East 4		108	38	0	1	1	1.000	23	9
	Seattle, West...4		105	42	1	3	0	.993	23	9
	Cleveland, Central...5		132	58	4	6	0	.979	20	9
	New York, East* 5		130	55	4	2	0	.979	25	10
998	Cleveland, Central...4		108	43	1	3	0	.993	22	11
	Boston, East* 4		105	33	0	4	2	1.000	24	10
	New York, East 3		81	28	1	2	0	.991	19	6
	Texas, West 3		75	31	1	4	1	.991	17	5
999	Boston, East* 5		130	45	3	3	3	.983	25	11
	Cleveland, Central...5		129	48	2	4	0	.983	25	11
	New York, East 3		81	29	2	5	0	.982	19	5
	Texas, West 3		75	27	3	1	0	.981	19	9
000	New York, East 5		132	56	2	7	0	.989	21	8
	Oakland, West...5		132	42	5	3	0	.972	24	9
	Seattle, West*...3		84	28	1	5	0	.991	22	8
	Chicago, Central 3		82	38	2	5	0	.984	24	10
001	New York, East 5		135	42	4	4	0	.978	21	9
	Oakland, West*...5		132	60	6	4	0	.970	25	11
	Seattle, West...5		132	43	5	5	1	.972	25	10
	Cleveland, Central...5		129	53	3	4	0	.984	22	10

Wild-card team.

NATIONAL LEAGUE

ear	Team, Division	G	PO	A	E	DP	PB	Fielding Avg.	Players Used	Pitchers Used
981	Los Angeles, West...5		139	57	3	2	0	.985	22	8
	Houston, West...5		132	46	5	1	0	.973	24	8
	Philadelphia, East 5		132	51	3	2	0	.984	23	8
	Montreal, East...5		132	55	6	5	0	.969	22	9
995	Cincinnati, Central...3		81	30	2	1	0	.982	18	6
	Los Angeles, West...3		78	19	3	2	0	.970	22	8
	Atlanta, East 4		111	49	2	5	0	.988	24	10
	Colorado, West* 4		108	50	7	5	0	.958	24	11
996	Atlanta, East 3		84	28	3	1	0	.974	19	6
	Los Angeles, West*...3		81	32	1	4	0	.991	23	10
	St. Louis, Central...3		81	18	2	0	0	.980	20	7
	San Diego, West..3		75	28	2	3	0	.972	23	9

DIVISION SERIES *General reference*

Year	Team, Division	G	PO	A	E	DP	PB	Fielding Avg.	Players Used	Pitchers Used
1997	Florida, East*	3	81	33	4	3	0	.966	19	6
	San Francisco, West	3	77	31	0	4	0	1.000	21	8
	Atlanta, East	3	81	33	3	2	0	.974	18	5
	Houston, Central	3	75	27	4	2	1	.962	24	9
1998	San Diego, West	4	104	37	3	5	2	.979	22	7
	Houston, Central	4	102	41	2	1	0	.986	21	8
	Atlanta, East	3	84	25	0	2	0	1.000	21	7
	Chicago, Central*	3	79	20	4	1	1	.961	22	8
1999	New York, East*	4	108	41	0	5	0	1.000	25	11
	Arizona, West	4	106	37	5	2	0	.966	23	10
	Atlanta, East	4	117	46	2	4	0	.988	23	9
	Houston, Central	4	114	50	4	4	0	.976	24	10
2000	New York, East*	4	120	33	0	1	0	1.000	24	10
	San Francisco, West	4	118	40	1	8	0	.994	25	11
	St. Louis, Central	3	81	29	1	2	0	.991	21	9
	Atlanta, East	3	75	28	5	0	0	.954	22	9
2001	Atlanta, East	3	81	32	1	5	0	.991	21	8
	Houston, Central	3	78	30	3	7	0	.973	22	9
	Arizona, West	5	132	54	4	4	0	.979	23	8
	St. Louis, Central*	5	131	50	3	4	0	.984	22	10

MANAGERIAL RECORDS

AMERICAN LEAGUE

	Series W	L	Games W	L
Mike Hargrove, Cleveland	3	2	12	9
Art Howe, Oakland	0	2	4	6
Dick Howser, Kansas City	0	1	0	3
Dave Johnson, Baltimore	2	0	6	2
Kevin Kennedy, Boston	0	1	0	3
Bob Lemon, New York	1	0	3	2
Charlie Manuel, Cleveland	0	1	2	3
Jerry Manuel, Chicago	0	1	0	3
Billy Martin, Oakland	1	0	3	0
John Oates, Texas	0	3	1	9
Lou Piniella, Seattle	3	1	10	7
Buck Rodgers, Milwaukee	0	1	2	3
Buck Showalter, New York	0	1	2	3
Joe Torre, New York	5	1	17	8
Jimy Williams, Boston	1	1	4	5

Total number of managers: 15

NATIONAL LEAGUE

	Series W	L	Games W	L
Dusty Baker, San Francisco	0	2	1	6
Don Baylor, Colorado	0	1	1	3
Bruce Bochy, San Diego	1	1	3	4

	Series W	L	Games W	L
Bob Brenly, Arizona	1	0	3	2
Bobby Cox, Atlanta	6	1	18	5
Larry Dierker, Houston	0	4	2	12
Jim Fanning, Montreal	1	0	3	2
Dallas Green, Philadelphia	0	1	2	3
Dave Johnson, Cincinnati	1	0	3	0
Tony LaRussa, St. Louis	2	1	8	3
Tom Lasorda, Los Angeles	1	1	3	5
Jim Leyland, Florida	1	0	3	0
Jim Riggleman, Chicago	0	1	0	3
Bill Russell, Los Angeles	0	1	0	3
Buck Showalter, Arizona	0	1	1	3
Bobby Valentine, New York	2	0	6	2
Bill Virdon, Houston	0	1	2	3

Total number of managers: 17

COMBINED RECORDS FOR BOTH LEAGUES

	Series W	L	Games W	L
Dave Johnson, Cincinnati N.L., Baltimore A.L.	3	0	9	2
Buck Showalter, New York A.L., Arizona N.L.	0	2	3	6

Total number of managers: 2

DIVISION SERIES *General reference*

CHAMPIONSHIP SERIES

Service (Individual, Club)

Batting (Individual, Club)

Baserunning (Individual, Club)

Pitching (Individual, Club)

Fielding (Individual, Club)

Miscellaneous

Non-Playing Personnel

General Reference

INDIVIDUAL SERVICE

ALL PLAYERS
SERIES AND CLUBS

Most series played

A.L.—11—Reggie Jackson, Oakland, 1971 through 1975; New York, 1977, 1978, 1980, 1981; California, 1982, 1986.

N.L.—9

Tom Glavine, Atlanta, 1991 through 2001, except 1994 and 2000.

John Smoltz, Atlanta, 1991 through 2001, except 1994 and 2000.

Most consecutive years played in series

A.L.—5—Sal Bando, Vida Blue, Bert Campaneris, Rollie Fingers, Reggie Jackson, Joe Rudi, Gene Tenace, Oakland, 1971 through 1975.

N.L.—5—Tom Glavine, Chipper Jones, Ryan Klesko, Greg Maddux and John Smoltz, Atlanta, 1995 through 1999.

Most series playing in all games

A.L.—9—Reggie Jackson, Oakland, 1971 through 1975; New York, 1977, 1978, 1980; California, 1982; 37 games.

N.L.—7—Pete Rose, Cincinnati, 1970, 1972, 1973, 1975, 1976; Philadelphia, 1980, 1983; 28 games.

Most series played with one club

N.L.—9

Tom Glavine, Atlanta, 1991 through 2001, except 1994 and 2000.
John Smoltz, Atlanta, 1991 through 2001, except 1994 and 2000.

A.L.—7—Jim Palmer, Baltimore, 1969, 1970, 1971, 1973, 1974, 1979, 1983.

Most series appeared in as pinch-hitter

Both leagues—4

Vic Davalillo, Pittsburgh N.L., 1971, 1972; Oakland A.L., 1973; Los Angeles N.L., 1977; five games.

Danny Heep, Houston N.L., 1980; New York N.L., 1986; Los Angeles N.L., 1988; Boston A.L., 1990; 10 games.

N.L.—4

Rick Monday, Los Angeles, 1977, 1978, 1981, 1983; four games.

Richie Hebner, Pittsburgh, 1971; Philadelphia, 1977, 1978; Chicago, 1984; five games.

Keith Lockhart, Atlanta, 1997, 1998, 1999, 2001; six games.

A.L.—3

Curt Motton, Baltimore, 1969, 1971, 1974; four games.

Jim Holt, Minnesota, 1970; Oakland, 1974, 1975; four games.

Cliff Johnson, New York, 1977, 1978; Toronto, 1985; five games.

Jamie Quirk, Kansas City, 1976, 1985; Oakland, 1990; four games.

Most times on series-winning club (playing one or more game each series)

Both leagues—6

David Justice, Atlanta N.L., 1991, 1992, 1995; Cleveland A.L., 1997; New York A.L., 2000, 2001.

Paul O'Neill, Cincinnati N.L., 1990; New York A.L., 1996, 1998 through 2001.

Mike Stanton, Atlanta N.L., 1991, 1992; New York A.L., 1998 through 2001.

A.L.—6—Reggie Jackson, Oakland, 1972, 1973, 1974; New York, 1977, 1978, 1981.

N.L.—6—Pete Rose, Cincinnati, 1970, 1972, 1975, 1976; Philadelphia, 1980, 1983.

Most times on series-losing club (playing one or more game each series)

N.L.—7—Richie Hebner, Pittsburgh, 1970, 1972, 1974, 1975; Philadelphia, 1977, 1978; Chicago, 1984.

A.L.—5

Bobby Grich, Baltimore, 1973, 1974; California, 1979, 1982, 1986.

Reggie Jackson, Oakland, 1971, 1975; New York, 1980; California, 1982, 1986.

Most clubs, career

A.L.—5—Don Baylor, Baltimore, 1973, 1974; California 1979, 1982; Boston, 1986; Minnesota, 1987; Oakland, 1988.

N.L.—3—Held by many players.

BY POSITION (EXCEPT PITCHERS)

Most series by first baseman

Both leagues—6—John Olerud, Toronto A.L., 1991, 1992, 1993; New York N.L., 1999; Seattle A.L., 2000, 2001; 34 games.

A.L.—6—Tino Martinez, Seattle, 1995; New York, 1996, 1998 through 2001; 33 games.

N.L.—5

Tony Perez, Cincinnati, 1970, 1972, 1973, 1975, 1976; 17 games.

Bob Robertson, Pittsburgh, 1970, 1971, 1972, 1974, 1975; 11 games.

Steve Garvey, Los Angeles, 1974, 1977, 1978, 1981; San Diego, 1984; 22 games.

Most series by second baseman

N.L.—7—Joe Morgan, Cincinnati, 1972, 1973, 1975, 1976, 1979; Houston, 1980; Philadelphia, 1983; 27 games.

A.L.—6—Frank White, Kansas City, 1976, 1977, 1978, 1980, 1984, 1985; 26 games.

Most series by third baseman

Both leagues—6—Graig Nettles, New York A.L., 1976, 1977, 1978, 1980, 1981; San Diego N.L., 1984; 23 games.

A.L.—6—George Brett, Kansas City, 1976, 1977, 1978, 1980, 1984, 1985; 27 games.

N.L.—6

Terry Pendleton, St. Louis, 1985, 1987; Atlanta, 1991, 1992, 1993, 1996; 34 games.

Chipper Jones, Atlanta, 1995 through 2001, except 2000; 34 games.

Most series by shortstop

Both leagues—6—Walt Weiss, Oakland A.L., 1988, 1989, 1990, 1992; Atlanta N.L., 1998, 1999.

A.L.—6

Mark Belanger, Baltimore, 1969, 1970, 1971, 1973, 1974, 1979; 21 games.

Bert Campaneris, Oakland, 1971, 1972, 1973, 1974, 1975; California, 1979; 18 games.

N.L.—6—Jeff Blauser, Atlanta, 1991, 1992, 1993, 1995, 1996, 1997; 29 games.

Most series by outfielder

A.L.—10—Reggie Jackson, Oakland, 1971, 1972, 1973, 1974, 1975; New York, 1977, 1978, 1980, 1981; California, 1982; 32 games.

N.L.—5

Cesar Geronimo, Cincinnati, 1972, 1973, 1975, 1976, 1979; 17 games.

Garry Maddox, Philadelphia, 1976, 1977, 1978, 1980, 1983; 17 games.

Ron Gant, Atlanta, 1991, 1992, 1993; Cincinnati, 1995; St. Louis, 1996; 31 games.

Andruw Jones, Atlanta, 1996 through 2001, except 2000; 27 games.

Most series by catcher

Both leagues—6—Bob Boone, Philadelphia N.L., 1976, 1977, 1978, 1980; California A.L., 1982, 1986; 27 games.

N.L.—6

Johnny Bench, Cincinnati, 1970, 1972, 1973, 1975, 1976, 1979; 22 games.

Steve Yeager, Los Angeles, 1974, 1977, 1978, 1981, 1983, 1985; 15 games.

Javy Lopez, Atlanta, 1992, 1995 through 1998, 2001; 27 games.

A.L.—5

Andy Etchebarren, Baltimore, 1969, 1970, 1971, 1973, 1974; 12 games.

YOUNGEST AND OLDEST NON-PITCHERS

Youngest championship series non-pitcher

N.L.—19 years, 5 months, 16 days—Andruw Jones, Atlanta, October 9, 1996.

A.L.—20 years, 1 month, 5 days—Claudell Washington, Oakland, October 5, 1974.

Oldest championship series non-pitcher

N.L.—42 years, 5 months, 24 days—Pete Rose, Philadelphia, October 8, 1983.

A.L.—41 years, 11 days—Dave Winfield, Toronto, October 14, 1992.

YEARS BETWEEN SERIES (INCLUDES PITCHERS)

Most years between first and second series

N.L.—14—Tony Gwynn, San Diego, 1984, 1998.

A.L.—12—Doyle Alexander, Baltimore, 1973; Toronto, 1985. (Bert Blyleven went 17 years between ALCS appearances with Minnesota in 1970 and 1987, but that span was interrupted by a 1979 NLCS appearance with Pittsburgh.)

Most years between first and last series

Both leagues—19—Dennis Martinez, Baltimore A.L., 1979; Atlanta N.L., 1998.

A.L.—19—Rickey Henderson, Oakland, 1981; Seattle, 2000.

N.L.—17—Nolan Ryan, New York, 1969; Houston, 1986.

POSITIONS

Most positions played, career

N.L.—4

Pete Rose, Cincinnati, 1970, 1972, 1973, 1975, 1976; Philadelphia, 1980; right field, left field, third base, first base; 24 games.

Pedro Guerrero, Los Angeles, 1981, 1983, 1985; right field, center field, third base, left field; 15 games.

Lloyd McClendon, Chicago, 1989; Pittsburgh, 1991, 1992; catcher, left field, first base, right field; 11 games.

A.L.—3—Held by many players.

Most positions played, series

A.L.—3

Cesar Tovar, Minnesota, 1970; center field, second base, left field; 3-game series, three games.

Stan Javier, Seattle, 2000; right field, center field, left field; 6-game series, four games.

Mark McLemore, Seattle, 2001; shortstop, left field, second base; 5-game series; five games.

N.L.—3

Melvin Mora, New York, 1999; left field, center field, right field; 6-game series, six games.

Joe McEwing, New York, 2000; left field, third base, right field; 5-game series, four games.

Craig Paquette, St. Louis, 2000; third base, left field, right field; 5-game series, four games.

PITCHERS
SERIES

Most series pitched

N.L.—9

Tom Glavine, Atlanta, 1991 through 2001, except 1994 and 2000; 15 games.

John Smoltz, Atlanta, 1991 through 2001, except 1994 and 2000; 17 games.

A.L.—6

Catfish Hunter, Oakland, 1971 through 1974; New York, 1976, 1978; 10 games.

Jim Palmer, Baltimore, 1969, 1970, 1971, 1973, 1974, 1979; eight games.

Roger Clemens, Boston, 1986, 1988, 1990; New York, 1999 through 2001; nine games.

Jeff Nelson, Seattle, 1995, 2001; New York, 1996, 1998, 1999, 2000; 15 games.

Most series pitched by relief pitcher

Both leagues—7

Rick Honeycutt, Los Angeles N.L., 1983, 1985; Oakland A.L., 1988, 1989, 1990, 1992; St. Louis, 1996; 20 games as a relief pitcher.

Mark Wohlers, Atlanta N.L., 1991 through 1997, except 1994; New York A.L., 2001; 19 games as a relief pitcher.

N.L.—6

Tug McGraw, New York, 1969, 1973; Philadelphia, 1976, 1977, 1978, 1980; 15 games as a relief pitcher.

Mark Wohlers, Atlanta, 1991, 1992, 1993, 1995, 1996, 1997; 18 games as a relief pitcher.

A.L.—6—Jeff Nelson, Seattle, 1995, 2001; New York, 1996, 1998, 1999, 2000; 15 games as a relief pitcher.

YOUNGEST AND OLDEST PITCHERS

Youngest championship series pitcher

A.L.—19 years, 5 months, 29 days—Bert Blyleven, Minnesota, October 5, 1970.

N.L.—19 years, 8 months, 28 days—Don Gullett, Cincinnati, October 4, 1970.

Oldest championship series pitcher

N.L.—43 years, 6 months, 8 days—Phil Niekro, Atlanta, October 9, 1982.

A.L.—41 years, 6 months, 13 days—Don Sutton, California, October 15, 1986.

CHAMPIONSHIP SERIES *Individual service*

CLUB SERVICE

PLAYERS USED

Most players, series
A.L.-N.L.—25—Held by many clubs.

For a list of players and pitchers used each series, see page 458.

Most players used by both clubs, series
3-game series
  A.L.—46—Oakland 24, New York 22, 1981.
  N.L.—42—Pittsburgh 24, Cincinnati 18, 1975.
4-game series
  N.L.—46—Cincinnati 24, Atlanta 22, 1995.
  A.L.—45—Chicago 23, Baltimore 22, 1983.
5-game series
  A.L.—49—Oakland 25, Detroit 24, 1972.
      New York 25, Boston 24, 1999.
      Seattle 25, New York 24, 2001.
  N.L.—49—St. Louis 25, New York 24, 2000.
6-game series
  A.L.—50—Cleveland 25, Seattle 25, 1995.
  N.L.—50—Atlanta 25, New York 25, 1999.
7-game series
  N.L.—50—Pittsburgh 25, Atlanta 25, 1992.
  A.L.—46—Toronto 24, Kansas City 22, 1985.

Fewest players, series
3-game series
  A.L.—14—Baltimore vs. Minnesota, 1970.
      Boston vs. Oakland, 1975.
  N.L.—15—St. Louis vs. Atlanta, 1982.
4-game series
  A.L.—20—Oakland vs. Baltimore, 1974.
      Kansas City vs. New York, 1978.
      Baltimore vs. California, 1979.
      Boston vs. Oakland, 1988.
  N.L.—20—Philadelphia vs. Los Angeles, 1983.
5-game series
  N.L.—17—New York vs. Cincinnati, 1973.
  A.L.—18—New York vs. Kansas City, 1977.
6-game series
  A.L.—19—Toronto vs. Chicago, 1993.
  N.L.—21—Houston vs. New York, 1986.
      Pittsburgh vs. Cincinnati, 1990.
7-game series
  A.L.—20—Boston vs. California, 1986.
  N.L.—22—New York vs. Los Angeles, 1988.

Fewest players used by both clubs, series
3-game series
  A.L.—35—Oakland 20, Baltimore 15, 1971.
      New York 20, Kansas City 15, 1980.
  N.L.—35—Atlanta 20, St. Louis 15, 1982.
4-game series
  A.L.—41—New York 21, Kansas City 20, 1978.
  N.L.—42—Los Angeles 22, Philadelphia 20, 1983.
5-game series
  A.L.—40—Kansas City 22, New York 18, 1977.
      Milwaukee 20, California 20, 1982.
  N.L.—41—Cincinnati 24, New York 17, 1973.
6-game series
  A.L.—41—Chicago 22, Toronto 19, 1993.
  N.L.—43—New York 22, Houston 21, 1986.
7-game series
  A.L.—44—California 24, Boston 20, 1986.
  N.L.—46—St. Louis 23, San Francisco 23, 1987.
      Los Angeles 24, New York 22, 1988.

Most times one club using only nine players in game, series
N.L.—3—New York vs. Cincinnati, 1973 (5-game series).
A.L.—2—Baltimore vs. Minnesota, 1970 (3-game series).

Most players, nine-inning game
N.L.—21—St. Louis vs. New York, October 16, 2000.
A.L.—20—Oakland vs. Detroit, October 10, 1972.

Most players, extra-inning game
N.L.—23—New York vs. Atlanta, October 17, 1999, 15 innings.
A.L.—20—Oakland vs. Detroit, October 11, 1972, 10 innings.

Most players used by both clubs, nine-inning game
N.L.—37
  Pittsburgh 20, Atlanta 17, October 7, 1992.
  St. Louis 19, Atlanta 18, October 14, 1996.
A.L.—36—New York 19, Seattle 17, October 20, 2001.

Most players used by both clubs, extra-inning game
N.L.—45—New York 23, Atlanta 22, October 17, 1999, 15 innings.
A.L.—37—Baltimore 19, Cleveland 18, October 11, 1997, 12 innings.

PINCH-HITTERS

Most pinch-hitters, series
N.L.—20—New York vs. Atlanta, 1999 (6-game series).
A.L.—14—Oakland vs. Detroit, 1972 (5-game series).

Most pinch-hitters used by both clubs, series
N.L.—32—New York 20, Atlanta 12, 1999 (6-game series).
A.L.—22—Oakland 14, Detroit 8, 1972 (5-game series).

Fewest pinch-hitters, series
A.L.-N.L.—0—Held by many clubs.

Fewest pinch-hitters used by both clubs, series
A.L.—2
  California 2, Milwaukee 0, 1982 (5-game series).
  Chicago 2, Toronto 0, 1993 (6-game series).

Most pinch-hitters, nine-inning game
A.L.—6—Oakland vs. Detroit, October 10, 1972.
N.L.—5—Held by many clubs.

Most pinch-hitters, extra-inning game
N.L.—6
  Los Angeles vs. New York, October 9, 1988, 12 innings.
  Atlanta vs. New York, October 19, 1999, 11 innings.
A.L.—Less than nine-inning record.

Most pinch-hitters used by both clubs, nine-inning game
A.L.—7—Oakland 6, Detroit 1, October 10, 1972.
N.L.—6—Occurred many times.

Most pinch-hitters used by both clubs, extra-inning game
N.L.—10—New York 5, Houston 5, October 15, 1986, 16 innings.
A.L.—Less than nine-inning record.

Most pinch-hitters, inning
A.L.—4—Baltimore vs. Chicago, October 7, 1983, ninth inning.
N.L.—4—Philadelphia vs. Los Angeles, October 5, 1983, ninth inning.

PINCH-RUNNERS

Most pinch-runners, series
A.L.—5
  Oakland vs. Baltimore, 1974 (4-game series).
  Oakland vs. Boston, 1990 (4-game series).
N.L.—4—New York vs. St. Louis, 2000 (5-game series).

Most pinch-runners used by both clubs, series
A.L.—8—Oakland 5, Baltimore 3, 1974 (4-game series).
N.L.—7—New York 4, St. Louis 3, 2000 (5-game series).

Fewest pinch-runners used, series
A.L.-N.L.—0—Held by many clubs.

Fewest pinch-runners used by both clubs, series
N.L.—0
  Philadelphia 0, Los Angeles 0, 1978 (4-game series).
  Florida 0, Atlanta 0, 1997 (6-game series).

A.L.—0
  Baltimore 0, Minnesota 0, 1969 (3-game series).
  Kansas City 0, New York 0, 1980 (3-game series).

Most pinch-runners, nine-inning game
A.L.-N.L.—2—Held by many clubs.

Most pinch-runners, extra-inning game
A.L.—3—Kansas City vs. Detroit, October 3, 1984, 11 innings.
N.L.—2—Held by many clubs.

Most pinch-runners used by both clubs, nine-inning game
A.L.-N.L.—3—Made in many games.

Most pinch-runners used by both clubs, extra-inning game
A.L.—4—Boston 2, California 2, October 12, 1986, 11 innings.
N.L.—3
  Philadelphia 2, Houston 1, October 12, 1980, 10 innings.
  Atlanta 2, New York 1, October 17, 1999, 15 innings.

Most pinch-runners, inning
A.L.—2
  Oakland vs. Detroit, October 7, 1972, 11th inning.
  Baltimore vs. Oakland, October 9, 1974, ninth inning.
  New York vs. Seattle, October 13, 2000, ninth inning.
N.L.—2—New York vs. St. Louis, October 11, 2000, ninth
  inning.

NUMBER OF PLAYERS USED BY POSITION
FIRST BASEMEN

Most first basemen, series
A.L.-N.L.—3—Held by many clubs.

Most first basemen used by both clubs, series
A.L.—5
  Oakland 3, Baltimore 2, 1973 (5-game series).
  California 3, Boston 2, 1986 (7-game series).
N.L.—5
  Pittsburgh 3, Cincinnati 2, 1990 (6-game series).
  Pittsburgh 3, Atlanta 2, 1991 (7-game series).

Most first basemen, game
N.L.—3
  Los Angeles vs. St. Louis, October 14, 1985.
  Atlanta vs. New York, October 12, 1999.
A.L.—2—Made in many games.

Most first basemen used by both clubs, game
N.L.—4
  Los Angeles 3, St. Louis 1, October 14, 1985.
  Atlanta 2, Pittsburgh 2, October 7, 1992.
  Atlanta 2, Pittsburgh 2, October 10, 1992.
  Atlanta 3, New York 1, October 12, 1999.
A.L.—3—Made in many games.

SECOND BASEMEN

Most second basemen, series
A.L.—4—Oakland vs. Detroit, 1972 (5-game series).
N.L.—3
  Atlanta vs. Pittsburgh, 1992 (7-game series).
  Atlanta vs. San Diego, 1998 (6-game series).

Most second basemen used by both clubs, series
A.L.—6—Oakland 4, Detroit 2, 1972 (5-game series).
N.L.—5
  Atlanta 3, Pittsburgh 2, 1992 (7-game series).
  Atlanta 3, St. Louis 2, 1996 (7-game series).

Most second basemen, game
A.L.—3
  Minnesota vs. Baltimore, October 3, 1970.
  Oakland vs. Detroit, October 7, 1972, 11 innings.
  Oakland vs. Detroit, October 10, 1972.
  Oakland vs. Boston, October 7, 1975.
  New York vs. Kansas City, October 4, 1978.
N.L.—2—Made in many games.

Most second basemen used by both clubs, game
A.L.—4
  Minnesota 3, Baltimore 1, October 3, 1970.
  Oakland 3, Detroit 1, October 7, 1972, 11 innings.
  Oakland 3, Detroit 1, October 10, 1972.
  Oakland 3, Boston 1, October 7, 1975.
  New York 3, Kansas City 1, October 4, 1978.
N.L.—3—Made in many games.

THIRD BASEMEN

Most third basemen, series
A.L.-N.L.—3—Held by many clubs.

Most third basemen used by both clubs, series
N.L.—6—San Francisco 3, Chicago 3, 1989 (5-game series).
A.L.—5—Detroit 3, Kansas City 2, 1984 (3-game series).

Most third basemen, game
A.L.—3
  Detroit vs. Kansas City, October 3, 1984, 11 innings.
  Minnesota vs. Toronto, October 8, 1991.
N.L.—2—Held by many clubs.

Most third basemen used by both clubs, game
A.L.—5—Detroit 3, Kansas City 2, October 3, 1984, 11 innings.
N.L.—4—Atlanta 2, St. Louis 2, October 14, 1996.

SHORTSTOPS

Most shortstops, series
A.L.—4—Oakland vs. Detroit, 1972 (5-game series).
N.L.—3
  Cincinnati vs. New York, 1973 (5-game series).
  Pittsburgh vs. Los Angeles, 1974 (4-game series).
  Pittsburgh vs. Cincinnati, 1975 (3-game series).

Most shortstops used by both clubs, series
A.L.—6—Oakland 4, Detroit 2, 1972 (5-game series).
N.L.—4—Made in many series.

Most shortstops, nine-inning game
N.L.—3—Pittsburgh vs. Los Angeles, October 6, 1974.
A.L.—2—Held by many clubs.

Most shortstops, extra-inning game
N.L.—3
  Cincinnati vs. New York, October 9, 1973, 12 innings.
  Pittsburgh vs. Cincinnati, October 7, 1975, 10 innings.
A.L.—3—Oakland vs. Detroit, October 11, 1972, 10 innings.

Most shortstops used by both clubs, game
A.L.-N.L.—4—Occurred in many games.

LEFT FIELDERS

Most left fielders, series
N.L.—5—Philadelphia vs. Houston, 1980 (5-game series).
A.L.—5
  Seattle vs. New York, 2000 (6-game series).
  Seattle vs. New York, 2001 (5-game series).

Most left fielders used by both clubs, series
A.L.—7
  Seattle 5, New York 2, 2000 (6-game series).
  Seattle 5, New York 2, 2001 (5-game series).
N.L.—6
  Cincinnati 4, Pittsburgh 2, 1970 (3-game series).
  Philadelphia 5, Houston 1, 1980 (5-game series).
  San Diego 3, Atlanta 3, 1998 (6-game series).
  St. Louis 4, New York 2, 2000 (5-game series).

Most left fielders, game
A.L.-N.L.—3—Held by many clubs.

Most left fielders used by both clubs, game
N.L.—5—Atlanta 3, San Diego 2, October 12, 1998.
A.L.—4—Occurred in many games.

CENTER FIELDERS

Most center fielders, series
N.L.—4—St. Louis vs. Atlanta, 1996 (7-game series).
A.L.—3
Oakland vs. Baltimore, 1973 (5-game series).
New York vs. Kansas City, 1978 (4-game series).

Most center fielders used by both clubs, series
A.L.—5—Oakland 3, Baltimore 2, 1973 (5-game series).
N.L.—5—St. Louis 4, Atlanta 1, 1996 (7-game series).

Most center fielders, game
N.L.—3—New York vs. Atlanta, October 17, 1999.
A.L.—2—Held by many clubs.

Most center fielders used by both clubs, game
A.L.-N.L.—3—Made in many games.

RIGHT FIELDERS

Most right fielders, series
N.L.—5—St. Louis vs. San Francisco, 1987 (7-game series).
A.L.—4
New York vs. Oakland, 1981 (3-game series).
Seattle vs. New York, 2000 (6-game series).

Most right fielders used by both clubs, series
N.L.—7—St. Louis 5, San Francisco 2, 1987 (7-game series).
A.L.—6—Seattle 4, New York 2, 2000 (6-game series).

Most right fielders, game
N.L.—4—St. Louis vs. San Francisco, October 11, 1987.
A.L.—3
New York vs. Oakland, October 14, 1981.
Seattle vs. New York, October 20, 2001.

Most right fielders used by both clubs, game
N.L.—5
St. Louis 4, San Francisco 1, October 11, 1987.
St. Louis 3, San Francisco 2, October 13, 1987.
A.L.—5—Seattle 3, New York 2, October 20, 2001.

CATCHERS

Most catchers, series
A.L.—3—Kansas City vs. New York, 1976 (5-game series).
N.L.—3
Philadelphia vs. Cincinnati, 1976 (3-game series).
Houston vs. Philadelphia, 1980 (5-game series).
Chicago vs. San Francisco, 1989 (5-game series).
Atlanta vs. Philadelphia, 1993 (6-game series).

Most catchers used by both clubs, series
N.L.—5
Houston 3, Philadelphia 2, 1980 (5-game series).
Chicago 3, San Francisco 2, 1989 (5-game series).
Atlanta 3, Philadelphia 2, 1993 (6-game series).
A.L.—4—Made in many series.

Most catchers, game
A.L.-N.L.—2—Held by many clubs.

Most catchers used by both clubs, nine-inning game
N.L.—4
Chicago 2, San Francisco 2, October 8, 1989.
Atlanta 2, St. Louis 2, October 14, 1996.
Atlanta 2, San Diego 2, October 10, 1998.
A.L.—4
New York 2, Boston 2, October 16, 1999.
Seattle 2, New York 2, October 20, 2001.

Most catchers used by both clubs, extra-inning game
A.L.—4—Baltimore 2, Minnesota 2, October 4, 1969, 12 innings.
N.L.—4
New York 2, Los Angeles 2, October 9, 1988, 12 innings.
Atlanta 2, New York 2, October 17, 1999, 15 innings.
Atlanta 2, New York 2, October 19, 1999, 11 innings.

PITCHERS

Most pitchers, series
3-game series
N.L.—10—Pittsburgh vs. Cincinnati, 1975.
A.L.—9—Minnesota vs. Baltimore, 1969, 1970.
4-game series
A.L.—10—Boston vs. Oakland, 1990.
N.L.—9—San Francisco vs. Pittsburgh, 1971.
Los Angeles vs. Philadelphia, 1977, 1978.
Cincinnati vs. Atlanta, 1995.
5-game series
A.L.—11—Seattle vs. New York, 2001.
N.L.—10—Pittsburgh vs. Cincinnati, 1972.
San Diego vs. Chicago, 1984.
St. Louis vs. New York, 2000.
New York vs. St. Louis, 2000.
Atlanta vs. Arizona, 2001.
6-game series
A.L.—11—Oakland vs. Toronto, 1992.
Cleveland vs. Seattle, 1995.
Cleveland vs. Baltimore, 1997.
Cleveland vs. New York, 1998.
N.L.—11—New York vs. Atlanta, 1999.
7-game series
N.L.—11—Pittsburgh vs. Atlanta, 1991.
A.L.—9—California vs. Boston, 1986.

For a list of players and pitchers used each series, see page 458.

Most pitchers used by both clubs, series
3-game series
N.L.—17—Pittsburgh 10, Cincinnati 7, 1975.
Cincinnati 9, Pittsburgh 8, 1979.
A.L.—16—Minnesota 9, Baltimore 7, 1969.
4-game series
N.L.—17—Los Angeles 9, Philadelphia 8, 1978.
Cincinnati 9, Atlanta 8, 1995.
A.L.—16—Oakland 9, Boston 7, 1988.
Boston 10, Oakland 6, 1990.
5-game series
N.L.—20—New York 10, Atlanta 10, 1999.
St. Louis 10, New York 10, 2000.
A.L.—20—Seattle 11, New York 9, 2001.
6-game series
A.L.—21—Cleveland 11, Seattle 10, 1995.
N.L.—19—San Diego 10, Atlanta 9, 1998.
7-game series
N.L.—20—Pittsburgh 11, Atlanta 9, 1991.
Pittsburgh 10, Atlanta 10, 1992.
Atlanta 10, St. Louis 10, 1996.
A.L.—16—California 9, Boston 7, 1986.

Fewest pitchers, series
A.L.—4
Baltimore vs. Minnesota, 1970 (3-game series).
Baltimore vs. Oakland, 1971 (3-game series).
Kansas City vs. New York, 1980 (3-game series).
N.L.—5
Pittsburgh vs. Cincinnati, 1970 (3-game series).
St. Louis vs. Atlanta, 1982 (3-game series).
Philadelphia vs. Los Angeles, 1983 (4-game series).

Fewest pitchers used by both clubs, series
A.L.—10—New York 6, Kansas City 4, 1980 (3-game series).
N.L.—12—Cincinnati 7, Pittsburgh 5, 1970 (3-game series).

Most pitchers, nine-inning game
A.L.—7—Minnesota vs. Baltimore, October 6, 1969.
N.L.—7
San Francisco vs. St. Louis, October 14, 1987.
Pittsburgh vs. Atlanta, October 7, 1992.
Atlanta vs. Arizona, October 19, 2001.

Most pitchers, extra-inning game

N.L.—9—New York vs. Atlanta, October 17, 1999, 15 innings.

A.L.—7

Cleveland vs. Baltimore, October 11, 1997, 12 innings.
Cleveland vs. New York, October 7, 1998, 12 innings.

Most pitchers used by winning club, nine-inning game

N.L.—6

Los Angeles vs. Philadelphia, October 7, 1977.
St. Louis vs. Atlanta, October 13, 1996.
Arizona vs. Atlanta, October 20, 2001.

A.L.—6

Oakland vs. Boston, October 8, 1988.
Cleveland vs. Baltimore, October 12, 1997.
New York vs. Boston, October 14, 1999.

Most pitchers used by winning club, extra-inning game

A.L.—9—New York vs. Atlanta, October 17, 1999, 15 innings.
N.L.—7—Los Angeles vs. New York, October 9, 1988, 12 innings.

Most pitchers used by losing club, nine-inning game

A.L.—7—Minnesota vs. Baltimore, October 6, 1969.
N.L.—7

San Francisco vs. St. Louis, October 14, 1987.
Pittsburgh vs. Atlanta, October 7, 1992.
Atlanta vs. Arizona, October 19, 2001.

Most pitchers used by losing club, extra-inning game

N.L.—8—New York vs. Atlanta, October 19, 1999, 11 innings.
A.L.—Less than nine-inning record.

Most pitchers used by both clubs, nine-inning game

N.L.—12

Pittsburgh 7, Atlanta 5, October 7, 1992.
Arizona 6, Atlanta 6, October 20, 2001.

A.L.—11

Baltimore 6, New York 5, October 12, 1996.
Cleveland 6, Baltimore 5, October 12, 1997.

Most pitchers used by both clubs, extra-inning game

N.L.—15—New York 9, Atlanta 6, October 17, 1999, 15 innings.
A.L.—13—Cleveland 7, Baltimore 6, October 11, 1997, 12 innings.

Most pitchers, inning

A.L.—5

Kansas City vs. New York, October 12, 1976, sixth inning.
New York vs. Boston, October 18, 1999, eighth inning.

N.L.—4

Los Angeles vs. New York, October 8, 1988, eighth inning.
New York vs. Atlanta, October 17, 1999, seventh inning.

SERIES

Most series played

N.L.—11—Atlanta, 1969, 1982, 1991, 1992, 1993, 1995 through 1999, 2001 (won five, lost six).

A.L.—10

Oakland, 1971, 1972, 1973, 1974, 1975, 1981, 1988, 1989, 1990, 1992 (won six, lost four).
New York, 1976 through 1978, 1980, 1981, 1996, 1998 through 2001 (won nine, lost one).

For a complete list of results and a complete list of series won and lost by teams, see page 451.

INDIVIDUAL BATTING

GAMES

Most games, career
Both leagues—46—David Justice, Atlanta N.L., 1991 through 1993, 1995; Cleveland A.L., 1997, 1998; New York A.L., 2000, 2001; eight series (23 in N.L., 23 in A.L.).
A.L.—45—Reggie Jackson, Oakland, 1971, 1972, 1973, 1974, 1975; New York, 1977, 1978, 1980, 1981; California, 1982, 1986; 11 series.
N.L.—38—Terry Pendleton, St. Louis, 1985, 1987; Atlanta, 1991, 1992, 1993, 1996; six series.

Most games with one club, career
N.L.—34—Chipper Jones, Atlanta, 1995 through 1999, 2001; six series.
A.L.—27
George Brett, Kansas City, 1976, 1977, 1978, 1980, 1984, 1985; six series.
Derek Jeter, New York, 1996, 1998 through 2001; five series.
Tino Martinez, New York, 1996, 1998 through 2001; five series.
Bernie Williams, New York, 1996, 1998 through 2001; five series.

Most games by pinch-hitter, career
Both leagues—10—Danny Heep, Houston N.L., 1980 (1); New York N.L., 1986 (4); Los Angeles N.L., 1988 (3); Boston A.L., 1990 (2) (10 plate appearances, seven at-bats).
N.L.—8—Lee Mazzilli, New York, 1986 (5), 1988 (3) (eight plate appearances, seven at-bats).
A.L.—6—Dane Iorg, Kansas City, 1984 (2), 1985 (4) (six plate appearances, four at-bats).

Most games by pinch-hitter, series
N.L.—6—Lonnie Smith, Atlanta, 1992 (7-game series).
A.L.—4
George Hendrick, Oakland, 1972 (5-game series).
Dane Iorg, Kansas City, 1985 (7-game series).

Most games by pinch-runner, career
A.L.—4—Lance Blankenship, Oakland, 1990, 1992; two series.
N.L.—3—Dave Concepcion, Cincinnati, 1970, 1972; two series).

Most games by pinch-runner, series
A.L.—3
Dave Stapleton, Boston, 1986.
Lance Blankenship, Oakland, 1990.
Eric Fox, Oakland, 1992.
Ruben Amaro Jr., Cleveland, 1995.
Jose Vizcaino, New York, 2000.
N.L.—3
Marty Malloy, Atlanta, 1998.
Joe McEwing, New York, 2000.

BATTING AVERAGE

Highest batting average, career (50 or more at-bats)
N.L.—.468—Will Clark, San Francisco, 1987, 1989; St. Louis, 2000; three series, 17 games, 62 at-bats, 29 hits.
A.L.—.392—Devon White, California, 1986; Toronto, 1991, 1992, 1993; four series, 21 games, 74 at-bats, 29 hits.

For a list of batting leaders each series and a complete list of .450 hitters, see page 453.

Highest batting average, series (10 or more at-bats)
3-game series
A.L.—.583—Brooks Robinson, Baltimore, 1970.
N.L.—.538—Art Shamsky, New York, 1969.
(Jay Johnstone, Philadelphia, 1976, had a .778 batting average in nine at-bats. If under rule 10.23 (a) Johnstone were charged with another at-bat to give him enough to qualify, he would have a batting average of .700.)
4-game series
A.L.—.500—Ron Hassey, Oakland, 1988.
N.L.—.467—Dusty Baker, Los Angeles, 1978.
Mike Schmidt, Philadelphia, 1983.

5-game series
N.L.—.650—Will Clark, San Francisco, 1989.
A.L.—.611—Fred Lynn, California, 1982.
6-game series
N.L.—.500—Keith Lockhart, Atlanta, 1997.
Roger Cedeno, New York, 1999.
Eddie Perez, Atlanta, 1999.
A.L.—.458—Kenny Lofton, Cleveland, 1995.
7-game series
N.L.—.542—Javy Lopez, Atlanta, 1996.
A.L.—.455—Bob Boone, California, 1986.

SLUGGING AVERAGE

Highest slugging average, career (50 or more at-bats)
N.L.—.806—Will Clark, San Francisco, 1987, 1989; St. Louis, 2000; three series, 17 games, 62 at-bats, 29 hits, seven doubles, one triple, four home runs, 50 total bases.
A.L.—.728—George Brett, Kansas City, 1976, 1977, 1978, 1980, 1984, 1985; six series, 27 games, 103 at-bats, 35 hits, five doubles, four triples, nine home runs, 75 total bases).

Highest slugging average, series (10 or more at-bats)
3-game series
N.L.—1.182—Willie Stargell, Pittsburgh, 1979.
A.L.—.917—Tony Oliva, Minnesota, 1970.
Reggie Jackson, Oakland, 1971
Bob Watson, New York, 1980.
Graig Nettles, New York, 1981.
4-game series
N.L.—1.250—Bob Robertson, Pittsburgh, 1971.
A.L.—1.056—George Brett, Kansas City, 1978.
5-game series
N.L.—1.200—Will Clark, San Francisco, 1989.
A.L.—1.167—Darryl Strawberry, New York, 1996.
6-game series
N.L.—.900—Eddie Perez, Atlanta, 1999.
A.L.—.826—Jim Thome, Cleveland, 1998.
7-game series
N.L.—1.182—Lloyd McClendon, Pittsburgh, 1992.
A.L.—.826—George Brett, Kansas City, 1985.

AT-BATS AND PLATE APPEARANCES

Most at-bats, career
Both leagues—166—David Justice, Atlanta N.L., 1991 through 1993, 1995; Cleveland A.L., 1997, 1998; New York A.L., 2000, 2001; eight series (82 in N.L., 84 in A.L.).
A.L.—163—Reggie Jackson, Oakland, 1971, 1972, 1973, 1974, 1975; New York, 1977, 1978, 1980, 1981; California, 1982, 1986; 11 series, 45 games).
N.L.—135—Terry Pendleton, St. Louis, 1985, 1987; Atlanta, 1991, 1992, 1993, 1996; six series, 38 games).

Most at-bats by pinch-hitter, career
Both leagues—7—Danny Heep, Houston N.L., 1980 (1), New York N.L., 1986 (3), Los Angeles N.L., 1988 (1), Boston A.L., 1990 (2).
N.L.—7—Lee Mazzilli, New York, 1986 (5), 1988 (2).
A.L.—5—Cliff Johnson, New York, 1977 (1), 1978 (1), Toronto, 1985 (3).

Most plate appearances by pinch-hitter, career
Both leagues—10—Danny Heep, Houston N.L., 1980 (1), New York N.L., 1986 (4); Los Angeles N.L., 1988 (3); Boston A.L., 1990 (2).
N.L.—8—Lee Mazzilli, New York, 1986 (5), 1988 (3).
A.L.—6—Dane Iorg, Kansas City, 1984 (2), 1985 (4).

Most consecutive hitless times at bat, career
Both leagues—31—Billy North, Oakland A.L., 1974 (last 13 times at bat), 1975 (all 10 times at bat); Los Angeles N.L., 1978 (all eight times at bat).
N.L.—30—Cesar Geronimo, Cincinnati, 1973 (last 13 times at bat), 1975 (all 10 times at bat), 1976 (first seven times at bat).
A.L.—24—Bert Campaneris, Oakland, 1974 (last 13 times at bat), 1975 (all 11 times at bat); California, 1979 (no times at bat).

Most at-bats, series

3-game series
A.L.—15—Mark Belanger, Baltimore, 1969.
    Paul Blair, Baltimore, 1969.
N.L.—15—Ken Oberkfell, St. Louis, 1982.

4-game series
N.L.—19—Dave Cash, Pittsburgh, 1971.
    Garry Maddox, Philadelphia, 1978.
    Marquis Grissom, Atlanta, 1995.
A.L.—18—George Brett, Kansas City, 1978.
    Thurman Munson, New York, 1978.
    Rudy Law, Chicago, 1983.

5-game series
N.L.—24—Mike Schmidt, Philadelphia, 1980.
A.L.—24—Kirby Puckett, Minnesota, 1987.
    Derek Jeter, New York, 1996.
    Jose Offerman, Boston, 1999.

6-game series
N.L.—28—Gerald Williams, Atlanta, 1999.
A.L.—27—Joe Carter, Toronto, 1993.
    Tim Raines Sr., Chicago, 1993.
    Devon White, Toronto, 1993.
    Kenny Lofton, Cleveland, 1998.

7-game series
N.L.—35—Marquis Grissom, Atlanta, 1996.
A.L.—32—Doug DeCinces, California, 1986.

Most at-bats by pinch-hitter, series
N.L.—6—Lonnie Smith, Atlanta, 1992.
A.L.—4—George Hendrick, Oakland, 1972.

Most at-bats by player with no hits, career
A.L.—15
 Tom Brookens, Detroit, 1984 (2), 1987 (15).
 Ron Karkovice, Chicago, 1993.
N.L.—13—Ray Lankford, St. Louis, 1996.

Most at-bats, nine-inning game
A.L.—6
 Paul Blair, Baltimore, October 6, 1969.
 Kirby Puckett, Minnesota, October 12, 1987.
 Rickey Henderson, Toronto, October 5, 1993.
 Jose Offerman, Boston, October 16, 1999.
 John Valentin, Boston, October 16, 1999.
N.L.—6
 Marquis Grissom, Atlanta, October 14, 1996.
 Fred McGriff, Atlanta, October 14, 1996.
 Jermaine Dye, Atlanta, October 14, 1996.
 Marquis Grissom, Atlanta, October 17, 1996.
 Tony Womack, Arizona, October 20, 2001.
 Craig Counsell, Arizona, October 20, 2001.

Most at-bats, extra-inning game
N.L.—7
 Glenn Davis, Houston, October 15, 1986, 16 innings.
 Bill Doran, Houston, October 15, 1986, 16 innings.
 Billy Hatcher, Houston, October 15, 1986, 16 innings.
 Keith Hernandez, New York, October 15, 1986, 16 innings.
 Mookie Wilson, New York, October 15, 1986, 16 innings.
 Brian Jordan, Atlanta, October 17, 1999, 15 innings.
 Gerald Williams, Atlanta, October 17, 1999, 15 innings.
 Robin Ventura, New York, October 17, 1999, 15 innings.
A.L.—6—Held by many players.

Most at-bats by player with no hits, nine-inning game
A.L.—6—Rickey Henderson, Toronto, October 5, 1993.
N.L.—5—Held by many players.

Most at-bats by player with no hits, extra-inning game
A.L.—6
 Don Buford, Baltimore, October 4, 1969, 12 innings.
 Chuck Knoblauch, New York, October 7, 1998, 12 innings.
N.L.—6—Alan Ashby, Houston, October 15, 1986, 16 innings.

Most at-bats, inning
A.L.-N.L.—2—Held by many players.

Most times faced pitcher, inning
A.L.-N.L.—2—Held by many players.

RUNS

Most runs, career
Both leagues—24—David Justice, Atlanta N.L., 1991 through
 1993, 1995; Cleveland A.L., 1997, 1998; New York A.L., 2000,
 2001; eight series (12 in N.L., 12 in A.L.).
A.L.—22
 George Brett, Kansas City, 1976, 1977, 1978, 1980, 1984,
  1985; six series, 27 games.
 Bernie Williams, New York, 1996, 1998 through 2001; five
  series, 27 games.
N.L.—20—Chipper Jones, Atlanta, 1995 through 1999, 2001;
 six series, 34 games.

Most runs by pinch-hitter, career
N.L.—2—Ty Cline, Cincinnati, 1970; one series, two games.
A.L.—1—Held by many players.

Most runs by pinch-runner, career
A.L.—2
 Marshall Edwards, Milwaukee, 1982; one series, two games.
 Devon White, California, 1986; one series, two games.
N.L.—2
 Gene Clines, Pittsburgh, 1972, 1974; two series, two games.
 Rafael Landestoy, Houston, 1980; one series, two games.
 Jose Gonzalez, Los Angeles, 1988; one series, two games.
 Joe McEwing, New York, 2000; one series, three games.

Most runs, series

3-game series
A.L.—5—Mark Belanger, Baltimore, 1970.
N.L.—4—Held by many players.

4-game series
A.L.—7—George Brett, Kansas City, 1978.
N.L.—6—Steve Garvey, Los Angeles, 1978.

5-game series
A.L.—8—Rickey Henderson, Oakland, 1989.
N.L.—8—Will Clark, San Francisco, 1989.
    Timo Perez, New York, 2000.

6-game series
A.L.—7—Dave Winfield, Toronto, 1992.
    Paul Molitor, Toronto, 1993.
N.L.—6—Willie McGee, St. Louis, 1985.
    Fred McGriff, Atlanta, 1993.
    Gary Sheffield, Florida, 1997.

7-game series
A.L.—8—Jim Rice, Boston, 1986.
N.L.—8—Javy Lopez, Atlanta, 1996.

Most runs by pinch-hitter, series
N.L.—2—Ty Cline, Cincinnati, 1970; two games.
A.L.—1—Held by many players.

Most runs by pinch-runner, series
N.L.—2
 Rafael Landestoy, Houston, 1980; two games.
 Jose Gonzalez, Los Angeles, 1988; two games.
 Joe McEwing, New York, 2000; three games.
A.L.—2
 Marshall Edwards, Milwaukee, 1982; two games.
 Devon White, California, 1986; two games.

Most runs, game
N.L.—4
 Bob Robertson, Pittsburgh, October 3, 1971.
 Steve Garvey, Los Angeles, October 9, 1974.
 Will Clark, San Francisco, October 4, 1989.
 Javy Lopez, Atlanta, October 14, 1996.
 Fred McGriff, Atlanta, October 17, 1996.
A.L.—4
 Mark Brouhard, Milwaukee, October 9, 1982.
 Eddie Murray, Baltimore, October 7, 1983.
 George Brett, Kansas City, October 11, 1985.

Most runs, inning
A.L.-N.L.—1—Held by many players.

HITS
CAREER AND SERIES

Most hits, career
N.L.—45—Pete Rose, Cincinnati, 1970, 1972, 1973, 1975, 1976; Philadelphia, 1980, 1983 (seven series, 28 games).
A.L.—37—Reggie Jackson, Oakland, 1971, 1972, 1973, 1974, 1975; New York, 1977, 1978, 1980, 1981; California, 1982, 1986 (11 series, 45 games).

Most hits by pinch-hitter, career
N.L.—3
Paul Popovich, Pittsburgh, 1974 (one series, three games).
Manny Mota, Los Angeles, 1974, 1977, 1978 (three series, six games).
Francisco Cabrera, Atlanta, 1992, 1993 (two series, five games).
A.L.—2—Held by many players.

Most hits, series
3-game series
A.L.—7—Brooks Robinson, Baltimore, 1969, 1970.
N.L.—7—Art Shamsky, New York, 1969.
Jay Johnstone, Philadelphia, 1976.
4-game series
N.L.—8—Dave Cash, Pittsburgh, 1971.
A.L.—7—George Brett, Kansas City, 1978.
Rod Carew, California, 1979.
Rudy Law, Chicago, 1983.
Wade Boggs, Boston, 1990.
Carney Lansford, Oakland, 1990.
5-game series
N.L.—13—Will Clark, San Francisco, 1989.
A.L.—11—Chris Chambliss, New York, 1976.
Fred Lynn, California, 1982.
Jose Offerman, Boston, 1999.
6-game series
A.L.—12—Tim Raines Sr., Chicago, 1993.
Devon White, Toronto, 1993.
N.L.—10—Ozzie Smith, St. Louis, 1985.
Fred McGriff, Atlanta, 1993.
Eddie Perez, Atlanta, 1999.
7-game series
N.L.—13—Javy Lopez, Atlanta, 1996.
A.L.—11—Marty Barrett, Boston, 1986.

Most hits by pinch-hitter, series
N.L.—3—Paul Popovich, Pittsburgh, 1974 (three games).
A.L.—2—Held by many players.

Most hits, two consecutive series
N.L.—22—Will Clark, San Francisco, 1987 (9), 1989 (13).
A.L.—20
Roberto Alomar, Toronto, 1991 (9), 1992 (11).
Devon White, Toronto, 1992 (8), 1993 (12).

Most series with one or more hits
A.L.—10—Reggie Jackson, Oakland, 1971, 1972, 1973, 1974, 1975; New York, 1977, 1978, 1980; California, 1982, 1986.
N.L.—7
Richie Hebner, Pittsburgh, 1970, 1971, 1972, 1974, 1975; Philadelphia, 1977, 1978.
Pete Rose, Cincinnati, 1970, 1972, 1973, 1975, 1976; Philadelphia, 1980, 1983.

Most consecutive hits, career
N.L.—6—Steve Garvey, Los Angeles, October 9, 1974 (4), October 4, 1977 (2).
A.L.—6—Paul Molitor, Toronto, October 5 (4), 6 (2), 1993.

Most consecutive hits by pinch-hitter, career
N.L.—3—Paul Popovich, Pittsburgh, October 5, 6, 9, 1974.
A.L.—2—Held by many players.

Most consecutive hits, series
A.L.—6—Paul Molitor, Toronto, October 5 (4), 6 (2), 1993.
N.L.—5
Gary Matthews, Philadelphia, October 5 (1), 7 (3), 8 (1), 1983 (one base on balls during streak).
Will Clark, San Francisco, October 4 (4), 5 (1), 1989 (two bases on balls during streak).
Steve Buechele, Pittsburgh, October 12 (2), 13 (3), 1991.
Javy Lopez, Atlanta, October 14 (4), 16 (1), 1996.

GAME AND INNING

Most hits, game
A.L.—5—Paul Blair, Baltimore, October 6, 1969.
N.L.—4—Held by many players.

Most times reached base safely, game (batting 1.000)
A.L.—5
Reggie Jackson, New York, October 3, 1978 (two bases on balls, one single, one double, one home run).
Graig Nettles, New York, October 14, 1981 (one hit by pitch, three singles, one home run).
Don Baylor, Boston, October 8, 1986 (two singles, three bases on balls).
Rich Gedman, Boston, October 12, 1986 (two singles, one double, one home run, one hit by pitch).
Frank Thomas, Chicago, October 5, 1993 (one single, four bases on balls).
Roberto Alomar, Toronto, October 10, 1993 (three singles, two bases on balls).
Kenny Lofton, Cleveland, October 10, 1995 (two singles, one triple, two bases on balls).
Rafael Palmeiro, Baltimore, October 9, 1996 (two bases on balls, one single, one double, one home run).
N.L.—5
Felix Millan, Atlanta, October 5, 1969 (three bases on balls, two singles).
Will Clark, San Francisco, October 4, 1989 (one base on balls, one single, one double, two home runs).

Most hits accounting for all club's hits, game
N.L.—2
Roberto Clemente, Pittsburgh, October 10, 1972.
Andy Kosco, Cincinnati, October 7, 1973.
A.L.—2—Willie Wilson, Kansas City, October 12, 1985.

Most consecutive games with one or more hits, career
N.L.—15—Pete Rose, Cincinnati, 1973 (last 3), 1975 (3), 1976 (3); Philadelphia, 1980 (5), 1983 (first 1).
A.L.—12—Don Baylor, California, 1982 (last 3); Boston, 1986 (7); Minnesota, 1987 (2).

Most hits in two consecutive games, series
A.L.—7—Tim Raines Sr., Chicago, October 8 (4), October 9 (3), 1993.
N.L.—6—Held by many players.

Most hits, inning
A.L.—2
Graig Nettles, New York, October 14, 1981, fourth inning.
Rickey Henderson, Oakland, October 6, 1990, ninth inning.
N.L.—2
Jack Clark, St. Louis, October 13, 1985, second inning.
Tito Landrum, St. Louis, October 13, 1985, second inning.
Jerome Walton, Chicago, October 5, 1989, first inning.
Barry Bonds, Pittsburgh, October 13, 1992, second inning.
Lloyd McClendon, Pittsburgh, October 13, 1992, second inning.

SINGLES

Most singles, career
N.L.—34—Pete Rose, Cincinnati, 1970, 1972, 1973, 1975, 1976; Philadelphia, 1980, 1983; seven series, 28 games.
A.L.—24—Reggie Jackson, Oakland, 1971, 1972, 1973, 1974, 1975; New York, 1977, 1978, 1980, 1981; California 1982, 1986; 11 series, 45 games.

Most singles by pinch-hitter, career
N.L.—3—Paul Popovich, Pittsburgh, 1974; one series, three games.
A.L.—2—Held by many players.

Most singles, series
3-game series
N.L.—7—Art Shamsky, New York, 1969.
A.L.—6—Brooks Robinson, Baltimore, 1969.
4-game series
N.L.—7—Bill Russell, Los Angeles, 1974.
A.L.—6—Chris Chambliss, New York, 1978.
Rudy Law, Chicago, 1983.
Carney Lansford, Oakland, 1990.

5-game series
  A.L.—10—Jose Offerman, Boston, 1999.
  N.L.—8—Pete Rose, Philadelphia, 1980.
    Terry Puhl, Houston, 1980.
    Jerome Walton, Chicago, 1989.
6-game series
  A.L.—10—Tim Raines Sr., Chicago, 1993.
    Omar Vizquel, Cleveland, 1998.
  N.L.—7—Jack Clark, St. Louis, 1985.
    Ozzie Smith, St. Louis, 1985.
    Terry Pendleton, Atlanta, 1993.
    Fred McGriff, Atlanta, 1993.
7-game series
  A.L.—9—Marty Barrett, Boston, 1986.
    Bob Boone, California, 1986.
  N.L.—9—Jay Bell, Pittsburgh, 1991.
    Mark Lemke, Atlanta, 1996.
    Chipper Jones, Atlanta, 1996.

Most singles by pinch-hitter, series
N.L.—3—Paul Popovich, Pittsburgh, 1974 (three games).
A.L.—2—Held by many players.

Most singles, game
A.L.—4
  Brooks Robinson, Baltimore, October 4, 1969, 12 innings.
  Chris Chambliss, New York, October 4, 1978.
  Kelly Gruber, Toronto, October 7, 1989.
  Jerry Browne, Oakland, October 12, 1992.
N.L.—4
  Terry Puhl, Houston, October 12, 1980, 10 innings.
  Tito Landrum, St. Louis, October 13, 1985.
  Chipper Jones, Atlanta, October 9, 1996.

Most singles, inning
A.L.—2
  Graig Nettles, New York, October 14, 1981, fourth inning.
  Rickey Henderson, Oakland, October 6, 1990, ninth inning.
N.L.—2
  Jack Clark, St. Louis, October 13, 1985, second inning.
  Tito Landrum, St. Louis, October 13, 1985, second inning.
  Jerome Walton, Chicago, October 5, 1989, first inning.
  Lloyd McClendon, Pittsburgh, October 13, 1992, second inning.

DOUBLES

Most doubles, career
Both leagues—7
  Rickey Henderson, Oakland A.L., 1981, 1989, 1990, 1992; Toronto A.L., 1993; New York, 1999; Seattle, 2000; seven series, 33 games (6 in A.L., 1 in N.L.).
  David Justice, Atlanta N.L., 1991 through 1993, 1995; Cleveland A.L., 1997, 1998; New York A.L., 2000, 2001; eight series (3 in N.L., 4 in A.L.).
N.L.—7
  Pete Rose, Cincinnati, 1970, 1972, 1973, 1975, 1976; Philadelphia, 1980, 1983; seven series, 28 games.
  Richie Hebner, Pittsburgh, 1970, 1971, 1972, 1974, 1975; Philadelphia, 1977, 1978; Chicago, 1984; eight series, 27 games.
  Mike Schmidt, Philadelphia, 1976, 1977, 1978, 1980, 1983; five series, 20 games.
  Ron Cey, Los Angeles, 1974, 1977, 1978, 1981; Chicago, 1984; five series, 22 games.
  Fred McGriff, Atlanta, 1993, 1995, 1996, 1997; four series, 23 games.
  Javy Lopez, Atlanta, 1992, 1995, 1996, 1997, 1998; five series, 22 games.
  Will Clark, San Francisco, 1987, 1989; St. Louis, 2000; three series, 17 games.
  Chipper Jones, Atlanta, 1995 through 2001, except 2000; six series, 34 games.
A.L.—7
  Hal McRae, Kansas City, 1976, 1977, 1978, 1980, 1984, 1985; six series, 25 games.
  Reggie Jackson, Oakland, 1971, 1972, 1973, 1974, 1975; New York, 1977, 1978, 1980, 1981; California, 1982, 1986; 11 series, 45 games.

Chuck Knoblauch, Minnesota, 1991; New York, 1998 through 2001; five series, 27 games.

Most doubles by pinch-hitter, career
N.L.—2—Manny Mota, Los Angeles, 1974, 1977, 1978; three series, six games.
A.L.—1—Held by many players.

Most doubles, series
3-game series
  N.L.—3—Joe Morgan, Cincinnati, 1975.
    Darrell Porter, St. Louis, 1982.
  A.L.—3—Bob Watson, New York, 1980.
4-game series
  N.L.—4—Fred McGriff, Atlanta, 1995.
  A.L.—3—Rod Carew, California, 1979.
5-game series
  A.L.—4—Matty Alou, Oakland, 1972.
    Tom Brunansky, Minnesota, 1987.
  N.L.—4—Pete Rose, Cincinnati, 1972.
6-game series
  N.L.—4—Tom Herr, St. Louis, 1985.
    Edgardo Alfonzo, New York, 1999.
  A.L.—3—Brian Giles, Cleveland, 1997.
    Mark McLemore, Seattle, 2000.
    John Olerud, Seattle, 2000.
7-game series
  N.L.—5—Javy Lopez, Atlanta, 1996.
  A.L.—4—Damaso Garcia, Toronto, 1985.

Most doubles, game
N.L.—3—Fred McGriff, Atlanta, October 11, 1995, 10 innings.
A.L.—2—Held by many players.

Most doubles, inning
A.L.-N.L.—1—Held by many players.

TRIPLES

Most triples, career
A.L.—4—George Brett, Kansas City, 1976, 1977, 1978, 1980, 1984, 1985; six series, 27 games.
N.L.—3
  Willie McGee, St. Louis, 1982, 1985, 1987, 1996; four series, 22 games.
  Mariano Duncan, Los Angeles, Cincinnati, Philadelphia, 1985, 1990, 1993, 1995; four series, 17 games.

Most triples by pinch-hitter, career
N.L.—1
  Ty Cline, Cincinnati, 1970; one series, two games.
  Lenny Dykstra, New York, 1986; one series, two games.
  Lonnie Smith, Atlanta, 1992; one series, six games.
  Dmitri Young, St. Louis, 1996; one series, three games.
A.L.—1—Al Martin, Seattle, 2001; one series, two games.

Most triples, series
A.L.—2
  George Brett, Kansas City, 1977 (5-game series).
  Kenny Lofton, Cleveland, 1995 (6-game series).
N.L.—2
  Willie McGee, St. Louis, 1982 (3-game series).
  Mariano Duncan, Philadelphia, 1993 (6-game series).

Most triples, game
N.L.—2—Mariano Duncan, October 9, 1993.
A.L.—1—Held by many players.

Most bases-loaded triples, game
A.L.—1
  Jim Sundberg, Kansas City, October 16, 1985.
  Mark McLemore, Seattle, October 20, 2001.
N.L.—1—Tom Glavine, Atlanta, October 17, 1996.

HOME RUNS
CAREER AND SERIES

Most home runs, career
A.L.—9—George Brett, Kansas City, 1976, 1977, 1978, 1980, 1984, 1985; six series, 27 games.

N.L.—8—Steve Garvey, Los Angeles, 1974, 1977, 1978, 1981; San Diego, 1984; five series, 22 games.

For a list of all home runs each series and a complete list of players with four or more career home runs, see page 455.

Most home runs, series
3-game series
N.L.—3—Hank Aaron, Atlanta, 1969.
A.L.—2—Held by many players.
4-game series
N.L.—4—Bob Robertson, Pittsburgh, 1971.
Steve Garvey, Los Angeles, 1978.
A.L.—3—George Brett, Kansas City, 1978.
Jose Canseco, Oakland, 1988.
5-game series
N.L.—3—Rusty Staub, New York, 1973.
A.L.—3—Darryl Strawberry, New York, 1996.
Todd Zeile, Baltimore, 1996.
Bernie Williams, New York, 2001.
6-game series
A.L.—4—Jim Thome, Cleveland, 1998.
N.L.—3—Bill Madlock, Los Angeles, 1985.
7-game series
N.L.—4—Jeffrey Leonard, San Francisco, 1987.
A.L.—3—George Brett, Kansas City, 1985.

Most series with one or more home runs
N.L.—5—Johnny Bench, Cincinnati, 1970 (1), 1972 (1), 1973 (1), 1976 (1), 1979 (1).
A.L.—4
Graig Nettles, New York, 1976 (2), 1978 (1), 1980 (1), 1981 (1).
Reggie Jackson, Oakland, 1971 (2), 1975 (1); New York, 1978 (2); California, 1982 (1).
George Brett, Kansas City, 1976 (1), 1978 (3), 1980 (2), 1985 (3).
Eddie Murray, Baltimore, 1979, 1983, 1996; Cleveland, 1995.
Bernie Williams, New York, 1996 (2), 1999 (1), 2000 (1), 2001 (3).

Most series with two or more home runs
A.L.—3
George Brett, Kansas City, 1978 (3), 1980 (2), 1985 (3).
Manny Ramirez, Cleveland, 1995 (2), 1996 (2), 1998 (2).
N.L.—2
Steve Garvey, Los Angeles, 1974 (2), 1978 (4).
Willie Stargell, Pittsburgh, 1974 (2), 1979 (2).
Gary Matthews, Philadelphia, 1983 (3); Chicago, 1984 (2).
Ron Gant, Atlanta, 1992 (2); St. Louis, 1996.

GAME AND INNING

Most home runs, game
N.L.—3—Bob Robertson, Pittsburgh, October 3, 1971.
A.L.—3—George Brett, Kansas City, October 6, 1978.

Most grand slams, game
A.L.—1
Mike Cuellar, Baltimore, October 3, 1970, fourth inning.
Don Baylor, California, October 9, 1982, eighth inning.
Jim Thome, Cleveland, October 13, 1998, fifth inning.
Ricky Ledee, New York, October 17, 1999, ninth inning.
N.L.—1
Ron Cey, Los Angeles, October 4, 1977, seventh inning.
Dusty Baker, Los Angeles, October 5, 1977, fourth inning.
Will Clark, San Francisco, October 4, 1989, fourth inning.
Ron Gant, Atlanta, October 7, 1992, fifth inning.
Gary Gaetti, St. Louis, October 10, 1996, seventh inning.
Andres Galarraga, Atlanta, October 11, 1998, seventh inning.

Inside-the-park home runs
A.L.—Graig Nettles, New York, October 9, 1980, fifth inning (none on base).
Paul Molitor, Milwaukee, October 6, 1982, fifth inning (one on base).
N.L.—Never accomplished.

Most home runs by pinch-hitter, game
N.L.—1
Jerry Martin, Philadelphia, October 4, 1978, ninth inning.
Bake McBride, Philadelphia, October 7, 1978, seventh inning.
Harry Spilman, San Francisco, October 9, 1987, ninth inning.
Greg Myers, San Diego, October 12, 1998, ninth inning.
Erubiel Durazo, Arizona, October 21, 2001, fifth inning.
A.L.—1
John Lowenstein, Baltimore, October 3, 1979, 10th inning.
Pat Sheridan, Kansas City, October 9, 1985, ninth inning.
Mike Pagliarulo, Minnesota, October 11, 1991, 10th inning.
Eric Davis, Baltimore, October 13, 1997, ninth inning.
Ricky Ledee, New York, October 17, 1999, ninth inning.
Jay Buhner, Seattle, October 20, 2001, ninth inning.

Home runs by leadoff batter, start of game
A.L.—Bert Campaneris, Oakland, October 7, 1973 (at Baltimore).
George Brett, Kansas City, October 6, 1978 (at New York).
Brady Anderson, Baltimore, October 8, 1997 (at Baltimore).
Kenny Lofton, Cleveland, October 11, 1998 (at Cleveland).
N.L.—Bob Dernier, Chicago, October 2, 1984 (at Chicago).
Orlando Merced, Pittsburgh, October 12, 1991 (at Atlanta).
Marcus Giles, Atlanta, October 17, 2001 (at Arizona).

Home runs winning 1-0 games
A.L.—Sal Bando, Oakland, October 8, 1974, fourth inning.
Tony Fernandez, Cleveland, October 15, 1997, 11th inning.
N.L.—Mike Schmidt, Philadelphia, October 4, 1983, first inning.
Glenn Davis, Houston, October 8, 1986, second inning.

Most home runs by pitcher, game
A.L.—1—Mike Cuellar, Baltimore, October 3, 1970 (three on base).
N.L.—1
Don Gullett, Cincinnati, October 4, 1975 (one on base).
Steve Carlton, Philadelphia, October 6, 1978 (two on base).
Rick Sutcliffe, Chicago, October 2, 1984 (none on base).

Most home runs by rookie, game
A.L.-N.L.—1—Held by many players.

Most consecutive games hitting one or more home runs, series
N.L.—4—Jeffrey Leonard, San Francisco, October 6, 7, 9, 10, 1987.
A.L.—3—Bernie Williams, New York, October 20, 21, 22, 2001.

Most home runs in two consecutive games, series (homering each game)
N.L.—4—Bob Robertson, Pittsburgh, October 3 (3), October 5 (1), 1971.
A.L.—3
Jay Buhner, Seattle, October 11, 13 (2), 1995, second game 11 innings.
Darryl Strawberry, New York, October 12 (2), 13, 1996.

Hitting home run in first championship series at-bat
A.L.—Frank Robinson, Baltimore, October 4, 1969, fourth inning (received base on balls in first inning).
Norm Cash, Detroit, October 7, 1972, second inning.
Dan Ford, California, October 3, 1979, first inning.
John Lowenstein, Baltimore, October 3, 1979, 10th inning (pinch-hit).
Rich Cerone, New York, October 8, 1980, first inning.
Gorman Thomas, Milwaukee, October 5, 1982, second inning.
Gary Gaetti, Minnesota, October 7, 1987, second inning.
Mike Blowers, Seattle, October 10, 1995, second inning.
Rafael Palmeiro, Baltimore, October 9, 1996, fourth inning (received base on balls in second inning).
N.L.—Joe Morgan, Cincinnati, October 7, 1972, first inning.
Bob Dernier, Chicago, October 2, 1984, first inning.
Rick Sutcliffe, Chicago, October 2, 1984, third inning.
Glenn Davis, Houston, October 8, 1986, second inning.
Mark Grace, Chicago, October 4, 1989, first inning.
Orlando Merced, Pittsburgh, October 12, 1991, first inning.

Hitting home runs in first two championship series at-bats
A.L.—Gary Gaetti, Minnesota, October 7, 1987, second and fifth innings.
N.L.—Never accomplished.

Most home runs, inning
A.L.-N.L.—1—Held by many players.

Most home runs, two consecutive innings
N.L.—2
Rusty Staub, New York, October 8, 1973, first and second innings.
Will Clark, San Francisco, October 4, 1989, third and fourth innings.
A.L.—Never accomplished.

TOTAL BASES

Most total bases, career
A.L.—75—George Brett, Kansas City, 1976, 1977, 1978, 1980, 1984, 1985; six series, 27 games.
N.L.—63—Pete Rose, Cincinnati, 1970, 1972, 1973, 1975, 1976; Philadelphia, 1980, 1983; seven series, 28 games.

Most total bases by pinch-hitter, career
N.L.—6—Jerry Martin, Philadelphia, 1977, 1978; two series, three games.
A.L.—4
John Lowenstein, Baltimore, 1979; one series, two games.
Pat Sheridan, Kansas City, 1985; one series, two games.
Mike Pagliarulo, Minnesota, 1991; one series, one game.
Eric Davis, Baltimore, 1997; one series, three games.
Ricky Ledee, New York, 1998, 1999; two series, two games.
Jay Buhner, Seattle, 2000, 2001; two series, two games.

Most total bases, series
3-game series
N.L.—16—Hank Aaron, Atlanta, 1969.
A.L.—11—Held by many players.
4-game series
N.L.—22—Steve Garvey, Los Angeles, 1978.
A.L.—19—George Brett, Kansas City, 1978.
5-game series
N.L.—24—Will Clark, San Francisco, 1989.
A.L.—20—Chris Chambliss, New York, 1976.
6-game series
A.L.—19—Jim Thome, Cleveland, 1998.
N.L.—18—Bill Madlock, Los Angeles, 1985.
7-game series
N.L.—24—Javy Lopez, Atlanta, 1996.
A.L.—19—George Brett, Kansas City, 1985.

Most total bases by pinch-hitter, series
N.L.—6—Jerry Martin, Philadelphia, 1978; two games.
A.L.—4
John Lowenstein, Baltimore, 1979; two games.
Pat Sheridan, Kansas City, 1985; two games.
Mike Pagliarulo, Minnesota, 1991; two games.
Eric Davis, Baltimore, 1997; three games.
Ricky Ledee, New York, 1999; one game.
Jay Buhner, Seattle, 2001; one game.

Most total bases, game
N.L.—14—Bob Robertson, Pittsburgh, October 3, 1971 (one double, three home runs).
A.L.—12—George Brett, Kansas City, October 6, 1978 (three home runs).

Most total bases, inning
A.L.-N.L.—4—Held by many players.

LONG HITS

Most long hits, career
A.L.—18—George Brett, Kansas City, 1976, 1977, 1978, 1980, 1984, 1985; six series, 27 games.
N.L.—12
Steve Garvey, Los Angeles, 1974, 1977, 1978, 1981; San Diego, 1984; five series, 22 games.
Will Clark, San Francisco, 1987, 1989; St. Louis, 2000; three series, 17 games.
Javy Lopez, Atlanta, 1992, 1995 through 1998, 2001; six series, 27 games.

Most long hits, series
3-game series
N.L.—5—Hank Aaron, Atlanta, 1969.
A.L.—4—Bob Watson, New York, 1980.
4-game series
N.L.—6—Steve Garvey, Los Angeles, 1978.
A.L.—5—George Brett, Kansas City, 1978.
5-game series
A.L.—6—Tom Brunansky, Minnesota, 1987.
N.L.—6—Will Clark, San Francisco, 1989.
6-game series
N.L.—5—Tom Herr, St. Louis, 1985.
A.L.—5—Jay Buhner, Seattle, 1995.
7-game series
N.L.—7—Javy Lopez, Atlanta, 1996.
A.L.—5—George Brett, Kansas City, 1985.

Most long hits, game
N.L.—4—Bob Robertson, Pittsburgh, October 3, 1971 (one double, three home runs).
A.L.—3
Paul Blair, Baltimore, October 6, 1969 (two doubles, one home run).
George Brett, Kansas City, October 6, 1978 (three home runs).
George Brett, Kansas City, October 11, 1985 (one double, two home runs).
Alex Rodriguez, Seattle, October 17, 2000 (two doubles, one home run).

Most long hits in two consecutive games, series
N.L.—5—Bob Robertson, Pittsburgh, October 3 (4; one double, three home runs); October 5 (1; one home run), 1971.
A.L.—4—George Brett, Kansas City, October 6 (3; three home runs); October 7 (1; one triple), 1978.

Most long hits, inning
A.L.-N.L.—1—Held by many players.

RUNS BATTED IN

Most runs batted in, career
Both leagues—27—David Justice, Atlanta N.L., 1991 through 1993, 1995; Cleveland A.L., 1997, 1998; New York A.L., 2000, 2001; eight series (13 in N.L., 14 in A.L.).
N.L.—21—Steve Garvey, Los Angeles, 1974, 1977, 1978, 1981; San Diego, 1984; five series, 22 games.
A.L.—21—Bernie Williams, New York, 1996 through 2001, except 1997; five series, 27 games.

Most runs batted in by pinch-hitter, career
A.L.—4—Ricky Ledee, New York, 1998, 1999; two series, two games.
N.L.—2
J.C. Martin, New York, 1969; one series, two games.
Jerry Martin, Philadelphia, 1977, 1978; two series, three games.
Luis Quinones, Cincinnati, 1990; one series, three games.
Dmitri Young, St. Louis, 1996; one series, three games.
Greg Myers, San Diego, 1998; one series, two games.
Erubiel Durazo, Arizona, 2001; one series, two games.

Most runs batted in, series
3-game series
A.L.—9—Graig Nettles, New York, 1981.
N.L.—7—Hank Aaron, Atlanta, 1969.
4-game series
N.L.—8—Dusty Baker, Los Angeles, 1977.
Gary Matthews, Philadelphia, 1983.
A.L.—6—Reggie Jackson, New York, 1978.
5-game series
A.L.—10—Don Baylor, California, 1982.
N.L.—9—Matt Williams, San Francisco, 1989.
6-game series
A.L.—8—Jim Thome, Cleveland, 1998.
David Justice, New York, 2000.
N.L.—7—Bill Madlock, Los Angeles, 1985.
7-game series
A.L.—7—Brian Downing, California, 1986.
N.L.—7—Jeffrey Leonard, San Francisco, 1987.
Fred McGriff, Atlanta, 1996.

Most runs batted in by pinch-hitter, series
A.L.—4—Ricky Ledee, New York, 1999; one game.
N.L.—2
    J.C. Martin, New York, 1969; two games.
    Jerry Martin, Philadelphia, 1978; two games.
    Luis Quinones, Cincinnati, 1990; three games.
    Dmitri Young, St. Louis, 1996; three games.
    Greg Myers, San Diego, 1998; two games.
    Jose Hernandez, Atlanta, 1999; two games.
    Erubiel Durazo, Arizona, 2001; two games.

Most runs batted in, game
N.L.—6—Will Clark, San Francisco, October 4, 1989.
A.L.—5
    Paul Blair, Baltimore, October 6, 1969.
    Don Baylor, California, October 5, 1982.
    John Valentin, Boston, October 16, 1999.
    Bret Boone, Seattle, October 20, 2001.

Most runs batted in by pinch-hitter, game
A.L.—4—Ricky Ledee, New York, October 17, 1999, ninth inning.
N.L.—2
    J.C. Martin, New York, October 4, 1969, eighth inning.
    Dmitri Young, St. Louis, October 13, 1996, seventh inning.
    Greg Myers, San Diego, October 12, 1998, ninth inning.
    Jose Hernandez, Atlanta, October 19, 1999, sixth inning.
    Erubiel Durazo, Arizona, October 21, 2001, fifth inning.

Most consecutive games with one or more runs batted in, career
N.L.-A.L.—4—Held by many players.

Most runs batted in accounting for all club's runs, game
A.L.—3
    Bert Campaneris, Oakland, October 5, 1974.
    Graig Nettles, New York, October 13, 1981.
N.L.—3
    Keith Hernandez, New York, October 5, 1988.
    Jeff Blauser, Atlanta, October 13, 1993.
    Ron Gant, St. Louis, October 12, 1996.
    John Olerud, New York, October 16, 1999.
    Steve Finley, Arizona, October 19, 2001.

Most runs batted in, inning
A.L.—4
    Mike Cuellar, Baltimore, October 3, 1970, fourth inning.
    Don Baylor, California, October 9, 1982, eighth inning.
    Jim Thome, Cleveland, October 13, 1998, fifth inning.
    Ricky Ledee, New York, October 17, 1999, ninth inning.
N.L.—4
    Ron Cey, Los Angeles, October 4, 1977, seventh inning.
    Dusty Baker, Los Angeles, October 5, 1977, fourth inning.
    Will Clark, San Francisco, October 4, 1989, fourth inning.
    Ron Gant, Atlanta, October 7, 1992, fifth inning.
    Gary Gaetti, St. Louis, October 10, 1996, seventh inning.
    Andres Galarraga, Atlanta, October 11, 1998, seventh inning.

Most game-winning RBIs, career (1980-88)
A.L.—3—George Brett, Kansas City, 1980, 1985 (2).
N.L.—3—Gary Carter, Montreal, 1981; New York, 1986, 1988.

Most game-winning RBIs, series (1980-88)
N.L.—2
    Greg Luzinski, Philadelphia, 1980.
    Gary Carter, New York, 1986.
    Kirk Gibson, Los Angeles, 1988.
A.L.—2
    Cecil Cooper, Milwaukee, 1982.
    Al Oliver, Toronto, 1985.
    George Brett, Kansas City, 1985.

BASES ON BALLS

Most bases on balls, career
Both leagues—24—David Justice, Atlanta N.L., 1991 through 1993, 1995; Cleveland A.L., 1997, 1998; New York A.L., 2000, 2001; eight series (14 in N.L., 10 in A.L.).
N.L.—24—Chipper Jones, Atlanta, 1995 through 1999, 2001; six series, 34 games.
A.L.—22—Bernie Williams, New York, 1996, 1998 through 2001; five series, 27 games.

Most bases on balls, series
3-game series
    A.L.—6—Harmon Killebrew, Minnesota, 1969.
    N.L.—6—Joe Morgan, Cincinnati, 1976.
4-game series
    N.L.—9—Jim Wynn, Los Angeles, 1974.
    A.L.—5—Reggie Jackson, Oakland, 1974.
        Eddie Murray, Baltimore, 1979.
        Gary Roenicke, Baltimore 1983.
        Jose Canseco, Oakland, 1990.
5-game series
    N.L.—8—Jose Cruz, Houston, 1980.
    A.L.—7—Lou Whitaker, Detroit, 1987.
        Rickey Henderson, Oakland, 1989.
6-game series
    A.L.—10—Frank Thomas, Chicago, 1993.
    N.L.—9—Chipper Jones, Atlanta, 1999.
7-game series
    A.L.—7—George Brett, Kansas City, 1985.
    N.L.—6—Held by many players.

Most consecutive bases on balls, series
A.L.—4
    Harmon Killebrew, Minnesota, October 4 (3), 5 (1), 1969.
    Gary Roenicke, Baltimore, October 6 (1), 7 (1), 8 (2), 1983.
    Bernie Williams, New York, October 10 (3), 11 (1), 1998.
N.L.—4—Darren Daulton, Philadelphia, October 10 (3), 11 (1), 1993.

Most bases on balls, game
N.L.—4
    Darren Daulton, Philadelphia, October 10, 1993.
    Ken Caminiti, San Diego, October 8, 1998.
A.L.—4
    Ruppert Jones, California, October 11, 1986, 11 innings.
    Frank Thomas, Chicago, October 5, 1993.

Most bases on balls with bases filled, game
A.L.-N.L.—1—Held by many players.

Bases on balls with bases filled by pinch-hitters, game
N.L.—Duffy Dyer, Pittsburgh, October 7, 1975, ninth inning.
    Mike Sharperson, Los Angeles, October 8, 1988, eighth inning.
A.L.—Never accomplished.

Most bases on balls, two consecutive games
A.L.—5
    Harmon Killebrew, Minnesota, October 4 (3), October 5 (2), 1969, first game 12 innings, second game 11 innings.
    Frank Thomas, Chicago, October 5 (4), October 6 (1), 1993.
N.L.—5
    Jim Wynn, Los Angeles, October 5 (2), October 6 (3), 1974.
    Darren Daulton, Philadelphia, October 10 (4), October 11 (1), 1993, second game 10 innings.
    Chipper Jones, Atlanta, October 12 (3), October 13 (2), 1999.

Most bases on balls, inning
A.L.-N.L.—1—Held by many players.

STRIKEOUTS

Most strikeouts, career
A.L.—41—Reggie Jackson, Oakland, 1971, 1972, 1973, 1974, 1975; New York, 1977, 1978, 1980, 1981; California, 1982, 1986; 11 series, 45 games.
N.L.—26—Ran Gant, Atlanta, 1991, 1992, 1993; Cincinnati, 1995; St. Louis, 1996; five series, 31 games.

Most strikeouts, series
3-game series
    A.L.—7—Leo Cardenas, Minnesota, 1969.
    N.L.—7—Cesar Geronimo, Cincinnati, 1975.
4-game series
    N.L.—10—Reggie Sanders, Cincinnati, 1995.
    A.L.—7—Dave Henderson, Oakland, 1988.
5-game series
    N.L.—9—Jim Edmonds, St. Louis, 2000.
    A.L.—8—Kirk Gibson, Detroit, 1987.
        Chili Davis, Minnesota, 1991.

6-game series
N.L.—12—Darryl Strawberry, New York, 1986.
A.L.—10—Omar Vizquel, Cleveland, 1997.
Rafael Palmeiro, Baltimore, 1997.

7-game series
N.L.—12—John Shelby, Los Angeles, 1988.
A.L.—8—Steve Balboni, Kansas City, 1985.
Bobby Grich, California, 1986.
Jim Rice, Boston, 1986.

Most strikeouts by pinch-hitter, series
N.L.—3
Lee Mazzilli, New York, 1986; five games.
Curtis Wilkerson, Pittsburgh, 1991; four games.
A.L.—2
Matt Nokes, Detroit, 1987; two games.
Larry Parrish, Boston, 1988; three games.
Glenallen Hill, New York, 2000; two games.

Most consecutive strikeouts, series (consecutive at-bats)
N.L.—7—Cesar Geronimo, Cincinnati, October 4 (1), 5 (3), 7
(3), 1975, first game 10 innings (one base on balls during
streak).
A.L.—5
Ron Karkovice, Chicago, October 5 (1), 6 (1), 8 (3), 1993
(one sacrifice hit during streak).
Omar Vizquel, Cleveland, October 9 (2), 11 (3), 1997, second
game 12 innings.
Manny Ramirez, Cleveland, October 10 (3), 11 (2), 1998 (one
sacrifice fly during streak).
Scott Brosius, New York, October 18 (3), 20 (2), 2001.

Most consecutive strikeouts, series (consecutive plate appearances)
N.L.—5
Cesar Geronimo, Cincinnati, October 6 (1), 7 (3), 9 (1), 1973,
third game 12 innings.
Reggie Sanders, Cincinnati, October 11 (2), 13 (3), 1995, first
game 10 innings.
A.L.—5
Omar Vizquel, Cleveland, October 9 (2), 11 (3), 1997, second
game 12 innings.
Scott Brosius, New York, October 18 (3), 20 (2), 2001.

Most strikeouts, game
A.L.—4
Dave Boswell, Minnesota, October 5, 1969, 11 innings
(consecutive).
Bobby Bonilla, Baltimore, October 10, 1996 (consecutive).
Marquis Grissom, Cleveland, October 11, 1997, 12 innings
(consecutive).
Marquis Grissom, Cleveland, October 15, 1997, 11 innings
(consecutive).
N.L.—4—Gerald Williams, Atlanta, October 10, 1998 (consec-
utive).

Most strikeouts, inning
A.L.-N.L.—1—Held by many players.

SACRIFICE HITS

Most sacrifice hits, career
N.L.—6—Greg Maddux, Chicago, 1989; Atlanta, 1993, 1995,
1996, 1997, 1998, 1999, 2001; eight series; 15 games.
A.L.—3
Dick Green, Oakland, 1971, 1972, 1973, 1974; four series,
17 games.
Bob Boone, California, 1982, 1986; two series, 12 games.

Most sacrifice hits, series
A.L.—3—Enos Cabell, Houston, 1980 (5-game series).
N.L.—2—Held by many players.

Most sacrifice hits, game
A.L.-N.L.—2—Held by many players.

SACRIFICE FLIES

Most sacrifice flies, career
A.L.-N.L.—2—Held by many players.

Most sacrifice flies, series
A.L.-N.L.—2—Held by many players.

Most sacrifice flies, game
A.L.-N.L.—1—Held by many players.

HIT BY PITCH

Most hit by pitch, career
N.L.—4—Richie Hebner, Pittsburgh, 1971 (1), 1972 (1), 1974
(1); Chicago, 1984 (1).
A.L.—3
Hal McRae, Kansas City, 1976 (1), 1980 (1), 1985 (1).
Bobby Grich, California, 1982 (1), 1986 (2).
Don Baylor, Boston, 1986 (2); Minnesota, 1987 (1).
Joey Cora, Chicago, 1993 (1); Seattle, 1995 (2).
Tino Martinez, New York, 1996 (1), 1998 (1), 1999 (1).
David Justice, Cleveland, 1997 (1), 1998 (1), New York, 2001
(1).

Most hit by pitch, series
N.L.—2
Lenny Dykstra, New York, 1988.
Jeff Blauser, Atlanta, 1996.
A.L.—2
Don Baylor, Boston, 1986.
Bobby Grich, California, 1986.
Dan Gladden, Minnesota, 1987.
Pat Sheridan, Detroit, 1987.
Joey Cora, Seattle, 1995.

Most hit by pitch, game
A.L.—2
Dan Gladden, Minnesota, October 11, 1987.
Pat Sheridan, Detroit, October 12, 1987.
N.L.—1—Held by many players.

GROUNDING INTO DOUBLE PLAYS

Most grounding into double plays, career
N.L.—5—Pedro Guerrero, Los Angeles, 1981, 1983, 1985;
three series, 15 games.
A.L.—5
Willie Randolph, New York, 1976, 1977, 1980, 1981, 1990;
five series, 22 games.
Roberto Alomar, Toronto, 1991, 1992, 1993; Baltimore, 1996,
1997; five series, 28 games.
David Justice, Cleveland, 1997, 1998; New York, 2000, 2001;
four series, 23 games.

Most grounding into double plays, series
N.L.—4—Pedro Guerrero, Los Angeles, 1981 (5-game series).
A.L.—3
Tony Taylor, Detroit, 1972 (5-game series).
Doug DeCinces, California, 1986 (7-game series).
Paul Sorrento, Cleveland, 1995 (6-game series).
German Berroa, Baltimore, 1997 (6-game series).

Most grounding into double plays, game
A.L.—3—Tony Taylor, Detroit, October 10, 1972.
N.L.—2
Cleon Jones, New York, October 4, 1969.
Pedro Guerrero, Los Angeles, October 16, 1981.
Jerry Royster, Atlanta, October 10, 1982.
Chris Gomez, San Diego, October 7, 1998.
Damian Miller, Arizona, October 20, 2001.

REACHING BASE ON INTERFERENCE

Most times awarded first base on catcher's interference, game
N.L.—1
Richie Hebner, Pittsburgh, October 8, 1974, fifth inning.
Mike Scioscia, Los Angeles, October 14, 1985, fourth inning.
A.L.—Never accomplished.

CLUB BATTING

GAMES

Most games played, total series
N.L.—60—Atlanta; 11 series; won 27, lost 33.
A.L.—47—New York; 10 series; won 32, lost 15.

For complete lists of results, and series, games, and home and road games played by all teams, see page 451. For a list of batting statistics by teams each series, see page 456.

BATTING AVERAGE

Highest batting average, series
3-game series
  A.L.—.336—New York vs. Oakland, 1981.
  N.L.—.330—St. Louis vs. Atlanta, 1982.
4-game series
  A.L.—.300—New York vs. Kansas City, 1978.
  N.L.—.286—Los Angeles vs. Philadelphia, 1978.
5-game series
  A.L.—.316—New York vs. Kansas City, 1976.
  N.L.—.303—Chicago vs. San Francisco, 1989.
6-game series
  A.L.—.301—Toronto vs. Chicago, 1993.
  N.L.—.279—St. Louis vs. Los Angeles, 1985.
7-game series
  N.L.—.309—Atlanta vs. St. Louis, 1996.
  A.L.—.277—California vs. Boston, 1986.

Highest batting average by both clubs, series
3-game series
  N.L.—.292—New York .327, Atlanta .255, 1969.
  A.L.—.286—Baltimore .330, Minnesota .238, 1970.
4-game series
  A.L.—.282—New York .300, Kansas City .263, 1978.
  N.L.—.268—Los Angeles .286, Philadelphia .250, 1978.
5-game series
  N.L.—.285—Chicago .303, San Francisco .267, 1989.
  A.L.—.283—New York .316, Kansas City .247, 1976.
6-game series
  A.L.—.271—Toronto .301, Chicago .237, 1993.
  N.L.—.256—St. Louis .279, Los Angeles .234, 1985.
7-game series
  A.L.—.275—California .277, Boston .272, 1986.
  N.L.—.260—Atlanta .309, St. Louis .204, 1996.

Highest batting average by losing club, series
N.L.—.303—Chicago vs. San Francisco, 1989 (5-game series).
A.L.—.293—Boston vs. New York, 1999 (5-game series).

Lowest batting average, series
3-game series
  A.L.—.155—Minnesota vs. Baltimore, 1969.
  N.L.—.169—Atlanta vs. St. Louis, 1982.
4-game series
  A.L.—.177—Baltimore vs. Oakland, 1974.
  N.L.—.194—Pittsburgh vs. Los Angeles, 1974.
5-game series
  N.L.—.186—Cincinnati vs. New York, 1973.
  A.L.—.198—Detroit vs. Oakland, 1972.
6-game series
  A.L.—.184—Seattle vs. Cleveland, 1995.
  N.L.—.189—New York vs. Houston, 1986.
7-game series
  N.L.—.204—St. Louis vs. Atlanta, 1996.
  A.L.—.225—Kansas City vs. Toronto, 1985.

Lowest batting average by both clubs, series
3-game series
  A.L.—.202—Detroit .234, Kansas City .170, 1984.
  N.L.—.223—Pittsburgh .225, Cincinnati .220, 1970.
4-game series
  A.L.—.180—Oakland .183, Baltimore .177, 1974.
  N.L.—.232—Los Angeles .268, Pittsburgh .194, 1974.

5-game series
  N.L.—.203—New York .220, Cincinnati .186, 1973.
  A.L.—.205—Baltimore .211, Oakland .200, 1973.
6-game series
  N.L.—.204—Houston .218, New York .189, 1986.
  A.L.—.219—Cleveland .220, New York .218, 1998.
7-game series
  N.L.—.228—New York .242, Los Angeles .214, 1988.
    Atlanta .231, Pittsburgh .224, 1991.
  A.L.—.247—Toronto .269, Kansas City .225, 1985.

Lowest batting average by winning club, series
A.L.—.183—Oakland vs. Baltimore, 1974 (4-game series).
N.L.—.189—New York vs. Houston, 1986 (6-game series).

SLUGGING AVERAGE

Highest slugging average, series
3-game series
  N.L.—.575—New York vs. Atlanta, 1969.
  A.L.—.560—Baltimore vs. Minnesota, 1970.
4-game series
  N.L.—.544—Los Angeles vs. Philadelphia, 1978.
  A.L.—.511—Oakland vs. Boston, 1988.
5-game series
  A.L.—.497—Minnesota vs. Detroit, 1987.
    New York vs. Baltimore, 1996.
  N.L.—.494—Chicago vs. San Diego, 1984.
6-game series
  A.L.—.471—Toronto vs. Oakland, 1992.
  N.L.—.420—Philadelphia vs. Atlanta, 1993.
7-game series
  N.L.—.474—Atlanta vs. St. Louis, 1996.
  A.L.—.402—California vs. Boston, 1986.
    Boston vs. California, 1986.

Highest slugging average by both clubs, series
3-game series
  N.L.—.530—New York .575, Atlanta .481, 1969.
  A.L.—.476—Baltimore .560, Minnesota .386, 1970.
4-game series
  N.L.—.477—Los Angeles .544, Philadelphia .407, 1978.
  A.L.—.443—Kansas City .4436, New York .4428, 1978.
5-game series
  N.L.—.456—San Francisco .473, Chicago .440, 1989.
  A.L.—.448—New York .497, Baltimore .398, 1996.
6-game series
  N.L.—.415—Philadelphia .420, Atlanta .409, 1993.
  A.L.—.408—Toronto .471, Oakland .343, 1992.
7-game series
  N.L.—.409—Pittsburgh .433, Atlanta .385, 1992.
  A.L.—.402—California .402, Boston .402, 1986.

Lowest slugging average, series
3-game series
  N.L.—.180—Atlanta vs. St. Louis, 1982.
  A.L.—.198—Kansas City vs. Detroit, 1984.
4-game series
  A.L.—.241—Chicago vs. Baltimore, 1983.
  N.L.—.261—Cincinnati vs. Atlanta, 1995.
5-game series
  A.L.—.288—Oakland vs. Detroit, 1972.
  N.L.—.278—Montreal vs. Los Angeles, 1981.
6-game series
  N.L.—.260—Florida vs. Atlanta, 1997.
  A.L.—.299—Seattle vs. Cleveland, 1995.
7-game series
  N.L.—.288—Los Angeles vs. New York, 1988.
  A.L.—.366—Kansas City vs. Toronto, 1985.

Lowest slugging average by both clubs, series
3-game series
  A.L.—.300—Detroit .402, Kansas City .198, 1984.
  N.L.—.318—St. Louis .437, Atlanta .180, 1982.
4-game series
  A.L.—.283—Oakland .308, Baltimore .258, 1974.
  N.L.—.339—Los Angeles .391, Philadelphia .290, 1977.

5-game series
A.L.—.304—Detroit .321, Oakland .288, 1972.
N.L.—.307—Cincinnati .311, New York .304, 1973.
6-game series
N.L.—.288—Houston .311, New York .264, 1986.
A.L.—.351—Baltimore .394, Cleveland .304, 1997.
7-game series
N.L.—.325—New York .363, Los Angeles .288, 1988.
A.L.—.369—Toronto .372, Kansas City .366, 1985.

AT-BATS AND PLATE APPEARANCES

Most at-bats, total series
N.L.—2,040—Atlanta; 11 series, 60 games.
A.L.—1,617—New York; 10 series, 47 games.

Most at-bats, series
3-game series
A.L.—123—Baltimore vs. Minnesota, 1969.
N.L.—113—New York vs. Atlanta, 1969.
4-game series
N.L.—149—Atlanta vs. Cincinnati, 1995.
A.L.—140—New York vs. Kansas City, 1978.
5-game series
N.L.—190—Philadelphia vs. Houston, 1980.
A.L.—184—Boston vs. New York, 1999.
6-game series
N.L.—227—New York vs. Houston, 1986.
A.L.—218—Baltimore vs. Cleveland, 1997.
7-game series
A.L.—256—California vs. Boston, 1986.
N.L.—249—Atlanta vs. St. Louis, 1996.

Most at-bats by both clubs, series
3-game series
A.L.—233—Baltimore 123, Minnesota 110, 1969.
N.L.—219—New York 113, Atlanta 106, 1969.
4-game series
N.L.—287—Los Angeles 147, Philadelphia 140, 1978.
A.L.—273—New York 140, Kansas City 133, 1978.
5-game series
N.L.—362—Philadelphia 190, Houston 172, 1980.
A.L.—360—Boston 184, New York 176, 1999.
6-game series
N.L.—452—New York 227, Houston 225, 1986.
A.L.—425—Baltimore 218, Cleveland 207, 1997.
7-game series
A.L.—510—California 256, Boston 254, 1986.
N.L.—483—Los Angeles 243, New York 240, 1988.

Most at-bats by pinch-hitters, series
N.L.—15
Atlanta vs. Pittsburgh, 1992 (7-game series).
New York vs. Atlanta, 1999 (6-game series).
St. Louis vs. New York, 2000 (5-game series).
A.L.—13
Oakland vs. Detroit, 1972 (5-game series).
Toronto vs. Kansas City, 1985 (7-game series).

Most at-bats by pinch-hitters on both clubs, series
N.L.—25—Atlanta 15, Pittsburgh 10, 1992 (7-game series).
A.L.—20—Oakland 13, Detroit 7, 1972 (5-game series).

Most plate appearances by pinch-hitters, series
N.L.—18—New York vs. Atlanta, 1999 (6-game series).
A.L.—14—Oakland vs. Detroit, 1972.

Most plate appearances by pinch-hitters on both clubs, series
N.L.—29—New York 18, Atlanta 11, 1999 (6-game series).
A.L.—22—Oakland 14, Detroit 8, 1972 (5-game series).

Fewest at-bats, series
3-game series
N.L.—89—Atlanta vs. St. Louis, 1982.
A.L.—95—Baltimore vs. Oakland, 1971.
4-game series
A.L.—120—Oakland vs. Baltimore, 1974.
N.L.—129—Pittsburgh vs. Los Angeles, 1974.
Los Angeles vs. Philadelphia, 1983.
5-game series
A.L.—151—Milwaukee vs. California, 1982.
N.L.—155—San Diego vs. Chicago, 1984.

6-game series
N.L.—181—Florida vs. Atlanta, 1997.
A.L.—191—Seattle vs. New York, 2000.
7-game series
N.L.—215—St. Louis vs. San Francisco, 1987.
A.L.—227—Kansas City vs. Toronto, 1985.

Fewest at-bats by both clubs, series
3-game series
A.L.—191—Oakland 96, Baltimore 95, 1971.
N.L.—192—St. Louis 103, Atlanta 89, 1982.
4-game series
A.L.—244—Baltimore 124, Oakland 120, 1974.
N.L.—259—Philadelphia 130, Los Angeles 129, 1983.
5-game series
A.L.—308—California 157, Milwaukee 151, 1982.
N.L.—317—Chicago 162, San Diego 155, 1984.
6-game series
N.L.—375—Atlanta 194, Florida 181, 1997.
A.L.—395—New York 204, Seattle 191, 2000.
7-game series
N.L.—441—San Francisco 226, St. Louis 215, 1987.
A.L.—469—Toronto 242, Kansas City 227, 1985.

Most at-bats by club, nine-inning game
N.L.—47—Atlanta vs. St. Louis, October 14, 1996.
A.L.—45—Boston vs. New York, October 16, 1999.

Most at-bats by club, extra-inning game
N.L.—56—Houston vs. New York, October 15, 1986, 16 innings.
A.L.—49—Toronto vs. Oakland, October 11, 1992, 11 innings.

Most at-bats by both clubs, nine-inning game
A.L.—80—Baltimore 44, Minnesota 36, October 6, 1969.
N.L.—80
Atlanta 47, St. Louis 33, October 14, 1996.
Arizona 42, Atlanta 38, October 20, 2001.

Most at-bats by both clubs, extra-inning game
N.L.—110—Houston 56, New York 54, October 15, 1986, 16 innings.
A.L.—91—Toronto 49, Oakland 42, October 11, 1992, 11 innings.

Most at-bats by pinch-hitters, game
A.L.—6—Oakland vs. Detroit, October 10, 1972.
N.L.—5
Atlanta vs. Pittsburgh, October 14, 1992.
St. Louis vs. New York, October 16, 2000.

Most at-bats by pinch-hitters on both clubs, nine-inning game
A.L.—7—Oakland 6, Detroit 1, October 10, 1972.
N.L.—6
Pittsburgh 3, Cincinnati 3, October 4, 1990.
Atlanta 3, St. Louis 3, October 14, 1996.
New York 4, St. Louis 2, October 14, 2000.

Most at-bats by pinch-hitters on both clubs, extra-inning game
N.L.—8
New York 4, Houston 4, October 15, 1986, 16 innings.
New York 4, Atlanta 4, October 19, 1999, 11 innings.
A.L.—Less than nine-inning record.

Most plate appearances by pinch-hitters, game
A.L.—6—Oakland vs. Detroit, October 10, 1972.
N.L.—6—Pittsburgh vs. Cincinnati, October 4, 1990.

Most plate appearances by pinch-hitters on both clubs, nine-inning game
A.L.—7—Oakland 6, Detroit 1, October 10, 1972.
N.L.—6—Made in many games.

Most plate appearances by pinch-hitters on both clubs extra-inning game
N.L.—10
New York 5, Houston 5, October 15, 1986, 16 innings.
New York 5, Atlanta 5, October 19, 1999, 11 innings.
A.L.—Less than nine-inning record.

Fewest at-bats, game
N.L.—26
St. Louis vs. San Francisco, October 7, 1987.
Florida vs. Atlanta, October 12, 1997; batted eight innings.

A.L.—25
California vs. Milwaukee, October 6, 1982; batted
eight innings.
Toronto vs. Oakland, October 8, 1992; batted eight innings.
New York vs. Seattle, October 21, 2001.

Fewest at-bats by both clubs, game
A.L.—54—Seattle 29, New York 25, October 21, 2001.
N.L.—58 .
Cincinnati 30, New York 28, October 6, 1973.
New York 31, Cincinnati 27, October 7, 1973.
Chicago 29, San Diego 29, October 3, 1984.
St. Louis 30, San Francisco 28, October 11, 1987.
Atlanta 29, New York 29, October 16, 1999.

Most at-bats, inning
N.L.—12—St. Louis vs. Los Angeles, October 13, 1985,
second inning.
A.L.—10
New York vs. Oakland, October 14, 1981, fourth inning.
Toronto vs. Kansas City, October 11, 1985, fifth inning.

Most at-bats by both clubs, inning
A.L.—16—New York 10, Oakland 6, October 14, 1981,
fourth inning.
N.L.—15
Philadelphia 8, Houston 7, October 12, 1980, eighth inning.
St. Louis 12, Los Angeles 3, October 13, 1985, second inning.
Pittsburgh 8, Atlanta 7, October 7, 1992, seventh inning.

Most batters facing pitcher, inning
N.L.—14—St. Louis vs. Los Angeles, October 13, 1985,
second inning.
A.L.—12
New York vs. Oakland, October 14, 1981, fourth inning.
New York vs. Seattle, October 17, 2000, seventh inning.

Most batters facing pitcher by both clubs, inning
A.L.—19—New York 12, Oakland 7, October 14, 1981,
fourth inning.
N.L.—19—Atlanta 10, Pittsburgh 9, October 7, 1992,
seventh inning.

RUNS
SERIES AND GAMES

Most runs, total series
N.L.—247—Atlanta; 11 series, 60 games.
A.L.—222—New York; 10 series, 47 games.

Most runs, series
3-game series
A.L.—27—Baltimore vs. Minnesota, 1970.
N.L.—27—New York vs. Atlanta, 1969.
4-game series
A.L.—26—Baltimore vs. California, 1979.
N.L.—24—Pittsburgh vs. San Francisco, 1971.
5-game series
A.L.—34—Minnesota vs. Detroit, 1987.
N.L.—31—New York vs. St. Louis, 2000.
6-game series
N.L.—33—Atlanta vs. Philadelphia, 1993.
A.L.—31—Toronto vs. Oakland, 1992.
New York vs. Seattle, 2000.
7-game series
N.L.—44—Atlanta vs. St. Louis, 1996.
A.L.—41—Boston vs. California, 1986.

Most runs by both clubs, series
3-game series
N.L.—42—New York 27, Atlanta 15, 1969.
A.L.—37—Baltimore 27, Minnesota 10, 1970.
4-game series
A.L.—41—Baltimore 26, California 15, 1979.
N.L.—39—Pittsburgh 24, San Francisco 15, 1971.
5-game series
A.L.—57—Minnesota 34, Detroit 23, 1987.
N.L.—52—San Francisco 30, Chicago 22, 1989.
New York 31, St. Louis 21, 2000.
6-game series
N.L.—56—Atlanta 33, Philadelphia 23, 1993.
A.L.—55—Toronto 31, Oakland 24, 1992.

7-game series
A.L.—71—Boston 41, California 30, 1986.
N.L.—69—Pittsburgh 35, Atlanta 34, 1992.

Most runs by losing club, series
N.L.—35—Pittsburgh vs. Atlanta, 1992 (7-game series).
A.L.—30—California vs. Boston, 1986 (7-game series).

Fewest runs, series
3-game series
N.L.—3—Pittsburgh vs. Cincinnati, 1970.
A.L.—4—Oakland vs. New York, 1981.
Kansas City vs. Detroit, 1984.
4-game series
A.L.—3—Chicago vs. Baltimore, 1983.
N.L.—5—Cincinnati vs. Atlanta, 1995.
5-game series
N.L.—8—Cincinnati vs. New York, 1973.
A.L.—10—Detroit vs. Oakland, 1972.
6-game series
A.L.—12—Seattle vs. Cleveland, 1995.
N.L.—15—Pittsburgh vs. Cincinnati, 1990.
7-game series
N.L.—12—Pittsburgh vs. Atlanta, 1991.
A.L.—25—Toronto vs. Kansas Ctiy, 1985.

Fewest runs by both clubs, series
3-game series
N.L.—12—Cincinnati 9, Pittsburgh 3, 1970.
A.L.—18—Detroit 14, Kansas City 4, 1984.
4-game series
A.L.—18—Oakland 11, Baltimore 7, 1974.
N.L.—24—Atlanta 19, Cincinnati 5, 1995.
5-game series
A.L.—23—Oakland 13, Detroit 10, 1972.
N.L.—25—Los Angeles 15, Montreal 10, 1981.
6-game series
N.L.—35—Cincinnati 20, Pittsburgh 15, 1990.
A.L.—35—Cleveland 23, Seattle 12, 1995.
7-game series
N.L.—31—Atlanta 19, Pittsburgh 12, 1991.
A.L.—51—Kansas City 26, Toronto 25, 1985.

Most runs, game
N.L.—15—Atlanta vs. St. Louis, October 17, 1996.
A.L.—14—Seattle vs. New York, October 20, 2001.

Most earned runs, game
N.L.—15—Atlanta vs. St. Louis, October 17, 1996.
A.L.—13—New York vs. Oakland, October 14, 1981.

Most runs by both clubs, nine-inning game
N.L.—18—Atlanta 13, Pittsburgh 5, October 7, 1992.
A.L.—17
Baltimore 9, California 8, October 4, 1979.
Seattle 14, New York 3, October 20, 2001.

Most runs by both clubs, extra-inning game
N.L.—19—Atlanta 10, New York 9, October 19, 1999, 11
innings.
A.L.—Less than nine-inning record.

Largest score, shutout game
N.L.—15—Atlanta 15, St. Louis 0, October 17, 1996.
A.L.—Baltimore 8, California 0, October 6, 1979.

Most players scoring one or more runs, game
N.L.—11—Atlanta vs. Philadelphia, October 7, 1993.
A.L.—11—Seattle vs. New York, October 20, 2001.

Most players from both clubs scoring one or more runs, game
A.L.—14
Baltimore 9, Minnesota 5, October 3, 1970.
Baltimore 7, California 7, October 4, 1979.
Seattle 11, New York 3, October 20, 2001.
N.L.—14
Atlanta 10, Pittsburgh 4, October 7, 1992.
Atlanta 11, Philadelphia 3, October 7, 1993.
New York 7, Atlanta 7, October 19, 1999, 11 innings.

INNING

Most runs, inning
N.L.—9—St. Louis vs. Los Angeles, October 13, 1985, second inning.
A.L.—7
Baltimore vs. Minnesota, October 3, 1970, fourth inning.
Baltimore vs. Minnesota, October 4, 1970, ninth inning.
New York vs. Oakland, October 14, 1981, fourth inning.
Oakland vs. Boston, October 6, 1990, ninth inning.
New York vs. Seattle, October 11, 2000, eighth inning.
Seattle vs. New York, October 20, 2001, sixth inning.

Most runs by both clubs, inning
A.L.—9—New York 7, Oakland 2, October 14, 1981, fourth inning.
N.L.—9
St. Louis 9, Los Angeles 0, October 13, 1985, second inning.
Atlanta 5, Pittsburgh 4, October 7, 1992, seventh inning.

Most runs, extra inning
N.L.—4
Houston vs. Philadelphia, October 8, 1980, 10th inning.
Atlanta vs. Cincinnati, October 11, 1995, 10th inning.
A.L.—3
Detroit vs. Oakland, October 11, 1972, 10th inning.
Baltimore vs. California, October 3, 1979, 10th inning.
Baltimore vs. Chicago, October 8, 1983, 10th inning.
Seattle vs. Cleveland, October 13, 1995, 11th inning.
Cleveland vs. New York, October 7, 1998, 12th inning.

Most runs by both clubs, extra inning
A.L.—5—Detroit 3, Oakland 2, October 11, 1972, 10th inning.
N.L.—5
Houston 4, Philadelphia 1, October 8, 1980, 10th inning.
New York 3, Houston 2, October 15, 1986, 16th inning.

Most innings scored, game
N.L.—6
New York vs. Atlanta, October 5, 1969.
Los Angeles vs. Pittsburgh, October 9, 1974.
Atlanta vs. St. Louis, October 14, 1996.
A.L.—6
Detroit vs. Kansas City, October 2, 1984.
Boston vs. New York, October 16, 1999.

Most innings scored by both clubs, nine-inning game
A.L.—8
New York 4, Kansas City 4, October 6, 1978.
California 5, Baltimore 3, October 4, 1979.
Kansas City 4, Toronto 4, October 9, 1985.
Minnesota 5, Detroit 3, October 11, 1987.
Oakland 5, Boston 3, October 8, 1988.
Minnesota 5, Toronto 3, October 12, 1991.
Baltimore 4, Cleveland 4, October 12, 1997.
N.L.—8
New York 6, Atlanta 2, October 5, 1969.
Pittsburgh 5, San Francisco 3, October 3, 1971.
Los Angeles 5, Philadelphia 3, October 4, 1978.
Atlanta 5, Pittsburgh 3, October 12, 1991.
Atlanta 4, Arizona 4, October 20, 2001.

Most innings scored by both clubs, extra-inning game
A.L.—9—New York 5, Baltimore 4, October 9, 1996, 11 innings.
N.L.—9—Atlanta 5, New York 4, October 19, 1999, 11 innings..

Most runs, first inning
N.L.—6
Chicago vs. San Francisco, October 5, 1989.
Atlanta vs. St. Louis, October 17, 1996.
A.L.—5—New York vs. Cleveland, October 6, 1998.

Most runs, second inning
N.L.—9—St. Louis vs. Los Angeles, October 13, 1985.
A.L.—4
Kansas City vs. New York, October 4, 1978.
Baltimore vs. California, October 4, 1979.
California vs. Boston, October 7, 1986.
Minnesota vs. Detroit, October 12, 1987.
Oakland vs. Boston, October 8, 1988.

Most runs, third inning
N.L.—6—Atlanta vs. Philadelphia, October 7, 1993.
A.L.—6—New York vs. Baltimore, October 13, 1996.

Most runs, fourth inning
A.L.—7
Baltimore vs. Minnesota, October 3, 1970.
New York vs. Oakland, October 14, 1981.
N.L.—4
Los Angeles vs. Philadelphia, October 5, 1977.
San Francisco vs. St. Louis, October 11, 1987.
San Francisco vs. Chicago, October 4, 1989.
Atlanta vs. St. Louis, October 17, 1996.

Most runs, fifth inning
N.L.—6—Chicago vs. San Diego, October 2, 1984.
A.L.—5
Toronto vs. Kansas City, October 11, 1985.
Cleveland vs. New York, October 13, 1998.
Seattle vs. New York, October 15, 2000.

Most runs, sixth inning
A.L.—7—Seattle vs. New York, October 20, 2001.
N.L.—5
St. Louis vs. Atlanta, October 7, 1982.
Atlanta vs. Philadelphia, October 9, 1993.
San Diego vs. Atlanta, October 14, 1998.

Most runs, seventh inning
N.L.—6—Atlanta vs. San Diego, October 11, 1998.
A.L.—6—New York vs. Seattle, October 17, 2000.

Most runs, eighth inning
A.L.—7—New York vs. Seattle, October 11, 2000.
N.L.—5
New York vs. Atlanta, October 4, 1969.
Philadelphia vs. Houston, October 12, 1980.
New York vs. Los Angeles, October 8, 1988.
Atlanta vs. San Diego, October 12, 1998.
Atlanta vs. Arizona, October 17, 2001.

Most runs, ninth inning
A.L.—7
Baltimore vs. Minnesota, October 4, 1970.
Oakland vs. Boston, October 6, 1990.
N.L.—4
New York vs. Cincinnati, October 7, 1973.
Los Angeles vs. Montreal, October 17, 1981.
Arizona vs. Atlanta, October 20, 2001.

Most runs, 10th inning
N.L.—4
Houston vs. Philadelphia, October 8, 1980.
Atlanta vs. Cincinnati, October 11, 1995.
A.L.—3
Detroit vs. Oakland, October 11, 1972.
Baltimore vs. California, October 3, 1979.
Baltimore vs. Chicago, October 8, 1983.

Most runs, 11th inning
N.L.—3—Pittsburgh vs. Cincinnati, October 2, 1979.
A.L.—3—Seattle vs. Cleveland, October 13, 1995.

Most runs, 12th inning
A.L.—3—Cleveland vs. New York, October 7, 1998.
N.L.—1
Cincinnati vs. New York, October 9, 1973.
New York vs. Houston, October 14, 1986.
Los Angeles vs. New York, October 9, 1988.

Most runs, 14th inning
N.L.—1
Houston vs. New York, October 15, 1986.
New York vs. Houston, October 15, 1986.
A.L.—Never accomplished.

Most runs, 15th inning
N.L.—2—New York vs. Atlanta, October 17, 1999.
A.L.—Never accomplished.

Most runs, 16th inning
N.L.—3—New York vs. Houston, October 15, 1986.
A.L.—Never accomplished.

GAMES BEING SHUT OUT

Most times being shut out, total series
N.L.—5
Pittsburgh, 1970, 1974, 1991 (3).
Atlanta, 1982, 1991, 1998 (2), 2001.
A.L.—4—Baltimore, 1973, 1974 (2), 1997.

Most consecutive games without being shut out, total series
N.L.—33—Atlanta, October 16, 1991 through October 7, 1998.
A.L.—36—New York, October 9, 1976 through October 18, 1999.

HITS
SERIES

Most hits, total series
N.L.—507—Atlanta; 11 series, 60 games.
A.L.—439—New York; 10 series, 47 games.

Most hits, series
3-game series
N.L.—37—New York vs. Atlanta, 1969.
A.L.—36—Baltimore vs. Minnesota, 1969, 1970.
New York vs. Oakland, 1981.
4-game series
N.L.—42—Los Angeles vs. Philadelphia, 1978.
Atlanta vs. Cincinnati, 1995.
A.L.—42—New York vs. Kansas City, 1978.
5-game series
A.L.—55—New York vs. Kansas City, 1976.
N.L.—55—Philadelphia vs. Houston, 1980.
6-game series
A.L.—65—Toronto vs. Chicago, 1993.
N.L.—59—Atlanta vs. Philadelphia, 1993.
7-game series
N.L.—77—Atlanta vs. St. Louis, 1996.
A.L.—71—California vs. Boston, 1986.

Most hits by both clubs, series
3-game series
N.L.—64—New York 37, Atlanta 27, 1969.
A.L.—60—Baltimore 36, Minnesota 24, 1970.
4-game series
N.L.—77—Los Angeles 42, Philadelphia 35, 1978.
A.L.—77—New York 42, Kansas City 35, 1978.
5-game series
N.L.—97—Chicago 53, San Francisco 44, 1989.
A.L.—96—Boston 54, New York 42, 1999.
6-game series
A.L.—111—Toronto 59, Oakland 52, 1992.
Toronto 65, Chicago 46, 1993.
N.L.—106—Atlanta 59, Philadelphia 47, 1993.
7-game series
A.L.—140—California 71, Boston 69, 1986.
N.L.—122—Atlanta 77, St. Louis 45, 1996.

Fewest hits, series
3-game series
N.L.—15—Atlanta vs. St. Louis, 1982.
A.L.—17—Minnesota vs. Baltimore, 1969.
4-game series
A.L.—22—Baltimore vs. Oakland, 1974.
Oakland vs. Baltimore, 1974.
N.L.—25—Pittsburgh vs. Los Angeles, 1974.
5-game series
N.L.—30—Pittsburgh vs. Cincinnati, 1972.
A.L.—32—Detroit vs. Oakland, 1972.
Oakland vs. Baltimore, 1973.
6-game series
N.L.—36—Florida vs. Atlanta, 1997.
A.L.—37—Seattle vs. Cleveland, 1995.
7-game series
N.L.—45—St. Louis vs. Atlanta, 1996.
A.L.—51—Kansas City vs. Toronto, 1985.

Fewest hits by both clubs, series
3-game series
A.L.—43—Detroit 25, Kansas City 18, 1984.
N.L.—45—Pittsburgh 23, Cincinnati 22, 1970.

4-game series
A.L.—44—Baltimore 22, Oakland 22, 1974.
N.L.—62—Los Angeles 37, Pittsburgh 25, 1974.
5-game series
A.L.—68—Baltimore 36, Oakland 32, 1973.
N.L.—68—New York 37, Cincinnati 31, 1973.
6-game series
N.L.—85—Atlanta 49, Florida 36, 1997.
A.L.—88—Cleveland 45, New York 43, 1998.
7-game series
N.L.—104—Atlanta 53, Pittsburgh 51, 1991.
A.L.—116—Toronto 65, Kansas City 51, 1985.

Most hits by pinch-hitters, series
A.L.—6—Toronto vs. Kansas City, 1985 (7-game series).
N.L.—4—Occurred in many series.

Most hits by pinch-hitters on both clubs, series
N.L.—8—Pittsburgh 4, Los Angeles 4, 1974 (4-game series).
A.L.—8—Toronto 6, Kansas City 2, 1985 (7-game series).

GAME AND INNING

Most hits, game
N.L.—22—Atlanta vs. St. Louis, October 14, 1996.
A.L.—21—Boston vs. New York, October 16, 1999.

Most hits by both clubs, game
A.L.—30—New York 19, Oakland 11, October 14, 1981.
N.L.—29—Atlanta 22, St. Louis 7, October 14, 1996.

Most hits by pinch-hitters, game
A.L.—3—Kansas City vs. Detroit, October 3, 1984, 11 innings.
N.L.—3—New York vs. Atlanta, October 19, 1999, 11 innings.

Most hits by pinch-hitters on both clubs, game
N.L.—5—New York 3, Atlanta 2, October 19, 1999, 11 innings.
A.L.—3
Kansas City 3, Detroit 0, October 3, 1984, 11 innings.
Detroit 2, Minnesota 1, October 11, 1987.

Fewest hits, game
A.L.—1
Oakland vs. Baltimore, October 9, 1974.
Seattle vs. New York, October 14, 2000.
N.L.—1—Pittsburgh vs. Cincinnati, October 12, 1990.

Fewest hits by both clubs, game
A.L.—6
Oakland 4, Baltimore 2, October 8, 1974.
Baltimore 5, Oakland 1, October 9, 1974.
Detroit 3, Kansas City 3, October 5, 1984.
New York 5, Seattle 1, October 14, 2000.
New York 4, Seattle 2, October 21, 2001.
N.L.—7—Houston 4, New York 3, October 12, 1986.

Most players with one or more hits, game
N.L.—11
Chicago vs. San Diego, October 2, 1984.
Atlanta vs. St. Louis, October 14, 1996.
A.L.—10
New York vs. Oakland, October 14, 1981.
Toronto vs. Kansas City, October 11, 1985.

Most players with one or more hits by both clubs, game
A.L.—18
New York 10, Oakland 8, October 14, 1981.
Boston 9, California 9, October 12, 1986, 11 innings.
N.L.—17—Atlanta 11, St. Louis 6, October 14, 1996.

Most hits, inning
N.L.—8
St. Louis vs. Los Angeles, October 13, 1985, second inning.
Pittsburgh vs. Atlanta, October 13, 1992, second inning.
A.L.—8—New York vs. Seattle, October 11, 2000, eighth inning.

Most hits by pinch-hitters, inning
A.L.-N.L.—2—Occurred many times.

Most hits by both clubs, inning
A.L.—11—New York 7, Oakland 4, October 14, 1981, fourth inning.
N.L.—9—Philadelphia 5, Houston 4, October 12, 1980, eighth inning.

Most consecutive hits, inning (consecutive at-bats)
A.L.—7—Baltimore vs. Minnesota, October 3, 1970, fourth
inning (one sacrifice fly during streak).
N.L.—6
St. Louis vs. Atlanta, October 7, 1982, sixth inning (one base
on balls during streak).
Atlanta vs. Arizona, October 17, 2001, eighth inning (one base
on balls during streak).

Most consecutive hits, inning (consecutive plate appearances)
N.L.—5
Cincinnati vs. Pittsburgh, October 8, 1972, first inning.
Los Angeles vs. Pittsburgh, October 6, 1974, eighth inning.
St. Louis vs. San Francisco, October 9, 1987, seventh inning.
A.L.—5
New York vs. Oakland, October 14, 1981, fourth inning.
Toronto vs. Minnesota, October 8, 1991, sixth inning.

SINGLES

Most singles, total series
N.L.—357—Atlanta; 11 series, 60 games.
A.L.—303—New York; 10 series, 47 games.

Most singles, series
3-game series
A.L.—29—New York vs. Oakland, 1981.
N.L.—27—St. Louis vs. Atlanta, 1982.
4-game series
A.L.—34—Oakland vs. Boston, 1990.
N.L.—31—Atlanta vs. Cincinnati, 1995.
5-game series
N.L.—45—Philadelphia vs. Houston, 1980.
A.L.—37—Minnesota vs. Toronto, 1991.
6-game series
A.L.—52—Toronto vs. Chicago, 1993.
N.L.—42—St. Louis vs. Los Angeles, 1985.
7-game series
N.L.—55—Atlanta vs. St. Louis, 1996.
A.L.—53—California vs. Boston, 1986.

Most singles by both clubs, series
3-game series
A.L.—46—New York 29, Oakland 17, 1981.
N.L.—41—St. Louis 27, Atlanta 14, 1982.
4-game series
A.L.—55—New York 33, Kansas City 22, 1978.
N.L.—53—Atlanta 31, Cincinnati 22, 1995.
5-game series
N.L.—73—Philadelphia 45, Houston 28, 1980.
A.L.—73—Minnesota 37, Toronto 36, 1991.
6-game series
A.L.—87—Toronto 52, Chicago 35, 1993.
N.L.—79—San Diego 41, Atlanta 38, 1998.
7-game series
A.L.—103—California 53, Boston 50, 1986.
N.L.—90—Atlanta 55, St. Louis 35, 1996.

Fewest singles, series
3-game series
A.L.—10—Oakland vs. Baltimore, 1971.
N.L.—13—Atlanta vs. New York, 1969.
4-game series
A.L.—14—Oakland vs. Baltimore, 1974.
N.L.—19—Los Angeles vs. Philadelphia, 1983.
5-game series
N.L.—20—Pittsburgh vs. Cincinnati, 1972.
Cincinnati vs. New York, 1973.
A.L.—21—Detroit vs. Oakland, 1972.
Oakland vs. Baltimore, 1973.
6-game series
A.L.—24—Seattle vs. Cleveland, 1995.
Seattle vs. New York, 2000.
N.L.—25—Philadelphia vs. Atlanta, 1993.
7-game series
A.L.—34—Kansas City vs. Toronto, 1985.
N.L.—31—Pittsburgh vs. Atlanta, 1992.

Fewest singles by both clubs, series
3-game series
A.L.—24—Baltimore 14, Oakland 10, 1971.
N.L.—31—Philadelphia 17, Cincinnati 14, 1976.
4-game series
A.L.—32—Baltimore 18, Oakland 14, 1974.
N.L.—44—Philadelphia 25, Los Angeles 19, 1983.
5-game series
A.L.—47—Baltimore 26, Oakland 21, 1973.
N.L.—47—Cincinnati 27, Pittsburgh 20, 1972.
6-game series
A.L.—61—Cleveland 37, Seattle 24, 1995.
N.L.—63—Atlanta 36, Florida 27, 1997.
7-game series
N.L.—69—Atlanta 38, Pittsburgh 31, 1992.
A.L.—78—Toronto 44, Kansas City 34, 1985.

Most singles by pinch-hitters, series
N.L.—4
Pittsburgh vs. Los Angeles, 1974 (4-game series).
Cincinnati vs. Pittsburgh, 1990 (6-game series).
Atlanta vs. Philadelphia, 1993 (6-game series).
A.L.—4—Toronto vs. Kansas City, 1985 (7-game series).

Most singles by pinch-hitters on both clubs, series
N.L.—7—Pittsburgh 4, Los Angeles 3, 1974 (4-game series).
A.L.—4
Oakland 3, Detroit 1, 1972 (5-game series).
Toronto 4, Kansas City 0, 1985 (7-game series).
Detroit 3, Minnesota 1, 1987 (5-game series).

Most singles, game
A.L.—15—New York vs. Oakland, October 14, 1981.
N.L.—15—Atlanta vs. St. Louis, October 14, 1996.

Most singles by both clubs, game
A.L.—25—Kansas City 13, New York 12, October 4, 1978.
N.L.—22—Atlanta 15, St. Louis 7, October 14, 1996.

Fewest singles, game
A.L.—0
Oakland vs. Baltimore, October 9, 1974.
Seattle vs. New York, October 14, 2000.
N.L.—0—Pittsburgh vs. Cincinnati, October 12, 1990.

Fewest singles by both clubs, game
A.L.—2—Seattle 1, New York 1, October 21, 2001.
N.L.—4
New York 2, Cincinnati 2, October 6, 1973.
New York 3, Houston 1, October 12, 1986.

Most singles, inning
N.L.—8—St. Louis vs. Los Angeles, October 13, 1985, second
inning.
A.L.—6—New York vs. Cleveland, October 6, 1998, first inning.

Most singles by both clubs, inning
A.L.—9—New York 5, Oakland 4, October 14, 1981, fourth
inning.
N.L.—8
Philadelphia 4, Houston 4, October 12, 1980, eighth inning.
St. Louis 8, Los Angeles 0, October 13, 1985, second inning.

DOUBLES

Most doubles, total series
N.L.—86—Atlanta; 11 series, 60 games.
A.L.—77—New York; 10 series, 47 games.

Most doubles, series
3-game series
N.L.—9—Atlanta vs. New York, 1969.
A.L.—8—Baltimore vs. Minnesota, 1969.
Oakland vs. Baltimore, 1971.
Boston vs. Oakland, 1975.
4-game series
A.L.—9—Baltimore vs. Chicago, 1983.
N.L.—8—Los Angeles vs. Pittsburgh, 1974.
Los Angeles vs. Philadelphia, 1978.

5-game series
A.L.—13—New York vs. Kansas City, 1976.
  Minnesota vs. Detroit, 1987.
  Boston vs. New York, 1999.
N.L.—12—New York vs. St. Louis, 2000..
6-game series
N.L.—14—Atlanta vs. Philadelphia, 1993.
A.L.—12—Seattle vs. New York, 2000.
7-game series
N.L.—20—Pittsburgh vs. Atlanta, 1992.
A.L.—19—Toronto vs. Kansas City, 1985.

Most doubles by both clubs, series
3-game series
N.L.—17—Atlanta 9, New York 8, 1969.
A.L.—15—Oakland 8, Baltimore 7, 1971.
4-game series
A.L.—13—Baltimore 9, Chicago 4, 1983.
N.L.—11—Los Angeles 8, Philadelphia 3, 1978.
  Atlanta 6, Cincinnati 5, 1995.
5-game series
N.L.—23—New York 12, St. Louis 11, 2000.
A.L.—21—New York 12, Kansas City 9, 1977.
6-game series
N.L.—25—Atlanta 14, Philadelphia 11, 1993.
A.L.—22—Seattle 12, New York 10, 2000.
7-game series
N.L.—31—Pittsburgh 20, Atlanta 11, 1992.
A.L.—28—Toronto 19, Kansas City 9, 1985.

Fewest doubles, series
3-game series
N.L.—1—Atlanta vs. St. Louis, 1982.
A.L.—1—Kansas City vs. Detroit, 1984.
4-game series
A.L.—1—Baltimore vs. Oakland, 1974.
N.L.—1—Pittsburgh vs. Los Angeles, 1974.
5-game series
N.L.—3—Los Angeles vs. Montreal, 1981.
A.L.—4—Milwaukee vs. California, 1982.
  Detroit vs. Minnesota, 1987.
  Baltimore vs. New York, 1996.
  New York vs. Boston, 1999.
  Seattle vs. New York, 2001.
6-game series
A.L.—3—Cleveland vs. New York, 1998.
N.L.—4—New York vs. Houston, 1986.
  Atlanta vs. San Diego, 1998.
7-game series
N.L.—4—St. Louis vs. San Francisco, 1987.
  St. Louis vs. Atlanta, 1996.
A.L.—9—Kansas City vs. Toronto, 1985.

Fewest doubles by both clubs, series
3-game series
N.L.—5—St. Louis 4, Atlanta 1, 1982.
A.L.—5—Detroit 4, Kansas City 1, 1984.
4-game series
A.L.—5—Oakland 4, Baltimore 1, 1974.
N.L.—9—San Francisco 5, Pittsburgh 4, 1971.
  Los Angeles 8, Pittsburgh 1, 1974.
  Los Angeles 6, Philadelphia 3, 1977.
  Los Angeles 5, Philadelphia 4, 1983.
5-game series
N.L.—10—Montreal 7, Los Angeles 3, 1981.
A.L.—11—New York 7, Seattle 4, 2001.
6-game series
N.L.—10—Houston 6, New York 4, 1986.
A.L.—11—New York 8, Cleveland 3, 1998.
7-game series
N.L.—11—San Francisco 7, St. Louis 4, 1987.
A.L.—22—Boston 11, California 11, 1986.

Most doubles by pinch-hitters, series
N.L.—3—St. Louis vs. New York, 2000 (5-game series).
A.L.—2—Toronto vs. Kansas City, 1985 (7-game series).

Most doubles by pinch-hitters on both clubs, series
A.L.—3—Toronto 2, Kansas City 1, 1985 (7-game series).
N.L.—3—St. Louis 3, New York 0, 2000 (5-game series).

Most doubles, game
A.L.—6
Baltimore vs. Minnesota, October 6, 1969.
Boston vs. New York, October 16, 1999.
Seattle vs. New York, October 17, 2000.
N.L.—6
Philadelphia vs. Cincinnati, October 12, 1976.
New York vs. St. Louis, October 15, 2000.

Most doubles by both clubs, game
A.L.—9—Oakland 5, Baltimore 4, October 3, 1971.
N.L.—8
Los Angeles 5, St. Louis 3, October 12, 1985.
Philadelphia 5, Atlanta 3, October 6, 1993, 10 innings.
Atlanta 5, Philadelphia 3, October 9, 1993.
New York 6, St. Louis 2, October 15, 2000.

Most doubles, inning
N.L.—5—New York vs. St. Louis, October 15, 2000, first inning.
A.L.—3
Oakland vs. Baltimore, October 10, 1973, second inning.
Boston vs. Oakland, October 4, 1975, seventh inning.
Minnesota vs. Detroit, October 8, 1987, second inning.

TRIPLES

Most triples, total series
A.L.—13—Kansas City; six series, 27 games.
N.L.—11—Atlanta; 11 series, 60 games.

Most triples, series
3-game series
N.L.—3—Cincinnati vs. Philadelphia, 1976.
A.L.—1—Held by many clubs.
4-game series
A.L.—3—Kansas City vs. New York, 1978.
N.L.—3—Los Angeles vs. Philadelphia, 1978.
5-game series
N.L.—5—Houston vs. Philadelphia, 1980.
A.L.—4—Kansas City vs. New York, 1976.
6-game series
N.L.—4—Philadelphia vs. Atlanta, 1993.
A.L.—3—Toronto vs. Chicago, 1993.
  Cleveland 3, Seattle 0, 1995.
7-game series
N.L.—4—St. Louis vs. San Francisco, 1987.
A.L.—2—Boston vs. California, 1986.

Most triples by both clubs, series
3-game series
N.L.—4—Cincinnati 3, Philadelphia 1, 1976.
A.L.—2—Baltimore 1, Minnesota 1, 1969.
  Baltimore 1, Oakland 1, 1971.
  Kansas City 1, New York 1, 1980.
4-game series
N.L.—5—Los Angeles 3, Philadelphia 2, 1978.
A.L.—4—Kansas City 3, New York 1, 1978.
5-game series
A.L.—6—Kansas City 4, New York 2, 1976.
N.L.—6—Houston 5, Philadelphia 1, 1980.
6-game series
N.L.—4—Philadelphia 4, Atlanta 0, 1993.
A.L.—4—Toronto 3, Chicago 1, 1993.
7-game series
N.L.—5—St. Louis 4, San Francisco 1, 1987.
  Pittsburgh 3, Atlanta 2, 1992.
  Atlanta 3, St. Louis 2, 1996.
A.L.—2—Boston 2, California 0, 1986.

Fewest triples, series
A.L.-N.L.—0—Held by many clubs.

Fewest triples by both clubs, series
A.L.-N.L.—0—Occurred many times.

Most triples by pinch-hitters, series
N.L.—1
Cincinnati vs. Pittsburgh, 1970 (3-game series).
New York vs. Houston, 1986 (6-game series).

Atlanta vs. Pittsburgh, 1992 (7-game series).
St. Louis vs. Atlanta, 1996 (7-game series).
.L.—1—Seattle vs. New York, 2001 (5-game series).

Most triples, game
.L.—3—Philadelphia vs. Atlanta, October 9, 1993.
.L.—2
Kansas City vs. New York, October 13, 1976.
Kansas City vs. New York, October 8, 1977.
Seattle vs. New York, October 20, 2001.

Most triples by both clubs, game
.L.—3
Los Angeles 2, Philadelphia 1, October 4, 1978.
Philadelphia 3, Atlanta 0, October 9, 1993.
.L.—2
Baltimore 1, Minnesota 1, October 6, 1969.
Kansas City 1, New York 1, October 9, 1976.
Kansas City 2, New York 0, October 13, 1976.
Kansas City 2, New York 0, October 8, 1977.
Detroit 1, Kansas City 1, October 2, 1984.
Toronto 1, Chicago 1, October 9, 1993.
Seattle 2, New York 0, October 20, 2001.

Most triples, inning
.L.—2—Kansas City vs. New York, October 8, 1977, third inning.
.L.—2—Philadelphia vs. Atlanta, October 9, 1993, fourth inning.

HOME RUNS
SERIES

Most home runs, total series
.L.—53—Atlanta; 11 series, 60 games.
.L.—52—New York; 10 series, 47 games.

Most grand slams, total series
.L.—2
Los Angeles, 1977 (2).
Atlanta, 1992, 1997.
.L.—1
Baltimore, 1970.
California, 1982.
Cleveland, 1998.
New York, 1999.

Most home runs, series
3-game series
N.L.—6—New York vs. Atlanta, 1969.
A.L.—6—Baltimore vs. Minnesota, 1970.
4-game series
N.L.—8—Pittsburgh vs. San Francisco, 1971.
Los Angeles vs. Philadelphia, 1978.
A.L.—7—Oakland vs. Boston, 1988.
5-game series
A.L.—10—New York vs. Baltimore, 1996.
N.L.—9—Chicago vs. San Diego, 1984.
6-game series
A.L.—10—Toronto vs. Oakland, 1992.
N.L.—7—Philadelphia vs. Atlanta, 1993.
7-game series
N.L.—9—San Francisco vs. St. Louis, 1987.
A.L.—7—California vs. Boston, 1986.

Most home runs by both clubs, series
3-game series
N.L.—11—New York 6, Atlanta 5, 1969.
A.L.—9—Baltimore 6, Minnesota 3, 1970.
4-game series
N.L.—13—Pittsburgh 8, San Francisco 5, 1971.
Los Angeles 8, Philadelphia 5, 1978.
A.L.—9—New York 5, Kansas City 4, 1978.
Oakland 7, Boston 2, 1988.
5-game series
A.L.—19—New York 10, Baltimore 9, 1996.
N.L.—11—Chicago 9, San Diego 2, 1984.
San Francisco 8, Chicago 3, 1989.
6-game series
A.L.—14—Toronto 10, Oakland 4, 1992.
N.L.—12—Philadelphia 7, Atlanta 5, 1993.

7-game series
A.L.—13—California 7, Boston 6, 1986.
N.L.—12—Atlanta 8, St. Louis 4, 1996.

Fewest home runs, series
3-game series
N.L.—0—Pittsburgh vs. Cincinnati, 1970.
Atlanta vs. St. Louis, 1982.
A.L.—0—Oakland vs. New York, 1981.
Kansas City vs. Detroit, 1984.
4-game series
N.L.—0—Cincinnati vs. Atlanta, 1995.
A.L.—0—Chicago vs. Baltimore, 1983.
Oakland vs. Boston, 1990.
5-game series
N.L.—0—Houston vs. Philadelphia, 1980.
A.L.—1—Oakland vs. Detroit, 1972.
Toronto vs. Minnesota, 1991.
6-game series
N.L.—1—Florida vs. Atlanta, 1997.
A.L.—2—Toronto vs. Chicago, 1993.
7-game series
A.L.—2—Toronto vs. Kansas City, 1985.
N.L.—2—St. Louis vs. San Francisco, 1987.

Fewest home runs by both clubs, series
3-game series
N.L.—1—St. Louis 1, Atlanta 0, 1982.
A.L.—2—New York 2, Oakland 0, 1981.
4-game series
A.L.—1—Boston 1, Oakland 0, 1990.
N.L.—4—Atlanta 4, Cincinnati 0, 1995.
5-game series
N.L.—1—Philadelphia 1, Houston 0, 1980.
A.L.—4—Minnesota 3, Toronto 1, 1991.
6-game series
A.L.—7—Chicago 5, Toronto 2, 1993.
N.L.—7—Atlanta 6, Florida 1, 1997.
7-game series
N.L.—8—New York 5, Los Angeles 3, 1988.
Atlanta 5, Pittsburgh 3, 1991.
A.L.—9—Kansas City 7, Toronto 2, 1985.

Most grand slams, series
N.L.—2—Los Angeles vs. Philadelphia, 1977.
A.L.—1
Baltimore vs. Minnesota, 1970.
California vs. Milwaukee, 1982.
Cleveland vs. New York, 1998.
New York vs. Boston, 1999.

Most home runs by pinch-hitters, series
N.L.—2—Philadelphia vs. Los Angeles, 1978 (4-game series).
A.L.—1
Baltimore vs. California, 1979 (4-game series).
Kansas City vs. Toronto, 1985 (7-game series).
Minnesota vs. Toronto, 1991 (5-game series).
New York vs. Boston, 1999 (5-game series).
Seattle vs. New York, 2001 (5-game series).

GAME AND INNING

Most home runs, game
N.L.—5—Chicago vs. San Diego, October 2, 1984.
A.L.—4
Baltimore vs. Oakland, October 4, 1971.
Oakland vs. Baltimore, October 7, 1973.
Oakland vs. Boston, October 8, 1988.
New York vs. Baltimore, October 12, 1996.
Cleveland vs. New York, October 9, 1998.

Most home runs by both clubs, game
A.L.—6—New York 3, Baltimore 3, October 13, 1996.
N.L.—6—Atlanta 4, Philadelphia 2, 1993.

Most consecutive games with one or more home runs, total series
A.L.—10—Baltimore, last three games vs. Chicago, 1983 (three home runs), all five games vs. New York, 1996 (nine home runs); first two games vs. Cleveland, 1997 (three home runs).

N.L.—7—Philadelphia, all four games vs. Los Angeles, 1983 (five home runs), first three games vs. Atlanta, 1993 (four home runs).

Most consecutive games with one or more home runs, series
A.L.—6—Toronto vs. Oakland, October 7, 8, 10, 11, 12, 14, 1992 (10 home runs).
N.L.—5—San Francisco vs. St. Louis, October 6, 7, 9, 10, 11, 1987 (nine home runs).

Most home runs, inning
A.L.—3
Baltimore vs. Minnesota, October 3, 1970, fourth inning (first two consecutive).
New York vs. Baltimore, October 13, 1996, third inning (first two consecutive).
Baltimore vs. Cleveland, October 12, 1997, third inning (last two consecutive).
Cleveland vs. New York, October 9, 1998, fifth inning (last two consecutive).
N.L.—2
Cincinnati vs. Pittsburgh, October 5, 1970, first inning (consecutive).
San Francisco vs. Pittsburgh, October 2, 1971, fifth inning.
San Francisco vs. Pittsburgh, October 6, 1971, second inning.
Pittsburgh vs. Los Angeles, October 8, 1974, first inning.
Cincinnati vs. Philadelphia, October 12, 1976, ninth inning (consecutive).
Pittsburgh vs. Cincinnati, October 5, 1979, third inning.
Los Angeles vs. Montreal, October 13, 1981, eighth inning (consecutive).
Chicago vs. San Diego, October 2, 1984, first inning.
Chicago vs. San Diego, October 6, 1984, fourth inning (consecutive).
New York vs. Los Angeles, October 9, 1988, fourth inning (consecutive).
Pittsburgh vs. Atlanta, October 13, 1992, second inning.
Atlanta vs. Philadelphia, October 7, 1993, third inning.
Atlanta vs. San Diego, October 11, 1998, seventh inning.
Atlanta vs. New York, October 13, 1999, sixth inning.
New York vs. St. Louis, October 11, 2000, ninth inning.

Most home runs by both clubs, inning
A.L.—3
Baltimore 3, Minnesota 0, October 3, 1970, fourth inning.
Toronto 2, Kansas City 1, October 11, 1985, fifth inning.
Oakland 2, Boston 1, October 8, 1988, second inning.
New York 3, Baltimore 0, October 13, 1996, third inning.
Baltimore 3, Cleveland 0, October 12, 1997, third inning.
Cleveland 3, New York 0, October 9, 1998, fifth inning.
N.L.—3—San Francisco 2, Pittsburgh 1, October 6, 1971, second inning.

Most consecutive home runs, inning
A.L.—2
Baltimore (Cuellar and Buford) vs. Minnesota, October 3, 1970, fourth inning.
Minnesota (Killebrew and Oliva) vs. Baltimore, October 4, 1970, fourth inning.
Oakland (Rudi and Bando) vs. Baltimore, October 7, 1973, sixth inning.
New York (Cerone and Piniella) vs. Kansas City, October 8, 1980, second inning.
Oakland (McGwire and Steinbach) vs. Toronto, October 7, 1992, second inning.
New York (Fielder and Strawberry) vs. Baltimore, October 13, 1996, third inning.
Baltimore (Baines and Palmeiro) vs. Cleveland, October 12, 1997, third inning.
Cleveland (Thome and Whiten) vs. New York, October 9, 1998, fifth inning.
New York (Williams, T. Martinez) vs. Seattle, October 13, 2000, second inning.
Seattle (E. Martinez, Olerud) vs. New York, October 15, 2000, fifth inning.
N.L.—2
Cincinnati (Perez and Bench) vs. Pittsburgh, October 5, 1970, first inning.
Cincinnati (Foster and Bench) vs. Philadelphia, October 12, 1976, ninth inning.

Los Angeles (Guerrero and Scioscia) vs. Montreal, October 13, 1981, eighth inning.
Chicago (Davis and Durham) vs. San Diego, October 6, 1984, fourth inning.
New York (Strawberry and McReynolds) vs. Los Angeles, October 9, 1988, fourth inning.
Atlanta (Jordan and Klesko) vs. New York, October 16, 1999, eighth inning.

TOTAL BASES

Most total bases, total series
N.L.—774—Atlanta; 11 series, 60 games.
A.L.—686—New York; 10 series, 47 games.

Most total bases, series
3-game series
N.L.—65—New York vs. Atlanta, 1969.
A.L.—61—Baltimore vs. Minnesota, 1970.
4-game series
N.L.—80—Los Angeles vs. Philadelphia, 1978.
A.L.—70—Oakland vs. Boston, 1988.
5-game series
A.L.—91—New York vs. Baltimore, 1996.
N.L.—80—Chicago vs. San Diego, 1984.
6-game series
A.L.—99—Toronto vs. Oakland, 1992.
N.L.—88—Atlanta vs. Philadelphia, 1993.
7-game series
N.L.—118—Atlanta vs. St. Louis, 1996.
A.L.—103—California vs. Boston, 1986.

Most total bases by both clubs, series
3-game series
N.L.—116—New York 65, Atlanta 51, 1969.
A.L.—100—Baltimore 61, Minnesota 39, 1970.
4-game series
N.L.—137—Los Angeles 80, Philadelphia 57, 1978.
A.L.—121—New York 62, Kansas City 59, 1978.
5-game series
A.L.—161—New York 91, Baltimore 70, 1996.
N.L.—155—San Francisco 78, Chicago 77, 1989.
6-game series
N.L.—175—Atlanta 88, Philadelphia 87, 1993.
A.L.—170—Toronto 99, Oakland 71, 1992.
7-game series
A.L.—205—California 103, Boston 102, 1986.
N.L.—190—Pittsburgh 100, Atlanta 90, 1992.

Fewest total bases, series
3-game series
N.L.—16—Atlanta vs. St. Louis, 1982.
A.L.—21—Kansas City vs. Detroit, 1984.
4-game series
A.L.—31—Boston vs. Oakland, 1990.
N.L.—35—Pittsburgh vs. Los Angeles, 1974.
Cincinnati vs. Atlanta, 1995.
5-game series
N.L.—44—Montreal vs. Los Angeles, 1981.
A.L.—49—Oakland vs. Detroit, 1972.
6-game series
N.L.—47—Florida vs. Atlanta, 1997.
A.L.—60—Seattle vs. Cleveland, 1995.
7-game series
N.L.—65—St. Louis vs. Atlanta, 1996.
A.L.—83—Kansas City vs. Toronto, 1985.

Fewest total bases by both clubs, series
3-game series
N.L.—61—St. Louis 45, Atlanta 16, 1982.
A.L.—64—Detroit 43, Kansas City 21, 1984.
4-game series
A.L.—69—Oakland 37, Baltimore 32, 1974.
N.L.—91—Los Angeles 56, Pittsburgh 35, 1974.
5-game series
N.L.—99—Los Angeles 55, Montreal 44, 1981.
A.L.—101—Detroit 52, Oakland 49, 1972.
6-game series
N.L.—123—Atlanta 76, Florida 47, 1997
A.L.—142—Cleveland 77, New York 65, 1998.

7-game series
N.L.—150—Atlanta 80, Pittsburgh 70, 1991.
A.L.—173—Toronto 90, Kansas City 83, 1985.

Most total bases, game
A.L.—38—Boston vs. New York, October 16, 1999.
N.L.—34
Chicago vs. San Diego, October 2, 1984.
Atlanta vs. St. Louis, October 14, 1996.

Most total bases by both clubs, game
N.L.—47—Los Angeles 30, Philadelphia 17, October 4, 1978.
A.L.—47—Oakland 30, Boston 17, October 8, 1988.

Fewest total bases, game
N.L.—2
Cincinnati vs. New York, October 7, 1973.
St. Louis vs. San Francisco, October 7, 1987.
Pittsburgh vs. Cincinnati, October 12, 1990.
Atlanta vs. San Diego, October 14, 1998.
A.L.—2
Baltimore vs. Oakland, October 8, 1974.
Oakland vs. Baltimore, October 9, 1974.
Kansas City vs. Toronto, October 12, 1985.
Seattle vs. New York, October 14, 2000.

Fewest total bases by both clubs, game
A.L.—6—Detroit 3, Kansas City 3, October 5, 1984.
N.L.—10—New York 7, Atlanta 3, October 15, 1999.

Most total bases, inning
A.L.—16—Baltimore vs. Minnesota, October 3, 1970, fourth inning.
N.L.—16—Pittsburgh vs. Atlanta, October 13, 1992, second inning.

Most total bases by both clubs, inning
A.L.—18—Baltimore 16, Minnesota 2, October 3, 1970, fourth inning.
N.L.—17—San Francisco 11, Pittsburgh 6, October 6, 1971, second inning.

LONG HITS

Most long hits, total series
N.L.—150—Atlanta; 11 series, 60 games.
A.L.—136—New York; 10 series; 47 games.

Most long hits, series
3-game series
N.L.—15—New York vs. Atlanta, 1969.
A.L.—13—Baltimore vs. Minnesota, 1969, 1970.
4-game series
N.L.—19—Los Angeles vs. Philadelphia, 1978.
A.L.—15—Oakland vs. Boston, 1988.
5-game series
A.L.—22—Minnesota vs. Detroit, 1987.
N.L.—20—Chicago vs. San Diego, 1984.
6-game series
N.L.—22—Philadelphia vs. Atlanta, 1993.
A.L.—19—Toronto vs. Oakland, 1992.
7-game series
N.L.—28—Pittsburgh vs. Atlanta, 1992.
A.L.—21—Toronto vs. Kansas City, 1985.

Most long hits by both clubs, series
3-game series
N.L.—29—New York 15, Atlanta 14, 1969.
A.L.—24—Baltimore 12, Oakland 12, 1971.
4-game series
N.L.—29—Los Angeles 19, Philadelphia 10, 1978.
A.L.—22—Kansas City 13, New York 9, 1978.
5-game series
A.L.—33—Minnesota 22, Detroit 11, 1987.
New York 20, Baltimore 13, 1996.
Boston 20, New York 13, 1999.
N.L.—30—New York 17, St. Louis 13, 2000.
6-game series
N.L.—41—Philadelphia 22, Atlanta 19, 1993.
A.L.—33—Seattle 17, New York 16, 2000.

7-game series
N.L.—47—Pittsburgh 28, Atlanta 19, 1992.
A.L.—38—Toronto 21, Kansas City 17, 1985.

Fewest long hits, series
3-game series
N.L.—1—Atlanta vs. St. Louis, 1982.
A.L.—2—Kansas City vs. Detroit, 1984.
4-game series
N.L.—4—Pittsburgh vs. Los Angeles, 1974.
A.L.—4—Baltimore vs. Oakland, 1974.
Chicago vs. Baltimore, 1983.
Oakland vs. Boston, 1990.
5-game series
N.L.—8—New York vs. Cincinnati, 1973.
Los Angeles vs. Montreal, 1981.
Montreal vs. Los Angeles, 1981.
San Diego vs. Chicago, 1984.
Arizona vs. Atlanta, 2001.
A.L.—7—Toronto vs. Minnesota, 1991.
6-game series
N.L.—9—New York vs. Houston, 1986.
Florida vs. Atlanta, 1997.
Atlanta vs. San Diego, 1998.
A.L.—10—Oakland vs. Toronto, 1992.
7-game series
N.L.—10—St. Louis vs. San Francisco, 1987.
St. Louis vs. Atlanta, 1996.
A.L.—17—Kansas City vs. Toronto, 1985.

Fewest long hits by both clubs, series
3-game series
N.L.—8—St. Louis 7, Atlanta 1, 1982.
A.L.—11—Detroit 9, Kansas City 2, 1984.
4-game series
A.L.—10—Boston 6, Oakland 4, 1990.
N.L.—15—Los Angeles 10, Philadelphia 5, 1977.
5-game series
N.L.—16—Los Angeles 8, Montreal 8, 1981.
A.L.—20—Detroit 11, Oakland 9, 1972.
Minnesota 13, Toronto 7, 1991.
6-game series
N.L.—20—Houston 11, New York 9, 1986.
A.L.—24—Toronto 13, Chicago 11, 1993.
7-game series
N.L.—27—San Francisco 17, St. Louis 10, 1987.
A.L.—37—Boston 19, California 18, 1986.

Most long hits, game
A.L.—10—Boston vs. New York, October 16, 1999 (six doubles, one triple, three home runs).
N.L.—8
Cincinnati vs. Philadelphia, October 9, 1976 (five doubles, two triples, one home run).
Chicago vs. San Diego, October 2, 1984 (three doubles, five home runs).

Most long hits by both clubs, game
A.L.—12—Oakland 6 (five doubles, one home run), Boston 6 (four doubles, two home runs), October 5, 1975.
N.L.—12—Philadelphia 7 (three doubles, three triples, one home run), Atlanta 5 (five doubles), October 9, 1993.

EXTRA BASES ON LONG HITS

Most extra bases on long hits, total series
N.L.—267—Atlanta; 11 series, 60 games (86 on doubles, 22 on triples, 159 on home runs).
A.L.—247—New York; 10 series, 47 games (77 on doubles, 14 on triples; 156 on home runs).

Most extra bases on long hits, series
3-game series
N.L.—28—New York vs. Atlanta, 1969.
A.L.—25—Baltimore vs. Minnesota, 1970.
4-game series
N.L.—38—Los Angeles vs. Philadelphia, 1978.
A.L.—29—Oakland vs. Boston, 1988.
5-game series
A.L.—41—New York vs. Baltimore, 1996.
N.L.—38—Chicago vs. San Diego, 1984.

6-game series
A.L.—40—Toronto vs. Oakland, 1992.
N.L.—40—Philadelphia vs. Atlanta, 1993.
7-game series
N.L.—41—Pittsburgh vs. Atlanta, 1992.
Atlanta vs. St. Louis, 1996.
A.L.—33—Boston vs. California, 1986.

Most extra bases on long hits by both clubs, series
3-game series
N.L.—52—New York 28, Atlanta 24, 1969.
A.L.—40—Baltimore 25, Minnesota 15, 1970.
Baltimore 21, Oakland 19, 1971.
4-game series
N.L.—60—Los Angeles 38, Philadelphia 22, 1978.
A.L.—44—Kansas City 24, New York 20, 1978.
5-game series
A.L.—72—New York 41, Baltimore 31, 1996.
N.L.—58—San Francisco 34, Chicago 24, 1989.
6-game series
N.L.—69—Philadelphia 40, Atlanta 29, 1993.
A.L.—59—Toronto 40, Oakland 19, 1992.
7-game series
N.L.—74—Pittsburgh 41, Atlanta 33, 1992.
A.L.—65—Boston 33, California 32, 1986.

Fewest extra bases on long hits, series
3-game series
N.L.—1—Atlanta vs. St. Louis, 1982.
A.L.—3—Kansas City vs. Detroit, 1984.
4-game series
A.L.—4—Chicago vs. Baltimore, 1983.
Oakland vs. Boston, 1990.
N.L.—7—Cincinnati vs. Atlanta, 1995.
5-game series
A.L.—9—Toronto vs. Minnesota, 1991.
N.L.—10—Montreal vs. Los Angeles, 1981.
6-game series
N.L.—11—Florida vs. Atlanta, 1997.
A.L.—19—Oakland vs. Toronto, 1992.
7-game series
N.L.—18—St. Louis vs. San Francisco, 1987.
Los Angeles vs. New York, 1988.
A.L.—25—Toronto vs. Kansas City, 1985.

Fewest extra bases on long hits by both clubs, series
3-game series
N.L.—12—St. Louis 11, Atlanta 1, 1982.
A.L.—17—New York 11, Oakland 6, 1981.
4-game series
A.L.—12—Boston 8, Oakland 4, 1990.
N.L.—26—Los Angeles 17, Philadelphia 9, 1977.
5-game series
N.L.—27—Los Angeles 17, Montreal 10, 1981.
A.L.—29—Minnesota 20, Toronto 9, 1991.
6-game series
N.L.—38—Houston 21, New York 17, 1986.
Atlanta 27, Florida 11, 1997.
A.L.—42—Chicago 22, Toronto 20, 1993.
7-game series
N.L.—46—Atlanta 27, Pittsburgh 19, 1991.
A.L.—57—Kansas City 32, Toronto 25, 1985.

RUNS BATTED IN

Most runs batted in, total series
N.L.—235—Atlanta; 11 series, 60 games.
A.L.—206—New York; 10 series, 47 games.

Most runs batted in, series
3-game series
A.L.—24—Baltimore vs. Minnesota, 1970.
N.L.—24—New York vs. Atlanta, 1969.
4-game series
A.L.—25—Baltimore vs. California, 1979.
N.L.—23—Pittsburgh vs. San Francisco, 1971.
5-game series
A.L.—33—Minnesota vs. Detroit, 1987.
N.L.—29—San Francisco vs. Chicago, 1989.

6-game series
N.L.—32—Atlanta vs. Philadelphia, 1993.
A.L.—30—Toronto vs. Oakland, 1992.
7-game series
A.L.—35—Boston vs. California, 1986.
N.L.—43—Atlanta vs. St. Louis, 1996.

Most runs batted in by both clubs, series
3-game series
N.L.—39—New York 24, Atlanta 15, 1969.
A.L.—34—Baltimore 24, Minnesota 10, 1970.
4-game series
A.L.—39—Baltimore 25, California 14, 1979.
N.L.—37—Pittsburgh 23, San Francisco 14, 1971.
Los Angeles 21, Philadelphia 16, 1978.
5-game series
A.L.—54—Minnesota 33, Detroit 21, 1987.
N.L.—50—San Francisco 29, Chicago 21, 1989.
6-game series
N.L.—54—Atlanta 32, Philadelphia 22, 1993.
A.L.—53—Toronto 30, Oakland 23, 1992.
7-game series
A.L.—64—Boston 35, California 29, 1986.
N.L.—64—Atlanta 32, Pittsburgh 32, 1992.

Fewest runs batted in, series
3-game series
N.L.—3—Pittsburgh vs. Cincinnati, 1970.
Atlanta vs. St. Louis, 1982.
A.L.—4—Oakland vs. New York, 1981.
Kansas City vs. Detroit, 1984.
4-game series
A.L.—2—Chicago vs. Baltimore, 1983.
N.L.—4—Cincinnati vs. Atlanta, 1995.
5-game series
N.L.—8—Cincinnati vs. New York, 1973.
Montreal vs. Los Angeles, 1981.
A.L.—10—Oakland vs. Detroit, 1972.
Detroit vs. Oakland, 1972.
6-game series
A.L.—10—Seattle vs. Cleveland, 1995.
N.L.—17—Houston vs. New York, 1986.
Atlanta vs. San Diego, 1998.
7-game series
N.L.—11—Pittsburgh vs. Atlanta, 1991.
A.L.—23—Toronto vs. Kansas City, 1985.

Fewest runs batted in by both clubs, series
3-game series
N.L.—11—Cincinnati 8, Pittsburgh 3, 1970.
A.L.—18—Detroit 14, Kansas City 4, 1984.
4-game series
A.L.—18—Oakland 11, Baltimore 7, 1974.
N.L.—22—Philadelphia 15, Los Angeles 7, 1983.
5-game series
A.L.—20—Oakland 10, Detroit 10, 1972.
N.L.—23—Los Angeles 15, Montreal 8, 1981.
6-game series
A.L.—31—Cleveland 21, Seattle 10, 1995.
N.L.—36—New York 19, Houston 17, 1986.
7-game series
N.L.—30—Atlanta 19, Pittsburgh 11, 1991.
A.L.—49—Kansas City 26, Toronto 23, 1985.

Most runs batted in by pinch-hitters, series
A.L.—4
Baltimore vs. California, 1979 (4-game series).
Toronto vs. Kansas City, 1985 (7-game series).
Detroit vs. Minnesota, 1987 (5-game series).
New York vs. Boston, 1999 (5-game series).
N.L.—4—Philadelphia vs. Houston, 1980 (5-game series).

Most runs batted in by pinch-hitters on both clubs, series
A.L.—6—Detroit 4, Minnesota 2, 1987 (5-game series).
N.L.—5—Philadelphia 4, Houston 1, 1980 (5-game series).

Most runs batted in, game
N.L.—14
Atlanta vs. Philadelphia, October 7, 1993.
Atlanta vs. St. Louis, October 14, 1996.
Atlanta vs. St. Louis, October 17, 1996.

A.L.—13
　　New York vs. Oakland, October 14, 1981.
　　Seattle vs. New York, October 20, 2001.

Most runs batted in by both clubs, nine-inning game
N.L.—17
　　New York 11, Atlanta 6, October 5, 1969.
　　Atlanta 13, Pittsburgh 4, October 7, 1992.
　　Atlanta 14, Philadelphia 3, October 7, 1993.
A.L.—16
　　Baltimore 8, California 8, October 4, 1979.
　　New York 13, Oakland 3, October 14, 1981.
　　Oakland 10, Boston 6, October 8, 1988.
　　Seattle 13, New York 3, October 20, 2001.

Most runs batted in by both clubs, extra-inning game
N.L.—18—New York 9, Atlanta 9, October 19, 1999, 11 innings.
A.L.—Less than nine-inning record.

Fewest runs batted in by both clubs, game
N.L.—0—Atlanta 0, New York 0, October 15, 1999.
A.L.—1—Held by many clubs.

Most runs batted in, inning
N.L.—8—St. Louis vs. Los Angeles, October 13, 1985, second inning.
A.L.—7
　　Baltimore vs. Minnesota, October 3, 1970, fourth inning.
　　New York vs. Oakland, October 14, 1981, fourth inning.
　　New York vs. Seattle, October 11, 2000, eighth inning.

Most runs batted in by both clubs, inning
A.L.—9—New York 7, Oakland 2, October 14, 1981, fourth inning.
N.L.—8—St. Louis 8, Los Angeles 0, October 13, 1985, second inning.

Most runs batted in by pinch-hitters, inning
A.L.—4—New York vs. Boston, October 17, 1999, ninth inning.
N.L.—2—Held by many clubs.

BASES ON BALLS

Most bases on balls, total series
N.L.—215—Atlanta; 11 series, 60 games.
A.L.—172—New York; 10 series, 47 games.

Most bases on balls, series
3-game series
　　N.L.—15—Cincinnati vs. Philadelphia, 1976.
　　A.L.—13—Baltimore vs. Minnesota, 1969.
　　　　Baltimore vs. Oakland, 1971.
4-game series
　　N.L.—30—Los Angeles vs. Pittsburgh, 1974.
　　A.L.—22—Oakland vs. Baltimore, 1974.
5-game series
　　N.L.—31—Houston vs. Philadelphia, 1980.
　　A.L.—27—New York vs. Seattle, 2000.
6-game series
　　A.L.—35—New York vs. Cleveland, 1998.
　　N.L.—31—Atlanta vs. New York, 1999.
7-game series
　　N.L.—29—Atlanta vs. Pittsburgh, 1992.
　　　　Pittsburgh vs. Atlanta, 1992.
　　A.L.—22—Kansas City vs. Toronto, 1985.

Most bases on balls by both clubs, series
3-game series
　　N.L.—27—Cincinnati 15, Philadelphia 12, 1976.
　　A.L.—25—Baltimore 13, Minnesota 12, 1969.
4-game series
　　N.L.—38—Los Angeles 30, Pittsburgh 8, 1974.
　　A.L.—28—Baltimore 16, Chicago 12, 1983.
　　　　Boston 18, Oakland 10, 1988.
5-game series
　　N.L.—44—Houston 31, Philadelphia 13, 1980.
　　A.L.—41—New York 23, Seattle 18, 2001.
6-game series
　　A.L.—53—Chicago 32, Toronto 21, 1993.
　　N.L.—53—San Diego 27, Atlanta 26, 1998.

7-game series
　　N.L.—58—Atlanta 29, Pittsburgh 29, 1992.
　　A.L.—39—California 20, Boston 19, 1986.

Fewest bases on balls, series
3-game series
　　A.L.—3—Boston vs. Oakland, 1975.
　　N.L.—6—Atlanta vs. St. Louis, 1982.
4-game series
　　A.L.—5—Baltimore vs. Oakland, 1974.
　　N.L.—5—Pittsburgh vs. San Francisco, 1971.
5-game series
　　A.L.—9—New York vs. Kansas City, 1977.
　　N.L.—9—Pittsburgh vs. Cincinnati, 1972.
6-game series
　　N.L.—10—Cincinnati vs. Pittsburgh, 1990.
　　A.L.—15—Seattle vs. Cleveland, 1995.
7-game series
　　N.L.—11—St. Louis vs. Atlanta, 1996.
　　A.L.—16—Toronto vs. Kansas City, 1985.

Fewest bases on balls by both clubs, series
3-game series
　　A.L.—12—Oakland 9, Boston 3, 1975.
　　N.L.—18—St. Louis 12, Atlanta 6, 1982.
4-game series
　　N.L.—18—Los Angeles 9, Philadelphia 9, 1978.
　　A.L.—21—Kansas City 14, New York 7, 1978.
5-game series
　　N.L.—19—Cincinnati 10, Pittsburgh 9, 1972.
　　A.L.—24—Kansas City 15, New York 9, 1977.
6-game series
　　N.L.—31—Houston 17, New York 14, 1986.
　　A.L.—40—Cleveland 25, Seattle 15, 1995.
7-game series
　　N.L.—33—San Francisco 17, St. Louis 16, 1987.
　　A.L.—38—Kansas City 22, Toronto 16, 1985.

Most bases on balls by pinch-hitters, series
N.L.—4—Los Angeles vs. New York, 1988 (7-game series).
A.L.—2—Held by many clubs.

Most bases on balls by pinch-hitters on both clubs, series
N.L.—6—Los Angeles 4, New York 2, 1988 (7-game series).
A.L.—3
　　California 2, Baltimore 1, 1979 (4-game series).
　　Toronto 2, Minnesota 1, 1991 (5-game series).
　　Boston 2, New York 1, 1999 (5-game series).

Most bases on balls, game
A.L.—11
　　Oakland vs. Baltimore, October 9, 1974.
　　New York vs. Cleveland, October 11, 1998.
N.L.—11—Los Angeles vs. Pittsburgh, October 9, 1974.

Most bases on balls by both clubs, game
A.L.—15—New York 10, Seattle 5, October 21, 2001.
N.L.—13—Atlanta 8, Pittsburgh 5, October 7, 1992.

Fewest bases on balls, game
A.L.-N.L.—0—Held by many clubs.

Fewest bases on balls by both clubs, game
A.L.—1
　　Oakland 1, Baltimore 0, October 8, 1974.
　　New York 1, Kansas City 0, October 9, 1976.
N.L.—1—New York 1, Atlanta 0, October 16, 1999.

Most bases on balls by pinch-hitters, game
N.L.—2
　　Pittsburgh vs. Cincinnati, October 7, 1975, 10 innings.
　　Los Angeles vs. New York, October 8, 1988.
　　Los Angeles vs. New York, October 9, 1988, 12 innings.
A.L.—2
　　California vs. Baltimore, October 4, 1979.
　　Baltimore vs. Chicago, October 7, 1983.

Most bases on balls by pinch-hitters on both clubs, game
N.L.—3
　　Pittsburgh 2, Cincinnati 1, October 7, 1975, 10 innings.
　　Los Angeles 2, New York 1, October 8, 1988.

A.L.—2
Detroit 1, Oakland 1, October 11, 1972, 10 innings.
California 2, Baltimore 0, October 4, 1979.
Baltimore 2, Chicago 0, October 7, 1983.
Baltimore 1, Cleveland 1, October 9, 1997.

Most bases on balls, inning
A.L.—4—Oakland vs. Baltimore, October 9, 1974, fifth inning (consecutive).
N.L.—4
Philadelphia vs. Los Angeles, October 7, 1977, second inning (consecutive).
St. Louis vs. Los Angeles, October 12, 1985, first inning.
San Francisco vs. Chicago, October 9, 1989, eighth inning.

Most bases on balls by both clubs, inning
N.L.—6—St. Louis 4, Los Angeles 2, October 12, 1985, first inning.
A.L.—4—Made in many innings.

Most bases on balls by pinch-hitters, inning
N.L.—2
Pittsburgh vs. Cincinnati, October 7, 1975, ninth inning.
Los Angeles vs. New York, October 8, 1988, eighth inning.
A.L.—2—Baltimore vs. Chicago, October 7, 1983, ninth inning.

STRIKEOUTS

Most strikeouts, total series
N.L.—421—Atlanta; 11 series, 60 games.
A.L.—270—New York; 10 series, 47 games.

Most strikeouts, series
3-game series
N.L.—28—Cincinnati vs. Pittsburgh, 1975.
A.L.—27—Minnesota vs. Baltimore, 1969.
4-game series
A.L.—35—Oakland vs. Boston, 1988.
N.L.—33—Pittsburgh vs. San Francisco, 1971.
5-game series
A.L.—44—New York vs. Boston, 1999.
N.L.—42—Cincinnati vs. New York, 1973.
6-game series
A.L.—62—Cleveland vs. Baltimore, 1997.
N.L.—57—New York vs. Houston, 1986.
7-game series
N.L.—57—Pittsburgh vs. Atlanta, 1991.
A.L.—51—Kansas City vs. Toronto, 1985.

Most strikeouts by both clubs, series
3-game series
N.L.—46—Cincinnati 28, Pittsburgh 18, 1975.
A.L.—41—Minnesota 27, Baltimore 14, 1969.
Minnesota 22, Baltimore 19, 1970.
4-game series
N.L.—61—Pittsburgh 33, San Francisco 28, 1971.
A.L.—58—Oakland 35, Boston 23, 1988.
5-game series
A.L.—82—New York 44, Boston 38, 1999.
N.L.—71—Atlanta 39, Arizona 32, 2001.
6-game series
A.L.—109—Cleveland 62, Baltimore 47, 1997.
N.L.—105—Atlanta 54, Philadelphia 51, 1993.
7-game series
N.L.—104—St. Louis 53, Atlanta 51, 1996.
A.L.—88—Kansas City 51, Toronto 37, 1985.

Fewest strikeouts, series
N.L.—9—Philadelphia vs. Cincinnati, 1976.
A.L.—10—New York vs. Oakland, 1981.
4-game series
A.L.—13—California vs. Baltimore, 1979.
N.L.—16—Los Angeles vs. Pittsburgh, 1974.
5-game series
A.L.—15—New York vs. Kansas City, 1976.
N.L.—19—Houston vs. Philadelphia, 1980.
6-game series
A.L.—29—Toronto vs. Oakland, 1992.
N.L.—31—Los Angeles vs. St. Louis, 1985.

7-game series
N.L.—28—Atlanta vs. Pittsburgh, 1992.
A.L.—31—Boston vs. California, 1986.

Fewest strikeouts by both clubs, series
3-game series
N.L.—25—Cincinnati 16, Philadelphia 9, 1976.
A.L.—26—Oakland 14, Boston 12, 1975.
4-game series
N.L.—33—Pittsburgh 17, Los Angeles 16, 1974.
A.L.—36—Baltimore 20, Oakland 16, 1974.
5-game series
A.L.—33—Kansas City 18, New York 15, 1976.
N.L.—48—Montreal 25, Los Angeles 23, 1981.
6-game series
A.L.—62—Oakland 33, Toronto 29, 1992.
N.L.—65—St. Louis 34, Los Angeles 31, 1985.
7-game series
N.L.—70—Pittsburgh 42, Atlanta 28, 1992.
A.L.—75—California 44, Boston 31, 1986.

Most strikeouts by pinch-hitters, series
N.L.—7—Cincinnati vs. New York, 1973 (5-game series).
A.L.—4
Minnesota vs. Baltimore, 1970 (3-game series).
Oakland vs. Detroit, 1972 (5-game series).

Most strikeouts by pinch-hitters on both clubs, series
N.L.—11—New York 6, Atlanta 5, 1999 (6-game series).
A.L.—4
Minnesota 4, Baltimore 0, 1970 (3-game series).
Oakland 4, Detroit 0, 1972 (5-game series).

Most strikeouts, nine-inning game
N.L.—15
Philadelphia vs. Atlanta, October 10, 1993.
Atlanta vs. Florida, October 12, 1997.
A.L.—15—Seattle vs. New York, October 14, 2000.

Most strikeouts, extra-inning game
A.L.—21—Cleveland vs. Baltimore, October 11, 1997, 12 innings.
N.L.—15
Cincinnati vs. Pittsburgh, October 7, 1975, 10 innings.
New York vs. Houston, October 14, 1986, 12 innings.

Most strikeouts by pinch-hitters, game
A.L.—4—Oakland vs. Detroit, October 10, 1972.
N.L.—4—Pittsburgh vs. Atlanta, October 10, 1992.

Most strikeouts by both clubs, nine-inning game
N.L.—25—Atlanta 15, Florida 10, October 12, 1997.
A.L.—22—New York 13, Seattle 9, October 10, 2000.

Most strikeouts by both clubs, extra-inning game
A.L.—33—Cleveland 21, Baltimore 12, October 11, 1997, 12 innings.
N.L.—32—Atlanta 19, New York 13, October 17, 1999, 15 innings.

Fewest strikeouts, game
N.L.—0—Pittsburgh vs. Los Angeles, October 6, 1974.
A.L.—1
Baltimore vs. Oakland, October 11, 1973.
New York vs. Kansas City, October 13, 1976.
Kansas City vs. New York, October 4, 1978.
Toronto vs. Kansas City, October 12, 1985.
Boston vs. Oakland, October 10, 1990.

Fewest strikeouts by both clubs, game
A.L.—3
Oakland 2, Baltimore 1, October 11, 1973.
Kansas City 2, New York 1, October 13, 1976.
N.L.—4—Philadelphia 2, Cincinnati 2, October 12, 1976.

Most consecutive strikeouts, game
A.L.—5—Cleveland vs. Baltimore, October 11, 1997 (one in fifth inning, three in sixth inning, one in seventh inning).
N.L.—5—Atlanta vs. Philadelphia, October 6, 1993 (three in first inning, two in second inning).

Most strikeouts, inning
A.L.-N.L.—3—Held by many clubs.

Most strikeouts by both clubs, inning
A.L.-N.L.—5—Occurred in many innings.

Most strikeouts by pinch-hitters, inning
A.L.—2—Oakland vs. Baltimore, October 5, 1971, ninth inning (consecutive).
N.L.—2
  Cincinnati vs. New York, October 7, 1973, eighth inning (consecutive).
  Pittsburgh vs. Atlanta, October 10, 1992, eighth inning.
  Cincinnati vs. Atlanta, October 10, 1995, 10th inning (consecutive).
  Atlanta vs. San Diego, October 10, 1998, sixth inning (consecutive).
  New York vs. St. Louis, October 14, 2000, ninth inning (consecutive).

SACRIFICE HITS

Most sacrifice hits, total series
N.L.—31—Atlanta; 11 series, 60 games.
A.L.—22—Oakland; 10 series, 42 games.

Most sacrifice hits, series
N.L.—7
  Houston vs. Philadelphia, 1980 (5-game series).
  Atlanta vs. New York, 1999 (6-game series).
A.L.—5
  Boston vs. Oakland, 1975 (3-game series).
  California vs. Milwaukee, 1982 (5-game series).
  Chicago vs. Toronto, 1993 (6-game series).

Most sacrifice hits by both clubs, series
N.L.—12—Houston 7, Philadelphia 5, 1980 (5-game series).
A.L.—7
  Oakland 4, Detroit 3, 1972 (5-game series).
  California 5, Milwaukee 2, 1982 (5-game series).
  California 4, Boston 3, 1986 (7-game series).

Fewest sacrifice hits, series
A.L.-N.L.—0—Held by many clubs.

Fewest sacrifice hits by both clubs, series
N.L.—0—Cincinnati 0, Pittsburgh 0, 1975 (3-game series).
A.L.—0—Baltimore 0, New York 0, 1996 (5-game series).

Most sacrifice hits, game
N.L.—3
  Pittsburgh vs. Cincinnati, October 3, 1979, 10 innings.
  Philadelphia vs. Houston, October 8, 1980, 10 innings.
  Los Angeles vs. Montreal, October 17, 1981.
  St. Louis vs. Atlanta, October 9, 1982.
  Atlanta vs. New York, October 19, 1999, 11 innings.
A.L.—3
  California vs. Milwaukee, October 10, 1982.
  California vs. Boston, October 12, 1986, 11 innings.

Most sacrifice hits by both clubs, game
N.L.—4
  Pittsburgh 3, Cincinnati 1, October 3, 1979, 10 innings.
  Los Angeles 3, Montreal 1, October 17, 1981.
  St. Louis 2, Atlanta 2, October 9, 1982.
  Atlanta 2, Philadelphia 2, October 13, 1993.
  Atlanta 3, New York 1, October 19, 1999, 11 innings.
A.L.—3
  California 3, Milwaukee 0, October 10, 1982.
  Boston 2, California 1, October 11, 1986, 11 innings.
  California 3, Boston 0, October 12, 1986, 11 innings.
  Oakland 2, Boston 1, October 6, 1990.

Most sacrifice hits, inning
N.L.—2—Philadelphia vs. Cincinnati, October 10, 1976, fourth inning.
A.L.—1—Held by many clubs.

SACRIFICE FLIES

Most sacrifice flies, total series
N.L.—15—Atlanta; 11 series, 60 games.
A.L.—12
  Baltimore; nine series, 37 games.
  New York; 10 series, 47 games.

Most sacrifice flies, series
A.L.—4
  Kansas City vs. New York, 1976 (5-game series).
  Toronto vs. Oakland, 1992 (6-game series).
N.L.—4
  San Diego vs. Chicago, 1984 (5-game series).
  St. Louis vs. San Francisco, 1987 (7-game series).

Most sacrifice flies by both clubs, series
N.L.—6—San Diego 4, Chicago 2, 1984 (5-game series).
A.L.—6—Toronto 4, Oakland 2, 1992 (6-game series).

Most sacrifice flies, game
N.L.—3—St. Louis vs. Atlanta, October 7, 1982.
A.L.—2—Held by many clubs.

Most sacrifice flies by both clubs, game
N.L.—3
  St. Louis 3, Atlanta 0, October 7, 1982.
  St. Louis 2, San Francisco 1, October 11, 1987.
A.L.—2—Occurred many times.

Most sacrifice flies, inning
A.L.—2
  Baltimore vs. Chicago, October 7, 1983, ninth inning.
  Detroit vs. Minnesota, October 7, 1987, eighth inning.
N.L.—2—San Diego vs. Chicago, October 7, 1984, sixth inning.

HIT BY PITCH

Most hit by pitch, total series
N.L.—13—Atlanta; 11 series, 60 games.
A.L.—12
  Oakland; 10 series, 42 games.
  New York; 10 series, 47 games.

Most hit by pitch, series
A.L.—5
  Minnesota vs. Detroit, 1987 (5-game series).
  Cleveland vs. New York, 1998 (6-game series).
N.L.—4
  New York vs. Los Angeles, 1988 (7-game series).
  Atlanta vs. New York, 1999 (6-game series).

Most hit by pitch by both clubs, series
A.L.—8—Minnesota 5, Detroit 3, 1987 (5-game series).
N.L.—6—New York 4, Los Angeles 2, 1988 (7-game series).

Most hit by pitch, nine-inning game
A.L.—3
  Minnesota vs. Detroit, October 11, 1987.
  Cleveland vs. Baltimore, October 9, 1997.
N.L.—2
  New York vs. Los Angeles, October 12, 1988.
  Atlanta vs. St. Louis, October 16, 1996.
  Atlanta vs. Florida, October 7, 1997.

Most hit by pitch, extra-inning game
N.L.—3—Atlanta vs. New York, October 19, 1999, 11 innings.
A.L.—Less than nine-inning record.

Most hit by pitch by both clubs, game
A.L.—4
  Detroit 2, Minnesota 2, October 12, 1987.
  Cleveland 2, New York 2, October 11, 1998.
N.L.—3
  Atlanta 2, Florida 1, October 7, 1997.
  Atlanta 3, New York 0, October 19, 1999, 11 innings.

Most hit by pitch, inning
A.L.—3—Cleveland vs. Baltimore, October 9, 1997, first inning.
N.L.—2—Atlanta vs. New York, October 19, 1999, first inning.

INDIVIDUAL BASERUNNING

STOLEN BASES

Most stolen bases, career

A.L.—17—Rickey Henderson, Oakland A.L., 1981, 1989, 1990, 1992; Toronto A.L., 1993; New York N.L., 1999; Seattle A.L.; seven series, 33 games.

A.L.—16—Rickey Henderson, Oakland, 1981, 1989, 1990, 1992; Toronto, 1993; Seattle, 2000; six series, 27 games.

N.L.—9—Dave Lopes, Los Angeles, 1974, 1977, 1978, 1981; Chicago, 1984; Houston, 1986; six series, 22 games.

Most stolen bases, series

3-game series

  N.L.—4—Joe Morgan, Cincinnati, 1975.

  A.L.—2—Juan Beniquez, Boston, 1975.

      Amos Otis, Kansas City, 1980.

      Rickey Henderson, Oakland, 1981.

4-game series

  A.L.—4—Amos Otis, Kansas City, 1978.

  N.L.—3—Dave Lopes, Los Angeles, 1974.

5-game series

  A.L.—8—Rickey Henderson, Oakland, 1989.

  N.L.—5—Dave Lopes, Los Angeles, 1981.

6-game series

  A.L.—7—Willie Wilson, Oakland, 1992.

  N.L.—3—Billy Hatcher, Houston, 1986.

      Barry Larkin, Cincinnati, 1990.

      Chipper Jones, Atlanta, 1999.

      Gerald Williams, Atlanta, 1999.

7-game series

  N.L.—7—Ron Gant, Atlanta, 1991.

  A.L.—1—Held by many players.

Most stolen bases, game

A.L.—4—Rickey Henderson, Oakland, October 4, 1989.

N.L.—3

  Joe Morgan, Cincinnati, October 4, 1975.

  Ken Griffey Sr., Cincinnati, October 5, 1975.

  Steve Sax, Los Angeles, October 9, 1988, 12 innings.

  Ron Gant, Atlanta, October 10, 1991.

  Edgar Renteria, St. Louis, October 12, 2000.

Most stolen bases by pinch-runner, game

A.L.-N.L.—1—Held by many players.

Most times stealing home, game

A.L.—1

  Reggie Jackson, Oakland, October 12, 1972, second inning (front end of double steal).

  Marquis Grissom, Cleveland, October 11, 1997, 12th inning.

N.L.—1—Jeff Branson, Cincinnati, October 11, 1995, fifth inning.

Most stolen bases, inning

A.L.-N.L.—2—Held by many players.

CAUGHT STEALING

Most caught stealing, career

A.L.—6—Hal McRae, Kansas City, 1976, 1977, 1978, 1980, 1984, 1985; six series, 28 games.

N.L.—4

  Willie McGee, St. Louis, 1982, 1985, 1987, 1996; four series, 22 games.

  Vince Coleman, St. Louis, 1985, 1987; two series, 10 games.

Most caught stealing by pinch-runner, career

A.L.—2—Herb Washington, Oakland, 1974; one series, two games.

N.L.—Never accomplished.

Most caught stealing, series

A.L.—4—Devon White, Toronto, 1992 (no stolen bases; 6-game series).

N.L.—3

  Willie McGee, St. Louis, 1985 (two stolen bases; 6-game series).

  Kevin Bass, Houston, 1986 (two stolen bases; 6-game series).

Most caught stealing by pinch-runner, series

A.L.—2—Herb Washington, Oakland, 1974; two games.

N.L.—Never accomplished.

Most caught stealing, nine-inning game

A.L.-N.L.—1—Held by many players.

Most caught stealing, extra-inning game

A.L.—2—Brooks Robinson, Baltimore, October 4, 1969, 12 innings.

N.L.—2—Kevin Bass, Houston, October 15, 1986, 16 innings.

Most caught stealing by pinch-runner, game

A.L.—1

  Herb Washington, Oakland, October 6, 8, 1974.

  Sandy Alomar Sr., New York, October 14, 1976.

  Onix Concepcion, Kansas City, October 9, 1985.

N.L.—Never accomplished.

Most caught stealing, inning

A.L.-N.L.—1—Held by many players.

CLUB BASERUNNING

STOLEN BASES

Most stolen bases, total series
A.L.—54—Oakland; 10 series, 42 games.
N.L.—41—Atlanta; 11 series, 60 games.

Most stolen bases, series
3-game series
  N.L.—11—Cincinnati vs. Pittsburgh, 1975.
  A.L.—4—Detroit vs. Kansas City, 1984.
4-game series
  A.L.—9—Oakland vs. Boston, 1990.
  N.L.—5—Los Angeles vs. Pittsburgh, 1974.
5-game series
  A.L.—13—Oakland vs. Toronto, 1989.
  N.L.—7—Philadelphia vs. Houston, 1980.
6-game series
  A.L.—16—Oakland vs. Toronto, 1992.
  N.L.—14—Atlanta vs. New York, 1999.
7-game series
  N.L.—10—Atlanta vs. Pittsburgh, 1991.
  A.L.—2—Kansas City vs. Toronto, 1985.
      Toronto vs. Kansas City, 1985.

Most stolen bases by both clubs, series
3-game series
  N.L.—11—Cincinnati 11, Pittsburgh 0, 1975.
  A.L.—4—New York 2, Oakland 2, 1981.
      Detroit 4, Kansas City 0, 1984.
4-game series
  A.L.—10—Oakland 9, Boston 1, 1990.
  N.L.—6—Los Angeles 5, Pittsburgh 1, 1974.
      Cincinnati 4, Atlanta 2, 1995.
5-game series
  A.L.—24—Oakland 13, Toronto 11, 1989.
  N.L.—11—Philadelphia 7, Houston 4, 1980.
6-game series
  A.L.—23—Oakland 16, Toronto 7, 1992.
  N.L.—21—Atlanta 14, New York 7, 1999.
7-game series
  N.L.—16—Atlanta 10, Pittsburgh 6, 1991.
  A.L.—4—Toronto 2, Kansas City 2, 1985.

Fewest stolen bases, series
A.L.-N.L.—0—Held by many clubs.

Fewest stolen bases by both clubs, series
3-game series
  A.L.—0—Baltimore 0, Oakland 0, 1971.
  N.L.—1—Cincinnati 1, Pittsburgh 0, 1970.
4-game series
  N.L.—2—Los Angeles 2, Philadelphia 0, 1978.
  A.L.—1—Oakland 1, Boston 0, 1988.
5-game series
  N.L.—0—Cincinnati 0, New York 0, 1973.
  A.L.—3—Milwaukee 2, California 1, 1982.
      New York 3, Baltimore 0, 1996.
6-game series
  N.L.—2—Philadelphia 2, Atlanta 0, 1993.
  A.L.—7—New York 4, Seattle 3, 2000.
7-game series
  A.L.—2—Boston 1, California 1, 1986.
  N.L.—5—Atlanta 4, St. Louis 1, 1996.

Most stolen bases, game
N.L.—7—Cincinnati vs. Pittsburgh, October 5, 1975.
A.L.—6
  Oakland vs. Toronto, October 4, 1989.
  Oakland vs. Toronto, October 8, 1992.

Most stolen bases by both clubs, nine-inning game
A.L.—8
  Oakland 6, Toronto 2, October 4, 1989.
  Oakland 6, Toronto 2, October 8, 1992.
N.L.—7—Cincinnati 7, Pittsburgh 0, October 5, 1975.

Most stolen bases by both clubs, extra-inning game
N.L.—8—Atlanta 6, New York 2, October 19, 1999, 11 innings.
A.L.—Less than nine-inning record.

Longest game with no stolen bases
N.L.—16 innings—New York vs. Houston, October 15, 1986.
A.L.—12 innings
  Baltimore vs. Minnesota, October 4, 1969.
  Cleveland vs. New York, October 7, 1998.

Longest game with no stolen bases by either club
N.L.—12 innings—New York 0, Cincinnati 0, October 9, 1973.
A.L.—11 innings
  Detroit 0, Oakland 0, October 7, 1972.
  Baltimore 0, Oakland 0, October 9, 1973.
  Boston 0, California 0, October 11, 1986.
  Boston 0, California 0, October 12, 1986.
  Baltimore 0, New York 0, October 9, 1996.

Most stolen bases, inning
A.L.—3
  Oakland vs. Detroit, October 12, 1972, second inning.
  Oakland vs. Toronto, October 8, 1992, fifth inning.
N.L.—2—Held by many clubs.

CAUGHT STEALING

Most caught stealing, series
3-game series
  A.L.—5—Kansas City vs. New York, 1980.
  N.L.—2—Pittsburgh vs. Cincinnati, 1970.
      Cincinnati vs. Pittsburgh, 1979.
      Atlanta vs. St. Louis, 1982.
4-game series
  A.L.—3—Oakland vs. Baltimore, 1974.
      Baltimore vs. Oakland, 1974.
      Kansas City vs. New York, 1978.
      Oakland vs. Boston, 1988, 1990.
  N.L.—3—Cincinnati vs. Atlanta, 1995.
5-game series
  A.L.—5—Kansas City vs. New York, 1976.
  N.L.—3—Philadelphia vs. Houston, 1980.
      Chicago vs. San Diego, 1984.
6-game series
  N.L.—6—St. Louis vs. Los Angeles, 1985.
  A.L.—5—Toronto vs. Oakland, 1992.
7-game series
  A.L.—4—Kansas City vs. Toronto, 1985.
      California vs. Boston, 1986.
  N.L.—4—San Francisco vs. St. Louis, 1987.
      St. Louis vs. San Francisco, 1987.
      Atlanta vs. Pittsburgh, 1991.

Most caught stealing by both clubs, series
3-game series
  A.L.—5—Kansas City 5, New York 0, 1980.
  N.L.—3—Pittsburgh 2, Cincinnati 1, 1970.
4-game series
  A.L.—6—Oakland 3, Baltimore 3, 1974.
  N.L.—4—Cincinnati 3, Atlanta 1, 1995.
5-game series
  A.L.—8—Kansas City 5, New York 3, 1976.
  N.L.—5—Chicago 3, San Diego 2, 1984.
6-game series
  N.L.—7—St. Louis 6, Los Angeles 1, 1985.
  A.L.—7—Toronto 5, Oakland 2, 1992.
7-game series
  N.L.—8—San Francisco 4, St. Louis 4, 1987.
  A.L.—6—Kansas City 4, Toronto 2, 1985.

Fewest caught stealing, series
A.L.-N.L.—0—By many clubs.

Fewest caught stealing by both clubs, series
A.L.-N.L.—0—Occurred in many series.

Most caught stealing, game
A.L.-N.L.—2—Held by many clubs.

Most caught stealing by both clubs, game
A.L.—3
Baltimore 2, Oakland 1, October 10, 1973.
Kansas City 2, New York 1, October 12, 1976.
Milwaukee 2, California 1, October 9, 1982.
N.L.—3
Chicago 2, San Diego 1, October 7, 1984.
St. Louis 2, Los Angeles 1, October 12, 1985.

Most caught stealing, inning
N.L.—2
St. Louis vs. Los Angeles, October 10, 1985, first inning.
St. Louis vs. Los Angeles, October 12, 1985, second inning.
A.L.—1—Held by many clubs.

LEFT ON BASE

Most left on base, total series
N.L.—441—Atlanta; 11 series, 60 games.
A.L.—367—New York; 10 series, 47 games.

Most left on base, series
3-game series
N.L.—31—St. Louis vs. Atlanta, 1982.
A.L.—30—New York vs. Oakland, 1981.
4-game series
N.L.—44—Los Angeles vs. Pittsburgh, 1974.
A.L.—35—Chicago vs. Baltimore, 1983.
Oakland vs. Boston, 1990.
5-game series
N.L.—45—Houston vs. Philadelphia, 1980.
A.L.—45—Boston vs. New York, 1999.
6-game series
A.L.—56—Toronto vs. Chicago, 1993.
N.L.—52—Philadelphia vs. Atlanta, 1993.
San Diego vs. Atlanta, 1998.
7-game series
A.L.—60—California vs. Boston, 1986.
N.L.—58—Atlanta vs. St. Louis, 1996.

Most left on base by both clubs, series
3-game series
A.L.—50—Baltimore 28, Minnesota 22, 1969.
New York 30, Oakland 20, 1981.
N.L.—49—Cincinnati 25, Pittsburgh 24, 1979.
4-game series
N.L.—68—Los Angeles 44, Pittsburgh 24, 1974.
A.L.—59—Chicago 35, Baltimore 24, 1983.
5-game series
N.L.—88—Houston 45, Philadelphia 43, 1980.
A.L.—87—Boston 45, New York 42, 1999.
6-game series
A.L.—106—Toronto 56, Chicago 50, 1993.
N.L.—99—Philadelphia 52, Atlanta 47, 1993.
7-game series
A.L.—108—California 60, Boston 48, 1986.
N.L.—105—Pittsburgh 54, Atlanta 51, 1991.

Fewest left on base, series
3-game series
N.L.—12—Atlanta vs. St. Louis, 1982.
A.L.—14—Boston vs. Oakland, 1975.
4-game series
A.L.—16—Baltimore vs. Oakland, 1974.
N.L.—22—Los Angeles vs. Philadelphia, 1977.
5-game series
A.L.—22—Kansas City vs. New York, 1976.
N.L.—24—Pittsburgh vs. Cincinnati, 1972.
6-game series
N.L.—33—Cincinnati vs. Pittsburgh, 1990.
A.L.—38—Seattle vs. New York, 2000.
7-game series
N.L.—34—St. Louis vs. Atlanta, 1996.
A.L.—44—Kansas City vs. Toronto, 1985.

Fewest left on base by both clubs, series
3-game series
A.L.—33—Oakland 19, Boston 14, 1975.
N.L.—38—Pittsburgh 21, Cincinnati 17, 1975.
4-game series
A.L.—45—Baltimore 23, California 22, 1979.
N.L.—52—Los Angeles 28, Philadelphia 24, 1978.
5-game series
N.L.—54—Cincinnati 30, Pittsburgh 24, 1972.
A.L.—62—New York 34, Kansas City 28, 1977.
6-game series
N.L.—74—Pittsburgh 41, Cincinnati 33, 1990.
A.L.—87—New York 48, Cleveland 39, 1998.
7-game series
N.L.—80—San Francisco 43, St. Louis 37, 1987.
A.L.—94—Toronto 50, Kansas City 44, 1985.

Most left on bases, nine-inning game
N.L.—15—Philadelphia vs. Atlanta, October 10, 1993.
A.L.—15—New York vs. Seattle, October 15, 2000.

Most left on base, extra-inning game
N.L.—19—Atlanta vs. New York, October 17, 1999; 15 innings.
A.L.—Less than nine-inning record.

Most left on base by both clubs, nine-inning game
N.L.—26—Philadelphia 15, Atlanta 11, October 10, 1993.
A.L.—25—Chicago 13, Toronto 12, October 5, 1993.

Most left on base by both clubs, extra-inning game
N.L.—31—Atlanta 19, New York 12, October 17, 1999, 15 innings.
A.L.—25—Toronto 14, Oakland 11, October 11, 1992, 11 innings.

Fewest left on base, game
N.L.—0—Atlanta vs. New York, October 16, 1999.
A.L.—1—Baltimore vs. New York, October 11, 1996.

Fewest left on base by both clubs, game
N.L.—3—New York 3, Atlanta 0, October 16, 1999.
A.L.—6
Oakland 4, Detroit 2, October 8, 1972.
New York 5, Baltimore 1, October 11, 1996.

Most left on base, nine-inning shutout defeat
A.L.—10—Oakland vs. Detroit, October 10, 1972 (lost 3-0).
N.L.—10
Los Angeles vs. Pittsburgh, October 8, 1974 (lost 7-0).
San Diego vs. Chicago, October 2, 1984 (lost 13-0).

Most left on base, extra-inning shutout defeat
A.L.—14—Baltimore vs. Cleveland, October 15, 1997, 11 innings (lost 1-0).
N.L.—11—Philadelphia vs. Houston, October 10, 1980, 11 innings (lost 1-0).

Most left on base, two consecutive games (18 innings)
N.L.—25—Los Angeles vs. Pittsburgh, October 5 (13), October 6 (12), 1974.
A.L.—23
Minnesota vs. Detroit, October 11 (11), October 12 (12), 1987.
Chicago vs. Toronto, October 5 (13), October 6 (10), 1993.
Boston vs. New York, October 14 (13), October 16 (10), 1999.
New York vs. Seattle, October 15 (15), October 17 (8), 2000.

Most left on base, two consecutive games (more than 18 innings)
N.L.—28—Atlanta vs. New York, October 17 (19), October 19 (12), 1999; 26 innings.
A.L.—24—New York vs. Baltimore, October 9 (13), October 10 (11), 1996; 20 innings.

INDIVIDUAL PITCHING

GAMES

Most games pitched, career
Both leagues—20—Rick Honeycutt, Los Angeles N.L., 1983, 1985; Oakland A.L., 1988, 1989, 1990, 1992; St. Louis N.L., 1996; seven series.
N.L.—18—Mark Wohlers, Atlanta, 1991, 1992, 1993, 1995, 1996, 1997; six series.
A.L.—16—Mariano Rivera, New York, 1996, 1998 through 2001; five series.

Most games pitched, series
3-game series
   A.L.-N.L.—3—Held by many pitchers.
4-game series
   N.L.—4—Dave Giusti, Pittsburgh, 1971.
           Mark Wohlers, Atlanta, 1995.
   A.L.—4—Dennis Eckersley, Oakland, 1988.
5-game series
   N.L.—5—Tug McGraw, Philadelphia, 1980.
   A.L.—5—Jim Acker, Toronto, 1989.
6-game series
   N.L.—6—John Rocker, Atlanta, 1998.
           John Rocker, Atlanta, 1999.
   A.L.—5—Paul Assenmacher, Cleveland, 1997.
           Mike Jackson, Cleveland, 1997.
           Paul Shuey, Cleveland, 1998.
           Jose Paniagua, Seattle, 2000.
7-game series
   N.L.—6—Mark Petkovsek, St. Louis, 1996.
   A.L.—4—Held by many pitchers.

Most consecutive games pitched, series
N.L.—6
   John Rocker, Atlanta, October 7, 8, 10, 11, 12, 14, 1998.
   John Rocker, Atlanta, October 12, 13, 15, 16, 17, 19, 1999.
A.L.—5
   Jim Acker, Toronto, October 3, 4, 6, 7, 8, 1989.
   Paul Assenmacher, Cleveland, October 9, 11, 12, 13, 15, 1997.
   Mike Jackson, Cleveland, October 9, 11, 12, 13, 15, 1997.

GAMES STARTED

Most games started, career
N.L.—15—Tom Glavine, Atlanta, 1991, 1992, 1993, 1995, 1996, 1997, 1998, 1999, 2001; nine series.
A.L.—10
   Catfish Hunter, Oakland, 1971, 1972, 1973, 1974; New York, 1976, 1978; six series.
   Dave Stewart, Oakland, 1988, 1989, 1990, 1992; Toronto, 1993; five series.

Most opening games started, career
Both leagues—4—Don Gullett, Cincinnati N.L., 1972, 1975, 1976; New York A.L., 1977 (won 2, lost 2).
N.L.—4
   Steve Carlton, Philadelphia, 1976, 1977, 1980, 1983 (won 2, lost 1).
   Greg Maddux, Chicago, 1989; Atlanta, 1997, 1999, 2001 (won 1, lost 3).
A.L.—4—Dave Stewart, Oakland, 1988, 1989, 1990, 1992 (won 2).

Most games started, series
A.L.-N.L.—3—Held by many pitchers.

GAMES RELIEVED AND FINISHED

Most games by relief pitcher, career
Both leagues—20—Rick Honeycutt, Los Angeles N.L., 1983, 1985; Oakland A.L., 1988, 1989, 1990, 1992; St. Louis N.L., 1996; 14.1 innings.
N.L.—18—Mark Wohlers, Atlanta, 1991, 1992, 1993, 1995, 1996, 1997; 19 innings.

A.L.—16—Mariano Rivera, New York, 1996, 1998 through 2001; 23.2 innings.

Most games by relief pitcher, series
N.L.—6
   Mark Petkovsek, St. Louis, 1996 (7-game series).
   John Rocker, Atlanta, 1998 (6-game series).
   John Rocker, Atlanta, 1999 (6-game series).
A.L.—5
   Jim Acker, Toronto, 1989 (5-game series).
   Paul Assenmacher, Cleveland, 1997 (6-game series).
   Mike Jackson, Cleveland, 1997 (6-game series).
   Paul Shuey, Cleveland, 1998 (6-game series).
   Jose Paniagua, Seattle, 2000 (6-game series).

Most games finished, career
Both leagues—16—Dennis Eckersley, Oakland A.L., 1988, 1989, 1990, 1992; St. Louis N.L., 1996; five series, 17 games.
N.L.—14—Mark Wohlers, Atlanta, 1991, 1992, 1993, 1995, 1996, 1997; six series, 18 games.
A.L.—14—Mariano Rivera, New York, 1996, 1998 through 2001; five series, 16 games.

Most games finished, series
A.L.-N.L.—4—Held by many pitchers.

COMPLETE GAMES

Most complete games pitched, career
A.L.—5—Jim Palmer, Baltimore, 1969, 1970, 1971, 1973, 1974.
N.L.—2—Held by many pitchers.

Most consecutive complete games pitched, career
A.L.—4—Jim Palmer, Baltimore, 1969 (1), 1970 (1), 1971 (1), 1973 (1; won four).
N.L.—2
   Tommy John, Los Angeles, 1977 (1), 1978 (1; won two).
   Mike Scott, Houston, 1986 (2; won two).
   Danny Cox, St. Louis, 1987 (2; won one, lost one).
   Tim Wakefield, Pittsburgh, 1992 (2; won two).

Most complete games, series
N.L.—2
   Mike Scott, Houston, 1986 (6-game series).
   Danny Cox, St. Louis, 1987 (7-game series).
   Tim Wakefield, Pittsburgh, 1992 (7-game series).
A.L.—1—Held by many pitchers.

INNINGS

Most innings pitched, career
N.L.—95.1—John Smoltz, Atlanta, 1991, 1992, 1993, 1995, 1996, 1997, 1998, 1999, 2001; nine series, 17 games.
A.L.—75.1—Dave Stewart, Oakland, 1988, 1989, 1990, 1992; Toronto, 1993; five series, 10 games.

Most innings pitched, series
3-game series
   A.L.—11—Dave McNally, Baltimore, 1969.
              Ken Holtzman, Oakland, 1975.
   N.L.—9.2—Dock Ellis, Pittsburgh, 1970.
4-game series
   N.L.—17—Don Sutton, Los Angeles, 1974.
   A.L.—16—Dave Stewart, Oakland, 1990.
5-game series
   A.L.—19—Mickey Lolich, Detroit, 1972.
   N.L.—17—Ray Burris, Montreal, 1981.
6-game series
   N.L.—18—Mike Scott, Houston, 1986.
   A.L.—16.2—Dave Stewart, Oakland, 1992.
7-game series
   N.L.—24.2—Orel Hershiser, Los Angeles, 1988.
   A.L.—22.2—Roger Clemens, Boston, 1986.

Most innings pitched, game

A.L.—11

Dave McNally, Baltimore, October 5, 1969 (complete game, won 1-0).

Ken Holtzman, Oakland, October 9, 1973 (complete game, won 2-1).

N.L.—10

Joe Niekro, Houston, October 10, 1980 (incomplete game, no decision).

Dwight Gooden, New York, October 14, 1986 (incomplete game, no decision).

GAMES WON

Most games won, career

A.L.—8—Dave Stewart, Oakland, 1988, 1989, 1990, 1992; Toronto, 1993; five series, 10 games (lost none).

N.L.—6—John Smoltz, Atlanta, 1991, 1992, 1993, 1995, 1996, 1997, 1998, 1999; eight series, 15 games (lost two).

For a complete list of pitchers with four or more victories, see page 456.

Most games won by undefeated pitcher, career

A.L.—8—Dave Stewart, Oakland, 1988, 1989, 1990, 1992; Toronto, 1993.

N.L.—3—Jesse Orosco, New York, 1986; Los Angeles, 1988.

Most opening games won, career

N.L.—2

Don Gullett, Cincinnati, 1975, 1976.

Steve Carlton, Philadelphia, 1980, 1983.

John Smoltz, Atlanta, 1992, 1996.

A.L.—2

Dick Hall, Baltimore, 1969, 1970.

Tommy John, New York, 1981; California, 1982.

Dave Stewart, Oakland, 1989, 1990.

Jack Morris, Detroit, 1984; Minnesota, 1991.

Mariano Rivera, New York, 1996, 1999.

Most consecutive games won, career

A.L.—8—Dave Stewart, Oakland, October 9, 1988; October 3, 8, 1989; October 6, 10, 1990; October 12, 1992; Toronto, October 6, 12, 1993 (one complete).

N.L.—4

Steve Carlton, Philadelphia, October 6, 1978; October 7, 1980; October 4, 8, 1983 (one complete).

John Smoltz, Atlanta, October 6, 10, 1991; October 6, 10, 1992 (none complete).

Most consecutive complete games won, career

A.L.—4—Jim Palmer, Baltimore, October 6, 1969; October 5, 1970; October 5, 1971; October 6, 1973.

N.L.—2

Tommy John, Los Angeles, October 8, 1977; October 5, 1978.

Mike Scott, Houston, October 8, 12, 1986.

Tim Wakefield, Pittsburgh, October 9, 13, 1992.

Most games won, series

N.L.—3—Jesse Orosco, New York, 1986 (6-game series).

A.L.—2—Held by many pitchers.

Most games won by relief pitcher, series

N.L.—3—Jesse Orosco, New York, 1986 (6-game series).

A.L.—2

Sparky Lyle, New York, 1977 (5-game series).

Tom Henke, Toronto, 1985 (7-game series).

Jeff Reardon, Minnesota, 1987 (5-game series).

SAVES

Most saves, career

Both leagues—11—Dennis Eckersley, Oakland A.L., 1988, 1989, 1990, 1992; St. Louis N.L., 1996.

A.L.—10—Dennis Eckersley, Oakland, 1988, 1989, 1990, 1992.

N.L.—5—Tug McGraw, New York, 1969, 1973; Philadelphia, 1977, 1980.

Most saves, series

3-game series

A.L.—2—Dick Drago, Boston, 1975.

N.L.—2—Don Gullett, Cincinnati, 1970.

4-game series

A.L.—4—Dennis Eckersley, Oakland, 1988.

N.L.—3—Dave Giusti, Pittsburgh, 1971.

5-game series

N.L.—3—Steve Bedrosian, San Francisco, 1989.

A.L.—3—Dennis Eckersley, Oakland, 1989.

Rick Aguilera, Minnesota, 1991.

6-game series

N.L.—3—Randy Myers, Cincinnati, 1990.

A.L.—3—Tom Henke, Toronto, 1992.

7-game series

N.L.—3—Alejandro Pena, Atlanta, 1991.

A.L.—1—Held by many pitchers.

GAMES LOST

Most games lost, career

N.L.—9—Tom Glavine, Atlanta, 1991, 1992, 1993, 1995, 1996, 1997, 1998, 1999, 2001; nine series, 15 games.

A.L.—4—Doyle Alexander, Baltimore, 1973; Toronto, 1985; Detroit, 1987; three series, five games (won none).

Most games lost by winless pitcher, career

N.L.—7—Jerry Reuss, Pittsburgh, 1974 (2), 1975; Los Angeles, 1981, 1983 (2), 1985.

A.L.—4—Doyle Alexander, Baltimore, 1973; Toronto, 1985; Detroit, 1987 (2).

Most consecutive games lost, career

N.L.—7—Jerry Reuss, Pittsburgh, 1974 (2), 1975; Los Angeles, 1981, 1983 (2), 1985.

A.L.—4—Doyle Alexander, Baltimore, 1973; Toronto, 1985; Detroit, 1987 (2).

Most games lost, series

N.L.—3—Doug Drabek, Pittsburgh, 1992.

A.L.—2—Held by many pitchers.

RUNS

Most runs allowed, career

N.L.—50—Greg Maddux, Chicago, 1989; Atlanta, 1993, 1995, 1996, 1997, 1998, 1999, 2001; eight series, 15 games.

A.L.—25—Catfish Hunter, Oakland, 1971, 1972, 1973, 1974; New York, 1976, 1978; six series, 10 games.

Most runs allowed, series

3-game series

A.L.—9—Jim Perry, Minnesota, 1970.

N.L.—9—Phil Niekro, Atlanta, 1969.

4-game series

N.L.—11—Gaylord Perry, San Francisco, 1971.

A.L.—10—Dave Frost, California, 1979.

5-game series

N.L.—12—Greg Maddux, Chicago, 1989.

A.L.—10—Doyle Alexander, Detroit, 1987.

6-game series

N.L.—10—Joaquin Andujar, St. Louis, 1985.

Tommy Greene, Philadelphia, 1993.

A.L.—10—Jack McDowell, Chicago, 1993.

7-game series

A.L.—13—Kirk McCaskill, California, 1986.

N.L.—11—Doug Drabek, Pittsburgh, 1992.

Tom Glavine, Atlanta, 1992.

Todd Stottlemyre, St. Louis, 1996.

Most runs allowed, game

N.L.—9—Phil Niekro, Atlanta, October 4, 1969.

A.L.—8

Jim Perry, Minnesota, October 3, 1970.

Roger Clemens, Boston, October 7, 1986.

Hideki Irabu, New York, October 16, 1999.

Most runs allowed, inning
A.L.—8—Tom Glavine, Atlanta, October 13, 1992, second inning.
N.L.—6
Jim Perry, Minnesota, October 3, 1970, fourth inning.
Scott Erickson, Baltimore, October 13, 1996, third inning.

EARNED RUNS

Most earned runs allowed, career
N.L.—36—Greg Maddux, Chicago, 1989; Atlanta, 1993, 1995, 1996, 1997, 1998, 1999, 2001; eight series, 15 games.
A.L.—25—Catfish Hunter, Oakland, 1971, 1972, 1973, 1974; New York, 1976, 1978; six series, 10 games.

Most earned runs allowed, series
3-game series
A.L.—8—Jim Perry, Minnesota, 1970.
N.L.—6—Jerry Koosman, New York, 1969.
        Pat Jarvis, Atlanta, 1969.
4-game series
N.L.—10—Gaylord Perry, San Francisco, 1971.
A.L.— 9—Dave Frost, California, 1979.
5-game series
N.L.—11—Greg Maddux, Chicago, 1989.
A.L.—10—Doyle Alexander, Detroit, 1987.
6-game series
N.L.—10—Tommy Greene, Philadelphia, 1993.
A.L.—10—Jack McDowell, Chicago, 1993.
7-game series
A.L.—11—Roger Clemens, Boston, 1986.
N.L.—11—Todd Stottlemyre, St. Louis, 1996.

Most earned runs allowed, game
A.L.—7
Jim Perry, Minnesota, October 3, 1970.
Roger Clemens, Boston, October 7, 1986.
Jack McDowell, Chicago, October 5, 1993.
Hideki Irabu, New York, October 16, 1999.
N.L.—7
Gaylord Perry, San Francisco, October 6, 1971.
Greg A. Harris, San Diego, October 2, 1984.
Tom Glavine, Atlanta, October 13, 1992.
Tommy Greene, Philadelphia, October 7, 1993.
Todd Stottlemyre, St. Louis, October 14, 1996.
Tom Glavine, Atlanta, October 14, 1997.
Darryl Kile, St. Louis, October 15, 2000.

Most earned runs allowed, inning
N.L.—7—Tom Glavine, Atlanta, October 13, 1992, second inning.
A.L.—6—Jim Perry, Minnesota, October 3, 1970, fourth inning.

SHUTOUTS AND SCORELESS INNINGS

Most shutouts, series
A.L.-N.L.—1—Held by many pitchers.

For a complete list of shutouts, see page 452.

Most consecutive scoreless innings, career
N.L.—22.1—Steve Avery, Atlanta, October 10 (8.1 innings), October 16 (eight innings), 1991; October 7 (six innings), 1992.
A.L.—18—Ken Holtzman, Oakland, October 9, 1973 (nine innings); October 6 (nine innings), 1974.

Most consecutive scoreless innings, series
N.L.—16.1—Steve Avery, Atlanta, October 10, 16, 1991.
A.L.—11—Dave McNally, Baltimore, October 5, 1969.

HITS

Most hits allowed, career
N.L.—91—Tom Glavine, Atlanta, 1991, 1992, 1993, 1995, 1996, 1997, 1998, 1999, 2001; nine series, 15 games.
A.L.—57—Catfish Hunter, Oakland, 1971, 1972, 1973, 1974; New York, 1976, 1978; six series, 10 games.

Most consecutive hitless innings, career
A.L.—10—Dave McNally, Baltimore, October 5 (7 innings), 1969; October 4 (3 innings), 1970.
N.L.—7—Randy Johnson, Arizona, October 16 (7 innings), 2001.

Most hits allowed, series
3-game series
A.L.—12—Ken Holtzman, Oakland, 1975.
N.L.—10—Pat Jarvis, Atlanta, 1969.
4-game series
N.L.—19—Gaylord Perry, San Francisco, 1971.
A.L.—13—Dennis Leonard, Kansas City, 1978.
5-game series
A.L.—18—Larry Gura, Kansas City, 1976.
N.L.—16—Nolan Ryan, Houston, 1980.
        Scott Garrelts, San Francisco, 1989.
6-game series
A.L.—18—Jack McDowell, Chicago, 1993.
N.L.—17—Orel Hershiser, Los Angeles, 1985.
7-game series
A.L.—22—Roger Clemens, Boston, 1986.
N.L.—19—Andy Benes, St. Louis, 1996.

Most hits allowed, game
A.L.—13
Jack McDowell, Chicago, October 5, 1993.
Hideki Irabu, New York, October 16, 1999.
N.L.—11—Kevin Brown, Florida, October 14, 1997.

Most consecutive hitless innings, game
A.L.—7—Dave McNally, Baltimore, October 5, 1969, 11-inning game.
N.L.—7—Randy Johnson, Arizona, October 16, 2001.

Fewest hits allowed, nine-inning game
A.L.—1—Roger Clemens, New York, October 14, 2000.
N.L.—2
Ross Grimsley, Cincinnati, October 10, 1972.
Jon Matlack, New York, October 7, 1973.
Dave Dravecky, San Francisco, October 7, 1987.

Most hits allowed, inning
A.L.—6
Jim Perry, Minnesota, October 3, 1970; fourth inning.
Kirk McCaskill, California, October 14, 1966, third inning.
N.L.—6
Greg A. Harris, San Diego, October 2, 1984, fifth inning.
Tom Glavine, Atlanta, October 13, 1992, second inning.
Todd Stottlemyre, St. Louis, October 14, 1996, first inning.

Most consecutive hits allowed, inning (consecutive at-bats)
A.L.—6—Jim Perry, Minnesota, October 3, 1970, fourth inning (sacrifice fly during streak).
N.L.—5—Bob Moose, Pittsburgh, October 8, 1972, first inning.

Most consecutive hits allowed, inning (consecutive plate appearances)
N.L.—5—Bob Moose, Pittsburgh, October 8, 1972, first inning.
A.L.—5
Dave Beard, Oakland, October 14, 1981, fourth inning.
Jack Morris, Minnesota, October 8, 1991, sixth inning.

DOUBLES, TRIPLES AND HOME RUNS

Most doubles allowed, game
N.L.—6—Darryl Kile, St. Louis, October 15, 2000.
A.L.—4
Dave McNally, Baltimore, October 3, 1971.
Vida Blue, Oakland, October 3, 1971.
Hideki Irabu, New York, October 16, 1999.
Orlando Hernandez, New York, October 17, 2000.

Most triples allowed, game
A.L.—2—Ed Figueroa, New York, October 8, 1977.
N.L.—2
Steve Carlton, Philadelphia, October 9, 1976.
Larry Christenson, Philadelphia, October 4, 1978.
Tom Glavine, Atlanta, October 9, 1993.

– 427 –

Most home runs allowed, career
A.L.—12—Catfish Hunter, Oakland, 1971 (4), 1972 (2), 1974 (3); New York, 1978 (3).
N.L.—8
  John Smoltz, Atlanta, 1991 (2), 1992, 1997, 1998 (2), 1999 (2).
  Tom Glavine, Atlanta, 1991, 1992 (3), 1993, 1996 (2), 2001.

Most home runs allowed, series
3-game series
  A.L.—4—Catfish Hunter, Oakland, 1971.
  N.L.—3—Pat Jarvis, Atlanta, 1969.
4-game series
  N.L.—4—Steve Blass, Pittsburgh, 1971.
  A.L.—3—Catfish Hunter, Oakland, 1974; New York, 1978.
      Mike Boddicker, Boston, 1988.
5-game series
  N.L.—5—Eric Show, San Diego, 1984.
  A.L.—4—Dave McNally, Baltimore, 1973.
      Andy Pettitte, New York, 1996.
6-game series
  A.L.—4—Andy Pettitte, New York, 1998.
  N.L.—3—Tommy Greene, Philadelphia, 1993.
7-game series
  A.L.—4—Doyle Alexander, Toronto, 1985.
  N.L.—4—Tim Wakefield, Pittsburgh, 1992.

Most home runs allowed, game
A.L.—4
  Catfish Hunter, Oakland, October 4, 1971.
  Dave McNally, Baltimore, October 7, 1973.
  Andy Pettitte, New York, October 9, 1998.
N.L.—3
  Pat Jarvis, Atlanta, October 6, 1969.
  Eric Show, San Diego, October 2, 1984.
  Danny Cox, St. Louis, October 10, 1987.

Most grand slams allowed, game
A.L.—1
  Jim Perry, Minnesota, October 3, 1970, fourth inning.
  Moose Haas, Milwaukee, October 9, 1982, eighth inning.
  David Cone, New York, October 13, 1998, fifth inning.
  Rod Beck, Boston, October 17, 1999, ninth inning.
N.L.—1
  Steve Carlton, Philadelphia, October 4, 1977, seventh inning.
  Jim Lonborg, Philadelphia, October 5, 1977, fourth inning.
  Greg Maddux, Chicago, October 4, 1989, fourth inning.
  Bob Walk, Pittsburgh, October 7, 1992, fifth inning.
  Greg Maddux, Atlanta, October 10, 1996, seventh inning.
  Dan Miceli, San Diego, October 11, 1998, seventh inning.

Most home runs allowed, inning
A.L.—3
  Scott Erickson, Baltimore, October 13, 1996, third inning.
  Jaret Wright, Cleveland, October 12, 1997, third inning.
  Andy Pettitte, New York, October 9, 1998, fifth inning.
N.L.—2—Held by many pitchers.

Most consecutive home runs allowed, inning
A.L.-N.L.—2—Held by many pitchers.

TOTAL BASES

Most total bases allowed, game
A.L.—23—Hideki Irabu, New York, October 16, 1999.
N.L.—22—Pat Jarvis, Atlanta, October 6, 1969.

BASES ON BALLS

Most bases on balls, career
N.L.—37—Tom Glavine, Atlanta, 1991, 1992, 1993, 1995, 1996, 1997, 1998, 1999, 2001; nine series, 15 games.
A.L.—25—Dave Stewart, Oakland, 1988, 1989, 1990, 1992; Toronto, 1993; five series, 10 games.

Most bases on balls, series
3-game series
  A.L.—7—Dave Boswell, Minnesota, 1969.
  N.L.—5—Fred Norman, Cincinnati, 1975.
      Steve Carlton, Philadelphia, 1976.
4-game series
  A.L.—13—Mike Cuellar, Baltimore, 1974.
  N.L.— 8—Jerry Reuss, Pittsburgh, 1974.
      Steve Carlton, Philadelphia, 1977.
5-game series
  A.L.—8—Jim Palmer, Baltimore, 1973.
      Paul Abbott, Seattle, 2001.
  N.L.—8—Steve Carlton, Philadelphia, 1980.
      Rick Sutcliffe, Chicago, 1984.
6-game series
  N.L.—11—Tom Glavine, Atlanta, 1997.
  A.L.— 9—Jack Morris, Toronto, 1992.
      Juan Guzman, Toronto, 1993.
7-game series
  A.L.—10—Dave Stieb, Toronto, 1985.
  N.L.—10—John Smoltz, Atlanta, 1992.

Most bases on balls, game
A.L.—9—Mike Cuellar, Baltimore, October 9, 1974.
N.L.—8—Fernando Valenzuela, Los Angeles, October 14, 1985.

Most bases on balls, inning
A.L.—4—Mike Cuellar, Baltimore, October 9, 1974, fifth inning (consecutive).
N.L.—4
  Burt Hooton, Los Angeles, October 7, 1977, second inning (consecutive).
  Bob Welch, Los Angeles, October 12, 1985, first inning.

Most consecutive bases on balls, inning
A.L.—4—Mike Cuellar, Baltimore, October 9, 1974, fifth inning.
N.L.—4—Burt Hooton, Los Angeles, October 7, 1977, second inning.

STRIKEOUTS

Most strikeouts, career
N.L.—89—John Smoltz, Atlanta, 1991, 1992, 1993, 1995, 1996, 1997, 1998, 1999, 2001; nine series, 17 games.
A.L.—53—Roger Clemens, Boston, 1986, 1988, 1990; New York, 1999 through 2001; six series, nine games.

Most strikeouts, series
3-game series
  N.L.—14—John Candelaria, Pittsburgh, 1975.
  A.L.—12—Jim Palmer, Baltimore, 1970.
4-game series
  A.L.—14—Mike Boddicker, Baltimore, 1983.
  N.L.—13—Don Sutton, Los Angeles, 1974.
      Steve Carlton, Philadelphia, 1983.
      Pete Schourek, Cincinnati, 1995.
5-game series
  N.L.—19—Randy Johnson, Arizona, 2001.
  A.L.—15—Jim Palmer, Baltimore, 1973.
6-game series
  A.L.—25—Mike Mussina, Baltimore, 1997.
  N.L.—19—Mike Scott, Houston, 1986.
      Curt Schilling, Philadelphia, 1993.
7-game series
  N.L.—20—Dwight Gooden, New York, 1988.
  A.L.—18—Dave Stieb, Toronto, 1985.

Most strikeouts, game
A.L.—15
  Mike Mussina, Baltimore, October 11, 1997, pitched first seven innings of nine-inning game.
  Roger Clemens, New York, October 14, 2000.
N.L.—15—Livan Hernandez, Florida, October 12, 1997.

For a complete list of pitchers with 10 or more strikeouts in a game, see page 456.

Most strikeouts, game, relief pitcher
A.L.—8—Wes Gardner, Boston, October 8, 1988, pitched 4.2 innings.
N.L.—7—Nolan Ryan, New York, October 6, 1969, pitched seven innings.

Most consecutive strikeouts, game

N.L.—5—Curt Schilling, Philadelphia, October 6, 1993 (three in first inning, two in second inning).

A.L.—5—Mike Mussina, Baltimore, October 11, 1997 (one in fifth inning, three in sixth inning, one in seventh inning).

Most consecutive strikeouts from start of game

N.L.—5—Curt Schilling, Philadelphia, October 6, 1993 (three in first inning, two in second inning).

A.L.—4—Nolan Ryan, California, October 3, 1979.

Most strikeouts, inning

A.L.-N.L.—3—Held by many pitchers.

HIT BATSMEN, WILD PITCHES AND BALKS

Most hit batsmen, career

N.L.—5
Tom Glavine, Atlanta, 1992 (2), 1995, 1996, 1997.
Greg Maddux, Chicago, 1989; Atlanta, 1995, 1997, 1998, 2001.

A.L.—4
Frank Tanana, California, 1979; Detroit, 1987 (3).
Mike Boddicker, Baltimore, 1983 (2); Boston, 1990 (2).

Most hit batsmen, series

A.L.—3
Frank Tanana, Detroit, 1987 (5-game series).
Jimmy Key, Baltimore, 1997 (6-game series).

N.L.—2
Tommy John, Los Angeles, 1977 (4-game series).
Orel Hershiser, Los Angeles, 1988 (7-game series).
Tom Glavine, Atlanta, 1992 (7-game series).
Al Leiter, New York, 1999 (6-game series).

Most hit batsmen, game

A.L.—3
Frank Tanana, Detroit, October 11, 1987.
Jimmy Key, Baltimore, October 9, 1997.

N.L.—2
Orel Hershiser, Los Angeles, October 12, 1988.
Al Leiter, New York, October 19, 1999.

Most hit batsmen, inning

A.L.—3—Jimmy Key, Baltimore, October 9, 1997, first inning.
N.L.—2—Al Leiter, New York, October 19, 1999, first inning.

Most wild pitches, career

A.L.—4
Tommy John, New York, 1980; California, 1982.
Juan Guzman, Toronto, 1991, 1992, 1993.

N.L.—4
Alejandro Pena, Los Angeles, 1983; Atlanta 1991.
Rick Ankiel, St. Louis, 2000.

Most wild pitches, series

N.L.—4—Rick Ankiel, St. Louis, 2000 (5-game series).
A.L.—3
Tommy John, California, 1982 (5-game series).
Juan Guzman, Toronto, 1993 (6-game series).

Most wild pitches, game

A.L.—3
Tommy John, California, October 9, 1982.
Juan Guzman, Toronto, October 5, 1993.

N.L.—2—Held by many pitchers.

Most wild pitches, inning

A.L.—2
Chris Zachary, Detroit, October 8, 1972, fifth inning.
Tommy John, California, October 9, 1982, fourth inning.
Juan Guzman, Toronto, October 5, 1993, first inning.
Mariano Rivera, New York, October 17, 2001, ninth inning.

N.L.—2
Jeff Calhoun, Houston, October 15, 1986, 16th inning.
Sterling Hitchcock, San Diego, October 14, 1998, second inning.
Rick Ankiel, St. Louis, October 12, 2000, first inning.
Rick Ankiel, St. Louis, October 16, 2000, seventh inning.

Most balks, game

A.L.-N.L.—1—Held by many pitchers.

CLUB PITCHING

APPEARANCES

Most appearances by pitchers, series
3-game series
A.L.—14—Minnesota vs. Baltimore, 1970.
N.L.—13—Cincinnati vs. Pittsburgh, 1979.
4-game series
A.L.—16—Oakland vs. Boston, 1988.
N.L.—16—Atlanta vs. Cincinnati, 1995.
5-game series
A.L.—24—Baltimore vs. New York, 1996.
N.L.—22—St. Louis vs. New York, 2000.
6-game series
N.L.—30—New York vs. Atlanta, 1999.
A.L.—29—Cleveland vs. Baltimore, 1997.
7-game series
N.L.—32—St. Louis vs. Atlanta, 1996.
A.L.—22—California vs. Boston, 1986.

Most appearances by pitchers of both clubs, series
3-game series
N.L.—25—Cincinnati 13, Pittsburgh 12, 1979.
A.L.—18—Minnesota 11, Baltimore 7, 1969.
Minnesota 14, Baltimore 4, 1970.
4-game series
N.L.—30—Atlanta 16, Cincinnati 14, 1995.
A.L.—26—Oakland 16, Boston 10, 1988.
Boston 15, Oakland 11, 1990.
5-game series
A.L.—41—Baltimore 24, New York 17, 1996.
N.L.—39—St. Louis 22, New York 17, 2000.
6-game series
N.L.—55—Atlanta 28, San Diego 27, 1998.
A.L.—52—Cleveland 29, Baltimore 23, 1997.
7-game series
N.L.—53—St. Louis 32, Atlanta 21, 1996.
A.L.—40—California 22, Boston 18, 1986.

COMPLETE GAMES

Most complete games, series
A.L.-N.L.—2—Held by many clubs.

Most complete games by both clubs, series
A.L.—4—Baltimore 2, Oakland 2, 1973 (5-game series).
N.L.—4—San Francisco 2, St. Louis 2, 1987 (7-game series).

SAVES

Most saves, series
3-game series
N.L.—3—Cincinnati vs. Pittsburgh, 1970.
A.L.—2—Boston vs. Oakland, 1975.
4-game series
A.L.—4—Oakland vs. Boston, 1988.
N.L.—3—Pittsburgh vs. San Francisco, 1971.
5-game series
A.L.—3—Milwaukee vs. California, 1982.
Minnesota vs. Detroit, 1987.
Oakland vs. Toronto, 1989.
Minnesota vs. Toronto, 1991.
New York vs. Boston, 1999.
N.L.—3—San Francisco vs. Chicago, 1989.
6-game series
N.L.—4—Cincinnati vs. Pittsburgh, 1990.
A.L.—3—Toronto vs. Oakland, 1992.
7-game series
N.L.—3—St. Louis vs. San Francisco, 1987.
Los Angeles vs. New York, 1988.
Atlanta vs. Pittsburgh, 1991.
A.L.—1—Held by many clubs.

Most saves by both clubs, series
3-game series
N.L.—3—Cincinnati 3, Pittsburgh 0, 1970.
A.L.—2—Boston 2, Oakland 0, 1975.
4-game series
A.L.—4—Oakland 4, Boston 0, 1988.
N.L.—3—Pittsburgh 3, San Francisco 0, 1971.
5-game series
N.L.—5—Houston 3, Philadelphia 2, 1980.
A.L.—4—Minnesota 3, Toronto 1, 1991.
6-game series
N.L.—6—Cincinnati 4, Pittsburgh 2, 1990.
A.L.—4—Toronto 3, Oakland 1, 1992.
7-game series
N.L.—5—Atlanta 3, Pittsburgh 2, 1991.
A.L.—2—California 1, Boston 1, 1986.

Fewest saves by one and both clubs, series
A.L.-N.L.—0—Held by many clubs.

RUNS AND SHUTOUTS

Most runs allowed, total series
N.L.—224—Atlanta; 11 series, 60 games.
A.L.—181—New York; 10 series, 47 games.

Most shutouts won, total series
N.L.—9—Atlanta, 1991 (3), 1995, 1996 (2), 1997, 1999, 2001.
A.L.—6—Baltimore, 1969, 1973, 1979, 1983 (2), 1997.

For a complete list of shutouts, see page 452.

Most shutouts won, series
N.L.—3—Atlanta vs. Pittsburgh, 1991 (7-game series).
A.L.—2
Oakland vs. Baltimore, 1974 (4-game series).
Baltimore vs. Chicago, 1983 (4-game series).
Cleveland vs. Seattle, 1995 (6-game series).

Most consecutive shutouts won, series
A.L.—2—Oakland vs. Baltimore, October 6, 8, 1974.
N.L.—2
St. Louis vs. San Francisco, October 13, 14, 1987.
Atlanta vs. Pittsburgh, October 16, 17, 1991.

Most shutouts by both clubs, series
N.L.—4—Atlanta 3, Pittsburgh 1, 1991 (7-game series).
A.L.—2
Oakland 1, Detroit 1, 1972 (5-game series).
Oakland 1, Baltimore 1, 1973 (5-game series).
Oakland 2, Baltimore 0, 1974 (4-game series).
Baltimore 2, Chicago 0, 1983 (4-game series).
Cleveland 2, Seattle 0, 1995 (6-game series).
Seattle 1, New York 1, 2000 (6-game series).

Largest score, shutout game
N.L.—15-0—Atlanta 15, St. Louis 0, October 17, 1996.
A.L.—8-0—Baltimore 8, California 0, October 6, 1979.

Longest shutout game
A.L.—11 innings
Baltimore 1, Minnesota 0, October 5, 1969.
Cleveland 1, Baltimore 0, October 15, 1997.
N.L.—11 innings—Houston 1, Philadelphia 0, October 10, 1980.

Most consecutive innings shutting out opponent, total series
A.L.—30—Oakland vs. Baltimore, October 5 (sixth inning) through October 9 (eighth inning), 1974.
N.L.—26—Pittsburgh vs. Atlanta, October 13 (second inning) through October 16 (eighth inning), 1991.

Most consecutive innings shutting out opponent, series
A.L.—30—Oakland vs. Baltimore, October 5 (sixth inning) through October 9 (eighth inning), 1974.

N.L.—26—Pittsburgh vs. Atlanta, October 13 (second inning) through October 16 (eighth inning), 1991.

WILD PITCHES AND BALKS

Most wild pitches, series
A.L.—5—Toronto vs. Chicago, 1993 (6-game series).
N.L.—5—St. Louis vs. New York, 2000 (5-game series).

Most wild pitches by both clubs, series
A.L.—7—Toronto 5, Chicago 2, 1993 (6-game series).
N.L.—7—St. Louis 5, New York 2, 2000 (5-game series).

Most balks, series
A.L.—2—Baltimore vs. Chicago, 1983 (4-game series).

N.L.—2
   Pittsburgh vs. Cincinnati, 1975 (3-game series).
   New York vs. Los Angeles, 1988 (7-game series).

Most balks by both clubs, series
N.L.—2
   Pittsburgh 2, Cincinnati 0, 1975 (3-game series).
   Philadelphia 1, Los Angeles 1, 1977 (4-game series).
   New York 2, Los Angeles 0, 1988 (7-game series).
A.L.—2
   Baltimore 2, Chicago 0, 1983 (4-game series).
   Boston 1, Oakland 1, 1988 (4-game series).

INDIVIDUAL FIELDING

FIRST BASEMEN
GAMES

Most games played, career
Both leagues—34—John Olerud, Toronto A.L., 1991, 1992, 1993; New York N.L., 1999; Seattle A.L., 2000, 2001; six series (28 in A.L., 6 in N.L.).
A.L.—33—Tino Martinez, Seattle, 1995; New York, 1996, 1998 through 2001; six series.
N.L.—23—Fred McGriff, Atlanta, 1993, 1995, 1996, 1997; four series.

PUTOUTS, ASSISTS AND CHANCES ACCEPTED

Most putouts, career
Both leagues—288—John Olerud, Toronto A.L., 1991, 1992, 1993; New York N.L., 1999; Seattle A.L., 2000, 2001; six series, 34 games (229 in A.L., 59 in N.L.).
A.L.—256—Tino Martinez, Seattle, 1995; New York, 1996, 1998 through 2001; six series; 33 games.
N.L.—208—Steve Garvey, Los Angeles, 1974, 1977, 1978, 1981; San Diego, 1984; five series, 22 games.

Most putouts, series
3-game series
N.L.—35—Keith Hernandez, St. Louis, 1982.
A.L.—34—Boog Powell, Baltimore, 1969.
4-game series
N.L.—44—Steve Garvey, Los Angeles, 1978.
A.L.—44—Eddie Murray, Baltimore, 1979.
5-game series
A.L.—55—Mike Epstein, Oakland, 1972.
N.L.—53—Pete Rose, Philadelphia, 1980.
6-game series
N.L.—67—Keith Hernandez, New York, 1986.
A.L.—55—Rafael Palmeiro, Baltimore, 1997.
7-game series
A.L.—72—Steve Balboni, Kansas City, 1985.
N.L.—63—Will Clark, San Francisco, 1987.

Most putouts, nine-inning game
N.L.—17—Andres Galarraga, Atlanta, October 14, 1998.
A.L.—15
  Chris Chambliss, New York, October 14, 1976.
  Mark McGwire, Oakland, October 4, 1989.

Most putouts, extra-inning game
N.L.—21—Glenn Davis, Houston, October 15, 1986, 16 innings.
A.L.—16—John Olerud, Toronto, October 11, 1991, 10 innings.

Fewest putouts, nine-inning game
N.L.—1—Bob Robertson, Pittsburgh, October 2, 1971.
A.L.—2
  Norm Cash, Detroit, October 8, 1972.
  Cecil Cooper, Boston, October 4, 1975.
  Carlos Quintana, Boston, October 6, 1990.

Most putouts, inning
A.L.-N.L.—3—Held by many first basemen.

Most assists, career
Both leagues—27—John Olerud, Toronto A.L., 1991, 1992, 1993; New York N.L., 1999; Seattle A.L., 2000, 2001; six series, 34 games (23 in A.L., 4 in N.L.).
A.L.—27—Tino Martinez, Seattle, 1995; New York, 1996, 1998 through 2001; six series, 33 games.
N.L.—17—Keith Hernandez, St. Louis, 1982; New York, 1986, 1988; three series, 16 games.

Most assists, series
3-game series
A.L.—5—Rich Reese, Minnesota, 1969.
      Bob Watson, New York, 1980.
N.L.—5—Tony Perez, Cincinnati, 1975.
      Chris Chambliss, Atlanta, 1982.

4-game series
N.L.—5—Steve Garvey, Los Angeles, 1978.
A.L.—3—Eddie Murray, Baltimore, 1979, 1983.
      Tom Paciorek, Chicago, 1983.
5-game series
A.L.—8—Kent Hrbek, Minnesota, 1991.
N.L.—7—Pete Rose, Philadelphia, 1980.
      Julio Franco, Atlanta, 2001.
6-game series
N.L.—12—Keith Hernandez, New York, 1986.
A.L.—9—John Olerud, Toronto, 1993.
7-game series
A.L.—7—Steve Balboni, Kansas City, 1985.
      Willie Upshaw, Toronto, 1985.
N.L.—7—Will Clark, San Francisco, 1987.

Most assists, nine-inning game
A.L.—4—Steve Balboni, Kansas City, October 12, 1985.
N.L.—4—Andres Galarraga, Atlanta, October 10, 1998.

Most assists, extra-inning game
N.L.—7—Keith Hernandez, New York, October 15, 1986, 16 innings.
A.L.—Less than nine-inning record.

Most assists, inning
A.L.-N.L.—2—Held by many first basemen.

Most chances accepted, career
Both leagues—315—John Olerud, Toronto A.L., 1991, 1992, 1993; New York N.L., 1999; Seattle A.L., 2000, 2001; six series, 34 games (252 in A.L., 63 in N.L.).
A.L.—283—Tino Martinez, Seattle, 1995; New York, 1996, 1998 through 2001; six series; 33 games.
N.L.—221—Steve Garvey, Los Angeles, 1974, 1977, 1978, 1981; San Diego, 1984; five series, 22 games.

Most chances accepted, series
3-game series
N.L.—36—Keith Hernandez, St. Louis, 1982.
A.L.—34—Boog Powell, Baltimore, 1969.
4-game series
N.L.—49—Steve Garvey, Los Angeles, 1978.
A.L.—47—Eddie Murray, Baltimore, 1979.
5-game series
N.L.—60—Pete Rose, Philadelphia, 1980.
A.L.—57—Mike Epstein, Oakland, 1972.
6-game series
N.L.—79—Keith Hernandez, New York, 1986.
A.L.—57—John Olerud, Toronto, 1993.
      Rafael Palmeiro, Baltimore, 1997.
7-game series
A.L.—79—Steve Balboni, Kansas City, 1985.
N.L.—70—Will Clark, San Francisco, 1987.

Most chances accepted, nine-inning game
N.L.—18—Steve Garvey, Los Angeles, October 6, 1978 (16 putouts, two assists).
A.L.—16
  Steve Balboni, Kansas City, October 12, 1985 (12 putouts, four assists).
  George Hendrick, California, October 11, 1986, 11 innings (14 putouts, two assists).

Most chances accepted, extra-inning game
N.L.—27—Keith Hernandez, New York, October 15, 1986, 16 innings (20 putouts, seven assists).
A.L.—16—John Olerud, Toronto, October 11, 1991, 10 innings (16 putouts).

Fewest chances offered, nine-inning game
N.L.—2—Bob Robertson, Pittsburgh, October 2, 1971 (one putout, one assist).
A.L.—2—Carlos Quintana, Boston, October 6, 1990 (two putouts).

Most chances accepted, inning
A.L.-N.L.—3—Held by many first basemen.

ERRORS AND DOUBLE PLAYS

Most errors, career
N.L.—4—Andres Galarraga, Atlanta, 1998; one series, six games.
A.L.—3
  Cecil Cooper, Boston, 1975; Milwaukee, 1982; two series, eight games.
  Eddie Murray, Baltimore, 1979, 1983; two series, eight games.
  Steve Balboni, Kansas City, 1984, 1985; two series, 10 games.

Most consecutive errorless games, career
A.L.—20—Tino Martinez, New York, October 9, 1998 through October 22, 2001.
N.L.—19—Steve Garvey, Los Angeles, San Diego, October 9, 1974 through October 7, 1984.

Most errors, series
N.L.—4—Andres Galarraga, Atlanta, 1998 (6-game series).
A.L.—2—Held by many first basemen.

Most chances accepted, errorless series
N.L.—79—Keith Hernandez, New York, 1986 (6-game series).
A.L.—57
  Mike Epstein, Oakland, 1972 (5-game series).
  Rafael Palmeiro, Baltimore, 1997 (6-game series).

Most errors, nine-inning game
A.L.-N.L.—1—Held by many first basemen.

Most errors, extra-inning game
N.L.—2
  Andres Galarraga, Atlanta, October 7, 1998, 10 innings.
  Brian R. Hunter, Atlanta, October 17, 1999, 15 innings.
A.L.—1—Held by many first basemen.

Most double plays, career
Both leagues—28—John Olerud, Toronto A.L., 1991, 1992, 1993; New York N.L., 1999; Seattle A.L., 2000, 2001; six series, 34 games (23 in A.L., 5 in N.L.).
A.L.—27—Tino Martinez, Seattle, 1995; New York, 1996, 1998 through 2001; six series; 33 games.
N.L.—21—Steve Garvey, Los Angeles, 1974, 1977, 1978, 1981; San Diego, 1984; five series, 22 games.

Most double plays, series
N.L.—10—Will Clark, San Francisco, 1987 (7-game series).
A.L.—8—Jim Thome, Cleveland, 1997 (6-game series).

Most double plays started, series
N.L.-A.L.—1—Held by many first basemen.

Most double plays, game
N.L.—4—Will Clark, San Francisco, October 10, 1987.
A.L.—3—Held by many first basemen.

Most double plays started, game
A.L.-N.L.—1—Held by many first basemen.

Most unassisted double plays, game
A.L.—1
  Tino Martinez, New York, October 11, 1996.
  Tino Martinez, New York, October 22, 2001.
N.L.—1—John Mabry, St. Louis, October 14, 1996.

SECOND BASEMEN
GAMES

Most games played, career
N.L.—31—Mark Lemke, Atlanta, 1991, 1992, 1993, 1995, 1996; five series.
A.L.—28—Roberto Alomar, Toronto, 1991, 1992, 1993; Baltimore, 1996, 1997; five series.

PUTOUTS, ASSISTS AND CHANCES ACCEPTED

Most putouts, career
A.L.—69—Roberto Alomar, Toronto, 1991, 1992, 1993; Baltimore, 1996, 1997; five series, 28 games.

N.L.—63—Joe Morgan, Cincinnati, 1972, 1973, 1975, 1976, 1979; Houston, 1980; Philadelphia, 1983; seven series, 27 games.

Most putouts, series
3-game series
  N.L.—12—Joe Morgan, Cincinnati, 1979.
  A.L.—12—Willie Randolph, New York, 1981.
4-game series
  A.L.—13—Bobby Grich, Baltimore, 1974.
  N.L.—13—Mark Lemke, Atlanta, 1995.
5-game series
  N.L.—18—Manny Trillo, Philadelphia, 1980.
  A.L.—16—Bobby Grich, Baltimore, 1973.
6-game series
  N.L.—19—Jose Lind, Pittsburgh, 1990.
  A.L.—18—Joey Cora, Chicago, 1993.
7-game series
  A.L.—19—Marty Barrett, Boston, 1986.
  N.L.—16—Jose Lind, Pittsburgh, 1992.

Most putouts, nine-inning game
A.L.—7—Bobby Grich, Baltimore, October 6, 1974.
N.L.—6
  Dave Cash, Philadelphia, October 12, 1976.
  Dave Lopes, Los Angeles, October 13, 1981.

Most putouts, extra-inning game
A.L.—8—Roberto Alomar, Toronto, October 11, 1992, 11 innings.
N.L.—7—Steve Sax, Los Angeles, October 9, 1988, 12 innings.

Most putouts, inning
N.L.—3
  Joe Morgan, Cincinnati, October 10, 1976, eighth inning.
  Ryne Sandberg, Chicago, October 4, 1984, fifth inning.
A.L.—3
  Bobby Grich, Baltimore, October 11, 1973, third inning.
  Dick Green, Oakland, October 8, 1974, seventh inning.

Most assists, career
A.L.—86—Roberto Alomar, Toronto, 1991, 1992, 1993; Baltimore, 1996, 1997; five series, 28 games.
N.L.—85—Joe Morgan, Cincinnati, 1972, 1973, 1975, 1976, 1979; Houston, 1980; Philadelphia, 1983; seven series, 27 games.

Most assists, series
3-games series
  N.L.—12—Tommy Helms, Cincinnati, 1970.
  A.L.—12—Willie Randolph, New York, 1981.
4-game series
  N.L.—18—Dave Lopes, Los Angeles, 1974.
  A.L.—14—Julio Cruz, Chicago, 1983.
5-game series
  N.L.—27—Joe Morgan, Cincinnati, 1973.
  A.L.—25—Roberto Alomar, Baltimore, 1996.
6-game series
  N.L.—21—Steve Sax, Los Angeles, 1985.
  A.L.—22—Carlos Baerga, Cleveland, 1995.
7-game series
  A.L.—28—Frank White, Kansas City, 1985.
  N.L.—24—Jose Lind, Pittsburgh, 1991.

Most assists, nine-inning game
A.L.—9—Joey Cora, Chicago, October 6, 1993.
N.L.—8—Manny Trillo, Philadelphia, October 7, 1980.

Most assists, extra-inning game
N.L.—9—Wally Backman, October 14, 1986, 12 innings.
A.L.—Less than nine-inning record.

Most assists, inning
A.L.-N.L.—2—Held by many second basemen.

Most chances accepted, career
A.L.—155—Roberto Alomar, Toronto, 1991, 1992, 1993; Baltimore, 1996, 1997; five series, 28 games.
N.L.—148—Joe Morgan, Cincinnati, 1972, 1973, 1975, 1976, 1979; Houston, 1980; Philadelphia, 1983; seven series, 27 games.

Most chances accepted, series
3-game series
A.L.—24—Willie Randolph, New York, 1981.
N.L.—23—Tommy Helms, Cincinnati, 1970.
Joe Morgan, Cincinnati, 1979.
4-game series
N.L.—29—Mark Lemke, Atlanta, 1995.
A.L.—25—Bobby Grich, Baltimore, 1974.
5-game series
N.L.—43—Manny Trillo, Philadelphia, 1980.
A.L.—40—Roberto Alomar, Baltimore, 1996.
6-game series
N.L.—38—Jose Lind, Pittsburgh, 1990.
A.L.—38—Joey Cora, Chicago, 1993.
7-game series
N.L.—39—Jose Lind, Pittsburgh, 1992.
A.L.—37—Frank White, Kansas City, 1985.

Most chances accepted, nine-inning game
N.L.—13—Manny Trillo, Philadelphia, October 7, 1980 (five putouts, eight assists).
A.L.—12—Bobby Grich, Baltimore, October 6, 1974 (seven putouts, five assists, one error).

Most chances accepted, extra-inning game
A.L.—13—Roberto Alomar, Toronto, October 11, 1992 (eight putouts, five assists).
N.L.—Less than nine-inning record.

Fewest chances offered, game
A.L.—0
Danny Thompson, Minnesota, October 4, 1970.
Bobby Grich, California, October 10, 1986.
N.L.—0—Ryne Sandberg, Chicago, October 9, 1989.

Most chances accepted, inning
A.L.-N.L.—3—Held by many second basemen.

ERRORS AND DOUBLE PLAYS

Most errors, career
A.L.—4
Dick Green, Oakland, 1971, 1972, 1973, 1974; four series, 17 games.
Bobby Grich, Baltimore, 1973, 1974; California, 1979, 1982, 1986; five series, 21 games.
Joey Cora, Chicago, 1993; Seattle, 1995; Cleveland, 1998; three series, 14 games.
Roberto Alomar, Toronto, 1991, 1992, 1993; Baltimore, 1996, 1997; five series, 28 games.
N.L.—4—Dave Lopes, Los Angeles, 1974, 1977, 1978, 1981; four series, 17 games.

Most consecutive errorless games, career
N.L.—27—Joe Morgan, Cincinnati, Houston, Philadelphia, October 7, 1972 through October 8, 1983.
A.L.—20—Willie Randolph, New York, Oakland, October 9, 1976 through October 10, 1990.

Most errors, series
A.L.—3—Joey Cora, Chicago, 1993 (6-game series).
N.L.—2—Held by many second basemen.

Most chances accepted, errorless series
A.L.—40—Marty Barrett, Boston, 1986 (7-game series).
N.L.—39—Joe Morgan, Cincinnati, 1973 (5-game series).

Most errors, game
A.L.—2
Dick Green, Oakland, October 9, 1973, 11 innings.
Dick Green, Oakland, October 8, 1974.
Lance Blankenship, Oakland, October 10, 1992.
N.L.—1—Held by many second basemen.

Most errors, inning
A.L.-N.L.—1—Held by many second basemen.

Most double plays, career
A.L.—20—Roberto Alomar, Toronto, 1991, 1992, 1993; Baltimore, 1996, 1997; five series, 28 games.

N.L.—14
Joe Morgan, Cincinnati, 1972, 1973, 1975, 1976, 1979; Houston, 1980; Philadelphia, 1983; seven series, 27 games.
Mark Lemke, Atlanta, 1991, 1992, 1993, 1995, 1996; five series, 31 games.

Most double plays, series
N.L.—7—Rodney Scott, Montreal, 1981 (5-game series).
A.L.—7—Roberto Alomar, Baltimore, 1996 (5-game series).

Most double plays started, series
N.L.—5—Steve Sax, Los Angeles, 1988 (7-game series).
A.L.—3—Bret Boone, Seattle, 2001 (5-game series).

Most double plays, game
N.L.—4—Dave Lopes, Los Angeles, October 13, 1981.
A.L.—3
Rob Wilfong, California, October 14, 1986.
Bip Roberts, Cleveland, October 11, 1997.

Most double plays started, game
N.L.—2—Held by many second basemen.
A.L.—1—Held by many second basemen.

Most unassisted double plays, game
N.L.—1—Joe Morgan, Cincinnati, October 10, 1976.
A.L.—Never accomplished.

THIRD BASEMEN
GAMES

Most games played, career
N.L.—34
Terry Pendleton, St. Louis, 1985, 1987; Atlanta, 1991, 1992, 1993, 1996; six series.
Chipper Jones, Atlanta, 1995 through 2001, except 2000; six series.
A.L.—27—George Brett, Kansas City, 1976, 1977, 1978, 1980, 1984, 1985; six series.

PUTOUTS, ASSISTS AND CHANCES ACCEPTED

Most putouts, career
A.L.—25—Sal Bando, Oakland, 1971, 1972, 1973, 1974, 1975; five series, 20 games.
N.L.—25—Terry Pendleton, St. Louis, 1985, 1987; Atlanta, 1991, 1992, 1993, 1996; six series, 34 games.

Most putouts, series
3-game series
A.L.—6—Brooks Robinson, Baltimore, 1969.
Harmon Killebrew, Minnesota, 1969.
Sal Bando, Oakland, 1971.
N.L.—5—Tony Perez, Cincinnati, 1970.
4-game series
N.L.—7—Ron Cey, Los Angeles, 1977.
A.L.—7—Carney Lansford, Oakland, 1988.
5-game series
A.L.—9—Doug DeCinces, California, 1982.
N.L.—5—Richie Hebner, Pittsburgh, 1972.
Ron Cey, Los Angeles, 1981.
Graig Nettles, San Diego, 1984.
Matt Williams, San Francisco, 1989.
6-game series
N.L.—7—Terry Pendleton, Atlanta, 1993.
A.L.—6—Matt Williams, Cleveland, 1997.
7-game series
N.L.—11—Jeff King, Pittsburgh, 1992.
A.L.—7—George Brett, Kansas City, 1985.
Wade Boggs, Boston, 1986.
Mike Blowers, Seattle, 1995.

Most putouts, game
A.L.—4
Carney Lansford, California, October 6, 1979.
Wade Boggs, Boston, October 10, 1990.
N.L.—3—Held by many players.

Most putouts, inning
A.L.-N.L.—2—Held by many third basemen.

Most assists, career
N.L.—66—Mike Schmidt, Philadelphia, 1976, 1977, 1978, 1980, 1983; five series, 20 games.
A.L.—49
  Brooks Robinson, Baltimore, 1969, 1970, 1971, 1973, 1974; five series, 18 games.
  George Brett, Kansas City, 1976, 1977, 1978, 1980, 1984, 1985; six series, 27 games.

Most assists, series
3-game series
  A.L.—11—Sal Bando, Oakland, 1975.
  N.L.—9—Mike Schmidt, Philadelphia, 1976.
4-game series
  N.L.—18—Mike Schmidt, Philadelphia, 1978.
  A.L.—13—Brooks Robinson, Baltimore, 1974.
    Todd Cruz, Baltimore, 1983.
5-game series
  N.L.—17—Mike Schmidt, Philadelphia, 1980.
  A.L.—16—Sal Bando, Oakland, 1972.
6-game series
  N.L.—19—Ray Knight, New York, 1986.
  A.L.—18—Matt Williams, Cleveland, 1997.
7-game series
  N.L.—19—Jeff King, Pittsburgh, 1992.
  A.L.—18—Doug DeCinces, California, 1986.

Most assists, nine-inning game
N.L.—8—Ron Cey, Los Angeles, October 16, 1981.
A.L.—6
  Sal Bando, Oakland, October 8, 1972.
  Todd Cruz, Baltimore, October 5, 1983.
  Tom Brookens, Detroit, October 11, 1987.
  Wade Boggs, New York, October 13, 1996.

Most assists, extra-inning game
A.L.—7—Aurelio Rodriguez, Detroit, October 11, 1972, 10 innings.
N.L.—Less than nine-inning record.

Most assists, inning
N.L.—3
  Ron Cey, Los Angeles, October 4, 1977, fourth inning.
  Ron Cey, Los Angeles, October 16, 1981, eighth inning.
A.L.—3—Todd Cruz, Baltimore, October 5, 1983, fifth inning.

Most chances accepted, career
N.L.—89—Terry Pendleton, St. Louis, 1985, 1987; Atlanta, 1991, 1992, 1993, 1996; six series, 34 games.
A.L.—72—Sal Bando, Oakland, 1971, 1972, 1973, 1974, 1975; five series, 20 games.

Most chances accepted, series
3-game series
  A.L.—16—Brooks Robinson, Baltimore, 1969.
  N.L.—13—Mike Schmidt, Philadelphia, 1976.
4-game series
  N.L.—21—Ron Cey, Los Angeles, 1977.
    Mike Schmidt, Philadelphia, 1978.
  A.L.—19—Todd Cruz, Baltimore, 1983.
5-game series
  A.L.—22—Sal Bando, Oakland, 1972.
  N.L.—21—Ron Cey, Los Angeles, 1981.
6-game series
  N.L.—24—Terry Pendleton, St. Louis, 1985.
    Ray Knight, New York, 1986.
  A.L.—24—Matt Williams, Cleveland, 1997.
7-game series
  A.L.—24—Doug DeCinces, California, 1986.
  N.L.—22—Steve Buechele, Pittsburgh, 1991.

Most chances accepted, game
N.L.—10—Ron Cey, Los Angeles, October 16, 1981 (two putouts, eight assists).
A.L.—9
  Todd Cruz, Baltimore, October 5, 1983 (three putouts, six assists).
  Wade Boggs, Boston, October 10, 1990 (four putouts, five assists).

Fewest chances offered, game
A.L.-N.L.—0—Held by many players.

Most chances accepted, inning
A.L.-N.L.—3—Held by many third basemen.

ERRORS AND DOUBLE PLAYS

Most errors, career
A.L.—8—George Brett, Kansas City, 1976, 1977, 1978, 1980, 1984, 1985; six series, 27 games.
N.L.—5—Mike Schmidt, Philadelphia, 1976, 1977, 1978, 1980, 1983; five series, 20 games.

Most consecutive errorless games, career
N.L.—33—Terry Pendleton, St. Louis, Atlanta, October 10, 1985 through October 17, 1996.
A.L.—17
  Sal Bando, Oakland, October 3, 1971 through October 9, 1974.
  Carney Lansford, California, Oakland, October 3, 1979 through October 8, 1992.

Most errors, series
A.L.—3
  George Brett, Kansas City, 1976 (5-game series).
  Doug DeCinces, California, 1982 (5-game series).
  Kelly Gruber, Toronto, 1991 (5-game series).
N.L.—3—Matt Williams, Arizona, 2001 (5-game series).

Most chances accepted, errorless series
A.L.—22—Sal Bando, Oakland, 1972 (5-game series).
N.L.—22
  Steve Buechele, Pittsburgh, 1991 (7-game series).
  Terry Pendleton, Atlanta, 1992 (7-game series).

Most errors, game
A.L.—2
  George Brett, Kansas City, October 9, 1976.
  Doug DeCinces, California, October 9, 1982.
  Darrell Evans, Detroit, October 11, 1987.
  Kelly Gruber, Toronto, October 8, 1991.
N.L.—2
  Ron Cey, Los Angeles, October 5, 1974.
  Fernando Tatis, St. Louis, October 15, 2000.

Most errors, inning
A.L.—2—George Brett, Kansas City, October 9, 1976, first inning.
N.L.—2—Fernando Tatis, St. Louis, October 15, 2000, sixth inning.

Most double plays, career
N.L.—8—Terry Pendleton, St. Louis, 1985, 1987; Atlanta, 1991, 1992, 1993, 1996; six series, 34 games.
A.L.—7—Doug DeCinces, Baltimore, 1979; California, 1982, 1986; three series, 16 games.

Most double plays, series
N.L.—5—Jeff King, Pittsburgh, 1992 (7-game series).
A.L.—3
  Carney Lansford, California, 1979 (4-game series).
  Doug DeCinces, California, 1982 (5-game series).
  Cal Ripken Jr., Baltimore, 1997 (6-game series).
  Matt Williams, Cleveland, 1997 (6-game series).

Most double plays started, series
N.L.—5—Jeff King, Pittsburgh, 1992 (7-game series).
A.L.—3
  Carney Lansford, California, 1979 (4-game series).
  Cal Ripken Jr., Baltimore, 1997 (6-game series).
  Matt Williams, Cleveland, 1997 (6-game series).

Most double plays, game
A.L.-N.L.—2—Held by many third basemen.

Most double plays started, game
A.L.-N.L.—2—Held by many third basemen.

Most unassisted double plays, game
N.L.—1
  Mike Schmidt, Philadelphia, October 9, 1976.
  Jeff King, Pittsburgh, October 14, 1992.
A.L.—Never accomplished.

SHORTSTOPS
GAMES

Most games played, career
N.L.—29—Jeff Blauser, Atlanta, 1991, 1992, 1993, 1995, 1996, 1997; six series.
A.L.—27—Derek Jeter, New York, 1996, 1998 through 2001; five series.

PUTOUTS, ASSISTS AND CHANCES ACCEPTED

Most putouts, career
N.L.—42—Bill Russell, Los Angeles, 1974, 1977, 1978, 1981, 1983; five series, 21 games.
A.L.—40—Derek Jeter, New York, 1996, 1998 through 2001; five series, 27 games.

Most putouts, series
3-game series
A.L.—13—Leo Cardenas, Minnesota, 1969.
N.L.—6—Held by many shortstops.
4-game series
N.L.—13—Bill Russell, Los Angeles, 1974.
A.L.—9—Fred Patek, Kansas City, 1978.
5-game series
N.L.—19—Garry Templeton, San Diego, 1984.
A.L.—13—Fred Patek, Kansas City, 1976.
6-game series
N.L.—21—Barry Larkin, Cincinnati, 1990.
A.L.—16—Omar Vizquel, Cleveland, 1997.
7-game series
N.L.—17—Alfredo Griffin, Los Angeles, 1988.
A.L.—13—Dick Schofield, California, 1986.

Most putouts, game
N.L.—7—Garry Templeton, San Diego, October 4, 1984.
A.L.—6
Mark Belanger, Baltimore, October 5, 1974.
Bucky Dent, New York, October 5, 1977.
Fred Patek, Kansas City, October 5, 1977.
Manny Lee, Toronto, October 8, 1992.

Most putouts, inning
A.L.—3
Mark Belanger, Baltimore, October 5, 1974, third inning.
Fred Patek, Kansas City, October 5, 1977, second inning.
N.L.—3—Chris Speier, Montreal, October 14, 1981, fifth inning.

Most assists, career
N.L.—70—Larry Bowa, Philadelphia, 1976, 1977, 1978, 1980; Chicago, 1984; five series, 21 games.
A.L.—69—Mark Belanger, Baltimore, 1969, 1970, 1971, 1973, 1974, 1979; six series, 21 games.

Most assists, series
3-game series
A.L.—14—Mark Belanger, Baltimore, 1970.
N.L.—14—Dave Concepcion, Cincinnati, 1979.
4-game series
A.L.—17—Bert Campaneris, Oakland, 1974.
N.L.—17—Larry Bowa, Philadelphia, 1977.
5-game series
A.L.—18—Fred Patek, Kansas City, 1976, 1977.
N.L.—16—Darrel Chaney, Cincinnati, 1972.
Chris Speier, Montreal, 1981.
6-game series
A.L.—26—Omar Vizquel, Cleveland, 1998.
N.L.—24—Rey Ordonez, New York, 1999.
7-game series
A.L.—23—Dick Schofield, California, 1986.
N.L.—20—Jose Uribe, San Francisco, 1987.

Most assists, game
N.L.—9—Bill Russell, Los Angeles, October 5, 1978.
A.L.—9—Kiko Garcia, Baltimore, October 4, 1979.

Most assists, inning
A.L.-N.L.—3—Held by many shortstops.

Most chances accepted, career
N.L.—107—Bill Russell, Los Angeles, 1974, 1977, 1978, 1981, 1983; five series, 21 games.
A.L.—101—Derek Jeter, New York, 1996, 1998 through 2001; five series, 27 games.

Most chances accepted, series
3-game series
A.L.—25—Leo Cardenas, Minnesota, 1969.
N.L.—17—Dave Concepcion, Cincinnati, 1979.
4-game series
N.L.—29—Bill Russell, Los Angeles, 1974.
A.L.—22—Kiko Garcia, Baltimore, 1979.
5-game series
A.L.—31—Fred Patek, Kansas City, 1976.
N.L.—31—Chris Speier, Montreal, 1981.
6-game series
A.L.—37—Omar Vizquel, Cleveland, 1998.
N.L.—36—Barry Larkin, Cincinnati, 1990.
7-game series
A.L.—36—Dick Schofield, California, 1986.
N.L.—32—Jay Bell, Pittsburgh, 1991.

Most chances accepted, game
N.L.—13—Bill Russell, Los Angeles, October 8, 1974 (six putouts, seven assists).
A.L.—11
Leo Cardenas, Minnesota, October 5, 1969, 11 innings (six putouts, five assists, one error).
Kiko Garcia, Baltimore, October 4, 1979 (two putouts, nine assists).

Fewest chances offered, game
A.L.-N.L.—0—Held by many shortstops.

Most chances accepted, inning
A.L.-N.L.—3—Held by many shortstops.

ERRORS AND DOUBLE PLAYS

Most errors, career
A.L.—5—Spike Owen, Boston, 1986; one series, seven games.
N.L.—5—Jeff Blauser, Atlanta, 1991, 1992, 1993, 1995, 1996, 1997; six series, 29 games.

Most consecutive errorless games, career
A.L.—17
Mark Belanger, Baltimore, October 4, 1969 through October 8, 1974.
Omar Vizquel, Cleveland, October 10, 1995 through October 11, 1998.
N.L.—13—Bill Russell, Los Angeles, October 5, 1977 through October 4, 1983.

Most errors, series
A.L.—5—Spike Owen, Boston, 1986 (7-game series).
N.L.—3—Darrel Chaney, Cincinnati, 1972 (5-game series).

Most chances accepted, errorless series
A.L.—31
Fred Patek, Kansas City, 1976 (5-game series).
Omar Vizquel, Cleveland, 1997 (6-game series).
N.L.—31
Rafael Santana, New York, 1986 (6-game series).
Rey Ordonez, New York, 1999 (6-game series).

Most errors, game
A.L.—2
Leo Cardenas, Minnesota, October 4, 1970.
Manny Lee, Toronto, October 11, 1992, 11 innings.
Nomar Garciaparra, Boston, October 13, 1999, 10 innings.
N.L.—2
Gene Alley, Pittsburgh, October 10, 1972.
Bill Russell, Los Angeles, October 4, 1977.
Kevin Elster, New York, October 9, 1988; 12 innings.
Rey Sanchez, Atlanta, October 20, 2001.

Most errors, inning
N.L.—2
Gene Alley, Pittsburgh, October 10, 1972, fourth inning.
Kevin Elster, New York, October 9, 1988, fifth inning.
A.L.—1—Held by many shortstops.

Most double plays, career
N.L.—18—Bill Russell, Los Angeles, 1974, 1977, 1978, 1981, 1983; five series, 21 games.
A.L.—18—Omar Vizquel, Cleveland, 1995, 1997, 1998; three series, 18 games.

Most double plays, series
A.L.—8—Omar Vizquel, Cleveland, 1997 (6-game series).
N.L.—7
    Jose Uribe, San Francisco, 1987 (7-game series).
    Alfredo Griffin, Los Angeles, 1988 (7-game series).

Most double plays started, series
A.L.—5—Omar Vizquel, Cleveland, 1997 (6-game series).
N.L.—3—Held by many shortstops.

Most double plays, game
A.L.—3
    Bert Campaneris, Oakland, October 5, 1975.
    Omar Vizquel, Cleveland, October 11, 1997, 12 innings.
    Omar Vizquel, Cleveland, October 13, 1997.
    Omar Vizquel, Cleveland, October 9, 1998.
N.L.—3
    Bill Russell, Los Angeles, October 8, 1974.
    Bill Russell, Los Angeles, October 5, 1983.
    Jose Uribe, San Francisco, October 10, 1987.
    Ozzie Smith, St. Louis, October 14, 1987.
    Jeff Blauser, Atlanta, October 10, 1995, 11 innings.

Most double plays started, game
N.L.—3—Bill Russell, Los Angeles, October 5, 1983.
A.L.—3—Omar Vizquel, Cleveland, October 13, 1997.

Most unassisted double plays, game
A.L.-N.L.—1—Held by many shortstops.

OUTFIELDERS
GAMES

Most games played, career
Both leagues—33—Rickey Henderson, Oakland A.L., 1981, 1989, 1990, 1992; Toronto A.L., 1993; New York N.L., 1999; Seattle A.L., 2000; seven series, 33 games (27 in A.L., 6 in N.L.).
A.L.—32—Reggie Jackson, Oakland, 1971, 1972, 1973, 1974, 1975; New York, 1977, 1978, 1980, 1981; California, 1982; 10 series.
N.L.—31—Ron Gant, Atlanta, 1991, 1992, 1993; Cincinnati, 1995; St. Louis, 1996; five series.

PUTOUTS, ASSISTS AND CHANCES ACCEPTED

Most putouts, career
A.L.—70—Bernie Williams, New York, 1996, 1998 through 2001; five series, 27 games.
N.L.—62
    Garry Maddox, Philadelphia, 1976, 1977, 1978, 1980, 1983; five series, 17 games.
    Ron Gant, Atlanta, 1991, 1992, 1993; Cincinnati, 1995; St. Louis, 1996; five series, 31 games.
    Andruw Jones, Atlanta, 1996 through 2001, except 2000; five series, 27 games.

Most putouts, series
3-game series
    N.L.—13—Cesar Geronimo, Cincinnati, 1975.
                 Dave Parker, Pittsburgh, 1975.
    A.L.—12—Fred Lynn, Boston, 1975
4-game series
    N.L.—16—Garry Maddox, Philadelphia, 1978.
    A.L.—14—Bill North, Oakland, 1974.
5-game series
    N.L.—23—Garry Maddox, Philadelphia, 1980.
    A.L.—22—Dave Henderson, Oakland, 1989.
6-game series
    N.L.—18—Willie McGee, St. Louis, 1985.
    A.L.—16—Devon White, Toronto, 1992.
                 Kenny Lofton, Cleveland, 1995.
7-game series
    A.L.—28—Gary Pettis, California, 1986.
    N.L.—20—Andy Van Slyke, Pittsburgh, 1992.

Most putouts by left fielder, game
A.L.—7—Roy White, New York, October 13, 1976.
N.L.—7
    Rennie Stennett, Pittsburgh, October 7, 1972.
    Jose Cruz, Houston, October 10, 1980, 11 innings.

Most putouts by center fielder, game
A.L.—9—Gary Pettis, California, October 10. 1986.
N.L.—8
    Al Oliver, Pittsburgh, October 7, 1972.
    Don Hahn, New York, October 8, 1973.

Most putouts by right fielder, game
A.L.—9—Jesse Barfield, Toronto, October 11, 1985.
N.L.—8—Brian Jordan, Atlanta, October 21, 2001.

Most consecutive putouts, game
A.L.—4
    Oscar Gamble, New York, October 15, 1981, 3 in sixth inning, 1 in seventh inning (right fielder).
    Dan Gladden, Minnesota, October 9, 1991, 3 in eighth inning, 1 in ninth inning (left fielder).
N.L.—4—Andre Dawson, Montreal, October 19, 1981, 1 in sixth inning, 3 in seventh inning (center fielder).

Most putouts, inning
A.L.-N.L.—3—Held by many outfielders.

Most assists, career
Both leagues—6—Lonnie Smith, Philadelphia N.L., 1980; St. Louis N.L., 1982; Kansas City A.L., 1985; Atlanta N.L., 1991; four series, 19 games.
N.L.—5—Bake McBride, Philadelphia, 1977, 1978, 1980; three series, 11 games.
A.L.—3
    Tony Oliva, Minnesota, 1969, 1970; two series, six games.
    Reggie Jackson, Oakland, 1971, 1972, 1973, 1974, 1975; New York, 1977, 1978, 1980, 1981; nine series, 27 games.
    Lonnie Smith, Kansas City, 1985; one series, seven games.

Most games played with no assists, career
A.L.—24—Paul Blair, Baltimore, 1969, 1970, 1971, 1973, 1974; New York, 1977, 1978; seven series.
N.L.—21—Willie McGee, St. Louis, 1982, 1985, 1987, 1996; four series.

Most assists, series
3-game series
    N.L.—2—George Foster, Cincinnati, 1979.
    A.L.—2—Tony Oliva, Minnesota, 1970.
                 Carl Yastrzemski, Boston, 1975.
                 Tony Armas, Oakland, 1981.
4-game series
    N.L.—2—Bake McBride, Philadelphia, 1977.
    A.L.—2—Rick Miller, California, 1979.
5-game series
    N.L.—3—Bake McBride, Philadelphia, 1980.
    A.L.—1—Held by many outfielders.
6-game series
    N.L.—2—Paul O'Neill, Cincinnati, 1990.
                 Wes Chamberlain, Philadelphia, 1993.
                 Gary Sheffield, Florida, 1997.
                 Rickey Henderson, New York, 1999.
    A.L.—1—Held by many outfielders.
7-game series
    A.L.—3—Lonnie Smith, Kansas City, 1985.
    N.L.—3—David Justice, Atlanta, 1992.

Most assists, game
A.L.—2—Tony Oliva, Minnesota, October 4, 1970.
N.L.—2
    George Foster, Cincinnati, October 3, 1979, 10 innings.
    Bake McBride, Philadelphia, October 11, 1980, 10 innings.
    Rickey Henderson, New York, October 15, 1999.

Most chances accepted, career
A.L.—72—Reggie Jackson, Oakland, 1971, 1972, 1973, 1974, 1975; New York, 1977, 1978, 1980, 1981; California, 1982; 10 series, 32 games.
N.L.—65—Ron Gant, Atlanta, 1991, 1992, 1993; Cincinnati, 1995; St. Louis, 1996; five series, 31 games.

Most chances accepted, series

3-game series
 N.L.—14—Dave Parker, Pittsburgh, 1975.
 A.L.—13—Fred Lynn, Boston, 1975.
4-game series
 N.L.—16—Garry Maddox, Philadelphia, 1978.
 A.L.—16—Rick Miller, California, 1979.
5-game series
 N.L.—23—Garry Maddox, Philadelphia, 1980.
 A.L.—22—Dave Henderson, Oakland, 1989.
6-game series
 N.L.—18—Willie McGee, St. Louis, 1985.
 A.L.—16—Devon White, Toronto, 1992.
    Willie Wilson, Oakland, 1992.
    Kenny Lofton, Cleveland, 1995.
7-game series
 A.L.—28—Gary Pettis, California, 1986.
 N.L.—22—David Justice, Atlanta, 1992.

Most chances accepted by left fielder, game

A.L.—7
 Roy White, New York, October 13, 1976 (seven putouts).
 Clint Hurdle, Kansas City, October 6, 1978 (six putouts, one assist).
N.L.—7
 Rennie Stennett, Pittsburgh, October 7, 1972 (seven putouts).
 Jose Cruz, Houston, October 10, 1980 (seven putouts).
 Kevin Mitchell, San Francisco, October 7, 1989 (six putouts, one assist).

Most chances accepted by center fielder, game

A.L.—9—Gary Pettis, California, October 10, 1986 (nine putouts).
N.L.—8
 Al Oliver, Pittsburgh, October 7, 1972 (eight putouts).
 Don Hahn, New York, October 8, 1973 (eight putouts).

Most chances accepted by right fielder, game

A.L.—9—Jesse Barfield, Toronto, October 11, 1985 (nine putouts).
N.L.—8—Brian Jordan, Atlanta, October 21, 2001 (eight putouts).

Longest game with no chances offered to outfielder

N.L.—12 innings
 Don Hahn, New York, October 9, 1973.
 Billy Hatcher, Houston, October 14, 1986.
A.L.—12 innings—Brian Giles, Cleveland, October 11, 1997.

Most chances accepted, inning

A.L.-N.L.—3—Held by many players.

ERRORS AND DOUBLE PLAYS

Most errors, career

Both leagues—7—Rickey Henderson, Oakland A.L., 1981, 1989, 1990, 1992; Toronto A.L., 1993; New York N.L., 1999; Seattle A.L., 2000; seven series, 33 games (6 in A.L., 1 in N.L.).
A.L.—6—Rickey Henderson, Oakland, 1981, 1989, 1990, 1992; Toronto, 1993; Seattle, 2000; six series, 27 games.
N.L.—2
 Reggie Smith, Los Angeles, 1977, 1978; two series, eight games.
 Willie McGee, St. Louis, 1982, 1985, 1987, 1996; four series, 21 games.
 Kenny Lofton, Atlanta, 1997; one series, six games.

Most consecutive errorless games, career

Both leagues—31—Paul O'Neill, Cincinnati N.L., New York A.L., October 4, 1990 through October 22, 2001.
A.L.—26—Paul O'Neill, New York, October 9, 1996 through October 22, 2001.
N.L.—27—Andruw Jones, Atlanta, October 9, 1996 through October 21, 2001.

Most errors, series

A.L.—3—Rickey Henderson, Oakland, 1992 (6-game series).
N.L.—2—Kenny Lofton, Atlanta, 1997 (6-game series).

Most chances accepted, errorless series

N.L.—23—Garry Maddox, Philadelphia, 1980 (5-game series).
A.L.—22—Dave Henderson, Oakland, 1989 (5-game series).

Most errors, game

A.L.—2
 Tony Oliva, Minnesota, October 6, 1969.
 Ben Oglivie, Milwaukee, October 10, 1982.
N.L.—1—Held by many outfielders.

Most errors, inning

A.L.-N.L.—1—Held by many outfielders.

Most double plays, career

N.L.—3—Bake McBride, Philadelphia, 1977, 1978, 1980; three series, 11 games.
A.L.—2—Rick Miller, California, 1979; one series, four games.

Most double plays, nine-inning game

A.L.-N.L.—1—Held by many outfielders.

Most double plays, extra-inning game

N.L.—2—Bake McBride, Philadelphia, October 11, 1980, 10 innings.
A.L.—1—Held by many outfielders.

Most double plays started, nine-inning game

A.L.-N.L.—1—Held by many outfielders.

Most double plays started, extra-inning game

N.L.—2—Bake McBride, Philadelphia, October 11, 1980, 10 innings.
A.L.—1—Held by many outfielders.

Most unassisted double plays, game

A.L.-N.L.—Never accomplished.

CATCHERS
GAMES

Most games caught, career

Both leagues—27—Bob Boone, Philadelphia N.L., 1976, 1977, 1978, 1980; California A.L., 1982, 1986; six series.
N.L.—27—Javy Lopez, Atlanta, 1992, 1995, 1996, 1997, 1998, 2001; six series.
A.L.—19—Jorge Posada, New York, 1998 through 2001; four series.

PUTOUTS, ASSISTS AND CHANCES ACCEPTED

Most putouts, career

N.L.—183—Javy Lopez, Atlanta, 1992, 1995, 1996, 1997, 1998, 2001; six series, 27 games.
A.L.—140—Jorge Posada, New York, 1998 through 2001; four series, 19 games.

Most putouts, series

3-game series
 N.L.—29—Manny Sanguillen, Pittsburgh, 1975.
 A.L.—23—Rick Cerone, New York, 1981.
4-game series
 N.L.—34—Dick Dietz, San Francisco, 1971.
 A.L.—34—Rich Gedman, Boston, 1988.
5-game series
 A.L.—44—Jason Varitek, Boston, 1999.
 N.L.—42—Jerry Grote, New York, 1973.
6-game series
 N.L.—59—Alan Ashby, Houston, 1986.
 A.L.—51—Jorge Posada, New York, 2000.
7-game series
 N.L.—62—Greg Olson, Atlanta, 1991.
 A.L.—50—Ernie Whitt, Toronto, 1985.

Most putouts, nine-inning game

A.L.—15
 Rick Dempsey, Baltimore, October 6, 1983.
 Jorge Posada, New York, October 14, 2000.
N.L.—15—Charles Johnson, Florida, October 12, 1997.

Most putouts, extra-inning game

A.L.—15—Chris Hoiles, Baltimore, October 11, 1997, caught first eight innings of 12-inning game).

N.L.—16—Mike Piazza, New York, October 17, 1999, 15 innings.

Fewest putouts, game

N.L.—1—Terry Kennedy, San Diego, October 3, 1984.

A.L.—1
Ray Fosse, Oakland, October 11, 1973.
Buck Martinez, Kansas City, October 13, 1976.
Jim Sundberg, Kansas City, October 12, 1985.
Terry Steinbach, Oakland, October 10, 1990.

Most putouts, inning

A.L.-N.L.—3—Held by many catchers.

Most assists, career

N.L.—18—Johnny Bench, Cincinnati, 1970, 1972, 1973, 1975, 1976, 1979; six series, 22 games.
A.L.—14—Thurman Munson, New York, 1976, 1977, 1978; three series, 14 games.

Most assists, series

3-game series
  A.L.—4—George Mitterwald, Minnesota, 1969.
        Rick Cerone, New York, 1980.
  N.L.—4—Johnny Bench, Cincinnati, 1975, 1976.

4-game series
  A.L.—5—Rick Dempsey, Baltimore, 1983.
        Rich Gedman, Boston, 1988.
  N.L.—2—Held by many catchers.

5-game series
  A.L.—6—Thurman Munson, New York, 1976.
  N.L.—4—Terry Kennedy, San Diego, 1984.

6-game series
  A.L.—7—Terry Steinbach, Oakland, 1992.
  N.L.—5—Gary Carter, New York, 1986.

7-game series
  N.L.—5—Tony Pena, St. Louis, 1987.
        Don Slaught, Pittsburgh, 1991.
  A.L.—4—Rich Gedman, Boston, 1986.

Most assists, game

N.L.—3
Johnny Bench, Cincinnati, October 3, 1970, 10 innings.
Johnny Bench, Cincinnati, October 5, 1975.
Gary Carter, New York, October 15, 1986, 16 innings.

A.L.—3
Rich Gedman, Boston, October 8, 1988.
Terry Steinbach, Oakland, October 10, 1992.
Pat Borders, Toronto, October 8, 1993.
Dan Wilson, Seattle, October 11, 2000.

Most assists, inning

N.L.—2
Johnny Bench, Cincinnati, October 7, 1973, eighth inning.
Mike Scioscia, Los Angeles, October 10, 1985, first inning.
Gary Carter, New York, October 15, 1986, 12th inning.
A.L.—2—Rich Gedman, Boston, October 8, 1988, first inning.

Most chances accepted, career

N.L.—193—Javy Lopez, Atlanta, 1992, 1995, 1996, 1997, 1998, 2001; six series, 27 games.
A.L.—148—Jorge Posada, New York, 1998 through 2001; four series, 19 games.

Most chances accepted, series

3-game series
  N.L.—30—Manny Sanguillen, Pittsburgh, 1975.
  A.L.—25—Rick Cerone, New York, 1981.

4-game series
  A.L.—39—Rich Gedman, Boston, 1988.
  N.L.—36—Dick Dietz, San Francisco, 1971.

5-game series
  A.L.—45—Jason Varitek, Boston, 1999.
  N.L.—43—Jerry Grote, New York, 1973.

6-game series
  N.L.—60—Alan Ashby, Houston, 1986.
  A.L.—54—Jorge Posada, New York, 2000.

7-game series
  N.L.—62—Greg Olson, Atlanta, 1991.
  A.L.—53—Ernie Whitt, Toronto, 1985.

Most chances accepted, nine-inning game

A.L.—16—Rick Dempsey, Baltimore, October 6, 1983 (15 putouts, 1 assist).
N.L.—16—Charles Johnson, Florida, October 12, 1997 (15 putouts, 1 assist).

Most chances accepted, extra-inning game

N.L.—18—Mike Piazza, New York, October 17, 1999, 15 innings (16 putouts, 2 assists).
A.L.—16—Chris Hoiles, Baltimore, October 11, 1997, caught first eight innings of 12-inning game (15 putouts, 1 assist).

Fewest chances offered, game

A.L.-N.L.—2—Held by many catchers.

Most chances accepted, inning

A.L.-N.L.—3—Held by many catchers.

ERRORS AND PASSED BALLS

Most errors, career

N.L.—5—Manny Sanguillen, Pittsburgh, 1970, 1971, 1972, 1974, 1975; five series, 19 games.
A.L.—3
Don Slaught, Kansas City, 1984; one series, three games.
Pat Borders, Toronto, 1989, 1991, 1992, 1993; four series, 18 games.
Sandy Alomar, Cleveland, 1995, 1997, 1998; three series, 16 games.

Most consecutive errorless games, career

Both leagues—18—Darrell Porter, Kansas City A.L., October 5, 1977 through October 10, 1980, 12 games; St. Louis N.L., October 7, 1982 through October 12, 1985, six games.
N.L.—18—Gary Carter, Montreal, New York, October 13, 1981 through October 12, 1988.
A.L.—15—Terry Steinbach, Oakland, October 5, 1988 through October 14, 1992.

Most errors, series

A.L.—3—Don Slaught, Kansas City, 1984 (3-game series).
N.L.—3—Mike Piazza, New York, 1999 (6-game series).

Most chances accepted, errorless series

N.L.—63—Greg Olson, Atlanta, 1991 (7-game series).
A.L.—54—Jorge Posada, New York, 2000 (6-game series).

Most errors, game

A.L.—2
Thurman Munson, New York, October 10, 1976.
Don Slaught, Kansas City, October 5, 1984.
Sandy Alomar, Cleveland, October 10, 1998.
N.L.—2
Manny Sanguillen, Pittsburgh, October 6, 1974.
Mike Piazza, New York, October 19, 1999, 11 innings.

Most errors, inning

A.L.-N.L.—1—Held by many catchers.

Most passed balls, career

Both leagues—4—Bob Boone, Philadelphia N.L., 1976, 1977, 1978, 1980; California A.L., 1982, 1986; six series, 27 games.
N.L.—4—Manny Sanguillen, Pittsburgh, 1970, 1971, 1972, 1974, 1975; five series, 19 games.
A.L.—3
Bob Boone, California, 1982, 1986; two series, 12 games.
Pat Borders, Toronto, 1989, 1991, 1992, 1993; four series, 18 games.

Most passed balls, series

A.L.—3—Pat Borders, Toronto, 1992 (6-game series).
N.L.—2
Manny Sanguillen, Pittsburgh, 1975 (3-game series).
Alan Ashby, Houston, 1986 (6-game series).
Don Slaught, Pittsburgh, 1992 (7-game series).
Darren Daulton, Philadelphia, 1993 (6-game series).

CHAMPIONSHIP SERIES *Individual fielding*

Most passed balls, game
N.L.—2
Manny Sanguillen, Pittsburgh, October 4, 1975.
Alan Ashby, Houston, October 11, 1986.
Don Slaught, Pittsburgh, October 13, 1992.
A.L.—2—Pat Borders, Toronto, October 14, 1992.

Most passed balls, inning
A.L.-N.L.—1—Held by many catchers.

DOUBLE PLAYS AND RUNNERS CAUGHT STEALING

Most double plays, career
A.L.—4—Ray Fosse, Oakland, 1973, 1974, 1975; three series, 10 games.
N.L.—3
Manny Sanguillen, Pittsburgh, 1970, 1971, 1972, 1974, 1975; five series, 19 games.
Terry Kennedy, San Diego, 1984; San Francisco, 1989; two series, 10 games.

Most double plays, series
A.L.—2
George Mitterwald, Minnesota, 1970 (3-game series).
Ray Fosse, Oakland, 1973 (5-game series).
N.L.—2
Terry Kennedy, San Francisco, 1989 (5-game series).
Javy Lopez, Atlanta, 1997 (6-game series).
Mike Piazza, New York, 1999 (6-game series).

Most double plays started, series
A.L.—2—Ray Fosse, Oakland, 1973 (5-game series).
N.L.—1—Held by many catchers.

Most double plays, game
A.L.-N.L.—1—Held by many catchers.

Most double plays started, game
A.L.-N.L.—1—Held by many catchers.

Most unassisted double plays, game
A.L.-N.L.—Never accomplished.

Most runners caught stealing, career
A.L.—12—Thurman Munson, New York, 1976, 1977, 1978; three series, 14 games.
N.L.—6—Mike Scioscia, Los Angeles, 1981, 1985, 1988; three series, 18 games.

Most runners caught stealing, series
A.L.—5
Thurman Munson, New York, 1976 (5-game series).
Terry Steinbach, Oakland, 1992 (6-game series).
N.L.—4—Mike Scioscia, Los Angeles, 1985 (6-game series).

Most runners caught stealing, game
A.L.-N.L.—2—Held by many catchers.

Most runners caught stealing, inning
N.L.—2—Mike Scioscia, Los Angeles, October 10, 1985, first inning.
A.L.—1—Held by many catchers.

PITCHERS
GAMES

Most games pitched, career
Both leagues—20—Rick Honeycutt, Los Angeles N.L., 1983, 1985; Oakland A.L., 1988, 1989, 1990, 1992; St. Louis N.L.; seven series.
N.L.—18—Mark Wohlers, Atlanta, 1991, 1992, 1993, 1995, 1996, 1997; six series.
A.L.—16—Mariano Rivera, New York, 1996, 1998 through 2001; five series.

Most games pitched, series
3-game series
A.L.-N.L.—3—Held by many pitchers.
4-game series
N.L.—4—Dave Giusti, Pittsburgh, 1971.
Mark Wohlers, Atlanta, 1995.
A.L.—4—Dennis Eckersley, Oakland, 1988.

5-game series
N.L.—5—Tug McGraw, Philadelphia, 1980.
A.L.—5—Jim Acker, Toronto, 1989.
6-game series
N.L.—6—John Rocker, Atlanta, 1998.
John Rocker, Atlanta, 1999.
A.L.—5—Paul Assenmacher, Cleveland, 1997.
Mike Jackson, Cleveland, 1997.
Paul Shuey, Cleveland, 1998.
Jose Paniagua, Seattle, 2000.
7-game series
N.L.—6—Mark Petkovsek, St. Louis, 1996.
A.L.—4—Held by many pitchers.

PUTOUTS, ASSISTS AND CHANCES ACCEPTED

Most putouts, career
N.L.—11—Greg Maddux, Chicago, 1989; Atlanta, 1993, 1995, 1996, 1997, 1998, 1999, 2001; eight series, 15 games.
A.L.—9—Mariano Rivera, New York, 1996, 1998 through 2001; five series, 16 games.

Most putouts, series
3-game series
N.L.—4—Don Gullett, Cincinnati, 1975.
A.L.—2—Rick Wise, Boston, 1975.
Milt Wilcox, Detroit, 1984.
4-game series
A.L.—3—Catfish Hunter, Oakland, 1974.
N.L.—2—Juan Marichal, San Francisco, 1971.
Don Sutton, Los Angeles, 1974.
Jeff Brantley, Cincinnati, 1995.
5-game series
A.L.—4—Mariano Rivera, 2001.
N.L.—2—Tug McGraw, New York, 1973.
Dick Ruthven, Philadelphia, 1980.
Miguel Batista, Arizona, 2001.
Tom Glavine, Atlanta, 2001.
Greg Maddux, Atlanta, 2001.
6-game series
N.L.—4—Greg Maddux, Atlanta, 1993.
Andy Ashby, San Diego, 1998.
A.L.—4—Brett Tomko, Seattle, 2000.
7-game series
N.L.—4—Danny Cox, St. Louis, 1987.
A.L.—3—Charlie Leibrandt, Kansas City, 1985.

Most putouts, game
N.L.—4—Don Gullett, Cincinnati, October 4, 1975.
A.L.—3
Tommy John, California, October 5, 1982.
Charlie Leibrandt, Kansas City, October 12, 1985.
Charles Nagy, Cleveland, October 7, 1998.

Most putouts, inning
A.L.—2
Mike Torrez, New York, October 7, 1977, second inning.
Charlie Leibrandt, Kansas City, October 12, 1985, fifth inning.
Mike Witt, California, October 12, 1986, first inning.
Mariano Rivera, New York, October 17, 2001, ninth inning.
N.L.—2
Don Gullett, Cincinnati, October 4, 1975, third inning.
Roger McDowell, New York, October 15, 1986, 10th inning.

Most assists, career
N.L.—25—Greg Maddux, Chicago, 1989; Atlanta, 1993, 1995, 1996, 1997, 1998, 1999, 2001; eight series, 15 games.
A.L.—12—Mike Cuellar, Baltimore, 1969, 1970, 1971, 1973, 1974; five series, six games.

Most assists, series
3-game series
A.L.—4—Dave Boswell, Minnesota, 1969.
Paul Lindblad, Oakland, 1975.
N.L.—3—Phil Niekro, Atlanta, 1969.
Dock Ellis, Pittsburgh, 1970.
Pat Zachry, Cincinnati, 1976.

4-game series
    A.L.—5—Mike Cuellar, Baltimore, 1974.
    N.L.—5—Steve Carlton, Philadelphia, 1983.
5-game series
    N.L.—4—Darryl Kile, St. Louis, 2000.
    A.L.—3—Held by many pitchers.
6-game series
    N.L.—7—Greg Maddux, Atlanta, 1997.
    A.L.—5—Scott Erickson, Baltimore, 1997.
7-game series
    A.L.—7—Charlie Leibrandt, Kansas City, 1985.
    N.L.—5—Danny Cox, St. Louis, 1987.

Most assists, game
A.L.—5—Charlie Leibrandt, Kansas City, October 12, 1985.
N.L.—4
    Juan Marichal, San Francisco, October 5, 1971.
    Greg Maddux, Atlanta, October 7, 1997.
    Greg Maddux, Atlanta, October 12, 1999.

Most assists, inning
N.L.—3—Pat Zachry, Cincinnati, October 10, 1976,
    fourth inning.
A.L.—2—Held by many pitchers.

Most chances accepted, career
N.L.—35—Greg Maddux, Chicago, 1989; Atlanta, 1993, 1995,
    1996, 1997, 1998, 1999, 2001; eight series, 15 games.
A.L.—15—Mariano Rivera, New York, 1996, 1998 through
    2001; five series, 16 games.

Most chances accepted, series
3-game series
    N.L.—5—Don Gullett, Cincinnati, 1975.
    A.L.—5—Dave Boswell, Minnesota, 1969.
            Rick Wise, Boston, 1975.
            Paul Lindblad, Oakland, 1975.
4-game series
    N.L.—6—Juan Marichal, San Francisco, 1971.
            Steve Carlton, Philadelphia, 1983.
    A.L.—5—Catfish Hunter, Oakland, 1974.
            Mike Cuellar, Baltimore, 1974.
            Larry Gura, Kansas City, 1978.
5-game series
    N.L.—5—Darryl Kile, St. Louis, 2000.
            Tom Glavine, Atlanta, 2001.
            Greg Maddux, Atlanta, 2001.
    A.L.—5—Mike Flanagan, Toronto, 1989.
            Mariano Rivera, New York, 2001.
6-game series
    N.L.—9—Greg Maddux, Atlanta, 1993.
    A.L.—5—Scott Erickson, Baltimore, 1997.
7-game series
    A.L.—10—Charlie Leibrandt, Kansas City, 1985.
    N.L.—9—Danny Cox, St. Louis, 1987.

Most chances accepted, game
A.L.—8—Charlie Leibrandt, Kansas City, October 12, 1985.
N.L.—6—Juan Marichal, San Francisco, October 5, 1971.

Most chances accepted, inning
N.L.—3—Pat Zachry, Cincinnati, October 10, 1976,
    fourth inning.
A.L.—3—Mariano Rivera, New York, October 17, 2001, ninth
    inning.

ERRORS AND DOUBLE PLAYS

Most errors, career
N.L.—3—Greg Maddux, Chicago, 1989; Atlanta, 1993, 1995,
    1996, 1997, 1998, 1999, 2001; eight series, 15 games.
A.L.—1—Held by many pitchers.

Most consecutive errorless games, career
Both leagues—20—Rick Honeycutt, Los Angeles N.L., Oakland
    A.L., St. Louis N.L., October 7, 1983 through October 17,
    1996.
N.L.—18—Mark Wohlers, Atlanta, October 9, 1991 through
    October 8, 1997.
A.L.—16—Mariano Rivera, New York, October 9, 1996 through
    October 22, 2001.

Most errors, series
N.L.—2—Joaquin Andujar, St. Louis, 1985.
A.L.—1—Held by many pitchers.

Most chances accepted, errorless series
A.L.—10—Charlie Leibrandt, Kansas City, 1985 (7-game
    series).
N.L.—9—Danny Cox, St. Louis, 1987 (7-game series).

Most errors, game
A.L.-N.L.—1—Held by many pitchers.

Most double plays, career
N.L.—3—Greg Maddux, Chicago, 1989; Atlanta, 1993 through
    2001, except 1994 and 2000; eight series, 15 games.
A.L.—2
    Mike Flanagan, Baltimore, 1979, 1983; Toronto, 1989;
        three series, three games.
    Jeff Nelson, Seattle, 1995, 2001; New York, 1997 through
        2000; six series, 15 games.

Most double plays started, career
N.L.—3—Greg Maddux, Chicago, 1989; Atlanta, 1993 through
    2001, except 1994 and 2000; eight series, 15 games.
A.L.—2
    Mike Flanagan, Baltimore, 1979, 1983; Toronto, 1989;
        three series, three games.
    Jeff Nelson, Seattle, 1995, 2001; New York, 1997 through
        2000; six series, 15 games.

Most double plays, series
A.L.—2
    Mike Flanagan, Toronto, 1989 (5-game series).
    Jeff Nelson, Seattle, 1995 (6-game series).
N.L.—2
    Pat Mahomes, New York, 1999 (6-game series).
    Greg Maddux, Atlanta, 2001 (5-game series).

Most double plays started, series
A.L.—2
    Mike Flanagan, Toronto, 1989 (5-game series).
    Jeff Nelson, Seattle, 1995 (6-game series).
N.L.—2
    Pat Mahomes, New York, 1999 (6-game series).
    Greg Maddux, Atlanta, 2001 (5-game series).

Most double plays, game
A.L.—2—Jeff Nelson, Seattle, October 14, 1995.
N.L.—2—Greg Maddux, Atlanta, October 16, 2001.

Most unassisted double plays, game
A.L.-N.L.—Never accomplished.

CLUB FIELDING

AVERAGE

Highest fielding average, series

3-game series
A.L.—1.000—Baltimore vs. Minnesota, 1970.
    Oakland vs. Baltimore, 1971.
N.L.—1.000—Pittsburgh vs. Cincinnati, 1979.
4-game series
A.L.—.993—New York vs. Kansas City, 1978.
    Boston vs. Oakland, 1988.
    Oakland vs. Boston, 1990.
N.L.—.993—Los Angeles vs. Philadelphia, 1983.
5-game series
A.L.—.995—New York vs. Baltimore, 1996.
N.L.—.994—San Diego vs. Chicago, 1984.
6-game series
N.L.—.996—New York vs. Houston, 1986.
    San Diego vs. Atlanta, 1998.
A.L.—.995—New York vs. Seattle, 2000.
7-game series
N.L.—.992—Atlanta vs. Pittsburgh, 1992.
A.L.—.984—Toronto vs. Kansas City, 1985.

For a list of fielding statistics by teams each series, see page 458.

Highest fielding average by both clubs, series

3-game series
N.L.—.996—Pittsburgh 1.000, Cincinnati .992, 1979.
A.L.—.995—Oakland 1.000, Baltimore .991, 1971.
4-game series
A.L.—.986—Boston .993, Oakland .979, 1988.
N.L.—.985—Cincinnati .987, Atlanta .983, 1995.
5-game series
N.L.—.989—San Diego .994, Chicago .983, 1984.
A.L.—.987—New York .995, Baltimore .980, 1996.
6-game series
A.L.—.991—New York .995, Seattle .986, 2000.
N.L.—.985—New York .996, Houston .973, 1986.
7-game series
N.L.—.986—Atlanta .992, Pittsburgh .980, 1992.
A.L.—.981—Toronto .984, Kansas City .979, 1985.

Lowest fielding average, series

3-game series
A.L.—.940—Kansas City vs. Detroit, 1984.
N.L.—.950—Atlanta vs. New York, 1969.
4-game series
N.L.—.957—Los Angeles vs. Pittsburgh, 1974.
A.L.—.968—Boston vs. Oakland, 1990.
5-game series
A.L.—.945—Boston vs. New York, 1999.
N.L.—.962—St. Louis vs. New York, 2000.
6-game series
A.L.—.966—Toronto vs. Oakland, 1992.
N.L.—.968—Philadelphia vs. Atlanta, 1993.
7-game series
N.L.—.969—New York vs. Los Angeles, 1988.
A.L.—.971—California vs. Boston, 1986.

Lowest fielding average by both clubs, series

3-game series
A.L.—.958—Boston .966, Oakland .950, 1975.
N.L.—.965—New York .981, Atlanta .950, 1969.
4-game series
N.L.—.964—Pittsburgh .973, Los Angeles .957, 1974.
A.L.—.978—California .986, Baltimore .970, 1979.
5-game series
A.L.—.961—New York .977, Boston .945, 1999.
N.L.—.970—New York .978, St. Louis .962, 2000.
6-game series
A.L.—.967—Oakland .969, Toronto .966, 1992.
N.L.—.971—Atlanta .971, New York .970, 1999.

7-game series
A.L.—.973—Boston .975, California .971, 1986.
N.L.—.975—New York .969, Los Angeles .981, 1988.

PUTOUTS

Most putouts, total series

N.L.—1,620—Atlanta; 11 series, 60 games.
A.L.—1,263—New York; 10 series, 47 games.

Most putouts, series

3-game series
A.L.—96—Baltimore vs. Minnesota, 1969.
N.L.—90—Pittsburgh vs. Cincinnati, 1979.
4-game series
N.L.—117—Atlanta vs. Cincinnati, 1995.
A.L.—111—Baltimore vs. Chicago, 1983.
5-game series
N.L.—148—Philadelphia vs. Houston, 1980.
A.L.—141—New York vs. Baltimore, 1996.
6-game series
N.L.—189—New York vs. Houston, 1986.
A.L.—174—Baltimore vs. Cleveland, 1997.
    Cleveland vs. Baltimore, 1997.
7-game series
A.L.—196—Boston vs. California, 1986.
N.L.—195—Los Angeles vs. New York, 1988.

Most putouts by both clubs, series

3-game series
A.L.—190—Baltimore 96, Minnesota 94, 1969.
N.L.—177—Pittsburgh 90, Cincinnati 87, 1979.
4-game series
N.L.—228—Atlanta 117, Cincinnati 111, 1995.
A.L.—219—Baltimore 111, Chicago 108, 1983.
5-game series
N.L.—295—Philadelphia 148, Houston 147, 1980.
A.L.—279—New York 141, Baltimore 138, 1996.
6-game series
N.L.—377—New York 189, Houston 188, 1986.
A.L.—348—Baltimore 174, Cleveland 174, 1997.
7-game series
A.L.—388—Boston 196, California 192, 1986.
N.L.—387—Los Angeles 195, New York 192, 1988.

Fewest putouts, series

3-game series
A.L.—75—Oakland vs. Baltimore, 1971.
    Oakland vs. Boston, 1975.
    New York vs. Kansas City, 1980.
    Oakland vs. New York, 1981.
N.L.—76—Atlanta vs. St. Louis, 1982.
4-game series
A.L.—102—Kansas City vs. New York, 1978.
    Boston vs. Oakland, 1988, 1990.
N.L.—102—San Francisco vs. Pittsburgh, 1971.
    Los Angeles vs. Philadelphia, 1983.
5-game series
A.L.—126—California vs. Milwaukee, 1982.
N.L.—126—Chicago vs. San Francisco, 1989.
6-game series
N.L.—154—Los Angeles vs. St. Louis, 1985.
A.L.—156—Seattle vs. New York, 2000.
7-game series
N.L.—180—San Francisco vs. St. Louis, 1987.
    St. Louis vs. Atlanta, 1996.
A.L.—186—Toronto vs. Kansas City, 1985.

Fewest putouts by both clubs, series

3-game series
A.L.—156—Baltimore 81, Oakland 75, 1971.
    Boston 81, Oakland 75, 1975.
    Kansas City 81, New York 75, 1980.
    New York 81, Oakland 75, 1981.
N.L.—157—St. Louis 81, Atlanta 76, 1982.

4-game series
 A.L.—207—New York 105, Kansas City 102, 1978.
 N.L.—207—Pittsburgh 105, San Francisco 102, 1971.
  Philadelphia 105, Los Angeles 102, 1983.
5-game series
 A.L.—255—Milwaukee 129, California 126, 1982.
 N.L.—256—Chicago 129, San Diego 127, 1984.
6-game series
 N.L.—310—St. Louis 156, Los Angeles 154, 1985.
 A.L.—315—New York 159, Seattle 156, 2000.
7-game series
 N.L.—363—St. Louis 183, San Francisco 180, 1987.
  Atlanta 183, St. Louis 180, 1996.
 A.L.—374—Kansas City 188, Toronto 186, 1985.

Most players with one or more putouts, nine-inning game
A.L.—11
 Oakland vs. New York, October 14, 1981.
 Toronto vs. Oakland, October 7, 1989.
 Seattle vs. New York, October 17, 2000.
N.L.—11—Atlanta vs. San Diego, October 10, 1998.

Most players with one or more putouts, extra-inning game
N.L.—14—New York vs. Houston, October 15, 1986, 16 innings.
A.L.—11
 Kansas City vs. Detroit, October 3, 1984, 11 innings.
 California vs. Boston, October 12, 1986, 11 innings.
 Boston vs. California, October 12, 1986, 11 innings.

Most players with one or more putouts by both clubs, nine-inning game
N.L.—21—Atlanta 11, San Diego 10, October 10, 1998.
A.L.—21—Seattle 11, New York 10, October 17, 2000.

Most players with one or more putouts by both clubs, extra-inning game
N.L.—23
 New York 14, Houston 9, October 15, 1986, 16 innings.
 Atlanta 12, New York 11, October 19, 1999, 11 innings.
A.L.—22—Boston 11, California 11, October 12, 1986, 11 innings.

Most putouts by outfield, game
N.L.—18—Pittsburgh vs. Cincinnati, October 7, 1972.
A.L.—14
 Boston vs. Oakland, October 4, 1975.
 New York vs. Kansas City, October 13, 1976.

Most putouts by outfield of both clubs, game
A.L.—26—New York 14, Kansas City 12, October 13, 1976.
N.L.—25—Pittsburgh 18, Cincinnati 7, October 7, 1972.

Fewest putouts by outfield, nine-inning game
N.L.—1
 Atlanta vs. New York, October 4, 1969.
 Cincinnati vs. Pittsburgh, October 5, 1970.
 Montreal vs. Los Angeles, October 16, 1981.
A.L.—2
 Oakland vs. Boston, October 5, 1975; fielded eight innings.
 Milwaukee vs. California, October 8, 1982.
 Baltimore vs. Chicago, October 5, 1983.
 Boston vs. Oakland, October 10, 1990; fielded eight innings.
 Cleveland vs. Seattle, October 10, 1995; fielded eight innings.
 Cleveland vs. New York, October 11, 1998.

Fewest putouts by outfield, extra-inning game
N.L.—3—Cincinnati vs. Pittsburgh, October 3, 1970, 10 innings.
A.L.—3—Baltimore vs. Cleveland, October 11, 1997, fielded 11.1 innings of 12-inning game.

Fewest putouts by outfield of both clubs, nine-inning game
N.L.—5—Pittsburgh 4, Cincinnati 1, October 5, 1970.
A.L.—7—Minnesota 4, Baltimore 3, October 3, 1970.

Fewest putouts by outfield of both clubs, extra-inning game
A.L.—9—Cleveland 6, Baltimore 3, October 11, 1997, 12 innings.
N.L.—11—Cincinnati 9, Atlanta 2, October 10, 1995, 11 innings.

Most putouts by outfield, inning
A.L.-N.L.—3—Held by many clubs.

Most putouts by outfield of both clubs, inning
A.L.—6—Baltimore 3, Oakland 3, October 11, 1973, seventh inning.
N.L.—5
 New York 3, Atlanta 2, October 5, 1969, seventh inning.
 Pittsburgh 3, Cincinnati 2, October 7, 1972, third inning.
 Los Angeles 3, Philadelphia 2, October 7, 1978, third inning.
 St. Louis 3, Atlanta 2, October 9, 1996, sixth inning.

Most putouts by catchers of both clubs, inning
A.L.-N.L.—5—Occurred in many innings.

ASSISTS

Most assists, total series
N.L.—613—Atlanta; 11 series, 60 games.
A.L.—454—New York; 10 series, 47 games.

Most assists, series
3-game series
 A.L.—41—New York vs. Kansas City, 1980.
 N.L.—39—Cincinnati vs. Pittsburgh, 1970, 1979.
  Atlanta vs. St. Louis, 1982.
4-game series
 N.L.—54—Atlanta vs. Cincinnati, 1995.
 A.L.—52—Baltimore vs. California, 1979.
5-game series
 N.L.—71—Philadelphia vs. Houston, 1980.
 A.L.—60—New York vs. Kansas City, 1976.
6-game series
 N.L.—94—New York vs. Houston, 1986.
 A.L.—77—Cleveland vs. New York, 1998.
7-game series
 A.L.—87—Kansas City vs. Toronto, 1985.
 N.L.—77—San Francisco vs. St. Louis, 1987.

Most assists by both clubs, series
3-game series
 N.L.—76—Cincinnati 39, Pittsburgh 37, 1970.
 A.L.—73—Oakland 40, Boston 33, 1975.
4-game series
 A.L.—100—Chicago 51, Baltimore 49, 1983.
 N.L.—97—Atlanta 54, Cincinnati 43, 1995.
5-game series
 N.L.—123—Philadelphia 71, Houston 52, 1980.
 A.L.—111—New York 60, Kansas City 51, 1976.
6-game series
 N.L.—160—New York 94, Houston 66, 1986.
 A.L.—131—Cleveland 77, New York 54, 1998.
7-game series
 A.L.—151—California 78, Boston 73, 1986.
 N.L.—144—San Francisco 77, St. Louis 67, 1987.

Fewest assists, series
3-game series
 A.L.—15—Oakland vs. Baltimore, 1971.
 N.L.—20—Pittsburgh vs. Cincinnati, 1975.
4-game series
 A.L.—30—Oakland vs. Boston, 1988.
 N.L.—32—Pittsburgh vs. San Francisco, 1971.
5-game series
 N.L.—38—Pittsburgh vs. Cincinnati, 1972.
 A.L.—38—New York vs. Boston, 1999.
6-game series
 N.L.—45—Cincinnati vs. Pittsburgh, 1980.
 A.L.—54—New York vs. Cleveland, 1998.
  New York vs. Seattle, 2000.
7-game series
 N.L.—55—Atlanta vs. St. Louis, 1996.
 A.L.—61—Toronto vs. Kansas City, 1985.

Fewest assists by both clubs, series
3-game series
 A.L.—46—Baltimore 31, Oakland 15, 1971.
 N.L.—51—Cincinnati 31, Pittsburgh 20, 1975.

4-game series
A.L.—64—Boston 34, Oakland 30, 1988.
N.L.—69—San Francisco 37, Pittsburgh 32, 1971.
5-game series
A.L.—78—New York 40, Boston 38, 1999.
N.L.—88—St. Louis 49, New York 39, 2000.
6-game series
N.L.—101—Atlanta 54, Philadelphia 47, 1993.
A.L.—112—Seattle 58, New York 54, 2000.
7-game series
N.L.—117—St. Louis 62, Atlanta 55, 1996.
A.L.—148—Kansas City 87, Toronto 61, 1985.

Most assists, nine-inning game
N.L.—21—Los Angeles vs. Philadelphia, October 5, 1978.
A.L.—18—Boston vs. Oakland, October 7, 1975.

Most assists, extra-inning game
N.L.—31—New York vs. Houston, October 15, 1986, 16 innings.
A.L.—18—Toronto vs. Oakland, October 11, 1992, 11 innings.

Most assists by both clubs, nine-inning game
A.L.—33—Boston 18, Oakland 15, October 7, 1975.
N.L.—30—Los Angeles 21, Philadelphia 9, October 5, 1978.

Most assists by both clubs, extra-inning game
N.L.—56—New York 31, Houston 25, October 15, 1986, 16 innings.
A.L.—Less than nine-inning record.

Most players with one or more assists, nine-inning game
N.L.—9
Los Angeles vs. Montreal, October 14, 1981.
Atlanta vs. Pittsburgh, October 13, 1992.
A.L.—9—Oakland vs. New York, October 14, 1981.

Most players with one or more assists, extra-inning game
N.L.—10—New York vs. Houston, October 15, 1986, 16 innings.
A.L.—Less than nine-inning record.

Most players with one or more assists by both clubs, nine-inning game
N.L.—13
New York 7, Atlanta 6, October 4, 1969.
Pittsburgh 7, Cincinnati 6, October 9, 1972.
Cincinnati 8, New York 5, October 10, 1973.
Los Angeles 9, Montreal 4, October 14, 1981.
Atlanta 7, St. Louis 6, October 9, 1982.
San Francisco 7, St. Louis 6, October 14, 1987.
A.L.—15—Oakland 9, New York 6, October 14, 1981.

Most players with one or more assists by both clubs, extra-inning game
N.L.—19—New York 10, Houston 9, October 15, 1986, 16 innings.
A.L.—Less than nine-inning record.

Fewest assists, game
A.L.—2—Boston vs. Oakland, October 4, 1975.
N.L.—2
Pittsburgh vs. Cincinnati, October 7, 1972.
Pittsburgh vs. Cincinnati, October 7, 1975, 10 innings.

Fewest assists by both clubs, game
N.L.—7—Atlanta 4, St. Louis 3, October 9, 1996.
A.L.—10
Toronto 6, Oakland 4, October 3, 1989.
Seattle 5, New York 5, October 14, 2000.

Most assists by outfield, nine-inning game
N.L.—3—New York vs. Atlanta, October 15, 1999.
A.L.—2
Minnesota vs. Baltimore, October 4, 1970.
Boston vs. Oakland, October 5, 1975.
Baltimore vs. California, October 5, 1979.

Most assists by outfield, extra-inning game
N.L.—3—Philadelphia vs. Houston, October 11, 1980, 10 innings.
A.L.—Less than nine-inning record.

Most assists by outfield of both clubs, nine-inning game
N.L.—3
Pittsburgh 2, Cincinnati 1, October 9, 1972.
New York 3, Atlanta 0, October 15, 1999.
A.L.—3
Minnesota 2, Baltimore 1, October 4, 1970.
Boston 2, Oakland 1, October 5, 1975.
Baltimore 2, California 1, October 5, 1979.

Most assists by outfield of both clubs, extra-inning game
N.L.—4—Philadelphia 3, Houston 1, October 11, 1980, 10 innings.
A.L.—Less than nine-inning record.

Most assists by outfield, inning
N.L.—2—Cincinnati vs. New York, October 10, 1973, fifth inning.
A.L.—1—Held by many clubs.

CHANCES OFFERED

Fewest chances offered to outfield, nine-inning game
N.L.—1
Cincinnati vs. Pittsburgh, October 5, 1970.
Montreal vs. Los Angeles, October 16, 1981.
A.L.—2
Kansas City vs. New York, October 7, 1978.
Milwaukee vs. California, October 8, 1982.
Cleveland vs. New York, October 11, 1998.

Fewest chances offered to outfield, extra-inning game
N.L.—3—Cincinnati vs. Pittsburgh, October 3, 1970, 10 innings.
A.L.—3—Baltimore vs. Cleveland, October 11, 1997, fielded 11.1 innings of 12-inning game.

Fewest chances offered to outfields of both clubs, nine-inning game
N.L.—5—Pittsburgh 4, Cincinnati 1, October 5, 1970.
A.L.—7—Minnesota 4, Baltimore 3, October 3, 1970.

Fewest chances offered to outfields of both clubs, extra-inning game
A.L.—9—Cleveland 6, Baltimore 3, October 11, 1997, 12 innings.
N.L.—12—Cincinnati 7, Pittsburgh 5, October 2, 1979, 11 innings.

ERRORS

Most errors, total series
N.L.—51—Atlanta; 11 series, 60 games.
A.L.—33—Oakland; 10 series, 42 games.

Most errors, series
3-game series
A.L.—7—Kansas City vs. Detroit, 1984.
N.L.—6—Atlanta vs. New York, 1969.
4-game series
N.L.—7—Los Angeles vs. Pittsburgh, 1974.
A.L.—5—Baltimore vs. California, 1979.
Boston vs. Oakland, 1990.
5-game series
A.L.—10—Boston vs. New York, 1999.
N.L.—7—St. Louis vs. New York, 2000.
Atlanta vs. Arizona, 2001.
6-game series
A.L.—8—Toronto vs. Oakland, 1992.
N.L.—8—Atlanta vs. San Diego, 1998.
New York vs. Atlanta, 1999.
7-game series
A.L.—8—California vs. Boston, 1986.
N.L.—8—New York vs. Los Angeles, 1988.

Most errors by both clubs, series
3-game series
A.L.—10—Oakland 6, Boston 4, 1975.
N.L.—8—Atlanta 6, New York 2, 1969.

-game series
  N.L.—11—Los Angeles 7, Pittsburgh 4, 1974.
  A.L.—7—Baltimore 5, California 2, 1979.
-game series
  A.L.—14—Boston 10, New York 4, 1999.
  N.L.—11—St. Louis 7, New York 4, 2000.
-game series
  A.L.—15—Toronto 8, Oakland 7, 1992.
  N.L.—15—New York 8, Atlanta 7, 1999.
-game series
  A.L.—15—California 8, Boston 7, 1986.
  N.L.—13—New York 8, Los Angeles 5, 1988.

Fewest errors, series
3-game series
  A.L.—0—Baltimore vs. Minnesota, 1970.
        Oakland vs. Baltimore, 1971.
  N.L.—0—Pittsburgh vs. Cincinnati, 1970.
4-game series
  A.L.—1—New York vs. Kansas City, 1978.
        Boston vs. Oakland, 1988.
        Oakland vs. Boston, 1990.
  N.L.—1—Los Angeles vs. Philadelphia, 1983.
5-game series
  N.L.—1—San Diego vs. Chicago, 1984.
  A.L.—1—New York vs. Baltimore, 1996.
        Seattle vs. New York, 2001.
6-game series
  N.L.—1—New York vs. Houston, 1986.
        San Diego vs. Atlanta, 1998.
  A.L.—1—New York vs. Seattle, 2000.
7-game series
  N.L.—3—St. Louis vs. San Francisco, 1987.
  A.L.—4—Toronto vs. Kansas City, 1985.

Fewest errors by both clubs, series
3-game series
  A.L.—1—Baltimore 1, Oakland 0, 1971.
  N.L.—1—Cincinnati 1, Pittsburgh 0, 1979.
4-game series
  A.L.—4—Oakland 3, Boston 1, 1988.
  N.L.—5—Atlanta 3, Philadelphia 2, 1995.
5-game series
  N.L.—4—Chicago 3, San Diego 1, 1984.
  A.L.—5—Oakland 3, Toronto 2, 1989.
        Baltimore 4, New York 1, 1996.
        New York 4, Seattle 1, 2001.
6-game series
  A.L.—4—Seattle 3, New York 1, 2000.
  N.L.—7—Pittsburgh 5, Cincinnati 2, 1990.
        Atlanta 4, Florida 3, 1997.
7-game series
  N.L.—9—San Francisco 6, St. Louis 3, 1987.
  A.L.—10—Kansas City 6, Toronto 4, 1985.

Most errors, game
  A.L.—5—New York vs. Kansas City, October 10, 1976.
  N.L.—5—Los Angeles vs. Pittsburgh, October 8, 1974.

Most errors by both clubs, game
  A.L.—7—Oakland 4, Boston 3, October 4, 1975.
  N.L.—5—Los Angeles 5, Pittsburgh 0, October 8, 1974.

Most errors by infield, game
  A.L.—3
  Oakland vs. Baltimore, October 9, 1973, 11 innings.
  California vs. Boston, October 8, 1986.
  N.L.—3—Atlanta vs. Arizona, October 20, 2001.

Most errors by infields of both clubs, game
  A.L.—5—California 3, Boston 2, October 8, 1986.
  N.L.—3
  Atlanta 2, New York 1, October 5, 1969.
  Pittsburgh 2, Cincinnati 1, October 10, 1972.
  New York 2, Los Angeles 1, October 9, 1988, 12 innings.
  Atlanta 3, Arizona 0, October 20, 2001.

Most errors by outfield, game
  A.L.—2
  Minnesota vs. Baltimore, October 6, 1969.
  Oakland vs. Boston, October 4, 1975.
  Milwaukee vs. California, October 10, 1982.
  Cleveland vs. Seattle, October 16, 1995.
  Cleveland vs. Baltimore, October 9, 1997.
  New York vs. St. Louis, October 11, 2000.
  N.L.—1—Held by many clubs.

Most errors by outfields of both clubs, game
  A.L.—3
  Oakland 2, Boston 1, October 4, 1975.
  Cleveland 2, Seattle 1, October 16, 1995.
  N.L.—1—Made in many games.

Longest errorless game
  N.L.—16 innings—New York vs. Houston, October 15, 1986.
  A.L.—12 innings—Cleveland vs. Baltimore, October 11, 1997.

Longest errorless game by both clubs
  N.L.—11 innings
  Pittsburgh vs. Cincinnati, October 2, 1979.
  Atlanta vs. Cincinnati, October 16, 1995.
  A.L.—11 innings
  California vs. Boston, October 12, 1986.
  Cleveland vs. Baltimore, October 15, 1997.

Most errors, inning
  A.L.—3
  Oakland vs. Boston, October 4, 1975, first inning.
  California vs. Boston, October 8, 1986, seventh inning.
  N.L.—3—Atlanta vs. Arizona, October 20, 2001, third inning.

PASSED BALLS

Most passed balls, total series
  N.L.—6
  Pittsburgh; nine series, 42 games.
  Atlanta; 11 series, 60 games.
  A.L.—4
  Oakland; 10 series, 42 games.
  Toronto; four series, 23 games.
  New York; 10 series, 47 games.

Most passed balls, series
  A.L.—3—Toronto vs. Oakland, 1992 (6-game series).
  N.L.—2
  Pittsburgh vs. Cincinnati, 1975 (3-game series).
  Houston vs. New York, 1986 (6-game series).
  Chicago vs. San Francisco, 1989 (5-game series).
  Pittsburgh vs. Atlanta, 1992 (7-game series).
  Philadelphia vs. Atlanta, 1993 (6-game series).

Most passed balls by both clubs, series
  N.L.—3
  Chicago 2, San Francisco 1, 1989 (5-game series).
  Pittsburgh 2, Atlanta 1, 1992 (7-game series).
  A.L.—3—Toronto 3, Oakland 0, 1992 (6-game series).

Most passed balls, game
  N.L.—2
  Pittsburgh vs. Cincinnati, October 4, 1975.
  Houston vs. New York, October 11, 1986.
  Pittsburgh vs. Atlanta, October 13, 1992.
  A.L.—2—Toronto vs. Oakland, October 14, 1992.

Most passed balls, inning
  A.L.-N.L.—1—Held by many clubs.

DOUBLE AND TRIPLE PLAYS

Most double plays, total series
  N.L.—47—Atlanta; 11 series, 60 games.
  A.L.—39—Oakland; 10 series, 42 games.

Most double plays, series
3-game series
  A.L.—6—New York vs. Oakland, 1981.
  N.L.—4—Atlanta vs. New York, 1969.

4-game series
N.L.—8—Los Angeles vs. Pittsburgh, 1974.
A.L.—7—California vs. Baltimore, 1979.
5-game series
N.L.—8—Montreal vs. Los Angeles, 1981.
A.L.—7—Baltimore vs. New York, 1996.
New York vs. Boston, 1999.
6-game series
A.L.—11—Cleveland vs. Baltimore, 1997.
N.L.—9—New York vs. Atlanta, 1999.
7-game series
N.L.—10—San Francisco vs. St. Louis, 1987.
A.L.—7—Kansas City vs. Toronto, 1985.
California vs. Boston, 1986.

Most double plays by both clubs, series
3-game series
A.L.—8—Minnesota 5, Baltimore 3, 1970.
N.L.—6—Atlanta 4, New York 2, 1969.
Cincinnati 3, Philadelphia 3, 1976.
4-game series
A.L.—12—California 7, Baltimore 5, 1979.
N.L.—11—Atlanta 7, Cincinnati 4, 1995.
5-game series
N.L.—13—Montreal 8, Los Angeles 5, 1981.
A.L.—9—Oakland 5, Detroit 4, 1972.
Toronto 5, Oakland 4, 1989.
Seattle 5, New York 4, 2001.
6-game series
A.L.—15—Cleveland 11, Baltimore 4, 1997.
N.L.—13—New York 9, Atlanta 4, 1999.
7-game series
N.L.—15—San Francisco 10, St. Louis 5, 1987.
A.L.—12—California 7, Boston 5, 1986.

Fewest double plays, series
3-game series
N.L.—0—Atlanta vs. St. Louis, 1982.
A.L.—0—Detroit vs. Kansas City, 1984.
4-game series
N.L.—0—Philadelphia vs. Los Angeles, 1983.
A.L.—2—New York vs. Kansas City, 1978.
Boston vs. Oakland, 1988.
5-game series
A.L.—0—Boston vs. New York, 1999.
N.L.—1—Chicago vs. San Francisco, 1989.
New York vs. St. Louis, 2000.

6-game series
N.L.—1—Atlanta vs. Philadelphia, 1993.
A.L.—4—Cleveland vs. Seattle, 1995.
Baltimore vs. Cleveland, 1997.
Seattle vs. New York, 2000.
7-game series
N.L.—2—New York vs. Los Angeles, 1988.
A.L.—4—Toronto vs. Kansas City, 1985.

Fewest double plays by both clubs, series
3-game series
A.L.—2—Kansas City 2, Detroit 0, 1984.
N.L.—3—St. Louis 3, Atlanta 0, 1982.
4-game series
N.L.—3—Los Angeles 3, Philadelphia 0, 1983.
A.L.—6—Kansas City 4, New York 2, 1978.
5-game series
A.L.—4—Kansas City 2, New York 2, 1977.
Minnesota 3, Detroit 1, 1987.
N.L.—4—St. Louis 3, New York 1, 2000.
6-game series
N.L.—3—Philadelphia 2, Atlanta 1, 1993.
A.L.—9—New York 5, Seattle 4, 2000.
7-game series
N.L.—9—Atlanta 6, Pittsburgh 3, 1991.
Pittsburgh 6, Atlanta 3, 1992.
A.L.—10—Boston 5, California 5, 1986.

Most double plays, nine-inning game
N.L.—4
Los Angeles vs. Montreal, October 13, 1981.
San Francisco vs. St. Louis, October 10, 1987.
A.L.—4—Oakland vs. Boston, October 5, 1975.

Most double plays, extra-inning game
N.L.—5—Atlanta vs. Cincinnati, October 10, 1995, 11 innings.
A.L.—4—Cleveland vs. Baltimore, October 11, 1997, 12 innings.

Most double plays by both clubs, game
A.L.—6—Oakland 4, Boston 2, October 5, 1975.
N.L.—6—Atlanta 5, Cincinnati 1, October 10, 1995, 11 innings.
N.L. nine-inning record—5—Pittsburgh 3, Cincinnati 2, October 5, 1975.

Most triple plays, series
A.L.-N.L.—Never accomplished.

CHAMPIONSHIP SERIES *Club fielding*

MISCELLANEOUS

CLUB AND DIVISION
ONE-RUN DECISIONS

Most one-run games won, series
N.L.—3
  New York vs. Houston, 1986 (6-game series).
  Atlanta vs. New York, 1999 (6-game series).
A.L.—4—Cleveland vs. Baltimore, 1997 (6-game series).

Most one-run games by both clubs, series
N.L.—5—Atlanta (won three) vs. New York (won two), 1999 (6-game series).
A.L.—4—Cleveland (won four) vs. Baltimore, 1997 (6-game series).

LENGTH OF GAMES
BY INNINGS

Longest game
N.L.—16 innings—New York 7, Houston 6, October 15, 1986 (at Houston).
A.L.—12 innings
  Baltimore 4, Minnesota 3, October 4, 1969 (at Baltimore).
  Cleveland 2, Baltimore 1, October 11, 1997 (at Cleveland).
  Cleveland 4, New York 1, October 7, 1998 (at New York).

For a complete list of extra-inning games, see page 452.

Most extra-inning games, total series
A.L.—8—Baltimore; nine series, 37 games (won four, lost four).
N.L.—8—Atlanta; 11 series, 60 games (won three, lost five).

Most extra-inning games won, total series
A.L.—4—Baltimore; nine series, 37 games; lost four.
N.L.—4—Philadelphia; six series, 26 games; lost none.

Most extra-inning games lost, total series
N.L.—5—Atlanta; 11 series, 60 games; won three.
A.L.—4—Baltimore; nine series, 37 games; won four.

Most extra-inning games, series
N.L.—4—Philadelphia vs. Houston, 1980 (5-game series).
A.L.—2—Occurred often.

BY TIME

Longest nine-inning game
A.L.—4 hours, 14 minutes—Seattle 6, New York 2, October 15, 2000 (at Seattle).
N.L.—3 hours, 59 minutes—New York 6, St. Louis 5, October 12, 2000 (at St. Louis).

Longest extra-inning game
N.L.—5 hours, 46 minutes—New York 4, Atlanta 3, October 17, 1999, 15 innings (at New York).
A.L.—4 hours, 51 minutes—Cleveland 2, Baltimore 1, October 11, 1997, 12 innings (at Cleveland).

Shortest game
A.L.—1 hour, 57 minutes—Oakland 1, Baltimore 0, October 8, 1974 (at Baltimore).
N.L.—1 hour, 57 minutes—Pittsburgh 5, Cincinnati 1, October 7, 1972 (at Pittsburgh).

SERIES STARTING AND FINISHING DATES

Earliest date for series game
N.L.—October 2, 1971—Pittsburgh at San Francisco.
  October 2, 1979—Pittsburgh at Cincinnati, 11 innings.
  October 2, 1984—San Diego at Chicago.
A.L.—October 2, 1984—Detroit at Kansas City.

Earliest date for series final game
N.L.—October 5, 1970—Pittsburgh at Cincinnati (3-game series).
  October 5, 1979—Cincinnati at Pittsburgh (3-game series).
A.L.—October 5, 1970—Minnesota at Baltimore (3-game series).
  October 5, 1971—Baltimore at Oakland (3-game series).
  October 5, 1984—Kansas City at Detroit (3-game series).

Latest date for series start
A.L.—October 17, 2001—New York at Seattle.
N.L.—October 16, 2001—Atlanta at Arizona.

Latest date for series finish
A.L.—October 22, 2001—Seattle at New York (5-game series).
N.L.—October 21, 2001—Arizona at Atlanta (5-game series).

SERIES AND GAMES WON

Most series won
A.L.—9—New York, 1976, 1977, 1978, 1981, 1996, 1998, 1999, 2000, 2001 (lost one).
N.L.—5
  Los Angeles, 1974, 1977, 1978, 1981, 1988 (lost two).
  Cincinnati, 1970, 1972, 1975, 1976, 1990 (lost three).
  Atlanta, 1991, 1992, 1995, 1996, 1999 (lost six).

For complete lists of results, and series played by all teams, see page 451.

Most consecutive years winning series
A.L.—4—New York, 1998 through 2001.
N.L.—2
  Cincinnati, 1975, 1976.
  Los Angeles, 1977, 1978.
  Atlanta, 1991, 1992; 1995, 1996.

Most consecutive series won, division
N.L.—5
  West Division, 1974, 1975, 1976, 1977, 1978.
  West Division, 1988, 1989, 1990, 1991, 1992.
A.L.—5
  East Division, 1975, 1976, 1977, 1978, 1979.
  West Division, 1987, 1988, 1989, 1990, 1991.

Most times winning series in four consecutive games
A.L.—2—Oakland, 1988, 1990.
N.L.—1—Atlanta, 1995.

Most times winning series in three consecutive games
A.L.—3—Baltimore, 1969, 1970, 1971.
N.L.—3—Cincinnati, 1970, 1975, 1976.

Winning series after winning first game
A.L—Accomplished 21 times.
N.L.—Accomplished 22 times.

Winning series after losing first game
A.L.—Accomplished 11 times.
N.L.—Accomplished 10 times.

Winning series after trailing two games to one
N.L.—Cincinnati vs. Pittsburgh, 1972 (5-game series).
  Philadelphia vs. Houston, 1980 (5-game series).
  Los Angeles vs. Montreal, 1981 (5-game series).
  San Diego vs. Chicago, 1984 (5-game series).
  St. Louis vs. Los Angeles, 1985 (5-game series).
  Los Angeles vs. New York, 1988 (7-game series).
  Philadelphia vs. Atlanta, 1993 (6-game series).
  Atlanta vs. St. Louis, 1996 (7-game series).
A.L.—New York vs. Kansas City, 1977 (5-game series).
  Milwaukee vs. California, 1982 (5-game series).
  Kansas City vs. Toronto, 1985 (7-game series).
  Boston vs. California, 1986 (7-game series).
  Cleveland vs. Seattle, 1995 (6-game series).
  New York vs. Cleveland, 1998 (6-game series).

Winning series after trailing three games to one

A.L.—Kansas City vs. Toronto, 1985.
    Boston vs. California, 1986.
N.L.—Atlanta vs. St. Louis, 1996.

Winning series after losing first two games

A.L.—Milwaukee vs. California, 1982 (5-game series).
    Kansas City vs. Toronto, 1985 (7-game series).
N.L.—San Diego vs. Chicago, 1984 (5-game series).
    St. Louis vs. Los Angeles, 1985 (6-game series).

Most games won, total series

A.L.—32—New York; 10 series; won 32, lost 15.
N.L.—27—Atlanta; 11 series; won 27, lost 33.

**For complete lists of results, and games
played by all teams, see page 451.**

Most consecutive games won, total series

A.L.—10—Baltimore, 1969 (3), 1970 (3), 1971 (3), 1973 (first 1).
N.L.—6—Cincinnati, 1975 (3), 1976 (3).

Most consecutive games won, division

A.L.—9—East Division, 1969 (3), 1970 (3), 1971 (3).
N.L.—7—West Division, 1974 (last 1), 1975 (3), 1976 (3).

SERIES AND GAMES LOST

Most series lost

N.L.—7—Pittsburgh, 1970, 1972, 1974, 1975, 1990, 1991, 1992; won two.
A.L.—4
    Kansas City, 1976, 1977, 1978, 1984; won two.
    Oakland, 1971, 1975, 1981, 1992; won six.
    Baltimore, 1973, 1974, 1996, 1997; won five.

**For complete lists of results, and series
played by all teams, see page 451.**

Most consecutive years losing series

A.L.—3—Kansas City, 1976, 1977, 1978.
N.L.—3
    Philadelphia, 1976, 1977, 1978.
    Pittsburgh, 1990, 1991, 1992.

Most games lost, total series

N.L.—33—Atlanta; 11 series; won 27, lost 33.
A.L.—19—Oakland; 10 series; won 23, lost 19.

**For complete lists of results, and games
played by all teams, see page 451.**

Most consecutive games lost, total series

A.L.—8—Boston, 1988 (4), 1990 (4).
N.L.—7—Atlanta, 1969 (3), 1982 (3), 1991 (1).

ATTENDANCE

Largest attendance, series

3-game series
    N.L.—180,338—Cincinnati vs. Philadelphia, 1976.
    A.L.—151,539—Oakland vs. New York, 1981.
4-game series
    N.L.—240,584—Philadelphia vs. Los Angeles, 1977.
    A.L.—195,748—Baltimore vs. Chicago, 1983.
5-game series
    A.L.—284,691—California vs. Milwaukee, 1982.
    N.L.—271,558—New York vs. St. Louis, 2000.
6-game series
    N.L.—343,046—Philadelphia vs. Atlanta, 1993.
    A.L.—309,828—New York vs. Seattle, 2000.

7-game series
    N.L.—396,597—St. Louis vs. San Francisco, 1987.
    A.L.—324,430—Boston vs. California, 1986.

**For a list of attendance each series, see
page 453.**

Smallest attendance, series

3-game series
    A.L.—81,945—Baltimore vs. Minnesota, 1970.
    N.L.—112,943—Pittsburgh vs. Cincinnati, 1970.
4-game series
    A.L.—144,615—Baltimore vs. Oakland, 1974.
    N.L.—157,348—San Francisco vs. Pittsburgh, 1971.
5-game series
    A.L.—175,833—Baltimore vs. Oakland, 1973.
    N.L.—206,630—Arizona vs. Atlanta, 2001.
6-game series
    A.L.—282,431—Cleveland vs. Baltimore, 1997.
    N.L.—299,316—New York vs. Houston, 1986.
7-game series
    A.L.—264,167—Kansas City vs. Toronto, 1985.
    N.L.—369,443—Atlanta vs. Pittsburgh, 1991.

Largest attendance, game

N.L.—65,042—At San Diego, October 11, 1998 (Atlanta 8, San Diego 3).
A.L.—64,406—At California, October 5, 1982 (California 8, Milwaukee 3).

Smallest attendance, game

A.L.—24,265—At Oakland, October 11, 1973 (Oakland 3, Baltimore 0).
N.L.—33,088—At Pittsburgh, October 3, 1970 (Cincinnati 3, Pittsburgh 0).

Largest attendance by each club, game

AMERICAN LEAGUE

Club	Attendance	Date
Baltimore	52,787	Oct. 3, 1979
Boston	35,578	Oct. 4, 1975
		Oct. 5, 1975
California	64,406	Oct. 5, 1982
Chicago	46,635	Oct. 7, 1983
Cleveland	45,081	Oct. 12, 1997
Detroit	52,168	Oct. 5, 1984
Kansas City	42,633	Oct. 9, 1980
Milwaukee	54,968	Oct. 10, 1982
Minnesota	55,245	Oct. 8, 1987
New York	57,181	Oct. 13, 1999
Oakland	49,444	Oct. 4, 1989
Seattle	58,489	Oct. 17, 1995
Toronto	51,889	Oct. 9, 1993

NATIONAL LEAGUE

Club	Attendance	Date
Arizona	49,334	Oct. 17, 2001
Atlanta	52,335	Oct. 19, 1999
Chicago	39,195	Oct. 4, 1989
		Oct. 5, 1989
Cincinnati	56,079	Oct. 12, 1990
Florida	54,890	Oct. 11, 1997
Houston	45,718	Oct. 15, 1986
Los Angeles	55,973	Oct. 5, 1977
Montreal	54,499	Oct. 17, 1981
New York	55,911	Oct. 15, 1999
Philadelphia	65,476	Oct. 8, 1980
Pittsburgh	57,533	Oct. 10, 1991
St. Louis	56,782	Oct. 14, 1996
San Diego	62,779	Oct. 10, 1998
San Francisco	62,084	Oct. 9, 1989

AMERICAN LEAGUE

Club	Attendance	Date
Baltimore	27,608	Oct. 5, 1970
Boston	32,786	Oct. 8, 1986
California	43,199	Oct. 5, 1979
		Oct. 6, 1979
Chicago	45,477	Oct. 8, 1983
Cleveland	43,607	Oct. 16, 1995
Detroit	37,615	Oct. 11, 1972
Kansas City	40,046	Oct. 13, 1985
Milwaukee	50,135	Oct. 8, 1982
Minnesota	26,847	Oct. 3, 1970
New York	48,497	Oct. 14, 1981
Oakland	24,265	Oct. 11, 1973
Seattle	47,644	Oct. 17, 2001
Toronto	32,084	Oct. 16, 1985

NATIONAL LEAGUE

Club	Attendance	Date
Arizona	37,729	Oct. 16, 2001
Atlanta	35,652	Oct. 21, 2001
Chicago	36,282	Oct. 2, 1984
		Oct. 3, 1984
Cincinnati	39,447	Oct. 10, 1972
Florida	51,982	Oct. 12, 1997
Houston	44,131	Oct. 8, 1986
Los Angeles	49,963	Oct. 4, 1983
Montreal	36,491	Oct. 19, 1981
New York	44,672	Oct. 8, 1988
Philadelphia	53,490	Oct. 7, 1983
Pittsburgh	33,088	Oct. 3, 1970
St. Louis	52,250	Oct. 12, 2000
San Diego	58,346	Oct. 4, 1984
San Francisco	40,977	Oct. 2, 1971

NON-PLAYING PERSONNEL

MANAGERS

Most series by manager
Both leagues—10—Bobby Cox, Toronto A.L., 1985; Atlanta N.L.,
1991 through 2001, except 1994 and 2000 (won five, lost five).
N.L.—9—Bobby Cox, Atlanta, 1991 through 2001, except 1994
and 2000 (won five, lost four).
A.L.—6—Earl Weaver, Baltimore, 1969, 1970, 1971, 1973,
1974, 1979 (won four, lost two).

**For a complete list of managers and their
records, see page 460.**

Most championship series winners managed
Both leagues—5—Sparky Anderson, Cincinnati N.L., 1970,
1972, 1975, 1976; Detroit A.L., 1984.
N.L.—5—Bobby Cox, Atlanta, 1991, 1992, 1995, 1996, 1999.
A.L.—5—Joe Torre, New York, 1996, 1998 through 2001.

Most championship series losers managed
Both leagues—5—Bobby Cox, Toronto A.L., 1985; Atlanta N.L.,
1993, 1997, 1998, 2001.
A.L.—3
Whitey Herzog, Kansas City, 1976, 1977, 1978.
Billy Martin, Minnesota, 1969; Detroit, 1972; Oakland, 1981.
Lou Piniella, Seattle, 1995, 2000, 2001.
N.L.—4—Bobby Cox, Atlanta, 1993, 1997, 1998, 2001.

Most different clubs managed, league
A.L.—4—Billy Martin, Minnesota 1970; Detroit 1972; New York
1976, 1977; Oakland 1981.
N.L.—2
Bill Virdon, Pittsburgh 1972; Houston 1980.
Dave Johnson, New York 1986, 1988; Cincinnati 1995.

UMPIRES

Most series umpired
N.L.—10—Bruce Froemming; 52 games.
A.L.—7
Larry Barnett; 36 games.
Jim Evans; 34 games.

Most games umpired
N.L.—52—Bruce Froemming; 10 series.
A.L.—36—Larry Barnett; seven series.

GENERAL REFERENCE

RESULTS
YEAR BY YEAR

*Wild-card team.

AMERICAN LEAGUE

Year	Winner	Loser	Games
1969	Baltimore (East)	Minnesota (West)	3-0
1970	Baltimore (East)	Minnesota (West)	3-0
1971	Baltimore (East)	Oakland (West)	3-0
1972	Oakland (West)	Detroit (East)	3-2
1973	Oakland (West)	Baltimore (East)	3-2
1974	Oakland (West)	Baltimore (East)	3-1
1975	Boston (East)	Oakland (West)	3-0
1976	New York (East)	Kansas City (West)	3-2
1977	New York (East)	Kansas City (West)	3-2
1978	New York (East)	Kansas City (West)	3-1
1979	Baltimore (East)	California (West)	3-1
1980	Kansas City (West)	New York (East)	3-0
1981	New York (East)	Oakland (West)	3-0
1982	Milwaukee (East)	California (West)	3-2
1983	Baltimore (East)	Chicago (West)	3-1
1984	Detroit (East)	Kansas City (West)	3-0
1985	Kansas City (West)	Toronto (East)	4-3
1986	Boston (East)	California (West)	4-3
1987	Minnesota (West)	Detroit (East)	4-1
1988	Oakland (West)	Boston (East)	4-0
1989	Oakland (West)	Toronto (East)	4-1
1990	Oakland (West)	Boston (East)	4-0
1991	Minnesota (West)	Toronto (East)	4-1
1992	Toronto (East)	Oakland (West)	4-2
1993	Toronto (East)	Chicago (West)	4-2
1994	No series played.		
1995	Cleveland (Central)	Seattle (West)	4-2
1996	New York (East)	Baltimore (East)*	4-1
1997	Cleveland (Central)	Baltimore (East)	4-2
1998	New York (East)	Cleveland (Central)	4-2
1999	New York (East)	Boston (East)*	4-1
2000	New York (East)	Seattle (West)*	4-2
2001	New York (East)	Seattle (West)	4-1

NATIONAL LEAGUE

Year	Winner	Loser	Games
1969	New York (East)	Atlanta (West)	3-0
1970	Cincinnati (West)	Pittsburgh (East)	3-0
1971	Pittsburgh (East)	San Francisco (West)	3-1
1972	Cincinnati (West)	Pittsburgh (East)	3-2
1973	New York (East)	Cincinnati (West)	3-2
1974	Los Angeles (West)	Pittsburgh (East)	3-1
1975	Cincinnati (West)	Pittsburgh (East)	3-0
1976	Cincinnati (West)	Philadelphia (East)	3-0
1977	Los Angeles (West)	Philadelphia (East)	3-1
1978	Los Angeles (West)	Philadelphia (East)	3-1
1979	Pittsburgh (East)	Cincinnati (West)	3-0
1980	Philadelphia (East)	Houston (West)	3-2
1981	Los Angeles (West)	Montreal (East)	3-2
1982	St. Louis (East)	Atlanta (West)	3-0
1983	Philadelphia (East)	Los Angeles (West)	3-1
1984	San Diego (West)	Chicago (East)	3-2
1985	St. Louis (East)	Los Angeles (West)	4-2
1986	New York (East)	Houston (West)	4-2
1987	St. Louis (East)	San Francisco (West)	4-3
1988	Los Angeles (West)	New York (East)	4-3
1989	San Francisco (West)	Chicago (East)	4-1
1990	Cincinnati (West)	Pittsburgh (East)	4-2
1991	Atlanta (West)	Pittsburgh (East)	4-3
1992	Atlanta (West)	Pittsburgh (East)	4-3
1993	Philadelphia (East)	Atlanta (West)	4-2
1994	No series played.		
1995	Atlanta (East)	Cincinnati (Central)	4-0
1996	Atlanta (East)	St. Louis (Central)	4-3
1997	Florida (East)*	Atlanta (East)	4-2
1998	San Diego (West)	Atlanta (East)	4-2
1999	Atlanta (East)	New York (East)*	4-2
2000	New York (East)*	St. Louis (Central)	4-1
2001	Arizona (West)	Atlanta (East)	4-1

SERIES WON AND LOST BY TEAMS

AMERICAN LEAGUE

	W	L	Pct.
Milwaukee	1	0	1.000
New York	9	1	.900
Cleveland	2	1	.667
Oakland	6	4	.600
Baltimore	5	4	.556
Minnesota	2	2	.500
Boston	2	3	.400
Toronto	2	3	.400
Detroit	1	2	.333
Kansas City	2	4	.333
Chicago	0	2	.000
California	0	3	.000
Seattle	0	3	.000
Totals	32	32	.500

NATIONAL LEAGUE

	W	L	Pct.
San Diego	2	0	1.000
Arizona	1	0	1.000
Florida	1	0	1.000
Los Angeles	5	2	.714
New York	4	2	.667
Cincinnati	5	3	.625
St. Louis	3	2	.600
Philadelphia	3	3	.500
Atlanta	5	6	.455
San Francisco	1	2	.333
Pittsburgh	2	7	.222
Montreal	0	1	.000
Chicago	0	2	.000
Houston	0	2	.000
Totals	32	32	.500

GAMES WON AND LOST BY TEAMS

AMERICAN LEAGUE

	W	L	Pct.
New York	32	15	.681
Milwaukee	3	2	.600
Baltimore	21	16	.568
Cleveland	10	8	.556
Oakland	23	19	.548
Minnesota	8	8	.500
Detroit	6	7	.462
Toronto	13	16	.448
Kansas City	12	15	.444
California	6	10	.375
Boston	8	15	.348
Seattle	5	12	.294
Chicago	3	7	.300
Totals	150	150	.500

NATIONAL LEAGUE

	W	L	Pct.
Arizona	4	1	.800
Florida	4	2	.667
San Diego	7	4	.636
New York	19	13	.594
Cincinnati	18	14	.563
Los Angeles	19	15	.559
St. Louis	15	13	.536
San Francisco	8	8	.500
Philadelphia	12	14	.462
Atlanta	27	33	.450
Pittsburgh	17	25	.405
Montreal	2	3	.400
Houston	4	7	.364
Chicago	3	7	.300
Totals	159	159	.500

CHAMPIONSHIP SERIES *General reference*

HOME AND ROAD GAMES BY TEAMS

AMERICAN LEAGUE

	Years	Games	Home	Away
New York	10	47	23	24
Oakland	10	42	19	23
Baltimore	9	37	19	18
Toronto	5	29	16	13
Kansas City	6	27	14	13
Boston	5	23	13	10
Cleveland	3	18	9	9
Seattle	3	17	8	9
Minnesota	4	16	7	9
California	3	16	7	9
Detroit	3	13	7	6
Chicago	2	10	5	5
Milwaukee	1	5	3	2
Totals	32	150	150	150

NATIONAL LEAGUE

	Years	Games	Home	Away
Atlanta	11	60	30	30
Pittsburgh	9	42	20	22
Los Angeles	7	34	17	17
Cincinnati	8	32	16	16
New York	6	32	16	16
St. Louis	5	28	14	14
Philadelphia	6	26	13	13
San Francisco	3	16	8	8
Houston	2	11	6	5
San Diego	2	11	6	5
Chicago	2	10	4	6
Florida	1	6	3	3
Arizona	1	5	2	3
Montreal	1	5	3	2
Totals	32	159	159	159

SHUTOUTS

AMERICAN LEAGUE

Oct. 5, 1969   Dave McNally, Baltimore 1, Minnesota 0, 11 innings (three hits).
Oct. 8, 1972   Blue Moon Odom, Oakland 5, Detroit 0 (three hits).
Oct. 10, 1972   Joe Coleman, Detroit 3, Oakland 0 (seven hits).
Oct. 6, 1973   Jim Palmer, Baltimore 6, Oakland 0 (five hits).
Oct. 11, 1973   Catfish Hunter, Oakland 3, Baltimore 0 (five hits).
Oct. 6, 1974   Ken Holtzman, Oakland 5, Baltimore 0 (five hits).
Oct. 8, 1974   Vida Blue, Oakland 1, Baltimore 0 (two hits).
Oct. 6, 1979   Scott McGregor, Baltimore 8, California 0 (six hits).
Oct. 15, 1981   Dave Righetti, Ron Davis and Rich Gossage, New York 4, Oakland 0 (five hits).
Oct. 6, 1983   Mike Boddicker, Baltimore 4, Chicago 0 (five hits).
Oct. 8, 1983   Storm Davis and Tippy Martinez, Baltimore 3, Chicago 0, 10 innings (10 hits).
Oct. 5, 1984   Milt Wilcox and Willie Hernandez, Detroit 1, Kansas City 0 (three hits).
Oct. 13, 1985   Danny Jackson, Kansas City 2, Toronto 0 (eight hits).
Oct. 14, 1995   Ken Hill, Jim Poole, Chad Ogea and Alan Embree, Cleveland 7, Seattle 0 (six hits).
Oct. 17, 1995   Dennis Martinez, Julian Tavares and Jose Mesa, Cleveland 4, Seattle 0 (four hits).
Oct. 8, 1997   Scott Erickson and Randy Myers, Baltimore 3, Cleveland 0 (four hits).
Oct. 15, 1997   Charles Nagy, Paul Assenmacher, Mike Jackson, Brian Anderson and Jose Mesa, Cleveland 1, Baltimore 0, 11 innings (10 hits).
Oct. 10, 1998   Orlando Hernandez, New York 4, Cleveland 0, (four hits).
Oct. 10, 2000   Freddy Garcia, Jose Paniagua, Arthur Rhodes and Kazuhiro Sasaki, Seattle 2, New York 0 (six hits).
Oct. 14, 2000   Roger Clemens, New York 5, Seattle 0 (one hit).
Total number of shutouts: 20

NATIONAL LEAGUE

Oct. 3, 1970   Gary Nolan and Clay Carroll, Cincinnati 3, Pittsburgh 0, 10 innings (eight hits).
Oct. 7, 1973   Jon Matlack, New York 5, Cincinnati 0 (two hits).
Oct. 5, 1974   Don Sutton, Los Angeles 3, Pittsburgh 0 (four hits)
Oct. 8, 1974   Bruce Kison and Ramon Hernandez, Pittsburgh 7, Los Angeles 0 (four hits).
Oct. 4, 1978   Tommy John, Los Angeles 4, Philadelphia 0 (four hits).
Oct. 10, 1980   Joe Niekro and Dave Smith, Houston 1, Philadelphia 0, 11 innings (seven hits).
Oct. 14, 1981   Ray Burris, Montreal 3, Los Angeles 0 (five hits).
Oct. 7, 1982   Bob Forsch, St. Louis 7, Atlanta 0 (three hits).
Oct. 4, 1983   Steve Carlton and Al Holland, Philadelphia 1, Los Angeles 0 (seven hits).
Oct. 2, 1984   Rick Sutcliffe and Warren Brusstar, Chicago 13, San Diego 0 (six hits).
Oct. 8, 1986   Mike Scott, Houston 1, New York 0 (five hits).
Oct. 7, 1987   Dave Dravecky, San Francisco 5, St. Louis 0 (two hits).
Oct. 13, 1987   John Tudor, Todd Worrell and Ken Dayley, St. Louis 1, San Francisco 0 (four hits).
Oct. 14, 1987   Danny Cox, St. Louis 6, San Francisco 0 (eight hits).
Oct. 12, 1988   Orel Hershiser, Los Angeles 6, New York 0 (five hits).
Oct. 10, 1991   Steve Avery and Alejandro Pena, Atlanta 1, Pittsburgh 0 (six hits).
Oct. 14, 1991   Zane Smith and Roger Mason, Pittsburgh 1, Atlanta 0 (nine hits).
Oct. 16, 1991   Steve Avery and Alejandro Pena, Atlanta 1, Pittsburgh 0 (four hits).
Oct. 17, 1991   John Smoltz, Atlanta 4, Pittsburgh 0 (six hits).
Oct. 14, 1995   Steve Avery, Greg McMichael, Alejandro Pena and Mark Wohlers, Atlanta 6, Cincinnati 0 (three hits).
Oct. 14, 1996   John Smoltz, Mike Bielecki, Terrell Wade and Brad Clontz, Atlanta 14, St. Louis 0 (seven hits).
Oct. 17, 1996   Tom Glavine, Mike Bielecki and Steve Avery, Atlanta, 15, St. Louis 0 (four hits).
Oct. 11, 1997   Denny Neagle, Atlanta 4, Florida 0 (four hits).
Oct. 8, 1998   Kevin Brown, San Diego 3, Atlanta 0 (three hits).
Oct. 14, 1998   Sterling Hitchcock, Brian Boehringer, Mark Langston, Joey Hamilton and Trevor Hoffman, San Diego 5, Atlanta 0 (two hits).
Oct. 15, 1999   Tom Glavine, Mike Remlinger and John Rocker, Atlanta 1, New York 0 (seven hits).
Oct. 16, 2000   Mike Hampton, New York 7, St. Louis 0 (three hits).
Oct. 16, 2001   Randy Johnson, Arizona 2, Atlanta 0 (three hits).
Total number of shutouts: 28

EXTRA-INNING GAMES

AMERICAN LEAGUE

Oct. 4, 1969   12 innings, Baltimore 4, Minnesota 3.
Oct. 5, 1969   11 innings, Baltimore 1, Minnesota 0.
Oct. 7, 1972   11 innings, Oakland 3, Detroit 2.
Oct. 11, 1972   10 innings, Detroit 4, Oakland 3.
Oct. 9, 1973   11 innings, Oakland 2, Baltimore 1.
Oct. 3, 1979   10 innings, Baltimore 6, California 3.
Oct. 8, 1983   10 innings, Baltimore 3, Chicago 0.
Oct. 3, 1984   11 innings, Detroit 5, Kansas City 3.
Oct. 9, 1985   10 innings, Toronto 6, Kansas City 5.
Oct. 11, 1986   11 innings, California 4, Boston 3.
Oct. 12, 1986   11 innings, Boston 7, California 6.
Oct. 11, 1991   10 innings, Minnesota 3, Toronto 2.
Oct. 11, 1992   11 innings, Toronto 7, Oakland 6.
Oct. 13, 1995   11 innings, Seattle 5, Cleveland 2.
Oct. 9, 1996   11 innings, New York 5, Baltimore 4.
Oct. 11, 1997   12 innings, Cleveland 2, Baltimore 1.
Oct. 15, 1997   11 innings, Cleveland 1, Baltimore 0.
Oct. 7, 1998   12 innings, Cleveland 4, New York 1.
Oct. 13, 1999   10 innings, New York 4, Boston 3.
Total number of extra-inning games: 19

NATIONAL LEAGUE

Oct. 3, 1970 10 innings, Cincinnati 3, Pittsburgh 0.
Oct. 9, 1973 12 innings, Cincinnati 2, New York 1.
Oct. 7, 1975 10 innings, Cincinnati 5, Pittsburgh 3.
Oct. 7, 1978 10 innings, Los Angeles 4, Philadelphia 3.
Oct. 2, 1979 11 innings, Pittsburgh 5, Cincinnati 4.
Oct. 3, 1979 10 innings, Pittsburgh 3, Cincinnati 2.
Oct. 8, 1980 10 innings, Houston 7, Philadelphia 4.
Oct. 10, 1980 11 innings, Houston 1, Philadelphia 0.
Oct. 11, 1980 10 innings, Philadelphia 5, Houston 3.
Oct. 12, 1980 10 innings, Philadelphia 8, Houston 7.
Oct. 14, 1986 12 innings, New York 2, Houston 1.
Oct. 15, 1986 16 innings, New York 7, Houston 6.
Oct. 9, 1988 12 innings, Los Angeles 5, New York 4.
Oct. 13, 1991 10 innings, Pittsburgh 3, Atlanta 2.
Oct. 6, 1993 10 innings, Philadelphia 4, Atlanta 3.
Oct. 11, 1993 10 innings, Philadelphia 4, Atlanta 3.
Oct. 10, 1995 11 innings, Atlanta 2, Cincinnati 1.
Oct. 11, 1995 10 innings, Atlanta 6, Cincinnati 2.
Oct. 7, 1998 10 innings, San Diego 3, Atlanta 2.
Oct. 17, 1999 15 innings, New York 4, Atlanta 3.
Oct. 19, 1999 11 innings, Atlanta 10, New York 9.

Total number of extra-inning games: 21

ATTENDANCE

AMERICAN LEAGUE

Year	Games	Total
1969	3	113,763
1970	3	81,945
1971	3	110,800
1972	5	189,671
1973	5	175,833
1974	4	144,615
1975	3	120,514
1976	5	252,152
1977	5	234,713
1978	4	194,192
1979	4	191,293
1980	3	141,819
1981	3	151,539
1982	5	284,691
1983	4	195,748
1984	3	136,160
1985	7	264,167
1986	7	324,430
1987	5	257,631
1988	4	167,376
1989	5	249,247
1990	4	168,340
1991	5	263,987
1992	6	293,086
1993	6	292,921
1995	6	304,634
1996	5	259,254
1997	6	282,431
1998	6	323,007
1999	5	214,726
2000	6	309,828
2001	5	264,697

NATIONAL LEAGUE

Year	Games	Total
1969	3	153,587
1970	3	112,943
1971	4	157,348
1972	5	234,814
1973	5	262,548
1974	4	200,262
1975	3	155,740
1976	3	180,338
1977	4	240,584
1978	4	234,269
1979	3	152,246
1980	5	264,950
1981	5	250,098
1982	3	158,589
1983	4	223,914
1984	5	247,623
1985	6	326,824
1986	6	299,316
1987	7	396,597
1988	7	373,695
1989	5	264,617
1990	6	310,528
1991	7	369,443
1992	7	374,599
1993	6	343,046
1995	4	188,497
1996	7	375,202
1997	6	309,352
1998	6	306,259
1999	6	308,637
2000	5	271,558
2001	5	206,630

INDIVIDUAL BATTING
LEADING BATTERS

(Playing in all games, each series, with four or more hits)

AMERICAN LEAGUE

Year	Player, Club	AB	H	TB	Avg.
1969	Brooks Robinson, Baltimore	14	7	8	.500
1970	Brooks Robinson, Baltimore	12	7	9	.583
1971	Brooks Robinson, Baltimore	11	4	8	.364
	Sal Bando, Oakland	11	4	9	.364
1972	Matty Alou, Oakland	21	8	12	.381
1973	Bert Campaneris, Oakland	21	7	14	.333
1974	Ray Fosse, Oakland	12	4	8	.333
1975	Sal Bando, Oakland	12	6	8	.500
1976	Chris Chambliss, New York	21	11	20	.524
1977	Hal McRae, Kansas City	18	8	14	.444
1978	Reggie Jackson, New York	13	6	13	.462
1979	Eddie Murray, Baltimore	12	5	8	.417
1980	Frank White, Kansas City	11	6	10	.545
1981	Graig Nettles, New York	12	6	11	.500
	Jerry Mumphrey, New York	12	6	7	.500
1982	Fred Lynn, California	18	11	16	.611
1983	Cal Ripken Jr., Baltimore	15	6	8	.400
1984	Kirk Gibson, Detroit	12	5	9	.417
1985	Cliff Johnson, Toronto	19	7	9	.368
1986	Bob Boone, California	22	10	13	.455
1987	Tom Brunansky, Minnesota	17	7	17	.412
1988	Ron Hassey, Oakland	8	4	8	.500
1989	Rickey Henderson, Oakland	15	6	15	.400
1990	Wade Boggs, Boston	16	7	11	.438
	Carney Lansford, Oakland	16	7	8	.438
1991	Roberto Alomar, Toronto	19	9	9	.474
1992	Harold Baines, Oakland	25	11	16	.440
1993	Tim Raines Sr., Chicago	27	12	14	.444
	Devon White, Toronto	27	12	18	.444
1994	No series played.				
1995	Kenny Lofton, Cleveland	24	11	15	.458
1996	Bernie Williams, New York	19	9	18	.474
1997	Brady Anderson, Baltimore	25	9	17	.360
1998	Omar Vizquel, Cleveland	25	11	13	.440
1999	Jose Offerman, Boston	24	11	13	.458
2000	Bernie Williams, New York	23	10	14	.435
2001	Paul O'Neill, New York	12	5	11	.417

NATIONAL LEAGUE

Year	Player, Club	AB	H	TB	Avg.
1969	Art Shamsky, New York	13	7	7	.538
1970	Willie Stargell, Pittsburgh	12	6	7	.500
1971	Bob Robertson, Pittsburgh	16	7	20	.438
1972	Pete Rose, Cincinnati	20	9	13	.450
1973	Pete Rose, Cincinnati	21	8	15	.381
1974	Willie Stargell, Pittsburgh	15	6	12	.400
1975	Richie Zisk, Pittsburgh	10	5	6	.500
1976	Jay Johnstone, Philadelphia	9	7	10	.778
1977	Bob Boone, Philadelphia	10	4	4	.400
1978	Dusty Baker, Los Angeles	15	7	9	.467
1979	Willie Stargell, Pittsburgh	11	5	13	.455
1980	Terry Puhl, Houston	19	10	12	.526
1981	Gary Carter, Montreal	16	7	8	.438
1982	Darrell Porter, St. Louis	9	5	8	.556
	Ozzie Smith, St. Louis	9	5	5	.556
1983	Mike Schmidt, Philadelphia	15	7	12	.467
1984	Steve Garvey, San Diego	20	8	12	.400
1985	Ozzie Smith, St. Louis	23	10	16	.435
1986	Lenny Dykstra, New York	23	7	13	.304
1987	Jeffrey Leonard, San Francisco	24	10	22	.417
1988	Lenny Dykstra, New York	14	6	12	.439
1989	Will Clark, San Francisco	20	13	24	.650
1990	Mariano Duncan, Cincinnati	20	6	9	.300
1991	Jay Bell, Pittsburgh	29	12	17	.414
1992	Mark Lemke, Atlanta	21	7	8	.333
1993	Fred McGriff, Atlanta	23	10	15	.435
1994	No series played.				
1995	Chipper Jones, Atlanta	16	7	10	.438
	Fred McGriff, Atlanta	16	7	11	.438
1996	Javy Lopez, Atlanta	24	13	24	.542
1997	Keith Lockhart, Atlanta	16	8	11	.500
1998	Michael Tucker, Atlanta	13	5	9	.385
1999	Eddie Perez, Atlanta	20	10	18	.500
	Roger Cedeno, New York	12	6	7	.500
2000	Edgardo Alfonzo, New York	18	8	11	.444
2001	Craig Counsell, Arizona	21	8	11	.381

CHAMPIONSHIP SERIES *General reference*

.450 HITTERS

(Playing in all games and having nine or more at-bats)

AMERICAN LEAGUE

Player, Club	Year	AB	H	TB	Avg.
Fred Lynn, California	1982	18	11	16	.611
Brooks Robinson, Baltimore	1970	12	7	9	.583
Frank White, Kansas City	1980	11	6	10	.545
Chris Chambliss, New York	1976	21	11	20	.524
Brooks Robinson, Baltimore	1969	14	7	8	.500
Tony Oliva, Minnesota	1970	12	6	11	.500
Sal Bando, Oakland	1975	12	6	8	.500
Bob Watson, New York	1980	12	6	11	.500
Graig Nettles, New York	1981	12	6	11	.500
Jerry Mumphrey, New York	1981	12	6	7	.500
Roberto Alomar, Toronto	1991	19	9	9	.474
Bernie Williams, New York	1996	19	9	18	.474
Reggie Jackson, New York	1978	13	6	13	.462
Larry Milbourne, New York	1981	13	6	6	.462
Charlie Moore, Milwaukee	1982	13	6	6	.462
Jose Offerman, Boston	1999	24	11	13	.458
Carl Yastrzemski, Boston	1975	11	5	9	.455
Mickey Rivers, New York	1978	11	5	5	.455
Bob Boone, California	1986	22	10	13	.455

Total number of occurrences: 19

NATIONAL LEAGUE

Player, Club	Year	AB	H	TB	Avg.
Jay Johnstone, Philadelphia	1976	9	7	10	.778
Will Clark, San Francisco	1989	20	13	24	.650
Mark Grace, Chicago	1989	17	11	19	.647
Darrell Porter, St. Louis	1982	9	5	8	.556
Ozzie Smith, St. Louis	1982	9	5	5	.556
Javy Lopez, Atlanta	1996	24	13	24	.542
Art Shamsky, New York	1969	13	7	7	.538
Terry Puhl, Houston	1980	19	10	12	.526
Keith Lockhart, Atlanta	1997	16	8	11	.500
Eddie Perez, Atlanta	1999	20	10	18	.500
Willie Stargell, Pittsburgh	1970	12	6	7	.500
Roger Cedeno, New York	1999	12	6	7	.500
Richie Zisk, Pittsburgh	1975	10	5	6	.500
Dusty Baker, Los Angeles	1978	15	7	9	.467
Mike Schmidt, Philadelphia	1983	15	7	12	.467
Orlando Cepeda, Atlanta	1969	11	5	10	.455
Dave Concepcion, Cincinnati	1975	11	5	8	.455
Willie Stargell, Pittsburgh	1979	11	5	13	.455
Pete Rose, Cincinnati	1972	20	9	13	.450

Total number of occurrences: 19

HOME RUNS

AMERICAN LEAGUE

1969—4—Baltimore (East), Frank Robinson, Mark Belanger, Boog Powell, Paul Blair.
　1—Minnesota (West), Tony Oliva.
1970—6—Baltimore (East), Dave Johnson 2, Mike Cuellar, Don Buford, Boog Powell, Frank Robinson.
　3—Minnesota (West), Harmon Killebrew 2, Tony Oliva.
1971—4—Baltimore (East), Boog Powell 2, Brooks Robinson, Elrod Hendricks.
　3—Oakland (West), Reggie Jackson 2, Sal Bando.
1972—4—Detroit (East), Norm Cash, Al Kaline, Bill Freehan, Dick McAuliffe.
　1—Oakland (West), Mike Epstein.
1973—5—Oakland (West), Sal Bando 2, Bert Campaneris 2, Joe Rudi.
　3—Baltimore (East), Earl Williams, Andy Etchebarren, Bobby Grich.
1974—3—Baltimore (East), Paul Blair, Brooks Robinson, Bobby Grich.
　3—Oakland (West), Sal Bando 2, Ray Fosse.
1975—2—Boston (East), Carl Yastrzemski, Rico Petrocelli.
　1—Oakland (West), Reggie Jackson.
1976—4—New York (East), Graig Nettles 2, Chris Chambliss 2.
　2—Kansas City (West), John Mayberry, George Brett.

1977—3—Kansas City (West), Hal McRae, John Mayberry, Al Cowens.
　2—New York (East), Thurman Munson, Cliff Johnson.
1978—5—New York (East), Reggie Jackson 2, Thurman Munson, Graig Nettles, Roy White.
　4—Kansas City (West), George Brett 3, Fred Patek.
1979—3—Baltimore (East), John Lowenstein, Eddie Murray, Pat Kelly.
　3—California (West), Dan Ford 2, Don Baylor.
1980—3—New York (East), Rick Cerone, Lou Piniella, Graig Nettles.
　3—Kansas City (West), George Brett 2, Frank White.
1981—3—New York (East), Lou Piniella, Graig Nettles, Willie Randolph.
　0—Oakland (West).
1982—5—Milwaukee (East), Paul Molitor 2, Gorman Thomas, Mark Brouhard, Ben Oglivie.
　4—California (West), Fred Lynn, Reggie Jackson, Bob Boone, Don Baylor.
1983—3—Baltimore (East), Gary Roenicke, Eddie Murray, Tito Landrum.
　0—Chicago (West).
1984—4—Detroit (East), Kirk Gibson, Larry Herndon, Lance Parrish, Alan Trammell.
　0—Kansas City (West).
1985—7—Kansas City (West), George Brett 3, Pat Sheridan 2, Willie Wilson, Jim Sundberg.
　2—Toronto (East), Jesse Barfield, Rance Mulliniks.
1986—7—California (West), Bob Boone, Doug DeCinces, Brian Downing, Bobby Grich, Wally Joyner, Gary Pettis, Dick Schofield.
　6—Boston (East), Jim Rice 2, Don Baylor, Dwight Evans, Rich Gedman, Dave Henderson.
1987—8—Minnesota (West), Tom Brunansky 2, Gary Gaetti 2, Greg Gagne 2, Kent Hrbek, Kirby Puckett.
　7—Detroit (East), Chet Lemon 2, Kirk Gibson, Mike Heath, Matt Nokes, Pat Sheridan, Lou Whitaker.
1988—7—Oakland (West), Jose Canseco 3, Ron Hassey, Dave Henderson, Carney Lansford, Mark McGwire.
　2—Boston (East), Rich Gedman, Mike Greenwell.
1989—7—Oakland (West), Rickey Henderson 2, Dave Parker 2, Jose Canseco, Dave Henderson, Mark McGwire.
　3—Toronto (East), George Bell, Lloyd Moseby, Ernie Whitt.
1990—1—Boston (East), Wade Boggs.
　0—Oakland (West).
1991—3—Minnesota (West), Kirby Puckett 2, Mike Pagliarulo.
　1—Toronto (East), Joe Carter.
1992—10—Toronto (East), Roberto Alomar 2, Candy Maldonado 2, Dave Winfield 2, Pat Borders, Joe Carter, Kelly Gruber, John Olerud.
　4—Oakland (West), Harold Baines, Mark McGwire, Ruben Sierra, Terry Steinbach.
1993—5—Chicago (West), Ellis Burks, Lance Johnson, Warren Newson, Frank Thomas, Robin Ventura.
　2—Toronto (East), Paul Molitor, Devon White.
1994—No series played.
1995—7—Cleveland (Central), Manny Ramirez 2, Jim Thome 2, Carlos Baerga, Albert Belle, Eddie Murray.
　5—Seattle (West), Jay Buhner 3, Mike Blowers, Ken Griffey Jr.
1996—10—New York (East), Darryl Strawberry 3, Cecil Fielder 2, Bernie Williams 2, Derek Jeter 2, Jim Leyritz, Paul O'Neill.
　9—Baltimore (East), Todd Zeile 3, Rafael Palmeiro 2, Brady Anderson, Bobby Bonilla, Chris Hoiles, Eddie Murray.
1997—7—Baltimore (East), Brady Anderson 2, Roberto Alomar, Harold Baines, Eric Davis, Rafael Palmeiro, Cal Ripken Jr.
　5—Cleveland (Central), Manny Ramirez 2, Sandy Alomar Jr., Tony Fernandez, Marquis Grisson.
1998—9—Cleveland (Central), Jim Thome 4, Manny Ramirez 2, David Justice, Kenny Lofton, Mark Whiten.
　4—New York (East), Scott Brosius, Chili Davis, Paul O'Neill, Jorge Posada.

1999—8—New York (East), Scott Brosius 2, Derek Jeter, Ricky Ledee, Tino Martinez, Jorge Posada, Darryl Strawberry, Bernie Williams.

5—Boston (East), Nomar Garciaparra 2, Brian Daubach, John Valentin, Jason Varitek.

2000—6—New York (East), Derek Jeter 2, David Justice 2, Tino Martinez, Bernie Williams.

5—Seattle (West), Alex Rodriguez 2, Carlos Guillen, Edgar Martinez, John Olerud.

2001—7—New York (East), Bernie Williams 3, Paul O'Neill 2, Tino Martinez, Alfonso Soriano.

5—Seattle (West), Bret Boone 2, Jay Buhner, Stan Javier, John Olerud.

Total number of home runs: 268

NATIONAL LEAGUE

1969—6—New York (East), Tommie Agee 2, Ken Boswell 2, Cleon Jones, Wayne Garrett.

5—Atlanta (West), Hank Aaron 3, Tony Gonzalez, Orlando Cepeda.

1970—3—Cincinnati (West), Bobby Tolan, Tony Perez, Johnny Bench.

0—Pittsburgh (East).

1971—8—Pittsburgh (East), Bob Robertson 4, Richie Hebner 2, Gene Clines, Al Oliver.

5—San Francisco (West), Willie McCovey 2, Tito Fuentes, Willie Mays, Chris Speier.

1972—4—Cincinnati (West), Joe Morgan 2, Cesar Geronimo, Johnny Bench.

3—Pittsburgh (East), Al Oliver, Manny Sanguillen, Roberto Clemente.

1973—5—Cincinnati (West), Pete Rose 2, Johnny Bench, Denis Menke, Tony Perez.

3—New York (East), Rusty Staub 3.

1974—3—Los Angeles (West), Steve Garvey 2, Ron Cey.

3—Pittsburgh (East), Willie Stargell 2, Richie Hebner.

1975—4—Cincinnati (West), Don Gullett, Tony Perez, Dave Concepcion, Pete Rose.

1—Pittsburgh (East), Al Oliver.

1976—3—Cincinnati (West), George Foster 2, Johnny Bench.

1—Philadelphia (East), Greg Luzinski.

1977—3—Los Angeles (West), Dusty Baker 2, Ron Cey.

2—Philadelphia (East), Greg Luzinski, Bake McBride.

1978—8—Los Angeles (West), Steve Garvey 4, Dave Lopes 2, Steve Yeager, Ron Cey.

5—Philadelphia (East), Greg Luzinski 2, Jerry Martin, Steve Carlton, Bake McBride.

1979—4—Pittsburgh (East), Willie Stargell 2, Phil Garner, Bill Madlock.

2—Cincinnati (West), George Foster, Johnny Bench.

1980—1—Philadelphia (East), Greg Luzinski.

0—Houston (West).

1981—4—Los Angeles (West), Pedro Guerrero, Mike Scioscia, Steve Garvey, Rick Monday.

1—Montreal (East), Jerry White.

1982—1—St. Louis (East), Willie McGee.

0—Atlanta (West).

1983—5—Philadelphia (East), Gary Matthews 3, Mike Schmidt, Sixto Lezcano.

2—Los Angeles (West), Mike A. Marshall, Dusty Baker.

1984—9—Chicago (East), Jody Davis 2, Leon Durham 2, Gary Matthews 2, Ron Cey, Bob Dernier, Rick Sutcliffe.

2—San Diego (West), Steve Garvey, Kevin McReynolds.

1985—5—Los Angeles (West), Bill Madlock 3, Greg Brock, Mike A. Marshall.

3—St. Louis (East), Jack Clark, Tom Herr, Ozzie Smith.

1986—5—Houston (West), Alan Ashby, Glenn Davis, Bill Doran, Billy Hatcher, Dickie Thon.

3—New York (East), Darryl Strawberry 2, Lenny Dykstra.

1987—9—San Francisco (West), Jeffrey Leonard 4, Bob Brenly, Will Clark, Kevin Mitchell, Harry Spilman, Robby Thompson.

2—St. Louis (East), Jim Lindeman, Jose Oquendo.

1988—5—New York (East), Kevin McReynolds 2, Lenny Dykstra, Keith Hernandez, Darryl Strawberry.

3—Los Angeles (West), Kirk Gibson 2, Mike Scioscia.

1989—8—San Francisco (West), Will Clark 2, Kevin Mitchell 2, Robby Thompson 2, Matt Williams 2.

3—Chicago (East), Mark Grace, Luis Salazar, Ryne Sandberg.

1990—4—Cincinnati (West), Mariano Duncan, Billy Hatcher, Paul O'Neill, Chris Sabo.

3—Pittsburgh (East), Jay Bell, Sid Bream, Jose Lind.

1991—5—Atlanta (West), Sid Bream, Ron Gant, Brian Hunter, David Justice, Greg Olson.

3—Pittsburgh (East), Jay Bell, Orlando Merced, Andy Van Slyke.

1992—6—Atlanta (West), Ron Gant 2, David Justice 2, Jeff Blauser, Sid Bream.

5—Pittsburgh (East), Jay Bell, Barry Bonds, Jose Lind, Lloyd McClendon, Don Slaught.

1993—7—Philadelphia (East), Lenny Dykstra 2, Dave Hollins 2, Darren Daulton, Pete Incaviglia, John Kruk.

5—Atlanta (West), Jeff Blauser 2, Damon Berryhill, Fred McGriff, Terry Pendleton.

1994—No series played.

1995—4—Atlanta (East), Mike Devereaux, Chipper Jones, Javy Lopez, Charlie O'Brien.

0—Cincinnati (Central).

1996—8—Atlanta (East), Javy Lopez 2, Fred McGriff 2, Marquis Grissom, Andruw Jones, Ryan Klesko, Mark Lemke.

4—St. Louis (Central), Ron Gant 2, Gary Gaetti, Brian Jordan.

1997—6—Atlanta (East), Chipper Jones 2, Ryan Klesko 2, Jeff Blauser, Michael Tucker.

1—Florida (East), Gary Sheffield.

1998—5—San Diego (West), Ken Caminiti 2, Jim Leyritz, Greg Myers, John Vander Wal.

4—Atlanta (East), Andres Galarraga, Andruw Jones, Javy Lopez, Michael Tucker.

1999—5—Atlanta (East), Brian Jordan 2, Eddie Perez 2, Ryan Klesko.

4—New York (East), John Olerud 2, Melvin Mora, Mike Piazza.

2000—4—New York (East), Mike Piazza 2, Jay Payton, Todd Zeile.

2—St. Louis (Central), Will Clark, Jim Edmonds.

2001—5—Atlanta (East), Julio Franco, Marcus Giles, Andruw Jones, Javy Lopez, B.J. Surhoff.

2—Arizona (West), Erubiel Durazo, Luis Gonzalez.

Total number of home runs: 244

PLAYERS WITH FOUR HOME RUNS

BOTH LEAGUES

Player	Series	No.
Darryl Strawberry	4	7
David Justice	8	6
John Olerud	6	5
Paul O'Neill	6	6
Kirk Gibson	3	4

Total number of players: 5

AMERICAN LEAGUE

Player	Series	No.
George Brett	6	9
Bernie Williams	5	7
Jim Thome	3	6
Manny Ramirez	3	6
Reggie Jackson	11	6
Sal Bando	5	5
Graig Nettles	6	5
Darryl Strawberry	2	4
Jay Buhner	3	4
Jose Canseco	3	4
Eddie Murray	4	4
Derek Jeter	5	4
Paul O'Neill	5	4
Boog Powell	5	4

Total number of players: 14

NATIONAL LEAGUE

Player	Series	No.
Steve Garvey	5	8
Gary Matthews	2	5
Ron Gant	5	5
Greg Luzinski	5	5
Johnny Bench	6	5
Javy Lopez	6	5
Jeffrey Leonard	2	4
Bill Madlock	2	4
Will Clark	3	4
Lenny Dykstra	3	4
Ron Cey	5	4
Ryan Klesko	5	4
Bob Robertson	5	4
Jeff Blauser	6	4
Willie Stargell	6	4

Total number of players: 15

INDIVIDUAL PITCHING
PITCHERS WITH FOUR VICTORIES
BOTH LEAGUES

Pitcher, Club	Yrs.	W	L
Bruce Kison, Pit. N.L., Cal. A.L.	5	4	0
Orel Hershiser, L.A. N.L., Cle. A.L., N.Y. N.L.	5	4	0
Tommy John, L.A. N.L., N.Y. A.L., Cal. A.L.	5	4	1
Don Sutton, L.A. N.L., Mil. A.L., Cal. A.L.	5	4	1

Total number of pitchers: 4

AMERICAN LEAGUE

Pitcher, Club	Yrs.	W	L
Dave Stewart, Oakland, Toronto	5	8	0
Juan Guzman, Toronto	3	5	0
Orlando Hernandez, New York	4	4	0
Andy Pettitte, New York	5	5	1
Jim Palmer, Baltimore	6	4	1
Catfish Hunter, Oakland, New York	6	4	3

Total number of pitchers: 6

NATIONAL LEAGUE

Pitcher, Club	Yrs.	W	L
John Smoltz, Atlanta	9	6	2
Steve Avery, Atlanta	5	4	1
Steve Carlton, Philadelphia	5	4	2
Greg Maddux, Chicago, Atlanta	7	4	6
Tom Glavine, Atlanta	9	5	9

Total number of pitchers: 5

10-STRIKEOUT GAMES BY PITCHERS
AMERICAN LEAGUE

Date	Pitcher, Club	No
Oct. 5, 1969	Dave McNally, Bal. vs. Min. (11 inn.)	11
Oct. 5, 1970	Jim Palmer, Bal. vs. Min.	12
Oct. 10, 1972	Joe Coleman, Det. vs. Oak.	14
Oct. 6, 1973	Jim Palmer, Bal. vs. Oak.	12
Oct. 9, 1973	Mike Cuellar, Bal. vs. Oak. (10 inn.)	11
Oct. 6, 1983	Mike Boddicker, Bal. vs. Chi.	14
Oct. 11, 1997	Mike Mussina, Bal. vs. Cle. (7 inn.)	15
Oct. 15, 1997	Mike Mussina, Bal. vs. Cle. (7 inn.)	10
Oct. 11, 1998	David Wells, N.Y. vs. Cle. (7.1 inn.)	11
Oct. 16, 1999	Pedro Martinez, Bos. vs. N.Y. (7 inn.)	12
Oct. 14, 2000	Roger Clemens, N.Y. vs. Sea.	15

Total number of occurrences: 11

NATIONAL LEAGUE

Date	Pitcher, Club	No
Oct. 6, 1973	Tom Seaver, N.Y. vs. Cin. (8.1 inn.)	13
Oct. 7, 1975	John Candelaria, Pit. vs. Cin. (7.2 inn.)	14
Oct. 8, 1986	Mike Scott, Hou. vs. N.Y.	14
Oct. 14, 1986	Nolan Ryan, Hou. vs. N.Y.	12
Oct. 4, 1988	Dwight Gooden, N.Y. vs. L.A.	10
Oct. 5, 1988	Tim Belcher, L.A. vs. N.Y.	10
Oct. 6, 1993	Curt Schilling, Phi. vs. Atl. (8 inn.)	10
Oct. 10, 1993	John Smoltz, Atl. vs. Phi. (6.1 inn.)	10
Oct. 12, 1997	Livan Hernandez, Fla. vs. Atl.	15
Oct. 8, 1998	Kevin Brown, S.D. vs. Atl.	11
Oct. 16, 2001	Randy Johnson, Ari. vs. Atl.	11
Oct. 19, 2001	Curt Schilling, Ari. vs. Atl.	12

Total number of occurrences: 12

CLUB BATTING
AMERICAN LEAGUE

Year	Team, Division	G	AB	R	H	TB	2B	3B	HR	SH	SF	SB	BB	SO	RBI	Avg.	LOB
1969	Baltimore, East	3	123	16	36	58	8	1	4	2	0	0	13	14	15	.293	28
	Minnesota, West	3	110	5	17	25	3	1	1	0	1	2	12	27	5	.155	22
1970	Baltimore, East	3	109	27	36	61	7	0	6	1	2	1	12	19	24	.330	20
	Minnesota, West	3	101	10	24	39	4	1	3	1	0	0	9	22	10	.238	20
1971	Baltimore, East	3	95	15	26	47	7	1	4	0	1	0	13	22	14	.274	19
	Oakland, West	3	96	7	22	41	8	1	3	2	0	0	5	16	7	.229	15
1972	Detroit, East	5	162	10	32	52	6	1	4	3	0	0	13	25	10	.198	30
	Oakland, West	5	170	13	38	49	8	0	1	4	1	7	12	35	10	.224	38
1973	Baltimore, East	5	171	15	36	52	7	0	3	0	0	1	16	25	15	.211	36
	Oakland, West	5	160	15	32	54	5	1	5	4	1	3	17	39	15	.200	34
1974	Baltimore, East	4	124	7	22	32	1	0	3	2	0	0	5	20	7	.177	16
	Oakland, West	4	120	11	22	37	4	1	3	2	1	3	22	16	11	.183	30
1975	Boston, East	3	98	18	31	45	8	0	2	5	1	3	3	12	14	.316	14
	Oakland, West	3	98	7	19	28	6	0	1	0	0	0	9	14	7	.194	19
1976	New York, East	5	174	23	55	84	13	2	4	2	1	4	16	15	21	.316	41
	Kansas City, West	5	162	24	40	60	6	4	2	0	4	5	11	18	24	.247	22
1977	New York, East	5	175	21	46	64	12	0	2	1	2	2	9	16	17	.263	34
	Kansas City, West	5	163	22	42	66	9	3	3	2	2	5	15	22	21	.258	28
1978	New York, East	4	140	19	42	62	3	1	5	0	1	0	7	18	18	.300	27
	Kansas City, West	4	133	17	35	59	6	3	4	1	2	6	14	21	16	.263	28
1979	Baltimore, East	4	133	26	37	53	5	1	3	1	3	5	18	24	25	.278	23
	California, West	4	137	15	32	48	7	0	3	0	2	2	7	13	14	.234	22
1980	New York, East	3	102	6	26	44	7	1	3	1	0	0	6	16	5	.255	22
	Kansas City, West	3	97	14	28	45	6	1	3	0	0	3	9	15	14	.289	18
1981	New York, East	3	107	20	36	49	4	0	3	2	1	2	13	10	20	.336	22
	Oakland, West	3	99	4	22	28	4	1	0	0	0	2	6	23	4	.222	20
1982	Milwaukee, East	5	151	23	33	52	4	0	5	2	3	2	15	28	20	.219	24
	California, West	5	157	23	40	62	8	1	4	5	2	1	16	34	23	.255	29

Year	Team, Division	G	AB	R	H	TB	2B	3B	HR	SH	SF	SB	BB	SO	RBI	Avg.	LOB
1983	Baltimore, East	4	129	19	28	46	9	0	3	1	3	2	16	24	17	.217	24
	Chicago, West	4	133	3	28	32	4	0	0	1	0	4	12	26	2	.211	35
1984	Detroit, East	3	107	14	25	43	4	1	4	2	1	4	8	17	14	.234	20
	Kansas City, West	3	106	4	18	21	1	1	0	0	0	0	6	21	4	.170	21
1985	Toronto, East	7	242	25	65	90	19	0	2	0	2	2	16	37	23	.269	50
	Kansas City, West	7	227	26	51	83	9	1	7	4	2	2	22	51	26	.225	44
1986	Boston, East	7	254	41	69	102	11	2	6	3	2	1	19	31	35	.272	48
	California, West	7	256	30	71	103	11	0	7	4	2	1	20	44	29	.277	60
1987	Detroit, East	5	167	23	40	65	4	0	7	2	2	5	18	35	21	.240	37
	Minnesota, West	5	171	34	46	85	13	1	8	2	2	4	20	25	33	.269	37
1988	Boston, East	4	126	11	26	36	4	0	2	2	2	0	18	23	10	.206	30
	Oakland, West	4	137	20	41	70	8	0	7	0	1	1	10	35	20	.299	26
1989	Toronto, East	5	165	21	40	54	5	0	3	0	3	11	15	24	19	.242	30
	Oakland, West	5	158	26	43	75	9	1	7	3	2	13	20	32	23	.272	29
1990	Boston, East	4	126	4	23	31	5	0	1	1	2	1	6	16	4	.183	23
	Oakland, West	4	127	20	38	42	4	0	0	4	3	9	19	21	18	.299	35
1991	Toronto, East	5	173	19	43	52	6	0	1	3	1	7	15	30	18	.249	35
	Minnesota, West	5	181	27	50	70	9	1	3	1	2	8	15	37	25	.276	38
1992	Toronto, East	6	210	31	59	99	8	1	10	1	4	7	23	29	30	.281	45
	Oakland, West	6	207	24	52	71	5	1	4	3	2	16	24	33	23	.251	48
1993	Toronto, East	6	216	26	65	85	8	3	2	1	1	7	21	36	24	.301	56
	Chicago, West	6	194	23	46	68	5	1	5	5	1	3	32	43	22	.237	50
1994	No series played.																
1995	Cleveland, East	6	206	23	53	86	6	3	7	1	2	9	25	37	21	.257	50
	Seattle, West	6	201	12	37	60	8	0	5	1	0	9	15	46	10	.184	43
1996	New York, East	5	183	27	50	91	9	1	10	0	0	3	20	37	24	.273	40
	Baltimore, East	5	176	19	39	70	4	0	9	0	3	0	15	33	19	.222	34
1997	Baltimore, East	6	218	19	54	86	11	0	7	1	0	3	23	47	19	.248	50
	Cleveland, Central	6	207	18	40	63	8	0	5	2	0	5	23	62	15	.193	44
1998	New York, East	6	197	27	43	65	8	1	4	3	3	9	35	42	25	.218	48
	Cleveland, Central	6	205	20	45	77	3	1	9	0	1	6	16	51	19	.220	39
1999	New York, East	5	176	23	42	72	4	1	8	2	0	3	18	44	21	.239	42
	Boston, East	5	184	21	54	86	13	2	5	1	0	4	15	38	19	.293	45
2000	New York, East	6	204	31	57	85	10	0	6	1	3	4	25	41	31	.279	49
	Seattle, West	6	191	18	41	68	12	0	5	2	1	3	21	48	18	.215	38
2001	New York, East	5	159	25	42	70	7	0	7	4	1	3	23	31	24	.264	34
	Seattle, West	5	171	22	36	59	4	2	5	1	0	3	18	35	20	.211	34

NATIONAL LEAGUE

Year	Team, Division	G	AB	R	H	TB	2B	3B	HR	SH	SF	SB	BB	SO	RBI	Avg.	LOB
1969	New York, East	3	113	27	37	65	8	1	6	1	0	5	10	25	24	.327	19
	Atlanta, West	3	106	15	27	51	9	0	5	0	1	1	11	20	15	.255	23
1970	Pittsburgh, East	3	102	3	23	29	6	0	0	2	0	0	12	19	3	.225	29
	Cincinnati, West	3	100	9	22	36	3	1	3	0	0	1	8	12	8	.220	18
1971	Pittsburgh, East	4	144	24	39	67	4	0	8	1	0	2	5	33	23	.271	26
	San Francisco, West	4	132	15	31	51	5	0	5	4	0	2	16	28	14	.235	33
1972	Pittsburgh, East	5	158	15	30	47	6	1	3	2	0	0	9	27	14	.190	24
	Cincinnati, West	5	166	19	42	67	9	2	4	3	1	4	10	28	16	.253	30
1973	New York, East	5	168	23	37	51	5	0	3	3	1	0	19	28	22	.220	30
	Cincinnati, West	5	167	8	31	52	6	0	5	3	1	0	13	42	8	.186	35
1974	Pittsburgh, East	4	129	10	25	35	1	0	3	2	0	1	8	17	10	.194	24
	Los Angeles, West	4	138	20	37	56	8	1	3	1	0	5	30	16	19	.268	44
1975	Pittsburgh, East	3	101	7	20	26	3	0	1	0	0	0	10	18	7	.198	21
	Cincinnati, West	3	102	19	29	45	4	0	4	0	3	11	9	28	18	.284	17
1976	Philadelphia, East	3	100	11	27	40	8	1	1	3	2	0	12	9	11	.270	25
	Cincinnati, West	3	99	19	25	45	5	3	3	1	3	5	15	16	17	.253	20
1977	Philadelphia, East	4	138	14	31	40	3	0	2	2	0	1	11	21	12	.225	32
	Los Angeles, West	4	133	22	35	52	6	1	3	2	0	3	14	22	20	.263	22
1978	Philadelphia, East	4	140	17	35	37	3	2	5	2	1	0	9	21	16	.250	24
	Los Angeles, West	4	147	21	42	80	8	3	8	2	0	2	9	22	21	.286	28
1979	Pittsburgh, East	3	105	15	28	47	3	2	4	5	3	4	13	13	14	.267	24
	Cincinnati, West	3	107	5	23	35	4	1	2	1	1	4	11	26	5	.215	25
1980	Philadelphia, East	5	190	20	55	68	8	1	1	5	1	7	13	37	19	.291	43
	Houston, West	5	172	19	40	57	7	5	0	7	2	4	31	19	18	.233	45
1981	Montreal, East	5	158	10	34	44	7	0	1	3	0	2	12	25	8	.215	31
	Los Angeles, West	5	163	15	38	55	3	1	4	4	0	5	12	23	15	.233	33
1982	St. Louis, East	3	103	17	34	45	4	2	1	5	3	1	12	16	16	.330	31
	Atlanta, West	3	89	5	15	16	1	0	0	2	1	1	6	15	3	.169	12
1983	Philadelphia, East	4	130	16	34	53	4	0	5	3	1	2	15	22	15	.262	31
	Los Angeles, West	4	129	8	27	40	5	1	2	2	0	3	11	31	7	.209	31
1984	Chicago, East	5	162	26	42	80	11	0	9	1	2	6	20	28	25	.259	32
	San Diego, West	5	155	22	41	54	5	1	2	2	4	2	14	22	20	.265	27
1985	St. Louis, East	6	201	29	56	77	10	1	3	2	1	6	30	34	26	.279	51
	Los Angeles, West	6	197	23	46	75	12	1	5	1	1	4	19	31	23	.234	40

Year	Team, Division	G	AB	R	H	TB	2B	3B	HR	SH	SF	SB	BB	SO	RBI	Avg.	LOB
1986	New York, East......6		227	21	43	60	4	2	3	1	3	4	14	57	19	.189	36
	Houston, West 6		225	17	49	70	6	0	5	2	0	8	17	40	17	.218	39
1987	St. Louis, East......7		215	23	56	74	4	4	2	5	4	4	16	42	22	.260	37
	San Francisco, West..7		226	23	54	90	7	1	9	3	1	5	17	51	20	.239	43
1988	New York, East......7		240	27	58	87	12	1	5	3	1	6	28	42	27	.242	54
	Los Angeles, West .7		243	31	52	70	7	1	3	1	2	9	25	54	30	.214	50
1989	Chicago, East........5		175	22	53	77	9	3	3	3	2	3	16	27	21	.303	43
	San Francisco, West 5		165	30	44	78	6	2	8	2	1	2	17	29	29	.267	30
1990	Pittsburgh, East......6		186	15	36	58	9	2	3	0	1	6	27	49	14	.194	41
	Cincinnati, West.....6		192	20	49	70	9	0	4	3	3	6	10	37	20	.255	33
1991	Pittsburgh, East......7		228	12	51	70	10	0	3	4	1	6	22	57	11	.224	54
	Atlanta, West.........7		229	19	53	80	10	1	5	5	1	10	22	42	19	.231	51
1992	Pittsburgh, East......7		231	35	59	100	20	3	5	3	3	1	29	42	32	.255	50
	Atlanta, West.........7		234	34	57	90	11	2	6	2	2	5	29	28	32	.244	51
1993	Philadelphia, East..6		207	23	47	87	11	4	7	3	2	2	26	51	22	.227	52
	Atlanta, West.........6		215	33	59	88	14	0	5	5	2	0	22	54	32	.274	47
1994	No series played.																
1995	Atlanta, East..........4		149	19	42	62	6	1	4	1	0	2	16	22	17	.282	36
	Cincinnati, Central..4		134	5	28	35	5	1	0	1	1	4	12	31	4	.209	28
1996	Atlanta, East..........7		249	44	77	118	11	3	8	2	3	4	25	51	43	.309	58
	St. Louis, Central ...7		221	18	45	65	4	2	4	1	1	1	11	53	15	.204	34
1997	Atlanta, East..........6		194	21	49	76	5	2	6	5	3	1	16	49	21	.253	40
	Florida, East..........6		181	20	36	47	8	0	1	5	0	2	23	52	20	.199	36
1998	San Diego, West...6		208	24	53	75	7	0	5	2	0	2	27	48	20	.255	52
	Atlanta, East..........6		200	18	47	65	4	1	4	2	1	3	26	54	17	.235	46
1999	Atlanta, East..........6		206	24	46	72	9	1	5	7	1	14	31	47	22	.223	47
	New York, East......6		225	21	49	70	9	0	4	3	2	7	14	49	21	.218	42
2000	New York, East......5		164	31	43	69	12	1	4	3	3	2	27	24	27	.262	40
	St. Louis, Central ...5		177	21	47	64	11	0	2	4	2	3	11	39	18	.266	39
2001	Atlanta, East..........5		169	15	35	56	6	0	5	0	0	0	11	39	14	.207	30
	Arizona, West........5		172	22	40	52	6	0	2	2	0	3	18	32	19	.233	39

CLUB FIELDING AND PLAYERS USED

AMERICAN LEAGUE

Year	Team, Division	G	PO	A	E	DP	PB	Fielding Avg.	Players Used	Pitchers Used
1969	Baltimore, East 3		96	31	1	2	0	.992	20	7
	Minnesota, West 3		94	34	5	3	0	.962	22	9
1970	Baltimore, East 3		81	29	0	3	0	1.000	14	4
	Minnesota, West 3		78	28	6	5	0	.946	24	9
1971	Baltimore, East 3		81	31	1	3	0	.991	15	4
	Oakland, West 3		75	15	0	4	0	1.000	20	7
1972	Detroit, East 5		139	48	7	4	0	.964	24	8
	Oakland, West 5		138	59	3	5	1	.985	25	8
1973	Baltimore, East 5		135	51	2	2	1	.989	23	7
	Oakland, West 5		138	47	4	4	0	.979	22	6
1974	Baltimore, East 4		105	50	4	4	0	.975	22	7
	Oakland, West 4		108	43	2	4	1	.987	20	5
1975	Boston, East 3		81	33	4	3	0	.966	14	5
	Oakland, West 3		75	40	6	4	0	.950	22	7
1976	New York, East 5		132	60	6	3	1	.970	22	6
	Kansas City, West 5		129	51	4	5	0	.978	24	9
1977	New York, East 5		132	51	2	2	0	.989	18	6
	Kansas City, West 5		132	54	5	2	0	.974	22	8
1978	New York, East 4		105	35	1	2	1	.993	21	8
	Kansas City, West 4		102	36	4	4	1	.972	20	7
1979	Baltimore, East 4		109	52	5	5	1	.970	20	5
	California, West 4		107	37	2	7	0	.986	23	9
1980	New York, East 3		75	42	1	2	0	.991	20	6
	Kansas City, West 3		81	29	1	3	0	.991	15	4
1981	New York, East 3		81	30	1	6	1	.991	22	6
	Oakland, West 3		75	33	4	1	0	.964	24	8
1982	Milwaukee, East 5		129	45	8	5	0	.956	20	8
	California, West 5		126	46	4	3	1	.977	20	7
1983	Baltimore, East 4		111	49	2	4	0	.988	22	6
	Chicago, West 4		108	51	3	5	0	.981	23	9
1984	Detroit, East 3		87	27	1	0	0	.991	20	5
	Kansas City, West 3		84	26	7	2	0	.940	22	6
1985	Toronto, East 7		186	61	4	4	0	.984	24	8
	Kansas City, West 7		188	87	6	7	0	.979	22	7
1986	Boston, East 7		196	73	7	5	0	.975	20	7
	California, West 7		192	78	8	5	2	.971	24	9
1987	Detroit, East 5		129	56	5	1	1	.974	24	10
	Minnesota, West 5		132	41	3	3	0	.983	21	7

Year	Team, Division	G	PO	A	E	DP	PB	Fielding Avg.	Players Used	Pitchers Used
1988	Boston, East	4	102	34	1	2	1	.993	20	7
	Oakland, West	4	108	30	3	5	1	.979	22	9
1989	Toronto, East	5	129	40	2	5	1	.988	22	9
	Oakland, West	5	132	45	3	4	1	.983	22	8
1990	Boston, East	4	102	47	5	6	1	.968	23	10
	Oakland, West	4	108	43	1	3	0	.993	21	6
1991	Toronto, East	5	135	49	7	4	0	.963	23	10
	Minnesota, West	5	138	51	4	3	0	.979	23	8
1992	Toronto, East	6	165	60	8	7	3	.966	21	9
	Oakland, West	6	162	55	7	5	0	.969	25	11
1993	Toronto, East	6	162	57	2	7	0	.991	19	10
	Chicago, West	6	159	56	7	5	0	.968	22	9
1994	No series played.									
1995	Cleveland, East	6	165	66	7	4	0	.971	25	11
	Seattle, West	6	162	59	6	7	1	.974	25	10
1996	New York, East	5	141	44	1	1	0	.995	24	9
	Baltimore, East	5	138	58	4	7	0	.980	23	10
1997	Baltimore, East	6	174	60	5	4	0	.979	23	9
	Cleveland, Central	6	174	61	5	11	0	.979	23	11
1998	New York, East	6	168	54	2	5	0	.991	24	9
	Cleveland, Central	6	165	77	7	7	0	.972	25	11
1999	New York, East	5	135	38	4	7	1	.977	25	10
	Boston, East	5	132	40	10	0	0	.945	24	10
2000	New York, East	6	159	54	1	5	0	.995	22	10
	Seattle, West	6	156	58	3	4	1	.986	25	10
2001	New York, East	5	135	47	4	4	0	.978	24	9
	Seattle, West	5	130	45	1	5	0	.994	25	11

NATIONAL LEAGUE

Year	Team, Division	G	PO	A	E	DP	PB	Fielding Avg.	Players Used	Pitchers Used
1969	New York, East	3	81	23	2	2	1	.981	17	6
	Atlanta, West	3	78	37	6	4	1	.950	23	9
1970	Pittsburgh, East	3	81	37	2	3	0	.983	18	5
	Cincinnati, West	3	84	39	1	1	0	.992	20	7
1971	Pittsburgh, East	4	105	32	3	3	1	.979	21	7
	San Francisco, West	4	102	37	4	1	1	.972	22	9
1972	Pittsburgh, East	5	131	38	4	3	0	.977	23	10
	Cincinnati, West	5	132	53	4	3	1	.979	21	8
1973	New York, East	5	142	44	4	3	0	.979	17	6
	Cincinnati, West	5	138	59	2	3	0	.990	24	9
1974	Pittsburgh, East	4	105	37	4	2	1	.973	22	8
	Los Angeles, West	4	108	46	7	8	1	.957	22	7
1975	Pittsburgh, East	3	78	20	2	3	2	.980	24	10
	Cincinnati, West	3	84	31	1	2	0	.991	18	7
1976	Philadelphia, East	3	79	34	2	3	0	.983	22	7
	Cincinnati, West	3	81	32	2	3	0	.983	18	6
1977	Philadelphia, East	4	105	49	3	3	1	.981	21	7
	Los Angeles, West	4	108	44	5	3	0	.968	23	9
1978	Philadelphia, East	4	110	46	4	4	0	.975	22	8
	Los Angeles, West	4	111	50	3	4	0	.982	22	9
1979	Pittsburgh, East	3	90	34	0	2	0	1.000	20	9
	Cincinnati, West	3	87	39	1	2	0	.992	20	9
1980	Philadelphia, East	5	148	71	6	7	0	.973	23	9
	Houston, West	5	147	52	3	4	1	.985	24	7
1981	Montreal, East	5	132	52	4	8	0	.979	19	7
	Los Angeles, West	5	132	53	2	5	1	.989	23	9
1982	St. Louis, East	3	81	35	2	3	0	.983	15	5
	Atlanta, West	3	76	39	1	0	1	.991	20	8
1983	Philadelphia, East	4	105	36	5	0	0	.966	20	5
	Los Angeles, West	4	102	38	1	3	1	.993	22	8
1984	Chicago, East	5	127	49	3	6	1	.983	23	8
	San Diego, West	5	129	43	1	4	0	.994	24	10
1985	St. Louis, East	6	156	54	4	4	1	.981	23	9
	Los Angeles, West	6	154	72	6	3	0	.974	25	9
1986	New York, East	6	189	94	1	6	0	.996	22	8
	Houston, West	6	188	66	7	3	2	.973	21	8
1987	St. Louis, East	7	183	67	3	5	0	.988	23	8
	San Francisco, West	7	180	77	6	10	1	.977	23	10
1988	New York, East	7	192	62	8	2	0	.969	22	8
	Los Angeles, West	7	195	61	5	9	1	.981	24	9
1989	Chicago, East	5	126	40	3	1	2	.982	24	9
	San Francisco, West	5	132	49	5	7	1	.973	24	9

– 459 –

Year	Team, Division	G	PO	A	E	DP	PB	Fielding Avg.	Players Used	Pitchers Used
1990	Pittsburgh, East	6	156	71	5	4	0	.978	21	8
	Cincinnati, West	6	159	45	2	3	0	.990	23	8
1991	Pittsburgh, East	7	189	75	6	3	0	.978	25	11
	Atlanta, West	7	189	62	4	6	0	.984	23	9
1992	Pittsburgh, East	7	182	63	5	6	2	.980	25	10
	Atlanta, West	7	183	74	2	3	1	.992	25	10
1993	Philadelphia, East	6	165	47	7	2	2	.968	25	10
	Atlanta, West	6	163	54	5	1	0	.977	23	8
1994	No series played.									
1995	Atlanta, East	4	117	54	3	7	0	.983	22	8
	Cincinnati, West	4	111	43	2	4	1	.987	25	10
1996	Atlanta, East	7	183	55	4	6	0	.983	24	10
	St. Louis, Central	7	180	61	6	4	0	.976	25	10
1997	Atlanta, East	6	156	57	4	7	0	.982	22	8
	Florida, East	6	159	57	3	4	0	.986	24	10
1998	San Diego, West	6	165	60	1	6	0	.996	24	10
	Atlanta, East	6	162	74	8	6	1	.967	24	9
1999	Atlanta, East	6	181	55	7	4	1	.971	25	9
	New York, East	6	178	82	8	9	0	.970	25	11
2000	New York, East	5	135	39	4	1	0	.978	24	10
	St. Louis, Central	5	129	49	7	3	1	.962	25	10
2001	Atlanta, East	5	132	52	7	5	1	.963	24	10
	Arizona, West	5	135	43	3	3	0	.983	23	9

MANAGERIAL RECORDS

AMERICAN LEAGUE

	Series W	L	Games W	L
Joe Altobelli, Baltimore	1	0	3	1
Sparky Anderson, Detroit	1	1	4	4
Bobby Cox, Toronto	0	1	3	4
Alvin Dark, Oakland	1	1	3	4
Jim Fregosi, California	0	1	1	3
Jim Frey, Kansas City	1	0	3	0
Cito Gaston, Toronto	2	2	10	12
Mike Hargrove, Cleveland	2	1	10	8
Whitey Herzog, Kansas City	0	3	5	9
Dick Howser, New York, Kansas City	1	2	4	9
Darrell Johnson, Boston	1	0	3	0
Dave Johnson, Baltimore	0	2	3	8
Tom Kelly, Minnesota	2	0	8	2
Harvey Kuenn, Milwaukee	1	0	3	2
Gene Lamont, Chicago	0	1	2	4
Tony La Russa, Chicago, Oakland	3	2	15	8
Bob Lemon, New York	2	0	6	1
Billy Martin, Minnesota, Detroit, New York, Oakland	2	3	8	13
Gene Mauch, California	0	2	5	7
John McNamara, Boston	1	0	4	3
Joe Morgan, Boston	0	2	0	8
Lou Piniella, Seattle	0	3	5	12
Bill Rigney, Minnesota	0	1	0	3
Joe Torre, New York	5	0	20	7
Earl Weaver, Baltimore	4	2	15	7
Dick Williams, Oakland	2	1	6	7
Jimy Williams, Boston	0	1	1	4

Total number of managers: 27

NATIONAL LEAGUE

	Series W	L	Games W	L
Walter Alston, Los Angeles	1	0	3	1
Sparky Anderson, Cincinnati	4	0	14	5
Yogi Berra, New York	1	0	3	2
Bruce Bochy, San Diego	1	0	4	2
Bob Brenly, Arizona	1	0	4	1
Bobby Cox, Atlanta	5	4	27	27
Roger Craig, San Francisco	1	1	7	5
Jim Fanning, Montreal	0	1	2	3
Jim Fregosi, Philadelphia	1	0	4	2
Jim Frey, Chicago	0	1	2	3
Charlie Fox, San Francisco	0	1	1	3
Dallas Green, Philadelphia	1	0	3	2
Lum Harris, Atlanta	0	1	0	3
Whitey Herzog, St. Louis	3	0	11	5
Gil Hodges, New York	1	0	3	0
Dave Johnson, New York, Cincinnati	1	2	7	10
Hal Lanier, Houston	0	1	2	4
Tony La Russa, St. Louis	0	2	4	8
Tom Lasorda, Los Angeles	4	2	16	14
Jim Leyland, Pittsburgh, Florida	1	3	12	14
John McNamara, Cincinnati	0	1	0	3
Danny Murtaugh, Pittsburgh	1	3	4	10
Paul Owens, Philadelphia	1	0	3	1
Danny Ozark, Philadelphia	0	3	2	9
Lou Piniella, Cincinnati	1	0	4	2
Chuck Tanner, Pittsburgh	1	0	3	0
Joe Torre, Atlanta	0	1	0	3
Bobby Valentine, New York	1	1	6	5
Bill Virdon, Pittsburgh, Houston	0	2	4	6
Dick Williams, San Diego	1	0	3	2
Don Zimmer, Chicago	0	1	1	4

Total number of managers: 31

COMBINED RECORDS FOR BOTH LEAGUES

	Series W	L	Games W	L
Sparky Anderson, Cincinnati N.L., Detroit A.L.	5	2	18	9
Bobby Cox, Toronto A.L., Atlanta N.L.	5	5	30	31
Jim Fregosi, California A.L., Philadelphia N.L.	1	1	5	5
Jim Frey, Kansas City A.L., Chicago N.L.	1	1	5	3
Whitey Herzog, Kansas City A.L., St. Louis N.L.	3	3	16	14
Dave Johnson, New York N.L., Cincinnati N.L., Baltimore A.L.	1	4	10	18
Tony La Russa, Chicago A.L., Oakland A.L., St. Louis N.L.	3	4	19	16
John McNamara, Cincinnati N.L., Boston A.L.	1	1	4	6
Lou Piniella, Cincinnati N.L., Seattle A.L.	1	3	9	14
Joe Torre, Atlanta N.L., New York A.L.	5	1	20	10
Dick Williams, Oakland A.L., San Diego N.L.	3	1	9	9

Total number of managers:

WORLD SERIES

Service (Individual, Club)

Batting (Individual, Club)

Baserunning (Individual, Club)

Pitching (Individual, Club)

Fielding (Individual, Club)

Miscellaneous

Non-Playing Personnel

General Reference

INDIVIDUAL SERVICE

ALL PLAYERS
SERIES AND CLUBS

Most series played
14—Yogi Berra, New York A.L., 1947, 1949, 1950, 1951, 1952, 1953, 1955, 1956, 1957, 1958, 1960, 1961, 1962, 1963, 75 games (65 consecutive).

Most series eligible, but did not play
6—Charlie Silvera, New York A.L., 1950, 1951, 1952, 1953, 1955, 1956, 37 games (played one game in 1949).

Most consecutive series played (17 times)
5—Hank Bauer, New York A.L., 1949 through 1953.
Yogi Berra, New York A.L., 1949 through 1953.
Ed Lopat, New York A.L., 1949 through 1953.
Johnny Mize, New York A.L., 1949 through 1953.
Vic Raschi, New York A.L., 1949 through 1953.
Allie Reynolds, New York A.L., 1949 through 1953.
Phil Rizzuto, New York A.L., 1949 through 1953.
Gene Woodling, New York A.L., 1949 through 1953.
Johnny Blanchard, New York A.L., 1960 through 1964.
Clete Boyer, New York A.L., 1960 through 1964.
Ralph Terry, New York A.L., 1960 through 1964.
Whitey Ford, New York A.L., 1960 through 1964.
Elston Howard, New York A.L., 1960 through 1964.
Hector Lopez, New York A.L., 1960 through 1964.
Mickey Mantle, New York A.L., 1960 through 1964.
Roger Maris, New York A.L., 1960 through 1964.
Bobby Richardson, New York A.L., 1960 through 1964.

Most series played with one club
14—Yogi Berra, New York A.L., 1947, 1949, 1950, 1951, 1952, 1953, 1955, 1956, 1957, 1958, 1960, 1961, 1962, 1963, 75 games (65 consecutive).

Most series playing in all games
10—Joe DiMaggio, New York A.L., 1936, 1937, 1938, 1939, 1941, 1942, 1947, 1949, 1950, 1951, 51 games.

Most times on series-winning club (playing one or more games each series)
10—Yogi Berra, New York A.L., 1947, 1949, 1950, 1951, 1952, 1953, 1956, 1958, 1961, 1962.

Most times on series-losing club (playing one or more games each series)
6—Pee Wee Reese, Brooklyn N.L., 1941, 1947, 1949, 1952, 1953, 1956.
Elston Howard, New York A.L., 1955, 1957, 1960, 1963, 1964; Boston A.L., 1967.

Most series played in first four major league seasons
4—Joe DiMaggio, New York A.L., 1936 through 1939.
Elston Howard, New York A.L., 1955 through 1958.
Johnny Kucks, New York A.L., 1955 through 1958.
Orlando Hernandez, New York A.L., 1998 through 2001.

Most clubs, career
4—Lonnie Smith, Philadelphia N.L., 1980; St. Louis N.L., 1982; Kansas City A.L., 1985; Atlanta N.L., 1991, 1992.

BY POSITION (EXCEPT PITCHERS)

Most series by first baseman
8—Bill Skowron, New York A.L., 1955, 1956, 1957, 1958, 1960, 1961, 1962; Los Angeles N.L., 1963, 37 games.

Most series by second baseman
7—Frankie Frisch, New York N.L., 1922, 1923, 1924; St. Louis N.L., 1928, 1930, 1931, 1934, 42 games.

Most series by third baseman
6—Red Rolfe, New York A.L., 1936, 1937, 1938, 1939, 1941, 1942, 28 games.

Most series by shortstop
9—Phil Rizzuto, New York A.L., 1941, 1942, 1947, 1949, 1950, 1951, 1952, 1953, 1955, 52 games.

Most series by outfielder
12—Mickey Mantle, New York A.L., 1951, 1952, 1953, 1955, 1956, 1957, 1958, 1960, 1961, 1962, 1963, 1964, 63 games.

Most series by catcher
12—Yogi Berra, New York A.L., 1947, 1949, 1950, 1951, 1952, 1953, 1955, 1956, 1957, 1958, 1960, 1962, 63 games.

YOUNGEST AND OLDEST NON-PITCHERS

Youngest World Series non-pitcher
18 years, 10 months, 13 days—Fred Lindstrom, New York N.L., October 4, 1924.

Oldest World Series non-pitcher
42 years, 6 months, 2 days—Pete Rose, Philadelphia N.L., October 16, 1983.

YEARS BETWEEN SERIES (INCLUDES PITCHERS)

Most years between first and second series
17—Jim Kaat, Minnesota A.L., 1965; St. Louis N.L., 1982.

Most years between first and last series
22—Willie Mays, New York Giants N.L., 1951; New York Mets N.L., 1973.

Most years played in majors before playing in series
21—Joe Niekro, Minnesota A.L., October 21, 1987.
Mike Morgan, Arizona N.L., October 27, 2001.

POSITIONS

Most positions played, career
4—Babe Ruth, Boston A.L., 1915, 1916, 1918; New York A.L., 1921, 1922, 1923, 1926, 1927, 1928, 1932, 41 games (pitcher, left field, right field, first base).
Jackie Robinson, Brooklyn N.L., 1947, 1949, 1952, 1953, 1955, 1956, 38 games (first base, second base, left field, third base).
Elston Howard, New York A.L., 1955, 1956, 1957, 1958, 1960, 1961, 1962, 1963, 1964; Boston A.L., 1967, 54 games (left field, right field, first base, catcher).
Tony Kubek, New York A.L., 1957, 1958, 1960, 1961, 1962, 1963, 37 games (left field, third base, center field, shortstop).
Pete Rose, Cincinnati N.L., 1970, 1972, 1975, 1976; Philadelphia N.L., 1980, 1983, 34 games (right field, left field, third base, first base).

Most positions played, series
3—Held by many players.

PITCHERS
SERIES

Most series pitched
11—Whitey Ford, New York A.L., 1950, 1953, 1955, 1956, 1957, 1958, 1960, 1961, 1962, 1963, 1964, 22 games.

Most series pitched by relief pitcher
6—Johnny Murphy, New York A.L., 1936, 1937, 1938, 1939, 1941, 1943, eight games as a relief pitcher.
Mike Stanton, Atlanta N.L., 1991, 1992; New York A.L., 1998 through 2001, 20 games as a relief pitcher.

YOUNGEST AND OLDEST PITCHERS

Youngest World Series pitcher
19 years, 20 days—Ken Brett, Boston A.L., October 8, 1967.

Oldest World Series pitcher
46 years, 2 months, 29 days—Jack Quinn, Philadelphia A.L., October 4, 1930.

CLUB SERVICE

PLAYERS USED

Most players, series
4-game series—25
  Oakland A.L. vs. Cincinnati N.L., 1990.
  Atlanta N.L. vs. New York A.L., 1999.
5-game series—25
  Brooklyn N.L. vs. New York A.L., 1949.
  New York N.L. vs. New York A.L., 2000.
6-game series—25
  Los Angeles N.L. vs. New York A.L., 1977.
  New York A.L. vs. Atlanta N.L., 1996.
7-game series—26
  Detroit A.L. vs. Chicago N.L., 1945.
  Boston A.L. vs. St. Louis N.L., 1946.
  Florida N.L. vs. Cleveland A.L., 1997.
8-game series—19
  Chicago A.L. vs. Cincinnati N.L., 1919.
  New York A.L. vs. New York N.L., 1921.

For a list of players and pitchers used each series, see page 515.

Most players used by both clubs, series
4-game series—48—Atlanta N.L. 25, New York A.L. 23, 1999.
5-game series—47
  New York N.L. 25, New York A.L. 22, 2000.
6-game series—49—New York A.L. 25, Atlanta N.L. 24, 1996.
7-game series—51—Detroit A.L. 26, Chicago N.L. 25, 1945.
8-game series—36—Chicago A.L. 19, Cincinnati N.L. 17, 1919.

Fewest players, series
4-game series—13
  Los Angeles N.L. vs. New York A.L., 1963.
  Baltimore A.L. vs. Los Angeles N.L., 1966.
5-game series—12
  New York N.L. vs. Philadelphia A.L., 1905.
  Philadelphia A.L. vs. Chicago N.L., 1910.
  Philadelphia A.L. vs. New York N.L., 1913.
6-game series—14
  Chicago N.L. vs. Chicago A.L., 1906.
  Philadelphia A.L. vs. New York N.L., 1911.
7-game series—16—Detroit A.L. vs. Pittsburgh N.L., 1909.
8-game series—13
  Boston A.L. vs. Pittsburgh N.L., 1903.
  New York N.L. vs. New York A.L., 1921.

Fewest players used by both clubs, series
4-game series—31—Philadelphia A.L. 16, Boston N.L. 15, 1914.
5-game series—25—Philadelphia A.L. 13, New York N.L. 12, 1905.
6-game series—29—New York N.L. 15, Philadelphia A.L. 14, 1911.
7-game series—33—Pittsburgh N.L. 17, Detroit A.L. 16, 1909.
8-game series—27—Pittsburgh N.L. 14, Boston A.L. 13, 1903.

Most times one club using only nine players in game, series
5-game series—5
  Philadelphia A.L. vs. Chicago N.L., 1910.
  Philadelphia A.L. vs. New York N.L., 1913.
7-game series—5—New York A.L. vs. Brooklyn N.L., 1956.
8-game series—6—Pittsburgh N.L. vs. Boston A.L., 1903.

Most times both clubs using only nine players in game, series
7-game series—7—New York A.L. 5, Brooklyn N.L. 2, 1956.
8-game series—11—Pittsburgh N.L. 6, Boston A.L. 5, 1903.

Most players, nine-inning game
21—New York A.L. vs. Brooklyn N.L., October 5, 1947.
  Cincinnati N.L. vs. New York A.L., October 9, 1961.

Most players, extra-inning game
23—Minnesota A.L. vs. Atlanta N.L., October 22, 1991, 12 innings.

Most players used by both clubs, nine-inning game
38—New York A.L. 21, Brooklyn N.L. 17, October 5, 1947.

Most players used by both clubs, extra-inning game
42—Minnesota A.L. 23, Atlanta N.L. 19, October 22, 1991, 12 innings.

PINCH-HITTERS

Most times pinch-hitters used, series
23—Baltimore A.L. vs. Pittsburgh N.L., 1979 (7-game series).

Most pinch-hitters used by both clubs, series
37—Minnesota A.L. 21, Atlanta N.L. 16, 1991 (7-game series).

Fewest times pinch-hitters used, series
0—Held by many clubs. Last club—Cincinnati N.L. vs. New York A.L., 1976 (4-game series).

Fewest pinch-hitters used by both clubs, series
2—New York N.L. 1, Philadelphia A.L. 1, 1905 (5-game series).

Most pinch-hitters, nine-inning game
6—Los Angeles N.L. vs. Chicago A.L., October 6, 1959.

Most pinch-hitters, extra-inning game
8—Minnesota A.L. vs. Atlanta N.L., October 22, 1991, 12 innings.

Most pinch-hitters used by both clubs, nine-inning game
8—Oakland A.L. 5, New York N.L. 3, October 14, 1973.
  Baltimore A.L. 4, Philadelphia N.L. 4, October 15, 1983.

Most pinch-hitters used by both clubs, extra-inning game
12—Minnesota A.L. 8, Atlanta N.L. 4, October 22, 1991, 12 innings.

Most pinch-hitters, inning
4—New York N.L. vs. Oakland A.L. October 13, 1973, ninth inning.
  Baltimore A.L. vs. Philadelphia N.L., October 15, 1983, sixth inning.
  Minnesota A.L. vs. St. Louis N.L., October 22, 1987, ninth inning.
  Atlanta N.L. vs. New York A.L., October 23, 1999, eighth inning.
  New York N.L. vs. New York A.L., October 25, 2000, seventh inning.

PINCH-RUNNERS

Most times pinch-runners used, series
8—Oakland A.L. vs. Cincinnati N.L., 1972 (7-game series).

Most pinch-runners used by both clubs, series
10—Oakland A.L. 8, Cincinnati N.L. 2, 1972 (7-game series).

Fewest times pinch-runners used, series
0—Held by many clubs.

Most pinch-runners, game
2—Made in many games.

Most pinch-runners used by both clubs, game
4—St. Louis N.L. 2, Kansas City A.L. 2, October 26, 1985.

Most pinch-runners, inning
2—Held by many clubs.

Most pinch-runners used by both clubs, inning
2—Made in many games.

NUMBER OF PLAYERS USED BY POSITION
FIRST BASEMEN

Most first basemen, series
4—New York A.L. vs. Milwaukee N.L., 1957 (7-game series).
  Oakland A.L. vs. New York N.L., 1973 (7-game series).

Most first basemen used by both clubs, series
6—New York A.L. 4, Milwaukee N.L. 2, 1957 (7-game series).

Most first basemen, game
3—New York A.L. vs. Milwaukee N.L., October 2, 1957.
  New York A.L. vs. Milwaukee N.L., October 5, 1957.
  Florida N.L. vs. Cleveland A.L., October 26, 1997, 11 innings.

Most first basemen used by both clubs, game
5—New York A.L. 3, Milwaukee N.L. 2, October 2, 1957.
  New York A.L. 3, Milwaukee N.L. 2, October 5, 1957.

SECOND BASEMEN

Most second basemen, series
3—Held by many clubs. Last club—New York A.L. vs. Atlanta N.L., 1996 (6-game series).

Most second basemen used by both clubs, series
5—Oakland A.L. 3, San Francisco N.L. 2, 1989 (4-game series).

Most second basemen, game
3—St. Louis N.L. vs. New York A.L., October 7, 1964.
Oakland A.L. vs. New York N.L., October 14, 1973, 12 innings.

Most second basemen used by both clubs, game
4—Made in many games. Last game—Oakland A.L. 2, San Francisco N.L. 2, October 27, 1989.

THIRD BASEMEN

Most third basemen, series
3—Held by many clubs. Last club—New York A.L. vs. Atlanta N.L., 1996 (6-game series).

Most third basemen used by both clubs, series
6—Oakland A.L. 3, San Francisco N.L. 3, 1989 (4-game series).

Most third basemen, game
3—Held by many clubs. Last club—New York A.L. vs. Atlanta N.L., October 23, 1996, 10 innings.

Most third basemen used by both clubs, nine-inning game
4—Made in many games.

Most third basemen used by both clubs, extra-inning game
5—New York A.L. 3, Atlanta N.L. 2, October 23, 1996, 10 innings.

SHORTSTOPS

Most shortstops, series
3—Held by many clubs. Last club—Atlanta N.L. vs. New York A.L., 1999 (4-game series).

Most shortstops used by both clubs, series
5—Chicago N.L. 3, Detroit A.L. 2, 1945 (7-game series).
New York A.L. 3, Pittsburgh N.L. 2, 1960 (7-game series).
Minnesota A.L. 3, Atlanta N.L. 2, 1991 (7-game series).

Most shortstops, game
3—New York A.L. vs. Pittsburgh N.L., October 13, 1960.
Cincinnati N.L. vs. Baltimore A.L., October 14, 1970.
Minnesota A.L. vs. Atlanta N.L. October 27, 1991, 10 innings.
Atlanta N.L. vs. New York A.L., October 23, 1996, 10 innings.

Most shortstops used by both clubs, nine-inning game
4—Made in many games.

Most shortstops used by both clubs, extra-inning game
5—Minnesota A.L. 3, Atlanta N.L. 2, October 27, 1991, 10 innings.

LEFT FIELDERS

Most left fielders, series
4—Held by many clubs. Last club—New York A.L. vs. Arizona N.L., 2001 (7-game series).

Most left fielders used by both clubs, series
7—Oakland A.L. 4, Los Angeles N.L. 3, 1988 (5-game series).
New York A.L. 4, Arizona N.L. 3, 2001 (7-game series).

Most left fielders, game
3—Held by many clubs. Last club—New York A.L. vs. New York N.L., October 21, 2000, 12 innings. Last club in nine-inning game—Atlanta N.L. vs. Cleveland A.L., October 22, 1995.

Most left fielders used by both clubs, game
5—Brooklyn N.L. 3, New York A.L. 2, October 5, 1947.
New York A.L. 3, New York N.L. 2, October 21, 2000, 12 innings.

CENTER FIELDERS

Most center fielders, series
4—Los Angeles N.L. vs. Chicago A.L., 1959 (6-game series).

Most center fielders used by both clubs, series
6—New York A.L. 3, Los Angeles N.L. 3, 1981 (6-game series).

Most center fielders, game
3—New York N.L. vs. New York A.L., October 5, 1922, 10 innings.

Most center fielders used by both clubs, game
4—Made in many games. Last game—New York A.L. 2, Los Angeles N.L. 2, October 24, 25, 1981.

RIGHT FIELDERS

Most right fielders, series
5—Los Angeles N.L. vs. Chicago A.L., 1959 (6-game series).

Most right fielders used by both clubs, series
9—Los Angeles N.L. 5, Chicago A.L. 4, 1959 (6-game series).

Most right fielders, game
3—Held by many clubs.

Most right fielders used by both clubs, game
5—Los Angeles N.L. 3, Chicago A.L. 2, October 8, 1959.

CATCHERS

Most catchers, series
4—Los Angeles N.L. vs. New York A.L., 1978 (6-game series).

Most catchers used by both clubs, series
6—New York A.L. 3, Pittsburgh N.L. 3, 1927 (4-game series).
Los Angeles N.L. 4, New York A.L. 2, 1978 (6-game series).
New York A.L. 3, Pittsburgh N.L. 3, 1960 (7-game series).

Most catchers, game
3—Philadelphia N.L. vs. New York A.L., October 5, 1950, 10 innings.
Los Angeles N.L. vs. New York A.L., October 13, 1978.

Most catchers used by both clubs, game
4—Made in many games.

PITCHERS

Most pitchers, series
4-game series—10
Oakland A.L. vs. Cincinnati N.L., 1990.
San Diego N.L. vs. New York A.L., 1998.
5-game series—10
San Diego N.L. vs. Detroit A.L., 1984.
Oakland A.L. vs. Los Angeles N.L., 1988.
New York N.L. vs. New York A.L., 2000.
6-game series—10—Held by many clubs. Last clubs—Atlanta N.L. vs. New York A.L., 1996; New York A.L. vs. Atlanta N.L., 1996.
7-game series—11
Boston A.L. vs. St. Louis N.L., 1946.
Cleveland A.L. vs. Florida N.L., 1997.
8-game series—8—New York A.L. vs. New York N.L., 1921.

For a list of players and pitchers used each series, see page 515.

Most pitchers used by both clubs, series
4-game series—19—San Diego N.L. 10, New York A.L. 9, 1998.
5-game series—18
Baltimore A.L. 9, Cincinnati N.L. 9, 1970.
New York N.L. 10, New York A.L. 8, 2000.
6-game series—20
Toronto A.L. 10, Philadelphia N.L. 10, 1993.
Atlanta N.L. 10, New York A.L. 10, 1996.
7-game series—21—Cleveland A.L. 11, Florida N.L. 10, 1997.
8-game series—12—New York A.L. 8, New York N.L. 4, 1921.

Fewest pitchers, series
2—Philadelphia A.L. vs. Chicago N.L. 1910 (5-game series).

Fewest pitchers used by both clubs, series
6—Philadelphia A.L. 3, New York N.L. 3, 1905 (5-game series).

Most different starting pitchers, series
6—Brooklyn N.L. vs. New York A.L., 1947.
Brooklyn N.L. vs. New York A.L., 1955.
Pittsburgh N.L. vs. Baltimore A.L., 1971.

Most different starting pitchers used by both clubs, series
11—Brooklyn N.L. 6, New York A.L. 5, 1955.

Most pitchers, game
8—Cincinnati N.L. vs. New York A.L., October 9, 1961.
St. Louis N.L. vs. Boston A.L., October 11, 1967.
Cincinnati N.L. vs. Boston A.L., October 21, 1975, 12 innings.

Most pitchers used by winning club, nine-inning game
6—Cincinnati N.L. vs. Oakland A.L., October 20, 1972 (won 5-4).
Most pitchers used by winning club, extra-inning game
7—Toronto A.L. vs. Atlanta N.L., October 24, 1992, 11 innings
   (won 4-3).
Most pitchers used by losing club, game
8—Cincinnati N.L. vs. New York A.L., October 9, 1961 (lost 13-5).
   St. Louis N.L. vs. Boston A.L., October 11, 1967 (lost 8-4).
   Cincinnati N.L. vs. Boston A.L., October 21, 1975, 12
      innings (lost 7-6).
Most pitchers used by both clubs, nine-inning game
11—St. Louis N.L. 8, Boston A.L. 3, October 11, 1967.
   San Francisco N.L. 6, Oakland A.L. 5, October 28, 1989.
Most pitchers used by both clubs, extra-inning game
13—Minnesota A.L. 7, Atlanta N.L. 6, October 22, 1991, 12 innings.
   New York A.L. 7, Atlanta N.L. 6, October 23, 1996, 10 innings.
Most pitchers, inning
5—Baltimore A.L. vs. Pittsburgh N.L., October 17, 1979, ninth inning.
   St. Louis N.L. vs. Kansas City A.L., October 27, 1985, fifth inning.

Most series played
38—New York A.L., 1921, 1922, 1923, 1926, 1927, 1928, 1932,
   1936, 1937, 1938, 1939, 1941, 1942, 1943, 1947,
   1949, 1950, 1951, 1952, 1953, 1955, 1956, 1957,
   1958, 1960, 1961, 1962, 1963, 1964, 1976, 1977,
   1978, 1981, 1996, 1998, 1999, 2000, 2001 (won 26,
   lost 12).
18—Brooklyn/Los Angeles N.L., 1916, 1920, 1941, 1947, 1949,
   1952, 1953, 1955, 1956, 1959, 1963, 1965, 1966,
   1974, 1977, 1978, 1981, 1988 (won 6, lost 12).

**For a complete list of results and a complete
list of series won and lost by teams, see
page 505.**

Most consecutive series played between same clubs
3—New York N.L. vs. New York A.L., 1921, 1922, 1923.

WORLD SERIES Club service

– 465 –

INDIVIDUAL BATTING

GAMES

Most games, career
75—Yogi Berra, New York A.L., 1947, 1949, 1950, 1951, 1952, 1953, 1955, 1956, 1957, 1958, 1960, 1961, 1962, 1963 (14 series, 65 consecutive games).

Most games with one club, career
75—Yogi Berra, New York A.L., 1947, 1949, 1950, 1951, 1952, 1953, 1955, 1956, 1957, 1958, 1960, 1961, 1962, 1963 (14 series, 65 consecutive games).

Most consecutive games played (in consecutive years)
30—Bobby Richardson, New York A.L., October 5, 1960 through October 15, 1964.

Most games by pinch-hitter, career
12—Luis Polonia, Oakland A.L., 1988 (2); Atlanta N.L., 1995 (2), 1996 (6); New York A.L., 2000 (2).

Most games by pinch-runner, career
9—Allan Lewis, Oakland A.L., 1972, 1973; two series (three runs).

Most games by pinch-hitter, series
6—Luis Polonia, Atlanta N.L., 1996.

Most games by pinch-runner, series
6—Allan Lewis, Oakland A.L., 1972 (scored two runs).

BATTING AVERAGE

Highest batting average, career (50 or more at-bats)
.418—Pepper Martin, St. Louis N.L., 1928, 1931, 1934; three series, 15 games (55 at-bats, 23 hits).
Paul Molitor, Milwaukee A.L., 1982; Toronto A.L., 1993; three series, 13 games (55 at-bats, 23 hits).

For a yearly list of batting leaders and a complete list of .450 hitters, see page 508.

Highest batting average, series
4-game series—.750—Billy Hatcher, Cincinnati N.L., 1990.
5-game series—.500
Larry McLean, New York N.L., 1913.
Joe Gordon, New York A.L., 1941.
6-game series—.500
Dave Robertson, New York N.L., 1917.
Billy Martin, New York A.L., 1953.
Paul Molitor, Toronto A.L., 1993.
7-game series—.500
Pepper Martin, St. Louis N.L., 1931.
Johnny Lindell, New York A.L., 1947 (played only six games due to broken rib).
Phil Garner, Pittsburgh N.L., 1979.
8-game series—.400—Buck Herzog, New York N.L., 1912.

Most series leading club in batting average
3—Home Run Baker, Philadelphia A.L., 1911, 1913, 1914.
Pee Wee Reese, Brooklyn N.L., 1947, 1949, 1952 (tied).
Duke Snider, Brooklyn N.L., 1952 (tied), 1955, 1956 (tied).
Gil Hodges, Brooklyn N.L., Los Angeles N.L., 1953, 1956 (tied), 1959.
Steve Garvey, Los Angeles N.L., 1974, 1977, 1981.

Most series batting .300 or over
6—Babe Ruth, New York A.L., 1921, 1923, 1926, 1927, 1928, 1932.

SLUGGING AVERAGE

Highest slugging average, career (20 or more games)
.755—Reggie Jackson, Oakland A.L., 1973, 1974; New York A.L., 1977, 1978, 1981; five series, 30 games (98 at-bats, 35 hits, seven doubles, one triple, 10 home runs, 74 total bases).

Highest slugging average, series
4-game series—1.727—Lou Gehrig, New York A.L., 1928.
5-game series—.929—Joe Gordon, New York A.L., 1941.
(Donn Clendenon, New York N.L., 1969, had slugging average of 1.071 but played only four games.)
6-game series—1.250—Reggie Jackson, New York A.L., 1977.
7-game series—.913—Gene Tenace, Oakland A.L., 1972.
8-game series—.600—Buck Herzog, New York N.L., 1912.

AT-BATS AND PLATE APPEARANCES

Most at-bats, career
259—Yogi Berra, New York A.L., 1947, 1949, 1950, 1951, 1952, 1953, 1955, 1956, 1957, 1958, 1960, 1961, 1962, 1963; 14 series, 75 games.

Most at-bats, series
4-game series—19
Mark Koenig, New York A.L., 1928.
Rickey Henderson, Oakland A.L., 1989.
Paul O'Neill, New York A.L., 1998.
5-game series—23
Hal Janvrin, Boston A.L., 1916.
Joe Moore, New York N.L., 1937.
Bobby Richardson, New York A.L., 1961.
6-game series—29—Mariano Duncan, Philadelphia N.L., 1993.
7-game series—33
Bucky Harris, Washington A.L., 1924.
Sam Rice, Washington A.L., 1925.
Omar Moreno, Pittsburgh N.L., 1979.
Devon White, Florida N.L., 1997.
8-game series—36—Jimmy Collins, Boston A.L., 1903.

Most at-bats, nine-inning game
6—Held by many players. Last player—Tony Womack, Arizona N.L., November 3, 2001.

Most at-bats, extra-inning game
7—Don Hahn, New York N.L., October 14, 1973, 12 innings.

Most times faced pitcher with no at-bats, game
5—Fred Clarke, Pittsburgh N.L., October 16, 1909 (four bases on balls, one sacrifice hit).

Most at-bats, inning
2—Held by many players. Last players—Matt Williams, Arizona N.L., November 3, 2001, third inning; Reggie Sanders, Arizona N.L., November 3, 2001, third inning.

Most times faced pitcher, inning
2—Held by many players. Last players—Greg Colbrunn, Arizona N.L., November 3, 2001, third inning; Matt Williams, Arizona N.L., November 3, 2001, third inning; Reggie Sanders, Arizona N.L., November 3, 2001, third inning.

Most at-bats by pinch-hitter, inning
2—George H. Burns, Philadelphia A.L., October 12, 1929, seventh inning.

Most times faced pitcher twice in an inning, career
3—Joe DiMaggio, New York A.L., October 6, 1936, ninth inning; October 6, 1937, sixth inning; September 30, 1947, fifth inning.

Most times faced pitcher twice in an inning, series
2—Stan Musial, St. Louis N.L., September 30, ninth inning; October 4, 1942, fourth inning.

RUNS

Most runs, career
42—Mickey Mantle, New York A.L., 1951, 1952, 1953, 1955, 1956, 1957, 1958, 1960, 1961, 1962, 1963, 1964; 12 series, 65 games.

Most runs, series

4-game series—9
Babe Ruth, New York A.L., 1928.
Lou Gehrig, New York A.L., 1932.
5-game series—6
Home Run Baker, Philadelphia A.L., 1910.
Dan Murphy, Philadelphia A.L., 1910.
Harry Hooper, Boston A.L., 1916.
Al Simmons, Philadelphia A.L., 1929.
Lee May, Cincinnati N.L., 1970.
Boog Powell, Baltimore A.L., 1970.
Lou Whitaker, Detroit A.L., 1984.
Derek Jeter, New York A.L., 2000.
6-game series—10
Reggie Jackson, New York A.L., 1977.
Paul Molitor, Toronto A.L., 1993.
7-game series—8
Tommy Leach, Pittsburgh N.L., 1909.
Pepper Martin, St. Louis N.L., 1934.
Billy Johnson, New York A.L., 1947.
Mickey Mantle, New York A.L., 1960.
Bobby Richardson, New York A.L., 1960.
Mickey Mantle, New York A.L., 1964.
Lou Brock, St. Louis N.L., 1967.
Jim Thome, Cleveland A.L., 1997.
Matt Williams, Cleveland A.L., 1997.
8-game series—8—Fred Parent, Boston A.L., 1903.

Most series with one or more runs

12—Yogi Berra, New York A.L., 1947, 1949, 1950, 1951, 1952,
1953, 1955, 1956, 1957, 1958, 1960, 1961.

Most at-bats without scoring a run, series

33—Devon White, Florida N.L., 1997 (7-game series).

Most consecutive games with one or more runs, career

9—Babe Ruth, New York A.L., 1927 (last 2), 1928 (4),
1932(first 3).

Most runs, game

4—Babe Ruth, New York A.L., October 6, 1926.
Earle Combs, New York A.L., October 2, 1932.
Frank Crosetti, New York A.L., October 2, 1936.
Enos Slaughter, St. Louis N.L., October 10, 1946.
Reggie Jackson, New York A.L., October 18, 1977.
Kirby Puckett, Minnesota A.L., October 24, 1987.
Carney Lansford, Oakland A.L., October 27, 1989.
Lenny Dykstra, Philadelphia N.L., October 20, 1993.

Most runs, inning

2—Frankie Frisch, New York N.L., October 7, 1921, seventh
inning.
Al Simmons, Philadelphia A.L., October 12, 1929, seventh
inning.
Jimmie Foxx, Philadelphia A.L., October 12, 1929, seventh
inning.
Dick McAuliffe, Detroit A.L., October 9, 1968, third inning.
Mickey Stanley, Detroit A.L., October 9, 1968, third inning.
Al Kaline, Detroit A.L., October 9, 1968, third inning.
Greg Colbrunn, Arizona N.L., November 3, 2001, third
inning.

HITS
CAREER AND SERIES

Most hits, career

71—Yogi Berra, New York A.L., 1947, 1949, 1950, 1951, 1952,
1953, 1955, 1956, 1957, 1958, 1960, 1961, 1962,
1963; 14 series, 75 games.

Most hits by pinch-hitter, career

3—Ken O'Dea, Chicago N.L., 1935 (1), 1938 (0); St. Louis N.L.,
1942 (1), 1943 (0), 1944 (1), 5 series, 8 games.
Bobby Brown, New York A.L., 1947 (3), 1949 (0), 1950 (0),
1951 (0), four series, seven games.
Johnny Mize, New York A.L., 1949 (2), 1950 (0), 1951 (0),
1952 (1), 1953 (0), five series, eight games.
Dusty Rhodes, New York N.L., 1954 (3), one series, three
games.

Carl Furillo, Brooklyn N.L., 1947 (2), 1949 (0); Los Angeles
N.L., 1959 (1), three series, seven games.
Bob Cerv, New York A.L., 1955 (1), 1956 (1), 1960 (1),
three series, three games.
John Blanchard, New York A.L., 1960 (1), 1961 (1), 1962
(0), 1964 (1), four series, 10 games.
Carl Warwick, St. Louis N.L., 1964 (3), one series, five games.
Gonzalo Marquez, Oakland A.L., 1972 (3), one series, five
games.
Ken Boswell, New York N.L., 1973 (3), one series, three games.

Most series with one or more hits

12—Yogi Berra, New York A.L., 1947, 1949, 1950, 1951, 1952,
1953, 1955, 1956, 1957, 1958, 1960, 1961.
Mickey Mantle, New York A.L., 1951, 1952, 1953, 1955,
1956, 1957, 1958, 1960, 1961, 1962, 1963, 1964.

Most consecutive games with one or more hits, career

17—Hank Bauer, New York A.L., 1956 (7), 1957 (7), 1958 (first 3).

Most hits, series

4-game series—10—Babe Ruth, New York A.L., 1928.
5-game series—9
Home Run Baker, Philadelphia A.L., 1910.
Eddie Collins, Philadelphia A.L., 1910.
Home Run Baker, Philadelphia A.L., 1913.
Heinie Groh, New York N.L., 1922.
Joe Moore, New York N.L., 1937.
Bobby Richardson, New York A.L., 1961.
Paul Blair, Baltimore A.L., 1970.
Brooks Robinson, Baltimore A.L., 1970.
Alan Trammell, Detroit A.L., 1984.
Derek Jeter, New York A.L., 2000.
Paul O'Neill, New York A.L., 2000.
6-game series—12
Billy Martin, New York A.L., 1953.
Paul Molitor, Toronto A.L., 1993.
Roberto Alomar, Toronto A.L., 1993.
Marquis Grissom, Atlanta N.L., 1996.
7-game series—13
Bobby Richardson, New York A.L., 1964.
Lou Brock, St. Louis N.L., 1968.
Marty Barrett, Boston A.L., 1986.
8-game series—12
Buck Herzog, New York N.L., 1912.
Joe Jackson, Chicago A.L., 1919.

Most hits by pinch-hitter, series

3—Bobby Brown, New York A.L., 1947 (consecutive; four
games; one base on balls, one single, two doubles, three
runs batted in).
Dusty Rhodes, New York N.L., 1954 (consecutive; three
games; one home run, two singles, six runs batted in).
Carl Warwick, St. Louis N.L., 1964 (consecutive; five
games; two singles, walk, single, one run batted in).
Gonzalo Marquez, Oakland A.L., 1972 (consecutive; three
games; three singles, one run batted in).
Ken Boswell, New York N.L., 1973 (consecutive; three
games; three singles).

Most consecutive hits, career

7—Thurman Munson, New York A.L., October 19 (2), October
21 (4), 1976, October 11 (1), 1977.
Billy Hatcher, Cincinnati N.L., October 16 (3), 17 (4), 1990.

Most hits, two consecutive series

25—Lou Brock, St. Louis N.L., 1967 (12), 1968 (13).

Most consecutive hits, series

7—Billy Hatcher, Cincinnati N.L., October 16 (3), 17 (4), 1990.

Most games with four or more hits, series

2—Robin Yount, Milwaukee A.L., October 12 (4), 16 (4), 1982.

Collecting one or more hits in each game, series

Held by many players.

Most at-bats without a hit, career

22—George Earnshaw, Philadelphia A.L., 1929 (5), 1930 (9),
1931 (8).

Most at-bats without a hit, series

22—Dal Maxvill, St. Louis N.L., 1968 (7-game series).

Most consecutive hitless times at bat, career
31—Marv Owen, Detroit A.L., 1934 (last 12), 1935 (first 19).

GAME AND INNING

Most hits, game
5—Paul Molitor, Milwaukee A.L., October 12, 1982.

Most times reached first base safely, nine-inning game (batting 1.000)
5—Babe Ruth, New York A.L., October 6, 1926 (three home runs, two bases on balls).
Babe Ruth, New York A.L., October 10, 1926 (one home run, four bases on balls).
Lou Brock, St. Louis N.L., October 4, 1967 (four singles, one base on balls).
Brooks Robinson, Baltimore A.L., October 11, 1971 (three singles, two bases on balls).
Rusty Staub, New York N.L., October 17, 1973 (three singles, one home run, one base on balls).
Kiko Garcia, Baltimore A.L., October 12, 1979 (two singles, one double, one triple, one base on balls).
Reggie Jackson, New York A.L., October 24, 1981 (two singles, one home run, two bases on balls).
George Brett, Kansas City A.L., October 22, 1985 (two singles, three bases on balls).
Kirby Puckett, Minnesota A.L., October 24, 1987 (four singles, one base on balls).
Billy Hatcher, Cincinnati N.L., October 17, 1990 (one single, two doubles, one triple, one base on balls).
Matt Williams, Cleveland A.L., October 22, 1997 (two singles, one home run, two bases on balls).

Most hits accounting for all club's hits, game
3—Irish Meusel, New York N.L., October 14, 1923 (one single, one double, one triple).
Dave Parker, Oakland A.L., October 16, 1988 (three singles).

Most at-bats with no hits, nine-inning game
5—Held by many players.

Most at-bats with no hits, extra-inning game
6—Travis Jackson, New York N.L., October 10, 1924, 12 innings.
Hughie Critz, New York N.L., October 6, 1933, 11 innings.
Felix Millan, New York N.L., October 14, 1973, 12 innings.
Mickey Rivers, New York A.L., October 11, 1977, 12 innings.
Ron Gant, Atlanta N.L., October 22, 1991, 12 innings.
Devon White, Florida N.L., October 26, 1997, 11 innings.
Craig Counsell, Arizona N.L., November 1, 2001, 12 innings.

Most hits in two consecutive games, series
7—Frank Isbell, Chicago A.L., October 13 (4), 14 (3), 1906.
Fred Lindstrom, New York N.L., October 7 (3), 8 (4), 1924.
Monte Irvin, New York N.L., October 4 (4), 5 (3), 1951.
Thurman Munson, New York A.L., October 19 (3), 21 (4), 1976.
Paul Molitor, Milwaukee A.L., October 12 (5), 13 (2), 1982.
Billy Hatcher, Cincinnati N.L., October 16 (3), 17 (4), 1990.

Most hits, inning (18 times)
2—Ross Youngs, New York N.L., October 7, 1921, seventh inning.
Al Simmons, Philadelphia A.L., October 12, 1929, seventh inning.
Jimmie Foxx, Philadelphia A.L., October 12, 1929, seventh inning.
Jimmie Dykes, Philadelphia A.L., October 12, 1929, seventh inning.
Joe Moore, New York N.L., October 4, 1933, sixth inning.
Dizzy Dean, St. Louis N.L., October 9, 1934, third inning.
Joe DiMaggio, New York A.L., October 6, 1936, ninth inning.
Hank Leiber, New York N.L., October 9, 1937, second inning.
Stan Musial, St. Louis N.L., October 4, 1942, fourth inning.
Elston Howard, New York A.L., October 6, 1960, sixth inning.
Bobby Richardson, New York A.L., October 6, 1960, sixth inning.
Bob Cerv, New York A.L., October 8, 1960, first inning.
Frank Quilici, Minnesota A.L., October 6, 1965, third inning.

Al Kaline, Detroit A.L., October 9, 1968, third inning.
Norm Cash, Detroit A.L., October 9, 1968, third inning.
Merv Rettenmund, Baltimore A.L., October 11, 1971, fifth inning.
Gary Gaetti, Minnesota A.L., October 17, 1987, fourth inning.
Matt Williams, Arizona N.L., November 3, 2001, third inning.

SINGLES

Most singles, career
49—Yogi Berra, New York A.L., 1947, 1949, 1950, 1951, 1952, 1953, 1955, 1956, 1957, 1958, 1960, 1961, 1962, 1963; 14 series, 75 games.

Most singles, series
4-game series—9—Thurman Munson, New York A.L., 1976.
5-game series—8
Frank Chance, Chicago N.L., 1908.
Home Run Baker, Philadelphia A.L., 1913.
Heinie Groh, New York N.L., 1922.
Joe Moore, New York N.L., 1937.
Bobby Richardson, New York A.L., 1961.
Paul Blair, Baltimore A.L., 1970.
Steve Garvey, Los Angeles N.L., 1974.
6-game series—10
Red Rolfe, New York A.L., 1936.
Monte Irvin, New York N.L., 1951.
7-game series—12—Sam Rice, Washington A.L., 1925.
8-game series—9
Jimmy Sebring, Pittsburgh N.L., 1903.
Chief Meyers, New York N.L., 1912.

Most singles, game
5—Paul Molitor, Milwaukee A.L., October 12, 1982.

Most singles, inning
2—Jimmie Foxx, Philadelphia A.L., October 12, 1929, seventh inning.
Joe Moore, New York N.L., October 4, 1933, sixth inning.
Joe DiMaggio, New York A.L., October 6, 1936, ninth inning.
Hank Leiber, New York N.L., October 9, 1937, second inning.
Bob Cerv, New York A.L., October 8, 1960, first inning.
Al Kaline, Detroit A.L., October 9, 1968, third inning.
Norm Cash, Detroit A.L., October 9, 1968, third inning.
Merv Rettenmund, Baltimore A.L., October 11, 1971, fifth inning.

DOUBLES

Most doubles, career
10—Frankie Frisch, New York N.L. (5), 1921, 1922, 1923, 1924; St. Louis N.L. (5), 1928, 1930, 1931, 1934; eight series, 50 games.
Yogi Berra, New York A.L., 1947, 1949, 1950, 1951, 1952, 1953, 1955, 1956, 1957, 1958, 1960, 1961, 1962, 1963; 14 series, 75 games.

Most doubles, series
4-game series—4—Billy Hatcher, Cincinnati, N.L., 1990.
5-game series—4
Eddie Collins, Philadelphia A.L., 1910.
Rick Dempsey, Baltimore A.L., 1983.
6-game series—5—Chick Hafey, St. Louis N.L., 1930.
7-game series—6—Pete Fox, Detroit A.L., 1934.
8-game series—4
Red Murray, New York N.L., 1912.
Buck Herzog, New York N.L., 1912.
Buck Weaver, Chicago A.L., 1919.
George J. Burns, New York N.L., 1921.

Most doubles, game
4—Frank Isbell, Chicago A.L., October 13, 1906.

Most doubles batting in three runs, game
1—Frankie Frisch, St. Louis N.L., October 9, 1934, third inning.
Paul Richards, Detroit A.L., October 10, 1945, first inning.
Lou Brock, St. Louis N.L., October 6, 1968, eighth inning.
Terry Pendleton, St. Louis N.L., October 20, 1985, ninth inning.

Most doubles, inning
2—Matt Williams, Arizona N.L., November 3, 2001, third inning.

TRIPLES

Most triples, career
4—Tommy Leach, Pittsburgh N.L., 1903, 1909; two series, 15
　　games.
　　Tris Speaker, Boston A.L. (3), 1912, 1915; Cleveland A.L.
　　　(1), 1920; three series, 20 games.
　　Billy Johnson, New York A.L., 1943, 1947, 1949, 1950; four
　　　series, 18 games.

Most games without a triple, career
75—Yogi Berra, New York A.L.; 14 series, 259 at-bats.

Most triples, series
4-game series—2
　Lou Gehrig, New York A.L., 1927.
　Tommy Davis, Los Angeles N.L., 1963.
　Rickey Henderson, Oakland A.L., 1989.
5-game series—2
　Eddie Collins, Philadelphia A.L., 1913.
　Bobby Brown, New York A.L., 1949.
　Paul O'Neill, New York A.L., 2000.
6-game series—2
　George Rohe, Chicago A.L., 1906.
　Bob Meusel, New York A.L., 1923.
　Billy Martin, New York A.L., 1953.
　Paul Molitor, Toronto A.L., 1993.
　Devon White, Toronto A.L., 1993.
7-game series—3
　Billy Johnson, New York A.L., 1947.
　Mark Lemke, Atlanta N.L., 1991.
8-game series—4—Tommy Leach, Pittsburgh N.L., 1903.

Most triples, game
2—Tommy Leach, Pittsburgh N.L., October 1, 1903.
　　Patsy Dougherty, Boston A.L., October 7, 1903.
　　Dutch Ruether, Cincinnati N.L., October 1, 1919.
　　Bobby Richardson, New York A.L., October 12, 1960.
　　Tommy Davis, Los Angeles N.L., October 3, 1963.
　　Mark Lemke, Atlanta N.L., October 24, 1991.

Most bases-loaded triples, game
1—George Rohe, Chicago A.L., October 11, 1906, sixth inning.
　　Ross Youngs, New York N.L., October 7, 1921, seventh inning.
　　Billy Johnson, New York A.L., October 7, 1943, eighth inning.
　　Bobby Brown, New York A.L., October 8, 1949, fifth inning.
　　Hank Bauer, New York A.L., October 10, 1951, sixth inning.
　　Billy Martin, New York A.L., September 30, 1953, first inning.
　　Kiko Garcia, Baltimore A.L., October 12, 1979, fourth inning.
　　Milt Thompson, Philadelphia N.L., October 20, 1993, first
　　　inning.

Most triples, inning
1—Held by many players.

HOME RUNS
CAREER AND SERIES

Most home runs, career
18—Mickey Mantle, New York A.L., 1951, 1952, 1953, 1955,
　　1956, 1957, 1958, 1960, 1961, 1962, 1963, 1964; 12
　　series, 65 games.

**For a list of all home runs each series and a
complete list of players with five or more
career home runs, see page 510.**

Most home runs by pitcher, career
2—Bob Gibson, St. Louis N.L., 1964 (0), 1967 (1), 1968 (1);
　　three series, nine games.
　　Dave McNally, Baltimore A.L., 1966 (0), 1969 (1), 1970 (1),
　　1971 (0); four series, nine games.

Most games without a home run, career
50—Frankie Frisch, New York N.L., St. Louis N.L.; eight series,
　　197 at-bats.

Most series with one or more home runs
9—Yogi Berra, New York A.L., 1947 (1), 1950 (1), 1952 (2),
　　　1953 (1), 1955 (1), 1956 (3), 1957 (1), 1960 (1), 1961 (1).
　　Mickey Mantle, New York A.L., 1952 (2), 1953 (2), 1955
　　　(1), 1956 (3), 1957 (1), 1958 (2), 1960 (3), 1963 (1),
　　　1964 (3).

Most home runs, four consecutive games (homering in each game)
6—Reggie Jackson, New York A.L., 1977 (5), last three games;
　　1978 (1), first game.

Hitting home runs for both leagues
Bill Skowron, A.L. (7), N.L. (1).
Frank Robinson, N.L. (1), A.L. (7).
Roger Maris, A.L. (5), N.L. (1).
Reggie Smith, A.L. (2), N.L. (4).
Enos Slaughter, N.L. (2), A.L. (1).
Kirk Gibson, A.L. (2), N.L. (1).
Matt Williams, N.L. (2), A.L. (1).

Most home runs, series
4-game series—4—Lou Gehrig, New York A.L., 1928.
5-game series—3—Donn Clendenon, New York N.L., 1969.
6-game series—5—Reggie Jackson, New York, 1977.
7-game series—4
　Babe Ruth, New York A.L., 1926.
　Duke Snider, Brooklyn N.L., 1952.
　Duke Snider, Brooklyn N.L., 1955.
　Hank Bauer, New York A.L., 1958.
　Gene Tenace, Oakland A.L., 1972.
8-game series—2—Patsy Dougherty, Boston A.L., 1903.

Most home runs by pinch-hitter, series
2—Chuck Essegian, Los Angeles N.L., 4 games, 1959.
　　Bernie Carbo, Boston A.L., 3 games, 1975.

Most home runs by rookie, series
3—Charlie Keller, New York A.L., 1939.

Most series with two or more home runs
6—Mickey Mantle, New York A.L., 1952 (2), 1953 (2), 1956 (3),
　　1958 (2), 1960 (3), 1964 (3).

Most series with three or more home runs
3—Babe Ruth, New York A.L., 1923 (3), 1926 (4), 1928 (3).
　　Mickey Mantle, New York A.L., 1956 (3), 1960 (3), 1964 (3).

Most series with four or more home runs
2—Duke Snider, Brooklyn N.L., 1952, 1955.

Most home runs, two consecutive series (two consecutive years)
7—Reggie Jackson, New York A.L., 1977 (5), 1978 (2).

Most home runs, three consecutive series (three consecutive years)
9—Babe Ruth, New York A.L., 1926 (4), 1927 (2), 1928 (3).

Most home runs in three consecutive games, series (homering each game)
5—Reggie Jackson, New York A.L., October 15 (1), 16 (1), 18
　　(3), 1977.

Most home runs in two consecutive games, series (homering each game)
4—Reggie Jackson, New York A.L., October 16 (1), 18 (3), 1977.

Most consecutive home runs in two consecutive games, series
4—Reggie Jackson, New York A.L., October 16 (1), 18 (3),
　　1977 (one base on balls included).

Most series with two or more home runs in a game
4—Babe Ruth, New York A.L., 1923, 1926, 1928, 1932 (two
　　home runs in one game twice, three home runs in one
　　game twice).

GAME AND INNING

Most home runs, game (3 homers, 3 times; 2 homers, 37 times; *consecutive)

3—Babe Ruth, New York A.L., October 6, 1926 (two consecutive).
Babe Ruth, New York A.L., October 9, 1928, (two consecutive).
Reggie Jackson, New York A.L., October 18, 1977 (each on first pitch).*

2—Patsy Dougherty, Boston A.L., October 2, 1903.
Harry Hooper, Boston A.L., October 13, 1915.
Benny Kauff, New York N.L., October 11, 1917.
Babe Ruth, New York A.L., October 11, 1923.*
Lou Gehrig, New York A.L., October 7, 1928.*
Lou Gehrig, New York A.L., October 1, 1932.*
Babe Ruth, New York A.L., October 1, 1932.
Tony Lazzeri, New York A.L., October 2, 1932.
Charlie Keller, New York A.L., October 7, 1939.
Bob Elliott, Boston N.L., October 10, 1948.*
Duke Snider, Brooklyn N.L., October 6, 1952.*
Joe Collins, New York A.L., September 28, 1955.*
Duke Snider, Brooklyn N.L., October 2, 1955.*
Yogi Berra, New York A.L., October 10, 1956.*
Tony Kubek, New York A.L., October 5, 1957.
Mickey Mantle, New York A.L., October 2, 1958.
Ted Kluszewski, Chicago A.L., October 1, 1959.*
Charlie Neal, Los Angeles N.L., October 2, 1959.*
Mickey Mantle, New York A.L., October 6, 1960.
Carl Yastrzemski, Boston A.L., October 5, 1967.
Rico Petrocelli, Boston A.L., October 11, 1967.*
Gene Tenace, Oakland A.L., October 14, 1972.*
Tony Perez, Cincinnati N.L., October 16, 1975.*
Johnny Bench, Cincinnati N.L., October 21, 1976.
Dave Lopes, Los Angeles N.L., October 10, 1978.*
Willie Aikens, Kansas City A.L., October 14, 1980.
Willie Aikens, Kansas City A.L., October 18, 1980.
Willie McGee, St. Louis N.L., October 15, 1982.*
Eddie Murray, Baltimore A.L., October 16, 1983.*
Alan Trammell, Detroit A.L., October 13, 1984.*
Kirk Gibson, Detroit A.L., October 14, 1984.
Gary Carter, New York N.L., October 22, 1986.
Dave Henderson, Oakland A.L., October 27, 1989.*
Chris Sabo, Cincinnati N.L., October 19, 1990.*
Andruw Jones, Atlanta N.L., October 20, 1996.*
Scott Brosius, New York A.L., October 20, 1998.*
Chad Curtis, New York A.L., October 26, 1999 (10 innings).

Most home runs by rookie, game

2—Charlie Keller, New York A.L., October 7, 1939.
Tony Kubek, New York A.L., October 5, 1957.
Willie McGee, St. Louis N.L., October 15, 1982.
Andruw Jones, Atlanta N.L., October 20, 1996.

Hitting home runs in first two World Series at-bats

Gene Tenace, Oakland A.L., October 14, 1972, second and fifth innings.
Andruw Jones, Atlanta N.L., October 20, 1996, second and third innings.

Hitting home run in first World Series at-bat (25 times; *not first plate appearance)

Joe Harris, Washington A.L., vs. Pittsburgh N.L., October 7, 1925, second inning.
George Watkins, St. Louis N.L., vs. Philadelphia A.L., October 2, 1930, second inning.
Mel Ott, New York N.L., vs. Washington A.L., October 3, 1933, first inning.
George Selkirk, New York A.L., vs. New York N.L., September 30, 1936, third inning.
Dusty Rhodes, New York N.L., vs. Cleveland A.L., September 29, 1954, 10th inning.
Elston Howard, New York A.L., vs. Brooklyn N.L. September 28, 1955, second inning.
Roger Maris, New York A.L., vs. Pittsburgh N.L., October 5, 1960, first inning.
Don Mincher, Minnesota A.L., vs. Los Angeles N.L., October 6, 1965, second inning.
Brooks Robinson, Baltimore A.L., vs. Los Angeles N.L., October 5, 1966, first inning.

Jose R. Santiago, Boston A.L., vs. St. Louis N.L., October 4, 1967, third inning.
Mickey Lolich, Detroit A.L., vs. St. Louis N.L., October 3, 1968, third inning.
Don Buford, Baltimore A.L., vs. New York N.L., October 11, 1969, first inning.
Gene Tenace, Oakland A.L., vs. Cincinnati N.L., October 14, 1972, second inning.
Jim Mason, New York A.L., vs. Cincinnati N.L., October 19, 1976, seventh inning.
Doug DeCinces, Baltimore A.L. vs. Pittsburgh N.L., October 10, 1979, first inning.
Amos Otis, Kansas City A.L. vs. Philadelphia N.L., October 14, 1980, second inning.
Bob Watson, New York A.L. vs. Los Angeles N.L., October 20, 1981, first inning.
Jim Dwyer, Baltimore A.L. vs. Philadelphia N.L., October 11, 1983, first inning.
Mickey Hatcher, Los Angeles N.L. vs. Oakland A.L., October 15, 1988, first inning.
Jose Canseco, Oakland A.L. vs. Los Angeles N.L., October 15, 1988, second inning.*
Bill Bathe, San Francisco N.L. vs. Oakland A.L., October 27, 1989, ninth inning.
Eric Davis, Cincinnati N.L. vs. Oakland A.L., October 16, 1990, first inning.
Ed Sprague Jr., Toronto A.L. vs. Atlanta N.L., October 18, 1992, ninth inning.
Fred McGriff, Atlanta N.L. vs. Cleveland A.L., October 21, 1995, second inning.
Andruw Jones, Atlanta N.L. vs. New York A.L., October 20, 1996, second inning.

Most times hitting home run winning a 1-0 game

1—Casey Stengel, New York N.L., October 12, 1923, seventh inning.
Tommy Henrich, New York A.L., October 5, 1949, ninth inning.
Paul Blair, Baltimore A.L., October 8, 1966, fifth inning.
Frank Robinson, Baltimore A.L., October 9, 1966, fourth inning.
David Justice, Atlanta N.L., October 28, 1995, sixth inning.

Most times homering as leadoff batter at start of game (16 times)

1—Patsy Dougherty, Boston A.L., October 2, 1903.
Davy Jones, Detroit A.L., October 13, 1909.
Phil Rizzuto, New York A.L., October 5, 1942.
Dale Mitchell, Cleveland A.L., October 10, 1948.
Gene Woodling, New York A.L., October 4, 1953.
Al Smith, Cleveland A.L., September 30, 1954.
Billy Bruton, Milwaukee N.L., October 2, 1958.
Lou Brock, St. Louis N.L., October 6, 1968.
Don Buford, Baltimore A.L., October 11, 1969.
Tommie Agee, New York N.L., October 14, 1969.
Pete Rose, Cincinnati N.L., October 20, 1972.
Wayne Garrett, New York N.L., October 16, 1973.
Dave Lopes, Los Angeles N.L., October 17, 1978.
Lenny Dykstra, New York N.L., October 21, 1986.
Rickey Henderson, Oakland A.L., October 28, 1989.
Derek Jeter, New York A.L., October 25, 2000.

Most home runs by pitcher, game (14 times)

1—Jim Bagby Sr., Cleveland A.L., October 10, 1920 (two on base).
Rosy Ryan, New York N.L., October 6, 1924 (none on base).
Jack Bentley, New York A.L., October 8, 1924 (one on base).
Jesse Haines, St. Louis N.L., October 5, 1926 (one on base).
Bucky Walters, Cincinnati N.L., October 7, 1940 (none on base).
Lew Burdette, Milwaukee N.L., October 2, 1958 (none on base).
Mudcat Grant, Minnesota A.L., October 13, 1965 (two on base).
Jose R. Santiago, Boston A.L., October 4, 1967 (none on base).
Bob Gibson, St. Louis N.L., October 12, 1967 (none on base).
Mickey Lolich, Detroit A.L., October 3, 1968 (none on base).
Bob Gibson, St. Louis N.L., October 6, 1968 (none on base).
Dave McNally, Baltimore A.L., October 16, 1969 (none on base).
Dave McNally, Baltimore A.L., October 13, 1970 (three on base).
Ken Holtzman, Oakland A.L., October 16, 1974 (none on base).

Most home runs by pinch-hitter, inning or game (17 times)

1—Yogi Berra, New York A.L., October 2, 1947, seventh inning (none on base).
Johnny Mize, New York A.L., October 3, 1952, ninth inning (none on base).
George Shuba, Brooklyn N.L., September 30, 1953, sixth inning (one on base).
Dusty Rhodes, New York N.L., September 29, 1954, 10th inning (two on base).
Hank Majeski, Cleveland A.L., October 2, 1954, fifth inning (two on base).
Bob Cerv, New York A.L., October 2, 1955, seventh inning (none on base).
Chuck Essegian, Los Angeles N.L., October 2, 1959, seventh inning (none on base).
Chuck Essegian, Los Angeles N.L., October 8, 1959, ninth inning (none on base).
Elston Howard, New York A.L., October 5, 1960, ninth inning (one on base).
John Blanchard, New York A.L., October 7, 1961, eighth inning (none on base).
Bernie Carbo, Boston A.L., October 14, 1975, seventh inning (none on base).
Bernie Carbo, Boston A.L., October 21, 1975, eighth inning (two on base).
Jay Johnstone, Los Angeles N.L., October 24, 1981, sixth inning (one on base).
Kirk Gibson, Los Angeles N.L., October 15, 1988, ninth inning (one on base).
Bill Bathe, San Francisco N.L., October 27, 1989, ninth inning (two on base).
Chili Davis, Minnesota A.L., October 22, 1991, eighth inning (one on base).
Ed Sprague Jr., Toronto A.L., October 18, 1992, ninth inning (one on base).
Jim Leyritz, New York A.L., October 27, 1999, eighth inning (none on base).

Most grand slams, game (17 times)

1—Elmer Smith, Cleveland A.L., October 10, 1920, first inning.
Tony Lazzeri, New York A.L., October 2, 1936, third inning.
Gil McDougald, New York A.L., October 9, 1951, third inning.
Mickey Mantle, New York A.L., October 4, 1953, third inning.
Yogi Berra, New York A.L., October 5, 1956, second inning.
Bill Skowron, New York A.L., October 10, 1956, seventh inning.
Bobby Richardson, New York A.L., October 8, 1960, first inning.
Chuck Hiller, San Francisco N.L., October 8, 1962, seventh inning.
Ken Boyer, St. Louis N.L., October 11, 1964, sixth inning.
Joe Pepitone, New York A.L., October 14, 1964, eighth inning.
Jim Northrup, Detroit A.L., October 9, 1968, third inning.
Dave McNally, Baltimore A.L., October 13, 1970, sixth inning.
Dan Gladden, Minnesota A.L., October 17, 1987, fourth inning.
Kent Hrbek, Minnesota A.L., October 24, 1987, sixth inning.
Jose Canseco, Oakland A.L., October 15, 1988, second inning.
Lonnie Smith, Atlanta N.L., October 22, 1992, fifth inning.
Tino Martinez, New York A.L., October 17, 1998, seventh inning.

Most home runs, inning

1—Held by many players.

Most home runs, two consecutive innings (nine times)

2—Babe Ruth, New York A.L., October 11, 1923, fourth and fifth innings.
Babe Ruth, New York A.L., October 9, 1928, seventh and eighth innings.
Ted Kluszewski, Chicago A.L., October 1, 1959, third and fourth innings.
Reggie Jackson, New York A.L., October 18, 1977, fourth and fifth innings.
Willie Aikens, Kansas City A.L., October 18, 1980, first and second innings.
Dave Henderson, Oakland A.L., October 27, 1989, fourth and fifth innings.

Chris Sabo, Cincinnati N.L., October 19, 1990, second and third innings.
Andruw Jones, Atlanta N.L., October 20, 1996, second and third innings.
Scott Brosius, New York A.L., October 20, 1998, seventh and eighth innings.

TOTAL BASES

Most total bases, career

123—Mickey Mantle, New York A.L., 1951, 1952, 1953, 1955, 1956, 1957, 1958, 1960, 1961, 1962, 1963, 1964; 12 series, 65 games.

Most total bases, series

4-game series—22—Babe Ruth, New York A.L., 1928.
5-game series—19—Derek Jeter, New York A.L., 2000.
6-game series—25—Reggie Jackson, New York A.L., 1977.
7-game series—25—Willie Stargell, Pittsburgh N.L., 1979.
8-game series—18
Buck Herzog, New York N.L., 1912.
Joe Jackson, Chicago A.L., 1919.

Most total bases by pinch-hitter, series

8—Chuck Essegian, Los Angeles N.L., 1959; four games (two home runs).
Bernie Carbo, Boston A.L., 1975; three games (two home runs).

Most total bases, game

12—Babe Ruth, New York A.L., October 6, 1926 (three home runs).
Babe Ruth, New York A.L., October 9, 1928 (three home runs).
Reggie Jackson, New York A.L., October 18, 1977 (three home runs).

Most total bases, inning

5—Ross Youngs, New York N.L., October 7, 1921, seventh inning (double and triple).
Al Simmons, Philadelphia A.L., October 12, 1929, seventh inning (home run and single).

LONG HITS

Most long hits, career

26—Mickey Mantle, New York A.L., 1951, 1952, 1953, 1955, 1956, 1957, 1958, 1960, 1961, 1962, 1963, 1964; 12 series, 65 games.

Most long hits, series

4-game series—6—Babe Ruth, New York A.L., 1928.
5-game series—5
Rick Dempsey, Baltimore A.L., 1983.
Derek Jeter, New York A.L., 2000.
6-game series—6
Reggie Jackson, New York A.L., 1977.
Paul Molitor, Toronto A.L., 1993.
Devon White, Toronto A.L., 1993.
7-game series—7—Willie Stargell, Pittsburgh N.L., 1979.
8-game series—5
Red Murray, New York N.L., 1912.
Buck Herzog, New York N.L., 1912.
Buck Weaver, Chicago A.L., 1919.
George J. Burns, New York N.L., 1921.

Most long hits, game

4—Frank Isbell, Chicago A.L., October 13, 1906 (four doubles).

Most long hits in two consecutive games, series

5—Lou Brock, St. Louis N.L., October 6 (3—double, triple, home run); October 7 (2—two doubles), 1968.

Most long hits, inning

2—Ross Youngs, New York N.L., October 7, 1921, seventh inning (double and triple).

EXTRA BASES ON LONG HITS

Most extra bases on long hits, career
64—Mickey Mantle, New York A.L., 1951, 1952, 1953, 1955, 1956, 1957, 1958, 1960, 1961, 1962, 1963, 1964; 12 series, 65 games.

Most extra bases on long hits, series
4-game series—13—Lou Gehrig, New York A.L., 1928 (one double, four home runs).
5-game series—10
Donn Clendenon, New York N.L., 1969 (one double, three home runs).
Derek Jeter, New York A.L., 2000 (two doubles, one triple, two home runs).
6-game series—16—Reggie Jackson, New York A.L. 1977 (one double, five home runs).
7-game series—14—Duke Snider, Brooklyn N.L., 1952 (two doubles, four home runs).
8-game series—10—Patsy Dougherty, Boston A.L., 1903 (two triples, two home runs).

RUNS BATTED IN

Most runs batted in, career
40—Mickey Mantle, New York A.L., 1951, 1952, 1953, 1955, 1956, 1957, 1958, 1960, 1961, 1962, 1963, 1964; 12 series, 65 games.

Most series with one or more runs batted in
11—Yogi Berra, New York A.L., 1947, 1949, 1950, 1952, 1953, 1955, 1956, 1957, 1958, 1960, 1961.

Most consecutive games with one or more RBIs, career
8—Lou Gehrig, New York A.L., 1928 (4), 1932 (4); total of 17 runs batted in.
Reggie Jackson, New York A.L., 1977 (4), 1978 (4); total of 14 runs batted in.

Most runs batted in, series
4-game series—9—Lou Gehrig, New York A.L., 1928.
5-game series—8
Dan Murphy, Philadelphia A.L., 1910.
Lee May, Cincinnati N.L., 1970.
6-game series—10—Ted Kluszewski, Chicago A.L., 1959.
7-game series—12—Bobby Richardson, New York A.L., 1960.
8-game series—8
Tommy Leach, Pittsburgh N.L., 1903.
Pat Duncan, Cincinnati N.L., 1919.

Most runs batted in by pinch-hitter, series
6—Dusty Rhodes, New York N.L., 1954; three games.

Most at-bats without a run batted in, series
34—Fred Clarke, Pittsburgh N.L., 1903; eight games.
Buck Weaver, Chicago A.L., 1919; eight games.

Most runs batted in, game
6—Bobby Richardson, New York A.L., October 8, 1960.

Most runs batted in accounting for all club's runs, game
4—Hank Bauer, New York A.L., October 4, 1958 (won 4-0).
Ken Boyer, St. Louis N.L., October 11, 1964 (won 4-3).
Ron Cey, Los Angeles N.L., October 11, 1978 (won 4-3).
Alan Trammell, Detroit A.L., October 13, 1984 (won 4-2).
Jose Canseco, Oakland A.L., October 15, 1988 (lost 5-4).

Most runs batted in, inning (17 times)
4—Elmer Smith, Cleveland A.L., October 10, 1920, first inning.
Tony Lazzeri, New York A.L., October 2, 1936, third inning.
Gil McDougald, New York A.L., October 9, 1951, third inning.
Mickey Mantle, New York A.L., October 4, 1953, third inning.
Yogi Berra, New York A.L., October 5, 1956, second inning.
Bill Skowron, New York A.L., October 10, 1956, seventh inning.
Bobby Richardson, New York A.L., October 8, 1960, first inning.
Chuck Hiller, San Francisco N.L., October 8, 1962, seventh inning.

Ken Boyer, St. Louis N.L., October 11, 1964, sixth inning.
Joe Pepitone, New York A.L., October 14, 1964, eighth inning.
Jim Northrup, Detroit A.L., October 9, 1968, third inning.
Dave McNally, Baltimore A.L., October 13, 1970, sixth inning.
Dan Gladden, Minnesota A.L., October 17, 1987, fourth inning.
Kent Hrbek, Minnesota A.L., October 24, 1987, sixth inning.
Jose Canseco, Oakland A.L., October 15, 1988, second inning.
Lonnie Smith, Atlanta N.L., October 22, 1992, fifth inning.
Tino Martinez, New York A.L., October 17, 1998, seventh inning.

BASES ON BALLS

Most bases on balls, career
43—Mickey Mantle, New York A.L., 1951, 1952, 1953, 1955, 1956, 1957, 1958, 1960, 1961, 1962, 1963, 1964; 12 series, 65 games.

Most bases on balls, series
4-game series—7—Hank Thompson, New York N.L., 1954.
5-game series—7
Jimmy Sheckard, Chicago N.L., 1910.
Mickey Cochrane, Philadelphia A.L., 1929.
Joe Gordon, New York A.L., 1941.
6-game series—9—Willie Randolph, New York A.L., 1981.
7-game series—11
Babe Ruth, New York A.L., 1926.
Gene Tenace, Oakland A.L., 1973.
8-game series—7
Josh Devore, New York N.L., 1912.
Ross Youngs, New York N.L., 1921.

Most series with one or more bases on balls, career
13—Yogi Berra, New York A.L., 1947, 1949, 1950, 1951, 1952, 1953, 1955, 1956, 1957, 1958, 1960, 1961, 1962.

Most bases on balls by pinch-hitter, series
3—Bennie Tate, Washington A.L., 1924; three games.

Most at-bats without a base on balls, series
34—Buck Weaver, Chicago A.L., 1919 (8-game series).

Most at-bats without a base on balls or strikeout, series
29—Billy Southworth, St. Louis N.L., 1926 (7-game series).

Most consecutive bases on balls, one series
5—Lou Gehrig, New York A.L., October 7 (2), October 9 (3), 1928.

Most bases on balls, game
4—Fred Clarke, Pittsburgh N.L., October 16, 1909.
Dick Hoblitzell, Boston A.L., October 9, 1916, 14 innings.
Ross Youngs, New York N.L., October 10, 1924, 12 innings.
Babe Ruth, New York A.L., October 10, 1926.
Jackie Robinson, Brooklyn N.L., October 5, 1952, 11 innings.
Doug DeCinces, Baltimore A.L., October 13, 1979.

Most bases on balls with bases filled, game
2—Jim Palmer, Baltimore A.L., October 11, 1971, fourth and fifth innings.

Most bases on balls, two consecutive games
6—Jimmy Sheckard, Chicago N.L., October 18 (3), October 20 (3), 1910.

Most bases on balls, inning
2—Lefty Gomez, New York A.L., October 6, 1937, sixth inning.
Dick McAuliffe, Detroit A.L., October 9, 1968, third inning.

STRIKEOUTS

Most strikeouts, career
54—Mickey Mantle, New York A.L., 1951, 1952, 1953, 1955, 1956, 1957, 1958, 1960, 1961, 1962, 1963, 1964; 12 series, 65 games.

Most strikeouts, series
4-game series—7
Bob Meusel, New York A.L., 1927.
Ken Caminiti, San Diego N.L., 1998.
5-game series—9—Carmelo Martinez, San Diego N.L., 1984.
6-game series—12—Willie Wilson, Kansas City A.L., 1980.

7-game series—11
  Eddie Mathews, Milwaukee N.L., 1958.
  Wayne Garrett, New York N.L., 1973.
  Luis Gonzalez, Arizona N.L., 2001.
  Damian Miller, Arizona N.L., 2001.
8-game series—10—George Kelly, New York N.L., 1921.

Most series with one or more strikeouts
12—Mickey Mantle, New York A.L., 1951, 1952, 1953, 1955,
    1956, 1957, 1958, 1960, 1961, 1963, 1964.

Most consecutive strikeouts, one series
5—Josh Devore, New York N.L., October 16 (4), 17 (1), 1911.
  George Mogridge, Washington A.L., October 7 (4), 10, (1),
    1924.
  George Pipgras, New York A.L., October 1 (5), 1932.
  Mickey Mantle, New York A.L., October 2 (4), 3 (1), 1953.
  Mike Shannon, St. Louis N.L., October 12 (2), 14 (3), 1964.
  Danny Jackson, Kansas City A.L., October 19 (2), 24 (3),
    1985.
  Devon White, Florida N.L., October 21 (1), 22 (4), 1997.
  David Justice, New York A.L., October 30 (2), 31 (3), 2001.
  Damian Miller, Arizona N.L., November 3 (2), 4 (3), 2001.

Most strikeouts by pinch-hitter, series
3—Gabby Hartnett, Chicago N.L., 1929; three games.
  Rollie Hemsley, Chicago N.L., 1932; three games.
  Otto Velez, New York A.L., 1976; three games.
  Luis Polonia, Atlanta N.L., 1996; six games.

Most at-bats without a strikeout, series
30—Tim Foli, Pittsburgh N.L., 1979 (7-game series).

Most strikeouts, game
5—George Pipgras, New York A.L., October 1, 1932 (consecutive).

Most strikeouts, inning
2—Edgar Renteria, Florida N.L., October 23, 1997, sixth inning.

SACRIFICE HITS AND FLIES

Most sacrifices, career (including flies)
8—Eddie Collins, Philadelphia A.L. (6), 1910, 1911, 1913, 1914;
    Chicago A.L. (2), 1917, 1919; six series, 34 games.

Most sacrifices, series (including flies)
4-game series—3—Wes Westrum, New York N.L., 1954 (one
    sacrifice hit and two sacrifice flies).
5-game series—4—Duffy Lewis, Boston A.L., 1916.
6-game series—3
  Jimmy Sheckard, Chicago N.L., 1906.
  Harry Steinfeldt, Chicago N.L., 1906.
  Joe Tinker, Chicago N.L., 1906.
  Jack Barry, Philadelphia A.L., 1911.
  Bill Lee, Chicago N.L., 1935.
7-game series—5—Fred Clarke, Pittsburgh N.L., 1909.
8-game series—5—Jake Daubert, Cincinnati N.L., 1919.

Most sacrifices, game (including flies)
3—Joe Tinker, Chicago N.L., October 12, 1906 (all sacrifice hits).
  Wes Westrum, New York N.L., October 2, 1954 (one sacrifice
    hit and two sacrifice flies).
  Craig Counsell, Arizona N.L., October 31, 2001 (all sacrifice
    hits).

Most sacrifice hits, inning
1—Held by many players.

Most sacrifice flies, career
4—Joe Carter, Toronto A.L., 1992 (1), 1993 (3); two series, 12
    games.

Most sacrifice flies, series
3—Joe Carter, Toronto A.L., 1993 (6-game series).

Most sacrifice flies, game
2—Wes Westrum, New York N.L., October 2, 1954.

Most sacrifice flies, inning
1—Held by many players.

Most runs batted in on sacrifice fly
2—Tommy Herr, St. Louis N.L., October 16, 1982, second inning.

HIT BY PITCH

Most hit by pitch, career
3—Frank Chance, Chicago N.L., 1906 (2), 1907 (1).
  Honus Wagner, Pittsburgh N.L., 1903 (1), 1909 (2).
  Fred Snodgrass, New York N.L., 1911 (2), 1912 (1).
  Max Carey, Pittsburgh N.L., 1925 (3).
  Yogi Berra, New York A.L., 1953 (2), 1955 (1).
  Elston Howard, New York A.L., 1960 (1), 1962 (1), 1964 (1).
  Frank Robinson, Cincinnati N.L., 1961 (2); Baltimore A.L.,
    1971 (1).
  Bert Campaneris, Oakland A.L., 1973 (2), 1974 (1).
  Reggie Jackson, New York A.L., 1977 (1), 1978 (2).

Most hit by pitch, series
3—Max Carey, Pittsburgh N.L., 1925 (7-game series).

Most hit by pitch, game
2—Max Carey, Pittsburgh N.L., October 7, 1925.
  Yogi Berra, New York A.L., October 2, 1953.
  Frank Robinson, Cincinnati N.L., October 8, 1961.
  Todd Pratt, New York N.L., October 21, 2000, 12 innings.

Most hit by pitch, inning
1—Held by many players.

GROUNDING INTO DOUBLE PLAYS

Most grounding into double play, career
7—Joe DiMaggio, New York A.L., 1936, 1937, 1938, 1939, 1941,
    1942, 1947, 1949, 1950, 1951; 10 series, 51 games.

Most grounding into double play, series
5—Irv Noren, New York A.L., 1955 (7-game series).

Most grounding into double play, game
3—Willie Mays, New York N.L., October 8, 1951.

REACHING ON ERRORS OR INTERFERENCE

Most times reaching first base on error, game
3—Fred Clarke, Pittsburgh N.L., October 10, 1903.

Most times awarded first base on catcher's interference, game
1—Roger Peckinpaugh, Washington A.L., October 15, 1925,
    first inning.
  Bud Metheny, New York A.L., October 6, 1943, sixth inning.
  Ken Boyer, St. Louis N.L., October 12, 1964, first inning.
  Pete Rose, Cincinnati N.L., October 10, 1970, fifth inning.
  George Hendrick, St. Louis N.L., October 15, 1982,
    ninth inning.

CLUB BATTING

GAMES

Most games played, total series
213—New York A.L.; 38 series (won 128, lost 84, tied 1).

For complete lists of results, and series, games, and home and road games played by all teams, see page 505. For a yearly list of batting statistics by teams, see page 513.

BATTING AVERAGE

Highest batting average, series
4-game series—.317—Cincinnati N.L. vs. Oakland A.L., 1990.
5-game series—.316—Philadelphia A.L. vs. Chicago N.L., 1910.
6-game series—.311—Toronto A.L. vs. Philadelphia N.L., 1993.
7-game series—.338—New York A.L. vs. Pittsburgh N.L., 1960.
8-game series—.270—New York N.L. vs. Boston A.L., 1912.

Highest batting average by both clubs, series
4-game series—.283—New York A.L. .313, Chicago N.L. .253, 1932.
5-game series—.272—Philadelphia A.L. .316, Chicago N.L. .222, 1910.
6-game series—.292
Philadelphia N.L. .294, Kansas City A.L. .290, 1980.
Toronto A.L. .311, Philadelphia N.L. .274, 1993.
7-game series—.300—New York A.L. .338, Pittsburgh N.L. .256, 1960.
8-game series—.245—New York N.L. .270, Boston A.L. .220, 1912.

Highest batting average by series loser
.338—New York A.L. vs. Pittsburgh N.L., 1960 (7-game series).

Lowest batting average, series
4-game series—.142—Los Angeles N.L. vs. Baltimore A.L., 1966.
5-game series—.146—Baltimore A.L. vs. New York N.L., 1969.
6-game series—.175—New York N.L. vs. Philadelphia A.L., 1911.
7-game series—.183—New York A.L. vs. Arizona N.L., 2001.
8-game series—.207—New York A.L. vs. New York N.L., 1921.

Lowest batting average by both clubs, series
4-game series—.171—Los Angeles N.L. .142, Baltimore A.L. .200, 1966.
5-game series—.184—Baltimore A.L. .146, New York N.L. .220, 1969.
6-game series—.197—Chicago A.L. .198, Chicago N.L. .196, 1906.
7-game series—.209—Oakland A.L. .209, Cincinnati N.L. .209, 1972.
8-game series—.239—Cincinnati N.L. .255, Chicago A.L. .224, 1919.

Lowest batting average by series winner
.186—Boston A.L. vs. Chicago N.L., 1918 (6-game series).

SLUGGING AVERAGE

Highest slugging average, series
4-game series—.582—Oakland A.L. vs. San Francisco N.L., 1989.
5-game series—.509—Baltimore A.L. vs. Cincinnati N.L., 1970.
6-game series—.510—Toronto A.L. vs. Philadelphia N.L., 1993.
7-game series—.528—New York A.L. vs. Pittsburgh N.L., 1960.
8-game series—.401—Boston A.L. vs. Pittsburgh N.L., 1903.

Highest slugging average by both clubs, series
4-game series—.468—Oakland A.L. .582, San Francisco N.L. .343, 1989.
5-game series—.433—Baltimore A.L. .509, Cincinnati N.L. .354, 1970.
6-game series—.467—Toronto A.L. .510, Philadelphia N.L. .425, 1993.
7-game series—.447—New York A.L. .528, Pittsburgh N.L. .355, 1960.
8-game series—.344—New York N.L. .361, Boston A.L. .326, 1912.

Lowest slugging average, series
4-game series—.192—Los Angeles N.L. vs. Baltimore A.L., 1966.
5-game series—.194—Philadelphia A.L. vs. New York N.L., 1905.
6-game series—.233—Boston A.L. vs. Chicago N.L., 1918.
7-game series—.237—Brooklyn N.L. vs. Cleveland A.L., 1920.
8-game series—.270—New York A.L. vs. New York N.L., 1921.

Lowest slugging average by both clubs, series
4-game series—.267—Baltimore A.L. .342, Los Angeles N.L. .192, 1966.
5-game series—.224—New York N.L. .255, Philadelphia A.L. .194, 1905.
6-game series—.241—Chicago N.L. .250, Boston A.L. .233, 1918.
7-game series—.285—Cleveland A.L. .332, Brooklyn N.L. .237, 1920.
8-game series—.323—New York N.L. .371, New York A.L. .270, 1921.

AT-BATS AND PLATE APPEARANCES

Most at-bats, total series
7,138—New York A.L.; 38 series, 213 games.

Most at-bats, series
4-game series—146
Chicago N.L. vs. New York A.L., 1932.
Oakland A.L. vs. San Francisco N.L., 1989.
5-game series—179—New York A.L. vs. New York N.L., 2000.
6-game series—222—New York A.L. vs. Los Angeles N.L., 1978.
7-game series—269—New York A.L. vs. Pittsburgh N.L., 1960.
8-game series—282—Boston A.L. vs. Pittsburgh N.L., 1903.

Most at-bats by both clubs, series
4-game series—290—Chicago N.L. 146, New York A.L. 144, 1932.
5-game series—354—New York A.L. 179, New York N.L. 175, 2000.
6-game series—421—New York A.L. 222, Los Angeles N.L. 199, 1978.
7-game series—512—St. Louis N.L. 262, Detroit A.L. 250, 1934.
8-game series—552—Boston A.L. 282, Pittsburgh N.L. 270, 1903.

Fewest at-bats, series
4-game series—117—Los Angeles N.L. vs. New York A.L., 1963.
5-game series—142—Oakland A.L. vs. Los Angeles N.L., 1974.
6-game series—172—Boston A.L. vs. Chicago N.L., 1918.
7-game series—215
Brooklyn N.L. vs. Cleveland A.L., 1920.
Brooklyn N.L. vs. New York A.L., 1956.
Minnesota A.L. vs. Los Angeles N.L., 1965.
8-game series—241—New York A.L. vs. New York N.L., 1921.

Fewest at-bats by both clubs, series
4-game series—240—Baltimore A.L. 120, Los Angeles N.L. 120, 1966.
5-game series—300—Los Angeles N.L. 158, Oakland A.L. 142, 1974.
6-game series—348—Chicago N.L. 176, Boston A.L. 172, 1918.
7-game series—432—Cleveland A.L. 217, Brooklyn N.L. 215, 1920.
8-game series—505—New York N.L. 264, New York A.L. 241, 1921.

Most at-bats, nine-inning game
46—Arizona N.L. vs. New York A.L., November 3, 2001.

Most at-bats, extra-inning game
54—New York N.L. vs. Oakland A.L., October 14, 1973, 12 innings.

Most at-bats by both clubs, nine-inning game
85—Toronto A.L. 44, Philadelphia 41, October 20, 1993.

Most at-bats by both clubs, extra-inning game
101—New York N.L. 54, Oakland A.L. 47, October 14, 1973, 12 innings.

Fewest official at-bats, nine-inning game
25—Philadelphia A.L. vs. Boston N.L., October 10, 1914.
 Atlanta N.L. vs. Cleveland A.L., October 21, 1995 (batted
 eight innings).

Fewest official at-bats by both clubs, nine-inning game
54—Chicago N.L. 27, Chicago A.L. 27, October 12, 1906.

Most at-bats, inning
13—Philadelphia A.L. vs. Chicago N.L., October 12, 1929,
 seventh inning.

Most at-bats by both clubs, inning
17—Philadelphia A.L. 13, Chicago N.L. 4, October 12, 1929,
 seventh inning.

Most men facing pitcher, inning
15—Philadelphia A.L. vs. Chicago N.L., October 12, 1929, seventh inning.
 Detroit A.L. vs. St. Louis N.L., October 9, 1968, third inning.

Most men facing pitcher by both clubs, inning
20—Philadelphia A.L. 15, Chicago N.L. 5, October 12, 1929,
 seventh inning.

RUNS
SERIES AND GAME

Most runs, total series
936—New York A.L.; 38 series, 213 games.

Most runs, series
4-game series—37—New York A.L. vs. Chicago N.L., 1932.
5-game series—35—Philadelphia A.L. vs. Chicago N.L., 1910.
6-game series—45—Toronto A.L. vs. Philadelphia N.L., 1993.
7-game series—55—New York A.L. vs. Pittsburgh N.L., 1960.
8-game series—39—Boston A.L. vs. Pittsburgh N.L., 1903.

Most runs by both clubs, series
4-game series—56—New York A.L. 37, Chicago N.L. 19, 1932.
5-game series—53—Baltimore A.L. 33, Cincinnati N.L. 20, 1970.
6-game series—81—Toronto A.L. 45, Philadelphia N.L. 36, 1993.
7-game series—82—New York A.L. 55, Pittsburgh N.L. 27, 1960.
8-game series—63—Boston A.L. 39, Pittsburgh N.L. 24, 1903.

Most runs by series loser
55—New York A.L. vs. Pittsburgh N.L., 1960 (7-game series).

Fewest runs, series
4-game series—2—Los Angeles N.L. vs. Baltimore A.L. 1966.
5-game series—3—Philadelphia A.L. vs. New York N.L. 1905.
6-game series—9—Boston A.L. vs. Chicago N.L., 1918.
7-game series—8—Brooklyn N.L. vs. Cleveland A.L., 1920.
8-game series—20—Chicago A.L. vs. Cincinnati N.L., 1919.

Fewest runs by both clubs, series
4-game series—15—Baltimore A.L. 13, Los Angeles N.L. 2, 1966.
5-game series—18—New York N.L. 15, Philadelphia A.L. 3, 1905.
6-game series—19—Chicago N.L. 10, Boston A.L. 9, 1918.
7-game series—29—Cleveland A.L. 21, Brooklyn N.L. 8, 1920.
8-game series—51—New York N.L. 29, New York A.L. 22, 1921.

Most runs, game
18—New York A.L. vs. New York N.L., October 2, 1936 (won
 18-4).

Most runs by pinch-hitters, game
3—New York A.L. vs. Brooklyn N.L., October 2, 1947.

Most earned runs, game
17—New York A.L. vs. New York N.L., October 2, 1936 (won
 18-4).

Most runs by both clubs, game
29—Toronto A.L. 15, Philadelphia N.L. 14, October 20, 1993.

Largest score, shutout game
12-0—New York A.L. 12, Pittsburgh N.L. 0, October 12, 1960.

Most players scoring one or more runs, game
9—St. Louis N.L. vs. Detroit A.L., October 9, 1934.
 New York A.L. vs. New York N.L., October 2, 1936.
 Milwaukee N.L. vs. New York A.L., October 2, 1958.

New York A.L. vs. Pittsburgh N.L., October 6, 1960.
Pittsburgh N.L. vs. New York A.L., October 13, 1960.
Toronto A.L. vs. Philadelphia N.L., October 20, 1993.

Most players from both clubs scoring one or more runs, game
16—Toronto A.L. 9, Philadelphia N.L. 7, October 20, 1993.

INNING

Most runs, inning
10—Philadelphia A.L. vs. Chicago N.L., October 12, 1929, seventh inning.
 Detroit A.L. vs. St. Louis N.L., October 9, 1968, third inning.

Most runs by both clubs, inning
11—Philadelphia A.L. 10, Chicago N.L. 1, October 12, 1929,
 seventh inning.
 Brooklyn N.L. 6, New York A.L. 5, October 5, 1956,
 second inning.

Most runs, extra inning
4—New York N.L. vs. Oakland A.L., October 14, 1973, 12th inning.

Most runs, two consecutive innings
12—Detroit A.L. vs. St. Louis N.L., October 9, 1968 (2 in
 second inning, 10 in third inning).

Most innings scored, game
6—New York A.L. vs. St. Louis N.L., October 6, 1926.
 New York A.L. vs. Brooklyn N.L., October 1, 1947.
 New York A.L. vs. Pittsburgh N.L., October 6, 1960.
 Philadelphia N.L. vs. Toronto A.L., October 20, 1993.

Most innings scored by both clubs, game
10—Philadelphia N.L. 6, Toronto A.L. 4, October 20, 1993.

Most runs, first inning
7—Milwaukee N.L. vs. New York A.L., October 2, 1958.

Most runs, second inning
6—New York A.L. vs. New York N.L., October 13, 1923.
 New York N.L. vs. New York A.L., October 9, 1937.
 Brooklyn N.L. vs. New York A.L., October 2, 1947.
 Brooklyn N.L. vs. New York A.L., October 5, 1956.

Most runs, third inning
10—Detroit A.L. vs. St. Louis N.L., October 9, 1968.

Most runs, fourth inning
7—Minnesota A.L. vs. St. Louis N.L., October 17, 1987.

Most runs, fifth inning
6—Baltimore A.L. vs. Pittsburgh N.L., October 11, 1971.
 Kansas City A.L. vs. St. Louis N.L., October 27, 1985.

Most runs, sixth inning
7—New York A.L. vs. New York N.L., October 6, 1937.
 New York A.L. vs. Pittsburgh N.L., October 6, 1960.

Most runs, seventh inning
10—Philadelphia A.L. vs. Chicago N.L., October 12, 1929.

Most runs, eighth inning
6—Chicago N.L. vs. Detroit A.L., October 11, 1908.
 Baltimore A.L. vs. Pittsburgh N.L., October 13, 1979.
 Toronto A.L. vs. Philadelphia N.L., October 20, 1993.

Most runs, ninth inning
7—New York A.L. vs. New York N.L., October 6, 1936.

Most runs with none on base and two out in ninth inning
4—New York A.L. vs. Brooklyn N.L., October 5, 1941.

Most runs, 10th inning
3—New York N.L. vs. Philadelphia A.L., October 8, 1913.
 New York A.L. vs. Cincinnati N.L., October 8, 1939.
 New York A.L. vs. Cleveland A.L., September 29, 1954.
 Milwaukee N.L. vs. New York A.L., October 6, 1957.
 St. Louis N.L. vs. New York A.L., October 12, 1964.
 New York N.L. vs. Boston A.L., October 25, 1986.

Most runs, 11th inning
2—Philadelphia A.L. vs. New York N.L., October 17, 1911.
 Toronto A.L. vs. Atlanta N.L., October 24, 1992.

Most runs, 12th inning
4—New York N.L. vs. Oakland A.L., October 14, 1973.

GAMES BEING SHUT OUT

Most times shut out, total series
15—New York A.L.

Most times shut out, series
4—Philadelphia A.L. vs. New York N.L., 1905.

Most consecutive times shut out, series
3—Philadelphia A.L. vs. New York N.L., October 12, 13, 14, 1905.
Los Angeles N.L. vs. Baltimore A.L., October 6, 8, 9, 1966.

Most consecutive games without being shut out, total series
42—New York A.L., October 6, 1926 through October 1, 1942.

HITS
SERIES

Most hits, total series
1,780—New York A.L.; 38 series, 213 games.

Most hits, series
4-game series—45
New York A.L. vs. Chicago N.L., 1932.
Cincinnati N.L. vs. Oakland A.L., 1990.
5-game series—56—Philadelphia A.L. vs. Chicago N.L., 1910.
6-game series—68—New York A.L. vs. Los Angeles N.L., 1978.
7-game series—91—New York A.L. vs. Pittsburgh N.L., 1960.
8-game series—74—New York N.L. vs. Boston A.L., 1912.

Most hits by both clubs, series
4-game series—82—New York A.L. 45, Chicago N.L. 37, 1932.
5-game series—91—Philadelphia A.L. 56, Chicago N.L. 35, 1910.
6-game series—122—Toronto A.L. 64, Philadelphia N.L. 58, 1993.
7-game series—151—New York A.L. 91, Pittsburgh N.L. 60, 1960.
8-game series—135—Boston A.L. 71, Pittsburgh N.L. 64, 1903.

Fewest hits, series
4-game series—17—Los Angeles N.L. vs. Baltimore A.L., 1966.
5-game series—23—Baltimore A.L. vs. New York N.L., 1969.
6-game series—32—Boston A.L. vs. Chicago N.L., 1918.
7-game series—40—St. Louis N.L. vs. Kansas City A.L., 1985.
8-game series—50—New York A.L. vs. New York N.L., 1921.

Fewest hits by both clubs, series
4-game series—41—Baltimore A.L. 24, Los Angeles N.L. 17, 1966.
5-game series—57—New York N.L. 32, Philadelphia A.L. 25, 1905.
6-game series—69—Chicago N.L. 37, Boston A.L. 32, 1918.
7-game series—92—Oakland A.L. 46, Cincinnati N.L. 46, 1972.
8-game series—121—New York N.L. 71, New York A.L. 50, 1921.

Most hits by pinch-hitters, series
6—New York A.L. vs. Brooklyn N.L., 1947 (7-game series).
New York A.L. vs. Pittsburgh N.L., 1960 (7-game series).
Oakland A.L. vs. Cincinnati N.L., 1972 (7-game series).
Baltimore A.L. vs. Pittsburgh N.L., 1979 (7-game series).

Most hits by pinch-hitters for both clubs, series
11—New York A.L. 6, Brooklyn N.L. 5, 1947 (7-game series).

Most players with one or more hits in each game, series
4—New York A.L. vs. Los Angeles N.L., 1978 (6-game series).

Most consecutive hitless innings, series
9—Brooklyn N.L. vs. New York A.L., October 8, 1956 (all 27 batters).

GAME AND INNING

Most hits, game
22—Arizona N.L. vs. New York A.L., November 3, 2001.

Most hits by losing club, game
17—Pittsburgh N.L. vs. Baltimore A.L., October 13, 1979.

Most hits by pinch-hitters, game
3—Oakland A.L. vs. Cincinnati N.L., October 19, 1972.
Baltimore A.L. vs. Pittsburgh N.L., October 13, 1979.

Most hits by both clubs, game
32—New York A.L. 19, Pittsburgh N.L. 13, October 6, 1960.
Toronto A.L. 18, Philadelphia 14, October 20, 1993.

Fewest hits, game
0—Brooklyn N.L. vs. New York A.L., October 8, 1956.

Fewest hits by both clubs, game
5—New York A.L. 3, New York N.L. 2, October 6, 1921.
New York A.L. 5, Brooklyn N.L. 0, October 8, 1956.
Atlanta N.L. 3, Cleveland A.L. 2, October 21, 1995.

Most players with one or more hits, game
11—New York A.L. vs. St. Louis N.L., October 9, 1928.
New York A.L. vs. Pittsburgh N.L., October 6, 1960.

Most players with one or more hits for either club, game
19—New York A.L. 11, Pittsburgh N.L. 8, October 6, 1960.

Most players with one or more hits and runs, game
9—New York A.L. vs. New York N.L., October 2, 1936.
New York A.L. vs. Pittsburgh N.L., October 6, 1960.

Most hits, inning
10—Philadelphia A.L. vs. Chicago N.L., October 12, 1929,
seventh inning.

Most hits by pinch-hitters, inning
3—Oakland A.L. vs. Cincinnati N.L., October 19, 1972,
ninth inning.

Most hits by both clubs, inning
12—Philadelphia A.L. 10, Chicago N.L. 2, October 12, 1929,
seventh inning.

Most consecutive hits, inning
8—New York N.L. vs. New York A.L., October 7, 1921,
seventh inning. (base on balls and sacrifice during streak.)

Most consecutive hits, inning (consecutive plate appearances)
6—Chicago N.L. vs. Detroit A.L., October 10, 1908, ninth inning (6 singles).

SINGLES

Most singles, total series
1,271—New York A.L.; 38 series, 213 games.

Most singles, series
4-game series—32—New York A.L. vs. San Diego N.L., 1998.
5-game series—46—New York N.L. vs. New York A.L., 1922.
6-game series—57—New York A.L. vs. Los Angeles N.L., 1978.
7-game series—64—New York A.L. vs. Pittsburgh N.L., 1960.
8-game series—55—New York N.L. vs. Boston A.L., 1912.

Most singles by both clubs, series
4-game series—55—New York A.L. 31, Chicago N.L. 24, 1932.
5-game series—70—New York N.L. 39, Washington A.L. 31, 1933.
6-game series—95—New York A.L. 57, Los Angeles N.L. 38, 1978.
7-game series—109—New York A.L. 64, Pittsburgh N.L. 45, 1960.
8-game series—96—Boston A.L. 49, Pittsburgh N.L. 47, 1903.

Fewest singles, series
4-game series—13
Philadelphia A.L. vs. Boston N.L., 1914.
Los Angeles N.L. vs. Baltimore A.L., 1966.
5-game series—19
Brooklyn N.L. vs. New York A.L., 1941.
Baltimore A.L. vs. New York N.L., 1969.
6-game series—17—Philadelphia A.L. vs. St. Louis N.L., 1930.
7-game series—27
Minnesota A.L. vs. Los Angeles N.L., 1965.
St. Louis N.L. vs. Kansas City A.L., 1985.
8-game series—39—Boston A.L. vs. New York N.L., 1912.

Fewest singles by both clubs, series
4-game series—29—Baltimore A.L. 16, Los Angeles N.L. 13, 1966.
5-game series—40—New York N.L. 21, Baltimore A.L. 19, 1969.
6-game series—42—St. Louis N.L. 25, Philadelphia A.L. 17, 1930.
7-game series—66—St. Louis N.L. 33, Boston A.L. 33, 1967.
8-game series—92
Cincinnati N.L. 47, Chicago A.L. 45, 1919.
New York N.L. 52, New York A.L. 40, 1921.

Most singles, game
6—New York A.L. vs. Los Angeles N.L., October 15, 1978.
  Arizona N.L. vs. New York A.L., November 3, 2001.

Most singles by both clubs, game
24—New York A.L. 16, Los Angeles N.L. 8, October 15, 1978.

Fewest singles, game
1—Philadelphia A.L. vs. St. Louis N.L., October 1, 1930 (batted
    eight innings).
  Philadelphia A.L. vs. St. Louis N.L., October 8, 1930 (batted
    eight innings).
  Brooklyn N.L. vs. New York A.L., October 3, 1947 (batted
    8.2 innings).
  New York A.L. vs. Brooklyn N.L., October 4, 1952 (batted
    eight innings).
  Brooklyn N.L. vs. New York A.L., October 8, 1956.
  St. Louis N.L. vs. Boston A.L., October 5, 1967.

Fewest singles by both clubs, game
2—St. Louis N.L. 2, Philadelphia A.L. 0, October 8, 1930.

Most singles, inning
7—Philadelphia A.L. vs. Chicago N.L., October 12, 1929, sev-
    enth inning.
  New York N.L. vs. Washington A.L., October 4, 1933, sixth
    inning.
  Brooklyn N.L. vs. New York A.L., October 8, 1949, sixth
    inning.

Most singles by both clubs, inning
8—Philadelphia A.L. 7, Chicago N.L. 1, October 12, 1929, sev-
    enth inning.
  New York N.L. 7, Washington A.L. 1, October 4, 1933, sixth
    inning.
  Brooklyn N.L. 7, New York A.L. 1, October 8, 1949, sixth
    inning.

DOUBLES

Most doubles, total series
254—New York A.L; 38 series, 213 games.

Most doubles, series
4-game series—9
  Philadelphia A.L. vs. Boston N.L., 1914.
  Cincinnati N.L. vs. Oakland A.L., 1990.
5-game series—19—Philadelphia A.L. vs. Chicago N.L., 1910.
6-game series—15—Philadelphia A.L. vs. New York N.L., 1911.
7-game series—19—St. Louis N.L. vs. Boston A.L., 1946.
8-game series—14
  Boston A.L. vs. New York N.L., 1912.
  New York N.L. vs. Boston A.L., 1912.

Most doubles by both clubs, series
4-game series—15—Philadelphia A.L. 9, Boston N.L. 6, 1914.
5-game series—30—Philadelphia A.L. 19, Chicago N.L. 11, 1910.
6-game series—26—Philadelphia A.L. 15, New York N.L. 11,
  1911.
7-game series—29—Detroit A.L. 16, Pittsburgh N.L. 13, 1909.
8-game series—28—Boston A.L. 14, New York N.L. 14, 1912.

Fewest doubles, series
4-game series—3
  Cincinnati N.L. vs. New York A.L., 1939.
  New York A.L. vs. Philadelphia N.L., 1950.
  New York N.L. vs. Cleveland A.L., 1954.
  Los Angeles N.L. vs. New York A.L., 1963.
  New York A.L. vs. Los Angeles N.L., 1963.
  Baltimore A.L. vs. Los Angeles N.L., 1966.
  Los Angeles N.L. vs. Baltimore A.L., 1966.
  New York A.L. vs. Cincinnati N.L., 1976.
5-game series—1
  Detroit A.L. vs. Chicago N.L., 1907.
  Baltimore A.L. vs. New York N.L., 1969.
6-game series—2
  Boston A.L. vs. Chicago N.L., 1918.
  New York N.L. vs. New York A.L., 1923.
7-game series—3—Baltimore A.L. vs. Pittsburgh N.L., 1971.
8-game series—4—Boston A.L. vs. Pittsburgh N.L., 1903.

Fewest doubles by both clubs, series
4-game series—6
  Los Angeles N.L. 3, New York A.L. 3, 1963.
  Baltimore A.L. 3, Los Angeles N.L. 3, 1966.
5-game series—6—Philadelphia N.L. 4, Boston A.L. 2, 1915.
6-game series—7—Chicago N.L. 5, Boston A.L. 2, 1918.
7-game series—11—St. Louis N.L. 7, Detroit A.L. 4, 1968.
8-game series—11—Pittsburgh N.L. 7, Boston A.L. 4, 1903.

Most doubles, game
8—Chicago A.L. vs. Chicago N.L., October 13, 1906.
  Pittsburgh N.L. vs. Washington A.L., October 15, 1925.

Most doubles by both clubs, game
11—Chicago A.L. 8, Chicago N.L. 3, October 13, 1906.

Most doubles, inning
3—Chicago A.L. vs. Chicago N.L., October 13, 1906,
    fourth inning.
  Philadelphia A.L. vs. Chicago N.L., October 18, 1910,
    seventh inning.
  Philadelphia A.L. vs. New York N.L., October 24, 1911,
    fourth inning (consecutive).
  Pittsburgh N.L. vs. Washington A.L., October 15, 1925,
    eighth inning.
  St. Louis N.L. vs. Detroit A.L., October 9, 1934, third inning.
  Brooklyn N.L. vs. New York A.L., October 2, 1947, second
    inning.
  Brooklyn N.L. vs. New York A.L., October 5, 1947, third
    inning (consecutive).
  New York A.L. vs. Brooklyn N.L., October 8, 1949, fourth
    inning.
  Chicago A.L. vs. Los Angeles N.L., October 1, 1959, third
    inning.
  Arizona N.L. vs. New York A.L., November 3, 2001, third
    inning.

TRIPLES

Most triples, total series
51—New York A.L.; 38 series, 213 games.

Most triples, series
4-game series—3
  Cincinnati N.L. vs. New York A.L., 1976.
  Oakland A.L. vs. San Francisco N.L., 1989.
5-game series—6—Boston A.L. vs. Brooklyn N.L., 1916.
6-game series—5—Toronto A.L. vs. Philadelphia N.L., 1993.
7-game series—5
  St. Louis N.L. vs. Detroit A.L., 1934.
  New York A.L. vs. Brooklyn N.L., 1947.
8-game series—16—Boston A.L. vs. Pittsburgh N.L., 1903.

Most triples by both clubs, series
4-game series—4
  Cincinnati N.L. 3, New York A.L. 1, 1976.
  Oakland A.L. 3, San Francisco N.L. 1, 1989.
5-game series—11—Boston A.L. 6, Brooklyn N.L. 5, 1916.
6-game series—7
  New York A.L. 4, New York N.L. 3, 1923.
  Toronto A.L. 5, Philadelphia N.L. 2, 1993.
7-game series—8—Atlanta N.L. 4, Minnesota A.L. 4, 1991.
8-game series—25—Boston A.L. 16, Pittsburgh N.L. 9, 1903.

Fewest triples, series
4-game series—0—Held by many clubs. Last club—New York
  A.L., 1999.
5-game series—0—Held by many clubs. Last club—Oakland
  A.L., 1988.
6-game series—0—Held by many clubs. Last club—New York
  N.L., 2000.
7-game series—0—Held by many clubs. Last clubs—Arizona
  N.L., 2001; New York A.L., 2001.
8-game series—1—New York A.L. vs. New York N.L., 1921.

Fewest triples by both clubs, series
4-game series—1
  St. Louis N.L. 1, New York A.L. 0, 1928.
  Cleveland A.L. 1, New York N.L. 0, 1954.

Baltimore A.L. 1, Los Angeles N.L. 0, 1966.
San Diego N.L. 1, New York A.L. 0, 1998.
Atlanta N.L. 1, New York A.L. 0, 1999.
5-game series—0
New York N.L. 0, Philadelphia A.L. 0, 1905.
New York N.L. 0, Washington A.L. 0, 1933.
New York N.L. 0, Baltimore A.L. 0, 1969.
Detroit A.L. 0, San Diego N.L. 0, 1984.
6-game series—0
Cleveland A.L. 0, Boston N.L. 0, 1948.
New York A.L. 0, Los Angeles N.L. 0, 1978.
Toronto A.L. 0, Atlanta N.L. 0, 1992.
7-game series—0
St. Louis N.L. 0, Philadelphia A.L. 0, 1931.
Arizona N.L. 0, New York A.L. 0, 2001.
8-game series—5—New York N.L. 4, New York A.L. 1, 1921.

Most triples, nine-inning game
5—Boston A.L. vs. Pittsburgh N.L., October 7, 1903.
   Boston A.L. vs. Pittsburgh N.L., October 10, 1903.

Most triples by both clubs, nine-inning game
7—Boston A.L. 5, Pittsburgh N.L. 2, October 10, 1903.

Most triples, inning
2—Boston A.L. vs. Pittsburgh N.L., October 7, 1903, eighth
      inning.
   Boston A.L. vs. Pittsburgh N.L., October 10, 1903, first
      inning, also fourth inning.
   Boston A.L. vs. New York N.L., October 12, 1912, third inning.
   Philadelphia A.L. vs. New York N.L., October 7, 1913,
      fourth inning.
   Boston A.L. vs. Chicago N.L., September 6, 1918, ninth inning.
   New York A.L. vs. Brooklyn N.L., October 1, 1947, third inning.
   New York A.L. vs. Brooklyn N.L., September 30, 1953,
      first inning.
   Detroit A.L. vs. St. Louis N.L., October 7, 1968, fourth inning.

HOME RUNS
SERIES

Most home runs, total series
204—New York A.L.; 38 series, 213 games.

Most grand slams, total series
8—New York A.L.; 38 series, 213 games.

Most home runs by pinch-hitters, total series
6—New York A.L.; 38 series, 213 games.

Most home runs, series
4-game series—9
New York A.L. vs. St. Louis N.L., 1928.
Oakland A.L. vs. San Francisco N.L., 1989.
5-game series—10—Baltimore A.L. vs. Cincinnati N.L., 1970.
6-game series—9
New York A.L. vs. Brooklyn N.L., 1953.
Los Angeles N.L. vs. New York A.L., 1977.
7-game series—12—New York A.L. vs. Brooklyn N.L., 1956.
8-game series—2
Boston A.L. vs. Pittsburgh N.L., 1903.
New York A.L. vs. New York N.L., 1921.
New York N.L. vs. New York A.L., 1921.

Most home runs by both clubs, series
4-game series—13—Oakland A.L. 9, San Francisco N.L. 4,
   1989.
5-game series—15—Baltimore A.L. 10, Cincinnati N.L. 5, 1970.
6-game series—17
New York A.L. 9, Brooklyn N.L. 8, 1953.
Los Angeles N.L. 9, New York A.L. 8, 1977.
7-game series—17—Brooklyn N.L. 9, New York A.L. 8, 1955.
8-game series—4—New York N.L. 2, New York A.L. 2, 1921.

Most grand slams, series
2—New York A.L. vs. Brooklyn N.L., 1956.
   Minnesota A.L. vs. St. Louis N.L., 1987.

Most grand slams by both clubs, series
2—New York A.L. 2, Brooklyn N.L. 0, 1956.
   St. Louis N.L. 1, New York A.L. 1, 1964.
   Minnesota A.L. 2, St. Louis N.L. 0, 1987.

Most home runs by pinch-hitters, series
2—Los Angeles N.L. vs. Chicago A.L., 1959.
   Boston A.L. vs. Cincinnati N.L., 1975.

Most home runs by pinch-hitters for both clubs, series
2—New York N.L. 1, Cleveland A.L. 1, 1954.
   Los Angeles N.L. 2, Chicago A.L. 0, 1959.
   Boston A.L. 2, Cincinnati N.L. 0, 1975.

Most home runs by pitchers as batters, series
2—New York N.L. vs. Washington A.L., 1924.

Most home runs by pitchers as batters for both clubs, series
2—New York N.L. 2, Washington A.L. 0, 1924.
   Boston A.L. 1, St. Louis N.L. 1, 1967.
   Detroit A.L. 1, St. Louis N.L. 1, 1968.

Fewest home runs, series
4-game series—0—Held by many clubs.
5-game series—0—Held by many clubs.
6-game series—0
Chicago N.L. vs. Chicago A.L., 1906.
Chicago A.L. vs. Chicago N.L., 1906.
New York N.L. vs. Philadelphia A.L., 1911.
Boston A.L. vs. Chicago N.L., 1918.
Chicago N.L. vs. Boston A.L., 1918.
7-game series—0—Brooklyn N.L. vs. Cleveland A.L., 1920.
8-game series—0—Cincinnati N.L. vs. Chicago A.L., 1919.

Fewest home runs by both clubs, series
4-game series—1—Boston N.L. 1, Philadelphia A.L. 0, 1914.
5-game series—0
New York N.L. 0, Philadelphia A.L. 0, 1905.
Chicago N.L. 0, Detroit A.L. 0, 1907.
6-game series—0
Chicago A.L. 0, Chicago N.L. 0, 1906.
Boston A.L. 0, Chicago N.L. 0, 1918.
7-game series—2—Cleveland A.L. 2, Brooklyn N.L. 0, 1920.
8-game series—1—Chicago A.L. 1, Cincinnati N.L. 0, 1919.

GAME

Most home runs, game
5—New York A.L. vs. St. Louis N.L., October 9, 1928.
   Oakland A.L. vs. San Francisco N.L., October 27, 1989.

Most home runs by both clubs, game
7—Oakland A.L. 5, San Francisco N.L. 2, October 27, 1989.

**Most consecutive games with one or more home runs, total
series**
9—New York A.L., last 2 games vs. Chicago N.L. in 1932 (seven
      home runs), all 6 games vs. New York N.L. in 1936
      (seven home runs) and first game vs. New York N.L. in
      1937 (one home run; total 15 home runs).
   New York A.L., all 7 games vs. Brooklyn N.L. in 1952 (10
      home runs) and first 2 games vs. Brooklyn N.L. in 1953
      (four home runs; total 14 home runs).

Most consecutive games with one or more home runs, series
7—Washington A.L. vs. Pittsburgh N.L., October 7 through 15,
      1925 (eight home runs).
   New York A.L. vs. Brooklyn N.L., October 1 through 7, 1952
      (10 home runs).

INNING

Most home runs, inning (two home runs, 35 times)
3—Boston A.L. vs. St. Louis N.L., October 11, 1967, fourth
      inning, Yastrzemski, Smith, Petrocelli (two consecutive).
2—New York N.L. vs. New York A.L., October 11, 1921, sec-
      ond inning.
   Washington A.L. vs. Pittsburgh N.L., October 11, 1925,
      third inning.

New York A.L. vs. St. Louis N.L., October 9, 1928, seventh inning.

New York A.L. vs. St. Louis N.L., October 9, 1928, eighth inning.

Philadelphia A.L. vs. Chicago N.L., October 12, 1929, seventh inning.

New York A.L. vs. Chicago N.L., October 1, 1932, fifth inning.

New York A.L. vs. Chicago N.L., October 2, 1932, ninth inning.

New York A.L. vs. Cincinnati N.L., October 7, 1939, fifth inning.

New York A.L. vs. Cincinnati N.L., October 8, 1939, seventh inning.

Detroit A.L. vs. Cincinnati N.L., October 4, 1940, seventh inning.

Brooklyn N.L. vs. New York A.L., October 7, 1949, ninth inning.

Brooklyn N.L. vs. New York A.L., September 30, 1953, sixth inning.

Brooklyn N.L. vs. New York A.L., October 1, 1955, fourth inning.

Milwaukee N.L. vs. New York A.L., October 6, 1957, fourth inning.

Milwaukee N.L. vs. New York A.L., October 2, 1958, first inning.

New York A.L. vs. Milwaukee N.L., October 2, 1958, ninth inning.

Los Angeles N.L. vs. Chicago A.L., October 2, 1959, seventh inning.

New York A.L. vs. St. Louis N.L., October 14, 1964, sixth inning.

New York A.L. vs. St. Louis N.L., October 15, 1964, ninth inning.

Baltimore A.L. vs. Los Angeles N.L., October 5, 1966, first inning.

Baltimore A.L. vs. New York N.L., October 16, 1969, third inning.

Oakland A.L. vs. New York N.L., October 21, 1973, third inning.

Cincinnati N.L. vs. Boston A.L., October 14, 1975, fifth inning.

New York A.L. vs. Los Angeles N.L., October 16, 1977, eighth inning.

Los Angeles N.L. vs. New York A.L., October 10, 1978, second inning.

Los Angeles N.L. vs. New York A.L., October 25, 1981, seventh inning.

Boston A.L. vs. New York N.L., October 27, 1986, second inning.

Oakland A.L. vs. San Francisco N.L., October 27, 1989, fourth and fifth innings.

Philadelphia N.L. vs. Toronto A.L., October 20, 1993, fifth inning.

Florida N.L. vs. Cleveland A.L., October 18, 1997, fourth inning.

San Diego N.L. vs. New York A.L., October 17, 1998, fifth inning.

New York A.L. vs. San Diego N.L., October 17, 1998, seventh inning.

New York N.L. vs. New York A.L., October 22, 2000, ninth inning.

Arizona N.L. vs. New York A.L., November 1, 2001, fifth inning.

Most home runs by both clubs, inning
3—New York N.L., 2, New York A.L., 1, October 11, 1921, second inning.
  Boston A.L., 3, St. Louis N.L. 0, October 11, 1967, fourth inning.

Most consecutive home runs, inning (12 times)
2—Washington A.L. vs. Pittsburgh N.L., October 11, 1925, third inning.
  New York A.L. vs. St. Louis N.L., October 9, 1928, seventh inning.
  New York A.L. vs. Chicago N.L., October 1, 1932, fifth inning.
  New York A.L. vs. St. Louis N.L., October 14, 1964, sixth inning.

Baltimore A.L. vs. Los Angeles N.L., October 5, 1966, first inning.

Boston A.L. vs. St. Louis N.L., October 11, 1967, fourth inning.

Cincinnati N.L. vs. Boston A.L., October 14, 1975, fifth inning.

New York A.L. vs. Los Angeles N.L., October 16, 1977, eighth inning.

Los Angeles N.L. vs. New York A.L., October 25, 1981, seventh inning.

Boston A.L. vs. New York N.L., October 27, 1986, second inning.

Florida N.L. vs. Cleveland A.L., October 18, 1997, fourth inning.

San Diego N.L. vs. New York A.L., October 17, 1998, fifth inning.

Most times hitting two home runs in an inning, total series
11—New York A.L., 1928 (2), 1932 (2), 1939 (2), 1958 (1), 1964 (2), 1977 (1), 1998 (1).

Most times hitting two home runs in an inning, series
2—New York A.L., 1928, 1932, 1939, 1964; Oakland A.L., 1989.

Most times hitting two home runs in an inning, game
2—New York A.L. vs. St. Louis N.L., October 9, 1928, seventh and eighth innings.
  Oakland A.L. vs. San Francisco N.L., October 27, 1989, fourth and fifth innings.

TOTAL BASES

Most total bases, total series
2,748—New York A.L.; 38 series, 213 games.

Most total bases, series
4-game series—85—Oakland A.L. vs. San Francisco N.L., 1989.
5-game series—87—Baltimore A.L. vs. Cincinnati N.L., 1970.
6-game series—105—Toronto A.L. vs. Philadelphia N.L., 1993.
7-game series—142—New York A.L. vs. Pittsburgh N.L., 1960.
8-game series—113—Boston A.L. vs. Pittsburgh N.L., 1903.

Most total bases by both clubs, series
4-game series—133—New York A.L. 75, Chicago N.L. 58, 1932.
5-game series—145—Baltimore A.L. 87, Cincinnati N.L. 58, 1970.
6-game series—200—Brooklyn N.L. 103, New York A.L. 97, 1953.
7-game series—225—New York A.L. 142, Pittsburgh N.L. 83, 1960.
8-game series—205—Boston A.L. 113, Pittsburgh N.L. 92, 1903.

Fewest total bases, series
4-game series—23—Los Angeles N.L. vs. Baltimore A.L., 1966.
5-game series—30—Philadelphia A.L. vs. New York N.L., 1905.
6-game series—40—Boston A.L. vs. Chicago N.L., 1918.
7-game series—51—Brooklyn N.L. vs. Cleveland A.L., 1920.
8-game series—65—New York A.L. vs. New York N.L., 1921.

Fewest total bases by both clubs, series
4-game series—64—Baltimore A.L. 41, Los Angeles N.L. 23, 1966.
5-game series—69—New York N.L. 39, Philadelphia A.L. 30, 1905.
6-game series—84—Chicago N.L. 44, Boston A.L. 40, 1918.
7-game series—123—Cleveland A.L. 72, Brooklyn N.L. 51, 1920.
8-game series—163—New York N.L. 98, New York A.L. 65, 1921.

Most total bases, game
34—Atlanta N.L. vs. Minnesota A.L., October 24, 1991.

Most total bases by both clubs, game
47—New York A.L. 27, Brooklyn N.L. 20, October 4, 1953.

Fewest total bases, game
0—Brooklyn N.L. vs. New York A.L., October 8, 1956.

Fewest total bases by both clubs, game
5—New York A.L. 3, New York N.L. 2, October 6, 1921.

Most total bases, inning
17—Philadelphia A.L. vs. Chicago N.L., October 12, 1929, seventh inning.

Most total bases by both clubs, inning
21—Philadelphia A.L. 17, Chicago N.L. 4, October 12, 1929, seventh inning.

LONG HITS

Most long hits, total series
509—New York A.L.; 38 series, 213 games.

Most long hits, series
4-game series—20—Oakland A.L. vs. San Francisco N.L., 1989.
5-game series—21—Philadelphia A.L. vs. Chicago N.L., 1910.
6-game series—24—Toronto A.L. vs. Philadelphia N.L., 1993.
7-game series—27—New York A.L. vs. Pittsburgh N.L., 1960.
8-game series—22—Boston A.L. vs. Pittsburgh N.L., 1903.

Most long hits by both clubs, series
4-game series—29—Oakland A.L. 20, San Francisco N.L. 9, 1989.
5-game series—33—Philadelphia A.L. 21, Chicago N.L. 12, 1910.
6-game series—41—Brooklyn N.L. 22, New York A.L. 19, 1953.
7-game series—42
New York A.L. 27, Pittsburgh N.L. 15, 1960.
St. Louis N.L. 23, Milwaukee A.L. 19, 1982.
Atlanta N.L. 22, Minnesota A.L. 20, 1991.
8-game series—40—Boston A.L. 21, New York N.L. 19, 1912.

Fewest long hits, series
4-game series—4
Cincinnati N.L. vs. New York A.L., 1939.
Los Angeles N.L. vs. Baltimore A.L., 1966.
5-game series—3—Detroit A.L. vs. Chicago N.L., 1907.
6-game series—5—Boston A.L. vs. Chicago N.L., 1918.
7-game series—6—Brooklyn N.L. vs. Cleveland A.L., 1920.
8-game series—10—New York A.L. vs. New York N.L., 1921.

Fewest long hits by both clubs, series
4-game series—12—Baltimore A.L. 8, Los Angeles N.L. 4, 1966.
5-game series—10—Chicago N.L. 7, Detroit A.L. 3, 1907.
6-game series—11—Chicago N.L. 6, Boston A.L. 5, 1918.
7-game series—19—Cleveland A.L. 13, Brooklyn N.L. 6, 1920.
8-game series—29—New York N.L. 19, New York A.L. 10, 1921.

Most long hits, game
9—Pittsburgh N.L. vs. Washington A.L., October 15, 1925 (8 doubles, 1 triple).

Most long hits by both clubs, game
11—Chicago A.L. 8 (eight doubles), Chicago N.L. 3 (3 doubles), October 13, 1906.
Pittsburgh N.L. 9 (8 doubles, 1 triple), Washington A.L. 2 (1 double, 1 home run), October 15, 1925.
New York A.L. 7 (4 doubles, 1 triple, 2 home runs), Cincinnati N.L. 4 (2 doubles, 2 home runs), October 9, 1961.
Oakland A.L. 7 (2 doubles, 5 home runs), San Francisco N.L. 4 (2 doubles, 2 home runs), October 27, 1989.
Atlanta N.L. 8 (2 doubles, 3 triples, 3 home runs), Minnesota A.L. 3 (1 double, 2 triples), October 24, 1991, 12 innings.

Longest extra-inning game without a long hit
12 innings—Chicago N.L. vs. Detroit A.L., October 8, 1907.
Detroit A.L. vs. Chicago N.L., October 8, 1907.

Longest extra-inning game without a long hit by either club
12 innings—Chicago N.L. 0, Detroit A.L. 0, October 8, 1907.

EXTRA BASES ON LONG HITS

Most extra bases on long hits, total series
968—New York A.L.; 38 series, 213 games (254 on doubles, 102 on triples, 612 on home runs).

Most extra bases on long hits, series
4-game series—41—Oakland A.L. vs. San Francisco N.L., 1989.
5-game series—37—Baltimore A.L. vs. Cincinnati N.L., 1970.
6-game series—41
New York A.L. vs. Brooklyn N.L., 1953.
Toronto A.L. vs. Philadelphia N.L., 1993.
7-game series—51—New York A.L. vs. Pittsburgh N.L., 1960.
8-game series—42—Boston A.L. vs. Pittsburgh N.L., 1903.

Most extra bases on long hits by both clubs, series
4-game series—59—Oakland A.L. 41, San Francisco N.L. 18, 1989.
5-game series—60—Baltimore A.L. 37, Cincinnati N.L. 23, 1970.
6-game series—80—New York A.L. 41, Brooklyn N.L. 39, 1953.
7-game series—82—Atlanta N.L. 42, Minnesota A.L. 40, 1991.
8-game series—70—Boston A.L. 42, Pittsburgh N.L. 28, 1903.

Fewest extra bases on long hits, series
4-game series—5—Cincinnati N.L. vs. New York A.L., 1939.
5-game series—5
Philadelphia A.L. vs. New York N.L., 1905.
Detroit A.L. vs. Chicago N.L., 1907.
Detroit A.L. vs. Chicago N.L., 1908.
6-game series—7—Chicago N.L. vs. Boston A.L., 1918.
7-game series—7—Brooklyn N.L. vs. Cleveland A.L., 1920.
8-game series—15—New York A.L. vs. New York N.L., 1921.

Fewest extra bases on long hits by both clubs, series
4-game series—19—New York A.L. 11, Philadelphia N.L. 8, 1950.
5-game series—12—New York N.L. 7, Philadelphia A.L. 5, 1905.
6-game series—15—Boston A.L. 8, Chicago N.L. 7, 1918.
7-game series—26—Cleveland A.L. 19, Brooklyn N.L. 7, 1920.
8-game series—42—New York N.L. 27, New York A.L. 15, 1921.

RUNS BATTED IN

Most runs batted in, total series
884—New York A.L.; 38 series, 213 games.

Most runs batted in, series
4-game series—36—New York A.L. vs. Chicago N.L., 1932.
5-game series—32—Baltimore A.L. vs. Cincinnati N.L., 1970.
6-game series—45—Toronto A.L. vs. Philadelphia N.L., 1993.
7-game series—54—New York A.L. vs. Pittsburgh N.L., 1960.
8-game series—35—Boston A.L. vs. Pittsburgh N.L., 1903.

Most runs batted in by both clubs, series
4-game series—52—New York A.L. 36, Chicago N.L. 16, 1932.
5-game series—52—Baltimore A.L. 32, Cincinnati N.L. 20, 1970.
6-game series—80—Toronto A.L. 45, Philadelphia N.L. 35, 1993.
7-game series—80—New York A.L. 54, Pittsburgh N.L. 26, 1960.
8-game series—58—Boston A.L. 35, Pittsburgh N.L. 23, 1903.

Fewest runs batted in, series
4-game series—2—Los Angeles N.L. vs. Baltimore A.L., 1966.
5-game series—2—Philadelphia A.L. vs. New York N.L., 1905.
6-game series—6—Boston A.L. vs. Chicago N.L., 1918.
7-game series—8—Brooklyn N.L. vs. Cleveland A.L., 1920.
8-game series—17—Chicago A.L. vs. Cincinnati N.L., 1919.

Fewest runs batted in by both clubs, series
4-game series—12—Los Angeles N.L. 2, Baltimore A.L. 10, 1966.
5-game series—15—Philadelphia A.L. 2, New York N.L. 13, 1905.
6-game series—16—Boston A.L. 6, Chicago N.L. 10, 1918.
7-game series—26—Brooklyn N.L. 8, Cleveland A.L. 18, 1920.
8-game series—46—Boston A.L. 21, New York N.L. 25, 1912.

Most runs batted in, game
18—New York A.L. vs. New York N.L., October 2, 1936.

Most runs batted in by both clubs, game
29—Toronto A.L. 15, Philadelphia N.L. 14, October 20, 1993.

Fewest runs batted in, game
0—Held by many clubs.

Most runs batted in, inning
10—Philadelphia A.L. vs. Chicago N.L., October 12, 1929, seventh inning.
Detroit A.L. vs. St. Louis N.L., October 9, 1968, third inning.

Most runs batted in by both clubs, inning
11—Philadelphia A.L. 10, Chicago N.L. 1, October 12, 1929, seventh inning.
Brooklyn N.L. 6, New York A.L. 5, October 5, 1956, second inning.

Fewest runs batted in by both clubs, game
0—New York N.L. 0, Philadelphia A.L. 0, October 13, 1905.
New York N.L. 0, New York A.L. 0, October 13, 1921.
Chicago A.L. 0, Los Angeles N.L. 0, October 6, 1959.
New York A.L. 0, San Francisco N.L. 0, October 16, 1962.

BASES ON BALLS

Most bases on balls, total series
45—New York A.L.; 38 series, 213 games.

Most bases on balls, series
4-game series—23—New York A.L. vs. Chicago N.L., 1932.
5-game series—25—New York A.L. vs. New York N.L., 2000.
6-game series—34—Philadelphia N.L. vs. Toronto A.L., 1993.
7-game series—40—Cleveland A.L. vs. Florida N.L., 1997.
8-game series—27—New York A.L. vs. New York N.L., 1921.

Most bases on balls by both clubs, series
4-game series—34—New York A.L. 23, Chicago N.L. 11, 1932.
5-game series—37—New York A.L. 23, Brooklyn N.L. 14, 1941.
6-game series—59—Philadelphia N.L. 34, Toronto A.L. 25, 1993.
7-game series—76—Cleveland A.L. 40, Florida N.L. 36, 1997.
8-game series—49—New York A.L. 27, New York N.L. 22, 1921.

Fewest bases on balls, series
4-game series—4—Pittsburgh N.L. vs. New York A.L., 1927.
5-game series—5—Philadelphia A.L. vs. New York N.L., 1905.
6-game series—4—Philadelphia A.L. vs. New York N.L., 1911.
7-game series—9—St. Louis N.L. vs. Philadelphia A.L., 1931.
8-game series—13—Boston A.L. vs. Pittsburgh N.L., 1903.

Fewest bases on balls by both clubs, series
4-game series—15—New York A.L. 9, Cincinnati N.L. 6, 1939.
5-game series—15—New York N.L. 8, Philadelphia A.L. 7, 1913.
6-game series—17—Chicago A.L. 11, New York N.L. 6, 1917.
7-game series—30—New York A.L. 18, Pittsburgh N.L. 12, 1960.
8-game series—27—Pittsburgh N.L. 14, Boston A.L. 13, 1903.

Most bases on balls, game
11—Brooklyn N.L. vs. New York A.L., October 5, 1956.
New York A.L. vs. Milwaukee N.L., October 5, 1957.
Detroit A.L. vs. San Diego N.L., October 12, 1984.

Most bases on balls by both clubs, game
19—New York A.L. 11, Milwaukee N.L. 8, October 5, 1957.

Longest game with no bases on balls
12 innings—St. Louis N.L. vs. Detroit A.L., October 4, 1934.

Fewest bases on balls by both clubs, game
0—Philadelphia A.L. 0, New York N.L. 0, October 16, 1911.
New York N.L. 0, Chicago A.L. 0, October 10, 1917.
New York N.L. 0, New York A.L. 0, October 9, 1921.
Boston A.L. 0, St. Louis N.L. 0, October 7, 1967.
Philadelphia N.L. 0, Baltimore A.L. 0, October 11, 1983.

Most bases on balls, inning
5—New York A.L. vs. St. Louis N.L., October 6, 1926, fifth inning.

Most bases on balls by both clubs, inning
6—New York A.L. 3, New York N.L. 3, October 7, 1921,
third inning.
New York A.L. 5, St. Louis N.L. 1, October 6, 1926, fifth inning.

Most bases on balls by pinch-hitters, inning
2—New York A.L. vs. New York N.L., October 15, 1923,
eighth inning.
Baltimore A.L. vs. Philadelphia N.L., October 15, 1983,
sixth inning.

STRIKEOUTS

Most strikeouts, total series
1,192—New York A.L.; 38 series, 213 games.

Most strikeouts, series
4-game series—37—New York A.L. vs. Los Angeles N.L., 1963.
5-game series—50—Chicago N.L. vs. Philadelphia A.L., 1929.
6-game series—50—Philadelphia N.L. vs. Toronto A.L., 1993.
7-game series—70—Arizona N.L. vs. New York A.L., 2001.
8-game series—45—Pittsburgh N.L. vs. Boston A.L., 1903.

Most strikeouts by both clubs, series
4-game series—62—New York A.L. 37, Los Angeles N.L. 25,
1963.

5-game series—88—New York N.L. 48, New York A.L., 40,
2000.
6-game series—92—St. Louis A.L. 49, St. Louis N.L. 43, 1944.
7-game series—113—Arizona N.L. 70, New York A.L. 63, 2001.
8-game series—82—New York A.L. 44, New York N.L. 38, 1921.

Fewest strikeouts, series
4-game series—7—Pittsburgh N.L. vs. New York A.L., 1927.
5-game series—15—New York N.L. vs. New York A.L., 1922.
6-game series—14—Chicago N.L. vs. Boston A.L., 1918.
7-game series—20—Brooklyn N.L. vs. Cleveland A.L., 1920.
8-game series—22—Cincinnati N.L. vs. Chicago A.L., 1919.

Fewest strikeouts by both clubs, series
4-game series—32
New York A.L. 25, Pittsburgh N.L. 7, 1927.
Cincinnati N.L. 16, New York A.L. 16, 1976.
5-game series—35
New York N.L. 19, Philadelphia A.L. 16, 1913.
New York A.L. 20, New York N.L. 15, 1922.
6-game series—35—Boston A.L. 21, Chicago N.L. 14, 1918.
7-game series—41—Cleveland A.L. 21, Brooklyn N.L. 20, 1920.
8-game series—52—Chicago A.L. 30, Cincinnati N.L. 22, 1919.

Most strikeouts, game
17—Detroit A.L. vs. St. Louis N.L., October 2, 1968.

Most strikeouts by pinch-hitters, game
4—St. Louis A.L. vs. St. Louis N.L., October 8, 1944
(consecutive) and October 9, 1944 (consecutive).

Most consecutive strikeouts, game
6—Chicago A.L. vs. Cincinnati N.L., October 6, 1919 (3 in second
inning, 3 in third inning).
Los Angeles N.L. vs. Baltimore A.L., October 5, 1966 (3 in
fourth inning, 3 in fifth inning).
Kansas City A.L. vs. St. Louis N.L., October 24, 1985 (3 in
sixth inning, 3 in seventh inning).

Most strikeouts by both clubs, nine-inning game
25—New York A.L. 15, Los Angeles N.L. 10, October 2, 1963.
New York N.L. 13, New York A.L. 12, October 24, 2000.

Most strikeouts by both clubs, extra-inning game
25—Oakland A.L. 15, New York N.L. 10, October 14, 1973,
12 innings.

Fewest strikeouts, game
0—Chicago N.L. vs. Boston A.L., September 6, 1918 (batted
eight innings).
Chicago N.L. vs. Boston A.L., September 9, 1918.
New York A.L. vs. New York N.L., October 6, 1921 (batted
eight innings).
New York A.L. vs. Philadelphia N.L., October 4, 1950.
Brooklyn N.L. vs. New York A.L., October 3, 1952.
Pittsburgh N.L. vs. New York A.L., October 6, 1960.
Pittsburgh N.L. vs. New York A.L., October 13, 1960.
New York A.L. vs. Pittsburgh N.L., October 13, 1960.

Fewest strikeouts by both clubs, game
0—Pittsburgh N.L. 0, New York A.L. 0, October 13, 1960.

Most consecutive strikeouts by pinch-hitters, two consecutive games
8—St. Louis A.L. vs. St. Louis N.L., October 8 (4), October 9
(4), 1944.

Most strikeouts, inning
4—Detroit A.L. vs. Chicago N.L., October 14, 1908, first inning.

Most strikeouts by pinch-hitters, inning
3—St. Louis A.L. vs. St. Louis N.L., October 8, 1944,
ninth inning.

Most strikeouts by both clubs, inning
6—Cincinnati N.L. 3, Oakland A.L. 3, October 18, 1972,
fifth inning.
Kansas City A.L. 3, St. Louis N.L. 3, October 24, 1985,
seventh inning.
New York A.L. 3, New York N.L. 3, October 24, 2000, second
inning.

SACRIFICE HITS

Most sacrifices, total series
116—New York A.L.; 38 series, 213 games.

Most sacrifices, series
14—Chicago N.L. vs. Chicago A.L., 1906 (6-game series).

Most sacrifices by both clubs, series
22—St. Louis N.L. 12, New York A.L. 10, 1926 (7-game series).

Fewest sacrifices, series
0—Held by many clubs. Last club—Atlanta N.L. vs. New York A.L., 1999.

Fewest sacrifices by both clubs, series
0—New York A.L. 0, Brooklyn N.L. 0, 1941 (5-game series).
Cincinnati N.L. 0, New York A.L. 0, 1976 (4-game series).
Baltimore A.L. 0, Philadelphia N.L. 0, 1983 (5-game series).
Oakland A.L. 0, San Francisco N.L. 0, 1989 (4-game series).

Most sacrifices, game
5—Chicago N.L. vs. Chicago A.L., October 12, 1906 (all sacrifice hits).
Chicago N.L. vs. Detroit A.L., October 10, 1908 (all sacrifice hits).
Pittsburgh N.L. vs. Detroit A.L., October 16, 1909 (4 sacrifice hits, 1 sacrifice fly).
New York N.L. vs. Cleveland A.L., October 2, 1954 (3 sacrifice hits, 2 sacrifice flies).

Most sacrifices by both clubs, game
7—Chicago N.L. 5, Detroit A.L. 2, October 10, 1908 (all sacrifice hits).

Most sacrifices, inning
3—Brooklyn N.L. vs. New York A.L., October 4, 1955, sixth inning (2 sacrifice hits, 1 sacrifice fly).

SACRIFICE FLIES (SINCE 1954)

Most sacrifice flies, total series
18—New York A.L.; 18 series, 106 games.

Most sacrifice flies, series
7—Toronto A.L. vs. Philadelphia N.L., 1993 (6-game series).

Most sacrifice flies by both clubs, series
8—Toronto A.L. 7, Philadelphia N.L. 1, 1993 (6-game series).

Most sacrifice flies, game
3—Toronto A.L. vs. Philadelphia N.L., October 19, 1993.

Most sacrifice flies by both clubs, game
3—Toronto A.L. 3, Philadelphia N.L. 0, October 19, 1993.
Toronto A.L. 2, Philadelphia N.L. 1, October 23, 1993.

Most sacrifice flies, inning
2—Baltimore A.L. vs. Pittsburgh N.L., October 13, 1971, first inning.

HIT BY PITCH

Most hit by pitch, total series
46—New York A.L.; 38 series, 213 games.

Most hit by pitch, series
6—Pittsburgh N.L. vs. Detroit A.L., 1909 (7-game series).
Arizona N.L. vs. New York A.L., 2001 (7-game series).

Most hit by pitch by both clubs, series
10—Pittsburgh N.L. 6, Detroit A.L. 4, 1909 (7-game series).

Fewest hit by pitch, series
0—Held by many clubs.

Most hit by pitch, game
3—Detroit A.L. vs. St. Louis N.L., October 9, 1968.
Baltimore A.L. vs. Pittsburgh N.L., October 13, 1971.

Most hit by pitch by both clubs, game
3—Philadelphia N.L. 2, Boston A.L. 1, October 13, 1915.
Cincinnati N.L. 2, Chicago A.L. 1, October 9, 1919.
Pittsburgh N.L. 2, Washington A.L. 1, October 7, 1925.
Detroit A.L. 3, St. Louis N.L. 0, October 9, 1968.
Baltimore A.L. 3, Pittsburgh N.L. 0, October 13, 1971.
New York N.L. 2, Oakland A.L. 1, October 14, 1973.
Minnesota A.L. 2, St. Louis N.L. 1, October 21, 1987.

Most hit by pitch, inning
2—Pittsburgh N.L. vs. Detroit A.L., October 11, 1909, second inning (consecutive).
Detroit A.L. vs. St. Louis N.L., October 9, 1968, eighth inning.
Pittsburgh N.L. vs. Baltimore A.L., October 17, 1979, ninth inning (consecutive).

REACHING BASE ON ERRORS

Most first on error, game
5—Chicago N.L. vs. Chicago A.L., October 13, 1906.

Most first on error by both clubs, game
6—Pittsburgh N.L. 4, Boston A.L. 2, October 10, 1903.
Chicago N.L. 4, Philadelphia A.L. 2, October 18, 1910.
New York N.L. 4, Philadelphia A.L. 2, October 26, 1911.

INDIVIDUAL BASERUNNING

STOLEN BASES

ost stolen bases, career
—Eddie Collins, Philadelphia A.L. (10), 1910, 1911, 1913, 1914; Chicago A.L. (4), 1917, 1919; six series, 34 games.
  Lou Brock, St. Louis N.L., 1964 (0), 1967 (7), 1968 (7); three series, 21 games.

ost stolen bases, series
game series—3
 Rickey Henderson, Oakland A.L., 1989, 1990.
 Derek Jeter, New York A.L., 1999.
game series—6—Jimmy Slagle, Chicago N.L., 1907.
game series—6—Kenny Lofton, Cleveland A.L., 1995.
game series—7
Lou Brock, St. Louis N.L., 1967.
Lou Brock, St. Louis N.L., 1968.
game series—4—Josh Devore, New York N.L., 1912.

ost stolen bases, game
—Honus Wagner, Pittsburgh N.L., October 11, 1909.
  Willie Davis, Los Angeles N.L., October 11, 1965.
  Lou Brock, St. Louis N.L., October 12, 1967.
  Lou Brock, St. Louis N.L., October 5, 1968.

ost times stealing home, game (13 times; *part of double steal)
—Bill Dahlen, New York N.L., October 12, 1905, fifth inning.*
  George Davis, Chicago A.L., October 13, 1906, third inning.*
  Jimmy Slagle, Chicago N.L., October 11, 1907, seventh inning.
  Ty Cobb, Detroit A.L., October 9, 1909, third inning.
  Buck Herzog, New York N.L., October 14, 1912, first inning.*
  Butch Schmidt, Boston N.L., October 9, 1914, eighth inning.*
  Mike McNally, New York A.L., October 5, 1921, fifth inning.
  Bob Meusel, New York A.L., October 6, 1921, eighth inning.
  Bob Meusel, New York A.L., October 7, 1928, sixth inning.*
  Hank Greenberg, Detroit A.L., October 6, 1934, eighth inning.*
  Monte Irvin, New York N.L., October 4, 1951, first inning.
  Jackie Robinson, Brooklyn N.L., September 28, 1955, eighth inning.
  Tim McCarver, St. Louis N.L., October 15, 1964, fourth inning.*

Most stolen bases, inning (nine times)
2—Jimmy Slagle, Chicago N.L., October 8, 1907, 10th inning.
  George Browne, New York N.L., October 12, 1905, ninth inning.
  Ty Cobb, Detroit A.L., October 12, 1908, ninth inning.
  Eddie Collins, Chicago A.L., October 7, 1917, sixth inning.
  Babe Ruth, New York A.L., October 6, 1921, fifth inning.
  Lou Brock, St. Louis N.L., October 12, 1967, fifth inning.
  Dave Lopes, Los Angeles N.L., October 15, 1974, first inning.
  Kenny Lofton, Cleveland A.L., October 21, 1995, first inning.
  Omar Vizquel, Cleveland A.L., October 26, 1997, fifth inning.

CAUGHT STEALING

Most caught stealing, career
9—Frank Schulte, Chicago N.L., 1906, 1907, 1908, 1910; four series, 21 games.

Most caught stealing, series
5—Frank Schulte, Chicago N.L., 1910 (5-game series).

Most times caught stealing, game
2—Frank Schulte, Chicago N.L., October 17, 1910.
  Frank Schulte, Chicago N.L., October 23, 1910.
  Fred Luderus, Philadelphia N.L., October 8, 1915.
  Jimmy Johnston, Brooklyn N.L., October 9, 1916.
  Mickey Livingston, Chicago N.L., October 3, 1945.
  Billy Martin, New York A.L., September 28, 1955.

Most times caught stealing, inning
1—Held by many players.

Most times caught off base, game
2—Max Flack, Chicago N.L., September 9, 1918 (first base in first inning, second base in third inning).

CLUB BASERUNNING

STOLEN BASES

Most stolen bases, total series
72—New York A.L.; 38 series, 213 games.

Most stolen bases, series
4-game series—9—Boston N.L. vs. Philadelphia A.L., 1914.
5-game series—18—Chicago N.L. vs. Detroit A.L., 1907.
6-game series—15—Atlanta N.L. vs. Toronto A.L., 1992.
7-game series—18—Pittsburgh N.L. vs. Detroit A.L., 1909.
8-game series—12—New York N.L. vs. Boston A.L., 1912.

Most stolen bases by both clubs, series
4-game series—11—Boston N.L. 9, Philadelphia A.L. 2, 1914.
5-game series—25—Chicago N.L. 18, Detroit A.L. 7, 1907.
6-game series—20—Atlanta N.L. 15, Toronto A.L. 5, 1992.
7-game series—24—Pittsburgh N.L. 18, Detroit A.L. 6, 1909.
8-game series—18—New York N.L. 12, Boston A.L. 6, 1912.

Fewest stolen bases, series
4-game series—0—Held by many clubs.
5-game series—0—Held by many clubs.
6-game series—0—Held by many clubs.
7-game series—0
Philadelphia A.L. vs. St. Louis N.L., 1931.
Detroit A.L. vs. Cincinnati N.L., 1940.
New York A.L. vs. Pittsburgh N.L., 1960.
Detroit A.L. vs. St. Louis N.L., 1968.
New York N.L. vs. Oakland A.L., 1973.
Boston A.L. vs. Cincinnati N.L., 1975.
Pittsburgh N.L. vs. Baltimore A.L., 1979.
Boston A.L. vs. New York N.L., 1986.
8-game series—5
Boston A.L. vs. Pittsburgh N.L., 1903.
Chicago A.L. vs. Cincinnati N.L., 1919.

Fewest stolen bases by both clubs, series
4-game series—1
Cincinnati N.L. 1, New York A.L. 0, 1939.
New York N.L. 1, Cleveland A.L. 0, 1954.
Los Angeles N.L. 1, Baltimore A.L. 0, 1966.
5-game series—1
Chicago N.L. 1, Philadelphia A.L. 0, 1929.
Washington A.L. 1, New York N.L. 0, 1933.
New York N.L. 1, New York A.L. 0, 1937.
New York A.L. 1, Cincinnati N.L. 0, 1961.
Cincinnati N.L. 1, Baltimore A.L. 0, 1970.
New York A.L. 1, New York N.L. 0, 2000.
6-game series—0—St. Louis N.L. 0, St. Louis A.L. 0, 1944.
7-game series—1—Cincinnati N.L. 1, Detroit A.L. 0, 1940.
8-game series—12
Pittsburgh N.L. 7, Boston A.L. 5, 1903.
Cincinnati N.L. 7, Chicago A.L. 5, 1919.

Most stolen bases, nine-inning game
5—New York N.L. vs. Philadelphia A.L., October 12, 1905.
Chicago N.L. vs. Chicago A.L., October 10, 1906.
Chicago N.L. vs. Detroit A.L., October 9, 1907.
St. Louis N.L. vs. Minnesota A.L., October 22, 1987.
Atlanta N.L. vs. Toronto A.L., October 18, 1992.

Most stolen bases, extra-inning game
7—Chicago N.L. vs. Detroit A.L., October 8, 1907, 12 innings.

Most stolen bases by both clubs, nine-inning game
6—New York N.L. 5, Philadelphia A.L. 1, October 12, 1905.
Pittsburgh N.L. 4, Detroit A.L. 2, October 13, 1909.
New York N.L. 3, Philadelphia A.L. 3, October 9, 1913.
St. Louis N.L. 5, Minnesota A.L. 1, October 22, 1987.

Most stolen bases by both clubs, extra-inning game
11—Chicago N.L. 7, Detroit A.L. 4, October 8, 1907, 12 innings.

Longest extra-inning game with no stolen bases
14 innings—Boston A.L. vs. Brooklyn N.L., October 9, 1916.
Brooklyn N.L. vs. Boston A.L., October 9, 1916.

Longest extra-inning game with no stolen bases by either club
14 innings—Boston A.L. vs. Brooklyn N.L., October 9, 1916.

Most stolen bases, inning
3—Pittsburgh N.L. vs. Boston A.L., October 1, 1903, first inning.
New York N.L. vs. Philadelphia A.L., October 12, 1905, ninth inning.
Chicago N.L. vs. Detroit A.L., October 8, 1907, 10th inning.
Chicago N.L. vs. Detroit A.L., October 11, 1908, eighth inning.
New York N.L. vs. Boston A.L., October 14, 1912, first inning.
Chicago A.L. vs. New York N.L., October 7, 1917, sixth inning.

CAUGHT STEALING

Most caught stealing, series
4-game series—5
Boston N.L. vs. Philadelphia A.L., 1914.
Cincinnati N.L. vs. New York, A.L., 1976.
5-game series—8—Chicago N.L. vs. Philadelphia A.L. 1910.
6-game series—13—New York N.L. vs. Philadelphia A.L. 1911.
7-game series—7
Cleveland A.L. vs. Brooklyn N.L., 1920.
Washington A.L. vs. Pittsburgh N.L., 1925.
St. Louis N.L. vs. Detroit A.L., 1968.
8-game series—11—New York N.L. vs. Boston A.L., 1912.

Most caught stealing by both clubs, series
4-game series—7—Cincinnati N.L. 5, New York A.L. 2, 1976.
5-game series—15—Chicago N.L. 8, Philadelphia A.L. 7, 1910.
6-game series—19—New York N.L. 13, Philadelphia A.L. 6, 1911.
7-game series—11—Pittsburgh N.L. 6, Detroit A.L. 5, 1909.
8-game series—16—New York N.L. 11, Boston A.L. 5, 1912.

Fewest caught stealing, series
0—Held by many clubs.

Fewest caught stealing by both clubs, series
4-game series—1—New York A.L. 1, Pittsburgh N.L. 0, 1927.
Cincinnati N.L. 1, New York A.L. 0, 1939.
New York A.L. 1, Philadelphia N.L. 0, 1950.
New York N.L. 1, Cleveland A.L. 0, 1954.
New York A.L. 1, San Diego N.L. 0, 1998.
5-game series—0—New York A.L. 0, Brooklyn N.L. 0, 1949.
6-game series—1
St. Louis N.L. 1, St. Louis A.L. 0, 1944.
Cleveland A.L. 1, Boston N.L. 0, 1948.
7-game series—0—St. Louis N.L. 0, New York A.L. 0, 1964.
8-game series—6—Pittsburgh N.L. 4, Boston A.L. 2, 1903.

Most caught stealing, nine-inning game
3—Made in many games. Last time—Los Angeles N.L. vs. Oakland A.L., October 19, 1988.

Most caught stealing, extra-inning game
5—New York N.L. vs. Philadelphia A.L., October 17, 1911, 11 innings (0 stolen bases).

Most caught stealing by both clubs, nine-inning game
5—Philadelphia A.L. 3, Chicago N.L. 2, October 17, 1910.

Most caught stealing, inning
2—Made in many innings.

LEFT ON BASE

Most left on base, total series
1,471—New York A.L.; 38 series, 213 games.

Most left on base, series
4-game series—37—Cleveland A.L. vs. New York N.L., 1954.
5-game series—52—New York A.L. vs. New York N.L., 2000.
6-game series—55—New York A.L. vs. Los Angeles N.L., 1981.
7-game series—72—New York N.L. vs. Oakland A.L., 1973.
8-game series—55
Boston A.L. vs. Pittsburgh N.L., 1903.
Boston A.L. vs. New York N.L., 1912.

Most left on base by both clubs, series

4-game series—65—Cleveland A.L. 37, New York N.L. 28, 1954.
5-game series—88—New York A.L. 52, New York N.L. 36, 2000.
6-game series—101—New York A.L. 55, Los Angeles N.L. 46, 1981.
7-game series—130—New York N.L. 72, Oakland A.L. 58, 1973.
8-game series—108—Boston A.L. 55, New York N.L. 53, 1912.

Fewest left on base, series

4-game series—16—New York A.L. vs. Cincinnati N.L., 1939.
5-game series—23—Philadelphia N.L. vs. Baltimore A.L., 1983.
6-game series—29—Philadelphia A.L. vs. New York N.L., 1911.
7-game series—36—Minnesota A.L. vs. Los Angeles N.L., 1965.
8-game series—43—New York A.L. vs. New York N.L., 1921.

Fewest left on base by both clubs, series

4-game series—39—Cincinnati N.L. 23, New York A.L. 16, 1939.
5-game series—51—Baltimore A.L. 28, Philadelphia N.L. 23, 1983.
6-game series—60—New York N.L. 31, Philadelphia A.L. 29, 1911.
7-game series—82
    Cleveland A.L. 43, Brooklyn N.L. 39, 1920.
    Brooklyn N.L. 42, New York A.L. 40, 1956.
    New York A.L. 43, San Francisco N.L. 39, 1962.
8-game series—97—New York N.L. 54, New York A.L. 43, 1921.

Most left on base, nine-inning game

14—Chicago N.L. vs. Philadelphia A.L., October 18, 1910.
    Detroit A.L. vs. Cincinnati N.L., October 6, 1940 (batted eight innings).
    Milwaukee N.L. vs. New York A.L., October 5, 1957.
    Pittsburgh N.L. vs. Baltimore A.L., October 11, 1971.
    St. Louis N.L. vs. Milwaukee A.L., October 20, 1982 (batted eight innings).
    Detroit A.L. vs. San Diego N.L., October 12, 1984.

Most left on base, extra-inning game

15—New York N.L. vs. Oakland A.L., October 14, 1973, 12 innings.
    Philadelphia N.L. vs. Kansas City A.L., October 17, 1980, 10 innings.
    New York A.L. vs. New York N.L., October 21, 2000, 12 innings.

Most left on base, two consecutive nine-inning games

26—Cleveland A.L. vs. New York N.L. September 29 (13), September 30 (13), 1954.

Most left on base, nine-inning shutout defeat

11—Philadelphia A.L. vs. St. Louis N.L., October 4, 1930 (lost 5-0).
    St. Louis N.L. vs. New York A.L., October 11, 1943 (lost 2-0).
    Los Angeles N.L. vs. Chicago A.L., October 6, 1959 (lost 1-0).
    Baltimore A.L. vs. New York N.L., October 14, 1969 (lost 5-0).

Most left on base by both clubs, nine-inning game

24—Detroit A.L. 14, San Diego N.L. 10, October 12, 1984.

Most left on base by both clubs, extra-inning game

27—New York N.L. 15, Oakland A.L. 12, October 14, 1973, 12 innings.

Fewest left on base, game

0—Brooklyn N.L. vs. New York A.L., October 8, 1956.
    Los Angeles N.L. vs. New York A.L., October 6, 1963 (batted eight innings).

Fewest left on base by both clubs, game

3—New York A.L. 3, Brooklyn N.L. 0, October 8, 1956.

INDIVIDUAL PITCHING

GAMES

Most games pitched, career
22—Whitey Ford, New York A.L., 1950, 1953, 1955, 1956, 1957, 1958, 1960, 1961, 1962, 1963, 1964; 11 series.

Most games pitched, series
4-game series—4—Jeff Nelson, New York A.L., 1999 (2.2 innings).
5-game series—5—Mike G. Marshall, Los Angeles N.L., 1974 (nine innings).
6-game series—6—Dan Quisenberry, Kansas City A.L., 1980 (10.1 innings).
7-game series—7—Darold Knowles, Oakland A.L., 1973 (6.1 innings).
8-game series—5—Deacon Phillippe, Pittsburgh N.L., 1903 (44 innings).

Most consecutive games pitched, series
7—Darold Knowles, Oakland A.L., October 13, 14, 16, 17, 18, 20, 21, 1973.

GAMES STARTED

Most games started, career
22—Whitey Ford, New York A.L., 1950, 1953, 1955, 1956, 1957, 1958, 1960, 1961, 1962, 1963, 1964; 11 series.

Most opening games started, career
8—Whitey Ford, New York A.L., 1955, 1956, 1957, 1958, 1961, 1962, 1963, 1964 (won 4, lost 3).

Most consecutive games started, series
2—Deacon Phillippe, Pittsburgh N.L., October 3, 6, 1903.
Deacon Phillippe, Pittsburgh N.L., October 10, 13, 1903.
Jack Coombs, Philadelphia A.L., October 18, 20, 1910.
Christy Mathewson, New York N.L., October 17, 24, 1911.
George Earnshaw, Philadelphia A.L., October 9, 11, 1929.
George Earnshaw, Philadelphia A.L., October 6, 8, 1930.

Most series with three games started, career
3—Bob Gibson, St. Louis N.L., 1964, 1967, 1968.

Most games started, series
5—Deacon Phillippe, Pittsburgh N.L., 1903 (8-game series).

Oldest pitcher to start a game
45 years, 3 months, 7 days—Jack Quinn, Philadelphia A.L., October 12, 1929 (pitched five innings).

GAMES RELIEVED AND FINISHED

Most games by relief pitcher, career
20—Mike Stanton, Atlanta N.L., 1991, 1992; New York A.L., 1998 through 2001 (23.1 innings).

Most games pitched by relief pitcher, series
7—Darold Knowles, Oakland A.L., 1973 (7-game series).

Most games finished, series
6—Hugh Casey, Brooklyn N.L., 1947 (7-game series).
Dan Quisenberry, Kansas City A.L., 1980 (6-game series).

Oldest pitcher to finish game
46 years, 2 months, 29 days—Jack Quinn, Philadelphia A.L., October 4, 1930 (pitched two innings).

COMPLETE GAMES

Most complete games pitched, career
10—Christy Mathewson, New York N.L. 1905, 1911, 1912, 1913.

Most consecutive complete games pitched, career
8—Bob Gibson, St. Louis N.L., 1964, 1967, 1968 (won 7, lost 1).

Most consecutive complete games won, career
7—Bob Gibson, St. Louis N.L., October 12, 15, 1964; October 4, 8, 12, 1967; October 2, 6, 1968.

Most complete games, series
5—Deacon Phillippe, Pittsburgh N.L., 1903 (8-game series).

Youngest pitcher to pitch a complete game
20 years, 10 months, 12 days—Joe Bush, Philadelphia A.L., October 9, 1913 (Philadelphia A.L. 8, New York N.L. 2).

Youngest pitcher to win a complete game
20 years, 10 months, 12 days—Joe Bush, Philadelphia A.L., October 9, 1913 (Philadelphia A.L. 8, New York N.L. 2)

Oldest pitcher to pitch a complete game
39 years, 7 months, 13 days—Grover Alexander, St. Louis N.L., October 9, 1926 (St. Louis N.L. 10, New York A.L. 2).

INNINGS

Most innings pitched, career
146—Whitey Ford, New York A.L., 1950, 1953, 1955 through 1964, except 1959; 11 series, 22 games.

Most innings pitched, series
4-game series—18
Dick Rudolph, Boston N.L., 1914.
Waite Hoyt, New York A.L., 1928.
Red Ruffing, New York A.L., 1938.
Sandy Koufax, Los Angeles N.L., 1963.
5-game series—27
Christy Mathewson, New York N.L., 1905.
Jack Coombs, Philadelphia A.L., 1910.
6-game series—27
Christy Mathewson, New York N.L. 1911.
Red Faber, Chicago A.L., 1917.
Hippo Vaughn, Chicago N.L., 1918.
7-game series—32—George Mullin, Detroit A.L., 1909.
8-game series—44—Deacon Phillippe, Pittsburgh N.L., 1903.

Most innings pitched, game
14—Babe Ruth, Boston A.L., October 9, 1916 (complete game, won 2-1).

GAMES WON

Most games won, career
10—Whitey Ford, New York A.L., 1950, 1953, 1955, 1956, 1957, 1958, 1960, 1961, 1962, 1963, 1964; 11 series, 22 games (lost 8).

For a complete list of pitchers with five or more victories, see page 512.

Most consecutive games won, career
7—Bob Gibson, St. Louis N.L., October 12, 15, 1964; October 4, 8, 12, 1967; October 2, 6, 1968 (seven complete).

Most games won by undefeated pitcher, career
6—Lefty Gomez, New York A.L., 1932, 1936, 1937, 1938.

Most series-opening games won, career
5—Red Ruffing, New York A.L., 1932, 1938, 1939, 1941, 1942, four complete (lost complete-game opener in 1936).

Most games won, series
4-game series—2—Held by many pitchers.
5-game series—3
Christy Mathewson, New York N.L., 1905.
Jack Coombs, Philadelphia A.L., 1910.
6-game series—3—Red Faber, Chicago A.L., 1917.
7-game series—3
Babe Adams, Pittsburgh N.L., 1909.
Stan Coveleski, Cleveland A.L., 1920.

Harry Brecheen, St. Louis N.L., 1946.
Lew Burdette, Milwaukee N.L., 1957.
Bob Gibson, St. Louis N.L., 1967.
Mickey Lolich, Detroit A.L., 1968.
Randy Johnson, Arizona N.L., 2001.
-game series—3
Bill Dinneen, Boston A.L., 1903.
Deacon Phillippe, Pittsburgh N.L., 1903.
Joe Wood, Boston A.L., 1912.

Most games won by relief pitcher, series
—Jesse Barnes, New York N.L., 1921 (8-game series).
Hugh Casey, Brooklyn N.L., 1947 (7-game series).
Larry Sherry, Los Angeles N.L., 1959 (6-game series).
Ross Grimsley, Cincinnati N.L., 1972 (6-game series).
Rawly Eastwick, Cincinnati N.L., 1975 (7-game series).
Duane Ward, Toronto A.L., 1992 (6-game series).
Mike Stanton, New York A.L., 2000 (5-game series).

Most games won by undefeated pitcher, series
-game series—2—Held by many pitchers.
-game series—3
Christy Mathewson, New York N.L., 1905.
Jack Coombs, Philadelphia N.L., 1910.
-game series—2—Held by many pitchers.
-game series—3
Babe Adams, Pittsburgh N.L., 1909.
Stan Coveleski, Cleveland A.L., 1920.
Harry Brecheen, St. Louis N.L., 1946.
Lew Burdette, Milwaukee N.L., 1957.
Bob Gibson, St. Louis N.L., 1967.
Mickey Lolich, Detroit A.L., 1968.
Randy Johnson, Arizona N.L., 2001.
3-game series—2
Rube Marquard, New York N.L., 1912.
Hod Eller, Cincinnati N.L., 1919.
Dickie Kerr, Chicago A.L., 1919.
Jesse Barnes, New York N.L., 1921.

SAVES (SINCE 1969)

Most saves, career
3—Mariano Rivera, New York A.L., 1996, 1998 through 2001.

Most saves, series
4—John Wetteland, New York A.L., 1996 (6-game series).

GAMES LOST

Most games lost, career
8—Whitey Ford, New York A.L., 1950, 1953, 1955, 1956, 1957, 1958, 1960, 1961, 1962, 1963, 1964; 11 series, 22 games (won 10).

Most consecutive games lost, career
5—Joe Bush, Philadelphia A.L., 1914 (1), Boston A.L., 1918 (1), New York A.L., 1922 (2), 1923 (1).

Most games lost by winless pitcher, career
4—Ed Summers, Detroit A.L., 1908 (2), 1909 (2).
Willie Sherdel, St. Louis N.L., 1926 (2), 1928 (2).
Don Newcombe, Brooklyn N.L., 1949 (2), 1955 (1), 1956 (1).
Charlie Leibrandt, Kansas City A.L., 1985 (1); Atlanta N.L., 1991 (2), 1992 (1).

Most games lost, series
4-game series—2—Held by many pitchers.
5-game series—2—Held by many pitchers.
6-game series—3—George Frazier, New York A.L., 1981.
7-game series—2—Held by many pitchers
8-game series—3—Lefty Williams, Chicago A.L., 1919.

RUNS, EARNED RUNS AND ERA

Most runs allowed, series
4-game series—11
Grover Alexander, St. Louis N.L., 1928.
Bob Lemon, Cleveland A.L., 1954.
5-game series—16—Mordecai Brown, Chicago N.L., 1910.

6-game series—10
Slim Sallee, New York N.L., 1917.
Red Ruffing, New York A.L., 1936.
Don Gullett, New York A.L., 1977.
Don Sutton, Los Angeles N.L., 1978.
Jack Morris, Toronto A.L., 1992.
7-game series—17—Lew Burdette, Milwaukee N.L., 1958.
8-game series—19—Deacon Phillippe, Pittsburgh N.L., 1903.

Most runs allowed, nine-inning game
10—Bill Kennedy, Pittsburgh N.L., October 7, 1903.

Most earned runs allowed, nine-inning game
8—Jay Witasick, New York A.L., November 3, 2001.

Most runs allowed, inning
7—Hooks Wiltse, New York N.L., October 26, 1911, seventh inning.
Carl Hubbell, New York N.L., October 6, 1937, sixth inning.

Most earned runs allowed, inning
6—Hooks Wiltse, New York N.L., October 26, 1911, seventh inning.
Danny Cox, St. Louis N.L., October 18, 1987, fourth inning.
Jay Witasick, New York A.L., November 3, 2001, third inning.

Lowest earned-run average, series (14 or more innings)
0.00—Christy Mathewson, New York N.L., 1905 (27 innings).
Waite Hoyt, New York A.L., 1921 (27 innings).
Carl Hubbell, New York N.L., 1933 (20 innings).
Whitey Ford, New York A.L., 1960 (18 innings).
Joe McGinnity, New York N.L., 1905 (17 innings).
Duster Mails, Cleveland A.L., 1920 (15.2 innings).
Rube Benton, New York N.L., 1917 (14 innings).
Whitey Ford, New York A.L., 1961 (14 innings).

SHUTOUTS AND SCORELESS INNINGS

Most shutouts won, career
4—Christy Mathewson, New York N.L., 1905 (3), 1913 (1).

For a complete list of shutouts, see page 506.

Most shutouts won, series
3—Christy Mathewson, New York N.L., October 9, 12, 14, 1905 (consecutive).

Most 1-0 shutouts won, career
2—Art Nehf, New York N.L., October 13, 1921, October 12, 1923.

Most shutouts lost, career
3—Eddie Plank, Philadelphia A.L., 1905 (2), 1914 (1).

Most 1-0 shutouts lost, career
2—Eddie Plank, Philadelphia A.L., October 13, 1905, October 10, 1914.

Youngest pitcher to win a complete World Series shutout game
20 years, 11 months, 21 days—Jim Palmer, Baltimore A.L., October 6, 1966; Baltimore A.L., 6, Los Angeles N.L., 0.

Oldest pitcher to win a complete World Series shutout game
38 years, 1 month, 18 days—Randy Johnson, Arizona N.L., October 28, 2001; Arizona N.L. 4, New York A.L. 0.

Most consecutive scoreless innings, career
33—Whitey Ford, New York A.L., October 8, 1960 (9); October 12, 1960 (9); October 4, 1961 (9) innings; October 8, 1961 (5); October 4, 1962 (1).

Most consecutive scoreless innings, series
27—Christy Mathewson, New York N.L., October 9, 12, 14, 1905.

Retiring side on three pitched balls
Christy Mathewson, New York N.L., October 9, 1912, 11th inning.
Christy Mathewson, New York N.L., October 16, 1912, fifth inning.
Rube Walberg, Philadelphia A.L., October 14, 1929, seventh inning.
Tiny Bonham, New York A.L., October 6, 1941, seventh inning.

HITS

Most hits allowed, series
4-game series—17—Red Ruffing, New York A.L., 1938.
5-game series—23
Jack Coombs, Philadelphia A.L., 1910.
Mordecai Brown, Chicago N.L., 1910.
6-game series—25—Christy Mathewson, New York N.L., 1911.
7-game series—30—Walter Johnson, Washington A.L., 1924.
8-game series—38—Deacon Phillippe, Pittsburgh N.L., 1903.

Most hits allowed, nine-inning game
15—Walter Johnson, Washington A.L., October 15, 1925.

Fewest hits allowed, nine-inning game
0—Don Larsen, New York A.L., October 8, 1956 (perfect game).

One and two-hit games of nine innings (pitching complete game)
1—Ed Reulbach, Chicago N.L., October 10, 1906 (hit came with
none out in seventh).
Claude Passeau, Chicago N.L., October 5, 1945 (hit came
with two out in second).
Bill Bevens, New York A.L., October 3, 1947 (hit came with
two out in ninth).
Jim Lonborg, Boston A.L., October 5, 1967 (hit came with
two out in eighth).
2—Ed Walsh, Chicago A.L., October 11, 1906.
Mordecai Brown, Chicago N.L., October 12, 1906.
Eddie Plank, Philadelphia A.L., October 11, 1913.
Bill James, Boston N.L., October 10, 1914.
Waite Hoyt, New York A.L., October 6, 1921.
Burleigh Grimes, St. Louis N.L., October 5, 1931.
George Earnshaw, Philadelphia A.L., October 6, 1931.
Monte Pearson, New York A.L., October 5, 1939.
Mort Cooper, St. Louis N.L., October 4, 1944.
Bob Feller, Cleveland A.L., October 6, 1948.
Allie Reynolds, New York A.L., October 5, 1949.
Vic Raschi, New York A.L., October 4, 1950.
Warren Spahn, Milwaukee N.L., October 5, 1958.
Whitey Ford, New York A.L., October 4, 1961.
Nelson Briles, Pittsburgh N.L., October 14, 1971.
Greg Maddux, Atlanta N.L., October 21, 1995.

Fewest hits allowed, two consecutive complete games
4—Jim Lonborg, Boston A.L., October 5 (1), October 9 (3), 1967.

Fewest hits allowed, three consecutive complete games
14—Christy Mathewson, New York N.L., October 5 (4), October
12 (4), October 14 (6), 1905.
Bob Gibson, St. Louis N.L., October 4 (6), October 8 (5),
October 12 (3), 1967.

Most consecutive hitless innings, career
11—Don Larsen, New York A.L., October 8, 1956 (9), October
5, 1957 (2).

Most consecutive hitless innings, game
9—Don Larsen, New York A.L., October 8, 1956.

Most consecutive innings allowing no players to reach first base, career
11—Don Larsen, New York A.L., October 8, 1956 (9), October
5, 1957 (2).

Most consecutive innings allowing no players to reach first base, series
9—Don Larsen, New York A.L., October 8, 1956.

Most consecutive innings allowing no player to reach first base, game
9—Don Larsen, New York A.L., October 8, 1956 (perfect game).

Most hits allowed, inning
8—Jay Witasick, New York A.L., November 3, 2001, third
inning.

Most consecutive hits allowed, inning (consecutive plate appearances)
6—Ed Summers, Detroit A.L., October 10, 1908, ninth inning (6
singles).

DOUBLES, TRIPLES AND HOME RUNS

Most doubles allowed, game
8—Walter Johnson, Washington A.L., October 15, 1925.

Most triples allowed, game
5—Deacon Phillippe, Pittsburgh N.L., October 10, 1903.

Most home runs allowed, career
9—Catfish Hunter, Oakland A.L., 1972, 1973, 1974; New York
A.L., 1976, 1977, 1978; six series, 12 games.

Most home runs allowed, series
4-game series—4
Willie Sherdel, St. Louis N.L., 1928.
Charlie Root, Chicago N.L., 1932.
Junior Thompson, Cincinnati N.L., 1939.
Scott Garrelts, San Francisco N.L., 1989.
5-game series—4
Gary Nolan, Cincinnati N.L., 1970.
Charles Hudson, Philadelphia N.L., 1983.
6-game series—4—Allie Reynolds, New York A.L., 1953.
7-game series—5
Lew Burdette, Milwaukee N.L., 1958.
Dick Hughes, St. Louis N.L., 1967.
8-game series—2
Babe Adams, Pittsburgh N.L., 1909.
Harry Harper, New York A.L., 1921.

Most home runs allowed, game
4—Charlie Root, Chicago N.L., October 1, 1932.
Junior Thompson, Cincinnati N.L., October 7, 1939.
Dick Hughes, St. Louis N.L., October 11, 1967.

Most home runs allowed, inning
3—Dick Hughes, St. Louis N.L., October 11, 1967, fourth inning.

Most consecutive home runs allowed, inning (10 times)
2—Emil Yde, Pittsburgh N.L., October 11, 1925, third inning.
Bill Sherdel, St. Louis N.L., October 9, 1928, seventh inning.
Charlie Root, Chicago N.L., October 1, 1932, fifth inning.
Curt Simmons, St. Louis N.L., October 14, 1964, sixth inning.
Don Drysdale, Los Angeles N.L., October 5, 1966, first inning.
Dick Hughes, St. Louis N.L., October 11, 1967, fourth inning.
Rick Wise, Boston A.L., October 14, 1975, fifth inning.
Don Sutton, Los Angeles N.L., October 16, 1977, eighth inning.
Ron Guidry, New York A.L., October 25, 1981, seventh inning.
Ron Darling, New York N.L., October 27, 1986, second inning.
Orel Hershiser, Cleveland A.L., October 18, 1997, fourth inning.
David Wells, New York A.L., October 17, 1998, fifth inning.

TOTAL BASES AND LONG HITS

Most total bases allowed, game
25—Walter Johnson, Washington A.L., October 15, 1925.

Most long hits allowed, game
9—Walter Johnson, Washington A.L., October 15, 1925.

BASES ON BALLS

Most bases on balls, career
34—Whitey Ford, New York A.L., 1950, 1953, 1955, 1956,
1957, 1958, 1960, 1961, 1962, 1963, 1964; 11 series,
22 games.

Most innings pitched without allowing a base on balls, series
26—Carl Mays, New York A.L., 1921.

Most bases on balls, series
4-game series—8—Bob Lemon, Cleveland A.L., 1954.
5-game series—14—Jack Coombs, Philadelphia A.L., 1910.
6-game series—11
Lefty Tyler, Chicago N.L., 1918.
Lefty Gomez, New York A.L., 1936.
Allie Reynolds, New York A.L., 1951.
7-game series—11
Walter Johnson, Washington A.L., 1924.
Bill Bevens, New York A.L., 1947.
8-game series—13—Art Nehf, New York N.L., 1921.

Most bases on balls, game
10—Bill Bevens, New York A.L., October 3, 1947.

Longest game without allowing base on balls
12 innings—Schoolboy Rowe, Detroit A.L., October 4, 1934.

Most bases on balls, inning
—Bill Donovan, Detroit A.L., October 16, 1909, second inning.
   Art Reinhart, St. Louis N.L., October 6, 1926, fifth inning
     (one base on balls with bases full).
   Guy Bush, Chicago N.L., September 28, 1932, sixth inning.
   Don Gullett, Cincinnati N.L., October 22, 1975, third inning
     (two bases on balls with bases full).
   Tom Glavine, Atlanta N.L., October 24, 1991, sixth inning
     (one base on balls with bases full).
   Todd Stottlemyre, Toronto A.L., October 20, 1993, first
     inning (one base on balls with bases full).
   Al Leiter, Florida N.L., October 21, 1997, fourth inning (one
     base on balls with bases full).

Most consecutive bases on balls, inning
—Bob Shawkey, New York A.L., October 7, 1921, fourth inning
     (two bases on balls with bases full).
   Art Reinhart, St. Louis N.L., October 6, 1926, fifth inning
     (one base on balls with bases full).
   Guy Bush, Chicago N.L., September 28, 1932, sixth inning.
   Joe Hoerner, St. Louis N.L., October 3, 1968, ninth inning
     (two bases on balls with bases full).
   Tom Glavine, Atlanta N.L., October 24, 1991, sixth inning
     (two bases on balls with bases full).
   Todd Stottlemyre, Toronto A.L., October 20, 1993, first
     inning (one base on balls with bases full).
   Charles Nagy, Cleveland A.L., October 21, 1997, third inning
     (one base on balls with bases full).

STRIKEOUTS

Most strikeouts, career
94—Whitey Ford, New York A.L., 1950, 1953, 1955, 1956,
     1957, 1958, 1960, 1961, 1962, 1963, 1964; 11 series,
     22 games.

Most strikeouts, series
4-game series—23—Sandy Koufax, Los Angeles N.L., 1963.
5-game series—18—Christy Mathewson, New York N.L., 1905.
6-game series—20—Chief Bender, Philadelphia A.L., 1911.
7-game series—35—Bob Gibson, St. Louis N.L., 1968.
8-game series—28—Bill Dinneen, Boston A.L., 1903.

Most strikeouts, game
17—Bob Gibson, St. Louis N.L., October 2, 1968.

**For a complete list of pitchers with 10 or
more strikeouts in a game, see page 512.**

For a complete list of pitchers with 10 or
more strikeouts in a game, see page 512.

Most games with 10 or more strikeouts, career
5—Bob Gibson, St. Louis N.L., 1964 (1), 1967 (2), 1968 (2).

Most strikeouts by losing pitcher, nine-inning game
12—Orlando Hernandez, New York A.L., October 24, 2000,
     pitched first 7.1 innings.

Most strikeouts by losing pitcher, extra-inning game
12—Walter Johnson, Washington A.L., October 4, 1924, 12
     innings.

Most strikeouts by relief pitcher, game
11—Moe Drabowsky, Baltimore A.L., October 5, 1966, pitched
     6.2 innings.

Most consecutive strikeouts, game
6—Hod Eller, Cincinnati N.L., October 6, 1919 (three in second
     inning, three in third inning).
   Moe Drabowsky, Baltimore A.L., October 5, 1966 (three in
     fourth inning, three in fifth inning).
   Todd Worrell, St. Louis N.L., October 24, 1985 (three in
     sixth inning, three in seventh inning).

Most consecutive strikeouts at start of game
5—Mort Cooper, St. Louis N.L., October 11, 1943.
   Sandy Koufax, Los Angeles N.L., October 23, 1963.

Most innings with one or more strikeouts, nine-inning game
9—Ed Walsh, Chicago A.L., October 11, 1906 (12 strikeouts).
   Bob Gibson, St. Louis N.L., October 2, 1968 (17 strikeouts).

Most strikeouts, inning
4—Orval Overall, Chicago N.L., October 14, 1908, first inning.

HIT BATSMEN, WILD PITCHES AND BALKS

Most hit batsmen, career
4—Bill Donovan, Detroit A.L., 1907 (3), 1908 (0), 1909 (1).
   Eddie Plank, Philadelphia A.L., 1905 (1), 1911 (1), 1913 (1),
     1914 (1).

Most hit batsmen, series
3—Bill Donovan, Detroit A.L., 1907 (5-game series).
   Bruce Kison, Pittsburgh N.L., 1971 (7-game series).

Most hit batsmen, game
3—Bruce Kison, Pittsburgh N.L., October 13, 1971, 6.1 innings.

Most hit batsmen, inning
2—Ed Willett, Detroit A.L., October 11, 1909, second inning
     (consecutive).
   Wayne Granger, St. Louis N.L., October 9, 1968, eighth
     inning.

Most wild pitches, career
5—Hal Schumacher, New York N.L., 1933 (2), 1936 (2), 1937 (1).

Most wild pitches, series
3—Jeff Tesreau, New York N.L., 1912.
   John Stuper, St. Louis N.L., 1982.

Most wild pitches, game
2—Jeff Tesreau, New York N.L., October 15, 1912.
   Jeff Pfeffer, Brooklyn N.L., October 12, 1916.
   Bob Shawkey, New York A.L., October 5, 1922.
   Vic Aldridge, Pittsburgh N.L., October 15, 1925.
   Johnny Miljus, Pittsburgh N.L., October 8, 1927.
   Tex Carleton, Chicago N.L., October 9, 1938.
   Jim Bouton, New York A.L., October 5, 1963.
   John Stuper, St. Louis N.L., October 13, 1982.
   George Medich, Milwaukee A.L., October 19, 1982.
   Jack Morris, Detroit A.L., October 13, 1984.
   Ron Darling, New York N.L., October 18, 1986.
   Mike Moore, Oakland A.L., October 15, 1989.
   John Smoltz, Atlanta N.L., October 18, 1992.
   Glendon Rusch, New York N.L., October 21, 2000.

Most wild pitches, inning
2—Bob Shawkey, New York A.L., October 5, 1922, fifth inning.
   Vic Aldridge, Pittsburgh N.L., October 15, 1925, first inning.
   Johnny Miljus, Pittsburgh N.L., October 8, 1927, ninth
     inning.
   Tex Carleton, Chicago N.L., October 9, 1938, eighth inning.
   Doc Medich, Milwaukee A.L., October 19, 1982, sixth inning.

Most balks, inning, game, series or career
1—Held by many pitchers.

CLUB PITCHING

APPEARANCES

Most appearances by pitchers, series
4-game series—19—San Francisco N.L. vs. Oakland A.L., 1989.
5-game series—21—New York N.L. vs. New York A.L., 2000.
6-game series—27—New York A.L. vs. Atlanta N.L., 1996.
7-game series—33—Cleveland A.L. vs. Florida N.L., 1997.
8-game series—14—Boston A.L. vs. New York N.L., 1912.

Most appearances by pitchers from both clubs, series
4-game series—32—San Francisco N.L. 19, Oakland A.L. 13, 1989.
5-game series—38—New York N.L. 21, New York A.L. 17, 2000.
6-game series—48—New York A.L. 27, Atlanta N.L. 21, 1996.
7-game series—60—Cleveland A.L. 33, Florida N.L. 27, 1997.
8-game series—25—Chicago A.L. 13, Cincinnati N.L. 12, 1919.

COMPLETE GAMES

Most complete games, series
7—Boston A.L. vs. Pittsburgh N.L., 1903 (8-game series).

Most complete games from both clubs, series
13—Boston A.L. 7, Pittsburgh N.L. 6, 1903 (8-game series).

Fewest complete games, series
0—Held by many clubs.

Fewest complete games by both clubs, series
0—Occurred many times. Last time—New York A.L. 0, New
York N.L. 0, 2000 (5-game series).

SAVES (SINCE 1969)

Most saves, series
4-game series—3—New York A.L. vs. San Diego N.L., 1998.
5-game series—3—Oakland A.L. vs. Los Angeles N.L., 1974.
6-game series—4—New York A.L. vs. Atlanta N.L., 1996.
7-game series—4—Oakland A.L. vs. New York N.L., 1973.

Most saves by both clubs, series
4-game series—3—New York A.L. 3, San Diego N.L. 0, 1998.
5-game series—4—Oakland A.L. 3, Los Angeles N.L. 1, 1974.
6-game series—4
   Philadelphia N.L. 3, Kansas City A.L. 1, 1980.
   Toronto A.L. 3, Atlanta N.L. 1, 1992.
   Atlanta N.L. 3, Cleveland A.L. 1, 1995.
   New York A.L. 4, Atlanta N.L. 0, 1996.
7-game series—7—Oakland A.L. 4, New York N.L. 3, 1973.

Fewest saves, series
0—Held by many clubs.

Fewest saves by both clubs, series
0—New York A.L. 0, Los Angeles N.L. 0, 1977 (6-game series).

RUNS AND SHUTOUTS

Most runs allowed, total series
752—New York A.L.; 38 series, 213 games.

Most shutouts won, total series
17—New York A.L.

For a complete list of shutouts, see page 506.

Most shutouts won, series
4—New York N.L. vs. Philadelphia A.L., 1905.

Most consecutive shutouts won, series
3—New York N.L. vs. Philadelphia A.L., October 12, 13, 14, 1905.
   Baltimore A.L., vs. Los Angeles N.L., October 6, 8, 9, 1966.

Most shutouts by both clubs, series
5—New York N.L. 4, Philadelphia A.L. 1, 1905.

Fewest shutouts, series
0—Held by many clubs in series of all lengths.

Fewest shutouts by both clubs, series
0—Held by many clubs in series of all lengths.

Longest shutout game
10 innings—New York N.L. 3, Philadelphia A.L. 0, October 8, 1913
   Brooklyn N.L. 1, New York A.L. 0, October 9, 1956
   Minnesota A.L. 1, Atlanta N.L. 0, October 27, 1991

Largest score, shutout game
12-0—New York A.L. 12, Pittsburgh N.L. 0, October 12, 1960.

Most consecutive innings shut out opponents, total series
39—Baltimore A.L., October 5, 1966, fourth inning, through
   October 11, 1969, first six innings.

Most consecutive innings shut out opponent, series
33—Baltimore A.L. vs. Los Angeles N.L., October 5, fourth
   inning, through end of game, October 6, 8, 9, 1966.

1-0 GAMES

Most 1-0 games won, total series
4—New York A.L.

Most 1-0 games won, series
2—Baltimore A.L. vs. Los Angeles N.L., 1966.

Most 1-0 games won by both clubs, series
2—New York A.L. 1, Brooklyn N.L. 1, 1949.
   Baltimore A.L. 2, Los Angeles N.L. 0, 1966.

WILD PITCHES AND BALKS

Most wild pitches, series
5—Pittsburgh N.L. vs. New York A.L., 1960.

Most wild pitches by both clubs, series
8—New York A.L. 4, Brooklyn N.L. 4, 1947.

Fewest wild pitches by both clubs, series
0—Made in series of all lengths.

Most balks, series
2—Cleveland A.L. vs. Boston N.L., 1948.
   Minnesota A.L. vs. St. Louis N.L., 1987.

Most balks by both clubs, series
2—Cleveland A.L. 2, Boston N.L. 0, 1948.
   Minnesota A.L. 2, St. Louis N.L. 0, 1987.
   Los Angeles N.L. 1, Oakland A.L. 1, 1988.

Fewest balks by both clubs, series
0—Made in series of all lengths.

INDIVIDUAL FIELDING

FIRST BASEMEN
GAMES

ost games played, career
3—Gil Hodges, Brooklyn N.L., Los Angeles N.L., 1949, 1952,
1953, 1955, 1956, 1959; six series.

PUTOUTS, ASSISTS AND CHANCES ACCEPTED

Most putouts, career
26—Gil Hodges, Brooklyn N.L., Los Angeles N.L., 1949, 1952,
1953, 1955, 1956, 1959; six series, 38 games.

Most putouts, series
-game series—52—Butch Schmidt, Boston N.L., 1914.
-game series—69—Dick Hoblitzel, Boston A.L., 1916.
-game series—79—Jiggs Donahue, Chicago A.L., 1906.
-game series—79—Jim Bottomley, St. Louis N.L., 1926.
-game series—92—Wally Pipp, New York A.L., 1921.

Most putouts, nine-inning game
9—George Kelly, New York N.L., October 15, 1923.
Fred McGriff, Atlanta N.L., October 21, 1995.

ewest putouts, nine-inning game
—Orlando Cepeda, St. Louis N.L., October 2, 1968.

Most putouts, inning
—Held by many first basemen.

Most assists, career
9—Bill Skowron, New York A.L., 1955, 1956, 1957, 1958,
1960, 1961, 1962; Los Angeles N.L., 1963; eight series,
37 games.

Most assists, series
-game series—6
Vic Wertz, Cleveland A.L., 1954.
Joe Pepitone, New York A.L., 1963.
-game series—5
Claude Rossman, Detroit A.L., 1908.
Dolph Camilli, Brooklyn N.L., 1941.
Ray Sanders, St. Louis N.L., 1943.
Bill Skowron, New York A.L., 1961.
-game series—9—Fred Merkle, Chicago N.L., 1918.
-game series—10—Cecil Cooper, Milwaukee A.L., 1982.
-game series—7—George Kelly, New York N.L., 1921.

Most assists, nine-inning game
4—Marv Owen, Detroit A.L., October 6, 1935.
Don Mincher, Minnesota A.L., October 7, 1965.

Most assists, inning
2—Held by many first basemen.

Most chances accepted, career
850—Gil Hodges, Brooklyn N.L., Los Angeles N.L., 1949, 1952,
1953, 1955, 1956, 1959; six series, 38 games.

Most chances accepted, series
4-game series—55—Butch Schmidt, Boston N.L., 1914.
5-game series—73—Dick Hoblitzel, Boston A.L., 1916.
6-game series—87—Jiggs Donahue, Chicago A.L., 1906.
7-game series—81—Cecil Cooper, Milwaukee A.L., 1982.
8-game series—93
George Kelly, New York N.L., 1921.
Wally Pipp, New York A.L., 1921.

Most chances accepted, nine-inning game
20—Fred McGriff, Atlanta N.L., October 21, 1995 (19 putouts, 1
assist).

Fewest chances offered, nine-inning game
2—Wally Pipp, New York A.L., October 11, 1921 (2 putouts).
Orlando Cepeda, St. Louis N.L., October 2, 1968 (1 putout,
1 assist).

Most chances accepted, inning
3—Held by many first basemen.

ERRORS AND DOUBLE PLAYS

Most errors, career
8—Fred Merkle, New York N.L., 1911, 1912, 1913 (7); Brooklyn
N.L., 1916 (1), Chicago N.L., 1918 (0); five series,
25 games.

Most consecutive errorless games, career
31—Bill Skowron, New York A.L., Los Angeles N.L., October 10,
1956 through October 6, 1963.

Most errors, series
4-game series—2
Mark McGwire, Oakland A.L., 1990.
Brian R. Hunter, Atlanta N.L., 1999.
5-game series—3
Frank Chance, Chicago N.L., 1908.
Harry Davis, Philadelphia A.L., 1910.
6-game series—3—Hank Greenberg, Detroit A.L., 1935.
7-game series—5—Bill Abstein, Pittsburgh N.L., 1909.
8-game series—3—Fred Merkle, New York N.L., 1912.

Most chances accepted, errorless series
93—George Kelly, New York N.L., 1921 (8-game series).
Wally Pipp, New York A.L., 1921 (8-game series).

Most errors, nine-inning game
2—Held by many first basemen.

Most errors, inning
2—Hank Greenberg, Detroit A.L., October 3, 1935, fifth inning.
Johnny McCarthy, New York N.L., October 8, 1937,
fifth inning.
Frank Torre, Milwaukee N.L., October 9, 1958, second inning.
Brian R. Hunter, Atlanta N.L., October 23, 1999, eighth inning.

Most double plays, career
31—Gil Hodges, Brooklyn N.L., Los Angeles N.L., 1949, 1952,
1953, 1955, 1956, 1959; six series, 38 games.

Most double plays, series
11—Gil Hodges, Brooklyn N.L., 1955 (7-game series).

Most double plays started, series
3—Gil Hodges, Brooklyn N.L., 1955 (7-game series).

Most double plays, nine-inning game
4—Stuffy McInnis, Philadelphia A.L., October 9, 1914.
Joe Collins, New York A.L., October 8, 1951.
Gene Tenace, Oakland A.L., October 17, 1973.
Pete Rose, Philadelphia N.L., October 15, 1980.

Most double plays started, game
2—Eddie Murray, Baltimore A.L., October 11, 1979.

Most unassisted double plays, game
1—Held by many first basemen.

SECOND BASEMEN
GAMES

Most games played, career
42—Frankie Frisch, New York N.L. (18), 1922, 1923, 1924; St.
Louis N.L. (24), 1928, 1930, 1931, 1934; seven series.

PUTOUTS, ASSISTS AND CHANCES ACCEPTED

Most putouts, career
104—Frankie Frisch, New York N.L., St. Louis N.L., 1922, 1923,
1924, 1928, 1930, 1931, 1934; seven series, 42 games.

Most putouts, series
4-game series—14—Willie Randolph, Oakland A.L., 1990.
5-game series—20—Joe Gordon, New York A.L., 1943.

6-game series—26—Dave Lopes, Los Angeles N.L., 1981.
7-game series—26—Bucky Harris, Washington A.L., 1924.
8-game series—22—Morrie Rath, Cincinnati N.L., 1919.

Most putouts, nine-inning game
8—Bucky Harris, Washington A.L., October 8, 1924.
Dave Lopes, Los Angeles N.L., October 16, 1974.

Most putouts, extra-inning game
9—Hughie Critz, New York N.L., October 6, 1933, 11 innings.

Most putouts, inning
3—Larry Doyle, New York N.L., October 9, 1913, seventh inning.
Bill Wambsganss, Cleveland A.L., October 10, 1920,
    fifth inning.
Johnny Rawlings, New York N.L., October 11, 1921,
    ninth inning.
Dave Lopes, Los Angeles N.L., October 16, 1974, sixth inning.
Dave Lopes, Los Angeles N.L., October 21, 1981,
    fourth inning.

Most assists, career
135—Frankie Frisch, New York N.L., St. Louis N.L., 1922, 1923,
    1924, 1928, 1930, 1931, 1934; seven series, 42 games.

Most assists, series
4-game series—18—Tony Lazzeri, New York A.L., 1927.
5-game series—23—Joe Gordon, New York A.L., 1943.
6-game series—27—Aaron Ward, New York A.L., 1923.
7-game series—33—Jim Gantner, Milwaukee A.L., 1982.
8-game series—34—Aaron Ward, New York A.L., 1921.

Most assists, nine-inning game
8—Claude Ritchey, Pittsburgh, N.L., October 10, 1903.
Germany Schaefer, Detroit A.L., October 12, 1907.
Hal Janvrin, Boston A.L., October 7, 1916.
Eddie Collins, Chicago A.L., October 15, 1917.
Bucky Harris, Washington A.L., October 7, 1924.
Joe Gordon, New York A.L., October 5, 1943.
Bobby Doerr, Boston A.L., October 9, 1946.
Mark Lemke, Atlanta N.L., October 21, 1995.

Most assists, inning
3—Eddie Collins, Philadelphia A.L., October 12, 1914,
    fourth inning.
Pete Kilduff, Brooklyn N.L., October 10, 1920, third inning.
Aaron Ward, New York A.L., October 12, 1921, sixth inning.
Joe Gordon, New York A.L., October 11, 1943, eighth inning.
Jackie Robinson, Brooklyn N.L., October 8, 1949,
    seventh inning.
Phil Garner, Pittsburgh N.L., October 13, 1979, ninth inning.
Marty Barrett, Boston A.L., October 23, 1986; first inning.

Most chances accepted, career
239—Frankie Frisch, New York N.L., St. Louis N.L., 1922, 1923,
    1924, 1928, 1930, 1931, 1934; seven series, 42 games.

Most chances accepted, series
4-game series—28—Tony Lazzeri, New York A.L., 1927.
5-game series—30—Joe Gordon, New York A.L., 1943.
6-game series—40—Dave Lopes, Los Angeles N.L., 1981.
7-game series—54—Bucky Harris, Washington A.L., 1924.
8-game series—52
Eddie Collins, Chicago A.L., 1919.
Aaron Ward, New York A.L., 1921.

Most chances accepted, nine-inning game
13—Claude Ritchey, Pittsburgh N.L., October 10, 1903 (5
    putouts, 8 assists).
Bucky Harris, Washington A.L., October 11, 1925 (6
    putouts, 7 assists).
Dave Lopes, Los Angeles N.L., October 16, 1974 (8
    putouts, 5 assists).

Most chances accepted, extra-inning game
14—Hughie Critz, New York N.L., October 6, 1933, 11 innings
    (9 putouts, 5 assists).

Fewest chances offered, nine-inning game
0—Charlie Pick, Chicago N.L., September 7, 1918.
Max Bishop, Philadelphia A.L., October 6, 1931.

Jerry Coleman, New York A.L., October 8, 1949.
Willie Randolph, New York A.L., October 25, 1981.
Frank White, Kansas City A.L., October 20, 1985.
Mariano Duncan, Cincinnati N.L., October 19, 1990.

Most chances accepted, inning
3—Held by many second basemen.

ERRORS AND DOUBLE PLAYS

Most errors, career
8—Larry Doyle, New York N.L., 1911, 1912, 1913; three series,
    19 games.
Eddie Collins, Philadelphia A.L., 1910, 1911, 1913, 1914,
    Chicago A.L., 1917, 1919; six series, 34 games.

Most consecutive errorless games, career
23—Billy Martin, New York A.L., October 5, 1952 through
    October 10, 1956.

Most errors, series
4-game series—2
Tony Lazzeri, New York A.L., 1928.
Joe Gordon, New York A.L., 1938.
Billy Herman, Chicago N.L., 1938.
Joe Morgan, Cincinnati N.L., 1976.
5-game series—4—Danny Murphy, Philadelphia A.L., 1905.
6-game series—6—Dave Lopes, Los Angeles N.L., 1981.
7-game series—5—Jim Gantner, Milwaukee A.L., 1982.
8-game series—4—Larry Doyle, New York N.L., 1912.

Most chances accepted, errorless series
49—Bobby Doerr, Boston A.L., 1946 (7-game series).

Most errors, nine-inning game
3—Danny Murphy, Philadelphia A.L., October 12, 1905.
Buddy Myer, Washington A.L., October 3, 1933.
Dave Lopes, Los Angeles N.L., October 25, 1981.

Most errors, inning
2—Danny Murphy, Philadelphia A.L., October 12, 1905, fifth
    inning.
Mike Andrews, Oakland A.L., October 14, 1973, 12th inning.
Dave Lopes, Los Angeles N.L., October 25, 1981, fourth
    inning.

Most double plays, career
24—Frankie Frisch, New York N.L., St. Louis N.L., 1922, 1923,
    1924, 1928, 1930, 1931, 1934; seven series, 42 games.

Most double plays, series
9—Phil Garner, Pittsburgh N.L., 1979 (7-game series).

Most double plays started, series
5—Billy Herman, Chicago N.L., 1932 (4-game series).
Tom Herr, St. Louis N.L., 1985 (7-game series).

Most double plays, nine-inning game
3—Held by many second basemen.

Most double plays started, nine-inning game
3—Dick Green, Oakland A.L., October 15, 1974.

Most unassisted double plays, game
1—Hobe Ferris, Boston A.L., October 2, 1903.
Larry Doyle, New York N.L., October 9, 1913.
Buck Herzog, New York N.L., October 7, 1917.
Frank White, Kansas City A.L., October 17, 1980.
Mark Lemke, Atlanta N.L., October 27, 1991, 10 innings.

Unassisted triple play
1—Bill Wambsganss, Cleveland A.L., October 10, 1920.

THIRD BASEMEN
GAMES

Most games played, career
31—Gil McDougald, New York A.L., 1951, 1952, 1953, 1955,
    1960; five series.

PUTOUTS, ASSISTS AND CHANCES ACCEPTED

Most putouts, career
37—Home Run Baker, Philadelphia A.L., New York A.L., 1910, 1911, 1913, 1914, 1921; five series, 22 games.

Most putouts, series
4-game series—10—Home Run Baker, Philadelphia A.L., 1914.
5-game series—10—Harry Steinfeldt, Chicago N.L., 1907.
6-game series—14—Red Rolfe, New York A.L. 1936.
7-game series—13—Whitey Kurowski, St. Louis N.L., 1946.
8-game series—13—Frankie Frisch, New York N.L., 1921.

Most putouts, nine-inning game
4—Art Devlin, New York N.L., October 13, 1905.
Bill Coughlin, Detroit A.L., October 10, 1907.
Bobby Byrne, Pittsburgh N.L., October 9, 1909.
Tommy Leach, Pittsburgh N.L., October 16, 1909.
Home Run Baker, Philadelphia A.L., October 24, 1911.
Heinie Zimmerman, New York N.L., October 7, 1917.
Jimmie Dykes, Philadelphia A.L., October 2, 1930.
Bob Elliott, Boston N.L., October 11, 1948.
Willie Jones, Philadelphia N.L. October 4, 1950.

Most putouts, inning
2—Held by many third basemen.

Most assists, career
68—Graig Nettles, New York A.L., 1976, 1977, 1978, 1981; San Diego N.L., 1984; five series, 24 games.

Most assists, series
4-game series—15—Home Run Baker, Philadelphia A.L., 1914.
5-game series—18—Larry Gardner, Boston A.L., 1916.
6-game series—20—Graig Nettles, New York A.L., 1977.
7-game series—30—Pinky Higgins, Detroit A.L., 1940.
8-game series—24—Frankie Frisch, New York N.L., 1921.

Most assists, nine-inning game
9—Pinky Higgins, Detroit A.L., October 5, 1940.

Most assists, inning
3—Jose Pagan, Pittsburgh N.L., October 14, 1971, ninth inning.
Sal Bando, Oakland A.L., October 16, 1974, sixth inning.
Wade Boggs, Boston A.L., October 19, 1986, third inning.
Terry Pendleton, Atlanta N.L., October 27, 1991, seventh inning.

Most chances accepted, career
96—Graig Nettles, New York A.L., 1976, 1977, 1978, 1981; San Diego N.L., 1984; five series, 24 games.

Most chances accepted, series
4-game series—25—Home Run Baker, Philadelphia A.L., 1914.
5-game series—25—Larry Gardner, Boston A.L., 1916.
6-game series—27—Bobby Thomson, New York N.L., 1951.
7-game series—34—Pinky Higgins, Detroit A.L., 1940.
8-game series—37—Frankie Frisch, New York N.L., 1921.

Most chances accepted, nine-inning game
10—Pinky Higgins, Detroit A.L., October 5, 1940 (1 putout, 9 assists).
Chris Sabo, Cincinnati N.L., October 19, 1990 (3 putouts, 7 assists).

Fewest chances offered, nine-inning game
0—Held by many third basemen.

Most chances accepted, inning
4—Eddie Mathews, Milwaukee N.L., October 5, 1957, third inning.

ERRORS AND DOUBLE PLAYS

Most errors, career
8—Larry Gardner, Boston A.L., 1912, 1915, 1916 (6); Cleveland A.L., 1920 (2); four series, 25 games.

Most consecutive errorless games, career
22—Ron Cey, Los Angeles N.L., October 13, 1974 through October 28, 1981.

Most errors, series
4-game series—2
Red Rolfe, New York A.L., 1938.
Ken Caminiti, San Diego N.L., 1998.
5-game series—4—Harry Steinfeldt, Chicago N.L., 1910.
6-game series—3
George Rohe, Chicago A.L., 1906.
Buck Herzog, New York N.L., 1911.
Travis Jackson, New York N.L., 1936.
Bob Elliott, Boston N.L., 1948.
7-game series—4
Pepper Martin, St. Louis N.L., 1934.
Gil McDougald, New York A.L., 1952.
8-game series—4
Tommy Leach, Pittsburgh N.L., 1903.
Larry Gardner, Boston A.L., 1912.

Most chances accepted, errorless series
29—Denis Menke, Cincinnati N.L., 1972 (7-game series).

Most errors, nine-inning game
3—Pepper Martin, St. Louis N.L., October 6, 1934.

Most errors, inning
2—Harry Steinfeldt, Chicago N.L., October 18, 1910, third inning.
Doug DeCinces, Baltimore A.L., October 10, 1979, sixth inning.

Most double plays, career
7—Graig Nettles, New York A.L., 1976, 1977, 1978, 1981; San Diego N.L., 1984; five series, 24 games.

Most double plays, series
4—Jim Davenport, San Francisco N.L., 1962 (7-game series).
Bill Madlock, Pittsburgh N.L., 1979 (7-game series).

Most double plays started, series
4—Jim Davenport, San Francisco N.L., 1962 (7-game series).

Most double plays, nine-inning game
2—Held by many third basemen.

Most double plays started, nine-inning game
2—Fred McMullin, Chicago A.L., October 13, 1917.
Ossie Bluege, Washington A.L., October 5, 1924.
Whitey Kurowski, St. Louis N.L., October 13, 1946.
Clete Boyer, New York A.L., October 12, 1960.
Dalton Jones, Boston A.L., October 4, 1967.
Graig Nettles, New York A.L., October 19, 1976.
Bobby Bonilla, Florida N.L., October 19, 1997.

Most unassisted double plays, game
Never accomplished.

SHORTSTOPS
GAMES

Most games played, career
52—Phil Rizzuto, New York A.L., 1941, 1942, 1947, 1949, 1950, 1951, 1952, 1953, 1955; nine series.

PUTOUTS, ASSISTS AND CHANCES ACCEPTED

Most putouts, career
107—Phil Rizzuto, New York A.L., 1941, 1942, 1947, 1949, 1950, 1951, 1952, 1953, 1955; nine series, 52 games.

Most putouts, series
4-game series—16—Frank Crosetti, New York A.L., 1938.
5-game series—15
Joe Tinker, Chicago N.L., 1907.
Phil Rizzuto, New York A.L., 1942.
6-game series—16—Billy Jurges, Chicago N.L., 1935.
7-game series—22—Ozzie Smith, St. Louis N.L., 1982.
8-game series—24—Heinie Wagner, Boston A.L., 1912.

Most putouts, nine-inning game
7—Buck Weaver, Chicago A.L., October 7, 1917.
Phil Rizzuto, New York A.L., October 5, 1942.

Most putouts, inning
3—Mickey Stanley, Detroit A.L., October 10, 1968, sixth inning.

Most assists, career
143—Phil Rizzuto, New York A.L., 1941, 1942, 1947, 1949,
1950, 1951, 1952, 1953, 1955; nine series, 52 games.

Most assists, series
4-game series—21—Jack Barry, Philadelphia A.L., 1914.
5-game series—25—Everett Scott, Boston A.L., 1916.
6-game series—26—Bill Russell, Los Angeles N.L., 1981.
7-game series—32—Tim Foli, Pittsburgh N.L., 1979.
8-game series—30—Freddy Parent, Boston A.L., 1903.

Most assists, nine-inning game
9—Roger Peckinpaugh, New York A.L., October 5, 1921.

Most assists, extra-inning game
10—Johnny Logan, Milwaukee N.L., October 6, 1957, 10 innings.

Most assists, inning
3—Dave Bancroft, New York N.L., October 8, 1922, third inning.
Ossie Bluege, Washington, A.L., October 7, 1924,
  sixth inning.
Glenn Wright, Pittsburgh N.L., October 8, 1927,
  second inning.
Blondy Ryan, New York N.L., October 7, 1933, third inning.
Phil Rizzuto, New York A.L., October 3, 1942,
  second inning.
Ernie Bowman, San Francisco N.L., October 8, 1962,
  ninth inning.
Bud Harrelson, New York N.L., October 14, 1969, fifth inning.
Mark Belanger, Baltimore A.L., October 16, 1971,
  seventh inning.
Bud Harrelson, New York N.L., October 13, 1973,
  seventh inning.
Tim Foli, Pittsburgh N.L., October 12, 1979, second inning.

Most chances accepted, career
250—Phil Rizzuto, New York A.L., 1941, 1942, 1947, 1949,
1950, 1951, 1952, 1953, 1955; nine series, 52 games.

Most chances accepted, series
4-game series—27—Maury Wills, Los Angeles N.L., 1966.
5-game series—38—Joe Tinker, Chicago N.L., 1907.
6-game series—37—Phil Rizzuto, New York A.L., 1951.
7-game series—42—Charlie Gelbert, St. Louis N.L., 1931.
8-game series—51—Swede Risberg, Chicago A.L., 1919.

Most chances accepted, nine-inning game
13—Buck Weaver, Chicago A.L., October 7, 1917 (7 putouts, 6
assists).

Fewest chances offered, nine-inning game
0—Joe Boley, Philadelphia A.L., October 8, 1929.
Phil Rizzuto, New York A.L., October 7, 1949.
Zoilo Versalles, Minnesota A.L., October 7, 1965.
Rico Petrocelli, Boston A.L., October 4, 1967.
Bert Campaneris, Oakland A.L., October 18, 1972.
Dave Concepcion, Cincinnati N.L., October 16, 1975.
Ozzie Smith, St. Louis N.L., October 23, 1985.
Omar Vizquel, Cleveland A.L., October 19, 1997.

Fewest chances offered, eight-inning game
0—Dave Bancroft, New York N.L., October 12, 1915.
Pee Ree Reese, Brooklyn N.L., October 1, 1947.

Most chances accepted, inning
3—Held by many shortstops.

ERRORS AND DOUBLE PLAYS

Most errors, career
12—Art Fletcher, New York N.L., 1911, 1912, 1913, 1917; four
series, 25 games.

Most consecutive errorless games, career
21—Phil Rizzuto, New York A.L., October 3, 1942 through
October 5, 1951.

Most errors, series
4-game series—4—Frank Crosetti, New York A.L., 1932.

5-game series—4
Ivy Olson, Brooklyn N.L., 1916.
Woody English, Chicago N.L., 1929.
6-game series—4
Art Fletcher, New York N.L., 1911.
Buck Weaver, Chicago A.L., 1917.
7-game series—8—Roger Peckinpaugh, Washington A.L., 1925.
8-game series—6—Honus Wagner, Pittsburgh N.L., 1903.

Most chances accepted, errorless series
42—Charlie Gelbert, St. Louis N.L., 1931 (7-game series).

Most errors, nine-inning game
3—Jack Barry, Philadelphia A.L., October 26, 1911.
Art Fletcher, New York N.L., October 9, 1912.
Buck Weaver, Chicago A.L., October 13, 1917.

Most errors, inning
2—Roger Peckinpaugh, Washington A.L., October 8, 1925,
  eighth inning.
Woody English, Chicago N.L., October 8, 1929, ninth inning.
Dick Bartell, New York N.L., October 9, 1937, third inning.
Pee Wee Reese, Brooklyn N.L., October 2, 1941, eighth
  inning.

Most double plays, career
32—Phil Rizzuto, New York A.L., 1941, 1942, 1947, 1949,
1950, 1951, 1952, 1953, 1955; nine series, 52 games.

Most double plays, series
8—Phil Rizzuto, New York A.L., 1951 (6-game series).

Most double plays started, series
7—Larry Bowa, Philadelphia N.L., 1980 (6-game series).

Most unassisted double plays, series
2—Joe Tinker, Chicago N.L., October 10, 11, 1907.

Most double plays, nine-inning game
4—Phil Rizzuto, New York A.L., October 8, 1951.

Most double plays started, nine-inning game
3—Phil Rizzuto, New York A.L., October 10, 1951.
Maury Wills, Los Angeles N.L., October 11, 1965.
Larry Bowa, Philadelphia N.L., October 15, 1980.

Most unassisted double plays, game
1—Joe Tinker, Chicago N.L., October 10, 1907
Joe Tinker, Chicago N.L., October 11, 1907.
Charlie Gelbert, St. Louis N.L., October 2, 1930.
Eddie Kasko, Cincinnati N.L., October 7, 1961.
Greg Gagne, Minnesota N.L., October 26, 1991, 11 innings.

OUTFIELDERS
GAMES

Most games played, career
63—Mickey Mantle, New York A.L., 1951, 1952, 1953, 1955, 1956,
1957, 1958, 1960, 1961, 1962, 1963, 1964; 12 series.

PUTOUTS, ASSISTS AND CHANCES ACCEPTED

Most putouts, career
150—Joe DiMaggio, New York A.L., 1936, 1937, 1938, 1939, 1941,
1942, 1947, 1949, 1950, 1951; 10 series, 51 games.

Most putouts, series
4-game series—16—Earle Combs, New York A.L., 1927.
5-game series—20—Joe DiMaggio, New York A.L., 1942.
6-game series—24—Mickey Rivers, New York A.L., 1977.
7-game series—25—Dan Gladden, Minnesota A.L., 1991.
8-game series—30—Edd Roush, Cincinnati N.L., 1919.

Most putouts, game
8—Edd Roush, Cincinnati N.L., October 1, 1919.
George Foster, Cincinnati N.L., October 21, 1976.

Most putouts by left fielder, game
8—George Foster, Cincinnati N.L., October 21, 1976.

Most putouts by center fielder, game
9—Amos Otis, Kansas City A.L., October 17, 1980, 10 innings.
8—Edd Roush, Cincinnati N.L., October 1, 1919.

Most putouts by right fielder, game

7—Red Murray, New York N.L., October 14, 1912.
Bing Miller, Philadelphia A.L., October 5, 1930.
Ray Blades, St. Louis N.L., October 5, 1930.
Tony Oliva, Minnesota A.L., October 6, 1965.
Al Kaline, Detroit A.L., October 9, 1968.
Frank Robinson, Baltimore A.L., October 14, 1969.

Most consecutive putouts, game

4—Mike Donlin, New York N.L., October 13, 1905 (1 in third
inning, 3 in fourth inning, center field).
Dode Paskert, Philadelphia N.L., October 11, 1915 (3 in
fourth inning, 1 in fifth inning, center field).
Charlie Keller, New York A.L., October 1, 1941 (1 in second
inning, 3 in third inning, left field).
Monte Irvin, New York N.L., September 29, 1954 (1 in
eighth inning, 3 in ninth inning, left field; Irvin dropped
fly for error after second putout in ninth inning).
Tommie Agee, New York N.L., October 14, 1969 (3 in seventh
inning, 1 in eighth inning, center field).
Ben Oglivie, Milwaukee A.L., October 19, 1982 (1 in sixth
inning, 3 in seventh inning, left field).

Most putouts by left fielder, inning

3—Charlie Keller, New York A.L., October 1, 1941, third inning.
Monte Irvin, New York N.L., September 29, 1954,
ninth inning.
Tommy Davis, Los Angeles N.L., October 3, 1963,
seventh inning.
Ben Oglivie, Milwaukee A.L., October 19, 1982, seventh inning.
Deion Sanders, Atlanta N.L., October 22, 1992, fifth inning.

Most putouts by center fielder, inning

3—Mike Donlin, New York N.L., October 13, 1905, fourth inning.
Dode Paskert, Philadelphia N.L., October 11, 1915,
fourth inning.
Ernie Orsatti, St. Louis N.L., October 8, 1934, fifth inning.
Joe DiMaggio, New York A.L., October 2, 1936,
ninth inning, and October 7, 1937, sixth inning.
Roger Maris, New York A.L., October 11, 1964, third inning.
Reggie Smith, Boston A.L., October 11, 1967, seventh inning.
Tommie Agee, New York N.L., October 14, 1969,
seventh inning.
Willie McGee, St. Louis N.L., October 22, 1987, eighth inning.
Andruw Jones, Atlanta N.L., October 24, 1999, seventh
inning.

Most putouts right fielder, inning

3—Mel Ott, New York N.L., October 4, 1933, seventh inning.
Bob Hazle, Milwaukee N.L., October 10, 1957, fourth inning.
Ron Swoboda, New York N.L., October 15, 1969, ninth inning.
Charlie Moore, Milwaukee A.L., October 12, 1982,
eighth inning.

Most assists, career

5—Harry Hooper, Boston A.L., 1912, 1915, 1916, 1918; four
series, 24 games.
Ross Youngs, New York N.L., 1921, 1922, 1923, 1924; four
series, 26 games.

Most games by outfielder with no assists, career

51—Joe DiMaggio, New York A.L., 1936, 1937, 1938, 1939,
1941, 1942, 1947, 1949, 1950, 1951; 10 series.

Most assists, series

4-game series—2—Joe Connally, Boston, N.L., 1914.
5-game series—2—Held by many outfielders.
6-game series—2—Held by many outfielders.
7-game series—4—Edgar Rice, Washington A.L., 1924.
8-game series—3
Patsy Dougherty, Boston A.L., 1903.
Harry Hooper, Boston A.L., 1912.
Edd Roush, Cincinnati N.L., 1919.

Most assists, game

2—Held by many outfielders.

Most chances accepted, career

150—Joe DiMaggio, New York A.L., 1936, 1937, 1938, 1939, 1941,
1942, 1947, 1949, 1950, 1951; 10 series, 51 games.

Most chances accepted, series

4-game series—16—Earle Combs, New York A.L., 1927.
5-game series—20—Joe DiMaggio, New York A.L., 1942.
6-game series—25—Mickey Rivers, New York A.L., 1977.
7-game series—26
Andy Pafko, Chicago N.L., 1945.
Dan Gladden, Minnesota A.L., 1991.
8-game series—33—Edd Roush, Cincinnati N.L., 1919.

Most chances accepted by left fielder, game

8—George Foster, Cincinnati N.L., October 21, 1976 (8 putouts).

Most chances accepted by center fielder, nine-inning game

8—Edd Roush, Cincinnati N.L., October 1, 1919 (8 putouts).
Hank Leiber, New York N.L., October 2, 1936 (7 putouts,
1 assist).

Most chances accepted by center fielder, extra-inning game

9—Edd Roush, Cincinnati N.L., October 7, 1919, 10 innings (7
putouts, 2 assists).
Amos Otis, Kansas City A.L., October 17, 1980, 10 innings
(9 putouts).

Most chances accepted by right fielder, game

7—Red Murray, New York N.L., October 14, 1912 (7 putouts).
Bing Miller, Philadelphia A.L., October 5, 1930 (7 putouts).
Ray Blades, St. Louis N.L., October 5, 1930 (7 putouts).
Tony Oliva, Minnesota A.L., October 6, 1965 (7 putouts).
Al Kaline, Detroit A.L., October 9, 1968 (7 putouts).
Frank Robinson, Baltimore A.L., October 14, 1969 (7 putouts).

Longest game with no chances offered

12 innings—Ty Cobb, Detroit A.L., right field, October 8, 1907
(right field).
Earl McNeely, Washington A.L., October 10, 1924
(center field).
Joe Medwick, St. Louis N.L., October 4, 1934
(played 11.1 innings in left field).
Don Hahn, New York N.L., October 14, 1973
(center and right field).
Cleon Jones, New York N.L., October 14, 1973 (left
field).
Ken Griffey Sr., Cincinnati N.L., October 21, 1975
(played 11 innings in right field).

Fewest chances offered, three consecutive games

0—George Browne, New York N.L., October 12, 1905 (nine
innings); October 13, 1905 (nine innings); October 14,
1905 (nine innings; right field).
Max Carey, Pittsburgh N.L., October 11, 1925 (eight
innings); October 12, 1925 (nine innings); October 13,
1925 (nine innings; center field).
Al Simmons, Philadelphia A.L., October 11, 1929 (nine
innings); October 12, 1929 (nine innings); October 14,
1929 (nine innings; left field).
Chief Wilson, Pittsburgh N.L., October 8, 1909 (nine
innings); October 9, 1909 (nine innings); October 11,
1909 (nine innings; right field).

Fewest chances offered, four consecutive games

0—Chief Wilson, Pittsburgh N.L., October 8, 1909 (nine
innings); October 9, 1909 (nine innings); October 11,
1909 (nine innings); October 12, 1909 (eight innings;
right field).

Most chances accepted, inning

3—Held by many outfielders.

ERRORS AND DOUBLE PLAYS

Most errors, career

4—Ross Youngs, New York N.L., 1921, 1922, 1923, 1924; four
series, 26 games.

Most consecutive errorless games, career

45—Joe DiMaggio, New York A.L., October 6, 1937 through
October 10, 1951.

Most errors, series

4-game series—3—Willie Davis, Los Angeles N.L., 1966.
5-game series—2—Held by many outfielders.

6-game series—3
Red Murray, New York N.L., 1911.
Shano Collins, Chicago A.L., 1917.
7-game series—2
Zack Wheat, Brooklyn N.L., 1920.
Ernie Orsatti, St. Louis N.L., 1934.
Goose Goslin, Detroit A.L., 1934.
Mickey Mantle, New York A.L., 1964.
Jim Northrup, Detroit A.L., 1968.
8-game series—2—Held by many outfielders.

Most chances accepted, errorless series
25—Mickey Rivers, New York A.L., 1977 (6-game series).

Most errors, game
3—Willie Davis, Los Angeles N.L., October 6, 1966.

Most errors, inning
3—Willie Davis, Los Angeles N.L., October 6, 1966, fifth inning.

Most double plays, career
2—Held by many outfielders.

Most double plays, series
2—Danny Murphy, Philadelphia A.L., 1910 (5-game series).
Tris Speaker, Boston A.L., 1912 (8-game series).
Edd Roush, Cincinnati N.L., 1919 (8-game series).
Elston Howard, New York A.L., 1958 (7-game series).

Most double plays started, series
2—Danny Murphy, Philadelphia A.L., 1910 (5-game series).
Tris Speaker, Boston A.L., 1912 (8-game series).
Edd Roush, Cincinnati N.L., 1919 (8-game series).
Elston Howard, New York A.L., 1958 (7-game series).

Most double plays, game
2—Edd Roush, Cincinnati N.L., October 7, 1919 (fifth and eighth innings of 10-inning game).

Most double plays started, game
2—Edd Roush, Cincinnati N.L., October 7, 1919 (fifth and eighth innings of 10-inning game).

Most unassisted double plays, game
1—Tris Speaker, Boston A.L., October 15, 1912.

CATCHERS
GAMES

Most games caught, career
63—Yogi Berra, New York A.L., 1947, 1949, 1950, 1951, 1952, 1953, 1955, 1956, 1957, 1958, 1960, 1962; 12 series.

PUTOUTS, ASSISTS AND CHANCES ACCEPTED

Most putouts, career
421—Yogi Berra, New York A.L., 1947, 1949, 1950, 1951, 1952, 1953, 1955, 1956, 1957, 1958, 1960, 1962; 12 series, 63 games.

Most putouts, series
4-game series—43—John Roseboro, Los Angeles N.L., 1963.
5-game series—59—Mickey Cochrane, Philadelphia A.L., 1929.
6-game series—55—Walker Cooper, St. Louis N.L., 1944.
7-game series—69—Jorge Posada, New York A.L., 2001.
8-game series—54—Lou Criger, Boston A.L., 1903.

Most putouts, nine-inning game
18—John Roseboro, Los Angeles N.L., October 2, 1963 (15 strikeouts).

Fewest putouts, nine-inning game
1—Held by many catchers.

Most putouts, inning
3—Held by many catchers.

Most assists, career
36—Yogi Berra, New York A.L., 1947, 1949, 1950, 1951, 1952, 1953, 1955, 1956, 1957, 1958, 1960, 1962; 12 series, 63 games.

Most assists, series
4-game series—7—Thurman Munson, New York A.L., 1976.
5-game series—9
Boss Schmidt, Detroit A.L., 1907.
Johnny Kling, Chicago N.L., 1907.
Ed Burns, Philadelphia N.L., 1915.
6-game series—12—Chief Meyers, New York N.L., 1911.
7-game series—11—Boss Schmidt, Detroit A.L., 1909.
8-game series—15—Ray Schalk, Chicago A.L., 1919.

Most assists, nine-inning game
4—Johnny Kling, Chicago N.L., October 9, 1907.
Boss Schmidt, Detroit A.L., October 11, 1907.
Boss Schmidt, Detroit A.L., October 14, 1908.
George Gibson, Pittsburgh N.L., October 12, 1909.
Bill Rariden, New York N.L., October 10, 1917.
Sam Agnew, Boston A.L., September 6, 1918.
Bill DeLancey, St. Louis N.L., October 8, 1934.

Most assists, extra-inning game
6—Jack Lapp, Philadelphia A.L., October 17, 1911, 11 innings.

Most assists, inning
2—Held by many catchers.

Most chances accepted, career
457—Yogi Berra, New York A.L., 1947, 1949, 1950, 1951, 1952, 1953, 1955, 1956, 1957, 1958, 1960, 1962; 12 series, 63 games.

Most chances accepted, series
4-game series—43—John Roseboro, Los Angeles N.L., 1963.
5-game series—61—Mickey Cochrane, Philadelphia A.L., 1929.
6-game series—56
Johnny Kling, Chicago N.L., 1906.
Roy Campanella, Brooklyn N.L., 1953.
7-game series—73—Jorge Posada, New York A.L., 2001.
8-game series—62—Lou Criger, Boston A.L., 1903.

Most chances accepted, nine-inning game
18—John Roseboro, Los Angeles N.L., October 2, 1963, (18 putouts, 15 strikeouts).
Tim McCarver, St. Louis N.L., October 2, 1968 (17 putouts, 1 assist, 17 strikeouts).

Fewest chances offered, nine-inning game
1—Wally Schang, Philadelphia A.L., October 11, 1913 (strikeout).
Wally Schang, New York A.L., October 11, 1923 (strikeout).
Muddy Ruel, Washington A.L., October 5, 1924 (strikeout).
Mickey Cochrane, Detroit A.L., October 6, 1934 (strikeout).
Gabby Hartnett, Chicago N.L., October 2, 1935 (strikeout).
Sherm Lollar, Chicago A.L., October 6, 1959 (strikeout).
Elston Howard, New York A.L., October 6, 1960.

Fewest chances offered, eight-inning game
1—Bill Killefer, Chicago N.L., September 9, 1918 (strikeout).

Most chances accepted, inning
4—Tim McCarver, St. Louis N.L., October 9, 1967, ninth inning (3 putouts, 1 assist; 2 strikeouts).

ERRORS AND PASSED BALLS

Most errors, career
7—Boss Schmidt, Detroit A.L., 1907, 1908, 1909; three series, 13 games.

Most consecutive errorless games, career
30—Yogi Berra, New York A.L., October 4, 1952 through October 9, 1957.

Most errors, series
4-game series—3—Joe Oliver, Cincinnati N.L., 1990.
5-game series—2
Boss Schmidt, Detroit A.L., 1907.
Walker Cooper, St. Louis N.L., 1943.
Joe Ferguson, Los Angeles N.L., 1974.
6-game series—2—Ray Schalk, Chicago A.L., 1917.
7-game series—5—Boss Schmidt, Detroit A.L., 1909.
8-game series—3—Lou Criger, Boston A.L., 1909.

Most chances accepted, errorless series
71—Jerry Grote, New York N.L., 1973 (7-game series).

Most errors, nine-inning game
—Lou Criger, Boston A.L., October 1, 1903.
  Jimmie Wilson, St. Louis N.L., October 7, 1928.
  Joe Ferguson, Los Angeles N.L., October 15, 1974.
  Carlton Fisk, Boston A.L., October 14, 1975, 9.1 innings.

Most errors, inning
—Lou Criger, Boston A.L., October 1, 1903, first inning.
  Jimmie Wilson, St. Louis N.L., October 7, 1928, sixth inning.

Most passed balls, career
—Johnny Kling, Chicago N.L., 1906 (3), 1907, 1908.

Most passed balls, series
—Johnny Kling, Chicago N.L., 1906.
  Smoky Burgess, Pittsburgh N.L., 1960.
  Elston Howard, New York A.L., 1964.

Most passed balls, nine-inning game
—Johnny Kling, Chicago N.L., October 9, 1906.
  Bill Killefer, Chicago N.L., September 9, 1918.
  Paul Richards, Detroit A.L., October 3, 1945.
  Bruce Edwards, Brooklyn N.L., October 4, 1947.
  Smoky Burgess, Pittsburgh N.L., October 6, 1960.
  Elston Howard, New York A.L., October 7, 1964.

Most passed balls, inning
—Held by many catchers.

DOUBLE PLAYS, RUNNERS CAUGHT STEALING

Most double plays, career
—Yogi Berra, New York A.L., 1947, 1949, 1950, 1951, 1952,
  1953, 1955, 1956, 1957, 1958, 1960, 1962; 12 series,
  63 games.
  Johnny Bench, Cincinnati N.L., 1970 (1), 1972 (2), 1975
  (3), 1976 (0); four series, 23 games.

Most double plays, series
3—Johnny Kling, Chicago N.L., 1906 (6-game series).
  Boss Schmidt, Detroit A.L., 1909 (7-game series).
  Wally Schang, New York A.L., 1921 (8-game series).
  Johnny Bench, Cincinnati N.L., 1975 (7-game series).

Most double plays started, series
3—Wally Schang, New York A.L., 1921 (8-game series).

Most double plays, nine-inning game
2—Boss Schmidt, Detroit A.L., October 14, 1909.
  Wally Schang, New York A.L., October 11, 1921.
  Gabby Hartnett, Chicago N.L., September 29, 1932.
  Del Rice, Milwaukee N.L., October 9, 1957.
  Rich Gedman, Boston A.L., October 22, 1986.

Most double plays started, nine-inning game
2—Boss Schmidt, Detroit A.L., October 14, 1909.
  Wally Schang, New York A.L., October 11, 1921.

Most unassisted double plays, game
—Never accomplished.

Most runners caught stealing, career
20—Wally Schang, Philadelphia A.L., 1913, 1914; Boston A.L.,
  1918; New York A.L., 1921, 1922, 1923, six series,
  32 games.

Most runners caught stealing, series
10—Ray Schalk, Chicago A.L., 1919 (8-game series).

Most runners caught stealing, nine-inning game
3—Performed nine times by eight catchers. Last time—Terry
  Steinbach, Oakland A.L., October 19, 1988.

Most runners caught stealing, extra-inning game
5—Jack Lapp, Philadelphia A.L., October 17, 1911, 11 innings.

Most runners caught stealing, inning
2—Jack Lapp, Philadelphia A.L., October 17, 1911, 10th inning.
  Aaron Robinson, New York A.L., October 6, 1947, first inning.
  Bill Carrigan, Boston A.L., October 9, 1912, 11th inning.
  Roy Campanella, Brooklyn N.L., October 2, 1952,
  first inning.

Most games pitched, career
22—Whitey Ford, New York A.L., 1950, 1953, 1955, 1956,
  1957, 1958, 1960, 1961, 1962, 1963, 1964; 11 series.

Most games pitched, series
4-game series—4—Jeff Nelson, New York A.L., 1999, 2.2
  innings.
5-game series—5—Mike G. Marshall, Los Angeles N.L., 1974,
  nine innings.
6-game series—6—Dan Quisenberry, Kansas City A.L., 1980,
  10.1 innings.
7-game series—7—Darold Knowles, Oakland A.L., 1973,
  6.1 innings.
8-game series—5—Deacon Phillippe, Pittsburgh N.L., 1903,
  44 innings.

PUTOUTS, ASSISTS AND CHANCES ACCEPTED

Most putouts, career
11—Whitey Ford, New York A.L., 1950, 1953, 1955, 1956,
  1957, 1958, 1960, 1961, 1962, 1963, 1964; 11 series,
  22 games.

Most putouts, series
4-game series—3—Whitey Ford, New York A.L., 1963.
5-game series—5—Jack Morris, Detroit, A.L., 1984.
6-game series—6
  Nick Altrock, Chicago A.L., 1906.
  Hippo Vaughn, Chicago N.L., 1918.
7-game series—5—Jim Kaat, Minnesota A.L., 1965.
8-game series—2
  Deacon Phillippe, Pittsburgh N.L., 1903.
  Phil Douglas, New York N.L., 1921.

Most putouts, nine-inning game
5—Jim Kaat, Minnesota A.L., October 7, 1965.

Most putouts, inning
2—Johnny Beazley, St. Louis N.L., October 5, 1942, eighth inning.
  Bob Turley, New York A.L., October 9, 1957, seventh inning.
  Whitey Ford, New York A.L., October 8, 1960, ninth inning.
  Bob Purkey, Cincinnati N.L., October 7, 1961, ninth inning.
  John Denny, Philadelphia N.L., October 15, 1983, fifth inning.
  Dave Stewart, Oakland A.L., October 16, 1990, third inning.

Most assists, career
34—Christy Mathewson, New York N.L., 1905, 1911, 1912,
  1913; four series, 11 games.

Most assists, series
4-game series—5
  Joe Bush, Philadelphia A.L., 1914.
  Lefty Tyler, Boston N.L., 1914.
  Bill James, Boston N.L., 1914.
  Wilcy Moore, New York A.L., 1927.
  Monte Pearson, New York A.L., 1939.
5-game series—10—Mordecai Brown, Chicago N.L., 1910.
6-game series—12—Mordecai Brown, Chicago N.L., 1906.
7-game series—12—George Mullin, Detroit A.L., 1909.
8-game series—12—Christy Mathewson, New York N.L., 1912.

Most assists, nine-inning game
8—Nick Altrock, Chicago A.L., October 12, 1906.
  Lon Warneke, Chicago N.L., October 2, 1935.

Most assists, inning
3—Eddie Plank, Philadelphia A.L., October 13, 1905,
  eighth inning.
  Rube Marquard, New York N.L., October 7, 1913,
  fourth inning.
  Lon Warneke, Chicago N.L., October 2, 1935, third inning.
  Johnny Murphy, New York A.L., October 8, 1939,
  eighth inning.
  Bob Rush, Milwaukee N.L., October 4, 1958, third inning.

Most chances accepted, career
40—Christy Mathewson, New York N.L., 1905, 1911, 1912, 1913; four series, 11 games.

Most chances accepted, series
4-game series—6
Lefty Tyler, Boston N.L., 1914.
Red Ruffing, New York A.L., 1938.
5-game series—10
Christy Mathewson, New York N.L., 1905.
Mordecai Brown, Chicago N.L., 1910.
6-game series—17
Nick Altrock, Chicago A.L., 1906.
Hippo Vaughn, Chicago N.L., 1918.
7-game series—12—George Mullin, Detroit A.L., 1909.
8-game series—13—Christy Mathewson, New York N.L., 1912.

Most innings pitched with no chances offered, series
26—Lefty Grove, Philadelphia A.L., 1931; three games.

Most chances accepted, nine-inning game
11—Nick Altrock, Chicago A.L., October 12, 1906 (3 putouts, 8 assists).

Fewest chances offered, extra-inning game
0—Howie Pollet, St. Louis N.L., October 6, 1946, 10 innings.
Robin Roberts, Philadelphia N.L., October 5, 1950, 10 innings.

Most chances accepted, inning
3—Held by many pitchers.

ERRORS AND DOUBLE PLAYS

Most errors, career
3—Deacon Phillippe, Pittsburgh N.L., 1903, 1909; two series, seven games.
Ed Cicotte, Chicago A.L., 1917, 1919; two series, six games.
Max Lanier, St. Louis N.L., 1942, 1943, 1944; three series, seven games.

Most errors, series
4-game series—1—Held by many pitchers.
5-game series—2
Jack Coombs, Philadelphia A.L., 1910.
Max Lanier, St. Louis N.L., 1942.
6-game series—2—Nels Potter, St. Louis A.L., 1944.

7-game series—2
Deacon Phillippe, Pittsburgh N.L., 1909.
Allie Reynolds, New York A.L., 1952.
8-game series—2—Ed Cicotte, Chicago A.L., 1919.

Most chances accepted, errorless series
17—Nick Altrock, Chicago A.L., 1906 (6-game series).
Hippo Vaughn, Chicago N.L., 1918 (6-game series).

Most errors, nine-inning game
2—Deacon Phillippe, Pittsburgh N.L., October 12, 1909.
Jack Coombs, Philadelphia A.L., October 18, 1910.
Ed Cicotte, Chicago A.L., October 4, 1919.
Max Lanier, St. Louis N.L., September 30, 1942.
Nels Potter, St. Louis A.L., October 5, 1944.

Most errors, inning
2—Jack Coombs, Philadelphia A.L., October 18, 1910, fifth inning.
Ed Cicotte, Chicago A.L., October 4, 1919, fifth inning.
Max Lanier, St. Louis N.L., September 30, 1942, ninth inning.
Nels Potter, St. Louis A.L., October 5, 1944, third inning.

Most consecutive errorless games, career
20—Mike Stanton, Atlanta N.L., New York A.L., October 19, 1991 through November 4, 2001.

Most double plays, career
3—Chief Bender, Philadelphia A.L., 1905, 1910, 1911, 1913, 1914; five series, 10 games.
Joe Bush, Philadelphia A.L., Boston A.L., New York A.L., 1913, 1914, 1918, 1922, 1923; five series, nine games.
Allie Reynolds, New York A.L., 1947, 1949, 1950, 1951, 1952, 1953; six series, 15 games.

Most double plays, series
2—Held by many pitchers.

Most double plays started, series
2—Held by many pitchers.

Most unassisted double plays, game
Never accomplished.

Most double plays started, game
2—Chief Bender, Philadelphia A.L., October 9, 1914.
Joe Bush, New York A.L., October 8, 1922.
Allie Reynolds, New York A.L., October 8, 1951.

CLUB FIELDING

AVERAGE

Highest fielding average, series
4-game series—1.000—Baltimore A.L. vs. Los Angeles N.L., 1966.
5-game series—1.000—New York A.L. vs. New York N.L., 1937.
6-game series—.996
 Boston A.L. vs. Chicago N.L., 1918.
 St. Louis N.L. vs. St. Louis A.L., 1944.
 Los Angeles N.L. vs. New York A.L., 1977.
7-game series—.993—Cincinnati N.L. vs. Boston A.L., 1975.
8-game series—.984—New York N.L. vs. New York A.L., 1921.

**For a list of fielding statistics by teams each
series, see page 515.**

Highest fielding average by both clubs, series
4-game series—.986—New York A.L. .993, Los Angeles N.L.
 .979, 1963.
5-game series—.986—Oakland A.L. .989, Los Angeles N.L.
 .983, 1988.
6-game series—.991—Los Angeles N.L. .996, New York A.L.
 .987, 1977.
7-game series—.990—St. Louis N.L. .992, Kansas City A.L.
 .989, 1985.
8-game series—.983—New York N.L. .984, New York A.L.
 .981, 1921.

Lowest fielding average, series
4-game series—.949—New York A.L. vs. Chicago N.L., 1932.
5-game series—.942—Brooklyn N.L. vs. Boston A.L., 1916.
6-game series—.938—New York N.L. vs. Philadelphia A.L., 1911.
7-game series—.934—Detroit A.L. vs. Pittsburgh N.L., 1909.
8-game series—.944—Pittsburgh N.L. vs. Boston A.L., 1903.

Lowest fielding average by both clubs, series
4-game series—.954—Chicago N.L. .959, New York A.L.
 .949, 1932.
5-game series—.946—Philadelphia A.L. .947, Chicago N.L.
 .946, 1910.
6-game series—.947—Philadelphia A.L. .956, New York N.L.
 .938, 1911.
7-game series—.941—Pittsburgh N.L. .947, Detroit A.L.
 .934, 1909.
8-game series—.951—Boston A.L. .957, Pittsburgh N.L. .944, 1903.

PUTOUTS

Most putouts, total series
5,698—New York A.L.; 38 series, 213 games.

Most putouts, series
4-game series—117—Boston N.L. vs. Philadelphia A.L., 1914.
5-game series—147—Boston A.L. vs. Brooklyn N.L., 1916.
6-game series—168—New York A.L. vs. Los Angeles N.L., 1977.
7-game series—202—Minnesota A.L. vs. Atlanta N.L., 1991.
8-game series—222—Boston A.L. vs. New York N.L., 1912.

Most putouts by both clubs, series
4-game series—228—Boston N.L. 117, Philadelphia A.L.
 111, 1914.
5-game series—289—Boston A.L. 147, Brooklyn N.L. 142, 1916.
6-game series—333—New York A.L. 168, Los Angeles N.L.
 165, 1977.
7-game series—401—Washington A.L. 201, New York N.L.
 200, 1924.
8-game series—443—Boston A.L. 222, New York N.L. 221, 1912.

Fewest putouts, series
4-game series—102
 St. Louis N.L. vs. New York A.L., 1928.
 Chicago N.L. vs. New York A.L., 1932.
 Chicago N.L. vs. New York A.L., 1938.
 New York A.L. vs. Los Angeles N.L., 1963.
 Los Angeles N.L. vs. Baltimore A.L., 1966.

San Francisco N.L. vs. Oakland A.L., 1989.
 San Diego N.L. vs. New York A.L., 1998.
5-game series—126
 Los Angeles N.L. vs. Oakland A.L., 1974.
 San Diego N.L. vs. Detroit A.L., 1984.
6-game series—153
 New York N.L. vs. Chicago A.L., 1917.
 St. Louis N.L. vs. Philadelphia A.L., 1930.
 New York N.L. vs. Los Angeles N.L., 1981.
7-game series—177
 Brooklyn N.L. vs. Cleveland A.L., 1920.
 St. Louis N.L. vs. Minnesota A.L., 1987.
8-game series—210
 Pittsburgh N.L. vs. Boston A.L., 1903.
 New York A.L. vs. New York N.L., 1921.

Fewest putouts by both clubs, series
4-game series—210
 New York A.L. 108, St. Louis N.L. 102, 1928.
 New York A.L. 108, Chicago N.L. 102, 1932.
 New York A.L. 108, Chicago N.L. 102, 1938.
 Los Angeles N.L. 108, New York A.L. 102, 1963.
 Baltimore A.L. 108, Los Angeles N.L. 102, 1966.
 Oakland A.L. 108, San Francisco N.L. 102, 1989.
 New York A.L. 108, San Diego N.L. 102, 1998.
5-game series—258
 Oakland A.L. 132, Los Angeles N.L. 126, 1974.
 Detroit A.L. 132, San Diego N.L. 126, 1984.
6-game series—309
 Chicago A.L. 156, New York N.L. 153, 1917.
 Philadelphia A.L. 156, St. Louis N.L. 153, 1930.
 Los Angeles N.L. 156, New York A.L. 153, 1981.
7-game series—357—Minnesota A.L. 180, St. Louis N.L.
 177, 1987.
8-game series—422—New York N.L. 212, New York A.L.
 210, 1921.

Most players with one or more putouts, nine-inning game
11—New York A.L. vs. Milwaukee N.L., October 2, 1957.
 Baltimore A.L. vs. Pittsburgh N.L., October 16, 1979.

Most players with one or more putouts by both clubs, nine-inning game
19—New York A.L. 11, Milwaukee N.L. 8, October 2, 1957.
 Baltimore A.L. 10, Pittsburgh N.L. 9, October 11, 1971.
 Florida N.L. 10, Cleveland A.L. 9, October 19, 1997.

Most players with one or more putouts by both clubs, extra-inning game
20—Chicago N.L. 10, Detroit A.L. 10, October 8, 1945, 12 innings.

Most putouts by outfield, nine-inning game
15—New York N.L. vs. Boston A.L., October 14, 1912.
 Boston N.L. vs. Cleveland A.L., October 6, 1948.

Most putouts by outfield, extra-inning game
16—Brooklyn N.L. vs. New York A.L., October 5, 1952,
 11 innings.

Most putouts by outfields of both clubs, game
23—Pittsburgh N.L. 13, New York A.L. 10, October 6, 1927.
 Brooklyn N.L. 16, New York A.L. 7, October 5, 1952,
 11 innings.

Fewest putouts by outfield, nine-inning game
0—New York N.L. vs. New York A.L., October 5, 1921.
 New York N.L. vs. New York A.L., September 30, 1936.
 Cleveland A.L. vs. Atlanta N.L., October 21, 1995 (fielded
 eight innings).

Fewest putouts by outfield, extra-inning game
1—New York N.L. vs. Oakland A.L., October 14, 1973, 12 innings.

Fewest putouts by outfields of both clubs, nine-inning game
2—Atlanta N.L. 2, Cleveland A.L. 0, October 21, 1995
 (Cleveland fielded eight innings).
3—New York A.L. 2, Brooklyn N.L. 1, October 10, 1956.

Most putouts by outfield, inning
3—Made in many games.

Most putouts by outfields of both clubs, inning
6—Kansas City A.L. 3, St. Louis N.L. 3, October 27, 1985, seventh inning.

Most putouts by catchers of both clubs, inning
6—Chicago A.L. 3, Cincinnati N.L. 3, October 6, 1919, second inning.
Cincinnati N.L. 3, Oakland A.L. 3, October 18, 1972, fifth inning.
St. Louis N.L. 3, Kansas City A.L. 3, October 24, 1985, seventh inning.
New York N.L. 3, New York A.L. 3, October 24, 2000, second inning.

ASSISTS

Most assists, total series
2,246—New York A.L.; 38 series, 213 games.

Most assists, series
4-game series—67—Philadelphia A.L. vs. Boston N.L., 1914.
5-game series—90—Boston A.L. vs. Brooklyn N.L., 1916.
6-game series—99—Chicago A.L. vs. Chicago N.L., 1906.
7-game series—99
Washington A.L. vs. New York N.L., 1924.
St. Louis N.L. vs. New York A.L., 1926.
8-game series—116—Chicago A.L. vs. Cincinnati N.L., 1919.

Most assists by both clubs, series
4-game series—129—Philadelphia A.L. 67, Boston N.L. 62, 1914.
5-game series—160—Boston A.L. 90, Brooklyn N.L. 70, 1916.
6-game series—183—Chicago A.L. 99, Chicago N.L. 84, 1906.
7-game series—193—Washington A.L. 99, New York N.L. 94, 1924.
8-game series—212—Chicago A.L. 116, Cincinnati N.L. 96, 1919.

Fewest assists, series
4-game series—28—New York A.L. vs. St. Louis N.L., 1928.
5-game series—36—Los Angeles N.L. vs. Oakland A.L., 1988.
6-game series—41—Philadelphia A.L. vs. St. Louis N.L., 1930.
7-game series—48—St. Louis N.L. vs. Detroit A.L., 1968.
8-game series—96
Pittsburgh N.L. vs. Boston A.L., 1903.
Cincinnati N.L. vs. Chicago A.L., 1919.

Fewest assists by both clubs, series
4-game series—64—St. Louis N.L. 36, New York A.L. 28, 1928.
5-game series—79—Oakland A.L. 43, Los Angeles N.L. 36, 1988.
6-game series—96—St. Louis N.L. 55, Philadelphia A.L. 41, 1930.
7-game series—120—Detroit A.L. 72, St. Louis N.L. 48, 1968.
8-game series—198—Boston A.L. 102, Pittsburgh N.L. 96, 1903.

Most players with one or more assists, nine-inning game
9—Chicago A.L. vs. New York N.L., October 7, 1917.
New York A.L. vs. New York N.L., October 6, 1922.
Chicago N.L. vs. Detroit A.L., October 8, 1945, 12 innings.
Brooklyn N.L. vs. New York A.L., October 3, 1947.

Most players with one or more assists by both clubs, nine-inning game
15—New York A.L. 9, New York N.L. 6, October 6, 1922.
Chicago N.L. 9, Detroit A.L. 6, October 8, 1945, 12 innings.

Most players with one or more assists by both clubs, extra-inning game
16—Los Angeles N.L. 9, New York A.L. 7, October 11, 1977, 12 innings.

Most assists, nine-inning game
21—Chicago A.L. vs. New York N.L., October 7, 1917.
Boston A.L. vs. Chicago N.L., September 9, 1918.

Most assists by both clubs, nine-inning game
38—Chicago A.L. 20, Chicago N.L. 18, October 12, 1906.

Fewest assists, nine-inning game
2—St. Louis N.L. vs. Detroit A.L., October 2, 1968.

Fewest assists by both clubs, nine-inning game
8—Philadelphia A.L. 5, St. Louis N.L. 3, October 2, 1930.
Boston A.L. 5, Cincinnati N.L. 3, October 16, 1975.

Fewest assists by infield, nine-inning game
1—St. Louis N.L. vs. Detroit A.L., October 2, 1968.

Most assists by outfield, inning
2—Boston A.L. vs. St. Louis N.L., October 10, 1946, fifth inning.

CHANCES OFFERED

Fewest chances offered to outfield, nine-inning game
0—New York N.L. vs. New York A.L., September 30, 1936.
Cleveland A.L. vs. Atlanta N.L., October 21, 1995 (fielded eight innings).

Fewest chances offered to outfield, extra-inning game
1—New York N.L. vs. Oakland A.L., October 14, 1973, 12 innings.

Fewest chances offered to outfield by both clubs, nine-inning game
2—Atlanta N.L. 2, Cleveland A.L. 0, October 21, 1995 (Cleveland fielded eight innings).
3—New York A.L. 2, Brooklyn N.L. 1, October 10, 1956.

Fewest chances offered to infield, game (excluding first base)
2—Philadelphia A.L. vs. St. Louis N.L., October 6, 1931.

ERRORS

Most errors, total series
158—New York A.L.; 38 series, 213 games.

Most errors, series
4-game series—8—New York A.L. vs. Chicago N.L., 1932.
5-game series—13—Brooklyn N.L. vs. Boston A.L., 1916.
6-game series—16—New York N.L. vs. Philadelphia A.L., 1911.
7-game series—19—Detroit A.L. vs. Pittsburgh N.L., 1909.
8-game series—18—Pittsburgh N.L. vs. Boston A.L., 1903.

Most errors by both clubs, series
4-game series—14—New York A.L. 8, Chicago N.L. 6, 1932.
5-game series—23—Chicago N.L. 12, Philadelphia A.L. 11, 1910
6-game series—27—New York N.L. 16, Philadelphia A.L. 11, 1911
7-game series—34—Detroit A.L. 19, Pittsburgh N.L. 15, 1909.
8-game series—32—Pittsburgh N.L. 18, Boston A.L. 14, 1903.

Fewest errors, series
4-game series—0—Baltimore A.L. vs. Los Angeles N.L., 1966.
5-game series—0—New York A.L. vs. New York N.L., 1937.
6-game series—1
Boston A.L. vs. Chicago N.L., 1918.
St. Louis N.L. vs. St. Louis A.L., 1944.
New York A.L. vs. Brooklyn N.L., 1953.
Los Angeles N.L. vs. New York A.L., 1977.
7-game series—2—Held by many clubs.
8-game series—5—New York N.L. vs. New York A.L., 1921.

Fewest errors by both clubs, series
4-game series—4—Los Angeles N.L. 3, New York A.L. 1, 1963.
5-game series—5—Los Angeles N.L. 3, Oakland A.L. 2, 1988.
6-game series—4—New York A.L. 3, Los Angeles N.L. 1, 1977.
7-game series—5—Kansas City A.L. 3, St. Louis N.L. 2, 1985.
8-game series—11—New York A.L. 6, New York N.L. 5, 1921.

Most errors, nine-inning game
6—Chicago A.L. vs. Chicago N.L., October 13, 1906.
Pittsburgh N.L. vs. Detroit A.L., October 12, 1909.
Chicago A.L. vs. New York N.L., October 13, 1917.
Los Angeles N.L. vs. Baltimore A.L., October 6, 1966.

Most errors by both clubs, nine-inning game
9—Chicago A.L. 6, New York N.L. 3, October 13, 1917.

Most errors by outfield, game
4—Los Angeles N.L. vs. Baltimore A.L., October 6, 1966.

Most errors by outfields of both clubs, game
4—Los Angeles N.L. 4, Baltimore A.L. 0, October 6, 1966.

Most errors by infield, game

5—Chicago A.L. vs. Chicago N.L., October 13, 1906.
    New York N.L. vs. Philadelphia A.L., October 17, 1911, 11
       innings.
    Detroit A.L. vs. St. Louis N.L., October 3, 1934.

Most errors by infields of both clubs, game

7—New York N.L. 5, Philadelphia A.L. 2, October 17, 1911, 11
    innings.
    Chicago A.L. 4, New York N.L. 3, October 13, 1917.

Most errors, inning

3—Chicago A.L., October 13, 1917, fourth inning.
    New York N.L., October 8, 1937, fifth inning.
    New York N.L., October 9, 1937, third inning.
    Cincinnati N.L., October 8, 1939, 10th inning.
    Los Angeles N.L., October 1, 1959, third inning.
    Los Angeles N.L., October 6, 1966, fifth inning.
    Cleveland A.L., October 21, 1997, ninth inning.

Most errorless games, total series

100—New York A.L; 38 series, 213 games.

Most consecutive errorless games, total series

7—Philadelphia A.L. vs. St. Louis N.L., October 6, 7, 1930;
    October 1, 2, 5, 6, 7, 1931.

Most errorless games, series

4-game series—4—Baltimore A.L. vs. Los Angeles N.L., 1966.
5-game series—5—New York A.L. vs. New York N.L., 1937.
6-game series—5
    Boston A.L. vs. Chicago N.L., 1918.
    St. Louis N.L. vs. St. Louis A.L., 1944.
    New York A.L. vs. Brooklyn N.L., 1953.
    Los Angeles N.L. vs. New York A.L., 1977.
7-game series—6—Arizona N.L. vs. New York A.L., 2001.
8-game series—5—New York N.L. vs. New York A.L., 1921.

Most consecutive errorless games, series

5—Philadelphia A.L. vs. St. Louis N.L., October 1, 2, 5, 6, 7,
    1931 (first five games).
    New York A.L. vs. New York N.L., October 6, 7, 8, 9, 10,
      1937 (full series).
    New York A.L. vs. Brooklyn N.L., September 29, 30, October
      1, 2, 3, 1955.

Most errorless games by both clubs, series

4-game series—7—Baltimore A.L. 4, Los Angeles N.L. 3, 1966.
5-game series—7—New York A.L. 5, New York N.L. 2, 1937.
6-game series—9—Los Angeles N.L. 5, New York A.L. 4, 1977.
7-game series—10—St. Louis N.L. 5, Kansas City A.L. 5, 1985.
8-game series—8—New York N.L. 5, New York A.L. 3, 1921.

Fewest errorless games, series

0—Held by many clubs.

Longest errorless game

12 innings—Detroit A.L. vs. St. Louis N.L., October 4, 1934.
             New York A.L. vs. Los Angeles N.L., October 11, 1977.
             New York A.L. vs. New York N.L., October 21, 2000.
             Arizona N.L. vs. New York A.L., November 1, 2001.

Longest errorless game by both clubs

12 innings—New York A.L. vs. Los Angeles N.L., October 11,
             1977 (Los Angeles fielded 11 innings).
             New York A.L. vs. New York N.L., October 21, 2000
             (New York N.L. fielded 11.2 innings).

PASSED BALLS

Most passed balls, total series

14—New York A.L.; 38 series, 213 games.

Most passed balls, series

3—Chicago N.L. vs. Chicago A.L., 1906.
    Pittsburgh N.L. vs. New York A.L., 1960.
    New York A.L. vs. St. Louis N.L., 1964.

Most passed balls by both clubs, series

4—Chicago N.L., 3, Chicago A.L., 1, 1906 (6-game series).
    New York A.L. 2, Brooklyn N.L. 2, 1947 (7-game series).

Fewest passed balls, series

0—Held by many clubs.

Fewest passed balls by both clubs, series

0—Held by many clubs.

DOUBLE AND TRIPLE PLAYS

Most double plays, total series

187—New York A.L.; 38 series, 213 games.

Most double plays, series

4-game series—7
    Chicago N.L. vs. New York A.L., 1932.
    New York A.L. vs. Los Angeles N.L., 1963.
5-game series—7
    New York A.L. vs. New York N.L., 1922.
    New York A.L. vs. Brooklyn N.L., 1941.
    Cincinnati N.L. vs. New York A.L., 1961.
6-game series—10—New York A.L. vs. New York N.L., 1951.
7-game series—12—Brooklyn N.L. vs. New York A.L., 1955.
8-game series—9—Chicago A.L. vs. Cincinnati N.L., 1919.

Most double plays by both clubs, series

4-game series—10—New York A.L. 6, Cincinnati N.L. 4, 1976.
5-game series—12—New York A.L. 7, Brooklyn N.L. 5, 1941.
6-game series—16—Philadelphia N.L. 8, Kansas City A.L. 8, 1980.
7-game series—19—Brooklyn N.L. 12, New York A.L. 7, 1955.
8-game series—16—Chicago A.L. 9, Cincinnati N.L. 7, 1919.

Fewest double plays, series

4-game series—1
    New York A.L. vs. Chicago N.L., 1932.
    Cincinnati N.L. vs. New York A.L., 1939.
    Philadelphia N.L. vs. New York A.L., 1950.
    Los Angeles N.L. vs. New York A.L., 1963.
    Oakland A.L. vs. San Francisco N.L., 1989.
5-game series—0—New York N.L. vs. Baltimore A.L., 1969.
6-game series—2
    Chicago A.L. vs. Chicago N.L., 1906.
    New York N.L. vs. Philadelphia A.L., 1911.
    Philadelphia A.L. vs. New York N.L., 1911.
    Philadelphia A.L. vs. St. Louis N.L., 1930.
    New York A.L. vs. New York N.L., 1936.
    Chicago A.L. vs. Los Angeles N.L., 1959.
    New York A.L. vs. Los Angeles N.L., 1977, 1981.
7-game series—2
    St. Louis N.L. vs. Detroit A.L., 1934.
    Baltimore A.L. vs. Pittsburgh N.L., 1971.
    St. Louis N.L. vs. Minnesota A.L., 1987.
8-game series—4—New York N.L. vs. Boston A.L., 1912.

Fewest double plays by both clubs, series

4-game series—4
    New York N.L. 2, Cleveland A.L. 2, 1954.
    San Francisco N.L. 3, Oakland A.L. 1, 1989.
5-game series—4
    New York N.L. 2, Philadelphia A.L. 2, 1905.
    Baltimore A.L. 4, New York N.L. 0, 1969.
    New York N.L. 3, New York A.L. 1, 2000.
6-game series—4—Philadelphia A.L. 2, New York N.L. 2, 1911.
7-game series—6—Minnesota A.L. 4, St. Louis N.L. 2, 1987.
8-game series—9—Boston A.L. 5, New York N.L. 4, 1912.

Most double plays, nine-inning game

4—Philadelphia A.L. vs. Boston N.L., October 9, 1914.
    Boston A.L. vs. Brooklyn N.L., October 7, 1916.
    Chicago N.L. vs. New York A.L., September 29, 1932.
    Cleveland A.L. vs. Boston N.L., October 11, 1948.
    New York A.L. vs. New York N.L., October 8, 1951.
    Oakland A.L. vs. New York N.L., October 17, 1973.
    Philadelphia N.L. vs. Kansas City A.L., October 15, 1980.

Most double plays by both clubs, nine-inning game

6—New York A.L. 3, Brooklyn N.L. 3, September 29, 1955.
    Philadelphia N.L. 4, Kansas City A.L. 2, October 15, 1980.

Most triple plays, series

1—Cleveland A.L. vs. Brooklyn N.L., 1920.

MISCELLANEOUS

CLUB

ONE-RUN DECISIONS

Most one-run games, total series
67—New York A.L.; 38 series; won 36 lost 31.

Most one-run games won, total series
36—New York A.L.; 38 series; lost 31.

Most one-run games lost, total series
31—New York A.L.; 38 series; won 36.

Most one-run games won, series
4—Boston A.L. vs. Philadelphia N.L., 1915 (lost one).
Boston A.L. vs. Chicago N.L., 1918 (lost none).
Oakland A.L. vs. Cincinnati N.L., 1972 (lost two).

Most one-run games by both clubs, series
4-game series—3—New York A.L. (won three) vs. Philadelphia N.L., 1950.
5-game series—4
Boston A.L. (won four) vs. Philadelphia N.L., 1915.
Oakland A.L. (won three) vs. Los Angeles N.L. (won one), 1974.
6-game series—5—Atlanta N.L. (won three) vs. Cleveland A.L. (won two), 1995.
7-game series—6—Oakland A.L. (won four) vs. Cincinnati N.L (won two), 1972.
8-game series—4—Boston A.L. (won three) vs. New York N.L. (won one), 1912.

Most one-run games won, series
4-game series—3—New York A.L. vs. Philadelphia N.L., 1950.
5-game series—4—Boston A.L. vs. Philadelphia N.L., 1915.
6-game series—4
Boston A.L. vs. Chicago N.L., 1918.
Toronto A.L. vs. Atlanta N.L., 1992.
7-game series—4—Oakland A.L. vs. Cincinnati N.L., 1972.
8-game series—3—Boston A.L. vs. New York N.L., 1912.

Most consecutive one-run games won, total series
6—Boston A.L., 1915 (last 4), 1916 (first 2).

Most consecutive one-run games lost, total series
7—Philadelphia N.L., 1915 (last 4), 1950 (first 3).

LENGTH OF GAMES

BY INNINGS

Longest game
14 innings—Boston A.L. 2, Brooklyn N.L. 1, October 9, 1916 (at Boston).

For a complete list of extra-inning games, see page 507.

Longest tie game
12 innings—Chicago N.L. 3, Detroit A.L. 3, October 8, 1907 (at Chicago).

Most extra-inning games, total series
18—New York A.L.; 38 series, 213 games (won 11, lost six, tied one).

Most extra-inning games won, total series
11—New York A.L.; 38 series, 213 games (won 11, lost six, tied one).

Most extra-inning games lost, total series
6—New York A.L.; 38 series, 213 games (won 11 lost six, tied one).

Most extra-inning games, series
4-game series—1
Boston N.L. vs. Philadelphia A.L., 1914.
New York A.L. vs. Cincinnati N.L., 1939.

New York A.L. vs. Philadelphia N.L., 1950.
New York N.L. vs. Cleveland A.L., 1954.
5-game series—2—New York N.L. vs. Washington A.L., 1933.
6-game series—2—Philadelphia A.L. vs. New York N.L., 1911.
7-game series—3—Minnesota A.L. vs. Atlanta N.L., 1991.
8-game series—2—Boston A.L. vs. New York N.L., 1912.

BY TIME

Longest average time per game, series
4-game series—3 hours, 14 minutes—New York A.L. vs. San Diego N.L., 1998.
5-game series—3 hours, 46 minutes—New York A.L. vs. New York N.L., 2000.
6-game series—3 hours, 29 minutes—Toronto A.L. vs. Philadelphia N.L., 1993.
7-game series—3 hours, 30 minutes—Florida N.L. vs. Cleveland A.L., 1997.
8-game series—2 hours, 14 minutes—Boston A.L. vs. New York N.L., 1912.

Shortest average time per game, series
4-game series—1 hour, 46 minutes—New York A.L. vs. Cincinnati N.L., 1939.
5-game series—1 hour, 46 minutes—Detroit A.L. vs. Chicago N.L., 1908.
6-game series—1 hour, 49 minutes—Philadelphia A.L. vs. St. Louis N.L., 1930.
7-game series—1 hour, 47 minutes—Cleveland A.L. vs. Brooklyn N.L., 1920.
8-game series—1 hour, 48 minutes—Boston A.L. vs. Pittsburgh N.L., 1903.

Shortest game
1 hour, 25 minutes—Chicago N.L., 2, Detroit A.L., 0, October 14, 1908 (at Detroit).

Longest nine-inning day game
3 hours, 48 minutes—Baltimore A.L., 9, Pittsburgh N.L., 6, October 13, 1979 (at Pittsburgh).

Longest nine-inning night game
4 hours, 14 minutes—Toronto A.L., 15, Philadelphia N.L., 14, October 20, 1993 (at Philadelphia).

Longest extra-inning day game
4 hours, 13 minutes—New York N.L., 10, Oakland A.L., 7, October 14, 1973, 12 innings (at Oakland).

Longest extra-inning night game
4 hours, 51 minutes—New York A.L. 4, New York N.L. 3, October 21, 2000, 12 innings (at New York A.L.).

SERIES STARTING AND FINISHING DATES

Earliest date for series game (except 1918)
September 28, 1932—Chicago N.L. at New York A.L.
September 28, 1955—Brooklyn N.L. at New York A.L.

Earliest date for series final game (except 1918)
October 2, 1932—New York A.L. at Chicago N.L. (4-game series).
October 2, 1954—New York N.L. at Cleveland A.L. (4-game series).

Latest date for series start
October 27, 2001—New York A.L. at Arizona N.L.

Latest date for series finish
November 4, 2001—New York A.L. at Arizona N.L. (7-game series).

NIGHT GAMES

First night game
October 13, 1971—Pittsburgh N.L., 4, Baltimore A.L., 3 (at Pittsburgh).

First year the entire series played at night
1985—St. Louis N.L. vs. Kansas City A.L., October 19 through 27 (7-game series).

SERIES AND GAMES WON

Most series won
26—New York A.L., 1923, 1927, 1928, 1932, 1936, 1937, 1938, 1939, 1941, 1943, 1947, 1949, 1950, 1951, 1952, 1953, 1956, 1958, 1961, 1962, 1977, 1978, 1996, 1998, 1999, 2000 (lost 12).

For complete lists of results, and series played by all teams, see page 505.

Most consecutive series won
8—New York A.L., 1927, 1928, 1932, 1936, 1937, 1938, 1939, 1941.

Most consecutive years winning series
5—New York A.L., 1949, 1950, 1951, 1952, 1953.

Most times winning series in four consecutive games
8—New York A.L., 1927, 1928, 1932, 1938, 1939, 1950, 1998, 1999.

Winning series after winning first game
Accomplished 59 times.

Winning series after losing first game
Accomplished 38 times.

Winning series after winning one game and losing three
Boston A.L. vs. Pittsburgh N.L., 1903 (8-game series; needed five wins).
Pittsburgh N.L. vs. Washington A.L., 1925 (7-game series).
New York A.L. vs. Milwaukee N.L., 1958 (7-game series).
Detroit A.L. vs. St. Louis N.L., 1968 (7-game series).
Pittsburgh N.L. vs. Baltimore A.L., 1979 (7-game series).
Kansas City A.L. vs. St. Louis N.L., 1985 (7-game series).

Winning series after losing first two games
New York N.L. vs. New York A.L., 1921 (8-game series; needed five wins).
Brooklyn N.L. vs. New York A.L., 1955 (7-game series).
New York A.L. vs. Brooklyn N.L., 1956 (7-game series).
New York A.L. vs. Milwaukee N.L., 1958 (7-game series).
Los Angeles N.L. vs. Minnesota A.L., 1965 (7-game series).
Pittsburgh N.L. vs. Baltimore A.L., 1971 (7-game series).
New York A.L. vs. Los Angeles N.L., 1978 (6-game series).
Los Angeles N.L. vs. New York A.L., 1981 (6-game series).
Kansas City A.L. vs. St. Louis N.L., 1985 (7-game series).
New York N.L. vs. Boston A.L., 1986 (7-game series).
New York A.L. vs. Atlanta N.L., 1996 (6-game series).

Winning series after losing first three games
Never accomplished.

Most games won, total series
128—New York A.L.; 38 series; lost 84, tied one.

For complete lists of results, and games played by all teams, see page 505.

Most consecutive games won, total series
14—New York A.L., 1996 (last 4), 1998 (4), 1999 (4), 2000 (first 2).

SERIES AND GAMES LOST

Most series lost
12—Brooklyn/Los Angeles N.L., 1916, 1920, 1941, 1947, 1949, 1952, 1953, 1956, 1966, 1974, 1977, 1978 (won six).
12—New York A.L., 1921, 1922, 1926, 1942, 1955, 1957, 1960, 1963, 1964, 1976, 1981, 2001 (won 26).

Most consecutive series lost
7—Chicago N.L., 1910, 1918, 1929, 1932, 1935, 1938, 1945.
Brooklyn N.L., 1916, 1920, 1941, 1947, 1949, 1952, 1953.

Most consecutive years losing series
3—Detroit A.L., 1907, 1908, 1909.
New York N.L., 1911, 1912, 1913.

Most games lost, total series
84—New York A.L.; 38 series, won 128, tied one.

For complete lists of results, and games played by all teams, see page 505.

Most consecutive games lost, total series
8—New York A.L., 1921 (last 3), 1922 (4; one tie during streak), 1923 (first 1).
Philadelphia N.L., 1915 (last 4), 1950 (4).

ATTENDANCE

Largest attendance, series
4-game series—251,507—New York N.L. vs. Cleveland A.L., 1954.
5-game series—304,139—Baltimore A.L. vs. Philadelphia N.L., 1983.
6-game series—420,784—Los Angeles N.L. vs. Chicago A.L., 1959.
7-game series—403,617—Florida N.L. vs. Cleveland A.L., 1997.
8-game series—269,976—New York N.L. vs. New York A.L., 1921.

For list of attendance by series each series, see page 508.

Smallest attendance, series
4-game series—111,009—Boston N.L. vs. Philadelphia A.L., 1914.
5-game series—62,232—Chicago N.L. vs. Detroit A.L., 1908.
6-game series—99,845—Chicago A.L. vs. Chicago N.L., 1906.
7-game series—145,295—Pittsburgh N.L. vs. Detroit A.L., 1909.
8-game series—100,429—Pittsburgh N.L. vs. Boston A.L., 1903.

Largest attendance, game
92,706—At Los Angeles, October 6, 1959, Chicago A.L. 1, Los Angeles N.L. 0.

Smallest attendance, game
6,210—At Detroit, October 14, 1908; Chicago N.L. 2, Detroit A.L. 0.

LEAGUE
SERIES AND GAMES WON AND LOST

Most consecutive series won, league
7—American League, 1947, 1948, 1949, 1950, 1951, 1952, 1953.

Most consecutive series lost, league
7—National League, 1947, 1948, 1949, 1950, 1951, 1952, 1953.

Most consecutive games won, league
10—American League, 1927 (4) 1928 (4), 1929 (first 2).
American League, 1937 (last 1), 1938 (4), 1939 (4), 1940 (first 1).
American League, 1998 (4), 1999 (4), 2000 (first 2).

SHUTOUTS

Most consecutive series with shutouts
9—1955 through 1963.

Most consecutive series ending in shutouts
3—1907, 1908, 1909.
1955, 1956, 1957.

Most consecutive series without shutouts
3—1910, 1911, 1912.
1927, 1928, 1929.
1936, 1937, 1938.
1976, 1977, 1978.

NON-PLAYING PERSONNEL

MANAGERS AND COACHES

Most series by manager
10—Casey Stengel, New York A.L., 1949, 1950, 1951, 1952, 1953, 1955, 1956, 1957, 1958, 1960 (won seven, lost three).

For a complete list of managers and their records, see page 518.

Most series by coach
15—Frank Crosetti, New York A.L., 1947, 1949, 1950, 1951, 1952, 1953, 1955, 1956, 1957, 1958, 1960, 1961, 1962, 1963, 1964 (10 World Series winners).

Most series eligible as player and coach
23—Frank Crosetti, New York A.L., 1932, 1936, 1937, 1938, 1939, 1941, 1942, 1943 (eight series as player, seven winners); 1947, 1949, 1950, 1951, 1952, 1953, 1955, 1956, 1957, 1958, 1960, 1961, 1962, 1963, 1964 (15 series as coach, 10 winners).

Most series winners managed
7—Joe McCarthy, New York A.L., 1932, 1936, 1937, 1938, 1939, 1941, 1943.
  Casey Stengel, New York A.L., 1949, 1950, 1951, 1952, 1953, 1956, 1958.

Most consecutive years managing series winners
5—Casey Stengel, New York A.L., 1949, 1950, 1951, 1952, 1953 (his first five years as New York A.L. manager).

Most consecutive series winners managed, career
6—Joe McCarthy, New York A.L., 1932, 1936, 1937, 1938, 1939, 1941.

Most series losers managed
6—John McGraw, New York N.L., 1911, 1912, 1913, 1917, 1923, 1924.

Most consecutive years managing series losers
3—Hughey Jennings, Detroit A.L., 1907, 1908, 1909.
  John McGraw, New York N.L., 1911, 1912, 1913.

Most consecutive series losers managed, career
4—John McGraw, New York N.L., 1911, 1912, 1913, 1917.

Most different series winners managed
2—Bill McKechnie, Pittsburgh N.L., 1925; Cincinnati N.L., 1940.
  Bucky Harris, Washington A.L., 1924; New York A.L., 1947.
  Sparky Anderson, Cincinnati N.L., 1975, 1976; Detroit A.L., 1984.

Most different clubs managed
3—Bill McKechnie, Pittsburgh N.L., 1925; St. Louis N.L., 1928; Cincinnati N.L., 1939, 1940.
  Dick Williams, Boston A.L., 1967; Oakland A.L., 1972, 1973; San Diego N.L., 1984.

Most games by manager
63—Casey Stengel, New York A.L., 10 series.

Most games won by manager
37—Casey Stengel, New York A.L., 10 series.

Most games lost by manager
28—John McGraw, New York N.L., 10 series.

Youngest manager
26 years, 11 months, 21 days—Joe Cronin, Washington A.L. vs. New York N.L., October 3, 1933.

Youngest manager of a series winner
27 years, 11 months, 2 days—Bucky Harris, Washington A.L. vs. New York N.L., October 10, 1924.

UMPIRES

Most series umpired
18—Bill Klem, 1908, 1909, 1911, 1912, 1913, 1914, 1915, 1917, 1918, 1920, 1922, 1924, 1926, 1929, 1931, 1932, 1934, 1940.

Most consecutive series umpired
5—Bill Klem, 1911, 1912, 1913, 1914, 1915.

Most games umpired
104—Bill Klem, 18 series.

GENERAL REFERENCE

RESULTS
YEAR BY YEAR

Includes one tie.

Year	Winner	Loser	Games
903	Boston A.L.	Pittsburgh N.L.	5-3
904	No series played.		
905	New York N.L.	Philadelphia A.L.	4-1
906	Chicago A.L.	Chicago N.L.	4-2
907	Chicago N.L.	Detroit A.L.	*4-0
908	Chicago N.L.	Detroit A.L.	4-1
909	Pittsburgh N.L.	Detroit A.L.	4-3
910	Philadelphia A.L.	Chicago N.L.	4-1
911	Philadelphia A.L.	New York N.L.	4-2
912	Boston A.L.	New York N.L.	*4-3
913	Philadelphia A.L.	New York N.L.	4-1
914	Boston N.L.	Philadelphia A.L.	4-0
915	Boston A.L.	Philadelphia N.L.	4-1
916	Boston A.L.	Brooklyn N.L.	4-1
917	Chicago A.L.	New York N.L.	4-2
918	Boston A.L.	Chicago N.L.	4-2
919	Cincinnati N.L.	Chicago A.L.	5-3
920	Cleveland A.L.	Brooklyn N.L.	5-2
921	New York N.L.	New York A.L.	5-3
922	New York N.L.	New York A.L.	*4-0
923	New York A.L.	New York N.L.	4-2
924	Washington A.L.	New York N.L.	4-3
925	Pittsburgh N.L.	Washington A.L.	4-3
926	St. Louis N.L.	New York A.L.	4-3
927	New York A.L.	Pittsburgh N.L.	4-0
928	New York A.L.	St. Louis N.L.	4-0
929	Philadelphia A.L.	Chicago N.L.	4-1
930	Philadelphia A.L.	St. Louis N.L.	4-2
931	St. Louis N.L.	Philadelphia A.L.	4-3
932	New York A.L.	Chicago N.L.	4-0
933	New York N.L.	Washington A.L.	4-1
934	St. Louis N.L.	Detroit A.L.	4-3
935	Detroit A.L.	Chicago N.L.	4-2
936	New York A.L.	New York N.L.	4-2
937	New York A.L.	New York N.L.	4-1
938	New York A.L.	Chicago N.L.	4-0
939	New York A.L.	Cincinnati N.L.	4-0
940	Cincinnati N.L.	Detroit A.L.	4-3
941	New York A.L.	Brooklyn N.L.	4-1
942	St. Louis N.L.	New York A.L.	4-1
943	New York A.L.	St. Louis N.L.	4-1
944	St. Louis N.L.	St. Louis A.L.	4-2
945	Detroit A.L.	Chicago N.L.	4-3
946	St. Louis N.L.	Boston A.L.	4-3
947	New York A.L.	Brooklyn N.L.	4-3
948	Cleveland A.L.	Boston N.L.	4-2
949	New York A.L.	Brooklyn N.L.	4-1
950	New York A.L.	Philadelphia N.L.	4-0
951	New York A.L.	New York N.L.	4-2
952	New York A.L.	Brooklyn N.L.	4-3
953	New York A.L.	Brooklyn N.L.	4-2
954	New York N.L.	Cleveland A.L.	4-0
955	Brooklyn N.L.	New York A.L.	4-3
956	New York A.L.	Brooklyn N.L.	4-3
957	Milwaukee N.L.	New York A.L.	4-3
958	New York A.L.	Milwaukee N.L.	4-3
959	Los Angeles N.L.	Chicago A.L.	4-2
960	Pittsburgh N.L.	New York A.L.	4-3
961	New York A.L.	Cincinnati N.L.	4-1
962	New York A.L.	San Francisco N.L.	4-3
963	Los Angeles N.L.	New York A.L.	4-0
964	St. Louis N.L.	New York A.L.	4-3
965	Los Angeles N.L.	Minnesota A.L.	4-3
966	Baltimore A.L.	Los Angeles N.L.	4-0
967	St. Louis N.L.	Boston A.L.	4-3
968	Detroit A.L.	St. Louis N.L.	4-3
969	New York N.L.	Baltimore A.L.	4-1
970	Baltimore A.L.	Cincinnati N.L.	4-1

Year	Winner	Loser	Games
1971	Pittsburgh N.L.	Baltimore A.L.	4-3
1972	Oakland A.L.	Cincinnati N.L.	4-3
1973	Oakland A.L.	New York N.L.	4-3
1974	Oakland A.L.	Los Angeles N.L.	4-1
1975	Cincinnati N.L.	Boston A.L.	4-3
1976	Cincinnati N.L.	New York A.L.	4-0
1977	New York A.L.	Los Angeles N.L.	4-2
1978	New York A.L.	Los Angeles N.L.	4-2
1979	Pittsburgh N.L.	Baltimore A.L.	4-3
1980	Philadelphia N.L.	Kansas City A.L.	4-2
1981	Los Angeles N.L.	New York A.L.	4-2
1982	St. Louis N.L.	Milwaukee A.L.	4-3
1983	Baltimore A.L.	Philadelphia N.L.	4-1
1984	Detroit A.L.	San Diego N.L.	4-1
1985	Kansas City A.L.	St. Louis N.L.	4-3
1986	New York N.L.	Boston A.L.	4-3
1987	Minnesota A.L.	St. Louis N.L.	4-3
1988	Los Angeles N.L.	Oakland A.L.	4-1
1989	Oakland A.L.	San Francisco N.L.	4-0
1990	Cincinnati N.L.	Oakland A.L.	4-0
1991	Minnesota A.L.	Atlanta N.L.	4-3
1992	Toronto A.L.	Atlanta N.L.	4-2
1993	Toronto A.L.	Philadelphia N.L.	4-2
1994	No series played.		
1995	Atlanta N.L.	Cleveland A.L.	4-2
1996	New York A.L.	Atlanta N.L.	4-2
1997	Florida N.L.	Cleveland A.L.	4-3
1998	New York A.L.	San Diego N.L.	4-0
1999	New York A.L.	Atlanta N.L.	4-0
2000	New York A.L.	New York N.L.	4-1
2001	Arizona N.L.	New York A.L.	4-3

SERIES WON AND LOST BY TEAMS

AMERICAN LEAGUE

	W	L	Pct.
Toronto	2	0	1.000
New York	26	12	.684
Oakland	4	2	.667
Minnesota	2	1	.667
Philadelphia	5	3	.625
Boston	5	4	.556
Baltimore	3	3	.500
Chicago	2	2	.500
Kansas City	1	1	.500
Detroit	4	5	.444
Cleveland	2	3	.400
Washington	1	2	.333
Milwaukee	0	1	.000
St. Louis	0	1	.000
Totals	57	40	.588

NATIONAL LEAGUE

	W	L	Pct.
Arizona	1	0	1.000
Florida	1	0	1.000
Pittsburgh	5	2	.714
St. Louis	9	6	.600
Cincinnati	5	4	.556
Los Angeles	5	4	.555
New York Mets	2	2	.500
Boston	1	1	.500
Milwaukee	1	1	.500
New York Giants	5	9	.357
Atlanta	1	4	.200
Philadelphia	1	4	.200
Chicago	2	8	.200
Brooklyn	1	8	.111
San Diego	0	2	.000
San Francisco	0	2	.000
Totals	40	57	.412

GAMES WON AND LOST BY TEAMS

*Includes one tie per asterisk.

AMERICAN LEAGUE

	W	L	Pct.
Toronto	8	4	.667
New York*	128	84	.604
Baltimore	19	14	.576
Boston*	33	26	.559
Philadelphia	24	19	.558
Oakland	17	15	.531
Minnesota	11	10	.524
Chicago	13	13	.500
Detroit*	26	29	.473
Cleveland	14	16	.467
Kansas City	6	7	.462
Milwaukee	3	4	.429
Washington	8	11	.421
St. Louis	2	4	.333
Totals	312	256	.549

NATIONAL LEAGUE

	W	L	Pct.
Boston	6	4	.600
Arizona	4	3	.571
Florida	4	3	.571
Los Angeles	25	24	.510
Cincinnati	26	25	.510
St. Louis	48	48	.500
New York Mets	12	12	.500
Milwaukee	7	7	.500
Pittsburgh	23	24	.489
New York Giants**	39	41	.488
Atlanta	11	18	.379
Chicago*	19	33	.365
Brooklyn	20	36	.357
Philadelphia	8	18	.308
San Francisco	3	8	.273
San Diego	1	8	.111
Totals	256	312	.451

HOME AND ROAD GAMES BY TEAMS

AMERICAN LEAGUE

	Years	Games	Home	Away
New York	38	213	103	110
Boston	9	60	31	29
Detroit	9	56	28	28
Philadelphia	8	43	20	23
Baltimore	6	33	17	16
Oakland	6	32	17	15
Chicago	4	26	13	13
Cleveland	5	30	15	15
Minnesota	3	21	12	9
Washington	3	19	10	9
Kansas City	2	13	7	6
Toronto	2	12	6	6
Milwaukee	1	7	3	4
St. Louis	1	6	3	3
Totals	97	571	285	286

NATIONAL LEAGUE

	Years	Games	Home	Away
St. Louis	15	96	47	49
New York Giants	14	82	41	41
Brooklyn	9	56	28	28
Chicago	10	53	27	26
Cincinnati	9	51	26	25
Los Angeles	9	49	23	26
Pittsburgh	7	47	23	24
Philadelphia	5	26	14	12
Atlanta	5	29	14	15
New York Mets	4	24	13	11
Milwaukee	2	14	7	7
San Francisco	2	11	6	5
Boston	2	10	5	5
San Diego	2	9	4	5
Arizona	1	7	4	3
Florida	1	7	4	3
Totals	97	571	286	285

TIE GAMES

Oct. 8, 1907—12 innings, Chicago N.L. 3, Detroit A.L. 3.
Oct. 9, 1912—11 innings, Boston A.L. 6, New York N.L. 6.
Oct. 5, 1922—10 innings, New York A.L. 3, New York N.L. 3.
Total number of ties: 3

SHUTOUTS

Oct. 2, 1903 Bill Dinneen, Boston A.L. 3, Pittsburgh N.L. 0 (three hits).

Oct. 13, 1903 Bill Dinneen, Boston A.L. 3, Pittsburgh N.L. 0 (four hits).

Oct. 9, 1905 Christy Mathewson, New York N.L. 3, Philadelphia A.L. 0 (four hits).

Oct. 10, 1905 Chief Bender, Philadelphia A.L. 3, New York N.L. 0 (four hits).

Oct. 12, 1905 Christy Mathewson, New York N.L. 9, Philadelphia A.L. 0 (four hits).

Oct. 13, 1905 Joe McGinnity, New York N.L. 1, Philadelphia A.L. 0 (five hits).

Oct. 14, 1905 Christy Mathewson, New York N.L. 2, Philadelphia A.L. 0 (six hits).

Oct. 11, 1906 Ed Walsh, Chicago A.L. 3, Chicago N.L. 0 (two hits).

Oct. 12, 1906 Mordecai Brown, Chicago N.L. 1, Chicago A.L. 0 (two hits).

Oct. 12, 1907 Mordecai Brown, Chicago N.L. 2, Detroit A.L. 0 (seven hits).

Oct. 13, 1908 Mordecai Brown, Chicago N.L. 3, Detroit A.L. 0 (four hits).

Oct. 14, 1908 Orval Overall, Chicago N.L. 2, Detroit A.L. 0 (three hits).

Oct. 12, 1909 George Mullin, Detroit A.L. 5, Pittsburgh N.L. 0 (five hits).

Oct. 16, 1909 Babe Adams, Pittsburgh N.L. 8, Detroit A.L. 0 (six hits).

Oct. 8, 1913 Christy Mathewson, New York N.L. 3, Philadelphia A.L. 0, 10 innings (eight hits).

Oct. 10, 1914 Bill James, Boston N.L. 1, Philadelphia A.L. 0 (two hits).

Oct. 10, 1917 Rube Benton, New York N.L. 2, Chicago A.L. 0 (five hits).

Oct. 11, 1917 Ferdie Schupp, New York N.L. 5, Chicago A.L. 0 (seven hits).

Sept. 5, 1918 Babe Ruth, Boston A.L. 1, Chicago N.L. 0 (six hits).

Sept. 10, 1918 Hippo Vaughn, Chicago N.L. 3, Boston A.L. 0 (five hits).

Oct. 3, 1919 Dickie Kerr, Chicago A.L. 3, Cincinnati N.L. 0 (three hits).

Oct. 4, 1919 Jimmy Ring, Cincinnati N.L. 2, Chicago A.L. 0 (three hits).

Oct. 6, 1919 Hod Eller, Cincinnati N.L. 5, Chicago A.L. 0 (three hits).

Oct. 6, 1920 Burleigh Grimes, Brooklyn N.L. 3, Cleveland A.L. 0 (seven hits).

Oct. 11, 1920 Duster Mails, Cleveland A.L. 1, Brooklyn N.L. 0 (three hits).

Oct. 12, 1920 Stan Coveleski, Cleveland A.L. 3, Brooklyn N.L. 0 (five hits).

Oct. 5, 1921 Carl Mays, New York A.L. 3, New York N.L. 0 (five hits).

Oct. 6, 1921 Waite Hoyt, New York A.L. 3, New York N.L. 0 (two hits).

Oct. 13, 1921 Art Nehf, New York N.L. 1, New York A.L. 0 (four hits).

Oct. 6, 1922 Jack Scott, New York N.L. 3, New York A.L. 0 (four hits).

Oct. 12, 1923 Art Nehf, New York N.L. 1, New York A.L. 0 (six hits).

Oct. 11, 1925 Walter Johnson, Washington A.L. 4, Pittsburgh N.L. 0 (six hits).

Oct. 5, 1926 Jesse Haines, St. Louis N.L. 4, New York A.L. 0 (five hits).

Oct. 4, 1930 Bill Hallahan, St. Louis N.L. 5, Philadelphia A.L. 0 (seven hits).

Oct. 6, 1930 George Earnshaw and Lefty Grove, Philadelphia A.L. 2, St. Louis N.L. 0 (three hits).

Oct. 2, 1931 Bill Hallahan, St. Louis N.L. 2, Philadelphia A.L. 0 (three hits).

Oct. 6, 1931 George Earnshaw, Philadelphia A.L. 3, St. Louis N.L. 0 (two hits).

Oct. 5, 1933 Earl Whitehill, Washington A.L. 4, New York N.L. 0 (five hits).

Oct. 9, 1934 Dizzy Dean, St. Louis N.L. 11, Detroit A.L. 0 (six hits).

Oct. 2, 1935 Lon Warneke, Chicago N.L. 3, Detroit A.L. 0 (four hits).

Oct. 5, 1939 Monte Pearson, New York A.L. 4, Cincinnati N.L. 0 (two hits).

Oct. 6, 1940 Bobo Newsom, Detroit A.L. 8, Cincinnati N.L. 0 (three hits).

Oct. 7, 1940 Bucky Walters, Cincinnati N.L. 4, Detroit A.L. 0 (five hits).

Oct. 3, 1942 Ernie White, St. Louis N.L. 2, New York A.L. 0 (six hits).

Oct. 11, 1943 Spud Chandler, New York A.L. 2, St. Louis N.L. 0 (10 hits).

Oct. 8, 1944 Mort Cooper, St. Louis N.L. 2, St. Louis A.L. 0 (seven hits).

Oct. 3, 1945 Hank Borowy, Chicago N.L. 9, Detroit A.L. 0 (six hits).

Oct. 5, 1945 Claude Passeau, Chicago N.L. 3, Detroit A.L. 0 (one hit).

Oct. 7, 1946 Harry Brecheen, St. Louis N.L. 3, Boston A.L. 0 (four hits).

Oct. 9, 1946 Boo Ferriss, Boston A.L. 4, St. Louis N.L. 0 (six hits).

Oct. 6, 1948 Johnny Sain, Boston N.L. 1, Cleveland A.L. 0 (four hits).

Oct. 8, 1948 Gene Bearden, Cleveland A.L. 2, Boston N.L. 0 (five hits).

Oct. 5, 1949 Allie Reynolds, New York A.L. 1, Brooklyn N.L. 0 (two hits).

Oct. 6, 1949 Preacher Roe, Brooklyn N.L. 1, New York A.L. 0 (six hits).

Oct. 4, 1950 Vic Raschi, New York A.L. 1, Philadelphia N.L. 0 (two hits).

Oct. 4, 1952 Allie Reynolds, New York A.L. 2, Brooklyn N.L. 0 (four hits).

Oct. 4, 1955 Johnny Podres, Brooklyn N.L. 2, New York A.L. 0 (eight hits).

Oct. 8, 1956 Don Larsen, New York A.L. 2, Brooklyn N.L. 0 (no hits).

Oct. 9, 1956 Clem Labine, Brooklyn N.L. 1, New York A.L. 0, 10 innings (seven hits).

Oct. 10, 1956 Johnny Kucks, New York A.L. 9, Brooklyn N.L. 0 (three hits).

Oct. 7, 1957 Lew Burdette, Milwaukee N.L. 1, New York A.L. 0 (seven hits).

Oct. 10, 1957 Lew Burdette, Milwaukee N.L. 5, New York A.L. 0 (seven hits).

Oct. 4, 1958 Don Larsen and Ryne Duren, New York A.L. 4, Milwaukee N.L. 0 (six hits).

Oct. 5, 1958 Warren Spahn, Milwaukee N.L. 3, New York A.L., 0 (two hits).

Oct. 6, 1958 Bob Turley, New York A.L. 7, Milwaukee N.L. 0 (five hits).

Oct. 1, 1959 Early Wynn and Gerry Staley, Chicago A.L. 11, Los Angeles N.L. 0 (eight hits).

Oct. 6, 1959 Bob Shaw, Billy Pierce and Dick Donovan, Chicago A.L. 1, Los Angeles N.L. 0 (nine hits).

Oct. 8, 1960 Whitey Ford, New York A.L. 10, Pittsburgh N.L. 0 (four hits).

Oct. 12, 1960 Whitey Ford, New York A.L. 12, Pittsburgh N.L. 0 (seven hits).

Oct. 4, 1961 Whitey Ford, New York A.L. 2, Cincinnati N.L. 0 (two hits).

Oct. 8, 1961 Whitey Ford and Jim Coates, New York A.L. 7, Cincinnati N.L. 0 (five hits).

Oct. 5, 1962 Jack Sanford, San Francisco N.L. 2, New York A.L. 0 (three hits).

Oct. 16, 1962 Ralph Terry, New York A.L. 1, San Francisco N.L. 0 (four hits).

Oct. 5, 1963 Don Drysdale, Los Angeles N.L. 1, New York A.L. 0 (three hits).

Oct. 9, 1965 Claude Osteen, Los Angeles N.L. 4, Minnesota A.L. 0 (five hits).

Oct. 11, 1965 Sandy Koufax, Los Angeles N.L. 7, Minnesota A.L. 0 (four hits).

Oct. 14, 1965 Sandy Koufax, Los Angeles N.L. 2, Minnesota A.L. 0 (three hits).

Oct. 6, 1966 Jim Palmer, Baltimore A.L. 6, Los Angeles N.L. 0 (four hits).

Oct. 8, 1966 Wally Bunker, Baltimore A.L. 1, Los Angeles N.L. 0 (six hits).

Oct. 9, 1966 Dave McNally, Baltimore A.L. 1, Los Angeles N.L. 0 (four hits).

Oct. 5, 1967 Jim Lonborg, Boston A.L. 5, St. Louis N.L. 0 (one hit).

Oct. 8, 1967 Bob Gibson, St. Louis N.L. 6, Boston A.L. 0 (five hits).

Oct. 2, 1968 Bob Gibson, St. Louis N.L. 4, Detroit A.L. 0 (five hits).

Oct. 14, 1969 Gary Gentry and Nolan Ryan, New York N.L. 5, Baltimore A.L. 0 (four hits).

Oct. 14, 1971 Nelson Briles, Pittsburgh N.L. 4, Baltimore A.L. 0 (two hits).

Oct. 18, 1972 Jack Billingham and Clay Carroll, Cincinnati N.L. 1, Oakland A.L. 0 (three hits).

Oct. 18, 1973 Jerry Koosman and Tug McGraw, New York N.L. 2, Oakland A.L. 0 (three hits).

Oct. 11, 1975 Luis Tiant, Boston A.L. 6, Cincinnati N.L. 0 (five hits).

Oct. 16, 1979 John Candelaria and Kent Tekulve, Pittsburgh N.L. 4, Baltimore A.L. 0 (seven hits).

Oct. 21, 1981 Tommy John and Rich Gossage, New York A.L., 3 Los Angeles N.L. 0 (four hits).

Oct. 12, 1982 Mike Caldwell, Milwaukee A.L. 10, St. Louis N.L. 0 (three hits).

Oct. 16, 1983 Scott McGregor, Baltimore A.L. 5, Philadelphia N.L. 0 (five hits).

Oct. 23, 1985 John Tudor, St. Louis N.L. 3, Kansas City A.L. 0 (five hits).

Oct. 27, 1985 Bret Saberhagen, Kansas City A.L. 11, St. Louis N.L. 0 (five hits).

Oct. 18, 1986 Bruce Hurst and Calvin Schiraldi, Boston A.L. 1, New York N.L. 0 (five hits).

Oct. 16, 1988 Orel Hershiser, Los Angeles N.L. 6, Oakland A.L. 0 (three hits).

Oct. 14, 1989 Dave Stewart, Oakland A.L. 5, San Francisco N.L. 0 (five hits).

Oct. 16, 1990 Jose Rijo, Rob Dibble and Randy Myers, Cincinnati N.L. 7, Oakland A.L. 0 (nine hits).

Oct. 27, 1991 Jack Morris, Minnesota A.L. 1, Atlanta N.L. 0, 10 innings (seven hits).

Oct. 21, 1993 Curt Schilling, Philadelphia N.L. 2, Toronto A.L. 0 (five hits).

Oct. 28, 1995 Tom Glavine, Atlanta N.L. 1, Cleveland A.L. 0 (one hit).

Oct. 21, 1996 Greg Maddux, Atlanta N.L. 4, New York A.L. 0 (seven hits).

Oct. 24, 1996 Andy Pettitte and John Wetteland, New York A.L. 1, Atlanta N.L. 0 (seven hits).

Oct. 21, 1998 Andy Pettitte, Jeff Nelson and Mariano Rivera, New York A.L. 3, San Diego N.L. 0 (seven hits).

Oct. 28, 2001 Randy Johnson, Arizona N.L. 4, New York A.L. 0 (three hits).

Total number of shutouts: 105

EXTRA-INNING GAMES

Oct. 8, 1907 12 innings, Chicago N.L. 3, Detroit A.L. 3 (tie).

Oct. 22, 1910 10 innings, Chicago N.L. 4, Philadelphia A.L. 3.

Oct. 17, 1911	11 innings, Philadelphia A.L. 3, New York N.L. 2.
Oct. 25, 1911	10 innings, New York N.L. 4, Philadelphia A.L. 3.
Oct. 9, 1912	11 innings, Boston A.L., 6, New York N.L. 6 (tie).
Oct. 16, 1912	10 innings, Boston A.L. 3, New York N.L. 2.
Oct. 8, 1913	10 innings, New York N.L. 3, Philadelphia A.L. 0.
Oct. 12, 1914	12 innings, Boston N.L. 5, Philadelphia A.L. 4.
Oct. 9, 1916	14 innings, Boston A.L. 2, Brooklyn N.L. 1.
Oct. 7, 1919	10 innings, Chicago A.L. 5, Cincinnati N.L. 4.
Oct. 5, 1922	10 innings, New York N.L. 3, New York A.L. 3 (tie).
Oct. 4, 1924	12 innings, New York N.L. 4, Washington A.L. 3.
Oct. 10, 1924	12 innings, Washington A.L. 4, New York N.L. 3.
Oct. 7, 1926	10 innings, New York A.L. 3, St. Louis N.L. 2.
Oct. 6, 1933	11 innings, New York N.L. 2, Washington A.L. 1.
Oct. 7, 1933	10 innings, New York N.L. 4, Washington A.L. 3.
Oct. 4, 1934	12 innings, Detroit A.L. 3, St. Louis N.L. 2.
Oct. 4, 1935	11 innings, Detroit A.L. 6, Chicago N.L. 5.
Oct. 5, 1936	10 innings, New York A.L. 5, New York A.L. 4.
Oct. 8, 1939	10 innings, New York A.L. 7, Cincinnati N.L. 4.
Oct. 5, 1944	11 innings, St. Louis N.L. 3, St. Louis A.L. 2.
Oct. 8, 1945	12 innings, Chicago N.L. 8, Detroit A.L. 7.
Oct. 6, 1946	10 innings, Boston A.L. 3, St. Louis N.L. 2.
Oct. 5, 1950	10 innings, New York A.L. 2, Philadelphia N.L. 1.
Oct. 5, 1952	11 innings, Brooklyn N.L. 6, New York A.L. 5.
Sept. 29, 1954	10 innings, New York N.L. 5, Cleveland A.L. 2.
Oct. 9, 1956	10 innings, Brooklyn N.L. 1, New York A.L. 0.
Oct. 6, 1957	10 innings, Milwaukee N.L. 7, New York A.L. 5.
Oct. 1, 1958	10 innings, Milwaukee N.L. 4, New York A.L. 3.
Oct. 8, 1958	10 innings, New York A.L. 4, Milwaukee N.L. 3.
Oct. 12, 1964	10 innings, St. Louis N.L. 5, New York A.L. 2.
Oct. 15, 1969	10 innings, New York N.L. 2, Baltimore A.L. 1.
Oct. 16, 1971	10 innings, Baltimore A.L. 3, Pittsburgh N.L. 2.
Oct. 14, 1973	12 innings, New York N.L. 10, Oakland A.L. 7.
Oct. 16, 1973	11 innings, Oakland A.L. 3, New York N.L. 2.
Oct. 14, 1975	10 innings, Cincinnati N.L. 6, Boston A.L. 5.
Oct. 21, 1975	12 innings, Boston A.L. 7, Cincinnati N.L. 6.
Oct. 11, 1977	12 innings, New York A.L. 4, Los Angeles N.L. 3.
Oct. 14, 1978	10 innings, New York A.L. 4, Los Angeles N.L. 3.
Oct. 17, 1980	10 innings, Kansas City A.L. 4, Philadelphia N.L. 3.
Oct. 25, 1986	10 innings, New York N.L. 6, Boston A.L. 5.
Oct. 17, 1990	10 innings, Cincinnati N.L. 5, Oakland A.L. 4.
Oct. 22, 1991	12 innings, Atlanta N.L. 5, Minnesota A.L. 4.
Oct. 26, 1991	11 innings, Minnesota A.L. 4, Atlanta N.L. 3.
Oct. 27, 1991	10 innings, Minnesota A.L. 1, Atlanta N.L. 0.
Oct. 24, 1992	11 innings, Toronto A.L. 4, Atlanta N.L. 3.
Oct. 24, 1995	11 innings, Cleveland A.L. 7, Atlanta N.L. 6.
Oct. 23, 1996	10 innings, New York A.L. 8, Atlanta N.L. 6.
Oct. 26, 1997	11 innings, Florida N.L. 3, Cleveland A.L. 2.
Oct. 26, 1999	10 innings, New York A.L. 4, Atlanta N.L. 5.
Oct. 21, 2000	12 innings, New York A.L. 4, New York N.L. 3.
Oct. 31, 2001	10 innings, New York A.L. 4, Arizona N.L. 3.
Nov. 1, 2001	12 innings, New York A.L. 3, Arizona N.L. 2.

Total number of occurrences: 52

ATTENDANCE

Year	Games	Total	Year	Games	Total
1903	8	100,429	1925	7	282,848
1905	5	91,723	1926	7	328,051
1906	6	99,845	1927	4	201,705
1907	5	78,068	1928	4	199,072
1908	5	62,232	1929	5	190,490
1909	7	145,295	1930	6	212,619
1910	5	124,222	1931	7	231,567
1911	6	179,851	1932	4	191,998
1912	8	252,037	1933	5	163,076
1913	5	151,000	1934	7	281,510
1914	4	111,009	1935	6	286,672
1915	5	143,351	1936	6	302,924
1916	5	162,859	1937	5	238,142
1917	6	186,654	1938	4	200,833
1918	6	128,483	1939	4	183,849
1919	8	236,928	1940	7	281,927
1920	7	178,737	1941	5	235,773
1921	8	269,976	1942	5	277,101
1922	5	185,947	1943	5	277,312
1923	6	301,430	1944	6	206,708
1924	7	283,665	1945	7	333,457

Year	Games	Total	Year	Games	Total
1946	7	250,071	1974	5	260,004
1947	7	389,763	1975	7	308,272
1948	6	358,362	1976	4	223,009
1949	5	236,716	1977	6	337,708
1950	4	196,009	1978	6	337,304
1951	6	341,977	1979	7	367,597
1952	7	340,706	1980	6	324,516
1953	6	307,350	1981	6	338,081
1954	4	251,507	1982	7	384,570
1955	7	362,310	1983	5	304,139
1956	7	345,903	1984	5	271,820
1957	7	394,712	1985	7	327,494
1958	7	393,909	1986	7	321,774
1959	6	420,784	1987	7	387,138
1960	7	349,813	1988	5	259,984
1961	5	223,247	1989	4	222,843
1962	7	376,864	1990	4	208,544
1963	4	247,279	1991	7	373,160
1964	7	321,807	1992	6	311,460
1965	7	364,326	1993	6	344,394
1966	4	220,791	1994		No World Series
1967	7	304,085	1995	6	286,385
1968	7	379,670	1996	6	324,685
1969	5	272,378	1997	7	403,617
1970	5	253,183	1998	4	243,498
1971	7	351,091	1999	4	216,114
1972	7	363,149	2000	5	277,853
1973	7	358,289	2001	7	366,289

INDIVIDUAL BATTING
LEADING BATTERS

(Playing in all games, each series; capitalized name denotes leader o
tied for series lead, both teams)

AMERICAN LEAGUE

Year	Player, Club	AB	H	TB	Avg
1903	Chick Stahl, Boston	33	10	17	.30.
1904	No series played.				
1905	Topsy Hartsel, Philadelphia	17	5	6	.294
1906	GEORGE ROHE, Chicago	21	7	12	.33.
	JIGGS DONAHUE, Chicago	18	6	10	.33.
1907	Claude Rossman, Detroit	20	8	10	.40.
1908	Ty Cobb, Detroit	19	7	8	.36.
1909	JIM DELAHANTY, Detroit	26	9	13	.34.
1910	EDDIE COLLINS, Philadelphia	21	9	13	.42.
1911	HOME RUN BAKER, Philadelphia	24	9	17	.375
1912	Tris Speaker, Boston	30	9	14	.30.
1913	Home Run Baker, Philadelphia	20	9	12	.45.
1914	Home Run Baker, Philadelphia	16	4	6	.25.
1915	DUFFY LEWIS, Boston	18	8	12	.444
1916	DUFFY LEWIS, Boston	17	6	10	.353
1917	Eddie Collins, Chicago	22	9	10	.40.
1918	Stuffy McInnis, Boston	20	5	5	.25.
	George Whiteman, Boston	20	5	7	.25.
1919	JOE JACKSON, Chicago	32	12	18	.375
1920	STEVE O'NEILL, Cleveland	21	7	10	.33.
1921	Wally Schang, New York	21	6	9	.296
1922	Bob Meusel, New York	20	6	7	.30.
1923	AARON WARD, New York	24	10	13	.417
1924	JOE JUDGE, Washington	26	10	11	.385
1925	Bucky Harris, Washington	25	11	22	.44.
1926	Earle Combs, New York	28	10	12	.357
1927	MARK KOENIG, New York	18	9	11	.50.
1928	BABE RUTH, New York	16	10	22	.625
1929	Jimmie Dykes, Philadelphia	19	8	9	.421
1930	AL SIMMONS, Philadelphia	22	8	16	.364
1931	Jimmie Foxx, Philadelphia	23	8	11	.348
1932	LOU GEHRIG, New York	17	9	19	.529
1933	Fred Schulte, Washington	21	7	21	.333
1934	CHARLIE GEHRINGER, Detroit	29	11	15	.379
1935	PETE FOX, Detroit	26	10	15	.385
1936	JAKE POWELL, New York	22	10	14	.455
1937	TONY LAZZERI, New York	15	6	11	.400
1938	Bill Dickey, New York	15	6	9	.400
	Joe Gordon, New York	15	6	11	.400

Year	Player, Club	AB	H	TB	Avg.
1939	CHARLIE KELLER, New York	16	7	19	.438
1940	Bruce Campbell, Detroit	25	9	13	.360
1941	JOE GORDON, New York	14	7	13	.500
1942	PHIL RIZZUTO, New York	21	8	11	.381
1943	Billy Johnson, New York	20	6	9	.300
1944	GEORGE McQUINN, St. Louis	16	7	12	.438
1945	Roger Cramer, Detroit	29	11	11	.379
1946	Rudy York, Boston	23	6	15	.261
1947	TOMMY HENRICH, New York	31	10	15	.323
1948	Larry Doby, Cleveland	22	7	11	.318
1949	Tommy Henrich, New York	19	5	8	.263
1950	GENE WOODLING, New York	14	6	6	.429
1951	Phil Rizzuto, New York	25	8	11	.320
1952	GENE WOODLING, New York	23	8	14	.348
1953	BILLY MARTIN, New York	24	12	23	.500
1954	VIC WERTZ, Cleveland	16	8	15	.500
1955	YOGI BERRA, New York	24	10	14	.417
1956	YOGI BERRA, New York	25	9	20	.360
1957	Jerry Coleman, New York	22	8	10	.364
1958	Hank Bauer, New York	31	10	22	.323
1959	TED KLUSZEWSKI, Chicago	23	9	19	.391
1960	MICKEY MANTLE, New York	25	10	20	.400
1961	BOBBY RICHARDSON, New York	23	9	10	.391
1962	Tom Tresh, New York	28	9	13	.321
1963	Elston Howard, New York	15	5	5	.333
1964	Bobby Richardson, New York	32	13	15	.406
1965	Zoilo Versalles, Minnesota	28	8	14	.286
	Harmon Killebrew, Minnesota	21	6	9	.286
1966	BOOG POWELL, Baltimore	14	5	6	.357
1967	Carl Yastrzemski, Boston	25	10	21	.400
1968	Norm Cash, Detroit	26	10	13	.385
1969	Boog Powell, Baltimore	19	5	5	.263
1970	PAUL BLAIR, Baltimore	19	9	10	.474
1971	Brooks Robinson, Baltimore	22	7	7	.318
1972	Gene Tenace, Oakland	23	8	21	.348
1973	Joe Rudi, Oakland	27	9	11	.333
1974	Bert Campaneris, Oakland	17	6	8	.353
1975	Carl Yastrzemski, Boston	29	9	9	.310
1976	Thurman Munson, New York	17	9	9	.529
1977	REGGIE JACKSON, New York	20	9	25	.450
1978	BRIAN DOYLE, New York	16	7	8	.438
1979	Ken Singleton, Baltimore	28	10	11	.357
1980	AMOS OTIS, Kansas City	23	11	22	.478
1981	LOU PINIELLA, New York	16	7	8	.438
1982	ROBIN YOUNT, Milwaukee	29	12	18	.414
1983	JOHN SHELBY, Baltimore	9	4	4	.444
1984	ALAN TRAMMELL, Detroit	20	9	16	.450
1985	GEORGE BRETT, Kansas City	27	10	11	.370
1986	MARTY BARRETT, Boston	30	13	15	.433
1987	Kirby Puckett, Minnesota	28	10	13	.357
1988	Dave Henderson, Oakland	20	6	8	.300
1989	RICKEY HENDERSON, Oakland	19	9	17	.474
1990	Rickey Henderson, Oakland	15	5	10	.333
1991	BRIAN HARPER, Minnesota	21	8	10	.381
1992	PAT BORDERS, Toronto	20	9	15	.450
1993	PAUL MOLITOR, Toronto	24	12	24	.500
1994	No series played.				
1995	Albert Belle, Cleveland	17	4	10	.235
1996	Cecil Fielder, New York	23	9	11	.391
1997	Matt Williams, Cleveland	26	10	14	.385
1998	RICKY LEDEE, New York	10	6	9	.600
1999	Scott Brosius, New York	16	6	7	.375
2000	PAUL O'NEILL, New York	19	9	15	.474
2001	Alfonso Soriano, New York	25	6	9	.240

NATIONAL LEAGUE

Year	Player, Club	AB	H	TB	Avg.
1903	JIMMY SEBRING, Pittsburgh	30	11	16	.367
1904	—No series played.				
1905	MIKE DONLIN, New York	19	6	7	.316
1906	Solly Hofman, Chicago	23	7	8	.304
1907	HARRY STEINFELDT, Chicago	17	8	11	.471
1908	FRANK CHANCE, Chicago	19	8	8	.421
1909	Honus Wagner, Pittsburgh	24	8	12	.333
1910	Frank Schulte, Chicago	17	6	9	.353
	Frank Chance, Chicago	17	6	9	.353
1911	Larry Doyle, New York	23	7	12	.304
1912	BUCK HERZOG, New York	30	12	18	.400
1913	LARRY McLEAN, New York	12	6	6	.500
1914	HANK GOWDY, Boston	11	6	14	.545
1915	Fred Luderus, Philadelphia	16	7	12	.438
1916	Ivy Olson, Brooklyn	16	4	6	.250
1917	DAVE ROBERTSON, New York	22	11	14	.500
1918	CHARLIE PICK, Chicago	18	7	8	.389
1919	Greasy Neale, Cincinnati	28	10	13	.357
1920	ZACH WHEAT, Brooklyn	27	9	11	.333
1921	IRISH MEUSEL, New York	29	10	17	.345
1922	HEINIE GROH, New York	19	9	11	.474
1923	CASEY STENGEL, New York	12	5	11	.417
1924	Frankie Frisch, New York	30	10	16	.333
	Fred Lindstrom, New York	30	10	12	.333
1925	MAX CAREY, Pittsburgh	24	11	15	.458
1926	TOMMY THEVENOW, St. Louis	24	10	14	.417
1927	Lloyd Waner, Pittsburgh	15	6	9	.400
1928	Rabbit Maranville, St. Louis	13	4	5	.308
1929	Hack Wilson, Chicago	17	8	10	.471
1930	Charlie Gelbert, St. Louis	17	6	8	.353
1931	PEPPER MARTIN, St. Louis	24	12	19	.500
1932	Riggs Stephenson, Chicago	18	8	9	.444
1933	MEL OTT, New York	18	7	13	.389
1934	JOE MEDWICK, St. Louis	29	11	16	.379
1935	Billy Herman, Chicago	24	8	15	.333
1936	Dick Bartell, New York	21	8	14	.381
1937	Joe Moore, New York	23	9	10	.391
1938	STAN HACK, Chicago	17	8	9	.471
1939	Frank McCormick, Cincinnati	15	6	7	.400
1940	BILL WERBER, Cincinnati	27	10	14	.370
1941	Joe Medwick, Brooklyn	17	4	5	.235
1942	Jimmy Brown, St. Louis	20	6	6	.300
1943	MARTY MARION, St. Louis	14	5	10	.357
1944	Emil Verban, St. Louis	17	7	7	.412
1945	PHIL CAVARRETTA, Chicago	26	11	16	.423
1946	HARRY WALKER, St. Louis	17	7	9	.412
1947	Pee Wee Reese, Brooklyn	23	7	8	.304
1948	BOB ELLIOTT, Boston	21	7	13	.333
1949	PEE WEE REESE, Brooklyn	19	6	10	.316
1950	GRANNY HAMNER, Philadelphia	14	6	10	.429
1951	MONTE IRVIN, New York	24	11	13	.458
1952	Duke Snider, Brooklyn	29	10	24	.345
	Pee Wee Reese, Brooklyn	29	10	13	.345
1953	Gil Hodges, Brooklyn	22	8	11	.364
1954	Alvin Dark, New York	17	7	7	.412
1955	Duke Snider, Brooklyn	25	8	21	.320
1956	Duke Snider, Brooklyn	23	7	11	.304
	Gil Hodges, Brooklyn	23	7	12	.304
1957	HANK AARON, Milwaukee	28	11	22	.393
1958	BILL BRUTON, Milwaukee	17	7	10	.412
1959	GIL HODGES, Los Angeles	23	9	14	.391
1960	Bill Mazeroski, Pittsburgh	25	8	16	.320
1961	Wally Post, Cincinnati	18	6	10	.333
1962	JOSE PAGAN, San Francisco	19	7	10	.368
1963	TOMMY DAVIS, Los Angeles	15	6	10	.400
1964	TIM McCARVER, St. Louis	23	11	17	.478
1965	RON FAIRLY, Los Angeles	29	11	20	.379
1966	Lou Johnson, Los Angeles	15	4	5	.267
1967	LOU BROCK, St. Louis	29	12	19	.414
1968	LOU BROCK, St. Louis	28	13	24	.464
1969	AL WEIS, New York	11	5	8	.455
1970	Lee May, Cincinnati	18	7	15	.389
1971	ROBERTO CLEMENTE, Pittsburgh	29	12	22	.414
1972	TONY PEREZ, Cincinnati	23	10	12	.435
1973	RUSTY STAUB, New York	26	11	16	.423
1974	STEVE GARVEY, Los Angeles	21	8	8	.381
1975	PETE ROSE, Cincinnati	27	10	13	.370
1976	JOHNNY BENCH, Cincinnati	15	8	17	.533
1977	Steve Garvey, Los Angeles	24	9	15	.375
1978	Bill Russell, Los Angeles	26	11	13	.423
1979	PHIL GARNER, Pittsburgh	24	12	16	.500
1980	Bob Boone, Philadelphia	17	7	9	.412
1981	Steve Garvey, Los Angeles	24	10	11	.417
1982	George Hendrick, St. Louis	28	9	9	.321
	Lonnie Smith, St. Louis	28	9	15	.321

Year	Player, Club	AB	H	TB	Avg.
1983	Bo Diaz, Philadelphia	15	5	6	.333
1984	Kurt Bevacqua, San Diego	17	7	15	.412
1985	Tito Landrum, St. Louis	25	9	14	.360
1986	Lenny Dykstra, New York	27	8	14	.296
1987	TONY PENA, St. Louis	22	9	10	.409
1988	MICKEY HATCHER, Los Angeles	19	7	14	.368
1989	Ken Oberkfell, San Francisco	6	2	2	.333
1990	BILLY HATCHER, Cincinnati	12	9	15	.750
1991	Rafael Belliard, Atlanta	16	6	7	.375
1992	Otis Nixon, Atlanta	27	8	9	.296
1993	Lenny Dykstra, Philadelphia	23	8	21	.348
	John Kruk, Philadelphia	23	8	9	.348
1994	No series played.				
1995	MARQUIS GRISSOM, Atlanta	25	9	10	.360
1996	MARQUIS GRISSOM, Atlanta	27	12	16	.444
1997	DARREN DAULTON, Florida	18	7	12	.389
1998	Tony Gwynn, San Diego	16	8	11	.500
1999	BRET BOONE, Atlanta	13	7	11	.538
2000	Todd Zeile, New York	20	8	10	.400
2001	STEVE FINLEY, Arizona	19	7	10	.368

.450 HITTERS

(Playing in all games and having 10 or more at-bats)

Player, Club	Year	AB	H	TB	Avg.
Billy Hatcher, Cincinnati N.L.	1990	12	9	15	.750
Babe Ruth, New York A.L.	1928	16	10	22	.625
Ricky Ledee, New York A.L.	1998	10	6	9	.600
Chris Sabo, Cincinnati N.L.	1990	16	9	16	.563
Hank Gowdy, Boston N.L.	1914	11	6	14	.545
Lou Gehrig, New York A.L.	1928	11	6	19	.545
Bret Boone, Atlanta N.L.	1999	13	7	11	.538
Johnny Bench, Cincinnati N.L.	1976	15	8	17	.533
Lou Gehrig, New York A.L.	1932	17	9	19	.529
Thurman Munson, New York A.L.	1976	17	9	9	.529
Larry McLean, New York N.L.	1913	12	6	6	.500
Dave Robertson, New York N.L.	1917	22	11	14	.500
Mark Koenig, New York A.L.	1927	18	9	11	.500
Pepper Martin, St. Louis N.L.	1931	24	12	19	.500
Joe Gordon, New York A.L.	1941	14	7	13	.500
Billy Martin, New York A.L.	1953	24	12	23	.500
Vic Wertz, Cleveland A.L.	1954	16	8	15	.500
Phil Garner, Pittsburgh N.L.	1979	24	12	16	.500
Paul Molitor, Toronto A.L.	1993	24	12	24	.500
Tony Gwynn, San Diego N.L.	1998	16	8	11	.500
Roberto Alomar, Toronto A.L.	1993	25	12	16	.480
Tim McCarver, St. Louis N.L.	1964	23	11	17	.478
Amos Otis, Kansas City A.L.	1980	23	11	22	.478
Heinie Groh, New York N.L.	1922	19	9	11	.474
Paul Blair, Baltimore A.L.	1970	19	9	10	.474
Rickey Henderson, Oakland A.L.	1989	19	9	17	.474
Paul O'Neill, New York A.L.	2000	19	9	15	.474
Harry Steinfeldt, Chicago N.L.	1907	17	8	11	.471
Frankie Frisch, New York N.L.	1922	17	8	9	.471
Hack Wilson, Chicago N.L.	1929	17	8	10	.471
Stan Hack, Chicago N.L.	1938	17	8	9	.471
Scott Brosius, New York A.L.	1998	17	8	14	.471
Lou Brock, St. Louis N.L.	1968	28	13	24	.464
Phil Cavarretta, Chicago N.L.	1938	13	6	7	.462
Max Carey, Pittsburgh N.L.	1925	24	11	15	.458
Monte Irvin, New York N.L.	1951	24	11	13	.458
Jake Powell, New York A.L.	1936	22	10	14	.455
Al Weis, New York N.L.	1969	11	5	8	.455
Home Run Baker, Phil. A.L.	1913	20	9	12	.450
Reggie Jackson, New York A.L.	1977	20	9	25	.450
Alan Trammell, Detroit A.L.	1984	20	9	16	.450
Pat Borders, Toronto A.L.	1992	20	9	15	.450

Total number of occurrences: 42

HOME RUNS

AMERICAN LEAGUE

1903—2—Boston, Patsy Dougherty 2.
1904—No series played.
1905—0—Philadelphia.
1906—0—Chicago.
1907—0—Detroit.
1908—0—Detroit.
1909—2—Detroit, Davy Jones, Sam Crawford.
1910—1—Philadelphia, Danny Murphy.
1911—3—Philadelphia, Home Run Baker 2, Rube Oldring.
1912—1—Boston, Larry Gardner.
1913—2—Philadelphia, Home Run Baker, Wally Schang.
1914—0—Philadelphia.
1915—3—Boston, Harry Hooper 2, Duffy Lewis.
1916—2—Boston, Larry Gardner 2.
1917—1—Chicago, Happy Felsch.
1918—0—Boston.
1919—1—Chicago, Joe Jackson.
1920—2—Cleveland, Elmer Smith, Jim Bagby.
1921—2—New York, Babe Ruth, Chick Fewster.
1922—2—New York, Aaron Ward 2.
1923—5—New York, Babe Ruth 3, Aaron Ward, Joe Dugan.
1924—5—Washington, Goose Goslin 3, Bucky Harris 2.
1925—8—Washington, Bucky Harris 3, Goose Goslin 3, Joe Judge, Roger Peckinpaugh.
1926—4—New York, Babe Ruth 4.
1927—2—New York, Babe Ruth 2.
1928—9—New York, Lou Gehrig 4, Babe Ruth 3, Bob Meusel, Cedric Durst.
1929—6—Philadelphia, Jimmie Foxx 2, Al Simmons 2, Mule Haas 2.
1930—6—Philadelphia, Mickey Cochrane 2, Al Simmons 2, Jimmie Foxx, Jimmie Dykes.
1931—3—Philadelphia, Al Simmons 2, Jimmie Foxx.
1932—8—New York, Lou Gehrig 3, Babe Ruth 2, Tony Lazzeri 2, Earle Combs.
1933—2—Washington, Goose Goslin, Fred Schulte.
1934—2—Detroit, Hank Greenberg, Charlie Gehringer.
1935—1—Detroit, Hank Greenberg.
1936—7—New York, Lou Gehrig 2, George Selkirk 2, Tony Lazzeri, Bill Dickey, Jake Powell.
1937—4—New York, Tony Lazzeri, Lou Gehrig, Myril Hoag, Joe DiMaggio.
1938—5—New York, Frank Crosetti, Joe DiMaggio, Joe Gordon, Bill Dickey, Tommy Henrich.
1939—7—New York, Charlie Keller 3, Bill Dickey 2, Babe Dahlgren, Joe DiMaggio.
1940—4—Detroit, Bruce Campbell, Rudy York, Pinky Higgins, Hank Greenberg.
1941—2—New York, Joe Gordon, Tommy Henrich.
1942—3—New York, Charlie Keller 2, Phil Rizzuto.
1943—2—New York, Joe Gordon, Bill Dickey.
1944—1—St. Louis, George McQuinn.
1945—2—Detroit, Hank Greenberg 2.
1946—4—Boston, Rudy York 2, Bobby Doerr, Leon Culberson.
1947—4—New York, Joe DiMaggio 2, Tommy Henrich, Yogi Berra.
1948—4—Cleveland, Larry Doby, Dale Mitchell, Jim Hegan, Joe Gordon.
1949—2—New York, Tommy Henrich, Joe DiMaggio.
1950—2—New York, Joe DiMaggio, Yogi Berra.
1951—5—New York, Joe Collins, Gene Woodling, Joe DiMaggio, Gil McDougald, Phil Rizzuto.
1952—10—New York, Johnny Mize 3, Mickey Mantle 2, Yogi Berra 2, Gil McDougald, Billy Martin, Gene Woodling.
1953—9—New York, Mickey Mantle 2, Gil McDougald 2, Billy Martin 2, Yogi Berra, Joe Collins, Gene Woodling.
1954—3—Cleveland, Al Smith, Vic Wertz, Hank Majeski.
1955—8—New York, Joe Collins 2, Yogi Berra, Bob Cerv, Elston Howard, Mickey Mantle, Gil McDougald, Bill Skowron.
1956—12—New York, Mickey Mantle 3, Yogi Berra 3, Billy Martin 2, Enos Slaughter, Hank Bauer, Elston Howard, Bill Skowron.
1957—7—New York, Hank Bauer 2, Tony Kubek 2, Mickey Mantle, Yogi Berra, Elston Howard.
1958—10—New York, Hank Bauer 4, Gil McDougald 2, Mickey Mantle 2, Bill Skowron 2.
1959—4—Chicago, Ted Kluszewski 3, Sherm Lollar.

1960—10—New York, Mickey Mantle 3, Roger Maris 2, Bill Skowron 2, Yogi Berra, Elston Howard, Bobby Richardson.
1961—7—New York, Johnny Blanchard 2, Yogi Berra, Elston Howard, Hector Lopez, Roger Maris, Bill Skowron.
1962—3—New York, Tom Tresh, Roger Maris, Clete Boyer.
1963—2—New York, Tom Tresh, Mickey Mantle.
1964—10—New York, Mickey Mantle 3, Phil Linz 2, Tom Tresh 2, Roger Maris, Joe Pepitone, Clete Boyer.
1965—6—Minnesota, Zoilo Versalles, Tony Oliva, Harmon Killebrew, Don Mincher, Bob Allison, Mudcat Grant.
1966—4—Baltimore, Frank Robinson 2, Brooks Robinson, Paul Blair.
1967—8—Boston, Carl Yastrzemski 3, Reggie Smith 2, Rico Petrocelli 2, Jose Santiago.
1968—8—Detroit, Al Kaline 2, Jim Northrup 2, Norm Cash, Willie Horton, Mickey Lolich, Dick McAuliffe.
1969—3—Baltimore, Don Buford, Dave McNally, Frank Robinson.
1970—10—Baltimore, Boog Powell 2, Frank Robinson 2, Brooks Robinson 2, Don Buford, Elrod Hendricks, Dave McNally, Merv Rettenmund.
1971—5—Baltimore, Don Buford 2, Frank Robinson 2, Merv Rettenmund.
1972—5—Oakland, Gene Tenace 4, Joe Rudi.
1973—2—Oakland, Bert Campaneris, Reggie Jackson.
1974—4—Oakland, Ray Fosse, Ken Holtzman, Reggie Jackson, Joe Rudi.
1975—6—Boston, Bernie Carbo 2, Carlton Fisk 2, Dwight Evans, Fred Lynn.
1976—1—New York, Jim Mason.
1977—8—New York, Reggie Jackson 5, Chris Chambliss, Thurman Munson, Willie Randolph.
1978—3—New York, Reggie Jackson 2, Roy White.
1979—4—Baltimore, Doug DeCinces, Eddie Murray, Benny Ayala, Rich Dauer.
1980—8—Kansas City, Willie Aikens 4, Amos Otis 3, George Brett.
1981—6—New York, Willie Randolph 2, Bob Watson 2, Rich Cerone, Reggie Jackson.
1982—5—Milwaukee, Ted Simmons 2, Cecil Cooper, Ben Oglivie, Robin Yount.
1983—6—Baltimore, Eddie Murray 2, Jim Dwyer, John Lowenstein, Dan Ford, Rick Dempsey.
1984—7—Detroit, Kirk Gibson 2, Alan Trammell 2, Marty Castillo, Larry Herndon, Lance Parrish.
1985—2—Kansas City, Frank White, Darryl Motley.
1986—5—Boston, Dwight Evans 2, Dave Henderson 2, Rich Gedman.
1987—7—Minnesota, Don Baylor, Gary Gaetti, Greg Gagne, Dan Gladden, Kent Hrbek, Tim Laudner, Steve Lombardozzi.
1988—2—Oakland, Jose Canseco, Mark McGwire.
1989—9—Oakland, Dave Henderson 2, Jose Canseco, Rickey Henderson, Carney Lansford, Dave Parker, Tony Phillips, Terry Steinbach, Walt Weiss.
1990—3—Oakland, Harold Baines, Jose Canseco, Rickey Henderson.
1991—8—Minnesota, Chili Davis 2, Kirby Puckett 2, Greg Gagne, Kent Hrbek, Scott Leius, Mike Pagliarulo.
1992—6—Toronto, Joe Carter 2, Pat Borders, Kelly Gruber, Candy Maldonado, Ed Sprague.
1993—6—Toronto, Joe Carter 2, Paul Molitor 2, John Olerud, Devon White.
1994—No series played.
1995—5—Cleveland, Albert Belle 2, Eddie Murray, Manny Ramirez, Jim Thome.
1996—2—New York, Jim Leyritz, Bernie Williams.
1997—7—Cleveland, Sandy Alomar Jr. 2, Manny Ramirez 2, Jim Thome 2, Matt Williams.
1998—6—New York, Scott Brosius 2, Chuck Knoblauch, Tino Martinez, Jorge Posada, Bernie Williams.
1999—5—New York, Chad Curtis 2, Chuck Knoblauch, Jim Leyritz, Tino Martinez.
2000—4—New York, Derek Jeter 2, Scott Brosius, Bernie Williams.
2001—6—New York, Scott Brosius, Derek Jeter, Tino Martinez, Jorge Posada, Alfonso Soriano, Shane Spencer.

Total number of home runs: 430

NATIONAL LEAGUE

1903—1—Pittsburgh, Jimmy Sebring.
1904—No series played.
1905—0—New York.
1906—0—Chicago.
1907—0—Chicago.
1908—1—Chicago, Joe Tinker.
1909—2—Pittsburgh, Fred Clarke 2.
1910—0—Chicago.
1911—0—New York.
1912—1—New York, Larry Doyle.
1913—1—New York, Fred Merkle.
1914—1—Boston, Hank Gowdy.
1915—1—Philadelphia, Fred Luderus.
1916—1—Brooklyn, Hy Myers.
1917—2—New York, Benny Kauff 2.
1918—0—Chicago.
1919—0—Cincinnati.
1920—0—Brooklyn.
1921—2—New York, Frank Snyder, Irish Meusel.
1922—1—New York, Irish Meusel.
1923—5—New York, Casey Stengel 2, Irish Meusel, Ross Youngs), Frank Snyder.
1924—4—New York, George Kelly, Bill Terry), Rosy Ryan, Jack Bentley.
1925—4—Pittsburgh, Pie Traynor, Glenn Wright, Kiki Cuyler, Eddie Moore.
1926—4—St. Louis, Billy Southworth, Tommy Thevenow, Jesse Haines, Les Bell.
1927—0—Pittsburgh.
1928—1—St. Louis, Jim Bottomley.
1929—1—Chicago, Charlie Grimm.
1930—2—St. Louis, George Watkins, Taylor Douthit.
1931—2—St. Louis, Pepper Martin, George Watkins.
1932—3—Chicago, Kiki Cuyler, Gabby Hartnett, Frank Demaree.
1933—3—New York, Mel Ott 2, Bill Terry.
1934—2—St. Louis, Joe Medwick, Bill DeLancey.
1935—5—Chicago, Frank Demaree 2, Gabby Hartnett, Chuck Klein, Billy Herman.
1936—4—New York, Dick Bartell, Jimmy Ripple, Mel Ott, Joe Moore.
1937—1—New York, Mel Ott.
1938—2—Chicago, Joe Marty, Ken O'Dea.
1939—0—Cincinnati.
1940—2—Cincinnati, Jimmy Ripple, Bucky Walters.
1941—1—Brooklyn, Pete Reiser.
1942—2—St. Louis, Enos Slaughter, Whitey Kurowski.
1943—2—St. Louis, Marty Marion, Ray Sanders.
1944—3—St. Louis, Stan Musial, Ray Sanders, Danny Litwhiler.
1945—1—Chicago, Phil Cavarretta.
1946—1—St. Louis, Enos Slaughter.
1947—1—Brooklyn, Dixie Walker.
1948—4—Boston, Bob Elliott 2, Marv Rickert, Bill Salkeld.
1949—4—Brooklyn, Pee Wee Reese, Luis Olmo, Roy Campanella, Gil Hodges.
1950—0—Philadelphia.
1951—2—New York, Alvin Dark, Whitey Lockman.
1952—6—Brooklyn, Duke Snider 4, Jackie Robinson, Pee Wee Reese.
1953—8—Brooklyn, Jim Gilliam 2, Roy Campanella, Billy Cox, Carl Furillo, Gil Hodges, George Shuba, Duke Snider.
1954—2—New York, Dusty Rhodes 2.
1955—9—Brooklyn, Duke Snider 4, Roy Campanella 2, Sandy Amoros, Carl Furillo, Gil Hodges.
1956—3—Brooklyn, Duke Snider, Jackie Robinson, Gil Hodges.
1957—8—Milwaukee, Hank Aaron 3, Frank Torre 2, Eddie Mathews, Johnny Logan, Del Crandall.
1958—3—Milwaukee, Del Crandall, Bill Bruton, Lew Burdette.
1959—7—Los Angeles, Charlie Neal 2, Chuck Essegian 2, Wally Moon, Duke Snider, Gil Hodges.
1960—4—Pittsburgh, Bill Mazeroski 2, Rocky Nelson, Hal Smith.
1961—3—Cincinnati, Gordy Coleman, Wally Post, Frank Robinson.
1962—5—San Francisco, Chuck Hiller, Willie McCovey, Tom Haller, Ed Bailey, Jose Pagan.

1963—3—Los Angeles, John Roseboro, Bill Skowron, Frank Howard.
1964—5—St. Louis, Ken Boyer 2, Lou Brock, Mike Shannon, Tim McCarver.
1965—5—Los Angeles, Ron Fairly 2, Lou Johnson 2, Wes Parker.
1966—1—Los Angeles, Jim Lefebvre.
1967—5—St. Louis, Lou Brock, Bob Gibson, Julian Javier, Roger Maris, Mike Shannon.
1968—7—St. Louis, Lou Brock 2, Orlando Cepeda 2, Bob Gibson, Tim McCarver, Mike Shannon.
1969—6—New York, Donn Clendenon 3, Tommie Agee, Ed Kranepool, Al Weis.
1970—5—Cincinnati, Lee May 2, Johnny Bench, Pete Rose, Bobby Tolan.
1971—5—Pittsburgh, Bob Robertson 2, Roberto Clemente 2, Richie Hebner.
1972—3—Cincinnati, Johnny Bench, Denis Menke, Pete Rose.
1973—4—New York, Wayne Garrett 2, Cleon Jones, Rusty Staub.
1974—4—Los Angeles, Bill Buckner, Willie Crawford, Joe Ferguson, Jim Wynn.
1975—7—Cincinnati, Tony Perez 3, Cesar Geronimo 2, Johnny Bench, David Concepcion.
1976—4—Cincinnati, Johnny Bench 2, Dan Driessen, Joe Morgan.
1977—9—Los Angeles, Reggie Smith 3, Steve Yeager 2, Dusty Baker, Ron Cey, Steve Garvey, Dave Lopes.
1978—6—Los Angeles, Dave Lopes 3, Dusty Baker, Ron Cey, Reggie Smith.
1979—3—Pittsburgh, Willie Stargell 3.
1980—3—Philadelphia, Mike Schmidt 2, Bake McBride.
1981—6—Los Angeles, Pedro Guerrero 2, Steve Yeager 2, Ron Cey, Jay Johnstone.
1982—4—St. Louis, Willie McGee 2, Keith Hernandez, Darrell Porter.
1983—4—Philadelphia, Joe Morgan, Garry Maddox, Gary Matthews.
1984—3—San Diego, Kurt Bevacqua 2, Terry Kennedy.
1985—2—St. Louis, Tito Landrum, Willie McGee.
1986—7—New York, Gary Carter 2, Lenny Dykstra 2, Ray Knight, Darryl Strawberry, Tim Teufel.
1987—2—St. Louis, Tom Herr, Tom Lawless.
1988—5—Los Angeles, Mickey Hatcher 2, Mike Davis, Kirk Gibson, Mike A. Marshall.
1989—4—San Francisco, Bill Bathe, Greg Litton, Kevin Mitchell, Matt Williams.
1990—3—Cincinnati, Chris Sabo 2, Eric Davis.
1991—8—Atlanta, Lonnie Smith 3, David Justice 2, Terry Pendleton 2, Brian Hunter.
1992—3—Atlanta, Damon Berryhill, David Justice, Lonnie Smith.
1993—7—Philadelphia, Lenny Dykstra 4, Darren Daulton, Jim Eisenreich, Milt Thompson.
1994—No series played.
1995—8—Atlanta, Ryan Klesko 3, Fred McGriff 2, David Justice, Javier Lopez, Luis Polonia.
1996—4—Atlanta, Andruw Jones 2, Fred McGriff 2.
1997—8—Florida, Moises Alou 3, Bobby Bonilla, Darren Daulton, Jim Eisenreich, Charles Johnson, Gary Sheffield.
1998—3—San Diego, Greg Vaughn 2, Tony Gwynn.
1999—1—Atlanta, Chipper Jones.
2000—4—New York, Mike Piazza 2, Jay Payton, Robin Ventura.
2001—6—Arizona, Rod Barajas, Craig Counsell, Steve Finley, Luis Gonzalez, Mark Grace, Matt Williams.

Total number of home runs: 315

PLAYERS WITH FIVE HOME RUNS

Player	Series	No.
Mickey Mantle	12	18
Babe Ruth	10	15
Yogi Berra	14	12
Duke Snider	6	11
Reggie Jackson	5	10
Lou Gehrig	7	10
Frank Robinson	5	8

Player	Series	No.
Bill Skowron	8	8
Joe DiMaggio	10	8
Goose Goslin	5	7
Gil McDougald	8	7
Hank Bauer	9	7
Lenny Dykstra	2	6
Al Simmons	4	6
Reggie Smith	4	6
Roger Maris	7	6
Charlie Keller	4	5
Hank Greenberg	4	5
Johnny Bench	4	5
Billy Martin	5	5
Gil Hodges	7	5
Bill Dickey	8	5
Elston Howard	9	5

Total number of players: 23

INDIVIDUAL PITCHING
PITCHERS WITH FIVE VICTORIES

Pitcher, Club	Yrs.	W	L
Whitey Ford, New York A.L.	11	10	8
Red Ruffing, New York A.L.	7	7	2
Allie Reynolds, New York A.L.	6	7	2
Bob Gibson, St. Louis N.L.	3	7	2
Lefty Gomez, New York A.L.	4	6	0
Chief Bender, Philadelphia A.L.	5	6	4
Waite Hoyt, New York A.L., Philadelphia A.L.	6	6	4
Jack Coombs, Philadelphia A.L., Brooklyn N.L.	3	5	0
Herb Pennock, New York A.L.	3	5	0
Vic Raschi, New York A.L.	5	5	3
Catfish Hunter, Oakland A.L., New York A.L.	6	5	3
Mordecai Brown, Chicago N.L.	4	5	4
Christy Mathewson, New York N.L.	4	5	5

Total number of pitchers: 13

10-STRIKEOUT GAMES BY PITCHERS

Date	Pitcher, Club	No.
Oct. 1,1903	Deacon Phillippe, Pit. N.L. vs. Bos. A.L.	10
Oct. 2,1903	Bill Dinneen, Bos. A.L. vs. Pit. N.L.	11
Oct. 11,1906	Ed Walsh, Chi. A.L. vs. Chi. N.L.	12
Oct. 8,1907	Bill Donovan, Det. A.L. vs. Chi. N.L. (12 innings)	12
Oct. 14,1908	Orval Overall, Chi. N.L. vs. Det. A.L.	10
Oct. 12,1909	George Mullin, Det. A.L. vs. Pit. N.L.	10
Oct. 14,1911	Chief Bender, Phi. A.L. vs. N.Y. N.L. (eight innings)	11
Oct. 8,1912	Joe Wood, Bos. A.L. vs. N.Y. N.L.	11
Oct. 11,1921	Jesse Barnes, N.Y. N.L. vs. N.Y. A.L.	10
Oct. 24,1924	Walter Johnson, Was. A.L. vs. N.Y. N.L. (12 innings)	12
Oct. 7,1925	Walter Johnson, Was. A.L. vs. Pit. N.L.	10
Oct. 3,1926	Grover Alexander, St.L. N.L. vs. N.Y. A.L.	10
Oct. 8,1929	Howard Ehmke, Phi. A.L. vs. Chi. N.L.	13
Oct. 11,1929	George Earnshaw, Phi. A.L. vs. Chi. N.L.	10
Sept.28,1932	Red Ruffing, N.Y. A.L. vs. Chi. N.L.	10
Oct. 3,1933	Carl Hubbell, N.Y. N.L. vs. Was. A.L.	10
Oct. 5,1936	Hal Schumacher, N.Y. N.L. vs. N.Y. A.L. (10 innings)	10
Oct. 6,1944	Jack Kramer, St.L. A.L. vs. St.L. N.L.	10
Oct. 8,1944	Denny Galehouse, St.L. A.L. vs. St.L. N.L.	10
Oct. 8,1944	Mort Cooper, St.L. N.L. vs. St.L. A.L.	12
Oct. 10,1945	Hal Newhouser, Det. A.L. vs. Chi. N.L.	10
Oct. 5,1949	Don Newcombe, Bkn. N.L. vs. N.Y. A.L. (eight innings)	11
Oct. 4,1952	Allie Reynolds, N.Y. A.L. vs. Bkn. N.L.	10
Oct. 2,1953	Carl Erskine, Bkn. N.L. vs. N.Y. A.L.	14
Oct. 3,1956	Sal Maglie, Bkn. N.L. vs. N.Y. A.L.	10
Oct. 9,1956	Bob Turley, N.Y. A.L. vs. Bkn. N.L.	11
Oct. 6,1958	Bob Turley, N.Y. A.L. vs. Mil. N.L.	10
Oct. 10,1962	Jack Sanford, S.F. N.L. vs. N.Y. A.L.	10
Oct. 2,1963	Sandy Koufax, L.A. N.L. vs. N.Y. A.L.	15
Oct. 12,1964	Bob Gibson, St.L. N.L. vs. N.Y. A.L. (10 innings)	13

Date	Pitcher, Club	No.
Oct. 10,1965	Don Drysdale, L.A. N.L. vs. Min. A.L.	11
Oct. 11,1965	Sandy Koufax, L.A. N.L. vs. Min. A.L.	10
Oct. 14,1965	Sandy Koufax, L.A. N.L. vs. Min. A.L.	10
Oct. 5,1966	Moe Drabowsky, Bal. A.L. vs. L.A. N.L.	11
Oct. 4,1967	Bob Gibson, St.L. N.L. vs. Bos. A.L.	10
Oct. 12,1967	Bob Gibson, St.L. N.L. vs. Bos. A.L.	10
Oct. 2,1968	Bob Gibson, St.L. N.L. vs. Det. A.L.	17
Oct. 6,1968	Bob Gibson, St.L. N.L. vs. Det. A.L.	10
Oct. 11,1971	Jim Palmer, Bal. A.L. vs. Pit. N.L.	10
Oct. 18,1972	Blue Moon Odom, Oak. A.L. vs. Cin. N.L. (seven innings)	11
Oct. 16,1973	Tom Seaver, N.Y. N.L. vs. Oak. A.L. (eight innings)	12
Oct. 15,1980	Steve Carlton, Phi. N.L. vs. K.C. A.L. (eight innings)	10
Oct. 24,1996	John Smoltz, Atl. N.L. vs. N.Y. A.L. (eight innings)	10
Oct. 23,1999	Orlando Hernandez, N.Y. A.L. vs. Atl. N.L. (seven innings)	10
Oct. 27,1999	John Smoltz, Atl. N.L. vs. N.Y. A.L. (seven innings)	11
Oct. 24,2000	Orlando Hernandez, N.Y. A.L. vs. N.Y. N.L.	12
Oct. 28,2001	Randy Johnson, Ariz. N.L. vs. N.Y. A.L.	11
Nov. 1,2001	Mike Mussina, N.Y. A.L. vs. Ariz. N.L. (eight innings)	10
Nov. 3,2001	Roger Clemens, N.Y. A.L. vs. Ariz. N.L. (6.1 innings)	10

Total number of performances: 49

INDIVIDUAL FIELDING
UNASSISTED TRIPLE PLAYS

Bill Wambsganss, second baseman, Cleveland A.L. vs. Brooklyn N.L. at Cleveland, October 10, 1920, fifth inning. Wambsganss caught Clarence Mitchell's line drive, stepped on second to retire Pete Kilduff, then tagged Otto Miller coming from first. (This unassisted triple play was made with runners on first and second bases only.)

Total number of occurrences: 1

CLUB BATTING

Year	Club, League	G	AB	R	H	TB	2B	3B	HR	SB	BB	SO	RBI	Avg.	LOB
1903	Pittsburgh N.L.	8	270	24	64	92	7	9	1	7	14	45	23	.237	51
	Boston A.L.	8	282	39	71	113	4	16	2	5	13	27	35	.252	55
1904	No series played.														
1905	New York N.L.	5	153	15	32	39	7	0	0	11	15	26	13	.209	31
	Philadelphia A.L.	5	155	3	25	30	5	0	0	2	5	25	2	.161	26
1906	Chicago N.L.	6	184	18	36	45	9	0	0	8	18	27	11	.196	37
	Chicago A.L.	6	187	22	37	53	10	3	0	6	18	35	19	.198	33
1907	Chicago N.L.	5	167	19	43	51	6	1	0	18	12	25	16	.257	35
	Detroit A.L.	5	173	6	36	41	1	2	0	7	9	21	6	.208	36
1908	Chicago N.L.	5	164	24	48	59	4	2	1	13	13	26	21	.293	30
	Detroit A.L.	5	158	15	32	37	5	0	0	5	12	26	14	.203	27
1909	Pittsburgh N.L.	7	223	34	49	70	12	1	2	18	20	34	26	.220	44
	Detroit A.L.	7	234	28	55	77	16	0	2	6	20	22	25	.235	50
1910	Chicago N.L.	5	158	15	35	48	11	1	0	3	18	31	13	.222	31
	Philadelphia A.L.	5	177	35	56	80	19	1	1	7	17	24	29	.316	36
1911	New York N.L.	6	189	13	33	46	11	1	0	4	14	44	10	.175	31
	Philadelphia A.L.	6	205	27	50	74	15	0	3	4	4	31	21	.244	29
1912	New York N.L.	8	274	31	74	99	14	4	1	12	22	39	25	.270	53
	Boston A.L.	8	273	25	60	89	14	6	1	6	19	36	21	.220	55
1913	New York N.L.	5	164	15	33	41	3	1	1	5	8	19	15	.201	24
	Philadelphia A.L.	5	174	23	46	64	4	4	2	5	7	16	21	.264	30
1914	Boston N.L.	4	135	16	33	46	6	2	1	9	15	18	14	.244	27
	Philadelphia A.L.	4	128	6	22	31	9	0	0	2	13	28	5	.172	21
1915	Philadelphia N.L.	5	148	10	27	36	4	1	1	2	10	25	9	.182	23
	Boston A.L.	5	159	12	42	57	2	2	3	1	11	25	11	.264	35
1916	Brooklyn N.L.	5	170	13	34	49	2	5	1	1	14	19	11	.200	32
	Boston A.L.	5	164	21	39	64	7	6	2	1	18	25	18	.238	31
1917	New York N.L.	6	199	17	51	70	5	4	2	4	6	27	16	.256	37
	Chicago A.L.	6	197	21	54	63	6	0	1	6	11	28	18	.274	37
1918	Chicago N.L.	6	176	10	37	44	5	1	0	3	18	14	10	.210	31
	Boston A.L.	6	172	9	32	40	2	3	0	3	16	21	6	.186	32
1919	Cincinnati N.L.	8	251	35	64	88	10	7	0	7	25	22	34	.255	46
	Chicago A.L.	8	263	20	59	78	10	3	1	5	15	30	17	.224	52
1920	Brooklyn N.L.	7	215	8	44	51	5	1	0	1	10	20	8	.205	39
	Cleveland A.L.	7	217	21	53	72	9	2	2	2	21	21	18	.244	43
1921	New York N.L.	8	264	29	71	98	13	4	2	7	22	38	28	.269	54
	New York A.L.	8	241	22	50	65	7	1	2	6	27	44	20	.207	43
1922	New York N.L.	5	162	18	50	57	2	1	1	1	12	15	18	.309	32
	New York A.L.	5	158	11	32	46	6	1	2	2	8	20	11	.203	25
1923	New York N.L.	6	201	17	47	70	2	3	5	1	12	18	17	.234	35
	New York A.L.	6	205	30	60	91	8	4	5	1	20	22	29	.293	43
1924	New York N.L.	7	253	27	66	91	9	2	4	3	25	40	22	.261	59
	Washington A.L.	7	248	26	61	85	9	0	5	5	29	34	23	.246	57
1925	Pittsburgh N.L.	7	230	25	61	89	12	2	4	7	17	32	25	.265	54
	Washington A.L.	7	225	26	59	91	8	0	8	2	17	32	25	.262	46
1926	St. Louis N.L.	7	239	31	65	91	12	1	4	2	11	30	30	.272	43
	New York A.L.	7	223	21	54	78	10	1	4	1	31	31	19	.242	55
1927	Pittsburgh N.L.	4	130	10	29	37	6	1	0	0	4	7	10	.223	23
	New York A.L.	4	136	23	38	54	6	2	2	2	13	25	19	.279	29
1928	St. Louis N.L.	4	131	10	27	37	5	1	1	3	11	29	9	.206	27
	New York A.L.	4	134	27	37	71	7	0	9	4	13	12	25	.276	24

Year	Club, League	G	AB	R	H	TB	2B	3B	HR	SB	BB	SO	RBI	Avg.	LOB
1929	Chicago N.L.	5	173	17	43	56	6	2	1	1	13	50	15	.249	36
	Philadelphia A.L.	5	171	26	48	71	5	0	6	0	13	27	26	.281	35
1930	St. Louis N.L.	6	190	12	38	56	10	1	2	1	11	33	11	.200	37
	Philadelphia A.L.	6	178	21	35	67	10	2	6	0	24	32	21	.197	36
1931	St. Louis N.L.	7	229	19	54	71	11	0	2	8	9	41	17	.236	40
	Philadelphia A.L.	7	227	22	50	64	5	0	3	0	28	46	20	.220	52
1932	Chicago N.L.	4	146	19	37	58	8	2	3	2	11	24	16	.253	31
	New York A.L.	4	144	37	45	75	6	0	8	0	23	26	36	.313	33
1933	New York N.L.	5	176	16	47	61	5	0	3	0	11	21	16	.267	39
	Washington A.L.	5	173	11	37	47	4	0	2	1	13	25	11	.214	37
1934	St. Louis N.L.	7	262	34	73	103	14	5	2	2	11	31	32	.279	49
	Detroit A.L.	7	250	23	56	76	12	1	2	4	25	43	20	.224	64
1935	Chicago N.L.	6	202	18	48	73	6	2	5	1	11	29	17	.238	33
	Detroit A.L.	6	206	21	51	67	11	1	1	1	25	27	18	.248	51
1936	New York N.L.	6	203	23	50	71	9	0	4	0	21	33	20	.246	46
	New York A.L.	6	215	43	65	96	8	1	7	1	26	35	41	.302	43
1937	New York N.L.	5	169	12	40	49	6	0	1	1	11	21	12	.237	36
	New York A.L.	5	169	28	42	68	6	4	4	0	21	21	25	.249	36
1938	Chicago N.L.	4	136	9	33	45	4	1	2	0	6	26	8	.243	26
	New York A.L.	4	135	22	37	60	6	1	5	3	11	16	21	.274	24
1939	Cincinnati N.L.	4	133	8	27	32	3	1	0	1	6	22	8	.203	23
	New York A.L.	4	131	20	27	54	4	1	7	0	9	20	18	.206	16
1940	Cincinnati N.L.	7	232	22	58	78	14	0	2	1	15	30	21	.250	49
	Detroit A.L.	7	228	28	56	83	9	3	4	0	30	30	24	.246	50
1941	Brooklyn N.L.	5	159	11	29	43	7	2	1	0	14	21	11	.182	27
	New York A.L.	5	166	17	41	54	5	1	2	2	23	18	16	.247	42
1942	St. Louis N.L.	5	163	23	39	53	4	2	2	0	17	19	23	.239	32
	New York A.L.	5	178	18	44	59	6	0	3	3	8	22	14	.247	34
1943	St. Louis N.L.	5	165	9	37	48	5	0	2	1	11	26	8	.224	37
	New York A.L.	5	159	17	35	50	5	2	2	2	12	30	14	.220	29
1944	St. Louis N.L.	6	204	16	49	69	9	1	3	0	19	43	15	.240	51
	St. Louis A.L.	6	197	12	36	50	9	1	1	0	23	49	9	.183	44
1945	Chicago N.L.	7	247	29	65	90	16	3	1	2	19	48	27	.263	50
	Detroit A.L.	7	242	32	54	70	10	0	2	3	33	22	32	.223	53
1946	St. Louis N.L.	7	232	28	60	86	19	2	1	3	19	30	27	.259	50
	Boston A.L.	7	233	20	56	77	7	1	4	2	22	28	18	.240	53
1947	Brooklyn N.L.	7	226	29	52	70	13	1	1	7	30	32	26	.230	46
	New York A.L.	7	238	38	67	100	11	5	4	2	38	37	36	.282	63
1948	Boston N.L.	6	187	17	43	61	6	0	4	1	16	19	16	.230	34
	Cleveland A.L.	6	191	17	38	57	7	0	4	2	12	26	16	.199	34
1949	Brooklyn N.L.	5	162	14	34	55	7	1	4	1	15	38	14	.210	31
	New York A.L.	5	164	21	37	57	10	2	2	2	18	27	20	.226	32
1950	Philadelphia N.L.	4	128	5	26	34	6	1	0	1	7	24	3	.203	26
	New York A.L.	4	135	11	30	41	3	1	2	1	13	12	10	.222	33
1951	New York N.L.	6	194	18	46	61	7	1	2	2	25	22	15	.237	45
	New York A.L.	6	199	29	49	75	7	2	5	0	26	23	25	.246	41
1952	Brooklyn N.L.	7	233	20	50	75	7	0	6	5	24	49	18	.215	52
	New York A.L.	7	232	26	50	89	5	2	10	1	31	32	24	.216	48
1953	Brooklyn N.L.	6	213	27	64	103	13	1	8	2	15	30	26	.300	49
	New York A.L.	6	201	33	56	97	6	4	9	2	25	43	32	.279	47
1954	New York N.L.	4	130	21	33	42	3	0	2	1	17	24	20	.254	28
	Cleveland A.L.	4	137	9	26	42	5	1	3	0	16	23	9	.190	37
1955	Brooklyn N.L.	7	223	31	58	95	8	1	9	2	33	38	30	.260	55
	New York A.L.	7	222	26	55	87	4	2	8	3	22	39	25	.248	41
1956	Brooklyn N.L.	7	215	25	42	61	8	1	3	1	32	47	24	.195	42
	New York A.L.	7	229	33	58	100	6	0	12	2	21	43	33	.253	40
1957	Milwaukee N.L.	7	225	23	47	79	6	1	8	1	22	40	22	.209	46
	New York A.L.	7	230	25	57	87	7	1	7	1	22	34	25	.248	49
1958	Milwaukee N.L.	7	240	25	60	81	10	1	3	1	27	56	24	.250	58
	New York A.L.	7	233	29	49	86	5	1	10	1	21	42	29	.210	40
1959	Los Angeles N.L.	6	203	21	53	79	3	1	7	5	12	27	19	.261	42
	Chicago A.L.	6	199	23	52	74	10	0	4	2	20	33	19	.261	43
1960	Pittsburgh N.L.	7	234	27	60	83	11	0	4	2	12	26	26	.256	42
	New York A.L.	7	269	55	91	142	13	4	10	0	18	40	54	.338	51
1961	Cincinnati N.L.	5	170	13	35	52	8	0	3	0	8	27	11	.206	33
	New York A.L.	5	165	27	42	73	8	1	7	1	24	25	26	.255	34
1962	San Francisco N.L.	7	226	21	51	80	10	2	5	1	12	39	19	.226	39
	New York A.L.	7	221	20	44	61	6	1	3	4	21	39	17	.199	43
1963	Los Angeles N.L.	4	117	12	25	41	3	2	3	2	11	25	12	.214	17
	New York A.L.	4	129	4	22	31	3	0	2	0	5	37	4	.171	24
1964	St. Louis N.L.	7	240	32	61	90	8	3	5	3	18	39	29	.254	47
	New York A.L.	7	239	33	60	101	11	0	10	2	25	54	33	.251	47
1965	Los Angeles N.L.	7	234	24	64	91	10	1	5	9	13	31	21	.274	52
	Minnesota A.L.	7	215	20	42	71	7	2	6	2	19	54	19	.195	36
1966	Los Angeles N.L.	4	120	2	17	23	3	0	1	1	13	28	2	.142	24
	Baltimore A.L.	4	120	13	24	41	3	1	4	0	11	17	10	.200	18

Year	Club, League	G	AB	R	H	TB	2B	3B	HR	SB	BB	SO	RBI	Avg.	LOB
1967	St. Louis N.L.	7	229	25	51	81	11	2	5	7	17	30	24	.223	40
	Boston A.L.	7	222	21	48	80	6	1	8	1	17	49	19	.216	43
1968	St. Louis N.L.	7	239	27	61	95	7	3	7	11	21	40	27	.255	49
	Detroit A.L.	7	231	34	56	90	4	3	8	0	27	59	33	.242	44
1969	New York N.L.	5	159	15	35	61	8	0	6	1	15	35	13	.220	34
	Baltimore A.L.	5	157	9	23	33	1	0	3	1	15	28	9	.146	29
1970	Cincinnati N.L.	5	164	20	35	58	6	1	5	1	15	23	20	.213	28
	Baltimore A.L.	5	171	33	50	87	7	0	10	0	20	33	32	.292	31
1971	Pittsburgh N.L.	7	238	23	56	84	9	2	5	5	26	47	21	.235	63
	Baltimore A.L.	7	219	24	45	65	3	1	5	1	20	35	22	.205	39
1972	Cincinnati N.L.	7	220	21	46	65	8	1	3	12	27	46	21	.209	49
	Oakland A.L.	7	220	16	46	65	4	0	5	1	21	37	16	.209	45
1973	New York N.L.	7	261	24	66	89	7	2	4	0	26	36	16	.253	72
	Oakland A.L.	7	241	21	51	75	12	3	2	3	28	62	20	.212	58
1974	Los Angeles N.L.	5	158	11	36	54	4	1	4	3	16	32	10	.228	36
	Oakland A.L.	5	142	16	30	46	4	0	4	3	16	42	14	.211	26
1975	Cincinnati N.L.	7	244	29	59	95	9	3	7	9	25	30	29	.242	50
	Boston A.L.	7	239	30	60	89	7	2	6	0	30	40	30	.251	52
1976	Cincinnati N.L.	4	134	22	42	70	10	3	4	7	12	16	21	.313	22
	New York A.L.	4	135	8	30	38	3	1	1	1	12	16	8	.222	33
1977	Los Angeles N.L.	6	208	28	48	86	5	3	9	2	16	36	28	.231	31
	New York A.L.	6	205	26	50	84	10	0	8	1	11	37	25	.244	32
1978	Los Angeles N.L.	6	199	23	52	78	8	0	6	5	20	31	22	.261	38
	New York A.L.	6	222	36	68	85	8	0	3	5	16	40	34	.306	47
1979	Pittsburgh N.L.	7	251	32	81	110	18	1	3	0	16	35	32	.323	60
	Baltimore A.L.	7	233	26	54	78	10	1	4	2	26	41	23	.232	49
1980	Philadelphia N.L.	6	201	27	59	81	13	0	3	3	15	17	26	.294	41
	Kansas City A.L.	6	207	23	60	97	9	2	8	6	26	49	22	.290	54
1981	Los Angeles N.L.	6	198	27	51	77	6	1	6	6	20	44	26	.258	46
	New York A.L.	6	193	22	46	74	8	1	6	4	33	24	22	.238	55
1982	St. Louis N.L.	7	245	39	67	101	16	3	4	7	20	26	34	.273	49
	Milwaukee A.L.	7	238	33	64	95	12	2	5	1	19	28	29	.269	44
1983	Philadelphia N.L.	5	159	9	31	49	4	1	4	1	7	29	9	.195	23
	Baltimore A.L.	5	164	18	35	61	8	0	6	1	10	37	17	.213	28
1984	San Diego N.L.	5	166	15	44	60	7	0	3	2	11	26	14	.265	34
	Detroit A.L.	5	158	23	40	65	4	0	7	7	24	27	23	.253	39
1985	St. Louis N.L.	7	216	13	40	58	10	1	2	2	28	42	13	.185	38
	Kansas City A.L.	7	236	28	68	90	12	2	2	7	18	56	26	.288	56
1986	New York N.L.	7	240	32	65	92	6	0	7	7	21	43	29	.271	50
	Boston A.L.	7	248	27	69	99	11	2	5	0	28	53	26	.278	69
1987	St. Louis N.L.	7	232	26	60	74	8	0	2	12	13	44	25	.259	43
	Minnesota A.L.	7	238	38	64	101	10	3	7	6	29	36	38	.269	56
1988	Los Angeles N.L.	5	167	21	41	66	8	1	5	4	13	36	19	.246	30
	Oakland A.L.	5	158	11	28	37	3	0	2	3	17	41	11	.177	34
1989	San Francisco N.L.	4	134	14	28	46	4	1	4	2	8	27	14	.209	21
	Oakland A.L.	4	146	32	44	85	8	3	9	4	18	22	30	.301	31
1990	Cincinnati N.L.	4	142	22	45	67	9	2	3	2	15	9	22	.317	32
	Oakland A.L.	4	135	8	28	41	4	0	3	7	12	28	8	.207	31
1991	Atlanta N.L.	7	249	29	63	105	10	4	8	5	26	39	29	.253	52
	Minnesota A.L.	7	241	24	56	96	8	4	8	7	21	48	24	.232	47
1992	Atlanta N.L.	6	200	20	44	59	6	0	3	15	20	48	19	.220	40
	Toronto A.L.	6	196	17	45	71	8	0	6	5	18	33	17	.230	38
1993	Philadelphia N.L.	6	212	36	58	90	7	2	7	7	34	50	35	.274	54
	Toronto A.L.	6	206	45	64	105	13	5	6	7	25	30	45	.311	39
1994	No series played.														
1995	Atlanta N.L.	6	193	23	47	81	10	0	8	5	25	34	23	.244	44
	Cleveland A.L.	6	195	19	35	59	7	1	5	8	25	37	17	.179	39
1996	Atlanta N.L.	6	201	26	51	74	9	1	4	3	23	36	26	.254	41
	New York A.L.	6	199	18	43	57	6	1	2	4	26	43	16	.216	48
1997	Florida N.L.	7	250	37	68	106	12	1	8	4	36	48	34	.272	62
	Cleveland A.L.	7	247	44	72	107	12	1	7	5	40	51	42	.291	59
1998	San Diego N.L.	4	134	13	32	50	7	1	3	1	12	29	11	.239	27
	New York A.L.	4	139	26	43	66	5	0	6	1	20	29	25	.309	34
1999	Atlanta N.L.	4	130	9	26	36	5	1	1	1	15	26	9	.200	25
	New York A.L.	4	137	21	37	57	5	0	5	5	13	31	20	.270	27
2000	New York N.L.	5	175	16	40	60	8	0	4	0	11	48	15	.229	36
	New York A.L.	5	179	19	47	73	8	3	4	1	25	40	18	.263	52
2001	Arizona N.L.	7	246	37	65	97	14	0	6	2	17	70	36	.264	49
	New York A.L.	7	229	14	42	66	6	0	6	1	16	63	14	.183	38

CLUB FIELDING AND PLAYERS USED

Year	Club, League	G	PO	A	E	DP	PB	Fielding Avg.	Players Used	Pitchers Used	PH	PR
1903	Pittsburgh N.L.	8	210	96	18	5	0	.944	14	5	1	0
	Boston A.L.	8	213	102	14	6	2	.957	13	3	4	0

Year	Club, League	G	PO	A	E	DP	PB	Fielding Avg.	Players Used	Pitchers Used	PH	PR
1904	No series played.											
1905	New York N.L. 5		135	78	6	2	0	.973	12	3	1	0
	Philadelphia A.L........5		129	56	9	2	0	.954	13	3	1	0
1906	Chicago N.L. 6		159	84	7	4	3	.972	14	4	4	0
	Chicago A.L. 6		162	99	14	2	1	.949	16	4	2	1
1907	Chicago N.L. 5		144	65	10	6	1	.954	15	4	2	0
	Detroit A.L. 5		138	70	9	2	0	.959	14	4	1	1
1908	Chicago N.L. 5		135	74	5	4	1	.977	13	4	1	0
	Detroit A.L. 5		131	63	10	5	1	.951	16	5	4	1
1909	Pittsburgh N.L. 7		182	88	15	3	0	.947	17	6	3	0
	Detroit A.L. 7		183	87	19	4	1	.934	16	5	5	0
1910	Chicago N.L. 5		132	77	12	3	0	.946	18	7	6	1
	Philadelphia A.L........5		136	59	11	6	0	.947	12	2	0	0
1911	New York N.L. 6		162	79	16	2	1	.938	15	5	4	0
	Philadelphia A.L........6		167	72	11	2	0	.956	14	3	0	1
1912	New York N.L. 8		221	108	17	4	0	.951	17	5	5	3
	Boston A.L.................8		222	101	14	5	0	.958	17	5	5	1
1913	New York N.L. 5		135	67	7	1	1	.967	20	5	6	5
	Philadelphia A.L........5		138	54	5	6	0	.975	12	3	0	0
1914	Boston N.L. 4		117	62	4	4	0	.978	15	3	3	1
	Philadelphia A.L........4		111	66	3	4	1	.983	16	6	1	0
1915	Philadelphia N.L. 5		131	54	3	3	0	.984	16	4	2	2
	Boston A.L.................5		132	58	4	2	0	.979	17	3	3	1
1916	Brooklyn N.L..............5		142	70	13	2	2	.942	20	7	6	1
	Boston A.L.................5		147	90	6	5	1	.975	20	5	3	1
1917	New York N.L. 6		153	72	11	3	1	.953	17	6	3	0
	Chicago A.L. 6		156	82	12	7	1	.952	16	5	5	0
1918	Chicago N.L. 6		156	76	5	7	2	.979	17	4	8	2
	Boston A.L.................6		159	88	1	4	1	.996	15	4	5	0
1919	Cincinnati N.L. 8		216	96	12	7	0	.963	17	6	3	1
	Chicago A.L. 8		213	116	12	9	1	.965	19	7	6	0
1920	Brooklyn N.L..............7		177	91	6	5	2	.978	21	7	7	3
	Cleveland A.L............7		182	89	12	8	0	.958	20	5	12	1
1921	New York N.L. 8		212	102	5	5	2	.984	13	4	2	0
	New York A.L............8		210	106	6	8	0	.981	19	8	3	2
1922	New York N.L. 5		138	70	6	4	0	.972	16	5	3	1
	New York A.L............5		129	62	1	7	1	.995	17	5	4	0
1923	New York N.L. 6		159	80	6	8	0	.976	22	8	9	3
	New York A.L............6		162	77	3	6	0	.988	17	5	4	2
1924	New York N.L. 7		200	94	6	4	0	.980	21	9	7	3
	Washington A.L........7		201	99	12	10	1	.962	21	8	8	2
1925	Pittsburgh N.L. 7		182	89	7	4	0	.980	18	7	5	2
	Washington A.L........7		180	75	9	8	1	.966	21	6	7	4
1926	St. Louis N.L. 7		189	99	5	6	0	.983	19	8	6	0
	New York A.L............7		189	82	7	3	1	.975	19	7	7	2
1927	Pittsburgh N.L. 4		104	46	6	2	0	.962	21	7	5	1
	New York A.L............4		108	44	3	4	0	.981	15	4	1	0
1928	St. Louis N.L. 4		102	36	5	3	0	.965	20	6	6	1
	New York A.L............4		108	28	6	3	0	.958	16	3	4	0
1929	Chicago N.L. 5		131	44	7	4	0	.962	19	6	8	0
	Philadelphia A.L........5		135	40	4	2	6	.978	17	6	3	0
1930	St. Louis N.L. 6		153	55	5	4	1	.977	21	7	7	0
	Philadelphia A.L........6		156	41	3	2	0	.985	15	5	3	0
1931	St. Louis N.L. 7		186	73	4	7	0	.985	21	6	6	1
	Philadelphia A.L........7		183	69	2	4	0	.992	20	6	8	1
1932	Chicago N.L. 4		102	40	6	7	0	.959	22	8	6	1
	New York A.L............4		108	41	8	1	0	.949	16	6	6	1
1933	New York N.L. 5		141	67	4	5	0	.981	15	5	2	0
	Washington A.L........5		138	65	4	4	0	.981	10	7	5	1
1934	St. Louis N.L. 7		196	73	15	2	0	.947	20	8	5	2
	Detroit A.L. 7		195	70	12	6	0	.957	17	6	4	0
1935	Chicago N.L. 6		164	74	6	5	0	.975	18	7	5	0
	Detroit A.L. 6		165	72	9	7	1	.963	15	5	2	0
1936	New York N.L. 6		159	62	7	7	0	.969	22	8	10	2
	New York A.L............6		162	57	6	2	0	.973	16	6	2	2
1937	New York N.L. 5		129	46	9	5	0	.951	20	7	7	0
	New York A.L............5		132	47	0	2	0	1.000	17	7	1	0
1938	Chicago N.L. 4		102	35	3	3	0	.979	20	8	8	0
	New York A.L............4		108	39	6	4	0	.961	14	4	1	0
1939	Cincinnati N.L. 4		106	34	4	1	0	.972	18	5	3	2
	New York A.L............4		111	50	2	5	0	.988	15	7	0	0
1940	Cincinnati N.L. 7		183	67	8	9	1	.969	23	9	9	1
	Detroit A.L. 7		180	80	4	4	0	.985	20	8	6	0
1941	Brooklyn N.L..............5		132	60	4	5	0	.980	20	7	6	0
	New York A.L............5		135	55	2	7	0	.990	18	7	2	1

Year	Club, League	G	PO	A	E	DP	PB	Fielding Avg.	Players Used	Pitchers Used	PH	PR
1942	St. Louis N.L.	5	135	45	10	3	0	.947	18	6	4	1
	New York A.L.	5	132	45	5	2	0	.973	20	7	4	2
1943	St. Louis N.L.	5	129	53	10	4	0	.948	20	6	6	1
	New York A.L.	5	135	63	5	3	0	.975	16	5	2	0
1944	St. Louis N.L.	6	165	59	1	3	1	.996	20	8	7	0
	St. Louis A.L.	6	163	60	10	4	0	.957	22	7	13	1
1945	Chicago N.L.	7	195	78	6	5	1	.978	25	8	14	3
	Detroit A.L.	7	197	85	5	4	2	.983	26	9	11	1
1946	St. Louis N.L.	7	186	68	4	7	1	.984	19	7	5	0
	Boston A.L.	7	183	76	10	5	0	.963	26	11	10	3
1947	Brooklyn N.L.	7	180	71	8	8	2	.969	24	8	19	5
	New York A.L.	7	185	70	4	4	2	.985	24	9	11	0
1948	Boston N.L.	6	156	54	6	3	0	.972	20	6	8	4
	Cleveland A.L.	6	159	72	3	9	0	.987	23	8	3	0
1949	Brooklyn N.L.	5	132	40	5	1	0	.972	25	9	11	0
	New York A.L.	5	135	44	3	5	0	.984	20	5	4	2
1950	Philadelphia N.L.	4	107	35	4	1	0	.973	20	5	6	4
	New York A.L.	4	111	41	2	4	0	.987	18	5	2	2
1951	New York N.L.	6	156	65	10	4	0	.957	24	9	10	2
	New York A.L.	6	159	67	4	10	1	.982	21	8	5	2
1952	Brooklyn N.l.	7	192	71	4	4	0	.985	19	6	8	1
	New York A.L.	7	192	66	10	7	1	.963	19	8	6	1
1953	Brooklyn N.L.	6	154	62	7	3	0	.969	23	10	8	0
	New York A.L.	6	156	60	1	5	0	.995	20	9	7	0
1954	New York N.L.	4	111	40	7	2	0	.955	15	6	3	0
	Cleveland A.L.	4	106	40	4	2	0	.973	24	7	16	2
1955	Brooklyn N.L.	7	180	84	6	12	0	.978	22	10	6	1
	New York A.L.	7	180	72	2	7	0	.992	24	9	12	3
1956	Brooklyn N.L.	7	183	69	2	8	0	.992	21	8	9	0
	New York A.L.	7	185	66	6	7	0	.977	22	8	6	0
1957	Milwaukee N.L.	7	186	93	3	10	1	.989	23	8	9	2
	New York A.L.	7	187	72	6	5	0	.977	23	9	10	2
1958	Milwaukee N.L.	7	189	78	7	5	0	.974	19	6	8	5
	New York A.L.	7	191	65	3	5	1	.988	22	9	9	0
1959	Los Angeles N.L.	6	159	69	4	7	0	.983	24	9	13	4
	Chicago A.L.	6	156	62	4	2	1	.982	21	7	9	2
1960	Pittsburgh N.L.	7	186	67	4	7	3	.984	25	10	9	2
	New York A.L.	7	183	93	8	9	0	.972	25	10	11	3
1961	Cincinnati N.L.	5	132	42	4	7	1	.978	24	9	15	1
	New York A.L.	5	135	50	5	1	1	.974	18	6	4	1
1962	San Francisco N.L.	7	183	67	8	9	1	.969	21	7	7	1
	New York A.L.	7	183	67	5	5	0	.980	18	6	4	0
1963	Los Angeles N.L.	4	108	31	3	1	0	.979	13	4	1	0
	New York A.L.	4	102	49	1	7	0	.993	20	7	7	0
1964	St. Louis N.L.	7	189	64	4	6	0	.984	21	8	12	3
	New York A.L.	7	186	82	9	6	3	.968	21	9	8	1
1965	Los Angeles N.L.	7	180	72	6	7	0	.977	20	7	7	1
	Minnesota A.L.	7	180	58	5	3	0	.979	21	9	7	0
1966	Los Angeles N.L.	4	102	44	6	4	0	.961	23	8	8	1
	Baltimore A.L.	4	108	33	0	4	0	1.000	13	4	0	0
1967	St. Louis N.L.	7	183	66	4	3	0	.984	23	10	8	0
	Boston A.L.	7	183	66	4	4	1	.984	25	10	13	1
1968	St. Louis N.L.	7	186	48	2	7	0	.992	25	10	8	1
	Detroit A.L.	7	186	72	11	4	0	.959	24	9	8	1
1969	New York N.L.	5	135	42	2	0	0	.989	21	6	4	1
	Baltimore A.L.	5	129	51	4	4	0	.978	21	7	5	3
1970	Cincinnati N.L.	5	129	50	3	4	0	.984	24	9	13	0
	Baltimore A.L.	5	135	43	5	3	0	.973	21	9	3	0
1971	Pittsburgh N.L.	7	185	70	3	7	1	.988	25	10	8	1
	Baltimore A.L.	7	183	69	9	2	0	.966	21	10	6	1
1972	Cincinnati N.L.	7	187	89	5	5	0	.982	22	8	16	2
	Oakland A.L.	7	186	65	9	4	0	.965	23	8	13	8
1973	New York N.L.	7	195	72	10	3	1	.964	22	7	15	3
	Oakland A.L.	7	198	79	9	8	1	.969	24	8	20	4
1974	Los Angeles N.L.	5	126	50	6	5	0	.967	19	6	9	2
	Oakland A.L.	5	132	51	5	6	0	.973	20	5	6	4
1975	Cincinnati N.L.	7	195	76	2	8	0	.993	22	9	8	0
	Boston A.L.	7	196	72	6	6	0	.978	23	10	13	0
1976	Cincinnati N.L.	4	108	36	5	4	0	.966	16	7	0	0
	New York A.L.	4	104	41	2	6	0	.986	21	7	9	0
1977	Los Angeles N.L.	6	165	69	1	4	0	.996	25	9	10	1
	New York A.L.	6	168	68	3	2	1	.987	20	7	6	0
1978	Los Angeles N.L.	6	158	64	7	4	0	.969	23	8	4	0
	New York A.L.	6	159	54	2	9	1	.991	24	8	5	2
1979	Pittsburgh N.L.	7	186	79	9	11	0	.967	24	9	11	1
	Baltimore A.L.	7	186	85	9	5	0	.968	25	9	23	2

Year	Club, League	G	PO	A	E	DP	PB	Fielding Avg.	Players Used	Pitchers Used	PH	PR
1980	Philadelphia N.L.	6	161	68	2	8	0	.991	22	10	4	1
	Kansas City A.L.	6	156	72	7	8	0	.970	21	7	3	3
1981	Los Angeles N.L.	6	156	65	9	6	0	.961	24	10	14	2
	New York A.L.	6	153	55	4	2	1	.981	24	9	10	5
1982	St. Louis N.L.	7	183	74	7	9	0	.973	22	8	8	3
	Milwaukee A.L.	7	180	81	11	3	0	.960	21	9	2	1
1983	Philadelphia N.L.	5	132	42	3	3	0	.983	23	8	12	3
	Baltimore A.L.	5	135	51	4	5	0	.979	23	7	13	2
1984	San Diego N.L.	5	126	40	4	5	0	.976	24	10	4	3
	Detroit A.L.	5	132	52	4	2	0	.979	22	7	10	1
1985	St. Louis N.L.	7	184	60	2	9	1	.992	24	9	8	2
	Kansas City A.L.	7	186	80	3	3	1	.989	22	6	13	3
1986	New York N.L.	7	189	63	5	4	0	.981	22	8	11	2
	Boston A.L.	7	188	79	4	7	1	.985	21	8	6	3
1987	St. Louis N.L.	7	177	69	6	2	1	.976	24	9	4	1
	Minnesota A.L.	7	180	74	3	4	0	.988	24	9	15	2
1988	Los Angeles N.L.	5	133	36	3	3	1	.983	22	7	11	0
	Oakland A.L.	5	131	43	2	2	1	.989	24	10	4	3
1989	San Francisco N.L.	4	102	40	4	3	0	.973	24	9	10	0
	Oakland A.L.	4	108	35	1	1	1	.993	19	6	4	0
1990	Cincinnati N.L.	4	111	42	4	2	0	.975	21	8	6	0
	Oakland A.L.	4	106	46	5	5	0	.968	25	10	8	1
1991	Atlanta N.L.	7	196	86	5	9	0	.983	25	10	16	1
	Minnesota A.L.	7	202	75	5	6	1	.982	25	9	21	2
1992	Atlanta N.L.	6	163	68	2	7	0	.991	22	8	7	3
	Toronto A.L.	6	165	47	4	5	0	.981	23	10	8	0
1993	Philadelphia N.L.	6	157	54	2	5	1	.991	23	10	7	1
	Toronto A.L.	6	159	45	7	5	0	.967	23	10	3	3
1994	No series played.											
1995	Atlanta N.L.	6	162	69	6	2	0	.975	23	10	9	0
	Cleveland A.L.	6	159	73	6	8	1	.975	23	9	6	2
1996	Atlanta N.L.	6	162	73	4	6	0	.983	24	10	10	3
	New York A.L.	6	165	63	5	7	0	.979	25	10	8	1
1997	Florida N.L.	7	192	82	8	9	0	.972	25	10	17	2
	Cleveland A.L.	7	191	64	5	8	0	.981	23	11	5	0
1998	San Diego N.L.	4	102	41	3	5	0	.979	24	10	9	2
	New York A.L.	4	108	36	2	4	1	.986	21	9	3	2
1999	Atlanta N.L.	4	105	31	4	4	0	.971	25	9	11	1
	New York A.L.	4	111	48	1	5	0	.994	23	9	4	1
2000	New York N.L.	5	140	47	5	3	0	.974	25	10	11	2
	New York A.L.	5	141	46	2	1	1	.989	22	8	8	1
2001	Arizona N.L.	7	195	61	3	6	0	.988	25	10	5	4
	New York A.L.	7	190	75	8	7	0	.971	25	10	8	2

MANAGERIAL RECORDS

AMERICAN LEAGUE

	Series W	L	Games W	L
Joe Altobelli, Baltimore	1	0	4	1
Sparky Anderson, Detroit	1	0	4	1
Del Baker, Detroit	0	1	3	4
Ed Barrow, Boston	1	0	4	2
Hank Bauer, Baltimore	1	0	4	0
Yogi Berra, New York	0	1	3	4
Lou Boudreau, Cleveland	1	0	4	2
Bill Carrigan, Boston	2	0	8	2
Mickey Cochrane, Detroit	1	1	7	6
Jimmy Collins, Boston	1	0	5	3
Joe Cronin, Washington, Boston	0	2	4	8
Alvin Dark, Oakland	1	0	4	1
Jim Frey, Kansas City	0	1	2	4
Cito Gaston, Toronto	2	0	8	4
Kid Gleason, Chicago	0	1	3	5
Mike Hargrove, Cleveland	0	2	5	8
Bucky Harris, Washington, New York	2	1	11	10
Ralph Houk, New York	2	1	8	8
Dick Howser, Kansas City	1	0	4	3
Miller Huggins, New York*	3	3	18	15
Hughey Jennings, Detroit*	0	3	4	12
Darrell Johnson, Boston	0	1	3	4
Fielder Jones, Chicago	1	0	4	2
Tom Kelly, Minnesota	2	0	8	6
Harvey Kuenn, Milwaukee	0	1	3	4
Tony La Russa, Oakland	1	2	5	8
Bob Lemon, New York	1	1	6	6
Al Lopez, Cleveland, Chicago	0	2	2	8
Connie Mack, Philadelphia	5	3	24	19
Billy Martin, New York	1	1	4	6
Joe McCarthy, New York	7	1	29	9
John McNamara, Boston	0	1	3	4
Sam Mele, Minnesota	0	1	3	4
Steve O'Neill, Detroit	1	0	4	3
Pants Rowland, Chicago	1	0	4	2
Luke Sewell, St. Louis	0	1	2	4
Mayo Smith, Detroit	1	0	4	3
Tris Speaker, Cleveland	1	0	5	2
Jake Stahl, Boston*	1	0	4	3
Joe Torre, New York	4	1	19	7
Casey Stengel, New York	7	3	37	26
Earl Weaver, Baltimore	1	3	11	13
Dick Williams, Boston, Oakland	2	1	11	10

Total number of managers: 43
*Includes one tie per asterisk.

NATIONAL LEAGUE

	Series W	L	Games W	L
Walter Alston, Brooklyn, Los Angeles	4	3	20	20
Sparky Anderson, Cincinnati	2	2	12	11
Yogi Berra, New York	0	1	3	4
Bruce Bochy, San Diego	0	1	0	4
Bob Brenly, Arizona	1	0	4	3
Donie Bush, Pittsburgh	0	1	0	4
Frank Chance, Chicago*	2	2	11	9
Fred Clarke, Pittsburgh	1	1	7	8
Bobby Cox, Atlanta	1	4	11	18
Roger Craig, San Francisco	0	1	0	4
Alvin Dark, San Francisco	0	1	3	4
Charlie Dressen, Brooklyn	0	2	5	8
Leo Durocher, Brooklyn, New York	1	2	7	8
Eddie Dyer, St. Louis	1	0	4	3
Jim Fregosi, Philadelphia	0	1	2	4
Frank Frisch, St. Louis	1	0	4	3
Dallas Green, Philadelphia	1	0	4	2
Chuck Grimm, Chicago	0	3	5	12
Fred Haney, Milwaukee	1	1	7	7
Gabby Hartnett, Chicago	0	1	0	4
Whitey Herzog, St. Louis	1	2	10	11
Gil Hodges, New York	1	0	4	1
Rogers Hornsby, St. Louis	1	0	4	3
Fred Hutchinson, Cincinnati	0	1	1	4
Dave Johnson, New York	1	0	4	3
Johnny Keane, St. Louis	1	0	4	3
Tom Lasorda, Los Angeles	2	2	12	11
Jim Leyland, Florida	1	0	4	3
Joe McCarthy, Chicago	0	1	1	4
John McGraw, New York**	3	6	26	28
Bill McKechnie, Pittsburgh, St. Louis, Cincinnati	2	2	8	14
Fred Mitchell, Chicago	0	1	2	4
Pat Moran, Philadelphia, Cincinnati	1	1	6	7
Danny Murtaugh, Pittsburgh	2	0	8	6
Paul Owens, Philadelphia	0	1	1	4
Lou Piniella, Cincinnati	1	0	4	0
Wilbert Robinson, Brooklyn	0	2	3	9
Eddie Sawyer, Philadelphia	0	1	0	4
Red Schoendienst, St. Louis	1	1	7	7
Burt Shotton, Brooklyn	0	2	4	8
Billy Southworth, St. Louis, Boston	2	2	11	11
George Stallings, Boston	1	0	4	0
Gabby Street, St. Louis	1	1	6	7
Chuck Tanner, Pittsburgh	1	0	4	3
Bill Terry, New York	1	2	7	9
Bobby Valentine, New York	0	1	1	4
Dick Williams, San Diego	0	1	1	4

Total number of managers: 47

COMBINED RECORDS FOR BOTH LEAGUES

	Series W	L	Games W	L
Joe McCarthy, Chicago N.L., New York A.L.	7	2	30	13
Yogi Berra, New York A.L., New York N.L.	0	2	6	8
Alvin Dark, San Francisco N.L., Oakland A.L.	1	1	7	5
Sparky Anderson, Cincinnati N.L., Detroit A.L.	3	2	16	12
Dick Williams, Boston A.L., Oakland A.L., San Diego N.L.	2	2	12	14

Total number of managers: 5

ALL-STAR GAME

Service (Individual, Club)

Batting (Individual, Club)

Baserunning (Individual, Club)

Pitching (Individual, Club)

Fielding (Individual, Club)

Miscellaneous

Non-Playing Personnel

General Reference

SERVICE

INDIVIDUAL
CLUBS

Most clubs represented, career
4—Rich Gossage, Chicago A.L., 1975; Pittsburgh N.L., 1977;
New York A.L., 1978, 1980; San Diego N.L., 1984, 1985
(six games).
Roberto Alomar, San Diego N.L., 1990; Toronto A.L., 1991
through 1995; Baltimore A.L., 1996 through 1998;
Cleveland A.L., 1999, through 2001 (12 games).
Kevin Brown, Texas A.L., 1992; Florida N.L., 1996, 1997; San
Diego N.L., 1998; Los Angeles N.L., 2000 (five games).

PLAYING ON WINNING AND LOSING CLUBS

Most times playing on winning club
17—Willie Mays, N.L., 1955, 1956, 1959 (first game), 1960
(both games), 1961 (first game), 1962 (first game),
1963 through 1970, 1972, 1973 (one tie—1961, second game).
Hank Aaron, N.L., 1955, 1956, 1959 (first game), 1960,
1960, 1961 (first game), 1963 through 1970, 1972
through 1974 (one tie—1961, second game).

Most times playing on losing club
15—Brooks Robinson, A.L., 1960, 1960, 1961 (first game),
1962 (first game), 1963 through 1970, 1972 through
1974 (one tie—1961, second game).

YOUNGEST AND OLDEST PLAYERS

Youngest player
19 years, 7 months, 24 days—Dwight Gooden, N.L., 1984.
Oldest player
47 years, 7 days—Satchel Paige, A.L., 1953.

POSITIONS

Most fielding positions played, career
5—Pete Rose, N.L. (second base, left field, right field, third
base, first base; 16 games).

Most fielding positions played, game
2—Held by many players.

CLUB
PLAYERS USED

Most players, game
29—N.L., August 9, 1981.
A.L., July 11, 2000.
A.L., July 10, 2001.
N.L., July 10, 2001.

Most players by both clubs, game
58—N.L. (29), A.L. (29), July 10, 2001.

Fewest players, game
11—A.L., July 6, 1942.

Fewest players by both clubs, game
27—A.L. (15), N.L. (12), July 1, 1938.

PINCH-HITTERS

Most pinch-hitters, nine-inning game
8—N.L., July 9, 1957.

Most pinch-hitters by both clubs, game
11—N.L. (7), A.L. (4), July 24, 1973.
N.L. (7), A.L. (4), August 9, 1981.
N.L. (6), A.L. (5), July 11, 1967, 15 innings.

Fewest pinch-hitters, game
0—A.L., July 8, 1935.
N.L., July 9, 1940.
A.L., July 8, 1980.

Fewest pinch-hitters by both clubs, game
1—A.L. (1), N.L. (0), July 9, 1940.

INDIVIDUAL BATTING

GAMES

Most games played

24—Stan Musial, N.L., 1943, 1944, 1946 through 1958, 1959, 1959, 1960, 1960, 1961, 1961, 1962, 1962, 1963 (consecutive).

Willie Mays, N.L., 1954 through 1958, 1959, 1959, 1960, 1960, 1961, 1961, 1962, 1962, 1963 through 1973 (consecutive).

Hank Aaron, N.L., 1955 through 1958, 1959, 1959, 1960, 1960, 1961, 1961, 1962, 1963 through 1974 (23 games); A.L., 1975 (one game).

Most games by pinch-hitter

10—Stan Musial, 1947, 1955, 1959 (first game), 1960, 1960, 1961, 1961, 1962, 1962, 1963 (10 pinch-hit at-bats).

BATTING AVERAGE AND AT-BATS

Highest batting average, career (five or more games)

.500—Charlie Gehringer, A.L., 1933 through 1938 (six games, 20 at-bats).

Most at-bats, career

75—Willie Mays, N.L., 1954 through 1958, 1959, 1959, 1960, 1960, 1961, 1961, 1962, 1962, 1963 through 1973 (24 games).

Most at-bats, nine-inning game

5—Held by many players. Last players—Cal Ripken, A.L., July 12, 1994; Ivan Rodriguez, A.L., July 12, 1994; Tony Gwynn, N.L., July 12, 1994.

Most at-bats, extra-inning game

7—Willie Jones, N.L., July 11, 1950, 14 innings.

Most at-bats, inning

2—Jim Rice, A.L., July 6, 1983, third inning.

Most times faced pitcher, inning

2—Babe Ruth, A.L., July 10, 1934, fifth inning.
Lou Gehrig, A.L., July 10, 1934, fifth inning.
Jim Rice, A.L., July 6, 1983, third inning.

RUNS

Most runs, career

20—Willie Mays, N.L., 1954 through 1958, 1959, 1959, 1960, 1960, 1961, 1961, 1962, 1962, 1963 through 1973 (24 games).

Most runs, game

4—Ted Williams, A.L., July 9, 1946.

Most runs, inning

1—Held by many players.

HITS

Most hits, career

23—Willie Mays, N.L., 1954 through 1958, 1959, 1960, 1960, 1961, 1961, 1962, 1962, 1963 through 1973 (24 games).

Most hits by pinch-hitter, career

3—Stan Musial, N.L., 1943, 1944, 1946 through 1958, 1959, 1959, 1960, 1960, 1961, 1962, 1962, 1963 (24 games).

Most consecutive games batted safely

7—Mickey Mantle, A.L., 1954 through 1958, 1959 (second game), 1960, second game. (Pinch-ran in 1959, first game, and received two bases on balls in 1960, first game.)

Joe Morgan, N.L., 1970, 1972 through 1977 (was not on team in 1971).
Dave Winfield, A.L., 1982 through 1988.

Most at-bats without a hit, career

10—Terry Moore, N.L., 1939 through 1942 (four games).

Most hits, game

4—Joe Medwick, N.L., July 7, 1937 (two singles, two doubles; consecutive).
Ted Williams, A.L., July 9, 1946 (two singles, two home runs, also one base on balls; consecutive).
Carl Yastrzemski, A.L., July 14, 1970, 12 innings (three singles, one double).

Most times reached first base safely, game

5—Charlie Gehringer, A.L., July 10, 1934 (three bases on balls, two singles).
Phil Cavarretta, N.L., July 11, 1944 (three bases on balls, one single, one triple).
Ted Williams, A.L., July 9, 1946 (two singles, two home runs, one base on balls).

Most hits, inning

1—Held by many players.

SINGLES

Most singles, game

3—Charlie Gehringer, A.L., July 7, 1937.
Billy Herman, N.L., July 9, 1940.
Stan Hack, N.L., July 13, 1943.
Bobby Avila, A.L., July 13, 1954.
Ken Boyer, N.L., July 10, 1956.
Harmon Killebrew, A.L., July 7, 1964.
Carl Yastrzemski, A.L., July 14, 1970, 12 innings.
Rickey Henderson, A.L., July 13, 1982.
Ivan Rodriguez, A.L., July 7, 1998.

Most singles, inning

1—Held by many players.

DOUBLES

Most doubles, career

7—Dave Winfield, N.L., 1977 through 1980; A.L., 1981 through 1988 (12 games).

Most doubles, game

2—Joe Medwick, N.L., July 7, 1937.
Al Simmons, A.L., July 10, 1934.
Ted Kluszewski, N.L., July 10, 1956.
Ernie Banks, N.L., July 7, 1959.
Barry Bonds, N.L., July 13, 1993.

Most doubles, inning

1—Held by many players.

Most doubles driving in three runs, inning

Never accomplished.

TRIPLES

Most triples, career

3—Willie Mays, N.L., 1954 through 1958, 1959, 1959, 1960, 1960, 1961, 1961, 1962, 1962, 1963 through 1973 (24 games).
Brooks Robinson, A.L., 1960, 1960, 1961, 1961, 1962, 1962, 1963 through 1974 (18 games).

Most triples, game

2—Rod Carew, A.L., July 11, 1978.

Most triples, inning

1—Held by many players.

Most triples driving in three runs, inning
Never accomplished.

HOME RUNS

Most home runs, career
6—Stan Musial, N.L., 1943, 1944, 1946 through 1958, 1959, 1959, 1960, 1960, 1961, 1961, 1962, 1962, 1963 (24 games).

For a complete list of All-Star Game home runs, see page 539.

Most home runs, game
2—Arky Vaughan, N.L., July 8, 1941 (consecutive).
Ted Williams, A.L., July 9, 1946.
Al Rosen, A.L., July 13, 1954 (consecutive).
Willie McCovey, N.L., July 23, 1969 (consecutive).
Gary Carter, N.L., August 9, 1981 (consecutive).

Most home runs by pinch-hitter, game (16)
1—Mickey Owen, N.L., July 6, 1942, eighth inning.
Gus Bell, N.L., July 13, 1954, eighth inning.
Larry Doby, A.L., July 14, 1954, eighth inning.
Willie Mays, N.L., July 10, 1956, fourth inning.
Stan Musial, N.L., July 13, 1960, seventh inning.
Harmon Killebrew, A.L., July 11, 1961, sixth inning.
George Altman, N.L., July 11, 1961, eighth inning.
Pete Runnels, A.L., July 30, 1962, third inning.
Reggie Jackson, A.L., July 13, 1971, third inning.
Cookie Rojas, A.L., July 25, 1972, eighth inning.
Willie Davis, N.L., July 24, 1973, sixth inning.
Carl Yastrzemski, A.L., July 15, 1975, sixth inning.
Lee Mazzilli, N.L., July 17, 1979, eighth inning.
Frank White, A.L., July 15, 1986, seventh inning.
Fred McGriff, N.L., July 12, 1994, ninth inning.
Jeff Conine, N.L., July 11, 1995, sixth inning.

Most home runs as leadoff batter, start of game
1—Frankie Frisch, N.L., July 10, 1934.
Lou Boudreau, A.L., July 6, 1942.
Willie Mays, N.L., July 13, 1965.
Joe Morgan, N.L., July 19, 1977.
Bo Jackson, A.L., July 11, 1989.

Hitting home run in first at-bat (11)
Max West, N.L., July 9, 1940, first inning.
Hoot Evers, A.L., July 13, 1948, second inning.
Jim Gilliam, N.L., Aug. 3, 1959, seventh inning.
George Altman, N.L., July 11, 1961, eighth inning.
Johnny Bench, N.L., July 23, 1969, second inning.
Dick Dietz, N.L., July 14, 1970, ninth inning.
Lee Mazzilli, N.L., July 17, 1979, eighth inning.
Terry Steinbach, A.L., July 12, 1988, third inning.
Bo Jackson, A.L., July 11, 1989, first inning.
Jeff Conine, N.L., July 11, 1995, eighth inning.
Javy Lopez, N.L., July 8, 1997, seventh inning.

Most grand slams, game
1—Fred Lynn, A.L., July 6, 1983, third inning.

Most home runs, inning
1—Held by many players.

TOTAL BASES

Most total bases, career
40—Stan Musial, N.L., 1943, 1944, 1946 through 1958, 1959, 1959, 1960, 1960, 1961, 1961, 1962, 1962, 1963 (24 games).
Willie Mays, N.L., 1954 through 1958, 1959, 1959, 1960, 1960, 1961, 1961, 1962, 1962, 1963 through 1973 (24 games).

Most total bases, game
10—Ted Williams, A.L., July 9, 1946.

Most total bases, inning
4—Held by many players.

LONG HITS

Most long hits, career
8—Stan Musial, N.L., 1943, 1944, 1946 through 1958, 1959, 1959, 1960, 1960, 1961, 1961, 1962, 1962, 1963 (24 games; two doubles, six home runs).
Willie Mays, N.L., 1954 through 1958, 1959, 1959, 1960, 1960, 1961, 1961, 1962, 1962, 1963 through 1973 (24 games; two doubles, three triples, three home runs.)

Most long hits, game
2—Held by many players.

Most long hits, inning
1—Held by many players.

RUNS BATTED IN

Most runs batted in, career
12—Ted Williams, A.L., 1940 through 1942, 1946 through 1951, 1954 through 1958, 1959, 1959, 1960, 1960 (18 games).

Most runs batted in, game
5—Ted Williams A.L., July 9, 1946.
Al Rosen, A.L., July 13, 1954.

Most runs batted in, inning
4—Fred Lynn, A.L., July 6, 1983, third inning.

BASES ON BALLS

Most bases on balls, career
11—Ted Williams, A.L., 1940 through 1942, 1946 through 1951, 1954 through 1958, 1959, 1959, 1960, 1960 (18 games).

Most bases on balls, game
3—Charlie Gehringer, A.L., July 10, 1934.
Phil Cavarretta, N.L., July 11, 1944 (also one single, one triple).

Most bases on balls, inning
1—Held by many players.

STRIKEOUTS

Most strikeouts, career
17—Mickey Mantle, A.L., 1953 through 1958, 1959, 1959, 1960, 1960, 1961, 1961, 1962, 1964, 1967, 1968 (16 games).

Most strikeouts, nine-inning game
3—Lou Gehrig, A.L., July 10, 1934.
Bob L. Johnson, A.L., July 8, 1935.
Stan Hack, N.L., July 11, 1939.
Joe Gordon, A.L., July 6, 1942.
Ken Keltner, A.L., July 13, 1943.
Jim Hegan, A.L., July 11, 1950.
Mickey Mantle, A.L., July 10, 1956.
Johnny Roseboro, N.L., July 31, 1961.
Willie McCovey, N.L., July 9, 1968.
Johnny Bench, N.L., July 14, 1970.
Albert Belle, A.L., July 9, 1996.
Craig Biggio, N.L., July 7, 1998.

Most strikeouts, extra-inning game
4—Roberto Clemente, N.L., July 11, 1967 (consecutive).

Most strikeouts, inning
1—Held by many players.

SACRIFICE HITS AND FLIES

Most sacrifice hits, career
1—Held by many players.

ost sacrifice hits, game or inning
—Held by many players.

ost sacrifice flies, career
—George Brett, A.L., 1976 through 1979, 1981 through 1985,
    1988 (10 games).

ost sacrifice flies, game or inning
—Held by many players.

HIT BY PITCH, GROUNDING INTO DOUBLE PLAYS

ost hit by pitch, career
—Held by many players.

Most grounding into double plays, career
3—Joe DiMaggio, A.L., 1936 through 1942, 1947 through 1950
    (11 games).
  Pete Rose N.L., 1965, 1967, 1969 through 1971, 1973
    through 1982, 1985 (16 games).

Most grounding into double plays, game
2—Bobby Richardson, A.L., July 9, 1963.

REACHING ON ERRORS OR INTERFERENCE

Most times reaching base on catcher's interference, game
1—Paul Molitor, A.L., July 9, 1991.

ALL-STAR GAME *Individual batting*

CLUB BATTING

BATTING AVERAGE

Highest batting average, game
.442—A.L., July 7, 1998 (43 at-bats, 19 hits).

Lowest batting average, game
.069—N.L., July 10, 1990 (29 at-bats, two hits).

AT-BATS AND PLATE APPEARANCES

Most at-bats, nine-inning game
44—A.L., July 14, 1992.

Most at-bats by both clubs, nine-inning game
83—A.L. 44, N.L. 39, July 14, 1992.

Fewest at-bats, nine-inning game
27—N.L., July 9, 1968 (batted eight innings).
29—Held by many clubs. Last club: N.L., July 10, 2001.

Fewest at-bats by both clubs, nine-inning game
57—A.L. 30, N.L. 27, July 9, 1968.

Most consecutive batters facing pitcher with none reaching base, game
20—A.L., July 9, 1968 (Jim Fregosi doubled to start game, then 20 consecutive batters were retired before Tony Oliva doubled in seventh inning).

Most batters facing pitcher, inning
11—A.L., July 10, 1934, fifth inning.

Most batters facing pitcher by both clubs, inning
19—A.L. 11, N.L. 8, July 10, 1934, fifth inning.

RUNS

Most runs, game
13—A.L., July 6, 1983.
A.L., July 14, 1992.
A.L., July 7, 1998.

Most runs by both clubs, game
21—A.L. 13, N.L. 8, July 7, 1998.

Most runs, inning
7—A.L., July 6, 1983, third inning.

Most runs by both clubs, inning
9—A.L. 6, N.L. 3, July 10, 1934, fifth inning.

Most innings scored, game
6—A.L., July 7, 1998.

Most innings scored by both clubs, game
10—A.L. 6, N.L. 4, July 7, 1998.

Most consecutive scoreless innings by one league, total games
19—A.L.; last nine innings, 1967; all nine innings, 1968; first inning, 1969.

EARNED RUNS

Most earned runs, game
13—A.L., July 14, 1992.

Most earned runs by both clubs, game
20—A.L. 11, N.L. 9, July 13, 1954.

Fewest earned runs, game
0—N.L., July 11, 1939; A.L., July 9, 1940; N.L., July 9, 1946; A.L., July 13, 1960; A.L., July 9, 1968; N.L., July 9, 1968; A.L., July 16, 1985; A.L., July 14, 1987; N.L., July 10, 1990; A.L., July 9, 1996.

Fewest earned runs by both clubs, game
0— A.L. 0, N.L. 0, July 9, 1968.

HITS

Most hits, game
19—A.L., July 14, 1992.

Most hits by both clubs, game
31—A.L. 17, N.L. 14, July 13, 1954.
A.L. 19, N.L. 12, July 14, 1992.
A.L. 19, N.L. 12, July 7, 1998.

Fewest hits, game
2—N.L., July 10, 1990.

Fewest hits by both clubs, game
8—N.L. 5, A.L. 3, July 9, 1968.

SINGLES

Most singles, game
16—A.L., July 7, 1998.

Most singles by both clubs, game
26—A.L. 16, N.L. 10, July 7, 1998.

Fewest singles, game
0—A.L., July 9, 1968.
N.L., July 11, 1995.

Fewest singles by both clubs, game
4—N.L. 4, A.L. 0, July 9, 1968.

DOUBLES

Most doubles, game
5—A.L., July 10, 1934.
A.L., July 12, 1949.

Most doubles by both clubs, game
7—A.L. 5, N.L. 2, July 12, 1949.
A.L. 4, N.L. 3, July 13, 1993.

Fewest doubles, game
0—Made in many games.

Fewest doubles by both clubs, game
0—July 6, 1942; July 9, 1946; July 13, 1948; July 8, 1958, July 13, 1976.

TRIPLES

Most triples, game
2—A.L., July 10, 1934; A.L., July 10, 1951; N.L., July 13, 1976 A.L., July 11, 1978; A.L., July 6, 1983.

Most triples by both clubs, game
3—A.L. 2, N.L. 1, July 11, 1978.

Fewest triples, game
0—Made in many games.

Fewest triples by both clubs, game
0—Made in many games.

HOME RUNS

Most home runs, game
4—N.L., July 10, 1951; A.L., July 13, 1954; N.L., July 13, 1960 N.L., August 9, 1981.

Most home runs by both clubs, game
6—N.L. 4, A.L. 2, July 10, 1951.
A.L. 4, N.L. 2, July 13, 1954.
A.L. 3, N.L. 3, July 13, 1971.

Most home runs accounting for all runs by both clubs, extra-inning game
3—N.L. 2, A.L. 1, July 11, 1967.

Fewest home runs, game
0—Made in many games.

Fewest home runs by both clubs, game
0—Made in many games.

Most consecutive games, one or more home runs
4—N.L., 1969 through 1977.

Most consecutive home runs from start of game
2—A.L., July 11, 1989 (Jackson, Boggs).

Most home runs, inning (13 times; *consecutive)
2—A.L., July 6, 1942, first inning (Boudreau, York).
    N.L., July 10, 1951, fourth inning (Musial, Elliott).
    A.L., July 13, 1954, third inning* (Rosen, Boone).
    A.L., July 10, 1956, sixth inning* (Williams, Mantle).
    N.L., July 7, 1964, fourth inning (Williams, Boyer).
    N.L., July 13, 1965, first inning (Mays, Torre).
    A.L., July 13, 1965, fifth inning (McAuliffe, Killebrew).
    A.L., July 13, 1971, third inning (Jackson, F. Robinson).
    N.L., July 15, 1975, second inning* (Garvey, Wynn).
    N.L., July 19, 1977, first inning (Morgan, Luzinski).
    A.L., July 6, 1983, third inning (Rice, Lynn).
    A.L., July 11, 1989, first inning* (Jackson, Boggs).
    A.L., July 10, 2001, sixth inning* (Jeter, Ordonez).

Most home runs by both clubs, inning
3—N.L. 2 (Musial, Elliott), A.L. 1 (Wertz), July 10, 1951, fourth
    inning.
    A.L. 2 (Jackson, F. Robinson), N.L. 1 (Aaron), July 13, 1971,
    third inning.

TOTAL BASES

Most total bases, game
29—A.L., July 13, 1954.

Most total bases by both clubs, game
52—A.L. 29, N.L. 23, July 13, 1954.

Fewest total bases, game
2—N.L., July 10, 1990.

Fewest total bases by both clubs, game
12—A.L. 6, N.L. 6, 1968.

LONG HITS

Most long hits, game
7—A.L., July 10, 1934 (five doubles, two triples).
    A.L., July 6, 1983 (three doubles, two triples, two home runs).

Most long hits by both clubs, game
10—N.L. 5 (one double, four home runs); A.L. 5 (one double,
    two triples, two home runs), July 10, 1951.
    A.L. 6 (four doubles, two home runs); N.L. 4 (three
    doubles, one home run), July 13, 1993.

Fewest long hits, game
0—A.L., July 11, 1944; N.L., July 9, 1946; A.L., July 14, 1953;
    N.L., July 8, 1958; A.L., July 8, 1958; N.L., July 9, 1963;
    A.L., July 16, 1985; N.L., July 12, 1988; N.L., July 11,
    1989; N.L., July 10, 1990; A.L., July 13, 1999.

Fewest long hits by both clubs, game
0—July 8, 1958.

EXTRA BASES ON LONG HITS

Most extra bases on long hits, game
14—N.L., August 9, 1981.

Most extra bases on long hits by both clubs, game
24—N.L. 13, A.L. 11, July 10, 1951.

Fewest extra bases on long hits, game
0—A.L., July 11, 1944; N.L., July 9, 1946; A.L., July 14, 1953;
    N.L., July 8, 1958; A.L., July 8, 1958; N.L., July 9, 1963;
    A.L., July 16, 1985; N.L., July 12, 1988; N.L., July 11,
    1989; N.L., July 10, 1990; A.L., July 13, 1999.

Fewest extra bases on long hits by both clubs, game
0—July 8, 1958.

RUNS BATTED IN

Most runs batted in, game
13—A.L., July 6, 1983.
    A.L., July 14, 1992.

Most runs batted in by both clubs, game
20—A.L. 11, N.L. 9, July 13, 1954.

Fewest runs batted in, game
0—A.L., July 9, 1940; N.L., July 9, 1946; A.L., July 13, 1960;
    A.L., July 12, 1966; A.L., July 9, 1968; N.L., July 9,
    1968; A.L., July 14, 1987; N.L., July 12, 1988; N.L., July
    10, 1990; A.L., July 9, 1996.

Fewest runs batted in, game, both clubs
0—A.L. 0, N.L. 0, July 9, 1968.

BASES ON BALLS

Most bases on balls, game
9—A.L., July 10, 1934.

Most bases on balls by both clubs, game
13—N.L. 8, A.L. 5, July 12, 1949.

Fewest bases on balls, game
0—N.L., July 6, 1933; N.L., July 7, 1937; N.L., July 6, 1938; A.L.,
    July 6, 1942; A.L., July 10, 1956; N.L., July 11, 1967, 15
    innings; A.L., July 9, 1968; N.L., July 15, 1975; A.L., July
    9, 1996; N.L., July 9, 1996; A.L., July 10, 2001.

Fewest bases on balls by both clubs, nine-inning game
0—A.L. 0, N.L. 0, July 9, 1996.

Fewest bases on balls by both clubs, extra-inning game
2—A.L. 2, N.L. 0, July 11, 1967, 15 innings.

STRIKEOUTS

Most strikeouts, nine-inning game
12—A.L., July 10, 1934; N.L., July 10, 1956; A.L., August 3,
    1959; A.L., July 15, 1986; N.L., July 13, 1999.

Most strikeouts, extra-inning game
17—A.L., July 11, 1967, 15 innings.

Most strikeouts by both clubs, nine-inning game
22—N.L. 12, A.L. 10, July 13, 1999.

Most strikeouts by both clubs, extra-inning game
30—A.L. 17, N.L. 13, July 11, 1967, 15 innings.

Fewest strikeouts, game
0—N.L., July 7, 1937.

Fewest strikeouts by both clubs, game
6—A.L. 4, N.L. 2, July 8, 1958.

SACRIFICE HITS

Most sacrifice hits, nine-inning game
3—N.L., July 11, 1944.

Most sacrifice hits by both clubs, nine-inning game
3—N.L. 3, A.L. 0, July 11, 1944.

Fewest sacrifice hits, game
0—Made in many games.

Fewest sacrifice hits by both clubs, game
0—Made in many games.

HIT BY PITCH

Most hit by pitch, game
2—A.L., July 10, 1962.

Most hit by pitch by both clubs, game
2—A.L. 2, N.L. 0, July 10, 1962.
    A.L. 1, N.L. 1, July 15, 1975.
    A.L. 1, N.L. 1, July 19, 1977.

BASERUNNING

INDIVIDUAL

Most stolen bases, career
6—Willie Mays, N.L., 1954 through 1958, 1959, 1959, 1960, 1960, 1961, 1961, 1962, 1962, 1963 through 1973 (24 games).

Most stolen bases, game
2—Willie Mays, N.L., July 9, 1963.
Kelly Gruber, A.L., July 10, 1990.
Roberto Alomar, A.L., July 14, 1992.
Kenny Lofton, A.L., July 9, 1996.

Stealing home, game
1—Pie Traynor, N.L., July 10, 1934, fifth inning (front end of a double steal with Mel Ott).

Most times caught stealing, nine-inning game
1—Held by many players.

Most times caught stealing, extra-inning game
2—Tony Oliva, A.L., July 11, 1967, 15 innings.

CLUB

Most stolen bases, game
5—A.L., July 7, 1998.

Most stolen bases by both clubs, game
5—A.L. 3, N.L. 2, July 16, 1985.
A.L. 4, N.L. 1, July 10, 1990.
A.L. 5, N.L. 0, July 7, 1998.

Fewest stolen bases, game
0—Made in many games.

Fewest stolen bases by both clubs, game
0—Made in many games.

Most left on base, game
12—A.L., July 10, 1934.
N.L., July 12, 1949.
A.L., July 13, 1960.

Most left on base by both clubs, game
20—N.L. 12, A.L. 8, July 12, 1949.

Fewest left on bases, game
0—N.L., July 11, 1995.

Fewest left on base by both clubs, game
4—N.L. 2, A.L. 2, July 13, 1971.

PITCHING

GAMES

Most games pitched

8—Jim Bunning, A.L., 1957, 1959 (first game), 1961, 1961, 1962 (first game), 1963; N.L., 1964, 1966.
  Don Drysdale, N.L., 1959, 1959, 1962 (first game), 1963 through 1965, 1967, 1968.
  Juan Marichal, N.L., 1962, 1962, 1964, through 1968, 1971.
  Tom Seaver, N.L., 1967, 1968, 1970, 1973, 1975 through 1977, 1981.

Most consecutive games pitched

6—Ewell Blackwell, N.L., 1946 through 1951.
  Early Wynn, A.L., 1955 through 1958, 1959, 1959.

GAMES STARTED AND FINISHED

Most games started

5—Lefty Gomez, A.L., 1933 through 1935, 1937, 1938.
  Robin Roberts, N.L., 1950, 1951, 1953 through 1955.
  Don Drysdale, N.L. 1959, 1959, 1962 (first game), 1964, 1968.

Most games finished

6—Rich Gossage, A.L., 1975, 1978, 1980; N.L., 1977, 1984, 1985.

INNINGS

Most innings pitched, career

19.1—Don Drysdale, N.L., 1959, 1959, 1962 (first game), 1963, 1964, 1965, 1967, 1968 (eight games).

Most innings, game

6—Lefty Gomez, A.L., July 8, 1935.

GAMES WON AND LOST

Most games won

3—Lefty Gomez, A.L., 1933, 1935, 1937.

Most games lost

2—Mort Cooper, N.L., 1942, 1943.
  Claude Passeau, N.L., 1941, 1946.
  Whitey Ford, A.L., 1959 (first game), 1960 (second game).
  Luis Tiant, A.L., 1968, 1974.
  Catfish Hunter, A.L., 1967, 1975.
  Dwight Gooden, N.L., 1986, 1988.

RUNS AND EARNED RUNS

Most runs allowed, career

13—Whitey Ford, A.L., 1954 through 1956, 1959, 1960, 1961.

Most earned runs allowed, career

11—Whitey Ford, A.L., 1954 through 1956, 1959, 1960, 1961.

Most runs allowed, game

7—Atlee Hammaker, N.L., July 6, 1983.

Most earned runs allowed, game

7—Atlee Hammaker, N.L., July 6, 1983.

Most runs allowed, inning

7—Atlee Hammaker, N.L., July 6, 1983, third inning.

Most earned runs allowed, inning

7—Atlee Hammaker, N.L., July 6, 1983, third inning.

HITS

Most hits allowed, total games

19—Whitey Ford, A.L., 1954 through 1956, 1959, 1960, 1961.

Most hits allowed, game

9—Tom Glavine, N.L., July 14, 1992.

Most hits allowed, inning

7—Tom Glavine, N.L., July 14, 1992, first inning (consecutive).

HOME RUNS

Most home runs allowed, career

4—Vida Blue, A.L., 1971, 1975.
  Catfish Hunter, A.L., 1967, 1970, 1973 through 1976.

Most home runs allowed, game

3—Jim Palmer, A.L., July 19, 1977.

Most home runs allowed, inning (12 times; *consecutive)

2—Mort Cooper, N.L., July 6, 1942, first inning.
  Eddie Lopat, A.L., July 10, 1951, fourth inning.
  Robin Roberts, N.L., July 13, 1954, third inning*.
  Warren Spahn, N.L., July 10, 1956, sixth inning*.
  John Wyatt, A.L., July 7, 1964, fourth inning.
  Milt Pappas, A.L., July 13, 1965, first inning.
  Jim Maloney, N.L., July 13, 1965, fifth inning.
  Dock Ellis, N.L., July 13, 1971, third inning.
  Vida Blue, A.L., July 15, 1975, second inning*.
  Jim Palmer, A.L., July 19, 1977, first inning.
  Atlee Hammaker, A.L., July 6, 1983, third inning.
  Rick Reuschel, N.L., July 11, 1989, first inning*.
  Jon Lieber, N.L., July 10, 2001, sixth inning*.

BASES ON BALLS

Most bases on balls, career

7—Jim Palmer, A.L., 1970 through 1972, 1977, 1978.

Most bases on balls, game

5—Bill Hallahan, N.L., July 6, 1933 (two innings).

Most bases on balls, inning (*consecutive)

3—Early Wynn, A.L., August 3, 1959, fifth inning.
  Jim Palmer, A.L., July 11, 1978, third inning*.
  Jim Kern, A.L., July 17, 1979, ninth inning.
  Dan Petry, A.L., July 16, 1985, ninth inning.
  Kevin Brown, N.L., July 11, 2000, third inning.

STRIKEOUTS

Most strikeouts, career

19—Don Drysdale, N.L., 1959, 1959, 1962 (first game), 1963 through 1965, 1967, 1968 (eight games).

Most strikeouts, game

6—Carl Hubbell, N.L., July 10, 1934 (three innings).
  Johnny Vander Meer, N.L., July 13, 1943 (2.2 innings).
  Larry Jansen, N.L., July 11, 1950 (five innings).
  Ferguson Jenkins, N.L., July 11, 1967 (three innings).

Most consecutive strikeouts, game

5—Carl Hubbell, N.L., July 10, 1934; three in first inning, two in second inning (Ruth, Gehrig, Foxx, Simmons, Cronin).
  Fernando Valenzuela, N.L., July 15, 1986; three in fourth inning, two in fifth inning (Mattingly, Ripken, Barfield, Whitaker, Higuera).

Most consecutive strikeouts from start of game

4—Pedro Martinez, A.L., July 13, 1999; three in first inning, one in second inning (Larkin, Walker, Sosa, McGwire).

HIT BATSMEN, WILD PITCHES AND BALKS

Most hit batsmen, inning or game

1—Held by many pitchers.

Most wild pitches, career

2—Ewell Blackwell, N.L., 1946 through 1951.
  Robin Roberts, N.L., 1950, 1951, 1953 through 1955.
  Tom Brewer, A.L., 1956.
  Juan Marichal, N.L., 1962, 1962, 1964 through 1968, 1971.
  Dave Stieb, A.L., 1980, 1981.
  Steve Rogers, N.L., 1978, 1979, 1982.
  John Smoltz, N.L., 1989, 1992, 1993.

Most wild pitches, game

2—Tom Brewer, A.L., July 10, 1956, sixth and seventh innings.
    Juan Marichal, N.L., July 30, 1962, ninth inning.
    Dave Stieb, A.L., July 8, 1980, seventh inning.
    John Smoltz, N.L., July 13, 1993, sixth inning.

Most wild pitches, inning

2—Juan Marichal, N.L., July 30, 1962, ninth inning.
    Dave Stieb, A.L., July 8, 1980, seventh inning.
    John Smoltz, N.L., July 13, 1993, sixth inning.

Most balks, career

2—Dwight Gooden, N.L., 1984, 1986, 1988.

Most balks, inning or game

1—Bob Friend, N.L., July 11, 1960.
    Stu Miller, N.L., July 11, 1961.
    Steve Busby, A.L., July 15, 1975.
    Jim Kern, A.L., July 17, 1979.
    Dwight Gooden, N.L., July 15, 1986; July 12, 1988.
    Charlie Hough, A.L., July 15, 1986.

INDIVIDUAL FIELDING

FIRST BASEMEN

Most games played
10—Steve Garvey, N.L., 1974 through 1981, 1984, 1985.

Most putouts, career
53—Lou Gehrig, A.L., 1933 through 1938.

Most putouts, nine-inning game
14—George McQuinn, A.L., July 13, 1948.

Most putouts, extra-inning game
15—Harmon Killebrew, A.L., July 11, 1967.

Most assists, career
6—Steve Garvey, N.L., 1974 through 1981, 1984, 1985.

Most assists, game
3—Rudy York, A.L., July 6, 1942.
    Bill White, N.L., July 9, 1963.

Most chances accepted, career
55—Lou Gehrig, A.L., 1933 through 1938.
    Steve Garvey, N.L., 1974 through 1981, 1984, 1985.

Most chances accepted, nine-inning game
14—Rudy York, A.L., July 6, 1942.
    George McQuinn, A.L., July 13, 1948.

Most chances accepted, extra-inning game
16—Harmon Killebrew, A.L., July 11, 1967.

Most errors, career
2—Lou Gehrig, A.L., 1933 through 1938.

Most errors, game
1—Held by many players.

Most double plays, career
6—Bill White, N.L., 1960, 1960, 1961, 1961, 1963.
    Harmon Killebrew, A.L., 1965, 1967, 1968, 1971.

Most double plays, game
3—Stan Musial, N.L., July 8, 1958.

Most unassisted double plays, game
1—Pete Runnels, A.L., August 3, 1959, second inning.
    Lee May, N.L., July 25, 1972, third inning.

SECOND BASEMEN

Most games played
13—Nellie Fox, A.L., 1951, 1953 through 1958, 1959, 1959,
    1960, 1960, 1961, 1963.

Most putouts, career
25—Nellie Fox, A.L., 1951, 1953 through 1958, 1959, 1959,
    1960, 1960, 1961, 1963.

Most putouts, nine-inning game
5—Frankie Frisch, N.L., July 6, 1933.

Most putouts, extra-inning game
7—Juan Samuel, N.L., July 14, 1987, 13 innings.

Most assists, career
23—Billy Herman, N.L., 1934 through 1938, 1940 through
    1943.

Most assists, game
6—Willie Randolph, A.L., July 19, 1977.

Most chances accepted, career
39—Nellie Fox, A.L., 1951, 1953 through 1958, 1959, 1959,
    1960, 1960, 1961, 1963.

Most chances accepted, game
9—Bill Mazeroski, N.L., July 8, 1958.
    Juan Samuel, N.L., July 14, 1987, 13 innings.

Most errors, career
2—Billy Herman, N.L., 1934 through 1938, 1940 through 1943.
    Nellie Fox, A.L., 1951, 1953 through 1958, 1959, 1959,
    1960, 1960, 1961, 1963.
    Willie Randolph, A.L., 1977, 1980, 1981, 1987, 1989.
    Steve Sax, N.L., 1982, 1983, 1986, 1989, 1990.

Most errors, game
2—Billy Herman, N.L., July 13, 1943.
    Willie Randolph, A.L., July 8, 1980.

Most double plays, career
5—Roberto Alomar, N.L., 1990; A.L. 1991 through 2001.

Most double plays, game
3—Billy Herman, N.L., July 13, 1943.
    Bill Mazeroski, N.L., July 8, 1958.

Most unassisted double plays, game
Never accomplished.

THIRD BASEMEN

Most games played
18—Brooks Robinson, A.L., 1960, 1960, 1961, 1961, 1962,
    1962, 1963 through 1974 (consecutive).

Most putouts, career
11—Brooks Robinson, A.L., 1960, 1960, 1961, 1961, 1962,
    1962, 1963 through 1974.

Most putouts, game
4—George Kell, A.L., July 10, 1951.
    Brooks Robinson, A.L., July 12, 1966, 9.1 innings.

Most assists, career
32—Brooks Robinson, A.L., 1960, 1960, 1961, 1961, 1962,
    1962, 1963 through 1974.

Most assists, game
6—Ken Keltner, A.L., July 13, 1948.
    Frank Malzone, A.L., August 3, 1959.

Most chances accepted, career
43—Brooks Robinson, A.L., 1960, 1960, 1961, 1961, 1962,
    1962, 1963 through 1974.

Most chances accepted, nine-inning game
7—Ken Keltner, A.L., July 13, 1948.
    Frank Malzone, A.L., August 3, 1959.

Most chances accepted, extra-inning game
8—Brooks Robinson, A.L., July 12, 1966, 9.1 innings.

Most errors, career
6—Eddie Mathews, N.L., 1953, 1955, 1957, 1959, 1960, 1960,
    1961, 1961, 1962 (second game).

Most errors, game
2—Red Rolfe, A.L., July 7, 1937.
    Eddie Mathews, N.L., July 11, 1960; July 30, 1962.
    Ken Boyer, N.L., July 11, 1961, 10 innings.

Most errors, inning
2—Eddie Mathews, N.L., July 30, 1962, ninth inning.

Most double plays, career
3—Frank Malzone, A.L., 1957, 1958, 1959, 1959, 1960, 1960,
    1963.
    Brooks Robinson, A.L., 1960, 1960, 1961, 1961, 1962,
    1962, 1963 through 1974.
    George Brett, A.L., 1976 through 1979, 1981 through 1983.

Most double plays, game
1—Held by many players.

Most unassisted double plays, game
Never accomplished.

SHORTSTOPS

Most games played
15—Cal Ripken Jr., A.L., 1983 through 1996, 2001.

Most putouts, career
16—Ozzie Smith, N.L., 1981 through 1992, 1994, 1996.

Most putouts, nine-inning game
5—Chico Carrasquel, A.L., July 13, 1954.

Most assists, career
24—Joe Cronin, A.L., 1933 through 1935, 1937 through 1939, 1941.

Most assists, nine-inning game
8—Joe Cronin, A.L., July 10, 1934.

Most chances accepted, career
39—Ozzie Smith, N.L., 1981 through 1992, 1994, 1996.

Most chances accepted, nine-inning game
10—Joe Cronin, A.L., July 10, 1934.
    Marty Marion, N.L., July 9, 1946.

Most errors, career
2—Joe Cronin, A.L., 1933 through 1935, 1937 through 1939, 1941.
    Ernie Banks, N.L., 1955, 1957, 1958, 1959, 1959, 1960, 1960, 1961.
    Nomar Garciaparra, A.L., 1997, 1999, 2000.

Most errors, game
2—Nomar Garciaparra, A.L., July 11, 2000.

Most double plays, career
6—Ernie Banks, N.L., 1955, 1957, 1958, 1959, 1959, 1960, 1960, 1961.

Most double plays, game
2—Lou Boudreau, A.L., July 6, 1942.
    Marty Marion, N.L., July 9, 1946.
    Eddie Joost, A.L., July 12, 1949.
    Ernie Banks, N.L., July 8, 1958; July 13, 1960.
    Eddie Kasko, N.L., July 31, 1961.
    Luis Aparicio, A.L., July 30, 1962.
    Dick Groat, N.L., July 9, 1963.
    Tony Fernandez, A.L., July 11, 1989.

Most unassisted double plays, game
Never accomplished.

OUTFIELDERS

Most games played
22—Willie Mays, N.L., 1954 through 1958, 1959, 1959, 1960, 1960, 1961, 1961, 1962, 1962, 1963 through 1972.

Most putouts, career
55—Willie Mays, N.L., 1954 through 1958, 1959, 1959, 1960, 1960, 1961, 1961, 1962, 1962, 1963 through 1972.

Most putouts, center fielder, nine-inning game
7—Chet Laabs, A.L., July 13, 1943.
    Willie Mays, N.L., July 7, 1964.

Most putouts, center fielder, extra-inning game
9—Larry Doby, A.L., July 11, 1950, 14 innings.

Most putouts, left fielder, nine-inning game
5—Sammy West, A.L., July 7, 1937.
    Frank Robinson, N.L., July 9, 1957.
    Joe Rudi, A.L., July 15, 1975.

Most putouts, right fielder, nine-inning game
4—Charlie Keller, A.L., July 9, 1940.
    Enos Slaughter, N.L., July 14, 1953.
    Darryl Strawberry, N.L., July 12, 1988.

Most putouts, right fielder, extra-inning game
6—Roberto Clemente, N.L., July 11, 1967, 15 innings.

Most assists, career
3—Stan Musial, N.L., 1943, 1944, 1946, 1948, 1949, 1951 through 1956, 1962 (second game).

Most assists, center fielder, game
1—Held by many players.

Most assists, left fielder, game
1—Held by many players.

Most assists, right fielder, game
2—Dave Parker, N.L., July 17, 1979.
    Tony Gwynn, N.L., July 14, 1992.

Most chances accepted, career
55—Willie Mays, N.L., 1954 through 1958, 1959, 1959, 1960, 1960, 1961, 1961, 1962, 1962, 1963 through 1972.

Most chances accepted, center fielder, nine-inning game
7—Chet Laabs, A.L., July 13, 1943.
    Willie Mays, N.L., July 7, 1964.

Most chances accepted, center fielder, extra-inning game
9—Larry Doby, A.L., July 11, 1950, 14 innings.

Most chances accepted, left fielder, game
5—Samny West, A.L., July 7, 1937.
    Joe Rudi, A.L., July 15, 1975.

Most chances accepted, right fielder, game
4—Charlie Keller, A.L., July 9, 1940.
    Enos Slaughter, N.L., July 14, 1953.
    Darryl Strawberry, N.L., July 12, 1988.

Most errors, career
2—Pete Reiser, N.L., 1941, 1942.
    Joe DiMaggio, A.L., 1936 through 1942, 1947, 1949, 1950.

Most errors, center fielder, game
2—Pete Reiser, N.L., July 8, 1941.

Most errors, left fielder, game
1—Held by many players.

Most errors, right fielder, game
1—Held by many players.

Most double plays, career
1—Stan Spence, A.L., 1944, 1946, 1947.
    Tommy Davis, N.L., 1962, 1962, 1963.
    Darryl Strawberry, N.L., 1984 through 1988, 1990.

Most double plays, center fielder, game
Never accomplished.

Most double plays, left fielder, game
1—Tommy Davis, N.L., July 9, 1963.

Most double plays, right fielder, game
1—Stan Spence, A.L., July 11, 1944.
    Darryl Strawberry, N.L., July 10, 1990.

Most unassisted double plays
Never accomplished.

CATCHERS

Most games played
14—Yogi Berra, A.L., 1949 through 1958, 1959, 1960, 1960, 1961.

Most innings caught, game
15—Bill Freehan, A.L., July 11, 1967 (complete game).

Most putouts, career
61—Yogi Berra, A.L., 1949 through 1958, 1959, 1960, 1960, 1961.

Most putouts, nine-inning game
10—Bill Dickey, A.L., July 11, 1939.
    Yogi Berra, A.L., July 10, 1956.
    Del Crandall, N.L., July 7, 1959.
    Johnny Bench, N.L., July 15, 1975.
    Ivan Rodriguez, A.L., July 13, 1999.

Most putouts, extra-inning game
13—Roy Campanella, N.L., July 11, 1950, 14 innings.
Smoky Burgess, N.L., July 11, 1961, 10 innings.
Bill Freehan, A.L., July 11, 1967, 15 innings.

Most assists, career
7—Yogi Berra, A.L., 1949 through 1958, 1959, 1960, 1960, 1961.

Most assists, game
3—Lance Parrish, A.L., July 13, 1982.

Most chances accepted, career
68—Yogi Berra, A.L., 1949 through 1958, 1959, 1960, 1960, 1961.

Most chances accepted, nine-inning game
11—Yogi Berra, A.L., July 10, 1956.
Johnny Bench, N.L., July 15, 1975.
Ivan Rodriguez, A.L., July 13, 1999.

Most chances accepted, extra-inning game
15—Roy Campanella, N.L., July 11, 1950, 14 innings.

Most errors, career
2—Smoky Burgess, N.L., 1954, 1955, 1960, 1960, 1961, 1961.

Most errors, game
1—Held by many players.

Most passed balls, career and game
1—Held by many catchers.

Most double plays, career
2—Ivan Rodriguez, A.L., 1992 through 2001.

Most double plays, game
1—Held by many catchers.

Most unassisted double plays, game
Never accomplished.

PITCHERS

Most games pitched
8—Jim Bunning, A.L., 1957, 1959 (first game), 1961, 1961, 1962 (first game), 1963; N.L., 1964, 1966.
Don Drysdale, N.L., 1959, 1959, 1962 (first game), 1963, 1964, 1965, 1967, 1968.
Juan Marichal, N.L., 1962, 1962, 1964 through 1968, 1971.
Tom Seaver, N.L., 1967, 1968, 1970, 1973, 1975 through 1977, 1981.

Most putouts, career
3—Spud Chandler, A.L., 1942.

Most putouts, game
3—Spud Chandler, A.L., July 6, 1942.

Most assists, career
5—Johnny Vander Meer, N.L., 1938, 1942, 1943.

Most assists, game
3—Johnny Vander Meer, N.L., July 6, 1938.
Don Drysdale, N.L., July 7, 1964.
Mickey Lolich, A.L., July 13, 1971.

Most chances accepted, career
5—Mel Harder, A.L., 1934, 1935, 1936, 1937.
Johnny Vander Meer, N.L., 1938, 1942, 1943.
Don Drysdale, N.L., 1959, 1959, 1962 (first game), 1963 through 1965, 1967, 1968.

Most chances accepted, game
4—Spud Chandler, A.L., July 6, 1942.

Most errors, career and game
1—Held by many pitchers.

Most double plays, career and game
1—Held by many pitchers.

Most unassisted double plays, game
Never accomplished.

ALL-STAR GAME Individual fielding

CLUB FIELDING

NUMBER OF PLAYERS AT POSITIONS
INFIELDERS

Most infielders, game
10—N.L., July 13, 1960 (second game).
N.L., July 14, 1970, 12 innings.
N.L., July 13, 1976.
A.L., July 11, 2000.
A.L., July 10, 2001.

Most infielders by both clubs, game
19—A.L. 10, N.L. 9, July 11, 2000.

Most first basemen, nine-inning game
3—N.L., July 9, 1946.
N.L., July 13, 1960 (second game).
N.L., July 24, 1973.
A.L., July 11, 2000.
A.L., July 10, 2001.

Most first basemen by both clubs, nine-inning game
5—N.L. 3, A.L. 2, July 9, 1946.
N.L. 3, A.L. 2, July 13, 1960 (second game).
A.L. 3, N.L. 2, July 11, 2000.
N.L. 3, A.L. 2, July 10, 2001.

Most second basemen, nine-inning game
3—N.L., July 13, 1960 (second game).
N.L., August 9, 1981.
A.L., July 14, 1992.
A.L., July 8, 1997.
N.L., July 11, 2000.

Most second basemen by both clubs, nine-inning game
5—N.L. 3, A.L. 2, July 13, 1960 (second game).
N.L. 3, A.L. 2, August 9, 1981.
A.L. 3, N.L. 2, July 14, 1992.
A.L. 3, N.L. 2, July 8, 1997.
N.L. 3, A.L. 2, July 11, 2000.

Most third basemen, nine-inning game
3—Held by many clubs.

Most third basemen by both clubs, nine-inning game
6—A.L. 3, N.L. 3, July 10, 2001.

Most shortstops, nine-inning game
3—Held by many clubs.

Most shortstops by both clubs, nine-inning game
6—A.L. 3, N.L. 3, July 13, 1976.

OUTFIELDERS

Most outfielders, nine-inning game
8—N.L., July 24, 1973.

Most outfielders by both clubs, game
14—N.L. 7, A.L. 7, July 8, 1980.

Most right fielders, nine-inning game
4—N.L., July 13, 1976.

Most right fielders by both clubs, nine-inning game
6—N.L. 4, A.L. 2, July 13, 1976.

Most center fielders, nine-inning game
3—Occurred many times.

Most center fielders by both clubs, nine-inning game
5—Occurred many times.

Most left fielders, nine-inning game
3—Occurred many times.

Most left fielders by both clubs, nine-inning game
5—Occurred many times.

Most left fielders by both clubs, extra-inning game
6—N.L. 3, A.L. 3, July 14, 1970, 12 innings.

BATTERY

Most catchers, nine-inning game
3—Occurred many times.

Most catchers by both clubs, nine-inning game
6—Occurred many times.

Most pitchers, game
10—A.L., July 14, 1992.

Most pitchers by both clubs, nine-inning game
18—A.L. 10, N.L. 8, July 14, 1992.
A.L. 9, N.L. 9, July 10, 2001.

Fewest pitchers, game
2—A.L., July 8, 1935.
A.L., July 6, 1942.

Fewest pitchers by both clubs, game
6—Occurred many times.

PUTOUTS, ASSISTS

Most players with one or more putouts, nine-inning game
14—N.L., July 13, 1976; A.L., July 6, 1983; A.L., July 14, 1992;
A.L., July 10, 2001.

Most players with one or more putouts by both clubs, nine-inning game
25—N.L. 14, A.L. 11, July 13, 1976.
A.L. 13, N.L. 12, July 16, 1985.
A.L. 14, N.L. 11, July 14, 1992.

Most assists, nine-inning game
16—A.L., July 6, 1942.
A.L., August 9, 1981.

Most assists by both clubs, nine-inning game
26—A.L. 15, N.L. 11, July 12, 1949.
A.L. 16, N.L. 10, August 9, 1981.
A.L. 14, N.L. 12, July 8, 1997.

Fewest assists, eight-inning game
4—A.L., July 9, 1940.
N.L., July 13, 1948.

Fewest assists, nine-inning game
5—N.L., July 10, 1934.
N.L., July 9, 1957.
N.L., July 23, 1969.
N.L., July 13, 1999.

Fewest assists by both clubs, nine-inning game
11—N.L. 6, A.L. 5, July 7, 1959.

Most players one or more assists, nine-inning game
10—N.L., July 24, 1973.

Most players one or more assists by both clubs, nine-inning game
19—N.L. 10, A.L. 9, July 24, 1973.

ERRORS, DOUBLE PLAYS

Most errors, game
5—N.L., July 12, 1949.
N.L., July 11, 1961.

Most errors by both clubs, nine-inning game
6—N.L. 5, A.L. 1, July 12, 1949.

Most errors by both clubs, extra-inning game
7—N.L. 5, A.L. 2, July 11, 1961, 10 innings.

Fewest errors, game
0—Occurred many times.

Fewest errors by both clubs, game
0—Occurred many times.

Most consecutive errorless games
11—N.L., 1963 through 1973.

Most double plays, game
3—Occurred many times.

Most double plays by both clubs, game
4—Occurred many times.

Fewest double plays, game
0—Occurred many times.

Fewest double plays by both clubs, game
0—Occurred many times.

MISCELLANEOUS

EARLIEST AND LATEST GAME DATES

Earliest date for All-Star Game
July 6, 1933 at Comiskey Park, Chicago.
July 6, 1938 at Crosley Field, Cincinnati.
July 6, 1942 at Polo Grounds, New York.
July 6, 1983 at Comiskey Park, Chicago.

Latest date for All-Star Game
August 9, 1981 at Municipal Stadium, Cleveland.

NIGHT GAMES

First night game
July 13, 1943 at Shibe Park, Philadelphia.

LENGTH OF GAMES

Longest game, by innings
15 innings—at Anaheim Stadium, California, July 11, 1967.

Shortest game, by innings
5 innings—at Shibe Park, Philadelphia, July 8, 1952 (rain).

Longest nine-inning game, by time
3 hours, 38 minutes—at Coors Field, Colorado, July 7, 1998.

Shortest nine-inning game, by time
1 hour, 53 minutes—at Sportsman's Park, St. Louis, July 9, 1940.

Longest extra-inning game, by time
3 hours, 41 minutes—at Anaheim Stadium, California, July 11, 1967, 15 innings.

GAMES WON AND LOST

All-Star games won
40—National League (lost 31, tied one).
31—American League (lost 40, tied one).

For a complete list of All-Star Game results, see page 538.

Most consecutive All-Star games won
11—National League, 1972 through 1982.

Most consecutive All-Star games lost
11—American League, 1972 through 1982.

ATTENDANCE

Largest attendance, game
72,086—at Municipal Stadium, Cleveland, August 9, 1981.

Smallest attendance, game
25,556—at Braves Field, Boston, July 7, 1936.

NON-PLAYING PERSONNEL

MANAGERS
GAMES

Most All-Star games managed
10—Casey Stengel, A.L., 1950 through 1954, 1956, 1957, 1958, 1959, 1959 (won four, lost six).

Most consecutive All-Star games managed
5—Casey Stengel, A.L., 1950, through 1954; also 1956, 1957, 1958, 1959, 1959.

GAMES WON

Most All-Star games won as manager
7—Walter Alston, N.L., 1956, 1960, 1960, 1964, 1966, 1967, 1975 (lost two).

Most All-Star games won as undefeated manager
4—Joe Torre, A.L., 1997, 1999 through 2001.

Most consecutive victories as All-Star manager
6—Walter Alston, N.L., 1960, 1960, 1964, 1966, 1967, 1975.

Most consecutive years managing All-Star winners
3—Tony La Russa, A.L., 1989 through 1991.
Joe Torre, A.L., 1999 through 2001.

Most All-Star games won as manager, one season
2—Walter Alston, N.L., July 11, July 13, 1960.

GAMES LOST

Most All-Star games lost as manager
6—Casey Stengel, A.L., 1950 through 1953, 1956, 1959, first game (won four).

Most All-Star games lost as winless manager
5—Al Lopez, A.L., 1955, 1960, 1960, 1964, 1965.

Most consecutive defeats as All-Star manager
5—Al Lopez, A.L., 1955, 1960, 1960, 1964, 1965.

Most consecutive years managing All-Star losers
4—Casey Stengel, A.L., 1950 through 1953.

Most All-Star games lost as manager, one season
2—Al Lopez, A.L., July 11, July 13, 1960.

UMPIRES

Most games umpired
7—Al Barlick, N.L., 1942, 1949, 1952, 1955, 1959, 1966, 1970.

Most consecutive games umpired
2—Held by many umpires

GENERAL REFERENCE

RESULTS

Year	Date	Site	Winner	Manager	Loser	Manager	Score
1933	July 6	Comiskey Park, Chicago ...............A.L.	Connie Mack, Phi.	N.L.	John McGraw, N.Y.	4-2
1934	July 10	Polo Grounds, New York ...............A.L.	Joe Cronin, Was.	N.L.	Bill Terry, N.Y.	9-7
1935	July 8	Cleveland Stadium, Cleveland........A.L.	Mickey Cochrane, Det.	N.L.	Frankie Frisch, St.L.	4-1
1936	July 7	Braves Field, Boston ....................N.L.	Charley Grimm, Chi.	A.L.	Joe McCarthy, N.Y.	4-3
1937	July 7	Griffith Stadium, Washington .......A.L.	Joe McCarthy, N.Y.	N.L.	Bill Terry, N.Y.	8-3
1938	July 6	Crosley Field, Cincinnati...............N.L.	Bill Terry, N.Y.	A.L.	Joe McCarthy, N.Y.	4-1
1939	July 11	Yankee Stadium, New York...........A.L.	Joe McCarthy, N.Y.	N.L.	Gabby Hartnett, Chi.	3-1
1940	July 9	Sportsman's Park, St. Louis .........N.L.	Bill McKechnie, Cin.	A.L.	Joe Cronin, Bos.	4-0
1941	July 8	Briggs Stadium, Detroit ................A.L.	Del Baker, Det.	N.L.	Bill McKechnie, Cin.	7-5
1942	July 6	Polo Grounds, New York ...............A.L.	Joe McCarthy, N.Y.	N.L.	Leo Durocher, Bkn.	3-1
1943	July 13	Shibe Park, Philadelphia ..............A.L.	Joe McCarthy, N.Y.	N.L.	Billy Southworth, St.L.	5-3
1944	July 11	Forbes Field, Pittsburgh................N.L.	Billy Southworth, St.L.	A.L.	Joe McCarthy, N.Y.	7-1
1945		Game canceled due to wartime travel restrictions.				
1946	July 9	Fenway Park, Boston ....................A.L.	Steve O'Neill, Det.	N.L.	Charley Grimm, Chi.	12-0
1947	July 8	Wrigley Field, Chicago ..................A.L.	Joe Cronin, Bos.	N.L.	Eddie Dyer, St.L.	2-1
1948	July 13	Sportsman's Park, St. Louis .........A.L.	Bucky Harris, N.Y.	N.L.	Leo Durocher, Bkn.	5-2
1949	July 12	Ebbets Field, Brooklyn ..................A.L.	Lou Boudreau, Cle.	N.L.	Billy Southworth, Bos.	11-7
1950	July 11	Comiskey Park, Chicago ...............N.L.	Burt Shotton, Bkn.	A.L.	Casey Stengel, N.Y.	4-3, 14 inn.
1951	July 10	Briggs Stadium, Detroit .................N.L.	Eddie Sawyer, Phi.	A.L.	Casey Stengel, N.Y.	8-3
1952	July 8	Shibe Park, Philadelphia................N.L.	Leo Durocher, N.Y.	A.L.	Casey Stengel, N.Y.	3-2, five inn.
1953	July 14	Crosley Field, Cincinnati................N.L.	Charlie Dressen, Bkn.	A.L.	Casey Stengel, N.Y.	5-1
1954	July 13	Cleveland Stadium, Cleveland........A.L.	Casey Stengel, N.Y.	N.L.	Walter Alston, Bkn.	11-9
1955	July 12	County Stadium, Milwaukee ..........N.L.	Leo Durocher, N.Y.	A.L.	Al Lopez, Cle.	6-5, 12 inn.
1956	July 10	Griffith Stadium, Washington ........N.L.	Walter Alston, Bkn.	A.L.	Casey Stengel, N.Y.	7-3
1957	July 9	Busch Stadium, St. Louis ..............A.L.	Casey Stengel, N.Y.	N.L.	Walter Alston, Bkn.	6-5
1958	July 8	Memorial Stadium, Baltimore .......A.L.	Casey Stengel, N.Y.	N.L.	Fred Haney, Mil.	4-3
1959	July 7	Forbes Field, Pittsburgh................N.L.	Fred Haney, Mil.	A.L.	Casey Stengel, N.Y.	5-4
	August 3	Memorial Coliseum, Los Angeles ..A.L.	Casey Stengel, N.Y.	N.L.	Fred Haney, Mil.	5-3
1960	July 11	Municipal Stadium, Kansas City ....N.L.	Walter Alston, L.A.	A.L.	Al Lopez, Chi.	5-3
	July 13	Yankee Stadium, New York...........N.L.	Walter Alston, L.A.	A.L.	Al Lopez, Chi.	6-0
1961	July 11	Candlestick Park, San Francisco ....N.L.	Danny Murtaugh, Pit.	A.L.	Paul Richards, Bal.	5-4, 10 inn.
	July 31	Fenway Park, Boston	Paul Richards, Bal. (A.L.), Danny Murtaugh, Pit. (N.L.)			1-1 (tie)
1962	July 10	District of Columbia Stad., Was. ...N.L.	Fred Hutchinson, Cin.	A.L.	Ralph Houk, N.Y.	3-1
	July 30	Wrigley Field, Chicago ..................A.L.	Ralph Houk, N.Y.	N.L.	Fred Hutchinson, Cin.	9-4
1963	July 9	Cleveland Stadium, Cleveland........N.L.	Alvin Dark, S.F.	A.L.	Ralph Houk, N.Y.	5-3
1964	July 7	Shea Stadium, New York ...............N.L.	Walter Alston, L.A.	A.L.	Al Lopez, Chi.	7-4
1965	July 13	Metropolitan Stad., Bloomington...N.L.	Gene Mauch, Phi.	A.L.	Al Lopez, Chi.	6-5
1966	July 12	Busch Memorial Stad., St. Louis ...N.L.	Walter Alston, L.A.	A.L.	Sam Mele, Min.	2-1, 10 inn.
1967	July 11	Anaheim Stadium, Anaheim...........N.L.	Walter Alston, L.A.	A.L.	Hank Bauer, Bal.	2-1, 15 inn.
1968	July 9	Astrodome, Houston......................N.L.	Red Schoendienst, St.L.	A.L.	Dick Williams, Bos.	1-0
1969	July 23	Robt. F. Kennedy Mem. Stad., Was...N.L.	Red Schoendienst, St.L.	A.L.	Mayo Smith, Det.	9-3
1970	July 14	Riverfront Stadium, Cincinnati.......N.L.	Gil Hodges, N.Y.	A.L.	Earl Weaver, Bal.	5-4, 12 inn.
1971	July 13	Tiger Stadium, Detroit ..................A.L.	Earl Weaver, Bal.	N.L.	Sparky Anderson, Cin.	6-4
1972	July 25	Atlanta Stadium, Atlanta ...............N.L.	Danny Murtaugh, Pit.	A.L.	Earl Weaver, Bal.	4-3, 10 inn.
1973	July 24	Royals Stadium, Kansas City .........N.L.	Sparky Anderson, Cin.	A.L.	Dick Williams, Oak.	7-1
1974	July 23	Three Rivers Stadium, Pittsburgh..N.L.	Yogi Berra, N.Y.	A.L.	Dick Williams, Cal.	7-2
1975	July 15	County Stadium, Milwaukee ..........N.L.	Walter Alston, L.A.	A.L.	Alvin Dark, Oak.	6-3
1976	July 13	Veterans Stadium, Philadelphia .....N.L.	Sparky Anderson, Cin.	A.L.	Darrell Johnson, Bos.	7-1
1977	July 19	Yankee Stadium, New York...........N.L.	Sparky Anderson, Cin.	A.L.	Billy Martin, N.Y.	7-5
1978	July 11	San Diego Stadium, San Diego......N.L.	Tom Lasorda, L.A.	A.L.	Billy Martin, N.Y.	7-3
1979	July 17	Kingdome, Seattle........................N.L.	Tom Lasorda, L.A.	A.L.	Bob Lemon, N.Y.	7-6
1980	July 8	Dodger Stadium, Los Angeles .......N.L.	Chuck Tanner, Pit.	A.L.	Earl Weaver, Bal.	4-2
1981	August 9	Cleveland Stadium, Cleveland........N.L.	Dallas Green, Phi.	A.L.	Jim Frey, K.C.	5-4
1982	July 13	Olympic Stadium, Montreal ...........N.L.	Tom Lasorda, L.A.	A.L.	Billy Martin, N.Y.	4-1
1983	July 6	Comiskey Park, Chicago ...............A.L.	Harvey Kuenn, Mil.	N.L.	Whitey Herzog, St.L.	13-3
1984	July 10	Candlestick Park, San Francisco ....N.L.	Paul Owens, Phi.	A.L.	Joe Altobelli, Bal.	3-1
1985	July 16	Metrodome, Minneapolis ...............N.L.	Dick Williams, S.D.	A.L.	Sparky Anderson, Det.	6-1
1986	July 15	Astrodome, Houston......................A.L.	Dick Howser, K.C.	N.L.	Whitey Herzog, St.L.	3-2
1987	July 14	Oakland Coliseum, Oakland ...........N.L.	Dave Johnson, N.Y.	A.L.	John McNamara, Bos.	2-0, 13 inn.
1988	July 12	Riverfront Stadium, Cincinnati.......A.L.	Tom Kelly, Min.	N.L.	Whitey Herzog, St.L.	2-1
1989	July 11	Anaheim Stadium, Anaheim...........A.L.	Tony La Russa, Oak.	N.L.	Tom Lasorda, L.A.	5-3
1990	July 10	Wrigley Field, Chicago ..................A.L.	Tony La Russa, Oak.	N.L.	Roger Craig, S.F.	2-0
1991	July 9	SkyDome, Toronto ........................A.L.	Tony La Russa, Oak.	N.L.	Lou Piniella, Cin.	4-2
1992	July 14	Jack Murphy Stadium, San Diego .A.L.	Tom Kelly, Min.	N.L.	Bobby Cox, Atl.	13-6
1993	July 13	Oriole Park at Camden Yards, Bal. A.L.	Cito Gaston, Tor.	N.L.	Bobby Cox, Atl.	9-3
1994	July 12	Three Rivers Stadium, Pittsburgh..N.L.	Jim Fregosi, Phi.	A.L.	Cito Gaston, Tor.	8-7, 10 inn.
1995	July 11	The Ballpark in Arlington, Texas ....N.L.	Felipe Alou, Mon.	A.L.	Buck Showalter, N.Y.	3-2

Year	Date	Site	Winner	Manager	Loser	Manager	Score
1996	July 9	Veterans Stadium, Philadelphia .....N.L.	Bobby Cox, Atl.		A.L.	Mike Hargrove, Cle.	6-0
1997	July 8	Jacobs Field, Cleveland..................A.L.	Joe Torre, N.Y.		N.L.	Bobby Cox, Atl.	3-1
1998	July 7	Coors Field, Colorado ....................A.L.	Mike Hargrove, Cle.		N.L.	Jim Leyland, Fla.	13-8
1999	July 13	Fenway Park, Boston ....................A.L.	Joe Torre, N.Y.		N.L.	Bruce Bochy, S.D.	4-1
2000	July 11	Turner Field, Atlanta....................A.L.	Joe Torre, N.Y.		N.L.	Bobby Cox, Atl.	6-3
2001	July 10	Safeco Field, Seattle....................A.L.	Joe Torre, N.Y.		N.L.	Bobby Valentine, N.Y.	4-1

HOME RUNS (154)

(Numbers in parentheses indicate cumulative totals by batters or pitchers)

Player	Date	Inning	On	Pitcher
Babe Ruth, A.L. ....July 6, 1933		3	1	Bill Hallahan
Frankie Frisch, N.L.................July 6, 1933		6	0	Alvin Crowder
Frankie Frisch, N.L. (2).........July 10, 1934		1	0	Lefty Gomez
Joe Medwick, N.L. ....July 10, 1934		3	2	Lefty Gomez (2)
Jimmie Foxx, A.L. ....July 8, 1935		1	1	Bill Walker
Augie Galan, N.L....................July 7, 1936		5	0	Schoolboy Rowe
Lou Gehrig, A.L. ....July 7, 1936		7	0	Curt Davis
Lou Gehrig, A.L. (2)................July 7, 1937		3	1	Dizzy Dean
Joe DiMaggio, A.L. ....July 11, 1939		5	0	Bill C. Lee
Max West, N.L. ....July 9, 1940		1	2	Red Ruffing
Arky Vaughan, N.L..................July 8, 1941		7	1	Sid Hudson
Arky Vaughan, N.L. (2)...........July 8, 1941		8	1	Eddie Smith
Ted Williams, A.L....................July 8, 1941		9	2	Claude Passeau
Lou Boudreau, A.L...................July 6, 1942		1	0	Mort Cooper
Rudy York, A.L. ....July 6, 1942		1	1	Mort Cooper (2)
Mickey Owen, N.L....................July 6, 1942		8	0	Al Benton
Bobby Doerr, A.L.....................July 13, 1943		2	2	Mort Cooper (3)
Vince DiMaggio, N.L................July 13, 1943		9	0	Cecil Hughson
Charlie Keller, A.L....................July 9, 1946		1	1	Claude Passeau
Ted Williams, A.L. (2)..............July 9, 1946		4	0	Kirby Higbe
Ted Williams, A.L. (3)..............July 9, 1946		8	2	Rip Sewell
Johnny Mize, N.L. ....July 8, 1947		4	0	Spec Shea
Stan Musial, N.L. ....July 13, 1948		1	1	Walt Masterson
Hoot Evers, A.L.......................July 13, 1948		2	0	Ralph Branca
Stan Musial, N.L. (2)...............July 12, 1949		1	1	Mel Parnell
Ralph Kiner, N.L. ....July 12, 1949		6	1	Lou Brissie
Ralph Kiner, N.L. (2)...............July 11, 1950		9	0	Art Houtteman
Red Schoendienst, N.L. ....July 11, 1950		14	0	Ted Gray
Stan Musial, N.L. (3) ....July 10, 1951		4	0	Eddie Lopat
Bob Elliott, N.L. ....July 10, 1951		4	1	Eddie Lopat (2)
Vic Wertz, A.L.........................July 10, 1951		4	0	Sal Maglie
George Kell, A.L.......................July 10, 1951		5	0	Sal Maglie (2)
Gil Hodges, N.L.......................July 10, 1951		6	1	Fred Hutchinson
Ralph Kiner, N.L. (3)...............July 10, 1951		8	0	Mel Parnell (2)
Jackie Robinson, N.L...............July 8, 1952		1	0	Vic Raschi
Hank Sauer, N.L......................July 8, 1952		4	1	Bob Lemon
Al Rosen, A.L..........................July 13, 1954		3	2	Robin Roberts
Ray Boone, A.L........................July 13, 1954		3	0	Robin Roberts (2)
Ted Kluszewski, N.L................July 13, 1954		5	1	Bob Porterfield
Al Rosen, A.L. (2)....................July 13, 1954		5	1	Johnny Antonelli
Gus Bell, N.L...........................July 13, 1954		8	1	Bob Keegan
Larry Doby, A.L.......................July 13, 1954		8	0	Gene Conley
Mickey Mantle, A.L. ....July 12, 1955		1	2	Robin Roberts (3)
Stan Musial, N.L. (4) ....July 12, 1955		12	0	Frank Sullivan
Willie Mays, N.L......................July 10, 1956		4	1	Whitey Ford
Ted Williams, A.L. (4).............July 10, 1956		6	1	Warren Spahn
Mickey Mantle, A.L. (2)...........July 10, 1956		6	0	Warren Spahn (2)
Stan Musial, N.L. (5)...............July 10, 1956		7	0	Tom Brewer
Eddie Mathews, N.L................July 7, 1959		1	0	Early Wynn
Al Kaline, A.L. ....July 7, 1959		4	0	Lew Burdette
Frank Malzone, A.L.................Aug. 3, 1959		2	0	Don Drysdale
Yogi Berra, A.L. ....Aug. 3, 1959		3	1	Don Drysdale (2)
Frank Robinson, N.L................Aug. 3, 1959		5	0	Early Wynn (2)
Jim Gilliam, N.L.......................Aug. 3, 1959		7	0	Billy O'Dell
Rocky Colavito, A.L..................Aug. 3, 1959		8	0	Roy Face
Ernie Banks, N.L. ....July 11, 1960		1	1	Bill Monbouquette
Del Crandall, N.L. ....July 11, 1960		2	0	Bill Monbouquette (2)
Al Kaline, A.L. (2)....................July 11, 1960		8	0	Bob Buhl
Eddie Mathews, N.L. (2).........July 13, 1960		2	1	Whitey Ford (2)
Willie Mays, N.L. (2)...............July 13, 1960		3	0	Whitey Ford (3)
Stan Musial, N.L. (6)...............July 13, 1960		7	0	Gerry Staley
Ken Boyer, N.L.........................July 13, 1960		9	1	Gary Bell

ALL-STAR GAME *General reference*

– 539 –

Player	Date	Inning	On	Pitcher
Harmon Killebrew, A.L.	July 11, 1961	6	0	Mike McCormick
George Altman, N.L.	July 11, 1961	8	0	Mike Fornieles
Rocky Colavito, A.L. (2)	July 31, 1961	1	0	Bob Purkey
Pete Runnels, A.L.	July 30, 1962	3	0	Art Mahaffey
Leon Wagner, A.L.	July 30, 1962	4	1	Art Mahaffey (2)
Rocky Colavito, A.L. (3)	July 30, 1962	7	2	Dick Farrell
Johnny Roseboro, N.L.	July 30, 1962	9	0	Milt Pappas
Billy Williams, N.L.	July 7, 1964	4	0	John Wyatt
Ken Boyer, N.L. (2)	July 7, 1964	4	0	John Wyatt (2)
Johnny Callison, N.L.	July 7, 1964	9	2	Dick Radatz
Willie Mays, N.L. (3)	July 13, 1965	1	0	Milt Pappas (2)
Joe Torre, N.L.	July 13, 1965	1	1	Milt Pappas (3)
Willie Stargell, N.L.	July 13, 1965	2	1	Mudcat Grant
Dick McAuliffe, A.L.	July 13, 1965	5	1	Jim Maloney
Harmon Killebrew, A.L. (2)	July 13, 1965	5	1	Jim Maloney (2)
Dick Allen, N.L.	July 11, 1967	2	0	Dean Chance
Brooks Robinson, A.L.	July 11, 1967	6	0	Ferguson Jenkins
Tony Perez, N.L.	July 11, 1967	15	0	Catfish Hunter
Johnny Bench, N.L.	July 23, 1969	2	1	Mel Stottlemyre
Frank Howard, A.L.	July 23, 1969	2	0	Steve Carlton
Willie McCovey, N.L.	July 23, 1969	3	1	Blue Moon Odom
Bill Freehan, A.L.	July 23, 1969	3	0	Steve Carlton (2)
Willie McCovey, N.L. (2)	July 23, 1969	4	0	Denny McLain
Dick Dietz, N.L.	July 14, 1970	9	0	Catfish Hunter (2)
Johnny Bench, N.L. (2)	July 13, 1971	2	1	Vida Blue
Hank Aaron, N.L.	July 13, 1971	3	0	Vida Blue (2)
Reggie Jackson, A.L.	July 13, 1971	3	1	Dock Ellis
Frank Robinson, A.L. (2)	July 13, 1971	3	1	Dock Ellis (2)
Harmon Killebrew, A.L. (3)	July 13, 1971	6	1	Ferguson Jenkins
Roberto Clemente, N.L.	July 13, 1971	8	0	Mickey Lolich
Hank Aaron, N.L. (2)	July 25, 1972	6	1	Gaylord Perry
Cookie Rojas, A.L.	July 25, 1972	8	1	Bill Stoneman
Johnny Bench, N.L. (3)	July 24, 1973	4	0	Bill Singer
Bobby Bonds, N.L.	July 24, 1973	5	1	Bill Singer (2)
Willie Davis, N.L.	July 24, 1973	6	1	Nolan Ryan
Reggie Smith, N.L.	July 23, 1974	7	0	Catfish Hunter (3)
Steve Garvey, N.L.	July 15, 1975	2	0	Vida Blue (3)
Jimmy Wynn, N.L.	July 15, 1975	2	0	Vida Blue (4)
Carl Yastrzemski, A.L.	July 15, 1975	6	2	Tom Seaver
George Foster, N.L.	July 13, 1976	3	1	Catfish Hunter (4)
Fred Lynn, A.L.	July 13, 1976	4	0	Tom Seaver (2)
Cesar Cedeno, N.L.	July 13, 1976	8	1	Frank Tanana
Joe Morgan, N.L.	July 19, 1977	1	0	Jim Palmer
Greg Luzinski, N.L.	July 19, 1977	1	1	Jim Palmer (2)
Steve Garvey, N.L. (2)	July 19, 1977	3	0	Jim Palmer (3)
George Scott, A.L.	July 19, 1977	9	1	Rich Gossage
Fred Lynn, A.L. (2)	July 17, 1979	1	1	Steve Carlton (3)
Lee Mazzilli, N.L.	July 17, 1979	8	0	Jim Kern
Fred Lynn, A.L. (3)	July 8, 1980	5	1	Bob Welch
Ken Griffey Sr., N.L.	July 8, 1980	5	0	Tommy John
Ken Singleton, A.L.	Aug. 9, 1981	2	0	Tom Seaver (3)
Gary Carter, N.L.	Aug. 9, 1981	5	0	Ken Forsch
Dave Parker, N.L.	Aug. 9, 1981	6	0	Mike Norris
Gary Carter, N.L. (2)	Aug. 9, 1981	7	0	Ron Davis
Mike Schmidt, N.L.	Aug. 9, 1981	8	1	Rollie Fingers
Dave Concepcion, N.L.	July 13, 1982	2	1	Dennis Eckersley
Jim Rice, A.L.	July 6, 1983	3	0	Atlee Hammaker
Fred Lynn, A.L. (4)	July 6, 1983	3	3	Atlee Hammaker (2)
George Brett, A.L.	July 10, 1984	2	0	Charlie Lea
Gary Carter, N.L. (3)	July 10, 1984	2	0	Dave Stieb
Dale Murphy, N.L.	July 10, 1984	8	0	Guillermo Hernandez
Lou Whitaker, A.L.	July 15, 1986	2	1	Dwight Gooden
Frank White, A.L.	July 15, 1986	7	0	Mike Scott
Terry Steinbach, A.L.	July 12, 1988	3	0	Dwight Gooden (2)
Bo Jackson, A.L.	July 11, 1989	1	0	Rick Reuschel
Wade Boggs, A.L.	July 11, 1989	1	0	Rick Reuschel (2)
Cal Ripken Jr., A.L.	July 9, 1991	3	2	Dennis Martinez
Andre Dawson, N.L.	July 9, 1991	4	0	Roger Clemens
Ken Griffey Jr., A.L.	July 14, 1992	3	0	Greg Maddux
Ruben Sierra, A.L.	July 14, 1992	6	1	Bob Tewksbury
Will Clark, N.L.	July 14, 1992	8	2	Rick Aguilera
Gary Sheffield, N.L.	July 13, 1993	1	1	Mark Langston
Kirby Puckett, A.L.	July 13, 1993	2	0	Terry Mulholland

Player	Date	Inning	On	Pitcher
Roberto Alomar, A.L.	July 13, 1993	3	0	Andy Benes
Marquis Grissom, N.L.	July 12, 1994	6	0	Randy Johnson
Fred McGriff, N.L.	July 12, 1994	9	1	Lee Smith
Frank Thomas, A.L.	July 11, 1995	4	1	John Smiley
Craig Biggio, N.L.	July 11, 1995	6	0	Dennis Martinez (2)
Mike Piazza, N.L.	July 11, 1995	7	0	Kenny Rogers
Jeff Conine, N.L.	July 11, 1995	8	0	Steve Ontiveros
Mike Piazza, N.L. (2)	July 9, 1996	2	0	Charles Nagy
Ken Caminiti, N.L.	July 9, 1996	6	0	Roger Pavlik
Edgar Martinez, A.L.	July 8, 1997	2	0	Greg Maddux (2)
Javy Lopez, N.L.	July 8, 1997	7	0	Jose Rosado
Sandy Alomar Jr., A.L.	July 8, 1997	7	1	Shawn Estes
Alex Rodriguez, A.L.	July 7, 1998	5	0	Andy Ashby
Barry Bonds, N.L.	July 7, 1998	5	2	Bartolo Colon
Roberto Alomar, A.L. (2)	July 7, 1998	7	0	Trevor Hoffman
Chipper Jones, N.L.	July 11, 2000	3	0	James Baldwin
Cal Ripken Jr., A.L. (2)	July 10, 2001	3	0	Chan Ho Park
Derek Jeter, A.L.	July 10, 2001	6	0	Jon Lieber
Magglio Ordonez, A.L.	July 10, 2001	6	0	Jon Lieber (2)

MANAGERIAL RECORDS

AMERICAN LEAGUE

	Games W	L
Joe Altobelli, Baltimore	0	1
Sparky Anderson, Detroit	0	1
Del Baker, Detroit	1	0
Hank Bauer, Baltimore	0	1
Lou Boudreau, Cleveland	1	0
Mickey Cochrane, Detroit	1	0
Joe Cronin, Boston, Washington	2	1
Alvin Dark, Oakland	0	1
Jim Frey, Kansas City	0	1
Cito Gaston, Toronto	1	1
Mike Hargrove, Cleveland	1	1
Bucky Harris, New York	1	0
Ralph Houk, New York	1	2
Dick Howser, Kansas City	1	0
Darrell Johnson, Boston	0	1
Tom Kelly, Minnesota	2	0
Harvey Kuenn, Milwaukee	1	0
Tony La Russa, Oakland	3	0
Bob Lemon, New York	0	1
Al Lopez, Cleveland-Chicago	1	5
Connie Mack, Philadelphia	1	0
Billy Martin, New York	0	3
Joe McCarthy, New York	4	3
John McNamara, Boston	0	1
Sam Mele, Minnesota	0	1
Steve O'Neill, Detroit	1	0
Paul Richards, Baltimore*	0	1
Buck Showalter, New York	0	1
Mayo Smith, Detroit	0	1
Casey Stengel, New York	4	6
Joe Torre, New York	4	0
Earl Weaver, Baltimore	1	3
Dick Williams, Boston, Oakland, California	0	3

Total number of managers: 33
*Includes one tie per asterisk.

NATIONAL LEAGUE

	Games W	L
Felipe Alou, Montreal	1	0
Walter Alston, Brooklyn, Los Angeles	7	2
Sparky Anderson, Cincinnati	3	1
	Games W	L
Yogi Berra, New York	1	0
Bruce Bochy, San Diego	0	1
Bobby Cox, Atlanta	1	4
Roger Craig, San Francisco	0	1
Alvin Dark, San Francisco	1	0
Charlie Dressen, Brooklyn	1	0
Leo Durocher, Brooklyn	2	2
Eddie Dyer, St. Louis	0	1
Jim Fregosi, Philadelphia	1	0
Frankie Frisch, St. Louis	0	1
Dallas Green, Philadelphia	1	0
Charley Grimm, Chicago	1	1
Fred Haney, Milwaukee	1	2
Gabby Hartnett, Chicago	0	1
Whitey Herzog, St. Louis	0	3
Gil Hodges, New York	1	0
Fred Hutchinson, Cincinnati	1	1
Dave Johnson, New York	1	0
Tom Lasorda, Los Angeles	3	1
Jim Leyland, Florida	0	1
Gene Mauch, Philadelphia	1	0
John McGraw, New York	0	1
Bill McKechnie, Cincinnati	1	1
Danny Murtaugh, Pittsburgh*	2	0
Paul Owens, Philadelphia	1	0
Lou Piniella, Cincinnati	0	1
Eddie Sawyer, Philadelphia	1	0
Red Schoendienst, St. Louis	2	0
Burt Shotton, Brooklyn	1	0
Billy Southworth, St. Louis	1	2
Chuck Tanner, Pittsburgh	1	0
Bill Terry, New York	1	2
Bobby Valentine, New York	0	1
Dick Williams, San Diego	1	0

Total number of managers: 37

COMBINED RECORDS FOR BOTH LEAGUES

	Games W	L
Sparky Anderson, Cincinnati N.L., Detroit A.L.	3	2
Alvin Dark, San Francisco N.L., Oakland A.L.	1	1
Dick Williams, Boston, Oakland, California	1	3

Total number of managers: 3

INDEX

REGULAR SEASON

SERVICE

Category	Individual	Club	League
PLAYERS USED		16	19
Pinch-Hitters		16	
Pinch-Runners		16	
YEARS PLAYED	14	18	
20-Year Players	170		
Youngest and Oldest Players	14		
LEAGUES AND CLUBS PLAYED FOR	14		
YEARS PITCHED	15		
20-Year Pitchers	170		
Youngest and Oldest Pitchers	15		

BATTING

Category	Individual	Club	League
GAMES PLAYED	20	48	68
2,400 or More	170		
500 or More Consecutive	170		
BATTING AVERAGE	20	48	68
Yearly Leaders	143		
Batting .300, 10 Times	171		
.300 Lifetime Average	171		
.400 Hitters	182		
Triple Crown Hitters	182		
SLUGGING AVERAGE	22	48	68
Yearly Leaders	144		
Of Players with 4,000 Total Bases	172		
AT-BATS AND PLATE APPEARANCES	22	48	68
9,000 or More	172		
RUNS	23		68
Yearly Leaders	146		
1,500 or More	172		
Season and Month		49	
Game and Doubleheader, One Club		49	
Game and Doubleheader, Both Clubs		50	
Inning		51	
Most, First Through 26th Innings		52	
Games Being Shut Out		53	
HITS			68
Career	24		
2,500 or More	172		
Season	24	54	
Yearly Leaders	147		
200 or More, Four Times	173		
200 or More by Rookies	182		
Game	25	54	
Six Hits in Game	191		
Hitting for Cycle	26, 189		
Doubleheader	25	55	
Inning	26	56	
Batting Streaks	26	55	
30-Game Streaks	182		
DiMaggio's 56-Game Streak	197		
SINGLES	27	56	69
Yearly Leaders	149		
2,000 or More	173		
DOUBLES	28	56	69
Yearly Leaders	150		
450 or More	173		
TRIPLES	29	57	69
Yearly Leaders	152		
150 or More	173		
HOME RUNS			
Career	30		
300 or More	174		
10 or More by Pinch-Hitter	174		
Season	31	57	69
Yearly Leaders	154		
Home and Road	32		
By Clubs, Each Year		198	
50, 40, 30 and 20 in Season	32, 182		

Category	Individual	Club	League
50 Homers, 20 Stolen Bases	189		
40 Homers, 40 Stolen Bases	188		
30 Homers, 30 Stolen Bases	188		
20 Homers, 50 Stolen Bases	189		
Bonds' 73 in 2001	193		
McGwire's 70 in 1998	194		
Maris' 61 in 1961	195		
Ruth's 60 in 1927	196		
Two Consecutive Seasons	32		
Month	33	57	
Week	33		
Game	33	58	
Four and Three in Game	33, 184		
Two in Game	35		
25 Multiple-Homer Games	174		
Consecutive and in Consecutive Games	36	59	
Doubleheader	33	59	
One Day			70
Inning	33	60	
Five and Four in Inning		201	
Three Consecutive in Inning		202	
GRAND SLAMS	37	61	70
10 or More	175		
TOTAL BASES	38	62	70
Yearly Leaders	156		
400 in Season	189		
4,000 or More	175		
LONG HITS	38	62	70
100 in Season	189		
800 or More	175		
EXTRA BASES ON LONG HITS	40	62	70
1,500 or More	175		
RUNS BATTED IN	41	63	71
Yearly Leaders	157		
1,200 or More	176		
Game-Winning RBIs	42	63	
BASES ON BALLS	42	63	71
Yearly Leaders	158		
1,000 or More	176		
Intentional	43	64	71
STRIKEOUTS	43	64	71
Yearly Leaders	160		
1,200 or More	176		
SACRIFICE HITS	45	65	71
SACRIFICE FLIES	46	66	71
HIT BY PITCH	46	66	71
GROUNDING INTO DOUBLE PLAYS	47	67	71
REACHING BASE ON ERRORS	47	67	
REACHING BASE ON INTERFERENCE	47		

BASERUNNING

Category	Individual	Club	League
STOLEN BASES	72	74	76
Yearly Leaders	161		
400 or More	177		
50 Steals, 20 Homers	189		
40 Steals, 40 Homers	188		
30 Steals, 30 Homers	188		
20 Steals, 50 Homers	189		
Steals of Home	72	74	
10 or More	177		
CAUGHT STEALING	73	74	76
Caught off Base	73	74	
LEFT ON BASE		74	76

PITCHING

Category	Individual	Club	League
GAMES PITCHED	77		
700 or More	177		
GAMES STARTED	77		
500 or More	178		
GAMES RELIEVED	77		
GAMES FINISHED	78		

Category	Individual	Club	League
COMPLETE GAMES	78	93	96
300 or More	178		
INNINGS	78	93	96
3,500 or More	178		
WINNING PERCENTAGE	79		
Yearly Leaders	162		
GAMES WON		93	96
Career	79		
200 or More	178		
Season	79		
20 and 30-Victory Seasons	80		
Complete List	211		
20 Wins, Five Times	179		
30 Wins, Two Times	179		
Month	79		
Doubleheader	80, 209		
Consecutive	80		
12 Consecutive in Season	210		
SAVES	81	93	
Yearly Leaders	167		
150 or More	179		
GAMES LOST	81	93	96
12 Consecutive in Season	210		
AT-BATS AND PLATE APPEARANCES	82	93	
RUNS	82	93	96
1,800 or More	179		
EARNED RUNS	83	93	96
EARNED-RUN AVERAGE	83	93	96
Yearly Leaders	164		
3.50 or Under, Career	180		
SHUTOUTS	83	93	96
Yearly Leaders	165		
40 or More	180		
CONSECUTIVE SCORELESS INNINGS	85		
1-0 GAMES	85	94	96
10 or More	180		
HITS	85	94	
4,000 or More	180		
No-Hit Games	86	94	96
Complete List	204		
One-Hit Games	86	94	96
Singles	86		
Home Runs	87	94	97
Seven or More Grand Slams	181		
Long Hits and Total Bases	87		
BASES ON BALLS	88	95	97
1,200 or More	181		
STRIKEOUTS		95	97
Career	88		
2,000 or More	181		
Season	89		
Yearly Leaders	168		
Game and Inning	89		
Consecutive	90		
HIT BATSMEN	91	95	97
WILD PITCHES	91	95	97
SACRIFICE HITS	92	95	
SACRIFICE FLIES	92	95	
BALKS	92	95	97

FIELDING

| Category | Individual | | | | | | | Club | League |
	1B	2B	3B	SS	OF	C	P		
GAMES AND INNINGS	98	101	104	107	109	113	117		
AVERAGE	98	101	104	107	110	113	117	120	124
PUTOUTS	98	101	104	107	110	114	117	120	124
ASSISTS	99	102	105	107	111	114	118	120	124
CHANCES ACCEPTED AND OFFERED	99	102	105	108	111	115	118	121	124
ERRORS	100	103	105	108	112	115	118	122	124
PASSED BALLS						116		122	124
DOUBLE PLAYS	100	103	106	109	113	116	119	123	125

INDEX

Category	1B	2B	3B	SS	OF	C	P	Club	League
			Individual						
TRIPLE PLAYS							119	123	125
Unassisted	220	220		220				220	220
BASERUNNERS VS. CATCHERS						117			
NO-HITTERS CAUGHT						117			
NUMBER OF PLAYERS AT POSITIONS								17	

MISCELLANEOUS

Category	Individual	Club	League
HISTORIC FIRSTS	126	126	
NIGHT GAMES		130	137
POSTPONEMENTS		130	137
TIE GAMES		130	137
ONE-RUN DECISIONS		130	138
EXTRA-INNING GAMES			137
LENGTH OF GAMES			
By Innings		130	
Games of 18 or More Innings		225	
By Time		131	
GAMES WON		132	
Lifetime by Franchises		220	
90 and 100-Victory Seasons			137
100 or More in Season		222	
Home and Road Victories			137
Consecutive		133	
13 or More in Season		223	
First Eight or More in Season		225	
GAMES LOST		133	
Lifetime by Franchises		220	
90 and 100-Loss Seasons			137
100 or More in Season		222	
Consecutive		134	
13 or More in Season		224	
First Eight or More in Season		225	
WINNING PERCENTAGE			
Lifetime by Franchises		220	
Highest, Season and Month		134	
Lowest, Season and Month		134	
YEARLY PENNANT WINNERS		140	
YEARLY FINISHES, BY TEAMS		228	
CHAMPIONSHIPS AND FIRST-DIVISION FINISHES		135	
LAST PLACE AND SECOND-DIVISION FINISHES		135	
GAMES FINISHED AHEAD AND BEHIND		135	
PENNANT CLINCHING AND DAYS IN FIRST PLACE		136	
ATTENDANCE		136	138
3,200,000 or More in Season		226	
TEAM RECORDS	228	228	

NON-PLAYING PERSONNEL

Category	Individual	Club	League
COMMISSIONERS AND LEAGUE PRESIDENTS	226		
MANAGERS	139	139	139
UMPIRES	139		

DIVISION SERIES
SERVICE

Category	Individual	Club
PLAYERS USED		341
Pinch-Hitters		341
Pinch-Runners		341
SERIES PLAYED	340	341
Youngest and Oldest Players	340	
POSITIONS PLAYED	340	
SERIES PITCHED	340	
Youngest and Oldest Pitchers	340	

BATTING

Category	Individual	Club
GAMES PLAYED	344	351
BATTING AVERAGE	344	351

INDEX

Category	Individual	Club
By Team, Each Series		390
Leading Batters, Each Series	388	
.450 Hitters, Each Series	388	
SLUGGING AVERAGE	344	351
AT-BATS AND PLATE APPEARANCES	344	351
RUNS	345	352
Games Being Shut Out		354
HITS	345	354
SINGLES	346	355
DOUBLES	346	355
TRIPLES	346	356
HOME RUNS	347	356
Complete List	389	
Players With Four or More, Career	389	
TOTAL BASES	348	357
LONG HITS	348	358
EXTRA BASES ON LONG HITS		358
RUNS BATTED IN	348	358
BASES ON BALLS	349	359
STRIKEOUTS	349	360
SACRIFICE HITS	350	361
SACRIFICE FLIES	350	361
HIT BY PITCH	350	361
GROUNDING INTO DOUBLE PLAYS	350	
REACHING BASE ON INTERFERENCE	350	

BASERUNNING

Category	Individual	Club
STOLEN BASES	362	363
CAUGHT STEALING	362	363
LEFT ON BASE		364

PITCHING

Category	Individual	Club
GAMES PITCHED	365	370
GAMES STARTED	365	
GAMES RELIEVED AND FINISHED	365	
COMPLETE GAMES	365	370
INNINGS	365	
GAMES WON	365	
Pitchers With Three or More, Career	389	
SAVES	366	370
GAMES LOST	366	
RUNS	366	370
EARNED RUNS	367	
SHUTOUTS	367	370
Complete List	388	
HITS	367	
DOUBLES, TRIPLES AND HOMERS	367	
TOTAL BASES	368	
BASES ON BALLS	368	
STRIKEOUTS	368	
10-Strikeout Games by Pitchers	390	
HIT BATSMEN	369	
WILD PITCHES	369	370
BALKS	369	370

FIELDING

Category				Individual				Club
	1B	2B	3B	SS	OF	C	P	
SERIES	340	340	340	340	340	340	340	
GAMES	371	372	373	374	375	376	378	380
AVERAGE								391
By Team, Each Series								380
PUTOUTS	371	372	373	374	375	377	378	380
ASSISTS	371	372	373	374	375	377	378	381
CHANCES ACCEPTED	371	372	373	374	375	377	378	
CHANCES OFFERED	371	372	373	374	375	377	378	381
ERRORS	371	372	374	375	376	377	379	382
PASSED BALLS						377		382
RUNNERS CAUGHT STEALING						377		
DOUBLE PLAYS	371	372	374	375	376	377	379	382
NUMBER OF PLAYERS AT POSITIONS								341

INDEX

MISCELLANEOUS

Category	Club
SERIES RESULTS	387
ONE-RUN DECISIONS	384
LENGTH OF GAMES	
By Innings	384
By Time	384
SERIES WON	384, 387
SERIES LOST	385, 387
GAMES WON	384, 387
GAMES LOST	385, 387
SERIES STARTING AND FINISHING DATES	384
HOME AND ROAD GAMES, EACH TEAM	387
EXTRA-INNING GAMES—COMPLETE LIST	388
ATTENDANCE	385
Each Series	388

NON-PLAYING PERSONNEL

Category	Club
MANAGERS	386
Complete List With Won-Lost Records	392
UMPIRES	386

CHAMPIONSHIP SERIES
SERVICE

Category	Individual	Club
PLAYERS USED		396
Pinch-Hitters		396
Pinch-Runners		396
SERIES PLAYED	394	399
Youngest and Oldest Players	395	
POSITIONS PLAYED	395	
SERIES PITCHED	395	
Youngest and Oldest Pitchers	395	

BATTING

Category	Individual	Club
GAMES PLAYED	400	408
BATTING AVERAGE	400	408
By Team, Each Series		456
Leading Batters, Each Series	453	
.450 Hitters, Each Series	454	
SLUGGING AVERAGE	400	408
AT-BATS AND PLATE APPEARANCES	400	409
RUNS	401	410
Games Being Shut Out		412
HITS	402	412
SINGLES	402	413
DOUBLES	403	413
TRIPLES	403	414
HOME RUNS	403	415
Complete List	454	
Players With Four or More, Career	455	
TOTAL BASES	405	416
LONG HITS	405	417
EXTRA BASES ON LONG HITS		417
RUNS BATTED IN	405	418
BASES ON BALLS	406	419
STRIKEOUTS	406	420
SACRIFICE HITS	407	421
SACRIFICE FLIES	407	421
HIT BY PITCH	407	421
GROUNDING INTO DOUBLE PLAYS	407	
REACHING BASE ON INTERFERENCE	407	

BASERUNNING

Category	Individual	Club
STOLEN BASES	422	423
CAUGHT STEALING	422	423
LEFT ON BASE		424

PITCHING

Category	Individual	Club
GAMES PITCHED	425	430
GAMES STARTED	425	
GAMES RELIEVED AND FINISHED	425	
COMPLETE GAMES	425	430
INNINGS	425	
GAMES WON	426	
Pitchers With Four or More, Career	456	
SAVES	426	430
GAMES LOST	426	
RUNS	426	430
EARNED RUNS	427	
SHUTOUTS	427	430
Complete List	452	
HITS	427	
DOUBLES, TRIPLES AND HOMERS	427	
TOTAL BASES	428	
BASES ON BALLS	428	
STRIKEOUTS	428	
10-Strikeout Games by Pitchers	456	
HIT BATSMEN	429	
WILD PITCHES	429	431
BALKS	429	431

FIELDING

Category	1B	2B	3B	SS	OF	C	P	Club
SERIES	394	394	394	394	394	394	395	
GAMES	432	433	434	436	437	438	440	
AVERAGE								442
By Team, Each Series								458
PUTOUTS	432	433	434	436	437	438	440	442
ASSISTS	432	433	434	436	437	438	440	443
CHANCES ACCEPTED	432	433	434	436	437	438	440	
CHANCES OFFERED	432	433	434	436	437	438	440	444
ERRORS	433	434	435	436	438	439	441	444
PASSED BALLS						439		445
RUNNERS CAUGHT STEALING						440		
DOUBLE PLAYS		433	434	435	436	438	440	441	445
NUMBER OF PLAYERS AT POSITIONS								397

MISCELLANEOUS

Category	Club
SERIES RESULTS	451
ONE-RUN DECISIONS	447
LENGTH OF GAMES	
By Innings	447
By Time	447
SERIES WON	447, 451
SERIES LOST	448, 451
GAMES WON	447, 451
GAMES LOST	448, 451
SERIES STARTING AND FINISHING DATES	447
HOME AND ROAD GAMES, EACH CLUB	452
EXTRA-INNING GAMES—COMPLETE LIST	452
ATTENDANCE	449
Each Series	453

NON-PLAYING PERSONNEL

Category	Club
MANAGERS	450
Complete List With Won-Lost Records	460
UMPIRES	450

WORLD SERIES
SERVICE

Category	Individual	Club
PLAYERS USED		463
Pinch-Hitters		463
Pinch-Runners		463

INDEX

Category	Individual	Club
SERIES PLAYED	462	465
Youngest and Oldest Players	462	
CLUBS PLAYED FOR	462	
POSITIONS PLAYED	462	
SERIES PITCHED	462	
Youngest and Oldest Pitchers	462	

BATTING

Category	Individual	Club
GAMES PLAYED	466	474
BATTING AVERAGE	466	474
By Team, Each Series		513
Leading Batters, Each Series	508	
.450 Hitters, Each Series	510	
SLUGGING AVERAGE	466	474
AT-BATS AND PLATE APPEARANCES	466	474
RUNS	466	475
Games Being Shut Out		476
HITS	467	476
SINGLES	468	476
DOUBLES	468	477
TRIPLES	469	477
HOME RUNS	469	478
Complete List	510	
Players With Five or More, Career	512	
TOTAL BASES	471	479
LONG HITS	471	480
EXTRA BASES ON LONG HITS	472	480
RUNS BATTED IN	472	480
BASES ON BALLS	472	481
STRIKEOUTS	472	481
SACRIFICE HITS	473	482
SACRIFICE FLIES	473	482
HIT BY PITCH	473	482
GROUNDING INTO DOUBLE PLAYS	473	
REACHING BASE ON ERRORS	473	482
REACHING BASE ON INTERFERENCE	473	

BASERUNNING

Category	Individual	Club
STOLEN BASES	483	484
CAUGHT STEALING	483	484
LEFT ON BASE		484

PITCHING

Category	Individual	Club
GAMES PITCHED	486	490
GAMES STARTED	486	
GAMES RELIEVED AND FINISHED	486	
COMPLETE GAMES	486	490
INNINGS	486	
GAMES WON	486	
Pitchers With Five or More, Career	512	
SAVES	487	490
GAMES LOST	487	
RUNS	487	490
EARNED RUNS	487	
EARNED-RUN AVERAGE	487	
SHUTOUTS AND SCORELESS INNINGS	487	490
Complete List	506	
1-0 GAMES		490
HITS	488	
DOUBLES, TRIPLES AND HOMERS	488	
TOTAL BASES AND LONG HITS	488	
BASES ON BALLS	488	
STRIKEOUTS	489	
10-Strikeout Games by Pitchers	512	
HIT BATSMEN	489	
WILD PITCHES	489	490
BALKS	489	490

INDEX

FIELDING

Category	1B	2B	3B	SS	OF	C	P	Club
SERIES	462	462	462	462	462	462	462	
GAMES	491	491	492	493	494	496	497	
AVERAGE								499
By Team, Each Series								515
PUTOUTS	491	491	493	493	494	496	497	499
ASSISTS	491	491	493	493	494	496	497	500
CHANCES ACCEPTED	491	491	493	493	494	496	497	
CHANCES OFFERED	491	491	493	493	494	496	497	500
ERRORS	491	492	493	494	495	496	498	500
PASSED BALLS						496		501
RUNNERS CAUGHT STEALING						497		
DOUBLE PLAYS	491	492	493	494	495	497	498	501
TRIPLE PLAYS								501
NUMBER OF PLAYERS AT POSITIONS								463

MISCELLANEOUS

Category	Club
SERIES RESULTS	505
ONE-RUN DECISIONS	502
LENGTH OF GAMES	
By Innings	502
By Time	502
SERIES STARTING AND FINISHING DATES	502
SERIES WON	503, 505
SERIES LOST	503, 505
GAMES WON	503, 506
GAMES LOST	503, 506
NIGHT GAMES	502
HOME AND ROAD GAMES, EACH TEAM	506
TIE GAMES	506
EXTRA-INNING GAMES—COMPLETE LIST	507
ATTENDANCE	503
Each Series	508

NON-PLAYING PERSONNEL

Category	Club
MANAGERS	504
Complete List With Won-Lost Records	518
UMPIRES	504

ALL-STAR GAME
SERVICE

Category	Individual	Club
MOST CLUB REPRESENTED	522	
PLAYING ON WINNING AND LOSING CLUBS	522	
YOUNGEST AND OLDEST PLAYERS	522	
POSITIONS	522	
PLAYERS USED		522
Pinch-Hitters		522

BATTING

Category	Individual	Club
GAMES PLAYED	523	
BATTING AVERAGE	523	526
AT-BATS AND PLATE APPEARANCES	523	526
RUNS	523	526
EARNED RUNS		526
HITS	523	526
SINGLES	523	526
DOUBLES	523	526
TRIPLES	523	526
HOME RUNS	524	526
Complete List	539	
TOTAL BASES	524	527
LONG HITS	524	527

INDEX

Category	Individual	Club
EXTRA BASES ON LONG HITS		527
RUNS BATTED IN	524	527
BASES ON BALLS	524	527
STRIKEOUTS	524	527
SACRIFICE HITS	524	527
SACRIFICE FLIES	524	
HIT BY PITCH	525	527
GROUNDING INTO DOUBLE PLAYS	525	

BASERUNNING

Category	Individual	Club
STOLEN BASES	528	528
CAUGHT STEALING	528	
LEFT ON BASE		528

PITCHING

Category	Individual	Club
GAMES PITCHED	529	
GAMES STARTED AND FINISHED	529	
GAMES WON AND LOST	529	
INNINGS	529	
RUNS AND EARNED RUNS	529	
HITS	529	
HOME RUNS	529	
BASES ON BALLS	529	
STRIKEOUTS	529	
HIT BATSMEN	529	
WILD PITCHES	529	
BALKS	529	

FIELDING

Category	Individual	Club
FIRST, SECOND AND THIRD BASEMEN	531	
SHORTSTOPS AND OUTFIELDERS	532	
CATCHERS AND PITCHERS	532	
NUMBER OF PLAYERS AT POSITIONS		534

MISCELLANEOUS

Category	Club
GAME RESULTS	538
EARLIEST AND LATEST GAME DATES	536
NIGHT GAMES	536
LENGTH OF GAMES	536
GAMES WON AND LOST	536
ATTENDANCE	536

NON-PLAYING PERSONNEL

Category	Individual
MANAGERS AND UMPIRES	537
Complete List of Managers With Won-Lost Records	541